The Literature of
AUTOBIOGRAPHICAL NARRATIVE

The Literature of
AUTOBIOGRAPHICAL NARRATIVE

VOLUME 3

ORAL HISTORIES

THOMAS RIGGS, *editor*

ST. JAMES PRESS
A part of Gale, Cengage Learning

Detroit • New York • San Francisco • New Haven, Conn • Waterville, Maine • London

The Literature of Autobiographical Narrative
Thomas Riggs, Editor
Andrea Kovacs Henderson, Project Editor

Artwork and photographs for *The Literature of Autobiographical Narrative* covers were reproduced with the following kind permission.

Volume 1
For foreground painting "Chief Geronimo, 1899" by Elbridge Ayer Burbank. © Butler Institute of American Art, Youngstown, OH USA/Museum Purchase 1912/The Bridgeman Art Library.

For background image of a band of Apache Indian prisoners, 1886. The Art Archive/National Archives Washington DC.

Volume 2
For foreground portrait "Anne Frank, 1960" (coal with pastel on paper) by Ilya Glazunov (b. 1930). Private Collection/The Bridgeman Art Library.

For background image of 263 Prinsengracht in Amsterdam, the house where Anne Frank and her family spent two years in hiding during the German occupation of The Netherlands during World War II. The Art Archive/Culver Pictures.

Volume 3
For foreground "May the Whole Country from the Mountains to the Rivers be a Sea of Red, 1960" (colour litho). Private Collection/© The Chambers Gallery, London/The Bridgeman Art Library.

For background image of detail of Political Relief Sculpture in Tiananmen Square. © Brian A. Vikanders/CORBIS.

© 2013 Gale, Cengage Learning

ALL RIGHTS RESERVED. No part of this work covered by the copyright herein may be reproduced, transmitted, stored, or used in any form or by any means graphic, electronic, or mechanical, including but not limited to photocopying, recording, scanning, digitizing, taping, Web distribution, information networks, or information storage and retrieval systems, except as permitted under Section 107 or 108 of the 1976 United States Copyright Act, without the prior written permission of the publisher.

For product information and technology assistance, contact us at
Gale Customer Support, 1-800-877-4253.
For permission to use material from this text or product,
submit all requests online at **www.cengage.com/permissions**.
Further permissions questions can be emailed to
permissionrequest@cengage.com.

While every effort has been made to ensure the reliability of the information presented in this publication, Gale, a part of Cengage Learning, does not guarantee the accuracy of the data contained herein. Gale accepts no payment for listing; and inclusion in the publication of any organization, agency, institution, publication, service, or individual does not imply endorsement of the editors or publisher. Errors brought to the attention of the publisher and verified to the satisfaction of the publisher will be corrected in future editions.

Library of Congress Cataloging-in-Publication Data

The literature of autobiographical narrative / Thomas Riggs, editor.
   volumes cm
 Includes bibliographical references and indexes.
   ISBN 978-1-55862-870-0 (set : alk. paper) -- ISBN 978-1-55862-871-7 (vol. 1 : alk. paper) -- ISBN 978-1-55862-872-4 (vol. 2 : alk. paper) -- ISBN 978-1-55862-873-1 (vol. 3 : alk. paper)
 1. Autobiography. 2. Biography as a literary form. 3. Authors--Biography--History and criticism. 4. Literature--History and criticism. I. Riggs, Thomas, 1963-
 CT25.L58 2013
 920.02--dc23
                                                        2013002574

Gale
27500 Drake Rd.
Farmington Hills, MI, 48331-3535

ISBN-13: 978-1-55862-870-0 (set)   ISBN-10: 1-55862-870-3 (set)
ISBN-13: 978-1-55862-871-7 (vol. 1) ISBN-10: 1-55862-871-1 (vol. 1)
ISBN-13: 978-1-55862-872-4 (vol. 2) ISBN-10: 1-55862-872-X (vol. 2)
ISBN-13: 978-1-55862-873-1 (vol. 3) ISBN-10: 1-55862-873-8 (vol. 3)

This title will also be available as an e-book.
ISBN-13: 978-1-55862-881-6 ISBN-10: 1-55862-881-9
Contact your Gale, a part of Cengage Learning, sales representative for ordering information.

Printed in the United States of America
1 2 3 4 5 6 7 17 16 15 14 13

ADVISORY BOARD

CHAIR

Richard Bradford
Research Professor of English and Senior Distinguished Research Fellow, University of Ulster, Ulster, Northern Ireland. Author of *A Brief Life of John Milton* (2013); *The Odd Couple: The Curious Friendship between Kingsley Amis and Philip Larkin* (2012); *Martin Amis: The Biography* (2011); *The Life of a Long-Distance Writer: The Authorized Biography of Alan Sillitoe* (2008); *First Boredom, Then Fear: The Life of Philip Larkin* (2005); and *Lucky Him: The Life of Kingsley Amis* (2001). Editor of *Life Writing: Essays on Autobiography, Biography and Literature* (2010).

ADVISORS

Lynn Abram
Professor of Gender History, University of Glasgow, Glasgow, Scotland. Author of *Oral History Theory* (2010); *Myth and Materiality in a Woman's World: Shetland 1800–2000* (2005); *The Making of Modern Woman: Europe, 1789–1918* (2002); and *The Orphan Country: Children of Scotland's Broken Homes from 1800 to the Present Day* (1998). Series editor of Manchester University Press Gender in History series (2003–).

Suzanne Bunkers
Professor of English, Minnesota State University, Mankato, Mankato, Minnesota. Author of *In Search of Susanna* (1996). Coauthor, with Frank W. Klein, of *Good Earth, Black Soil* (1981). Editor of *Diaries of Girls and Women: A Midwestern American Sampler* (2001); *A Pioneer Farm Girl: The Diary of Sarah Gillespie, 1877–1878* (2000); *"All Will Yet Be Well": The Diary of Sarah Gillespie Huftalen, 1873–1952* (1993); and *The Diary of Caroline Seabury, 1854–1863* (1991). Coeditor, with Cynthia Huff, of *Inscribing the Daily: Critical Essays on Women's Diaries* (1996).

Cynthia Huff
Professor of English, Illinois State University, Normal, Illinois. Editor of *Towards a Geography of Women's Life Writing and Imagined Communities* (2005). Coeditor, with Suzanne Bunkers, of *Inscribing the Daily: Critical Essays on Women's Diaries* (1996). Contributor to the journals *Biography* and *a/b: Auto/Biography Studies*. Editorial board member of *a/b*.

ADVISORY BOARD

Geneva Cobb Moore
Professor of English, University of Wisconsin-Whitewater, Whitewater, Wisconsin. Contributor to *Inscribing the Daily: Critical Essays on Women's Diaries* (1996), edited by Suzanne Bunkers and Cynthia Huff; and to *The Oxford Companion to African American Literature,* edited by William L. Andrews, Frances Smith Foster, and Trudier Harris (1997). Contributor of essays on Africa, Zora Neale Hurston, Alice Walker, Harriet Jacobs, Toni Morrison, and Danzy Senna to journals including the *Southern Literary Journal,* the *Black Scholar,* and the *Western Journal of Black Studies.* Former Fulbright Scholar of American and African American Literature at the University of Ghana, West Africa. Recipient of grants and awards from the National Endowment for the Humanities and the Paul W. Mellon Foundation.

Harry Ross
Associate Professor of Secondary Education, National Louis University, Chicago, Illinois. Coauthor of *13 Steps to Teacher Empowerment: Taking a More Active Role in Your School Community* (2009). National presenter on life writing, multicultural literature, urban teacher preparation, and teacher collaboration and leadership. Lead scholar on a National Endowment for the Humanities grant to teach the life stories written by the 1930s Federal Writers' Project authors.

Amanda Rust
English and Theatre Librarian, Northeastern University, Boston, Massachusetts.

Sharon Cadman Seelig
Roe/Straut Professor in the Humanities, Smith College, Northampton, Massachusetts. Author of *Autobiography and Gender in Early Modern Literature: Reading Women's Lives, 1600–1680* (2006); *Generating Texts: The Progeny of Seventeenth-Century Prose* (1996); and *The Shadow of Eternity: Belief and Structure in Herbert, Vaughan, and Traherne* (1981). Editorial board member of *English Literary Renaissance.*

Eugene Stelzig
Distinguished Teaching Professor of English, State University of New York at Geneseo, Geneseo, New York. Author of *Henry Crabb Robinson in Germany: A Study in Nineteenth-Century Life Writing* (2010); *The Romantic Subject in Autobiography: Rousseau and Goethe* (2000); *Herman Hesse's Fictions of the Self: Autobiography and the Confessional Imagination* (1988); and *All Shades of Consciousness: Wordsworth's Poetry and the Self in Time* (1975). Contributor to journals in the areas of Romantic studies and autobiography studies. Editor of *Romantic Autobiography in England* (2009).

Editorial and Production Staff

Associate Publisher
Marc Cormier

Product Manager
Philip J. Virta

Project Editor
Andrea Kovacs Henderson

Editorial Support
Rebecca Parks

Editorial Assistance
Laura Avery, Lisa Kumar, Michelle Lee, Margaret Mazurkiewicz, Tracie Moy

Art Director
Kristine Julien

Composition and Imaging
Evi Seoud, John Watkins

Manufacturing
Wendy Blurton

Rights Acquisition and Management
Kimberly Potvin, Margaret Chamberlain-Gaston

Technical Support
Luann Brennan, Mike Weaver

Table of Contents

Introduction **xiii**

Editor's Note **xvii**

Contributors **xix**

Academic Reviewers **xxi**

Adversity and Resistance

Anarchist Voices: An Oral History of Anarchism in America by Paul Avrich **3**

Biography of a Runaway Slave by Miguel Barnet and Esteban Montejo **7**

Bitter Water: Diné Oral Histories of the Navajo-Hopi Land Dispute by Malcolm D. Benally **10**

Exodus to Shanghai: Stories of Escape from the Third Reich by Steve Hochstadt **14**

Gulag Voices: Oral Histories of Soviet Incarceration and Exile by Jehanne M. Gheith and Katherine R. Jolluck **17**

Head of the Class: An Oral History of African American Achievement in Higher Education and Beyond by Gabrielle Morris **20**

The History of Mary Prince, a West Indian Slave, Related by Herself by Mary Prince **23**

Ireland's Unfinished Revolution: An Oral History by Kenneth Griffith and Timothy O'Grady **27**

Massacre in Mexico by Elena Poniatowska **31**

Mothers, Sisters, Resisters: Oral Histories of Women Who Survived the Holocaust by Brana Gurewitsch **34**

Nisa: The Life and Words of a !Kung Woman by Marjorie Shostak **37**

Survivors: An Oral History of the Armenian Genocide by Donald E. Miller and Lorna Touryan Miller **40**

Voices of Freedom: An Oral History of the Civil Rights Movement from the 1950s through the 1980s by Henry Hampton and Steve Fayer **44**

Voices of Resistance: Oral Histories of Moroccan Women by Alison Baker **47**

Witnesses to the Holocaust: An Oral History by Rhoda Lewin **50**

Working-Class Childhood: An Oral History by Jeremy Seabrook **53**

Communities

Akenfield: Portrait of an English Village by Ronald Blythe **59**

Ask the Fellows Who Cut the Hay by George Ewart Evans **63**

Coal Hollow: Photographs and Oral Histories by Kenneth Light and Melanie Light **66**

Daring Hearts: Lesbian and Gay Lives of the 50s and 60s Brighton by Brighton Ourstory **70**

Doña María's Story: Life History, Memory and Political Identity by Daniel James **73**

Hill Country Teacher: Oral Histories from the One-Room School and Beyond by Diane Manning **77**

The Hood River Issei: An Oral History of Japanese Settlers in Oregon's Hood River Valley by Linda Tamura **80**

The Making of a Gay Asian Community: An Oral History of Pre-AIDS Los Angeles by Eric Wat **83**

Our Appalachia: An Oral History by Laurel Shackelford and Bill Weinberg **86**

The Saga of Coe Ridge: A Study in Oral History by William Lynwood Montell **90**

Swiftwater People: Lives of Old Timers on the Upper St. Joe & St. Maries Rivers by Bert Russell **93**

They Say in Harlan County: An Oral History by Alessandro Portelli **96**

Untold Tales, Unsung Heroes: An Oral History of Detroit's African-American Community, 1918–1967 by Elaine Latzman Moon **99**

TABLE OF CONTENTS

Voices from this Long Brown Land: Oral Recollections of Owens Valley Lives and Manzanar Pasts by Jane Wehrey **102**

Culture and Tradition

Always a People: Oral Histories of Contemporary Woodland Indians by Rita Kohn and William Lynwood Montell **107**

Black Elk Speaks: Being the Life Story of a Holy Man of the Oglala Sioux by Black Elk and John G. Neihardt **110**

Californio Voices: The Oral Memoirs of José María Amador and Lorenzo Asisara by Thomas Savage **114**

Growing Up Jewish in America by Myrna Katz Frommer and Harvey Frommer **118**

The Hispanic-American Entrepreneur: An Oral History of the American Dream by Beatrice Rodriguez Owsley **121**

In the Mansion of Confucius' Descendants: An Oral History by Kong Demao and Ke Lan **124**

Japanese War Brides in America: An Oral History by Miki Ward Crawford, Katie Kaori Hayashi, and Shizuko Suenaga **127**

Songs My Mother Sang to Me: An Oral History of Mexican American Women by Patricia Preciado Martin **131**

A Stranger's Supper: An Oral History of Centenarian Women in Montenegro by Zorka Milich **135**

Uqalurait: An Oral History of Nunavut by John Bennett and Susan Rowley **138**

When We Began, There Were Witchmen: An Oral History from Mount Kenya by Jeffrey A. Fadiman **141**

Women and Families: An Oral History, 1940–1970 by Elizabeth Roberts **144**

Women in the Chinese Enlightenment: Oral and Textual Histories by Wang Zheng **147**

Theories

Between Management and Labor: Oral Histories of Arbitration by Clara Friedman **153**

The Death of Luigi Trastulli and Other Stories by Alessandro Portelli **157**

Hard Times: An Oral History of the Great Depression by Louis "Studs" Terkel **161**

I, Rigoberta Menchú: An Indian Woman in Guatemala by Rigoberta Menchú **164**

Juan the Chamula: An Ethnological Re-creation of the Life of a Mexican Indian by Ricardo Pozas **167**

Oral History, Health and Welfare by Joanna Bornat, Robert Perks, Paul Thompson, and Jan Walmsley **170**

Oral History Theory by Lynn Abrams **173**

Popular Memory: Theory, Politics, Method by Popular Memory Group **176**

A Shared Authority: Essays on the Craft and Meaning of Oral and Public History by Michael Frisch **179**

The Story of a Shipwrecked Sailor by Gabriel García Márquez **183**

The Voice of the Past: Oral History by Paul Thompson **186**

Women's Words: The Feminist Practice of Oral History by Sherna Berger Gluck and Daphne Patai **190**

War Experiences

And Justice for All: An Oral History of the Japanese American Detention Camps by John Tateishi **195**

Bloods: An Oral History of the Vietnam War by Black Veterans by Wallace Terry **199**

Carrier Warfare in the Pacific: An Oral History Collection by E. T. Wooldridge **202**

El Salvador at War: An Oral History of Conflict from the 1979 Insurrection to the Present by Max G. Manwaring and Court Prisk **205**

Everything We Had: An Oral History of the Vietnam War by Al Santoli **209**

"The Good War": An Oral History of World War II by Louis "Studs" Terkel **212**

Japan at War: An Oral History by Haruko Taya Cook and Theodore F. Cook **215**

Memoirs of Fatemeh Pakravan by Habib Ladjevardi **218**

The Strength Not to Fight: An Oral History of Conscientious Objectors of the Vietnam War by James W. Tollefson **221**

The Unknown Internment: An Oral History of the Relocation of Italian Americans during World War II by Stephen Fox **224**

"We Have Just Begun to Not Fight": An Oral History of Conscientious Objectors in Civilian Public Service during World War II by Heather T. Frazer and John O'Sullivan **227**

What Was Asked of Us: An Oral History of the Iraq War by the Soldiers Who Fought It by Trish Wood **231**

The World at War by Richard Holmes **234**

Witnessing History

Children of Los Alamos: An Oral History of the Town Where the Atomic Bomb Began by Katrina Mason **239**

Country of My Skull: Guilt, Sorrow, and the Limits of Forgiveness in the New South Africa by Antjie Krog **242**

The Firm: The Inside Story of the Stasi by Gary Bruce **245**

Freedom Flyers: The Tuskegee Airmen of World War II by J. Todd Moye **248**

An Ill-Fated People: Zimbabwe before and after Rhodes by Lawrence Chinyani Vambe **251**

Launching the War on Poverty: An Oral History by Michael L. Gillette **254**

Machete Season: The Killers in Rwanda Speak by Jean Hatzfeld **257**

An Oral History of Abraham Lincoln: John G. Nicolay's Interviews and Essays by Michael Burlingame **261**

The Order Has Been Carried Out: History, Memory, and Meaning of a Nazi Massacre in Rome by Alessandro Portelli **265**

Peacework: Oral Histories of Women Peace Activists by Judith Porter Adams **268**

Shattered Dreams?: An Oral History of the South African AIDS Epidemic by Gerald M. Oppenheimer and Ronald Bayer **272**

Strange Ground: Americans in Vietnam 1945–1975: An Oral History by Harry Maurer **275**

Tears before the Rain: An Oral History of the Fall of South Vietnam by Larry Engelmann **279**

Voices from Chernobyl: The Oral History of a Nuclear Disaster by Svetlana Alexievich **282**

Voices from the Whirlwind: An Oral History of the Chinese Cultural Revolution by Feng Jicai **287**

The Witch Purge of 1878: Oral and Documentary History in the Early Navajo Reservation Years by Martha Blue **290**

Witnesses to Nuremberg: An Oral History of American Participants at the War Crimes Trials by Bruce M. Stave, Michele Palmer, and Leslie Frank **293**

Work and Family Life

Chinese Lives: An Oral History of Contemporary China by Zhang Xinxin and Sang Ye **299**

The First Agraristas: An Oral History of a Mexican Agrarian Reform Movement by Ann L. Craig **302**

Grandmothers, Mothers, and Daughters: Oral Histories of Three Generations of Ethnic American Women by Corinne Azen Krause **305**

Habits of Change: An Oral History of American Nuns by Carole Garibaldi Rogers **308**

Hooligans or Rebels?: An Oral History of Working-Class Childhood and Youth, 1889–1939 by Stephen Humphries **311**

Irish Days: Oral Histories of the Twentieth Century by Margaret Hickey **315**

Left Handed, Son of Old Man Hat: A Navajo Autobiography by Left Handed and Walter Dyk **318**

Let Me Speak!: Testimony of Domitila, a Woman of the Bolivian Mines by Moema Viezzer and Domitila Barrios de Chungara **322**

Long Journey Home: Oral Histories of Contemporary Delaware Indians by James W. Brown and Rita T. Kohn **325**

Solidarity Forever: An Oral History of the IWW by Stewart Bird, Dan Georgakas, and Deborah Shaffer **328**

Soviet Baby Boomers: An Oral History of Russia's Cold War Generation by Donald J. Raleigh **331**

Warlpiri Women's Voices: Our Lives, Our History by Petronella Vaarzon-Morel **334**

Women in the Mines: Stories of Life and Work by Marat Moore **337**

Workers of the Donbass Speak: Survival and Identity in the New Ukraine, 1989–1992 by Lewis H. Siegelbaum and Daniel J. Walkowitz **340**

Working: People Talk about What They Do All Day and How They Feel about What They Do by Louis "Studs" Terkel **343**

Subject Index **347**

Author Index **457**

Title Index **461**

INTRODUCTION

An autobiographical narrative is an account by the teller of some aspect of his or her life. Yet beneath this overarching definition lie myriad variations upon a theme. For the modern reader the best-known manifestations of the genre are book-length memoirs or autobiographies. Their authors usually feel that they have something significant to say about their private experiences or that their role as witnesses to moments in history merits permanent record. Classic instances, covered in the *Autobiography and Memoir* volume of *The Literature of Autobiographical Narrative,* include Rosa Parks's *My Story* (1992). Parks propelled herself into fame in 1955 when she, an African American, refused to give up her bus seat to a white passenger. As a resident of Montgomery, Alabama, she was subject to the legally legitimatized system of segregation enforced in virtually all parts of the southern states of the United States. Her memoir covers that incident and also offers an account of her early life of subjection and injustice and provides readers with an insight into the growth of the civil rights movement, in which she became an activist.

Generically, Vladimir Nabokov's *Speak, Memory* (1951) belongs in the same category as Parks's book, but it is difficult to conceive of two more contrasting volumes. Nabokov is best known for *Lolita* (1955), a controversial novel narrated by a self-confessed pedophile who spends most of the book reflecting upon his obsession with the eponymous schoolgirl, but *Speak, Memory,* ostensibly at least, is not concerned with its author's career as a novelist. It covers the first four decades of his life, in which he witnessed some of the key transformative events in European history, notably, as a child, the Bolshevik Revolution (1917) in his native Russia. In this respect Nabokov and Parks might seem, as autobiographers, similarly motivated. Despite the significance of what they experienced, however, they differ radically in the telling of their stories. As an author, Parks is largely unobtrusive and transparent, allowing where possible the events of her life to bear witness to their political and emotional resonance. For Parks, memory and history are indistinguishable. Nabokov, on the other hand, writes about his life in much the same way that, as a novelist, he would describe the worlds of his inventions. At one point he tells of how the Russian Imperial Minister of War, Aleksey Kuropatkin, a friend of the Nabokov family, would amuse young Vladimir with a trick involving a match box; Nabokov then connects this anecdote with the story of Kuropatkin, now in disguise and on the run from the Bolsheviks, surreptitiously asking his father for a light. Nabokov does not alter the facts; rather, he believes that memory should be treated as a series of episodes that depend as much upon the impressions of their perceiver for significance as upon objective description.

Maya Angelou's autobiography *I Know Why the Caged Bird Sings* (1969) should, we might assume, have more in common with Parks's than Nabokov's book: it is the searingly honest story of her own experiences of racist violence and oppression in the American South. However, it is celebrated as much for its formal literary qualities as for its revelations. Angelou's manner of relating her shared history lends the latter a special degree of vividness and durability, and in this respect Angelou invites comparison with Nabokov. Like both, Tepilit Ole Scitoti, in *The World of a Maasai Warrior* (1986), wraps an emotionally charged autobiography—specifically its author's crossing of the boundary between precolonial African tribal existence and Western society—in a text that bears a close resemblance to what we expect of fiction: dialogue, historical narrative and myth are blended in a less than predictable manner.

Such variations in manner and theme reflect the richness and diversity of autobiography as a genre, in terms of both its informative, even educational, power and its strength as a literary form in its own right. How, then, should we classify Adolf Hitler's *Mein Kamf* (1925) in relation to the books so far mentioned? In order to qualify for inclusion and coverage in these volumes, a work must at least enlighten us as to the mindset of its author and the circumstances that led to its composition. The fact is that were it not for Hitler's hideous acts and legacy subsequent to the publication of *Mein Kamf* the book would have disappeared from the landscape of twentieth century history of writing. It is poorly written, its author is at time deranged in his avowed worship of the Aryan race, and its purely autobiographical passages are littered with stories that have since been proved to be exaggerations at best and often outright falsehoods. Its endurance as a "significant" autobiographical work has been ensured by events that no sane or decent person would have wished upon those affected by them. Here we come upon the uniqueness and importance of autobiographical narrative. Hitler's book might well be a compendium of half-truths and evil avocations, but it adds something to our knowledge of how a particularly foul individual came to power and wreaked havoc on the world. Like every work covered in these volumes, it carries a trace of our past and in particular the imprint of its author's involvement therein.

The second volume of *The Literature of Autobiographical Narrative* covers diaries and letters. The most obvious difference between these and autobiography is that while virtually all of the latter are addressed to a general readership, the former are works generally underpinned by a notion of confidentiality, privacy or intimacy. In this regard the diary is a particularly troubling genre. It is, by its nature, a record—often a day-to-day record—of its author's activities, some of them utterly mundane, that typically contains observations on the events and moods of his or her world. The motive or impulse behind the keeping of a diary remains a matter for speculation, but most would agree that it is a private endeavor with the author also its single reader (though intimate friends or family members have on occasions been allowed access to entries). We might, therefore, expect from such documents a different level of candor than is generally found in autobiographies intended for publication. It is not that authors of the latter deliberately set out to mislead—with the exception of figures such as Hitler—but rather that, even in unadorned acts of truth-telling such as Parks's *My Story,* there is a degree of performance. Honesty might be maintained but consideration is also given to the experience of the reader. Diaries, being designed for self-consumption, carry no such responsibilities.

Two of the best-known early-modern examples of the form are *The Diary of John Evelyn* (1818) and *The Diary of Samuel Pepys* (1825). Both are treated an invaluable insights into the events and mannerisms of mid-to-late seventeenth-century Britain. The period involved momentous occurrences, most notably the Civil War, the execution of Charles I, the establishment of the first modern European republic and the Restoration of the Monarchy. The printing press was more than a century old, and for the first time in history an abundance of documents, including government statements, manifestos, and declarations by individuals with an interest in the future of society, became available for later scrutiny by historians. Evelyn and Pepys provide an invaluable supplement to the largely impersonal evidence of print, taking us on a tour of their particular worlds, from what they wore and ate to their encounters with epoch-making events; Evelyn's account of the return of the monarch, Charles II, to London contains everything from the minutiae of the floral decorations to his own understated reflections on the significance of the day. Diaries bridge the divide between introspective impressionistic records of a time and a state of mind—so often lacking in works intended for publication—and a more objective conception of a historical milieu. Diaries and notebooks are immensely important too in our broader appreciation of how writers work. Even if in, for instance, Joseph Conrad's *Congo Diary* (1952), there is little direct reference to how his experience influenced his fiction, the implied connections are self-evident.

We should, however, deal cautiously with the commonplace assumption that the diary is always an impeccably candid record of its author's thoughts and impressions. That Evelyn's and Pepys's works did not go into print until over a century after they had been completed would seem to testify to both men's sense of them as private documents. Yet it is possible to imagine that Anne Frank, hiding from the Nazis, harbored a sense of duty to those who would later try to document the horrors of World War II. Even if, as she feared, she would not live to adulthood, perhaps she hoped that her words would survive as a record of a fate she shared with so many others. The same can be said of Victor Klemperer as he composed his *Diary of the Nazi Years* (1995). In a different context George Gissing, who was at the center of the thriving cultural and literary life of Victorian England, was surely not so naïve as to believe that his *Diary* would remain forever untouched and unpublished.

The letter involves a different level of candor in that, once the piece is dispatched, the recipient is trusted as its sole reader, but in this respect correspondence can be just as revealing as the private diary or notebook. Sylvia Plath's *Letters Home* (1975), mostly addressed to her mother, tells us more about her state of distress and her sense of vocation as a writer than anything primarily intended for publication.

The third volume of *The Literature of Autobiographical Narrative* covers oral histories, and the best introduction to this complex means of recording and preserving the past is Lynn Abrams's *Oral History Theory* (2010). Abrams examines the tendentious issues that surround the collecting of oral histories, principally the implicit tension between a voluntary spoken testimony and the role of the person who asks questions, edits, and coordinates this material: how much does the latter impose upon the former? One of the most famous nonacademic examples of the form is Ronald Blythe's *Akenfield: Portrait of an English Village* (1969), in which Blythe attempts to capture life in a fictionalized rural English community through a set of interviews with individuals such as farmworkers and blacksmiths who have known of little more than their immediate environment since the nineteenth century. Blythe's *Akenfield* is not a real village but a fictionalized composite based on interviews with residents of various villages. Although he does his best to remain in the background, Blythe's editorial approach has led critics to wonder to what extent the "Portrait" carries something of his influence.

Oral histories that are more rigorous than Blythe's in their maintenance of objectivity include Jeremy Seabrook's *Working-Class Childhood* (1982), in which Seabrook, as interviewer, refrains from any prompts and directions in his recordings of British working-class individuals during the late 1970s and early 1980s. As Lynn Abrams argues, however, it is virtually impossible to claim that an exercise in oral history can be a purely objective record, unaffected by the presence of the interviewer or coordinator. For example, Rhoda Lewin's *Witnesses to the Holocaust* (1991) is composed of her interviews with sixty survivors and liberators of the Nazi concentration camps. While Lewin scrupulously avoids leading her interviewees, the fact that they were all then residents of Minnesota suggests that their testimonies may have been skewed by a shared experience of the postwar years. Similarly, in Alison Baker's *Voices of Resistance: Oral Histories of Moroccan Women* (1998), women involved in the Moroccan independence movement speak freely of their personal lives, but this material is embedded in contextual information on Moroccan society, history, and politics and quotations from songs and poems, largely for the benefit of Western readers unfamiliar with the region. In this respect, then, Baker's choice and use of contextual material will in some way inevitably affect the reader's impression of the women themselves.

Esteban Montejo's *Autobiography of a Runaway Slave* (1993) originates from a series of interviews given by Montejo in 1963 to Miguel Barnet, who subsequently transcribed them as a book with the former as first-person narrator. Montejo, then aged 103, was thought to be the last surviving ex-slave on the island of Cuba; his testimony provided one final opportunity to record this period in Caribbean history. The book blurs the distinction between autobiography and oral history. One assumes that it is placed in the latter category because, without Barnet's act of recording the oral testimony, it would not exist, yet its potential status as a hybrid form makes it all the more intriguing. Once again questions arise about the concepts of fact and truth and the extent to which they are influenced by oral testimony and conventional notions of writing.

Oral history is the most complex of the three categories of autobiographical narrative and for this reason it is one of the most richly rewarding. For all of its variety, at its heart is the quintessential notion of a voice unsullied by the formalities and conventions of writing and print.

Only a few pieces covered in these three volumes predate the history of the printing press, notably St. Augustine's *Confessions* (397 CE) and Marcus Aurelius's *Meditations* (180 CE). Some, such as Marco Polo's *Travels* (c. 1300) and King Henry VI's *Literary Remains* (1549), found their way into print well within a century of their composition, but the vast majority of the pieces were either spoken, recorded, written or published during or after the seventeenth century. Autobiographical narrative, including oral history, will always owe something to the mechanism of print, including its recent electronic form, but its value as a means of understanding the human condition and permutations through ethnicity, region, history, and culture remains uncorrupted by this.

These three volumes will stand as an invaluable tool for researchers who wish to locate a starting point for a detailed scrutiny of a place, an event, or a state of mind. Their structure, including the subclassification of each of the three forms according to context and frame of reference, will assist greatly in its function as a basis for curriculum building. Each volume can serve numerous and often overlapping disciplinary roles. Writers' autobiographies, diaries, and notebooks offer invaluable insights into the relationship between private inspiration and the unfolding of literary history. Throughout, students of history, politics, and society will find testimonies to personal experience that underpin and illuminate a broader perception of our pasts and differences.

It is a unique enterprise, gathering seemingly disparate elements within a space to which all human beings will at some point commit themselves: speaking or writing to someone, even to ourselves, of our lives and experiences.

Richard Bradford

Editor's Note

The Literature of Autobiographical Narrative, a three-volume reference guide, provides critical introductions to 300 autobiographies, memoirs, diaries, letters, and oral histories. All the works are based on the lives of the authors, but a wide variety of interests and ambitions, from the personal and artistic to the historical and political, motivated writers to share their intimate and exceptional memories.

An early memoir covered in the guide is *The Travels of Marco Polo,* which recounts the journey of the Venetian explorer in the 1290s to the Far East and the court of Kublai Khan. In 1298, three years after returning from Asia, Marco Polo was captured in a battle against the Genoese. Over several months in prison, with the help of his cellmate, Rustichiello of Pisa, he wrote his travelogue, filled with exotic tales set in a faraway land, which fascinated his European audience. Other works discussed in the guide had more private goals. Edgar Allan Poe's "Letter to Maria Clemm," written to his Aunt Maria on August 29, 1835, declares his love for her thirteen-year-old daughter, Virginia, and offers financial assistance to them both. Kept from publication for more than a century by Poe's family, the letter—in particular the passionate desire Poe expresses for his young cousin (later his wife)—is fundamental to the modern understanding of Poe as a transgressor of moral boundaries. *Japanese War Brides in America* (1998), an oral history of nineteen Japanese women who married American soldiers during the post-World War II occupation of Japan, is an example of an autobiographical work for which the motivation to publish was less an author's desire for self-expression than an outsider's interest in another person's story.

The structure and content of *The Literature of Autobiographical Narrative* was planned with the help of the project's advisory board, chaired by Richard Bradford, Professor of English and Senior Distinguished Research Fellow, University of Ulster, Northern Ireland. His introduction explains some of the concerns behind the development of the guide and provides a brief overview of autobiographical genres.

ORGANIZATION

All entries share a common structure, providing consistent coverage of the works and a simple way of comparing basic elements of one text with another. Each entry has six parts: overview, historical and literary context, themes and style, critical discussion, sources, and further reading. Entries also have either an excerpt from the original text or a sidebar discussing a related topic, such as the life of the author.

The Literature of Autobiographical Narrative is divided into three volumes, each with 100 entries organized into subject-oriented sections. The sections in volume 1, *Autobiographies and Memoirs,* are Adversity and Resistance, Between Cultures, Coming of Age, Contemplation and Confession, Theories, and War Experiences. Among the works representing "adversity" is *The Story of My Life* (1903), by Helen Keller, who describes her experience being a blind and deaf child in late-nineteenth-century Alabama. Her efforts to express herself and become educated came at a time when many disabled children in the United States were considered a lost cause and institutionalized. Volume 2, *Diaries and Letters,* includes the sections Adversity and Resistance, Historical Perspectives, Literary Lives, Theories, Travel and Exploration, War Experiences, and Work and Family Life. Under "Historical Perspectives" is *Jemima Condict,* the diary of young New Jersey maid during the American Revolution who records thoughts about her family, community life, and newly independent country. The works discussed in volume 3, *Oral Histories,* stand apart from the books in the other volumes in their absence of a premeditated written structure. The volume is divided into the sections Adversity and Resistance, Communities, Culture and Tradition, Theories, War Experiences, Witnessing History, and Work and Family Life. Covered in the latter section is *Soviet Baby Boomers* (2012), in which sixty men and women from two elite Russian schools discuss their lives in the late twentieth century; a major theme of the book is remembering things from the past that state propaganda tried to conceal.

Among the criteria for selecting entry topics were the importance of the work in university and high school curricula, the genre, the region and country of the author and text, and the time period. Entries can be looked up in the author and title indexes, as well as in the subject index.

ACKNOWLEDGMENTS

Many people contributed time, effort, and ideas to *The Literature of Autobiographical Narrative.* At Gale, Philip Virta, manager of new products, developed the original plan for the book, and Andrea Henderson, senior editor, served as the in-house manager for the project. *The Literature of Autobiographical Narrative* owes its existence to their ideas and involvement.

We would like to express our appreciation to the advisors, who, in addition to creating the organization of *The Literature of Autobiographical Narrative* and choosing the entry topics, identified other scholars to work on the project and answered many questions, both big and small. We would also like to thank the contributors for their accessible essays, often on difficult topics, as well as the scholars who reviewed the text for accuracy and coverage.

I am grateful to Greta Gard, project editor, and Erin Brown, senior project editor, especially for their work with the advisors and on the entry list; Mary Beth Curran, associate editor, who oversaw the editing process; David Hayes, associate editor, whose many contributions included organizing the workflow; and Hannah Soukup, assistant editor, who identified and corresponded with the academic reviewers. Other important assistance came from Mariko Fujinaka, managing editor; Anne Healey, senior editor; and Janet Moredock and Lee Esbenshade, associate editors. The line editors were Cheryl Collins, Chuong-Dai Vo, Constance Israel, Donna Polydoros, Harrabeth Haidusek, Holli Fort, Jane Kupersmith, Jill Oldham, Joan Hibler, Kathy Wilson Peacock, Kerri Kennedy, Laura Gabler, Lisa Trow, Natalie Ruppert, Tony Craine, and Will Wagner.

Thomas Riggs

CONTRIBUTORS

DAVID AITCHISON
Aitchison is a PhD candidate in literary studies and a university instructor.

GREG BACH
Bach holds an MA in classics and is a freelance writer.

KATHERINE BARKER
Barker has an MA in English literature.

CRAIG BARNES
Barnes holds an MFA in creative writing and has been a university instructor and a freelance writer.

KATHERINE BISHOP
Bishop is a PhD student in English literature and has been a university instructor.

ALLISON BLECKER
Blecker is a PhD candidate in Near Eastern languages.

WESLEY BORUCKI
Borucki holds a PhD in American history and is a university professor.

GERALD CARPENTER
Carpenter holds an MA in U.S. intellectual history and a PhD in early modern French history. He is a freelance writer.

ALEX COVALCIUC
Covalciuc is a PhD candidate in English literature. He has been a university instructor and a freelance writer.

JENNY DALE
Dale holds an MFA in creative writing and has been a university instructor.

FARNOOSH FATHI
Fathi has a PhD in English literature and creative writing and has been a university instructor.

JEN GANN
Gann holds an MFA in creative writing and has been a university instructor.

DAISY GARD
Gard is a freelance writer with a background in English literature.

GRETA GARD
Gard is a PhD candidate in English literature and has been a university instructor and a freelance writer.

TINA GIANOULIS
Gianoulis is a freelance writer with a background in English literature.

CYNTHIA GILES
Giles holds an MA in English literature and a PhD in interdisciplinary humanities. She has been a university instructor and a freelance writer.

KRISTEN GLEASON
Gleason holds an MFA in creative writing and has been a university instructor.

NICOLE GRANT
Grant holds an MA in English and has been a university instructor.

QUAN MANH HA
Ha holds a PhD in American literature and is a university professor.

IRENE HSIAO
Hsiao has a PhD in literature and has been a university instructor.

FRANKLIN HYDE
Hyde holds a PhD in English literature and is a university instructor.

ANNA IOANES
Ioanes is a PhD student in English language and literature and has been a university instructor.

LAURA JOHNSON
Johnson holds a PhD in English and has been a university instructor.

EMILY JONES
Jones holds an MFA in creative writing and has been a university instructor.

ALICIA KENT
Kent holds a PhD in English literature and is a university professor.

KRISTIN KING-RIES
King-Ries holds an MFA in creative writing and has been a university instructor.

LISE LALONDE
LaLonde holds MAs in English literature and translation and has been a university instructor.

GREGORY LUTHER
Luther holds an MFA in creative writing and has been a university instructor and freelance writer.

KATIE MACNAMARA
Macnamara holds a PhD in English literature and has been a university instructor.

MAGGIE MAGNO
Magno has an MA in education. She has been a high school English teacher and a freelance writer.

xix

CONTRIBUTORS

ABIGAIL MANN
Mann holds a PhD in English literature and is a university professor.

EMILY MANN
Mann has an MA in library and information science.

THEODORE MCDERMOTT
McDermott holds an MFA in creative writing and has been a university instructor and a freelance writer.

LISA MERTEL
Mertel holds an MA in library science and an MA in history.

RACHEL MINDELL
Mindell holds an MFA in creative writing and has been a freelance writer.

JIM MLADENOVIC
Mladenovic holds an MS in clinical psychology and is pursuing an MA in library science.

KATHRYN MOLINARO
Molinaro holds an MA in English literature and has been a university instructor and a freelance writer.

CAITIE MOORE
Moore holds an MFA in creative writing and has been a university instructor.

ROBIN MORRIS
Morris holds a PhD in English literature and has been a university instructor.

JANET MULLANE
Mullane is a freelance writer and has been a high school English teacher.

ELLIOTT NIBLOCK
Niblock holds an MTS in the philosophy of religion.

KATRINA OKO-ODOI
Oko-Odoi is a PhD candidate in Spanish language and literature and a university instructor.

JAMES OVERHOLTZER
Overholtzer holds an MA in English literature and has been a university instructor.

IOANA PATULEANU
Patuleanu holds a PhD in English literature and has been a university instructor.

EVELYN REYNOLDS
Reynolds is pursuing an MA in English literature and an MFA in creative writing and has been a freelance writer.

CHRIS ROUTLEDGE
Routledge holds a PhD in English literature and is a university lecturer and a freelance writer.

REBECCA RUSTIN
Rustin holds an MA in English literature and is a freelance writer.

ANTHONY RUZICKA
Ruzicka is pursuing an MFA in poetry and has worked as a university instructor.

CATHERINE E. SAUNDERS
Saunders holds a PhD in English literature and is a university professor.

CARINA SAXON
Saxon is a PhD candidate in English literature and has been a university instructor and a freelance editor.

JACOB SCHMITT
Schmitt holds an MA in English literature and has been a freelance writer.

NANCY SIMPSON-YOUNGER
Simpson-Younger is a PhD candidate in literary studies and a university instructor.

CLAIRE SKINNER
Skinner holds an MFA in creative writing and is a university instructor.

ROGER SMITH
Smith has an MA in media ecology and has been a university instructor and a freelance writer.

NICHOLAS SNEAD
Snead is a PhD candidate in French language and literature and has been a university instructor.

SARAH STOECKL
Stoeckl holds a PhD in English literature and is a university instructor and a freelance writer.

PAMELA TOLER
Toler has a PhD in history and is a freelance writer and former university instructor.

GRACE WAITMAN
Waitman is pursuing a PhD in educational psychology. She holds an MA in English literature and has been a university instructor.

ALLYNA WARD
Ward holds a PhD in English literature and is a university professor.

JENNA WILLIAMS
Williams holds an MFA in creative writing and has been a university instructor and a freelance writer.

 Academic Reviewers

BARBARA ALLEN
Associate Professor of History, La Salle University, Philadelphia, Pennsylvania.

KHALED AL-MASRI
Assistant Professor of Arabic, Swarthmore College, Swarthmore, Pennsylvania.

HOLLY ARROW
Professor of Psychology, Institute of Cognitive and Decision Sciences, University of Oregon, Eugene.

STEPHEN BEHRENDT
George Holmes Distinguished Professor of English, University of Nebraska-Lincoln.

WILLIAM BELDING
Professorial Lecturer, School of International Service, American University, Washington, D.C.

AMY BELL
Associate Professor of History, Huron University College, London, Ontario, Canada.

ALAN L. BERGER
Raddock Family Eminent Scholar Chair in Holocaust Studies; Professor of Jewish Studies, English Department; Director, the Center for the Study of Values and Violence after Auschwitz, Florida Atlantic University, Boca Raton.

MOULAY-ALI BOUÂNANI
Professor of Africana Studies, Binghamton University-State University of New York, Vestal.

CLAIRE BOYLE
Lecturer in French, University of Edinburgh, United Kingdom.

MICHAEL BREEN
Associate Professor of History and Humanities, Reed College, Portland, Oregon.

GERRY CANAVAN
Assistant Professor of English, Marquette University, Milwaukee, Wisconsin.

NATHAN CLARKE
Assistant Professor of History, Minnesota State University Moorhead.

WILLIAM CLEMENTE
Professor of Literature, Peru State College, Peru, Nebraska.

MARC CONNER
Ballengee Professor of English, Washington and Lee University, Lexington, Virginia.

JANE CRAWFORD
Faculty, History and Political Science Department, Mount St. Mary's College, Los Angeles, California.

SONJA DARLINGTON
Professor of Education and Youth Studies, Beloit College, Beloit, Wisconsin.

GABRIELE DILLMANN
Associate Professor of German, Denison University, Granville, Ohio.

JEANNE DUBINO
Professor of English and Global Studies, Appalachian State University, Boone, North Carolina.

ELIZABETH DUQUETTE
Associate Professor of English, Gettysburg College, Gettysburg, Pennsylvania.

BREANNE FAHS
Associate Professor of Women and Gender Studies, Arizona State University West, Glendale.

DANINE FARQUHARSON
Associate Professor of English, Memorial University of Newfoundland, St. John's.

LUANNE FRANK
Associate Professor of English, University of Texas at Arlington.

GREGORY FRASER
Professor of English, University of West Georgia, Carrollton.

JAMES GIGANTINO
Assistant Professor of History, University of Arkansas at Fayetteville.

QUAN MANH HA
Assistant Professor of American Literature and Ethnic Studies, University of Montana, Missoula.

KEVIN J. HAYES
Professor of English, University of Central Oklahoma, Edmond.

RICHARD HIGGINS
Lecturer in English, Franklin College, Franklin, Indiana.

NELS HIGHBERG
Associate Professor and Chair of Rhetoric and Professional Writing Department, University of Hartford, West Hartford, Connecticut.

xxi

ACADEMIC REVIEWERS

WALTER HÖLBLING
Professor of American Studies, Karl-Franzens-Universität Graz, Austria.

FRANKLYN HYDE
Adjunct Professor of English, University of Manitoba, Winnipeg.

PETER IVERSON
Regents' Professor of History, Arizona State University, Tempe.

KELLY JEONG
Assistant Professor of Comparative Literature and Korean Studies, University of California, Riverside.

A. YEMISI JIMOH
Professor of African American Literature and Culture, University of Massachusetts Amherst.

JEFFREY W. JONES
Associate Professor of History, University of North Carolina at Greensboro.

ALICIA A. KENT
Associate Professor of English, University of Michigan-Flint.

CHRISTOPHER KNIGHT
Professor of English, University of Montana, Missoula.

LEAH KNIGHT
Associate Professor of Literature, Brock University, St. Catharines, Ontario.

MARY LARSON
President of Oral History Association; Head of Oklahoma Oral History Research Program, Oklahoma State University, Stillwater.

CHANA KAI LEE
Associate Professor of History and of the Institute for African American Studies, University of Georgia, Athens.

WEIJING LU
Associate Professor of History, University of California, San Diego, La Jolla.

CAROL MACKAY
Professor of English, University of Texas at Austin.

BRIDGET MARSHALL
Associate Professor and Associate Chair of English Department, University of Massachusetts Lowell.

MARIA DEL CARMEN MARTINEZ
Assistant Professor of English, University of Wisconsin-Parkside.

LUCINDA MCCRAY
Professor and Chair of History Department, Appalachian State University, Boone, North Carolina.

CAROL MCFREDERICK
Adjunct Instructor of English, Florida International University, Miami.

GORDON MCKINNEY
Professor Emeritus, Berea College, Berea, Kentucky.

LAURIE MERCIER
Professor of History, Washington State University, Vancouver.

DANIEL METRAUX
Professor of Asian Studies, Mary Baldwin College, Staunton, Virginia.

GENEVA COBB MOORE
Professor of English and Women's Studies, University of Wisconsin-Whitewater.

EARL MULDERINK
Professor of History, Southern Utah University, Cedar City.

SHAKIR MUSTAFA
Visiting Associate Professor of Arabic, Northeastern University, Boston, Massachusetts.

SEIWOONG OH
Professor and Chair of English Department, Rider University, Lawrenceville, New Jersey.

MICHEL PHARAND
Director of the Disraeli Project, Queen's University, Kingston, Ontario, Canada.

JANET POWERS
Professor Emerita of Interdisciplinary Studies and Women, Gender, and Sexuality Studies, Gettysburg College, Gettysburg, Pennsylvania.

JOHN R. REED
Distinguished Professor of English, Wayne State University, Detroit, Michigan.

PATRICIO RIZZO-VAST
Instructor of Spanish and Portuguese, Northeastern Illinois University, Chicago.

ASHRAF RUSHDY
Professor and Chair of African American Studies Program; Professor of English, Wesleyan University, Middletown, Connecticut.

ANDRE SIMIĆ
Professor of Anthropology, University of Southern California, Los Angeles.

CARL SMELLER
Associate Professor of English and Humanities, Texas Wesleyan University, Fort Worth.

MARY ZEISS STANGE
Professor of Women's Studies and Religion, Skidmore College, Saratoga Springs, New York.

REBECCA JANE STANTON
Assistant Professor of Russian, Barnard College, New York, New York.

RICHARD STOFFLE
Professor of Anthropology, University of Arizona, Tucson.

BILINDA STRAIGHT
Professor of Anthropology, Western Michigan University, Kalamazoo.

GWEN TARBOX
Associate Professor of English, Western Michigan University, Kalamazoo.

BARBARA TRUESDELL
Assistant Director of the Center for the Study of History and Memory, Indiana University, Bloomington.

CHUONG-DAI VO
Visiting Scholar, Foreign Language and Literatures, Massachusetts Institute of Technology, Cambridge.

ALLYNA E. WARD
Assistant Professor of English, Booth University College, Winnipeg, Manitoba.

RICHARD WEIKART
Professor of History, California State University-Stanislaus, Turlock.

ACADEMIC REVIEWERS

DOROTHY WILLS
Professor of Anthropology, California State Polytechnic University, Pomona.

MICHAEL WILSON
Associate Professor of English, University of Wisconsin-Milwaukee.

SIMONA WRIGHT
Professor and Director of Italian Program, The College of New Jersey, Ewing.

PRISCILLA YBARRA
Assistant Professor of English, University of North Texas, Denton.

GERALD ZAHAVI
Professor of History; Director of Documentary Studies Program, University at Albany-State University of New York.

PIERANTONIO ZANOTTI
Adjunct Professor of Japanese Language, Università Ca' Foscari Venezia, Italy.

Adversity and Resistance

Anarchist Voices: An Oral History of Anarchism in America by Paul Avrich	3
Biography of a Runaway Slave by Miguel Barnet and Esteban Montejo	7
Bitter Water: Diné Oral Histories of the Navajo-Hopi Land Dispute by Malcolm D. Benally	10
Exodus to Shanghai: Stories of Escape from the Third Reich by Steve Hochstadt	14
Gulag Voices: Oral Histories of Soviet Incarceration and Exile by Jehanne M. Gheith and Katherine R. Jolluck	17
Head of the Class: An Oral History of African American Achievement in Higher Education and Beyond by Gabrielle Morris	20
The History of Mary Prince, a West Indian Slave, Related by Herself by Mary Prince	23
Ireland's Unfinished Revolution: An Oral History by Kenneth Griffith and Timothy O'Grady	27
Massacre in Mexico by Elena Poniatowska	31
Mothers, Sisters, Resisters: Oral Histories of Women Who Survived the Holocaust by Brana Gurewitsch	34
Nisa: The Life and Words of a !Kung Woman by Marjorie Shostak	37
Survivors: An Oral History of the Armenian Genocide by Donald E. Miller and Lorna Touryan Miller	40
Voices of Freedom: An Oral History of the Civil Rights Movement from the 1950s through the 1980s by Henry Hampton and Steve Fayer	44
Voices of Resistance: Oral Histories of Moroccan Women by Alison Baker	47
Witnesses to the Holocaust: An Oral History by Rhoda Lewin	50
Working-Class Childhood: An Oral History by Jeremy Seabrook	53

Anarchist Voices
An Oral History of Anarchism in America
Paul Avrich

OVERVIEW

Anarchist Voices: An Oral History of Anarchism in America (1995) comprises 180 interviews on the American anarchist movement of the late nineteenth and early twentieth centuries collected between 1963 and 1991 by historian Paul Avrich. Avrich, who was a leading scholar of the anarchist movement during its heyday, interviewed fifty-three individuals, many more than once. When possible he spoke with surviving anarchists in the United States who had been active between 1880 and 1930, supplementing firsthand reports with interviews with the anarchists' families and their associates. Many of the interviewees are immigrants of European descent, and more than half are Jewish—factors representational of the anarchist movement's popularity in the United States. The interviews are organized roughly into six categories: Pioneers; Emma Goldman; Sacco and Vanzetti; Schools and Colonies; Ethnic Anarchists; and the 1920s and After. In all, Avrich attempts to expand popular understanding of anarchists and anarchism, depicting both as more human and less abstract than they are commonly understood to be.

Avrich secured many varied perspectives on the anarchist movement as recalled by participants and those around them before they died, and critics lauded his creation of a collection that captures a hitherto unrecorded personal side. *Anarchist Voices* continues to be an important reference for historians of anarchism.

HISTORICAL AND LITERARY CONTEXT

Anarchist Voices reflects upon the recollections of and about activists primarily concerned with liberties, the treatment of workers, and class-based discrimination in the United States. Many of the anarchists whom Avrich interviewed extended ideas such as Jean-Jacques Rousseau's Enlightenment-era thoughts on freedom and French Revolutionists' demands for equality, brotherhood, and liberty. Events such as the assemblage of the International Workingmen's Association in 1864, too, spurred workers to greater solidarity and also influenced the developing school of anarchist thought.

The central participants in Avrich's book were active from the end of the nineteenth century through the first few decades of the twentieth century, when the anarchist movement was at its peak in the United States. He dates the time period of key activity for his subjects from the Paris Commune of 1871 to the end of the Spanish Revolution of the 1930s. Unprecedented immigration levels, increasing mobility for people and ideas, and heightened levels of totalitarianism across the world contributed to the growth of anarchism in the United States during this period. Anarchism dropped off as the designation began to be associated with terrorism, as immigration levels lowered, as the quality of life improved for citizens and immigrants in the United States, and as the majority of industrialized nations entered World War I and then World War II.

Anarchist Voices stands alone as a collection of oral histories of anarchists, though it joins works such as Daniel Guérin's *No Gods, No Masters* (1970) in presenting compilations of primary documents pertaining to the anarchist movement, as well as a number of memoirs written by individual anarchists. Notable among the latter is Goldman's two-volume autobiography *Living My Life* (1931). Already known as one of the top historians of anarchism, Avrich, before producing *Anarchist Voices,* had previously published six other well-regarded works, including *The Haymarket Tragedy* (1984), *Anarchist Portraits* (1988), and *Sacco and Vanzetti: The Anarchist Background* (1991).

Anarchist Voices remains the only oral history of the early anarchist movement in the United States, as well as a popular reference for later historians of anarchism. After its publication, Avrich continued to contribute to the field of anarchist history, though he returned to the more conventional history based on the documentary evidence that he favored. At his behest, Avrich's daughter Karen finished his final project after his death in 2006, publishing *Sasha and Emma: The Anarchist Odyssey of Alexander Berkman and Emma Goldman* in 2012.

THEMES AND STYLE

The central theme of *Anarchist Voices* is to show the anarchists' perspectives and their humanity. In doing this, Avrich extends the common conceptions of the anarchist movement, expanding the repertoire of

❖ Key Facts

Time Period:
Late 19th to Early 20th Century

Relevant Historical Events:
Paris Commune of 1871; Spanish Revolution in 1931; growth of anarchism in the United States

Nationality:
American

Keywords:
anarchism; industrialization; immigration

ADVERSITY AND RESISTANCE

"The Only Form of Trial That Would Satisfy the Chicago Anarchists -- A Trial by a Court of Their Peers," a political cartoon by Frederick Opper, *Puck* magazine, 1886. After the Haymarket Riot in Chicago in 1886, eight anarchists were put on trial, and seven of those were sentenced to death. The satirical illustration depicts how the trial might have looked if it had been conducted by anarchists instead of according to the rule of law. © THE ART ARCHIVE AT ART RESOURCE, NY

known players and their legacies. He writes, "Of all the major movements of social reform, anarchism has been subject to the grossest misunderstandings of its nature and objectives. No group has been more maligned and misrepresented by the authorities or more feared and detested by the public." Avrich suggests that aspects of anarchists' lives, such as their entertainments, literature, education, and community, have become overshadowed by their stigmatization as terrorists—obfuscations he set out to rectify in the volume.

As he maintains at the book's outset, Avrich began interviewing anarchists and those who knew them to capture previously unknown elements of the movement that had few other personal records. Each of the six sections begins with a historical note, and each entry—an edited transcription of compiled interviews—is preceded by a short biography and information on where and when the interview(s) took place. Avrich gave little information about the interviews themselves, though he did include many of the questions he asked in the preface, such as what kind of people the anarchists were, what motivated them

to align themselves with the movement, what they gained from it, how they participated in anarchism, how they dealt with its stigmatization, and how they felt about the anarchist movement in hindsight. Commenting that Avrich relies heavily on his own previous work on subjects related to the section topics, Steven Biel claims in his 1995 analysis in *Reviews in American History* that "on a number of occasions, it becomes evident that these interviews were not intended for an oral history; they were conducted to seek specific information for whatever book Avrich was working on at the time." However, Biel acknowledges that "most of the interviews are fluid and expansive despite the research agendas that helped shape them."

The language in *Anarchist Voices* is kept to standard English without dialect or foreign phrasing, despite the fact that many of Avrich's subjects were foreign-born and of advanced age and, as Avrich wrote in the book's preface, "a few [interviews] were in other languages, or in a mixture of languages, since the interviewees … sometimes lapsed into their native tongues." It is clear that Avrich smoothed and edited his transcriptions of single and multiple interviews into coherent narratives, though he does not discuss how or to what extent he edited the transcriptions or amended translations. This standardization coheres the interviews, lending them a stylistic unification that emphasizes the commonalities of the subjects rather than highlighting their differences.

CRITICAL DISCUSSION

Anarchist Voices was widely and positively reviewed upon its publication. Most reviewers agreed with Avrich's comment in the preface that the book was "in many ways … the most important" he had ever worked on. Bob Jones, writing for *Oral History Society* in 1996, observes that the book is "not only, as Avrich hopes, 'an invaluable source for all future students of anarchism,' but a potent inspiration to anarchists and libertarians everywhere." Gerald Sorin agrees, calling *Anarchist Voices* "a treasure trove of sources not only for students of anarchism but also for those interested in the history of labor, education, immigration, and ethics politics" in his review in *Journal of American Ethnic History*. Hugh Wilford adds in the *Journal of American Studies* that "as a documentary guide to American anarchism in its heyday it is matchless."

Reprinted in 2005 by AK Press, the collectively run anarchist and radical publisher, *Anarchist Voices* has continued to hold its place as the premier work on the early American anarchist movement, adding a "human dimension often lacking in scholarly monographs, not to mention the accounts of journalists, policemen, and officials, and of other, for the most part hostile, observers." Many scholars have appreciated Avrich's wide embrasure of the movement's social and cultural elements and have been inspired to continue looking at the broad, often excluded dimensions of anarchism. Biel writes that Avrich's collection "shows people living history in the fullest sense, struggling to be its subjects, even in small ways, rather than its objects alone," finding that the many voices Avrich included "challenge or complicate historical generalizations." Biel is particularly interested in how Avrich recovers the often unmentioned aspects of the anarchists' "alternative society" surrounding their movement, indicated in the schools, social activities, and literary world that the interviews frequently discuss.

Since its publication, scholars have relied on *Anarchist Voices* for its rare perspectives, though the work has been little analyzed in its own right. It has served as an invaluable reference for those who continue to study the golden age of American anarchism. Tom Goyens's *Beer and Revolution: The German Anarchist Movement in New York City, 1880–1914* (2007), which deals heavily with the connections between anarchism and the lifestyle surrounding it; studies of particular anarchists such as Nunzio Pernicone's *Carlo Tresca: Portrait of a Rebel* (2010); and Jennifer Guglielmo's *Living the Revolution: Italian Women's Resistance and Radicalism in New York* (2012) are just a few of many recent works that cite Avrich's collection of oral histories and that continue *Anarchist Voices*' work of including human elements in the history of anarchism.

SOCIAL CHANGE THROUGH EDUCATIONAL REFORM

In his interview with Paul Avrich, anarchist Valerio Isca reported, "For me anarchism is mainly a question of education." Like Isca, anarchist thinkers William Godwin, Emma Goldman, Francesco Ferrer, and Mikhail Bakunin believed education was paramount to their endeavors. Many argued that traditional schools socialized children to accept rather than question social inequalities and authorities, contending that revolutionizing schools was as vital to counteracting an early inculcation of conformity as to finally succeeding in creating widespread social change.

Modern schools, also known as free schools, were central to the anarchist movement's plan for long-term success in eradicating oppression, exploitation, and totalitarianism and for supporting freedom of expression and liberty. Dorothy Rick, an educator at the Mohegan Modern School whom Avrich interviewed in 1972, reports that the community and school were conjoined and that the students enjoyed learning in a structured but not constraining environment. Avrich writes that "such schools, in which the pupils learned how to think and live according to their own lights" were conducted in anarchist enclaves in several languages such as "Italian, Spanish, German, Yiddish, and Czech" and were popular until the 1930s when increasing assimilation and a decreasing immigrant population lowered interest in both the modern schools and the anarchist movement.

BIBLIOGRAPHY

Sources

Avrich, Paul. *Anarchist Voices: An Oral History of Anarchism in America*. Oakland, CA: AK Press, 1995. Print.

Biel, Steven. Rev. of *Anarchist Voices: An Oral History of Anarchism in America*, by Paul Avrich. *Reviews in American History* 23.4 (1995): 704–09. Project MUSE. Web. 2 Jan. 2013.

Goyens, Tom. *Beer and Revolution: The German Anarchist Movement in New York City, 1880–1914*. Urbana: University of Illinois Press, 2007. Print.

Jones, Bob. Rev. of *Anarchist Voices: An Oral History of Anarchism in America*, by Paul Avrich. *Oral History Society* 24.1 (1996): 101–02. JSTOR. Web. 24 Dec. 2012.

Sorin, Gerald. Rev. of *Anarchist Voices: An Oral History of Anarchism in America*, by Paul Avrich. *Journal of American Ethnic History* 15.4 (1996): 78–80. JSTOR. Web. 23 Dec. 2012.

Wilford, Hugh. Rev. of *Anarchist Voices: An Oral History of Anarchism in America*, by Paul Avrich. *Journal of American Studies* 30.1 (1996): 165–66. Print.

Further Reading

Avrich, Paul. *Anarchist Portraits*. Princeton, NJ: Princeton University Press, 1988. Print.

Goldman, Emma. *Living My Life*. 2 vols. New York: Knopf, 1931. Print.

Guérin, Daniel, ed. *Anarchism: From Theory to Practice*. Trans. Mary Klopper. New York: Monthly Review, 1970. Print.

———. *No Gods, No Masters: An Anthology of Anarchism*. Trans. Paul Sharkey. 1998. Oakland, CA: AK Press, 2005. Print.

Guglielmo, Jennifer. *Living the Revolution: Italian Women's Resistance and Radicalism in New York*. Chapel Hill: University of North Carolina Press, 2012. Print.

Woodcock, George. *Anarchism: A History of Libertarian Ideas and Movements*. Toronto: University of Toronto Press, 2004. Print.

Katherine Bishop

Biography of a Runaway Slave

Miguel Barnet, Esteban Montejo

OVERVIEW

Biography of a Runaway Slave (1968), the English version of anthropologist Miguel Barnet's edited first-person rendering of Esteban Montejo's life as a *cimarrón,* or runaway slave, was first published in 1966 as *Biografía de un cimarrón.* The book captures rare glimpses of the practice of slavery in Cuba, as well as its end in 1886, and it does so from the perspective of a former enslaved man fighting in the War for Cuban Independence. In 1963, after reading that there were several centenarians in a nursing room, Barnet arranged to meet with the 103-year-old Montejo, likely the only living cimarrón, to discuss his experiences during and after slavery in Cuba. Though a few of Montejo's recollections drift past the end of the war, Barnet's narrative concludes with the close of the nineteenth century and the death of the Cuban general Maximo Gomez.

Upon its publication, the book was a success both critically and commercially. As Michael Zeuske notes in a 1997 article for *New West Indian Guide,* "There is hardly any other book in Cuban historiography that has met with such wide circulation." The many reprintings of *Biography of a Runaway Slave*—first just a few years after it was first published and again in 1993 and 1994—are proof of its wide-ranging influence. The book continues to be recognized by scholars as an important record of the end of slavery in Cuba and for its place in the genre of oral history.

HISTORICAL AND LITERARY CONTEXT

The abolition of slavery was one of the many elements at stake during the three 19th-century wars for independence that Cuba fought against Spain, which had held the island nation as a territory since 1492. The Cubans lost the Ten Years' War (1868–78) for reasons including the sale of weapons by the United States to Spain. The Cubans were also defeated during the Small War (1879–80) but finally achieved liberation from Spain at the end of the Cuban War of Independence (1895–98), for which the United States joined them during the last three months. In the United States, this conflict became known as the Spanish-American War.

Slavery was abolished in Cuba in 1886, when Montejo was a young man. In his preface to a 1994 translation of *Biography of a Runaway Slave,* translator W. Nick Hill quotes Barnet as saying that Montejo was "an authentic actor in the process of history in Cuba." Montejo's oral history covers his early life on a sugar plantation in Cuba, the years that he spent as a cimarrón living in the woods, the time following the abolition of slavery that he spent working for various plantations, his roles during the Cuban War of Independence, and some of his reflections on those events.

Biography of a Runaway Slave is one of the few first-person accounts of slavery in Cuba. It joined Juan Francisco Manzano's *Autobiografía de un esclavo* (*The Autobiography of a Slave*), which was published in England in 1840 and Cuba in 1937. It was written in 1835 by a man who, like Montejo, had escaped slavery. Barnet's book can also be considered with Manuel Moreno Franglinal's *El ingenio: Complejo económico social cubano del azúcar* (1964), translated into English in 1976 as *The Sugarmill: The Socioeconomic Complex of Sugar in Cuba,* for its examination of the effects of the processes of labor on the culture of Cuba.

Barnet is known by scholars as the progenitor of testimonial fiction, or *testimonio,* in Latin American literature, which is said to have begun with his oral history work with Montejo. In *Against Literature,* John Beverley describes the testimonio as a longer work of fiction from a first-person perspective—usually mediated by an editor, a translator, or a writer—that bears witness to significant personal experiences that are understood to represent a group. In the testimonio tradition, Montejo represents former enslaved Cubans as well as the entirety of Cuba in its fight for liberation. Barnet's book has also sparked interdisciplinary explorations such as composer Hans Werner Henze's *El Cimarrón* (1969–70), a score for four musicians.

Cuban author/ethnologist Miguel Barnet in 1992. Barnet recorded the interviews that would form the core of Esteban Mesa Montejo's story as told in *The Autobiography of a Runaway Slave.* © PHILIPPE CARON/SYGMA/CORBIS

Key Facts

Time Period:
Late 19th to Early 20th Century

Relevant Historical Events:
End of slavery in Cuba; War of Cuban Independence

Nationality:
Cuban

Keywords:
slavery; liberation; independence

ON THE FORMAT OF *BIOGRAPHY OF A RUNAWAY SLAVE*

As Michael Zeuske notes in the journal *New West Indian Guide,* some scholars believe that the principal figure in *Biography of a Runaway Slave,* Esteban Montejo, was mostly or completely editor Miguel Barnet's invention, but the "very convincing historical date" verifies many of the details in the book and fills in many of its gaps. Sources on Montejo's life after the war show that he was a staunch supporter of revolutionary José Martí and may have been an active member of the *Partido Independiente de Color* (PIC), founded in 1908 by African veterans of wars for independence who were frustrated by their mistreatment at the hands of the often-racist government. Nevertheless, in light of Montejo's participation in further historical movements, Zeuske, like many other historians, asks why sixty years of Montejo's life are not "adapt[ed] … for his literary life and for posterity" and who elided these years—Montejo or Barnet?

In a 1989 *MLN* article, William Luis posits that in his construction of the narrative, Barnet was "reflecting a certain political reality imposed upon him by the Cuban Revolution," such as a pressure to conform to political agendas in order to overcome censorship or worse. Thus, Luis suggests that Barnet may have left Montejo's later life out of the narrative to end the novel with Cuban triumph rather than the later internecine conflict in order to increase his chances of being published and to decrease a danger of censure.

THEMES AND STYLE

The sharing of personal experiences and cultural elements, self-sufficiency, and liberty, especially among the Cuban people, are at the crux of *Biography of a Runaway Slave.* Concerning shared culture, Montejo argues that formally educated people are too often blinded by their prejudices to see the "customs that are more important than information. To be educated, not to meddle in other folks' problems, speak softly, be respectful, be religious, be a hard worker. … All of that the Africans taught me." At the end of his narrative, Montejo reports that, although he always kept quiet to avoid conflict, "if I could I would tell the whole story now, all of it." Barnet's book also centers on Montejo's quest for personal and national freedom. Speaking of the racial hierarchies in Cuban society that socially segregated people and limited opportunities, Montejo explains, "There was no freedom. That's why a war was necessary."

In the afterword, "The Alchemy of Memory," Barnet argues that the form of his book, testimonial literature, "will revise a mangled, deformed interpretation of the past to offer a vision from the perspective of the class struggle" as it "reworks several traditional concepts of literature: realism, autobiography, the relationship between fiction and history." In his 1966 introduction to *Biography of a Runaway Slave,* Barnet writes that he did not intend to create "a literary text, a novel." Instead, as Hill terms it, the book was meant to project "a voice that speaks for a whole people, and marks a whole epoch, an I that speaks a we."

The first English edition was titled *Autobiography of a Runaway Slave* because it appears narrated from a first-person perspective with no interjections by Barnet. Barnet's and Montejo's voices merge in the "I" of the text, led by questions based on Barnet's interests and further mediated by a translator in non-Spanish versions. Barnet obviously smoothed his questions out of Montejo's narrative and likely regulated his subject's voice somewhat. However, Hill reports that as the translator, he tried to "provide or suggest the sounds that come most directly from Montejo himself, the 'aroma' of the original." Still, Montejo speaks in more standard language than many of the others he quotes. For example, one woman says, "You is good and quiet. I going to be telling to you something." Another figure responds to questions about the war: "Cuba libre. Me's a liberator." Still another person says, "Ussens not fraid of da war. Ussens used to it. In Africa ussens fight a lot." This type of language has raised questions among historians about whose voice is dominant in the narrative, Montejo's or Barnet's.

CRITICAL DISCUSSION

Immediately popular upon its original publication, *Biography of a Runaway Slave* was translated and reprinted several times. However, the book sparked a great deal of controversy, as its categorization waffled between history and fiction. Quoting Ulrich Fleishmann, Zeuske observes that the majority of the objections to the book stemmed from Barnet's methodology, the use of first-person narration, the "mimesis of a black narrator on the part of a white writer," and the "hero-worship, anti-imperialism, and sexualization of freedom" indicated in the work.

Despite, or perhaps because of, the discussion surrounding Barnet's role in producing Montejo's life story, and because of interest in the form of testimonial literature that it introduced, *Biography of a Runaway Slave* has been widely taught. Dale Graden recommends the book in his 1996 review in *H-Ethnic* and reports that "most students who participate in my 'Comparative Slavery and Emancipation in the Atlantic World' seminar at Idaho cherish this book as much as I do. After reading the *Biography of a Runaway Slave,* one does not quickly forget about the extraordinary life of Esteban Montejo or the power of words, spoken or written." Barnet's intervention and moderation of Montejo's life is a crucial aspect of this text. His insistence on underlining the sense of collectivity in Montejo's voice has been widely examined by scholars, especially in discussions of voicing oppressed or marginalized people in oral history.

For the most part, scholars such as Graden and William Luis have considered *Biography of a Runaway Slave* as a representative of the genre of testimonial literature, weighing its values, validity, and effect upon the discussion on the intersection of literature and history. Others, such as Zeuske, have reevaluated the book's contribution to a historiography of Cuba in light of newly acquired resources on Montejo's life. Archival scholarship has revealed notarial records, payrolls, and newspapers that place him as an important figure in Cuban history.

BIBLIOGRAPHY

Sources

Barnet, Miguel. *Biography of a Runaway Slave.* Trans. W. Nick Hill. Willimantic, CT: Curbstone, 1994. Print.

———. "The Alchemy of Memory." *Biography of a Runaway Slave.* Trans. W. Nick Hill. Willimantic, CT: Curbstone, 1994.

Beverley, John. *Against Literature.* Minneapolis: University of Minnesota Press, 1993. Print.

Graden, Dale T. "Miguel Barnet's *Biography of a Runaway Slave:* Testimonial Literature as History." *H-Ethnic* October 1996. *H-Net Reviews.* Web. 26 Jan. 2013.

Hill, W. Nick. Translator's prologue. *Biography of a Runaway Slave,* by Miguel Barnet. Willimantic, CT: Curbstone, 1994. 11–13. Print.

Luis, William. "The Politics of Memory and Miguel Barnet's *The Autobiography of a Run Away Slave.*" *MLN* 104.2 (1989): 475–91. *JSTOR.* Web. 24 Jan. 2013.

Zeuske, Michael. "The *Cimarrón* in the Archives: A Re-reading of Miguel Barnet's Biography of Esteban Montejo." *New West Indian Guide/Nieuwe West-Indische Gids* 71.3–4 (1997): 265–79. *KITLV.* Web. 25 Jan. 2013.

Further Reading

García, Ana. "Miguel Barnet 1940– : Cuban Ethnographer, Poet and Prose Writer." *Encyclopedia of Latin American Literature.* Ed. Verity Smith. Chicago: Fitzroy Dearborn, 1997. 96–97. Print.

Helg, Aline. *Our Rightful Share: The Afro-Cuban Struggle for Equality 1886–1912.* Chapel Hill: University of North Carolina Press, 1995. Print.

Luis, William. *Literary Bondage: Slavery in Cuban Narrative.* Austin: University of Texas Press, 1990. Print.

Price, Richard, ed. *Maroon Society: Rebel Slave Communities in the Americas.* 3rd ed. Baltimore: Johns Hopkins University Press, 1996. Print.

Katherine Bishop

Bitter Water
Diné Oral Histories of the Navajo-Hopi Land Dispute
Malcolm D. Benally

✤ *Key Facts*

Time Period:
Early 21st Century

Relevant Historical Events:
Navajo-Hopi Settlement Act of 1974; struggle for land rights among Native Americans

Nationality:
American

Keywords:
Native Americans; land rights; civil rights

OVERVIEW

Transcribed from video, translated, and edited by Malcolm D. Benally, *Bitter Water: Diné Oral Histories of the Navajo-Hopi Land Dispute* (2011) offers monologues with Diné (Navajo) women who continue to struggle for land rights in northeastern Arizona. The twenty-five hours of transcribed interview footage from a failed documentary endeavor in 1998 provide testimonies in both English and Navajo from four Navajo elders in the Black Mesa area who reside in three different communities. They discuss the social, ethical, and environmental issues involved in the U.S. government's century-long relocation effort. The women are responsible for land passed down from ancestors that, since the Navajo-Hopi Settlement Act of 1974, legally belongs to the Hopi tribes. University of New Mexico history professor Jennifer Nez Denetdale offers a guiding foreword that presents a history of the Diné people, and traditional Navajo poems further frame the stories. Among other vignettes of voices from the region, Benally compiled four monologues that vary in tone and focus from matriarch to matriarch. Together these stories reveal the preventable trauma caused by repeated relocation, as well as a spiritual purpose and a strong resolve in resistance.

Published during the ongoing Navajo-Hopi land dispute, *Bitter Water* was immediately recognized as an important document, as it was the first major presentation of Navajo testimonials from those living in the area since the Navajo-Hopi Settlement Act. The interviews took place in the late 1990s and were captured on film before funding to produce the documentary faded. The book currently serves as a model for multilingual oral history texts.

HISTORICAL AND LITERARY CONTEXT

The narratives collected in *Bitter Water* expose the continuing problems caused by the shifts in legal land boundaries for native Navajo communities. In the mid-nineteenth century the Diné, having been cast by Americans as a violent group in the region, came under U.S. rule and were forcibly moved to the Bosque Redondo Reservation in New Mexico. In 1868 Diné leaders signed a treaty that allowed the tribe to return to its original land, and a period of Navajo population growth ensued. In 1882 President Chester Arthur carved out Navajo boundaries to create a reservation for Hopis and "such other Indians as the Secretary of the Interior may see fit to settle thereon." The order became problematic as the number of Navajo farmers and herders continued to grow and as they began to settle around the Hopi Mesa communities that had existed in the area for centuries.

While the relationship between the Hopi and Navajo in the Black Mesa area in the latter half of the nineteenth century into the mid-twentieth century was largely amiable (including trade and marriage between the groups), the growing populations increased tension over land. The two tribes sued one another in 1958 for the exclusive rights to the reservation area established in 1882. In the foreword to *Bitter Water*, Denetdale employs scholarship that maintains that "the imperative to address the complaints of the Navajos and Hopis over shared lands was not taken seriously until coal, gas, and water were discovered." This new government interest led to the 1974 Navajo-Hopi Land Settlement Act, which divided the reservation between the Hopi and Navajo tribes and displaced hundreds of Hopis and more than twelve thousand Navajos. The Diné women featured in *Bitter Water* have been resisting relocation for more than fifty years in an effort to preserve the Navajo culture that they see as inextricably interconnected with the land in question.

Bitter Water follows in the literary conversation regarding the Navajo-Hopi land problem. Other significant works on the subject include Ward Churchill's *Struggle for the Land* (1993), David M. Brugge's *The Navajo-Hopi Land Dispute: An American Land Tragedy* (1994), and Robert S. McPherson's *Navajo Land, Navajo Culture* (2001), which are all more academic perspectives on the struggle for land in the region. *Bitter Water* is also an important addition to the Navajo oral history tradition, along with Marsha L Weisiger's collection *Dreaming of Sheep in Navajo Country* (2009).

Bitter Water quickly became an influential model for the collection and presentation of American Indian oral histories. In addition, the book led Benally to continue to pursue funding for the documentary.

Bitter Water's refusal to make political judgments gives it authority in the ongoing discussion of land rights and nonviolent resistance in the Black Mesa area.

THEMES AND STYLE

The central themes of *Bitter Water* include cultural genocide in the service of acquisition of materials for modern convenience, nonviolent resistance to relocation, and the spiritual connection to inherited land. All four women express concern with the rapid decline of Navajo tradition and culture. Mae Tso comments on the loss of traditional Diné spiritual lands and resources, saying, "They desecrate *our* church and strip-mine the land. Medicinal plants on the land are gone forever because of strip mining." Some of the elders convey frustration with the U.S. government's misleading ultimatums to force the Navajo people off the land within seventy-five years, a contract signed by some of the representatives of the tribes. Pauline Whitesinger describes her anger with the Navajo leaders and the tribe's lawyers, explaining that "the relocation law said, 'The seventy-five-year lease has a deadline. Before the deadline you must sign your name.' So the Diné people sold out. Our lawyers sold us out." Whitesinger compares the connection to the area to a mother-daughter relationship and further explains that "the reason we will not relocate is because the land has become a part of us."

Benally writes in the introduction that he was compelled to assemble the collection of monologues, poems, and essays as "an earnest attempt to communicate cultural, political, and historical realities from an indigenous language and perspective." While he expresses regret in presenting the stories in a book format (because of the negative connotation of English-printed documents for the four Navajo subjects), his desire to release the interviews outweighed those considerations. The Diné elders' words are presented first in Navajo and then translated into English by Benally, a Diné tribal member himself whose grandmother is one of the interviewees. "The goal," Benally writes, "though never spoken of at length, is to repeal Public Law 93–531," which is more commonly referred to as the "relocation law."

The U.S. Department of the Interior gave its first "Gold" Good Neighbor Award to the Peabody Western Coal Company in 2003, citing benefits the coal mines had brought to communities in Arizona since the company opened two mines there in the 1960s. However, the mines also greatly depleted the groundwater in this desert region of Navajo and Hopi lands, causing decades of controversy. © PRNEWSFOTO/ PEABODY ENERGY

MALCOLM D. BENALLY AND THE DINÉ

Although *Bitter Water* provides perspectives from several other Diné tribal members, Benally himself was directly affected by the Navajo-Hopi land dispute. Before studying Navajo and English at Northern Arizona University, Benally grew up in Forest Lake, Arizona, where his family's property contained a fence separating the Navajo from the Hopi lands. After returning to his home from his studies, Benally saw, as he states in a 2011 interview with the *Navajo Times*, media representations of the story as "broken up into little bits. The big picture of what happens when you force people off their land was lost."

When he volunteered at the 1995 Sundance Film Festival, he acquired grant money to start filming those affected by the Navajo-Hopi land dispute. Despite working full time for community organizations, Benally found time to film interviews with those affected, including many of his own family members. After further funding fell through in postproduction, he decided to painstakingly transcribe and translate the audio recordings. He found that the elders provided a rendering of the Navajo language that was much more colloquial than the Navajo his parents' generation had studied. Benally continues to be recognized for advocating Diné cultural literacy.

The structure of *Bitter Water* is notable for its framing essays, photographs, and poetry. Benally uses Navajo language throughout the English translations in order to preserve Navajo colloquiums and dialect. The Navajo parts are meant to force further conversation and scholarship of Navajo language. The location of the interviews is an important aspect of the tone, as Benally explains that "the women speak out as leaders and matriarchs from their communities and from their homes (instead of in Washington, D.C., in front of investigative panels, before the United Nation's Council on Human Rights, or in front of a small audience in a U.S. courtroom)." Denetdale's historical contextualization in the foreword provides background for the issue, while the more lyrical "Sheep Is Life" section provides unmarked vignettes, snapshots of interviews with Diné people about their experiences with relocation.

CRITICAL DISCUSSION

The initial responses to *Bitter Water* were favorable, noting the book's important contribution as a text devoted to the Diné perspective. Charlotte Frisbie's 2011 piece in the *Journal of Folklore Research Reviews* is typical of early scholarship on the book: calling *Bitter Water* an "extremely important volume," it names Benally "the ideal person to pursue this project, having been born three years before the 1974 act and raised in Forest Lake, another community on partitioned land." In her 2012 review in *Southwestern American Literature*, Laura Woodworth-Ney says the book is "a lyrical must-read for any writer or scholar interested in federal relations, human rights, and the value of language."

Bitter Water continues to engage public interest in the political dispute in the Black Mesa area. The latter half of the book discusses ongoing political situations of the Navajo resisters and those who have been relocated. The appendix is the prepared testimony of Roman Bitsui, the executive director of the Navajo Hopi Land Commission Office, and Kenja Hassan, assistant director for the Office of Public Affairs at Arizona State University, for the U.S. House Committee on Resources; it provides a reiterated view of the history of the land dispute for a nonnative audience.

While the book's relatively recent publication has not allowed for great shifts in scholarly focus, criticisms have arisen concerning its presentation and citation practices. For example, there are translation discrepancies such as nonverbal cues that are noted in Navajo and not in English. Frisbie, however, claims that "few criticisms are warranted." Furthermore, Robert S. McPherson's 2012 review in *Western Historical Quarterly* argues that the book's current presentation offers a "glimpse into a different culture and time [and] challenges the reader to learn more about and better understand the Navajo perspective." Linda Lizut Helstern also praises Benally's selectivity in her 2013 review in *Southwestern American Literature*, contending that the lack of clearly defined voices in the "Sheep Is Life" section "allows these comments, like those of his featured speakers, to stand without explanation, requiring the reader/listener to make sense of them in the traditional way by using each subsequent story to interrogate previous stories."

BIBLIOGRAPHY

Sources

Benally, Malcolm D., ed. *Bitter Water: Diné Oral Histories of the Navajo-Hopi Land Dispute*. Tucson: University of Arizona Press, 2011. Print.

Frisbie, Charlotte. Rev. of *Bitter Water: Diné Oral Histories of the Navajo-Hopi Land Dispute*, by Malcolm D. Benally. *Journal of Folklore Research Reviews*. Journal of Folklore Research, 9 Nov. 2011. Web. 12 Jan. 2013.

Helstern, Linda Lizut. Rev. of *Bitter Water: Diné Oral Histories of the Navajo-Hopi Land Dispute*, by Malcolm D. Benally. *Southwestern American Literature* 37.2 (2012): 84. *Academic OneFile*. Web. 10 Jan. 2013.

McPherson, Robert S. Rev. of *Bitter Water: Diné Oral Histories of the Navajo-Hopi Land Dispute*, by Malcolm D. Benally. *Western Historical Quarterly* 43.1 (2012): 82. Web. 11 Jan. 2013.

Woodworth-Ney, Laura. Rev. of *Bitter Water: Diné Oral Histories of the Navajo-Hopi Land Dispute*, by Malcolm D. Benally. *Oral History Review* 39.2 (2012): 389–92. Web. 10 Jan. 2013.

Further Reading

Brugge, David M. *The Navajo-Hopi Land Dispute.* Albuquerque: University of New Mexico Press, 1994. Print.

Churchill, Ward. *Struggle for the Land.* Monroe, ME: Common Courage, 1993. Print.

Denetdale, Jennifer. *Reclaiming Diné History: The Legacies of Navajo Chief Manuelito and Juanita.* Tucson: University of Arizona Press, 2007. Print.

McPherson, Robert S. *Navajo Land, Navajo Culture.* Norman: University of Oklahoma Press, 2001. Print.

Rev. of *Bitter Water: Diné Oral Histories of the Navajo-Hopi Land Dispute,* by Malcolm D. Benally. *Reference & Research Book News* Aug. 2011. *Academic OneFile.* Web. 8 Jan. 2013.

Weisiger, Marsha L. *Dreaming of Sheep in Navajo Country.* Seattle: University of Washington Press, 2009. Print.

Yurth, Cindy. "New Book Gives Voice to Land Dispute Victims." *Navajo Times.* Navajo Times, 3 Mar. 2011. Web. 10 Jan. 2013.

Tony Ruzicka

Exodus to Shanghai
Stories of Escape from the Third Reich
Steve Hochstadt

✣ **Key Facts**

Time Period:
Mid-20th Century

Relevant Historical Events:
World War II; Holocaust; Jewish immigration to China

Nationality:
American

Keywords:
Judaism; genocide, exile

OVERVIEW

Exodus to Shanghai: Stories of Escape from the Third Reich (2012) is a collection of oral histories of the Jewish refugee community in Shanghai during World War II that was recorded, edited, and introduced by Steve Hochstadt. More than sixteen thousand Jews escaped from Nazi-held central Europe to Shanghai—mostly in the years 1938–40—where they were treated by the Japanese occupying authorities only as "stateless persons." Those who did not succumb to illness or injury, or who did not run afoul of the occupiers, typically survived to see the city liberated by Americans in 1945. Between 1989 and 1999 Hochstadt, a historian of Europe with a research focus on migration, conducted more than a hundred interviews with survivors of the experience and chose thirteen "narrators whose stories add up to a history of mass flight and community survival." Hochstadt says in his introduction that he is not entirely detached from his subject: "I grew up with the exodus to Shanghai on my mind. My father and his family were hounded out of Vienna by the Nazis; my father came to the United States, but his parents fled to Shanghai."

Because he began conducting his interviews some fifty years after the events involved, Hochstadt mainly spoke with men and women who had been children or adolescents at the time of their flight to, and residence in, Shanghai. Thanks to the hyper-emotionalism of youth, their memories were vivid and detailed, but their experiences were more circumscribed, and they saw and heard little beyond the bounds of their families and immediate circles. Hochstadt takes considerable care filling in the background. In the short time since the book's release, reviews in the popular media were positive, yet academic reviewers and journals have yet to assess Hochstadt's text.

HISTORICAL AND LITERARY CONTEXT

Adolf Hitler and the National Socialists (Nazis) seized power in Germany in 1933 and began a program of world conquest. At the furthest extent of their conquests, the Nazis controlled most of Europe from the English Channel to Leningrad (St. Petersburg) and from Norway and Denmark to the Mediterranean. At the same time, from 1933 onward, the Nazis began to impose their murderous regime of anti-Semitism, first in Germany, then, after the Anschluss, in Austria, followed by the Sudetenland and the rest of Czechoslovakia. Jews living in the lands conquered after September 1, 1939, had no chance to emigrate legally and little opportunity to escape, but before war began the German, Austrian, and Czech Jews had some—limited and unreliable—opportunities to flee. From forty thousand departures in 1933, the numbers leveled off at twenty thousand per year until 1937. After the passage of the repressive Nuremberg Laws, and the anti-Semitic violence known as "The Night of Breaking Glass" (Kristallnacht), even greater numbers of Jews attempted to emigrate, until the outbreak of war brought this to an end. Hochstadt estimates that "about half of the 525,000 German Jews and somewhat more than half of the 200,000 Austrian Jews escaped from the Third Reich."

Once out of Nazi-controlled territory, the problem for the Jewish exiles became the problem of destination—indeed, it was usually the case that they were not allowed to leave until a country had agreed to receive them or they had a valid boat ticket. Many settled in European countries that ultimately were overrun by Germany, and the majority of these were arrested, sent to camps, and killed. Of those who went beyond Europe, the majority hoped to reach the United States, and approximately eighty-five thousand managed to get there between March 1938 and September 1939. However, the United States refused to raise its quotas for German immigrants and found ways of keeping Jews out. During the 1930s more than sixty thousand German Jews went to Palestine (then under British mandate), but the British White Paper of May 1939 contained clauses that drastically restricted Jewish entry into Palestine. Other countries that accepted significant numbers of Jewish refugees were Switzerland (30,000), Spain and Portugal (100,000), and Bolivia (30,000). Shanghai was unique in that it required no entry visas, but the German Jews still needed some kind of papers to get out of the country. Ho Feng-Shan, the consul-general in Vienna of the Republic of China, signed thousands of visas—twelve hundred during his first three months in office—permitting thousands of Jews to escape. Most went to occupied Shanghai, one of the most cosmopolitan cities in the world.

Few, if any, historical episodes have been so thoroughly documented, analyzed, and dramatized as the twelve-year lifespan, 1933–1945, of the Third Reich.

View of a Jewish refugee camp in Shanghai during World War II.
© DIZ MUENCHEN GMBH, SUEDDEUTSCHE ZEITUNG PHOTO/ALAMY

In addition to a huge catalog of scholarly and popular histories of the period, there is a vast body of memoirs of escape from Europe before war began and as many memoirs of life in occupied territories and life in the concentration camps. Oral histories of the survivors began to be collected almost as soon as the war ended and have continued to this day. Yet the story of the escape to Shanghai, and the survival of the Jewish community in that city, remained largely untold until 1976, when David Kranzler published *Japanese, Nazis & Jews: The Jewish Refugee Community of Shanghai, 1938–1945*.

Exodus to Shanghai had little cultural or literary influence during its first year after publication. Since the book itself was conceived, written, and edited with skill and integrity—and the stream of new books about the Nazi genocides continued to attract mainstream attention—the reason for the book's relative obscurity is unclear.

THEMES AND STYLE
The main themes of *Exodus to Shanghai* are accelerating persecution, escape, hard travel, and life in Shanghai. Gérard Kohbieter, for instance, was not reassured by his parents' jokes and expressed confidence that the Nazis would be out of power before long (in 1938). "It felt dangerous," he says, "all those clowns walking around, man, with this super-masculinity, this marching, this macho thing, God in heaven, and it was directed at us. I wasn't particularly a religious Jew or anything like that. I felt unsafe." Much of each person's narrative concerns the difficulty of exiting the Reich. "We tried once to go across the border," says Alfred Kohn. "We wanted to go to Belgium, Switzerland. We had relatives in this country who came here [the United States] in 1848 already. But because of the quota system, we couldn't leave. Everything tried, nothing worked. And there was no place in the world to go except Shanghai at the very end." Every escape story is different, but once the refugees get to Shanghai, the narratives become more like each other, though the details are always interesting. "As the water always had to be boiled," remembers Ernest Culman, "at every street corner practically there was a place where you could buy boiling water."

Hochstadt's motive for writing *Exodus to Shanghai* was to tell an underreported and fascinating episode of the Nazi years in the words of those who lived through it. It was also a chance to apply his academic expertise—migrations of large groups of modern peoples—to a subject that bore directly on his own personal history. "This book offers a fresh way to read Holocaust oral history," he says in his introduction, "by allowing survivors to speak directly to us. Just as they told me, a stranger in their living rooms, their family stories, they now tell them to readers everywhere."

Exodus to Shanghai is organized into nine chapters that are arranged thematically, within a chronological framework, rather than presenting the personal narratives one at a time. Hochstadt has noted that he took editorial license with the interviews: "All the words quoted in these chapters were spoken by the narrators," he says. "But these stories do not appear here exactly as they were told." He has cut and pasted

THE JEWS OF SHANGHAI

When the German-speaking Jewish refugees arrived in Shanghai in 1938 and 1939, they found an established community of Russian Jews who had fled the tsarist pogroms and totalitarian oppression of the communists and Jews, mostly from Baghdad, who had fled to Shanghai shortly after 1900 to avoid military service under the Ottoman Empire. After the sixteen thousand Austrian-Czech-German Jews arrived at the close of the 1930s, they were followed by two thousand Polish and Lithuanian Jews who had escaped in 1941, just before the German invasion of the Soviet Union. Many of this last group were male *yeshiva* (school for the study of religious texts) students, and the great majority were strictly observant Orthodox Jews, who spoke Yiddish and considered the secular German-speaking Jews as scarcely Jews at all.

The pre-"exodus" Jews of Shanghai were very supportive of the German Jews and provided money, clothes, and housing for them. However, after the Japanese finally bowed, in 1943, to Nazi pressure and relocated the "stateless persons" who had arrived after 1938 into a "Designated Area" (a slum called "Hongkou"), the Russian and "Baghdadi" Jews were allowed to remain where they were. As the German Jews never attempted to assimilate into Shanghai or Chinese life, but set up their community as an island of German-Jewish culture in Asia, so the Orthodox Poles and Lithuanians kept to themselves and knit themselves together with religious observances: they considered themselves not as transients but permanently apart from whatever society the accidents of history had placed them in.

according to the demands of the story's dynamic. "For the structure and emphases of this history," he explains, "I take responsibility."

CRITICAL DISCUSSION

As noted, as of early 2013 *Exodus to Shanghai* has not been reviewed by any print media. Online reviews have been thoughtful and approving, however. Bill Purves, writing for the *Asian Review of Books,* finds it "a clear and engaging treatment of a little-known topic." Purves finds especially valuable Hochstadt's identification of the four Jewish groups in Shanghai—"the Germans and Austrians, the Poles, the white Russians and what Prof. Hochstadt terms the Baghdadi Jews"—and their relations with each other. In *History News Network,* Murray Polner praises Hochstadt for "deftly weaving in the personal and political." He continues, "What [Hochstadt] does best is thoroughly set the stage from the panicky departure of men, women and children from Nazi Europe to life in Shanghai." Without pronouncing on the merit of *Exodus to Shanghai* as a book, Hannah Lee, in *Philadelphia Jewish Voice,* spends most of her review underscoring the information she has found particularly interesting, such as the fact that "remarkably, these refugees, most of whom had been children or teens during the years in Shanghai, can even look back and say, as did Doris Grey, that they were 'the best years' of her life."

Except for the dramatic stories, early on, of persecution and escape, *Exodus to Shanghai* does not fit easily into any of the main narratives of Holocaust studies. After they left the Third Reich, for the most part the refugees ceased to be targets of Nazi persecution. Because of this, it is unlikely that *Exodus to Shanghai* will leave a broad social or political legacy.

Although further research and firsthand accounts of the Jews of Shanghai will be difficult (the majority of survivors with whom Hochstadt spoke are now deceased), *Exodus to Shanghai* will continue to be of interest for scholars and others seeking information on the general refugee experience. Hochstadt joined the faculty at Illinois College as a professor of history, after teaching for more than twenty-five years at Bates College in Maine. He is also involved in the Sino-Judaic Institute, a nondenominational, nonprofit organization that was formed in 1985 to promote cultural understanding between Jewish and Chinese people.

BIBLIOGRAPHY

Sources

Hochstadt, Steve. *Exodus to Shanghai: Stories of Escape from the Third Reich.* New York: Palgrave Macmillan, 2012. Print.

Kranzler, David. *Japanese, Nazis & Jews: The Jewish Refugee Community of Shanghai, 1938–1945.* Hoboken, NJ: KTAV, 1988. Print.

Lee, Hannah. Rev. of *Exodus to Shanghai: Stories of Escape from the Third Reich,* by Steve Hochstadt. *Philadelphia Jewish Voice.* Philadelphia Jewish Voice, 17 Jan. 2013. Web. 18 Jan. 2013.

Polner, Murray. Rev. of *Exodus to Shanghai: Stories of Escape from the Third Reich,* by Steve Hochstadt. *History News Network.* History News Network, 9 Sept. 2012. Web. 18 Jan. 2013.

Purvis, Bill. Rev. of *Exodus to Shanghai: Stories of Escape from the Third Reich,* by Steve Hochstadt. *Asian Review of Books.* Asian Review of Books, Sept. 2012. Web. 18 Jan. 2013.

United States Holocaust Memorial Museum. *Holocaust Encyclopedia.* Web. 13 Jan. 2013.

Further Reading

Breitman, Richard, and Alan M. Kraut. *American Refugee Policy and European Jewry, 1933–1945.* Bloomington: Indiana University Press, 1987. Print.

Hale, Edward E. *First Captured, Last Freed: Memoirs of a P.O.W. in World War II Guam and Japan.* Sebastopol, CA: Grizzly Bear Press, 1995. Print.

Koestler, Arthur. *Scum of the Earth.* New York: Macmillan, 1941. Print.

Laqueur, Walter. *Generation Exodus: The Fate of Young Jewish Refugees from Nazi Germany.* Waltham, MA: Brandeis University Press, 2001. Print.

Maugham, W. Somerset. *Strictly Personal.* Garden City, NY: Doubleday, Doran, 1941. Print.

Gerald Carpenter

GULAG VOICES
Oral Histories of Soviet Incarceration and Exile
Jehanne M. Gheith, Katherine R. Jolluck

OVERVIEW

Compiled by Jehanne M. Gheith and Katherine R. Jolluck, *Gulag Voices: Oral Histories of Soviet Incarceration and Exile* (2011) presents firsthand accounts of the suffering and injustice endured by prisoners of the Gulag, the prison and labor camp system that arose in the Soviet Union under the dictatorship of Joseph Stalin. The anthology, which consists of ten interviews, draws on a range of subjects with differing experiences with the Soviet prison system: Some were prisoners in the Gulag; others were children of prisoners. It is estimated that under Joseph Stalin the Gulag imprisoned twenty-five million people of numerous ethnicities and faiths, and the interviews in *Gulag Voices* were conducted with a representative cross section of men and women of Russian, Polish, Tatar, German, Romanian, Jewish, and Muslim descent. The stories collected reflect the cruelty and inhumanity of the Soviet prison system, as well as the prisoners' capacity for endurance and survival.

Published in 2011, more than two decades after the fall of the Soviet Union, the accounts in *Gulag Voices* were collected from interviews with prisoners, some of whom had first been exiled or imprisoned more than seventy years prior. *Gulag Voices* was heralded as the first book of oral history to emerge out of the prison system, and it documents the nonliterary voices that emerged from the Soviet labor camps and the aftermath of the Gulag. While it has not received broad popular reception, *Gulag Voices* is widely recognized as an important document for scholars and students of Soviet history.

HISTORICAL AND LITERARY CONTEXT

The stories collected in *Gulag Voices* chronicle the shifting conditions of, and changing reasons for, imprisonment and forced labor during the roughly fifty-year existence of the Gulag prison system. Gulag, an acronym for *Glavnoe Upravlenie Lagerei* (Main Camp Administration), was initially the agency that administered the Soviet penal labor camp system established in the early 1920s, but in contemporary usage the word "Gulag" has come to represent not only the administrative body but also the prisons, labor camps, special exile settlements, and general phenomena of imprisonment in the system. The agency itself was established in 1929, following Stalin's decision to industrialize the Soviet Union. His unflinching demands for industrialization as well as the collectivization of agriculture led to an increasing use of forced labor. Prisoners of the Gulag, some of whom had been arrested for no legitimate reason, were forced to labor for the regime. As Gheith and Jolluck note in their introduction, "Prisoners built cities in brutal climes, they mined gold and uranium, built railroad and canals, and worked with peat and timber and in many other industries."

Gulag Voices focuses on a broad range of experiences. Three of the stories recount forced labor in the Perm region of Russia, where many of the first labor camps were established in the 1920s. Several of the other stories were told by children whose parents were imprisoned or killed in the Gulag. The interviews were conducted in 2004, several decades after Mikhail Gorbachev initiated a period of reform known as *perestroika*, which allowed the release and pardon of political prisoners. The reforms also allowed Soviet citizens to openly converse and write about the Gulag for the first time.

Gulag Voices falls into the Soviet literary tradition that has emerged out of the experiences of Gulag prisoners. The most notable literary figure to chronicle his suffering, and the suffering of his compatriots, is Aleksandr Solzhenitsyn, whose famous works *One Day in the Life of Ivan Denisovich* (1962) and *Gulag Archipelago* (1973) were some of the earliest accounts of the atrocities endured in the Gulag. *One Day in the Life* chronicles the experiences of a fictional character in a forced labor camp, while *Gulag Archipelago* draws on the true accounts of hundreds of citizens who suffered the atrocities of forced labor and starvation under Stalin's regime.

Gulag Voices attempts to broaden the literary discussion of the Gulag and its legacy, although, due to the recency of its publication, it has not yet exerted significant literary or cultural influence. Much of the previous literary and historical work surrounding the Soviet prison system emphasizes the suffering and experiences of the prisoners, but *Gulag Voices* opens the door to a broader discussion of the psychological and sociological aftermath experienced by Russian citizens. In addition, the work includes discussion of ethnic groups, such as the Tatars, that have historically received scant attention despite their oppression and imprisonment under Stalin.

❖ **Key Facts**

Time Period:
Mid-20th to Early 21st Century

Relevant Historical Events:
Stalin's establishment of the Gulag system; *perestroika*

Nationality:
Russian

Keywords:
incarceration; *perestroika*; totalitarianism

Caricature depicting a Siberian gulag, 1931. © PRIVATE COLLECTION/ ARCHIVES CHARMET/THE BRIDGEMAN ART LIBRARY

THEMES AND STYLE

The central themes of *Gulag Voices* are the experiences of daily life in prison, the suffering the prisoners of the Gulag endured, and their political views of Stalin and the Soviet Union, as well as the legacy and psychological effect of such imprisonment. Nina Ivanovna Rodina describes being shipped by train as a sixteen-year-old to a Gulag prison in 1950, where she was retained for three years under accusation of spying for Nazi Germany. "You're in a train car for goods, not for people. … There was no water and they gave us a piece of brown bread and this herring. And you go for thousands of kilometers beyond the Urals." Despite the cruelty and difficulty of life, and much to the surprise of Western readers, many of the interviewees express fealty to Stalin. Others, such as Valeria Mikhailovna Gerlin, whose parents were imprisoned (and her father murdered) in the Gulag, are bitter. Gerlin recalls that upon Stalin's death she felt "nothing but joy."

In compiling the series of interviews, Gheith and Jolluck intended to shed light on the less-studied people and aspects of the Gulag. As they write in the book's introduction, "The scope of the Gulag … is immense yet relatively little known." Because the personal oral accounts are often rambling, the editors excerpted the interviews, and in some cases rearranged passages for clarity, but they have attempted to "keep the essence of the interview" and "provide enough information and continuity for interviewees' comments to be clear." By acknowledging all alterations to the original transcripts, Gheith and Jolluck have attempted to avoid the controversy and questions of authenticity and intention that often arise with excerpted oral histories.

While many works on the Gulag prison system have incorporated oral histories and interviews, they have primarily been used as evidence in interpretive works. *Gulag Voices* differs in that it directly presents the nonliterary and nonacademic voices of imprisoned citizens. As pieces of oral history, the interviews have not been extensively revised or edited, and they often lack narrative structure. Many stories deviate from chronological narration, but the immediacy of the form, and the unedited and often unexpected and associative thought processes of the narrators, imbue the text with a raw emotional power. Furthermore, the troubled stories and tumultuous forms of narration attest to the psychological trauma of imprisonment in such harsh conditions: "And with the black walls in the cell, the walking courtyard was covered in black paint, the fence was three meters high, also all black, you only see the sky for 20 minutes on a walk."

CRITICAL DISCUSSION

Initial critical reception of *Gulag Voices* was highly complimentary but limited. K. C. O'Connor writes in a 2011 review for *Choice* that the "compelling aspect of their interviews is less the direct (and somewhat familiar) experience of incarceration and exile, than their widely varying attitudes toward Soviet power … and recollections of how their experiences continued to shape their lives." Nanci Adler, of the Netherlands Institute for War, Holocaust and Genocide Studies, argues that *Gulag Voices* stands as a "powerful testimony to the enduring legacy of state sponsored repression"; it is "an homage to survivors and those who did not survive."

Gulag Voices has yet to establish a broad social legacy, but its early recognition is promising. As O'Connor implies, "Scholars and students of Soviet history will appreciate" the work of the editors, and the book should continue to exert scholarly and popular influence on the perception of the Gulag. In a 2011 review for the *Journal of Modern History*, Steven A. Barnes celebrates the editors' decision to arrange "the most diverse group of Gulag voices that we have yet heard, including three Tatars, a group little studied despite their wholesale deportation in the Stalin Era." With such a varied study, *Gulag Voices* seeks to broaden scholarly discussion of the people oppressed by the Soviet prison system.

The limited scholarship regarding *Gulag Voices* has emphasized the role and efficacy of oral histories in research. As Gheith and Jolluck note in their introduction, "Distortions and overlays enter people's memories over time and in the former USSR, personal memory had to evolve in relation to a cultural narrative that often denied Gulag survivors' experiences." While the editors do not attempt to argue whether document-based or oral-based history is more efficacious, they rightly note that in light of the paucity of "information about the Gulag, both written and oral sources are necessary in order to (re)construct a fuller picture of the workings and effects of the Gulag."

BIBLIOGRAPHY

Sources

Barnes, Steven A. Rev. of *Gulag Voices*, by Jehanne M. Gheith and Katherine R. Jolluck. *Journal of Modern History* 84.3 (2012): 782–87. JSTOR. Web. 2 Jan. 2013

Conquest, Robert. *Harvest of Sorrow: Soviet Collectivization and the Terror-Famine*, Oxford: Oxford University Press, 1987. Print.

Gheith, Jehanne M., and Katherine R. Jolluck. *Gulag Voices: Oral Histories of Soviet Incarceration and Exile*. New York: Palgrave MacMillan, 2011. Print.

O'Connor, K. C. Rev. of *Gulag Voices*, by Jehanne M. Gheith and Katherine R. Jolluck. *Choice: Current Reviews for Academic Libraries* 49.2 (2011): 373. *Academic OneFile*. Gale. Web. 2 Jan. 2013.

Further Reading

Applebaum, Anne. *Gulag: A History*. New York: Anchor, 2003. Print.

———. *Gulag Voices: An Anthology.* New Haven, CT: Yale University Press, 2011. Print.

Ginzburg, Eugenia Semyonovna. *Journey into the Whirlwind*. New York: Harcourt, 1967. Print.

Grossman, Vasily. *Everything Flows*. New York: NYRB Classics, 2009. Print.

Klevniuk, Oleg V. *The History of the Gulag*. New Haven, CT: Yale University Press, 2004. Print.

Scammell, Michael. "Circles of Hell." *New York Review of Books*. NYREV, 28 Apr. 2011. Web. 2 Jan. 2013.

Shalamov, Varlam. *Kolyma Tales*. New York: Penguin, 1994. Print.

Snyder, Timothy. "Holocaust: The Ignored Reality." *New York Review of Books*. NYREV, 16 July 2009. Web. 13 Feb. 2013.

Solzhenitsyn, Aleksandr I. *Gulag Archipelago*. New York: Harper & Row, 1976. Print.

Tertz, Abram (Andrei Sinyavsky). *A Voice from the Chorus*. New Haven, CT: Yale University Press, 1995. Print.

———. *One Day in the Life of Ivan Denisovich*. New York: Knopf, Everyman's Library, 1995. Print.

Greg Luther

HOLODOMOR

The Gulag represents one of the most harrowing stories of the Joseph Stalin–controlled Soviet Union, but it is just one example of the atrocities the regime visited upon the Soviet people. Another is the Holodomor, also known as the Great Famine of 1932–33, during which millions of Ukrainians (estimates range from roughly 1.5 to 7.5 million people) starved to death. There is some debate about the extent to which natural causes contributed to the famine, but many scholars argue that the famine was the result of Soviet industrialization; the collectivization of agriculture; and, possibly, although it is hotly debated, a calculated genocide of the Ukrainian people implemented by the Stalin regime.

Despite the debates over the causes, nature, and scope of the famine, a general scholarly and political consensus has developed that the famine was indeed genocide. Some suggest that Stalin utilized the mass starvation as a tool to suppress Ukrainian nationalism. Others argue it was a tool against the peasantry in general who resisted the collectivization of agriculture. Robert Conquest, scholar and author of *Harvest of Sorrow*, goes so far as to call it a "mass murder." In the last several years, numerous countries have denounced the famine as an act of genocide, but Russia has made no formal apology or admittance.

HEAD OF THE CLASS

An Oral History of African American Achievement in Higher Education and Beyond

Gabrielle Morris

❖ **Key Facts**

Time Period:
Early to Mid-20th Century

Relevant Historical Events:
Burgeoning of the civil rights movement

Nationality:
American

Keywords:
segregation; racism; civil rights

OVERVIEW

Conducted and edited by oral historian Gabrielle Morris, *Head of the Class: An Oral History of African American Achievement in Higher Education and Beyond* (1995) presents a composite portrait of African American graduates of predominantly white colleges during the first half of the twentieth century. The collection includes a preface and a conclusion by prominent administrators from the University of California (UC) at Berkeley. Morris, an oral historian with UC Berkeley's Regional Oral History Office, drew on her decades of experience as an interviewer when composing *Head of the Class*. The narratives in this volume are direct, honest reports about a group of people who succeeded in spite of tough odds. Interviewees offer a candid picture of life in those decades, when high grades and a diploma were neither a safeguard against racism nor a guarantee of professional employment. The interviews are divided into three groups and are presented in chronological order. Morris names the groups Pioneers, Trail Blazers, and Bridge Builders. Their stories are intended to inspire and to set standards for future students, particularly African Americans to whom a college education seems impossible. Through the work Morris also hopes to provide insight into African American culture.

Published seventeen years after the landmark U.S. Supreme Court case on higher education *Regents of the University of California v. Bakke* (which outlawed the use of strict racial quotas in college admissions) and two years prior to the passage of Proposition 209 (a California law that banned all forms of affirmative action in the state), *Head of the Class* attempted to shift public and media attention from stories of reverse discrimination and academically less-qualified African American students to stories of African American achievement in higher education. The book was hailed by some as an inspirational account that brought readers into direct contact with the past, although other scholars described Morris's approach to oral history as dated. *Head of the Class* continues to appeal to readers interested in African American history, particularly in the context of California, as well as those interested in the history of higher education.

HISTORICAL AND LITERARY CONTEXT

The stories collected in *Head of the Class* reflect the sweeping social changes in higher education in the United States between the early twentieth century and the burgeoning civil rights movement of the 1950s. In 1914 the vast majority of U.S. schools and universities were racially segregated. The rest of American society was segregated as well; in places where Jim Crow laws were in effect the segregation was *de jure* and elsewhere it was *de facto*. This situation did not noticeably improve for many decades. At UC Berkeley the first African American professor was hired in 1954, and until the late 1960s whites made up 98 percent of the student body.

Moved by a thirst for education and a desire to improve their lives and their community, the interviewees in this book took the bold step of enrolling in predominantly white colleges. Faced with racism and economic hardship, these men and women made significant personal sacrifices to obtain their degrees only to be faced with more discrimination in hiring and in the workplace. Scholarships, federal aid, and affirmative action were virtually unobtainable. The interviewees, particularly those who went to school in the 1910s and 1920s, recall there being only a handful of other African Americans on campus. As Troy Duston observes in his conclusion to *Head of the Class*, the numbers do not fully capture the apartheid of the times. White students and faculty members felt free to insult the African American students and to block their advancement. Thelton Henderson, who went on to become chief judge for the U.S. Court of Appeals for the Ninth Circuit, went to Berkeley as a freshman in 1951 and played on the baseball team. In his interview he recalls the coach urging his players to run fast by saying, "The last one back is a nigger baby."

Head of the Class falls into the literary tradition of American oral histories, a genre that was viewed with skepticism by early twentieth-century scholars and relegated to the category of folklore until the 1930s but that has since the 1960s become an increasingly well-regarded source of popular history. Oral histories of African American education during the first half of the twentieth century that predate

Morris's book include *My Soul Is My Own: Oral Narratives of African American Women in the Professions* (1993) by G. Etter-Lewis and *Along Freedom Road: Hyde County, North Carolina, and the Fate of Black Schools in the South* (1994) by David Cecelski. *Blacks at Harvard* (1993), edited by Werner Sollors, Caldwell Titcomb, Thomas Underwood, and Randall Kennedy, examines African American experiences at a predominantly white college and covers some of the same ground but draws on speeches, stories, and newspaper articles rather than interviews. In addition to the interviews Morris conducted, her book draws on material from other oral history projects around the United States, including the Black Women Oral History Project at Radcliffe College, the Black Leadership Project at UCLA, and the Negro Political Leaders Project.

Since its publication, Morris's book has served as primary source material for scholars writing about the history of African American education. Subsequent oral historians have been influenced by its colloquial style. For most of her career as an oral historian, Morris has worked at the Regional Oral History Office at UC Berkeley, digging deep into local history by conducting countless interviews. She has continued to make use of these interviews in a series of oral history collections on popular history.

THEMES AND STYLE

The central themes of *Head of the Class* are the tradition of excellence established by African Americans in higher education in the United States during the first half of the twentieth century, the racial discrimination and economic hardships they endured, and how an understanding of this history can increase the aspirations of current and future students—especially African American students. *Head of the Class* records a UC Berkeley alumna's explanation that she put up with all manner of discrimination in order to earn her college degree because her father told her: "Get an education. It's the one thing the white man can't take from you." Concerning the aspirations of the next generations, students of today who feel under the microscope in class and are expected to do poorly can find parallels between their experiences and those of their predecessors and feel heartened by these early students' ability to overcome discrimination and to succeed in the world. Russ Ellis sums up beautifully the benefits of these interviews in the preface to *Head of the Class*: "There is support for the ambition of any American in the oral histories in this volume. We are mostly strangers in this baby nation."

As she writes in her introduction, Morris compiled this volume in response to urgent issues around ethnicity and race in the United States. She argues that the stories in her book are instructive for all Americans. "Because African Americans have played significant roles in the nation's history since its early days, their experiences are especially important as we seek to understand and deal with an ever more complex society." The author uses her own interviews as well as previously untapped materials found in archives around the country, letting the interviewees speak for themselves to capture the feeling of a one-to-one conversation with an older friend or relative. Her book is an example of a trend in oral history during the 1980s and 1990s of presenting a composite picture of a time and place through multiple individual accounts.

The language of *Head of the Class* is immediate and conversational. The intelligent and articulate interviewees are candid, sometimes using what the author calls "salty terms." Morris writes, "Perhaps because of their success in later life, they are objective in relating experiences of rejection and discrimination that can make the reader cringe." The honesty and humor of the narrators allows their personal charm to come through and makes for engaging reading.

CRITICAL DISCUSSION

Initial reception of *Head of the Class* was generally approving. In a 1997 article for *Oral American Historians Magazine,* Donald Ritchie included the book in a list of engaging oral histories, noting that they were "generally more casual, colorful and entertaining than formal written language." A 1998 article by Harry Schreiber praised Morris's work, particularly her interview with Allen Broussard, a justice on the California Supreme Court, describing it as "full and especially searching and evocative."

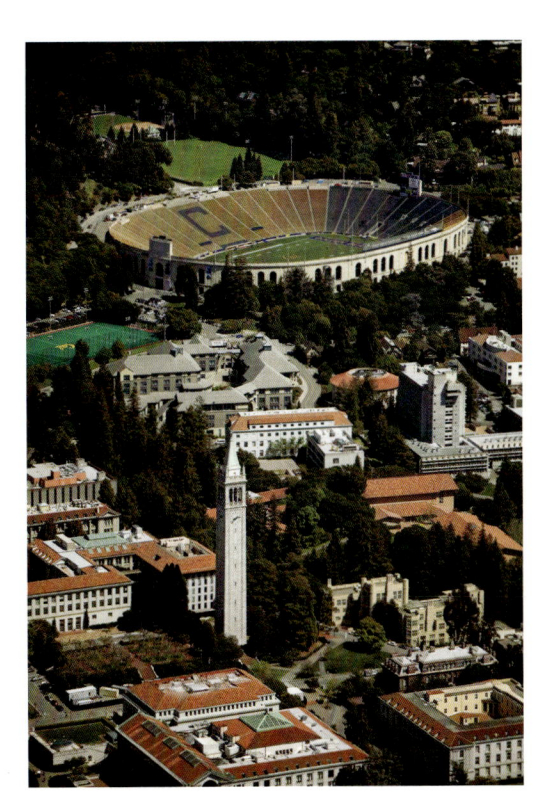

Aerial photo of the University of California at Berkeley campus. In *Head of the Class*, Gabrielle Morris interviews some of the first African American students to graduate from Berkeley. © AERIAL ARCHIVES/ALAMY

ADVERSITY AND RESISTANCE

THE FEDERAL WRITERS' PROJECT AND AMERICAN ORAL HISTORY

One of the earliest and most wide-reaching oral history projects in American history was undertaken by the Federal Writers' Project (FWP), a division of the Depression-era Works Progress Administration. Between 1936 and 1940, employees of the FWP conducted and recorded more than 10,000 interviews with people from all parts of the country, including 2,300 former slaves.

One of the goals of the project was to address questions on the nature of American identity, nationality, and culture. The pluralistic vision of nationalism that emerged saw diversity as a virtue and celebrated difference as a source of national vitality. The project aimed to broaden the definition of who and what was American. All groups were to be taken into account. The task was to introduce America to Americans in order to overcome differences in region, class, race, and religion. According to Jerrold Hirsch in his 2003 book *Portrait of America: A Cultural History of the Federal Writers' Project,* the directors hoped that oral history would allow people "to speak for themselves and the published results would create an encounter between the reader and narrator in which the reader could see things from the perspective of the speaker."

Although *Head of the Class* continues to be cited in works on the history of African American higher education, the history of African American leaders, and the history of higher education in the United States, changes in the field of oral history have called into question the value of the book except as primary source material. In a 1999 essay in *Journal of American History,* Jack Dougherty compares *Head of the Class* unfavorably with other oral history scholarship, suggesting that Morris failed to address important questions, including the role of the narrator in the collection and the ways in which the present circumstances of interviewees influenced their accounts of the past. An anthology of oral history education edited by Peter Lau and published in 2006 notes that oral histories like Morris's, though entertaining, "often privilege local over national, social over institutional."

Because of the lingering questions about the methodology Morris used for *Head of the Class,* no recent scholarship of the work exists; its use in a scholarly context is limited to its value as primary source material. The interviews remain valuable, however, as a kind of road map on diversity for future leaders who will be dealing with a complex world in which no one racial group dominates. For, as Ellis notes in his preface to the book, "The struggle of black people to have their genius acknowledged and expressed is a particularly distilled and intense version of all American stories."

BIBLIOGRAPHY

Sources

Anderson, Noel S., and Haroon Kharem, eds. *Education as Freedom: African American Educational Thought and Activism.* Plymouth, UK: Livingston, 2009. Print.

Dougherty, Jack. "From Anecdote to Analysis: Oral History Interviews and the New School in Educational History." *Journal of American History* 86.2 (1999): 712–23. *JSTOR.* Web. 28 Jan. 2013.

Etter-Lewis, G. *My Soul Is My Own: Oral Narratives of African American Women in the Professions.* New York: Routledge, 1993. Print.

Hirsch, Jerrold. *Portrait of America: A Cultural History of the Federal Writers' Project.* Chapel Hill: University of North Carolina Press, 2003. Print.

Morris, Gabrielle. "Asking Personal Questions." *Oral History Review* 29.2 (2002): 57–59. *JSTOR.* Web. 28 Jan. 2013.

———. *Head of the Class: An Oral History of African-American Achievement in Higher Education and Beyond.* New York: Twayne, 1995. Print.

O'Connor, Carla. "Black Women Beating the Odds from One Generation to the Next." *American Educational Research Journal* 39.4 (2002): 855–903. *JSTOR.* Web. 28 Jan. 2013.

Ritchie, Donald A. "Oral History: From Sound to Print and Back Again." *Oral American Historians Magazine* 11.3 (1997): 6–8. *JSTOR.* Web. 28 Jan. 2013.

Schreiber, Harry N. "On the Broussard Oral History Interview: Editor's Note." *The California Supreme Court Historical Society Yearbook.* Vol. 4. *JSTOR.* Web. 28 Jan. 2013.

Sollars, Werner, et al. *Blacks at Harvard: A Documentary History of African-American Experience at Harvard and Radcliffe.* New York: New York University Press, 1993. Print.

Walker, Vanessa S. *Their Highest Potential: An African American School Community in the Segregated South.* Chapel Hill: University of North Carolina Press, 1996. Print.

Further Reading

Banks, Ann. *First-Person America.* New York: Norton, 1990. Print.

Bowen, W. G., and Derek Bok. *The Shape of the River: Race in Admissions at Princeton.* Princeton, NJ: Princeton University Press, 1998. Print.

Gasman, Marybeth, and Christopher L. Tudico. *Historically Black Colleges and Universities.* New York: Palgrave, 2008. Print.

Kim, Mikyong Minsun. "The Impact of Historically Black Colleges and Universities on the Academic Success of African-American Students." *Researchers on Higher Education* 47.4 (2006): 399–427. *JSTOR.* Web. 28 Jan. 2013.

Newby, A. *Plain Folks in the New South: Social Change and Cultural Persistence, 1880–1915.* Baton Rouge: Louisiana State University Press, 1989. Print.

Thomson, Alastair. "Four Paradigms: Transformation in Oral History." *Oral History Review* 34.1 (2007): 49–70. *JSTOR.* Web. 29 Jan. 2013.

Kristin King-Ries

The History of Mary Prince, a West Indian Slave, Related by Herself

Mary Prince

OVERVIEW

Published in London in 1831, *The History of Mary Prince, a West Indian Slave, Related by Herself* represents an attempt by Mary Prince, her editor and employer Thomas Pringle, and her transcriber Susanna Strickland to provide evidence in support of the abolition of slavery in the British colonies. Born circa 1788 into slavery in Bermuda, Prince experienced great physical suffering from hard labor, harsh punishments, and illness brought on by overwork before leaving her last master's household during an 1828 trip to England. In its published form, *The History of Mary Prince* is a collaborative work, reflecting the combined efforts of—and some of the tensions among—Prince, Strickland, and Pringle as they seek to present Prince's history in a way that supports their individual and collective agendas.

Appearing during the last years of the antislavery struggle in Britain, *The History of Mary Prince* was controversial both for its portrayal of her last owners, the Woods, and for its criticism of the slavery-driven colonial economy of the West Indies. Prince's moral character, especially the details of her sexual history, received intense public scrutiny in an attempt to discredit her work. In recent years the struggle over who would tell Prince's story, and how, has itself been the subject of close study, as scholars seek to understand the complex power dynamics among a former slave, her former owners, and the British abolitionists for and with whom she worked.

HISTORICAL AND LITERARY CONTEXT

The History of Mary Prince was published with the purpose of supporting the final stages of the campaign to abolish slavery in the British colonies. Slavery was effectively outlawed in the British Isles by the 1789 Mansfield decision, which dictated that masters could not force slaves brought to Britain from the colonies to return. However, slaveholding was woven into the fabric of eighteenth-century British economic life: the wealth of both the aristocracy and the Church of England came in part from slave labor on West Indian plantations, and many Britons of all walks of life also profited directly or indirectly from the Atlantic slave trade. After a protracted battle, that trade was finally outlawed in 1807.

When Prince arrived in London in 1828, antislavery activists were intent on their ultimate goal: abolishing the institution throughout the British Empire. After she claimed her freedom, Prince went to work for Pringle, who was the secretary of the Anti-Slavery Society and eventually became her editor. Strickland, the white woman who transcribed and undoubtedly helped to shape Prince's story, was a guest in Pringle's home. Although Pringle, Strickland, and Prince had differing individual perspectives and agendas, they were apparently united in viewing Prince's life story, especially the cruelties she had suffered as a slave in the West Indies, as potentially valuable evidence in support of the abolitionist campaign.

Although *The History of Mary Prince* is the earliest-known first-person account of an enslaved woman's life to be published in English, it joined an existing tradition of works from the late eighteenth century illustrating the intellectual and spiritual capabilities of British subjects of African descent, including Olaudah Equiano's *Interesting Narrative* (1989). In the American colonies, Phillis Wheatley had written short spiritual autobiographies in poetic form, as well as poems and letters that commented on political events of her day. Like many of their predecessors, Prince and Strickland drew on a variety of genres, including spiritual autobiography,

❖ **Key Facts**

Time Period:
Late 18th to Early 19th Century

Relevant Historical Events:
Growth of abolitionism in Britain

Nationality:
Bermudan

Keywords:
slavery; abolition; colonialism

Plaque commemorating the burial ground for slaves and free blacks of St. George's Parish, in St. Peter's Church graveyard, Bermuda. © WHITE WINDMILL/ALAMY

ADVERSITY AND RESISTANCE

PRIMARY SOURCE

EXCERPT FROM *THE HISTORY OF MARY PRINCE, A WEST INDIAN SLAVE, RELATED BY HERSELF*

I am often much vexed, and I feel great sorrow when I hear some people in this country say, that the slaves do not need better usage, and do not want to be free. They believe the foreign people, who deceive them, and say slaves are happy. I say, Not so. How can slaves be happy when they have the halter round their neck and the whip upon their back? and are disgraced and thought no more of than beasts?—and are separated from their mothers, and husbands, and children, and sisters, just as cattle are sold and separated? Is it happiness for a driver in the field to take down his wife or sister or child, and strip them, and whip them in such a disgraceful manner?—women that have had children exposed in the open field to shame! There is no modesty or decency shown by the owner to his slaves; men, women, and children are exposed alike. Since I have been here I have often wondered how English people can go out into the West Indies and act in such a beastly manner. But when they go to the West Indies, they forget God and all feeling of shame, I think, since they can see and do such things. They tie up slaves like hogs—moor them up like cattle, and they lick them, so as hogs, or cattle, or horses never were flogged;—and yet they come home and say, and make some good people believe, that slaves don't want to get out of slavery. But they put a cloak about the truth. It is not so. All slaves want to be free—to be free is very sweet. I will say the truth to English people who may read this history that my good friend, Miss S, is now writing

captivity narratives by white authors such as Mary Rowlandson, and travel literature.

In the decades that followed the publication of *The History of Mary Prince,* other women of African descent made their livings through travel and by marketing records of their experiences. Nancy Prince (no relation), a free-born African American, published an account in 1841 of a missionary trip to Jamaica, which was later incorporated into her 1850 *Narrative of the Life and Travels of Mrs. Nancy Prince.* West Indian Mary Jane Seacole published *Wonderful Adventures of Mrs. Seacole in Many Lands* in 1857. Throughout the twentieth century autobiography remained an important genre for women of African descent; authors including Zora Neale Hurston, Maya Angelou, and Audre Lorde told their life stories as examples of and protests against the social and political constraints affecting African American women's lives.

THEMES AND STYLE

Much of *The History of Mary Prince* is devoted to detailing Prince's suffering from both harsh punishment and bodily illnesses brought on by unremitting hard labor. While her childhood was relatively carefree, the master and mistress to whom she was sold as a young teenager were especially cruel. Mrs. I—, Prince writes, "caused me to know the exact difference between the smart of the rope, the cart-whip, and the cow-skin, when applied to my naked body by her own cruel hand." Prince welcomes being "sent … away to Turk's Island," only to find work and the living conditions in a salt mine there even worse and the punishments equally severe. As she grows into young womanhood, she begins to resist, both verbally and by leaving her masters' houses for a time. She has some success, but the abuse she suffers becomes more psychological and often sexual: one master "ha[s] an ugly fashion of stripping himself quite naked and then ordering [Prince] to wash him in a tub of water."

Prince describes the purpose of her narrative in the text's final sentence: "I tell it [the story] to let the English people know the truth; and I hope they will never leave off to pray God, and to call loud to the great King of England, till all the poor blacks be given free, and slavery done up for evermore." Pringle describes Prince's purpose similarly: "she wished it to be done … that good people in England might hear from a slave what a slave had felt and suffered." As for the process of transcription, Pringle writes that "the narrative was taken down from Mary's own lips by a lady who happened at that time to be residing in my family as a visitor." While Pringle insists that "no fact of importance has been omitted, and not a single circumstance or sentiment has been added," recent critics suggest that Pringle and Strickland played an active role in shaping the published narrative.

Pringle's influence is especially evident in the structure of the published volume. It contains not only Prince's narrative, accompanied by editorial notes written by Pringle, but also a preface, a supplement, and the life story of another slave, Louis Asa-Asa, all of which were added by Pringle. Later editions include additional appendices. Modern critics find Pringle's presence intrusive. For example, Barbara Baumgartner writes in *Callaloo* that "with his numerous and lengthy explanations, additions, and interruptions … Pringle … appears to down for me. I have been a slave myself—I know what slaves feel—I can tell by myself what other slaves feel, and by what they have told me. The man that says slaves be quite happy in slavery—that they don't want to be free—that man is either ignorant or a lying person. I never heard a slave say so. I never heard a Buckra man say so, till I heard tell of it in England. Such people ought to be ashamed of themselves. They can't do without slaves, they say. What's the reason they can't do without slaves as well as in England? No slaves here—no whips—no stocks—no punishment, except for wicked people. They hire servants in England; and if they don't like them, they send them away: they can't lick them. Let them work ever so hard in England, they are far better off than slaves. If they get a bad master, they give warning and go hire to another. They have their liberty. That's just what we want. We don't mind hard work, if we had proper treatment, and proper wages like English servants, and proper time given in the week to keep us from breaking the Sabbath. But they won't give it; they will have work—work—work, night and day, sick or well, till we are quite done up; and we must not speak up nor look amiss, however much we be abused. And then when we are quite done up, who cares for us, more than for a lame horse? This is slavery. I tell it to let English people know the truth; and I hope they will never leave off to pray God, and call loud to the great King of England, till all the poor blacks be given free, and slavery done up for evermore.

SOURCE: Prince, Mary. *The History of Mary Prince, A West Indian Slave, Related by Herself.* London: F. Westley and A.H. Davis, 3rd Edition, 1831.

compete with Prince for control over her story and its meaning." As Baumgartner points out, Pringle's decision to publish, in the supplement, a letter from Prince's last master, John Wood, is especially puzzling, since the letter attacks Prince's moral character, alluding to aspects of her sexual history that Strickland had deliberately omitted from the narrative.

CRITICAL DISCUSSION

Reaction to *The History of Mary Prince* reflected the highly mediated nature of the work, with challenges to the veracity of her story directed as much at Pringle as at Prince herself. After James Macqueen, in an 1833 letter published in *Blackwood's Edinburgh Magazine,* accused Pringle of using Prince as a "despicable tool" for his own propagandistic purposes, Pringle successfully sued the publisher of *Blackwood's* for libel. Later the same year Prince's former master, Wood, successfully sued Pringle for libel. While testimony at the trial did not refute Prince's claims of abuse at the Woods' hands, it did reveal that her sexual history was more complicated than what was reported in the book.

In abolitionist circles, *The History of Mary Prince* continued to serve as evidence of the brutality of slavery in the West Indies and possibly also as a source of material support for Prince herself, who disappears from the historical record after the libel trials but is described by Pringle in a postscript to the second edition and a preface to the third as suffering from a "disease of the eyes" that "may terminate in total blindness," in addition to the rheumatism that had long interfered with her ability to work. An appendix to the third edition, a letter by Mrs. Pringle describing the "marks of severe punishment on Mary Prince's body," has been of particular interest to recent scholars. Some, such as A. M. Rauwerda, have seen the appendix as reflecting the skepticism with which even Prince's supporters treated her story, while others, such as Baumgartner, have read it as evidence of a female solidarity that contrasts with the tendency of Pringle's notes to undermine Prince's credibility.

Recent critics, including Rauwerda, Baumgartner, and Gillian Whitlock, have focused on the relationships between Prince, Pringle, and Strickland and the ways those relationships shaped, and are reflected in, the published text. As the number of critical editions has grown, scholars have also turned their attention to each other's work, reflecting on how the critical apparatus produced in the late twentieth and early twenty-first centuries continues the process of authorizing, shaping, and at times appropriating Prince's story.

BIBLIOGRAPHY

Sources

Baumgartner, Barbara. "The Body as Evidence: Resistance, Collaboration, and Appropriation in *The History of Mary Prince.*" *Callaloo* 24.1 (2001): 253–75. JSTOR. Web. 22 Jan. 2013.

Macqueen, James. "The Colonial Empire of Great Britain." *Blackwood's Edinburgh Magazine* 30.5 (1831): 744–64. *Hathi Trust Digital Library.* Web. 1 Feb. 2013.

Prince, Mary. *The History of Mary Prince, A West Indian Slave, Related by Herself.* 1831. Ed. Moira Ferguson. Ann Arbor: University of Michigan Press, 1993. Print.

Rauwerda, A. M. "Naming, Agency, and 'A Tissue of Falsehoods' in *The History of Mary Prince.*" *Victorian Literature and Culture* 29.2 (2001): 397–411. *JSTOR.* Web. 22 Jan. 2013.

Whitlock, Gillian. "Volatile Subjects: *The History of Mary Prince.*" *Literature of the Early Black Atlantic.* Ed. Vincent Carretta and Philip Gould. Lexington: University Press of Kentucky, 2001. 72–86. Print.

Further Reading

Gilroy, Paul. *The Black Atlantic: Modernity and Double-Consciousness.* Cambridge, MA: Harvard University Press, 1993. Print.

Hochschild, Adam. *Bury the Chains: Prophets and Rebels in the Fight to Free an Empire's Slaves.* Boston: Houghton Mifflin, 2005. Print.

Paquet, Sandra Pouchet. *Caribbean Autobiography: Cultural Identity and Self-Representation.* Madison: University of Wisconsin Press, 2002. Print.

Sharpe, Jenny. *Ghosts of Slavery: A Literary Archaeology of Black Women's Lives.* Minneapolis: University of Minnesota Press, 2003. Print.

Whitlock, Gillian. *The Intimate Empire: Reading Women's Autobiography.* New York: Cassell, 2000. Web. *Ebrary.* 22 January 2013.

Cathy Saunders

Ireland's Unfinished Revolution

An Oral History

Kenneth Griffith, Timothy O'Grady

Key Facts

Time Period:
Early 20th Century

Relevant Historical Events:
Easter Rising; Irish War for Independence; Irish Civil War

Nationality:
Irish

Keywords:
colonialism; independence; civil war

OVERVIEW

Kenneth Griffith and Timothy O'Grady's biographical study *Ireland's Unfinished Revolution: An Oral History* (1999) tells the story of the Irish fight for independence from 1916 to 1924 through the recollections of nine activists who were deeply involved in the struggle. During the late 1970s Griffith compiled more than a hundred hours of interviews with aging Irish activists, while O'Grady created a narrative that links the interviews with historical background and the authors' pro-independence political viewpoint. *Ireland's Unfinished Revolution* provides an insider's view of the Irish resistance to British rule through the personal stories of a handful of movement foot soldiers. In addition, the author/editors weave their interviewees' memories into compelling portraits of some of the most famous movement leaders of the era, including Michael Collins, Patrick Pearse, and Eamon de Valera.

First published in 1982 as *Curious Journey: An Oral History of Ireland's Unfinished Revolution,* the book became both a popular success and a groundbreaking work of validation for Irish oral history. Welsh-born filmmaker and historian Griffith gathered the source material for use in his documentary film *Curious Journey.* However, when British television refused to air the film for political reasons, Griffith joined forces with Irish American author O'Grady to reproduce his documentary in book form, ensuring that this intimate view of Irish insurrection would not be prevented from reaching a wide audience. Still viewed as an important historical source about the Irish republican movement, the book was reissued in Ireland in 1998 and in the United States in 1999.

HISTORICAL AND LITERARY CONTEXT

The Easter Rising of 1916 had its roots in deep mistrust between the Irish people and the British, who had attempted to exert control over them for centuries. Hostilities worsened during the 1840s, when a devastating famine resulted in starvation for the impoverished Irish while much of the nation's food was exported to England. During the last half of the nineteenth century, a number of resistance groups were formed. Some, such as the Gaelic League, promoted pride in Irish language and culture, while others, such as the Irish Republican Brotherhood, prepared for armed conflict. This tense atmosphere exploded in a number of divisive confrontations. The seven-day Easter Rising was followed by the guerrilla War of Independence from 1919 to 1921. These military actions exposed deep divisions within the movement for Irish independence, resulting in a bitter civil war that raged from 1921 to 1923 and left scars that would affect Irish society into the next century.

Though an independent republic was achieved in the southern part of the country by 1948, tensions persisted in British-occupied Northern Ireland between a largely working-class Catholic republican minority and a wealthier Protestant loyalist majority. By the late 1970s conflict over Irish independence had reached a new level of intensity. The three decades of civil unrest—popularly dubbed the "Troubles"—began during the late 1960s with a loyalist attack on a Catholic civil rights demonstration and peaked during the mid-1970s with almost three hundred deaths a year. At this painful moment in Irish history, Griffith resolved to record the experiences and perspectives of the men and women who had begun the struggle for Irish sovereignty.

Because the island faced frequent assault from neighboring invaders, it was perhaps inevitable that Irish literature would involve strong patriotic and political components. Personal experience of resistance to British rule became the basis for a literature of defiance, which included such writers as Sean O'Casey (*Shadow of a Gunman,* 1923). Tom Barry, one of Griffith's interviewees in *Ireland's Unfinished Revolution,* recalls the early struggle for independence in *Guerilla Days in Ireland* (1949), and Ernie O'Malley's 1978 autobiography *The Singing Flame* recounts his experiences during the early 1920s Irish Civil War. Irish historian David Fitzpatrick collected oral testimonies as source material for his 1977 *Politics and Irish Life, 1913–1921.* More strictly defined oral history is seen in Uinseann MacEoin's 1980 study *Survivors: The Story of Ireland's Struggle as Told through Some of Her Outstanding Living People.*

Capturing as it did the personal recollections of a dying generation of Irish revolutionaries, Griffith

ADVERSITY AND RESISTANCE

British soldiers patrol the rubble-filled streets of Dublin, Ireland, after the Easter Uprising of 1916. © POPPERFOTO/GETTY IMAGES

and O'Grady's work was well received upon its original publication and quickly became an important primary resource for studies of a pivotal time in Irish history. Though Griffith's first attempt to disseminate the stories of the fight for Irish independence on film had been stymied by British censorship during the late 1970s, by 2013 the British Broadcasting Corporation was using excerpts from *Ireland's Unfinished Revolution* as part of its website on Irish history.

THEMES AND STYLE

Ireland's Unfinished Revolution traces the realities of civil conflict, underscoring both the patriotic zeal of those who believed their work would liberate Ireland and the deep contradictions inherent in revolutionary politics. Martin Walton poignantly describes his baptism of blood at the age of fifteen: "I remember my knees nearly going out from under me. I would have sold my mother and father and the Pope just to get out of that bloody place. But you recover after a few minutes." Walton also attests to the sheer boredom of war, saying, "I always thought that was the great test of a man—if he was able to keep coming to meetings, without any arms and with nothing happening, just drilling and going through the long haul until he could see combat." The narrative explores the agonizing choices of civil war as well. Sean Harling relates, "Now when a civil war breaks out, it's brother against brother, and there's no saying what way you'd go. … Most of the lads … were just depressed that there was any split at all, you see."

In his linking narrative, O'Grady frames the focus of the text, writing, "The purpose of this book has been to somehow find the present through the past." Creating their book at a time of intense political unrest, the authors seek to link past and present through three basic interview questions: Why did each interviewee feel compelled to fight the British? What actions did each personally take? How does he or she feel those actions shaped the future of the state of Ireland? By choosing to interview two women and seven men "from all parts of Ireland and most social classes" who were deeply involved in the fighting, Griffith and O'Grady attempt to explore the Irish drive for independence and the historical and social roots of the bitterness and bloodshed.

Throughout *Ireland's Unfinished Revolution*, Griffith and O'Grady display frankly republican leanings, convictions that had triggered the British government's reluctance to air Griffith's original documentary film. Their sympathy with the Irish men and women who resisted British rule is evident in O'Grady's explanatory narrative, such as his response to a common perception of the Irish Republican Army as thugs and killers: "Motivated entirely by ideals, the Volunteers tended on the contrary to be the more sensitive members of the community." In the interviews themselves, Griffith preserves Irish vernacular without caricature, giving the oral narratives authority and intimacy. Joseph Sweeney brings a machine gun fight to life, saying, "I got a right belt from a bit of granite on top of my head." Maire Comerford describes republican response to U.S. President Woodrow Wilson's 1918 Fourteen Points statement, claiming that "everything that Wilson said—government by consent of the governed, war for small nations, open agreements openly arrived at … it was a litany of things which stirred up the Irish people right through."

CRITICAL DISCUSSION

Ronnie Munck, writing one of the earliest reviews of the 1982 edition of *Curious Journey* for the journal *Oral History*, noted that the work's political analysis is "frankly simplistic" and its oral history methodology "disarmingly naïve" but concluded positively, writing, "What we have essentially is an exciting story well told." Reviewers of the 1999 edition indicated that the work had lost little of its dramatic impact. Emer Mullins, writing for the *Irish Voice* in 1999, asserted that "from armed raids to kidnappings, prison breaks to secret agents, one could almost be forgiven for mistaking this novel for fiction. … This account of the founding of the Irish nation is a riveting read and a valuable historical archive." Pauline Ferrie of the *Boston Irish Reporter* agreed, claiming, "The firsthand commentaries, collected during interviews carried out by Griffith, are woven into O'Grady's narrative to produce a compelling account of what it meant to live and fight through the years from 1916 to 1922."

In his 1983 review of *Curious Journey*, Munck outlined Griffith and O'Grady's contribution to the use of oral history in Irish historical research, writing, "Apart from its intrinsic value this book has helped put oral history on the map in Ireland taking it beyond the realm of academia and folklorists." The volatile interactions of British occupiers, Irish loyalists, and Irish republicans form a complex web that connects the history of Ireland to the nation's present and future. Griffith and O'Grady's foresight in capturing the personal experiences of those who lived through the significant events at the turn of the twentieth century gives their work a unique and enduring place in the historical record of Ireland.

Though there has been little direct scholarly study of *Ireland's Unfinished Revolution* in the decades since its publication, the work has been an important primary source for historians researching Ireland's troubled past. David Leeson, for example, used information from a number of Griffith and O'Grady's interviews to piece together the chronology of a key event of the War of Independence for his 2003 *Canadian Journal of History* article about the 1920 Croke Park massacre. *Ireland's Unfinished Revolution* appears in numerous bibliographies, including such respected works as John T. Koch's 2006 *Celtic Culture: A Historical Encyclopedia*.

THE POLITICS OF ORAL HISTORY

The BBC's 1976 refusal to air Kenneth Griffith's film documentary *Curious Journey* is only one example of the political volatility of Irish republican oral history. During the early 2000s the historically Irish American Boston College launched an ambitious oral history project to expand and preserve the record of the Irish struggle for independence. Promising to keep the stories secret until after interviewees' deaths, historians compiled confidential interviews with dozens of militant activists from both the republican and the loyalist camps. Many candidly revealed carefully guarded details of their involvement in illegal paramilitary actions during the Troubles of the 1970s. After the deaths of the first two interviewees, a 2010 book and documentary film, both titled *Voices from the Grave*, showcased their stories.

In March 2011 British authorities, through a U.S. prosecutor, subpoenaed two confidential interviews from the Boston College archive to aid the government in prosecuting the kidnapping and murder of alleged loyalist informers during the 1970s. Opponents of the subpoena asserted that not only did the British government's demand threaten the future of the field of oral history by compromising the historian's right to guarantee confidentiality, but it also could actually damage the hard-won peace process itself. In December 2011 a judge ordered Boston College to hand over the documents, but both the institution and individual oral historians appealed the decision; a number of U.S. senators and representatives have also protested the ruling. The legal debate continued to develop into the 2010s.

BIBLIOGRAPHY

Sources

Ferrie, Pauline. "Book News and Reviews Direct from Ireland." Rev. of *Ireland's Unfinished Revolution: An Oral History*, by Kenneth Griffith and Timothy O'Grady. *Boston Irish Reporter* 1 Sept. 1998: 37. *ProQuest*. Web. 14 Jan. 2013.

Mullins, Emer. "Talking about a Revolution." Rev. of *Ireland's Unfinished Revolution: An Oral History*, by Kenneth Griffith and Timothy O'Grady. *Irish Voice* 13 Apr 1999: 28. *ProQuest*. Web. 14 Jan. 2013.

Munck, Ronnie. Rev. of *Curious Journey: An Oral History of Ireland's Unfinished Revolution*, by Kenneth Griffith and Timothy O'Grady. *Oral History* 11.2 (1983): 84. *JSTOR*. Web. 15 Jan. 2013.

"Sean Kavanagh—An Irish Patriot." *Clann Caomhánach*. Web. 14 Jan. 2013.

Further Reading

Beiner, Guy. "Bodhaire Uí Laoire: Oral History and Contemporary Irish Historiography." *University College Dublin*. Web. 14 Jan. 2013.

Dwyer, Jim. "Secret Archive of Ulster Troubles Faces Subpoena." *New York Times*. New York Times, 13 May 2011. Web. 18 Jan. 2013.

Ellis, Peter Berresford. *Eyewitness to Irish History*. Hoboken, NJ: Wiley, 2004. Print.

Griffith, Kenneth. *The Fool's Pardon: The Autobiography of Kenneth Griffith*. London: Little, Brown, 1994. Print.

Koch, John T. *Celtic Culture: A Historical Encyclopedia*. Santa Barbara, CA: ABC-CLIO, 2006. Print.

Leeson, David. "Death in the Afternoon: The Croke Park Massacre, 21 November 1920." *Canadian Journal of History* 38.1 (2003): 43–67. *ProQuest*. Web. 15 Jan. 2013.

Moloney, Ed. *Voices from the Grave: Two Men's War in Ireland*. New York: Public Affairs, 2010. Print.

Wharton, Kenneth. *Bloody Belfast: An Oral History of the British Army's War against the IRA*. Stroud, UK: Spellmount: History, 2010. Print.

Tina Gianoulis

Massacre in Mexico
Elena Poniatowska

OVERVIEW

First published in 1971, *La noche de Tlatelolco* (*Massacre in Mexico,* 1975) is Elena Poniatowska's account of the 1968 massacre in which the Mexican military and police opened fire on a group of students engaged in a peaceful protest against the government. Poniatowska, a Mexican journalist and novelist, compiled what she referred to as a "collage of voices," spinning a tapestry of the months leading up to the massacre at the Plaza de las Tres Culturas in Tlatelolco, Mexico City, and a vivid description of the night itself. She wove together testimony from witnesses of a variety of political affiliations, including both students and parents, and used newspaper headlines, tape recordings, and army dispatches, as well as her own account. The result is expertly moving and presents a complex understanding of all the forces that contributed to this gruesome chapter of Mexican history.

Because of government censorship, *La noche de Tlatelolco* received little publicity and was only reviewed by one poet, José Emilio Pacheco. Instead, the book gained readership by word of mouth. Some prominent politicians, trying to suppress news of the massacre, were eager to remove the text from circulation and threatened the publishing house. Worried that the book would fall out of print, supporters began buying multiple copies and the work sold quickly. By the early twenty-first century, the text had seen more than fifty editions, and many critics regarded it as an extraordinary piece of journalism and testimony.

HISTORICAL AND LITERARY CONTEXT

Massacre in Mexico offers a vivid account of the government's brutal assault on the student movement of 1968. After World War II, Mexico experienced rapid economic growth and industries boomed. Subsequent economic mishandling, however, caused the country to go deep into debt. While the Mexican government was able to project an image of Mexico as a peaceful and prosperous place, a different story was brewing on college campuses where the students wanted a real discussion of the issues facing their country, including severe poverty and political oppression. Unlike revolutions of the past, it was not the uprising of a class of serfs but of an empowered youth who believed their ideas would be heard.

By July 1968 students had organized a strike protesting governmental repression and violence and included demands such as monetary compensation for students injured because of the fighting and the release of students being held as political prisoners over previous political opposition. Tensions escalated, resulting in the military occupation of the National Autonomous University campus. On October 2, 1968, about 15,000 students gathered at the Plaza de las Tres Culturas to protest. By late afternoon, some 5,000 students and family members remained. Although organizers grew increasingly concerned about the strong military presence and attempted to stop the rally, they were unsuccessful; soon shots were fired into the crowd, killing and wounding hundreds of people. Many of the survivors were illegally dragged to prison. *Massacre in Mexico* uses interviews as a mode to document the rising political climate in the weeks just before the massacre as well as follows many narratives of the massacre itself.

Many of Poniatowska's interviewing methodologies were formulated during her time as an assistant to American anthropologist Oscar Lewis, whose book *Children of Sanchez* (1961) documents the life of a Mexican family living in poverty. Poniatowska worked with Lewis on his book *Pedro Martinez: A Mexican Peasant and His Family* (1964), and shortly after she altered the social emphasis of her work from Mexico's upper and middle classes to the urban poor.

The publication of *Massacre in Mexico* made a substantial contribution to the canon of Latin American oral discourse and gained Poniatowska recognition in the United States. The text is part of the genre of testimonial literature, which functions with the explicit purpose to "denounce repression and abuse of authority, raise the consciousness of its readers about situations of political, economic and cultural terror, and offer an alternative view to official, hegemonic history," explains Beth Ellen Jörgensen, author of *The Writing of Elena Poniatowska* (1994). As such, *Massacre in Mexico* offers more than just an exploration of the events of the student movement; it functions as a boldly critical text of Mexican politics in a time when critical voices were being staunchly silenced by the Mexican government.

THEMES AND STYLE

The central themes of *Massacre in Mexico* are divisions of class, gender inequity, and political repression.

❖ *Key Facts*

Time Period:
Mid-20th Century

Relevant Historical Events:
Government assault on the Mexican student movement; student occupation of UNAM and subsequent massacre

Nationality:
Mexican

Keywords:
student movement; massacre; revolution

Author Elena Poniatowska in 2012. © AP IMAGES/GDA

Poniatowska challenged the government's silence of the Tlatelolco massacre by weaving many fragments of testimonies that prevent the text from being dominated by one voice; instead, it is the compilation of the voices of many. A mother signs her letter, "hoping that you will continue to kill students and teachers with the same furious passion, love mom"; this piece is juxtaposed with newspaper ads taken out by parents still searching for their son a month after the massacre. One prisoner muses, "if the one thing the Student Movement has accomplished is to strip the Mexican Revolution bare, to show that it was a filthy, corrupt, old whore, that alone is enough to justify it. … " Though the text clearly privileges the voices of the defeated movement, it allows an exploration of bias and challenges its credibility by allowing contradictory narratives of the massacre to be presented throughout the text.

One of Poniatowska's motivations for compiling the text was the government's censorship and prevention of an investigation of the massacre. She was struck by how quickly life "went back to normal." Only a week after the massacre, the Summer Olympics, held in Mexico City, began, and Poniatowska was "outraged … that such a thing had happened and yet everyone was so absorbed in watching the Olympics on the TV." Immediately, Poniatowska began collecting testimonies from anyone related to the events. She visited the military camps and the campus dorms and interviewed professors, students, and parents, interspersing testimonies with newspaper clippings, photographs, and recollections of the chants and songs and graffiti associated with the student movement.

Stylistically, *Massacre in Mexico* rejects the modes of traditional nonfiction and journalism. It rejects convention and presents a nonlinear presentation of what Poniatowska calls "sound bites," which effectively record the silence and marginalization of the 1968 social and political climate. In the middle of the text, Poniatowska weaves sixteenth-century indigenous poems of Mexico's conquest to fuse an intertextual relationship between the voices of past and present. Mostly, the testimonials are quite short, a couple of sentences to a page long, and she frequently brackets headlines, banners, chants, and graffiti into the text, as in "NOTHING THROUGH FORCE, EVERYTHING THROUGH REASON" or "MEXICO—FREEDOM—MEXICO—FREEDOM—MEXICO—FREEDOM." Taken together, the author seeks to give an initial sketch of the devastation that culminates as more and more voices add to the resounding cries of those who suffered.

CRITICAL DISCUSSION

Because of the threat of government censorship, *Massacre in Mexico* was published quietly. Within a few months, however, the book gained enough notoriety that President Luis Echeverría, wishing to dissociate himself and public officials with the massacre, offered Poniatowska the esteemed Xavier Villaurrutia literary award. She declined the prize, asking, "Who will give literary awards to the dead?" José Emilio Pacheco, editor in chief of *La Cultura en México*, noted when *Massacre in Mexico* was published that "Elena Poniatowska has erased the distance between those who read the book and the events it recounts." In an introduction to the English translation, Mexican writer and diplomat Octavio Paz wrote that "the passion that suffuses all her pages is the passion for justice, the same burning ideal that inspired the students' demonstrations and protests." *La noche de Tlatelolco* has seen forty-eight Spanish editions, has sold almost one-quarter million copies, and has been translated into English, Czech, and Polish.

Since its 1971 publication, *Massacre in Mexico* has slowly spread awareness of the events and has served as a voice for the marginalized. Because of government censorship—and the insistence that the casualities of that night were very few—there has never been any official investigation into the hundreds of deaths and the inhumane treatment of the remaining prisoners. Scholars continue to examine *Massacre in Mexico* for the relationships between the compiler and the subject matter; it is also read through the lens of Latin American feminism, as discussed by María Teresa Medeiros-Lichem in *Reading the Feminine Voice in Latin American Women's Fiction: From Teresa De La Parra to Elena Poniatowska and Luisa Valenzuela* (2002).

Most scholarship of *Massacre in Mexico* relies on biographical information and compares the text to many of Poniatowska's other prominent works, including *Hasta no verte Jesús mío* (1969; Here's to you, Jesus), a hybrid fictional and nonfictional text about the life of a laundress in Mexico. Scholar Jörgensen explores the "framing questions" that Poniatowska used to compile the text, "which reminds us that the editorial function is neither neutral nor transparent but charged with meaning and the making of meaning." In her 2009 article "Print the Myth: Elena

Poniatowska's Biographical Fiction," Clary Loisel argues that the author writes herself into the work and locates the text on a spectrum of Latin American fictional and historic mythology.

BIBLIOGRAPHY

Sources

Fraiser, Ronald. "Foreword." *1968: A Student Generation in Revolt*. New York: Pantheon, 1988. 1–15. Print.

Gardner, Nathanial Eli. *Through Their Eyes: Marginality in the Works of Elena Poniatowska, Silvia Molina and Rosa Nissán*. Bern, Switzerland: Peter Lang, 2007. Print.

Jörgensen, Beth Ellen. *The Writing of Elena Poniatowska: Engaging Dialogues*. Austin: University of Texas Press, 1994. Print.

Loisel, Clary. "Print the Myth: Elena Poniatowska's Biographical Fiction." *Confluencia* 24.2 (2009): 83+. *JSTOR*. Web. 8 Feb. 2013.

Peden, Margaret Sayers. *Mexican Writers on Writing*. San Antonio, TX: Trinity University Press, 2007. Print.

Poniatowska, Elena. *Lilus Kikus and Other Stories*. Trans. Elizabeth Coonrod Martínez. Albuquerque: University of New Mexico Press, 2005. Print.

———. *Massacre in Mexico*. Trans. Helen R. Lane. New York: Viking, 1975. Print.

Schuessler, Michael Karl. *Elena Poniatowska: An Intimate Biography*. Tucson: University of Arizona Press, 2007. Print.

Further Reading

Brewster, Claire. *Responding to Crisis in Contemporary Mexico: The Political Writings of Paz, Fuentes, Monsiváis, and Poniatowska*. Tucson: University of Arizona Press, 2005. Print.

Carey, Elaine. *Plaza of Sacrifices: Gender, Power, and Terror in 1968 Mexico*. Albuquerque: University of New Mexico Press, 2005. Print.

Coerver, Don M., Suzanne B. Pasztor, and Robert Buffington. *Mexico: An Encyclopedia of Contemporary Culture and History*. Santa Barbara, CA: ABC-CLIO, 2004. Print.

1968: STUDENT MOVEMENTS

The year 1968 was important in terms of student protests. Students across the world were standing against oppression and for democracy, engaging in peaceful—and sometimes not-so-peaceful—protests. Largely because of the post-war influx of wealth, youth in the United States and Europe were prospering more than ever before. Television was readily accessible, families were traveling abroad, more students were ending up on college campuses, and, as a result, students were becoming more globally minded, aware of the oppression that was occurring elsewhere. In Germany, students were revolting against their poor living conditions and the government's silence surrounding the Holocaust. In France, university students were at a standoff with officials over the perceived lack of participatory university government, resulting in a march of 20,000 students at the Sorbonne, where hundreds were forcefully arrested. In the United States, the University of California at Berkeley had become a hub for protesting the Vietnam War. In Czechoslovakia, an attempt at democratization known as the Prague Spring concluded when the Soviets invaded the country and overthrew the government. Globally, 1968 was a devastatingly violent year, as many of the outbreaks between students and their government resulted in catastrophe, but it was also an important year, as a culture of the new revolutionary ethic fought for substantive social change.

García, Kay S. *Broken Bars: New Perspectives from Mexican Women Writers*. Albuquerque: University of New Mexico Press, 1994. Print.

Medeiros-Lichem, María Teresa. *Reading the Feminine Voice in Latin American Women's Fiction: From Teresa De La Parra to Elena Poniatowska and Luisa Valenzuela*. New York: Lang, 2002. Print.

Tuckman, Jo. *Mexico: Democracy Interrupted*. New Haven, CT: Yale University Press, 2012. Print.

Greg Luther

Mothers, Sisters, Resisters
Oral Histories of Women Who Survived the Holocaust
Brana Gurewitsch

Key Facts

Time Period:
Mid- to Late 20th Century

Relevant Historical Events:
Holocaust; World War II

Nationality:
American

Keywords:
genocide; holocaust; survival

OVERVIEW

Mothers, Sisters, Resisters: Oral Histories of Women Who Survived the Holocaust is a collection of twenty-five interviews edited by Brana Gurewitsch and published in 1998. The interviews were collected anywhere from twenty to forty years after World War II. Many contain dramatic testimony of conditions in the ghettoes of Eastern Europe and in Nazi concentration and extermination camps from 1940 to 1945. Some of the women also discuss their postwar experiences. As the title suggests, the women interviewed share not only the fact of having lived through one of the worst events in human history but also the distinctively feminine experiences of motherhood, daughterhood, and sisterhood. Their commentaries highlight the difficult choices Jewish women had to make during this period, as well as the qualities and strategies that enabled them to survive.

Although there were a number of memoirs written by Holocaust survivors in the first two decades after the war, organized collections of oral histories did not take shape in the United States until the mid-1970s, when Yaffa Eliach began to archive survivor interviews at the first Center for Holocaust Studies in the country. Many of the interviews included in *Mothers, Sisters, Resisters* come from the Eliach collection. The publication of Gurewitsch's carefully edited volume in the late 1990s coincided with an increasing focus among Holocaust scholars on the experiences of women—a subject that had previously been either neglected or rejected. *Mothers, Sisters, Resisters* is widely regarded as an important contribution both to Holocaust studies and to the documentation of women in history.

HISTORICAL AND LITERARY CONTEXT

The interviews in *Mothers, Sisters, Resisters* capture varied aspects of the efforts made during Adolf Hitler's regime to eliminate the Jewish population of Europe. Although there had been periods of intense and even deadly anti-Semitism in Europe for many centuries, there had also been long periods during which Jews were accepted—and at the beginning of the twentieth century, a flourishing Jewish culture had grown in several European countries. Some extreme groups, however, persisted in blaming Jews for a variety of social and economic problems. With the rise of Hitler's National Socialist Party in Germany during the 1930s, the rights of Jews were progressively restricted, and the German government introduced programs designed to reduce the Jewish population, ranging from euthanasia and sterilization to group executions.

As other European countries fell under German rule in the late 1930s, their Jewish populations were confined in ghettoes and concentration camps, and beginning in 1941 the German government implemented a secretive extermination program. Jews from all over Europe were transported to specialized extermination facilities located in Poland, and most were killed in gas chambers soon after arrival. Many others were sent to labor camps, where the majority of workers died from disease, starvation, and maltreatment. Some Jews avoided deportation to the camps by hiding, with the help of courageous non-Jews. Some managed by various means to stay alive in the camps until 1945, when they were liberated by U.S. and Soviet forces. The interview subjects in *Mothers, Sisters, Resisters* were among the one-quarter of European Jews who survived Hitler's attempted genocide.

Although an extensive tradition of Holocaust survivor literature had developed over fifty years, at the time of its publication *Mothers, Sisters, Resisters* reflected a relatively new interest in the experience of female survivors. With a few exceptions—such as Charlotte Delbo's trilogy, *Auschwitz and After* (1995)—most of the many memoirs, autobiographies, and fictionalized accounts by Holocaust survivors had been written by men and reflected the male experience. Initially, attempts to explore gender aspects of the Holocaust experience drew criticism from commentators who believed such efforts might take the focus of Holocaust studies away from the key factor of Jewish heritage or might set up a counterproductive contrast between men's behavior and women's. So it was not until 1983 that even one scholarly event (the Conference on Women Surviving the Holocaust) focused specifically on women and the Holocaust. Ten more years elapsed before publication of the pathbreaking anthology *Different Voices: Women and the Holocaust*, edited by Carol Rittner and John Roth.

In the late 1990s several new books—including *Mothers, Sisters, Resisters*—established gender as an important topic in Holocaust studies. Other works from this period include Judith Baumel's *Double Jeopardy: Gender and the Holocaust* (1998), Esther Fuchs's *Women and the Holocaust: Narrative and Representation* (1999), and Joy E. Miller's *Love Carried Me Home: Women Surviving Auschwitz* (2000). Although oral histories gathered from women contributed in some measure to all these works, *Mothers, Sisters, Resisters* was distinguished by its focus on that material and by the range and quality of the included interviews. The evolving importance of Gurewitsch's work is reflected in contemporary analyses such as Anne Cubilié's *Women Witnessing Terror: Testimony and the Cultural Politics of Human Rights* (2005), which considers the common aspects of feminine experience in various events of traumatic violence ranging from the Holocaust to ongoing conflicts in Afghanistan.

THEMES AND STYLE

The title *Mothers, Sisters, Resisters* encapsulates the thematic structure of Gurewitsch's collection. Many of the interviews share all three aspects—motherhood, sisterhood, and resistance—and as Gurewitsch points out, the themes are intimately intertwined: "By refusing to be separated, mother and daughters or sisters resisted the isolation that was the first step in the dehumanization process [that was practiced in the camps]. By taking risks for each other, they fought the system and their own despair." In order to clarify each of the three themes, however, Gurewitsch groups the interviews in separate sections, each with its own introduction. In addition, she traces associations that go beyond literal mother-daughter or sibling relationships to encompass symbolic connections, such as the bond established among "camp sisters" (*Lager Schwestern*). Several interviews illuminate what Gurewitsch describes as the "tendency of women to form close and long-lasting relationships that become a source of mutual assistance and strength."

Gurewitsch compiled *Mothers, Sisters, Resisters* in order to make available oral history material that reflects the gender-specific experiences of female Holocaust survivors. In addition, the volume demonstrates some of the "best practices" developed by Gurewitsch, who is not only archivist and curator at the Museum of Jewish Heritage in New York City but also coauthor (with Yaffa Eliach) of the *Holocaust Oral History Manual* (1991). Although the oral histories were taken by a variety of interviewers at different times, Gurewitsch made extensive attempts to "verify and corroborate" the stories, and the collection is supplemented with extensive footnotes that contextualize the material.

The stories told in *Mothers, Sisters, Resisters* cover a wide range of experiences and reflect the varied personalities of the interviewees. For example, Eva Schonbrun remembers her sister, who refused to leave her siblings and save herself; Rose Meth and Anna Heilman tell the story of four women who were hanged for their role in sabotaging gas chambers at one extermination facility. Bronislawa Feinesser, alias Marysia, discusses the dangerous missions she undertook smuggling weapons and food in and out of the Warsaw ghetto: "Today I would be very scared. At that time when I was twenty something; I wasn't scared. I wanted to do it. I wanted to be active, to help people." Gurewitsch provides perspective and analysis in the introductions to each section, and every entry begins with a description of the interview subject.

CRITICAL DISCUSSION

By 1998 popular interest in Holocaust memoirs had waned, but among scholars *Mothers, Sisters, Resisters* was generally regarded as a useful contribution to Holocaust studies. In a 2001 review for the *Journal of Contemporary History*, Mark Roseman approves of the fact that Gurewitsch's collection "reproduces lengthy extracts from a variety of different female voices and allows the women to speak for themselves." Roseman was critical of Gurewitsch's introductory sections, however, characterizing them as "rather uncritical and hagiographical." Rose M. Cichy's review for *Library Journal* in 1999 found the groupings used in *Mothers, Sisters, Resisters* to be "of only tangential significance" and observed that because of the length of time that had elapsed between the original experiences and the interviews, some of the stories are "so compressed that the impact and clarity of events are diminished."

When *Mothers, Sisters, Resisters* was published, the value of gender-specific analysis was still not widely recognized in Holocaust studies. In *Women in the Holocaust*, another pioneering work that appeared in 1998, Dalia Ofer and Lenore J. Weitzman observe that "the discussion of women's unique experiences provides a missing element of what we must now see as an incomplete picture of Jewish life during the Holocaust." In the same volume, however, Joan Ringelheim notes a "general reluctance to explore the questions about gender, including sexual exploitation amid the other horrors of the Holocaust—whether because it is

A death sign stands outside the Auschwitz concentration camp museum, Krakow, Poland, March 16, 2006. © ALEX MASI/CORBIS

THE TERRIBLE REALITY: *SOPHIE'S CHOICE*

Although the Holocaust took place during World War II, it was not a cause or a consequence of war. It was a separate, secretive undertaking that followed no rules or conventions and had only one goal: the annihilation of those groups regarded as inferior by Germany's racial purists. The largest proportion of those killed were Jews, but many Poles were also sent to extermination facilities, along with members of several other ethnic and religious groups. In modern warfare most casualties had traditionally been healthy men—soldiers—while women and children had been viewed as noncombatants, who were, if not protected, at least not targeted. The Holocaust machine, however, was designed to kill everyone, without regard to sex or age. In fact, the weakest died first and in greater numbers, while the strongest were often kept alive for slave labor.

The special plight of mothers deported to camps with their children was dramatized in William Styron's 1979 novel *Sophie's Choice*, the story of a Polish Catholic woman forced to choose which of her two children would be killed immediately and which would remain alive for a time. For many Americans Styron's book and the acclaimed motion picture version that appeared in 1982 provided an introduction to the extreme and pervasive cruelty practiced during the Holocaust.

thought to be trivial in comparison with genocide per se or because it is thought to be banal, or because it is too close to what we know in everyday life."

Since the late 1990s gender-specific studies have become a more accepted part of Holocaust scholarship, and aspects of the female experience highlighted in Gurewitsch's analysis of women's oral histories have become topics for further investigation. As a result, *Mothers, Sisters, Resisters* is frequently referenced by other authors. In Elizabeth R. Baer and Myrna Goldenberg's 2003 anthology *Experience and Expression: Women, the Nazis, and the Holocaust*, for example, several essays point to material from Gurewitsch's book. Goldenberg quotes Gurewitsch's broadened definition of Holocaust resistance—"any act or course of action taken between 1933 and May 8, 1945 that directly defied Nazi laws, policies, and ideology and that endangered the lives of those who engaged in such actions"—as a foundation for identifying and interpreting the heroism of women who worked inside the Holocaust landscape to save and sustain lives.

BIBLIOGRAPHY

Sources

Baer, Elizabeth R., and Myrna Goldenberg. *Experience and Expression: Women, the Nazis, and the Holocaust.* Detroit: Wayne State University Press, 2003. Print.

Cichy, Rose M. Rev. of *Mothers, Sisters, Resisters: Oral Histories of Women Who Survived the Holocaust*, by Brana Gurewitsch. *Library Journal* 124.1 (1999). 123. Print.

Gurewitsch, Brana. *Mothers, Sisters, Resisters: Oral Histories of Women Who Survived the Holocaust.* Tuscaloosa: University of Alabama Press, 1998. Print.

Ofer, Dalia, and Lenore J. Weitzman. *Women in the Holocaust.* New Haven, CT: Yale University Press, 1998. Print.

Ringelheim, Joan. "The Split between Gender and the Holocaust." *Women in the Holocaust.* By Dalia Ofer and Lenore J. Weitzman. New Haven, CT: Yale University Press, 1998. Print.

Roseman, Mark. "Recent Writing on the Holocaust." *Journal of Contemporary History* 36.2 (2001): 361–72. Print.

Further Reading

Baumel-Schwartz, Judith T. *Double Jeopardy: Gender and the Holocaust.* London: Vallentine, 1998. Print.

Cubilié, Anne. *Women Witnessing Terror: Testimony and the Cultural Politics of Human Rights.* New York: Fordham University Press, 2005. Print.

Delbo, Charlotte. *Auschwitz and After.* New Haven, CT: Yale University Press, 1995. Print.

Eliach, Yaffa, and Bonnie Gurewitsch. *Holocaust Oral History Manual.* Brooklyn, NY: Center for Holocaust Studies, 1992. Print.

Fuchs, Esther. *Women and the Holocaust: Narrative and Representation.* Lanham, MD: University Press of America, 1999. Print.

Kremer, S. L. *Women's Holocaust Writing: Memory and Imagination.* Lincoln: University of Nebraska Press, 1999. Print.

Miller, Joy E. *Love Carried Me Home: Women Surviving Auschwitz.* Deerfield Beach, FL: Simcha, 2000. Print.

Reading, Anna. *The Social Inheritance of the Holocaust: Gender, Culture, and Memory.* New York: Palgrave-Macmillan, 2002. Print.

Tec, Nechama. *Resilience and Courage: Women, Men, and the Holocaust.* New Haven, CT: Yale University Press, 2003. Print.

Waxman, Zoë. *Writing the Holocaust: Identity, Testimony, Representation.* Oxford: Oxford University Press, 2006. Web. 2 Feb. 2013.

Cynthia Giles

Nisa
The Life and Words of a !Kung Woman
Marjorie Shostak

OVERVIEW

Nisa: The Life and Words of a !Kung Woman, first published in 1981, is the life story of a woman who lived in the Kalahari bush, as recorded in a series of interviews with Marjorie Shostak. Shostak was not a trained anthropologist, but she had accompanied her anthropologist husband on a twenty-month ethnographic trip to the Dobe region of Africa in 1969. The book consists of a long introduction by Shostak; fifteen chapters—one for each interview—in which Nisa (a pseudonym) tells her story; and an epilogue, written after Shostak made a return visit to the region in 1975. Shostak interviewed several women of the hunter-gatherer clan to which Nisa belonged, intending a broader study of the tribal society, or at least a group portrait of the life of bush females. However, Nisa's personality was so vivid, her storytelling ability so exceptional, and her life history so dramatic and varied that Shostak made her the protagonist of the book.

Though her story was a trove of ethnographic detail, Nisa's frankness about her sexual experiences—five marriages and numerous affairs, both heterosexual and homosexual—and her tragic fate as a mother (all of her children were dead) appealed not only to the anthropological studies market but also to burgeoning feminists of the 1970s and 1980s. The book sold two hundred thousand copies in its first twenty years in print and has been a popular text in ethnography and women's studies curricula ever since.

HISTORICAL AND LITERARY CONTEXT

Europeans and people of central and eastern Asia have been exploring and settling the coast of Africa since ancient times, but until the nineteenth century most of the interior of sub-Saharan Africa was left untouched by European colonizers. By the time Europeans did enter the interior—as missionaries spreading the gospel, prospectors looking for gold, and settlers in search of arable land and suitable pasturage, among others—relatively advanced African tribes such as the Zulu and Masai had pushed the hunter-gatherers into the most desolate and unproductive regions of southeastern Africa. While the Europeans fought with and eventually conquered the more powerful tribes that stood in their way, the hunter-gatherers of the Kalahari went about their lives with little interference from the outside world until after World War II.

One of these hunter-gatherer groups, the !Kung people, first became the subject of anthropological interest when they were visited and studied in 1963 by American anthropologists Richard Lee and Irven DeVore. In 1966 Lee and DeVore organized a symposium in Chicago called "Man the Hunter," at which they called for, among other things, intensive studies of the Kalahari societies. (The proceedings of the symposium, which was a foundational event in modern ethnographic studies, were published in 1968 in a book of the same name.) In 1969 a young anthropologist named Melvin Konner heeded this call and set off for Africa with his new wife, Marjorie Shostak, who was not only a good writer but also a gifted photographer.

Shostak's book represents the confluence of a number of important streams of literary and cultural history. During the late 1940s, under the leadership of historian Allan Nevins, the development of inexpensive portable voice-recording devices made systematic oral history possible. In France Claude Lévi-Strauss had published *Tristes Tropiques* in 1955, in which he posits, based on his experiences with natives of the Amazon Basin, that the so-called "primitive" mind is structured exactly like the so-called "civilized" mind. James Watson and Francis Crick had discerned the chemical structure of DNA in 1953, and in the 1960s their discoveries contributed to the transformation of the life sciences, including anthropology. Furthermore, in the 1960s and 1970s feminism had become a global force, producing an expanding body of literature that included not just the explicitly feminist books of Betty Friedan, Germaine Greer, Kate Millett, and Shulamith Firestone but also the implicitly feminist perspective of field studies by biologists such as Jane Goodall, Diane Fossey, and others.

Nisa's success, coupled with Shostak's linguistic integrity, broadened the range of acceptable research in ethnographic studies and demonstrated the value of focus on a specific individual. Shostak's work also demonstrates the potential for a crossover of insights between ethnography, gender studies, and women's studies. In the introduction to *Nisa* and in the prefaces to each chapter, Shostak carefully frames Nisa's

⁘ Key Facts

Time Period:
Late 20th Century

Relevant Historical Events:
Increased anthropological interest in the !Kung; Shostak's ethnographic field trip to the Dobe region

Nationality:
Botswanan/South African

Keywords:
feminism; ethnography; tribalism

story as an ethnographic study and presents Nisa herself as a representative !Kung woman. However, the influence of the book and its ubiquity in a variety of academic areas derives from Nisa's uniqueness as an individual and Shostak's capacity for sympathy and understanding.

THEMES AND STYLE

Nisa is essentially two stories, each with its own themes. One is a written memoir by Shostak of her ethnographic expedition and her interviews with !Kung women. Shostak's themes include the status of women in !Kung society and their relative equality with men; the disappearance of the !Kung way of life; the intricacy and improvisational quality of social relationships among the !Kung; and what lessons modern society can learn from them—as when she states, in her introduction, "Here, in a society of ancient traditions, men and women live together in a nonexploitative manner, displaying a striking degree of equality between the sexes—perhaps a lesson for our own society." The parallel story is Nisa's oral memoir of her life, and her themes are the persistence and power of sexual desire, the tragedy of losing her children, and the overall pain and sorrow of life. As Nisa says, "When your child dies, you think ... 'This God ... his ways are foul! Why did he give me a little one and then take her away?'"

Nisa and Shostak each have their own reasons for telling their story. Nisa is something of an exhibitionist. She wants to tell her story, to be the center of attention, and to bear witness, but she also hopes that by telling her story she will then be free of it, so she can find peace and not have to drag it around with her. "I will break open the story," she tells Shostak, "and tell you what is there. Then, like the others that have fallen out onto the sand, I will finish with it, and the wind will take it away." Shostak's initial motive for the interviews was to collect ethnographic information about the life of !Kung women, but she was inspired by the richness of the data she gathered to tell Nisa's story.

Shostak and Nisa's stories are inextricably linked; once they bonded as women, their stories became the same story. Yet the structure of Shostak's book is academic, with a long introduction focused on methodology and the framing prefaces that are almost clinical in tone, while Nisa's story is literary, free-swinging. Although the book is mostly chronological, Nisa feels at liberty to take whatever side road invites, to get ahead of her story with foreshadowing, to disrupt the flow of her narrative with philosophical asides. Shostak's literary training shows through on occasion; for example, her "I don't remember the first time I met Nisa" is reminiscent of Edgar Allan Poe's "Ligeia," which begins with the narrator professing not to remember when and where he met his heroine. At the same time some of Nisa's descriptions of giving birth or making love have an almost clinical detachment. "They both touch it and try to have sex," she says, speaking of an affair gone stale for the man, "but the spilling of semen is all that happens. It never really becomes erect because, although the woman was excited, the man wasn't."

CRITICAL DISCUSSION

Nisa was enthusiastically embraced by several disciplines and struck a chord with the general reader as well. As Meredith Small stated in *Natural History*, "I doubt there is a single anthropology or women's studies student in the past two decades who hasn't been assigned this book." The book seemed to all but bypass the review process, and it found an immediate seat on the reference shelf, a model for future works. Shostak had made herself fluent in !Kung, which was not a written language, and all of her interviews were conducted in that tongue, later transcribed and edited by her. There was almost no one at the time who could check Shostak's work for accuracy, and *Nisa* was accepted as a definitive study by the ethnological community.

Since its first publication, *Nisa* has proved one of the most admired and influential of ethnographic studies. Shostak wrote only two books, the second of which, *Return to Nisa,* was published after her death of breast cancer in 1996. *Nisa* has also been valuable as an educational tool. In the *Encyclopedia of Anthropology,* Keridwen Luis states, "The classic example of [one kind] of ethnography is Marjorie Shostak's *Nisa: The Life and Words of a !Kung Woman* (1981). Shostak's ethnography is not only Nisa's life story; Shostak also provides chapter introductions that are intended to produce a larger ethnographic explanation of !Kung life." Students in women's studies programs, anthropology, and psychology have been inspired by *Nisa* to conduct fieldwork in remote regions, learn obscure dialects, and live in uncomfortable conditions.

Shostak's dedication to learning the !Kung language was a critical part of the book's success and influenced future approaches to ethnographic fieldwork. The only divergent views come from scholars in various fields who state that *Nisa* is more valuable in their field than in others.

BIBLIOGRAPHY

Sources

Lee, Richard B., and Irven DeVore, eds. *Kalahari Hunter-Gatherers: Studies of the !Kung San and Their Neighbors.* 2nd ed. Cambridge, MA: Harvard University Press, 1998. Print.

———. *Man the Hunter.* Chicago: Aldine, 1968. Print.

Luis, Keridwen N. "Anthropology of Women." *Encyclopedia of Anthropology* 1 (2006): 132–38. *Gale Virtual Reference Library.* Web. 23 Oct. 2012.

Shostak, Marjorie. *Nisa, the Life and Words of a !Kung Woman.* Cambridge, MA: Harvard University Press, 1981. Print.

Small, Meredith F. "Nisa: The Life and Words of a !Kung Woman." *Natural History* (2001): 76. *General OneFile.* Web. 23 Oct. 2012.

Further Reading

"Gender." *New Encyclopedia of Africa.* Ed. John Middleton and Joseph C. Miller. 2nd ed. Vol. 2. Detroit: Charles Scribner, 2008. 440–52. *Gale Virtual Reference Library.* Web. 23 Oct. 2012.

"Nisa." *Third World Women's Literatures: A Dictionary and Guide to Materials in English.* Barbara Fister. Westport, CT: Greenwood Press, 1995. 221. *Gale Virtual Reference Library.* Web. 23 Oct. 2012.

Schalge, Susan L. "Cross-Cultural Perspectives on Motherhood." *Encyclopedia of Motherhood.* Vol 1. Thousand Oaks, CA: Sage Reference, 2010. 256–59. *Gale Virtual Reference Library.* Web. 23 Oct. 2012.

Shostak, Marjorie. "In Short: Nonfiction." Rev. of *Testament to the Bushmen,* by Laurens van der Post and Jane Taylor. *New York Times Book Review* 7 July 1985. *General OneFile.* Web. 23 Oct. 2012.

———. *Return to Nisa.* Cambridge, MA: Harvard University Press, 2000. Print.

Thomas, Elizabeth Marshall. *The Harmless People.* New York: Knopf, 1959.

———. *Reindeer Moon.* Boston: Houghton-Mifflin, 1987.

Gerald Carpenter

Survivors

An Oral History of the Armenian Genocide

Donald E. Miller, Lorna Touryan Miller

❖ **Key Facts**

Time Period:
Early 20th Century

Relevant Historical Events:
Armenian genocide of 1915; World War I

Nationality:
Armenian

Keywords:
genocide; war; empire

OVERVIEW

Survivors: An Oral History of the Armenian Genocide (1993) is an oral history compiled by Donald E. Miller and Lorna Touryan Miller that discusses the survivors' memories of the 1915 Armenian genocide by the Ottoman Empire—a genocide that is still denied by the Turkish government. The Armenian people were Apostolic Christians who lived as a religious minority among the predominantly Muslim Turks. For 2,500 years, the two peoples lived in relative peace, until the human rights revolutions of the late eighteenth century began to influence Armenian ideas of national identity, and Armenians began to rebel against Ottoman authority. *Survivors* presents information gathered through interviews, research, and historical accounts of the genocide to produce a text sympathetic to the Armenian cause and backed by historical evidence.

The events of 1915 are a source of dispute between Armenian survivors and the Turkish government, which admits to an astounding loss of Armenian lives but attributes that loss to consequences of war rather than to a planned genocide. When the Millers began compiling evidence from Armenian survivors that pointed to organized massacres, their project received positive support from survivors of the genocide and the academic community. The book remains an influential source for historians, humanitarians, and psychologists looking for a primary source on the causes and effects of genocide.

HISTORICAL AND LITERARY CONTEXT

The 1915 Armenian genocide was a culmination of events that began in the late eighteenth century when Armenian nationalists, after witnessing the success of the French Revolution, demanded greater autonomy within their own country. The Ottomans retaliated with a series of massacres between 1894 and 1896 that resulted in two hundred thousand Armenian deaths. Political leadership in the Ottoman Empire was usurped by a reformist group known as the Young Turks, but a series of lost battles in 1912 and 1913 allowed the uprising of a radical section of Young Turks who labeled the Armenians dangerous to the empire's security because of religious differences and their supposed alliance with Russia. The outbreak of World War I provided the pretext necessary to formally declare the Armenians traitors and to initiate an organized genocide campaign.

The genocide itself took place in four stages. Despite survivor accounts, there is no official estimate of how many Armenians were killed. During the first stage, all able-bodied men between the ages of twenty and forty-five were conscripted to fight for the Ottoman Empire and were later disarmed and executed, their deaths explained under the pretext of war. The second stage, beginning in April 1915, saw the deportation or execution of important figures in the community, such as priests, intellectuals, and politicians, and the disarmament of the rest of the Armenian population. In May 1915 the Ottomans began the third stage of the genocide, which was the deportation of all remaining Armenian people into the deserts of Mesopotamia. During this stage thousands died from exposure, starvation, and raids on traveling caravans. The fourth stage was a final cleanup, during which the remaining population was murdered by mass drowning, burning, or beating with clubs.

Survivors belongs to a tradition of memoirs and historical texts that spotlight the brutal realities of the Armenian genocide from personal accounts and historical documents. Memoirs such as Kerop Bedoukian's *The Urchin: An Armenian's Escape* (1978) and Ramela Martin's *Out of Darkness* (1989) describe some gruesome events suffered by the authors as children and provide testimony to organized mass murder. Collections of historical documents verifying the Armenian genocide include Aram Andonian's *The Memoirs of Naim Bey* (1920) and Herbert Adams Gibbons's *The Blackest Page in Modern History* (1916).

Survivors is an influential text that provides scholars with firsthand accounts of the Armenian massacres interspersed with historical evidence to validate the memories. Scholars frequently use it as a primary text about Armenian history, and it presents a solid argument for the existence of the Armenian genocide. Moreover, it serves as a warning to the contemporary world about the evils humankind can commit—the genocide itself as well as the institutionalized denials and cover-ups by political officials.

Photographs of victims of the 1915 Armenian genocide, on display at the Armenian Genocide Museum in Yerevan, Armenia, 2012.
© MARTYN AIM/ZUMA PRESS/CORBIS

THEMES AND STYLE

The central theme of *Survivors* is the recognition of the 1915 Armenian massacres as an act of genocide and the preservation of the stories of the survivors. Donald Miller explains, "Given the amount of world press coverage of the massacres of Armenians at the time of the deportations, it is difficult to believe that fifty years later the same newspapers … would refer to the genocide of the Armenians as 'alleged.'" For the Millers, the position of denial became harder to believe as they further researched historical accounts of the genocide and official documents from the era recounting the atrocities. One participant remembers how the men were killed on the long deportation marches: "As soon as they separated the men, a group of armed men came from the other side of a kill and killed all the men right in front of our eyes. They killed them with bayonets at the end of their rifles, sticking them in their stomachs." The testimony of the survivors gathered through the interview process struck a chord with Donald Miller: "[T]he more I learned about this first genocide of the twentieth century, the more convinced I became that the story of the Armenian Genocide should be told through the experience of survivors."

The authors' motivations for producing the text stem from personal interactions with Lorna Touryan Miller's parents, who were both survivors of the genocide. After recording initial interviews with the Touryans for the benefit of their young children, the Millers began to expand their project: "[W]e interviewed a family friend who told a deeply moving story of the genocide. That was the turning point, and we launched a project that eventually led to interviewing more than one hundred people." With the interviews recorded and transcribed, the Millers began the research component of their project, finding historical documents that verified the personal accounts they had already collected. Armed with both individual and official documents, the Millers constructed a narrative that recounts the Armenian genocide from the perspective of the persecuted people.

Written in an academic style, the text offers a chronological narrative of events intermingled with firsthand accounts and official documents. The editorial process is transparent, and the questions asked during the interviews are provided. While the quotations appear in English, the interviews themselves were mostly conducted in Armenian, translated and transcribed by Lorna Touryan Miller. The decision to interview in Armenian and translate into English was established early in the interview process because "it soon became clear that survivors felt more comfortable talking about their experiences in their mother tongue." This level of comfort was important to allow the survivors to share such deeply personal memories. For example, one participant witnessed the abuse suffered by his uncle, who was too elderly to be conscripted to war and who liked to sit on the front porch. One day "four or five armed Turks came" looking for more men and "proceeded to say that they haven't seen an old man dance in a long time." In front of the family, "they tied his hands and began to cut him up with a knife so that he would jump around." Despite the necessary act of translation, the quotations preserve the individual voices of the survivors and set the somber tone that persists throughout the oral histories.

CRITICAL DISCUSSION

The initial reaction to *Survivors* was one of general acclaim. Harold Takooshian, in a 1995 review in the *Oral History Review,* praises the work: "This book might be regarded as oral history at its best—trained interviewers eliciting new information from eyewitnesses to tragedy in their own words." In a 1993 review in *Journal for the Scientific Study of Religion,* Eileen Barker notes the quality of the editing process, although she laments the terrible nature of its subject matter: "This is a well-written book, but it is not a pleasure to read."

THE FLIP SIDE: TURKISH DENIAL OF THE ARMENIAN GENOCIDE

Denial is often the final phase of genocide. When the premeditated extermination of an ethnic group is denied, the recorded past is rewritten to exclude the ethnicity altogether, and the present and future are structured as though that ethnicity never existed. Some scholars and the Turkish government continue to deny the Armenian genocide of 1915, which the Millers see as the final stage of their genocidal campaign. This denial of the genocide is facilitated by lack of structural evidence of premeditated extermination. There are no concentration camps, gas chambers, or crematory ovens to validate survivor narratives as there are for the Jewish Holocaust of World War II. Instead the cover of World War I and the nature of the organized massacres leave little physical evidence to justify the claims of survivors against the contradictory narratives of government officials.

The official Turkish position on the Armenian genocide is that it never occurred and that the number of Armenian deaths and their circumstances are exaggerated for the purposes of propaganda. Instead many Turks believe that the Armenians posed a threat to national security during the war and were subsequently deported. Moreover, the government claims that their deaths were the result of war, and many Turks and Kurds were also killed at the same time. Thus, the official narrative remains that accusations of genocide have been leveled for political and economic benefit rather than as an accurate description of events.

Although *Survivors* remains an influential resource for scholars studying the Armenian genocide, questions have been raised about the validity of the interviewees' memories considering the time that has passed since the events described in the text. Justin McCarthy discusses these ideas in his 1995 review in the *American Historical Review*: "The primary question is the reliability of evidence taken sixty or seventy years after the fact from witnesses who 'were, on average, eleven or twelve years old in 1915.'" In *The Armenian Massacres in Ottoman Turkey* (2005), Guenter Lewy discusses the inherent problems of memory, writing about "current empirical research" that reveals that "memory suffers as a result of traumatic events." He explains that this is no reason to discredit the accounts gathered by the Millers for *Survivors*, but it "does mean that survivor accounts, like all other historical evidence, must be analyzed carefully and critically." Despite its usefulness in documenting the survival narratives of the Armenian genocide, *Survivors* is generally mentioned but not thoroughly discussed by scholars because of the inherent complications of memory and the guided discussion of the interview process.

Trends in scholarship about *Survivors* include discussion of the validity of oral history as a historical document. Lorne Shirinian in an essay for *Remembrance and Denial: The Case of the Armenian Genocide* (1999) praises the Millers by saying they "have done excellent work on the oral testimony of the survivors in their book" but excludes *Survivors* from his study because oral histories "developed from a different dynamic and very different process." Shirinian writes that this process includes "a performative aspect that is part of the oral testimony given by the survivor" and an inherent bias because "the interviewer stimulates a response from the interviewee through direct questioning." Lewy demonstrates this trend by discussing the responses of "Turkish critics" who "have alleged that the aged survivors have been coached by their Armenian nationalist interviewers to relate tales of horror" that "are of no use whatsoever for historical research." While Lewy goes on to admit "survivor testimony is another valuable type of evidence that can help throw light on the tragic events of 1915–16," the criticism leveled against the interview process follows current trends in questioning the objectivity of oral history.

BIBLIOGRAPHY

Sources

Barker, Eileen. Rev. of *Survivors: An Oral History of the Armenian Genocide,* by Donald E. Miller and Lorna Touryan Miller. *Journal for the Scientific Study of Religion* 32.4 (1993): 422. *JSTOR*. Web. 8 Jan. 2013.

Lewy, Guenter. *The Armenian Massacres in Ottoman Turkey: A Disputed Genocide*. Salt Lake City: University of Utah Press, 2005. Print.

McCarthy, Justin. Rev. of *Survivors: An Oral History of the Armenian Genocide,* by Donald E. Miller and Lorna Touryan Miller. *American Historical Review* 99.2 (1994): 605–06. *JSTOR*. Web. 8 Jan. 2013.

Miller, Donald E., and Lorna Touryan Miller. *Survivors: An Oral History of the Armenian Genocide*. Berkeley: University of California Press, 1993. Print.

Shirinian, Lorne. "Survivor Memoirs of the Armenian Genocide as Cultural History." *Remembrance and Denial: The Case of the Armenian Genocide*. Ed. Richard G. Hovannisian. Detroit: Wayne State University Press, 1999. 165–75. Print.

Takooshian, Harold. Rev. of *Survivors: An Oral History of the Armenian Genocide,* by Donald E. Miller and Lorna Touryan Miller. *Oral History Review* 22.1 (1995): 158–61. *JSTOR*. Web. 8 Jan. 2013.

Further Reading

Akçam, Taner. *From Empire to Republic: Turkish Nationalism and the Armenian Genocide*. London: Zed, 2004. Print.

Andonian, Aram, ed. *The Memoirs of Naim Bey*. London: Hodder & Stoughton, 1920. Print.

Bedoukian, Kerop. *The Urchin: An Armenian's Escape*. London: John Murray, 1989. Print.

Bloxham, Donald. *The Great Game of Genocide: Imperialism, Nationalism and the Destruction of the*

Ottoman Armenians. Oxford: Oxford University Press, 2007. Print.

Gibbons, Herbert Adams. *The Blackest Page in Modern History: Events in Armenia in 1915: The Facts and the Responsibilities*. New York: Putnam's, 1916. Web. 10 Jan. 2013.

Gunter, Michael M. *Armenian History and the Question of Genocide*. New York: Palgrave MacMillan, 2011. Print.

Hovannisian, Richard D. "Denial of the Armenian Genocide in Comparison with Holocaust Denial." *Remembrance and Denial: The Case of the Armenian Genocide*. Ed. Richard G. Hovannisian. Detroit: Wayne State University Press, 1999. 201–36. Print.

Martin, Ramela. *Out of Darkness*. Arlington, MA: Zoryan Institute, 1989. Print.

Katherine Barker

VOICES OF FREEDOM
An Oral History of the Civil Rights Movement from the 1950s through the 1980s
Henry Hampton, Steve Fayer

Key Facts

Time Period:
Mid- to Late 20th Century

Relevant Historical Events:
Civil rights movement

Nationality:
American

Keywords:
civil rights; race; activism

OVERVIEW

Voices of Freedom: An Oral History of the Civil Rights Movement from the 1950s through the 1980s (1990) by Henry Hampton and Steve Fayer with Sarah Flynn is the by-product of the documentary television series *Eyes on the Prize,* produced by PBS, which discusses the events of the American civil rights movement from the firsthand perspectives of people affected by it. The oral history subjects come from an archive of nearly one thousand interviews conducted during the 1970s and 1980s during which participants were either filmed or recorded answering direct questions about their thoughts, feelings, locations, and actions in connection to specific historical events or movement organizations and leaders. The surplus of material excluded from the series was revisited and published in book form in *Voices of Freedom.* The book, like the series, reflects the subjects' personal lives and experiences in such turbulent times.

The successful *Eyes on the Prize* series reached millions of viewers and received critical acclaim for its portrayal of the civil rights movement. The array of voices produced an authentic mosaic of the thoughts and feelings of the times. Riding on the success of the series, and not wanting to discard the countless interviews that could not be included because of the timing restrictions of film, the authors composed *Voices of Freedom* in order to present the remaining material in an accessible format that offers a personalized oral history of the movement and creates a new way in which to access those perspectives. The text was praised by critics and scholars alike for its impactful presentation of personal narratives and for its significance as a scholarly resource.

HISTORICAL AND LITERARY CONTEXT

The main activity in the civil rights movement in the United States is generally dated to the 1950s and 1960s, although previous events foreshowed its development. By the end of the nineteenth century, most southern states had passed Jim Crow laws, which imposed segregation in public places. Civil rights organizations such as the National Association for the Advancement of Colored People (NAACP), formed in 1909, began to challenge racism in the United States. In 1936 African American voters were instrumental in electing President Franklin Delano Roosevelt, who in 1941 signed Executive Order 8802, which banned prejudice in the workplace and in the military based on race. During the postwar years the movement firmly took hold, when African American veterans who had fought in World War II for freedom abroad came home to a country that denied their basic rights.

In 1954 the U.S. Supreme Court overturned the previously accepted "separate but equal" doctrine for the education system in *Brown v. Board of Education.* For the first time African Americans could attend the same schools and colleges as white Americans. This motivated additional protests and energized the movement to support social change across the country. *Voices of Freedom* begins with the *Brown* decision and continues to document the personal recollections of African Americans as they experience other events of the movement, including the Montgomery Bus Boycott, the Little Rock Crisis, and the 1963 March on Washington. The book also discusses public opinions of such prominent people and organizations as Martin Luther King Jr., Malcolm X, Muhammad Ali, and the Black Panthers.

Voices of Freedom is one among many personal histories about the civil rights movement, including *Lay Bare the Heart: An Autobiography of the Civil Rights Movement* (1985) by James Farmer and *The Autobiography of Malcolm X* (1989), edited by Alex Haley. The book also resembles oral history adaptations from other media sources, such as *Living Atlanta: An Oral History of the City, 1914–1948* (1990) by Clifford Kuhn, Harlon Joye, and E. Bernard West, a text based on a program aired by Radio Free Atlanta about living in the city during the interwar years.

Although it did not gain the popularity of the television series, *Voices of Freedom* is still an acclaimed representation of the personal experiences of people during the turbulent times of the 1950s and 1960s in the racially divided United States. Its success allowed the authors to further publish in the field. Hampton's *The Black Chronicle,* published posthumously in 1999, replicates newspapers from the days of legalized slavery to the height of the civil rights movement. Fayer also continued to write television scripts for PBS about racism and civil rights, including an episode of *The American Experience* titled "Malcolm X: Make It Plain" (1994) and a miniseries, *Africans in America: America's Journey through Slavery* (1998).

THEMES AND STYLE

Of the many themes throughout *Voices of Freedom,* one that emerges to the forefront is the multiplicity of people involved in the civil rights movement on the most personal level. From political leaders to hardworking mothers, everybody did what they could to help the fight for their civil rights. The theme of personal involvement emerges from numerous voices, including Gussie Nesbitt, who remembers the Montgomery Bus Boycott: "I wanted to cooperate with the majority of the people that had [been] on the boycott. I wanted to be one of them that tried to make it better. I didn't want somebody else to make it better for me." Andrew Young remembers the riots in Chicago in 1966: "I was standing there in the middle of Gage Park when there was just a rain of rocks and cherry bombs. We were ducking because we didn't know whether it was a hand grenade or some more serious explosion, or a rock or a bottle." Not all people agreed with everything that happened in the movement, however. Richard Hatcher recollects how "many people who came to Gary [the Gary Convention of 1972] thought that the whole purpose of the convention was to form a third party," but "there were many individuals, and I include myself in that number, who were not convinced that that was the best strategy for us to take."

Hampton states in the introduction that the purpose of composing *Voices of Freedom* was to "capture the American civil rights movement in the voices of those who were there, and thereby give younger citizens who had not lived that struggle, or those who never understood, some idea of the raging torrents that had engulfed America in the fifties, sixties, and seventies." In order to make the voices of the movement known to readers, the editors transcribed the interview participants in an effort to retain their individual voice and diction. The participants vary in age, gender, class, and education, offering perspectives from all parts of society.

The book is stylized to mimic the television series, and individual experiences are edited and collated in thematic chapters that discuss the history of the movement in roughly chronological order. Ronald J. Grele notes the style in his 1991 review "Useful Discoveries," writing, "The interview segments are organized along the lines of the original series in which various sections were clipped and arranged according to topic." This style is often praised by critics, such as Jonathan Kirsch, who observes in his 1990 review in the *Los Angeles Times,* "What makes the material so compelling is the use of documentary-film editing techniques: the voices of various eyewitnesses are intercut into a single, seamless story."

CRITICAL DISCUSSION

Following the success of *Eyes on the Prize, Voices of Freedom* received praise from reviewers and critics, including Gwen Salama, who, writing in 1992 in *School Library Journal,* classifies the book as a "must purchase" as "a companion to the PBS series." Henry Mayer agrees, noting in a 1990 *New York Times Book Review* the "often eloquent, though occasionally diffuse" stories that reveal "the momentous work of the civil rights struggle in the words of its participants."

The book continues to be associated with the television series, and many critics dwell on this relationship and the effects it has on both the book and the show. Mayer believes that despite the success of both mediums, their "treatment of complex policy questions, such as affirmative action, is sketchy" and they ignore "a number of important issues, such as the growing disparity between the black middle class and underclass" because these issues "cannot be epitomized by a filmed event or an oral history." Kirsch also addresses the connection between the series and the book: "The very notion of turning outtakes into a book suggests something improvised and superficial, a cut-and-paste job, but the opposite is true of *Voices of Freedom.*" Grele prefers the book, writing, "The lack of the televised voice-over narration has eliminated the authorial voice Henry Hampton and his associates imposed upon the original."

Trends in scholarship discussing *Voices of Freedom* praise the work for successfully incorporating such a wide array of voices from ordinary people. Kirsch and Mayer both exemplify this trend, with Kirsch stating, "The most vivid and stirring words" in the book "are those of the less celebrated men and women whose bodies and souls were on the line in countless incidents of struggle, confrontation and protest." Mayer notes, "We hear ordinary people speaking and feel the sense of empowerment that is the movement's continuing legacy." Patrick H. Samway also follows this trend in his

Statue of Rosa Parks at the Birmingham Civil Rights Institute. Parks was a civil rights activist whose refusal to give up her seat on a bus to a white passenger in 1955 in Montgomery, Alabama, was a catalyst for many in the civil rights movement. © RAYMOND GEHMAN/CORBIS

EYES ON THE PRIZE: THE CIVIL RIGHTS MOVEMENT IN FILM

The television documentary series *Eyes on the Prize* first appeared on PBS stations in the United States in 1987 with the first phase, *Eyes on the Prize: America's Civil Rights Years 1954–1964*. This season consisted of six 1-hour episodes covering events such as the murder of Emmett Till and the passing of the Voting Rights Act. The success of the first installment allowed the producers to develop the second phase of the project, *Eyes on the Prize II: America at the Racial Crossroads 1965–1985*, which aired in 1990. This season consisted of eight 1-hour episodes covering the emergence of movement leaders such as Malcolm X and the internal struggles of the movement itself, including the strife between the middle and working classes, as well as the other human rights movements developing during this time.

The series received critical acclaim from scholars and reviewers alike, garnering numerous awards, including Program of the Year in News and Information from the Television Critics Association in 1987, the Erik Barnouw Award from the Organization of American Historians in 1991, an International Documentary Association award in 1987, and two Outstanding Individual Achievement in a Craft: Writers awards from the News and Documentary Emmys in 1988 and 1991. One episode was also nominated for an Academy Award for Best Documentary in 1988.

1990 "Summer Reading" review in *America*, stating, "The voices of these men and women, black and white, old and young resonate with an authenticity often lost in more abstract studies of the crucial period."

BIBLIOGRAPHY

Sources

Grele, Ronald J. "Useful Discoveries: Oral History, Public History, and the Dialectic of Narrative." *Public Historian* 13.2 (1991): 61–84. *JSTOR*. Web. 30 Jan. 2013.

Hampton, Henry, and Steve Fayer with Sarah Flynn. *Voices of Freedom: An Oral History of the Civil Rights Movement from the 1950s through the 1980s*. New York: Bantam, 1990. Print.

Kirsch, Jonathan. "A Stirring Saga of the Civil Rights Movement." Rev. of *Voices of Freedom: An Oral History of the Civil Rights Movement from the 1950s through the 1980s*, by Henry Hampton and Steve Fayer with Sarah Flynn. *Los Angeles Times*. Los Angeles Times, 31 Jan. 1990. Web. 29 Jan. 2013.

Mayer, Henry. "With Eyes Still on the Prize." Rev. of *Voices of Freedom: An Oral History of the Civil Rights Movement from the 1950s through the 1980s*, by Henry Hampton and Steve Fayer with Sarah Flynn. *New York Times Book Review* 28 Jan. 1990. *Lots of Newspapers*. Web. 29 Jan. 2013.

Salama, Gwen. Rev. of *Voices of Freedom: An Oral History of the Civil Rights Movement from the 1950s through the 1980s*, by Henry Hampton and Steve Fayer with Sarah Flynn. *School Library Journal* 36.5 (1990): 138. Print.

Samway, Patrick H. "Summer Reading." *America* 162.18 (1990): 479–83. *ProQuest*. Web. 30 Jan. 2013.

Further Reading

Alvah, Donna. "Civil Rights Movement." *Dictionary of American History*. Ed. Stanley I. Kutler. 3rd ed. Vol. 2. New York: Charles Scribner's Sons, 2003. 200–06. *Gale U.S. History in Context*. Web. 31 Jan. 2013.

Farmer, James. *Lay Bare the Heart: An Autobiography of the Civil Rights Movement*. New York: Arbor House, 1985. Print.

Hampton, Henry. *Black Chronicle*. Pittsburgh: Wilson, 1999. Print.

Kuhn, Clifford M., Harlon E. Joye, and E. Bernard West. *Living Atlanta: An Oral History of the City, 1914–1948*. Atlanta, GA: Atlanta Historical Society and University of Georgia Press, 1990. Print.

Malcolm X. *The Autobiography of Malcolm X*. 1965. Ed. Alex Haley. New York: Ballantine, 1992. Print.

Katherine Barker

Voices of Resistance
Oral Histories of Moroccan Women
Alison Baker

OVERVIEW

Published in 1998, Alison Baker's *Voices of Resistance: Oral Histories of Moroccan Women* collects oral accounts from female members of Morocco's national independence movement, which culminated in 1956 with the end of the French and Spanish Protectorates and the founding of an independent Moroccan state. Featuring interviews with nationalist women within the bourgeoisie as well as testimony from members of the largely proletarian armed resistance, the text discusses the various ways in which women contributed to the nationalist cause—whether through political activism, militant protest, or active involvement in rebellious operations (such as by transporting weapons). Also touched upon are such related issues as the education of women, the relationship between Moroccan nationalism and women's rights, and the aftermath of Morocco's newfound independence. The book as a whole provides valuable insight into an important aspect of the Moroccan resistance that had previously received relatively little attention.

Published at a time when historical writing on Moroccan nationalism was fairly uncommon, *Voices of Resistance* was hailed as an important and illuminating contribution to Moroccan history and anthropology. The book represents a uniquely personal documentation of a crucial but largely unknown part of the Moroccan resistance; consequently, it became an important resource for subsequent historical works and set the stage for further volumes scrutinizing Moroccan society and the place of women within it. It remains a widely cited and influential work within Moroccan studies.

HISTORICAL AND LITERARY CONTEXT

The narratives collected in *Voices of Resistance* are strongly informed by Morocco's colonial history. In 1912 Morocco officially became protectorates of France and Spain, with the majority of the country falling under French jurisdiction. In the following decades the increasingly autocratic influence of French administrators helped to bring about a large number of modernizing reforms in the Moroccan infrastructure as well as establishing a relatively high degree of political stability. Nevertheless, the French encroachment on both Moroccan rights (including freedom of speech and travel) and traditional Moroccan culture—as well as a growing nationalist displeasure at seeing Morocco transformed into what was essentially a French colony—precipitated a widespread sense of discontentment with life under the protectorate. Guerrilla warfare sometimes broke out, and an uprising in the Spanish-controlled Rif region precipitated a lengthy war (1920–1926) that ended in a victory for the colonial forces.

In 1930 the French administration introduced the Berber Dahir, a decree that attempted to excise areas inhabited by Morocco's indigenous Berber population from the jurisdiction of the Moroccan sultan. This attempt to increase French control and divide segments of the Moroccan population against one another in fact served to galvanize Morocco's organized independence movement, leading to political action and strife over the following decades. The women interviewed for *Voices of Resistance* were extensively involved in this activity, and their oral accounts elucidate their participation in it. In 1953 the French-appointed Sultan Mohammed V was exiled for advocating the nationalist cause and failing to cooperate with French authorities, sparking active, violent rebellion by the Moroccan armed resistance. In 1955 he was permitted to return, and the following year the protectorates were officially dissolved, making Morocco a free state once again.

Voices of Resistance is part of the literary tradition of Moroccan oral history and is also part of a more broad tradition of scholarly and journalistic writing about Morocco. Works such as Henry Munson Jr.'s *The House of Si Abd Allah: The Oral History of a Moroccan Family* (1984) and Vincent Crapanzano's ethnographical study *Tuhami: Portrait of a Moroccan* (1980) stand as noteworthy precursors to Baker's project. Other important antecedents include writings on Morocco by Moroccans themselves, including Latifa Akharbach and Narjis Rerhaye's French-language volume *Femmes et Politique* (1992), as well as the interviews with Moroccan nationalist women published in the Arabic feminist journal *8 mars*, which Baker quotes in *Voices of Resistance*.

Baker's volume represented a substantial addition to Moroccan scholarship. Along with other works of its kind—including Baker's own contemporaneous

❖ **Key Facts**

Time Period:
Early to Mid-20th Century

Relevant Historical Events:
Colonization of Morocco; Berber Dahir; rise of the Moroccan independence movement

Nationality:
Moroccan

Keywords:
colonialism; independence; women's rights

Voices of Resistance looks at the contributions of women to the Moroccan independence movement and explores their personal lives. Here, a Moroccan woman celebrates the fiftieth anniversary of independence, holding a picture of King Mohammed VI. © AP IMAGES/JALIL BOUNHAR

documentary film, *Still Ready: Three Women from the Moroccan Resistance*—it helped to pave the way for future studies of both the Moroccan struggle for independence (as in Spencer D. Segalla's 2009 volume *The Moroccan Soul: French Education, Colonial Ethnology, and Muslim Resistance, 1912–1956*) and the role of women within Moroccan society (as in Doris H. Gray's 2007 book *Muslim Women on the Move: Moroccan Women and French Women of Moroccan Origin Speak Out*). The book continues to be frequently cited in Moroccan historical scholarship.

THEMES AND STYLE

The primary theme of *Voices of Resistance* is the impact of the Moroccan independence movement on the lives of women. This impact differed significantly depending on the socioeconomic class of the women involved; the narratives of bourgeois nationalists tend to stress the pivotal role of female education, as when interviewee Zhor Lazraq asserts, "The Moroccan woman opened a door that had not yet been opened in the Islamic world. We entered the Qaraouine university, because one of the Istiqlal [Freedom] Party's main aims concerning women was that they should learn and educate themselves, which was what would permit women to liberate themselves." In contrast the much poorer women from the armed resistance are less emphatic about the movement's feminist potential, which for them was largely rescinded following Morocco's independence. Their accounts are more focused on the details of specific missions. For example, Saadia Bouhaddou begins one such reminiscence by stating that "one time before independence I went to Fez to get some weapons—five pistols and two machine guns."

Voices of Resistance was compiled to shed light on an important but underreported aspect of Moroccan history. As Baker notes in the preface, "The women's narratives reconstruct the little-known history of Moroccan feminism and nationalism, and take us into the lives of a remarkable group of Islamic women whose voices have never been heard." The interviews were conducted in a variety of settings, with narratives delivered in a group setting and then often followed up with a more intimate interview in the respondent's home. Though Baker is clearly engaged with Moroccan historical and anthropological scholarship and makes ample use of those resources in her contextual commentary, she also notes that the book is intended to be "accessible to the general reader and not conventionally academic. I have not tried overly hard to maintain a critical distance or scholarly objectivity in relation to the women themselves. The book as a whole is unabashedly celebratory."

The language of the interviews varies significantly between the bourgeois nationalist women and the women in the armed resistance. The former are often somewhat formal, as in Malika El Fassi's assertion that "it is no secret that the Moroccan woman's life is stillness and languor." The latter group, meanwhile, tends toward extensively detailed, somewhat repetitive tales of rebellious exploits punctuated with religious and nationalistic pieties, as in Ghalia Moujahide's remarks: "And, blessings from God, we worked, and worked, may God bestow barraka [blessing] on the king, our health, our children." Baker attempts to preserve the interviews' rhetorical tenor, noting, "If some of the interviews with nationalist women seem impersonal, stiff, and formal, and some of the interviews with women in the armed resistance seem repetitious, that is how the women presented themselves." The interviews were edited "to improve coherence and the flow of narrative," but Baker asserts, "I have kept the written text as close to the original spoken language as possible."

CRITICAL DISCUSSION

Voices of Resistance was highly praised upon its publication in 1998, with reviewers lauding it for granting a unique glimpse into the lives of women whose important work had gone largely unnoticed. Susan Schaefer Davis, writing in the *Middle East Studies Association Bulletin* (1999), calls the book "a wonderful collection of previously unexplored information that sheds light on women's roles in resisting the colonial occupation of Morocco." Likewise, Sondra Hale's review in *The Women's Review of Books* (1999), while taking issue with some of the generalized historical judgments Baker makes in her scholarly commentary, ultimately concludes, "In spite of some flaws, this is a powerful and readable book. … *Voices of Resistance* fills an important gap in our understanding of Moroccan and other African and Middle Eastern societies by linking, through oral narratives, two fields: the ethnography of Moroccan women and the history of Morocco."

In the years since its release *Voices of Resistance* has continued to play a significant role in the shaping of contemporary perceptions of both the lives of Moroccan women and the history of the Moroccan independence movement. It is a frequently assigned text in Moroccan and Middle Eastern history classes—particularly those that focus on the roles of women within traditional Islamic societies—and it is often cited (or listed as further reading in a bibliography) in recent works of historical scholarship on the Middle East. It is largely in its capacity as a historical resource that the book continues to attract interest from scholars.

Scholarly writing that discusses *Voices of Resistance* tends to do so by incorporating the book—often mentioned only in passing—into a larger scholarly argument, with Baker's text being mined for contextual information or used as supporting evidence for the author's assertions. Bruce Maddy-Weitzman, writing in *Middle East Journal* in 2005 about the legal status of women in Morocco, cites *Voices of Resistance* as a historical source during an explication of the struggles over women's rights legislation. In analyzing a memoir by the Moroccan writer Leila Abouzeid, Diya M. Abdo argues in an article written in 2009 for *Frontiers* that Abouzeid's book "joins a growing body of work whose authors aim to uncover Moroccan women's marginalized and forgotten efforts, whether in academic or popular writing," and Abdo cites *Voices of Resistance* as an example of this trend.

BIBLIOGRAPHY

Sources

Abdo, Diya M. "Textual Migration: Self-Translation and Translation of the Self in Leila Abouzeid's *Return to Childhood: The Memoir of a Modern Moroccan Woman* and *Ruju' 'Ila Al-Tufulah.*" *Frontiers* 30.2 (2009): 1–42. *JSTOR.* Web. 30 Jan. 2013.

Baker, Alison. *Voices of Resistance: Oral Histories of Moroccan Women.* Albany: State University of New York Press, 1998. Print.

Davis, Susan Schaefer. Rev. of *Voices of Resistance,* by Alison Baker. *Middle East Studies Association Bulletin* 33.1 (1999): 98–9. *JSTOR.* Web. 30 Jan. 2013.

Hale, Sondra. "Women Warriors." Rev. of *Voices of Resistance,* by Alison Baker. *Women's Review of Books* 16.12 (1999): 20–2. *JSTOR.* Web. 30 Jan. 2013.

Maddy-Weitzman, Bruce. "Women, Islam, and the Moroccan State: The Struggle over the Personal Status Law." *Middle East Journal* 59.3 (2005): 393–410. *JSTOR.* Web. 30 Jan. 2013.

PRINCESS LALLA AICHA

One of the primary inspirational touchstones for the nationalist women interviewed in *Voices of Resistance* is the example of Princess Lalla Aicha, the oldest daughter of Morocco's sultan, Mohammed V. The education of girls was fairly uncommon in Morocco at the time, and Mohammed's public advocacy of female education, which he exemplified by having his own daughters educated, turned Lalla Aicha into a living embodiment of women's liberation. To that end the princess traveled to Morocco's major cities, urging people to send their daughters to school and extolling the principles of equality.

On April 11, 1947, Mohammed gave a speech in Tangier in which he publicly broke with the administration of the French protectorate in favor of Moroccan nationalism. His daughter gave a speech as well, again endorsing the cause of education for women and tying the need for women's emancipation into the nationalist struggle against the French. The speech had a germinal effect on female members of the independence movement, serving to mobilize political action on behalf of nationalism and women's rights. Lalla Aicha became a supremely important symbol for the women's movement, and from 1969 she served as honorary president of the National Union of Moroccan Women. She died in 2011.

Further Reading

Abouzeid, Leila. *Return to Childhood: The Memoir of a Modern Moroccan Woman.* Austin: University of Texas Press, 1998. Print.

Crapanzano, Vincent. *Tuhami: Portrait of a Moroccan.* Chicago: University of Chicago Press, 1980. Print.

Gershovich, Moshe. *French Military Rule in Morocco: Colonialism and Its Consequences.* London: Frank Cass, 2000. Print.

Gray, Doris H. *Muslim Women on the Move: Moroccan Women and French Women of Moroccan Origin Speak Out.* Lanham, MD: Lexington, 2007. Print.

Mernissi, Fatima. *Doing Daily Battle: Interviews with Moroccan Women.* Trans. Mary Jo Lakeland. London: Women's Press, 1988. Print.

Munson, Henry, Jr., ed. *The House of Si Abd Allah: The Oral History of a Moroccan Family.* New Haven, CT: Yale University Press, 1984. Print.

Newcomb, Rachel. *Women of Fes: Ambiguities of Urban Life in Morocco.* Philadelphia: University of Pennsylvania Press, 2009. Print.

Segalla, Spencer D. *The Moroccan Soul: French Education, Colonial Ethnology, and Muslim Resistance, 1912–1956.* Lincoln: University of Nebraska Press, 2009. Print.

James Overholtzer

Witnesses to the Holocaust
An Oral History
Rhoda Lewin

✣ Key Facts

Time Period:
Mid- to Late 20th Century

Relevant Historical Events:
Holocaust; World War II

Nationality:
American

Keywords:
genocide; holocaust; survival

OVERVIEW

Collected and edited by Rhoda Lewin, *Witnesses to the Holocaust: An Oral History* (1990) presents sixty poignant testimonies of Holocaust survivors and witnesses. A journalism professor at the University of Minnesota, Lewin began the interviewing process in April 1982. The collection gathers accounts from U.S. residents who relate their stories of deportation, concentration camps, and liberation in Europe during World War II. This collection also presents interviews from people who were not sent to the concentration camps as well as from the liberators. Lewin is connected to the events through her husband, whose grandmother Recha Lewin was deported to Auschwitz in 1943 and sent to the gas chamber. Lewin's collection is at once a compelling indictment of Holocaust deniers, a powerful reminder of events, and a carefully designed teaching tool.

Immediately after World War II, silence prevailed between Holocaust survivors and the rest of the world; informal interviews started to take place in the mid-1970s. Lewin's gathering of eyewitness testimonies also took place in the early 1980s at a time of important political change in Eastern Europe that included the fall of the Berlin Wall. *Witnesses to the Holocaust* was well received in the academic world, and the work was praised for the humanity of its approach. Indeed, the collection focuses on the personal experience of each interviewee rather than on facts and numbers. Its continued popularity in and out of the classroom is a testament to both the power of the historical accounts and Lewin's rigorous scholarship.

HISTORICAL AND LITERARY CONTEXT

The accounts collected in *Witnesses to the Holocaust* document the experiences of survivors and witnesses to the atrocities committed against Jews in Europe in the 1930s and 1940s. During the decades after the end of World War II, several scholarly theories were published that denied the Holocaust entirely. These theories, along with the motivating factor of an aging population of survivors, prompted Lewin and other historians to conduct interviews with survivors beginning in 1982 in order to document their experiences. These personal eyewitness accounts, taken together, present a counterpoint to Holocaust denial.

Witnesses to the Holocaust focuses on the personal experiences of residents of the Midwest who witnessed and survived the Nazi genocide during World War II in eastern and northern Europe. Adolf Hitler, leader of the National Socialist German Workers Party, or Nazi Party, which controlled Germany, implemented the systematic extermination of Jews and of anyone who did not fit the Nazi racial ideal (among others, the Romani people, homosexuals, the handicapped, and political prisoners). To this end, the Nazis in Germany and in the occupied countries established thousands of concentration camps and ghettos. The book presents the stories of survivors from slave-labor camps, prison camps, and extermination camps, where an estimated six million Jews and five million non-Jews were put to death between 1939 and 1945. After the war, tens of thousands of survivors came to the United States.

In the 1970s and 1980s, oral histories of the Holocaust began to appear in the United States as survivors come forward to speak about their experiences. *Witnesses to the Holocaust* belongs to a literary tradition of oral histories of genocide that includes *Survivors: An Oral History of the Armenian Genocide* (1993), by Donald Miller and Lorna Touryan Miller, which presents a study of the Armenian genocide based on survivor testimonies. Other Holocaust oral histories predating Lewin's collection include *Voices of the Holocaust* (1981), by Sylvia Rothchild, and *Shoah* (1985), by Claude Lanzmann. *Witnesses to the Holocaust* distinguishes itself from these collections in that it is designed as a guide for teaching and discussing the Holocaust in the classroom.

Witnesses to the Holocaust has influenced the methodology of oral history in its careful editing and the documentation of its interview processes in the preface. The quality of its design and content has also made it a widely used textbook in high schools and colleges. Lewin's interest as a historian lay in twentieth-century Jewish immigration, and ten years after publishing *Witnesses to the Holocaust* she published *The Jewish Community of North Minneapolis,* a small book of historic photographs of the Jewish community of North Minneapolis from the early 1800s to the early 2000s.

THEMES AND STYLE

The central themes of *Witnesses to the Holocaust* are the atrocities suffered during the Holocaust, survival skills, the difficulty of talking about the experiences, and the question of responsibility. For example, a survivor from Auschwitz describes what happened to sick prisoners: "At the sick barracks were long lines of guys that had swellings on their bellies … huge growths. … This doctor would take his fist and smash the guy. … Then he would take his knife and just slit the growth open." Concerning the lengths people went to in order to survive, an Auschwitz survivor talks about the ghetto: "In the ghetto, when one father's son died, he kept him in the cellar for weeks, to collect the kid's rations." A survivor from Bergen-Belsen comments on the difficulty of talking about his experience: "I even avoided talking to my own children about the Holocaust. But lately I have felt an absolute need" to share the experience. Regarding the question of responsibility, a survivor from the Mauthausen concentration camp comments: "You cannot blame a Hitler when millions of people were taken by trains, 'assisted' by local guards and train engineers. Roosevelt knew exactly what was happening."

As she explains in the preface, Lewin was prompted to compile *Witnesses* in part to "create teaching materials for high schools and colleges" and in part "to discredit the so-called scholars who were saying that the Holocaust was wholly imaginary." She designed the book to be the epitome of "what oral history is meant to be—'history as if people mattered.'" To preserve the authenticity and unique voice of each story, and "to let that person tell the story in his or her own words," Lewin kept the editing of the transcripts to a minimum, not correcting syntax. She corrected factual errors when necessary, but she notes that she did not try to replicate accents and that she translated most foreign terms into English. Most importantly, she focused on the eyewitness testimonies and left out hearsay.

The language of *Witnesses to the Holocaust* is notable for the personal and unbearably graphic images that bring to life the events narrated. One example comes from Lewin's interview with an entertainer attached to Special Forces who participated in the liberation of Buchenwald: "Not far from the ovens was a cement torture chamber. The walls were three feet thick to muffle the screams. There was a drain in the cement floor so they could hose down the blood. On the walls were great meat hooks where they hung prisoners like chunks of beef until they died." This account further contributes to the overall purpose of the book as presented in the foreword, which is for the readers to share the human experience to turn them into witnesses of the horrors as well, so that they may never forget.

CRITICAL DISCUSSION

Upon publication, *Witnesses to the Holocaust* was well received. Reviewers generally praised the book for the power of the emotions it elicits in the reader, and Lewin was lauded for her unobtrusive and careful editing of the interviews. Edward Nelson, in a 1992 review in *Minnesota History*, calls the book "a well-organized and readable work," while Ava Kahn in a 1990 review in *Oral History Review* offers that "*Witnesses* provides an excellent model for other oral history works." In his 1991 review of various oral histories, "Useful Discoveries: Oral History, Public History, and the Dialectic of Narrative," Ronald Grele is much less complimentary and rather deplores Lewin's minimal editing. While others such as Janine Bauman see historical credibility in the uniformity of narration found in the survivors' stories, Grele finds the book "historiographically dull."

Witnesses to the Holocaust has made a lasting impact as an oral history that connects modern readers viscerally with what Nelson calls "a tribute to human endurance and will to live." Nelson adds that "one cannot help be moved deeply by reading these stories." Kahn notes that the book "produce[s] powerful images that serve to pull the reader into the narratives." The power of the collection also lies in Lewin's rigorous journalistic

Holocaust Memorial in Miami Beach, Florida, designed by Kenneth Treister. © JAMES KIRKIKIS/ALAMY

SHOAH

In 1985, French documentary filmmaker Claude Lanzmann produced the critically acclaimed *Shoah,* a film about the Holocaust, which features interviews from witnesses and visits to places where the Holocaust took place in fourteen countries. Much like Lewin, Lanzmann spent years creating his documentary and carefully organized his interviews in three categories: survivors, bystanders, and perpetrators. Lanzmann brings a new dimension to his work, however, by presenting interviews with people directly involved in the implementation of the Holocaust.

Shoah was conceived in the same spirit as *Witnesses to the Holocaust* in the sense that it is an act of witnessing designed to awaken viewers' minds to the fact of unspeakable inhumanity. Much like Lewin, Lanzmann does not focus on historical facts and figures but rather on the raw and unfiltered power of the human experience. Lanzmann explains how he conceived of his work as "more powerful than history," which is why he did not use historical footage. Instead, he reconstructed the Holocaust entirely from memories (stories and images), showing how the horrific Nazi machinery worked in general but through individual human experiences. As a *New York Times* review notes, "the film has been noted as a bold new approach, ... striving ... in Mr. Lanzmann's words, 'to reincarnate' the Jewish tragedy."

training. As Kahn notes, the "oral history methodology and the publication of interview transcripts are again validated," as the careful recording and transcription of the stories presents the reader with overwhelming factual evidence. In this way, the work also serves as an enduring, personal, and powerful repudiation of Holocaust deniers.

While *Witnesses to the Holocaust* produced little to no scholarship, its main strength (and purpose) lies in its educational design, and it continues to have a lasting impact, particularly in high school and college classrooms. Reviewers unanimously agree that the book is a well-thought-out teaching tool, praising Lewin for the care she takes in explaining her methodology and giving the reader an opportunity to build a relationship with the stories. As Kahn notes, "the guide includes questions that ask the reader ... to create interest in ... people and events ... and stimulate the reader to make value judgments." Grele, meanwhile, concedes that "it contains an interesting afterword and a useful teacher's guide on how to use the interviews for further discussion," but finds Lewin's endeavor to "let the stories speak for themselves" detrimental to the book. He comments that the reader cannot get the whole experience from the testimonies alone and that the historian needs to actively engage with and interpret the interview material.

BIBLIOGRAPHY

Sources

Bauman, Janine. Rev. of *Witnesses to the Holocaust: An Oral History,* by Rhoda Lewin. *Oral History Society* 21.1 (1993): 88. *JSTOR.* Web. 28 Jan. 2013.

Grele, Ronald J. "Useful Discoveries: Oral History, Public History, and the Dialectic of Narrative." Rev. of *Witnesses to the Holocaust: An Oral History,* by Rhoda G. Lewin. *The Public Historian* 13.2 (1991): 61–74. Print.

Kahn, Ava. Rev. of *Witnesses to the Holocaust: An Oral History,* by Rhoda G. Lewin. *Oral History Review* 18.2 (1990): 172–74. *JSTOR.* Web. 28 Jan. 2013.

Lewin, Rhoda G. *Witnesses to the Holocaust: An Oral History.* Boston: Twayne, 1990. Print.

Nelson, Edward P. Rev. of *Witnesses to the Holocaust: An Oral History,* by Rhoda G. Lewin. *Minnesota History* 52.2 (1990): 83. *JSTOR.* Web. 28 Jan. 2013.

Further Reading

Chandler, Sally. "Oral History across Generations: Age, Generational Identity and Oral Testimony." *Oral History Society* 33.2 (2005): 48–56. *JSTOR.* Web. 30 Jan. 2013.

Lanzmann, Claude. *Shoah: An Oral History of the Holocaust: The Complete Text of the Film.* New York: Pantheon, 1985. Print.

Lewin, Rhoda G. "Each of Us Sees History through Our Own Eyes." *Oral History Review* 29.2 (2002): 47–51. *JSTOR.* Web. 28 Jan. 2013.

———. *Jewish Community of North Minneapolis.* Chicago: Arcadia, 2001. Print.

———. "Stereotype and Reality in the Jewish Immigrant Experience in Minneapolis." *Oral History Review* 29.7 (1979): 258–73. *JSTOR.* Web. 28 Jan. 2013.

Miller, Donald E., and Lorna Touryan Miller. *Survivors: An Oral History of the Armenian Genocide.* Berkeley: University of California Press, 1993. Print.

Rothchild, Sylvia. *Voices from the Holocaust.* New York: New American Library, 1981. Print.

Shaftel, Anna, and Stacy Zembrzycki. "Only Human: A Reflection on the Ethical and Methodological Challenges of Working with 'Difficult' Stories." *Oral History Review* 37.2 (2010): 191–214. *MLA International Bibliography.* Web. 28 Jan. 2013.

Terkel, Studs. *The Good War: An Oral History of World War II.* New York: New Press, 1984. Print.

Lise LaLonde

Working-Class Childhood
An Oral History
Jeremy Seabrook

OVERVIEW

Compiled and edited by author and journalist Jeremy Seabrook, *Working-Class Childhood: An Oral History*, published in 1982, includes reflections on childhood in Great Britain from the 1930s through the 1970s. Alongside transcribed interviews, Seabrook includes his own theories about the working class and the economy, especially as they relate to childhood. He uses oral histories as evidence of what he sees as the result of an advancing and increasingly powerful form of capitalism, one that drives working-class communities apart and increases the likelihood that children from these communities will define themselves through material goods rather than their accomplishments and actions.

Working-Class Childhood explores the social, cultural, and economic changes impacting lower-income neighborhoods in twentieth-century Britain. Having already written about the working class for a number of publications and in other books (such as *What Went Wrong: Working People and the Ideals of the Labour Movement*, published in 1978), Seabrook further cemented his reputation as a social journalist with the publication of *Working-Class Childhood*. Though some critics found his thesis lacking complexity and his editing of the oral histories to be too self-serving, *Working-Class Childhood* raised important questions about the effects of class and the economy on several generations of British citizens.

HISTORICAL AND LITERARY CONTEXT

From the 1930s through the 1970s, the working class witnessed a number of changes, including increased opportunities for women and minorities within the workforce, new governmental regulation of the workplace, and a diminishing need for manual labor. During the Great Depression food shortages caused children to face illnesses brought on by malnutrition, such as scurvy and tuberculosis. With World War II came evacuations and the separation of children from their families, the London Blitz, and inconsistent and often interrupted educations. After the war ended, children were encouraged to maintain a stoic attitude about their wartime experiences; later, changes in technology and industry altered the face of the workforce, leaving the parents of many working-class children unemployed.

In *Working-Class Childhood* Seabrook suggests that working-class children of the 1980s will be inclined toward a less community-oriented solution to poverty. He believes an increase in the capitalist marketplace over the fifty years his book chronicles has led to an attempt among working-class parents to mollify their children with material goods rather than stressing social or educational goals.

Many of Seabrook's ideas come from the work of Richard Hoggart, a British academic known for his work in sociology, literature, and cultural studies. Four years after the publication of *Working-Class Childhood*, Hoggart himself published a book using similar methods and concentrating on similar themes called *The Worst of Times: An Oral History of the Great Depression in Britain*. Within *Working-Class Childhood*, Seabrook uses the term "primary poverty," coined by British sociologist Seebohm Rowntree, to indicate the condition of lacking essentials. Rowntree's writings are based on his long-term research on poverty in the city of York, England, in 1899, 1935, and 1951. Rowntree compiled his experiences and theories in *Poverty, A Study of Town Life* (1901), *The Human Needs of Labour* (1918), and *English Life and Leisure: A Social Study* (1951).

The content of *Working-Class Childhood* continues to influence others working in a similar vein. One prominent example is Michael Apted's *Up* documentary series, which has chronicled the lives of fourteen British children since 1964. The series began when the children were seven. Since then Apted has shot a new episode at seven-year intervals, with the newest episode, *56 Up*, appearing in 2013. *Up* deals with many of the same themes that *Working-Class Childhood* does, including the influence of social class on childhood.

THEMES AND STYLE

The themes of *Working-Class Childhood* are capitalist domination, the influence of social and economic factors on childhood, and the fate of the working class. Seabrook alternates between the oral histories and his own commentary, allowing people to speak for themselves in places and further expounding their words in others. *Working-Class Childhood* repeatedly returns to its central themes, whether voiced by those recounting their experiences or by the author himself. For example, supporting Seabrook's point about material items

❖ **Key Facts**

Time Period:
Mid- to Late 20th Century

Relevant Historical Events:
Advancement of capitalism; deterioration of the British working class

Nationality:
British

Keywords:
labor rights; socialism; working class

Children enjoying a water ride in the northern seaside resort of Scarborough, New Yorkshire, England. In *Working-Class Childhood: An Oral History,* Jeremy Seabrook argues that modern children have had all of their needs and wants passively satisfied, creating a poverty of values. © RICHARD BAKER/IN PICTURES/CORBIS

serving as replacements for long-term solutions, an eighty-two-year-old woman describes the junk food she sees schoolchildren eating as "comforts for all the things they will never know, never learn."

Seabrook does not go into detail about his methods for transcribing and editing the oral histories. As a result, some critics believe that his oral histories might be edited with an eye toward making select points rather than authentically portraying what the individuals meant to convey. The debate about how much, or how little, to edit oral histories is common to the genre. In the continuation of his studies on the working class, Seabrook also published *Unemployment* (1982), which presents oral histories and observations about the jobless. Like some critics of *Working-Class Childhood,* Huw Benyon of the *Socialist Register* finds fault with Seabrook's oral histories in *Unemployment,* stating that "he builds his argument around a mixture of carefully worded, tape-recorded testimony and noted observation of spontaneous comment and interaction."

While *Working-Class Childhood* does contain sections written entirely in Seabrook's voice and in the authorial tone he created, it also contains entire chapters consisting only of oral histories. When describing the working-class world within which the oral histories take place, Seabrook's language paints a bleak picture. In a 1983 review of *Working-Class Childhood* for *History Workshop,* Jerry White concludes that "Seabrook's tone … is at once mournful and hopeful and bitter, deadening the spirit like sleet." White goes on to note Seabrook's use of somber words to describe working-class neighborhoods: "bricks 'bleed' in the rain; the poor sit on their split rexene sofas; children's bedrooms are 'grottoes of fantasy' already 'discarded, used up, disregarded.'" The oral histories from the older generations often express nostalgia for the past and distaste for the present. According to Seabrook, "There has been a loss of the human comforts of the formerly poor. … All this has been usurped by the power of money and the promise of what it can buy." Illustrating this point, one mother told Seabrook that "I was brought up poor and I made up my mind I was going to buy [my daughter] the best childhood there is."

CRITICAL DISCUSSION

Initial critical reactions to *Working-Class Childhood* were mixed, with most reviewers disagreeing somewhat with Seabrook's theories while also acknowledging the validity of the questions he raises. In his review for *Oral History,* Philip Corrigan finds that "there is a lot of truth here" but "there is also much that is too one-sided, totally fixed; closing down upon the vibrancy and creativity through which people relate to consumption, to style, to goods, and thus to the marketplace." In her review for the *Times Literary Supplement,* Nesta Roberts finds that Seabrook has "a tendency to say the same thing thrice over, not in strikingly different ways." Roberts concludes, however, that "the occasional verbosity of the argument does not invalidate the thesis, that today's young have been freed from primary poverty only to become market-fodder."

Since the publication of *Working-Class Childhood,* Seabrook has written a number of other works that touch on the same social and developmental issues. In a review of Seabrook's book *In the Cities of the South: Scenes from a Developing World, Publishers Weekly* describes how "Seabrook compares the plight of the industrialized Third World poor and his own upbringing in the industrialized Midlands of Britain while acknowledging how remote the two experiences are." Though the issues and questions raised in *Working-Class Childhood* continue to live on in the work of Seabrook and his peers, the book itself does not have the legacy belonging to works by Seabrook's predecessors such as Hoggart and Rowntree.

Working-Class Childhood has not received much critical attention in recent years. In the decades after the book was published, Seabrook wrote more than twenty books, including *Victims of Development: Resistance and Alternatives* (1993), *Children of Other Worlds: Exploitation in the Global Market* (2001), and *The Refuge and the Fortress: Britain and the Flight from Tyranny* (2008). Whether or not a contemporary reader agrees with Seabrook's depictions of working-class childhoods in twentieth-century Britain, he or she can still look to *Working-Class Childhood* for reflections about how class, the economy, and childhood have intersected and influenced one another—and how they continue to do so.

BIBLIOGRAPHY

Sources

Benyon, Huw. "Jeremy Seabrook and the British Working Class." Rev. of *Unemployment,* by Jeremy Seabrook. *Socialist Register.* Socialist Register, 1982. Web. 7 Jan. 2013.

Corrigan, Philip. Rev. of *Working-Class Childhood*, by Jeremy Seabrook. *Oral History* 11.2 (1983): 86–88. *JSTOR*. Web. 7 Jan. 2013.

Rev. of *In the Cities of the South: Scenes from a Developing World*, by Jeremy Seabrook. *Publishers Weekly* 18 Mar. 1996: 62. *Literature Resource Center*. Web. 8 Jan. 2013.

Roberts, Nesta. "Cold Comforts." Rev. of *Working-Class Childhood*, by Jeremy Seabrook. *Times Literary Supplement* 12 Nov. 1982: 1240. *Times Literary Supplement Historical Archive*. Web. 7 Jan. 2013.

Seabrook, Jeremy. *Working-Class Childhood: An Oral History*. London: Gallancz, 1982. Print.

White, Jerry. Rev. of *Working-Class Childhood*, by Jeremy Seabrook. *History Workshop* Spring 1983: 183–87. *JSTOR*. Web. 8 Jan. 2013.

Further Reading

Braun, Annette, Carol Vincent, and Stephen J. Ball. "Working-Class Fathers and Childcare: The Economic and Family Contexts of Fathering in the UK." *Community, Work & Family* 14.1 (2011): 19–37. *Academic Search Premier*. Web. 27 Jan. 2013.

Burnett, John. *Destiny Obscure: Autobiographies of Childhood, Education and Family from the 1820s to the 1920s*. London: Routledge, 1994. Print.

Engels, Friedrich. "Voices from the Past. The Condition of the Working Class in England." *American Journal of Public Health* 93.8 (2003): 1246–49. *CINAHL Plus with Full Text*. Web. 27 Jan. 2013.

Read, Jane. "Gutter to Garden: Historical Discourses of Risk in Interventions in Working Class Children's Street Play." *Children & Society* 25.6 (2011): 421–34. *ERIC*. Web. 27 Jan. 2013.

Scott, Peter. "Did Owner-Occupation Lead to Smaller Families for Interwar Working-Class Households?" *Economic History Review* 61.1 (2008): 99–124. *Business Source Complete*. Web. 27 Jan. 2013.

Seabrook, Jeremy. *Children of Other Worlds: Exploitation in the Global Market*. London: Pluto, 2001. Print.

JEREMY SEABROOK: A MULTIGENRE WRITER

Although Jeremy Seabrook mentions his own working-class origins in *Working-Class Childhood* and in his other books, he largely concentrates on others' experiences and on wider social issues. However, Seabrook is also the author of memoirs, stage plays, and scripts for both television and radio. His first book, in fact, was a memoir. Titled *The Unprivileged* (1967), it details his family's history, includes elements of oral history, and touches on many of the same class and social issues the author has explored in the course of his long and illustrious career.

In 1979 Seabrook published *Mother and Son: An Autobiography*, which concentrates on his upbringing as it relates to his class and his relationship to his mother. His plays for stage, television, and radio were mostly written with Michael O'Neill, whom Seabrook has known since they were in school together at the University of Cambridge. Like his journalistic work and even his memoirs, Seabrook's plays also deal with social issues and raise important questions about class.

———. *The Refuge and the Fortress: Britain and the Flight from Tyranny*. London: Palgrave Macmillan, 2008. Print.

———. *Unemployment*. London: Quartet, 1982. Print.

Siraj-Blatchford, Iram. "Learning in the Home and at School: How Working Class Children 'Succeed against the Odds.'" *British Educational Research Journal* 36.3 (2010): 463–82. *Academic Search Premier*. Web. 27 Jan. 2013.

Jen Gann

COMMUNITIES

Akenfield: Portrait of an English Village by Ronald Blythe	59
Ask the Fellows Who Cut the Hay by George Ewart Evans	63
Coal Hollow: Photographs and Oral Histories by Kenneth Light and Melanie Light	66
Daring Hearts: Lesbian and Gay Lives of the 50s and 60s Brighton by Brighton Ourstory	70
Doña María's Story: Life History, Memory and Political Identity by Daniel James	73
Hill Country Teacher: Oral Histories from the One-Room School and Beyond by Diane Manning	77
The Hood River Issei: An Oral History of Japanese Settlers in Oregon's Hood River Valley by Linda Tamura	80
The Making of a Gay Asian Community: An Oral History of Pre-AIDS Los Angeles by Eric Wat	83
Our Appalachia: An Oral History by Laurel Shackelford and Bill Weinberg	86
The Saga of Coe Ridge: A Study in Oral History by William Lynwood Montell	90
Swiftwater People: Lives of Old Timers on the Upper St. Joe & St. Maries Rivers by Bert Russell	93
They Say in Harlan County: An Oral History by Alessandro Portelli	96
Untold Tales, Unsung Heroes: An Oral History of Detroit's African-American Community, 1918–1967 by Elaine Latzman Moon	99
Voices from this Long Brown Land: Oral Recollections of Owens Valley Lives and Manzanar Pasts by Jane Wehrey	102

AKENFIELD
Portrait of an English Village
Ronald Blythe

OVERVIEW

Collected and edited by Ronald Blythe, *Akenfield: Portrait of an English Village* (1969) is an oral history capturing the essence of life in an English village from 1880 to 1966, as told by the villagers and farmers themselves. The fictional Suffolk village, which Blythe calls "Akenfield," is actually a composite of several rural communities in East Anglia, located approximately ninety miles northeast of London. In 1966–67 Blythe interviewed forty-nine villagers about a variety of topics, including farming, class, education, religion, and welfare, in what he describes as "a kind of natural conversation with three generations." He assigned interviewees fictionalized names and compiled their stories into a rich portrait of the Suffolk people and "the nature of rural life in England at a time of great change," according to Craig Taylor in *Return to Akenfield: Portrait of an English Village in the 21st Century* (2012).

Akenfield became an international best seller with critics praising Blythe's acute eye for detail. The book garnered the 1969 Heinemann Award, and it inspired a film directed by Sir Peter Hall. *Akenfield* has remained in print since its initial publication and has been translated into more than twenty languages. Although its validity as a sociological text has been called into question, it continues to be a popular example of the oral history genre and rural community literature. In a 2006 review of *Return to Akenfield* in the *New Statesman,* Robert Winder notes that "Akenfield was especially beloved in North America, where it came to represent Olde England, and perhaps even Old Europe." Winder also claims that Blythe made Suffolk "into the most famous slice of little England in the world."

HISTORICAL AND LITERARY CONTEXT

In *Return to Akenfield,* Taylor quotes Blythe as explaining that the vast majority of English villages began in the late Anglo-Saxon and Norman period as communities with "one or two fields, usually with moorland or woodland all around them, and they just spread out over the centuries." Eventually the villages developed manor houses, thatched cottages, medieval churches, "and the pub of course," writes Blythe. The villages became home to farmers, blacksmiths, millers, and wheelwrights whose faces "are familiar to us as the flowers in our garden. … We know everyone, are known to everyone," explains Mary Russell Mitford in *Our Village* (1830). These rural settlements operated as independent communities and derived their primary source of income from agriculture.

Although the villages may have appeared idyllic, with their picturesque buildings and close-knit communities, reality was often much harsher. As late as 1900 many farm workers remained poorly paid, fed, and housed. Cottages were often overcrowded; many were in decay and lacked proper sanitation services. In the late nineteenth and early twentieth centuries, people began to leave the villages for towns. Indeed, according to Blythe, Akenfield was home to only 298 villagers in 1961. This rural depopulation coincided with an agricultural recession that lasted from the end of the nineteenth century until World War II. A native of Suffolk, Blythe describes being brought up "in a kind of beautiful, ruinous landscape of great rural poverty." *Akenfield* appeared at a time of great change in English agriculture: technological advances such as large combines meant that fewer farm laborers were needed, making jobs associated with farming less secure. In 2012 Blythe told the *Spectator,* "When I wrote *Akenfield,* I had no idea that anything particular was happening, but it was the last days of the old traditional life in Britain. And it vanished."

Akenfield is often compared to George Ewart Evans's scholarly oral histories. Evans was a dedicated collector of oral history in the East Anglian countryside from the 1940s to the 1970s. According to Paul Thompson in *The Voice of the Past: Oral History* (2000), Evans's books are "direct yet subtle intertwinings of agricultural and economic history with cultural and community studies, portraits of individuals, and stories." Thompson goes on to state that Evans "set an exacting standard for what has become one of the best-known areas for oral history." A notable example of Evans's work is *Ask the Fellows Who Cut the Hay* (1956), in which the author explores the social structure of a Suffolk village. Blythe has also been compared to John Updike. In a *Times Literary Supplement* article, cited in *Contemporary Authors Online,* Valentine Cunningham asserts that Blythe does "for the honeysuckled ambience of unfervid village Anglicans what Updike

❖ *Key Facts*

Time Period:
Late 19th to Mid-20th Century

Relevant Historical Events:
Agricultural recession of the early 20th century; rural depopulation of Britain

Nationality:
English

Keywords:
agriculture; tradition; depopulation

COMMUNITIES

In East Anglia (a region of England that includes Norfolk and Suffolk), cereal grains have traditionally been among the most important crops. By 1969 new owners had planted much of the land in fruit orchards. Ronald Blythe calls this "the greatest farming change which Akenfield can have seen for hundreds of years."
© JARROLD PUBLISHING/ THE ART ARCHIVE AT ART RESOURCE, NY

seeks to do for their white clapboard counterparts in Lutheran North America."

Akenfield's unique blend of literature, history, and sociology became very popular and inspired writers around the world to explore both oral history and rural social history in new ways. The success of the work led Blythe to compose another oral history a decade later—*The View in Winter: Reflections on Old Age* (1979). With interview methods similar to those he used for *Akenfield,* he records his conversations with the elderly residents of East Anglia and a mining community in Wales, discussing what it is like to be old. In the *New York Review of Books,* V. S. Pritchett praises *The View in Winter* for being "an unflinching, inquiring, and reflective essay … brought sharply to life by interviews in which the old cottager, farmer, miner, the matron, the nurse, and others of all classes talk about their experiences and their dreads." At the age of ninety, Blythe continues to write and has composed a great variety of texts, but he is best known for his two oral histories.

THEMES AND STYLE

Central to *Akenfield* is both its homage to the countryside and its portrayal of the brutality of village life. Blythe's interviewees were typical villagers—farmers, blacksmiths, and thatchers—recounting their lives and giving their views on various topics. The blacksmith recalls forging his own nails, while the thatcher describes the joy of a completed roof where "the reeds shine silver and grey, and the deep eaves are cut razor sharp." Taylor notes that the farm laborers express their "connection to the old clay of Suffolk's soil—how they coaxed it, marked it, ploughed it, cursed it and occasionally questioned its worth altogether—and revealed stores of knowledge that technological progress was beginning to erase." Blythe's villagers also express a desire to escape the village and its limited opportunities. Thompson states that "the hard reality of a village labourer's life at once breaks through the first section of recollections by the older farm workers. It also becomes possible to see the community from conflicting standpoints, both of generation and of class."

In the mid-1960s, while living in a Suffolk village, Blythe was contacted by two publishers, Penguin in London and Pantheon in New York, about a project concerning how village life was changing on a global scale. Blythe recalls, "When they came to me and said that I should do one about Britain, I told them I was not a sociologist remotely, nor had I heard of the term oral history at the time." Although Blythe did not see his small village as particularly interesting, he agreed to the project. However, when he struggled to get started, he "went for a walk around Akenfield. It was an awful February day." He spoke first to the village nurse, whom he thought he knew very well, but he was astonished by the interview: "I soon realized I didn't know her at all. Once she started speaking about her own life, another person emerged." Now that he had direction, Blythe cycled around Suffolk, interviewing the residents and recording the conversations: "I would ask somebody to talk to me about keeping pigs—and suddenly he would tell me something astonishing about himself, or be so open about his emotional life that I was astounded. Often I hardly asked any questions at all, I just listened."

Stylistically, *Akenfield* is marked by its attention to detail and the vivid descriptions of the locale. Blythe writes, "The village lies folded away in one of the shallow valleys which dip into the East Anglian coastal plain. It is not a particularly striking place and says little at first meeting. … Centuries of traffic must have passed within yards of Akenfield without noticing it." Although Blythe may have altered the language of the residents while editing the transcripts, the voices of the villagers still manage to shine through in an often poetic tone. For example, at the very end of the book, the gravedigger muses, "I want to be cremated and my ashes thrown in the air. Straight from the flames to the winds, and let that be that."

CRITICAL DISCUSSION

Upon publication, *Akenfield* garnered instant critical acclaim for chronicling the changing rhythms and character of life in English villages. In a 1969 review in the *Atlantic*, for example, Yorick Blumenfeld describes *Akenfield* as a "superb documentation of the changes which have revolutionized modern England." Blythe was praised for his master craftsmanship and ability to bring the interviewees to life. In a 1969 review in *Life*, Melvin Maddocks declares, "With wit and with affection, Blythe has composed a little tragi-comic masterpiece on the ironies of progress: the reasonable profits and the often unreasonable costs." In a review for the *New Republic* (1969), Roger Starr characterizes the book as "a self-portrait so artfully drawn by the writer that it appears artless." Writing for the *Times Literary Supplement*, Paul Fussell observes that Blythe has a "talent for celebrating admirable people."

According to Thompson, Blythe's work proved "indisputably successful in popularizing a new form of rural literature, a cross between the interview documentary and the novel." *Akenfield* was followed by several other community studies, including *Il mondo dei vinti* (*The World of the Defeated*, 1977) by Nuto Revelli and *Le cheval d'orgueil* (*The Horse of Pride*, 1978) by Pierre Jakez Hélias, which offer authentic voices from the Italian and French peasantry, respectively. Mary Chamberlain's *Fenwomen* (1975) is a village study influenced by *Akenfield* but based entirely on the stories of women. A longtime admirer of *Akenfield*, Taylor continued Blythe's work in his 2006 oral history *Return to Akenfield*. Although Taylor spoke with some of the *Akenfield* interviewees, he focused more on the development of the village than on how the villagers had aged. In praise of Taylor's text, Winder declares that "it is oral history at its best: direct yet full of charm; at once sentimental and austere."

Although *Akenfield* was tremendously popular and garnered great praise, Blythe's method for collecting, editing, and arranging the oral evidence has been criticized. Thompson argues that *Akenfield* "cut too many corners" to be considered as a model text of sociology or history, asserting that "not only the language of the transcripts, but even its attachment to particular informants, cannot be trusted." However, Thompson also comments that there can be no "doubt that oral evidence constitutes [the book's] real strength." Despite its weakness as a strictly historical or sociological text, *Akenfield* is considered a modern classic. Taylor describes it as "vivid in the detail it accorded everyday tasks and poignant in its evocation of a disappearing past."

BIBLIOGRAPHY

Sources

Blumenfeld, Yorick. Rev. of *Akenfield: Portrait of an English Village*, by Ronald Blythe. *Atlantic* Sept. 1969. Print.

A PORTRAIT OF RONALD BLYTHE

On November 6, 1922, Ronald Blythe was born in Acton, a typical Suffolk village. The eldest of six children, he grew up during the time of the great agricultural depression. Although the country was ravaged by poverty, Blythe states that "we didn't know it, because the fields were full of wild flowers." Blythe's father, a farmhand, served at Gallipoli and in the Middle East during World War I. Although farm workers were not called to serve until 1917, Blythe's father entered service in 1914. Many young villagers volunteered early for military service because traveling abroad was a romantic notion for impoverished country boys who had seen little. When the elder Blythe returned to Suffolk, he recommenced working on a farm as a stockman and married Blythe's mother, a well-read Londoner who deeply loved the country.

In Taylor's *Return to Akenfield*, Blythe describes his childhood self as "a great watcher and listener," saying, "I loved history and looking at old churches." An avid reader, he spent ten years working as a reference librarian in Colchester after a brief military service in World War II. Blythe became close friends with the artist John Nash and his wife, Christine, who encouraged Blythe to become a writer. In 1960 Blythe published his first book, a novel titled *A Treasonable Growth*. His 1963 book *The Age of Illusion* led to a job with Penguin editing a series of classics. As of 2013, Blythe lives at Bottengoms Farm—the home Nash bequeathed to him—and continues to write. He is the author of a long-running column, *Word from Wormingford*, in the *Church Times*.

Blythe, Ronald. *Akenfield: Portrait of an English Village*. New York: Pantheon, 1969. Print.

Fussell, Paul. Rev. of *Akenfield: Portrait of an English Village*, by Ronald Blythe. *Times Literary Supplement* 6 June 1969. Print.

Maddocks, Melvin. "*Akenfield*." Rev. of *Akenfield: Portrait of an English Village*, by Ronald Blythe. *Life* 14 Nov. 1969: 23. Print.

Mitford, Mary Russell. *Our Village*. London: Whittaker, Treacher, 1830. *Project Gutenberg*. Web. 16 Jan. 2012.

Mount, Harry. "Rural Idol: Ronald Blythe, Author of *Akenfield*, at 90." *Spectator* 13 Oct. 2012: 23. *Literature Resource Center*. Web. 16 Jan. 2012.

Pritchett, V. S. Rev. of *The View of Winter: Reflections on Old Age*, by Ronald Blythe. *New York Review of Books* 8 Nov. 1979. Print.

"Ronald (George) Blythe." *Contemporary Authors Online*. Detroit: Gale, 2005. *Literature Resource Center*. Web. 7 Jan. 2013.

Starr, Roger. Rev. of *Akenfield: Portrait of an English Village*, by Ronald Blythe. *New Republic* 4 Oct. 1969. Print.

Taylor, Craig. *Return to Akenfield: Portrait of an English Village in the 21st Century*. London: Granta, 2012. Print.

Thompson, Paul. *Voice of the Past: Oral History*. Oxford: Oxford University Press, 2000. Print.

Winder, Robert. Rev. of *Return to Akenfield,* by Craig Taylor. *New Statesman* 13 Mar. 2006: 50+. *Literature Resource Center.* Web. 7 Jan. 2013.

Further Reading

Abrams, Lynn. "Revisiting *Akenfield:* 40 Years of an Iconic Text." *Oral History* 37.1 (2009): 33–42. Web. 7 Jan. 2013.

Barkham, Patrick. "A Life in Writing: Ronald Blythe." *Guardian.* Guardian News and Media, 21 Oct 2011. Web. 7 Jan. 2013.

Blythe, Ronald. *The View in Winter: Reflections on Old Age.* London: Penguin, 1979. Print.

House, Christian. "Ronald Blythe: My Not So Quiet Village Life." *Independent.* Independent, 11 Nov. 2012. Web. 7 Jan. 2013.

Rowley, Trevor. *English Landscape in the 20th Century.* London: Hambledon Continuum, 2006. Print.

Weiss, Robert S. *Learning from Strangers: The Art and Method of Qualitative Interview Studies.* New York: Free Press, 1994. Print.

Maggie Magno

Ask the Fellows Who Cut the Hay
George Ewart Evans

OVERVIEW
Compiled by George Ewart Evans from the testimony of people who farmed and lived in Suffolk, England, in the early part of the twentieth century, *Ask the Fellows Who Cut the Hay* (1956) records a way of life in rural England that had all but disappeared in one generation. Born in Wales, Evans moved with his wife and children to Blaxhall, a tiny village in Suffolk, after World War II and tried to make a living writing fiction. He soon realized that he was surrounded by older people who had fascinating stories to tell from their childhoods and young adulthood about a way of life that would soon be forgotten.

Published in postwar Britain, where food rationing had only just ended, *Ask the Fellows Who Cut the Hay* looked back to a period fifty years earlier, before mechanization and intensive farming had transformed the English landscape and put an end to traditional ways of life that had lasted hundreds of years. It was a pioneering work of social history, making its author one of the most influential British historical writers of the time. It remains a popular early example of British oral history and an important record of English rural life and customs.

HISTORICAL AND LITERARY CONTEXT
The personal testimonies, reminiscences, and stories collected and presented in *Ask the Fellows Who Cut the Hay* refer back to the years before World War I, when local customs in the village of Blaxhall, and much of southern rural England, were largely unchanged since the sixteenth century. The loss of many young farmworkers in the war and the growing cities of the early twentieth century put great strain on British agriculture, which even as late as the 1940s still depended on the power of the horse rather than the tractor. Shortages in World War II forced British agriculture to become more productive, and in the process of modernization many of the traditions surrounding activities such as plowing and harvest were lost.

While Blaxhall remained a small rural village in 1956, Evans found that contemporary life had diverged from life in the village at the beginning of the century and earlier. For example, the loss of agricultural jobs meant that harvest was no longer a "ritual" that involved the whole village but "merely an incident in the more mechanical and depersonalised round of the farm." Evans discovered that the oral tradition of the older inhabitants, in which they passed on stories and events from the past, had all but gone, and that for the younger generation the disappearance of old skills had created a complete break with the past.

Ask the Fellows Who Cut the Hay was a pioneering work of British oral history that, while unsentimental itself, fed the nostalgia with which the English view their rural landscapes. Evans used tape recordings as well as written interviews, setting different testimonies alongside one another with the explicit purpose of using the past to understand the present. While reminiscences had long been popular with the British reading public, Evans's methodical approach to collecting stories and his interest in every aspect of rural life, from farming methods to the language of his subjects, made his book original and unique.

Evans's book is generally seen as inaugurating an approach to studying the past that later found its way into academic history, popular writing, and by the 1980s the school curriculum. In schools, studying local history and the lives of working people was a radical departure from the history of "kings and queens" that had dominated British historical education up to that point. *Ask the Fellows Who Cut the Hay* was the first of ten books Evans published with Faber & Faber, including his autobiography.

THEMES AND STYLE
The central themes of *Ask the Fellows Who Cut the Hay* are the impact of mechanization on farming and farming communities in eastern England and the social change brought about by the loss of an oral tradition and traditional social structures. On farming methods, for example, Evans writes: "Some of these local beliefs and practices may appear to be simple superstition; but it must not be forgotten that superstition is often a primitive attempt at science." More practically, he observes that "a farm-worker of the old school, a horseman for instance, had latterly no apprentice to take up his lore"; if not written down, his experience and knowledge were lost. Although the book focuses on the village of Blaxhall, it is possible to extrapolate many of its conclusions to English villages of the time more generally. Evans documents social change in his own time and records the past. For example, he worries about whether communities can sustain

Key Facts

Time Period:
Early 20th Century

Relevant Historical Events:
Mechanization of agricultural production; World War I

Nationality:
British

Keywords:
pastoralism; agriculture; tradition

COMMUNITIES

Women pause for lunch while harvesting hay near Hawkshead, Lancashire, England, in 1928. © NGS IMAGE COLLECTION/THE ART ARCHIVE AT ART RESOURCE, NY

themselves when most people work outside the village and the shared daily experience of working the land is no longer the norm.

Evans's primary concern when writing *Ask the Fellows Who Cut the Hay* was to record the memories of people whose way of life had all but disappeared and, because few written records of it existed, would soon be forgotten. He notes that it is his "conviction that the oral tradition is at this time of the greatest historical importance" and that "old people in this countryside are survivors from another era." Evans used their stories to structure his book, but he understood the need to contextualize them. Striving for accuracy, he supports the oral testimony with evidence from manuscripts and written records wherever possible.

The written style of *Ask the Fellows Who Cut the Hay* is informative and factual, but it includes extensive use of direct quotation and stories from the Suffolk villagers Evans interviewed. For example, Evans goes into great detail on the technical process of beer brewing, noting that the yeast was shared among neighbors and that everyone would know who had brewed last and would have the freshest "barm" (yeast). The importance of beer to the community becomes clear when Evans explains that on brew day the wife of the household could only go to bed when she knew that "the beer is a-smiling." Dialect words often appear in the work—for example, in the advice of Priscilla Savage to her neighbor, who was making wine: "'You want to take that there mould off the top right quick, you dew! Thet will spoil it.'" Such direct speech adds authenticity to Evans's interviews and lightens the book's often serious tone.

CRITICAL DISCUSSION

Evans struggled to find a publisher for *Ask the Fellows Who Cut the Hay*, but after publication it was popular enough for Faber & Faber to commission further books from him. There is little scholarly criticism of the work, in part because oral history was not considered a serious approach to history at the time. Evans himself wrote letters to the *Times* calling for the University of Cambridge to establish research into East Anglian studies. Historians such as Asa Briggs and Elizabeth Roberts used recordings and interviews to document working-class life in the 1960s, but it was not until the 1970s that oral history became a respected academic discipline in Britain.

Ask the Fellows Who Cut the Hay is a landmark book, widely credited as the first work of British oral history, and an important record of East Anglian farming tradition and folklore. However, as the focus of scholarly interest shifted to recording the histories of women and ethnic and minority groups, the so-called "folklore studies" of writers such as Evans fell out of favor. In the 1980s oral historians were considered to have been too ready to accept what they were told by their interviewees. Indeed, Evans's work often takes the form of storytelling rather than rigorous recording. However, as Alun Howkins points out in *Labour History Review*, such criticism "misunderstands the roots of much of that work, which was within a 'people's history' tradition." Evans's histories were meant to be read and understood by the people who helped him write them.

Reflecting the growing importance of oral history in universities at the time, Evans was made a visiting fellow at Essex University from 1973 to 1978. He was a founding member of the Oral History Society, which was established in 1973. Since his death in 1988 Evans's work has become more closely associated with folklore and storytelling and with his Welsh roots; his name has been given to the George Ewart Evans Centre for Storytelling at the University of Glamorgan, Wales.

BIBLIOGRAPHY

Sources

Evans, George Ewart. *Ask the Fellows Who Cut the Hay.* London: Faber & Faber, 1956. Print.

———. *The Strength of the Hills; An Autobiography.* London: Faber & Faber, 1983. Print.

Howkins, Alun. "George Ewart Evans." *Labour History Review* 58.1 (1993): 90. *Business Source Complete.* Web. 29 Jan. 2013.

———. "Inventing Everyman: George Ewart Evans, Oral History and National Identity." *Oral History* 22.2 (1994). Web. 29 Jan. 2013.

Williams, Gareth. *George Ewart Evans.* Cardiff: University of Wales Press, 1993. Print.

Further Reading

Abrams, Lynn. *Oral History Theory.* Abingdon, UK: Routledge, 2010. Print.

Ely, Geoff. "The Generations of Social History." *Encyclopedia of European Social History.* Ed. Peter N. Stearns. Vol. 1. Detroit: Charles Scribner's Sons, 2001. *Gale Virtual Reference Library.* Web. 29 Jan. 2013.

Evans, George Ewart. *The Pattern under the Plough: Aspects of the Folk-life of East Anglia.* London: Faber, 1966. Print.

———. *Where Beards Wag All: The Relevance of the Oral Tradition.* London: Faber & Faber, 1970. Print.

THE GEORGE EWART EVANS COLLECTION

Throughout his career George Ewart Evans identified first and foremost as a writer. Much of his early oral history work was recorded by hand in notebooks. In 1956 his work as a radio writer brought him in contact with BBC producer David Bryson, who took an interest in his work and encouraged him to use a portable recorder. Beginning with a series of oral histories collected in the village of Blaxhall in 1956, Evans made a total of eight tapes. Unconvinced of their value, however, he put aside the recorder and returned to print recording. In 1963, however, David Thomson, another producer at the BBC, encouraged Evans to reconsider the benefits of audio recording. Over time Evans, who had at first seen the recordings as useful only for radio broadcast, began to see their value as part of his own process—one that would allow him to create authentic transcriptions of the stories he collected. Audio recording would come to play an important role in his later books. Comprising both interviews and songs, the recordings made by Evans between 1956 and 1977 are now part of a collection housed by the British Library. The entire collection is accessible to the public online through the library's website.

Gentleman, David, ed. *The Crooked Scythe: An Anthology of Oral History.* London: Faber & Faber, 1993. Print.

Howkins, Alun. *The Death of Rural England: A Social History of the Countryside since 1900.* London: Routledge, 2003. Print.

Thompson, E. P. *The Making of the British Working Class.* London: Gollancz, 1963. Print.

Thompson, Paul. *The Voices of the Past: Oral History.* 2nd. ed. New York: Oxford University Press, 1988. Print.

Chris Routledge

Coal Hollow
Photographs and Oral Histories
Kenneth Light, Melanie Light

✦ Key Facts

Time Period:
Early 21st Century

Relevant Historical Events:
Increasing awareness of the environmental and human costs of coal mining

Nationality:
American

Keywords:
mining; environmentalism; photography

OVERVIEW

A visual and written portrait of coal mining communities in West Virginia, *Coal Hollow: Photographs and Oral Histories* (2006) is a joint project of the husband-and-wife team of photographer Kenneth Light and writer Melanie Light. Traveling through southern West Virginia from 2000 to 2002, Kenneth used his camera to record images of daily life in pictures such as "Bryan at the swimming hole," "Hollie's hair cut," and "Wedding day." In order to expand and develop her husband's portrayal of families in Appalachia, Melanie recorded the stories of local people, including a journalist, a mayor, a retired miner, and a Pentecostal snake handler, in their own words. Using the name "Coal Hollow" to represent a composite of eight impoverished West Virginia counties, the Lights combined almost a hundred photos with eleven oral histories to create a bleak picture of coal industry exploitation leading to widespread poverty and desolation.

Published at a time of heightened public awareness about the human and environmental costs of coal mining, *Coal Hollow* was generally well received by readers outraged by corporate indifference and regulatory inadequacy. Critics who examined the book for scholarly objectivity and academic methodology were more critical of the Lights' photographic subjects and interviewing choices. However, most critics agree that *Coal Hollow* makes a powerful political statement, and the book has continued to stand as a significant documentation of the effects of the coal mining industry on modern Appalachian society.

HISTORICAL AND LITERARY CONTEXT

Occupied by native tribes since at least 1000 BCE, West Virginia began its colonial life as the western frontier of the sprawling territory of Virginia. The only state lying entirely in the Appalachian Mountains, the area was settled by fiercely independent immigrants, often from hilly regions in Scotland, Switzerland, and Germany. In 1861, when slave-owning Virginia seceded from the Union, the subsistence farmers of the rugged western counties voted to secede from Virginia, forming the state of West Virginia. The industrialization of the late 1800s led to expansion of the coal industry in the Appalachians, bringing enormous wealth to mine owners and grinding poverty to those forced to work in dangerous and unhealthy conditions, with thousands killed in accidents and disasters since the industry began. Where once family farms had supported generations of West Virginians, children began to follow their parents into the mines.

The release of *Coal Hollow* in 2006 had a particular resonance in U.S. society because it coincided with a well-publicized mine disaster the same year. The January 2006 mine explosion in the small town of Sago, West Virginia, came to represent many of the industry's problems, from unsafe working conditions to uncaring, greedy management. Twelve men were killed after being trapped in a collapsed shaft in Sago, a loss made more dramatic and painful by a false company report that all had survived. Investigation of the disaster revealed that the mining company had received hundreds of citations for safety violations in the years preceding the explosion, many of which had been ignored. The anger and grief of the survivors focused international attention on the hardships of Appalachian coal miners.

Politically conscious authors have long found the hard lives of coal miners exemplary of the need for social change. In *The Road to Wigan Pier* (1937), George Orwell explains his advocacy of socialism by describing his personal experience living among miners in an English coal town. Harry Caudill's *Night Comes to the Cumberlands: A Biography of a Depressed Area* (1962) focused national attention on the poverty and environmental destruction caused by the mining industry in the Appalachians of Kentucky. Coal mining also looms large in the personal stories in the 1977 oral history *Our Appalachia,* edited by Laurel Shackelford and Bill Weinberg. In 2007 photographer Thorney Lieberman initiated a project to show Appalachian coal miners in a different light, highlighting their pride and family connections. Photos from his life-sized exhibition were published in book form in 2012 as *Honoring America's Coal Miners.*

Upon its publication, the Lights' work filled a public desire for a personal look into the lives of those who work in the nation's coal mines. Readers and critics who were outraged by the working conditions dramatically illustrated by the Sago disaster welcomed *Coal Hollow*'s stark photographs and progressive political statement, though some questioned the book's methodology. In 2012 the Lights continued their

A 2000 photograph showing the effects of mountaintop removal mining near Kayford, West Virginia. The accounts of West Virginia miners appear in Melanie Light and Ken Light's *Coal Hollow: Photographs and Oral Histories.* © AP IMAGES/BOB BIRD, FILE

exploration of labor and poverty with *Valley of Shadows and Dreams,* a study of California farm workers.

THEMES AND STYLE

The major focus of both Kenneth's photographs and Melanie's text is the destruction of human lives that has been a by-product of the coal mining industry. Melanie's introduction compares this human waste with the environmental waste of mining: "Along with mineral debris, the coal companies left behind human slag. The broken earth and the broken people await reclamation." Kenneth's photos echo this theme by presenting stark black-and-white images of miners and their families, often in alienated poses and almost always unsmiling. In the photograph "Wedding day," for example, a bride in a white dress and lace veil stands alone on a dusty roadside, eyes cast down. "Laura, 45 years old, laundry day," shows a woman in front of a trailer home, laden clotheslines criss-crossing behind her, one hand on her hip and the other on her cheek, brow creased, as she gazes down in worry or despair.

The Lights intended their book to be a documentary exposé of life in Appalachian coal towns, with the underlying goal of provoking public outrage over the living conditions there and with the ultimate hope of creating social change. However, several critics have commented on an apparent lack of accountability and diversity in the Lights' choice of interviewees. Though Melanie mentions "the functioning universe of employed West Virginians," her text does not elaborate on their lives, focusing only on those living in extreme poverty. Mildred Beik, in a 2007 piece for the *Oral History Review,* points out limitations in that focus:

"No African Americans and only one person from a southern and eastern European ethnic background appear in the work, although both groups once had sizable populations in the region." Beik adds, "There is no way to know what the role of the interviewer was or what questions were asked or how the editing was done … or how or if the people shown and quoted gave consent through an Institutional Review Board process."

The fact that *Coal Hollow* is intended as a general indictment of the effects of the mining industry rather than a portrait of a particular community is immediately apparent in the work's name. There is no town of Coal Hollow; the Lights invented the name to represent all the West Virginia towns where life was shaped by mining. In the same way, the photographs and many of the interviews are depersonalized as if to make them archetypes of Appalachian poverty. The book begins with Kenneth's photographs, taken during the early 2000s. Most are identified only with the first name and age of the subject. Some, such as "Bryan at the swimming hole," which depicts an unsmiling boy in his underpants by a creek, and "Road kill," of a dead fox, seem to offer editorial comment on the bleakness of mountain life.

CRITICAL DISCUSSION

Coal Hollow struck a chord with a public still appalled by the Sago mine disaster. Arthur Salm, reviewing the work in 2006 for the *San Diego Union-Tribune,* describes it as a "devastating, deeply moving chronicle of threadbare lives and pitiless plunder." *Choice*'s review of the work calls it "a haunting profile of hardworking folks living on the margins. A singular accomplishment!" Norman

PRIMARY SOURCE

EXCERPT FROM *COAL HOLLOW*

FAYE, 65, MOUNTAIN WOMAN

Faye lives in a house next to an abandoned gas station deep in the West Virginia hills. She has cobbled together a life and a living from scavenging things and reselling them. Most recently, she and her grandson, Ray, were selling miner's overalls out of an abandoned yellow school bus on the side of the road for ten dollars a pair. She would scavenge discarded overalls, mend and clean them and sell them right back to the miners. Faye is a mountain woman, entrepreneur and a serious packrat.

"I'm Indian and Irish, mixed together. Dad died when we was all little. I was about nine when Daddy died. He was a farmer. He was out in the dankness and wet weather so much he took something called TB and pneumonia and it killed him when we was all real young.

"We had our own mountain water. We didn't have electricity 'till I was a great big girl. I was about eleven or twelve years old before we had electricity. We used oil lamps, and a lot of times nothing. The house was three rooms, made of logs cut, hewed and notched and stacked up.

"Either you worked or you didn't eat. They did not keep no sorry people around. They wouldn't fool with you. What food we had to eat when I was a kid, we had to raise in the hills. If we didn't raise something to eat in the summer, we had to do without when winter come. All of us had to work 'cause Mommy only had a little bit of money coming in to

---

Wirzba, writing in 2007 in *Books & Culture,* agrees: "It successfully makes a personal connection in a way that facts and statistics simply cannot." Those who examined the work from a scholarly perspective had sharper criticism. Barbara Howe, in a 2007 piece in the *Public Historian,* writes, "There is absolutely no balance to this book. … Public historians using this book to teach local history or oral history would be irresponsible not to balance it with scholarly histories of the state [and] oral histories from the state's archives."

Though less than a decade after its publication the work was not widely available in bookstores or libraries, Joan Hill, writing for the *Labor Studies Journal,* describes the lasting value of *Coal Hollow:* "Ken and Melanie Light's book is a true example of documentary journalism," which "bears witness to the struggles of those unique inhabitants of this geographic area of Appalachia." In spite of her criticism of the creators' methodology, Beik also asserts, "The aim of *Coal Hollow* was to bear witness to one of the nation's most devastated and forgotten regions today. The beautiful photographs and readable interviews certainly accomplish that goal."

Critique of *Coal Hollow* has been divided between those who admire the Lights' dedication to their progressive interpretation and those who find their approach simplistic and biased. In a 2009 study in the *Journal of Appalachian Studies,* Rebecca Scott argues that the work reinforces stereotypes that define Appalachian culture as defective and menacing. Comparing the work's "tropes of Appalachian cultural marginalization" to such "hillbilly" horror films as John Boorman's 1972 *Deliverance* and Rob Schmidt's 2003 *Wrong Turn,* Scott concludes, "Despite the intentions of the authors, *Coal Hollow* reiterates the traditional representation of Appalachian difference that has been essential to its status as a national sacrifice zone."

BIBLIOGRAPHY

Sources

Beik, Mildred Allen. Rev. of *Coal Hollow: Photographs and Oral Histories,* by Ken Light and Melanie Light. *Oral History Review* 34.1 (2007): 152–54. *JSTOR.* Web. 24 Jan. 2013.

Greenwald, M. Rev. of *Coal Hollow: Photographs and Oral Histories,* by Ken Light and Melanie Light. *Choice* 44.1 (2006): 182. *ProQuest.* Web. 27 Jan. 2013.

Hill, Joan G. Rev. of *Coal Hollow: Photographs and Oral Histories,* by Ken Light and Melanie Light. *Labor Studies Journal* 31. 4 (2007): 87–88. *Project MUSE.* Web. 27 Jan. 2013.

Howe, Barbara J. Rev. of *Coal Hollow: Photographs and Oral Histories,* by Ken Light and Melanie Light. *Public Historian* 29.2 (2007): 121–23. *JSTOR.* Web. 24 Jan. 2013.

Salm, Arthur. "Desolation Row: *Coal Hollow* Captures Lives of Quiet Desperation." *San Diego Union-Tribune* 30 July 2006: BOOKS-2. *ProQuest.* Web. 27 Jan. 2013.

Scott, Rebecca. "The Sociology of *Coal Hollow:* Safety, Othering, and Representations of Inequality." *Journal of Appalachian Studies* 15.1–2 (2009): 7–25. *EBSCOhost.* Web. 26 Jan. 2013.

Wirzba, Norman. "Throwaway People, Throwaway Land." *Books & Culture* Nov–Dec. 2007: 44+. *Literature Resource Center.* Web. 27 Jan. 2013.

buy the flour, the sugar, the coffee and a little bit, not much of nothing, for clothes.

"And if one didn't have something, the others would share. You'd give them a piece of the pig for a sack of potatoes or a piece of the pig for a sack of corn. Today, the mountains are all growed up and there ain't no food being grown out there. And if you got sick, you doctored yourself, 'cause there wasn't no hospital. If you broke a leg, you fixed it yourself. Two or three people'd come along and you'd slap that person upside the head [to give] him a pain shot. If it was broke to where you could see, you'd stretch it back—splintin' it.

"I just moved aways and got married and didn't better myself. Getting married with four kids was just a rough, rough life. I was married twice and neither husband was any good. They just wouldn't work and what work they worked, they didn't put to benefit toward the kids. I'd pick up stuff and recycle it. Wash it, clean it up, take it to the yard sale and sell it, like, for a quarter, fifty-cent and feed my kids. Same way my mother raised me.

"I don't have anything. I'm broke now. I got hit with this flood this spring and part of my garden down there washed away. Now I've got a few volunteer tomato plants and I've got some onions down there and something else is growing. I believe it's squash or a pumpkin … and potatoes, come back from last year. … I'm not gonna go hungry."

SOURCE: Light, Ken, and Melanie Light. *Coal Hollow.* Berkeley: University of California Press, 2006. All rights reserved. Reproduced by permission.

Further Reading

Batteau, Allen. *The Invention of Appalachia.* Tucson: University of Tucson Press, 1990. Print.

Corbin, David Alan, ed. *The West Virginia Mine Wars: An Anthology.* Charleston: Appalachian Editions, 1990. Print.

Harkins, Anthony. *Hillbilly: A Cultural History of an American Icon.* New York: Oxford University Press, 2004. Print.

"Honoring America's Coal Miners: A Photographic Project." *America's Coal Miners.* Web. 31 Jan. 2013.

Wray, Matt. *Not Quite White: White Trash and the Boundaries of Whiteness.* Durham, NC: Duke University Press, 2006. Print.

Tina Gianoulis

DARING HEARTS
Lesbian and Gay Lives of 50s and 60s Brighton
Brighton Ourstory

❖ Key Facts

Time Period:
Mid-20th Century

Relevant Historical Events:
Growth of gay rights movement; decriminalization of homosexuality in Britain

Nationality:
British

Keywords:
gay rights; civil rights; sexuality

OVERVIEW

Compiled and edited by Brighton Ourstory, a group that collects gay, lesbian, and bisexual history, *Daring Hearts: Lesbian and Gay Lives of 50s and 60s Brighton* (1992) presents the memories of twenty lesbians and twenty-one gay men for whom Brighton, England, was a significant place in the development of their social, sexual, and sometimes political selves. Though it focuses on a period, the 1950s and 1960s, when homosexuality was still forced underground, *Daring Hearts* traces a growing sense of possibility as individuals formed networks of friendship and support, becoming more visible as they began to sense a change in the larger English culture.

Published during a time when the gay community was being devastated by AIDS, *Daring Hearts* is a nostalgic, sometimes pained look back at an era that was quickly receding into history. The book was well reviewed upon its publication, and it has, along with its Brighton Ourstory authors, become an important model of oral history production for other lesbian, gay, bisexual, and transgender (LGBT) communities in the United Kingdom. In addition, the text is frequently cited in discussions of community oral history and in conversations regarding the historiography of queer studies in Great Britain.

HISTORICAL AND LITERARY CONTEXT

The closeted nature of many of the gay and lesbian relationships described in *Daring Hearts* is a reflection of legal and social prohibitions that were deeply rooted in English life. By decree of the Buggery Act of 1533, instituted during the reign of Henry VIII, anal intercourse and other sexual acts presumed to be "unnatural" were subject to the death penalty. While the Offences Against the Person Act of 1861 eliminated capital punishment for anal sex, it also criminalized all other sexual activity between men. Though not targeted by specific legislation, lesbians were subjected to social censure, as sexuality in a culture ruled predominantly by the Church of England was still firmly connected to marriage and reproduction well into the twentieth century.

Daring Hearts reflects the experiences of lesbians and gay men coming to terms with their sexuality and attempting to form relationships in this repressive climate. During the 1950s and 1960s, Brighton, described in the book's introduction as "a gay Mecca" in England's conservative landscape, became a destination for many of these women and men, who congregated in pubs and clubs such as the Spotted Dog, the Argyle, and the Greyhound. The 1957 release of the Report of the Departmental Committee on Homosexual Offences and Prostitution, which recommended decriminalizing sexual behavior between consenting adults in private, spurred some segments of the gay community to become more visible and politically active. Seminal organizations such as the lesbian Minorities Research Group and publications such as the gay magazine *Spartacus* emerged, laying the groundwork for an articulated queer consciousness and "out" community in the 1970s.

Daring Hearts arose from a tradition of community-based oral history that became increasingly popular in England in the 1970s. This movement was influenced by earlier folklore studies, especially those that sought to record the vanishing traditions of various minority groups, such as Gaelic speakers. This type of history was often collected and archived locally, and published works such as *A Bristol Childhood* (1976) also began to appear. In Brighton, QueenSpark Books began publishing a number of local histories, including *Backyard Brighton: Photographs and Memories of Brighton in the Thirties* (1988) and *Back Street Brighton: Photographs & Memories: A Sequel to Backyard Brighton* (1989).

Brighton Ourstory inspired the formation of OurStory Scotland, which began to collect LGBT testimonies in 2002. OurStory Scotland has received government funding and has mounted exhibits at a number of national museums, including the Gallery of Modern Art in Glasgow. A number of queer oral histories have appeared since the publication of *Daring Hearts*, including the community-based *Rainbow City: Stories from Lesbian, Gay, Bisexual and Transgender Edinburgh* (2007) and *Queer Twin Cities* (2010) in the United States.

THEMES AND STYLE

The stories of the women and men in Brighton in the early days of the gay movement—the ways they found to meet, fall in love, and fashion identities in the broader context of a repressive society—are the focus of *Daring Hearts*. Opening with an unattributed list of people, things, and sensations evoking a bygone era, the book segues into a series of reflections from the subjects on their impressions of the city. One of the book's subjects, Sandie, remembers, "There were so many gay people and they seemed to be accepted and there were clubs for gay people … ohh wonderful." At the same time, as George recalls, even in the comparatively liberal society of Brighton, "you never discussed where you worked, you never gave your real name, you'd be Bill or Harry. … I was terrified of the law, terrified of them." Still, there were meeting places known by word of mouth, such as "the very famous cottage down Black Lion Street," mentioned by Harry, and subtle ways to signify orientation and interests. Barbara notes that "you always had a little finger ring, whether you were butch or fem." The narratives toward the end of the book reflect the transition from the secrecy of the 1950s to the increasing openness of the 1960s. According to Janine, "Everything was fun then really. You've got to remember that in the sixties everything was new."

Daring Hearts includes a description of Brighton OurStory, whose stated purpose is "ensuring that our lesbian and gay lives are recoded, known and valued." Moreover, in collecting the oral histories in the book, the group aims at "making our roots and experiences accessible to all generations of ourselves." Unlike more traditional oral histories produced for an academic audience, *Daring Hearts* does not include an extensive historical context, nor does it provide an explanation of the methodology employed in constructing the history. While these conventions might have made the book more accessible to a broader audience, *Daring Hearts* caters to an audience that participated in, or would at least be familiar with, the production of the text.

The phrase "gone are those days," which appears at the beginning of *Daring Hearts,* sets the book's tone, which is notably nostalgic. People and places are remembered with affection, and the photos and bits of ephemera appearing in the margins give the book the air of a family scrapbook. At the same time, the narratives recall the persecution, fear, and alienation that many in the LGBT community endured before the advent of legal protections. These details illuminate the experience of being gay in the 1950s and 1960s.

CRITICAL DISCUSSION

The response to *Daring Hearts* within Brighton has not been well documented, although the spread of Brighton Ourstory's practices to other LGBT communities speaks to the book's resonance. Don Milligan,

A pink Union Jack flag and a rainbow flag are flown at Brighton, England's 2007 Gay Pride Parade. Members of Brighton's gay and lesbian community recall their histories in the Brighton Ourstory Project's 1992 work *Daring Hearts.* © HOWARD DAVIES/ALAMY

THE SIGNIFICANCE OF BRIGHTON

Brighton has been referred to as the gay capital of England, and its lesbian, gay, bisexual, and transgender (LGBT) community is often compared to that of San Francisco in the United States. Brighton's position on the south coast of Great Britain may have been a factor in its evolution as a queer Shangri-La, as historians have noted that gay men were drawn to Brighton by the large numbers of soldiers stationed there during the Napoleonic Wars and again during World War II. Its liberal reputation seems to have also drawn large numbers of lesbians, who enjoyed women-only tea dances at the Royal Albion Hotel.

In the period following the narratives in *Daring Hearts*, the Gay Liberation Front arrived on the British shores and, with its orientation toward coming out, was instrumental in making the LGBT community in Brighton visible. The city's first gay pride parade was held in 1973, and the Brighton Gay Switchboard, a community helpline, was formed in 1975. While the community was affected by a countrywide backlash against gay rights in the conservative 1980s, it came together to fight restrictive legislation, as well as to help those afflicted with AIDS. The members of Brighton OurStory, originally brought together in a community action group addressing discriminatory legislation, remain active in the field of community-based oral history.

in a review of the book for *Oral History*, notes that while he initially thought the text was "unreadable" due to its lack of a clear thematic or chronological structure, he later "found it to be full of incredible truths and infamous legends." Milligan also praises it for having "a good feel of its period." In his view, the shaping of the stories to emphasize brave struggle creates an "essential rhythm for a book concerned with *daring* hearts."

Daring Hearts is valuable as a record of the birth in Brighton of the lesbian and gay communities. In addition, commentators have suggested that it created a new model of oral history for members of marginalized groups. By abandoning what oral historian Joanna Bornat describes in *Oral History* as the "more conventional process of editorial collection and anthologizing," *Daring Hearts* illustrated how community-based collaborative oral history practices can not only be politically empowering but can also "offer located experience with an intensity and authenticity which the commercial medium cannot reproduce."

In his review in *GLQ: A Journal of Lesbian and Gay Studies Volume* of a wave of books he characterizes as part of "the new British queer history," Chris Waters analyzes the manner in which scholars such as Matt Houlbrook and Morris Kaplan look nostalgically at and identify with homosexual relations in the late nineteenth and early twentieth centuries. While these contemporary scholars are looking to a past even further removed from modern notions of a gay identity, Waters sees a common thread between their work and "the subtle admixture of nostalgia and regret that peppers the reminiscences" in *Daring Hearts*. According to Waters, the project of examining the past "by distancing it radically from our own understandings and categories of identity" is a valuable way to glean a more complete view.

BIBLIOGRAPHY

Sources

Bornat, Joanna. "The Communities of Community Publishing" *Oral History* 20.2 (1992): 23–31. *JSTOR*. Web. 1 Feb. 2013.

Brighton Ourstory Project. *Daring Hearts: Lesbian and Gay Lives of 50s and 60s Brighton*. Brighton, UK: QueenSpark, 1992. Print.

Milligan, Don. Rev. of *Daring Hearts: Lesbian and Gay Lives of 50s and 60s Brighton*, by Brighton Ourstory Project. *Oral History* 21.1 (1993): 82–83. *JSTOR*. Web. 1 Feb. 2013.

Waters, Chris. "Distance and Desire in the New British Queer History." *GLQ: A Journal of Lesbian and Gay Studies* 14.1 (2008): 139–55. Print.

Further Reading

Galford, Ellen, Ken Wilson, and Remember When Project. *Rainbow City: Stories from Lesbian, Gay, Bisexual and Transgender Edinburgh*. Edinburgh, UK: Word Power, 2006. Print.

Herzog, Dagmar. *Sexuality in Europe: A Twentieth-Century History*. Cambridge, UK: Cambridge University Press, 2011. Print.

Houlbrook, Matt. *Queer London: Perils and Pleasures in the Sexual Metropolis, 1918–1957*. Chicago: University of Chicago Press, 2005. Print.

Kaplan, Morris. *Sodom on the Thames: Sex, Love, and Scandal in Wilde Times*. Ithaca, NY: Cornell University Press, 2005. Print.

Katz, Jonathan Ned. *Love Stories: Sex between Men before Homosexuality*. Chicago: University of Chicago Press, 2001. Print.

Queer Twin Cities GLBT Project. *Queer Twin Cities*. Minneapolis: University of Minnesota Press, 2010. Print.

Stanley, Liz. *Sex Surveyed, 1949–1994: From Mass-Observation's "Little Kinsey" to the National Survey and the Hite Reports*. London: Taylor & Francis, 1995. Print.

Weeks, Jeffrey. *Coming Out: Homosexual Politics in Britain, from the Nineteenth Century to the Present*. London: Quartet, 1983. Print.

Daisy Gard

Doña María's Story
Life History, Memory and Political Identity
Daniel James

OVERVIEW

Doña María's Story: Life History, Memory and Political Identity (2000), by Daniel James, is a book of oral history that incorporates the testimony of Argentine meatpacker and union leader Doña María Roldán. The book, covering the time that Roldán worked at the Swift meatpacking plant in the town of Berisso (near La Plata, Argentina) from the 1930s through the 1980s, addresses issues including the exploitation of industrial workers by foreign companies and their collective organizing to attain better labor rights, as well as the rise to power of Juan and Evita Perón. Unlike other oral histories that focus solely on one individual's testimony, such as Theodore Rosengarten's *All God's Dangers: The Life of Nate Shaw* (1974), James combines Roldán's testimony with a theoretical reflection on the genre of oral history, an analysis of Roldán's story, and an exploration of his own experience as ethnographer and researcher in Berisso. Roldán's testimony reflects her pride in her role as a union leader in Berisso, her loyalty to the Peróns, and her feeling of betrayal at being eventually excluded from the Labor Party (Partido Laborista).

Doña María's Story covers the social and political impact of increasing European immigration in Argentina during the early to the mid-twentieth century, combined with the dominance of foreign companies in the country's meatpacking industry and the issue of gender relations within the Peronist movement. Critics praised the book for its unique blend of oral history and scholarly reflection along with the new contributions made by James to ethnographic theory. Upon its publication in Spanish in 2004, the book was highly regarded by Latin American scholars for the valuable analysis it provides of the gender dynamics in Peronism. James's book continues to be a popular reference in scholarship on ethnography and oral history as well as studies of the Argentine labor movement.

HISTORICAL AND LITERARY CONTEXT

Born in 1915, Doña María Roldán was the daughter of an Italian immigrant, who worked as a bricklayer in Buenos Aires. Roldán moved to Berisso in 1931 and began working in the meat factories in 1944. Her testimony covers a significant period in Argentine politics, in which Roldán herself was actively involved: the presidency of Colonel Juan Perón (1946–53) and the emergence of "Peronism"—the populist political ideology of aiding urban industrialism and facilitating cooperation between businesses and labor that was espoused by Perón and his followers, among them Roldán, who was instrumental in the unionization of Argentina's meatpacking laborers and appreciated Perón's concern for workers' rights. After playing a significant role in the success of the military coup of 1943, Perón was named Argentina's minister of labor, and he enacted several social reforms to aid the nation's growing industrial working class. Perón quickly gained the support of the Argentine public—particularly of workers in the nation's prominent meatpacking industry—due to his interest in the lower and middle classes and the industrial sector.

Perón's popularity gained him the presidency in 1946, and he benefited from the strong support of the labor unions and their workers. As the site of both the Swift and Armour meatpacking plants, Roldán's hometown of Berisso was the heart of the meatpacking industry, the "cradle of Peronism," as Catherine Davies explains in her 2002 review of *Doña María's Story* in *Biography*. Berisso workers were invaluable to the success of the protest of October 17, 1945, in the Plaza de Mayo, during which Roldán delivered a rousing speech and which brought about Perón's release from prison. Roldán played a leadership role in the town's staunchly Peronist labor union—the first labor union in Argentina, *Sindicato Autónomo*, which later became a national political party, the Partido Laborista. Roldán's story reveals the complex politics of the Peronist era in an intensely personal manner, providing the reader with insight into the contradictions inherent in the left-leaning labor movement's alignment with the Perón government, which often employed authoritarian—some even say fascistic—tactics to achieve its aims, leaving many Argentinians to feel a sense of disillusionment and betrayal with Perón later in his presidency.

Doña María's Story is a relatively unique text due to its combination of personal testimony, literary analysis, and ethnographic theory. Although first published in English, the book does follow a rich tradition of *testimonios* within Latin American literature. Influential testimonios include Rigoberta

❖ **Key Facts**

Time Period:
Mid- to Late 20th Century

Relevant Historical Events:
Rise of Juan and Evita Perón; industrialization in Argentina; growth of labor unions in Argentina

Nationality:
Argentine

Keywords:
labor; unionism; industrialization

COMMUNITIES

Political propaganda postcard (1954) for the "Campana Pro-Ayuda Social" with a portrait of Eva Perón, Argentina's first lady and minister of health and labor. Like many working-class Argentines, Doña María Roldán was a strong supporter of Juan and Eva Perón. © PRIVATE COLLECTION/ ARCHIVES CHARMET/THE BRIDGEMAN ART LIBRARY

Menchú's *I, Rigoberta Menchú: An Indian Woman in Guatemala* (1983, edited by Elisabeth Burgos-Debray) and Domitila Barrios de Chungara's *"Si me permiten hablar ...": Testimonio de Domitila, una mujer de las minas de Bolivia* (1977; Let Me Speak! Testimony of Domitila, a Woman of the Bolivian Mines). *Doña María's Story* differs from many testimonios, however, in that Roldán's text does not communicate an urgent message regarding experiences of "repression, poverty, subalternity, imprisonment, struggle for survival," as John Beverley characterized the genre in a 1989 article in *Modern Fiction Studies*. While it does address the Argentine labor movement and the history of Berisso, the text reads more as a personal memoir than a politicized testimonio. The scholarly portion of the book was influenced by the work of cultural anthropologists including Clifford Geertz and oral historians such as Luisa Passerini, both figures known for their penetrating ethnographic studies and concern with the anthropologist's role in shaping and interpreting the meaning of cultural movements for the world at large.

James's approach to oral history in *Doña María's Story* has influenced the work of contemporary scholars of Latin American history as well as oral historians and cultural anthropologists. The book has had the most impact within Peronist studies, influencing a new generation of scholars including Oscar Chamosa and Matthew Karush, whose 2010 *The New Cultural History of Peronism* follows in James's footsteps in its interdisciplinary theoretical approach to Peronism, and Mark Healey, a student of James and author of *The Ruins of the New Argentina: Peronism and the Remaking of San Juan after the 1944 Earthquake* (2011). As James's second book, *Doña María's Story* earned the historian further acclaim, and he is regarded as a leading scholar in the emerging field of new cultural history. James continued his studies of Berisso and oral history, publishing the article "Family Photographs and Ethnic Identity: The Ukrainians of Berisso" in collaboration with Mirta Zaida Lobato in 2004.

THEMES AND STYLE

Doña María's Story addresses the political tensions experienced by Roldán as a Peronist and union activist, as well as the effects of deindustrialization and the emergence of neoliberalism on the Berisso working class. In his first of four interpretive essays included in the book, James reflects, "Part of the crisis of contemporary memory in working-class communities is precisely the crisis of such social spaces [Berisso] that have fallen victim to the destructive power of de-industrialization, social dislocation, and simple irrelevance." James's analysis of the testimony in historical and economic terms adds another layer to the text. In her testimony Roldán expresses disillusionment with the political system of Peronism: "Politics has corners where they can hide things. ... There is lying, there is betrayal. ... Peronism, and I say this as a woman of the Peronist movement, was just as bad in this."

As James explains in the introduction to part three of *Doña María's Story*, his approach to oral history aims at exploring "the problem of memory, its limits, its failing, and its distortions," as well as entering into an interdisciplinary dialogue that brings the field of Latin American history together with oral history, literary criticism, and cultural anthropology. Prior to writing his book, James recorded more than thirty hours of interview in Spanish with Roldán, which amounted to more than six hundred pages of transcript that he then translated into English and pared down to the ninety pages of testimony that were ultimately included in *Doña María's Story*. While James did shorten Roldán's story considerably and reordered certain parts of her testimony, the fact that he clearly states this when introducing her narrative thus avoids any later confusion and controversy that has often arisen with other oral history texts in the past.

Doña María's Story is divided into four parts: a prologue that introduces the history of Berisso; Roldán's testimony; a third part that is divided into four different interpretive essays; and an epilogue. The language employed in Roldán's actual testimony is formal and reserved. She explains her role as a union leader in precise terms: "The delegate has to ensure that there is humane treatment of the worker in all things. ... So for the delegate who really knew what her obligations were it was very special work." Roldán does, however, speak with passion at times, revealing her feelings of betrayal and disillusionment at the abrupt end to her political career. Regarding her replacement by a rich woman as a political candidate, Roldán spoke with a mixture of anger and cynicism: "So, was it [Peronism] becoming bourgeois, or not? Because they installed in the legislature a woman with money and not a working woman from Berisso? There you have the why."

CRITICAL DISCUSSION

Doña María's Story was acclaimed by both U.S. and Latin American scholars and was reviewed extensively in the initial years following its publication. Davies praised it as "an exceptional book, a joy to read," while Elizabeth Dore, writing for *American Historical Review*, lauded its "original contributions to oral history" and other disciplines. Jose C. Moya's response to the book in the *Journal of Social History*, however, was much more mixed: "At its worst, it degenerates into a self-indulgent confessional that seems to push Doña María out of center stage." Nevertheless, an overwhelming majority of scholars celebrated James's book for opening up new avenues of dialogue between the field of Latin American history and numerous other disciplines.

James's approach to the oral history genre has been more influential with later scholars than the content of Roldán's narrative in itself. In particular, *Doña María's Story* has inspired more interdisciplinary approaches to Peronist studies, including the work of Anahi Ballent that incorporates visual art into its analysis of Peronist culture ("Unforgettable Kitsch: Images around Eva Peron," 2010), as well as Eduardo Elena's analysis of Peronism in print sources in "Peronism in 'Good Taste': Culture and Consumption in the Magazine *Argentina*" (2010). *Doña María's Story* has strongly impacted the work of Latin American historian Mirta Zaida Lobato, whose 2001 book *La vida en las fábricas. Trabajo, protesta y política en una comunidad obrera, Berisso (1904–1970)* takes up James's study of the labor movement in Berisso. Lobato and James have since collaborated on subsequent studies within the community of Berisso.

Certain scholars interested in Argentine labor history, including Jan Lucassen in his 2008 *Global Labour History: A State of the Art*, have analyzed the work of James and Lobato in conjunction as examples of a new trend in labor studies of "examining the slow agony of decline and disintegration, not only of an occupation or a class but of the communities which had been given life by these factories or mines."

THE LEGEND OF EVITA PERÓN

María Eva Duarte de Perón, more commonly known as Eva or Evita Perón, was the first lady of Argentina from 1946 until her death in 1952, as well as a popular political leader beloved by the Argentine public. Born in rural Argentina in 1919, Eva quickly transcended her humble origins after becoming a well-known actress in Buenos Aires by the 1940s. She met Colonel Juan Perón in 1944 and married the burgeoning politician the following year. Eva became first lady of Argentina when her husband was elected president in 1946, and she quickly gained power with the trade unions and much of the Argentine working class that supported Peronism.

During her six years as first lady, Eva also established her own charitable foundation; led the Argentine ministries of labor and health; and founded the Female Peronist Party, the first female political party to gain prominence in Argentina. In 1951 she became a candidate for the nation's vice presidency and received widespread support from loyal Peronists and the working-class public, whom she affectionately referred to as *descamisados* (literally, "the shirtless"), identifying with their impoverishment, which she had endured as a child. Eva was unable to run for the office, however, facing opposition from the Argentine military and elite and because of her own failing health. She succumbed to cancer in 1952, shortly after the Argentine Congress named her the Spiritual Leader of the Nation. Eva's death was mourned by millions, and she remains a prominent figure in both Argentine and international popular culture, having several plays and movies dedicated to her life story.

Other critics, such as Chamosa and Karush, emphasize James's consideration of "the ways rank and file workers understood Peronism" in *Doña María's Story* as an important approach to Peronist studies that goes beyond the traditional analysis of the "emission side" of the Peronist discourse.

BIBLIOGRAPHY

Sources

Beverley, John. "The Margin at the Center: On Testimonio (Testimonial Narrative)." *Modern Fiction Studies* 35.1 (1989): 11–28. Print.

Chamosa, Oscar, and Matthew Karush, eds. *The New Cultural History of Peronism: Power and Identity in Mid-Twentieth-Century Argentina*. Durham, NC: Duke University Press, 2010. Print.

Davies, Catherine. Rev. of *Doña María's Story: Life History, Memory and Political Identity*, by Daniel James. *Biography* 25.3 (2002): 531–35. Print.

Dore, Elizabeth. Rev. of *Doña María's Story: Life History, Memory and Political Identity*, by Daniel James. *American Historical Review* 107.5 (2002): 1615–16. Print.

James, Daniel. *Doña María's Story: Life History, Memory and Political Identity*. Durham, NC: Duke University Press, 2000. Print.

Lucassen, Jan. *Global Labour History: A State of the Art.* New York: Lang, 2008. Print.

Moya, Jose. Rev. of *Doña María's Story: Life History, Memory and Political Identity,* by Daniel James. *Journal of Social History* 36.2 (2002): 514–16. Print.

Further Reading

Arbena, Joseph L. Rev. of *Doña María's Story: Life History, Memory and Political Identity,* by Daniel James. *Americas* 58.4 (2002): 655–56. Print.

Cohen, Deborah. Rev. of *Doña María's Story: Life History, Memory and Political Identity,* by Daniel James. *Hispanic American Historical Review* 85.3 (2005), 540–41. Print.

French, John D., and D. James, eds. *The Gendered Worlds of Latin American Women Workers: From Household and Factory to the Union Hall and Ballot Box.* Durham, NC: Duke University Press, 1997. Print.

James, Daniel and Mirta Zaida Lobato. "Family Photographs and Ethnic Identity: The Ukrainians of Berisso." *Hispanic American Historical Review* 84.1 (2004): 5–36. Print.

———. *Resistance and Integration: Peronism and the Argentine Working Class, 1946–1976.* Cambridge, UK: Cambridge University Press, 1988. Print.

Ranis, Peter. *Argentine Workers: Peronism and Contemporary Class Consciousness.* Pittsburgh, PA: University of Pittsburgh Press, 1992. Print.

Rosemblatt, Karin Alejandra. Rev. of *Doña María's Story: Life History, Memory and Political Identity,* by Daniel James. *Social History* 27.2 (2002): 225–27. Print.

Katrina White

Hill Country Teacher
Oral Histories from the One-Room School and Beyond
Diane Manning

OVERVIEW

In *Hill Country Teacher: Oral Histories from the One-Room School and Beyond* (1990), Diane Manning preserves narratives of eight teachers who worked in rural Texas from the 1920s through the 1960s. Manning selected her subjects based on the commonality of their experience: all careers began in one-room schools, and all spanned the period from the 1920s or 1930s through desegregation. Manning's introduction details her methodology and rationale and traces "the common threads of [teachers'] experiences," which stem from "a degree of intimacy between teachers and community that is unparalleled today." Teachers often boarded with local families, received fatherly advice from principals and superintendents, and were seen as "surrogate mother[s]" for their students, making community a prevalent theme in their memoirs.

The teaching careers narrated in *Hill Country Teacher* spanned a time of "great and rapid … change" for education, in Geraldine Jonçich Clifford's words in her review of the work for *Teachers College Record;* one gets the sense that Manning's goal was to preserve such stories while their tellers were still alive. Although reviewers commended her for this goal and for the analyses in her introduction and conclusion, their reviews are nevertheless not glowingly positive. Multiple critics express disappointment in a lack of editorial guidance on Manning's part; because she allowed subjects to speak until they began to repeat themselves, the oral histories sometimes seem to ramble unnecessarily. Nevertheless, as a firsthand archive of the experience of women teachers during this time, *Hill Country Teacher* finds an enduring legacy.

HISTORICAL AND LITERARY CONTEXT

Throughout Texas's colorful history, public education has been a source of controversy and conflict, a tumultuous pattern Manning's informants inherited. As far back as 1836, when Texas declared independence from Mexico, one of its cited grievances was Mexico's failure to establish a system of public schooling for Texans. During its years as a republic, Texas was governed by a constitution that mandated public education, but attempts to establish school systems were mostly failures, creating more conflict. It was not until its annexation into the United States in 1854 that Texas' public education system was officially founded, yet there was little central organization or standardization. The years following the Civil War saw the establishment of schools for African Americans, and the segregated system remained in effect in many places until the 1960s. Thus the teachers Manning interviewed began their careers in a school system already characterized by fluctuation, controversy, and racial inequality.

Hill Country Teacher's narratives span an era of further change in education. The construction of one-room schools in conjunction with the "taming" of the West created professional opportunities for inexperienced teachers. Subsequently, the Great Depression reversed this trend by prioritizing teaching jobs for men over women. World War II brought many women back to the workforce, in education as much as in factories. Lastly, the integration of public schools, which did not occur in Kerrville—where the teachers profiled in *Hill Country Teacher* taught in and around—until the early 1960s, marked another radical change. Therefore, though there is commonality of experience among Manning's eight subjects, the general trend of the time period itself is one of frequent cultural shift.

Manning's introduction claims that "there is a remarkable paucity of memoirs and autobiographies [of women teachers] in which the subjects speak for themselves," indicating a niche for her work. Manning notes that the gap in the literature on this topic is the reason she "became an oral historian," which simultaneously speaks to the lack of precedent texts and to the "current vogue for history as narrative," according to Andrew Gulliford in his critique in the *Journal of American History*. As such, her method has more precedent than does her topic. Still, Manning acknowledges the influence of Nancy Hoffman's *Woman's "True" Profession: Voices from the History of Teaching* (1981)—which combines Hoffman's own essays with oral histories—and Frances R. Donovan's *The Schoolma'am* (1938).

Hill Country Teacher's most prominent legacy is its preservation of individual experiences of teaching in a specific time and place. As a compilation of primary texts, it attempts to archive rather than interpret. Manning hints at the utility of the work as archive when she opens her introduction with the observation

Key Facts

Time Period:
Mid-20th Century

Relevant Historical Events:
Desegregation; civil rights movement; Great Depression; World War II

Nationality:
American

Keywords:
education; desegregation; teachers

COMMUNITIES

Junction schoolhouse at Lyndon B. Johnson State Park and Historic Site near Johnson City, Texas. In Hill Country Teachers, *Diane Manning interviews those who taught in one-room schoolhouses in Texas.*
© LYROKY/ALAMY

that members of a graduate seminar did not believe a student who cited the historical ban on female teachers marrying. *Hill Country Teacher* provides the evidence the student cited to prove her point.

THEMES AND STYLE

A prominent theme that emerges in Manning's work is that of the teachers having to endure "a number of humiliating intrusions into [their] personal lives not extracted from women in other jobs." For example, the prohibition against marriage for women teachers is widely mentioned by critics. Sibyl Sutherland explains that she was required to sign a contract pledging not to marry. Gladys Peterson Meyers was forced to leave her job when she got married. Social restrictiveness went beyond marriage, however. Several teachers mention injunctions against dancing, and Witcher Teel, who later became an author, comments that other teachers in her school were fired for dancing. Beyond social restrictions, teachers endured economic hardship both personal and professional. Several mined their own meager salaries to clothe students from impoverished families (who often lived in tents). Most endured frustrations at school due to a lack of resources, including indoor plumbing; as Witcher Teel comments, "We had to do our own housecleaning, carry the wood, build the fire, take out the ashes, and get fresh water for our schoolroom."

Manning, an experienced teacher, teacher trainer, and researcher, compiled the volume to correct a perceived silence in the historical canon of autobiographical narratives of women teachers during this time. Manning explains, "As the first generation of the first profession where large numbers of women were able to combine careers and family life, they hold a unique place in the history of both education and working women"; their importance in history inspired her to "preserve their stories for successive generations of teachers." In keeping with the tenets of oral history, she empowers her subjects by recording their words directly, allowing them to speak for themselves.

Because her central methodological goal is to record her subjects' own voices, Manning contributes little in the way of directive interview questions, inserting her own voice only in the volume's introduction and conclusion, as well as in brief introductions to each narrative. Even for an oral history, Manning's methods are exceptionally noninterventionist, making the majority of the text the teachers' own words. Manning's contribution, particularly her conclusion, offers helpful analysis outlining common themes in teachers' experiences and speculating about teachers' complicity in the restrictive systems in which they taught.

CRITICAL DISCUSSION

Initial reaction to *Hill Country Teacher* was mixed, with reviewers noting Manning's contribution to historical literature while lamenting that the work contains relatively little of her writing. Most reviewers express desire for "a critical edge that might have given the reader better insight into what it meant to live and teach in rural west Texas during the middle years of this century," as Paul Theobald notes in his review of the book for *Educational Studies*. Linda McNeil, writing for the *Journal of Southern History*, argues that because Manning privileges biography, she fails to point to structural forces and resource deficiencies that speak to systemic flaws in the design of Texas education, making these flaws instead appear to be anomalies of individual experiences.

On the larger legacy of the work, most critics agree with Theobald, who observes, "The circumstances related in *Hill Country Teacher* that will likely engage scholars are those accounts of struggle and hardship on the part of most of these women." For preserving the voices of teachers whose careers spanned an important era in American education, Manning gets credit, yet criticism is more prevalent. Theobald in particular discusses interviewees' "very disconcerting propensity … to exhibit deeply internalized antipathies toward Blacks and Mexican Americans." For example, Sutherland identifies a group of communist protesters in San Antonio as "a bunch of pecan shellers"; Witcher Teel refers to two Mexicans as "these peons"; and Rachael Luna notes, "We had a good community of black people here, or else we would have had more trouble with things." Although Manning's final narrative by an African American couple is likely an attempt to balance the impression of prejudice left by her white informants, this final account is too brief and ends too abruptly to do so.

Critics agree that Manning inspires curiosities that her volume is insufficient to satisfy. Theobald argues that Manning could have pushed subjects to interrogate some of their assumptions; for example, multiple teachers express that teaching was the only career option for "ladies," without defining what being a "lady" meant in Texas in the 1930s. He further wishes that Manning had "ask[ed] subjects to explain the [racially] divided society they lived in." Although these larger items may have fallen outside Manning's agenda, she raises them as questions without addressing them directly, which likely explains widespread critical dissatisfaction with the range of her text as a work of historical scholarship.

BIBLIOGRAPHY

Sources

Clifford, Geraldine Jonçich. Rev. of *Hill Country Teacher: Oral Histories from the One-Room School and Beyond*, by Diane Manning. *Teachers College Record* 1 Sept. 1991: 177–80. *Academic Search Premier*. Web. 28 Jan. 2013.

Gulliford, Andrew. Rev. of *Hill Country Teacher: Oral Histories from the One-Room School and Beyond*, by Diane Manning. *Journal of American History* Sept. 1991: 716–17. *Academic Search Premier*. Web. 28 Jan. 2013.

Manning, Diane. *Hill Country Teacher: Oral Histories from the One-Room School and Beyond*. Boston: Twayne, 1990. Print.

McNeil, Linda. Rev. of *Hill Country Teacher: Oral Histories from the One-Room School and Beyond*, by Diane Manning. *Journal of Southern History* Feb. 1992: 164–65. *Academic Search Premier*. Web. 28 Jan. 2013.

Theobald, Paul. Rev. of *Hill Country Teacher: Oral Histories from the One-Room School and Beyond*, by Diane Manning. *Educational Studies* Summer 1991: 186–90. *Academic Search Premier*. Web. 28 Jan. 2013.

Further Reading

Abrams, Lynn. *Oral History Theory*. New York: Routledge, 2010.

Hoffman, Nancy. *Woman's "True" Profession: Voices from the History of Teaching*. 2nd ed. Cambridge, MA: Harvard Education Press, 2003.

Milewski, Patrice. "Perilous Times: A History of Teachers' Experience with School Inspection in the 1930s." *History of Education* 41.5 (2012): 637–56. Print.

Perks, Robert, and Alistair Thomson, eds. *The Oral History Reader*. 2nd ed. New York: Routledge, 2006.

Sarkar, Mahua. "Between Craft and Method: Meaning and Inter-subjectivity in Oral History Analysis." *Journal of Historical Sociology* 25.4 (2012): 578–600. Print.

MANNING'S VOICE

Diane Manning's conclusion in *Hill Country Teacher* represents the most thorough historical analysis in her volume, as the rest is mostly taken up by the words of her informants. In it she addresses restrictions on teachers' private lives before World War II and considers the possibility that these women were complicit in such restrictions because, in some ways, they benefited from them. Benefits included an excuse not to marry for teachers who preferred not to, economic independence from husbands or parents, and elevation of the status of teachers as a group by positioning the profession as one requiring sacrifice. In short, teaching offered a means for women who otherwise struggled to fit into the status quo—women who preferred to remain unmarried, desired professional lives, or wished to gain a degree of independence—an avenue by which to seamlessly integrate themselves into their communities.

None of this is to negate the real hardships women teachers of this era faced, but Manning's analysis invites consideration of some of the tangible benefits ironically derived from the restrictions female teachers endured. She thus concludes by returning to her theme of community: rural towns welcomed teachers into their communities and created a social niche for these unmarried women, in part as perpetuators of the standards of that community.

Laura Johnson

The Hood River Issei
An Oral History of Japanese Settlers in Oregon's Hood River Valley
Linda Tamura

❖ Key Facts

Time Period:
Late 19th to Late 20th Century

Relevant Historical Events:
Japanese immigration to Oregon; World War II; Japanese internment

Nationality:
American

Keywords:
internment; immigration; discrimination

OVERVIEW

The Hood River Issei: An Oral History of Japanese Settlers in Oregon's Hood River Valley (1993) is a collection of sixty-nine interviews with fourteen of the twenty Issei, or first-generation Japanese immigrants, still living in the Hood River Valley. The work was edited, translated, and thematically organized by Linda Tamura, the granddaughter of one of the interviewees, between October 1985 and May 1986. Working with a Nisei, or second-generation, Japanese translator who knew many of the interviewees, Tamura recorded issues pertaining to her subject's marriages, their motivations for and experiences with immigrating to the United States, their lives in the Hood River Valley, and their experiences during and after World War II. On the whole, Tamura allows the remembrances collected in *The Hood River Issei* to speak for themselves, though she does supplement the interviews with contextual information. Because most of the interviewees are women, the work contains rich details about the gender dimensions of immigration, work, family life, and internment.

During Tamura's collection period, fourteen of the twenty living Issei of the Hood River Valley—six of whom were interview subjects—died. This fact was not lost on reviewers of the collection. *The Hood River Issei* was consequently recognized as important documentation of life for Issei, records of whom would largely have been lost but for Tamura's project.

HISTORICAL AND LITERARY CONTEXT

The first Japanese immigrants settled in Oregon in 1880, and by the 1890s an increasing number were traveling to the United States to find work, though few intended to permanently emigrate. The "Gentlemen's Agreement" of 1907 between Japan and the United States slowed immigration, and the Immigration Act of 1924, which curtailed immigration to 2 percent of foreign-born residents from any country, effectively ended Japanese immigration for decades.

The twentieth century was a tumultuous time for Japanese immigrants and their families in the Hood River Valley of Oregon. The financial success of Japanese farmers exacerbated tensions with other landowners in the area. These mounting conflicts only grew with World War II. Tamura reports that in 1945 the Hood River's American Legion Post went so far as to remove the names of "all sixteen of the valley's Japanese American servicemen from the community's public roll of honor." However, such ill will eventually dissipated from the area, and in 1983, just two years before Tamura began collecting interviews, the federal government formally apologized to Japanese Americans for internment.

A number of scholars have set out to capture Japanese American experiences, though most are focused on a single family or narrowed to wartime experiences. One exception, the California State University at Fullerton, has been amassing oral histories for its Japanese American Oral History Project Collection since the 1970s and published *Voices Long Silent: Oral History and the Japanese American Evacuation* in 1974. As Arthur A. Hansen notes in his article for the *Journal of American History*, it is significant that four works dealing with the "semicentennial observance of [Japanese Americans'] eviction and detention … have been fashioned primarily from oral histories." Along with *The Hood River Issei,* Hansen reviews Lauren Kessler's *Stubborn Twig* (1993), in which she concentrates on the lives of the Yasui family, near Hood River, Oregon, from 1904 onward; Sandra Taylor's *Jewel of the Desert: Japanese American Internment at Topaz* (1993); and Valerie Matsumoto's *Farming the Home Place: A Japanese American Community in California, 1919–1982* (1993).

Because so many of Tamura's subjects were already quite elderly when she began working on *The Hood River Issei,* no similar projects with the Issei could have been undertaken in its wake. Her most recent work, *Nisei Soldiers Break Their Silence: Coming Home to Hood River* (2012), again uses oral history to concentrate upon how Nisei perceived World War II. Lawson Fusao Inada's anthology *Only What We Could Carry: The Japanese American Internment Experience* (2000) collects oral history with other artifacts such as cartoons, propaganda, and news articles.

THEMES AND STYLE

Capturing the Issei and their lives in the Hood River Valley as they would like to be represented is at the heart of *The Hood River Issei,* though Tamura does, as Hansen argues, emphasize "a community legacy of resistance to oppression, ethnic pride," and active participation in the arcs of her interviewees' lives. Though she is careful not to speak over her participants—rarely analyzing their words or silences—this constructed legacy does shape her responses to some issues. For example, in one of the few sections in which she offers interpretation, Tamura turns to social scientists such as Wendy Ng to explain her Issei subjects' reactions to internment, citing internalized racism in part for the "acceptance, submission, and rationalization" exhibited by the Issei during World War II. Most, like Itsu Akiyama, refused to speak too negatively of the experience, declaring that they were glad to be alive and that "probably it was better for us that we were evacuated, because we heard about Japanese being mistreated and shot."

Born and raised in the Hood River Valley herself, Tamura was close to several of her subjects, including her maternal grandmother, before beginning the project. Having recently finished her grandmother's biography, Tamura believed the recollections of the Issei, "their collective stories of perseverance," and their roles in the development of the community in which she grew up were too important to be lost. After mailing her subjects questionnaires in both English and Japanese, Tamura worked with a translator to break down questions and evoke answers in face-to-face interviews. When possible, Tamura completed follow-up interviews. Accurately transcribing the interviews posed a difficulty because many Japanese phrases and idioms have no English correlative and because the multiple interviews broke up answers related to the same question. In editing the transcriptions Tamura strove to maintain speech patterns as closely as possible while maximizing clarity.

After a brief section detailing her methodology and the history of the Hood River Issei, Tamura introduces each of her subjects with a brief biography before launching into the sections of her book. Within the ten chronologically and thematically cohered sections, individuals' statements on specific topics are interwoven with historical information and framing data such as population reports, earnings, translated poetry, and the Japanese Society Minutes on the construction of a community hall. As Karen Leonard writes in her review of *The Hood River Issei* for *American Anthropologist,* Tamura "weaves together economic, political, and social materials—primary and secondary, local and national—to set the context for quotations from the interviews." In the excerpted interviews, despite translation and editing, Tamura strives to "reproduce the Issei statements in English as accurately as possible" so that "they have ... provided the story of the Hood River Issei in their own words."

CRITICAL DISCUSSION

Critical reception of *The Hood River Issei* was initially positive, though reviewers such as Soofia Hussain, writing for the *International Migration Review,* found that Tamura's refusal to interrogate her participants'

Mount Hood and the Hood River Valley, Oregon. In the late nineteenth and early twentieth centuries, Japanese immigrants to this rural region often worked as farmers and orchardists. © CRAIG TUTTLE/CORBIS

responses left certain questions unanswered. Regardless, many critics agreed with Gordon Chang's assessment in the *Journal of American Ethnic History:* "the result is an important documentation of a people who are quickly disappearing." In addition to finding her research timely, many scholars, including Leonard and Hansen, laud Tamura's clear methodology, contextualization, and subject profiles as well as her adherence to oral history mores such as depositing copies of her tapes in a public repository (the Oregon Historical Society and the Hood River County Museum).

Leonard applauds the book for giving a voice to the Issei, writing, "Their remembrances are a valuable addition to the literature on Japanese Americans and, more generally, on the immigrant experience in the United States." Additionally, *The Hood River Issei* has been embraced by Oregon institutions as documentation of an often unfairly marginalized part of its history. Because it captures the Oregon experience of Issei so richly, Tamura's work has been placed on the Oregon State Library's list of 150 highly recommended sesquicentennial-related books.

The Hood River Issei is frequently cited in works tracing the effect of the Hood River Issei in the development of the Oregonian Japanese American community, the orchards and farms of the region, and reactions during and after Japanese internment—a theme continued in Tamura's most recent book project. Though there have not really been trends in scholarship about the text, Tamura's interviewees' reactions to internment and their refusal to speak poorly of anyone, even the U.S. government, are some of the most heavily cited sections of *The Hood River Issei*. Other projects pertaining to Oregon's Issei, such as Laurie Mercier's 2001 article, "Reworking Race, Class, and Gender into Pacific Northwest History," cite Tamura's book on the subject of Japanese gender roles and family dynamics at the beginning of the twentieth century.

BIBLIOGRAPHY

Sources

Azuma, Eiichiro. "A History of Oregon's Issei, 1880–1952." *Oregon Historical Quarterly* 94.4 (1993–94): 315–67. *JSTOR*. Web. 23 Dec. 2012.

JAPANESE SETTLEMENT IN OREGON: A SNAPSHOT

Although Japanese students had been traveling to the United States since 1866, Eiichiro Azuma writes in "A History of Oregon's Issei, 1880–1952" in the *Oregon Historical Quarterly* that when Miyo Iwakoshi, her younger brother, and her adopted daughter moved with Iwakoshi's husband, an Australian Scot, to the area in 1880, they became the first known Japanese immigrants to Oregon. Later, Iwakoshi's daughter would marry Shintaro Takaki, who, Azuma maintains, became the "first Japanese labor contractor in Oregon" in 1891. Japanese immigration to Oregon soared in the 1890s as work on railroads and for sawmills grew. Though Japanese workers were paid poorly as a whole, it was still more lucrative than working a farm in Japan. Many workers saw the increasingly cleared land, particularly of the Hood River Valley, as a place to settle and prosper. As a number of Issei became known for their fine produce, anti-Japanese sentiment—aimed at preventing the Japanese from owning land—increased in the area.

After being displaced by internment during World War II, only about half of the Issei returned to the Hood River Valley. Those who did often faced discrimination. However, some residents supported the Japanese American community. One, the Reverend Burgoyne, was recognized by the Council Against Intolerance in America in 1947 for his unflagging work to counter discrimination.

Chang, Gordon H. Rev. of *The Hood River Issei: An Oral History of Japanese Settlers in Oregon's Hood River Valley*, by Linda Tamura. *Journal of American Ethnic History* 15.3 (1996). *Academic Search Elite*. Web. 23 Dec. 2012.

Hansen, Arthur A. "Oral History and the Japanese American Evacuation." *Journal of American History* 82 (1995): 635–39. *JSTOR*. Web. 20 Jan. 2013.

Hussain, Soofia K. Rev. of *The Hood River Issei: An Oral History of Japanese Settlers in Oregon's Hood River Valley*, by Linda Tamura. *International Migration Review* 28.4 (1994): 898–900. *JSTOR*. Web. 12 Feb. 2013.

Leonard, Karen. Rev. of *The Hood River Issei: An Oral History of Japanese Settlers in Oregon's Hood River Valley*, by Linda Tamura. *American Anthropologist* 96.4 (1994): 1008–09. *JSTOR*. Web. 19 Jan. 2013.

Mercier, Laurie. "Reworking Race, Class, and Gender into Pacific Northwest History." *Frontiers: A Journal of Women's Studies* 22.3 (2001). *Project MUSE*. Web. 12 Feb. 2013.

Tamura, Linda. *The Hood River Issei: An Oral History of Japanese Settlers in Oregon's Hood River Valley.* Urbana: University of Illinois Press, 1993. Print.

Further Reading

Daniels, Roger. *Coming to America: A History of Immigration and Ethnicity in American Life.* 2nd ed. New York: HarperCollins, 2002. Print.

Dower, John. *War without Mercy: Race and Power in the Pacific War.* New York: Pantheon, 1986. Print.

Hegwood, Robert Alan. "Erasing the Space between Japanese and American: Progressivism, Nationalism, and Japanese American Resettlement in Portland, Oregon, 1945–1948." MA thesis. Portland State University, 2011. *Portland State University*. Web. 20 Jan. 2013.

Inada, Lawson Fusao. *Only What We Could Carry: The Japanese American Internment Experience.* Berkeley: California Historical Society, 2000. Print.

Kessler, Lauren. *Stubborn Twig: Three Generations in the Life of a Japanese American Family.* New York: Random House, 1993. Print.

Matsumoto, Valerie. *Farming the Home Place: A Japanese American Community in California, 1919–1982.* Ithaca, NY: Cornell University Press, 1993. Print.

Ng, Wendy. "Collective Memory, Social Networks, and Generations: The Japanese American Community in Hood River, Oregon." Diss. University of Oregon, 1989. *ProQuest*. Web. 20 Jan. 2013.

Taylor, Sandra. *Jewel of the Desert: Japanese American Internment at Topaz.* Berkeley: University of California Press, 1993. Print.

Katherine Bishop

The Making of a Gay Asian Community
An Oral History of Pre-AIDS Los Angeles
Eric Wat

OVERVIEW

Eric Wat's *The Making of a Gay Asian Community: An Oral History of Pre-AIDS Los Angeles* (2002) presents the narratives of twenty-four men and one woman as they shape, and are shaped by, the developing gay Asian American community in Los Angeles from the 1970s through the 1990s. A self-described "active member of the queer Asian community," Wat felt compelled to investigate and record its early history as told by the people who made it. Though generated by individuals of diverse ethnicities and backgrounds, *The Making of a Gay Asian Community* expresses a common need for an integrative identity that acknowledges both race and sexuality as orienting their social activities and political organization.

Published almost twenty-five years after the formation of Asian Pacific Lesbians and Gays (A/PLG), the community's seminal social and political organization, *The Making of a Gay Asian Community* describes the coalescence of a group that, after years of marginalization in both Asian American and gay rights communities, felt like a revelation to its members. Well received by its academic audience, the work provides an account of a previously obscure community. *The Making of a Gay Asian Community* is also notable in that it explicates the notion of community itself, unpacking the complex dynamics at play in a group that, while diverse, formed to address common struggles.

HISTORICAL AND LITERARY CONTEXT

The narratives in *The Making of a Gay Asian Community* describe the birth of an organized social and political community of gay Asian American men in Los Angeles. Prior to the 1970s, gay Asian men in L.A. were largely isolated from each other. Late in the decade, however, "rice bars," alternatives to the sometimes-exclusionary nightspots frequented by the largely Anglo gay community, brought Asians of various ethnicities into close proximity. Describing these establishments in *Global Divas: Filipino Gay Men in the Diaspora* (2003), Martin F. Manalansan IV notes, "Despite the camaraderie, fun and pleasure that can be found in these spaces … these same spaces were sites of alienation and exclusion" from the mainstream gay culture.

As gay Asian men began to meet and become part of each other's social circles, the desire to come together in a safe space resulted in the establishment of the A/PLG, a group initiated to provide a forum for airing grievances and to seek social support and political solutions to concerns within the developing community. Many of the narratives in *The Making of a Gay Asian Community* come from members of the A/PLG and describe their personal histories prior to and including their participation in the group, which was at times sharply divided over issues of membership and mission. By 1997, when the interviews for the book began, a new generation of activists had emerged. These younger men, who had inherited both the legacies of AIDS and an already established community, were less interested in identity politics and more geared toward working for equality.

The Making of a Gay Asian Community can be placed in several traditions of American oral history, including those that recount the experiences of gay men struggling to establish a community identity and those detailing the experiences of Asian Americans attempting to carve out a place in society. Eric Marcus's *The Struggle for Gay and Lesbian Equal Rights, 1945–1990: An Oral History* (1992) provides important background for Wat's book. Marcus offers a broad picture of the struggle for gay rights in the United States, from its beginnings in the post–World War II Mattachine Society, one of the earliest U.S. homophile organizations, through the Stonewall riots and AIDS activism. In addition, Joan Faung Jean Lee's *Oral Histories of First to Fourth Generation Americans from China, the Philippines, Japan, India, the Pacific Islands, Vietnam, and Cambodia* (1992) surveys a diversity of Asian Americans, describing, among other things, the racism and Orientalism impacting the narrators in Wat's book.

Following the publication of *The Making of a Gay Asian Community*, a number of other texts emerged that address the same theme. Kevin Kumashiro's *Restored Selves: Autobiographies of Queer Asian-Pacific-American Activists* (2004) tells the stories of a new generation of activists. *Gay L.A.: A History of Sexual Outlaws, Power Politics, and Lipstick Lesbians* (2006), edited by Lillian Faderman and Stuart Timmons, uses secondary literature, archival materials, and interviews to survey

❖ Key Facts

Time Period:
Mid- to Late 20th Century

Relevant Historical Events:
Formation of a gay Asian American community in Los Angeles; formation of Asian Pacific Lesbians and Gays; AIDS epidemic

Nationality:
American

Keywords:
gay rights; AIDS epidemic; identity

Gay Vietnamese man holds up sign for equal rights at the 2010 New Year celebration parade in Westminster, California. In *Making of a Gay Asian Community*, Eric Wat explores how gay Asian American men in Los Angeles have struggled to form a coherent community. © YOUNG-WOLFF PHOTOGRAPHY/ALAMY

the development of the wider queer community in Los Angeles. Faderman and Timmons reference Wat's work when describing discrimination against Asian Americans in the broader historical context.

THEMES AND STYLE

Edited into six roughly chronological chapters, the text uses the words of twenty-five "narrators" to explore how individual experiences of exclusion and difference from the mainstream, coupled with a shifting social landscape, led to the founding of the A/PLG. Both immigrants and American-born narrators echo Andy C.'s declaration that from an early age "I knew I was different." Many report feeling marginalized in both the broader gay community and in various Asian American organizations. However, a sense of community began to develop around rice bars and nightspots such as the River Club, as Paul Chen remembers: "I felt like this is the first time that all of me, all different parts of me fit in some place. I am Asian and I am gay." Realizing that there would be power in numbers against discrimination in clubs and elsewhere, a handful of men started the A/PLG. Says Tak Yamamoto, "We felt that we were empowered because we could now do things as a group."

As he writes in the book's introduction, Wat believed that "recovering this local history is essential to organizing the gay Asian community in Los Angeles" in part because the past is an "anchor of imagination" for shaping the future. In addition, Wat argues that "being gay is almost an ephemeral thing," which prompts questions such as "What have I inherited and to whom can I pass it on?" *The Making of a Gay Asian Community* seeks to answer such questions while also taking into consideration that being gay is only part of the equation. Finally, Wat uses the book to critique ethnic and gender stereotypes that he finds reflected in some of his narrators' stories. Noting that a number of narrators reject other Asians as partners, Wat theorizes that this reflects a residual privileging of heterosexual power dynamics, in which a couple needs to include both a male/white/top component and a female/"other"/bottom. He rejects this conception not only for its obvious stereotyping of Asian men as feminine but also for its antiquated expression of gender roles in relationships.

The Making of a Gay Asian Community is organized in a manner that itself replicates the "making" of a gay Asian community. Rather than devote chapters to individual stories, Wat organizes the chapters around themes that show common experiences across individual lives. This feeling of community is further emphasized by stories that dovetail into each other. Narrators reference each other, and in one segment Wat speaks with three of the men together. The work is also notable for its academic tone, with the interviews organized into chapters that are introduced, and sometimes concluded, with historical context and critical analysis. This structure serves to underline the legitimacy of the project, which can be viewed as an important redress to gay Asians' marginalization, both in life and in histories of the gay community and Asian Americans.

CRITICAL DISCUSSION

Largely reviewed by scholars in Asian American and queer studies, the text was well received. Writing in the *Journal of Asian American Studies*, Manalansan calls *The Making of a Gay Asian Community* "an important book that fills a long-standing gap in gay community history—the documentation of the emergence of Asian American gay communities." He adds, "The intricacies of these men's experiences sensitively elicited by Eric Wat are stunning reminders of the imaginative ways in which 'ordinary' life narratives can generate alternative worlds and histories." While slightly critical of the unbalanced structure of the book, Amy Suyeoshi, in her review for the *Journal of the History of Sexuality*, praises Wat's ability "to present convincing, unambiguous, and fluid accounts of desire and community."

The Making of a Gay Asian Community was the first significant chronicle of the gay Asian community as such, making it important as both historical record and a demonstration of how, as Suyeoshi writes, "both external and internal contradictions can fuel the formation of group identity." Wat's manner and accuracy in presenting the gay Asian community in Los Angeles, as well as the book's implications for oral history more generally, have been areas of recent scholarship.

Bodies of Evidence: The Practice of Queer Oral History (2012), edited by Nan Alamilla Boyyd and Horatio Roque Ramirez, explores the collaboration between researchers and narrators in the practice of queer oral history, devoting a chapter to *The Making of a Gay Asian Community*. *Bodies of Evidence* reprints Wat's interview with Ernest Wada, a Japanese American whose reflections are included in the book and who expressed distress over some of the contradictory self-revelations that came up during the session. In introductory and concluding text, Wat analyzes the interview and his own methods more generally, exploring the nature of the relationship between queer oral historians and their subjects. Manalansan, in his *Journal of Asian American Studies* review, discusses the problem created by generalizing about gay Asian men rather than differentiating between them, a weakness he sees in Wat's book. On a related note, he is critical of Wat's "strict chronological conception of 'generation,'" which he thinks could have been better defined "not as a marker of a cohort living in a specific time period but rather by cultural displacement and struggle."

THE EMERGENCE OF AIDS IN LOS ANGELES AND THE A/PLG

On June 5, 1981, the U.S. Centers for Disease Control and Prevention (CDC) published a report detailing five cases of a rare lung infection known as *Pneumocystis carinii pneumonia*. The five patients were gay men in Los Angeles, and the report, which appeared in the CDC's *Morbidity and Mortality Weekly*, marked the beginning of a national awareness of an emerging disease, AIDS, the first waves of which would devastate gay communities, especially those in urban centers such as New York, San Francisco, and Los Angeles.

While Eric Wat declares his subject in *The Making of a Gay Asian Community* to be "pre-AIDS" Los Angeles, the book is dedicated to Dennis Akazawa, a member of the A/PLG who died of AIDS in 1988. Additionally, the final chapter includes a narrative by Paul Bautista, who, along with his partner, tested HIV positive in 1987. Bautista's partner died the following year, at which time Bautista became actively involved in developing HIV support for the A/PLG community. Wat concludes the book by reflecting that AIDS had a transformative effect, "forcing the community to put aside some internal differences and come together."

BIBLIOGRAPHY

Sources

Boyd, Nan Alamilla, and Horatio N. Roque Ramirez, eds. *Bodies of Evidence: The Practice of Queer Oral History*. New York: Oxford University Press, 2012. Print.

Faderman, Lillian, and Stuart Timmons. *Gay L.A.: A History of Sexual Outlaws, Power Politics, and Lipstick Lesbians*. Berkeley: University of California Press, 2009. Print.

Manalansan, Martin. Rev. of *Take Out: Queer Writing from Asian Pacific America*, by Quang Bao, and *The Making of a Gay Asian Community: An Oral History of Pre-AIDS Los Angeles*, by Eric Wat. *Journal of Asian American Studies* 5.2 (2002): 182–85. Print.

———. *Global Divas: Filipino Gay Men in the Diaspora*. Durham, NC: Duke University Press, 2003. Print.

Suyeoshi, Amy. Rev. of *The Making of a Gay Asian Community: An Oral History of Pre-AIDS Los Angeles*, by Eric Wat. *Journal of the History of Sexuality* 12.3 (2003): 504+. Literature Resource Center. Web. 19 Jan. 2013.

Wat, Eric. *The Making of a Gay Asian Community: An Oral History of Pre-AIDS Los Angeles*. Lanham, MD: Rowman & Littlefield, 2002. Print.

Further Reading

Kumashiro, Kevin. *Restored Selves: Autobiographies of Queer Asian-Pacific-American Activists*. New York: Harrington Park, 2004. Print.

Lee, Joann Faung Jean. *Asian Americans: Oral Histories of First to Fourth Generation Americans from China, the Philippines, Japan, India, the Pacific Islands, Vietnam, and Cambodia*. New York: New Press, 1992. Print.

Marcus, Eric. *The Struggle for Gay and Lesbian Equal Rights, 1945–1990: An Oral History*. New York: HarperCollins, 1992. Print.

Sears, James. *Lonely Hunters: An Oral History of Lesbian and Gay Southern Life, 1948–1968*. Boulder, CO: Westview Press, 1997.

Daisy Gard

OUR APPALACHIA
An Oral History
Laurel Shackelford, Bill Weinberg

❖ *Key Facts*

Time Period:
20th Century

Relevant Historical Events:
Development of the coal industry; rising emigration from Appalachia; restoration of "hillbilly" culture

Nationality:
American

Keywords:
coal mining; emigration; exploitation

OVERVIEW

Created by the Appalachian Oral History Project, edited by Laurel Shackelford and Bill Weinberg, and published in 1977, *Our Appalachia: An Oral History* presents stories of the fiercely independent hill culture of the southeastern United States through the voices of forty-seven people with close ties to that culture. A joint project of several southern colleges and universities, the Appalachian Oral History Project conducted dozens of interviews in eastern Kentucky, western Virginia, and North Carolina during the late 1970s with the goal of preserving an authentic record of a unique society in transition. The resulting book includes historical and sociological analysis of the transition from subsistence farming to industrialization to economic depression, along with transcripts of interviews with a wide range of people of the central Appalachian Mountains who lived through those changes.

During the 1970s national movements for social change were felt even in the relatively isolated communities of Appalachia, where activists worked to increase awareness about the deep economic problems facing mountain communities. The authentic voices showcased in *Our Appalachia* captured the public imagination, making the book a popular success as well as a respected historical document. Reprinted in 1988, the book has continued to counter "hillbilly" stereotypes and to document the detrimental impact of the coal mining industry on both Appalachian society and the physical environment.

HISTORICAL AND LITERARY CONTEXT

First settled by the Cherokee, then by Scots, Irish, and German immigrants, the Appalachian region evolved into a distinct and colorful society. Rugged ridges and valleys were conducive to the development of small family farms and served to isolate communities, which as a result built their own religious and political institutions based on a meager, self-sufficient economy focused on agriculture, hunting, quilting, and distilling whiskey. Though observers as early as Thomas Jefferson noted rich coal deposits in the Appalachians, it was not until post–Civil War industrialization that commercial coal mining became a dominant feature of the mountain economy. Small local mining operations were soon replaced by a developed industry owned by "flatland" coal barons. During World War I rising demand for coal led to a dramatic increase in Appalachian mining and an influx of outside workers, both European immigrants and African Americans from the Deep South. In the North Carolina mountains, where coal was scarce, textile mills and tourism replaced subsistence farming as primary means of survival.

Families who had lived independently in the mountains for generations sold mineral rights to their land cheaply, often without understanding the implications, then found themselves seeking employment from the mine owners they felt had cheated them. The legendary freedom of the backwoodsman was soon traded for the unhealthy drudgery of the miner and, after demand for coal receded, the bleak hopelessness of unemployment. Thousands left the mountains and headed for urban centers to find work. Those who stayed faced the task of rebuilding communities, resisting further exploitation by outside mining interests, and restoring pride in "hillbilly" culture. When the Appalachian Oral History Project launched the series of interviews that would become *Our Appalachia,* this movement for renewal was flourishing in communities throughout the region.

The genre of oral history emerged from a socially progressive ideology that valued the personal recollections of ordinary citizens as both a legitimate contribution to the historical record and a tool for creating social change. Influential oral histories were created by the Federal Writer's Project during the Great Depression, such as the 1939 *These Are Our Lives,* compiled from interviews with dozens of southern workers. The social movements of the 1970s produced a new wave of politically focused oral history, including John Baskin's 1976 look at the destruction of an Ohio town, *New Burlington: The Life and Death of an American Village,* and Reed Wolcott's 1976 examination of small-town race relations in North Carolina, *Rose Hill.*

Published at a pivotal time in the history of the region, *Our Appalachia* remains an important reference and text in the study of Appalachian history. The work continues to be fresh and relevant because, as oral history, it captures the voices of the past. The Appalachian Oral History Project amassed more than six hundred archived interviews before the project ended in 1989. Its work has been carried on by such researchers as Italian historian Alessandro Portelli, who released his study of Appalachian coal country, *They Say in Harlan County: An Oral History,* in 2010.

THEMES AND STYLE

The themes of *Our Appalachia* are clearly delineated in the book's three-part format, with each section exploring a different theme. Part one, "A Simpler Time," is devoted to memories of an isolated and unspoiled Appalachia. This life was hard work: "If we needed anything done we did it, such as taking care of the stock, hoeing corn, plowing … raising everything we eat," says Delphia Ramey, born in 1906 in Kentucky. At the same time it was oriented toward community: "People had to take care of their neighbors. There was nobody else to do it," recalls Jim Byrd, who grew up in North Carolina during the early 1900s. Part two, "A Culture Under Attack," highlights the destructive force of the coal mining industry. Here the editors combine the recollections of those who made fortunes from the acquisition of mining rights with those of impoverished laborers. Henry La Viers, chair of the board of Kentucky's Southeast Coal Company, recalls coal speculator John Mayo as "a man of vision and he could see what the possibilities were." Steve Tomko, whose family emigrated from Austria-Hungary to the coal fields of Virginia, remembers the harsh reality of mining: "You'd tell the foreman, 'I just can't stand it. … There's no air in my place.' … They'd tell you, 'Well, there's a barefooted man outside waiting for your job if you want to quit." Part three, "Digging In," focuses on those who chose to remain in their mountain homes after unemployment and economic depression had forced many to leave. Robert Lampkins of southwestern Virginia works to improve conditions in the African American community: "My attitude is, I'm going to help the people I grew up with."

In their introduction to the work, the editors state that the "book grew out of the need for a social history of Central Appalachia," along with the opportunity for the people of the area to record their stories. Though drawn from interviews with a wide range of mountain residents, the book's demographics are somewhat limited—out of forty-seven interviewees, only ten are women and two African American. Because the Appalachian Oral History Project was a collaboration of area colleges, many of the interviews were conducted by college students who had roots in the region and "brought to each interview a knowledge and sensitivity that few people from outside the mountains could achieve."

The success of *Our Appalachia* as social history derives from both its cogent explanatory text and the authentically colloquial voices of its interviewees. The editors display obvious respect for Appalachian communities by recognizing that "mountain people had a history of adapting their surroundings into means for living." This indomitable spirit is echoed by interviewees such as Jim Byrd in their own vernacular: "They'd send one of us old boys out and invite everybody in the whole community to come to the working. … There was no overseer. They all knowed how to work." Resilience is apparent throughout the narrative, as in the words of Kentucky farmer Flora Rife, who told interviewers that "we had four children and another one on the road, and we didn't have no way of making ends meet … so my husband put up a moonshine still and made whiskey. … We had to do it to make a living."

Our Appalachia: An Oral History offers the stories of those who live there. Depicted here is a man on his porch in Appalachia, Virginia. © VISIONS OF AMERICA, LLC/ALAMY

CRITICAL DISCUSSION

Early critics admired the careful research and broad scope of *Our Appalachia.* H. L. Van Brunt praised the work in the *New York Times,* noting that there are "no one-dimensional characters in these tales" and adding that the "book reads with the cohesiveness of a good novel." In a review in the *Journal of American History,* Constance Myers asserts that "the reader of these carefully edited transcripts taken from taped personal histories of miners, loggers, still operators, coal camp widows, mountain migrants to the city, welfare recipients, and many more is bound to come away with a deeper perception and a sympathetic understanding of life in an environment that has undergone cataclysmic change in our century."

Myers articulated lasting value of Shackelford and Weinberg's work: "The book represents oral history technique artfully used to inform the lay reader as well as the serious student of southern social history." As a snapshot of a rural society undergoing painful industrial and economic transitions, *Our Appalachia* remains a significant historical document and reference. As a portrait of an American archetype of resourceful independence and determination, it is a riveting narrative that continues to attract readers into the twenty-first century.

Though not the subject of frequent scholastic examination, *Our Appalachia* remains a primary resource for information about Appalachian society and history. A 1979 article by Kenneth Kusmer in *Reviews in American History* cites the work for its

COMMUNITIES

PRIMARY SOURCE

EXCERPT FROM *OUR APPALACHIA*

VERNA MAE

It would take two years to tell about my daddy. He was a wonderful man. He was brilliant. That's why I hate all these stories and things that's told about us hillbillies that degrades him. I'd hate to have him labeled as a hillbilly because he was such a wonderful feller. He didn't have very much education, but he was brilliant in common sense, and he was the kindest, most generous person I ever knew. He had so many philosophies and so many sayings that were so wise. He said what made people fight was either that they were hungry or cold. If the kids got to yelling he'd build a big fire and go get us something to eat. He used it in some ways as a joke, but it was really true.

He taught me to love nature, to love thunder and lightning. And he'd teach me to [appreciate] the sunset and rainbow. I know when [Alice Lloyd] first [started her school] this teacher tried to tell him about the great paintings, the masterpieces and all that, and he said, "Listen, I look at pictures that was painted by the most wonderful master of all. Jesus. Did you ever see a sunset? Did you ever see a rainbow? Did you ever get up of the morning and see the whole world covered with snow? Nothing's more beautiful than that."

[…]

My father probably had about what would be the equivalent of the fifth or sixth grade. Mostly he taught hisself. He would kid and say he only went to school three days in his life and two of them he went in place of his brother.

My mother knew one letter, "O," and that was all of the education that she had, I mean book education. She knew how to do a lot of things like sew and how to keep a family together. She'd card, and spun, and wove. They dyed by hand. Onion hulls made yeller dye. Walnut hulls made a brown. They used things they could go out in the hills and get. They didn't use, as they say, "fotched-on" dyes.

scrutiny of the "contradictory characteristics of community." In a 1980 article in the *Journal of American Folklore*, Jeff Titon examines the difference between interview-based oral history and life story, referring to *Our Appalachia* as "the product of highly directed interviews" characterized by "leading questions." He describes the Appalachian Oral History Project's publication as "the result of a collaborative venture between the historians and the informants. This collaboration is the nature of oral history." Later works such as James C. Klotter's 1996 study *Kentucky: Portrait in Paradox, 1900–1950* and Catherine Lugo's article "The Fine Art of Moonshine" draw on the interviews in *Our Appalachia* in presenting their own depiction of the area.

BIBLIOGRAPHY

Sources

Kusmer, Kenneth L. "The Concept of 'Community' in American History." Rev. of *Community and Social Change in America*, by Thomas Bender, and *The Slum and the Ghetto: Neighborhood Deterioration and Middle-Class Reform, Chicago, 1880–1930*, by Thomas Lee Philpott. *Reviews in American History* 7.3 (1979): 380–86. *JSTOR*. Web. 22 Jan. 2013.

Myers, Constance Ashton. Rev. of *Our Appalachia: An Oral History*, ed. Laurel Shackelford and Bill Weinberg. *Journal of American History* 64.4 (1978): 1170–71. *JSTOR*. Web. 23 Jan. 2013.

Shackelford, Laurel, and Bill Weinberg, eds. *Our Appalachia: An Oral History*. Lexington: University Press of Kentucky, 1988. Print.

Titon, Jeff Todd. "The Life Story." *Journal of American Folklore* 93.369 (1980): 276–92. *JSTOR*. 22 Jan. 2013.

Van Brunt, H. L. "No Hillbillies in These Hills." Rev. of *Our Appalachia: An Oral History*, ed. Laurel Shackelford and Bill Weinberg. *New York Times* 3 Apr. 1977): 250. *ProQuest Historical Newspapers*. Web. 22 Jan. 2013.

Further Reading

Caudill, Henry M. *Night Comes to the Cumberlands: A Biography of a Depressed Area*. Ashland, KY: Jesse Stuart Foundation, 2001. Print.

Drake, Richard B. *A History of Appalachia*. Lexington: University Press of Kentucky, 2001. Print.

Klotter, James C. *Kentucky: Portrait in Paradox, 1900–1950*. Frankfort: Kentucky Historical Society, 1996. Print.

Lugo, Catherine. "The Fine Art of Moonshine." *Homestead*. Web. 23 Jan. 2013.

Portelli, Alessandro. *They Say in Harlan County*. New York: Oxford University Press, 2010. Print.

Weise, Robert S. *Grasping at Independence: Debt, Male Authority, and Mineral Rights in Appalachian Kentucky, 1850–1915*. Knoxville: University of Tennessee Press, 2001. Print.

Tina Gianoulis

They made their own. And she was a Christian. She joined the church.

My mother died [when I was five weeks old] and it was pretty hard for us girls because the older one was just fourteen and then I had one sister that was older than me that was mentally retarded. She wasn't born that way, she had rheumatic fever, "brain fever"'s what they called it then. And she finally just walked in the fire and got burned up.

From the time I could walk I was taught to be good to Sissie. The only candy that we had was big long red sticks of peppermint candy. My dad would bring me and her and my next older sister candy but she wouldn't eat it. So he would say, "Now you watch Sissie and when she lays hers down you have hers. [Do] not take it away from her." And I'd watch her, maybe follow her round for an hour or two and she'd lay it down. I'd grab it and run. She wouldn't eat it. It's probably because she had bad teeth. No matter what she wanted she got it first. And, you know, I didn't resent it. I knew that she was special, that [she wasn't] responsible for what she did.

[Sissie had a dress] she loved because it was red. And she was up close to the fire and it caught fire. That's the way she got burned up. I know my dad had gone to Wheelwright. It was at Easter and all the girls was outside watching the boys play ball. Heard her scream and run in and my older sister picked her up and carried her to the well and drawed water and poured it on her. She was burned so bad she died. I was scared to death. I can remember thinking, Now when Father comes back it'll all be okay. Of course, [the others] just forgot me and didn't pay any attention to me and I thought, now when he comes back. … The next thing I remember was him coming in and he hugged me so tight it hurt. After that I found out they had told him that I was the one that got burned up.

SOURCE: Shackelford, Laurel, and Bill Weinberg. *Our Appalachia: An Oral History.* Lexington: The University Press of Kentucky, 1977. All rights reserved. Reproduced by permission.

The Saga of Coe Ridge
A Study in Oral History
William Lynwood Montell

❖ **Key Facts**

Time Period:
Late 19th to Early 20th Century

Relevant Historical Events:
Establishment of Coe Ridge; Great Depression; collapse of Coe Ridge

Nationality:
American

Keywords:
race; community; Great Depression

OVERVIEW

The Saga of Coe Ridge: A Study in Oral History (1970), by William Lynwood Montell, is a grassroots history of a small African American community that was established in 1866 in the foothills of the Cumberland Mountains in southern Kentucky by former slaves of a white planter, John Coe. In its early days the colony thrived on its physical and cultural isolation and found a stable source of income in the timber industry. However, tensions with neighboring white communities escalated in the early decades of the twentieth century, when Coe Ridge became heavily involved in the moonshine trade. Federal revenue agents finally succeeded in shutting down the colony in 1958. *The Saga of Coe Ridge* is based on the author's interviews with seventeen surviving black members of the community and twenty-two of their white neighbors over a four-year span (1961–1965).

In addition to being a story about a legendary community, *The Saga of Coe Ridge* is noteworthy for being Montell's attempt to prove the validity of oral sources at a time when they were still considered suspect forms of evidence by many scholars. Containing a detailed theoretical analysis of oral forms, Montell's book was praised upon its publication as a work of pioneering analysis that admirably supported his claims for the historical legitimacy of oral testimony. He went on to author several more folk histories of the Cumberland River region in Kentucky and Tennessee, as well as a guide for field researchers, *From Memory to History* (1981), cowritten with Barbara Allen Bogart, to accommodate the growing numbers of professional historians in the United States who were accessing oral traditions.

HISTORICAL AND LITERARY CONTEXT

Coe Ridge (also known as Coe Town and Zeketown) was founded on several hundred acres of woodland purchased by Coe's former slaves after the Civil War. The residents initially found a ready source of income in cutting timber and rafting the logs down the Cumberland River. Conditions of poor communication and transportation favored the colony's clannish organization and shift to moonshining and bootlegging, activities it initially carried out freely and without reprisals from federal authorities, who were reluctant to ride horseback through an area notorious for successfully defending itself against attacks from outsiders. The settlement eventually collapsed, however, as a result of infighting, the Great Depression, migration to the industrial centers of the North, and sustained and frequent raids on the moonshiners (made possible by improved roads).

The colony of Coe Ridge is part of an area on the border between Kentucky and Tennessee for which few written records exist; most of the court records, as well as file copies of newspapers, were destroyed in fires. Montel had little corroborating evidence to substantiate the oral testimony save for census records, generalized data for Coe County, and a 1930 publication called *The Chronicles of Coe Country*, which was written by Samuel S. Coe in collaboration with another person. Because oral history as a discipline was in its infancy when Montell was working on the text, he devised a systematic approach to the collection and organization of his material that he hoped would demonstrate the usefulness of oral traditions to the reconstruction of the past in situations where written accounts were not available.

Oral history research in the United States was accorded academic legitimacy beginning in 1948 with the establishment of an Oral History Research Office at Columbia University. However, the discipline did not receive widespread institutionalization until the late 1960s, when it came to be regarded as fundamental to the documentation of the emerging civil rights, women's, and student protest movements. The academic emphasis on oral history suggested its usefulness as a means of recovering the forgotten histories of isolated communities and minorities throughout the country. This was especially true of Appalachia, which was largely known outside the region only on the basis of myths about its backward ways and the legendary feuding of its rival clans.

When the *Saga of Coe Ridge* was first published, many historians still questioned the authenticity of the folk tradition. Montell notes in his preface, "The utilization of oral traditions as undertaken here represents an area of open controversy and is severely attacked by some scholars who are accustomed to more conventional methods of documentation." Montell's painstaking methodology made a convincing argument for the insertion of folklore into the historical record and helped to open up to researchers an untapped reservoir of American history.

THEMES AND STYLE

The Saga of Coe Ridge consists of seven chapters that document the major phases in the social and economic development of Coe Ridge. The division reflects Montell's grouping of the oral narratives into three categories: local historical legends; universal tales; and tales joined by a motif element generally suggestive of racial solidarity (such as feats of cunning and strength directed at white interlopers by the blacks of Coe Ridge). The first category makes up the bulk of the testimony in the text. Through a comparative analysis of the interviews, Montell was able to identify consistent thematic strands that formed a cohesive chronology of the Coe community, from its plantation beginnings and entry into the logging business to the depletion of the land and the legendary transition to bootlegging. Testimony by both black and white informants blames the earliest racial feuding between the colony and the surrounding communities squarely on local roughnecks who could not accept the presence of a black enclave in their midst.

As he writes in his preface, Montell was "prepared to defend a thesis which holds that folk history can complement historical literature." His approach to his material is integrative, meshing oral testimony with authorial commentary and footnotes that appear directly alongside the text. In appendixes, Montell includes biographical sketches of his informants and genealogical charts of white and black Coe families. Montell's main editorial enhancement is a clustering of the narratives according to thematic preoccupation.

Montell claims to have reported the testimony of his subjects verbatim: "The oral accounts have been faithfully preserved in the same form in which they were collected from the people. Their words at all times have been transcribed as they sounded to this writer's ear. ... [Any] other manner of transcription would detract from the folk quality of the texts." In cases where the informant's testimony might cause embarrassment to persons still living, Montell uses fictitious names and records the alteration in a footnote. Montell was generally applauded for his rigorous standards of reporting and for restraining from making qualitative judgments on the testimony. However, some critics noticed inadequacies in the approach. Writing for the *Journal of Southern History* in 1971, Emma Lou Thornbrough observed, "[One] feels that he has perhaps placed so much emphasis on the explanation of his *methods* and has so conscientiously presented all the variants of an incident or tradition which he heard that the reader may lose sight of the *history* of Coe Ridge and its significance."

CRITICAL DISCUSSION

As one of the earliest published practical guides and folklore methodologies, *The Saga of Coe Ridge* was extensively reviewed in academic journals. In a 1970 review for the *Journal of American History,* Richard A. Van Orman enthuses, "The *Saga of Coe Ridge* marks a new and long-needed departure in American historiography. It introduces techniques for the study and writing of local history, grass roots history, folk history, oral history, and black history." Richard A. Reuss also predicted seminal influence for *The Saga of Coe Ridge* in a 1971 review for the *Journal of American Folklore:* "[Its] methodology, scope, and findings have implications far beyond the actual subject matter treated by the author. ... Montell's book ... is something of an historical landmark as far as most of the American historical profession is concerned."

Montell's field research in the 1960s formed an important complement to contemporaneous sociological studies of increasing poverty in Appalachia brought about by the loss of jobs to mechanization. *The Saga of Coe Ridge* helped to inspire a great deal of additional oral history research in the region. Appalachian

An African American coal miner in West Virginia in 2009. William Lynwood Montell's *The Saga of Coe Ridge* tells the story of an African American settlement in the Appalachian Mountains. © LES STONE/THE IMAGE WORKS

"THE WHITE GALS"

William Lynwood Montell devotes an entire chapter in *The Saga of Coe Ridge* to the various white women who developed relationships with the residents of Coe Ridge in the middle phase of the colony's development (1885–1920). Among these women are Molly Ballard and Nan Anderson, both from the nearby Mud Camp community. Late in the 1880s, Molly and Nan began sneaking out of their homes to meet with Calvin Coe and Little John Coe at the home of a sympathetic white neighbor. The two couples—Calvin and Molly, and Little John and Nan—decided to elope to Indiana, where they could marry without facing criminal penalties. The four only made it as far as Glasgow, Barren County, Kentucky, before they were apprehended by authorities at the train station.

Montell's interview subjects disagree on what caused the girls' white faces to become exposed from underneath their veils. The sources also call into question the fates of Calvin and Little John. However, according to the official records of Barren County for 1899, the men were arrested, fined $150 each, and imprisoned for fifty days on charges of unlawfully assembling "for the purpose of causing the marriage of a white woman to a Negro man." Two members of the Coe clan, Oleson Wilburn and Joe Coe, were killed by whites to avenge the sullying of the girls' reputations.

---

oral history projects were undertaken at universities throughout the South in the 1970s and 1980s and continue to flourish. Montell's native Kentucky boasts an independent state government agency dedicated to oral history, with more than fifty archival repositories.

The Saga of Coe Ridge has been reprinted several times since its original publication, and scholarship has confirmed its pioneering significance. In *The Voice of the Past* (1978), a publication highly important to legitimizing oral history, British folklorist Paul Thompson describes *The Saga of Coe Ridge* as "the leading American example of a serious fully documented community study, by its subject largely dependent on oral sources." Additionally, in a 1984 *Appalachian Journal* review of Montell's writings, Gordon B. McKinney writes, "In the introduction to his first book, [Montell] argues that oral sources are a legitimate means to recapture the past. Thirteen years later, Montell can virtually ignore that question, because historians, folklorists, and other scholars have embraced oral methods with enthusiasm. … [*The Saga of Coe Ridge*] has quickly become the classic study of a rural Southern black community."

BIBLIOGRAPHY

Sources

McKinney, Gordon B. "The World of William Lynwood Montell." *Appalachian Journal* 11.3 (1984): 255–59. *JSTOR.* Web. 5 Jan. 2013.

Montell, William Lynwood. *The Saga of Coe Ridge: A Study in Oral History.* Knoxville: University of Tennessee Press, 1970. Print.

Reuss, Richard A. Rev. of *The Saga of Coe Ridge,* by William Lynwood Montell. *Journal of American Folklore* 84.333 (1971): 351–53. *JSTOR.* Web. 5 Jan. 2013.

Smith, Robert Jerome. Rev. of *The Saga of Coe Ridge,* by William Lynwood Montell. *American Studies* 12.1 (1971): 78–79. *JSTOR.* Web. 5 Jan. 2013.

Thompson, Paul. *The Voice of the Past: Oral History.* 3rd ed. Oxford: Oxford University Press, 2000. Print.

Thornbrough, Emma Lou. Rev. of *The Saga of Coe Ridge,* by William Lynwood Montell. *Journal of Southern History* 37.1 (1971): 133–34. *JSTOR.* Web. 5 Jan. 2013.

Van Orman, Richard A. Rev. of *The Saga of Coe Ridge,* by William Lynwood Montell. *Journal of American History* 57.3 (1970): 725–26. *JSTOR.* Web. 5 Jan. 2013.

Further Reading

Coe, Samuel S., with R. A. Adams. *The Chronicles of Coe Colony.* Ed. Billy N. Guffey. Burkesville, KY: Xerxes, 2007. Print.

Montell, William Lynwood. "The Coe Ridge Colony: A Racial Island Disappears." *American Anthropologist* 74.3 (1972): 710–19. *JSTOR.* Web. 5 Jan. 2013.

———. *Ghosts along the Cumberland: Deathlore in the Kentucky Foothills.* Knoxville: University of Tennessee Press, 1975. Print.

———. *Don't Go Up Kettle Creek: Verbal Legacy of the Upper Cumberland.* Knoxville: University of Tennessee Press, 1983. Print.

———. *Grassroots Music in the Upper Cumberland.* Knoxville: University of Tennessee Press, 2006. Print.

Montell, William Lynwood, and Barbara Allen Bogart. *From Memory to History: Using Oral Sources in Local Historical Research.* Nashville, TN: American Association for State and Local History, 1981. Print.

Ritchie, Donald. *Doing Oral History. A Practical Guide: Using Interviews to Uncover the Past and Preserve It for the Future.* New York: Oxford University Press, 2003. Print.

Janet Mullane

Swiftwater People
Lives of Old Timers on the Upper St. Joe & St. Maries Rivers
Bert Russell

Key Facts

Time Period:
Early to Mid-20th Century

Relevant Historical Events:
Homesteading in northern Idaho; Great Depression; growth of the IWW

Nationality:
American

Keywords:
homesteading; labor; logging

OVERVIEW

The oral histories in *Swiftwater People: Lives of Old Timers on the Upper St. Joe & St. Maries Rivers* (1979), edited by Bert Russell, provide a diverse and detailed look into the everyday life of northern Idaho's early homesteaders and working people, with an emphasis on the 1920s–1940s. Teeming with memories of joy and triumph, hardship and tragedy, the personal histories in *Swiftwater People* span a wide range of life experiences. Russell's collection of nearly fifty narratives also conveys the tremendous impact that major industries, primarily logging, had on the lives of Idahoans during a time of significant development in the region.

When publishers were initially uninterested in *Swiftwater People*, Russell and his wife pressed onward through a self-publishing process in 1979. In 2001 a newer edition of the book was published by the Museum of North Idaho. Because of the title's relative obscurity, little is known about its initial public reception. Nonetheless Russell was popular among local Idahoans for his work in preserving the oral histories of early homesteaders and workers, and *Swiftwater People* remains notable for its highly personal exploration of life in Idaho in the early twentieth century.

HISTORICAL AND LITERARY CONTEXT

The oral histories in *Swiftwater People* illustrate the significance of northern Idaho's rich natural resources on the occupations and lifestyles of its people. In the late nineteenth century, northern Idaho's heavily forested terrain attracted timber companies that purchased the majority of the area's private forested land by the early 1900s. With the growth of the logging industry came the expansion of Idaho's railway system to better support the transportation of the state's commodities. The development of Idaho's major industries also contributed to the rise of powerful labor unions in the early 1900s.

The narratives in *Swiftwater People* bring to life the consequences of the Great Depression on the region's working class. Many of the book's narrators describe the struggle of finding and keeping a job. A large number secured employment in the region's growing timber industry, and their anecdotes vividly illustrate the risks that accompanied that work. It was not uncommon for loggers to be killed by falling timber or by logs that "jumped the chute" in transport, or for a man to drown in the river while driving or rolling logs. As the number of railroad camps and logging camps increased, so too did the influence of the Industrial Workers of the World (IWW), or "Wobblies." The Wobblies pushed hard for better working conditions, including an eight-hour workday (at the same pay as ten hours), "shower baths," and clean bedding at the camps. An interviewee named Russian Alec describes the conditions of the camps prior to and after the influence of the IWW: "Good camp after Wobbly strike 1917. Make 'em clean up. Furnish blankets. Before, you sleep on floor like cows and pigs. Everybody sleep in one bed with canvas over. Full of lice and bedbugs."

Few mainstream oral histories focus on the specific region and generation of people that Russell's does. The Museum of North Idaho continues to publish and sell a notable selection of lesser-known but related works on the area's history. Larry Strobel's *When the Mill Whistle Blew* (2009) also takes an inside look at the lives of homesteaders and timberworkers, focusing specifically on two families in the city of Coeur d'Alene. *Up the Swiftwater* (2003) by Sandra Crowell and David Asleson and *In All the West No Place Like This* (2009) by Simone Carbonneau Kincaid and Dorothy Dahlgren provide a photographic history of the Coeur d'Alene region's rich landscape, native people, and early American settlers.

As *Swiftwater People* has remained a relatively obscure title, little direct criticism exists to suggest its larger cultural or literary impact. However, Russell was relatively prolific, and with the help of his wife, Marie, he published five similar titles before his death in 1997. *Hardships and Happy Times* (1978) and *North Fork of the Coeur d'Alene River* (2003) both contain oral histories reflecting topics very similar to those of *Swiftwater People*. Russell's other titles include *Calked Boots and Other Northwest Writings* (1968), *The Sawdust Dream* (1990), and *Rock Burst* (1998). Although the age of the pioneers is long over, histories like the ones Russell edited remain relevant in the modern world as the timber industry continues to fill a significant role in Idaho's economy.

COMMUNITIES

Women fly-fishing on the Saint Joe River in Idaho amid snowlike debris from cottonwood trees, 2011. Residents of the Saint Joe and the Saint Maries River regions discuss their lives in *Swiftwater People,* edited by Bert Russell.
© JED CONKLIN/ NEWSPORT/CORBIS

THEMES AND STYLE

Several themes emerge in the narratives of *Swiftwater People,* chief among them the hardships and struggles inherent in daily life and the value of hard work. Russell's subjects recall flooding that drove families from their homes and destroyed everything they had. They tell of scarlet fever, typhoid fever, measles, and mumps. Clear in nearly every narrative are the trials of the Great Depression, which left people desperate for work in an ailing job market as they struggled to support their families. In spite of these troubles, or perhaps because of them, the importance of community and generosity shines through in the book. Genevieve Avery, who often assisted local women in delivering their children, recalls, "People may have [had] strong differences about some trifling matter and then the next day something happen[ed] and everyone help[ed]." During hard economic times, Oral Avery, who owned a town store, allowed customers to put items on credit, knowing he would likely never be paid. Bill Degen recalls how essential community was as he describes his decision to head east to Montana on the promise of employment: "If there was no job in Deer Lodge I was going to try to make it back home where I could at least starve among friends."

As noted on the dedication page of the 1979 printing of *Swiftwater People,* Russell's drive to record the stories of the region's "old timers" stemmed from his wish to preserve and spread their determined and gracious perspective on life. "In these unsettling times," Russell writes, "we need to draw from the reservoir of fortitude, humor and inventiveness handed down by river drivers and horse loggers, and by women and men homesteaders who made-do with what tools and food life offered and took their satisfactions and happiness in the accomplishments of hard work." It is unclear how much he edited the narratives in *Swiftwater People* to achieve this purpose, as he provides no introductory notes on his methodology. His editorial influence presents itself, however, through the insertion of explanations, related facts, and newspaper excerpts, which aid the reader in understanding the historical and cultural context of the narratives.

While Russell's editorial voice is relatively silent in *Swiftwater People,* his interest in personalizing the narratives is evident through the inclusion of each participant's photograph, as well as abundant snapshots of relevant people and places. Russell further individualizes the tales by deliberately keeping intact the speakers' grammatical errors, such as in "We was hauling timber" and "There was a lot of them old ones." Additionally, in the narratives of some immigrants, he deliberately misspells select words to convey the speaker's dialect or accent. For instance, in the narrative of Swedish immigrant Arvid Johnson, "that" becomes "dat," "thing" becomes "ting," "job" becomes "yob," and so on.

CRITICAL DISCUSSION

Having grown up near the St. Joe River in roughly the same period, Russell had a deeply rooted interest in the "old timers" of the Coeur d'Alene region. Longing to write down the people's stories, he organized the first annual Old Time Picnic in Harrison, Idaho, in

1953. The event attracted between four thousand and five thousand people and provided many stories for his oral history collections. Until his wife, Marie, took responsibility for his books near the end of his life, the publication of *Swiftwater People* and most of his other titles consisted primarily of self-publishing efforts. In 2001 the Museum of North Idaho republished *Swiftwater People*, which remains in print today.

Russell gained a solid reputation among locals for his interest in preserving oral histories of the pioneer days. "He devoted his lifetime to collecting and writing those tales," writes Cynthia Taggart in the *Spokesman Review* in 1997. When Alzheimer's disease diminished his mental faculties, Marie stepped up to finish compiling and editing the interviews and other materials needed to complete *Rock Burst*, Russell's sixth and final book.

Rock Burst brings into focus and personalizes the mining industry in the Coeur d'Alene region while shedding light on the inherent dangers of working in the mines. Published by University of Idaho Press in 1998, *Rock Burst* attracted more critical interest from historians than Russell's previous works. Reviewing the book in the *Oral History Review* in 2000, Mildred Allen Beik describes and criticizes Russell's work in ways that directly correlate to the content and style of *Swiftwater People*: "The character, mobility, and adaptability of the Idahoans emerges from their descriptions of their diverse work experiences in mining, railroading, logging, and homesteading." However, she notes, the editors' failure to address their purposes or methodology leaves the reader with a sense of "haphazard" organization and—most notably for oral historians—no "notion of a 'shared authority'" between editor and interviewee.

BIBLIOGRAPHY

Sources

Beik, Mildred Allen. "Rock Burst." *Oral History Review* 27.1 (2000): 181–83. *JSTOR*. Web. 27 Jan. 2013.

Bonner, Jeremy. "Idaho." *Dictionary of American History*. Ed. Stanley I. Kutler. 3rd ed. Vol. 4. New York: Scribner, 2003. 211–14. *Gale Power Search*. Web. 26 Jan. 2013.

"Books Online." *Museum of North Idaho*. Museum of North Idaho, n.d. Web. 26 Jan. 2013.

Russell, Bert. *Swiftwater People: Lives of Old Timers on the Upper St. Joe & St. Maries Rivers*. Harrison, ID: Lacon, 1979. Print.

"State of the Timber Industry 2011." *Idaho Forest Products Commission*. Idaho Forest Products Commission, 2011. Web. 29 Jan. 2013.

PROHIBITION IN IDAHO

The era of Prohibition emerges as a steady undercurrent throughout the narratives of *Swiftwater People*. Clandestine distilleries, or stills, were far from uncommon at the time, as was the undercover sale of moonshine to the locals. Law enforcement cracked down on the illegal trade, organizing posses to pursue the lawbreakers, but personal interests sometimes interfered with the success of those missions. One of the book's narrators, Wash Applegate, describes an inside deal between bootlegger Harry Burns and the sheriff wherein the sheriff would confiscate all of Burns's alcohol in transport, surrender one case to higher authorities, and hand the rest back to Burns for bootlegging, no doubt taking a cut for himself.

Another narrator, Walt Darry, recalls the time he and several others were arrested for selling booze. After pleading not guilty and being acquitted, he settled the bill with his lawyer in a two-part payment—fifty dollars and a gallon of whiskey. The rest of the men pleaded guilty and were punished accordingly. "The only way I can figure that I got free," Darry says, "was that I was a bigger liar than the rest of 'em."

Taggart, Cynthia. "Death Can't Silence Writer's Voice; Bert Russell's Wife Finishes His Idaho Tales." *Spokesman Review* 11 May 1997: A1. *LexisNexis*. Web. 6 Jan. 2013.

Further Reading

Andrews, Ralph W. *Timber: Loggers Challenge the Great Northwest Forests*. Atglen, PA: Schiffer, 2007. Print.

Arrington, Leonard J. *History of Idaho*. Moscow: University of Idaho Press, 1994. Print.

Crowell, Sandra, and David Asleson. *Up the Swiftwater: A Pictorial History of the Colorful Upper St. Joe River Country*. Coeur d'Alene: Museum of North Idaho, 2003. Print.

Dahlgren, Dorothy, and Simone Carbonneau Kincaid. *In All the West No Place Like This: A Pictorial History of the Coeur d'Alene Region*. Coeur d'Alene: Museum of North Idaho, 2009. Print.

LeMonds, James. *Deadfall: Generations of Logging in the Pacific Northwest*. Missoula, MT: Mountain, 2000. Print.

Russell, Bert, and Marie Russell. *Rock Burst*. Moscow: University of Idaho Press, 1998. Print.

Schwantes, Carlos A. *In Mountain Shadows: A History of Idaho*. Lincoln: University of Nebraska Press, 1991. Print.

Strobel, Larry. *When the Mill Whistle Blew: The Way It Was in Coeur d'Alene Country 1888–1955*. Coeur d'Alene: Museum of North Idaho, 2009. Print.

Jenna Williams

They Say in Harlan County
An Oral History
Alessandro Portelli

✧ **Key Facts**

Time Period:
Mid- to Late 20th Century

Relevant Historical Events:
Coal mining strikes in Harlan County; Great Depression

Nationality:
Italian

Keywords:
unionism; mining; workers' rights

OVERVIEW

In *They Say in Harlan County: An Oral History* (2011), Italian scholar and oral historian Alessandro Portelli explores the history of class struggle in the United States through the memory of coal-mining strikes in Harlan County, Kentucky. Portelli, a professor of American literature at the University of Rome and founder of the university's Center for Appalachian Studies, found his way to Harlan County via the folk music revival of the 1960s. From 1986 to 2009 he visited Harlan County every year, creating what he describes as "an unusual form of longitudinal study and, most important, a living personal relationship." The 150 narrators that he quotes in the book are varied in age, gender, and race. Although the views of union miners and other activists predominate, he also devotes time to what Allen Dieterich-Ward describes in *Comparative Studies of Society and History* in 2011 as "counter-voices": mine owners, scabs, and others needed to create a balanced narrative. Overall their stories combine to tell what Robert Weise summarizes in the *Journal of Southern History* in 2012 as "a long history of hard living."

Portelli first heard about Harlan County through the medium of strike songs. By his own account, he was "educated through music to the history of the American working class": a history of class conflict he had not known existed. In *They Say in Harlan County,* he places the Kentucky miners' strikes in an international context while retaining a powerful sense of place and local culture. Critics from both Appalachian studies and the oral history movement praised Portelli's skillful use of multiple voices to create a realistic portrait beyond the powerful stereotypes associated with Appalachia.

HISTORICAL AND LITERARY CONTEXT

The Great Depression devastated the previously booming coal mines of Harlan County. In February 1931, after several years of reducing miners' hours, mine owners announced a 10 percent wage reduction. In response, miners walked out in a wildcat strike. Union organizers soon arrived, and attempts to organize the miners led to violence on both sides. For ten years, Harlan County coal towns were armed camps—the scenes of beatings, shootings, looting, and at least two pitched battles. Newspapers nicknamed the region "Bloody Harlan."

In 1973, when Portelli first visited Harlan County, miners were again on strike over the right to unionize. The Brookfield strike of the 1970s was Bloody Harlan all over again, marked by "scabs, picketing, violence, state troopers and murder." Portelli, "on the track of the class struggle," interviewed modern-day strikers as well as those from the 1930s. He discovered that Harlan County's story centered not only on the mines but also on "the struggle to stay alive." The story as he tells it combines the union struggles of the 1930s and 1970s with the civil rights movement of the 1960s, welfare rights organization, strip mine protests, and environmental activism. The modern struggle in Harlan County is, according to Portelli, "[n]o longer, alas, in terms of the union, but against deadly drug merchants of many stripes, or the destruction of their homes, water, and air from strip mining, logging, pollution."

They Say in Harlan County is the latest in the tradition of oral histories dealing with the Harlan County strikes. While the strikes were still in progress, novelist Theodore Dreiser organized a report on the violence that was composed largely of firsthand narratives, published in 1932 as *Harlan Miners Speak*. After the rediscovery of Harlan County strike songs during the folk music revival of the 1960s, Harlan County became the subject of a growing body of scholarly literature based on oral history sources, including John W. Hevener's *Which Side Are You On?* (1978), Paul F. Taylor's *Bloody Harlan* (1990), and Shaunna L. Scott's *Two Sides to Everything* (1995).

Portelli had acquired a reputation as a leading figure in the oral history movement with his studies of Italian workers, such as *The Death of Luigi Trastulli and Other Stories* (1990). Although *They Say in Harlan County* was published after these groundbreaking studies, his more than twenty years of fieldwork in Harlan County was critical in shaping his influential theoretical work on the practice of oral history and the relationship between narrative and memory.

THEMES AND STYLE

Portelli sums up the central theme of *They Say in Harlan County* during an interview quoted late in the book: "the key word here is survival." The word appears

Coal miners entering a mine in Mayking, Kentucky, 1991. Coal mining is one of the topics discussed in *They Say in Harlan County: An Oral History* by Alessando Portelli.
© KAREN KASMAUSKI/CORBIS

repeatedly, in discussions that range from politics and the economy to the environment and culture. It is more than a metaphor. As one narrator tells Portelli early on, survival is "not just a word." Using the concept of survival, Portelli crafts a history of isolation, poverty, exploitation, and pride. For every narrator who repeats a variation on, "We're just a bunch of dumb hillbillies, they don't care if we die or not," there is another who displays "pride in the living they had achieved through hard work and hard struggles." It is this tension between pride and the struggle to survive that fascinates Portelli, who says, "I have always admired the way in which people fight back under great odds and survive, especially in the United States, where one is not supposed to be up against impossible odds."

In *The Battle of Valle Giula: Oral History and the Art of Dialogue* (1997), Portelli defines oral history as a dialogue "created not only by what the interviewees say, but also by what we as historians do—by the historian's presence in the field, and by the historian's presentation of the material." In the case of *They Say in Harlan County,* that dialogue is fundamentally shaped by the fact that "lines of age, class, gender, education, religion, language, color and nationality" separated Portelli from those he interviewed. Rather than blurring those distinctions, he learned to "think of the interview as an experiment in equality, where trust is achieved not by pretending we are all the same but by laying the difference and the inequality on the table and making it … the implicit subject of the conversation." Janet Wells Greene points out in her 2011 review in the *Public Historian* that in the resulting work, Portelli "presents his own master narrative in dialogue with both scholarship and the voices of the people."

They Say in Harlan County is notable for its experimental form, which Portelli describes as "history told through a multitude of stories spoken by a plurality of voices." Rather than presenting single stories told by a single narrator, he weaves quotations from multiple speakers into his own historical narrative, creating a coherent discourse from a multitude of voices. He compares his organizing principle to the Appalachian art of quilting— "a form of *bricolage* in which a new, significant whole is created out of an array of fragments." As David Cline describes it in *Labor* (2012), the intention is that "an entire community can be heard speaking as one voice, or since a community cannot really speak in one voice, we hear layers of individual contributions to the whole."

CRITICAL DISCUSSION

Initial critical reception of *They Say in Harlan County* was generally positive, though a few reviewers suggested that Portelli's experimental use of multiple voices created an occasional lack of clarity about narration and time period. Donna M. DeBlasio, writing in 2011 in *Oral History Review,* hailed the work as "a remarkable achievement that provides a fascinating glimpse into Appalachian life, history, work and culture." Weise offers concerns that Portelli ignored the region's growing middle class in favor of the standard academic tropes of Appalachian poverty and struggle but nonetheless concludes, "*They Say in Harlan County* is a stunningly effective, even beautiful, book." Ken Fones-Wolf, reviewing the work in 2011 for the

COMMUNITIES

BARBARA KOPPLE'S *HARLAN COUNTY, USA*

In 1977 Alessandro Portelli saw Barbara Kopple's documentary *Harlan County, USA* in a theater in Rome. The experience convinced him that "using music to educate myself about American struggles was not entirely a fantasy." Inspired by seeing an aging Florence Reese sing her iconic strike song "Which Side Are You On?" inspired him to return to Kentucky to study the subject and to later found an Appalachian studies collective at the University of Rome.

Kopple made the film in 1976 during the extended Brookside Mine strike over the right of miners to belong to a union of their own choosing. She captures the frustrations of United Mine Worker (UMW) members when they appear to be losing their strike and celebrates their courage in the face of violence. The film is particularly notable for its documentation of the moment when the miners' wives decide to sidestep court injunctions against union pickets and "woman" the picket lines. *Harlan County, USA* is unabashedly pro-union, but the film does not gloss over internal union problems, including the murder of union leader Jock Yablonski by killers hired by then-UMW president Tony Boyle. Despite its somber mood, *Harlan County, USA* competes with *Norma Rae* (1979) as one of the most popular labor films in the United States.

Journal of American History, describes it as "a powerful book from a distinguished oral historian."

While it is too early to determine the long-term legacy of *They Say in Harlan County*, reviewers have already identified the work as an important addition to the fields of oral history and Appalachian studies. Dieterich-Ward cites the book's last section, which deals with modern-day Harlan County, as potentially its most important contribution to the historical literature. Cline suggests that the book's major legacy may be its experimental form.

Portelli's theoretical discussions of the methodology and ethics of oral history are considered classics in the new field of oral history. Younger historians regularly cite his treatment of the relationship between memory and narrative construction. Linda Shopes, in her 2013 review of *They Say in Harlan County* in *Memory Studies,* sums up the importance of Portelli's work. She notes that Portelli's statement that "in an interview 'errors, inventions, and myths lead us through and beyond facts to their meanings' has become something of a mantra among oral historians."

BIBLIOGRAPHY

Sources

Cline, David. Rev. of *They Say in Harlan County*, by Alessandro Portelli. *Labor* 9.4 (2012): 103–04. *Duke Journals*. Web. 28 Jan. 2013.

DeBlasio, Donna M. Rev. of *They Say in Harlan County*, by Alessandro Portelli. *Oral History Review* 38.2 (2011): 374–76. *Oxford Journals*. Web. 28 Jan. 2013.

Dieterich-Ward, Allen. Rev. of *They Say in Harlan County*, by Alessandro Portelli. *Comparative Studies of Society and History* 53.4 (2011): 1014–15. *Cambridge Journals*. Web. 21 Jan. 2013.

Fones-Wolf, Ken. Rev. of *They Say in Harlan County*, by Alessandro Portelli. *Journal of American History* (2011): 263–64. *JSTOR*. Web. 28 Jan. 2013.

Greene, Janet Wells. Rev. of *They Say in Harlan County*, by Alessandro Portelli. *Public Historian* 33.4 (2011): 129–31. *JSTOR*. Web. 21 Jan. 2013.

Portelli, Alessandro. *The Battle of Valle Giulia: Oral History and the Art of Dialogue*. Madison: University of Wisconsin Press, 1997. Print.

———. *They Say in Harlan County: An Oral History*. Oxford: Oxford University Press, 2011. Print.

Shopes, Linda. Rev. of *They Say in Harlan County*, by Alessandro Portelli. *Memory Studies* 6.1 (2013): 115–16. *Sage*. Web. 28 Jan. 2013.

Weise, Robert S. Rev. of *They Say in Harlan County*, by Alessandro Portelli. *Journal of Southern History* 78.2 (2012): 506–7. *JSTOR*. Web. 28 Jan. 2013.

Further Reading

Brinson, Betsy, and Alessandro Portelli. "Crossing Cultures: An Interview with Alessandro Portelli." *Oral History Review* 28.1 (2001): 87–113. *JSTOR*. Web. 21 Jan. 2013.

Bubka, Tony. "The Harlan County Coal Strike of 1931." *Hitting Home: The Great Depression in Town and Country*. Ed. Bernard Sternsher. Chicago: Quadrangle, 1970. 181–99. Print.

Duff, Betty Parker. "Stand by Your Man: Gender and Class Formation in the Harlan County Coalfields." *Beyond Hill and Hollow: Original Readings in Appalachian Women's Studies*. Ed. Elizabeth S. D. Engelhardt. Athens: Ohio University Press, 2005. 152–69. Print.

Hevener, John W. *Which Side Are You On?: The Harlan County Coal Miners, 1931–39*. Urbana: University of Illinois Press, 1978. Print.

Jones, G. C. *Growing Up Hard in Harlan Country*. Lexington: University Press of Kentucky, 1985. Print.

Lynch, Timothy P. *Strike Songs of the Depression*. Jackson: University Press of Mississippi, 2001. Print.

National Committee for the Defense of Political Prisoners. *Harlan Miners Speak: A Report on Terrorism in the Kentucky Coal Fields*. New York: Harcourt, 1932. Print.

Portelli, Alessandro. *The Death of Luigi Trastulli and Other Stories: Form and Meaning in Oral History*. Albany: State University of New York Press, 1991. Print.

Scott, Shaunna L. *Two Sides to Everything: The Cultural Construction of Class Consciousness in Harlan County, Kentucky*. Albany: State University of New York Press, 1995. Print.

Taylor, Paul F. *Bloody Harlan: The United Mine Workers of America in Harlan County, Kentucky, 1931–1941*. Lanham, MD: University Press of America, 1990. Print.

Pamela Toler

UNTOLD TALES, UNSUNG HEROES
An Oral History of Detroit's African-American Community, 1918–1967
Elaine Latzman Moon

OVERVIEW

Untold Tales, Unsung Heroes: An Oral History of Detroit's African-American Community, 1918–1967 (1994), edited by historian and poet Elaine Latzman Moon, is a compilation of narratives from the people who were integral to the labor and civil rights movements in Detroit, Michigan, during the first half of the twentieth century. Moon began collecting narratives in 1989 in collaboration with the Detroit Urban League, which was founded in 1916 to help secure housing, employment, and a sense of community for the large influx of blacks migrating to Detroit from the South. The 110 interviews included in the text not only provide a comprehensive overview of the systemic discrimination experienced by African Americans but also their organized struggle to overcome adversity. Topics covered in the book include World War II, segregated and integrated housing, churches, law enforcement, and the riots of 1943 and 1967.

Published during a period of marked economic decline for Detroit, resulting in white flight and a depressed urban center, Moon's book presents a firsthand account from key activists and politicians whose stories are left out of other versions of Detroit's history. Moon allows these firsthand accounts to stand on their own; she provides only a brief introduction and short biography of each participant.

HISTORICAL AND LITERARY CONTEXT

The narratives in *Untold Tales* begin in the early twentieth century during the great migration of blacks to Detroit, a progressive city in contrast with much of the South. Many African Americans moved because they sought economic opportunities in the automobile industry or because they wanted to avoid the harsh conditions created by Jim Crow laws in the South. By 1920 the city was receiving a weekly influx of more than 1,000 black migrants. They found the North still segregated, but many men were able to secure good jobs assembling Model T Fords for $5 a day. With the onset of the Great Depression in 1929, however, many blacks were again out of work. Those who could get jobs through the Works Progress Administration were proscribed from upper-level positions. As recalled by Henry Biggs in *Untold Tales*, "I still couldn't get past the barrier that was there due to the color of my skin, not because of knowledge or of what I could do."

The austerity of the Great Depression and the racist practices of the Union of Automobile Workers gave way to the prosperity of World War II. Overwhelming demands for manpower enabled African American labor activists to successfully lobby for blacks in skilled labor positions. By 1943 racial tensions were high because of the growing integration, and a riot broke out on June 20. The three-day disturbance resulted in 34 dead and 675 wounded, according to a report that year in *The University of Chicago Law Review*. These racial tensions were sustained through the civil rights movement of the 1950s. They flared up again in 1967 during a five-day riot whose immediate cause was a police raid of a club on Twelfth Street.

Untold Tales is a typical example of an oral history that responds to the African American experience of urban areas in the twentieth century. Also in this vein, Robert Mast's book *Detroit Lives,* published the same year as Moon's text, examines issues concerning community organizing in the face of segregation by using interviews with the activists themselves.

Segregation and civil unrest in Detroit have been the focus of subsequent oral history projects, including the Detroit WestSiders, collected at the Walter P. Reuther Library at Wayne State University. In addition, *Freedom Flyers: The Tuskegee Airmen of World War II* (2012), by J. Todd Moye, takes up Moon's theme of military discrimination during World War II.

THEMES AND STYLE

The central themes of Moon's text focus on the enduring ties residents created even under adverse conditions. These ties sometimes extended across race lines, and *Untold Tales* includes a few interviews with white community builders. Famed labor organizer James Boggs notes that the struggle in Detroit was a "class struggle, which meant that I recognized that it wasn't just a black struggle. Blacks and whites were in the struggle." Similarly, activist Ernest Dillard recalls that it was a "white fellow" who tipped him off to the passage of the Michigan Equal Accommodations Act (1938), which outlawed discrimination in restaurants based on race. Noting his friend's insistence that "if the

❖ Key Facts

Time Period:
Mid-20th Century

Relevant Historical Events:
Civil rights movement; World War II; segregation; Detroit riots of 1943 and 1967

Nationality:
American

Keywords:
racism; civil rights; urbanism

Women passing a Detroit storefront in July 1967. The store displays signs reading "Soul Brother" to protect it from looters in the Detroit riots that occurred during that month. Detroit's African American history is the subject of *Untold Tales, Unsung Heroes* by Elaine Latzman Moon.
© BETTMANN/CORBIS

colored don't start going into these places, that law is just going to rust on the books," Dillard organized his community to start demanding service at every establishment in Detroit that still refused it to blacks.

As she mentions in her introduction, Moon was motivated to compile her text because "the African American community is not represented in the city's written history." Her editing strategy was to polish the interviews slightly and give them back to the participants for approval, which accounts for the discrepancies in different recollections of single events. Moon's conviction "that the reminiscence of African Americans has more validity than a history based on secondary research" led her to choose the oral history form as well as her moderate editorial style.

Moon arranges the interviews into five eras, which are characterized by the Great Migration; the Depression; World War II and the race riot of 1943; the "beginnings of civil unrest" between 1948 and 1957; and the Vietnam War, assassinations, and civil disturbances that marked the decade from 1958 to 1967. The text is notable for its candid narratives on community responses to racial tension. Regarding the riots of 1967, interviewee Ollie Foster recalls, "the word got out that they weren't going to burn any black guy's establishment because they said you were supposed to write on there 'soul brother.'" Concerning Detroit as a whole for the period between 1940 to 1970, Kermit G. Bailer relates how "blacks were having a terrible time with the administration of justice. The city had an all-white police department, all-white prosecutors, all-white judges, and all-white everything."

CRITICAL DISCUSSION

Initial reviews of *Untold Tales* praised Moon's oral history project while also taking issue with her chosen time frame and her editorial style. John Mort in *Booklist* (1994) argued that "by stopping at 1967, Moon avoids the period of Detroit's decline, occasioned by the automobile industry." In his 1994 article for the *Michigan Historical Review*, Charles F. Casey-Leininger noted that Moon's decision to rely "solely on oral history interviews to tell her story seriously undermines the book's value," arguing that "memories are notoriously unreliable." Casey-Leininger was also disoriented by the intimate nature of the oral histories and noted his "sense of listening to private conversations about people, places, and events for which he had been provided inadequate context."

Despite these issues, Casey-Leininger asserted that Moon's text furthers "our understanding of the history of the Detroit black community, and, indeed, of the place of African Americans in the twentieth-century United States." Historians and sociologists have drawn on the narratives in *Untold Tales* to examine the community strategies of both the labor movement and civil rights movement. Kevin Boyle, in "The Kiss: Racial and Gender Conflict in a 1950s Automobile Factory" (1997), employs Moon's text to demonstrate how "black auto workers supplemented individual struggles by turning to the community solidarity of independent social spaces." Boyle specifically references interviewee Shelton Tappes, who was let go from Ford Rouge in 1939 after marching in the Labor Day parade. Tappes was subsequently hired by the Local 600 Foundry Unit, where he served as chairman until his retirement in 1976.

Recent scholarship in the disciplines of history and critical race theory has utilized Moon's text to clarify perceptions of race and class tensions. Jeanne Theoharis, in her 2012 article in *OAH Magazine of History*, "The Northern Promised Land That Wasn't: Rosa Parks and the Black Freedom Struggle in Detroit," used the oral histories in *Untold Tales* to examine civil disobedience. Contrary to the myth of a "quiet seamstress tired from a day's work" that neutralizes Rosa Parks's actions, Theoharis finds that "it was Parks's agency as an activist and ordinary citizen—as well as the community-wide response following her arrest"—that sparked civil unrest in Montgomery. These community ties, Theoharis argues, similarly drove the movement in Detroit.

DETROIT AND COMMUNITY ACTIVISM

In the first half of the twentieth century, Detroit was nicknamed the Motor City, but the label morphed into the Murder City as auto factories closed and the African American, Polish, and Appalachian communities in the city became disenfranchised. The riot that began on June 23, 1967, foreshadowed what was in store for the African American community specifically; 5,000 people were arrested in the five-day period of civil unrest, most of them young black men. As Elaine Latzman Moon notes in *Untold Tales,* in 1967 "America was shaken by the upheaval of war … and Detroit marked by the violence of a civil disturbance."

Community organizations in the area, such as the Detroit Urban League and Detroit Summer, a youth empowerment program founded by activist Grace Lee Boggs, have stepped in to fill the gaps left by federal services and fleeing corporations. Both the Detroit Urban League and Detroit Summer emphasize an education that includes a focus on new media curriculum. The Detroit Urban League's programs cover a wide range of community needs, including housing, employment training programs, affordable food, and access to services. Detroit Summer, founded in 1982, harnesses the creativity of youth, providing a space for the next generation to lead the struggle for equality.

BIBLIOGRAPHY

Sources

Boyle, Kevin. "The Kiss: Racial and Gender Conflict in a 1950s Automobile Factory." *Journal of American History* 84.2 (1997): 496–523. JSTOR. Web. 26 Jan. 2013.

Casey-Leininger, Charles F. Rev. of *Untold Tales, Unsung Heroes: An Oral History of Detroit's African American Community, 1918–1967,* ed. Elaine Latzman Moon. *Michigan Historical Review* 20.2 (1994): 221–22. JSTOR. Web 23 Jan. 2013.

Moon, Elaine Latzman. *Untold Tales, Unsung Heroes: An Oral History of Detroit's African American Community, 1918–1967.* Detroit: Wayne State University Press, 1994. Print.

Mort, John. Rev. of *Untold Tales, Unsung Heroes: An Oral History of Detroit's African American Community, 1918–1967,* ed. Elaine Latzman Moon. *Booklist* 15 Apr. 1994: 1513. *Literature Resource Center.* Web. 26 Jan. 2013.

Theoharis, Jeanne. "The Northern Promised Land That Wasn't: Rosa Parks and the Black Freedom Struggle in Detroit." *OAH Magazine of History* 26.1 (2012): 23–27. Print.

Further Reading

"Elaine Latzman Moon." *Contemporary Authors Online.* Detroit: Gale, 2007. *Literature Resource Center.* Web. 26 Jan. 2013.

Georgakas, Dan, and Marvin Surkin. *Detroit: I Do Mind Dying.* Cambridge, MA: South End, 1998. Print.

Mast, Robert, ed. *Detroit Lives.* Philadelphia: Temple University Press, 1994. Print.

"The Report on the Detroit Race Riot." *University of Chicago Law Review* 10.4 (1943): 497–99. JSTOR. Web. 26 Jan. 2013.

Singer, Benjamin D. "Mass Media and Communication Processes in the Detroit Riot of 1967." *Public Opinion Quarterly* 34.2 (1970): 236–45. JSTOR. Web. 26 Jan. 2013.

Sugrue, Thomas J. *The Origins of the Urban Crisis: Race and Inequality in Postwar Detroit.* Princeton, NJ: Princeton University Press, 2005. Print.

Thompson, Heather Ann. *Whose Detroit?: Politics, Labor, and Race in a Modern City.* Ithaca, NY: Cornell University Press, 2001. Print.

Caitlin Moore

Voices from this Long Brown Land
Oral Recollections of Owens Valley Lives and Manzanar Pasts
Jane Wehrey

✣ Key Facts

Time Period:
Late 19th to Late 20th Century

Relevant Historical Events:
Settlement of Owens Valley; loss of water rights to Los Angeles; creation of Japanese internment camps in the valley

Nationality:
American

Keywords:
water rights; internment; settlement

OVERVIEW

Jane Wehrey's *Voices from this Long Brown Land: Oral Recollections of Owens Valley Lives and Manzanar Pasts* (2006) is an account of the experiences of men and women living in the Owens Valley region of California from the late nineteenth through the twentieth century. Culled from interviews collected from the 1950s through 1990s and archived in the Eastern California Museum (ECM), the narratives in *Voices* trace individual paths through a diversity of what Wehrey, in her book *Manzanar* (2008), calls "not simply a single community but many, whose pasts rest, often uneasily, one atop the other."

Voices was published in the wake of decades of scholarship on two significant features of Owens Valley's history: (1) the fight over water rights between local officials and the city of Los Angeles and (2) Manzanar's status as the site of the largest Japanese American internment camp during World War II. The latter in particular has made Manzanar a potent symbol of racial prejudice, and the area's designation as a historic site of remembrance has been a complicated issue in the valley. While well received as a more expansive view of Owens Valley than other, narrower considerations of the area, *Voices* has yet to gain a wide audience outside academia. The text is notable, however, for its accessibility and for its dissection of a significant community in the American West.

HISTORICAL AND LITERARY CONTEXT

Voices engages with Owens Valley from its hardscrabble frontier days of the late nineteenth century to its more prosperous years of ranching, agriculture, and tourism. Originally occupied by indigenous peoples including the Paiute Indian tribe, Owens Valley saw significant settlement by silver miners and homesteaders in the 1860s, at which time the U.S. government relocated the Paiute to reservations such as the one at Fort Tejon in California. Meanwhile, the city of Los Angeles, which had grown significantly by dint of the economic boom associated with the valley's mining operations, bought up large tracts of land there to gain control of the waters of the Owens River. The resulting drought in the valley caused agriculture to decline for a time, despite attempts to promote the city of Manzanar as a center for irrigated fruit farming. More infamously, Manzanar became the site of the largest internment camps during World War II, as around eleven thousand Japanese Americans were held there between 1942 and 1945. Manzanar was designated a National Historic Site in 1992, and in the decades since the camp itself closed, Owens Valley has prospered as a ski destination and as a center for farming and stock production, much of which takes place on land owned by Los Angeles.

In the mid-twentieth century historians associated with the ECM began conducting interviews with Owens Valley residents of varying backgrounds and occupations. Wehrey, who grew up in the valley, worked with the archived interviews in the early 1990s, becoming both familiar with and interested in the lives documented there, especially as many of these people were not represented in the specialized literature relating to water rights in the area and to the internment camp.

Each of these two historical occurrences has generated a substantial body of scholarship. John Walton's seminal *Western Times and Water Wars: State, Culture, and Rebellion in California* (1991) explores the history of Owens Valley and the manner in which the policies of the state of California affected not only the local economy but also spawned a culture of protest in response to the diversion of the valley's water to Los Angeles. Other notable books addressing the "water wars" include Abraham Hoffaman's *Vision or Villainy: Origins of the Owens Valley-Los Angeles Water Controversy* (1981) and Remi Nadeau's *The Water Seekers* (1950). Writings on the Manzanar camp include *Camp and Community: Manzanar and the Owens Valley* (1977), an oral history produced by the Japanese American Oral History Project at California State University, Fullerton. The text includes responses to the camp by twenty Owens Valley residents who were interviewed in 1975.

Following publication of *Voices,* Wehrey, again working with the ECM archives, published two additional works on Owens Valley. *Manzanar* contains an annotated photographic history of the community, including work by Ansel Adams. *The Owens Valley* (2013) similarly features text and photos relating to the larger region and includes works by Andrew Forbes and Burton Frasher.

Built in 1871, the American Hotel is in the ghost town of Cerro Gordo in the Owens Valley in California. In *Voices from This Long Brown Land,* Jane Wehrey argues that the Owens Valley has a storied history that is more than the region's water usage battles and its location as the Manzanar internment camp. © WITOLD SKRYPCZAK/ALAMY

THEMES AND STYLE

Wehrey focuses her book around Owens Valley and Manzanar as described by the voices of those she terms her "local companions"—men and women who, in sharing their recollections of daily life, also touch on "broad impulses in the history of the American West." The book is divided into fourteen sections, and each speaker, briefly introduced by Wehrey, discusses subjects ranging from early frontier life to the devastation of drought to the difficulties of being forced to live near the outsiders at the internment camp. Nettie Fausel, for example, describes how the frontier town of Independence was reduced to "live coals" when a fire started in the blacksmith shop and the town had "no fire service and no water service, nothing" to put out the blaze. Stub Lydston recounts the changes brought to the valley by the growth of Los Angeles and its consumption of the area's water: "The valley is nothin' like it was in the old days … no fruit, not much hay … all we've got left is the valley." Paiute Truman Buff remembers wondering about the internment camp: "Why is the government giving the Japs everything … three, four kinds of meat … [when] we couldn't buy no meat."

Voices is Wehrey's attempt to build a "more inclusive" account of the history of Owens Valley than had previously been expressed. Working from the thesis that the tellers shape the story as much as the subjects do, she attempts to achieve a certain degree of transparency and context by including the interviewer's questions in her oral history rather than simply the responses. It is a somewhat unusual move in the genre.

In the book's introduction, Wehrey describes the criteria she used in selecting her narratives as a certain "honesty of expression." This is reflected in the diversity of tone and subject matter across *Voices*' histories. Vic Taylor, a civil engineer and hydrographer, uses the technical language of engineering to describe the irrigation of the apple orchards on which he grew up. Connie Lozano, meanwhile, affectionately recounts the pans full of *bunuelos* (fried tortillas) her mother made for family and friends in the Mexican American community in Southern Inyo. Wehrey preserves the dialect and idioms of the original interviews, allowing words such as "Jap" to remain in the text despite their patent unacceptability to most contemporary readers.

CRITICAL DISCUSSION

Produced primarily for an academic audience, *Voices* was not widely reviewed, though the response it did receive was generally positive. Writing in *Oral History Review,* scholar Jacob Cohen dubs the book "well composed," lauding it as "a more inclusive, continuous, interwoven, and bottom-up account of the Owens Valley's past than any published to date." Cohen does, however, point out one of the book's "holes," such as a dearth of narratives from a Native American perspective. He notes that the lone Paiute in the text, Truman Buff, lived mostly among whites.

In their introduction to *Camp and Community: Manzanar and the Owens Valley,* Jessie Garrett and Ronald Larson assert that "what oral history demands with its emphasis on the person-to-person taped

MARY NOMURA: "THE SONGBIRD OF MANZANAR"

Following the bombing of Pearl Harbor in December 1941, President Franklin Delano Roosevelt issued U.S. Executive Order 9066, which allowed for the exclusion of persons from government-designated military zones. The order was used to relocate 110,000 Japanese Americans from coastal areas of California, Oregon, and Washington to internment camps, including the one located at Manzanar in California's Owens Valley. The camp, which occupied roughly six thousand acres, consisted of primitive living quarters, schools, shops, and other facilities and afforded its detainees little privacy or freedom.

To make their time in the camps more palatable, many of the internees took up sports or worked in the gardens. In addition, various musical groups formed to provide entertainment. At Manzanar, musicals were produced in the high school auditorium. Mary Nomura, who was sixteen when she arrived at the camp, participated in these productions and became known as "the Songbird of Manzanar." In *Voices from this Long Brown Land: Oral Recollections of Owens Valley Lives and Manzanar Pasts,* she states that these activities were a way "for people to keep their sanity going in that camp." Nomura met her future husband there, and in the 1970s he became involved in collecting artifacts for the site's museum.

interview is that the historian takes into consideration the thoughts, emotions and attitudes—in short, the perspectives—of historical actors." *Voices,* in some sense a descendent of this earlier type of oral history, has made available an account of Owens Valley that is shaped by the stories of a diversity of its inhabitants. These stories can be seen as adding to the previous histories of the area. As Garret and Larson point out regarding their own oral history, "Until the publication of this book, although there have been a number of studies dealing with the Manzanar camp—the first of the ten relocation centers administered by the War Relocation Authority—virtually nothing has been written about its impact on the surrounding Owens Valley communities." *Voices* is currently taught in university courses addressing the cultural and political history of the American West.

While *Voices* has received some critical treatment in book reviews, it has yet to generate a significant body of scholarship. Commentators have welcomed Wehrey's inclusion of narratives that speak to more than the symbolic resonance of Manzanar but may prefer the more complete source material from which Wehrey drew to make detailed studies of the Owens Valley community.

BIBLIOGRAPHY

Sources

Cohen, Jacob. Rev. of *Voices from this Long Brown Land,* by Jane Wehrey. *Oral History Review* 36.1 (2009): 98–100. Print.

Garrett, Jessie, and Ronald Larson. *Camp and Community: Manzanar and the Owens Valley.* Fullerton: California State University, Japanese American Oral History Project, 1977. *Calisphere.* Web. 15 Jan. 2013.

Wehrey, Jane. *Voices from this Long Brown Land: Oral Recollections of Owens Valley Lives and Manzanar Pasts.* New York: Palgrave Macmillan, 2006. Print.

———. *Manzanar.* Charleston, SC: Arcadia, 2008. Print.

Further Reading

Bahr, Diana Myers. *Viola Martinez, California Paiute: Living in Two Worlds.* Norman: University of Oklahoma Press, 2003. Print.

Ewan, Rebecca Fish. *A Land Between: Owens Valley, California.* Baltimore: Johns Hopkins University Press, 2000. Print.

Hoffman, Abraham. *Vision or Villainy: Origins of the Owens Valley-Los Angeles Water Controversy.* College Station: Texas A&M University Press, 1981. Print.

Inada, Lawson Fusoa. *Only What We Could Carry: The Japanese American Internment Experience.* San Francisco: California Historical Society, 2001. Print.

Knack, Martha. *Boundaries Between: The Southern Paiutes, 1775–1995.* Lincoln: University of Nebraska Press, 2004. Print.

Watson, John. *Western Times and Water Wars: State, Culture, and Rebellion in California.* Berkeley: University of California Press, 1993. Print.

Daisy Gard

CULTURE AND TRADITION

Always a People: Oral Histories of Contemporary Woodland Indians by Rita Kohn and William Lynwood Montell — 107

Black Elk Speaks: Being the Life Story of a Holy Man of the Oglala Sioux by Black Elk and John G. Neihardt — 110

Californio Voices: The Oral Memoirs of José María Amador and Lorenzo Asisara by Thomas Savage — 114

Growing Up Jewish in America by Myrna Katz Frommer and Harvey Frommer — 118

The Hispanic-American Entrepreneur: An Oral History of the American Dream by Beatrice Rodriguez Owsley — 121

In the Mansion of Confucius' Descendants: An Oral History by Kong Demao and Ke Lan — 124

Japanese War Brides in America: An Oral History by Miki Ward Crawford, Katie Kaori Hayashi, and Shizuko Suenaga — 127

Songs My Mother Sang to Me: An Oral History of Mexican American Women by Patricia Preciado Martin — 131

A Stranger's Supper: An Oral History of Centenarian Women in Montenegro by Zorka Milich — 135

Uqalurait: An Oral History of Nunavut by John Bennett and Susan Rowley — 138

When We Began, There Were Witchmen: An Oral History from Mount Kenya by Jeffrey A. Fadiman — 141

Women and Families: An Oral History, 1940–1970 by Elizabeth Roberts — 144

Women in the Chinese Enlightenment: Oral and Textual Histories by Wang Zheng — 147

Always a People
Oral Histories of Contemporary Woodland Indians
Rita Kohn, William Lynwood Montell

OVERVIEW

Always a People: Oral Histories of Contemporary Woodland Indians (1997, 2008), collected and edited by Rita Kohn and W. Lynwood Montell with oil portraits by Evelyn J. Ritter, consists of forty oral histories that provide a comprehensive overview of the diverse and changing culture of the Woodland Indians in the twentieth century. *Always a People* highlights the distinctive history and present-day society of this native people, historically less recognized and understood than other American Indian tribes. Interviews were conducted from 1992 to 1995; events recalled cover a time span from the early twentieth century to the mid-1990s. Although the oral histories reflect the individual differences of the narrators, the narratives are united by common themes and topics of concern, such as family life, tribal history and ancestry, retention of native language and traditions, issues of place and homeland, and assimilation into dominant American culture.

Always a People was directly inspired by Raymond O. White, a Miami tribal leader who was concerned about the dearth of accurate published information and literature about Woodland Indian people. In particular, White and the editors hoped that *Always a People* would carve out a place for Woodland Indian experience in literature about American Indians, as well as contribute to the continuing transmission of Woodland cultural practices and stories to future generations. As a result, much of the text explores how present-day Woodland Indians construct their identity as both tribal members and American citizens.

HISTORICAL AND LITERARY CONTEXT

Before colonization, present-day Ohio, Indiana, Illinois, Michigan, and Wisconsin were home to Woodland Indian people, which consisted of Peoria, Miami, Pokagon, Potawatomi, Delaware, Shawnee, Sauk and Fox, Chippewa, Ottawa, Winnebago, and Oneida tribes. In the seventeenth century the first wave of colonizers—primarily French traders, followed by Jesuits, who actively spread the Catholic faith among Woodland tribes—arrived in Woodland Indian territory. As American settlers moved westward in the 1800s, American Indians faced increasingly discriminatory legislation, such as 1830's Indian Removal Act and 1887's General Allotment Act (commonly known as the Dawes Act), which removed Indians from homelands, broke up tribes, and sunk many families into extreme poverty.

Despite such history, the speakers in *Always a People* remain unquestionably proud of their Indian heritage, committed to tribal affiliations, and determined to transmit their language and culture to future generations of Woodland Indians. The oral histories explore the evolution of Woodland Indians' lives throughout the twentieth century, a period that saw significant, if limited, advances for native peoples. The Indian Reorganization Act of 1934, for example, shifted some power back to Indian tribes. Further autonomy was gained in the 1970s when Congress began to support tribal courts, as well as in the 1990s when federal courts started to interpret treaties in favor of Indian rights.

Upon publication *Always a People* joined a diverse collection of oral histories, memoirs, and scholarly texts that investigated indigenous cultures after colonization. In particular, *Always a People* shares significant similarities with *Uqalurait: An Oral History of Nunavut,* edited by John Bennett and Susan Rowley; *Warlpiri Women's Voices: Our Lives Our History,* by Georgina Napangardi; and *Long Journey Home: Oral Histories of Contemporary Delaware Indians,* edited by James W. Brown and Rita Kohn. Similar to *Always a People,* these texts offer narratives about indigenous people's daily lives in the modern age. Throughout the twentieth century the oral history form—uniquely suited to capturing speakers' distinctive voices—emerged as a space for historically oppressed people to tell their own stories about topics that mattered to them.

Always a People directly inspired the creation of *Long Journey Home: Oral Histories of Contemporary Delaware Indians,* which was published in 2008 along with a paperback reissue of *Always a People.* As was true for *Always a People, Long Journey Home* is specifically concerned with native people's experiences as Indians in modern America. *Always a People* highlights the present-day culture of Woodland Indians, reminding readers that many native people continue to value their heritage, tribe, and culture, even though

❖ **Key Facts**

Time Period:
Early to Late 20th Century

Relevant Historical Events:
Indian Reorganization Act of 1934; increased Native American rights in the 20th century

Nationality:
American

Keywords:
Native Americans; civil rights; colonialism

CULTURE AND TRADITION

Drummers play a traditional song during a modern-day powwow on Shawnee homelands, Mohecan Park, Ohio. © MARILYN ANGEL WYNN/ GETTY IMAGES

they conduct "conventional" American lives in other respects. Narrator Phil Alexis (a businessman and Potawatomi tribe member) echoes this sentiment in an oral history: "Don't paint me as a 1700 or 1800 Indian. You have to paint me as who I am."

THEMES AND STYLE

The major topic discussed and analyzed in *Always a People* is the importance of retaining and transmitting Woodland Indian culture and history, with a special emphasis placed on the value of language use. Narrator Curtis Zunigha argues that language is the "foundation of our tribal identity" and that with loss of language may come "a loss of spirituality." Lucy Sadie Parks Blalock argues that preserving language is also a way of preserving history. In her narrative she advises future generations of Indians to "continue to learn their language. It is so important that [they] know about the way life used to be." Another topic addressed by most narrators is the importance of embracing and remaining proud of Woodland Indian heritage, despite historic prejudice. Rae Daugherty urges his children and grandchildren to "benefit from my pride of being who I am. Be proud, be proud." Narrator David Lee Smith exclaims, "Every one of us is proud to be an Indian. I can speak for the whole tribe."

As they write in the book's preface, Kohn and Montell produced *Always a People* to draw attention to "the vibrancy of the Woodland People as a distinctive, related, cohesive, Native American Culture." They also wanted to highlight the Woodland Indians' "tenacity to endure" as a unified community, despite centuries of targeted hostility from the U.S. government. The authors write that they chose the oral history format in order to allow Woodland Indians to "show us through their own words that their culture is alive and well." Kohn and Montell were inspired by what they describe as Raymond O. White's directions to "detail [Woodland Indians'] current accomplishments and future goals." In order to arrive at the final polished narratives, Kohn and Montell interviewed participants and afterward edited and narrativized the conversations.

Alphabetized by last name, the oral histories in *Always a People* are marked by a conversational tone, rich with the inflections and mannerisms of spoken language. The oral histories and the preface, introduction, and afterword are presented in a plainspoken language; Kohn writes that this stylistic choice was made so that the text could be "accessible to general readers who might be unfamiliar with Woodland history, culture, tradition, and geography." It is clear that the interviewers' questions (determined ahead of time with the help of Woodland Indian elders and interviewees themselves) have structured each oral history. The narratives generally begin with remembrances of childhood, early schooling, and family life and then move on to discussion of recent tribal history and cultural practices, as well as current activities of the tribe to preserve language and heritage.

CRITICAL DISCUSSION

Initial critical reception to *Always a People* was laudatory, although most reviewers noted that added information about Woodland Indian history would have been useful. Malea Powell writes in a review for *Studies in American Indian Literatures* that, while *Always a People* is not a "perfect book," it is "a piece of evidence that points to the continued existence of the Woodlands Nations and to the continued survival of the Woodlands cultures." Writing for the *Oral History Review* after the text's 2008 reprint, Barbara Sommer contends that the "editors and others associated with this project are to be commended" because the "book helps document first-person American history." On the whole reviewers celebrated *Always a People* as a much-needed addition to literature that explores the continuing presence and vitality of Woodland Indian culture.

A primary legacy of *Always a People* is its argument for Woodland Indians (and, by extension, all native peoples) to preserve their historic languages. In a review for the *Journal of American Folklore*, Marshall Joseph Becker writes that "most interesting in [*Always a People*] is the realization by the speakers that embedded within each language was the essence of true culture." Most narrators state that speaking their native language, passing it on to their children and grandchildren, and teaching it to the larger community via tribe-sponsored language classes is a necessary part of maintaining tribal cohesion and identity. Another legacy of *Always a People* is the narrators' unabashed pride in Woodland culture and history, despite centuries of directed persecution and forced assimilation programs.

While *Always a People* is often suggested as further reading in scholarly books on midwestern American Indians, the text has not received critical attention besides a handful of reviews. A general theme in every review is a mention of the text's chief limitation: the structure and exclusion of organized information (bibliography, footnotes, maps, further reading section, and so on) about Woodland Indians. In a review for the *Indiana Magazine of History*, Jennifer S. H. Brown writes, "Given that tribal identities have clearly remained important for the individuals involved, grouping them under those headings would have been helpful." Similarly Becker argues that "extracting the useful data [from the oral histories] is a task only a few will wish to pursue."

BIBLIOGRAPHY

Sources

Becker, Marshall Joseph. Rev. of *Always a People: Oral Histories of Contemporary Woodland Indians*, by Rita Kohn and W. Lynwood Montell. *Journal of American Folklore* 112.444 (1999): 222–23. JSTOR. Web. 10 Jan. 2013.

Brown, Jennifer S. H. Rev. of *Always a People: Oral Histories of Contemporary Woodland Indians*, by Rita Kohn and W. Lynwood Montell, and *Long Journey Home: Oral Histories of Contemporary Delaware Indians*, by Rita Kohn and James W. Brown. *Indiana Magazine of History* Mar. 2010: 115. JSTOR. Web. 10 Jan. 2013.

Kohn, Rita T., and W. Lynwood Montell. *Always a People: Oral Histories of Contemporary Woodland Indians.* Bloomington: Indiana University Press, 1997. Print.

WOODLAND INDIANS AND BOARDING SCHOOLS

Federally funded boarding schools became ubiquitous after the Civil War as the U.S. government attempted to implement a policy of incorporating Indians into American culture—as opposed to warring with them. The primary goal of these schools was simple: assimilate Indian youth into American culture by stripping them of family traditions, native language, and larger tribal community. Richard Henry Pratt, an influential proponent of the boarding school system, famously summarized the mission of boarding schools: "Kill the Indian in him, and save the man."

Many narrators in *Always a People* share bad memories of attending Indian boarding schools. In his oral history, Keller George says that Woodland Indians "lost all contact with family" while attending these schools. He continues, "The intention [of the schools] was to break that cycle, the tradition, learning who you were." He recalls a specific, painful memory of his boarding school days in the 1940s: "If we spoke our language we were punished by Tabasco sauce on our tongues." George notes that "all the teachers were non-Indians. The teachers called me racist names." It is even more remarkable, then, that Woodland Indians have retained so much of their culture and language in such a ruthlessly discriminatory environment.

Powell, Malea. Rev. of *Always a People: Oral Histories of Contemporary Woodland Indians*, by Rita Kohn and W. Lynwood Montell. *Studies in American Indian Literatures* 12.2 (2000): 97. JSTOR. Web. 10 Jan. 2013.

Sommer, Barbara. Rev. of *Always a People: Oral Histories of Contemporary Woodland Indians*, by Rita Kohn and W. Lynwood Montell. *Oral History Review* Summer/Fall 2009: 316. Project MUSE. Web. 10 January 2013.

Further Reading

Beatty Medina, Charles. *Contested Territories: Native Americans And Non-natives in the Lower Great Lakes, 1700–1850.* East Lansing: Michigan State University Press, 2012. Print.

Bennett, John, and Susan Diana Mary Rowley. *Uqalurait: An Oral History of Nunavut.* Montreal: McGill-Queen's University Press, 2004. Print.

Brown, James W., and Rita T. Kohn. *Long Journey Home: Oral Histories of Contemporary Delaware Indians.* Bloomington: Indiana University Press, 2008. Print.

Edmunds, R. David. *Enduring Nations: Native Americans in the Midwest.* Urbana: University of Illinois Press, 2008. Print.

Vaarzon-Morel, Petronella. *Warlpiri Women's Voices: Our Lives, Our History.* Alice Springs: Institute for Aboriginal Development, 1998. Print.

Volo, James M., and Dorothy Denneen Volo. *Family Life in Native America.* Westport, CT: Greenwood Press, 2007. Print.

Claire Skinner

BLACK ELK SPEAKS
Being the Life Story of a Holy Man of the Oglala Sioux
Black Elk, John G. Neihardt

❖ *Key Facts*

Time Period:
Late 19th to Mid-20th Century

Relevant Historical Events:
Wounded Knee; American expansion to, and population of, the West

Nationality:
American

Keywords:
Native Americans; reservations; colonialism

OVERVIEW

Compiled by poet John G. Neihardt, *Black Elk Speaks: Being the Life Story of a Holy Man of the Oglala Sioux* (1932) recounts the life of the Lakota medicine man Black Elk, from his childhood experiences in battles with the U.S. military to his participation in the massacre at Wounded Knee, when U.S. troops slaughtered 150 members of the Lakota-Sioux tribe. The book is based on a series of conversations translated by Black Elk's son Benjamin Black Elk to Neihardt. The result of a series of visions in the spirit world, the book deals with Black Elk's calling to be the savior of his people against their destruction by "white man's greed." At times playful, at other times richly steeped in Lakota mythology, the text reflects the daily life and struggles of the Lakota people.

The book was first published in 1932, a year after the interviews took place on the Pine Ridge Reservation in South Dakota. It received warm critical welcome but outside academia received little notice, and when publishers increased the price to forty-five cents a copy, the book fell out of print. In 1961 *Black Elk Speaks* was rereleased, and largely due to a cultural interest in Native American spirituality, the book found its way into mainstream media, where the *Christian Herald* called it a "current youth classic." Although the text has come under increasing critical scrutiny since its third publication in 1972, it remains poignantly powerful as a seminal Native American text.

HISTORICAL AND LITERARY CONTEXT

At the close of the Civil War, the country's attention turned toward the act of western expansion, and military focus switched to seizing control of the land. By 1886 Lakota lifestyles were changing, bringing an end to the era of nomadic ways. Mainstream western culture was infringing on Native American life, which led to a series of skirmishes with the U.S. military. Among these conflicts were the Battle of Little Big Horn, fought in 1876 between members of the Lakota and Cheyenne tribes and the army's Seventh Cavalry, and the massacre at Wounded Knee. *Black Elk Speaks* describes the massacre and the importance of the Ghost Dance. The Lakota Sioux believe that special garments, called ghost shirts, would protect them from injury during warfare. Consequently, 150 Sioux warriors were slaughtered by the Seventh Cavalry.

Between 1866 and 1891 the population of the western states quadrupled, resulting in tension over land ownership. The treaty of 1868 promised the Sioux people sole domain over the Black Hills, but when gold deposits were discovered in 1874 during an exploration of the Great Sioux Boundary led by General George Custer, the subsequent invasion of miners in violation of that treaty led to friction between the Sioux and the U.S. military. Tension climaxed in 1875 when the Indian Affairs Commissioner called for all Sioux to report to the reservation; the Lakota revolted, and the Battle of Little Big Horn ensued. From June 25 to 26 the military's death toll steadily rose, resulting in a victory for the Lakota and Cheyenne tribes. Though Black Elk was too young to participate in the fighting, he witnessed the two-day ordeal: "The valley went darker with dust and smoke, and there were only shadows and a big noise of many cries and hoofs and guns."

Black Elk Speaks draws on a tradition of Native American autobiography and storytelling that began in the late nineteenth century around the struggles and oppression of an infringing white populace. The book bears marked resemblance to *O-gi-maw-kwe Mit-I-gwa-ki* (*Queen of the Woods*; 1899) by Simon Pokagon, whose book was aimed at a white audience and intended to engender sympathy and awareness for the Potawatomi tribe. Special emphasis was given to the tribe's problems with alcohol. Although there is no direct connection between this work of fiction and *Black Elk Speaks,* the central concerns and thematic choices of the two texts are similar. As only the second novel ever written by a Native American author, *Queen of the Woods* is foundational to the entire genre.

Black Elk Speaks remains a canonical text in the study of religious thought in the United States. The text upholds a trend in American thinking that presents the natural world as a vehicle for religious and spiritual experience and positions Native Americans as the original drivers of this vehicle. *Black Elk Speaks* was the instrumental text in transforming the conception of Native American religion in the United States. Today scholars continue to examine this religion as the source for many current trends in mainstream culture, among them the interest in environmental preservation.

THEMES AND STYLE

The central themes of *Black Elk Speaks* are the religious teachings of the Lakota people, their oppression by western American culture, and being witness to a dying way of life. The text documents many religious visions that charge Black Elk with the responsibility of saving and healing his tribe; it also presents an unsparing look at the violence of Lakota warfare. In one example Black Elk is called to scalp a soldier, but his knife is so dull it requires that he first kill the soldier to complete the task. Despite the level of violence portrayed in the book, the text presents an unflinching and sympathetic look at the Sioux people's struggle to survive. The final revelation at Wounded Knee is that much more impactful: "And I can see that something else died there in the bloody mud, and was buried in the blizzard. A people's dream died there. It was a beautiful dream."

Black Elk's purpose in narrating *Black Elk Speaks* was to preserve a record of a dying culture and people. Within the Lakota tradition, autobiography was considered vain and largely not practiced; Black Elk broke with this tradition and tried to make the text about more than just himself. He viewed himself as an agent for the story of all Lakota people: "It is the story of all life that is holy and is good to tell." The book has a spiritual emphasis and uses visions as a mode of narration for the story of the tribe in general. The validity of the work as nonfiction and autobiography as well as Neihardt's intentions and methodology have been topics of much discussion. In assembling the text Neihardt admits to using artistic manipulation, some embellishment, and certainly some editing.

Black Elk Speaks opens with the reader being asked to sit down and share in smoking the peace pipe, and stylistically the book keeps to this tone of religious instruction by employing simple but reverent language. The text often relies on song and prayer: "With visible breath I am walking / A voice I am sending as I walk / In a sacred manner I am walking / With visible tracks I am walking." Occasionally the book will pass off the narrative to someone who is better equipped to tell a part of the story. In doing so it evokes the oral storytelling tradition of the Lakota people. The book also relies heavily on the interpretation of symbolic visions and dreams.

CRITICAL DISCUSSION

Though the initial reception of *Black Elk Speaks* was quite warm, it received little scholastic attention upon its 1932 publication, and the book might have been forgotten had it not been for psychologist Carl Jung, who translated the book into German, and Joseph Epes Brown's *The Sacred Pipe*, which was among the first pieces of popular scholarship about *Black Elk Speaks*. The book has had many champions over the years, including Native American activist Vine Deloria Jr., who, in his foreword to a 2000 version of the work, calls it "perhaps the only religious classic of this century" and fostered a Native American readership by urging young readers to "look into it for spiritual guidance, for sociological identity, for political insight, and for affirmation of the continuing substance of Indian tribal life." Much of the book's critical attention has come from the controversy surrounding Neihardt's manipulation of the text, particularly his treatment of Lakota religion. In an essay in *Social Text,* religious scholar William Powers sees *Black Elk Speaks* as being distinctly steeped in

Black Elk in 1936, shortly after the publication of *Black Elk Speaks*. © DENVER PUBLIC LIBRARY, WESTERN HISTORY COLLECTION/THE BRIDGEMAN ART LIBRARY

PRIMARY SOURCE

EXCERPT FROM *BLACK ELK SPEAKS*

They told Crazy Horse they would not harm him if he would go to the Soldiers' Town and have a talk with the Wasichu chief there. But they lied. They did not take him to the chief for a talk. They took him to the little prison with iron bars on the windows, for they had planned to get rid of him. And when he saw what they were doing, he turned around and took a knife out of his robe and started out against all those soldiers. Then Little Big Man, who had been his friend and was the one who told us boys that we were brave before my first fight when we attacked the wagons on War Bonnet Creek, took hold of Crazy Horse from behind and tried to get the knife away. And while they were struggling, a soldier ran a bayonet into Crazy Horse from one side at the back and he fell down and began to die. Then they picked him up and carried him into the soldier chief's office. The soldiers stood all around there and would not let anybody in and made the people go away. My father and I went back to our camp at Red Cloud Agency.

That night I heard mourning somewhere, and then there was more and more mourning, until it was all over the camp.

Crazy Horse was dead. He was brave and good and wise. He never wanted anything but to save his people, and he fought the Wasichus only when they came to kill us in our own country. He was only thirty years old. They could not kill him in battle. They had to lie to him and kill him that way.

I cried all night, and so did my father.

When it was day, Crazy Horse's father and mother brought him over to our camp in a wagon. Then they put him in a box, and I heard that they had to cut him in two because the box was not long enough. They fastened the box on a pony drag and went away alone toward the east and north. I saw the two old people going away alone

---

Christian mythology and damnation. Nevertheless, the book found a strong readership after Neihardt's 1971 appearance on *The Dick Cavett Show*.

Though *Black Elk Speaks* remains a core text for undergraduate students of religion, much discussion of the text has been mired in the controversy regarding the accuracy of Neihardt's portrayal, including his aim in creating the text. In his essay "Lakota Religion and Tragedy," Black Elk scholar Clyde Holler insists that "Neihardt was a literary artist, not an ethnologist, or comparative religionist, and *Black Elk Speaks* is not a work of scholarship." He attributes Black Elk as the creator of an "authentic Lakota Christianity." In Holler's eyes, this makes Black Elk "the greatest religious thinker yet produced by native North America." Yet many scholars feel that Black Elk's affiliation with Christianity weakens the text as a true representative of Lakota and Native American religion.

Many scholars seek to mitigate the controversial nature of *Black Elk Speaks* by placing the text in the crossroads of a Euro-American and Lakota culture. In "Black Elk Passes on the Power of the Earth," Ruth J. Heflin examines Black Elk's agency as an active contributor to the text, which, according to Heflin, mitigates Neihardt's manipulation. In particular, Heflin emphasizes Black Elk's choice to pass on his "great vision," which is considered a sacred Lakota experience. In her essay "Black Elk's Significance in American Culture," Amanda Porterfield examines Black Elk's larger influence, citing the intersection of Native American religion with mainstream culture as the necessary foundation for interest in environmental issues.

BIBLIOGRAPHY

Sources

Black Elk, and John G. Neihardt. *Black Elk Speaks: Being the Life Story of a Holy Man of the Oglala Sioux.* Albany: State University of New York Press, 2008. Print.

Deloria, Vine, Jr. Foreword. *Black Elk Speaks, Being the Life Story of a Holy Man of the Oglala Sioux.* By Black Elk and John G. Neihardt. Lincoln: University of Nebraska Press, 2000. Print.

Heflin, Ruth J. "Black Elk Passes on the Power of the Earth." *The Black Elk Reader.* Ed. Clyde Holler. Syracuse, NY: Syracuse University Press, 2000. 3–18. Print.

Holler, Clyde. "Lakota Religion and Tragedy: The Theology of Black Elk Speaks." *Journal of the American Academy of Religion* 52.1 (1984): 19–45. Print.

Porterfield, Amanda. "Black Elk's Significance in American Culture." *The Black Elk Reader.* Ed. Clyde Holler. Syracuse, NY: Syracuse University Press, 2000. 39–58. Print.

Powers, William. "When Black Elk Speaks, Everybody Listens." *Social Text* 24 (1990): 43–56. Print.

Sayre, Robert F. "Vision and Experience in Black Elk Speaks." *College English* 32 (1971): 509–35. Print.

Further Reading

Black Elk, Wallace H., and William S. Lyon. *Black Elk: The Sacred Ways of a Lakota.* San Francisco: HarperOne, 1991. Print.

with their son's body. Nobody followed them. They went all alone, and I can see them going yet. The horse that pulled the pony drag was a buckskin. Crazy Horse's father had a white-faced bay with white hind legs. His mother had a brown mare with a bay colt.

The old people never would tell where they took the body of their son. Nobody knows to-day where he lies, for the old people are dead too. Many have talked about the place, and some have said they knew where it was and would not tell, and many think it is somewhere on Bear Creek in the Badlands. I know one thing, and this is it. The old people came with the body right down Pepper Creek which is just a little way south across the hill from where we are. There were two hunters who were hunting along the creek there and they saw two old people coming with a pony drag, and when they told my father about this, they said a buckskin was pulling the drag that had a box on it; that the old man rode a white-faced bay with white hind legs and the old woman rode a brown mare with a bay colt. These hunters saw the old people coming down Pepper Creek, and later on they saw the old people again on White Horse Creek which is just a little way down Pepper Creek from where they were before. And the hunters said the box was not on the drag any more. So I think that maybe they hid the body somewhere on Pepper Creek over there because the hunters had seen them, and maybe they went back again at night and took the box away into the Badlands. But Crazy Horse might be lying over there just a little way from us right now on Pepper Creek across that hill yonder. I do not know.

It does not matter where his body lies, for it is grass; but where his spirit is, it will be good to be.

SOURCE: Black Elk and John G. Neihardt. *Black Elk Speaks: Being the Life Story of a Holy Man of the Oglala Sioux.* Albany: State University of New York Press, 2008. All rights reserved. Reproduced by permission.

Castro, Michael. Rev. of *Black Elk Speaks,* by John Neihardt. *Studies in American Indian Literatures* 4.4. (1980): 49–51. Print.

Feraca, Stephen E. *Wakinyan: Lakota Religion in the Twentieth Century.* Lincoln: University of Nebraska Press, 1998. Print.

Holler, Clyde. *Black Elk's Religion: The Sun Dance and Lakota Catholicism.* Syracuse, NY: Syracuse University Press, 1995. Print.

Petrillo, Larissa, Melda Trejo, and Lupe Trejo. *Being Lakota: Identity and Tradition on Pine Ridge Reservation.* Lincoln: University of Nebraska Press, 2007. Print.

Rice, Julian. *Black Elk's Story: Distinguishing Its Lakota Purpose.* Albuquerque: University of New Mexico Press, 1991. Print.

Steinmetz, Paul B. *Pipe, Bible, and Peyote among the Oglala Lakota: A Study in Religious Identity.* Knoxville: University of Tennessee Press, 1990. Print.

Young Bear, Severt, and R. D. Theisz. *Standing in the Light: A Lakota Way of Seeing.* Lincoln: University of Nebraska Press, 1994. Print.

Greg Luther

Californio Voices
The Oral Memoirs of José María Amador and Lorenzo Asisara
Thomas Savage

Key Facts

Time Period:
19th Century

Relevant Historical Events:
Mexican War of Independence; California Gold Rush; California's admission to the United States

Nationality:
American

Keywords:
statehood; colonialism; missionaries

OVERVIEW

Collected and transcribed by field historian Thomas Savage in 1877, *Californio Voices: The Oral Memoirs of José María Amador and Lorenzo Asisara* (2005) describes the experiences of two early Californians in Alta California. Savage, a research assistant to historian Hubert H. Bancroft, conducted the interviews under the auspices of Bancroft, who was gathering sources for his monumental research project on the history of California. The narratives of the two men—Amador, an ethnically Mexican Californio born in San Francisco, and Asisara, an indigenous American—provide diverse perspectives on the experiences of early Californians. Amador, the primary interviewee, and Asisara tell at times contrasting narratives about Northern California in the early and mid-1800s; their tales cover a wide breadth of the state's history: the Spanish and Mexican colonization, the role of the missions and missionaries, the annexation of California by the United States, and the California Gold Rush. Together the narratives reveal the frustration, bitterness, and chaos experienced by both Spanish-speaking Californios and indigenous peoples during the Anglo-American invasion of their homeland.

Published in its entirety for the first time in 2005, the oral histories contained in *Californio Voices* were initially used only as sources for Bancroft's massive *History of California* (1884) and his *California Pastoral* (1888). When scholar Gregorio Mora-Torres encountered the testimonials of Amador and Asisara while researching Mexican Californios of the Santa Clara Valley, he set about editing and translating the original source for publication. The resulting oral history, although considered what scholar Rosaura Sánchez, in *Telling Identities: The Californio Testimonios* (1995), would term a "mediated narrative" as a result of Bancroft's strict guidelines for the interviews, is an important record of the Spanish-speaking and indigenous Californian's experience of the nineteenth century in Alta California.

HISTORICAL AND LITERARY CONTEXT

The oral histories contained in *Californio Voices* describe the political and cultural climate of an area of Alta California encompassing modern-day Northern California. The narratives span the time of the area's transition from Spanish colony to Mexican territory to U.S. state. Alta California then boasted a diverse population of California Indians, European settlers, and *Californios*, which is a term used to refer to Spanish-speaking California natives of Latin American descent. The histories in the book touch on important events of the time, including the establishment of missions (Spanish Catholic outposts charged with converting Indians) and their accompanying presidios (military districts designed to protect the missions), the Mexican War of Independence (1810–21), and the California Gold Rush (1848–55).

The narratives highlight the difficulties for Californios and the area's indigenous peoples during this tumultuous period. For example, Amador discusses his experiences as a presidio soldier under both the Spanish and Mexican regimes. Presidio soldiers patrolled the San Francisco Bay region to protect settlers and missionaries against Indians and other invaders. Many of these surveys resulted in conflicts with Indians, with whom Spanish-speaking Californios had a complex relationship. Though he may have counted some Indians as friends, Amador showed little mercy to those he considered enemies: when instructed by his captain to discharge into the air during an encounter with natives, Amador chooses instead to "light the fuse of the cannon" and "hit seven Indians." Asisara, meanwhile, highlights the racial tension within the missions. He describes physical and sexual abuse by many Indians at the hands of the Spanish missionaries. Asisara writes that a Father Olbes would often order that children between the ages of eight and ten "receive twenty-five lashes at the hands of a strong man, on the buttocks or the belly."

Californio Voices is a narrative in the tradition of the Latin American *testimonio*, in which the subject dictates his or her first-person account of events to a transcriber. Famous examples of testimonios include *I, Rigoberta Ménchu* (1984)—dictated to anthropologist Elisabeth Burgos-Debray by Ménchu, an indigenous Guatemalan woman—and *Let Me Speak!*

Testimony of Domitila, a Woman of the Bolivian Mines (1978), coauthored by sociologist Moema Viezzer and the wife of a Bolivian tin miner, Domitila Barrios de Chúngara. Oral histories of early Californios that precede Mora-Torres's book include *The History of Alta California: A Memoir of Mexican California* (1996) by Antonio María Osio, Rose Marie Beebe, and Robert M. Senkewicz, and *Telling Identities* by Sánchez. In relation to these collections of testimonios, *Californio Voices* is unique in that the original Spanish appears alongside Mora-Torres's translation in an effort to best capture the voices of Amador and Asisara.

Californio Voices has been influential to oral history publication due to its dual-language format, and the text is often integral to university study of Mexican American history in California. A Mexican American studies professor at San Jose State University, Mora-Torres has garnered praise for his help in resurrecting the oral histories of Amador and Asisara, and he is often quoted as a scholarly source in news articles relating to Mexican American history.

THEMES AND STYLE

The central themes of *Californio Voices* are the strains between the area's Californio, indigenous, and Anglo-American populations, as well as an examination of the corruption and neglect of the time. Amador describes the poor conditions that presidio soldiers endured. He asserts that the only compensation he "received from the government (Spanish or Mexican) were the fourteen arrow holes that [he had] in [his] body." This does not stop Amador from completing his duties, as evidenced by his dispassionate description of how he and his company baptized their Indian prisoners so that they could be "executed from behind." Amador also describes the actions of the Anglo-Americans following the declaration of California's U.S. statehood, stating, "American troops confiscated from the ranches the horse herds, saddles, bridles, weapons, and whatever equipment was useful for war, leaving some of them lacking even the livestock that was vital for their maintenance or the weapons to defend themselves against Indians."

In the book's introduction, Mora-Torres writes that it was important to publish *Californio Voices* so that the testimonies of Amador and Asisara would no longer be "inaccessible to English language researchers and the general reader." Whereas the two oral histories had been largely regarded as historical sources (rather than primary texts), Mora-Torres identified the value of the distinctive voices of Amador and Asisara. To that end he includes the original Spanish alongside his translation. This is not to say that he hews exactly to the original text: Mora-Torres notes that he has reordered some of Amador's narrative to increase clarity, divided the manuscript into chapters, and altered Spanish accents in order to modernize the language. Such editing, however, is not uncommon in the oral history genre.

The language of *Californio Voices* is notable for Mora-Torres's decision to leave certain Spanish words in his English translation. For instance, in Amador's testimonio, Mora-Torres chooses to preserve a number of Spanish terms in the following description: "The jarabe was danced by men and women as partners—two, three, or four couples. They would make redobles or mudanzas with their feet to see who would make the most. Persons who were called cantadores would sit next to the vihuela to sing verses analogous to the dances." Maintaining original Spanish terms helps Mora-Torres capture the "unique flavor of Amador's *Memorias*."

Indigenous people of California listen to a Spanish missionary in this hand-colored woodcut of a nineteenth-century illustration. © AP IMAGES/NORTH WIND PICTURE ARCHIVES

WOMEN IN THE BANCROFT TESTIMONIOS

The testimonios featured in *Californio Voices* reveal little about the lives of women in early Alta California. Though Amador mentions feeling proud of his mother when presidio soldiers sought her tutelage in order to learn to read and earn a higher rank, he does not delve deeply into the lives of women in colonial California, despite having married three times. However, Hubert H. Bancroft's interviewers *did* interview thirteen women during their survey.

These interviewees came from a variety of social classes; some were landowners, some had worked at missions, and some were indigenous. Though the women were subject to the same limiting questions as the men, they managed to speak about their social situation and limited influence, as well as to denounce those in power. Throughout the women's testimonies—collected in Rose Marie Beebe and Robert M. Senkewicz's *Testimonios: Early California through the Eyes of Women, 1815–1848* (2006)—the women reveal their acuity regarding their social position, as when María Inocenta Pico states, "Many girls did not complete even … basic subjects because their mothers would take them out of school almost always to marry them off. The bad custom existed of marrying off very young girls, whenever men asked for their hands."

CRITICAL DISCUSSION

Early critical reception of *Californio Voices* was positive, although reviewers did make note of the sometimes harsh subject matter of the oral histories. Pedro Santoni, in his 2005 *Journal of Military History* review, indicated that the text had exposed the "physical and psychological harm" that some missionaries visited upon Indians in the region, as well as the fact that "presidio soldiers were poorly supplied, equipped, and paid." In his 2006 review in the *Americas,* Giorgio Perissinotto stated that the book should be "commended for the solid transcription, translation, and editing" and for "bringing back two *Californio* voices that needed to be heard." In general, the book was praised for its attention to detail, inclusion of the original Spanish transcription, and value as a record of the non-European experience in early California.

Californio Voices is one of the more recently published of the Bancroft Californio testimonios and as such has entered into a preexisting scholarly discussion about the extent to which these narratives have been mediated by interviewers, transcribers, editors, and translators. Sánchez asserts that "in accepting to speak through mediated narration there is an implicit concession to hegemonic policies toward Californios and contesting dominant historiography." James A. Sandos, in his 2008 *Reviews in American History* essay, examines the subaltern, or subordinate, nature of the original texts. He argues, "Californio testimonios, despite Sánchez's claims, cannot be so conveniently (mis)labeled as subaltern." Sandos claims that the difficulty of interpreting the validity of the testimonios in *Californio Voices* is partly the result of Mora-Torres's "presentation of documents without discourse," a mistake he asserts has not been made by other Bancroft testimonios translators and editors, such as Beebe and Senkewicz.

Current scholarship examines the book's depiction of mission culture and non-European social identities in early California. In a 2010 article for *Intertexts,* Deborah A. Miranda cites the oral histories contained in *Californio Voices* as evidence of the corruption of some missionaries, including Padre Real, who Asisara confirms had "problems with alcohol, gambling, and womanizing." In her 2008 article for the *Journal of Social Archaeology,* Barbara L. Voss uses one of the testimonios to examine how social identity was constructed in early California. She excerpts a section of Amador's oral history that concerns the soldier's acquisition of clothing from Fort Ross, a Russian outpost in early California. She asserts that Amador's history proves that though "clothing might at times transform poor people into gallant men … it was also used to 'fix' social identities through sumptuary laws, commodity trade, and government regulations."

BIBLIOGRAPHY

Sources

Miranda, Deborah A. "'Saying the Padre Had Grabbed Her': Rape Is the Weapon, Story Is the Cure" *Intertexts* 14.2 (2010): 93–112. *Project MUSE.* Web. 11 Jan. 2013.

Mora-Torres, Gregorio, ed. *Californio Voices: The Oral Memoirs of José María Amador and Lorenzo Asisara.* Trans. Mora-Torres. Denton: Universtiy of North Texas Press, 2005. Print.

Mora-Torres, Gregorio. Introduction. *Californio Voices: The Oral Memoirs of José María Amador and Lorenzo Asisara.* Ed. and Trans. Mora-Torres. Denton: University of North Texas Press, 2005. 1–25. Print.

Perissinotto, Giorgio. Rev. of *Californio Voices: The Oral Memoirs of José María Amador and Lorenzo Asisara,* ed. Gregorio Mora-Torres. *Americas* Jul. 2006: 162–64. *ProQuest Central.* Web. 11 Jan. 2013.

Sánchez, Rosaura. *Telling Identities: The Californio Testimonios.* Minneapolis: University of Minnesota Press, 1995. Print.

Sandos, James A. "Does the Term 'Subaltern' Apply to Colonial California? 'Testimonios' in Context." *Reviews in American History* 36 (2008): 160–70. *Project MUSE.* Web. 11 Jan. 2013.

Santoni, Pedro. Rev. of *Californio Voices: The Oral Memoirs of José María Amador and Lorenzo Asisara,* by Gregorio Mora-Torres. *Journal of Military History* Oct. 2005: 1211–12. *ProQuest Central.* Web. 11 Jan. 2013.

Voss, Barbara L. "'Poor People in Silk Shirts': Dress and Ethnogenesis in Spanish-Colonial San Francisco" *Journal of Social Archaeology* 8.3 (2008): 404–32. *SAGE Publications.* Web. 11 Jan. 2013.

Further Reading

Bancroft, Hubert Howe. *History of California, Volume I–VII.* San Francisco: History, 1890. *The Internet Archive.* Web. 11 Jan. 2013.

Beebe, Rose Marie, and Robert M. Senkewicz, trans. *Testimonios: Early California through the Eyes of Women, 1815–1848.* Berkeley: Heyday, 2006. Print.

Hackel, Steven. *Children of Coyote, Missionaries of Saint Francis: Indian-Spanish Relations in Colonial California, 1769–1850.* Chapel Hill: University of North Carolina Press, 2005. Print.

Sandos, James. *Converting California: Indian and Franciscans in the Missions.* New Haven, CT: Yale University Press, 2004. Print.

Voss, Barbara L. *The Archaeology of Ethnogenesis: Race and Sexuality in Colonial San Francisco.* Berkeley: University of California Press, 2008. Print.

Kristen Gleason

Growing Up Jewish in America

Myrna Katz Frommer, Harvey Frommer

❖ **Key Facts**

Time Period:
Early to Late 20th Century

Relevant Historical Events:
Great Depression; World War II; establishment of Israel; civil rights movement

Nationality:
American

Keywords:
Judaism; assimilation; civil rights

OVERVIEW

Collected by oral historians Myrna Katz Frommer and Harvey Frommer, *Growing Up Jewish in America* (1995) presents the memories and reflections of one hundred Jewish Americans who came of age during the twentieth century. Contributors include men and women of varying social classes, ethnicities, and religious commitments whose narratives range from humorous treatments of the eccentricities of beloved immigrant parents to serious reflections on the devastating impact of the Holocaust on Jewish American communities. Exploring challenges common to many immigrants—but particularly those felt by Jewish immigrants—the Frommers' book reflects the diverse lives of Jews in the United States.

Growing Up Jewish touches on many of the important historical events of the twentieth century, including the Great Depression, World War II, the establishment of the state of Israel, and the tumult of the civil rights movement. Appearing during a decade when memoir was the autobiographical genre of choice, the work received little critical or popular attention, although it was generally praised by critics. The book remains a valuable introduction to the lives of Jews in the United States, as well as a record of the experiences of several historically significant yet vanishing generations connected to the traditions of their countries of origin.

HISTORICAL AND LITERARY CONTEXT

Jews began immigrating to the New World in small numbers during the colonial period. Many of the earliest Jewish settlers were Sephardic, or Jews with roots in the Iberian Peninsula, whose ancestors had originally fled to South America during the Spanish Inquisition. Following the Revolutionary War, another wave of Jewish immigrants came to the United States, attracted by the political and religious freedom promised by the fledgling democracy. During the nineteenth century, poverty drove an increasing number of Yiddish-speaking Ashkenazic, or Eastern European, Jews to emigrate in search of economic opportunity. The first decade of the twentieth century witnessed yet another wave of Jewish immigrants, this time as they fled the pogroms in Russia that threatened their existence.

By the early twentieth century, Jewish Americans were settled throughout the United States, many of them clustered in New York City. The stories collected in *Growing Up Jewish* reflect their diverse circumstances: religious and secular, Orthodox and reform, urban and rural, prosperous and poor. While differing in their particulars, the voices in the text share an engagement with seminal events of the twentieth century. The Great Depression brought financial hardship to many and was also a factor in inflaming anti-Semitism against those who prospered. World War II and the Holocaust, even as experienced from the safety of the United States, devastated extended families and created for many Jewish Americans a profound sense of loss, which influenced them to work toward and celebrate the establishment of Israel in 1948. In the 1960s many Jews, victims of bigotry themselves, reported being sympathetic toward the plight of black Americans and toward the goals of the civil rights movement.

The Jewish community in the United States has a strong tradition of oral history. In the 1960s the Jewish American Committee engaged fifteen historians to supervise documentation of the stories of prominent Jewish Americans. Over the next three decades, thousands of interviews were recorded and transcribed, eventually detailing the memories of Jewish Americans from all walks of life. The resulting collection was donated to the New York Public Library, where it remains available to students and researchers. *Growing Up Jewish,* while exploring many of the same themes, focuses more narrowly on coming-of-age experiences. *It Happened in Brooklyn: An Oral History of Growing Up in the Borough in the 1940s, 1950s, and 1960s,* one of the authors' previous works (1993), shares this focus; it delves into a range of Brooklyn childhoods, including those of Jewish Americans, in the context of the mid-twentieth-century oral history of Brooklyn.

The 1990s and early 2000s witnessed the publication of a number of works that, like *Growing Up Jewish,* explore Jewishness in the United States through narratives of individual experience. Notable examples include *Nice Jewish Girls: Growing Up in America* (1996), *Matzo Balls for Breakfast and Other Memories of Growing Up Jewish* (2004), *From Baghdad to Brooklyn: Growing Up in a Jewish-Arabic Family in Midcentury America* (2005), and *A Jewish Feminine Mystique?: Jewish Women in Postwar America* (2010).

THEMES AND STYLE

Growing Up Jewish develops its central theme, the diversity of Jewish childhoods in twentieth-century America, using the voices of one hundred men and women including distinguished rabbis and community leaders, writers and entertainers, and average citizens. Divided by theme into three broad sections, the book describes regional differences in Jewish experience; the impact of major historical events on Jewish Americans; and the practice of Jewish cultural and religious traditions, distinct from and blended with, practices of the larger American society. In the book, writer Jim Sleeper describes both "want[ing] to speak the king's English" and wanting to preserve a sense of Jewishness, a recurrent subtheme in the narratives. Several generations were often involved in these struggles for identity, and different families took different approaches. Activist Phyllis Taylor recalls that "although all four grandparents were around, we were not allowed to mix languages. If unknowingly I'd say a Yiddish word, my mother would correct me." Astrophysicist Mike Lecar, on the other hand, remembers fighting to join the Boy Scouts of America rather than the Zionist Boy Scouts his father would have preferred. His father relented, but "it was a very big deal for him to get involved in what he called a *goyisha meshugas*, 'gentile craziness.'"

In their introduction to the text, the Frommers, both of whom are Jewish American, express a desire to capture "Jewish-American life in the twentieth-century with all its vibrancy, complexity and contradictions." To this end, they edited and organized individual histories by theme, with opposing viewpoints often juxtaposed back-to-back. Further, many of the individual stories suggest a certain amount of creative tension between an American identity and a Jewish identity. In the final section of the book, "Reflections," for example, writer Neil Postman reports, "Even in America, being Jewish means you're somewhat of an outsider. There's nothing more useful to someone who likes ideas … [than] to be able to step away and look at your own culture."

While the individual histories in *Growing Up Jewish* are diverse, the Frommers skew toward the now-majority Ashkenazic voices, creating a sense of commonality through the inclusion of shared Yiddish expressions, which are indexed at the back of the book. Words like *goyim* (Christian), *shul* (synagogue), and *Yiddishkeit* (Jewishness) recur throughout. In addition, memories are arranged to flow into each other so that references to an event or a place in one story are elaborated on by others who comment on the same event or place. Brooklynite Lucille Brody Noonan, for instance, describes being isolated from other Jewish kids in her Eastern Parkway neighborhood because she attended private school, and the other kids "thought [she] was exclusionary and would not play with [her]." In the next entry, Gail Eiseman Bernstein remembers "the kids who lived in beautiful apartments on Eastern Parkway" and the "temper tantrum" she threw when her father proposed sending her to school with "those snobs."

CRITICAL DISCUSSION

Growing Up Jewish received a mixed initial reception. A review in *Publishers Weekly* called the book "a rich mosaic portrait," and Helene Shrier, writing for the Women's League for Conservative Judaism's *Outlook*, praised the book as a "rich and personal view of history." A reviewer in *Kirkus*, however, wrote that "this badly organized (neither chronological, nor consistently thematic) and piecemeal conglomeration is unenlightening."

In addition to presenting the experiences of American Jews in the twentieth century, *Growing Up Jewish* also provides a link, as the Frommers write in their introduction, to "the still-recalled but soon-to-be-forgotten European past." Writing in the *Globe &*

Young Hasidic Jewish boys being lectured by their rabbi teacher, Brooklyn, New York, 1972. © NATHAN BENN/OTTOCHROME/CORBIS

JACK MARSHALL'S *FROM BAGHDAD TO BROOKLYN: GROWING UP IN A JEWISH-ARABIC FAMILY IN MIDCENTURY AMERICA*

American poet Jack Marshall, whose last name is an Anglicized version of Mash'aal, the name his father bore in his native Iraq, came of age in Brooklyn during the 1940s and 1950s. His parents, both born in Arab countries, were Sephardic Jews who immigrated to the United States seeking economic opportunity. Marshall was raised in a close-knit Syrian American community speaking Arabic, but he also attended Hebrew school, where he was the only Sephardic Jew. A self-described "American writing in English while having a mixed Jewish-Arabic heritage," Marshall describes his memoir as an attempt to "feed the twin streams (Jew, Arab) into one twined flowing river; not in order to *have* it both ways, but because of the fact of *being* both ways."

Like Myrna Katz Frommer and Harvey Frommer, Marshall attempts to describe the experience of Jewishness through a child's consciousness and as part of a multifaceted identity that also includes elements of the broader American culture. In Marshall's case, this includes his Syrian and Iraqi heritage. Combining boyhood memories with adult reflection, *From Baghdad to Brooklyn* provides another perspective on growing up Jewish in the United States.

Mail, Morton Ritts conceives of the book's reach even more broadly, arguing that "the various reminiscences illustrate an enduring theme of 4,000-year-old Jewish history—namely, the profound connection between irony and survival: The children of Israel were slaves in Egypt but Moses led them to freedom in Canaan; the Holocaust destroyed European Jewry but soon after the state of Israel was born."

The lack of scholarship on *Growing Up Jewish* may reflect critical perception of the book as broadly skimming the surface of a body of stories that are available in far greater number and detail elsewhere. Shrier, for instance, concludes her review of the text by noting, "This book is an accessible introduction to the varieties of the American Jewish experience, but the reader is reminded that there exists a rich body of reportage, fiction and memoir that delves far deeper into such stories." Given the many permutations of Jewish American life, the Frommers' decision to survey rather than specialize may make their book a less attractive subject for critical analysis.

BIBLIOGRAPHY

Sources

Frommer, Myrna Katz, and Harvey Frommer. *Growing Up Jewish in America.* New York: Harcourt, Brace, 1996. Print.

Marshall, Jack. *From Baghdad to Brooklyn: Growing Up in a Jewish-Arabic Family in Midcentury America.* Minneapolis, MN: Coffee House, 2005. Print

Rev. of *Growing Up Jewish in America,* by Myrna Katz Frommer and Harvey Frommer. *Kirkus Reviews.* Kirkus Media, 15 Sept. 1995. Web. 10 Jan. 2013.

Rev. of *Growing Up Jewish in America,* by Myrna Katz Frommer and Harvey Frommer. *Publishers Weekly.* PWxyz, 30 Sept. 1995. Web. 10 Jan. 2013.

Ritts, Morton. Rev. of *Growing Up Jewish in America,* by Myrna Katz Frommer and Harvey Frommer. *Globe & Mail* 23 Dec. 1995: C19. *Popular Magazines.* Web. 11 Jan. 2013.

Shrier, Helene. Rev. of *Growing Up Jewish in America,* by Myrna Katz Frommer and Harvey Frommer. *Women's League Outlook* 67.4 (1997): 27. *ProQuest.* Web. 11 Jan. 2013.

Further Reading

Ephross, Peter, and Martin Abramowitz. *Jewish Major Leaguers in Their Own Words: Oral Histories of 23 Players.* Jefferson, NC: McFarland, 2012. Print.

Frommer, Myrna Katz, and Harvey Frommer. *It Happened in Brooklyn: An Oral History of Growing Up in the Borough in the 1940s, 1950s, and 1960s.* New York: Harcourt Brace, 1993. Print.

Marks, Marlene Adler, ed. *Nice Jewish Girls: Growing Up in America.* New York: Plume, 1996. Print.

Moosnick, Nora Rose. *Arab and Jewish Women in Kentucky: Stories of Accommodation and Audacity.* Lexington: University Press of Kentucky, 2012. Print.

Rothchild, Sylvia. *A Special Legacy: An Oral History of Soviet Jewish Emigrés to the United States.* New York: Simon & Schuster, 1995. Print.

Daisy Gard

THE HISPANIC-AMERICAN ENTREPRENEUR
An Oral History of the American Dream
Beatrice Rodriguez Owsley

OVERVIEW

The Hispanic-American Entrepreneur: An Oral History of the American Dream (1992), by Beatrice Rodriguez Owsley, uses oral history to present the life histories of seventeen Hispanic American entrepreneurs in the New Orleans area. The narratives are part of a larger oral history project initiated by Owsley in 1985. *Hispanic-American Entrepreneur* examines the economic and social dynamics of the Hispanic immigrant community in Louisiana through the narratives of Hispanic businessmen and women in the sales, art, and food industries, as well as those of several professionals. The central themes of the text include the Hispanic entrepreneurs' shared pursuit of the "American dream" and their collective success in establishing themselves in the United States.

Published during a period of increased immigration of Latin Americans to the United States as a result of political and economic strife in the region during the 1980s, *Hispanic-American Entrepreneur* received mixed reviews from critics. While some reviewers praised the book for its new contributions to the study of Hispanic immigrant life in the United States, others criticized its lack of focus and depth as an oral history. Owsley's text contributed to a growing body of literature on U.S. immigrant entrepreneurship, as well as expanding scholarship on the experiences of Latinos in the American South.

HISTORICAL AND LITERARY CONTEXT

The narratives collected in *Hispanic-American Entrepreneur* span the second half of the twentieth century and address the diverse reasons for the individuals' immigration to the United States, as well as the challenges they faced upon arriving there. In broad terms, this was a period of political unrest and despotism in much of Latin America, especially Central America and the Hispanic Caribbean, where numerous countries endured a series of civil wars and dictatorships. Many of the immigrants, including some interviewed for Owsley's book, fled their home countries out of fear of political persecution, as well as a desire for better economic opportunities. Hundreds of thousands of Latin Americans arrived in the United States as undocumented persons, but the majority of the individuals in the oral histories were affluent enough to obtain legal immigration documents.

The Immigration Reform and Control Act of 1986 dramatically shifted U.S. immigration legislation, granting legal status to undocumented residents who entered the country prior to 1982 and had lived in the country continuously since their arrival. Though the law did not directly affect many of the entrepreneurs interviewed for Owsley's book, it did allow a large Hispanic population to legally join the workforce and travel more freely across state lines in search of better economic opportunities without fear of deportation. As a result, the Hispanic population in the South, specifically in New Orleans, grew substantially in the 1980s and early 1990s. *Hispanic-American Entrepreneur* addresses this period of burgeoning Hispanic entrepreneurship in New Orleans.

Owsley's text followed a growing body of work on Hispanic American culture and tradition based on the stories of individual community members, such as Patricia Preciado Martin's *Images and Conversations: Mexican Americans Recall a Southwestern Past* (1983). Martin's work records narratives of Hispanic immigrants and their struggles with dominant American culture, just as Owsley's *Hispanic-American Entrepreneur* does. Owsley's book also contributes to previous scholarship that addresses the cultural diversity of American entrepreneurs, including *Entrepreneurs in Cultural Context,* edited by Sidney Greenfield et al. (1979).

Since the publication of *Hispanic-American Entrepreneur,* many scholars in Hispanic American studies have collected the oral histories of a wide cross-section of the Latino community in the United States. They collect the life stories of immigrants of Hispanic origin, documenting their community's culture and traditions in much the same way as Owsley does in *Hispanic-American Entrepreneur.* Among these is *Californio Voices: The Oral Memoirs of José María Amador and Lorenzo Asisara* (2005) by Thomas Savage. In addition, Rosaura Sanchez's *Telling Identities: The Californio Testimonios* (1995) recreates the life stories of early Mexican residents of California in a manner similar to Owsley's documentation of the culture and

✣ **Key Facts**

Time Period:
Mid- to Late 20th Century

Relevant Historical Events:
Increased immigration to the United States from Latin America; Immigration Reform and Control Act

Nationality:
American

Keywords:
immigration; New Orleans; entrepreneurism

Downtown New Orleans at twilight. In her book *The Hispanic-American Entrepreneur*, Beatrice Rodriguez Owsley interviews seventeen Hispanic-American entrepreneurs from New Orleans. © ANDRIA PATINO/CORBIS

tradition of the Hispanic American community—the difference being that the subjects of Sanchez's narratives have been long deceased.

THEMES AND STYLE

The central themes of *Hispanic-American Entrepreneur* are the successes and challenges of these entrepreneurs in their goal of achieving the so-called American dream of economic prosperity and social mobility. As Owsley herself characterizes the narratives in her preface, each story "underscores entrepreneurial traits of foresight, tenacity, and individualism." Each individual's experiences echo those of the others in overcoming multiple odds and challenges to climb the social ladder and become established and respected leaders in their communities. Cuban American restaurateur Nancy Cortizas recalls having "difficulty speaking in English" but explains how she "learned [her] job quickly and in time handled responsible positions."

Owsley's motivation was to explore the economic and social circumstances of prominent individuals in the New Orleans Hispanic immigrant community. In the book's preface, she notes that she "chose the methodology of oral history, since prior ethnic studies using this approach had yielded rich testimony." Owsley wrote the oral histories based on the entrepreneurs' recorded interviews, interpreting and condensing their experiences in order to formulate brief narratives. The seventeen narratives presented in *Hispanic-American Entrepreneur* are selected from a total of 105 oral histories collected by Owsley during a project at the University of New Orleans in 1985.

Working from interviews that were conducted mostly in English, Owsley employs a formal, reserved language in her reconstruction of the entrepreneurs' stories. In this way she distances herself as the author of the narratives, which also takes away from the individual personalities of the entrepreneurs. Owsley writes in Jose "Pepe" Vasquez's personal history, "My other commercial pursuits started in response to needs expressed by family members." Instead of referring to his family in more personal terms, Owsley elects to use words that distance Vasquez's story from the emotions of his loved ones. The book is divided into six parts: a preface discussing methodology, an introduction, the oral histories, a conclusion, appendices with the questionnaire used for Owsley's interviews, and selected newspaper clippings on several of the entrepreneurs. The narratives themselves are organized thematically into four sections related to each individual's skills and/or interests: "The Marketplace," "Art in a Carnival Setting," "Professionals in the Gateway to America," and "A Creole Institution—Food."

CRITICAL DISCUSSION

Many critics responded to *Hispanic-American Entrepreneur* with certain reservations related to the detail and ethnographic insight provided in the text. In a 1993 review in the *Oral History Review,* Carolyn Mountain states that Owsley's book "lacks the focus required of good oral history," while Marcial Ocasio-Melendez opines in the *Hispanic American Historical Review* that the life stories presented are "not representative of the typical Latino immigrant." Nevertheless, certain critics, such as Lucy Cohen in a 1994 article in the *Journal of American History,* found value in the book's contribution to Hispanic American history. Cohen notes that "the narratives vividly highlight memories of long-standing connections that the peoples of Louisiana have had with Latin America."

While *Hispanic-American Entrepreneur* received initial scholarly attention within a limited academic sphere, there is little extant critical analysis of the book. The few sources that cite the text reference it in relation to a larger scholarly discourse on entrepreneurship. A 2007 *Urban Anthropology* article notes that "the literature on ethnic and immigrant entrepreneurship is vast. … From early collections on entrepreneurs in their cultural contexts to oral histories of Hispanic-American entrepreneurs in New Orleans (Owsley 1992) … anthropologists have developed a keen interest in the economic activities of populations desiring to retain their connections to their homelands." A professional archivist, Owsley has gone on to facilitate additional oral history projects at the University of New Orleans as well as the Amistad Research Center in New Orleans.

The little available scholarship on *Hispanic-American Entrepreneur* focuses on the subject of Latino businesspeople in Louisiana and the South. In *Racing the Storm: Racial Implications and Lessons Learned from Hurricane Katrina* (2007), Hillary Potter provides a historical background on minority groups in New Orleans, listing Owsley's book as part of the "limited published scholarship on Latinos in New Orleans" and noting that its oral histories "demonstrate that many Latino entrepreneurs … had arrived in New Orleans through social and commercial networks that resulted from trade between New Orleans and Latin America."

Mountain, in turn, questions the value of Owsley's approach to oral history, asking, "Where is the 'rich testimony' of struggle that the author promises, and where do the interviewees reflect on the political and social realities of immigration to New Orleans?"

BIBLIOGRAPHY

Sources

Cohen, Lucy. Rev. of *The Hispanic-American Entrepreneur: An Oral History of the American Dream,* by Beatrice Rodriguez Owsley. *Journal of American History* 81.1 (1994): 349. Print.

Kemper, R., et al. "From Undocumented Camionetas (Mini-Vans) to Federally Regulated Motor Carriers: Hispanic Transportation in Dallas, Texas, and Beyond." *Urban Anthropology and Studies of Cultural Systems and World Economic Development* 36.4 (2007): 381–423. Print.

Mountain, Carolyn. Rev. of *The Hispanic-American Entrepreneur: An Oral History of the American Dream,* by Beatrice Rodriguez Owsley. *Oral History Review* 21.2 (1993): 132–34. Print.

Ocasio-Melendez, Marcial. Rev. of *The Hispanic-American Entrepreneur: An Oral History of the American Dream,* by Beatrice Rodriguez Owsley. *Hispanic American Historical Review* 74.4 (1994): 758–60. Print.

Owsley, Beatriz Rodriguez. *The Hispanic-American Entrepreneur: An Oral History of the American Dream.* New York: Twayne, 1992. Print.

Potter, Hillary. *Racing the Storm: Racial Implications and Lessons Learned from Hurricane Katrina.* Lanham, MD: Lexington, 2007. Print.

Smith, Heather, and Owen Furuseth. *Latinos in the New South: Transformations of Place.* Burlington, UK: Ashgate, 2006. Print.

Further Reading

Bhachu, Parminder, and Ivan Light, eds. "Immigration and Entrepreneurship: Culture, Capital, and Ethnic Networks." *Journal of Economic Literature.* 32.2 (1994): 797. Print.

Brettell, Caroline, and Kristoffer Alstatt. "The Agency of Immigrant Entrepreneurs." *Journal of Anthropological Research* 93.3 (2007): 383–97. Print.

A HISTORY OF LATINOS IN THE SOUTH

Prior to the 1990s most scholars of Latino culture and history regarded the American South as "part of the Hispanic migration frontier—a place with incipient and uncertain settlement," as Heather Smith and Owen Furuseth explain in *Latinos in the New South: Transformations of Place* (2006). This absence of a large Latino presence in the South prior to 1990 was largely due to a lack of low-wage jobs, its geographical location, and migrants' own decisions not to settle there. However, in the past two decades, the history of Latinos in the South has changed substantially, transitioning into an experience of settlement and permanence.

In 1990 Hispanics made up only 3.8 percent of the total population in the South. In the band of mid-South states that stretches from Arkansas and Louisiana to Kentucky, Hispanics were under 1 percent of the population. By 2000 there had been a 104 percent increase in the Hispanic population in the southern states, with 1.15 million Hispanics residing in the ten states other than Florida (which has historically had a large Hispanic population). A primary characteristic of the Latino population in the South is a preference for settling in large metropolitan cities and in suburban and non-Latino neighborhoods, which defies the notion of immigrant ethnic clustering.

Kloosterman, Robert, and Jan Rath, eds. *Immigrant Entrepreneurs: Venturing Abroad in the Age of Globalization.* New York: Berg, 2003. Print.

Muñiz, Brenda. "In the Eye of the Storm: How the Government and Private Response to Hurricane Katrina Failed Latinos." *National Council of La Raza* 2006. Web. 15 Jan. 2013.

Robles, Barbara. "Latino Self-Employment and Entrepreneurship in the United States: An Overview of the Literature and Data Sources." *The Annals of the American Academy of Political and Social Science* 613.1 (2007): 18–31. Print.

Katrina White

IN THE MANSION OF CONFUCIUS' DESCENDANTS

An Oral History

Kong Demao, Ke Lan

Key Facts

Time Period:
Early to Late 20th Century

Relevant Historical Events:
End of dynastic rule in China; founding of the Republic of China; founding of the People's Republic of China

Nationality:
Chinese

Keywords:
Confucianism; aristocracy; revolution

OVERVIEW

First published in 1982, *In the Mansion of Confucius' Descendants: An Oral History* presents the childhood recollections of Kong Demao, who grew up in Qufu, China, within the legendary Kong mansion, the home of the lineal descendants of Chinese philosopher Confucius. Kong, who was born in 1917, chronicles the events of her own childhood—her brother, Kong Decheng (1920–2008), was the seventy-seventh heir of Confucius's line; she also details the mansion's flagging fortunes (economic and otherwise) during the social and ideological unrest of the early twentieth century. The book's narrative was recounted by Kong to her daughter Ke Lan, who prepared the manuscript for its initial Chinese publication. The text was later translated into English by Rosemary Roberts and published in 1984. It was reissued in English under the title *The House of Confucius* in 1988. Kong relates the history and immense cultural and political cachet of the mansion, as well as discusses its complex infrastructure and the ceremonial rites and rituals that shaped life on its grounds. The book as a whole serves as an intimate portrait of intense ritualism, as practiced by one of China's most prominent aristocratic families.

In the Mansion of Confucius' Descendants was published during a rebirth of interest in Confucianism and traditional Chinese belief systems, which had been suppressed during the Maoist Cultural Revolution (1966–76). (Kong herself was imprisoned in a labor camp during the revolution.) The work was received with considerable enthusiasm both in China and elsewhere, despite complaints about the book's lack of scholarly rigor. It inaugurated a great deal of historical fascination with the Kong mansion and its inhabitants, and it continues to attract interest as a unique personal reminiscence of important events in the mansion's history.

HISTORICAL AND LITERARY CONTEXT

Kong's narrative is strongly informed by the national prominence afforded to Confucius's descendants prior to the twentieth century. The Kong family had enjoyed political recognition ever since Confucius's teachings—which emphasize propriety, humanism, and veneration of one's elders—were designated as China's official ideology during the Han dynasty (206 BCE–220 CE). The sage's male heir even enjoyed a title of nobility that was eventually raised to the level of a dukedom. For centuries this dukedom had remarkable stability in the face of numerous shifts in political power. Kong notes in the book, "Imperial families retained their noble status only until the fall of a dynasty, but for the last two thousand years every generation of the family of Confucius had been high ranking aristocrats."

Kong's own life coincided with a precipitous decline in the Kong mansion's fortunes. The end of dynastic rule in 1911, followed by the founding of the Republic of China the next year, brought an end to the imperial stipends and gifts the mansion had previously relied upon. This loss, coupled with various difficulties in collecting rent, plunged the household into financial distress. The 1910s and 1920s also saw increased activism by anti-Confucian movements, as Confucianism had long been united with the ruling class. Kong explains, "Two thousand years of feudal rule had brought about changes in Confucius' doctrine, altering it as was necessary to maintain the power of the ruling class. Confucius had become a concrete symbol of rule by the feudal ethical code."

In the Mansion of Confucius' Descendants falls into the Chinese tradition of oral history. Following the founding of the People's Republic of China in 1949, a large number of oral history projects—often allied with the revolutionary ideals of the new communist regime—came into being, though they were eventually suspended with the advent of the Cultural Revolution. Kong's book is also a modern manifestation of the Kong family historiography and genealogy, which had been written over centuries and played a central role in shaping the family legacy. Indeed, many of Kong's recollections draw from this material.

The publication of Kong's book coincided with a revival of oral history in China in the years following the Cultural Revolution. The Kong family had suffered during the revolution, and this period of animosity saw the family mansion—along with the nearby Confucian temple and cemetery—ransacked by government forces. Eventually the family was seen by officials as largely rehabilitated, and many Chinese books about its history then appeared. Kong's narrative precipitated these works. Relatively few of them have been translated into English, an exception being Meng Jixin's *The First Household under Heaven* (1990). Kong's book, meanwhile, is still frequently cited in scholarly works on Chinese history.

THEMES AND STYLE

A major theme of *In the Mansion of Confucius' Descendants* is the pervasive influence of rigid ceremony and ritualism on life within the Kong mansion. Much of the text consists of lengthy descriptions of various rites and customs practiced within the household, including servant regulations, sacrificial rituals, funeral ceremonies, inner divisions within the mansion, and strict rules governing interpersonal interactions. Though Kong does not condemn Confucianism in itself, she does attest to the inertia and frequent dreariness of the complex ceremonialism of life in the Kong mansion, noting, "Generation after generation had lived here following the set routine, rarely implementing any changes. Life in the Inner Apartments was virtually cut off from the outside world, ultra-conservative and endlessly monotonous." She likewise recalls the impact of this atmosphere on her schooling: "The teacher rarely explained the texts we read. Since we were only required to learn them by heart—not only in the correct sentence order, but backwards as well—we had no idea of the meaning of what we recited."

Kong's narrative was produced to provide a personal account of life within the Kong mansion, giving insight into a hermetic, aristocratic social order that few had experienced and that had essentially disappeared in the wake of Chairman Mao Zedong and the Cultural Revolution. A publisher's note at the beginning of the text proclaims that Kong's "recollections here, as told to and collated by her daughter Ke Lan, grant an enticing glimpse into the private lives and affairs of an ancient and vanished elite." The specifics of the transcription process are (to the displeasure of some scholars) unclear beyond that mention. It is apparent from the text, however, that some of Kong's anecdotes are derived not from firsthand experience but from oral accounts Kong heard as a child from family members and servants, making the book a more multifaceted oral history than its single narrator may suggest.

The language of *In the Mansion of Confucius' Descendants,* as translated by Roberts, is characterized by a relatively detached and affectless tone. Much of Kong's narrative consists of a fairly dry, straightforward enumeration of facts pertaining to life in the mansion. More dramatic events carrying obvious emotional weight for Kong are discussed with only a slight increase in rhetorical intensity, and the book generally lacks the sense of emotional spontaneity that sometimes characterizes oral history. Kong's language is perhaps most heated when she discusses familial and domestic strife. For example, she says of her stepmother: "When I think of how she tormented and mistreated my real mother and finally drove her to her death, I can never bring myself to call her mother, so we shall simply refer to her here as Madame Tao." However, even Kong's harsh declamations of Madame Tao—whom the text depicts as a conniving, sadistic murderer—are more controlled than impassioned in their phrasing.

CRITICAL DISCUSSION

In the Mansion of Confucius' Descendants received mixed but generally positive reviews, with critics agreeing that its various shortcomings were outweighed by its status as a unique historical document. William W. Moss, writing for the *Oral History Review,* laments, "It is clearly a popular item for the tourist trade rather than a serious scholarly inquiry into a past that has been overtaken by revolution and plowed under in the remaking of Chinese society."

The Chinese philosopher Confucius, depicted here, was an ancestor of author Kong Demao (Te-Mao), who lived in the Confucius Mansion as a child. © PRIVATE COLLECTION/PETER NEWARK PICTURES/THE BRIDGEMAN ART LIBRARY

CULTURE AND TRADITION

ANTI-CONFUCIANISM IN PRE-MAO CHINA

Although Confucianism had enjoyed cultural and philosophical dominance in China for thousands of years, public criticism of Confucian doctrines and strictures became significantly more common with the end of Chinese imperial government and the founding of the Republic of China in 1912. Much anti-Confucian rhetoric of the time was associated with what came to be referred to as the New Culture Movement, which aligned itself against the cultural institutions of traditional Chinese culture—seen as excessively classicist, feudal, patriarchal, and resistant to change—in favor of egalitarianism, progressivism, openness to Western culture, and a general interest in intellectual and societal experimentation.

The New Culture Movement overlapped with—and is often conflated with—the populist, nationalistic May Fourth Movement, a more explicitly political movement that developed out of student protests in Beijing on May 4, 1919, over the Chinese response to the Treaty of Versailles. Neither of these movements, in themselves, had a significant impact on the structure of Chinese society, but they served as important precursors to the ideological background of the Chinese Civil War (1927–50). This war culminated in the establishment of the People's Republic of China in 1949, which (though largely outside the purview of Kong's narrative) made anti-Confucianism a matter of official policy.

Ultimately, however, Moss declares that "the book remains fascinating and is a useful contribution to history and to international understanding." Lillian Craig Harris, reviewing the retitled 1988 edition in the *Pacific Review,* similarly observes, "This is not a scholarly work ... and the story remains half-formed" but also notes that "in describing an antique world for us, the author has contributed uniquely to the historical record."

Kong's narrative contributes to a renewal of public interest in Confucianism in the decades since its governmental suppression. Since her release from a labor camp in 1979, Kong has served as a member of various public organizations, and in her old age she has, on the basis of her family background, been a sort of international ambassador of Confucian thought. Likewise, the book's publication in English (and other languages) has added to the increasing dissemination of Chinese culture in recent decades; Stephen Thompson and Paul Thompson, surveying Chinese oral history in 1987, take a dim view of aspects of this globalism, worrying that the book's English edition foretells a possibility "that the local men and women who once raised consciousness by telling their stories may now find their memories served up as curiosities for western tourists."

English-language scholarship discussing *In the Mansion of Confucius' Descendants* in detail is relatively uncommon. References to the work in scholarly writing often take the form of informational citations or brief, cursory descriptions rather than comprehensive analyses, with the book rarely becoming a particularly important part of the discussion. An exception is Christopher S. Agnew's 2009 *Journal of Family History* article, which incorporates Kong's narrative into an examination of the social and political ramifications of the Kong family historiography. Agnew asserts that the book "was the first in a wave of works on the Kong family that have been a part of the revival and reorganization of Kong kinship ties in an age of globalized capital."

BIBLIOGRAPHY

Sources

Agnew, Christopher S. "Memory and Power in Qufu: Inscribing the Past of Confucius' Descendants." *Journal of Family History* 34.4 (2009): 327–43. *SAGE Online Journals.* Web. 9 Jan. 2013.

Harris, Lillian Craig. Rev. of *The House of Confucius,* by Kong Demao and Ke Lan. *Pacific Review* 2.3 (1989): 273–74. *Taylor & Francis Online.* Web. 9 Jan. 2013.

Kong, Demao, and Ke Lan. *In the Mansion of Confucius' Descendants: An Oral History.* Trans. Rosemary Roberts. Beijing: New World, 1984. Print.

Moss, William W. Rev. of *In the Mansion of Confucius' Descendants: An Oral History,* by Kong Demao and Ke Lan. *Oral History Review* 13 (1985): 162–64. *JSTOR.* Web. 9 Jan. 2013.

Thompson, Stephen, and Paul Thompson. "Oral History in China." *Oral History* 15.1 (1987): 17–21. *JSTOR.* Web. 9 Jan. 2013.

Further Reading

Chow, Kai-wing. *The Rise of Confucian Ritualism in Late Imperial China: Ethics, Classics, and Lineage Discourse.* Stanford, CA: Stanford University Press, 1994. Print.

Hsü, Immanuel C. Y. *The Rise of Modern China.* Oxford: Oxford University Press, 2000. Print.

Jing, Jun. *The Temple of Memories: History, Power, and Morality in a Chinese Village.* Stanford, CA: Stanford University Press, 1996. Print.

Meng, Jixin. *The First Household under Heaven.* Trans. Sheng Wen and Wang Yong. Jinan: Shandong Friendship, 1993. Print.

Nylan, Michael, and Thomas Wilson. *Lives of Confucius: Civilization's Greatest Sage through the Ages.* New York: Doubleday, 2010. Print.

Wilson, Thomas A., ed. *On Sacred Grounds: Culture, Society, Politics, and the Formation of the Cult of Confucius.* Cambridge, MA: Harvard University Press, 2002. Print.

Zhang, Xinxin, and Sang Ye. *Chinese Lives: An Oral History of Contemporary China.* Ed. W. J. F. Jenner and Delia Davin. New York: Pantheon, 1987. Print.

James Overholtzer

Japanese War Brides in America
An Oral History
Miki Ward Crawford, Katie Kaori Hayashi, Shizuko Suenaga

OVERVIEW
Japanese War Brides in America: An Oral History (2010), compiled and edited by Miki Ward Crawford, Katie Kaori Hayashi, and Shizuko Suenaga, presents the stories of Japanese women who met and married American servicemen during the post–World War II occupation of Japan. The authors, two Japanese-born women and one American-born daughter of a Japanese war bride, draw out the stories of nineteen women who immigrated to the United States during the late 1940s and 1950s; these interviewees faced bureaucratic difficulties, social censure on both sides of the Pacific, and the challenges of raising families while mastering a new language and culture. In distinct but overlapping narratives, the war brides remember both the triumphs and struggles in their adopted homes.

Collected and published nearly half a century after these women began arriving on U.S. shores, *Japanese War Brides* is the first detailed account of the unique challenges these women confronted not only as immigrant wives and mothers but also, in some sense, as female representatives of a despised military enemy. Well received by its academic audience, this book is notable as an exploration of family, ethnicity, and identity issues in the twentieth-century United States, and it stands as an important source of information about an often neglected population of Japanese Americans.

HISTORICAL AND LITERARY CONTEXT
The economic and social demands of a wartime economy brought Japanese women, traditionally consigned to the domestic sphere, out into the world and into contact with American GIs. During World War II approximately four million Japanese women went to work in support of the war effort, typically holding positions in factories and offices. This trend continued during the postwar occupation from 1945 to 1952, and many women particularly sought employment with the U.S. military, which offered higher wages than most other employers. With American soldiers facing long deployments and Japanese women substantially outnumbering Japanese men, many of whom were lost during the war, a significant number of relationships developed. While these interracial relationships were generally condemned by Japanese society and legal marriages were made intentionally difficult to procure, a sizable number of couples did wed and eventually settled in the United States.

The narratives in *Japanese War Brides* reflect the experiences of some of the roughly fifty thousand Japanese women who arrived in the United States between 1947 and 1965. The earliest of these women were typically admitted through special individual congressional bills that overrode the Immigration Exclusion Act of 1924, which precluded Asians from entering the country. Attaining admission by this means was a lengthy process involving extensive lobbying by the petitioning serviceman and his family after he had returned to the United States without his Japanese wife. While the passage of Public Law 717 in 1950 and the Immigration and Nationality Act of 1952 made it much easier for war brides and their foreign-born children to enter the United States, many still faced the challenges of assimilation as well as the prejudice that was evident in the U.S. government's internment of thousands of Japanese Americans after the bombing of Pearl Harbor. These racist attitudes began to decline in the 1950s, whitewashed by what Carol Chung Simpson characterizes in *An Absent Presence* (2001) as images of war brides as "gracious and hard-working middle-class housewi[ves]." This characterization, while better than conceptions of war brides as former prostitutes or bar girls, continued to leave out important aspects of their experience.

Japanese War Brides is part of a small body of literature that offers a glimpse of Japanese war brides and the particular challenges these women faced as immigrants. An early work that provides useful comparative data, Elfreida Shukert and Barbara Scibetta's *War Brides of World War II* (1988), documents the experiences of a cross section of women from around the world who became war brides under varying circumstances. Several biographies have provided a more in-depth look at Japanese war brides and their families. Keiki Tamura's *Michi's Memories: The Story of a Japanese War Bride* (2001) recounts the life of a Japanese woman who married and immigrated to Australia, attempting to fit into that country's society as she and her husband raised seven children. Michael Forrester, a former U.S. airman, pays tribute to his own wife in *Tsuchino: My*

❖ **Key Facts**

Time Period:
Mid- to Late 20th Century

Relevant Historical Events:
World War II; interaction between Japanese women and U.S. soldiers in Japan; passage of the Immigration and Nationality Act

Nationality:
American

Keywords:
immigration; prejudice; ethnicity

CULTURE AND TRADITION

Japanese War Brides in America: An Oral History offers the firsthand stories of women who came to the United States after marrying American soldiers. Depicted here is the last couple to be married under a law that allowed marriages between soldiers and Japanese women, in 1951. © TAKAMASA INAMURA/CORBIS

Japanese War Bride (2005). Forrester attributes much of his postwar career success to his wife and provides not only a portrait of one war bride but also an example of the contributions made by many.

Sarah Kovner's *Occupying Power: Sex Workers and Servicemen in Postwar Japan* (2012), published two years after *Japanese War Brides,* provides an interesting counterpoint to the latter work as it documents relationships arising from the same milieu and subject to some of the same forces that led to marriages between Japanese women and American GIs. Indeed, many of the women interviewed for *Japanese War Brides* reported fighting against the stereotypical notion that any Japanese woman who married a GI had previously been a sex worker.

THEMES AND STYLE

Japanese War Brides focuses on the strength of character exhibited by each of the nineteen interviewed women as they faced obstacles not only in their unconventional marriages but also in their new lives in a country so unlike Japan. Divided into three sections, each representing one of the authors and comprising roughly six narratives each, the text documents the Japanese war bride experience from a variety of perspectives. The narrative of Fumiko Ward, mother of author Miki Ward Crawford, includes an account of Fumiko's early loneliness in the United States yet concludes with an affirmation of her decision to follow her husband to his home country: "So many nice things I have like children and friends. ... A lot of things trouble, usually forget them." Ayako Stevens, who relates the bombing of Hiroshima in harrowing detail, received family support for her marriage to a marine, despite the association between the U.S. military and the atomic bomb. The military, however, in effect still viewing all Japanese people as war enemies, resisted the marriage. The marine corps chaplain charged with screening the couple told Ayako, "You're Japanese and you take a bath, hot bath every day. He's from Pennsylvania, he's a farm boy. They only take a bath once a week." Kimiko Dardis's path to the United States involved difficulties learning English, which she eventually overcame. She comments that initially, "I didn't say what I wanted to say because I imagined others might laugh at me if my pronunciation was bad." After years "surrounded by all Americans," she continues, "now I do say what I want to say!"

In her author biography, Crawford, who originated the oral history project, characterizes her interest in these stories as an outgrowth of her interest in the Veterans History Project, an attempt by the Library of Congress's Institute for Folklife to collect and store the stories of U.S. military veterans. The impetus for that project, preserving the war experiences of a dying generation, also inspired Crawford to record the experiences of women like her mother, at least in part for the sake of their thousands of descendants. As Ann Marie Davis points out in her 2012 review of the book for *Oral History Review,* each of the book's three sections, while demonstrating continuity in overall themes and tone, reflect the backgrounds and approaches of the book's individual authors. Hayashi and Suenaga, for example, both of whom were born in Japan, elicited more details about the women's lives in Japan and fewer details about the problems of assimilation faced in the United States.

In the interest of creating a cohesive book from interviews conducted in both English and Japanese (which was then translated into English), the authors shaped the women's recollections into third-person narratives. They included direct quotes to retain each woman's unique voice while eliminating glaring differences in language use, particularly between those women who were interviewed in their native Japanese and those interviewed in English, a second language.

CRITICAL DISCUSSION

Although it has yet to garner mainstream attention in the United States, *Japanese War Brides* was positively reviewed by its small academic audience, particularly as it filled a gap in Japanese American literature, which has been dominated by work on the internment. Davis, who calls *Japanese War Brides* "a compelling new monograph," praises the authors for "bring[ing] a high degree of care and professionalism to their

PRIMARY SOURCE

EXCERPT FROM *JAPANESE WAR BRIDES IN AMERICA*

MEETING AND MARRIAGE TO LOUIS WARD

Fumi met Louis Ward, a corporal in the army, at the PX through a friend, Takeiko, and her boyfriend, Mansu-san (Mann), who was from California. Louis was the opposite of her—blond hair, blue eyes, and tall. Their first date was at a dance hall where most of the music was swing, which was popular at that time in the United States. Fumi begins to sing "Sentimental Journey" during this narrative to illustrate the type of music that she remembers. Going with another couple enabled the men and women to converse in their own languages. Conversation between the couple was a mixture of words and motions. They didn't dance on that first date, but just watched others and enjoyed the music. Fumi smiles, saying she was able to watch and learn the dance steps quickly. This was during the summer of 1946, when not many GIs and Japanese women socialized. The dance hall was a safe place for these couples and she describes Louis as a "real gentleman."

Every night at 5 p.m. Louis would wait outside the PX for Fumi. They would often get together with four or five other couples and go to Nakajima Park in Sapporo, where they would rent a rowboat for Sunday afternoon rides and enjoy picnics. Louis had learned some Japanese, but Fumi could not speak English, so they relied on his language skills at that time. It is interesting to note that he spoke feminine Japanese, as his conversations were basically with women. His word choices, tone, and inflections matched those of the women with whom he held conversations.

Louis had been in Sapporo almost a year before meeting Fumi. He worked as a corporal in the laundry in Sapporo, which enabled him to gain some Japanese language skills and the ability to converse. During their courtship, Fumi became employed at the laundry doing office work and taking care of the payroll for forty-eight people. They dated for about a year, and then Louis was transferred to Hachinohe, so he asked Fumi to move there with him. Her older brother, Tamotsu, helped her make the trip to Hachinohe to join Louis. They were married there on October 12, 1947, by an American preacher with Mrs. Abe, the interpreter for the laundry, as witness and interpreter of the ceremony for Fumi. This likely was not a legal Japanese or American wedding, but a simple ceremony that justified their union for their sakes. American marriages at that time were not permissible and Japanese marriages were not recognized by the United States. However, for Louis and Fumi, this sealed their fate as they would recognize this date as their first wedding anniversary for the rest of their lives.

While in Hachinohe, Louis attained the rank of sergeant. His next assignment was at Matsuyama where he was master sergeant and worked for the military government (MG) monitoring the immigration of Koreans. He also took part in discussions with Japanese land owners in the redistribution of land, which was part of the restructuring of Japan. Again, Tamotsu was instrumental in helping his sister move to Matsuyama. The military service did not provide aid with transitions as their marriage was not recognized. Louis enjoyed his service in Japan and he reenlisted for six years to stay with Fumi. His goal was to remain in the service and perhaps even in Japan.

SOURCE: Crawford, Miki Ward, Katie Kaori Hayashi, and Shizuko Suenaga. *Japanese War Brides in America: An Oral History.* Santa Barbara, CA: Praeger, 2010. All rights reserved. Reproduced by permission of ABC-CLIO, LLC, Santa Barbara, CA.

---

research … elevat[ing] the stories of the forgotten war brides to their rightful place in written history."

As Davis notes, *Japanese War Brides* and its tripartite structure also provides a unique opportunity to observe the influence of a historian's training and preoccupations upon the making of oral history. Crawford, she comments, approaches her interviews from the position as a daughter of a war bride, utilizing that association to make connections with her mother's friends and acquaintances. Her narratives mention the ongoing relationships that she has formed with several of these women. By contrast, Davis observes that Hayashi's training as a journalist is evident in the "fluid yet detached, journalistic narratives" present in her section of the book. Suenaga, a sociologist by training, "adopts the most reflective and ethnographic tone" and is the only one of the authors to explicitly discuss her interview methodology. Too, according to Davis, Suenaga's section provides the most "'raw' (yet translated) first-hand data" in the book, including large block quotations comprising about half of the text in her chapters. In addition to providing a window into the construction of oral history, the text is an example of what oral historian Alistair Thomson in *Oral History Review* (2007) calls "the increasing internationalism of oral history," a project influenced by the dual cultures and languages from which it has arisen.

Japanese War Brides has yet to generate a body of critical scholarship. Japanese historian Shigeyoshi Yasutomi has cited Crawford's research in his study of war brides and their relationship to the larger Japanese American community. While Yasutomi's research is primarily available in Japanese, he has presented his work in the United States and has conducted interviews of war brides facilitated by Crawford.

BIBLIOGRAPHY

Sources

Crawford, Miki Ward, Katie Kaori Hayashi, and Shizuko Suenaga. *Japanese War Brides in America: An Oral History.* Santa Barbara, CA: Praeger, 2010. Print.

Davis, Ann Marie. Rev. of *Japanese War Brides in America: An Oral History,* by Miki Ward Crawford, Katie Kaori Hayashi, and Shizuko Suenaga. *Oral History Review* 39.2 (2012): 340–42. Print.

Simpson, Caroline Chung. *An Absent Presence: Japanese Americans in Postwar American Culture, 1945–1960.* Durham, NC: Duke University Press, 2001. Print.

Thomson, Alistair. "Four Paradigm Transformations in Oral History." *Oral History Review* 34.1 (2007): 49–70. Print.

Further Reading

Bernstein, Gail Lee. *Recreating Japanese Women, 1600–1945.* Berkeley: University of California Press, 1991. Print.

Forrester, Michael. *Tsuchino: My Japanese War Bride.* Salt Lake City, UT: American Book Classics, 2005. Print.

Fujimura-Fanselow, Kumiko, and Atsuko Kameda. *Japanese Women: New Feminist Perspectives on the Past, Present, and Future.* New York: Feminist Press at the City University of New York, 1995. Print.

Glenn, Evelyn. *Issei, Nisei, War Bride: Three Generations of Japanese American Women in Domestic Service.* Philadelphia: Temple University Press, 2010. Print.

Shukert, Elfrieda Berthiaume, and Barbara Smith Scibetta. *War Brides of World War II.* New York: Penguin, 1988. Print.

Tamura, Keiko. *Michi's Memories: The Story of a Japanese War Bride.* Canberra, Australia: Pandanus, 2003. Print.

Zeiger, Susan. *Entangling Alliances: Foreign War Brides and American Soldiers in the Twentieth Century.* New York: New York University Press, 2010. Print.

Daisy Gard

Songs My Mother Sang to Me
An Oral History of Mexican American Women
Patricia Preciado Martin

OVERVIEW

Patricia Preciado Martin's *Songs My Mother Sang to Me: An Oral History of Mexican American Women* (1992) presents the stories of ten Mexican American women growing up in Arizona during the early part of the twentieth century. Focusing on the shift from rural to urban life of Chicana women in a way few works had done before and drawing on her own Mexican American heritage, Preciado Martin offers the stories of women from her mother's and grandmother's generation. The author's own background in both oral history and short fiction makes itself known and intertwines within the book. As the title suggests, song lyrics, poems, and prayers are interspersed with the oral histories along with personal photographs. While the oral histories themselves are presented in English, the songs are given in original Spanish alongside the translation. *Songs My Mother Sang to Me* presents the everyday life of Americans who were considered outsiders in their own time as well as in the twenty-first century.

Songs My Mother Sang to Me was seen by contemporary reviewers as a much-needed step between the rural lives of the nineteenth century and the more urban ones of the twentieth century. While the reviews were generally favorable, some scholars felt Preciado Martin edited too heavily, failed to offer analysis, and ended up with a more homogenized version of history than she may have intended. Regardless, she presented a well-rounded view of Mexican American women and helped bring closure to the often negative stereotypes presented in popular media.

HISTORICAL AND LITERARY CONTEXT

The histories of the ten women collected in *Songs My Mother Sang to Me* serve to combat stereotypes of Mexican American women in the past and present. As the Latino and Chicano population has continued to grow and become more firmly ingrained in American society, it has become essential to narrate their story in a truthful and equal manner. Chicano studies seeks to bring together and relate the Mexican and American sides of the story and of society. Since the Texas annexation of 1845 and the Mexican cession after the Mexican-American War, Mexican and American citizens have been narrowly separated both geographically and culturally. Yet, Mexicans and Mexican Americans continued to be stereotyped and lumped together as one single entity. Arizona, once a part of Mexico, continues to play an important role as a border between the two countries.

The women who tell their stories in *Songs My Mother Sang to Me* grew up in Arizona under diverse circumstances, with some having family that had lived in the area for years while others migrated after the Mexican Revolution of 1910. For example, one woman, Livia Leon Montiel, describes her family as true Tucson pioneers, having been in the area long before it was part of the United States, whereas others speak of moving across the border once it was established for reasons ranging from the revolution to run-ins with the local Yaqui Indians.

Published in the 1990s, when the Latino and Chicano populations were growing and racial tensions in the United States were volatile, *Songs My Mother Sang to Me* served to represent women who spoke a different language and identified with another culture yet were still U.S. citizens. Chicano studies, which began as a part of the Chicano rights movement in the 1960s and 1970s, serves as an interdisciplinary field that merges such subjects as anthropology, sociology, history, and literature. *Songs My Mother Sang to Me* demonstrates this interdisciplinary nature with its elements of oral history, social history, and music. While there are other oral histories of Chicana women, often they are lumped in with "multicultural women" or "Latino history." The history of the Chicano, however, is such a mix of Mexican and American traditions and stories that it needs its own discipline to be fully understood.

Though some argued it painted too rosy a picture, *Songs My Mother Sang to Me* gave Chicana women, particularly those outside California, a voice they had lacked in former oral and cultural histories. Preciado Martin continued her scholarly interest in oral history of Mexican Americans with her third oral history, *Beloved Land: An Oral History of Mexican Americans in Southern Arizona* (2004). The idea of Chicana women being a valid area of study has continued with books

❖ **Key Facts**

Time Period:
Early 20th Century

Relevant Historical Events:
Rise of Chicana studies; changes in Mexican American communities

Nationality:
American

Keywords:
identity; Chicanas; gender

CULTURE AND TRADITION

Female participants in Escaramuza Charros, part of a charreada, or Mexican rodeo, in Phoenix, Arizona, in 2001. Mexican American women tell their stories in *Songs My Mother Sang to Me*, by Patricia Preciado Martin. © JACK KURTZ/THE IMAGE WORKS

such as Debra J. Blake's *Chicana Sexuality and Gender: Cultural Reconfiguring in Literature, Oral History, and Art* (2008). Preciado Martin is deeply interdisciplinary, creating works in fiction and nonfiction alike, her mix of folklorist and historian backgrounds coming together in her oeuvre.

THEMES AND STYLE

While divided by cultural and socioeconomic lines, each oral history in *Songs My Mother Sang to Me* contains the themes of family, religion, women's place in and outside the home, and the ever-present connection to Mexican heritage. As the author notes, "These women document not only the rich details of their own lives, but also the histories of their ancestors, family and communities." The oral histories are meant to present not only the long-lasting effects that Mexican Americans, specifically Mexican American women, have had on the Arizona area of the United States. As one woman says, "We had to fill in and do the work of men." Especially in farming communities, women were essential workers, and everyone pitched in regardless of gender. Within the cities, women might take on more traditional roles, but they were actively involved in their communities in private and public. One woman describes how she became deeply involved in the community of Tucson through her activities with the church. She produced a Catholic radio show, was involved in church plays and clubs, and proudly states that "the church was always filled." Indeed, most of the stories involve religion, specifically Catholicism, as a part of daily life, with one woman describing herself as a "cradle Catholic"—"with my religion that is just no question; it's inbred in you." While these themes weave between the stories, Preciado Martin also highlights the differences between this group of women, who are often incorrectly viewed as homogenous.

Preciado Martin began her research for *Songs My Mother Sang to Me* in order to document the lives of "women of my mother's and grandmother's eras, before they were lost or forgotten." She describes the process of writing her book as being contingent on "references, determination, just plain luck and … not a small amount of miracles and coincidences." While she has cited her paternal grandparents, Mexican ranch owners, as having impacted her life, she notes that she never met her maternal grandmother. This fact becomes a major factor in prompting her research for the book, which she calls her "journey of the heart." In the preface, she describes her editing process, admitting to adding "transitional words" to aid in the "flow of the text."

The language of the book is a mixture of Spanish and English, with a poetic and lyrical undertone. Songs and prayers are presented apart from the text as if a poem. The original Spanish is always presented first, which serves to give non-Spanish speakers a feeling rather than an exact understanding of a culture different from their own. Each history begins with "My name is …" and then tells the story of the participant along with her entire family, with the stories, songs, and pictures interspersed to give a personal feeling to each oral history.

CRITICAL DISCUSSION

Initial reviews of *Songs My Mother Sang to Me* were positive and regarded the work as an important addition to Chicano studies, though there were some concerns about the overly positive view presented. Some critics felt that the lack of analysis within the text led to a lesser understanding of the subjects' lives. As Maria Montoya noted in her review for the *Western Historical Quarterly* (1993), "When reading, one often feels like an outsider—there is no map pointing out the locations of where the women lived, no annotation describing the people or historical events that influenced their lives." Reviewers stated that while Preciado Martin strove to give the women their voice, she failed to represent them fully in her lack of comments and history behind the oral histories themselves. As reviewer Ruth Behar observes in the *Women's Review of Books* in 1993, "[Preciado Martin] wanted to produce a book as lyrical as the lines from the poem by Lorna Dee Cervantes, and in this she has succeeded beautifully." As many reviewers remarked, *Songs My Mother Sang to Me* is written in a way that may not be overly analytical but is easily accessible to the public.

John Koegel, writing for *American Music,* points out that Chicano studies are interdisciplinary, and this combination can create disharmony for reviewers. In the decade or two since the book was released, the subject Preciado Martin tackles has been one of interest, but her work itself is not always highly cited. This lack of attention is perhaps because the book serves almost as a primary source with no secondary source study.

Scholars such as Debra Blake, who focus on Chicana women's and gender studies, have continued Preciado Martin's work. As Blake notes, few oral histories are available on working-class Chicana women. Preciado Martin set out to give a voice to an underserved population, and she succeeded and preserved their stories from which future scholars can study and learn.

BIBLIOGRAPHY

Sources

Aldama, Arturo J., and Naomi H. Quiñonez. *Decolonial Voices: Chicana and Chicano Cultural Studies in the 21st Century.* Bloomington: Indiana University Press, 2002. Print.

Behar, Ruth. "Journeys of the Heart." Rev. of *Songs My Mother Sang to Me: An Oral History of Mexican American Women,* by Patricia Preciado Martin. *Women's Review of Books* 10.6 (1993): 18–19. *JSTOR.* Web. 23 Jan. 2013.

Benson, Sonia. *The Hispanic American Almanac: A Reference Work on Hispanics in the United States.* Detroit: Gale, 2003. Print.

Koegel, John. Rev. of *Songs My Mother Sang to Me: An Oral History of Mexican American Women,* by Patricia Preciado Martin. *American Music* 13.3 (1995): 368. Print.

Montoya, Maria E. Rev. of *Songs My Mother Sang to Me: An Oral History of Mexican American Women,* by Patricia Preciado Martin. *Western Historical Quarterly* 24.3 (1993): 401–02. *JSTOR.* Web. 27 Jan. 2012.

Preciado Martin, Patricia. *Songs My Mother Sang to Me: An Oral History of Mexican American Women.* Tucson: University of Arizona Press, 1992. Print.

Rev. of *Songs My Mother Sang to Me: An Oral History of Mexican American Women,* by Patricia Preciado Martin. *Publishers Weekly* 12 Oct. 1992: 72. *Literature Resource Center.* Web. 4 Jan. 2013.

Smith, Roger. "Patricia Preciado Martin." *Guide to Literary Masters & Their Works* (2007): 1. *Literary Reference Center Plus.* Web. 22 Jan. 2013.

Further Reading

Bellver, Pilar. "La historia oral como autobiografía cultural: Dos ejemplos Chicanos." *Aztlán: A Journal of Chicano Studies* 24.2 (1999): 49–72. *MLA International Bibliography.* Web. 27 Jan. 2013.

Blake, Debra J. "Reading Dynamics of Power through Mexican-Origin Women's Oral Histories." *Frontiers: A Journal of Women Studies* 19.3 (1998): 24–41. *Academic Search Complete.* Web. 27 Jan. 2013.

———. *Chicana Sexuality and Gender: Cultural Refiguring in Literature, Oral History, and Art.* Durham, NC: Duke University Press, 2008. Print.

CHICANO MOVEMENT AND CHICANO STUDIES

The Chicano movement began in the late 1950s and early 1960s, much as the African American civil rights movement did. The term "Chicano" is steeped in some controversy and at one point was used as a derogatory slur but has since come to mean a person of Mexican descent living—or more often being born—in the United States. As the Mexican American generation commonly known as the baby boomers came to recognize themselves as both American and Mexican and at the same time as neither, they reclaimed the name Chicano. One early leader of this movement was Cesar Chavez, known for his labor organization, hunger strikes, and call for boycotts and protests to protect the rights of farm workers.

The Chicano movement focused on battling negative stereotypes about Mexicans and Chicanos socially as well as bringing Chicanos into the political field to influence laws and public policy. Chicano studies began as an academic discipline as an offshoot to the movement, with one of the first programs starting at the University of California at Santa Barbara in 1969. Beginning mainly in western states with traditionally large Chicano populations—such as California, Arizona, and Texas—Chicano studies programs in the twenty-first century can be found at universities throughout the country.

Cuádraz, Gloria Holguín. "Myths and the 'Politics of Exceptionality': Interpreting Chicana/o Narratives of Achievement." *Oral History Review* 33.1 (2006): 83–105. *Academic Search Complete*. Web. 27 Jan. 2013.

García, Alma M. *Narratives of Mexican American Women: Emergent Identities of the Second Generation.* Walnut Creek, CA: Altamira, 2004. Print.

Lima, L´zaro. *The Latino Body: Crisis Identities in American Literary and Cultural Memory.* New York: New York University Press, 2007. Print.

Preciado Martin, Patricia, and José Galvez. *Beloved Land: An Oral History of Mexican Americans in Southern Arizona.* Tucson: University of Arizona Press, 2004. Print.

Tywoniak, Frances E., and Mario T. García. *Migrant Daughter: Coming of Age as a Mexican American Woman.* Berkeley: University of California Press, 2000. *HighBeam Research*. Web. 4 Jan. 2013.

Emily Mann

A STRANGER'S SUPPER
An Oral History of Centenarian Women in Montenegro
Zorka Milich

OVERVIEW

In *A Stranger's Supper: An Oral History of Centenarian Women in Montenegro* (1995), scholar Zorka Milich provides insight into the culture and traditions of Montenegro by sharing the stories of ten rural Montenegrin women between the ages of 101 and 115. These ten subjects, selected from more than thirty whom Milich interviewed between January and June 1990, represent an ethnic and religious cross section of Montenegrin society: seven Orthodox Serbs, two Albanian Muslims, and one Albanian Catholic. Despite these differences in background, the stories collected in *A Stranger's Supper* reflect shared experiences of hardship and survival in the face of war, poverty, and harsh living conditions in the remote highlands of the rugged Dinaric Mountains east of the Adriatic Sea dating back to the nineteenth century.

Reviewers note the unique and specific nature of Milich's subject matter. Milich, herself of Montegrin descent, speaks the language and understands the customs of her interviewees, a fact that contributes to what critic E. C. Hawkesworth in a 1997 article for *Slavonic and East European Studies* calls the book's "particular flavour of intimacy and respect." This respect allows Milich the unique opportunity to give voice to the largely undocumented experience of female peasants in the deeply traditional and patriarchal Montenegrin society of the nineteenth and twentieth centuries.

HISTORICAL AND LITERARY CONTEXT

Although Milich conducted the interviews for *A Stranger's Supper* before the wars that led to the dissolution of Yugoslavia in the early 1990s, war and violence are major themes of Montenegrin history and of the book itself. Milich includes a timeline of wars and other conflicts in Montenegro dating back to 1042 to demonstrate how centuries of fighting contributed to a deeply rooted culture of war and violence in the country. According to Milich, "Montenegrins lived in a perpetual state of war or preparedness for war against the ever-threatening Turks. Among themselves, they had to contend with continual intertribal conflicts, often leading to blood vendettas." This tradition of violence in Montenegrin history is inextricably linked to a deeply ingrained culture of patriarchy: while men have been traditionally revered as warriors, women have been marginalized, valued primarily for their ability to produce sons.

The narratives collected in *A Stranger's Supper* cover more than a century of Montenegrin history from the perspective of the "women behind the warriors." All ten women speak of their wartime experiences, recalling lost loved ones and times of hunger and hardship. During their lives, all of these women endured major periods of conflict: the wars of liberation from Ottoman Turkish rule of their early youths, the Balkan Wars of 1912–13, World War I, World War II, and a civil war between Tito's Communist Partisans and the Royalist pro-Western Chetniks of general Draza Mihailovic. The interviewees lost fathers, brothers, husbands, and sons in these wars; yet their daily lives changed little during wartime. They were still expected to do the work required of Montenegrin wives and mothers, managing homes, caring for children, and working the difficult land.

A Stranger's Supper is rooted in the tradition of using oral history as a means of documenting the everyday experiences of "ordinary" people. According to Alistair Thompson in a 2007 article for the *Oral History Review,* the desire to document ordinary people's memories as historical sources was a major factor in the emergence of modern oral history practice. Thomson notes, "The lived experience of working class, women's or black history was undocumented or ill-recorded and oral history was an essential source for the 'history from below' fostered by politically-committed social historians in Britain and around the world from the 1960s onwards." Milich's meticulously documented oral histories are an example of this "history from below."

In *A Stranger's Supper* Milich captures a unique perspective while continuing the tradition of using oral history to offer insight into women's history. Nancy Grey Osterud and Lu Ann Jones, writing in *Oral History of Review* in 1989, before Milich began collecting her interviews, describe a tradition of oral histories of rural women, which Milich follows with her work: "Beyond simply documenting oppression, [oral history] illuminates the strategies women have adopted to cope with their situation, and the ways

❖ **Key Facts**

Time Period:
Late 19th to Late 20th Century

Relevant Historical Events:
The Balkan Wars; World War I; World War II; Yugoslavian civil war

Nationality:
Montenegrin

Keywords:
war; poverty; survival

CULTURE AND TRADITION

A woman in a monastery in Montenegro. Elderly women from Montenegro discuss their lives in *A Stranger's Supper: An Oral History of Centenarian Women in Montenegro* by Zorka Milich. © GAVIN HELLIER/GETTY IMAGES

they have come to terms with, compensated for, and even challenged the limitations they faced."

THEMES AND STYLE

The central themes of *A Stranger's Supper* are the patriarchal structure of Montenegrin society, marriage and familial relationships, loss, and the central importance of honor in Montenegrin culture. Milich notes, "[P]atrilineal practices resulted in the development of a cult of male superiority to an almost incomprehensible degree." The women's narratives clearly reflect this male superiority, particularly within marital relationships. Several interviewees speak of domestic violence as a common and even expected occurrence. One interviewee says of her husband, "He was a good man. He only hit me when I deserved it." Despite the fact that all of the marriages in the book were arranged as tradition demanded, most women report having loved their husbands. All of the marriages resulted in many children. Sons were much preferred: "Girls were not received in the same way as boys. … Mothers of sons are as happy as any woman can be in this land. And if she has no children at all, her life is a nightmare." The text frequently mentions the importance of family and personal honor as central values in the culture. For instance, a wife's infidelity or a sexual encounter by an unmarried woman could threaten the honor of the immediate family and the entire clan. In fact the need to defend and restore a clan's honor was one of the major causes for blood feuds.

As Milich writes in the preface, *A Stranger's Supper* grew out of her doctoral research. While studying Yugoslav author Ivo Andrić, she found that she "wanted to know the living history of those women born under oppression, survivors of years of foreign occupation: Ottoman and Austro-Hungarian." She had no prior experience with oral history but found the practice to be ideal for her research interests. She writes, "What I unveiled in Montenegro was life in a methodically circumscribed warrior patriarchy, revealed through the collective social and cultural memory of females more than a century old. The resonance of their heretofore unheard stories pervades this study." She describes her methodology in the preface, noting the striking similarities between each interview. In keeping with tradition, male relatives primarily arranged the interviews.

Describing her interactions with her interviewees (or narrators, as she refers to them), Milich writes, "To say I was humbled is to barely express my awe." This tone of humility permeates the text. After the preface and introduction, she includes an introductory chapter that provides a concise but comprehensive history of Montenegro. The next sections are all similarly structured, with a short introduction that prefaces the interviews and provides insight into the section's theme ("Sons and Brothers: Death in the Midst of Death," "The Honeymoon Must Wait," "The Friend of My Enemy Is My Enemy," and "We Are Sisters All"). An epilogue offers Milich's overall reflections on her experiences.

CRITICAL DISCUSSION

Perhaps because of the very specific and unique nature of the text, *A Stranger's Supper* has not sparked significant critical discussion. A 1995 review from *Publishers Weekly* notes, "It may seem a little eclectic, but in fact the recollections of 10 aged women reveal a fair amount about the misty, distant past and the very real present." This idea of timelessness is also reflected in Hawkesworth's review: "The lives these women describe, covering the hundred years up to 1990, have been essentially unchanged since people first settled the territory of Montenegro and began to strike a living from that harsh land. Most of the women interviewed live in remote, isolated areas where the changes brought by the twentieth century have only recently penetrated." Megan Hays's 1998 review in the *Journal of Women's History* sums up the wide variety of themes covered in *A Stranger's Supper*: "In intimate detail, [the women] describe ritualized weddings, childbirth experiences, losses of family to famine and war, bonds between brothers and sisters, the taboo against a mother's public grief for her son's death, and the overriding importance of honor."

There are no scholarly discussions of the long-term literary and historical significance of the text. However, this does not indicate that *A Stranger's Supper* has no lasting significance. In fact Hawkesworth praises it as making contributions "to several areas: it is a sound piece of oral history, painstakingly researched, with each testimony fully documented." Hawkesworth also praises Milich's "sound, scholarly approach" to her subject matter.

In the world of oral history, texts like *A Stranger's Supper* occupy an important space. Hawkesworth writes, "Zorka Milich's starting point is what has been omitted from conventional male authors' accounts of women's lives in both history and literature." This aligns with Osterud and Jones's assertion that "oral history is especially well-suited for women's history because it facilitates the recovery of individual and collective agency." By sharing their stories, the narrators featured in this text give voice to their personal histories and, in doing so, provide unique insight into the previously undocumented history of peasant women in the deeply traditional Montenegro of the nineteenth and twentieth centuries.

A STRANGER'S SUPPER AND MARRIAGE TRADITIONS IN OLD MONTENEGRO

In the deeply patriarchal "Old Montenegro" that Milich describes in her first chapter, a woman's primary purpose in life was to become a wife and ultimately a mother. The title of her book, *A Stranger's Supper*, refers to the transition that a woman underwent on the day she married. Traditionally women were strangers to their new families, their marriages arranged by future fathers-in-law. On her wedding day, a woman left her parents' home permanently, assuming her new role by tending to a *tudja večera*, or a "stranger's supper." According to tradition, a bride would prepare supper for her new family, which Milich describes as "a metaphor for her having to attend to the needs of her new, extended family for the remainder of her life." This symbolic act was one of many that were traditionally required in a new marriage.

Another practice that was still common when all of the women in *A Stranger's Supper* married was the bride spending her first night in bed, fully clothed, with her brother-in-law and not her husband. Only when she was given permission by an older female in the household was she allowed to consummate her marriage and begin sleeping in her husband's bed. While some scholars believe that this practice was abandoned in the nineteenth century, Milich's interviews suggest that it was still commonplace in tribal Montenegro well into the twentieth century.

BIBLIOGRAPHY

Sources

Hawkesworth, E. C. Rev. of *A Stranger's Supper: An Oral History of Centenarian Women in Montenegro*, by Zorka Milich. *Slavonic and East European Studies* 75.3 (1997): 536–37. *JSTOR*. Web. 27 Jan. 2013.

Hays, Megan. Rev. of *A Stranger's Supper: An Oral History of Centenarian Women in Montenegro*, by Zorka Milich. *Journal of Women's History* 10.1 (1998): 208. *JSTOR*. Web. 27 Jan. 2013.

Milich, Zorka. *A Stranger's Supper: An Oral History of Centenarian Women in Montenegro*. New York: Twayne, 1995. Print.

Osterud, Nancy Grey, and Lu Ann Jones. "'If I Must Say So Myself': Oral Histories of Rural Women." *Oral History Review* 17.2 (1989): 1–23. *JSTOR*. Web. 27 Jan. 2013.

Rev. of *A Stranger's Supper: An Oral History of Centenarian Women in Montenegro*, by Zorka Milich. *Publishers Weekly* 242.46 (1995): 59. *Literature Resources from Gale*. Web. 27 Jan. 2013.

Thompson, Alistair. "Paradigm Transformations in Oral History." *Oral History Review* 34.1 (2007): 49–70. *JSTOR*. Web. 24 Jan. 2013.

Further Reading

Andrić, Ivo. *The Slave Girl: And Other Stories about Women*. Budapest: Central European University Press, 2009. Print.

Boehn, Christopher. *Blood Revenge: The Enactment and Management of Conflict in Montenegro and Other Tribal Societies*. Philadelphia: University of Pennsylvania Press, 1987. Print.

Bornat, Joanna, and Hanna Diamond. "Women's History and Oral History: Developments and Debates." *Women's History Review* 16:1 (2007): 19–39. *Taylor & Francis Online*. Web. 24 Jan. 2013.

Djilas, Milovan. *Land without Justice*. New York: Harcourt Brace, 1958. Print.

Milich, Zorka, and Mark Milich, dir. *A Stranger's Supper: Centenarian Mountain Women of Montenegro*. Seattle, WA: Intermedia, 1999. Film.

Roberts, Elizabeth. *Realm of the Black Mountain: A History of Montenegro*. Ithaca, NY: Cornell University Press, 2007. Print.

Simic, Andrei. "The Blood Feud in Montenegro." *Essays in Balkan Ethnology*. Berkeley, CA: Kroeber Anthropological Society, 1967. 83–94. *AnthroHub*. Web. 8 Feb. 2013.

Zirin, Mary F. *Women & Gender in Central and Eastern Europe, Russia, and Eurasia: A Comprehensive Bibliography*. Armonk, NY: Sharpe, 2007. Print.

Jenny Dale

Uqalurait
An Oral History of Nunavut
John Bennett, Susan Rowley

✢ **Key Facts**

Time Period:
Late 19th to Early 20th Century

Relevant Historical Events:
Colonization of Inuit territory creation of Nunavut in 1999

Nationality:
Canadian

Keywords:
colonialism; cultural identity; history

OVERVIEW

Uqalurait: An Oral History of Nunavut (2004), compiled and edited by John Bennett and Susan Rowley, is a collection of images and quotations about the traditional history and cultural identity of Inuits living in the Canadian territory of Nunavut. A committee of Inuit elders comprises the participants for the book; they recall stories and research quotations from the time before European contact completely altered their lifestyle. The final work represents the Inuit idea of oral history, recorded in writing to preserve this knowledge before it disappears with the passing of the elders. The book strives to portray history from the perspective of the Inuit, therefore presenting a unique interpretation of history without the conventional linear progression of events and themes.

Despite its distinctive premise and honest attempts to produce history of the Inuit by the Inuit, *Uqalurait* was met with a lukewarm reception from scholars and reviewers alike. The work is largely criticized for its focus on the territory of Nunavut, which, although geographically central to the existing Inuit populations, excludes people living in Labrador, the Northwest Territories, and the Yukon who also fall under the category of Canadian Inuit and share common history, language, and cultural values. The book remains a significant effort to record Inuit oral history and is a notable text for initiating research into the preservation of traditional oral culture.

HISTORICAL AND LITERARY CONTEXT

The territory of Nunavut, officially created in 1999, is the newest addition to Canada's roster of provinces and territories. The largely Inuit population, however, have lived in the unforgiving arctic climate for generations before Europeans even discovered North America, and long before Canada was ever created. The introduction of European settlers in the late nineteenth century caused the Inuit to face massive changes to their culture as a result of residential schools and the introduction of English language. The Europeans also introduced writing and the development of written forms of the Inuit language of Inuktitut, a language that had previously existed in a purely oral form.

Uqalurait describes the period of the late nineteenth and early twentieth centuries, when the Inuit had acquired firearms through trade with whalers and other settlers but before they adopted Christianity and were subject to Canadian politics. Recorded by ethnographers, elders councils, historians, and others charged with preserving Inuit heritage, the quotations that make up the oral history come from people who lived through this period of time. By focusing on this specific time period, the editors hope to construct an image of traditional culture that is still remembered by community elders.

Uqalurait is not the first attempt at recording the history and culture of the arctic Inuit, although it is unique for its structure and approach to the project. *The Eskimo: Their Environment and Folkways* (1932) by Edward Moffat Weyer and *Never in Anger: Portrait of an Eskimo Family* (1970) by Jean L. Briggsoth present cultural accounts of the Inuit people but do so from the perspective of an outsider looking at the culture and describing its unique qualities. The researchers for *Uqalurait*, however, did not want to follow the outlines exemplified by studies such as these and therefore decided to record the Inuit perspective of their own history. By doing so, *Uqalurait* solidifies in writing many of the stories that were passed down orally in traditional oral stories but that run the risk of being forgotten because of changing political, social, and cultural climates.

Despite its lack of critical acclaim, the ideas behind the *Uqalurait* project—recording for posterity the oral histories of the Inuit people—have been continued by others in the attempt to preserve records of traditional culture. Keavy Martin discusses the effect of writing on Inuit oral histories in *Stories in a New Skin: Approaches to Inuit Literature* (2012), and Leo Tulugarjuk and Neil Christopher's compilation *Ilagiinniq: Interviews on Inuit Family Values from the Qikiqtani Region* (2011) includes facing-page English translations of interviews conducted in Inuktitut about aspects of traditional life. These texts work to preserve not only the stories of the Inuit people but also their language and identity.

THEMES AND STYLE

The editors mention five themes intentionally present in *Uqalurait*: "flexibility, sacrifice, social control, sharing, and respect." Taken together, these ideas create the central premise that unites the entire text: the presentation of the Inuit people as an autonomous culture with an active participation in the outcome of their lives. The editors explain in their introduction, "Arctic histories generally look through an 'outside' lens, focusing on the contact period and portraying Inuit as passive recipients of change rather than as active players in their own lives." By allowing the committee of elders the ultimate say in the material included within the oral history, *Uqalurait* represents a written version of traditional Inuit culture before the massive changes associated with European interference.

The editors of *Uqalurait* state two reasons for undertaking such a project. The "main goal of the project," they write in the introduction, "was to create a history of Nunavut for the people of Nunavut—written from their perspective." In addition, they wanted to "provide those outside Nunavut with an 'inside' view of Inuit history, one shaped by the Inuit themselves." The editors first gathered quotations from interviews and from previous records and organized them into chapters, discussing specific aspects of life such as family, animals, medicine, death, and the different seasons. Under the chapter heading "Death and Burial," for example, one participant discusses how "there is always the possibility that, should one mourn in private, trying to hide one's feelings, one's eyesight might get bad" or "it might cause a mental disorder." Another participant under the same heading explains, "The reason for the women to face southwards was because a woman gets cold easily, so they were always buried with their heads facing south." The editors also include brief explanatory paragraphs, interspersed with the quotations, which explain aspects of Inuit culture for non-Inuit readers. The result is not a fluid narrative or a series of memories that compose a linear progression of time but rather a montage of individual voices speaking about the way of life in the far north.

The overall style of *Uqalurait* was intended to be different from conventional histories, reflecting the Inuit perspective of cyclical time. The assembled quotations are accompanied by images, graphs, and drawings that help explain Inuit customs such as hunting practices and family structures. The plethora of voices that compose the oral history appear in English rather than in their native language of Inuktitut, although individual words that do not directly translate are preserved and followed by brief definitions. These words generally relate to traditional practices of which there was no European equivalent, such as *qimuguittuq,* which means when whales and walrus are harpooned, they "would not pull strongly on the harpoon line and attempt to flee, but instead would head towards land." Other words include garments, such as the *amauti,* a "parka with a pouch for carrying a baby on the back," and periods of life, such as the progression of a female infant from a *mirajuq,* or newborn, to *niuiassaaq,* a young girl, and *niviassaajjuqq,* a "big girl." The editors explain, "These terms indicate her age without having to use numbers," as was traditional for the Inuit.

CRITICAL DISCUSSION

The initial reaction to the publication of *Uqalurait* was generally unenthusiastic, with most reviewers feeling that, although the book is unique in its purpose and design, its narrow parameters of time and geography exclude many people as well as important cultural and political developments. John MacDonald in his 2005 review in *Arctic* credits the work for its "impressive assemblage of traditional knowledge," including "hundreds of attributed quotes from individual Inuit," despite their English translation. The "main limitation" of the work, MacDonald believes, is "the decision to focus almost entirely on 'the period before the Inuit adopted Christianity, but after they acquired firearms and traded regularly with whalers and others.'" MacDonald argues that by focusing exclusively on this stage, issues that have shaped the modern Inuit, such as Christianity, nationality, and government agencies, are not even mentioned, and therefore the overall image created for modern Inuit people is misleading and disassociated from their current lives. Another criticism is that, by only focusing on Nunavut—an area only recently designated a territory by the Canadian government—*Uqalurait* does not consider Inuit populations living in other territories of the arctic, even though they all have a common heritage and face similar hardships.

The broad social and political legacy of *Uqalurait* may become more apparent with time. The aging process is taking its toll on many community elders, and stories and lessons from the times before European contact risk being lost. The language of Inuktitut itself, although still widely spoken, is changing to suit a very different society. Guy Bordin's 2009

An Inuit hunter in Nunavut crouches with his dog sled team. In *Uqalurait: An Oral History of Nunavut,* hunting rituals are discussed. © ROB HOWARD/CORBIS

TRANSLATING ORAL SPEECH INTO WRITTEN WORDS

Writing was introduced to the Inuit people in the late nineteenth century when contact with European missionaries brought trade, including firearms, and new forms of education. Because Inuktitut existed purely as an oral language, it had many variations of dialect and pronunciations depending on the speaker's location. Thus, as the language was recorded in writing, it was done so phonetically in order to preserve the different dialects and be legible within each region.

Two systems of writing developed simultaneously: syllabics, or a system of symbols representing specific sounds, and a phonetic use of Roman orthography. Both of these systems have improved in accuracy since their initial development as native speakers of Inuktitut became literate and began recording their own vernacular rather than depending on Europeans who lacked an innate understanding of the sounds and nuances of the language. Two systems of spelling have emerged from users of Roman orthography: one by the speakers of Inuinnaqtun, a specific dialect, and the Inuit Cultural Institute Standard Orthography, which has become the standard for published texts and transliterates easily into syllabics.

study titled "Lexical Discontinuities" notes several Inuktitut words that are commonly used by elders but unknown to adults under forty years of age, suggesting that along with the stories and oral transmission of history from one generation to the next, much of the language itself is dying with the Inuit elders. The ideas behind *Uqalurait,* therefore, are an admirable attempt at conservation.

Current trends in scholarship tend to point out the shortcomings of the text while generally praising the attempt to compile Inuit oral history in a written format. Nelson Graburn, in his 2007 review in the *University of Toronto Quarterly,* follows this trend when he praises the "lively first-person accounts" but ultimately questions the exclusion of people in more urban areas of Nunavut: "Cape Dorset is hardly represented and there is almost nothing of the people of Sanikilluak (the Belchers), Kimmirut, and Iqaluit." Monika Rohlmann's 2004 review in the *Canadian Book Review Annual* praises the editors for creating a "pivotal text for the Inuit themselves" by "recording their oral history in a permanent form" but notices "there is little mention about fierce storms and snow or the beauty of the landscape"—features that are commonplace to the Inuit but that greatly interest tourists and non-Inuit readers.

BIBLIOGRAPHY

Sources

Bennett, John, and Susan Rowley, eds. *Uqalurait: An Oral History of Nunavut.* Montreal: McGill-Queen's University Press, 2004. Print.

Bordin, Guy. "Lexical Discontinuities between Generations: Recent Inuit Cases from North Baffin Island." *Anthropological Linguistics* 51 (2009): 191–208. *JSTOR.* Web. 26 Nov. 2012.

Graburn, Nelson. "*Uqalurait:* An Oral History of Nunavut." *University of Toronto Quarterly* 76.1 (2007): 346–47. Web. 26 Nov. 2012.

MacDonald, John. "*Uqalurait:* An Oral History of Nunavut." *Arctic* 58.4 (2005): 429+. *Canadian Periodicals Index Quarterly.* Web. 26 Nov. 2012.

Rohlmann, Monika. "*Uqalurait:* An Oral History of Nunavut." *Canadian Book Review Annual* 2004: 389. Web. 26 Nov. 2012.

Further Reading

Briggs, Jean L. *Never in Anger: Portrait of an Eskimo Family.* Cambridge, MA: Harvard University Press, 1970. Print.

Martin, Keavy. *Stories in a New Skin: Approaches to Inuit Literature.* Winnipeg, Canada: University of Manitoba Press, 2012. Print.

Tulugarjuk, Leo, and Neil Christopher, eds. *Ilagiinniq: Interviews on Inuit Family Values from the Qikiqtani Region.* Iqaluit, Canada: Inhabit Media, 2011. Print.

Weike, Wilhelm. *Inuit and Whalers on Baffin Island through German Eyes: Arctic Journal and Letters (1883–1884).* Ed. Ludger Müller-Wille and Bernd Gieseking. Trans. William Barr. Montreal: Baraka, 2011. Print.

Weyer, Edward Moffat. *The Eskimo: Their Environment and Folkways.* New Haven, CT: Yale University Press, 1932. Print.

Katherine Barker

When We Began, There Were Witchmen
An Oral History from Mount Kenya
Jeffrey A. Fadiman

OVERVIEW

When We Began, There Were Witchmen: An Oral History from Mount Kenya (1993), collected and edited by Jeffrey A. Fadiman, presents the history of the Meru people of Mount Kenya as told by Meru elders. Fadiman, educated in journalism and African studies, drew on his experience living on the slopes of Mount Kenya as a Fulbright Scholar in order to gain access to the elders whose stories are in *Witchmen*. While gathering data for the book, he interviewed more than one hundred of the oldest living Meru men, whose oral histories were in danger of disappearing because Christianity and colonization had eroded the traditional Meru social structure. As such, *Witchmen* narrates many significant developments in Meru society, including those related to enslavement, colonization, and *urogi*, or traditional witchcraft.

Published more than twenty years after Fadiman initially collected the oral histories, *Witchmen* presents a largely uncritical view of the stories related by the Meru elders. The text was praised but also derided for failing to acknowledge recent trends in historical African studies and ignoring recent scholarship on oral history. Some, such as scholar Jack Glazier, leveled accusations that Fadiman took a nostalgic or romantic view of colonialism. However, over time the book has come to be valued for its examination of how British colonialism shaped Meru institutions and for the information it provides on witchcraft. Today it remains a significant example of the genres of oral history and African preliterate history.

HISTORICAL AND LITERARY CONTEXT

Witchmen demonstrates the far-reaching effects of European colonization on African culture. The late nineteenth century saw Africa threatened by European imperialist forces from Great Britain, France, Portugal, and Belgium, among other countries. By the end of the nineteenth century, European powers had colonized most of Africa. Economic gain was a primary motivating factor behind colonization, and successful colonization required the assimilation of African peoples to European social institutions, resulting in social and cultural losses for Africans. While many Africans mounted resistance, they were largely unsuccessful against European military technology. Much of Africa, including Kenya, entered into an extended period of indirect rule by foreign colonizers. It was not until 1963 that Kenya, home of the Meru people, gained its independence from Great Britain.

The oral histories collected in *Witchmen* demonstrate the effects of enslavement, colonization, and conflict on the social structures of the Meru people. The Meru elders reported first contact with Europeans, or "red men," in the late nineteenth century, though their anxieties grew after the British conquest of neighboring Embu in 1906. The arrival of British colonizers and Methodist missionaries marked the beginning of the decline of traditional Meru social institutions, the warrior class, and practitioners of *urogi*. Missionaries gained a foothold in Meru culture by offering the eldest boys "stories, salt, bits of sugar, and strips of cloth." However, the 1920s saw a resurgence of local witchcraft and an increase in the strength of local societies of Meru elders, such as the A-Athi. Still, colonial persecution and religious conversion of Meru youth resulted in almost a complete disappearance of witchcraft in its traditional form.

Witchmen belongs to the literary tradition of African oral histories. Examples are collected in Philip D. Curtin's *Africa Remembered: Narratives by West Africans from the Era of the Slave Trade* (1967). *Akiga's Story: The Tiv Tribe as Seen by One of Its Members* (1965), compiled and edited by Rupert East, is a first-person oral narrative. A number of other African oral histories precede Fadiman's book, including Mary F. Smith's *Baba of Karo: A Woman of the Muslim Hausa* (1954) and Thomas Bluett's *Some Memories of the Life of Job, the Son of the Solomon High Priest of Boonda in Africa* (1734), which is a retelling of an oral narrative of a Senegalese man named Ayuba Suleiman Diallo. All of these oral histories are presented in mediated form, having been collected, edited, interpreted, or retold.

Witchmen has influenced the study and interpretation of African oral histories and is often assigned in U.S. college courses on folklore. The book is one of several that Fadiman wrote about Africa, including *The Moment of Conquest: Meru, Kenya, 1907* (1979) and *An Oral History of Tribal Warfare: The Meru of Mt. Kenya* (1982). After publishing *Witchmen*, he

❖ **Key Facts**

Time Period:
Late 19th to Early 20th Century

Relevant Historical Events:
British colonization of Kenya; success of Kenyan independence movement

Nationality:
Kenyan

Keywords:
colonization; witchcraft; independence

CULTURE AND TRADITION

A young Meru woman photographed in 1950. © W. ROBERT MOORE/ NATIONAL GEOGRAPHIC SOCIETY/CORBIS

wrote a book on African marketing methods titled *South Africa's "Black" Market: How to Do Business with Africans* (2000).

THEMES AND STYLE

The central theme of *Witchmen* is the effect of enslavement, colonization, and rebellion on traditional cultural and social institutions. Shortly after the arrival of the Europeans, young Meru warriors attacked in defense of their livestock, causing "an ominous split … between warriors and elders, with the former still seeking glory in traditional fashion and the latter forbidding them to do so. The result was a period … in which the entire Meru social system began to fray." Meru culture was further undermined when colonizers gathered the weapons and shields of the Meru warrior class and threw them into a river. The Meru, robbed of "their reasons for personal restraint, … began to question every facet of their previously inviolate codes of conduct." Colonizers assumed greater control, and "the impact on warrior behavior was devastating." When missionaries arrived with Western medicines and competed against traditional ritualists, successfully curing diseases that the local witchmen could not, "many of the aged who had previously enjoyed both financial security and community standing as healers became increasingly subject to verbal taunts and even physical abuse from youths."

As Fadiman notes in the book's introduction, he undertook *Witchmen* to preserve oral histories that "are folk art at its finest … [and] hold Africa's rich past." He acknowledges that "some traditions are fictional, others are based entirely on fact," but he feels that some traditions, specifically those related to witchcraft, are "windows that permit analysis of smaller segments of the social structure." He engages in a fair amount of authorial intervention, framing and paraphrasing the oral histories in the first third of the book and interpreting primary documents and historical records of colonists and missionaries later in the book. Such editing and rearranging of source material is not uncommon in the oral history genre. The mediated nature of the oral histories makes for a more cohesive narrative and a greater contextual framework, though some of the immediacy and authenticity of the oral histories is lost.

The language of *Witchmen* is distinguished by Fadiman's noncritical narrative tone. He presents, interprets, and paraphrases the oral histories without question. He introduces the Meru concepts of *ugwe* and *uroria*, "the Meru supernatural rituals … of prophecy, practiced by individuals whose contact with the supernatural enabled them to glimpse the future." Fadiman's straightforward retelling of Meru narratives works to imbue those narratives with historical, cultural, and social significance, though the original words of the Meru elders are not heavily represented in the text.

CRITICAL DISCUSSION

Early critical reception of *Witchmen* was mixed. Most reviewers agreed that the text offered interesting insight into the social institutions of the Meru people, while many took issue with the book's lack of direct narration and methodology. In a 1995 review for the *International Journal of African Historical Studies,* Bill Bravman states that the book "discusses the intricacies (and difficulties) of changes in authority relations, political economy, social life, religion, and cultural practices with an unusual and impressive sensitivity." In a 1995 review for the *Journal of the Royal Anthropological Institute,* Maia Green notes that *Witchmen* "contains material that is of interest to social historians of Kenya, but is weakened by a pervasive lack of analytical rigour and by the lack of comparative material which could help to place Meru history in a wider context." Nevertheless, critics praised the book for working to preserve Meru history. In a 1994 review for *Africa Today,* Maloba Wunyabari calls the book "an extremely valuable contribution to African studies."

While *Witchmen* is still appreciated as a folkloric text, its value as an oral history or historic record has been called into question. John Galaty, in a 1999 *American Ethnologist* article, notes that Fadiman's text fails to reflect "on the complex links between narrative and history." Anthropologist Brad Weiss, in a 1995 article in *American Anthropologist,* notes the absence of direct narrative in the book: "While the entire text has certainly been derived from oral reports … there are no quotations of any length … from any of these sources." Historian Thomas Spear notes that *Witchmen* distinguishes itself from other African oral histories because it allows Meru traditions to speak for themselves as interpretations of African history.

Recent scholarship focuses on the book's insight into the effect of colonial rule on Africa and the book's detailed examination of African witchcraft. Katherine Luongo, in her 2011 book *Witchcraft and Colonial Rule in Kenya, 1900–1955*, cites Fadiman's text as a rare example of a historical study of witchcraft that examines "witchcraft as part of larger histories of legal administration." In *A Historical Companion to Postcolonial Thought in English* (2005), editors David Johnson and Prem Poddar discuss the histories presented in *Witchmen* as demonstrating the "complex interplay of identities and ethnicities under colonial rule."

MERU WOMEN

The oral histories related by Jeffrey Fadiman in *When We Began, There Were Witchmen* (1993) are primarily the narratives of the male elders. As Fadiman explains, "My efforts to inquire among elderly women (about uniquely 'female' curses, for example) were usually rebuffed with declarations that I sought to learn things 'no man should know.' Only rarely did a woman of great age consent to talk to me, and then either in secrecy or with her husband present." However, Fadiman was able to glean some information about the history of the Meru women's social and cultural identity.

Traditionally the sexes were segregated and met separately in gender-specific councils to decide important matters, which meant that the women held separate *kiamas*, or associations. Women were considered capable of *urogi*, or witchcraft, but could only curse their own sex, while men were capable of cursing anyone. In general the home and the farm were considered the domain of women, and though women could be captured during war, there was a cultural admonition against either abusing or harming them. However, as with many Meru institutions, the traditional role of women was eroded under years of colonial and missionary influence.

BIBLIOGRAPHY

Sources

Bravman, Bill. Rev. of *When We Began, There Were Witchmen: An Oral History from Mount Kenya*, by Jeffrey A. Fadiman. *International Journal of African Historical Studies* 28.1 (1995): 185–86. *JSTOR*. Web. 1 Feb. 2013.

Fadiman, Jeffrey A. *When We Began, There Were Witchmen: An Oral History from Mount Kenya*. Berkeley: University of California Press, 1993. Print.

Galaty, John G. Rev. of *When We Began, There Were Witchmen: An Oral History from Mount Kenya*, by Jeffrey A. Fadiman. *American Ethnologist* 26.2 (1999): 507–8. *JSTOR*. Web. 31 Jan. 2013.

Green, Maia. Rev. of *When We Began, There Were Witchmen: An Oral History from Mount Kenya*, by Jeffrey A. Fadiman. *Journal of the Royal Anthropological Institute* 1.3 (1995): 641–42. *JSTOR*. Web. 1 Feb. 2013.

Johnson, David, and Prem Poddar, eds. *A Historical Companion to Postcolonial Thought in English*. New York: Columbia University Press, 2005. Print.

Luongo, Katherine. *Witchcraft and Colonial Rule in Kenya, 1900–1955*. New York: Cambridge University Press, 2011. Print.

Weiss, Brad. Rev. of *When We Began, There Were Witchmen: An Oral History from Mount Kenya*, by Jeffrey A. Fadiman. *American Anthropologist* 97.3 (1995): 625–26. *ProQuest*. Web. 1 Feb. 2013.

Wunyabari, Maloba. "Writing Oral History: A Valuable Effort." Rev. of *When We Began, There Were Witchmen: An Oral History from Mount Kenya*, by Jeffrey A. Fadiman. *Africa Today* 41.4 (1994): 77. *ProQuest*. Web. 31 Jan. 2013.

Further Reading

Ambler, Charles. "Oral History from Mount Kenya." Rev. of *When We Began, There Were Witchmen: An Oral History from Mount Kenya*, by Jeffrey A. Fadiman. *Journal of African History* 36.3 (1995): 513–14. *Cambridge Journals*. Web. 31 Jan. 2013.

Fadiman, Jeffrey A. *An Oral History of Tribal Warfare: The Meru of Mt. Kenya*. Athens: Ohio University Press, 1982. Print.

Finnegan, Ruth. *The Oral and Beyond: Doing Things with Words in Africa*. Chicago: University of Chicago Press, 2007. Print.

Greene, Sandra E. "Whispers and Silences: Explorations in African Oral History." *Africa Today* 50.2 (2003): 41–53. *Project Muse*. Web. 31 Jan. 2013.

Smith, James Howard. *Bewitching Development: Witchcraft and the Reinvention of Development in Neoliberal Kenya*. Chicago: University of Chicago Press, 2008. Print.

Tsey, Komla. *Re-thinking Development in Africa: An Oral History Approach from Botoku, Rural Ghana*. Bamenda, Cameroon: Langaa Rpcig, 2011. Print.

Kristen Gleason

Women and Families: An Oral History, 1940–1970

Elizabeth Roberts

Key Facts

Time Period:
Mid-20th Century

Relevant Historical Events:
Changes in the English working class

Nationality:
British

Keywords:
women; domesticity; working-class life

OVERVIEW

Written by Elizabeth Roberts and published in 1995, *Women and Families: An Oral History, 1940–1970* is a study of fifty-one women and forty-seven men of the working class from the North Lancashire towns of Barrow, Lancaster, and Preston in northwest England. Focusing principally on the lives of women, familial relationships, and domesticity, the text analyzes numerous elements of family life during the period in question—including household obligations, gender roles within marriage, changing approaches to childcare, and employment for married women—and quotes liberally from oral interviews (conducted from 1988 to 1990) to illustrate its assertions. Roberts's observations, along with the book's copious firsthand accounts, provide an illuminating glimpse into the social changes that occurred (or failed to occur) in British working-class families during the three decades under observation.

The long-awaited follow-up to Roberts's widely admired 1984 volume *A Woman's Place: An Oral History of Working Class Women 1890–1940*, *Women and Families* was hailed as a valuable contribution to both British social history and oral history, notwithstanding several notices about Roberts's cautious analytical approach. The book was particularly influential in undermining or complicating a number of widespread generalizations about changes in working-class life during and after World War II. Today it remains an important and frequently referenced work within the field of British scholarship on World War II.

HISTORICAL AND LITERARY CONTEXT

The oral narratives quoted in *Women and Families*—as well as Roberts's accompanying commentary—are heavily informed by the social conditions and customs that characterized working-class life in Great Britain during the first few decades of the twentieth century. These included husbands who worked in unskilled or semiskilled jobs and garnered a relatively low income compared to the postwar period. Gender roles within these families tended to be rigid, with husbands serving as the primary wage earners while wives managed the household and family finances. Neighborhood communities were close-knit, perpetuating a sense of solidarity beyond the nuclear family and reifying a commonly held set of traditional values and mores.

The years from 1940 to 1970 were marked by significant social changes, though the period was more transitional than revolutionary. Britain's significantly higher average income and lower unemployment rates—around 1 percent during the most prosperous years—coupled with new, labor-saving household appliances and the advent of the National Insurance Act, the National Assistance Act, and the National Health Service Act in 1948, resulted in an unprecedented amount of spending money and potential leisure time during the postwar decades. Communitarian values slowly eroded, with families becoming more private and individualistic, as well as more child focused. Gender roles began to blur, with fathers taking a more active role in the raising of children and the managing of family finances, while women entered the workforce in progressively greater numbers—though career opportunities for women remained severely circumscribed and full-time employment generally ended upon the birth of a first child. None of these changes represented a violent, unequivocal break with the past, however, and many of the practices and attitudes of the preceding decade continued to hold sway.

The book's most immediate predecessor is Roberts's *A Woman's Place: An Oral History of Working-Class Women, 1890–1940* (1984), but other noteworthy precursors within oral history include Melvyn Bragg's *Speak for England* (1976) and Stephen Humphries's *Hooligans or Rebels?: An Oral History of Working-Class Childhood and Youth, 1889–1939* (1981). Roberts's book was also prefigured by various scholarly works from outside oral history that addressed similar subjects, including Josephine Klein's *Samples from English Culture* (1965) and Ann Oakley's *The Sociology of Housework* (1974), both of which are cited multiple times in *Women and Families*.

Roberts's book helped shape historical perceptions of British working-class family life. Lucinda McCray Beier, who served as Roberts's research assistant and conducted many of the interviews in *Women and Families*, later used evidence contained in the Elizabeth Roberts Oral Archive at Lancaster University to expand on some of the issues that formed the basis of her 2008 study *For Their Own Good:*

The Transformation of English Working-Class Health Culture, 1880–1970. Likewise, Angela Davis's oral history–based study *Modern Motherhood: Women and Family in England, c. 1945–2000* (2012) may also be seen as a recent continuation of Roberts's work.

THEMES AND STYLE

Central to *Women and Families* is the significant inertia and change that characterized postwar England, along with a sense that some of the change was less dramatic than expected or had unexpected ramifications. Roberts observes that the period's partial blending of gender roles often increased the power of men while decreasing that of women: "In the post-war world the increasing number of women who worked outside the home were not able to replace the power and status they had lost in the home with equivalent power and status in the workplace." Likewise, the phenomenon of married women in the workplace was often incorporated into the dominant paradigm of women as homemakers and caregivers rather than in opposition to it. Hence one mother asserts, "[A]fter Ron was born I have only done little jobs like brewing tea at the British Legion, or cleaning up for someone. If it only bought the material for them to have some pants it was a big help, you know."

As a continuation of *A Woman's Place*, *Women and Families* focused on the same communities as the previous work in order to analyze "attitudes, behavior, and aspects of everyday life as recalled by witnesses living through a fascinating historical period." The book is clearly intended more as a historical study than a collection of personal stories; hence Roberts quotes from her interviewees—all of whom are referred to by pseudonyms—only in relatively brief excerpts as their statements illustrate her larger observations. (Tapes and transcripts of the full interviews, Roberts notes, are available to researchers.) Various statistical graphs and references to prior work in social history provide further context for the interviews.

The structure of *Women and Families* is straightforward and methodical, and Roberts's authorial tone is generally dispassionate and circumspect. Each chapter focuses on a specific aspect of family life—examples include "Homes and Houses," "Family Planning and Role Relationships in Marriage," and "Attitudes to Social Conditioning and Education"—which is then further divided into subheadings and followed by a synthesizing conclusion. Roberts is careful to avoid claims of her study's universality, noting that "this is a book based chiefly on oral evidence, [and] it is primarily concerned with the local and the personal. It would be unwise to draw from it too many conclusions about a wider society." Although Roberts inevitably discusses the broad implications of her interviewees' statements and notes where they seem to conflict with the findings of other researchers, the book's rhetorical approach generally avoids grandiosity, argumentativeness, and claims of profundity.

CRITICAL DISCUSSION

Women and Families was largely well received. Michael E. Rose, reviewing the book in *History* in 1997, declares it "a humane but serious chronicling and analysis of a social institution of central importance in a period of rapid and bewildering change." Ellen Ross, in a mixed but ultimately positive assessment in the *Journal of Social History* in 1997, laments Roberts's "squeamishness about making general claims for the validity of her research," a complaint echoed by other critics, some of whom feel that *Women and Families* was a less cohesive and rhetorically forceful work than its predecessor. Despite these objections, the book was generally praised as an impressive work of scholarship and as a substantial contribution to its field of inquiry.

Women and Families added significantly to the scholarly understanding of working-class England and generating context for further research. It remains one

A 1945 British poster for National Savings featuring a woman and her child. British women discuss their lives from the 1940s through the 1970s in *Women and Families: An Oral History, 1940–1970* by Elizabeth Roberts. © PRIVATE COLLECTION/ARCHIVES CHARMET/THE BRIDGEMAN ART LIBRARY

A WOMAN'S PLACE: AN ORAL HISTORY OF WORKING-CLASS WOMEN, 1890–1940

Women and Families was in large part a successor to Roberts's 1984 book *A Woman's Place*, which focuses on the same communities at an earlier point in time. In fact, eleven of the second book's interviewees were descendants of people interviewed for the first volume. Roberts drew from the testimony of a much larger group of respondents in composing *A Woman's Place* (around 160, as opposed to the 98 for *Women and Families*), but the portrait of working-class English domestic life that emerges from the book is much clearer, indicating the relative cultural stability that characterized that milieu during the late nineteenth and early twentieth centuries.

Roberts depicts her interviewees as holding strong communitarian values, with both neighbors and extended family members assuming roles in a given family's social structure. Likewise, familial roles tended to exhibit relatively little variance; the book's title betokens the specific, stabilizing role that women tended to hold within the typical household. Despite the rigidity of this role, Roberts emphasizes the level of power women were able to enjoy within it, which foreshadows the subtle loss of that power amid the societal changes detailed in *Women and Families*.

of the major oral history–based studies of British life in the twentieth century, particularly when considered alongside *A Woman's Place,* which together constitute a sustained examination of eighty years of family life within a specific group of communities. Both have been cited in numerous subsequent historical works as useful compilations of firsthand information and as sources of valuable sociological analysis. It continues to attract scholarly interest in this capacity.

Scholars who discuss *Women and Families* tend to do so in the context of larger historical statements. Claire Langhamer, writing in *History Workshop Journal* in 2006, repeatedly cites Roberts's work throughout her analysis of adultery in England during the postwar period: "Whilst studies by Roberts … have demonstrated how inconsistently the 'modern marriage' chimed with the specific experience of working-class couples, the *discursive* construction of marriage increasingly foregrounded love and sex." Likewise, Lynn Abrams's 1999 article in the *Scottish Historical Review* uses Roberts's research to contextualize an argument that "manhood and fatherhood were not mutually exclusive identities for working-class men in Scotland, and that … the country's experience of working-class fatherhood has been broadly similar to trends in the rest of Britain."

BIBLIOGRAPHY

Sources

Abrams, Lynn. "'There Was Nobody Like My Daddy': Fathers, the Family and the Marginalisation of Men in Modern Scotland." *Scottish Historical Review* 78.206 (1999): 219–42. *JSTOR.* Web. 23 Jan. 2013.

Langhamer, Claire. "Adultery in Post-War England." *History Workshop Journal* 62.1 (2006): 86–115. *Oxford Journals.* Web. 23 Jan. 2013.

Roberts, Elizabeth. *Women and Families: An Oral History, 1940–1970.* Oxford, UK: Blackwell, 1995. Print.

Rose, Michael E. Rev. of *Women and Families,* by Elizabeth Roberts. *History* 82.265 (1997): 187–89. *Academic Search Complete.* Web. 23 Jan. 2013.

Ross, Ellen. Rev. of *Women and Families,* by Elizabeth Roberts. *Journal of Social History* 31.1 (1997): 210–13. *JSTOR.* Web. 23 Jan. 2013.

Further Reading

Beier, Lucinda McCray. *For Their Own Good: The Transformation of English Working-Class Health Culture, 1880–1970.* Columbus: Ohio State University Press, 2008. Print.

Bragg, Melvyn. *Speak for England: An Oral History of England from 1900–1975, Based on Interviews with Inhabitants of Wigton, Cumberland.* New York: Knopf, 1976. Print.

Briggs, Asa. *A Social History of England.* 3rd ed. London: Weidenfeld and Nicolson, 1994. Print.

Davis, Angela. *Modern Motherhood: Women and Family in England, c. 1945–2000.* Manchester, UK: Manchester University Press, 2012. Print.

Fisher, Kate. *Birth Control, Sex and Marriage in Britain, 1918–1960.* New York: Oxford University Press, 2006. Print.

Klein, Josephine. *Samples from English Culture.* 2 vols. London: Routledge & Kegan Paul, 1965. Print.

Oakley, Ann. *The Sociology of Housework.* London: Martin Robertson, 1974. Print.

Roberts, Elizabeth. *A Woman's Place: An Oral History of Working-Class Women, 1890–1940.* Oxford, UK: Basil Blackwell, 1984. Print.

Summerfield, Penny. *Reconstructing Women's Wartime Lives.* Manchester, UK: Manchester University Press, 1998. Print.

Szreter, Simon, and Kate Fisher. *Sex before the Sexual Revolution: Intimate Life in England, 1918–1963.* Cambridge, UK: Cambridge University Press, 2010. Print.

Zweiniger-Bargielowska, Ina, ed. *Women in Twentieth-Century Britain.* Harlow, UK: Longman, 2001. Print.

James Overholtzer

Women in the Chinese Enlightenment
Oral and Textual Histories
Wang Zheng

OVERVIEW

Women in the Chinese Enlightenment: Oral and Textual Histories, compiled by historian Wang Zheng from 1993 to 1995 and published in 1999, offers five female perspectives on life and women's rights in China from 1915 to 1925—before, during, and after the May Fourth, or New Culture, era. Wang, who grew up in Shanghai fully entrenched in the era of the People's Republic, wanted to tell the forgotten stories of these women and "break the male monopoly of … the May Fourth era." This oral history involves five women born around the beginning of the twentieth century. They pursued diverse careers ranging from education to journalism to politics. Some were associated with the communists, some were with the nationalists, and some were apolitical. The only true similarities in the lives of these five women were that they all lived exceptional lives for Chinese women and their decisions were guided or shaped by the feminist ideals of the May Fourth era.

Writing the book during a time when China was emerging as a potential "global superpower" and had been firmly controlled by the People's Republic for decades, Wang chose to focus on women whose stories were left behind in the race toward advancement. The book was regarded highly in academic circles particularly for uncovering forgotten history, although some questioned Wang's objectivity. Working against both a Western stereotype of "subservient" Chinese women and the widespread belief circulated by the CCP that the Communist Party liberated Chinese women, Wang gives a forum to women whose liberation came mostly from their own efforts.

HISTORICAL AND LITERARY CONTEXT

In 1911, after millennia of rule by imperial dynasties, the Qing dynasty was overthrown and the Republic of China was established. This new government led to political instability and many questions about what the future of China would hold. Many people, particularly young people, began to feel that China's traditional culture was holding the nation back on the world stage and keeping China "backward" in comparison to the West. The May Fourth, or New Culture, movement arose as a reaction to the Treaty of Versailles, in which China had to submit to humiliating conditions toward its ancient rival, Japan.

One of the elements of Chinese culture that May Fourth activists attacked was traditional Chinese treatment of women. At the time, many women faced the common practices of foot-binding, forced marriage, and concubinage, and very few received an education or worked outside the home. The structures of the family and of society as a whole were built around Confucian ideals in which women depended entirely on their husbands. Both women and men involved in the New Culture movement advocated strongly for the "emancipation of women," in part as a crucial step toward a modern China. This flourishing of feminism, as Wang argues through her five testimonies, allowed women born near the turn of the twentieth century to have lives very different from the lives of their mothers and to understand themselves as individuals deserving of equality. *Women in the Chinese Enlightenment* is an oral history of five women who all pursued careers during the May Fourth era.

Wang's text builds on the work of other scholars. She explicitly cites a 1971 dissertation by Roxanne Witke called "Transformation of Attitudes towards Women during the May Fourth Era," which asked the same basic question that drove Wang's book: Why have women of this period been so forgotten? Another, more widely known work that paved the way for Wang was Elizabeth Kelley Gilmartin's *Engendering the Chinese Revolution: Radical Women, Communist Politics, and Mass Movements in the 1920s,* published in 1995, a constructed narrative of communist women based on interviews.

Although probably not well known outside academic circles, *Women in the Chinese Enlightenment* was well regarded when it came out and was reviewed in many prominent journals. Reviewers praised the author for writing about a fairly unknown subject, as well as for the interesting content of her interviews. On the book jacket, historian Dorothy Ko called the book a "milestone" that would "set the agenda for future scholars researching the relationship between feminism and nationalism in China."

THEMES AND STYLE

The central themes of the oral histories collected in *Women in the Chinese Enlightenment* are the changing nature of what it meant to be a woman in Chinese

❖ **Key Facts**

Time Period:
Early 20th Century

Relevant Historical Events:
New Culture era in China; modernization of China; rise of feminism in China

Nationality:
Chinese

Keywords:
feminism; intellectualism; women's rights

CULTURE AND TRADITION

A 2005 photograph of a Chinese man in front of a Beijing monument depicting the May Fourth Movement of 1919, which advocated political and social change. The histories of Chinese women active in the May Fourth Movement appear in *Women in the Chinese Enlightenment: Oral and Textual Histories* by Wang Zheng. © AP IMAGES/NG HAN GUAN

society, overcoming (or failing to overcome) barriers imposed by sexism. The five women interviewed all led unconventional lives and had successful careers: two were physical education teachers and the others an attorney, a journalist, and a career revolutionary. One recurring theme is an early dissatisfaction with women's status, whether that involved cutting bindings off of feet or disguising oneself as a boy to attend school, as was the case with Lu Lihua. Several of the women interviewed stated an attachment to the story of Hua Mulan, who dressed up as a man in her father's place to go to war. This early discovery of sexism fueled many of the career decisions of these women: "That is why I chose to study law," Zhu Su'e states, "to protect nüquan [women's rights]." Another recurring theme was political involvement and the changing political state. Many of the women were heavily involved in women's organizations, and one (Wang Yiwei) even founded a women's magazine. The author also tries to combat the theme of feminism having reached China only through the Communist Party. Only one of the interviewees, Huang Dinghui, is a member of the Communist Party, and she speaks of sexism within the party and feeling like a forgotten "ghost" in spite of being imprisoned for decades for her party allegiance.

Wang states that her interest in this period arose out of "both a political interest in deconstructing the CCP's myth of Chinese women's liberation and an intellectual dissatisfaction with stories about Chinese women that lacked women as protagonists." Although she spoke to many women born near the turn of the century, Wang chose five women who "had many accomplishments before 1949 but were reduced to marginal positions in the Mao era." She chose to "present their narratives in their entirety instead of selecting quotations from the narratives to suit [her] needs" and did not organize the narratives based around historical events.

The text is organized into two sections. The first section, called "The Setting," explains the background material necessary to understand the historical moment of these Chinese women. The second section, titled "Portraits," contains the oral histories of the five women, each organized by individual speaker. After each oral history Wang inserts a lengthy commentary, interpreting the particular oral history from a historical standpoint. Her choice of direct transcription limits her editorial intervention in the oral testimonies themselves, although she makes translation choices that can be more closely examined in a glossary of Chinese characters included at the end.

CRITICAL DISCUSSION

Early response to *Women in the Chinese Enlightenment* was largely positive, with many critics noting how interesting the book was. "The stories the women tell feel like novels," remarked Wendy Larson in the *Journal of Asian Studies,* adding that "Wang Zheng has selected, transcribed, and edited the stories with intelligence and sensitivity." Barbara Mittler, writing for the *American Historical Review,* commented that the book was "so gripping it keeps one up all night," although she noted that Wang's book may have "too one-sided" a view on liberal feminism, ignoring to some extent the class privilege needed to reap benefits from the May Fourth movement. In *Asian Studies Review,* Louise Edwards praised the book for its scholarship in a much-ignored field, predicting that "this book is destined to become a first reference for scholars and students working on women in twentieth-century China."

Today Wang's book is mainly known only in academic circles within the field, although it was still being reviewed in such journals as *Philosophy East and West* and *Journal of Asian and African Studies* in 2003, four years after its publication. *Women in the Chinese Enlightenment* continues to serve as an important text for other researchers. In a *Pacific Historical Review* article about woman suffrage in China, Edwards noted that, along with Ono Kazuko and Christina Gilmartin, Wang has "been particularly significant" in unearthing the forgotten feminist movement of the May Fourth era and "promoting this scholarship to the Western academy."

While most criticisms of the text are highly complimentary, some have found elements of Wang's book problematic. In a particularly negative review in the *China Journal*, Weili Ye accused Wang of inserting a "master narrative, that of 'liberal feminism,'" onto Chinese history and for inappropriately trying to separate the nationalist cause from that of women's rights. Paola Paderni, although praising the book in her review for *Social History*, had a similar complaint. She argued that "the author's reconstruction of this liberal feminism … is occasionally affected by prejudices or ingenuity which may derive from an excessive belief in the abstract concept of liberal humanism" and may have biased her explanation.

BIBLIOGRAPHY

Sources

Edwards, Louise. Rev. of *Women in the Chinese Enlightenment*, by Wang Zheng. *Asian Studies Review* 24.2 (2000): 279. *Academic Search Elite*. Web. 14 Jan. 2013.

———. "Women's Suffrage in China: Challenging Scholarly Conventions." *Pacific Historical Review* 69.4 (2000): 617–38. *JSTOR*. Web. 14 Jan. 2013.

Larson, Wendy. Rev. of *Women in the Chinese Enlightenment*, by Wang Zheng. *Journal of Asian Studies* 59.2 (2000): 423–24. *JSTOR*. Web. 14 Jan. 2013.

Mittler, Barbara. Rev. of *Women in the Chinese Enlightenment*, by Wang Zheng. *American Historical Review* 105.3 (2000): 906. Web. *JSTOR*. 14 Jan. 2013.

Paderni, Paola. Rev. of *Women in the Chinese Enlightenment*, by Wang Zheng. *Social History* 26.3 (2001): 378–80. Web. *JSTOR*. 14 Jan. 2013.

Wang, Zheng. *Women in the Chinese Enlightenment: Oral and Textual Histories*. Berkeley: University of California Press, 1999. Web. 14 Jan. 2013.

Ye, Weili. Rev. of *Women in the Chinese Enlightenment*, by Wang Zheng, and *Women of the Long March*, by Lily Xiao Hong Lee and Sue Wiles. *China Journal* 45 (2001): 262–64. Web. *JSTOR*. 14 Jan. 2013.

Further Reading

Gilmartin, Christina K. *Engendering the Chinese Revolution: Radical Women, Communist Politics, and Mass Movements in the 1920s*. Berkeley: University of California Press, 1995. Print.

MAY FOURTH AND MAY THIRTIETH

Wang Zheng dates the May Fourth era, or Chinese Enlightenment, as lasting from the May Fourth movement of 1919 to the May Thirtieth movement of 1925. The May Fourth protests occurred on May 4, 1919, in Beijing and began as student protests arising as a reaction to the World War I–ending Treaty of Versailles, which protesters believed forced China to give unfair concessions to Japan. This included giving Japan the Shadong province, even though China had supported the winning Allies under the condition that they would be allowed ownership of Shadong. The movement was rooted in anti-imperialism, science, democracy, and nationalism. Three thousand students protested in Tiananmen Square and strikes of workers and students continued in other cities until June. This event sparked a great deal of progressive thought in Chinese society, including questions concerning women's rights.

The May Thirtieth incident occurred during a protest on May 30, 1925. Workers in Shanghai were protesting an incident when a Japanese guard had shot a cotton worker dead while he was demonstrating. Thousands of protestors gathered outside the International Settlement. A British officer began to shoot into the crowd, killing thirteen people and wounding twenty. The incident horrified and angered China and begat many other protests and a strong nationalist sentiment. Wang argues that the nationalism following the May Thirtieth incident overpowered the other ideologies, including feminism, that had been an important part of the New Culture movement.

Hershatter, Gail. *Guide to Women's Studies in China*. Berkeley: University of California Press, 1998. Print.

Liu, Lydia He., Rebecca E. Karl, and Dorothy Ko. *The Birth of Chinese Feminism: Essential Texts in Transnational Theory*. New York: Columbia University Press, 2013. Print.

Wang, Zheng. *Never Forget National Humiliation: Historical Memory in Chinese Politics and Foreign Relations*. New York: Columbia University Press, 2012. Print.

Witke, Roxane H. "Transformation of Attitudes towards Women during the May Fourth Era." Ph.D. diss. Berkeley: University of California Press, 1971. Print.

Young, Marilyn Blatt. *Women in China: Studies in Social Change and Feminism*. Ann Arbor: University of Michigan Press, 1973. Print.

Zhou, Cezong. *The May Fourth Movement: Intellectual Revolution in Modern China*. Cambridge, MA: Harvard University Press, 1960. Print.

Emily Jones

THEORIES

Between Management and Labor: Oral Histories of Arbitration by Clara Friedman   153

The Death of Luigi Trastulli and Other Stories by Alessandro Portelli   157

Hard Times: An Oral History of the Great Depression by Louis "Studs" Terkel   161

I, Rigoberta Menchú: An Indian Woman in Guatemala by Rigoberta Menchú   164

Juan the Chamula: An Ethnological Re-creation of the Life of a Mexican Indian by Ricardo Pozas   167

Oral History, Health and Welfare by Joanna Bornat, Robert Perks, Paul Thompson, and Jan Walmsley   170

Oral History Theory by Lynn Abrams   173

Popular Memory: Theory, Politics, Method by Popular Memory Group   176

A Shared Authority: Essays on the Craft and Meaning of Oral and Public History by Michael Frisch   179

The Story of a Shipwrecked Sailor by Gabriel García Márquez   183

The Voice of the Past: Oral History by Paul Thompson   186

Women's Words: The Feminist Practice of Oral History by Sherna Berger Gluck and Daphne Patai   190

Between Management and Labor
Oral Histories of Arbitration
Clara Friedman

OVERVIEW

Between Management and Labor: Oral Histories of Arbitration (1995), compiled and edited by arbitrator Clara Friedman, uses oral history to follow the development of labor arbitration both as a legal practice and a profession. Developed from interviews conducted in 1983 and 1984, the book presents the narratives of fourteen arbitrators discussing their methods and recounting their most memorable cases. The arbitrators represent three generations of practice, starting with those who in the 1930s and 1940s heard a trickle of cases as a sideline to their main occupation and continuing through to the career arbitrators who heard numerous cases in the 1970s and early 1980s.

Initiated during a period when many of the arbitration pioneers were approaching retirement, *Between Management and Labor* reflects Friedman's commitment to preserve the wisdom of some of her field's earliest and most proficient practitioners, many of whom had written little of their work due to its delicate and often confidential nature. While well received in the few reviews published in the mainstream press, the work has proven useful to those interested in the history of arbitration between management and labor. The text is also notable in documenting important events in the twentieth century as they intertwine with and impact the development of arbitration.

HISTORICAL AND LITERARY CONTEXT

The histories collected in *Between Management and Labor* reflect the robust growth of the U.S. economy in the twentieth century and the attendant need for a variety of strategies to address disputes between labor and management in the country's private and public sectors. With roots dating back to the Revolutionary War era, the modern practice of arbitration emerged with the rapid increase in union membership from the dawn of the twentieth century to the early 1920s. The National War Labor Board (NWLB), initiated by President Woodrow Wilson during World War I, and its successor, created by President Franklin Roosevelt during World War II, were instrumental in developing standards that would govern arbitration practice in the decades that followed.

In the early years arbitrators often worked pro bono and generally had another primary occupation, typically in law or education. The U.S. Supreme Court's rulings in the so-called Steelworkers Trilogy in 1960 (*United Steelworkers of America v. American Manufacturing Co., United Steelworkers of America v. Warrior & Gulf Navigation Co.,* and *United Steelworkers of America v. Enterprise Wheel & Car Corp.*) served to reinforce the legitimacy of arbitration in labor-management disputes. This newfound legitimacy, in turn, made arbitration more viable as a primary career option and pulled more people into the field in general. Although the labor movement went into decline during the 1970s, leading to a decrease in the number of arbitration cases associated with private labor unions, arbitration surged in other areas, most notably related to collective-bargaining agreement cases in the public sector, service industry, and professional sports.

The National Academy of Arbitrators, a professional organization for those in the field, has a tradition of collecting oral histories from its members. A 1982 publication, *Oral History Project: The Early Days of Labor Arbitration as Recalled by G. Allan Dash, Jr., Sylvester Garrett, John Day Larkin, Harry H. Platt, Ralph T. Seward, William E. Simkin,* describes work by some of the trailblazers of the field. *Between Management and Labor* is also related to the tradition of oral histories of workers and labor union members. Peter Friedlander's *The Emergence of a UAW Local, 1936–1939: A Study in Class and Culture* (1976) documents the formation and development of a local United Automobile Workers union at a parts factory in Detroit in the 1930s. In Shelton Stromquist's *Solidarity and Survival* (1993), three generations of Iowa workers reflect on the struggle to create a labor movement in industries ranging from mining to construction. These and other texts, while not dealing directly with arbitration, give expressions to the sorts of concerns that prompt workers to unionize and to enter into disputes with management.

Since the publication of Friedman's oral history, a number of other books have appeared that provide additional context in understanding the forces that have, broadly speaking, shaped labor arbitration in the United States. Particularly notable is Valerie Jean Conner's *The National War Labor Board: Stability, Social Justice, and the Voluntary State in World War I* (1983),

⁜ Key Facts

Time Period:
Mid- to Late 20th Century

Relevant Historical Events:
Establishment of the National War Labor Board; 1960 Steelworkers Trilogy of Supreme Court cases

Nationality:
American

Keywords:
labor; unionism; arbitration

THEORIES

Pilots working for Delta Air Lines receive signs to display during picketing at the Greater Cincinnati/Northern Kentucky International Airport in Hebron, Kentucky, in 2006. The pilots' union threatened to strike if an arbitration panel let the airline reduce the salaries and benefits of the union's 6,000 members. The company contended that without those reductions it could not continue operations. © AP IMAGES/TOM UHLMAN

which examines the NWLB and the manner in which both labor and management groups attempted to profit from the strictures necessitated by U.S. involvement in World War I. Several of those interviewed for *Between Management and Labor* have gone on to lend their expertise to other publications. For instance, Robert Coulson recounts his tenure as president of the American Arbitration Association in *Family Mediation: Managing Conflict, Resolving Disputes* (1996).

THEMES AND STYLE

Between Management and Labor explores the nature of labor arbitration and its development in the United States, shaped as it was by the tumults of the world wars and rapid economic expansion in the private sector. The text also examines arbitration as it morphed from part-time obligation of a few select attorneys and professors to full-blown career option. Presenting the narratives of fourteen arbitrators, each with an individual chapter introduced by Friedman, *Between Management and Labor* concludes with a chapter by historian Irving Bernstein. Walter Gellhorn, an attorney and arbitrator who introduced the term *ombudsman* into the legal lexicon, attributes labor arbitration's basic philosophy of "avoiding the continuation of warfare about matters in contest" to the imperative of maintaining production during World Wars I and II. In terms of the practice of arbitration as a profession, Emmanuel Stein, in the book's opening narrative, remembers the early days when the phrase "Gee, I have two arbitrations booked for this month" indicated bounty and when arbitration was performed gratis or for "$25 or $30 for a case." Coulson, longtime administrator for the American Arbitration Association, describes subsequent generations of arbitrators hearing thirty-five to fifty cases a week.

Friedman conceives of "the window of oral history" as a way to access the experiences of skilled arbitrators without violating the confidential nature of their work. Further, she maintains that oral history interviews, while they "should not be vehicles for telling tales out of school," are well suited to summarizing insights in the process of narrating one's professional life and experiences. In the interest of providing narratives of historical import, Friedman includes in her history arbitrators at the top of the field rather than a representative sample from throughout the profession. This move is somewhat unusual in that oral histories tend to focus on everyday rather than especially illustrious lives.

The histories in *Between Management and Labor* vary in tone and style, but they similarly skirt around legal details and case specifics, veering instead toward the anecdotal and philosophical. In recalling his work as arbitrator of a dispute between the Jersey City Police Officer's Benevolent Association (JCPOBA) and Jersey City, for example, Irving Halevy recalls not the specifics of the case but his relationship with the police who donated blood when he had a heart attack following its settlement. "Approximately a month later," he remembers, "I received a note from the Jersey City PBA asking how it felt to have policemen's blood flowing through my veins." Similarly, recalling a defense plant election he refereed during his time with the National Labor Relations Board, Arthur Stark describes his puzzlement as he watched a young black man try to enter a voting booth by going to the back and climbing down over the top. Stark eventually realized that "his whole life [the young man] had been told that where white folks are involved he had to go around the back."

CRITICAL DISCUSSION

Between Management and Labor was written primarily for audiences in law and academia, and it was not widely reviewed on publication. Writing for *Booklist*, David Rouse praises the book's "fascinating" stories from arbitrators who "observed firsthand and even participated in—almost anonymously—major historic events of our time."

As Donald Ritchie notes in the book's foreword, Friedman's text makes available a succinct collection of labor arbitration narratives that would otherwise exist only "scattered in archives ... undiscovered or simply not used." While little critical work has been undertaken on *Between Management and Labor* as a standalone text, its histories constitute important source material for scholarship on arbitration.

Laura Cooper's book chapter "The Process of Process: The Historical Development of Procedure in Labor Arbitration," published in *Arbitration 2005: The Evolving World of Work: Proceedings of the Fifty-Eighth Annual Meeting, National Academy of Arbitrators* (2006), utilizes the accounts of Ida Klaus and Gellhorn to explore the ways in which the practice of arbitration evolved over decades in circumstances that, contrary to popular belief, did not always amount to the opposition of two equally powerful groups—labor unions and employers. In an era of diminished union participation, this fact, Cooper opines, can offer "reason to hope as we watch the now-ongoing, and often-discouraging, evolution of procedure in employment arbitration."

BIBLIOGRAPHY

Sources

Cooper, Laura. "The Process of Process: The Historical Development of Procedure in Labor Arbitration." *Arbitration 2005: The Evolving World of Work: Proceedings of the Fifty-Eighth Annual Meeting, National Academy of Arbitrators*. Ed. Charles Coleman. Washington, D.C.: Bureau of National Affairs, 2006. *National Academy of Arbitrators*. National Academy of Arbitrators. Web. 21 Jan. 2013.

Friedman, Clara, ed. *Between Management and Labor: Oral Histories of Arbitration*. New York: Twayne, 1995. Print.

ARBITRATION VERSUS MEDIATION

The terms *arbitrate* and *mediate* are often used almost interchangeably outside the strictures of law. However, within the legal system, these terms indicate distinct practices. While both practices are aimed at settling a dispute between parties without recourse to litigation, arbitration is more likely to result in a legally binding outcome. Generally conducted before a panel of three arbitrators, one chosen by each party and a third chosen by the other two, arbitration typically involves a presentation of evidence and a written decision prepared by the arbitrators. Mediation, on the other hand, is typically conducted by a single mediator and may follow a more informal procedure. Moreover, mediation can be applied to a broader variety of disputes and at a much earlier stage, before a lawsuit is likely to be imminent.

Although arbitration and mediation are typically practiced by different professionals, in his chapter in *Between Management and Labor* Benjamin Wolf recounts doing both, sometimes in the same case. Wolf relates his handling of a wildcat strike by black members of a union in a South Carolina shirt plant. In mediation, Wolf uncovered the reason for the strike, which violated the "no strike" clause of the union-management agreement in effect. The strike had been precipitated by the firing of a black man for falsifying his time sheet while a white woman caught doing the same in a previous week had gotten a weeklong suspension. Clarifying the nature of the disagreement and defining the outcomes each side hoped to receive during mediation smoothed the way for the arbitration hearing, which was settled by allowing the man to keep his job and giving the employer the option to make a new policy for future violations.

Ritchie, Donald. Foreword. *Between Management and Labor: Oral Histories of Arbitration*. Ed. Clara Friedman. New York: Twayne, 1995. Print.

Rouse, David. Rev. of *Between Management and Labor: Oral Histories of Arbitration*, ed. Clara Friedman. *Booklist* July 1995: 1846. *Literature Resource Center*. Web. 21 Jan. 2013.

Further Reading

Bennett, Stephan. *Arbitration: Essential Concepts*. New York: ALM, 2002. Print.

Buhl, Paul M. *Working Lives: An Oral History of Rhode Island Labor*. Providence: Rhode Island Historical Society, 1987. Print.

Conner, Valerie Jean. *The National War Labor Board: Stability, Social Justice, and the Voluntary State in World War I*. Chapel Hill: University of North Carolina Press, 1983. Print.

Coulson, Robert. *Family Mediation: Managing Conflict, Resolving Disputes*. San Francisco: Jossey-Bass, 1996. Print.

Dash, G. A. *Oral History Project: The Early Days of Labor Arbitration as Recalled by G. Allan Dash, Jr., Sylvester Garrett, John Day Larkin, Harry H. Platt, Ralph*

T. Seward, William E. Simkin. Washington, D.C.: Academy, 1982. Print.

Friedlander, Peter. *The Emergence of a UAW Local, 1936–1939: A Study in Class and Culture*. Pittsburgh: University of Pittsburgh Press, 1976. Print.

Hackett, Frank Warren. *Reminiscences of the Geneva Tribunal of Arbitration, 1872, the Alabama Claims*. Boston: Houghton Mifflin, 1911. Print.

Kuhn, Clifford M. *Contesting the New South Order: The 1914–1915 Strike at Atlanta's Fulton Mills*. Chapel Hill: University of North Carolina Press, 2002. Print.

Stromquist, Shelton. *Solidarity & Survival: An Oral History of Iowa Labor in the Twentieth Century*. Iowa City: University of Iowa Press, 1993. Print.

Terkel, Studs. *Working: People Talk about What They Do All Day and How They Feel about What They Do*. New York: Pantheon, 1974. Print.

Daisy Gard

The Death of Luigi Trastulli and Other Stories
Alessandro Portelli

OVERVIEW

The Death of Luigi Trastulli and Other Stories (1991) is a collection of essays about working-class communities in Terni, Italy, and Harlan County, Kentucky, written by Italian journalist, professor, former criminal lawyer, and oral historian Alessandro Portelli. The essays combine Portelli's historical analysis with transcribed portions of interviews with local narrators and verses from folk songs written in response to historical conditions. Portelli grew up in middle-class Terni but made friends with children from the city's working class, and those friends and their relatives provide many of the tales included in the volume. For the Harlan County essays, the author consulted local narrators, folk songs, and transcripts from a 1936 Senate subcommittee on freedom of speech and workers' rights. Portelli begins the work with an essay on the shooting death of factory worker Luigi Trastulli by local police at a 1949 anti-NATO (North Atlantic Treaty Organization) rally. Using this as a starting point, he investigates historical events and the conditions that occasioned them. The essays operate on two different levels: they illuminate history with stories and songs that aim at representing events in their many dimensions, and they demonstrate the power and relevance such narratives may have for historians.

Published for the most part in Italian academic journals during the 1980s, the essays cover events ranging from the 1920s clashes between police and labor activists in Terni to the intricate union politics of 1970s Kentucky. Portelli is admired for the compassion and affection he brings to his work and is respected for his efforts to understand the gap between scholars and the social questions they study. Thus, the volume continues to be a valuable resource for scholars of labor issues and oral history.

HISTORICAL AND LITERARY CONTEXT

The stories and songs collected in *Luigi Trastulli* reflect working-class life in the twentieth century. Both of the locales Portelli studies went through rapid industrialization in the late nineteenth century. With its proximity to Rome and distance from the sea, Terni was the ideal site for the recently united country to build its first ammunition factory. The construction of steel and textile mills and chemical and electricity plants rapidly followed. In Kentucky coal mines became the focal point for many communities. In both places the companies came to significantly affect the lives of the people who worked for them, with the factory whistle replacing the church bell, as one Italian folk song recalls.

Accelerating industrialization roughly coincided with the rise of the international labor movement. In Terni, in 1907, workers were locked out of the steelworks for three months, and five demonstrators died in clashes between workers and police in 1920, despite the United Nations' ratification of a workers' rights constitution in 1919. In 1931, when Harlan County miners tried to unionize, they faced staunch opposition from both employers and local police. That same year Kentucky folksinger Molly Jackson wrote: "I am a union woman, as brave as I can be, I do not like the bosses, and the bosses don't like me." Complicating matters on both sides of the Atlantic was the socialist ideology behind the workers' movement, which clashed with the more conservative values held by those in power.

Luigi Trastulli belongs to the literary tradition of working-class and labor movement oral histories. Notable examples include Clara Friedman's *Between Management and Labor: Oral Histories of Arbitration* (1995), a collection of oral histories from arbitrators who tried to broker agreements between unions and employers from the 1930s to the 1990s; Lewis H. Sigelbaum and Daniel J. Walkowitz's *Workers of the Donbass Speak: Survival and Identity in the New Ukraine, 1989–1992* (1995), which includes the testimony of coal miners who participated in the Soviet Union–wide strike during the summer of 1989; and Marat Moore's *Women in the Mines: Stories of Life and Work* (1996), a collection of oral histories of women who succeeded in altering the face of the U.S. mining industry and its union in the 1970s.

Luigi Trastulli has been credited as a great contribution to the relatively new field of oral history (it emerged as an academic discipline in the 1950s) and is often included in North American university class syllabi. Portelli continued to elaborate his methods in works such as *The Battle of Valle Giulia* (1997), which takes as its starting point 1960s Italian student protests;

❖ **Key Facts**

Time Period:
20th Century

Relevant Historical Events:
Labor struggles in Terni, Italy, and Harlan County, Kentucky

Nationality:
Italian

Keywords:
labor; unionism; industrialization

THEORIES

Striking Fiat workers in Rome in 2005. The 1949 murder of protesting Italian union member Luigi Trastulli is the focus of Alessandro Portelli's *The Death of Luigi Trastulli and Other Stories.* © SILVIA MORARA/CORBIS

The Order Has Been Carried Out (2003), about a Nazi massacre in Rome (winner of the 2005 Oral History Association Book Award); and *They Say in Harlan County* (2011), which defines oral history as simply "the telling of historical narratives in oral form." He has been a popular lecturer on oral history methodology.

THEMES AND STYLE

Portelli's aim with *Luigi Trastulli* is to suggest that truer versions of history can be made by including oral history. He examines how people arrange their memories to lessen the pain of distressing events and explores the tensions between working-class populations and the forces that govern their lives. Sante Carboni, a local worker, wrote these lyrics in an attempt to clarify the motive behind the anti-NATO demonstration in which Luigi Trastulli was killed: "The treaty you have signed / is a dark act of treason, / which will make Italy / a slave to foreigners." Portelli discovered that by the 1970s, when he was interviewing Terni locals, people telling the story of Trastulli's death often shifted it to the 1953 unrest involving thousands of layoffs or attributed the 1949 anti-NATO rally to workers' protests. Imagining the different levels of time or cause in which a narrator might place an event, Portelli observed that "the placing of one event on one level is not intrinsic to the event itself, but to the narrator's perspective."

Portelli, whose reputation as a leading oral historian is undisputed, has noted that he genuinely enjoys fieldwork and expresses gratitude in his foreword to *Luigi Trastulli* to "the hundreds of women and men from whom I received the gift of songs and stories" over the years. In a lecture at the University of London in 2012, he shared additional stories from the people he interviewed, expressing regret that he had to leave so many out of the volume.

Acknowledging the difficulties of transcribing the way people talk, particularly in dialect, Portelli makes every effort to render the narrators' words naturally. One of them, Elchide Trippa, "in wistful, faultless old-time dialect," said that he "would speak less and say more" if only he could speak that way for the whole interview. Through this exchange Portelli shows that some members of Terni's working class "had lost one language without mastering another." In Kentucky, Portelli captures Tillman Cadle describing a preacher: "And one day, we was havin' a big mass meeting in Pineville, and they was a fellow they called him the 'cussing preacher.'" In a chapter about a major Italian court case, a former criminal repeatedly uses the phrase "I confirm the transcript," explaining, "I have been in so many trials and heard it used so often that I thought it was a ritual formula." Portelli, a trained lawyer, uses the example to demonstrate the shortcomings of the Italian legal system's reliance on pretrial transcripts of testimony, which are often edited and selected by judges.

CRITICAL DISCUSSION

Although much of *Luigi Trastulli* had already been published in peer-reviewed journals by the time the book was released in 1991, it was the first time some of the essays appeared in English. Pioneering British oral historian Paul Thompson, reviewing the book for *Oral History* in 1991, called it "a future must for any oral historian" and praised Portelli's "fusion of history and comparative cultural studies." In the *Journal of American History*, in 1992, Paul Buhle applauded Portelli's commitment to "the scholar's fundamental obligation: justice to the subjects of our historical pursuits." Writing for the *Oral History Review* in 1993, Amy Shuman lamented a lack of more substantial links between the essays but concluded that they "made an important contribution to ongoing discussion of what it means to say—and whether it even can be said—that oral history is in any sense the people's history or that workers are creators of their own culture."

Luigi Trastulli is typically included in the collections of academic oral history centers, and Portelli may be called one of the discipline's few celebrities. The methodology and warmhearted approach that characterize the volume, as well as its elaboration of notions such as those of *événement* and *longue durée*—that is, a specific event versus long-term historical conditions, espoused by French historian Fernand Braudel—have earned widespread acclaim for *Luigi Trastulli*. In 1999 Betsy Brinson of the *Oral History Review* interviewed Portelli, the transcript of which was published in the journal in 2001.

Recent scholarship related to *Luigi Trastulli* continues to explore Portelli's methodology and the issues he studied. In a 2001 article published in the *New York Times*, Alexander Stille acknowledged Portelli as a major influence in the discipline of oral history and also drew a parallel between his work and that of Italian historian Luisa Passerini, who in 1979 "delivered a groundbreaking paper that examined the silences, discrepancies, irrelevancies and inconsistencies" she encountered while interviewing people who worked in Italy under fascist rule. Portelli himself did not turn his back on the workers of Terni after *Luigi Trastulli*. He returned to Terni in 1999 to investigate the closing of an electrical steel plant and a factory fire that killed seven people. He interviewed, among others, thirty-eight-year-old factory worker Giovanni Pignalosa, who described going on a coffee break: "And this young man runs up to me and says, 'Giovanni, Giovanni, come! Line number 5 blew up. They're all dead.'" As in Portelli's best interviews, the quote brings an immediacy and clarity to events. Moreover, it quotes another person, the "young man," showing how the best stories often contain the stories of others.

SONG OF CONSTANT SORROW

One of the folksingers who inspired Alessandro Portelli to become an oral historian was Sarah Ogan Gunning, who grew up in Kentucky coal country and was married to a miner. She adapted the song "Man of Constant Sorrow" as "I Am a Girl of Constant Sorrow" after mine-induced tuberculosis killed her husband, as it did her mother. Her arrangement appeared in *People's Songs Bulletin* in the 1940s. "Man of Constant Sorrow" was first published in a 1913 Richard Burnett songbook. The first verse goes: "I am a man of constant sorrow / I've seen trouble all my days / I'll bid farewell to old Kentucky / The place where I was born and raised." In a 1973 interview *Old Time Music* journalist Charles Wolfe asked Burnett if he had written the song. Burnett replied, "No, I think I got the ballet [sic] from somebody—I dunno. It may be my song." It may be that the song's simple, arresting melody had existed for a long time; many folk songs from the Appalachian region describing the protracted struggle between workers and coal barons were adapted from hymns.

In 1928 Kentucky singer Emry Arthur recorded another version, and in the 1960s folksingers Joan Baez and Bob Dylan also covered "Man/Girl of Constant Sorrow," Baez replacing "Kentucky" with "California" and turning it into a love song. It was restored to popularity once again in 2000 thanks to Dan Tyminski, Harley Allen, and Pat Enright's contribution to the film *O Brother, Where Art Thou?*

BIBLIOGRAPHY

Sources

Brinson, Betsy. "Crossing Cultures: An Interview with Alessandro Portelli." *Oral History Review* 28.1 (2001): 87–113. *JSTOR.* Web. 23 Jan. 2013.

Buhle, Paul. Rev. of *The Death of Luigi Trastulli and Other Stories*, by Alessandro Portelli. *Journal of American History* 78.4 (1992): 1404–5. *JSTOR.* Web. 23 Jan. 2013.

Friedman, Clara. *Between Management and Labor: Oral Histories of Arbitration.* New York: Twayne, 1995. Print.

Moore, Marat. *Women in the Mines: Stories of Life and Work.* New York: Twayne, 1996. Print.

Portelli, Alessandro. *The Death of Luigi Trastulli and Other Stories: Form and Meaning in Oral History.* Albany: State University of New York Press, 1991. Print.

———. "Italian Steel Workers in the Era of Supermechanisation and Globalisation: What Kinds of Creativity?" *Oral History* 37.2 (2009): 71–75. *JSTOR.* Web. 23 Jan. 2013.

———. "Reflecting on a Life in Progress and the Stories of Oral History." Royal Holloway, University of London Department of History. 6 Nov. 2012. Lecture. *Blackdoorbroadcasting.net.* Web. 22 Jan. 2013.

Shuman, Amy. Rev. of *The Death of Luigi Trastulli and Other Stories*, by Alessandro Portelli. *Oral History Review* 21.1 (1993): 119–21. *JSTOR.* Web. 22 Jan. 2013.

Sigelbaum, Lewis H., and Daniel J. Walkowitz. *Workers of the Donbass Speak: Survival and Identity in the New Ukraine, 1989–1992.* Albany: State University of New York Press, 1995. Print.

Stille, Alexander. "Prospecting for Truth in the Ore of Memory." *New York Times.* New York Times, 10 Mar. 2001. Web. 23 Jan. 2013.

Thompson, Paul. Rev. of *The Death of Luigi Trastulli and Other Stories*, by Alessandro Portelli. *Oral History* 19.2 (1991): 74–75. *JSTOR.* Web. 22 Jan. 2013.

United Nations International Labor Organization. "Origins and History." *International Labor Organization*. Web. 22 Jan. 2013.

Further Reading

Braudel, Fernand. *On History.* Trans. Sarah Matthews. Chicago: University of Chicago Press, 1980. Print.

Donaldson, Findlay. "Hard Times in These Mines." American Folklife Center, Library of Congress. 1938. Sound recording. 10-inch vinyl.

Gaventa, John. *Power and Powerlessness: Quiescence and Rebellion in an Appalachian Valley.* Oxford, UK: Clarendon Press, 1980. Print.

Goody, Jack, ed. *Literacy in Traditional Societies.* Cambridge: Cambridge University Press, 1968. Print.

Johnson, David W. *Lonesome Melodies: The Lives and Loves of the Stanley Brothers.* Jackson: University Press of Mississippi, 2013. Print.

Ong, Walter J. *Orality and Literacy: The Technologizing of the Word.* London: Routledge, 1982. Print.

Salstrom, Paul. *Appalachia's Path to Dependency: Rethinking a Region's Economic History, 1730–1940.* Lexington: University Press of Kentucky, 1994. Print.

Thompson, Paul. *Voices of the Past: Oral History.* Oxford, UK: Oxford University Press, 2000. Print.

Wolfe, Charles K. *Kentucky Country: Folk and Country Music of Kentucky.* Lexington: University Press of Kentucky, 1982. Print.

Rebecca Rustin

Hard Times
An Oral History of the Great Depression
Louis "Studs" Terkel

OVERVIEW

Published in 1970, Louis "Studs" Terkel's *Hard Times: An Oral History of the Great Depression* features the thoughts and memories of more than a hundred Americans on the subject of the Great Depression. The assembled narratives address a wide variety of Depression-oriented topics, including living in poverty, social activism, politics, labor unions, the New Deal, the likelihood of a future depression, and the lingering effects of the period on the outlooks of the interviewees. The book presents views from people of vastly different political, professional, religious, and socioeconomic backgrounds, including descendants of Americans who lived through the Depression. As a whole, *Hard Times* illuminates both the experiences of Americans during the Depression and their attempts to historicize it in the subsequent decades.

Appearing roughly three decades after the Great Depression ended, *Hard Times* was widely hailed as a significant cultural artifact. The second of Terkel's numerous compilations of oral testimonies—the first being *Division Street: America* (1967), a showcase of contemporary life in Chicago—the book contributed to his reputation as one of the eminent oral historians of the twentieth century and became a touchstone for critical discussions of oral history as a whole. *Hard Times* remains one of the most widely read works in the genre.

HISTORICAL AND LITERARY CONTEXT

The narratives gathered in *Hard Times* are informed not only by the Great Depression but also by the lengthy period of economic prosperity that preceded it. The 1920s in the United States began with a sharp recession that lasted until July 1921, but the bulk of the decade was marked by massive industrial expansion and a general increase in consumer affluence. The relative abundance of disposable income during this period, coupled with various advances in technology and mass production, resulted in an unprecedentedly "modern" cultural milieu that was reflected in the growing emphasis on luxury-status consumer products such as automobiles and radios. Thus, in addition to bringing about great suffering, the Depression represented a dramatic shift from a robust era.

In late October 1929 the U.S. stock market crashed, an event that is commonly cited as marking the beginning of the Depression. The U.S. economy deteriorated over the next few years—accompanied by similar declines in other countries—and reached its lowest point in 1933, when the unemployment rate hit 25 percent. The New Deal, a series of economic programs enacted under the aegis of President Franklin D. Roosevelt, provided a measure of relief for the poor and unemployed and attempted with some success to spur the economy to recovery (though this recovery was interrupted by a further downturn in 1937). However, it was not until the United States' entry into World War II, which produced an economic boost from defense spending, that the Depression finally ended in the United States.

An important predecessor to *Hard Times*—in terms of both the oral history tradition and subject matter—dates to the Depression itself, when the Federal Writers' Project dispatched writers to collect oral testimony from various Americans. Many of these narratives were eventually assembled in Ann Banks's 1980 volume *First Person America*. (This type of work, largely focused on ordinary people, contrasts with that begun by pioneering oral historian Allan Nevins at Columbia University in 1948, which concentrates on prominent national figures.) Likewise, Terkel's years of interviewing people on his long-running radio show, *The Studs Terkel Program* (1952–1997), undoubtedly contributed to his prowess in the field.

Hard Times provided readers with valuable insights into the thoughts and experiences of Americans whose lives were shaped by the Depression, and the book's considerable financial success contributed significantly to the popularization of the oral history genre. Terkel himself continued to add to the field with numerous subsequent volumes, most prominently *Working* (1974) and the Pulitzer Prize–winning *"The Good War": An Oral History of World War II* (1984). Likewise, the book's relatively populist, individualistic approach has influenced the editorial processes of other oral history projects, including James B. Lane's *Steel Shavings* magazine and Dave Eggers and Lola Vollen's *Voice of Witness* series.

❖ *Key Facts*

Time Period:
Mid-20th Century

Relevant Historical Events:
Great Depression; New Deal; World War II

Nationality:
American

Keywords:
unemployment; labor; unionism

People during the Great Depression line up for food in Seattle, in *Breadline on Western Avenue*, a watercolor by Ronald Debs Ginther. Americans recall their experiences during the Great Depression in Studs Terkel's *Hard Times: An Oral History of the Great Depression*. © WASHINGTON STATE HISTORICAL SOCIETY/ART RESOURCE, NY

THEMES AND STYLE

A central theme of *Hard Times* involves the degree to which individual perspectives on the Great Depression vary. Terkel begins by asserting, "This is a memory book, rather than one of hard fact and precise statistic." Oral history's subjective nature is emphasized throughout, with many of the interviewees contradicting each other both philosophically and on matters of empirical fact. Terkel disputes none of it. One anecdote, about an arrogant judge being threatened with hanging by angry farmers, is conveyed by multiple people, and the details of each telling differ: Oscar Heline asserts that "they drug him from his chair, pulled him down the steps of the courthouse, and shook a rope in front of his face. Then, tarred and feathered him." Frank and Rome Hentges claim that the judge was not tarred and feathered but that the farmers actually put the rope around his neck. Meanwhile, Orrin Kelly simply states that "they took him out in the country and threatened to lynch him, which they wouldn't have done, of course." No single account is deemed definitive, as Terkel attempts to show that people draw their own conclusions about history.

Hard Times was compiled, in Terkel's words, as "an attempt to get the story of the holocaust known as The Great Depression from an improvised battalion of survivors." To that end, the book contains a daunting number of interviews, which Terkel edited and truncated rigorously in order to preserve space and clarity. His interest in providing a broad portrait of the Depression extended to including the testimony of people who did not directly experience the event in order to contextualize the survivors' memories within the period they were transcribed. "There are young people in this book, too," he writes. "They did not experience the Great Depression. In many instances, they are wholly ignorant of it. It is no sign of their immaturity, but of ours."

The language in *Hard Times* varies greatly in tone, syntax, and diction, as befits a book composed of narratives from disparate sources. Despite Terkel's heavy editing of the transcripts, it is clear that he attempted to preserve the speech patterns of his interviewees. Hence the frequent use of colloquialisms and nonstandard grammar, as when Emma Tiller, an African American woman who worked as cook during the Depression, notes, "When you work for them rich people in the South, you don't go and buy no frozen peas and beans and rolls. Uh-uh, you cook them rolls, you shells them peas, you string them beans." Terkel's editorial presence is pervasive but not to the point of homogenizing the different voices.

CRITICAL DISCUSSION

Hard Times was a commercial success upon its initial publication. Reviewers, meanwhile, tended to praise the book as both a revelatory human document of the Depression's impact and a stirring, richly textured testament to the national character. Richard Rhodes, writing in the *New York Times*, stated, "Confronted with so immense a variety of people, you find yourself at last suspending judgment: These are the people; we are this various, this pungent, this tough. And these qualities of variety and strength range so wide a spectrum in 'Hard Times' that it puts fiction—most fiction—to shame." Although some reviewers were less enamored of Terkel's editorial decisions, the overall critical response to the book was highly favorable.

The book's status as one of the most prominent literary treatments of the Great Depression has not significantly faded in the decades since it was first published. James T. Baker states in his 1992 monograph on Terkel's work that "*Hard Times* proved to be one of Terkel's most influential works. Widely read (or at least scanned) and discussed (even if superficially), it helped to popularize oral history and consequently to make Terkel an important literary figure." Frequently assigned in college courses, the book has retained an air of relevance in contemporary society, particularly in light of the numerous lesser economic downturns that have occurred since its publication.

Scholarly writing on *Hard Times* frequently discusses the work in relation to oral history in general. In an article for *Red Buffalo*, Michael Frisch incorporates the book into an argument about the nature of oral history, asserting, "To the extent that *Hard Times* is any example, the interviews are nearly unanimous in showing the selective, synthetic, and generalizing nature of historical memory itself." Likewise, Andrea

Gustavson, writing in the *Journal of American Studies,* situates the book within a larger discussion of Terkel's methodology as an oral historian and the political ramifications of this approach: "Although he crafted his texts into seemingly unmediated documents, Terkel used his oral histories to comment on the current cultural and political context."

BIBLIOGRAPHY

Sources

Baker, James T. *Studs Terkel.* New York: Twayne, 1992. Print.

Frisch, Michael. "Oral History and *Hard Times:* A Review Essay." *Red Buffalo* 1.2–3 (1972): 217–31. Rpt. in *Oral History Review* 7 (1979): 70–79. *JSTOR.* Web. 16 Jan. 2013.

Gustavson, Andrea. "From 'Observer to Activist': Documentary Memory, Oral History, and Studs Terkel's 'Essence' Narratives." *Journal of American Studies* 46.1 (2012): 103–19. *Cambridge Journals Online.* Web. 16 Jan. 2013.

Rhodes, Richard. Rev. of *Hard Times,* by Studs Terkel. *New York Times.* New York Times, 19 Apr. 1970. Web. 16 Jan. 2013.

Terkel, Studs. *Hard Times: An Oral History of the Great Depression.* 1970. New York: New Press, 2005. Print.

Further Reading

Appel, Benjamin. *The People Talk: American Voices from the Great Depression.* New York: Simon and Schuster, 1982. Print.

Banks, Ann. *First Person America.* New York: Knopf, 1980. Print.

Bindas, Kenneth J. *Remembering the Great Depression in the Rural South.* Gainesville: University Press of Florida, 2007. Print.

Burg, David F. *The Great Depression: An Eyewitness History.* New York: Facts On File, 1996. Print.

Dunar, Andrew J., and Dennis McBride. *Building Hoover Dam: An Oral History of the Great Depression.* New York: Twayne, 1993. Print.

Grele, Ronald J., ed. *Envelopes of Sound: The Art of Oral History.* 2nd ed. Chicago: Precedent, 1985. Print.

McElvaine, Robert S., ed. *Down & Out in the Great Depression: Letters from the Forgotten Man.* Chapel Hill: University of North Carolina Press, 1983. Print.

Parker, Tony. *Studs Terkel: A Life in Words.* New York: Henry Holt, 1996. Print.

James Overholtzer

PRIMARY SOURCE

EXCERPT FROM *HARD TIMES*

SIDNEY J. WEINBERG

Senior partner, Goldman-Sachs Company, a leading investment house. He served during Roosevelt's first two Administrations as an industrial adviser.

OCTOBER 29, 1929—I remember that day very intimately. I stayed in the office a week without going home. The tape was running, I've forgotten how long that night. It must have been ten, eleven o'clock before we got the final reports. It was like a thunder clap. Everybody was stunned. Nobody knew what it was all about. The Street had general confusion. They didn't understand it any more than anybody else. They thought something would be announced.

Prominent people were making statements. John D. Rockefeller, Jr., announced on the steps of J.P. Morgan, I think, that he and his sons were buying common stock. Immediately, the market went down again. Pools combined to support the market, to no avail. The public got scared and sold. It was a very trying period for me. Our investment company went up to two, three hundred, and then went down to practically nothing. As all investment companies did.

Over-speculation was the cause, a reckless disregard of economics. There was a group ruthlessly selling short. You could sell anything and depress the market unduly. The more you depressed it, the more you created panic. Today we have protections against it. Call money went up—was it twenty percent?

No one was so sage that he saw this thing coming. You can be a Sunday morning quarterback. A lot of people have said afterwards, "I saw it coming, I sold all my securities." There's a credibility gap there. There are always some people who are conservative, who did sell out. I didn't know any of these.

I don't know anybody that jumped out of the window. But I know many who threatened to jump. They ended up in nursing homes and insane asylums and things like that. These were people who were trading in the market or in banking houses. They broke down physically, as well as financially.

Roosevelt saved the system. It's trite to say the system would have gone out the window. But certainly a lot of institutions would have changed. We were on the verge of something. You could have had a rebellion; you could have had a civil war.

SOURCE: Terkel, Studs. *Hard Times: An Oral History of the Great Depression.* New York: Pantheon Books, 1970. Reprinted by permission of International Creative Management, Inc.

I, Rigoberta Menchú

An Indian Woman in Guatemala

Rigoberta Menchú

✣ Key Facts

Time Period:
Mid- to Late 20th Century

Relevant Historical Events:
Guatemalan Civil War; genocide of indigenous people in Guatemala

Nationality:
Guatemalan

Keywords:
war; genocide; indigenous people

OVERVIEW

First published in 1984, *I, Rigoberta Menchú: An Indian Woman in Guatemala* is an oral history that documents the mistreatment and oppression of the indigenous people of Guatemala. Rigoberta Menchú, a member of the Quiche tribe, the largest of Guatemala's indigenous groups, tells the story of the human rights abuses that occurred in Guatemala before and during the civil war of 1960–1996, a genocide that claimed the life of her mother, father, and brother. Narrated in Paris when she was twenty-three and assembled by journalist and anthropologist Elisabeth Burgos-Debray, the book participates in a tradition of *testimonio* literature, speaking out against the oppression and enslavement of her people. The result is an account of daily life, culture, and ritual that is richly steeped in the collective memory of her people.

Published in the midst of Guatemala's civil war, the book achieved renown with Menchú's receipt of the Nobel Peace Prize in 1992. "Dante's *Inferno* 'is out,' *I, Rigoberta Menchu* 'is in'" wrote the *Wall Street Journal* in 1988 of Stanford University's decision to implement a stronger presence of Third World and feminist voices into its core curriculum. It was not until the late 1990s that the book came under serious critical scrutiny for possible embellishment and exaggeration. Yet despite the controversy, *I, Rigoberta Menchú* is still regarded as a primary source for the revolution and genocide that occurred in Guatemala, and it is widely considered a classic example of *testimonio* literature.

HISTORICAL AND LITERARY CONTEXT

For centuries Guatemala has suffered from a violence and instability, starting in the 1500s, when the Spanish invasion killed two and a half million people and virtually enslaved those who survived. In 1954 the U.S. Central Intelligence Agency subverted Guatemala's first attempt at democratization, installing an autocratic regime. The political climate in the country grew worse as radicalized Catholic groups, leftist political organizations, and indigenous activists, among others, took up arms. By the 1980s the government often relied upon death squads to murder political adversaries, including large populations of indigenous peoples.

When Menchú left Guatemala, the civil war was just coming to a head. The text describes an impoverished childhood, and it takes the reader through the government massacre at a protest in 1980 at the Spanish embassy, where her father died and her mother was kidnapped and later killed. That same year Menchú's village was attacked. Menchú captures the incredible suffering she experienced when she narrates how she was laid in bed for days at a time, sick with ulcers, awaiting flight to Mexico. In disbelief, she takes comfort knowing she "wasn't the only orphan." Later, she finds a different perspective: "What has happened is a sign of victory. A Revolution isn't born out of something good" but "wretchedness and bitterness."

I, Rigoberta Menchú falls into the Latin American oral literary tradition of *testimonio*. Always political in nature, *testimonio* functions with the intent to break oppressive silence. The text is often compared to the works of Carolina Maria de Jesus, whose book *Quarto de Despejo* (1960; *Child of the Dark*) documents the life of the rural poor outside of the Brazilian city of São Paulo. As *Quarto de Despejo* predates the Latin American literary boom, when writers such as Gabriel García Márquez and Julio Cortázar were becoming household literary names, it is considered foundational to the entire *testimonio* genre. Menchú would not likely have encountered the text at the time she narrated *I, Rigoberta Menchú,* but the indigenous storytelling culture of the Quiche would have immersed her in the genre from a young age.

I, Rigoberta Menchú has been an instrumental text in furthering the conversation of indigenous rights and human rights violations, and it is frequently assigned in college classes. Menchú's 1992 Nobel Peace Prize further catapulted the book to fame and made the author a sort of international celebrity. According to anthropologist David Stoll in *Rigoberta Menchú and the Story of All Poor Guatemalans* (1999), after the book's publication Menchú had the power to "call on the pope, presidents of important countries, and the UN-secretary-general." However, Stoll's scholarship exposed factual inconsistencies in Menchú's testimony, provoking often reactionary and sometimes unwarranted criticism from the popular media. Since the controversy, Menchú has distanced herself from the book, but she has continued her work as a Guatemalan peace activist.

THEMES AND STYLE

The central themes of *I, Rigoberta Menchú* are the oppression of the indigenous people of Guatemala,

Activist and Nobel Peace Prize–winner Rigoberta Menchú, an indigenous person of Guatemala, upon her return to Guatemala in 1998. Menchú recounts her life in *I, Rigoberta Menchu: An Indian Woman in Guatemala* (1984). © THE PRINT COLLECTOR/ALAMY

their extreme poverty, and the rampant racism and violence of a government dictatorship. In the text Menchú describes working on a plantation at the age of eight, where working conditions are so poor that a friend of hers dies from having been sprayed with pesticides. At thirteen Menchú becomes a maid and discovers the family she works for treats the dog better than her, giving it a bed to sleep on and plenty of food. "I was lower than the animals in the house," she recalls. Although the veracity of the chapter is debated, Menchú bears powerful witness to the torture and murder of her brother. "Everyone was weeping.... It's a reality I cannot forget."

In 1982 Menchú narrated her story to French journalist Elisabeth Burgos-Debray in order to pay witness to those who had lost their lives, she says. As Burgos-Debray writes in her introduction, "She is a privileged witness: she has survived the genocide that destroyed her family and community." Although there is some disagreement over exactly who was involved in various aspects of the editing process, it is known that over the course of a few weeks, Burgos-Debray taped and interviewed Menchú, and the transcripts were later typed and edited. After negative criticism of Menchú, she defended herself, saying, "My book was a cry in the silence."

The language used in *I, Rigoberta Menchú* reflects Menchú's process of language acquisition. She had learned Spanish only three years before narrating the book. As a result, the words she chooses are simple, and her Spanish reflects a biblical rhetoric that is juxtaposed with the language of political revolutionaries. She also calls upon her Quiche heritage and uses language full of natural imagery and tradition. The text was edited to reflect an oral speaker who pauses, starts sentences multiple times, and struggles to find the correct words. In her introduction Burgos-Debray describes a speaker "whose inner cadences are so pregnant with meaning that we … can almost hear her breathing."

CRITICAL DISCUSSION

Scholars disagree over the actual date of publication of *I, Rigoberta Menchú*, but it is known that the text was submitted by Burgos-Debray to the Casa de las Americas, a Latin American literary contest, and in 1983 it was awarded the best testimonial narrative. In 1986, after the Guatemalan political climate had relaxed, the book was allowed a freer circulation and began to find a Guatemalan readership. Even still, the book was largely unknown until Menchú won the Nobel Peace Prize in 1992. Soon thereafter Stoll sought to expose some discrepancies in Menchú's narrative. The *New York Review of Books*, *Time* magazine, and the *New York Post* ran feature-length stories about the controversy. David Horowitz, a conservative pundit, is quoted in Arturo Arias's introduction to *The Rigoberta Menchú Controversy* (2001) as calling the book "one of the greatest hoaxes of the twentieth century.… Virtually everything Menchú has written is a lie."

Despite the criticism surrounding factual inconsistencies of Menchú's story, her portrayal of the atrocities

GUATEMALAN CIVIL WAR AND U.S. INVOLVEMENT

The civil war in Guatemala, which erupted in 1960, was in part an expression of anger and frustration with the deeply rooted racism in the country. Mayans were living and working against their will in harsh conditions, often on coffee plantations that were owned by the Ladinos (or non-Mayan Guatemalans). In the 1970s the Mayans began to radicalize and form political organizations, among them the Committee for Peasant Unity, which was partly responsible for burning the Spanish embassy in 1980. The government launched "Project Sophia" in the 1980s, with the intent to end guerrilla warfare by destroying access to agriculture; among those chiefly targeted were Mayan communities. From 1980 to 1983 the army succeeded in destroying more than six hundred villages and killing twenty thousand people. A million and a half more fled for refuge in Mexico.

The U.S. government aided Guatemala under the guise of promoting an anticommunist agenda, providing financial backing and training to more than fifteen hundred Guatemalan soldiers on U.S. soil. A report issued by the United Nations' Historical Clarifications Commission revealed that the United States did have knowledge of gross human rights violations but continued to fund the war anyway. In 1999, three years after the war's end, the United States' president, Bill Clinton, apologized to the Guatemalan people, promising to support peace and reconciliation.

committed in the Guatemalan Civil War has not been called into question in the academic community; Stoll insists it was never his intention to discredit the book. However, since the 1990s the book has been the subject of a slew of criticism. Dinesh D'Souza, a conservative commentator, writes in *Illiberal Education* (1991) that "students do not read about Rigoberta because she has written a great and immortal book.... She simply happened to be in the right place at the right time." Others called Menchú a "Marxist terrorist" and demanded the renunciation of her Nobel Prize. Surprised by the media reaction to his book, Stoll defended Menchú's status as a Nobel laureate and asked that the media "keep focused on Guatemala."

Much scholarship of the book has attempted to situate the controversy in a larger historical and epistemological context. In "*I, Rigoberta Menchú* and the 'Culture Wars,'" Mary Louise Pratt locates the impetus for the controversy as a triumph for the political Right and offers a constructive reading of the text, which she claims "is worthwhile, especially given the international dimensions of the controversy and the serious stakes ... for the Guatemalan peace process." In her essay in *The Rigoberta Menchú Controversy,* Claudia Ferman calls for a clarification of the genre of *testimonio* when examining "the manner in which 'truth' is constructed in various discursive practices" and looks at the different ways we read and believe or disbelieve fiction, autobiography, and *testimonio*.

BIBLIOGRAPHY

Sources

Arias, Arturo. Introduction. *The Rigoberta Menchú Controversy.* Ed. Arias. Minneapolis: University of Minnesota Press, 2001. Print.

Bartow, Joanna R. *Subject to Change: The Lessons of Latin American Women's* Testimonio *for Truth, Fiction and Theory.* Chapel Hill: University of North Carolina Press, 2005. Print.

D'Souza, Dinesh. *Illiberal Education: The Politics of Race and Sex on Campus.* New York: Free Press, 1991. Print.

Ferman, Claudia. "Textual Truth, Historical Truth, and Media Truth." *The Rigoberta Menchú Controversy.* Ed. Arturo Arias. Minneapolis: University of Minnesota Press, 2001. 156–70. Print.

Gadin, Greg. *Who Is Rigoberta Menchú?* London: Verso, 2011. Print.

Kim, Lydia. "Overview of *I, Rigoberta Menchú.*" *Literature of Developing Nations for Students: Presenting Analysis, Context, and Criticism on Literature of Developing Nations.* Ed. Elizabeth Bellalouna, Michael L. LaBlanc, and Ira Mark Milne. Vol. 1. Detroit: Gale Group, 2000. *Literature Resource Center.* Web. 30 Jan. 2013.

Menchú, Rigoberta. *I, Rigoberta Menchú: An Indian Woman in Guatemala.* Ed. Elisabeth Burgos-Debray. Trans. Ann Wright. London: Verso, 1984. Print.

Pratt, Mary Louise. "*I, Rigoberta Menchú* and the 'Culture Wars.'" *The Rigoberta Menchú Controversy.* Ed. Arturo Arias. Minneapolis: University of Minnesota Press, 2001. 29–48. Print.

Stoll, David. *Rigoberta Menchú and the Story of All Poor Guatemalans.* Boulder, Colo.: Westview, 1999. Print.

Further Reading

Adams, Richard Newbold. *Crucifixion by Power: Essays on Guatemalan National Social Structure, 1944–1966.* Austin: University of Texas Press, 1970. Print.

Beverly, John. *Subalternity and Representation: Arguments in Cultural Theory.* Durham, N.C.: Duke University Press, 1999. Print.

Brintnall, Douglas E. *Revolt against the Dead: The Modernization of a Mayan Community in the Highlands of Guatemala.* New York: Gordon and Breach, 1979. Print.

Cullather, Nick. *Secret History: The CIA's Classified Account of Its Operations in Guatemala.* Stanford, Calif.: Stanford University Press, 1999. Print.

Kempen, Laura Charlotte. *Mariama Bâ, Rigoberta Menchú, and Postcolonial Feminism.* New York: Peter Lang, 2001. Print.

Zimmerman, Marc. *Literature and Resistance in Guatemala: Textual Modes and Cultural Politics from El Señor Presidente to Rigoberta Menchú.* Vol. 2. Athens: Ohio University Center for International Studies, 1995. Print.

Greg Luther

Juan the Chamula
An Ethnological Re-creation of the Life of a Mexican Indian

Ricardo Pozas

OVERVIEW

Juan the Chamula: An Ethnological Re-creation of the Life of a Mexican Indian (1962) is the English translation of Ricardo Pozas's classic anthropological study first published in Spanish in 1952 as *Juan Pérez Jolote: Biografía de un Tzotzil*. (Tzotzil here denotes a native of southern Mexico who speaks the Mayan language Tzotztil.) The text, translated by Lysander Kemp, is illustrated throughout with ink drawings by Alberto Beltrán. It is presented as if told in the first person by Pérez Jolote, a native of the village of San Juan Chamula in the highlands of the Mexican state of Chiapas. Pozas gives no details as to how or when he recorded the narrative or to what extent he intervened in Pérez Jolote's life story, which reaches back to a childhood during the Mexican Revolution (1910–1920) and ends with the mature Pérez Jolote assuming political leadership in his native village.

In his introduction, Pozas expresses interest in Chamula as a rustic locale undergoing change as its indigenous people increasingly come into contact with outside forces. He explicitly aligns himself and his readers with the "civilization" encroaching on this traditional, premodern culture and society. Early reviewers with knowledge of the region thought *Juan the Chamula* offered immense value for the anthropologist and the historian, though not all thought the English translation was an improvement on the original text. It remains an authoritative source for Mexican Indian studies, giving rich insights into the traditions and practices of the Chamulas, Chiapas's largest native population.

HISTORICAL AND LITERARY CONTEXT

Pérez Jolote's biography spans several decades in the early twentieth century, a period of great unrest and change for Mexico politically and economically. As a young adult, after running away from home, Pérez Jolote was pressed into military service in the Mexican Revolution, a civil war that began with Francisco Madero's revolt against Mexico's president Porfirio Díaz, whose urban, industrial, and agricultural reforms had boosted the national economy at the expense of small farmers and peasants. Pérez Jolote recounts fighting both for and against the forces led by revolutionaries such as Venustiano Carranza and Pancho Villa, sometimes a reluctant conscript, at other times a willing volunteer glad for the pay.

While the Mexican Revolution informs Pérez Jolote's journey to adulthood, it occupies only one episode in a narrative primarily concerned with more local goings-on around Chamula. The story he tells, after all, is one of leaving home as a boy to escape his abusive father, learning to support himself by his labor, and returning home to his village, where he settles down to marry and assume responsibilities in village governance. For the most part, it is a life story that resists conventional historicizing: it is clear that Pérez Jolote fights in the revolution and returns home in 1930, but otherwise the passing of time is unmarked. In fact, what he arrives at is a kind of timelessness, a return to the unchanging traditions of his fellow Chamulas.

Juan the Chamula is one of a number of oral histories taking ethnological interest in Mexico's indigenes. The year before it appeared, Calixta Guiteras-Holmes published *Perils of the Soul: The Worldview of a Tzotzil Indian* (1961), a study of another Mayan group from Chiapas, the Pedranos of San Pedro Chenalho; like Pozas, Guiteras-Holmes singles out one man (Manuel Arias Sohom) and takes his story to be typical. Ann L. Craig's *The First Agraristas: An Oral History of a Mexican Agrarian Reform Movement* (1983) is perhaps also comparable, to the extent that it sheds light on the land reform movement emerging from the Mexican Revolution. More recently Gary H. Gossen's *Telling Maya Tales: Tzotzil Identities in Modern Mexico* (1998) complements Pozas's earlier work by tracing the ongoing fragmentation of Chamula ethnicity in contact with nontraditional forces.

Pozas's has proven an influential work, a model approach to disclosing an indigenous people otherwise easily overlooked in conventional scholarship and a way of life endangered by encroaching modernity. Though the short introduction lays out Pozas's anthropological interests in the language of the social scientist (listing, for example, how Pérez Jolote's story gives evidence of "exogamous patrilineal clans"), the real achievement lies in his trusting Pérez Jolote's voice to reveal his culture and society

---

❖ Key Facts

Time Period:
Early to Mid-20th Century

Relevant Historical Events:
Mexican Revolution; increasing interaction between indigenous and colonial populations

Nationality:
Mexican

Keywords:
indigenous people; colonialism; revolution

THEORIES

Church and marketplace in San Juan Chamula, in the highlands of Chiapas, Mexico, 2005. © IMAGES & STORIES/ALAMY

in much plainer words. The resulting novelistic narrative has continuing relevance for readers in and beyond the scholarly community.

THEMES AND STYLE

One of Pérez Jolote's main themes is the constant dependence on paid work. The economy he describes is one in which the owners of large farms advance money to workers who contract to pay back with labor. When he runs away Pérez Jolote escapes his father's beatings by working for a woman in a neighboring village who passes him on to a widow, who in turn sells him (for a bottle of hard liquor) to an orchard-owning couple. This couple uses Pérez Jolote to work off debts to a corn planter: as he tells it, "we worked for three days, and then the parents went home with their two sons, leaving me to pay back what they still owed for the corn." Though this is apparently common practice, in time Pérez Jolote learns to work for himself and reap the benefits of his labor—borrowing to pay for his wedding and paying back with fieldwork.

As a cultural anthropologist Pozas is interested in Pérez Jolote's story to the extent that it reveals specific aspects of his society. As Pozas's introduction makes clear, what is special about Pérez Jolote is that he is "typical": "He exemplifies the conduct of many men of the group. His life is not exceptional; on the contrary, it is perfectly normal." Pozas's "ethnological re-creation" of Pérez Jolote's life is meant to lay bare the structure of Chamula society—economy, work practices, domestic relations, politics, and religion. Though Pozas does not explain what he means exactly by "ethnological re-creation," the phrase suggests that Pozas has remade Pérez Jolote's story in keeping with his own ethnological interests (yielding, that is, points of comparison between what he calls "our civilization" and Chamula culture and society).

The book comprises a brief introduction, an extended narrative from Pérez Jolote's point of view, a notes section, and a glossary of Spanish and Tzotzil words. Thematically the narrative falls into two parts: in the first, in which Pérez Jolote leaves home, grows up, and returns a working man, emphasis is on finding work and making money; in the second, in which he settles down, attention is given to traditions surrounding marriage, death, holidays, and religious beliefs. From first to last Pérez Jolote is plainspoken and matter-of-fact, even when recounting emotional episodes. Recalling his first night with his new wife, for instance, he explains, "I didn't say anything to Dominga, and she gave herself to me without saying a word. We did it slowly, so as not to make any noise that would wake my parents. That night I mounted her three times, once an hour. In the morning I woke her up early and said, 'It's daybreak.'" Here, as elsewhere, Pérez Jolote resorts to dispassionate language to account for the event without probing what it really means to him.

CRITICAL DISCUSSION

Pozas's book was released to critical acclaim. Writing for *Man*, Julian Pitt-Rivers describes it as "an important ethnographical document whose authenticity, whatever the extent of the editing may have been, impresses itself on anyone who knows the highlands of Chiapas." Pitt-Rivers does, however, think the English edition inferior to the Spanish because it "curtail[ed] the ethnographical footnotes published in the original." Frank Cancian, meanwhile, in an *American Anthropologist* review, thinks Kemp's translation an improvement for precisely the same reasons—that it reduced the footnotes and made room for the glossary. Cancian's only criticism is that the book, which he deems "excellent," is much too short.

Pérez Jolote's life story is cited widely in scholarship on southwestern Mexico: though brief, it is rich in insights into a number of aspects of Chamula society.

Pérez Jolote, for instance, not only works as a child servant for domestic and commercial concerns, but he is treated as currency used to pay off others' debts. Jailed as a young adult for refusing to testify against a murderer, he is similarly exploited by an army that presses native prisoners into service during the revolution. When he returns home and marries, he reveals a structure of social relations favoring male dominance and female subjugation. Finally, when he discusses his Chamula duties as "first mayor," "fiscal," and "*hábito*," he lays bare a fabric of beliefs indebted to European and native religious traditions. As such, *Juan the Chamula* has broad appeal for Mexican Indian studies.

Scholars rarely discuss *Juan the Chamula* as a work in its own right, though it is cited widely. Pitt-Rivers, for instance, exploring the relation between Tzotzil Indians and Ladinos (Spanish-speaking non-Indians), asks, "Why any Indians determine to remain in the subordinate status to which the ladinos relegate them and why we find men like Juan Perez Jolote who, after living for years as a ladino, return to their native village and way of life." More recently, Antonio Bolívar and Jesús Domingo have discussed the genre of "biographical-narrative inquiry," gauging the anthropological merits of Pozas's "cultural portrait" of Pérez Jolote. Meanwhile, scholars such as John B. Haviland have used Pérez Jolote's story to consider Spanish-speaking natives in Zinacantán.

BIBLIOGRAPHY

Sources

Bolívar, Antonio, and Jesús Domingo. "Biographical-Narrative Research in Iberoamerica: Areas of Development and the Current Situation." *Forum: Qualitative Social Research.* 7.4 (2006): n. pag. *Forum Qualitative Sozialforschung.* Web. 17 Jan. 2013.

Cancian, Frank. Rev. of *Juan the Chamula: An Ethnological Re-creation of the Life of a Mexican Indian,* by Ricardo Pozas. *American Anthropologist* 65.6 (1963): 1371–72. *JSTOR.* Web. 24 Jan. 2013.

Haviland, John B. "*Paisanos* and *Chamulitas:* Speech and Social Relations in (and around) Zinacantán." *Multilingua: Journal of Cross-Cultural and Interlanguage Communication* 8.4 (2009): 301–32. Print.

Pitt-Rivers, Julian. Rev. of *Juan the Chamula: An Ethnological Re-creation of the Life of a Mexican Indian,* by Ricardo Pozas. *Man* 64 (1964): 96–97. *JSTOR.* Web. 24 Jan 2013.

———. "Words and Deeds: The Ladinos of Chiapas" *Man* 2.1 (1967): 71–86. *JSTOR.* Web. 17 Jan. 2013.

Further Reading

Bricker, Victoria, and Gary H. Gossen, eds. *Ethnographic Encounters in Southern Mesoamerica: Essays in Honor of Evon Zartman Vogt, Jr.* Austin: University of Texas Press, 1989. Print.

Gossen, Gary H. *Chamulas in the World of the Sun: Time and Space in a Maya Oral Tradition.* Cambridge, Mass.: Harvard University Press, 1974. Print.

Gossen, Gary H. *Telling Maya Tales: Tzotzil Identities in Modern Mexico.* New York: Routledge, 1998. Print.

Moksnes, Heidi. *Maya Exodus: Indigenous Struggle for Citizenship in Chiapas.* Norman: University of Oklahoma Press, 2012. Print.

Rosenbaum, Brenda. *With Our Heads Bowed: The Dynamics of Gender in a Maya Community.* Austin: University of Texas Press, 1993. Print.

JUAN THE CHAMULA: A CLASSIC TEXT, AN INFAMOUS COVER

The paperback edition of *Juan the Chamula,* which was first published in 1962 and remains to this day the only edition in print, bears on its front cover an illustration of a Mexican Indian. A highly stylized, high-contrast image primarily in black and white, the picture shows a smiling man in what appears to be a traditional Mexican serape, his face partly in shadows from the wide brimmed hat perched high on his head. The problem, as reviewers noted when the book was released, is that the man is not wearing the garb of the Chamulas; rather, he is dressed in the style of a neighboring indigenous community from San Lorenzo Zinacantán, a town in Los Altos de Chiapas (the Chiapas highlands). Remarkably, the cover has never been changed, even though it constitutes a serious blunder for a work of scholarship on ethnic identity.

As Julian Pitt-Rivers sarcastically puts it in a 1964 review, it took some getting over "the initial shock of finding on the cover, rather than the drawing of a Chamula which graces the front of the Spanish paperback edition, a photograph of a Zinacanteco. Why worry about such fine points? Indians are all much the same!"

David Aitchison

Oral History, Health and Welfare

Joanna Bornat, Robert Perks, Paul Thompson, Jan Walmsley

❖ **Key Facts**

Time Period:
Mid-20th Century

Relevant Historical Events:
Rapid advancement in health-care technology; transformation of patient-practitioner relationships

Nationality:
British

Keywords:
health-care; theory; academia

OVERVIEW

Oral History, Health and Welfare (1999) is a collection of academic essays edited by Joanna Bornat, Robert Perks, Paul Thompson, and Jan Walmsley that discuss the application of oral history techniques to various aspects of the health-care industry, including patient care, the routines and workplace habits of medical professionals, and community welfare projects. The essays cover developments in medical history and generally focus on the mid-twentieth century. The text is the first to theorize about the application of oral history techniques, such as personal interviews and group seminars, to the study of the history of health and welfare in the United Kingdom. As such, it provides a unique insight into the usefulness of this endeavour in compiling historical data about health care that was previously unrecorded, such as the perspective of women and ethnic minorities, as well as the friendships developed among health-care workers.

The book was the product of a 1996 academic conference sponsored by the Oral History Society titled Cradle to Grave: Oral History, Health and Welfare. Of the papers, thirteen were collected and edited to produce this publication. Because of its theoretical content, the book received little attention from literary critics, although it generated some recognition among its academic readership. There is little scholarship about the book as a whole, but the specific implications of applying oral history techniques to various aspects of health care discussed in its chapters have been developed independently by further research and historical study.

HISTORICAL AND LITERARY CONTEXT

The twentieth century produced more radical advancements in medical technology than any century before it, including the development of diagnostic instruments such as ultrasound machines, refinement of medical practices such as open-heart surgery, and an increased success rate is dealing with such previously devastating diseases as syphilis and tuberculosis. Developments in contraceptives and inoculation medications have also greatly improved survival rates. In the United Kingdom, the Wellcome Trust was established in 1936 to provide funding for research into improvements for health-care practices, and the National Health Service was established in 1948 to provide publically funded medical care for British citizens.

Oral History, Health and Welfare focuses on the usefulness of first-person testimony about these developments during the mid-twentieth century, specifically the transformation in patient-practitioner relations and changing attitudes about health care and social welfare in general. By exploring the personalized effects of medical and social welfare advancements, such as public policies, advances in technology, and professional training, a broader and more in depth history of the vast changes of the health-care industry in the twentieth century can be developed and studied.

Although *Oral History, Health and Welfare* is a pioneering book on the theoretical benefits of utilizing oral history techniques on the history of medical practices in the United Kingdom, previous oral histories influenced its composition and the theories it develops. Oral histories from Britain such as Jocelyn Cornwell's *Hard-Earned Lives: Accounts of Health and Illness from East London* (1984) and J. Read and J. Reynolds's *Speaking Our Minds: An Anthology of Personal Experiences of Mental Distress and its Consequences* (1996) influenced the theoretical exploration of oral history as a feasible method to study the history of health care. American publications such as Gwendolyn Safier's *Contemporary American Leaders in Nursing: An Oral History* (1977) and Regina Morantz's *In Her Own Words: Oral Histories of Women Physicians* (1982) solidified the validity of the practice from international sources.

The publication of *Oral History, Health and Welfare* inspired additional research into the use of oral history practices to further study the history of health care and social welfare in the United Kingdom and other nations. Contributors to the volume published subsequent articles on the application of oral history in the health-care field, including Virginia Berridge's "History in the Public Health Toolkit" (2001) and Stuart Anderson's "Community Pharmacy and Public Health in Great Britain, 1936 to 2006" (2007).

THEMES AND STYLE

Although *Oral History, Health and Welfare* is a compilation of academic essays, there are several themes that unite the text as a whole. The most important of these is the recognition and development of a field of oral history research that focuses on the health-care system and issues of social welfare such as community health initiatives and the perspectives of patients receiving medical care. In the general introduction to the text, Paul Thompson states, "It is the first collection of new British work using oral history in the field" which makes the text, "an important reflection of the new atmosphere" in which this style of historical research is applied to health care from multiple angles. The contributors themselves also discuss this theme within their submissions. Stuart Anderson and Virginia Berridge, for example, mention the development of oral history techniques for the history of pharmacy in their chapter, stating, "The role of professions is well represented in historical writing about health and welfare" and there "has also been significant interest, particularly through oral history, in the continuing role of lay care," but "the role of the pharmacist in this area has been surprisingly neglected."

The authors' purpose in producing *Oral History, Health and Welfare* is one of academic advancement of the development of oral history as a viable practice in generating historical data about health and welfare. The book, therefore, does not includes first-person narratives transcribed to preserve the voices of speakers as they discuss issues related to their specific experiences. Rather, each chapter discusses the theoretical application of oral history in a specific field. Elizabeth Roberts, in her chapter, "The Recipients' View of Welfare," explains the relation of her research to the oral history subject: "As the chapter is a discussion of the views of the recipients of welfare it has been imperative to draw upon working class testimony" but "this chapter is an analysis and interpretation of the respondents' views" with only minimal "examples of them speaking for themselves."

In keeping with the theoretical material and its intended scholarly audience, *Oral History, Health and Welfare* is strictly academic in style, with each chapter professional in tone and organized in an acceptable format, including an introduction, analysis of data, and conclusion. Although the contributors discuss previous oral history studies, conducted by themselves or by others, the book itself is not an oral history per se but, rather, a discussion of oral history as it applies to the history of health and welfare in the United Kingdom.

CRITICAL DISCUSSION

Because of the book's strictly academic nature, it remained rather obscure and generated minimal reviews. Some academics, however, were positive in their criticism, including Graham Smith, who stated in his review (2001) that "above all this is a refreshing volume which, by combining the history of medicine and oral history, produces an electric mix that is both exciting and challenging." Lisa Bostock's review (2000) also praises the book by stating it "brings a human dimension to the study of health and social care developments in the UK."

Since the publication of *Oral History, Health and Welfare,* interest has developed in the historical exploration of health care and community welfare in the United Kingdom. S. Sheard in "Short Report: History in Health and Health Services" writes about the application of historical research in the healthcare field as a necessary step in improving services: "Historical skills—especially the methodologies involved in interpreting a wide range of sources—can provide a useful analysis of the structure and function of health services, and be used a s a means of improving public understanding of the expectations and experiences of health and health care." Sheard continues, "There is an increasing interest in history within public health and health services," but "there are few historians and health professionals who have direct experience of collaboration, and the potential benefits are only just beginning to be appreciated." Thus, while academic texts such as *Oral History, Health and Welfare* exist to explore the theoretical and practical benefits of oral history, more practical applications of historical research into health care and community welfare need to occur before the practice becomes publically accepted and the potential benefits of such research can be understood and applied.

Trends in discussing *Oral History, Health and Welfare* focus on the vast array of topics addressed in the volume. Smith comments on the diversity of the text: "The publication contains a variety of ways of utilizing oral history to investigate health and welfare, and a number of oral history's key concerns are present." Bostock discusses the "dizzying array of chapters" that make up the book and Amanda Vettini, in her review (2000) of the book, discusses the various chapters that "present interesting accounts both of their individual research topics and of the oral history

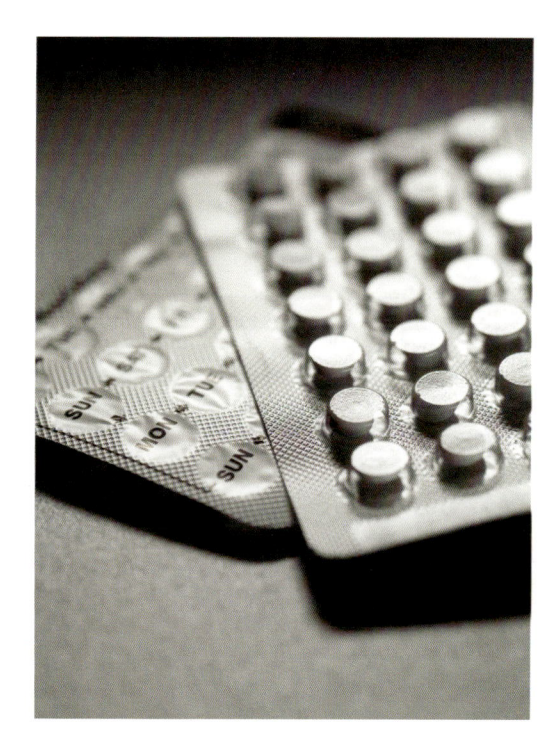

In *Oral History, Health and Welfare,* examines many topics and their significance to oral history, including birth control, like the oral contraceptives depicted here. © CORFIELD/ALAMY

THE ORAL HISTORY SOCIETY

The Oral History Society, founded in 1971 by a collection of academics from various fields including historians, folklorists, and ethnographers, is a British organization devoted to promoting the collection of personal memories from past events for preservation and research. To promote the use of oral history resources, the Oral History Society provides information about issues concerning oral history subjects, including gathering informed consent, current copyright laws in the United Kingdom, and moral considerations when conducting oral history research. The society also provides practical steps to follow when conducting such research and answers questions related to the research process and the practical application of findings.

In addition to information, the society also provides funding for oral history research projects through various heritage funds and grants and with support from academic and privately funded institutions. It also provides mediums in which to present such projects through its publications, including its quarterly periodical, and its annual academic conference. Selected conference proceedings are also edited and published in academic texts, including *Oral History, Health and Welfare*.

research method." Vettini goes on to suggest that the book "could have been more effectively divided into thematic sections" and that it "would have benefitted" from "a general overview by the editors."

BIBLIOGRAPHY

Sources

Bornat, Joanna. Robert Perks, Paul Thompson, and Jan Walmsley, eds. *Oral History, Health and Welfare*. London: Routledge, 1999. *Ebrary*. Web. 28 Jan. 2013.

Bostock, Lisa. Rev of *Oral History, Health and Welfare*, ed. by Joanna Bornat et al. *Sociology of Health and Illness* 22.3 (2000): 395–96. *Wiley Online Library*. Web. 30 Jan. 2013.

Sheard, S. "Short Report: History in Health and Health Services: Exploring the Possibilities." *Journal of Epidemiology and Community Health* 62.8 (2008): 740–44. *JSTOR*. 5 Dec. 2012.

Smith, Graham. Rev. of *Oral History, Health and Welfare*, ed. by Joanna Bornat et al. *Social History of Medicine* 14.2 (2001): 352–53. *Oxford Journals*. Web. 29 Jan. 2013.

Vettini, Amanda. Rev. of *Oral History, Health and Welfare*, ed. by Joanna Bornat et al. *Journal of Gender Studies* 9.2 (2000): 235–36. *MINDS@UW*. Web. 30 Jan 2013.

Further Reading

Anderson, Stuart. "Community Pharmacy and Public Health in Great Britain, 1936 to 2006: How a Phoenix Rose from the Ashes." *Journal of Epidemiology and Community Health* 61.10 (2007): 844–48. *JSTOR*. Web. 28 Jan. 2012.

Berridge, Virginia. "History in the Public Health Tool Kit." *Journal of Epidemiology and Community Health* 55.9 (2001): 611–12. *JSTOR*. Web. 5 Dec. 2012.

Cornwell, Jocelyn. *Hard-Earned Lives: Accounts of Health and Illness from East London*. London: Tavistock, 1984. Print.

Morantz, Regina Markell, Cynthia Stodola Pomerleau, and Carol Hansen Fenichel, eds. *In Her Own Words: Oral Histories of Women Physicians*. Westport, Conn.: Greenwood Press, 1982. Print.

Read, Jim, and Jill Reynolds, eds. *Speaking Our Minds: An Anthology of Personal Experiences of Mental Distress and Its Consequences*. Basingstoke, UK: Macmillan, 1996. Print.

Safier, Gwendolyn. *Contemporary American Leaders in Nursing: An Oral History*. New York: McGraw-Hill, 1977. Print.

Katherine Barker

Oral History Theory

Lynn Abrams

OVERVIEW

After teaching several classes on oral history at the University of Glasgow Lynn Abrams recognized the need for a comprehensive overview of oral history theory and published *Oral History Theory* in 2010. Rather than developing new theories or republishing extant pieces, Abrams traces the lineage of oral history as a field and outlines its generic markers, practices, and concerns as they have developed, primarily since the mid-twentieth century. Chapters on the self, subjectivity and intersubjectivity, memory, narrative, performance, and power delve into existing theories on each topic and reflect on how each topic is revealed in the past application of oral history work and how it could be realized in future practices of oral historiography.

Joining a range of texts on the theorization of history derived from oral sources, such as Michael Frisch's *A Shared Authority: Essays on the Craft and Meaning of Oral and Public History* (1990), Abrams's book has been appreciated as a teaching tool and has been warmly received. It has begun appearing on syllabi for diverse graduate and undergraduate courses that center on oral history in practice, as narrative, and in theory as well as for contemporary history classes.

HISTORICAL AND LITERARY CONTEXT

In *Oral History Theory,* Abrams limns the development of oral history as a field, hailing its origins in the United States in the late 1930s New Deal Federal Writers' Project (FWP), in the historian Allan Nevins's 1948 project using tape-recorded memories to document lives of people who made great contributions to a national or global society, and in the author and broadcaster Studs Terkel's radio shows and books, which concentrate on narratives derived from oral history. Abrams explains that in "Britain and the Nordic countries," an interest in oral history developed in the 1950s and 1960s and stemmed from a strong folklore tradition. After discussing these predecessors, Abrams points to the shift from social to cultural foci and the publication of "Work, Ideology and Consensus under Italian Fascism" (1979) by Luisa Passerini in *History Workshop Journal* as crucial catalysts in the development of the field of oral history. Alessandro Portelli's work—particularly the study of memory and its part in oral history—greatly influenced Abrams's project. Abrams notes that "by the 1980s, oral history had become the methodology of choice (and necessity) of a number of groups who had traditionally been disregarded by conventional histories."

As fields that historically lack an abundance of written documentation and that thus rely more heavily on orality and experiences—such as those pertaining to classically marginalized groups—have developed, oral history has become an increasingly valued and respected resource. It is becoming more accepted as a historiographical tool, and its concerns, such as memory, are now recognized as crucial to other disciplines. Thus the influence of oral history methods and elements on interdisciplinary projects is growing.

Oral History Theory uniquely combines theory and practice, whereas many of the preceding oral history readers represent theory more than practice. Such readers as Frisch's *Shared Authority* and Robert Perks and Alistair Thomson's *The Oral History Reader* (1998) tend to collect previous writings on oral history, whereas Abrams's book distills, interprets, and shows applications of much of the extant literature on oral history.

In her work Abrams is adept with both conventional historical methods and those derived from personal testimony and memory. In 2010, the same year in which she published *Oral History Theory,* Abrams also released *Everyday Life in Twentieth Century Scotland,* edited by C. G. Brown. Her website describes her current research projects, "Liberating the Female Self: Narratives of Women's Emancipation in Post-war Britain c. 1950–1975" and "Living the Modern Everyday: Gender and Home in Post-war Scotland," as drawing from oral history and addressing the intersection between gender and autonomy and of gender and modern landscapes, respectively.

THEMES AND STYLE

Stressing the importance of understanding the interconnectedness of theory and practice in oral history, Abrams focuses on "not just *what* is said, but also *how* it is said, *why* it is said and *what* it means" in oral history practice. She looks to both theories and observations by oral history practitioners to illustrate her text. Abrams also uses examples from actual interviews to illuminate issues pertinent to the study of oral history, such as incorporating dialect in transcriptions or standardizing language. She declares that theory and

❖ Key Facts

Time Period:
Early 21st Century

Relevant Historical Events:
Development of oral history as a field; New Deal Federal Writers' Project

Nationality:
Scottish

Keywords:
history; theory; subjectivity

Two teenagers interview each other in the StoryCorps interview booth in Grand Central Station, New York City, 2004. It is open to anyone who wants to record an interview, create an oral history, or record a personal story. Each recording will be archived in the Library of Congress's National Archives. The project, dependent on grants and donations, was created by David Isay. © ANDREW HOLBROOKE/CORBIS

practice are inextricably linked, that "oral history practice ... demands that one think about theory; indeed it is the practice, the doing of oral history, that leads to theoretical innovation."

Oral History Theory came from Abrams's experiences teaching an undergraduate course at the University of Glasgow that "combines the practical application of oral history techniques with theoretical analysis of the results." *Oral History Theory* was born of her desire for a text that comments accessibly on a range of theories and practices. Abrams uses a wealth of theories and examples in discussing the nuances of and concerns surrounding what she calls the four forms of oral history—"the original oral interview, the recorded version of the interview, the written transcript, and the interpretation of the interview material"—to show how oral historiography allows access to "not just information but also signification, interpretation and meaning."

After a few short chapters outlining what oral history is and does, defining its unique elements, and explaining how to move between theory and practice, Abrams moves into chapters that focus on a particular concern in the field, such as "self" and "power and empowerment." Each chapter begins with an introduction to the topic, followed by an overview of the theory related to the chapter's focus and multiple perspectives on the topic, practical applications, suggestions for future practice, and a conclusion. Abrams's language is aimed at an audience largely unfamiliar with the study of oral history and is for the most part free of jargon. What field-specific words she uses can be found in the glossary at the book's end.

CRITICAL DISCUSSION

Since its publication in 2010, *Oral History Theory* has been welcomed by educators and researchers and has received generally positive reviews. The reviewer Ronald Grele mentions in the *Oral History Review* that the provenance of the oral history field is more complex and global than Abrams indicates, citing such influences as a debate over narrative art and texts by Frisch in 1971, Peter Friedlander in 1975, and German and Latin American scholars and others; nevertheless, Grele admits, such points are minor, concluding positively that apart from taking a more concentrated look at conversation, *Oral History Theory* "outlines all of our current concerns, takes a wide purview of past and current work, provides a handy guide to relevant middle-level theories from a wide variety of perspectives, and yet leaves room for the engaged reader to explore beyond its boundaries." In her review in *Strata,* Kim Madsen voices the common praise of Abrams's thorough guidance through theories and practices as well as her attention to her audience, from the book's clarity and accessible style to the thoughtful glossary at the end.

Oral History Theory is entering discussions in academic work and in classrooms on approaches to historiography, pedagogy, and interdisciplinary concerns. Because historians have become more interested in what Anna Green calls the "creative" aspects of historiography that go beyond empirical data collection, "the strength of the book," Green notes, "lies in the clear exposition of some of the core theoretical dimensions that underpin this shift: composure, subjectivity and intersubjectivity, cultural discourse and the cultural circuit," though she questions where this shift leaves the relationship between oral and more traditional forms of history.

Because *Oral History Theory* is relatively new, trends in scholarship about the text may not have formed yet. However, such scholars as Jennifer Clary-Lemon and Lynne Williams find Abrams's presentation of oral history useful in conceiving of how to implement oral history in "opening up the concept of 'scholarship' in diverse ways" and uniquely allowing academics to cross disciplines as well as serving as a bridge between academics and their communities.

LYNN ABRAMS: BEYOND *ORAL HISTORY THEORY*

Not all of Abrams's work is based on personal testimony, in part because such an approach alone would not be able to capture the vast historical scope of some of her works, such as *The Orphan Country: Children of Scotland's Broken Homes, 1845 to the Present* (1998), *The Making of Modern Woman: Europe 1789–1918* (2002), and *Myth and Materiality in a Woman's World: Shetland 1800–2000* (2005). In *Myth and Materiality*, for example, Abrams highlights the important and relatively autonomous role of women in the unique environment of the Shetland Islands, relying on material evidence to supplement and reconstruct what interviews could not cover.

With Alex Shepard and Eleanor Gordon, Abrams coedits the journal *Gender & History* and is the series editor for the Manchester University Press series Gender in History. Other publications and projects include the collaboratively edited *A History of Everyday Life in Twentieth Century Scotland* (2010), a project with Shepard that examines Scottish masculinity historically, and an investigative project on East Kilbride residents' experiences with their housing. Abrams's work has been honored with the Scottish Innovation Fund First Step Award and the Royal Society of Edinburgh Arts and Humanities Workshop Award.

BIBLIOGRAPHY

Sources

Abrams, Lynn. *Oral History Theory.* New York: Routledge, 2010. Print.

Clary-Lemon, Jennifer, and Lynne Williams. "Teaching and Learning Oral History/Theory/Performance: A Case Study of the Scholarship of Discovery, Integration, Application, and Teaching." *Oral History Forum d'histoire orale* 32 (2012): 1–24. *Oral History Forum.* Web. 11 Jan. 2013.

Green, Anne. Rev. of *Oral History Theory,* by Lynn Abrams. *Bulletin of the International Oral History Association* 19.2 (2011): n. pag. *IOHA News.* Web. 5 Jan. 2013.

Grele, Ronald J. Rev. of *Oral History Theory,* by Lynn Abrams. *Oral History Review* 38.2 (2011): 354–59. *Project Muse.* Web. 3 Jan. 2013.

Madsen, Kim. Rev. of *Oral History Theory,* by Lynn Abrams. *Strata* 3 (2011): 137–40. University of Ottawa. Web. 14 Feb. 2013.

Further Reading

Abrams, Lynn. *Myth and Materiality in a Woman's World: Shetland 1800–2000.* Manchester, UK: Manchester University Press, 2005. Print.

Frisch, Michael. *A Shared Authority: Essays on the Craft and Meaning of Oral and Public History.* Albany: State University of New York Press, 1990. Print.

Grele, Ronald J., et al. *Envelopes of Sound: The Art of Oral History.* 2nd ed. New York: Greenwood Press, 1991. Print.

Jessee, Erin. "The Limits of Oral History: Ethics and Methodology amid Highly Politicized Research Settings." *Oral History Review* 38.2 (2011): 287–307. *Project Muse.* Web. 3 Jan. 2013.

Keulen, Sjoerd, and Ronald Kroeze. "Back to Business: A Next Step in the Field of Oral History—The Usefulness of Oral History for Leadership and Organizational Research." *Oral History Review* 39.1 (2012): 15–36. *Project Muse.* 11 Jan. 2013.

Passerini, Luisa. "Work, Ideology and Consensus under Italian Fascism." *History Workshop Journal* 8.1 (1979): 82–108. *JSTOR.* Web. 2 Jan. 2013.

Perks, Robert, and Alistair Thomson, eds. *The Oral History Reader.* London: Routledge, 1998. Print.

Yow, Valerie Raleigh. *Recording Oral History: A Guide for the Humanities and Social Sciences.* 2nd ed. Walnut Creek, CA: AltaMira, 2005. Print.

Katherine Bishop

Popular Memory
Theory, Politics, Method
Popular Memory Group

✧ Key Facts

Time Period:
Late 20th Century

Relevant Historical Events:
Increasing reliance on nonwritten sources by historians

Nationality:
British

Keywords:
socialism; feminism; theory

OVERVIEW

The collective essay "Popular Memory: Theory, Politics, Method," by the Popular Memory Group of Birmingham, England (a group of historians who worked together on collective projects at the University of Birmingham's Centre for Contemporary Cultural Study), was published in 1982 in a volume of essays called *Making History: Studies in History Writing and Politics*. It is an ambitious theoretical approach to history aimed at broadening perspective beyond the scope of the academic historian and at using history to promote socialist and feminist politics. Oral history is an important element of the group's exploration of the methodological difficulties involved in recording the past. Although the theoretical essay does not record an oral account of a specific event, the authors do cite and comment on historical projects that incorporate different oral histories from marginalized subjects. These include Paul Thompson's *The Edwardians*, which recorded early-twentieth-century experiences of England's working class, and Vera Brittain's *Testament of Youth*, her autobiographical account of World War I. Engagement with subjects such as Brittain and the workers Thompson had interviewed reflect the Popular Memory Group's political commitment to using a more democratic history to promote social causes.

With "Popular Memory," the group contributed to several ongoing debates among British historians over how to approach history from sociological, feminist, and Marxist angles. The essay responded in part to the way Thatcherite politics in the late 1970s and early 1980s used history to promote a conservative agenda. Initial reviews of "Popular Memory" from voices inside the oral history movement were mixed. However, the essay has had an important influence on the way historians have subsequently practiced oral and popular history.

HISTORICAL AND LITERARY CONTEXT

The accounts cited by the Popular Memory Group come from a diverse group of periods and nations. They include personal memories of life in Italy under fascist rule, firsthand accounts of the Spanish Civil War, and descriptions from the English working class of their first bosses. The Popular Memory Group's commentary on *Testament of Youth* provides a general idea of the kind of history the essay was promoting. During World War I England was engulfed in international conflict on the European mainland from 1914 to 1918. Millions of soldiers died in gruesome trench warfare, and the nation ultimately emerged victorious over the enemy. But this story of the military struggle and victory is only a part of English history from 1914 to 1918.

Brittain's account of the war recovers experiences, particularly women's experiences, absent from the traditional telling of the military progress of the war. Her work complicates the past considerably. "Popular Memory" asserts that her story of loss and her firsthand experience as a battlefield nurse emphasizes "the contrast between the idealistic hopes of young men going to the War and the physical and mental effects of their mutilation." Like Brittain's alternative war narrative, the other histories cited in the essay provide access in some way to lived experiences that do not typically figure into what the Popular Memory Group calls "dominant representations" of history.

The Popular Memory Group's approach had several important predecessors among British historians. The journals *Social History* and *History Workshop*, both launched in 1976, pursued similar historical perspectives. In the 1960s and 1970s British historians turned increasingly to individual oral accounts for documentation. Thompson's work is seen as the prototype for this shift to nonwritten source materials, and the Popular Memory Group also cite Roland Fraser's *Blood of Spain* (1979) as an exemplary forerunner of what they wanted history to be and do.

The work of the Popular Memory Group contributed to the growth of methodologies that explored the complexities of broadening historical perspective beyond written sources. An individual's relationship with the past is often amalgams of popular representation and personal recollection, and the Popular Memory Group sought to make readers more fully aware of these complexities through new forms of historical writing. Though the group disbanded in 1985, former members and historians influenced by the group used popular memory theory to structure, record, and interpret historical data in new ways. These historians focused on the ways popular culture, memory, subjectivity, and the past-present relationship interact to form fuller and admittedly more difficult meanings of the past. In a 1990 special issue of *Oral History* dedicated to popular memory, Alistair Thomson's article on Australian soldiers in World War I serves as an example of the type of inquiry "Popular Memory" inspired. Thomson demonstrates how cultural myth about Australian toughness collides in unsettling and contradictory ways with an individual soldier's memories and the way that soldier talks about his memories.

THEMES AND STYLE

The main argument in "Popular Memory" is that academic history is limited and incomplete. The essay calls for history to go "well beyond the limits of academic history-writing" and "include *all* the ways in which a sense of the past is constructed in our society." Professional historians record the past in the books and articles they write, but private citizens retain a different sense of the past in their "letters, diaries, photograph albums, and collections of things with past associations." The essay proposes bringing "private remembrance" into conversation with "dominant representations." In this manner, the Popular Memory Group hoped to move beyond simple "ideological" versions of the past and the "flattened stereotypes of myth" that simpler representations of the past promote. Oral history is an important avenue for recovering what "dominant memory" left out and glossed over. However, the practice of oral history presents a number of methodological difficulties. Class barriers between the interviewer and the subject pose problems. Even when historians turn to the accounts of the working class and other historically marginalized groups, the middle-class academic often still controls the process. "Popular Memory" acknowledges that it is difficult, if not impossible, to completely abolish the dominance of the academic perspective in some situations. Questions about the reliability of memory also complicate attempts to record the past through interviews with individual subjects. The Popular Memory Group wanted historians to acknowledge these difficulties and incorporate discussion of them into their historical writing.

The Popular Memory Group promoted their alternative history in order to raise social awareness among the forgotten voices of history and to increase the collective political power of groups pushing for change. They saw history as a unifying force for socialist and feminist causes that could foster connections by providing individuals a deeper understanding of the origins of their common struggles. They write that "[a sense of history] is one means by which an organic social group acquires a knowledge of the larger context of its collective struggles, and becomes capable of a wider transformative role in the society." History from a "socialist, feminist, and anti-racist" perspective would allow people to question and adapt "common-sense

AN AUSTRALIAN SOLDIER'S STRUGGLE WITH MEMORY

"ANZAC Memories: Putting Popular Memory Theory into Practice in Australia," written by Alistair Thomson for *Oral History* in 1990, helps bring some of the more abstract and theoretical points of "Popular Memory" into clearer focus. Thomson's article examines the experience of a World War I veteran named Fred Farral in light of postwar myths about soldiers from the Australian and New Zealand Army Corps (ANZAC). Thomson writes of the propaganda that created the stereotype of a "strong, sun-tanned, and resourceful" ANZAC soldier who was supposed to be "the best fighter in the war." Farral's war experience, however, was quite different from that heroic ideal: "He was young, naïve and under-confident, and wasn't very good at fighting and killing. Like many soldiers of all nationalities, he was terrified in battle and miserable in the trenches."

Farral returned from the fighting at the Somme traumatized and full of doubt after seeing many of his good friends die. It took him many years to come to terms with his war experience, and the ANZAC legend reinforced his feelings of doubt and inadequacy. In examining Farral's story and the ways his attitude about war changed over time, Thomson brings to light a very complex relationship between the past and the present and between private accounts of trauma on the battlefield and the public celebration of ANZAC heroes.

beliefs" about race, women, and the working class in ways that would contribute to "the struggle for a better world."

"Popular Memory" is a highly theoretical and challenging work that deals mainly in abstract terms with how history should and could be written. The writers begin with an organized summary of their argument in a brief introduction and then develop the details of the argument in subsequent sections. The essay engages with a number of previous works to provide concrete illustrations of theoretical points. The highly conceptual language draws on terms from sociology, psychology, the emerging fields of cultural and women's studies, and a Marxist tradition of historical study. The breadth and range of terminology accounts in part for the challenging nature of the text.

CRITICAL DISCUSSION

Initial critical response to "Popular Memory" highlighted the ways the essay had dealt with the complexities of recording the past through popular sources. The first scholarly reactions came in reviews of *Making History: Studies in History Writing and Politics*, the collection of essays in which "Popular Memory" first appeared. In a review for *Labour History*, John Buchanan and Bruce Smith praise the authors for systematically examining how public and private memory complicate oral history. They also write that the work provided "a basis upon which concrete studies can proceed." R. S. Neal's response in *Social History* was less favorable and reproached the group for failing to provide a workable solution for lessening the academic's dominant role in research.

Whether or not the essay solved all the problems it raised, the Popular Memory Group did succeed in bringing some of history's forgotten material and silenced voices out of the shadows of the past. Buchanan and Smith rightly saw the potential for concrete study. In addition to Thomson's writing on Australian soldiers, historians working in the popular-memory tradition have created richly nuanced accounts of English women enlisted in the military during World War II (Dorothy Sheridan), Britain's jazz musicians (Chris Clark), and the interactions of cultural representations with boyhood fantasies of war (Graham Dawson). These particular case studies can all be found in the 1990 issue of *Oral History* on popular memory. The trend of using "Popular Memory" as a secondary source for framing specific historical questions continues in contemporary practice.

The Popular Memory Group still informs historical methodology on a wide variety of subjects around the world. Recent examples include Melanie Tebbutt's work on the construction of family memory in Northampton, Pamela Sugiman's study of Japanese Canadians' narratives of World War II, and Aasim Sajjad Akhtar's investigation of Jihadist movements in northern Pakistan. The essay has appeared in extracted form in two editions of *The Oral History Reader,* a volume conceived by its editors "as a core text for undergraduate students who are using oral history, and as a resource for oral history practitioners working in a wide variety of fields." In addition, the essay figures in discussions of the development of thought about oral history.

BIBLIOGRAPHY

Sources

Buchanan, John, and Bruce Smith. "History and Socialist Politics." Rev. of *Making Histories: Studies in History-Writing and Politics,* ed. Richard Johnson et al. *Labour History* 47 (1984): 105–14. *JSTOR.* Web. 31 Jan. 2013.

Neal, R. S. Rev. of *Making Histories: Studies in History-Writing and Politics,* ed. Richard Johnson et al. *Social History* 9.3 (1984): 400–3. *JSTOR.* Web. 31 Jan. 2013.

Popular Memory Group. "Popular Memory: Theory, Politics, Method." *Making History: Studies in History Writing and Politics.* Ed. Richard Johnson et al. London: Hutchinson, 1982. 206–20. Print.

Thomson, Alistair. "ANZAC Memories: Putting Popular Memory Theory into Practice in Australia." *Popular Memory.* Spec. issue of *Oral History* 18.1 (1990): 25–31. *JSTOR.* Web. 31 Jan. 2013.

———. "Four Paradigm Transformations in Oral History." *Oral History Review* 34.1 (2007): 49–70. *JSTOR.* Web. 31 Jan. 2013.

Thomson, Alistair, Michael Frisch, and Paula Hamilton. "The Memory and History Debates: Some International Perspectives." *Oral History* 22.2 (1994): 33–43. *JSTOR.* Web. 31 Jan. 2013.

Further Reading

Akhtar, Aasim Sajjad. "Islam as Ideology of Tradition and Change: The 'New Jihad' in Swat, Northern Pakistan." *Comparative Studies of South Asia, Africa and the Middle East* 30.3 (2010): 595–609. *Project MUSE.* Web. 30 Jan. 2013.

Brittain, Vera. *Testament of Youth: An Autobiographical Study of the Years 1900–1925.* New York: Penguin, 1989. Print.

Clark, Chris. "An Oral History of Jazz in Britain." *Popular Memory.* Spec. issue of *Oral History* 18.1 (1990): 66–72. *JSTOR.* Web. 31 Jan. 2013.

Dawson, Graham. "Playing at War: An Autobiographical Approach to Boyhood Fantasy and Masculinity." *Popular Memory.* Spec. issue of *Oral History* 18.1 (1990): 44–53. *JSTOR.* Web. 31 Jan. 2013.

Fraser, Roland. *Blood of Spain: An Oral History of the Spanish Civil War.* New York: Pantheon, 1979. Print.

Sheridan, Dorothy. "Ambivalent Memories: Women and the 1939–1945 War in Britain." *Popular Memory.* Spec. issue of *Oral History* 18.1 (1990): 32–40. *JSTOR.* Web. 31 Jan. 2013.

Sugiman, Pamela. "'Life Is Sweet': Vulnerability and Composure in the Wartime Narratives of Japanese Canadians." *Journal of Canadian Studies* 43.1 (2009): 186–218. *Project MUSE.* Web. 30 Jan. 2013.

Tebbutt, Melanie. "Imagined Families and Vanished Communities: Memories of a Working-Class Life in Northampton." *History Workshop Journal* 73 (2012): 144–69. *Project MUSE.* Web. 31 Jan. 2013.

Thompson, Paul. *The Edwardians: The Remaking of British Society.* 2nd ed. New York: Routledge, 1992. Print.

Nicholas Snead

A Shared Authority
Essays on the Craft and Meaning of Oral and Public History
Michael Frisch

OVERVIEW

In *A Shared Authority: Essays on the Craft and Meaning of Oral and Public History* (1990), Michael Frisch brings together previously written essays—composed over the span of two decades—on oral and public history. Frisch, a professor, writes that oral and public memory—with their "processes of engagement, in the altered relationship between historian and 'source,' between scholarship and public discourse," and between cultural norms and alternatives to the status quo—"raise important issues of culture, communication, and politics." Frisch expresses an interest in reexamining what he calls a "split intellectual identity" that has room only for documentary or memory-based historiography and for the scholar or the subject. Such dichotomous thinking is unnecessary, he claims.

A Shared Authority immediately generated discussion within the fields of history and oral history. The book's title caught on as a useful way to describe one of the main issues of oral and public memory: authority. Frisch's book augmented discussions about how interviewers and interviewees can share authorship of a project as well as how to balance scholarly authority with empowering the people whose experiences are central to oral and public history projects. *A Shared Authority*'s lasting legacy and relevance are reflected in its continued place in dialogues related to history, such as the 2003 commentary issue on the book in the flagship journal for the field, the *Oral History Review*.

HISTORICAL AND LITERARY CONTEXT

The New Deal Federal Writers' Project (FWP)—begun to employ Great Depression–era writers, historians, and others—launched the fields of oral and public history in the United States. Historian Allan Nevins's 1948 project documenting the lives of "Great Men" and Studs Terkel's radio shows and books gave the burgeoning fields momentum. The earlier projects were billed more as "memory" than history projects, though later oral historians such as Frisch argue that how people remember, contextualize, and process history is a valuable lens through which to interpret the past and to understand the present.

A Shared Authority is arranged thematically rather than chronologically and represents nearly twenty years of work. The first section, for example, comprises both the oldest and the newest works at the time of the book's production. Many of the essays had been previously published and range from a 1972 piece on Terkel's seminal *Hard Times: An Oral History of the Great Depression* (1970) to an analysis of student responses to an in-class questionnaire Frisch had been developing and interpreting for years.

Frisch was initially moved to challenge traditional historical scholarship without neglecting all interpretation of history. As such, his collection represents an interest in finding a way to "transcend" the limitations of oral and traditional history as well as a quest to "discover the role for oral history in modern society." This interest came to be "propelled" by Terkel's *Hard Times* as well as by scholarly discussions in the 1960s and 1970s of the "critically analytic view of the cultural processes," Frisch writes, laid bare by oral history pioneers including Allan Nevins and the short-lived academic journal *Red Buffalo,* which transformed the roles and functions of historiography. He came to see that oral history provides "a capacity to redefine and redistribute intellectual authority" for communal empowerment and engagement with culture rather than maintaining a hierarchy of power. Among the many influences that impacted the essays in his collection, Frisch cites books such as *All God's Dangers: The Life of Nate Shaw* (1971), an oral history of the Alabama Sharecroppers' Union in the 1930s, and *Brass Valley* (1982), which covers 150 years of labor and community histories, along with films including *Union Maids* (1976), a film adaptation of Staughton and Alice Lynd's study of Chicago's 1930s labor, and *Rank and File: Histories of Working Class Organizers* (1973).

Aside from shaping the basic dialogue about the motivations for, players in, forms of, and assumptions in the field of oral history, *A Shared History* has been joined by many other collections on oral history, such as Robert Perks and Alistair Thomson's *The Oral History Reader* (1998) and by a growing school of related theories, many of which are distilled in Lynn Abrams's *Oral History Theory* (2010). The concepts central to Frisch's collection, particularly those of engagement, collaboration, and empowerment, continue to influence historiography. However, in

✤ Key Facts

Time Period:
Late 20th Century

Relevant Historical Events:
Development of oral history as a field; New Deal Federal Writers' Project

Nationality:
American

Keywords:
history; theory; subjectivity

THEORIES

The library of the Brooklyn Historical Society in Brooklyn, New York, circa 1989. As a university professor of American studies, Michael Frisch spent years analyzing the way historians document cultures and events. © JAMES MARSHALL/CORBIS

her 2011 article in *Oral History Review*, Erin Jessee writes that Frisch's term, "a shared authority," has often been morphed in recent years into "the more dynamic and process-oriented concept of 'sharing authority,' which implies an ongoing collaborative relationship and shared decision making between the interviewer and the interviewee."

THEMES AND STYLE

To better capture Frisch's "processes of engagement" with oral and public history, *A Shared Authority* is broken into three sections that emphasize the functions of memory, the connections between scholarship and the surrounding community, and the "various dimensions of shared and not-so-shared authority." In the overview, "Memory, History, and Cultural Authority," Frisch includes an analysis of his students' accrued historical memories, influenced, he posits, by culture as much as education. He turns to the power dynamics and effects of that cultural "packaging" in "publicly shared documentary forms" using a Public Broadcasting Service's television documentary as his case study in "Oral History, Documentary, and the Mystification of Power: A Critique of *Vietnam: A Television Series*" and coffee-table books on cities in upstate New York in "Get the Picture?: A Review Essay."

Frisch compiled the essays for *A Shared Authority* with the belief that a "shared reimagination of how the past connects to the present, and the possibilities this vantage suggests for the future," can help ameliorate the communication issues "eroding the binding values and symbols of American culture." He continues that this "shared reimagination" could come from reevaluating how history, memory, and one another are viewed. The essays reflect on the process of oral and public history rather than theories. Frisch notes that, although emergent theories of oral and public history exist, they, too, draw on "the applied level" where the majority of complexity and insights exist. Thus, he concludes, "There is something to be said for focusing discussion in concrete particulars" rather than abstract theorizations.

Beginning each section is an introductory headnote, discussing the section's themes, how the essays developed in general, and how they related to one another. Frisch writes that his organization was meant to encourage his readers to make connections "between the modes of historical practice being considered" without losing thematic arcs. In the structure of the book as well as its themes, Frisch bridges the gap between the academic world and several hierarchies of the public world at large: the organization, scope, and scholarly tone of the book remind the reader of Frisch's expertise on the subject of authority, while his deviation from heavy jargon, notes, and citations allude to his appeal to a wide readership.

CRITICAL DISCUSSION

A Shared Authority was greeted with enthusiastic reviews both for its provocative, thoughtful essays and for its title, which presented the oral and public history communities with an immediately adoptable and useful term. In his early review of *A Shared Authority* in the *Oral History Review*, a journal then edited by Frisch, David Thelen sums up his reaction to the book—an assessment he "imagine[s] … many readers already know—or at least suspect"—that "this is a great book." Paul Buhle begins his review in the *Journal of American History* with a nearly identical sentiment: "This is a remarkable book," lauding *A Shared Authority* for both its depth and its refusal to provide all the answers to the questions it raises, instead encouraging readers to engage personally with history because "the narrative is never quite what it seems."

Since the book first appeared in 1990, Frisch's notion of shared authority has become a central point in conversations on oral history. As Linda Shopes argues in a 2003 *Oral History Review* issue dedicated to discussing Frisch's book, "'Shared authority' has become something of a mantra among oral historians." Typical of work extending Frisch's original conception of shared authority is a 2009 article in the *Journal of Canadian Studies* on the continued quest to achieve a balance in authority; in it Alan Wong suggests that an interviewer's self-reflexivity and his or her willingness to be interviewed may allow the interviewer to share authority with his or her subjects more equitably.

Frisch's book is heavily cited in other works on oral history, such as Abrams's *Oral History Theory* and in conversations in which concerns central to history, oral history, and public history figure prominently. It is also shaping the discussion surrounding oral history as the technologies with which memories and narratives are captured change, a trend Joy Parr, Jessica Van Horssen, and Jon van der Veen discuss in relation to Frisch's book in their 2009 article in the *Journal of Canadian Studies*. Frisch himself considers the implications for oral history in a digital age in "Oral History and the Digital Revolution: Towards a Post-Documentary Sensibility," an essay featured in *The Oral History Reader*.

BIBLIOGRAPHY

Sources

Buhle, Paul. Rev. of *A Shared Authority: Essays on the Craft and Meaning of Oral and Public History*, by Michael Frisch. *Journal of American History* 78.2 (1991): 629–30. *JSTOR*. Web. 11 Jan. 2013.

ORAL HISTORY AND TECHNOLOGY

Discussion of the impact of technological changes has increasingly permeated conversations pertaining to many fields, including oral history. Like the tape recorders Allan Nevins deployed in his early "Great Men" project, advancing technology has always been a crucial part of capturing oral histories, aiding transcription and complicating interpretations thereof. The nuances of body language recorded in images, for example, can add another layer of narrative to dialect, pauses, and intonation.

Long before Frisch considered related issues in "Oral History and the Digital Revolution: Towards a Post-Documentary Sensibility" (2006), he was reflecting on how technological elements such as photography shape the deployment of oral history. With photographer Milton Rogovin, Frisch's *Portraits in Steel* (1993) captures steel workers dislocated by the devastation of the Buffalo, New York, steel industry. Though he does edit the responses heavily, rather than overlaying his interpretation of the photographs or the workers' responses to his questions, Frisch allows the images and words to speak for themselves, highlighting the collaborative nature of the project and working, as he reflects in *A Shared Authority*, "to document a contemporary crisis in a way that transcends the problem/victim focus of contemporary journalism, permitting the people at the center of these epochal changes to share their experience and perspective." *Portraits in Steel* won the 1995 Oral History Association Book Award.

Frisch, Michael. *A Shared Authority: Essays on the Craft and Meaning of Oral and Public History*. Albany: State University of New York Press, 1990. Print.

Jessee, Erin. "The Limits of Oral History: Ethics and Methodology amid Highly Politicized Research Settings." *Oral History Review* 38.2 (2011): 287–307. *Project MUSE*. Web. 3 Jan. 2013.

Parr, Joy, Jessica Van Horssen, and Jon van der Veen. "The Practice of History Shared across Differences: Needs, Technologies, and Ways of Knowing in the Megaprojects New Media Project." *Journal of Canadian Studies* 43.1 (2009): 35–58. *Literature Online*. Web. 14 Jan. 2013.

Perks, Robert, and Alistair Thomson, eds. *The Oral History Reader*. London: Routledge, 1998. Print.

Shopes, Linda. "Commentary: Sharing Authority." *Oral History Review* 30.1 (2003): 103–10. *JSTOR*. Web. 13 Jan. 2013.

Thelen, David. Rev. of *A Shared Authority: Essays on the Craft and Meaning of Oral and Public History*, by Michael Frisch. *Oral History Review* 18.2 (1990): 153–55. *JSTOR*. Web. 12 Jan. 2013.

Wong, Alan L. "Conversations for the Real World: Shared Authority, Self-Reflexivity, and Process in the Oral History Interview." *Journal of Canadian Studies* 43.1 (2009): 239–58. *JSTOR*. Web. 13 Jan. 2013.

Further Reading

Abrams, Lynn. *Oral History Theory*. New York: Routledge, 2010. Print.

Charlton, Thomas L., Lois E. Myers, and Rebecca Sharpless, eds. *Oral History: Foundations and Methodology.* Lanham, Md.: AltaMira, 2007. Print.

Dunar, Andrew J., ed. "Special Feature: Sharing Authority." *Oral History Review* 30.1 (2003): 23–113. *JSTOR.* Web. 13 Jan. 2013.

High, Steven, Lisa Ndejuru, and Kristen O'Hare, eds. "Special Issues on Sharing Authority: Community-University Collaboration in Oral History, Digital Storytelling, and Engaged Scholarship," *Journal of Canadian Studies* 43.1 (2009). *Project MUSE.* Web. 13 Jan. 2013.

Ritchie, Donald A. *Doing Oral History: A Practical Guide.* 2nd ed. Oxford, UK: Oxford University Press, 2003. Print.

Rogovin, Milton, and Michael Frisch. *Portraits in Steel.* Ithaca, N.Y.: Cornell University Press, 1993. Print.

Katherine Bishop

The Story of a Shipwrecked Sailor
Gabriel García Márquez

OVERVIEW

Collected and edited by Gabriel García Márquez, *Relato de un náufrago* (1970), or *The Story of a Shipwrecked Sailor* (1976), presents the firsthand account of the ten days that shipwrecked Colombian sailor Luis Alejandro Velasco spent alone on a lifeboat on the Caribbean Sea in 1955. Following his ordeal, he approached the liberal newspaper *El Espectador* to tell his story. Although much of the account focuses on the privations he endured at sea, *The Story of Shipwrecked Sailor* implicitly condemns the Colombian government's narrative of the event: it crowned Velasco a national hero in order to distract from its own negligence. In García Márquez's hands, Velasco's ordeal is a narrative of the suffering of an individual at sea and at the hands of a government concerned only with its image.

First published in serial form in the pages of *El Espectador* and later compiled as a book, *The Story of a Shipwrecked Sailor* stirred up political controversy for its depiction of the Colombian navy. After the story's publication, the government shut down the newspaper and forced Velasco out of the military. García Márquez subsequently fled in exile to France. Although significantly different in style and form from García Márquez's later literary works, the book continues to attract popular attention as a piece of García Márquez's apprentice work and as a depiction of the Colombian political climate in the mid-twentieth century.

HISTORICAL AND LITERARY CONTEXT

Although much of the narrative occurs at sea, thus ostensibly isolated from its politico-historical context, García Márquez imbues the text with implicit criticisms of the conservative government of President Gustavo Rojas Pinilla. Rojas Pinilla seized control of Colombia in 1953, wresting power from the brutal regime of President Laureano Gómez. Hopes were high with Rojas Pinilla's ascension to power: he promised greater peace and liberty by offering amnesty to various violent factions and by developing social work programs. However, by the end of 1953, rural violence was resurgent. Rojas Pinilla's regime cracked down on opposition in the press. As the economy deteriorated because of a drop in coffee prices, government graft was rampant. The popular tide soon turned against the regime.

In late 1954 and early 1955, the *Caldas*, a destroyer in the Colombian navy, was docked in Mobile, Alabama, for repairs to its gunnery and electronic equipment. The crew weighed anchor and departed on February 24, carrying illegal contraband on the deck of the ship. One day later five men, including Velasco, were tossed overboard. The Colombian government claimed that the men had fallen overboard during a storm, though Velasco stated that the men had been knocked overboard by illegal contraband that had not been properly secured and had broken free. His tale exposed the lack of safety equipment and preparation of the Colombian navy.

Although *The Story of a Shipwrecked Sailor* falls into the category of oral histories, it also is part of the tradition of maritime literature. In a 1986 *New York Times* review, Michiko Kakutani writes that, in the book, "conscious or unconscious, allusions are made to such sea literature as 'Robinson Crusoe' and 'The Rime of the Ancient Mariner,' and the book's subtitle, too, has the effect of making us see the protagonist … as the quintessential shipwrecked sailor." Like García Márquez, Daniel Defoe, author of *Robinson Crusoe*, was inspired by the experiences of a castaway—Scottish sailor Andrew Selkirk, who was trapped on a deserted island off the coast of Chile. However, García Márquez's book differs from the works of Defoe and Samuel Taylor Coleridge, author of *The Rime of the Ancient Mariner*, in that *The Story of a Shipwrecked Sailor*, though novelized, is not a fictional account.

In itself, *The Story of a Shipwrecked Sailor* has exerted little cultural or literary influence. The text was not published in book form until fifteen years after its serialization and was not translated into English until 1986. Although it was the first book that García Márquez wrote, it was the eighth to be translated from the original Spanish. Nevertheless, the work has proved to be an important early creation of one of Latin America's most distinguished novelists. In 1982 García Márquez was awarded the Nobel Prize in Literature for his body of fiction.

THEMES AND STYLE

The central theme of *The Story of a Shipwrecked Sailor* is the physical and emotional suffering that Velasco endured while lost at sea. The book chronicles the sailor's emotional vacillations, including his joy and

Key Facts

Time Period:
Mid-20th Century

Relevant Historical Events:
Government of Rojas Pinilla; the throwing overboard of five Colombian sailors

Nationality:
Colombian

Keywords:
shipping; politics; heroism

ROJAS PINILLA: LATIN AMERICAN DICTATOR

The twentieth century witnessed the rise of many right-wing dictators in Latin America. Although Gustavo Rojas Pinilla is less infamous than other Latin American dictators such as Chile's Augusto Pinochet, Argentina's Jorge Rafael Videla, or Nicaragua's Anastasio Somoza Debayle, Colombia nevertheless suffered under his reign. After graduating from the Colombia Military Academy in 1920, Rojas Pinilla quickly rose through the ranks of the Colombian Army. By 1948 he was a lieutenant general and had helped in the suppression of protests following the assassination of left-wing leader Jorge Eliécer Gaitán Ayala, who was favored to win the Colombian presidential election. Instead, Laureano Gómez, a supporter of Adolf Hitler and Francisco Franco, assumed the presidency following an election tainted by the imposition of martial law, severe press censorship, and the Liberal Party's refusal to participate.

Rojas Pinilla seized power in 1953. Many Colombians welcomed him because they believed he would bring peace and liberty following the oppressive Gómez presidency. Instead he cracked down on the freedom of the press, increased the size and power of the secret police, embezzled money, and provoked anti-Protestant sentiments that would eventually lead to violence. In 1957 he was ousted by his own people and fled in exile to the United States.

---

certainty of rescue as a plane flies overhead and his desperation and loneliness as he realizes that the plane has not seen him. Velasco tells of trying to fish with his bare hands. After eating three business cards he received in Mobile, he claims that he felt "stronger and more optimistic." While the textures of his daily experiences make up the bulk of the narrative, a subtle thread of political opposition is woven through the text. About the claims of military heroism and nobility that the government heaped upon him after his return, he states, "In my case, heroism consisted solely in not allowing myself to die of hunger and thirst for ten days."

While it seems likely that Velasco was primarily interested in telling his side of the story, García Márquez saw the piece as an opportunity to level criticism at the oppressive and conservative government of Rojas Pinilla. Based on 120 hours of interviews between Velasco and García Márquez, the text is closer to journalism than an unexpurgated oral history. Velasco approached *El Espectador* to tell his tale after initial interest in the story had waned, and in the hands of García Márquez the story became as remarkable for Velasco's tale of survival as the government's treatment of the sailor. García Márquez marvels at how Velasco "drifted on a life raft for ten days without food or water, was proclaimed a national hero, kissed by beauty queens, made rich through publicity, and then spurned by the government and forgotten for all time."

The structure of *The Story of a Shipwrecked Sailor* was influenced by its publication in serialized form. Many of the sections end with cliff-hangers to sustain audience interest. As Kakutani argues, the "flat reportorial language bears little resemblance to Mr. García Márquez's famous Faulknerian prose," though the story embodies "many of his mature concerns." However, the book differs from traditional oral histories in that García Márquez and Velasco worked together to novelize the story. As the author writes in the introduction to the 1989 edition, "We agreed that the story would be written in the first person and signed by him," thereby transforming García Márquez into Velasco's ghostwriter.

CRITICAL DISCUSSION

Upon its first serialized publication in the pages of *El Espectador*, *The Story of a Shipwrecked Sailor* was highly celebrated in the Colombian press. In his introduction, García Márquez claims that, after the story's publication, "the paper's circulation had almost doubled, and readers scrambled in front of the building to buy back issues in order to collect the entire series." Initially, the Colombian government issued only laudatory remarks about the story, but as inculpating details emerged—such as the fact that the navy ship had been carrying illegal contraband—the government grew hostile. Within a few months the newspaper was shut down. Velasco was offered a series of bribes, though he never recanted his story. As García Márquez writes, outside pressure forced Velasco "to leave the navy, the only career he had, and disappear into the oblivion of everyday life."

Although *The Story of a Shipwrecked Sailor* relates an interesting, if isolated, chapter of Colombian history, the book has not exerted lasting political or historical influence. In many ways the work, which is often read as an apprentice piece, has been overshadowed by García Márquez's later literary output. Nevertheless, *The Story of a Shipwrecked Sailor* was remarkable as a public relations debacle for an already unpopular dictatorial regime. For example, when the government responded that no contraband had been transported on the ship, *El Espectador* released photographs showing boxes of illegal American merchandise aboard the *Caldas*. Within two years of the story's publication, the Rojas Pinilla government collapsed.

Since its initial publication in 1955, *The Story of a Shipwrecked Sailor* has attracted limited scholarly inquiry. Most readers see it as an introduction to García Márquez's later work. Kakutani argues that the book, while lacking in literary style, capsulizes "in a very undeveloped form, themes addressed more fully in later novels and short stories," such as the "complicated questions about man's relationship with Nature and Fate." In *Chiasmus in the Works of Gabriel García Márquez* (2000), one of the few scholarly works to address *The Story of a Shipwrecked Sailor*, Rusel Everett Hays argues that certain parallel structures in several of

García Márquez's novels can be traced to oral storytelling traditions of Latin America.

BIBLIOGRAPHY

Sources

García Márquez, Gabriel. *The Story of a Shipwrecked Sailor.* Trans. Randolph Hogan. New York: Vintage, 1989. Print.

———. "The Story of This Story." *The Story of a Shipwrecked Sailor.* Trans. Randolph Hogan. New York: Vintage, 1989. v–ix. Print.

Hays, Rusel Everett. *Chiasmus in the Works of Gabriel García Márquez.* Dominguez Hills: California State University Press, 2000. *ProQuest.* Web. 31 Jan. 2012.

Kakutani, Michiko. "Early Garcia Marquez." Rev. of *The Story of a Shipwrecked Sailor,* by Gabriel García Márquez. *New York Times* 26 Apr. 1986. *ProQuest.* Web. 29 Jan. 2013.

Read, Piers Paul. "The Hero Who Lived to Regret It." Rev. of *The Story of a Shipwrecked Sailor,* by Gabriel García Márquez. *New York Times.* New York Times, 27 Apr. 1986. Web. 29 Jan. 2013.

Further Reading

García Márquez, Gabriel. *News of a Kidnapping.* New York: Penguin, 2008. Print.

Martin, Gerald. *Gabriel García Márquez.* New York: Knopf, 2009. Print.

Miles, Harvey. "Journeys to Hell." Rev. of *The Story of a Shipwrecked Sailor,* by Gabriel García Márquez. *Outside* 21.5 (1996): 69. Print.

Philbrick, Nathaniel. *In the Heart of the Sea: The Tragedy of the Whaleship* Essex. New York: Penguin, 2000. Print.

Stavans, Ilan. *Gabriel García Márquez: The Early Years.* New York: Palgrave Macmillan, 2010. Print.

Greg Luther

The Voice of the Past
Oral History
Paul Thompson

✥ Key Facts

Time Period:
Late 20th Century

Relevant Historical Events:
Increased validity of oral history after World War II

Nationality:
British

Keywords:
scholarship; theory; history

OVERVIEW

Written by British scholar Paul Thompson, *The Voice of the Past: Oral History* has provided foundational theory for oral history since its publication in 1978. In this monumental work, Thompson argues for oral history's value: it lets scholars collect more nuanced data; allows individuals from different races or economic classes to gain a better understanding of one another; permits students to learn historical techniques firsthand; and, most important, gives everyday people a voice in society. Not only does Thompson lay theoretical groundwork for oral history, but he also gives practical examples of possible projects and techniques. As a whole, *The Voice of the Past* demonstrates Thompson's belief that history should be an instrument of social change, using the stories of everyday people to improve society.

Thompson, a professor at the University of Exeter, wrote in an intellectual milieu that valued the working classes. He became well known for his groundbreaking use of oral history in his project *The Edwardians* (1975), which chronicled the experiences and opinions of people born between 1872 and 1906. This book served as Thompson's bridge into oral history, and *The Voice of the Past* solidified his place in the field. Just as Thompson had interviewed people from all walks of life for *The Edwardians,* so his socialist beliefs provide the theoretical underpinning for *The Voice of the Past.* Because of this, it initially received mixed reviews. Most scholars eagerly accepted Thompson's ideas and suggestions, but a few, such as Louis M. Starr, tempered their responses with cautions against accepting the author's socialist bent unreservedly. However, Thompson's work continues to be essential to practitioners of oral history and is often used as a textbook in college courses. *The Voice of the Past* entered its third edition in 2000 and is one of the most frequently cited works in scholarly writing about oral history.

HISTORICAL AND LITERARY CONTEXT

As Thompson and other oral historians, such as Bill Williams, have pointed out, oral history is an ancient practice, used by Herodotus, Tacitus, Bede, and other classical and medieval writers. However, by the early twentieth century most historians did not accept oral history as a valid source of facts, following nineteenth-century scholarship that valued archives and written texts more highly. After World War II historians once again began to accept living memory as a useful resource, and as portable tape recorders became more widely available, scholars turned to living people as resources. In the United States in the 1940s and 1950s, early oral history focused on recording the experiences of white male elites. For example, American historian Allan Nevins used correspondence and interviews to compose biographies about famous American leaders such as Grover Cleveland, Henry Ford, and John D. Rockefeller. To archive interviews about the lives of powerful men like these, in 1948 Nevins also started the first oral history project at Columbia University. In Britain, on the other hand, oral historians turned their attention to the laborer class thanks to the nation's politically charged atmosphere at the end of World War II. By the 1960s and 1970s this had also become more common in the United States, where essays such as "Black History, Oral History, and Genealogy" by Alex Haley, published in 1973, exemplified the turn toward underprivileged groups.

The Voice of the Past solidified oral history's attention to typically silenced members of society. Thompson argues that oral history should record the voices of "normal" people and use their experiences as a platform for radical social change. He writes that "history should not merely comfort; it should provide a challenge, and understanding which helps toward change.... It has to encompass the complexities of conflict."

The Voice of the Past stands in the genre of theoretical writing about history's subjects, practices, and purpose. Some historians writing in the 1970s criticized living memory as an accurate historical source. Barbara Tuchman, Enoch Powell, and Eric Hobsbawm, among others, claimed that people's memories were too subjective to be the proper material for history. Thompson argues, however, that oral history permits greater historical accuracy by allowing access to the nuanced, complex experiences of the masses. It also makes history more immediate for students and the public via television, radio, and film. Donald A. Ritchie's book *Doing Oral History: A Practical Guide,* published in its second edition in 2003, extends Thompson's ideas to explain basic techniques for collecting oral histories.

Scott County Historical Society director Kathy Kiehr conducting an oral history with Scott County Agricultural Society president Kevin Bailey in Jordan, Minnesota, in 2012. Paul Thompson explores the field of oral history in his book *The Voice of the Past: Oral History*. © ZUMA PRESS, INC./ALAMY

The Voice of the Past's emphasis on everyday people—workers, the elderly, women, indigenous tribes, socially denigrated groups—has become dominant in oral historical theory. The third edition has been updated to account for modern technology and is standard college reading. A prolific scholar, Thompson has continued to publish books and articles about oral history. His work includes essays in *Listening for a Change: Oral Testimony and Development* (1993), *Narrative and Genre: Contexts and Types of Communication* (1998), and *Environmental Consciousness: The Roots of a New Political Agenda* (2004), as well as the book *Sea-Change: Wivenhoe Remembered* (2006).

THEMES AND STYLE

The central theme of *The Voice of the Past* is that oral history allows historians to harness the nuance of individuals' experiences to create social change. Thompson notes that "even as the scope of history has widened, the original political and administrative focus has remained. Where ordinary people have been brought in, it has been generally as statistical aggregates derived from some earlier administrative investigation." Positing his own claims, he argues that oral history "is … built around people. … It brings history into, and out of, the community. It helps the less privileged, and especially the old, towards dignity and self-confidence. It makes for contact—and thence understanding—between social classes, and between generations." In addition to this theoretical framework, Thompson uses an extensive portion of his book to talk about specific facets of oral history. For example, the chapter "Memory and the Self" discusses the intersections between oral history and psychoanalysis. The chapters "Projects," "The Interview," and "Storing and Sifting" give practical suggestions for fieldwork. Overall, he emphasizes relationships—relationships between interviewer and interviewee and among teams of interviewers—as key to oral history's purpose of building better societies.

Thompson writes to provide a productive alternative to what he perceives as the stifling, elitist trend in mid-twentieth-century history. He believes oral history should offer "a challenge to the accepted myths of history, to the authoritarian judgment inherent in its tradition. It provides a means for a radical transformation of the social meaning of history." Instead of letting people simply receive history from elite academics, oral history should force society to revise its assumptions based on working-class experience, according to Thompson's argument. He claims that "if the full potential of oral history is realized, it will result not so much in a specific list of titles in a section of historical bibliographies, as in an underlying change in the ways in which history is written and learnt, in its questions and its judgments, and in its texture." To this end, *The Voice of the Past* includes an appendix called "A Life-Story Interview Guide," one of the features that has made the book most notable for students learning how to practice oral history as well as for experts in the field. The interview guide includes a questionnaire designed to help researchers glean comprehensive life histories from their interviewees.

Thompson's prose lends itself to his populist politics. From the title of his first chapter, "History and

THEORIES

PRIMARY SOURCE

EXCERPT FROM *THE VOICE OF THE PAST*

All history depends ultimately upon its social purpose. This is why in the past it has been handed down by oral tradition and written chronicle, and why today professional historians are supported from public funds, children are taught history in schools, amateur history societies blossom, and popular history books rank among the strongest bestsellers. Sometimes the social purpose of history is obscure. There are academics who pursue fact-finding research on remote problems, avoiding any entanglement with wider interpretations or contemporary issues, insisting only on the pursuit of knowledge for its own sake. They have one thing in common with the bland contemporary tourism which exploits the past as if it were another foreign country to escape to: a heritage of buildings and landscape so lovingly cared for that it is almost inhumanly comfortable, purged of social suffering, cruelty, and conflict to the point that a slavery plantation becomes a positive pleasure. Both look to their incomes free from interference, and in return stir no challenge to the social system. At the other extreme the social purpose of history can be quite blatant: used to provide justification for war and conquest, territorial seizure, revolution and counter-revolution, the rule of one class or race over another. Where no history is readily at hand, it will be created. South Africa's white rulers divide their urban blacks between tribes and "homelands"; Welsh nationalists gather at bardic eisteddfods; the Chinese of the cultural revolution were urged to construct the new "four histories" of grass-roots struggle; radical feminists looked to the history of wet-nursing in their search for mothers without maternal instinct. Between these two extremes are many other purposes, more or less obvious. For politicians the past is a quarry for supportive symbols: imperial victories, martyrs, Victorian values, hunger marches. And almost equally telling are the gaps in the public presentation of history: the silences in Russia on [Leon] Trotsky, in West Germany on the Nazi era, in France on the Algerian war.

Through history ordinary people seek to understand the upheavals and changes which they

---

the Community," he makes clear that his goal is to free history from the ivory tower. Although he sometimes cites academics, such as French psychoanalyst Jacques Lacan, who would be unfamiliar to the average reader, he also narrates anecdotes in a clear, conversational style. For instance, he recounts stories about class tensions in wealthy English and Italian households. Throughout the book Thompson quotes heavily from oral histories, including Isabelle Bertaux-Wiame's study of speech differences between men and women in France. His use of these sources lends legitimacy to his argument about oral history's usefulness for scholarly work and gives his text narrative power.

CRITICAL DISCUSSION

Initial responses to *The Voice of the Past* were mixed. In his 1978 review in *Oral History Review*, Starr called Thompson's socialist views "rank demagoguery," but most critics received the book as an important development in the field. Willa Baum and Amelia Fry, writing for *American Historical Review*, note that "this small volume is ideal for historians … who are grappling with the relative value of oral history as a primary source, for teachers in search of a basic text that will both inform and provoke lively classroom discussion, and for practitioners in other disciplines that use oral sources."

The Voice of the Past has remained a standard text on oral history. As Baum and Fry predicted, it is a textbook for students and a handbook for historians. The 2000 edition has been translated into Chinese, Greek, Portuguese, Spanish, Swedish, and Turkish, among others. In each new edition, Thompson has attempted to update his work to account for new technologies, new perspectives, and new uses for oral history. Paula Hamilton, reviewing the 2000 edition for *Oral History*, writes that despite oral history's "fragmented" nature, Thompson still helpfully "carries you right through to the end" of the interview process. At the same time, she complains that "the prescriptive tone [is] frankly irritating given the wide range of contexts within which oral history is used nowadays."

Critical discussions of *The Voice of the Past* mainly cite it as one of the first to provide guidelines for modern oral history. In his 2007 article "Four Paradigm Transformations in Oral History," Alistair Thomson begins his survey by discussing Thompson's book, and each of his subsequent sections demonstrates indirectly how oral history has used Thompson's ideas. Thompson's focus on oral history's social power has been inspirational for historians of marginalized groups. Sally Chandler's 2005 article "Oral History across Generations: Age, Generational Identity, and Oral Testimony," for instance—although it does not quote Thompson directly—uses his techniques. Paul Sandul, in a 2012 article on the folk songs of African Americans, often turns to Thompson's book as background. Thus, *The Voice of the Past* serves as a theoretical basis with which oral historians continue to work.

experience in their own lives: wars, social transformations like the changing position of youth, technological changes like the end of steam power, or personal migration to a new community. Family history especially can give an individual a strong sense of a much longer personal lifespan, which will even survive their own death. Through local history a village or town seeks meaning for its own changing character and newcomers can gain a sense of roots in personal historical knowledge. Through political and social history taught in schools, children are helped to understand, and accept, how the political and social system under which they live came about, and how force and conflict have played, and continue to play, their part in that evolution.

The challenge of oral history lies partly in relation to this essential social purpose of history. This is a major reason why it has so excited some historians, and so frightened others. In fact, fear of oral history as such is groundless. We shall see later that the use of interviews as a source by professional historians is long-standing and perfectly compatible with scholarly standards. American experience shows clearly enough that the oral history method can be regularly used in a socially and politically conservative manner; or indeed pushed as far as sympathy with Fascism in John Toland's portrait of *Adolf Hitler* (New York, 1976).

Oral history is not necessarily an instrument for change; it depends upon the spirit in which it is used. Nevertheless, oral history certainly can be a means for transforming both the content and the purpose of history. It can be used to change the focus of history itself, and open up new areas of inquiry; it can break down barriers between teachers and students, between generations, between educational institutions and the world outside; and in the writing of history—whether in books, or museums, or radio and film—it can give back to the people who made and experienced history, through their own words, a central place.

SOURCE: Thompson, Paul. *The Voice of the Past: Oral History.* 2nd ed. New York: Oxford University Press, 1988. By permission of Oxford University Press, USA.

BIBLIOGRAPHY

Sources

Baum, Willa, and Amelia Fry. Rev. of *The Voice of the Past: Oral History,* by Paul Thompson. *American Historical Review* 84.3 (1979): 711. *JSTOR.* Web. 10 Jan. 2013.

Hamilton, Paula. Rev. of *The Voice of the Past,* by Paul Thompson. *Oral History* 28.2 (2000): 103–4. *JSTOR.* Web. 10 Jan. 2013.

Rev. of *The Voice of the Past: Oral History,* by Paul Thompson. *History and Theory* 40.1 (2001): 151. *JSTOR.* Web. 10 Jan. 2013.

Starr, Louis M. Rev. of *The Voice of the Past: Oral History,* by Paul Thompson. *Oral History Review* 6 (1978): 67–68. *JSTOR.* Web. 10 Jan. 2013.

Thompson, Paul. *The Voice of the Past: Oral History.* Oxford, UK: Oxford University Press, 1978. *EBSCOhost.* Web. 10 Jan. 2013.

Thomson, Alistair. "Four Paradigm Transformations in Oral History." *Oral History Review* 34.1 (2007): 49–70. *JSTOR.* Web. 10 Jan. 2013.

Further Reading

Bauer, Elaine, and Paul Thompson. *Jamaican Hands across the Atlantic.* Kingston, Jamaica: Ian Randle, 2006. Print.

Chandler, Sally. "Oral History across Generations: Age, Generational Identity, and Oral Testimony." *Oral History* 33.2 (2005): 48–56. *JSTOR.* Web. 10 Jan. 2013.

Gluck, Sherna Berger, and Daphne Patai, eds. *Women's Words: The Feminist Practice of Oral History.* London: Routledge, 1991. Print.

Haley, Alex. "Black History, Oral History, and Genealogy." *Oral History Review* 1 (1973): 1–25. *JSTOR.* Web. 10 Jan. 2013.

Hussey, S., and Paul Thompson. *The Roots of Environmental Consciousness: Popular Tradition and Personal Experience.* London: Routledge, 2000. Print.

Neuenschwander, John A. *A Guide to Oral History and the Law.* New York: Oxford University Press, 2009. Print.

Perks, Robert, and Alistair Thomson, eds. *The Oral History Reader.* New York: Routledge, 2005. Print.

Ritchie, Donald A. *Doing Oral History: A Practical Guide.* Oxford, UK: Oxford University Press, 2003. Print.

Sandul, Paul, et al. "'In the Pines, Where the Sun Don't Ever Shine': Oral History, Community, and Race in Nacogdoches, East Texas." *East Texas Historical Journal* 50.1 (2012): 27–48. *Academic Search Premier.* Web. 10 Jan. 2013.

Williams, Bill. Rev. of *The Voice of the Past: Oral History,* by Paul Thompson. *Oral History* 7.1 (1979): 63–65. *JSTOR.* Web. 10 Jan. 2013.

Yow, Valerie Raleigh. *Recording Oral History: A Guide for the Humanities and Social Sciences,* 2nd ed. Walnut Creek, Calif.: AltaMira Press, 2005. Print.

Evelyn Reynolds

Women's Words
The Feminist Practice of Oral History
Sherna Berger Gluck, Daphne Patai

✣ Key Facts

Time Period:
Mid-20th Century

Relevant Historical Events:
Growth of feminism; rise of postmodern and postcolonial theory

Nationality:
American

Keywords:
postmodernism; postcolonialism; feminism; theory

OVERVIEW

Women's Words: The Feminist Practice of Oral History (1991), edited by Sherna Berger Gluck and Daphne Patai, is a landmark work in the field of oral history. The thirteen essays that appear in the book are written by scholars in a variety of fields, such as history, ethnography, literature, linguistics, and anthropology. Some of these scholars have interviewed women only in the United States, but many have worked in other countries with subjects of various races and ethnicities. The essays included in the anthology offer a self-critical assessment of the challenges, successes, and especially the failures that feminist scholars encounter in their work. The anthology reflects a growing awareness of the dangers of relying on feelings of empathy or the assumption of equality and the difficulty of separating questions of gender from questions of class, race, and ethnicity.

Published in the early 1990s, *Women's Words* reflects on almost two decades of feminist oral history. In the early 1970s feminist scholars challenged the validity of the positivistic approach to history practiced by their male peers, which imposed clear separation between researcher and informant, thinking and feeling. Instead feminist scholars emphasized empathy, relationships, and equality. Although the volume is dedicated to women's life stories and is designed to address feminist concerns, the contributors' poignant questions and interdisciplinary methodology have proved relevant to the field of oral history in general.

HISTORICAL AND LITERARY CONTEXT

The essays included in *Women's Words* were written at a time when American women demanded greater recognition of their lives and experiences. The notion of sisterhood seemed to be more powerful than issues of race and class or anything that might cause fissures in the united women's front. The essays were written at a time when activism, travel, and postmodern and postcolonial theory brought to the fore the articulation of women's selfhood in underdeveloped countries, where women's liberation was subordinated to political concerns. The essays also reflect the increased attention on the disparity of wealth between nations.

In the anthology several of the contributors discuss the difficulties and failures they registered in their attempts to relate as sisters in a common fight, especially when they interviewed women who found themselves in dangerous political contexts, such as in Palestine and Sudan. Patai writes of her concern that egregious economic disparities between her and the women she interviewed put her in the position of the colonizer, possibly making it appear that she was furthering a male, imperialist agenda.

The year before the anthology was published, professor Michael Frisch introduced the concept of shared authority between interviewer and narrator in his book *A Shared Authority: Essays on the Craft and Meaning of Oral and Public History* (1990). Most of the contributors to Gluck and Patai's anthology respond to the work of Ann Oakley, whose groundbreaking essay "Interviewing Women: A Contradiction in Terms" (1981) rejected the dispassionate, neutral methodology of the social sciences in favor of an engaged and empathetic relationship with the interviewed person. The authors of *Women's Words* also respond to Carole J. Spitzack's article "Body Talk: The Politics of Weight Loss and Female Identity" (1988), which explores the idea of universal sisterhood. Patai, reflecting on her experience in Brazil, argues that Oakley and Spitzack fail to consider the fact that an empathetic relationship between researcher and narrator can still be messy or even exploitative.

Women's Words was hailed as a major achievement in the field of oral history—in spite of the fact that it offers more questions than answers. Perhaps because it refuses to offer facile answers to the questions that it asks, it continues to be a reference text for oral historians. Even if the goal of the anthology is to discuss and promote a feminist agenda, it has quickly spread beyond its intended audience, informing the work of oral historians who research questions of race and ethnicity.

THEMES AND STYLE

In *Women's Words* the contributors give voice to the voiceless and record the lives of women who are marginalized by patriarchal societies and their economic status. At the same time, they raise questions about the ways these voices are to be transmuted to text, the ethics of interpreting and excerpting these voices,

Compiling oral histories at a nursing home in 1999, a university student reviews an elderly woman's photograph album. © JAMES MARSHALL/CORBIS

and the potentially positive or negative impact of the scholar on the community that he or she is studying. Some of the contributors discuss the extent to which scholars can combine research and advocacy, while others wonder what the researcher should do if he or she finds more differences than common ground with the interviewee.

The anthology is the product of the belief that—as Gluck and Patai observe in the introduction to *Women's Words*—"the telling of the story can be empowering, validating the importance of the speaker's life experience. This, indeed, is one of the reasons that oral history work with women was assumed to be inherently feminist." However, as most contributors point out, the process of "framing, presenting, interpreting, analyzing, and making [oral history] public" can put the women who are interviewed at risk of being misinterpreted. Scholars also risk betraying the narrators for the purpose of benefitting their academic career. Thus, in their introspective, self-critical, and careful analysis, the authors appeal to history, psychology, speech communication, and linguistics in order to define the complexities of the interview process and devise ethical and responsible approaches to conducting interviews and using recorded materials.

The clear, cogent essays in the anthology reflect an awareness that the tone and voice of the narrator is missing in many oral histories. Often the narrators' words are given only as translated by an interpreter. Claudia Salazar points out the inappropriate and naive manner in which the editor of *I, Rigoberta Menchú: An Indian Woman in Guatemala* (1984) reorganizes the autobiography of the Guatemalan advocate of human rights to fit certain themes. Moreover, Salazar points out that the editor takes the liberty of inserting "linking passages" in the manuscript in order to ensure fluidity of reading for the convenience of Western readers. In a different essay, Gwendolyn Etter-Lewis uses a sociolinguistic lens to show the wealth of information one can gather from narrative style. Through her research on the life stories of older, educated black women, she identifies "unified," "segmented," and "conversational" styles that allow her to better understand how her subjects choose to construct themselves in terms of gender, race, and class.

CRITICAL DISCUSSION

Gluck and Patai's anthology received a favorable response upon its publication. In a 1992 analysis in *Oral History Review*, Mary Chamberlain declares *Women's Words* "an exciting achievement. And a very important book." In a 1993 review for *Pennsylvania History*, Lori E. Cole commends the essays by Judith Stacey, Sondra Hale, and Daphne Patai, which are grouped in the anthology under the rubric of "Dilemmas and Contradictions," for their "multivariate approach to women's lives." Cole states that these essays "put the collection on the cutting edge of history." In a 1992 article for *Oral History Review*, Susan Armitage, George Lipsitz, and Gary R. Mormino call the book "pathbreaking." Nonetheless, Armitage offers the harshest criticism of the book, claiming that she "came to think of it as a 'how-*not*-to-do it' manual from which seasoned interviewers could learn a lot.

But as I read, I had the growing feeling that the main effect of his book on beginners might be to convince them that good oral history is impossible."

In the years since the publication of *Women's Words,* the ethical scrupulousness with which the contributors explore the composition of oral history has most resonated with oral historians. In a 1999 essay for *Oral History,* Lorraine Stizia uses the methodology provided by Frisch in *A Shared Authority* and Gluck and Patai in *Women's Words* to reflect on responsible ways of telling the story of a male World War II soldier who was also a communist, a pacifist, and a writer.

Women's Words continues to be a key influence on the methodology of oral history. In a 2007 article in *Oral History Review,* Alistair Thomson calls the essays included in *Women's Words* "core texts for feminist oral history." Jerrold Hirsch has pointed to Gluck and Patai's anthology as one of the texts that has helped to determine questions of validity in the field of history. Tracy E. K'Meyer and A. Glenn Crothers published an article in which they allayed some of Patai's fears of disempowering the interviewee, stating that quite often narrators see the interview process as an opportunity to give back to the community, thus sharing common ground with the researcher.

BIBLIOGRAPHY

Sources

Armitage, Susan, George Lipsitz, and Gary R. Mormino. "*Women's Words:* A Review Symposium." *Oral History Review* 20.1–2 (1992). 105–11. *JSTOR.* Web. 31 Jan. 2013.

Chamberlain, Mary. Rev. of *Women's Words: The Feminist Practice of Oral History,* ed. Sherna Berger Gluck and Daphne Patai. *Oral History Review.* Oxford University Press, Spring–Fall 1992. Web. 31 Jan. 2013.

Cole, Lori. Rev. of *Women's Words: The Feminist Practice of Oral History,* ed. Sherna Berger Gluck and Daphne Patai. *Pennsylvania History.* Penn State, October 1993. Web. 31 Jan. 2013.

Gluck, Sherna Berger, and Daphne Patai, eds. *Women's Words: The Feminist Practice of Oral History.* New York: Routledge, 1991. Print.

Stizia, Lorraine. "Telling Arthur's Story: Oral History Relationships and Shared Authority." *Oral History* 27.2 (1999): 58–67. Print.

Thomson, Alistair. "Four Paradigm Transformations in Oral History." *Oral History Review.* Oxford University Press, Winter–Spring 2007. Web. 31 Jan. 2013.

Further Reading

Frisch, Michael. *A Shared Authority: Essays on the Craft and Meaning of Oral and Public History.* Albany: State University of New York Press, 1990. Print.

K'Meyer, Tracy E., and A. Glenn Crothers. "'If I See Some of This in Writing, I'm Going to Shoot You': Reluctant Narrators, Taboo Topics, and the Ethical Dilemmas of the Oral Historian." *Oral History Review* 34.1 (2007): 71–93. Print.

Maksel, Rebecca. Rev. of *Women's Words: The Feminist Practice of Oral History,* ed. Sherna Berger Gluck and Daphne Patai. *Journal of American Folklore* 107.424 (1994): 332–35. Print.

Oakley, Ann. "Interviewing Women: A Contradiction in Terms." *Doing Feminist Research.* Ed. Helen Roberts. London: Routledge and Kegan Paul, 1981. 30–62. Print.

Perks, Robert, and Alistair Thomson, eds. *The Oral History Reader.* New York: Routledge, 1998. Print.

Spitzack, Carole J. "Body Talk: The Politics of Weight Loss and Female Identity." *Women Communicating: Studies of Women's Talk.* Ed. Barbara Bate and Anita Taylor. Norwood, N. J.: Ablex, 1988. 51–74. Print.

Sugiman, Pamela. "'These Feelings That Fill My Heart': Japanese Canadian Women's Memories of Internment." *Oral History* 34.2 (2006): 69–84. Print.

Ioana Pateleanu

War Experiences

And Justice for All: An Oral History of the Japanese American Detention Camps by John Tateishi	195
Bloods: An Oral History of the Vietnam War by Black Veterans by Wallace Terry	199
Carrier Warfare in the Pacific: An Oral History Collection by E. T. Wooldridge	202
El Salvador at War: An Oral History of Conflict from the 1979 Insurrection to the Present by Max G. Manwaring and Court Prisk	205
Everything We Had: An Oral History of the Vietnam War by Al Santoli	209
"The Good War": An Oral History of World War II by Louis "Studs" Terkel	212
Japan at War: An Oral History by Haruko Taya Cook and Theodore F. Cook	215
Memoirs of Fatemeh Pakravan by Habib Ladjevardi	218
The Strength Not to Fight: An Oral History of Conscientious Objectors of the Vietnam War by James W. Tollefson	221
The Unknown Internment: An Oral History of the Relocation of Italian Americans during World War II by Stephen Fox	224
"We Have Just Begun to Not Fight": An Oral History of Conscientious Objectors in Civilian Public Service during World War II by Heather T. Frazer and John O'Sullivan	227
What Was Asked of Us: An Oral History of the Iraq War by the Soldiers Who Fought It by Trish Wood	231
The World at War by Richard Holmes	234

And Justice for All
An Oral History of the Japanese American Detention Camps
John Tateishi

OVERVIEW

Compiled by John Tateishi and published in 1984, *And Justice for All: An Oral History of the Japanese American Detention Camps* presents the personal recollections of thirty Japanese Americans who were part of the forced relocation and incarceration of 120,000 Japanese American civilians during World War II. The book's interviewees vary widely in background and outlook, and their narratives touch on many different aspects of the internment experience, including camp conditions, wildly unreasonable governmental decrees, political disputes and conflicts among internees, camp riots, the widespread anti-Japanese sentiment in the wake of the attack on Pearl Harbor, the combat experiences of internees who served in the U.S. Army, and the legal travails of those who disobeyed orders to evacuate. As a whole, the interviews gathered in *And Justice for All* reflect the profound sense of injustice Japanese Americans feel about their treatment by the U.S. government, as well as the enduring impact the internment had on the shape of their lives.

Published during a time of widespread activism within the Japanese American community for the recognition and redress of the personal and financial hardships inflicted on interned civilians during World War II, *And Justice for All* was hailed by critics as an eye-opening testament to the experiences that prompted the current protests. It remains noteworthy as both a document of a seismic event in U.S. history and a sobering reminder of the extent to which racial prejudice has been institutionally sanctioned under the guise of national security, a fact that has grown newly relevant in light of the anti-Arab and anti-Muslim prejudice that proliferated in the wake of the attacks on September 11, 2001.

HISTORICAL AND LITERARY CONTEXT

The narratives collected in *And Justice for All* reflect the increasing sense of public animosity toward Japanese Americans in the decades leading up to the United States' entry into World War II. A growing unease—rooted partly in racial prejudice—at the burgeoning social and economic eminence of Japanese immigrants during the early twentieth century eventually resulted in the passage of the California Alien Land Law of 1913, preventing Japanese Americans (and other immigrants deemed ineligible for citizenship) from owning land in California. This was followed by the Immigration Act of 1924, which prohibited any further immigration from Japan (among many other countries). Meanwhile, the increasing discord between the United States and Japan on a national level led to widespread suspicions—fueled by racist media portrayals—that Japanese Americans were secretly planning or committing anti-American treachery.

The Japanese assault on Pearl Harbor on December 7, 1941, resulted in widespread distrust of Japanese Americans. Almost immediately after the attack, hundreds of Japanese American community leaders who had been previously identified by the Federal Bureau of Investigation as possible threats to national security were rounded up and detained. Then, on February 19, 1942, President Franklin Delano Roosevelt signed Executive Order 9066, which resulted in the forced relocation of approximately 120,000 Japanese American civilians—including the entire ethnic Japanese population residing on the West Coast—to ten isolated concentration camps located primarily in the western United States. The closing of the camps was not announced until December 17, 1944, with the final camp not shutting its doors until 1946.

And Justice for All emerged from a rich tradition of oral history, as well as from a much more sporadic sub-tradition focusing specifically on the Japanese American internment. Research for the book began during the internment period itself, with interviews conducted by social scientists for research purposes. Further oral history in this vein include the work done under the aegis of the Japanese American Oral History Project at California State University–Fullerton, which resulted in a number of published volumes, starting in 1974 with Arthur A. Hansen and Betty E. Mitson's *Voices Long Silent: An Oral Inquiry into the Japanese American Evacuation*. Prior to the 1980s, however, oral history of the internment was still relatively scarce, making *And Justice for All* a significant watershed within the field.

In the wake of the ongoing public debates over governmental redress during the 1980s, Tateishi's book helped launch a substantial increase in the

❖ *Key Facts*

Time Period:
Mid- to Late 20th Century

Relevant Historical Events:
Internment of Japanese Americans; World War II; Pearl Harbor

Nationality:
American

Keywords:
internment; war; racism

WAR EXPERIENCES

Photograph of a Japanese American internment camp at Tule Lake, California, in 1944. © CARL MYDANS/ TIME & LIFE PICTURES/ GETTY IMAGES

quantity of literature addressing the Japanese American internment, both within and outside of the oral history genre. Many additional historical volumes, either devoted specifically to oral history—as with Roger W. Axford's *Too Long Been Silent: Japanese-Americans Speak Out* (1986)—or making heavy use of it, appeared throughout the next several decades. *And Justice for All* remains a widely cited text in histories and studies of the internment period.

THEMES AND STYLE

A central theme of *And Justice for All* is the sense of profound betrayal experienced by Japanese Americans as a result of their mistreatment. Many internees identify the evacuation as a contravention of the nation's ideals, as when Paul Shinoda observes, "I didn't think they'd do it, because I thought American fair play was there, the Constitution too. And we had the right to the pursuit of happiness. Going to camp and being evacuated didn't fit that." This sense of betrayal is likewise reflected in the interviewees' discussions of the so-called loyalty questionnaire, which asked camp residents whether they would be willing disavow allegiance to Japan and serve in the U.S. armed forces. The issue of how to answer these questions was deeply controversial among the internees, hence Ben Takeshita's recollection that "when the no-no yes-yes questionnaire came out my oldest brother, who was about nineteen, thought it was absurd for people to answer those questions yes-yes and volunteer for the U.S. Army when our citizenship meant nothing."

As Tateishi—himself a former camp resident—indicates in the book's preface, *And Justice for All* is an attempt "to present for the first time in human and personal terms the experience of the only group of American citizens ever to be confined in concentration camps in the United States." The book's narratives are transcribed from recorded interviews conducted in the early 1980s, though Tateishi's editorial principles are somewhat unclear: the extent to which he condensed or rearranged his material is never specified, a fact that has been lamented by some critics. (The interview transcripts themselves were archived in the JACL Redress Collection at the Japanese American National Library in 2006, finally making it possible for researchers to compare the original interviews to the published versions.)

The language used throughout the book varies widely in tone and fluency depending on the speaker, a fact that reflects the diversity of viewpoints encompassed by the text. Some of the interviewees exhibit a thorough command of the English language, while others are obviously nonnative speakers, a distinction whose conspicuousness suggests that Tateishi generally attempted to preserve the original language of the transcripts. While the internees' feelings on their incarceration unsurprisingly tend to be similarly negative, the emotional tenor of their reactions varies considerably, with some, such as Helen Murao, conscientiously attempting to avoid bitterness: "So, you know, we never forget, but I'm all through being upset and angry. That's not productive, you know." Others, such as Mary Tsukamoto, emphasize the importance of not allowing the event to be forgotten:

> I know many Niseis [second-generation Japanese Americans] who say, That was all so long ago. Let's forget it and leave well enough alone. But I just say, we were the ones that went through it—the tears and the shame and the shock. We need to leave our legacy to our children. And also our legacy to America, from our tears, what we learned.

CRITICAL DISCUSSION

And Justice for All was generally well received upon its publication in 1984, with many reviewers noting its timeliness in relation to the redress movement as well as its unique historical value. Gary Y. Okihiro, writing for the *Oral History Review* in 1985, criticized the book's editorial ambiguity: "The conditions of the interview, the interviewer's questions, and even the rules followed in the transcriptions are not supplied in the book." Okihiro also objected to the work's overly general approach: "More serious shortcomings are the general tenor of the book and the absence of a systematic and directed inquiry." He nonetheless went on to affirm that "the book provides an ample feast for lay persons and scholars, and its appearance was timely for both the redress and reparations movement of the last three years." Other reviewers expressed similar sentiments.

Tateishi's book represented a significant contribution to the public redress debates of the 1980s. Philip Tajitsu Nash, reviewing the book for the *Yale Law Journal*, observed that "it is in the context of this redress movement that *And Justice for All* makes its most tangible contribution," going on to assert that "a presentation of the personal losses suffered improves the case for individualized compensation." After the passage of the Civil Liberties Act in 1988, the book's eminence faded somewhat, staying out of print for years before being reissued in 1999. However, the work remains a seminal and respected work within Japanese American studies and is still a widely cited scholarly resource on the internment experience.

Scholarly writing that addresses *And Justice for All* often incorporates it into larger discussions of the literary or historical tradition to which the book belongs. An example is Arthur A. Hansen's 1995 article in the *Journal of American History*, which uses Tateishi's book to illustrate the observation that "the CWRIC [redress] hearings had served Japanese Americans as a community catharsis became evident in the quickened oral history activity on the JAE [Japanese American Evacuation] that followed." However, the book is most

JOHN TATEISHI AND THE JAPANESE AMERICAN INTERNMENT

Although John Tateishi does not contribute a personal narrative of his own to *And Justice for All,* he was evacuated with the rest of his family to the Manzanar internment camp in California in 1942, when he was only three years old. (His mother, Yuri Tateishi, is among the book's interviewees, and she discusses, among other things, her husband's arrest and removal to an isolation center in the aftermath of a riot in the camp.) As an adult, Tateishi became a key member of the Japanese American Citizens League (JACL), serving as chairman of the National Redress Committee from 1978 to 1986.

After the signing of the Civil Liberties Act of 1988, which acknowledged the injustice of the internment and paid monetary reparations to former evacuees, Tateishi remained an important figure within Japanese American advocacy, eventually becoming national executive director of the JACL in 1999. In this capacity, he was among the most prominent critics of the encroachment of racial profiling policies directed at Arab and Muslim Americans in the wake of 9/11, believing that such policies, like those directed at Japanese Americans during World War II, both violated individual freedoms and undermined the constitutional integrity of the United States as a whole.

often used by scholars simply as a source of historical information, as in Russell Bearden's 1989 *Arkansas Historical Quarterly* article, which quotes at length from Tsukamoto's recollections of internees chopping, sawing, and hoarding wood in order to give a more tangible impression of the fact that at the Arkansas camps "the sole method of heating all buildings during the winters was by wood stoves."

BIBLIOGRAPHY

Sources

Bearden, Russell. "Life inside Arkansas's Japanese-American Relocation Centers." *Arkansas Historical Quarterly* 48.2 (1989): 169–96. *JSTOR.* Web. 2 Jan. 2013.

Hansen, Arthur A. "Oral History and the Japanese American Evacuation." *Journal of American History* 82.2 (1995): 625–39. *JSTOR.* Web. 2 Jan. 2013.

Nash, Philip Tajitsu. "Moving for Redress." Rev. of *And Justice for All: An Oral History of the Japanese American Detention Camps,* by John Tateishi. *Yale Law Journal* 94.3 (1985): 743–55. *JSTOR.* 2 Jan. 2013.

Okihiro, Gary Y. "Justice and Japanese Americans." Rev. of *Justice at War,* by Peter Irons, and *And Justice for All: An Oral History of the Japanese American Detention Camps,* by John Tateishi. *Oral History Review* 13 (1985): 137–44. *JSTOR.* Web. 2 Jan. 2013.

Tateishi, John. *And Justice for All: An Oral History of the Japanese American Detention Camps.* 1984. Seattle: University of Washington Press, 1999. Print.

Further Reading

Axford, Roger W. *Too Long Been Silent: Japanese-Americans Speak Out.* Lincoln, Neb.: Media Publishing & Marketing, 1986. Print.

Daniels, Roger. *Prisoners without Trial: Japanese Americans in World War II.* Rev. ed. New York: Hill and Wang, 2004. Print.

Daniels, Roger, Sandra C. Taylor, and Harry H. L. Kitano, eds. *Japanese Americans: From Relocation to Redress.* Rev. ed. Seattle: University of Washington Press, 1991. Print.

Fugita, Stephen S., and Marilyn Fernandez. *Altered Lives, Enduring Community: Japanese Americans Remember Their World War II Incarceration.* Seattle: University of Washington Press, 2004. Print.

Hansen, Arthur A., ed. *Japanese American World War II Evacuation Oral History Project.* 6 vols. Munich: K. G. Saur, 1991–94. Print.

Harth, Erica, ed. *Last Witnesses: Reflections on the Wartime Internment of Japanese Americans.* New York: Palgrave, 2001. Print.

Hausegger, Margret K. "Breaking the Silence: Third Generation Japanese American Poetry." MA thesis. Graz University, 2008. Print.

Inada, Lawson Fusao, ed. *Only What We Could Carry: The Japanese American Internment Experience.* Berkeley, Calif.: Heyday, 2000. Print.

Moertl, Susanne. "Japanese-American Literature from the Internment Camps of World War II." MA thesis. Graz University, 1998. Print.

Muller, Eric L. *American Inquisition: The Hunt for Japanese American Disloyalty in World War II.* Chapel Hill: University of North Carolina Press, 2007. Print.

Robinson, Greg. "What I Did in Camp: Interpreting Japanese American Internment Narratives of Isamu Noguchi, Miné Okubo, Jeanne Wakatsuki Houston, and John Tateishi." *Amerasia Journal* 30.2 (2004): 49–58. Print.

Shimabukuro, Robert Sadamu. *Born in Seattle: The Campaign for Japanese American Redress.* Seattle: University of Washington Press, 2001. Print.

James Overholtzer

BLOODS
An Oral History of the Vietnam War by Black Veterans
Wallace Terry

OVERVIEW
Collected and edited by journalist Wallace Terry, *Bloods: An Oral History of the Vietnam War by Black Veterans* (1984) presents the firsthand experiences of combat, racism, and the homecoming of twenty African American soldiers who served in the Vietnam War. The soldiers' narratives represent a cross section of black servicemen's experiences in Vietnam in all four branches of the armed forces, from enlisted men to officers and from those of rural and urban backgrounds. The term *bloods* originated in the black servicemen's community in Vietnam as a term of self-identification intended to foster solidarity in the face of ongoing racial discrimination within the U.S. military and as a reflection of the U.S. civil rights movement. In composing *Bloods,* Terry, a reporter for *Time* magazine, drew on his experience as one of the first black Vietnam war correspondents.

Published roughly ten years after the U.S. withdrawal from Vietnam and written in a dispassionate tone that was in contrast to the emotional, partisan prose of earlier chronicles of Vietnam, *Bloods* was heralded by critics for focusing on the overlooked experiences of black soldiers. The book established Terry's reputation as a preeminent journalist and was nominated for a Pulitzer Prize, although the validity of some accounts in the book and Terry's extensive editing were later called into question. The book continues to be a popular example of both the oral history genre and Vietnam War literature.

HISTORICAL AND LITERARY CONTEXT
During World War II, the U.S. military was racially segregated, with black soldiers serving in black units, usually under white officers—a structure that mirrored the segregationist nature of American society at the time. Motivated by the desire to increase efficiency and solidarity among armed forces members, President Harry Truman issued Executive Order 9981 in 1948, which called for the uniform desegregation of the military. However, Truman's order was not fulfilled until 1954, when increasing U.S. casualties in the Korean War necessitated the racial integration of military units.

Escalating U.S. involvement in the Vietnam War roughly coincided with the domestic civil rights movement, in which citizens of all races protested for the end of legal segregation and racial discrimination in the United States. Although the military was more integrated than many other segments of American society as a result of Truman's order, prejudicial attitudes remained; the result was de facto discrimination against black soldiers in the form of increased combat assignments, lack of promotions, and a perceived lack of concern for their welfare in comparison to their white comrades. The racial tension between black and white troops was further exacerbated by the disproportionate numbers of black men who were drafted for military service, the southern white backlash against the civil rights movement, black soldiers' identification with the Vietnamese people as another oppressed ethnicity, the lack of support from social institutions upon returning home, and the increasing perception of the war as unwinnable.

Bloods falls into the American literary tradition of oral histories. Notable examples include Studs Terkel's *Hard Times: An Oral History of the Great Depression* (1970) and *"The Good War" An Oral History of World War II* (1984), a Pulitzer Prize–winning collection of narratives about World War II; both featured the stories of everyday Americans told in their own words. Oral histories of the Vietnam War that predate Terry's book include Al Santoli's *Everything We Had: An Oral History of the Vietnam War* (1981); Mark Baker's *Nam: The Vietnam War in the Words of the Men and Women Who Fought There* (1981); and *Brothers: Black Soldiers in the Nam* (1982) by Stanley Goff, Robert Sanders, and Clark Smith. The latter, while also focusing on black soldiers' experiences in the war, offers less commentary on race relations than Terry's book and instead concentrates on racial unity in combat.

Bloods has influenced views of race relations in the military and remains a frequently assigned book in U.S. college courses about the Vietnam War. The book's popularity led Terry to write and edit a 1985 PBS *Frontline* documentary called *The Bloods of 'Nam* and to create a one-man show, *Bloods: An Evening with Wallace Terry,* in the mid-1980s. After Vietnam, Terry taught at Howard University; he later published *Missing Pages: Black Journalists of Modern America: An Oral History* (2007), which focuses on the experience of pioneering black American journalists such as Ethel

Key Facts

Time Period:
Mid- to Late 20th Century

Relevant Historical Events:
Vietnam War; civil rights movement

Nationality:
American

Keywords:
war; civil rights; racism

WAR EXPERIENCES

Frederick Hart's *The Three Soldiers* (1984), a sculpture that is part of the Vietnam Veterans Memorial in Washington, D.C. African Americans' military experiences in Vietnam are described in *Bloods: An Oral History of the Vietnam War by Black Veterans*, by Wallace Terry. © ALBUM/ART RESOURCE, NY

Payne of the *Chicago Defender*, Tom Johnson of the *New York Times*, and Ed Bradley of CBS.

THEMES AND STYLE

The central themes of *Bloods* are the racial discrimination experienced by black men in the U.S. military, the atrocities of war, conflicting views of the Vietnamese people, and the difficulty of returning to American society after combat duty. Terry includes one soldier's comment that because black soldiers were doing "first class dying" they resented their "second hand treatment" by the military. He also records another soldier who claimed that blacks and whites "had the utmost respect for each other, because when a fire fight is going on, and everybody's facing north, you don't want to see nobody looking around south." Concerning black soldiers' views of the Vietnamese, one soldier explained that he could not "go over there and degrade another human being" after experiencing the civil rights movement in the United States, but another soldier recalled his fear of being labeled a "gook lover" for identifying with the Vietnamese. The book includes several accounts of war atrocities, including graphic descriptions of the torture of U.S. and North Vietnamese soldiers and the rape of Vietnamese women by American servicemen, with one soldier explaining, "It's nothing civilized about war." Speaking about the difficulties of returning home, another soldier noted that U.S. employers were reluctant to hire him upon learning he was a veteran and that he joined the Black Panthers, a black nationalist organization, "basically because it was a war-like group."

As he writes in the book's foreword, Terry was prompted to compile *Bloods* to "help complete the missing pages of the American experience." In the interest of better telling this story, he heavily edited each soldier's account by reordering his transcribed interviews to produce coherent narratives; he was later criticized for not disclosing this fact at the time of the book's publication. The issue of editing transcribed interviews for better presentation is a long-running conflict within the oral history genre, of which Terry's *Bloods* is as much the rule as the exception.

The language of *Bloods* is notable for Terry's extensive use of dialect to represent the speech of his interview subjects. One example comes from his interview with Arthur E. "Gene" Woodley Jr. A former special forces combat paratrooper, Woodley speaks about his conflicted feelings upon encountering a Vietnamese grocery store owner in his native Baltimore after the war, saying, "I'm not angry 'cause he Vietn'ese. I don't have anything against the Vietn'ese. Nothin'. Not a damn thing. I'm angry with America." The dialectal spelling allows Terry to achieve a naturalistic effect that reflects the text's origin as an interview. This reflection contributes to the text's authenticity, even though the interview itself was heavily edited.

CRITICAL DISCUSSION

Initial critical reception to *Bloods* was highly complimentary, although many reviewers also noted its disturbing content. In his review in *Afro-Americans in New York Life and History*, Joseph Reidy calls the book "doubtlessly one of the most disturbing books yet to appear on Vietnam" and praises how Terry had "masterfully edited the narratives, giving them form while keeping himself invisible." Writing for the *New York Times,* Michiko Kakutani calls *Bloods* "a powerful and disturbing book" in which "Terry's determination to provide a perfectly balanced spectrum of viewpoints seems strained." *Time* magazine listed *Bloods* as one of the five best books of 1984, and the *New York Times* named it a notable book of the year.

Although *Bloods* remained one of the most frequently cited oral histories concerning the Vietnam War well into the 1990s, controversy over the stories' validity has overshadowed the book's earlier reputation. B. G. Burkett and Glenna Whitley's 1998 book, *Stolen Valor: How the Vietnam Generation Was Robbed of Its Heroes and Its History,* notes falsehoods and inventions in Harold "Light Bulb" Bryant's story as well as in the stories of some of the other veterans. Patrick Hagopian, in the *Journal of American History,* also questions the validity of Bryant's story of pulling another soldier off a mine with a rope. The book was banned from some Florida public schools in 1987 for its "harsh language" and because it was deemed a "moral danger to students." Hagopian notes that *Bloods* was not the only oral history of the Vietnam War to suffer from what he calls "wannabe" falsehoods perpetuated by the interview subjects, pointing to Santoli's *Everything We Had* as another example.

More recent scholarship has focused on the book's portrayal of racial minorities in the military. In her 2008 article for *Arizona Quarterly,* Jen Dunnaway notes how one soldier's account "describes the way basic training emphasized racialized characteristics in its war games, even designating as enemy certain ethnic Americans." She pointed to PFC Reginald "Malik" Edwards's comment: "if there were any Hawaiians and Asian Americans in the unit, they played the role of aggressors." Regarding the relative validity of each soldier's story, Hagopian argues that "the measure of such stories' interest may not be whether they are factually correct but whether they convey a moral or psychological truth important enough for the narrator to wish to share it." With this in mind, he points to the difference between what author and Vietnam veteran Tim O'Brien calls the difference between "story-truth" and "happening truth."

BIBLIOGRAPHY

Sources

Benedetto, Wendy, and Barbara Reynolds. "Military Worked Race-Relations 'Miracle.'" *USA Today* 18 Feb. 1991: 9A. *LexisNexis Academic.* Web. 12 Dec. 2012.

Burkett, B. G., and Glenna Whitley. *Stolen Valor: How the Vietnam Generation Was Robbed of Its Heroes and Its History.* Dallas: Verity, 1998. Print.

Dunnaway, Jen. "'One More Redskin Bites the Dirt': Racial Melancholy in Vietnam War Representation." *Arizona Quarterly* 64.1 (2008): 109–29. *Project MUSE.* Web. 12 Dec. 2012.

Hagopian, Patrick. "Voices from Vietnam: Veterans' Oral Histories in the Classroom." *Journal of American History* 87.2 (2000): 596–601. *JSTOR.* Web. 12 Dec. 2012.

Kakutani, Michiko. Rev. of *Bloods: An Oral History of the Vietnam War by Black Veterans,* by Wallace Terry. *New York Times* 27 Aug. 1984: C14. *ProQuest.* Web. 11 Dec. 2012.

Reidy, Joseph P. Rev. of *Bloods: An Oral History of the Vietnam War by Black Veterans,* by Wallace Terry. *Afro-Americans in New York Life and History (1977–1989)* 10.1 (1986): 76. *ProQuest.* Web. 11 Dec. 2012.

Terry, Wallace, ed. *Bloods: An Oral History of the Vietnam War by Black Veterans.* New York: Random House, 1984. Print.

Further Reading

Baker, Mark. *Nam: The Vietnam War in the Words of the Men and Women Who Fought There.* New York: Morrow, 1981. Print.

Budra, Paul Vincent, and Michael Zeitlin. *Soldier Talk: The Vietnam War in Oral Narrative.* Bloomington: Indiana University Press, 2004. Print.

George, Jerry E. M. "Black Amerasians: Forgotten Casualties of Vietnam." *Everybody's* 19.2 (1995): 43. *ProQuest.* Web. 12 Dec. 2012.

Goff, Stanley, Robert Sanders, and Clark Smith. *Brothers: Black Soldiers in the Nam.* Novato, Calif.: Presidio, 1982. Print.

O'Brien, Tim. *The Things They Carried.* New York: Broadway, 1990. Print.

Terkel, Studs. *"The Good War": An Oral History of World War II.* New York: New Press, 1984. Print.

Westheider, James E. *The Vietnam War.* Westport, Conn.: Greenwood Press, 2007. Print.

Craig Barnes

Carrier Warfare in the Pacific
An Oral History Collection
E. T. Wooldridge

✣ **Key Facts**

Time Period:
Mid-20th Century

Relevant Historical Events:
World War II; Pearl Harbor; increasing use of aircraft carriers

Nationality:
American

Keywords:
naval aviation; war; technology

OVERVIEW

A former member of the navy, Captain E. T. Wooldridge compiled *Carrier Warfare in the Pacific: An Oral History Collection* (1993) as part of his ongoing work in the field of U.S. naval aviation. Comprising over three hundred pages, *Carrier Warfare in the Pacific* contains more than thirty oral histories from those involved with naval aviation during World War II. Told from the perspective of pilots, captains, crew members, and others, the collected stories present a portrait of the drama, technology, and tragedies of naval aviation from those who witnessed them firsthand.

Published almost half a century after the conclusion of World War II, *Carrier Warfare in the Pacific* provides insight into a crucial aspect of Pacific War. As one of several books Wooldridge wrote for Smithsonian Books, it helped to cement the author's reputation as a naval historian. Six years after the original publication in 1993, Smithsonian Books issued a reprint of *Carrier Warfare in the Pacific*, reflecting the book's continued value as a record of the contributions of those who participated in U.S. naval aviation during World War II.

HISTORICAL AND LITERARY CONTEXT

On December 7, 1941, six Japanese aircraft carriers launched a military strike on the U.S. fleet stationed in Pearl Harbor, Hawaii. Japanese losses were light, while the United States lost more than one thousand men and women and sustained serious damage to its equipment. The next day the United States officially declared war on Japan. The oral histories in *Carrier Warfare in the Pacific* detail the ins and outs, the ups and downs, and the tragedies and triumphs of naval aviation's specific role within World War II.

In the book's introduction, Wooldridge explains that "in World War II, the aircrews flew into battle from the decks of ships that would not be in the same location—or possibly even afloat—when they returned hours later at the end of their mission." New technologies such as radar improved the effectiveness of naval aviation and increased its importance to the war. John B. Connally explains in the book's foreword that "had it not been for the atom bombs that were dropped on Nagasaki and Hiroshima and ended the war, the great story of World War II would have been the development of the radar." *Carrier Warfare in the Pacific* provides details for what it was like to be present for these technological advancements in naval aviation.

Carrier Warfare in the Pacific is part of the literary tradition of American oral histories about warfare. A number of oral histories of World War II predate Wooldridge's book, including Studs Terkel's *The "Good War": An Oral History of World War II* (1984), Archie Satterfield's *The Home Front: An Oral History of the War Years in America, 1941–1945* (1981), and *Remembering Pearl Harbor: Eyewitness Accounts by U.S. Military Men and Women* by Robert S. La Forte and Ronald E. Marcello (1991). Like Wooldridge's book, these titles seek to tell the story of World War II through the eyes of the men and women who were there.

Since the publication of *Carrier Warfare in the Pacific*, Wooldridge has continued his contributions to the study of U.S. naval aviation. A graduate of the U.S. Naval Academy, U.S. Navy Test Pilot School, and the National War College, he was once the commander of a carrier fighter squadron and served in the U.S. Navy until 1976. He went on to work at the National Air and Space Museum, where he has served as both the Admiral DeWitt C. Ramsey Fellow and the assistant director for museum operations.

THEMES AND STYLE

The main themes of *Carrier Warfare in the Pacific* involve the bravery, sacrifices, challenges, and triumphs of those involved with naval aviation during World War II. As one former naval aviator reflects, "A good fighter pilot has got to have a competitive spirit. He's got to want to do it more than anything else in the world." The oral histories often demonstrate a general sense of pride, with one soldier noting, "The pilots did their utmost, and there was nothing that I knew of that didn't reflect the greatest credit under the most difficult circumstances on the part of all hands." Another remembers a particular moment during the war with sobering honesty: "It was my first experience of real fear—being in the face of what you thought might be death at any moment, and I was interested in seeing how other people took it."

As the Admiral DeWitt C. Ramsey Fellow at the National Air and Space Museum, Woodridge was required to research and write about the field of U.S. naval aviation. He turned to the U.S. Naval Institute's Oral History Collection, where he selected interviews and edited them from their question-and-answer formats into the narratives that appear in *Carrier Warfare in the Pacific*. Though Wooldridge did not conduct the original interviews himself, it is perhaps his own navy experiences during the Vietnam War that allowed him to edit raw interviews into insightful narratives. When reflecting on them, he writes that the narratives "make history come alive, and give these valiant men their rightful place in the gallery of history." In his introduction, Wooldridge notes the fifty-year time gap between many of the recollected events and the interviews, explaining that, although he corrected misremembered historical facts and figures whenever possible, it is likely that the oral histories are colored by the passage of time and contain slight inaccuracies and incidents of misremembering.

Despite the high stakes of many of the events they depict, most of the oral histories in *Carrier Warfare in the Pacific* are relayed in calm, composed tones. In the book's foreword, Connally notes that "a reader will find examples of tragedy, of sorrow, disaster, and death—all told in a rather restrained, unemotional way." This frank, controlled language pervades the edited narratives and conjures up images of stoicism and bravery. Even when recounting a tense and dangerous battle, one soldier relates his experience in straightforward language that refrains from being overly dramatic: "I was scared. I couldn't believe this was happening to me."

CRITICAL DISCUSSION

The initial critical reactions to *Carrier Warfare in the Pacific* were mixed. In a 1993 review, *Publishers Weekly* described the book as "a story of guts, sacrifice, terror and exhilaration to be savored by anyone interested in the carrier as the ultimate war machine." On the other hand, in his 1995 review for *Naval Aviation News*, Peter Mersky finds *Carrier Warfare in the Pacific* "rather bland and only mildly interesting—certainly not as revealing as it could be." He goes on to acknowledge that "there are some interesting accounts and variations of well-known actions" but concludes that "the book disappoints, given the large, well-endowed collection of interviews and photos which the editor and book designers had at their disposal."

In the years following its publication, *Carrier Warfare in the Pacific* has not received critical attention. Instead, it most often appears in secondary sources as an entry in bibliographies or list of sources related to World War II, oral histories, or naval aviation. Using his long-standing expertise in the field, Wooldridge has gone on to publish other books about naval aviation, including *Night Fighters over Korea* (with G. G. O'Rourke, 1998), *The Golden Age Remembered: U.S. Naval Aviation, 1919–1941* (1998), and *Into the Jet Age: Conflict and Change in Naval Aviation, 1945–1975: An Oral History* (1996). Like *Carrier Warfare in the Pacific,* these titles serve as important historical records but have not received extensive critical attention.

In a *Booklist* review of *Into the Jet Age: Conflict and Change in Naval Aviation, 1945–1975: An Oral History,* Roland Green recognizes Wooldridge's editorial and writing skills: "Besides editing the testimonies, Wooldridge, a former naval aviator himself, contributes ably written background about the politics, economics, strategic considerations, and technology involved in each major change in naval jet aircraft." It is with the same editorial skills and knowledge of his subject that Wooldridge collected and edited *Carrier Warfare in the Pacific.*

BIBLIOGRAPHY

Sources

Connally, John B. Foreword. *Carrier Warfare in the Pacific: An Oral History Collection.* Ed. E. T. Wooldridge. Washington, D.C.: Smithsonian, 1993. Print.

Green, Roland. Rev. of *Into the Jet Age: Conflict and Change in Naval Aviation, 1945–1975: An Oral History,* ed. E. T. Wooldridge. *Booklist* 15 May 1995: 1616. *Literature Resource Center.* Web. 22 Jan. 2013.

Mersky, Peter. Rev. of *Carrier Warfare in the Pacific: An Oral History Collection,* ed. E. T. Wooldridge. *Naval Aviation News* 76.5 (1994): 40. *MasterFILE Premier.* Web. 22 Jan. 2013.

Rev. of *Carrier Warfare in the Pacific: An Oral History Collection,* ed. E. T. Wooldridge. *Publishers Weekly* 27 Sep. 1993: 54. *Literature Resource Center.* Web. 22 Jan. 2013.

The American cruiser USS *Santa Fe* (CL-60) comes to the aid of the burning aircraft carrier USS *Franklin* (CV-13), which was hit by two Japanese bombs on March 18, 1945. An estimated seven hundred to eight hundred sailors were killed and hundreds more injured in the explosions, but the remaining crew of the *Franklin* managed to save the ship and return to Hawaii for repairs. © US NAVY/TIME & LIFE PICTURES/GETTY IMAGES

CAPTAIN E. T. WOOLDRIDGE'S U.S. NAVAL CAREER

Although *Carrier Warfare in the Pacific* chronicles the stories of other men's service in the field of naval aviation, its author, E. T. Wooldridge, is a former naval aviator himself. During his time in the military, Wooldridge was the commander of a carrier fighter squadron and was involved with the creation of strategic plans and policy for staff overseas during the Vietnam War. In 1976 he retired from the U.S. Navy and went to work at the National Air and Space Museum, a position from which he penned many of his books about naval aviation.

In 1990 Wooldridge was awarded the Ramsey Fellowship in Naval Aviation History. He held the appointment until 1994, when he went on to serve as assistant director for museum operations. In 1998 his research and work in the field of naval aviation led him to be selected U.S. Naval Institute Author of the Year. Like his awards and positions, *Carrier Warfare in the Pacific* is a reflection of Wooldridge's sustained interest in and commitment to the field of naval aviation.

Wooldridge, E. T., ed. *Carrier Warfare in the Pacific: An Oral History Collection.* Washington, D.C.: Smithsonian, 1993. Print.

Further Reading

Chamberlain, Mary, and Paul Thompson, eds. *Narrative and Genre.* New York: Routledge, 1998. Print.

Erickson, Stacy, and Troy Reeves. *A Field Notebook for Oral History.* Boise: Idaho Oral History Center, 2002.

Mason, John T., Jr., ed. *The Pacific War Remembered: An Oral History Collection.* Annapolis, Md.: Naval Institute, 2003.

O'Donnell, Patrick, ed. *Into the Rising Sun: In Their Own Words, World War II's Pacific Veterans Reveal the Heart of Combat.* New York: Free Press, 1992. Print.

O'Rourke, G. G., and E. T. Wooldridge. *Night Fighters over Korea.* Annapolis, Md.: Naval Institute, 1998. Print.

Petty, Bruce M., ed. *Saipan: Oral Histories of the Pacific War.* Jefferson, N.C.: McFarland, 2002. Print.

Spiller, Harry, ed. *Pearl Harbor Survivors: An Oral History of 24 Servicemen.* Jefferson, N.C.: McFarland, 2002. Print.

Stillwell, Paul, ed. *The Golden Thirteen: Recollections of the First Black Naval Officers.* Annapolis, Md.: Naval Institute, 1993. Print.

Wooldridge, E. T., ed. *Into the Jet Age: Conflict and Change in Naval Aviation, 1945–1975.* Annapolis, Md.: Naval Institute, 1996. Print.

———. *The Golden Age Remembered: U.S. Naval Aviation, 1919–1941.* Annapolis, Md.: Naval Institute, 1998. Print.

Jen Gann

EL SALVADOR AT WAR
An Oral History of Conflict from the 1979 Insurrection to the Present
Max G. Manwaring, Court Prisk

OVERVIEW

Edited by former U.S. military members Max G. Manwaring and Court Prisk, *El Salvador at War: An Oral History of Conflict from the 1979 Insurrection to the Present* (1988) presents interviews conducted during El Salvador's civil war in the 1980s along with contextualizing commentary and interpretive observations. The book includes interviews excerpted and arranged by the editors, who worked as analysts linked to the U.S. Southern Command, the driving military force behind decisions in Central and South America. The work—which includes interviews with Salvadoran guerrillas, officers in the military, officials, and civilians as well as U.S. military officers assigned to El Salvador—was designed to deliver an evaluation of the civil war and to present a course of action to defeat insurgency in El Salvador and beyond. While the book and its discussion of counterinsurgency measures remain influential in some circles, some academics struggle with what appears to be a bias on the part of the editors and with some problematic methodologies.

El Salvador at War was published by the National Defense University Press while the U.S. military was still heavily involved in providing military and financial aid to the acting government in El Salvador. After the book's initial publication, critics questioned the lack of disclosed motives of the editors and also disputed the historical accuracy of information provided by the interviewed subjects. The book remains a polemic yet popular source of personal testimony from some of whom the editors refer to as the "key participants" in the Salvadoran civil war.

HISTORICAL AND LITERARY CONTEXT

The insurgency in El Salvador formed in 1980 when several smaller groups united to become the Farabundo Marti National Liberation Front (FMLN), a political-military alliance of the country's opposition groups. The group converged after a decade of coups, assassinations, and government-funded "death squads" that killed primarily indigenous people. The FMLN led the struggle against the government's repressive military control and received some aid from Cuba and the Soviet Union. The civil war coincided with continuing U.S. Cold War tensions with the Soviet Union and other communist entities. The United States retained a policy of containment in regards to the spread of communism and—to ensure noncommunist governments retained control—offered military support to countries such as Guatemala and Nicaragua, which were facing insurgencies. The FMLN continued to struggle against the U.S.-supported National Republican Alliance (ARENA) until 1991, when the FMLN was recognized as a political party within the Salvadoran government, and they signed a peace accord sponsored by the United Nations.

From the perspective of the U.S. military, the country's interest in El Salvador boiled down to what U.S. ambassador to El Salvador Edwin G. Corr describes in the book's preface as the struggle between "Salvadoran democrats and the Cuban-Nicaraguan supported Marxist-Leninist guerrillas." The majority of the Salvadorans saw the war as a struggle between classes for governmental control and—ultimately—for basic human rights. Much of the text is devoted to political and military officials and their assessments of the political history and methodology of the ongoing war against the insurgency. General Fred F. Woerner of the U.S. Infantry Brigade offers one such reflection: "The major lesson to be learned is the viability of the U.S. strategy of assisting host countries to fight their own wars of counterinsurgency." Some opinions from the insurgency side are also provided, including that of the president of the Revolutionary Democratic Front (FDR), a group that—at the time of publication—was allied with the FMLN. FDR President Guillermo M. Ungo assesses that the problems in El Salvador forced insurgents "to fight back and risk death in resistance or to submit and risk death from hunger, poverty, or political repression."

El Salvador at War is one among many oral history texts exploring the conflict in El Salvador. Books approaching larger political and social effects of the war include *Places of Origin: The Repopulation of Rural El Salvador* (1991) by Beatrice Edwards and Gretta Tovar Siebentritt, which uses case studies on repopulation projects, and Riordan Roett and Frank Smyth's *Dialogue and Armed Conflict: Negotiating the Civil War in El Salvador* (1988), which explores the nebulous nature of the war's stalemated resolution. Other prominent examples of oral histories on the Salvadoran Civil War include Jenny Pearce's *Promised Land: Peasant*

+ Key Facts

Time Period:
Late 20th Century

Relevant Historical Events:
El Salvador's civil war; Cold War

Nationality:
El Salvadoran

Keywords:
war; colonialism; communism

WAR EXPERIENCES

A young female guerrilla fighter in the jungles of El Salvador instructs comrades in the use of an American-made automatic rifle during El Salvador's civil war in 1982. This war is the focus of *El Salvador at War*. © SEBASTIAN RICH/CORBIS

Rebellion in Chalatenango, El Salvador (1986), which consists of interviews in insurgent-controlled Chalatenango Province, and Joe Fish and Cristina Sganga's photography and interviews in war-torn El Salvador in *El Salvador: Testament of Terror* (1986).

El Salvador at War remains a significant source for parties interested in the mind-set of political and military officials involved in the deadly conflict in El Salvador. The collection of high-ranking, firsthand military and political perspectives provides the authors an opportunity to approach counterinsurgency strategy from a new angle. Both Manwaring and Prisk continue to write on the subject of insurgency and "low-impact conflicts." Manwaring published *Small Wars & Insurgencies* in 2011.

THEMES AND STYLE

One key theme of *El Salvador at War* is the government's struggles against the insurgents. Deane Hinton, the ambassador to El Salvador in 1982 and 1983, recalls that his mission, "given to me by the government, the Secretary, and to some extent directly from the President, was to make sure the guerrillas and communists didn't take over El Salvador." By the late 1980s—when the book was published—it had become obvious both sides needed to reexamine their positions. Former insurgent leader Miguel Castellanos explains that it became clear that total military victory was not feasible and instead insurgents should seek to "share in the power that allows them to remain in the rural zones with their armed forces." Colonel Lyman C. Duryea, a U.S. defense attaché from 1983 to 1985, suggests that it had become obvious that "additional infusions of training, material, and various other elements of security assistance [wouldn't] move us toward the ultimate goal of defeating the insurgency."

The editors of *El Salvador at War* produced the collection of interviews in response to a request from Corr for a contemporary history of the conflict and also one from Commander-in-Chief of the U.S. Southern Command General John Galvin to generate new strategies for dealing with insurgencies. Manwaring and Prisk arrange excerpts to develop a selective history aimed at refining U.S. and Salvadoran military strategy. In the final editorial notes, the editors expound on counterinsurgency possibilities: "The primary objective of the insurgents is to destroy [the government's] legitimacy—this is the heart of the concept of a 'Prolonged People's War.' The primary objective of the Salvadoran government must then be to protect, maintain, and enhance its legitimacy."

The structure of *El Salvador at War* is notable for its six titled parts with twenty-four titled chapters containing guiding editorial notes for the portions of thirty-three interviews. The backgrounds of the editors account for the systemized approach to oral history as well as to what some critics call a bias toward the Salvadoran government. The first chapter, "Prone to Violence," sets the book's tone, painting a picture of a consistently warring El Salvador, while the last section, "Thoughts for the Future," gives glimpses at different approaches to war.

CRITICAL DISCUSSION

The publication of *El Salvador at War* corresponded with ongoing conflict in El Salvador in addition to continuing Cold War tensions, and its initial reception was divided. Praise for the work stems from its use in understanding the major figures in the conflict. As Richard Salisbury writes in his 1990 piece for *Oral History Review*, "Leading figures on both sides of the struggle articulate what is at times more than just self-serving rhetoric." However, Salisbury also calls the book "a piece of advocacy literature as reflected both by the professional background of the editors and the thrust of the study itself." Many critics object to a guise of the book's impartiality. Thomas P. Anderson, in his 1990 *Journal of Conflict Studies* review, calls it "an unabashedly partisan work composed of interviews with United States military and diplomatic personnel and Salvadoran army officers" with "a sprinkling of commentaries" by oppositional figures.

While *El Salvador at War* continues to be a frequently cited oral history regarding the civil war, the critical observations concerning the book's bias linger. In their 1990 *Armed Forces & Society* review, Robert Perrucci and Gladys C. Rivas numerate problems with the book, citing issues such as "the editors' unspecified method for selecting key participants," the insurgent interviews having been taken "primarily in 1981 and 1982," while the "Salvadoran participants were conducted mostly in 1987 and partly in 1986," and "the fact that the so-called 'interviews' with the U.S. and Salvadoran generals, colonels, ambassadors, defense intellectuals, intelligence operatives, and presidents are completely out of context" and "without any indication of the questions." Viberto Selochan also questions the text's validity in a 1990 *Australian Journal of International Affairs* review, claiming interviews "are presented without any attempt to challenge or analyze the statements, many of which are grossly inaccurate."

More recent scholarship places the book in the context of the most recent insurgencies, especially the wars in Iraq and Afghanistan. David Pedersen recognizes the work in his 2003 article, "As Irrational as Bert and Bin Laden: The Production of Categories, Commodities, and Commensurability in the Era of Globalization," as a significant resource for the U.S. Southern Command. Pedersen claims the book—along with other reports—"effected General Galvin's call for a new paradigm of counterinsurgency."

BIBLIOGRAPHY

Sources

Anderson, Thomas P. Rev. of *El Salvador at War: An Oral History of Conflict from the 1979 Insurrection to the Present,* by Max Manwaring and Court Prisk. *Journal of Conflict Studies.* Gregg Center for the Study of War and Society, 10 June 1990. Web. 25 Jan. 2013.

Jaksic, Ivan. "Oral History in the Americas." *Journal of American History* 79.2 (1992): 590–600. Print.

Manwaring, Max G., and Court Prisk. *El Salvador at War: An Oral History of Conflict from the 1979 Insurrection to the Present.* Washington, D.C.: National Defense University Press, 1988. Print.

Pedersen, David. "As Irrational as Bert and Bin Laden: The Production of Categories, Commodities, and Commensurability in the Era of Globalization." *Public Culture.* Public Culture and Duke University Press, Spring 2003. Web. 23 Jan. 2013.

Perrucci, Robert, and Gladys C. Rivas. Rev. of *El Salvador at War: An Oral History of Conflict from the 1979 Insurrection to the Present,* by Max Manwaring and Court Prisk. *Armed Forces & Society* 16.3 (1990): 458–60. *Academic Search Complete.* Web. 26 Jan. 2013.

Salisbury, Richard. Rev. of *El Salvador at War: An Oral History of Conflict from the 1979 Insurrection to the Present,* by Max Manwaring and Court Prisk. *Oral History Review* 18 (1990): 168–170. Web. 24 Jan. 2013.

Selochan, Viberto. Rev. of *El Salvador at War: An Oral History of Conflict from the 1979 Insurrection to the Present,* by Max Manwaring and Court Prisk. *Australian Journal of International Affairs* 44.1 (1990): 99. *Taylor Francis Online.* Web. 24 Jan. 2013.

Further Reading

Fish, Joe, and Cristina Sganga. *El Salvador Testament of Terror.* New York: Olive Branch, 1988. Print.

Gettleman, Marvin, et al., eds. *El Salvador: Central America in the New Cold War.* New York: Grove, 1986. Print.

Lowenthal, Abraham F. Rev. of *El Salvador at War: An Oral History of Conflict from the 1979 Insurrection*

THE MANWARING PARADIGM

In 1991 Max G. Manwaring published a collection of essays titled *Uncomfortable Wars: Toward a New Paradigm of Low Intensity Conflict.* Manwaring, who had worked with politics in Central and South America since 1964, sought to create a theoretical framework for addressing "low-intensity" conflicts. The book's essays were collected from several authors (including former collaborator Court Prisk), although the bulk of the writing is from Manwaring himself.

Manwaring's work—known as Small Wars Operations Research Directorate (SWORD), or as the Manwaring Paradigm—presents a model for approaching "low-intensity conflicts"; that is, wars that are not considered "major wars." In creating the paradigm, Manwaring studied forty-three different insurgencies to arrive at seven leading principles or "dimensions" to consider when approaching a counterinsurgency conflict, including whether the major struggle is over governmental legitimacy and whether military force should not be applied ad hoc.

Manwaring's work placed emphasis on the political aspect of insurgency, touting the importance of sound policy over tactical success. In 2006 Manwaring and John T. Fishel released *Uncomfortable Wars Revisited,* an updated paradigm with consideration of global changes and refinements since publication of the original text.

to the Present, by Max Manwaring and Court Prisk. *Foreign Affairs* 68.3 (1989): 174. *Academic Search Complete.* Web. 26 Jan. 2013.

Manwaring, Max, and Court Prisk. "A Strategic View of Insurgencies: Insights from El Salvador." *Small Wars & Insurgencies* 4.1 (1993): 53–72. *Taylor Francis Online.* Web. 25 Jan. 2013.

Montgomery, Tommie Sue. *Revolution in El Salvador.* Boulder, Colo.: Westview, 1995. Print.

Pearce, Jenny. *Promised Land: Peasant Rebellion in Chalatenango, El Salvador.* London: Latin American Bureau, 1986. Print.

Roett, Riordan, and Frank Smyth. *Dialogue and Armed Conflict: Negotiating the Civil War in El Salvador.* Washington, D.C.: Johns Hopkins Foreign Policy Institute, 1988. Print.

Tony Ruzicka

EVERYTHING WE HAD
An Oral History of the Vietnam War
Al Santoli

OVERVIEW

Collected by Vietnam War veteran Al Santoli and published in 1981, the oral histories that make up *Everything We Had: An Oral History of the Vietnam War* offer diverse perspectives on U.S. involvement in a controversial war. Collected after the conflict, the accounts detail the wartime experiences of soldiers of varied ranks and branches of the military. The book is arranged roughly chronologically, with veterans recalling events from the arrival of U.S. combat troops in 1965 through the fall of Saigon a decade later. Taken collectively, the stories of ordinary people placed in extraordinary circumstances attempt, in the words of Santoli, to help readers "see what we saw, do what we did, feel what we felt."

Everything We Had appeared at a time when Americans were struggling to come to terms with the massive loss of life and social upheaval left in the war's wake. Published by a major publisher (Random House) and aimed at a general audience, Santoli's book was one of the earliest to offer accounts of the war by the men and women who experienced it firsthand. The book struck an immediate chord with readers hungry for a more personal account of the war than what was broadcast on television or written about in newspapers. Although critics have raised questions regarding the authenticity of some of the stories collected, the book is considered among important texts treating the Vietnam War and is among the best-known oral histories of the conflict.

HISTORICAL AND LITERARY CONTEXT

Everything We Had reflects the tumult of the Vietnam War era, beginning with the arrival of U.S. combat troops in Vietnam, who encountered an inhospitable climate, unfamiliar terrain, and guerrilla warfare. The book opens with the experiences of medic David Ross, who arrived in Vietnam in 1965. Ross recalls the shock of the difficult conditions and devastating casualties that were not yet widely known to the American public. It concludes with Navy Hospital Corpsman Stephen Klinkhammer's account of the fall of Saigon. Throughout the book veterans detail aspects of life in Vietnam, from combat and the constant fear of attack to common vices such as alcohol and drugs. Many of the narratives reflect a sense of frustration with the war: Communications Officer Karl Phaler describes most of the operations he witnessed in Vietnam as "terminally fruitless," while Rifleman John Muir worries that the ultimate failure of U.S. intervention occluded the heroism and triumphs of those who served.

Everything We Had was published at a time when Americans were still reeling from a war in which more than fifty-eight thousand U.S. service members were killed. As Santoli's book makes clear, many of the men and women who returned from the war were profoundly changed by it, often struggling to return to their prewar lives. Sergeant Lee Childress reflects, "Today I go down the street and see things in a way that nobody else sees them." Even those who had watched the conflict unfold on television struggled to make sense of a war that saw a massive loss of American life without a U.S. victory. In a 1991 article in *History Workshop,* Patrick Hagopian suggests that the popular appeal of *Everything We Had* and other roughly contemporaneous Vietnam oral histories is that "they function cathartically for those whose stories have previously been ignored, both the speakers and the readers who may recognize their own experiences in what is narrated" and by providing a means of social healing.

The years leading up to the publication of *Everything We Had* saw the beginnings of an extensive American tradition of Vietnam War literature. Among the earliest successes in this vein were memoirs such as Ron Kovic's *Born on the Fourth of July* (1976), Philip Caputo's *A Rumor of War* (1977), and Michael Herr's *Dispatches* (1977). During the same period that Vietnam War literature was establishing its hold on the marketplace, oral history was also emerging as a credible historical genre, due in part to the work of Paul Thompson, whose landmark 1978 text *The Voice of the Past* challenges the belief that the genre is suspect or lowbrow and emphasizes its value as a means of spotlighting traditionally underrepresented populations. The success of Thompson's work helped pave the way for a new wave of oral histories.

Although Vietnam War literature was beginning to flourish in the years leading up to the publication of *Everything We Had,* Santoli's text and Mark Baker's *Nam* (1981) are often credited with opening the door to further oral histories of the conflict, in part by demonstrating that there was a popular audience for such work. The years following the success of Santoli's and Baker's texts saw growing interest in oral history

Key Facts

Time Period:
Mid-20th Century

Relevant Historical Events:
Vietnam War

Nationality:
American

Keywords:
war; intervention; heroism

Wounded American soldiers waiting to be evacuated during the Vietnam War, April 4, 1968. © BETTMANN/CORBIS

and an increase in the number of oral histories specific to the Vietnam War. Among the best known of these are Wallace Terry's *Bloods* (1984), which examines the experiences of African American soldiers, and Larry Engelmann's *Tears before the Rain* (1990), which focuses on the fall of South Vietnam. Santoli followed up the success of *Everything We Had* with the oral histories *To Bear Any Burden* (1985), about the war's impacts in the United States and Southeast Asia, and *Leading the Way* (1993), which focuses on the role of Vietnam veterans in shaping the postwar U.S. military.

THEMES AND STYLE

The central theme of *Everything We Had* is that the trauma of the Vietnam War requires individual and national healing, a process Santoli implies begins with the sharing and understanding of individual experiences. In his preface he explains that "until the broader public fully comprehends the nameless soldier, once an image on your television screen, the nation's resolution of the experience called Vietnam will be less than adequate." The oral histories reveal service members' struggles to come to terms with the horrors they witnessed, as well as the changes they saw in themselves during the war. Nurse Gayle Smith recalls that during the war she did not see the Vietnamese as people: "They were human, but they weren't people. They weren't like us, so it was okay to kill them. It was okay to hate them. I see now that they're people just like us. But at that moment …" Smith's narrative invites readers to understand how she came to feel that way and to sympathize with a perspective that they might otherwise find reprehensible. Throughout the collection descriptions of terrifying situations, civilian deaths, and difficult choices help to explain the ongoing struggles of veterans.

Presenting the stories of his fellow Vietnam veterans as oral history allows Santoli to depict a wide range of experiences with detail and emotion. His preface describes spending "countless hours, talking, crying, and laughing with other veterans and their families" and suggests that such moments are vital to the healing process. Speaking for his fellow veterans, he notes, "We feel an obligation … to say what we could not or did not say in the past," and oral history is offered as the ideal medium for conveying those untold stories. In order to preserve the feel of the war experience, Santoli retains the veterans' use of popular slang such as "gooks" to refer to the Vietnamese people and often incorporates military terminology. The book includes a glossary to aid readers unfamiliar with these terms.

The structure and language of *Everything We Had* reflect Santoli's desire to present the experiences of the "nameless soldier." The stories reveal the unique character and speech patterns of their subjects. There are notable distinctions, for example, between the casual language and tone of Medic David Ross, who describes "joking, smoking cigarettes, playing grab-ass in the line" and those of CIA Case Officer Bruce Lawlor, who explains, "That's what pacification was all about. The buzzword was 'root out.' We tried to go on and neutralize their political structure." The book includes wartime photographs that depict Santoli's subjects in a variety of settings and poses, from holding machine guns in the jungle to relaxing in camp with a pet dog. Many of the photos are also reminders of the soldiers' youth, which stands in stark contrast to their stories of wartime atrocities and lost innocence.

CRITICAL DISCUSSION

Upon publication, *Everything We Had* was well reviewed, winning the praise of both oral historians and journalists. In a 1982 review in *Oral History Review*, Charles R. Shrader, noting similarities between the book and Baker's *Nam*, suggests that "the selection of interview segments in both books are well balanced and adequately represent the wide variety of attitudes toward the Vietnam War," going on to note that "none of the accounts seems contrived." Santoli also won praise for including female veterans in his interviews, as this population had been underrepresented in other accounts of the war. Not all reactions were entirely positive, however. Reviewing the book for the *New York Times,* Marc Leepson, while granting that the book "accomplishes what oral history is meant to do," complained that "too many of these first-person accounts are pointlessly anecdotal, and a few are barely intelligible."

Santoli's book remained popular well after its initial publication, with new editions appearing periodically in the decades that followed. The text has been widely excerpted in periodicals and anthologies, including Stewart O'Nan's *The Vietnam Reader* (1998), and is frequently taught in college courses treating the war. The success of the book helped to establish Santoli as an important oral historian.

Despite—or perhaps because of—its popularity with lay audiences, *Everything We Had* has not attracted a significant body of academic criticism. Scholarly works treating the oral history have tended to focus on questions of memory and authenticity, and some critics have questioned the veracity of its accounts. Hagopian, for example, has raised concerns regarding the degree to which Santoli's and other Vietnam oral histories can truly claim the "ideological innocence" implied in their choice of "ordinary people, rather than politicians, strategists and others with axes to grind." He points out that Santoli, who has elsewhere been critical of the government's handling of the war, personally selected the interview subjects and notes that "what is offered as raw has in fact been diced and cooked in accordance with recipes concocted by the editors and publishers." B. G. Burkett and Glenna Whitley's 1998 book *Stolen Valor* offers a more biting indictment of Santoli's project, identifying what they believed were embellishments and fabrications in some of the book's eyewitness accounts, most notably the story of Mike Beamon, who is identified by Santoli as a scout for the U.S. Navy SEALs, but for whom no military records exist. Despite such controversies, *Everything We Had* remains popular, attesting to the emotional power of its testimony.

ORAL HISTORY, MEMORY, AND COMBAT

In a 2004 article in *Oral History Review,* Fred H. Allison, an oral historian and a former marine, examines how combat experience is remembered and retold. He compares an interview with a marine recorded two days after a traumatic firefight with the same man's account of the events more than three decades later. The marine, PFC Michael Nation, was part of an eight-man patrol that attempted to ambush a group of North Vietnamese soldiers, not realizing that several hundred of the men's comrades were nearby. Nation was one of only three men to survive the ensuing firefight.

Allison notes several significant differences in the two interviews. While, for example, the first account was confused and disjointed, Nation's later version was dramatic and cohesive, and he was more clearly engaged in storytelling. Moreover, some of the specific details of the earlier account gave way in the later interview to general observations. For example, while Nation initially focused on losing his military knife and borrowing one to cut a tourniquet for a wounded comrade, he omitted this detail in the later interview, focusing instead on the wounded man. Allison suggests that such changes reflect Nation's ongoing attempts to attach significance to and make sense of the traumatic event. He concludes that, while both accounts are valuable, the earlier one, though disjointed, is more accurate.

BIBLIOGRAPHY

Sources

Allison, Fred H. "Remembering a Vietnam War Firefight: Changing Perspectives over Time." *Oral History Review* 31.2 (2004): 69–83. Print.

Burkett, B. G., and Glenna Whitley. *Stolen Valor: How the Vietnam Generation Was Robbed of Its Heroes and Its History.* Dallas: Verity, 1998. Print.

Hagopian, Patrick. "Oral Narratives: Secondary Revision and the Memory of the Vietnam War." *History Workshop* 32 (1991): 134–50. Print.

Leepson, Marc. "Vietnam Voices." Rev. of *Everything We Had,* by Al Santoli, and *Nam,* by Mark Baker. *New York Times* 17 May 1981: BR3. Print.

Santoli, Al, ed. *Everything We Had: An Oral History of the Vietnam War.* New York: Random House, 1981. Print.

Shrader, Charles R. Rev. of *Everything We Had,* by Al Santoli, and *Nam,* by Mark Baker. *Oral History Review* 10 (1982): 157–60. Print.

Further Reading

Baker, Mark. *Nam: The Vietnam War in the Words of the Men and Women Who Fought There.* New York: Morrow, 1981. Print.

Brinker, William J. "Oral History and the Vietnam War." *Organization of American Historians: Magazine of History* 11.3 (1997): 15–19. Print.

Budra, Paul, and Michael Zeitlin, eds. *Soldier Talk: The Vietnam War in Oral Narrative.* Bloomington: Indiana University Press, 2004. Print.

Engelmann, Larry. *Tears before the Rain: An Oral History of the Fall of South Vietnam.* New York: Oxford University Press, 1990. Print.

O'Nan, Stewart, ed. *The Vietnam Reader: The Definitive Collection of American Fiction and Nonfiction on the War.* New York: Anchor, 1998. Print.

Santoli, Al, ed. *To Bear Any Burden: The Vietnam War and Its Aftermath in the Words of Americans and Southeast Asians.* New York: Dutton, 1985. Print.

———. *Leading the Way: How Vietnam Veterans Rebuilt the U.S. Military: An Oral History.* New York: Ballantine, 1993. Print.

Terry, Wallace, ed. *Bloods: An Oral History of the Vietnam War by Black Veterans.* New York: Random House, 1984. Print.

Greta Gard

"The Good War"
An Oral History of World War II
Louis "Studs" Terkel

✧ Key Facts

Time Period:
Mid- to Late 20th Century

Relevant Historical Events:
World War II; growth of the U.S. economy

Nationality:
American

Keywords:
war; militarization; industrialization

OVERVIEW

"The Good War": An Oral History of World War II was published in 1984 by oral historian and radio journalist Louis "Studs" Terkel. The collection, which Terkel introduces as "a memory book, rather than one of hard fact or precise statistic," showcases the experiences of more than a hundred people who lived through World War II. While a few of Terkel's interview subjects were in positions of power during the war—such as Telford Taylor, the chief U.S. prosecutor at the Nuremberg trials—most were ordinary people on whom the conflict had a profound effect. Terkel's work broke new ground by featuring the seldom-heard voices of African Americans and Japanese Americans as well as those of the working class and the poor.

Published almost four decades after the war, *"The Good War"* provides a deeply personal take on World War II at a time when public awareness about that period had begun to fade. Though some critics questioned Terkel's objectivity as a historian, many readers and scholars were enthusiastic about *"The Good War,"* finding its dozens of perspectives compelling and poignant. The work received the Pulitzer Prize for nonfiction in 1985, and a theatrical version appeared in 1988. *"The Good War"* has continued to be viewed as an authoritative depiction of the personal side of World War II.

HISTORICAL AND LITERARY CONTEXT

In the late 1920s a massive stock market crash followed by a wave of bank closures propelled an already unstable U.S. economy into a full-blown depression. By 1933 unemployment had reached 25 percent, and newly elected Democratic president Franklin D. Roosevelt began implementing strategies to spark an economic recovery. In Japan, Germany, Italy, and Spain, economic recession and depression led to increased militarization and the installation of repressive fascist governments. As these governments, especially in Germany and Japan, began to employ aggressive tactics to increase their territories and resources, it began to appear that the United States would be drawn into a world war.

On December 7, 1941, Japanese air forces launched a surprise attack on the U.S. Navy at Pearl Harbor, Hawaii, and the nation was soon at war in both Asia and Europe. The war transformed the United States, boosting the economy out of the Great Depression and engaging much of American society in military action and in military-related industries. When World War II ended, many of those who had participated in the conflict returned to "normal" life, and the U.S. population began the process of forgetting the war. By the early 1980s what Terkel called "the disremembrance of World War Two" was widespread, and the oral historian began the process of compiling the stories of those who lived through the transformative war years from 1939 to 1945.

Though the war had been deeply influential, stoic silence permeated American culture during the 1940s and 1950s. Some personal accounts—such as Ross S. Carter's *Those Devils in Baggy Pants* (1951), which recounts the author's experience as a paratrooper, and Charles E. Francis's *The Tuskegee Airmen: The Men Who Changed America* (1955), which explores the contributions of African American aviators—appeared shortly after the war's end. However, the confessional era that began in the mid-1970s introduced a new wave of literature that sought to uncover the experience of the often-forgotten ordinary individual during the war. In 1975 Mary Penick Motley compiled an oral history titled *The Invisible Soldier: The Experience of the Black Soldier, World War II,* and in 1976 Michi Weglyn published the first memoir of an interned Japanese American citizen, *Years of Infamy: The Untold Story of America's Concentration Camps.*

"The Good War," with its broadly diverse pool of interviewees and the progressive focus of its critique, brought the war to a new generation with unprecedented immediacy. Terkel's ability to elicit compelling narratives from his subjects had enlivened his earlier works, including *Hard Times* (1970), which focuses on the Great Depression. With *"The Good War,"* he was confirmed as an innovator in the modern genre of oral history. His work influenced subsequent oral historians, such as Mark Kukis (*Voices from Iraq,* 2011), and even inspired science fiction writer Max Brooks's 2007 *World War Z: An Oral History of the Zombie War.*

THEMES AND STYLE

Except for a brief author introduction, *"The Good War"* is a collection of the words of its subjects, but Terkel nevertheless uses a variety of techniques to insert his own thematic ideas. The title itself acts as a subtle reflection of the complexity of war, with the term *the good war* placed in quotes. In a 2004 *American Theatre* interview, Terkel explains, "There ain't no such animal as a good war. Even World War II, the most justifiable, made savages of otherwise young decent men and women." It is the effect of the war on these ordinary people that forms the central focus of Terkel's work. Some who joined the war in patriotic fervor found themselves confronting the darker sides of their own natures. "A lot of my buddies hit, the fatigue, the stress," says one such person. "After a while, the veneer of civilization wore pretty thin."

Terkel's purpose in creating *"The Good War"* goes beyond presenting an objective history. In choosing to showcase the memories of a broad cross section of society, and in his editing choices, he advances a progressive examination of the ramifications of the war. African American narratives reveal both segregation in the military and the unprecedented opportunity for advancement that army training provided, a sometimes ironic combination. "In the beginning, they didn't know what to do with us, so they just kept on training and training and training us," says an African American interviewee. "When we went overseas, most of our fliers had three times the flying training that white pilots had." Terkel's emphasis is on common humanity, and he reinforces this theme by also including histories from Japanese, German, and Russian perspectives. All of these narratives are touchingly similar: "We sent off our relatives and friends with cheery smiles and military songs," a Japanese man recalls, while a Russian declares, "As a former soldier, who saw thousands of deaths, I don't want any war repeated."

Terkel's editing is skillful and so subtle that it seems almost invisible. His use of dialect and colloquial phrasing not only brings his interviews to life but also adds an authenticity that draws the reader in and builds trust in the narrative: "I got one eye. My feet hangs down. I got a joint mashed in my back. I got a shoulder been broke." In his introduction Terkel points out the tendency of interviewees to refer to themselves and their comrades as "boys" and "kids," which heightens the innocence of the times.

CRITICAL DISCUSSION

Upon its publication, *"The Good War"* received positive notices from critics and readers alike, though some reviewers complained that Terkel's "memory book" lacked a solid historical foundation. Among the detractors was Barry Gewen of the *New Leader,* who wrote, "Reading this book is like chewing water.... The problem is that everything is presented uncritically, on its own terms." Others, however, appreciated Terkel's populist approach. Jonathan Yardley, writing for the *Washington Post Book World,* called *"The Good War"* a "clangorous but carefully orchestrated jumble of voices." Loudon Wainwright in a *New York Times Book Review* asserted, "In terms of plain human interest, Mr. Terkel may well have put together the most vivid collection of World War II sketches ever gathered between covers."

Author Studs Terkel in 1985. © BETTMANN/CORBIS

Wainwright, for one, sensed that the book would have a powerful legacy: "It is hard to see how any reader now or then can fail to benefit from its 600 pages. For Mr. Terkel … has turned an oral history into a popular literary form [and] has captured an especially broad and impressive chorus of voices." In a way not possible in a traditional historical narrative, Terkel's carefully orchestrated oral history keeps alive the individual experience of World War II in both its particularity and its universality.

Scholars have continued to analyze *"The Good War"* both in terms of its subject matter and its innovative literary form. Early critics such as Philip Greasley, writing in the *Great Lakes Review* in 1985, examined Terkel's "imperceptible yet highly effective narrative management." Historian William Moss proposed in the *Oral History Review* that Terkel belongs to "a tradition of writers emerged from journalism that goes back at least to Mark Twain." The study of Terkel's contribution to oral history has continued to evolve in the twenty-first century with scholars such as Andrea Gustavson, who, in a 2012 *Journal of American Studies* article, named his narratives "documentary memory," adding, "Terkel believed telling stories of the past to be a form of social action, and he used his texts about the past to comment politically on his present."

STUDS TERKEL: A HISTORIAN MAKING HISTORY

Far from being a bookish historian, Louis Terkel (1912–2008), nicknamed "Studs" after the hero of the popular Depression-era novel *Studs Lonigan,* lived a life as colorful as any he recorded in his numerous oral history books. Born in New York, Terkel and his family moved to Chicago in 1920. There he developed his skill at listening to the stories of ordinary working people while growing up in his parents' boardinghouse. Though Terkel earned a law degree from the University of Chicago, he never practiced law. Instead he became a performer, first onstage and then in the new medium of television. When his leftist politics ended his television career during the anticommunist 1950s, Terkel turned to radio, developing a successful interview program that aired for more than four decades.

Along with the oral histories that made him famous, Terkel wrote two memoirs, *Talking to Myself: A Memoir of My Times* (1977) and *Touch and Go: A Memoir* (2007). Terkel was also a lover of jazz, the rhythmic, improvisational music that has its roots in Africa, the American South, and urban centers such as Chicago. His writing style has drawn comparisons to the lively polyphony of jazz, especially in *Touch and Go,* which replaces traditional chronology with a nonlinear stream of consciousness that parallels the energetic movement of Terkel's life.

BIBLIOGRAPHY

Sources

Gewen, Barry. "Facts Are Not Enough." *New Leader* 67.20 (1984): 12–13. Rpt. in *Contemporary Literary Criticism.* Ed. Daniel G. Marowski and Roger Matuz. Vol. 38. Detroit: Gale Research, 1986. *Literature Resource Center.* Web. 2 Jan. 2013.

Greasley, Philip A. "Ripples on the Water: Studs Terkel's 'The Good War.'" Rev. of *"The Good War": An Oral History of World War II,* by Studs Terkel. *Great Lakes Review* 11.1 (1985): 23–31. *JSTOR.* Web. 3 Jan. 2013.

Gustavson, Andrea. "From 'Observer to Activist': Documentary Memory, Oral History, and Studs Terkel's 'Essence' Narratives." *Journal of American Studies* 46.1 (2012): 103–19. *JSTOR.* Web. 2 Jan. 2013.

Moss, William W. "Oral History or Literary Impressionism?" Rev. of *"The Good War": An Oral History of World War II,* by Studs Terkel. *Oral History Review* 13 (1985): 131–35. *JSTOR.* Web. 31 Dec. 2013.

Terkel, Studs. *"The Good War": An Oral History of World War II.* New York: Pantheon, 1984. Print.

Terkel, Studs. "Twenty Questions." *American Theatre* May–June 2004: 80. *Literature Resource Center.* Web. 2 Jan. 2013.

Wainwright, Loudon. "I Can Remember Every Hour." *New York Times Book Review.* New York Times, 7 Oct. 1984. Web. 3 Jan. 2013.

Yardley, Jonathan. Rev. of *"The Good War": An Oral History of World War II,* by Studs Terkel. *Washington Post Book World* 14.40 (1984): 3. Print.

Further Reading

de Graaf, John, and Alan Harris Stein. "The Guerrilla Journalist as Oral Historian: An Interview with Louis 'Studs' Terkel." *Oral History Review* 29.1 (2002): 87–107. *JSTOR.* Web. 2 Jan. 2013.

Frisch, Michael. "Studs Terkel, Historian." *History Workshop Journal* 69 (2010): 189–98. *JSTOR.* Web. 3 Jan. 2013.

Gregson, Sarah. "Oral Historian and Activist, 'Studs' Terkel (1912–2008)." *Labour History: A Journal of Labour and Social History* 96 (2009): 233+. *Academic OneFile.* Web. 3 Jan. 2013.

Stein, Alan Harris. "Old Stubborn Guts." *Oral History Review* 28.1 (2001): 121. *Academic OneFile.* Web. 3 Jan. 2013.

Terkel, Studs. *Hard Times: An Oral History of the Great Depression.* New York: Pantheon, 1970. Print.

Terkel, Studs, and Sydney Lewis. *Touch and Go: A Memoir.* New York: New Press, 2007. Print.

Tina Gianoulis

Japan at War
An Oral History
Haruko Taya Cook, Theodore F. Cook

OVERVIEW

Japan at War: An Oral History (1992) is a collection of stories gathered by the spousal team Haruko Taya Cook and Theodore F. Cook that portray Japanese experiences of World War II among a cross section of people, including military officers, soldiers, nurses, housewives, children, and prisoners. The interview process began in the late 1980s, after the death of Emperor Hirohito, when the Japanese people approached a new political order and were ready to discuss the war of the 1930s and 1940s. Their personal memories do not necessarily form a coherent narrative, however, and although the Cooks have done their best to construct a chronological sequence of events, the personal focus of the collected memories defies the traditional American narrative of war, which has a distinctive beginning and end.

Although the interviews were primarily conducted by the Cooks in Japanese, the book was published in English in the United States; as of early 2013, a Japanese edition has never been released. This curiosity has often been mentioned by critics, even though the text received mostly positive reviews from American critics and quickly became a valuable resource among educators. *Japan at War* continues to be a significant text for studying wartime experiences and the historical and cultural significance of World War II.

HISTORICAL AND LITERARY CONTEXT

What North Americans and Europeans know as World War II has several different names in Japan, including the Greater East Asia War, the Pacific War, and the Fifteen-Year War. This war officially began for Japan in 1931 with the so-called Manchurian Incident, during which Japan invaded northern China. A series of smaller battles between the two nations over the nature of political power in China continued for nearly a decade. In 1941, the official start of World War II for many Western nations, Japan retaliated against U.S. interference with its plans to dominate Southeast Asia through warfare, and the Japanese attack on Pearl Harbor in Hawaii initiated direct conflict between Japan and the United States.

Japan at War describes Japanese experiences throughout the entirety of the war, beginning with memories of campaigns in China and concluding with stories of homecomings after the war's conclusion, as well as the lingering physical and psychological effects of a war that included the atomic bombings of Hiroshima and Nagasaki. The selected stories cover various wartime subjects, from the atrocities committed by Japanese officers to the trials of young brides trying to maintain their households while their husbands were off fighting. The Cooks were clearly trying to provide an overview of the feelings and memories about the war from a broad base of Japanese society.

Japan at War is categorized as both a Japanese oral history and an oral history of World War II. Previously published texts that deal with the Japanese experience of the war include *Soldiers of the Sun* (1991) by Meirion and Susie Harries and Arthur A. Hansen's *Japanese American World War II Evacuation Oral History Project* (1991). *Japan at War* fits into a tradition of other World War II oral histories that portray a variety of international perspectives, including Johannes Steinhoff's *Voices from the Third Reich: An Oral History* (1989) and Stephen Fox's *The Unknown Internment: An Oral History of the Relocation of Italian Americans during World War II* (1990).

Since its publication, *Japan at War* has influenced American views on Japanese experiences during World War II; the work has also inspired the Cooks to continue writing on the subject. They collaborated to produce the academic article "A Lost War in Living Memory: Japan's Second World War" (2003), and they published several works separately, including Theodore Cook's "Tokyo, December 8, 1941" (2001) and Haruko Taya Cook's "Turning Women into Weapons: Japan's Women, the Battle of Saipan, and the 'Nature of the Pacific War'" (1999).

THEMES AND STYLE

The central themes of *Japan at War* are the preservation of Japanese wartime memories and the deconstruction of American stereotypes about World War II Japan. The Cooks explain, "The country so often portrayed in the West as a fanatical, suicidal nation, united in purpose by their Emperor, looks more like a collection of confused, terrorized, and desperate individuals beaten down by overwhelming force." The memories of soldiers are included in the oral history,

❖ **Key Facts**

Time Period:
Mid-20th Century

Relevant Historical Events:
World War II; Pearl Harbor; bombings of Hiroshima and Nagasaki

Nationality:
Japanese

Keywords:
war; stereotypes; memory

although they are not the primary focus; soldier Tanisuga Shizuo admits to using poison gas on a Chinese village: "I was glad to see the conditions were favorable—the weather cloudy, wind blowing toward the other side.... One after the other, I threw the canisters toward the enemy.... I ordered the men to charge into the village. Their soldiers, and most everyone else, had already run off." The personal stories of civilians left in Japan are also included in an attempt to portray a balanced representation of Japanese society during the war. For example, Tanaka Toki, a young newlywed whose husband is away fighting, relates, "There were many hardships, but the hardest was to keep the family together."

The authors' purpose in composing *Japan at War* is primarily to record Japanese memories of war for posterity but also to present them to an American audience in order to open channels of communication between the two nations and their vastly different views of war. In the introduction, the Cooks state:

> It is our belief that the living will not rest easy in the public sphere until that increasingly ancient, but still living, war is no longer avoided, but instead faced and examined in public, and until the complex Japanese experiences of war are opened to all and become a matter of public discussion and public understanding, in both the U.S. and Japan.

Japan at War is structured in roughly chronological order, with the stories of each participant working to create a sense of the beginning, middle, and end of the war on a very personal level. While each interview is preceded by a brief description of the participant, the translation process—the interviews were conducted primarily in Japanese and were later translated into English for the benefit of an American audience—eliminates most of the personal voice of each speaker, creating a text that reads more like a composed history than a collection of individual memories. The Cooks' translation and publication decisions are often questioned by critics, who suggest a Japanese edition might be more effective for the people involved in the composition of the book.

CRITICAL DISCUSSION

Japan at War initially received positive reviews for its ability to present a Japanese perspective of the war without American interjection or prejudice. Stanley Falk, in a 1993 review in *Journal of Military History*, praises how the Cooks "arranged and annotated the interviews with compassion and sympathetic yet perceptive understanding" and included "poignant stories of individual or group suffering mixed with gruesome testimony of widespread atrocities."

Japan at War is often used as a primary source for educators to illustrate for their students the Japanese perspective of World War II. In a 1994 review in *Journal of Japanese Studies,* Andrew Gordon notes that the "Cooks have constructed a resource of tremendous value" for "all of us who teach and study the history of Japan, or the modern world." He continues, *Japan at War* is not written in "the measured prose of academic monographs" but rather is directly presentable to a student. Despite the usefulness of the text as a teaching tool, Gordon questions the Cooks' decision to publish it only in English, suggesting that this "risks merely promoting an unreflective criticism of the Japanese 'other'" by promoting the idea "that 'we Americans' should be troubled about the way 'those Japanese' have avoided coming to terms with World War II."

Trends in discussing *Japan at War* tend to focus on the opaque editorial process and the overall purpose of the book as a historical text. Gordon follows this trend by stating, "The editors give inadequate attention to reflecting on their own position and the contemporary meaning of their undertaking," and "they tell us nothing of the mechanics of the book's production," including "the question of what it means to publish *Japan at War* in English, in America." Alvin Coox, in his 1995 analysis of the book in *Oral History Review,* follows a similar vein of thought when he writes, "Most distressing is the implicit question as to what the Japanese as a whole really learned from their painful wartime trauma," concluding that "Japan has still not come to grips with the vexing question of wartime guilt and responsibility."

BIBLIOGRAPHY

Sources

Cook, Haruko Taya, and Theodore F. Cook. *Japan at War: An Oral History.* New York: New Press, 1992. Print.

Coox, Alvin D. Rev. of *Japan at War: An Oral History,* by Haruko Taya Cook and Theodore F. Cook, and *Soldiers of the Sun: The Rise and Fall of the Imperial Japanese Army,* by Meirion Harries and Susie Harries. *Oral History Review* 22.1 (1995): 161–64. JSTOR. Web. 12 Jan. 2013.

Falk, Stanley L. Rev. of *Japan at War: An Oral History,* by Haruko Taya Cook and Theodore F. Cook. *Journal of Military History* 57.3 (1993): 564–65. JSTOR. Web. 12 Jan. 2013.

Gordon, Andrew. Rev. of *Japan at War: An Oral History,* by Haruko Taya Cook and Theodore F. Cook. *Journal of Japanese Studies* 20.2 (1994): 551–56. JSTOR. Web. 12 Jan. 2013.

Further Reading

Cook, Haruko Taya. "Turning Women into Weapons: Japan's Women, the Battle of Saipan, and the 'Nature of the Pacific War.'" *Women and War in the 20th Century, Enlisted with or without Consent.* Ed. Nicole A. Dombrowski. New York: Garland, 1999. 240–61. Print.

Cook, Haruko Taya, and Theodore F. Cook. "A Lost War in Living Memory: Japan's Second World War." *European Review* 11.4 (2003): 573–93. Web. 15 Jan. 2013.

Cook, Theodore F. "Tokyo, December 8, 1941." *No End Save Victory. Perspectives on World War II.* Ed. Robert Cowley. New York: Putnam, 2001. 131–43. Print.

Dower, John W. *Ways of Forgetting, Ways of Remembering: Japan in the Modern World.* New York: New Press, 2012. Print.

Fox, Stephen R. *The Unknown Internment: An Oral History of the Relocation of Italian Americans during World War II.* Boston: Twayne, 1990. Print.

Hansen, Arthur A. *Japanese American World War II Evacuation Oral History Project.* Westport, Conn.: Meckler, 1991. Print.

Harries, Meirion, and Susie Harries. *Soldiers of the Sun: The Rise and Fall of the Imperial Japanese Army.* New York: Random House, 1991. Print.

Mawdsley, Evan. *World War II: A New History.* Cambridge: Cambridge University Press, 2009. Print.

Soka Gakkai Youth Division. *Cries for Peace: Experiences of Japanese Victims of World War II.* Tokyo: Japan Times, 1978. Print.

Steinhoff, Johannes, Peter Pechel, and Dennis Showalter. *Voices from the Third Reich: An Oral History.* Washington, D.C.: Regnery Gateway, 1989. Print.

Katherine Barker

Memoirs of Fatemeh Pakravan

Habib Ladjevardi

❖ **Key Facts**

Time Period:
Mid-20th Century

Relevant Historical Events:
Allied occupation of Iran during World War II; White Revolution; Iranian Revolution

Nationality:
Iranian

Keywords:
revolution; occupation; government

OVERVIEW

Part of a series of transcribed interviews conducted for Harvard University's Iranian Oral History Project (HIOHP) led by scholar Habib Ladjevardi, *Memoirs of Fatemeh Pakravan* (1998) provides an insider's account of a life lived close to the powerful elite of Iran, from the 1940s until 1979, when Fatemeh Pakravan's husband, longtime government official general Hassan Pakravan, was executed by the revolutionary government of Ayatollah Ruhollah Khomeini. Ladjevardi interviewed Fatemeh Pakravan at her residence in Paris "in two sessions lasting a total of three and one-half hours" in March 1983, during which Pakravan described growing up in Tehran and Paris and returning to Iran after studies in France to work in the Iranian hospital system. Her first employer in the 1940s was Mohammad Mossadegh, who would become prime minister of Iran in 1951, only to be overthrown by a British- and American-backed coup in 1953. In the memoirs, General Pakravan, who worked for several heads of state, emerges as a gentle, thoughtful person, whose execution was not because of any wrongdoing but because of the revolutionary government's determination to start anew.

Published nearly twenty years after the revolution took her husband's life, Fatemeh Pakravan's memoirs reflect the attitude of a proud wife and mother; a privileged, educated woman with ideas about how her country might have been improved; and an Iranian citizen concerned about the fate of her country. Today *Memoirs of Fatemeh Pakravan* is seen as a valuable resource for scholars of Iranian history and a fine example of oral history.

HISTORICAL AND LITERARY CONTEXT

Pakravan's recollections cover the many shifts in Iranian politics that occurred over the course of her marriage to General Pakravan. The two married in Tehran during World War II. When the Allies deemed Iran of strategic importance, they occupied the country, with the Soviet Army leading the way. Along with the British, the Soviets—as the Russians before them—had long exerted influence in the country. Since 1909 the British-owned Anglo-Iranian Oil Company had been profiting from Iran's rich oil supplies. But in the 1950s, the Iranian oil industry was successfully nationalized, largely thanks to the efforts of Mossadegh. By 1954 the Anglo-Iranian Oil Company, which later became British Petroleum, began to seek revenue elsewhere.

In 1963 Mohammad Reza Shah Pahlavi (shah from 1941 to 1979) initiated the White Revolution, a series of reforms intended to modernize and strengthen the country—for example, by enshrining women's rights in national law. The reforms were opposed by the large religiously conservative population, led by Khomeini, who was not yet ayatollah. He led an uprising against the reforms in June 1963 and was imprisoned as a result. General Pakravan intervened to ensure Khomeini was not condemned to death by arranging to have him declared an ayatollah. Instead Khomeini was sent into exile, returning in 1979 to overthrow the government. General Pakravan insisted that his wife and their children go to Paris while he stayed behind.

The inclusion of *Memoirs of Fatemeh Pakravan* in HIOHP places the work in the literary tradition of twentieth-century accounts of exile by members of Iran's foreign-educated elite, as well as among works examining the causes of the revolution. Pakravan speaks admiringly of *Faces in a Mirror: Memoirs from Exile* (1980) by Ashraf Pahlavi, Mohammad Reza's twin sister, perhaps because Pahlavi was vice president of the Iranian Red Cross, in which Pakravan was active. Pakravan is less approving of Soraya Esfandiary's *The Autobiography of H.I.H. Soraya* (1963), which Pakravan calls a "stupid book" after witnessing Esfandiary refuse to address a reception held in her honor. *The Shah's Story* (1980) is an English translation of Reza's memoir, while *The Persian Sphinx* (2000), written by Abbas Milani, is a biography of Amir Abbas Hoveyda, who was prime minister of Iran from 1965 to 1977. Hoveyda's brother Fereydoun, who replaced the shah at the United Nations after Reza fled in 1979, rebukes him and his regime in the book *Fall of the Shah* (1980).

Memoirs of Fatemeh Pakravan is valued as a source of information about the years leading up to Khomeini's takeover, cited in works by scholars such as Milani, the director of Iranian Studies at Stanford University. Esmail Salemi translated Pakravan's memoirs into Persian in *Khaterat* (1999). In addition to an interview for HIOHP, Pakravan with the help of her daughter Saïdeh also wrote her own memoirs in French: *Ombre du vent: Lumière de mes yeux* (2007) (Shadow of the wind: Light of my eye). Ladjevardi's HIOHP includes 150 transcribed interviews recorded all over the world and narrated by Iranian political figures, academics, businesspeople, activists, and relatives of influential members of a vanished Iranian society.

THEMES AND STYLE

The main themes of Pakravan's narrative are the discrepancies between the Iranian elite and the country's majority, the difficulties General Pakravan faced in his various governmental posts, and the ever-present option, sometimes expressed as a need or desire, to live outside of Iran in places deemed safe—Paris in the case of the Pakravans. Recalling Khomeini's imprisonment after the June 1963 uprising, Fatemeh Pakravan relates how her husband "knew that, after all, the population of the country is not its elite. It's the real people. They are not very literate. They are simple. They are full of superstition." General Pakravan observes of Khomeini, "His ignorance in history and philosophy is something unbelievable." Maintaining an active career as a hospital administrator throughout her time in Iran, Fatemeh Pakravan describes in the early 1950s trying to contain "a typhus epidemic … because of the Poles. The Poles, who had been kept in camps in Russia and were going through Iran to be settled all over the world, brought all kinds of diseases with them." She asked that extra showers be built, but Mossadegh, then head of the hospital, stubbornly refused.

Ladjevardi was approached in 1980 by Harvard dean Edward N. Keenan "to collect and preserve personal accounts of individuals who played significant roles in important political events and decisions in Iran during their careers." Ladjevardi succeeded in interviewing 133 narrators from an initial list of 350. Pakravan's written comments on the transcript of her interview, quoted in the preface, indicate that she was motivated by a desire to honor her husband and to give her opinion on the political landscape. Her husband "led a very rich life of service and devotion to duty," she writes, criticizing the fact that the memoir seems to overemphasize his role in SAVAK, the organization that Milani refers to as "the much-despised secret police." She notes that "the fathers of this organization, justly criticized in later years, were the United States of America with the help of Israel."

In her narrative, Pakravan comes across as reserved, dignified, and hesitant to spread—or appear to spread—gossip. Her insight into the inner workings of Iranian government often comes in the form of direct quotes from conversations she had with her husband. In his final post, in which he felt that other members of the government were interfering, General Pakravan told his wife, "'You know, we don't have one shah.' I said, 'What do you mean?' He said, 'We have at least twelve of them. And the weakest is the one who wears the crown!'" When asked about General Pakravan's successor as head of SAVAK, General Nematollah Nassiri, who had a reputation for being financially corrupt, Fatemeh Pakravan comments, "Personally, I didn't like him very much.… There was a very sad story of a child of his being [pause] … I don't want to repeat them, because I don't believe in spreading rumors." Ladjevardi often includes pauses in parentheses and also parenthesizes words that appear to have been expressed by gesture, a nod of the head, or a facial expression. As such, the transcript tries to remain faithful to the interview.

In *Memoirs of Fatemeh Pakravan*, the subject, the wife of General Hassan Pakravan, describes life in Iran under the rule of Shah Mohammad Reza Pahlavi, pictured here in 1967.
© AP IMAGES/CHARLES TASNADI

CRITICAL DISCUSSION

Memoirs of Fatemeh Pakravan was greeted as one of the more useful examples of Ladjevardi's project in terms of understanding Iran's political history. In a 1999 review, Ibrahim Kilinc of *Middle East Journal* calls it "informative.… [It] contributes to the reader's understanding of the revolutionary process in Iran. The book contains a number of fascinating accounts, including the discussion of the relationship between General Pakravan and Ayatollah Ruhollah Khomeini during the latter's detention (prior to his exile in 1963)." Other memoirs in the project were not as warmly described. Writing for *Iranian Studies* in 1999, Anna Vanzan notes of *Memoirs of Prince Hamid Kadjar,* "The reader who evaluates the book for its possible value as firsthand historic material will be rather disappointed." Despite questioning the value of autobiography as historical document (Ladjevardi's introduction to *Memoirs of Prince Hamid Kadjar* describes the interviewer's role as ensuring that each recorded memoir serves as "a good substitute for an autobiography if the narrator had the time and interest to write it"), Vanzan concludes, "Often, when new events overturn the existing situation, we lack the documents that show us how the change developed. Autobiography can help us in understanding this process, as it enables us to see the mechanism of change while it is in progress."

While *Memoirs of Fatemeh Pakravan* is not frequently cited by scholars of the period, other memoirs in the HIOHP regularly appear in scholarly works.

AN EARTHQUAKE AND A LEGENDARY TRIBESWOMAN

In her memoirs, Fatemeh Pakravan recalls the devastation wreaked by an earthquake that struck late at night on September 1, 1962, just south of Qazvin, a densely populated region that lies west of Tehran. The earthquake killed 12,200 people and destroyed or damaged three hundred villages. In its aftermath, the Pakravans' friend Mary (Mehri) Gharagozlou, the daughter of a large landowning family who was raised in a mountain village in the province directly south of Qazvin, ensured the land was plowed and seeds were planted for the spring harvest. Pakravan estimates that Gharagozlou "saved the day for many, many peasants."

According to Pakravan, her husband was so impressed with Gharagozlou that he found a position for her in the Ministry of Housing, which "started building very nice houses with bazaars and mosques in the south of Tehran." However, Antony Wynn's 2001 obituary for Gharagozlou in the *Independent* has General Pakravan hiring her well before the earthquake to act as an intermediary between rural tribesmen and the Tehran government, which was trying to impose sweeping agrarian reforms and wanted to "settle the nomad tribes, who were seen as too independent." Gharagozlou successfully defended the nomadic shepherds who provided the nation with meat and whose flocks would have died had they been forced to settle.

As Ali R. Abootalebi observes in a 1999 review in *Middle East Studies Association Bulletin* of HIOHP's *Memoirs of Shapour Bakhtiar*, Bakhtiar's failure to provide any new information or insight "is not due to the questions asked in the interview but to the subject of the interview itself. Those interested in modern Iranian history will find this and other published texts of the Oral History Project extremely valuable."

Pakravan's memoirs are a valuable addition to a repository of personal accounts that will likely continue to yield useful information to future generations of scholars. In a 2010 essay on historiographical methodology for the *International Journal of Middle East Studies*, Cyrus Schayegh cites several taped HIOHP interviews, including one conducted in 1981 with Abolbashar Farmanfarmian, a prince of the Qajar dynasty that ruled Iran from 1796 until 1921. Farmanfarmian's testimony would otherwise have been lost—along with that of the many people who were forced to flee or who were rendered silent by the Iranian Revolution of 1979.

BIBLIOGRAPHY

Sources

Abootalebi, Ali R. Rev. of *Khaterat-e Shapour Bakhtiar* (*Memoirs of Shapour Bakhtiar*), ed. Habib Ladjevardi. *Middle East Studies Association Bulletin* 33 (1999): 130. Print.

Gharagozlou, Mary. "Introducing the Asil Horse of Khuzestan (Iran)." *World Arabian Horse Organization*. Web. 1 Feb. 2013.

Kilinc, Ibrahim. Rev. of *Memoirs of Fatemeh Pakravan*, ed. Habib Ladjevardi. *Middle East Journal* 53.3 (1999): 505. JSTOR. Web. 29 Jan. 2013.

Milani, Abbas. *The Persian Sphinx: Amir Abbas Hoveyda and the Riddle of the Iranian Revolution*. Washington, D.C.: Mage, 2000. Print.

Pakravan, Fatemeh. *Memoirs of Fatemeh Pakravan, Wife of General Hassan Pakravan: Army Officer, Chief of State Intelligence and Security Organization, Cabinet Minister, and Diplomat*. Ed. Habib Ladjevardi. Cambridge, Mass.: Iranian Oral History Project, Center for Middle Eastern Studies, and Harvard University, 1998. Print.

Vanzan, Anna. Rev. of *Memoirs of Prince Hamid Kadjar: Son of the Last Qajar Crown Prince*, ed. Habib Ladjevardi. *Iranian Studies* 32.1 (1999): 118–20. JSTOR. Web. 1 Feb. 2013.

Wynn, Antony. "Obituary—Mary Gharagozlou." *Independent* 2 Sept. 2001: 6. Questia. Web. 1 Feb. 2013.

Further Reading

De Bellaigue, Christopher. *Patriot of Persia: Muhammad Mossadegh and a Very British Coup*. London: Bodley Head, 2012. Print.

Ladjevardi, Habib. *Labor Unions and Autocracy in Iran*. Syracuse, N.Y.: Syracuse University Press, 1985. Print.

Lie, Trygve. *In the Cause of Peace: Seven Years with the United Nations*. New York: Macmillan, 1954. Print.

Moaddel, Mansoor. *Class, Politics, and Ideology in the Iranian Revolution*. New York: Columbia University Press, 1993. Print.

Pahlavi, Princess Ashraf. *Faces in a Mirror: Memoirs from Exile*. Englewood Cliffs, N.J.: Prentice, 1980. Print.

Pakravan, Saïdeh. *The Arrest of Hoveyda: Stories of the Iranian Revolution*. Costa Mesa, Calif.: Blind Owl, 1998. Print.

Samii, Abbas William. "The Shah's Lebanon Policy: The Role of SAVAK." *Middle Eastern Studies* 33.1 (1997): 66–91. JSTOR. Web. 1 Feb. 2013.

Schayegh, Cyrus. "'Seeing Like a State': An Essay on the Historiography of Modern Iran." *International Journal of Middle East Studies* 42.1 (2010): 37–61. JSTOR. Web. 1 Feb. 2013.

Rebecca Rustin

The Strength Not to Fight
An Oral History of Conscientious Objectors of the Vietnam War
James W. Tollefson

Key Facts

Time Period:
Mid-20th Century

Relevant Historical Events:
Vietnam War; antiwar movement; implementation of the military draft

Nationality:
American

Keywords:
conscientious objection; pacifism; war

OVERVIEW

In *The Strength Not to Fight* (1993), James W. Tollefson weaves together the testimony of roughly forty men whose opposition to the United States war in Vietnam led them to apply for conscientious objector (CO) status or to resist the draft by other means. Some of these men went to prison for their beliefs; some went underground and hid from the authorities. Still others escaped the country into Canada or elsewhere, or entered the military and served in noncombatant roles. Many of the subjects reveal deep personal losses, such as estrangement from their families and loved ones, that resulted from their principled stand. Their stories, collected two decades or more after the Vietnam War, reveal the myriad ways the decisions Tollefson's subjects made during the war years shaped their lives.

Tollefson, who received a CO deferment after demonstrating to his draft board that his pacifism was founded on genuine religious conviction, published *The Strength Not to Fight* two decades after the United States withdrew its troops from Vietnam and ended the military draft. However, the cultural divisions over the unpopular war remained a source of bitter conflict and reemerged during the 1992 presidential campaign after it was revealed that Bill Clinton had actively avoided the draft for several years. By drawing attention to the COs, *The Strength Not to Fight* has filled a niche in the extensive literature about the Vietnam antiwar movement and draft resistance.

HISTORICAL AND LITERARY CONTEXT

The military draft was reinstated at the end of the Korean War in 1953 and remained in effect through the end of the Vietnam War. All males were obligated to register with the Selective Service upon reaching eighteen years of age and to serve for a minimum of two years if called. Conscription rates increased after 1965, when the United States escalated its involvement in the Vietnam conflict. The draft became a focal point of generational conflict as students began protesting the war on campuses across the nation.

More than ten million Americans served in the military between 1964 and 1973, about 2.6 million of them in Vietnam. But many young men searched for alternatives to conscription into a war they bitterly opposed. At the time, the law stipulated that draft boards could exempt a draftee "who, by reason of religious training or belief, is conscientiously opposed to participation in war in any form." Approximately 170,000 applicants were granted CO status during the Vietnam period, while nearly twice that many had their applications rejected. Many who could afford to pursue higher education received student deferments. More than a half million men, according to Tollefson's research, chose to evade the draft by illegal means such as by crossing the border into Canada. Conscription came to an end in 1973, and President Gerald Ford proclaimed a conditional amnesty for draft evaders and military deserters one year later. His successor, Jimmy Carter, turned that amnesty into an unconditional pardon upon assuming the presidency in January 1977.

In presenting the stories of COs and other draft resisters, Tollefson offers a comparatively late addition to the literature concerning the Vietnam War. Many historians have recounted the experiences of those who fought in the war and those who fought against it. Among the Vietnam-related oral histories published prior to *The Strength Not to Fight* were ones collecting the stories of war veterans, such as *Nam* (1981) by Mark Baker; African American war veterans, such as *Bloods* (1984) by Wallace Terry; women in the U.S. military, such as *In the Combat Zone* (1987) by Kathryn Marshall; antiwar protesters and draft dodgers; and COs, such as Gerald P. Gioglio's *Days of Decision: An Oral History of Conscientious Objectors in the Military during the Vietnam War* (1988).

In addition to its contribution to scholarship on the Vietnam War, *The Strength Not to Fight* offers a useful introduction to an important stage in the history of ethical resistance to war and militarism. The end of the draft and the nation's transition to an all-volunteer army spurred a sea change in the military's role in American society. In subsequent periods of war, the number of CO applicants was drastically lower than during the Vietnam years, with most applications coming from those already serving in the military.

THEMES AND STYLE

The central theme of *The Strength Not to Fight* is elegantly expressed in the book's title. Each of Tollefson's subjects chose to act in accordance with his conscience,

Vietnam War protesters hoist a peace sign in a demonstration on Capitol Hill, circa 1970. Conscientious objectors to the Vietnam War recount their experiences in James W. Tollefson's *The Strength Not to Fight*. © WALLY MCNAMEE/CORBIS

even though most were vividly aware that there would be a price to pay. In many ways the opening chapter, "Deciding Not to Fight," contains the heart of the book's message. In story after story, the subjects describe how they made up their minds to refuse military service or to apply for CO status. In many cases their choices put them in bitter confrontation with their fathers, some of whom had served in World War II and had accused their sons of lacking patriotism or even of treason. Subsequent chapters elaborate on the theme of consequences, with detailed narratives by men who faced arrest, trial, and incarceration; who performed alternative forms of service as medics in uniform or as members of civilian programs such as the Peace Corps; or who migrated to Canada or other foreign lands, living as fugitives.

In the book's introduction, Tollefson asserts that COs for the most part have been left out of the lingering national debate over the Vietnam intervention and the antiwar movement. Knowing that having been granted a CO deferment made him "one of the privileged few," Tollefson set out to gain a broader view of this subset of his generation. He states that he did not aim to politicize his subjects' experiences: "I was not interested in praising them or condemning them or apologizing for them. My goal was to understand and to accurately convey their experiences." He also expanded his range of interviewees beyond those who achieved CO status, including men who refused to register or report for induction.

Perhaps Tollefson's most important stylistic decision in constructing the book was not to identify his subjects by name. Anonymous interview excerpts, ranging in length from a few brief sentences to many pages, appear in a loose, impressionistic sequence. The oral testimony is organized under five chapter headings: "Deciding Not to Fight," "Trial and Imprisonment," "Serving My Country," "A Country Not My Own," and "Making Peace," which covers the men's "efforts to reconcile themselves with their parents, with their country, and with themselves, and to find their way in a future after Vietnam." Tollefson explains that his intention "was not to glorify individuals" but to tell a collective story. This editorial choice prevents the reader from following the development of any one man in particular; instead, the voices blend together in a kind of chorus.

CRITICAL DISCUSSION

Initial response to the book's publication, while mixed, was generally positive. In a review published on July 4, 1993, in the *Philadelphia Inquirer*, poet John Balaban, a Vietnam CO, states the book "reminds us that there are many kinds of courage." A 1993 article in *Kirkus Reviews* concludes that the book is "quiet, simple, disturbing: An invaluable contribution to the cultural history of the '60s." The reviewer notes that the stories included in the book were "to some extent depersonalized" because Tollefson declines to attribute the words. In a 1993 *Los Angeles Times* review, Chris Goodrich faults Tollefson for organizing the book thematically rather than through distinctive individual stories: "There's great material here, but its power is diluted" because "instead of start-to-finish narratives we get puzzle pieces that fit together only haphazardly."

The Strength Not to Fight appears in many bibliographies and resource lists pertaining to Vietnam, draft resistance, nonviolence, and oral history. Selections from the book have appeared in several anthologies. Most prominently, two excerpts appear in *Echoes from the Wall: History, Learning, and Leadership* (2001), a hefty curriculum guide distributed freely to every high school in the United States by the Vietnam Veterans Memorial Fund, the organization responsible for the Vietnam Veterans Memorial Wall next to the National Mall in Washington, D.C. Tollefson, a longtime professor of English, linguistics, and education, contributed the entry "Draft Resistance and Evasion" to *The Oxford Companion to American Military History* (2000).

Scholars have taken an interest in Tollefson's text as an example of an informal, "impressionistic and meditative" approach to the presentation of collected oral accounts. Writing in the *Oral History Review* in 1996, Jo Ann O. Robinson characterizes *The Strength Not to Fight* as "less an oral history than a mosaic of remembrances ... a concert of mixed voices and feelings." Tollefson's subjective treatment of the interview material is bound to frustrate researchers seeking more systematic access to the data, Robinson concedes. Yet she counters, "By random sampling, blurring of identities, avoidance of judgmental conclusions, and empathy, Tollefson captured contradictions, complexities, and depths of feeling that might well have escaped a more formal methodology."

BIBLIOGRAPHY

Sources

Balaban, John. Rev. of *The Strength Not to Fight: An Oral History of Conscientious Objectors of the Vietnam War*, by James W. Tollefson. *Philadelphia Inquirer* 4 July 1993: L3. Print.

Goodrich, Chris. Rev. of *The Strength Not to Fight: An Oral History of Conscientious Objectors of the Vietnam War*, by James W. Tollefson. *Los Angeles Times*. Los Angeles Times, 17 Oct. 1993. Web. 30 Jan. 2013.

Rev. of *The Strength Not to Fight: An Oral History of Conscientious Objectors of the Vietnam War*, by James W. Tollefson. *Kirkus Reviews*. Kirkus Reviews, 1 May 1993. Web. 1 Feb. 2013.

Robinson, Jo Ann O. "The Strength Not to Fight." *Oral History Review* (1996): 107–10. *Infotrac*. Web. 30 Jan. 2013.

Scruggs, Jan C., ed. *Echoes from the Wall: History, Learning, and Leadership*. Washington, D.C.: Vietnam Veterans Memorial Fund, 2001. Web. 30 Jan. 2013.

Tollefson, James W. *The Strength Not to Fight: An Oral History of Conscientious Objectors of the Vietnam War*. Boston: Little, Brown, 1993. Print.

Further Reading

Baskir, Lawrence M., and William A. Strauss. *Chance and Circumstance: The Draft, the War and the Vietnam Generation*. New York: Knopf, 1978. Print.

CONSCIENTIOUS OBJECTION

Throughout most of U.S. history, conscientious objection to armed service was predominantly associated with the so-called peace churches, principally the Religious Society of Friends (the Quakers), the Mennonites, and the Church of the Brethren. These faiths consistently maintained a religiously based condemnation of all forms of warfare. During the Revolutionary War, patriot authorities fined many Quakers—and imprisoned some—for seeking exemption from serving in the militia. The federal government first instituted the draft in 1863, during the Civil War (the Confederate government passed a conscription law in 1862). Exemption from service was limited to members of the pacifist religious denominations, provided that the applicant could either hire a substitute combatant or pay a sum of $300. During World War I, roughly four thousand conscientious objectors (COs) were sent to army camps for noncombatant service or, if they refused, were sequestered in prisons. After the United States entered the war in 1917, Quakers organized the American Friends Service Committee in order to create alternative service opportunities, including humanitarian work in France. Civilian Public Service camps in the United States provided similar work for twelve thousand COs during World War II.

In the Vietnam era, conscientious objection and draft resistance grew much more widespread. Two Supreme Court cases helped expand the possible routes to CO status. In *Seeger v. United States* (1965), the court ruled that while objection must be founded on religious conviction, an applicant could not be required to believe in a supreme being. The case of *Welsh v. United States* (1970) allowed draft boards to grant CO status to applicants based on fervently held ethical and moral, rather than strictly religious, principles.

Foley, Michael S. *Confronting the War Machine: Draft Resistance during the Vietnam War*. Chapel Hill: University of North Carolina Press, 2003. Print.

Gioglio, Gerald P. *Days of Decision: An Oral History of Conscientious Objectors in the Military during the Vietnam War*. Trenton, N.J.: Broken Rifle, 1988. Print.

Schlissel, Lillian, ed. *Conscience in America: A Documentary History of Conscientious Objection in America, 1757–1967*. New York: Dutton, 1968. Print.

Small, Melvin. *Antiwarriors: The Vietnam War and the Battle for America's Hearts and Minds*. Wilmington, Del.: Scholarly Resources, 2002. Print.

Stacewicz, Richard. *Winter Soldiers: An Oral History of the Vietnam Veterans against the War*. Chicago: Haymarket, 2008. Print.

Surrey, David Sterling. *Choice of Conscience: Vietnam Era Military and Draft Resisters in Canada*. New York: Praeger, 1982. Print.

Tollefson, James W. "Draft Resistance and Evasion." *The Oxford Companion to American Military History*. Ed. John W. Chambers II. New York: Oxford University Press, 2000. 236–38. Print.

Roger Smith

The Unknown Internment
An Oral History of the Relocation of Italian Americans during World War II
Stephen Fox

✣ Key Facts

Time Period:
Mid-20th Century

Relevant Historical Events:
World War II; internment of Italian Americans

Nationality:
American

Keywords:
internment; war; discrimination

OVERVIEW

Stephen Fox's *The Unknown Internment: An Oral History of the Relocation of Italian Americans during World War II* (1990) tells the little-known story of how Franklin Roosevelt's Executive Order 9066 affected the Italian American community in California. Rather than offering a collection of stand-alone oral histories, Fox intertwines throughout his narrative interviews with forty-three individuals who suffered curfews, relocation, loss of livelihood, separation from family, and even suicide as a result of this order. The stories serve to personalize a more general narrative about the U.S. treatment of "enemy aliens." The immigrants involved recount tales of loss, shame, and humiliation, while simultaneously exhibiting a remarkable degree of American patriotism despite their treatment.

Based upon interviews conducted in the mid-1980s and published in 1990, *The Unknown Internment* was generally welcomed by critics as an integral (yet heretofore ignored) piece of World War II home-front history. Hailed for its groundbreaking subject matter, Fox's book remains unique, as publications dealing with the plight of Italian Americans during World War II are few. While some early criticism of *The Unknown Internment* calls into question the factual validity of information included in certain interviews, the book continues to be a valuable source for those exploring lesser-known aspects of World War II.

HISTORICAL AND LITERARY CONTEXT

Executive Order 9066, signed by Roosevelt on February 19, 1942, authorized the removal of individuals with German, Italian, or Japanese origins living within fifty or sixty miles of the West Coast in the states of Washington, Oregon, California, and Arizona. While the discrimination against and internment of Japanese Americans as a result of this order are more widely known, German Americans and Italian Americans also suffered—at least initially. The relocation of these groups lasted only a short while (February to October 1942) and was not as extreme in numbers or severity as that of Japanese Americans; as a result, it remained a largely unknown chapter of U.S. history until the publication of Fox's book in 1990.

With World War II still raging in Europe and the United States entering the war after the Japanese attack on Pearl Harbor on December 7, 1941, fear and suspicion of "enemy aliens" ran deep on the West Coast of the United States. Although most citizens were chiefly suspect of Japanese Americans, Fox notes that "the most vocal Californians … wanted all of the enemy aliens out without delay." The War Department, represented by General John L. DeWitt, and the Federal Bureau of Investigation put pressure on the Justice Department, represented by Attorney General Francis Biddle, to take measures against "internal enemies"—Germans, Italians, and Japanese. Public hysteria and fear grew. Biddle had been reluctant to agree to the relocation project, but he capitulated under the pressure, paving the way for Executive Order 9066.

The Unknown Internment is not strict oral history in that it does not convey unmediated, unedited first-person narratives. (In this way, it is similar to Sherna B. Gluck's 1987 oral history, *Rosie the Riveter Revisited*.) However, it still fits comfortably into the tradition of American oral history, as Fox uses the stories of ordinary individuals to document his narrative. *The Unknown Internment* focuses on the issue of ethnic discrimination—similar to John Tateishi's *And Justice for All* (1984) and David Mas Masumoto's *Country Voices* (1987), which compile oral histories from the World War II–era Japanese American community. There are no comparable earlier works relaying the Italian American experience; until Fox's publication of *The Unknown Internment*, scholars had left the subject unexplored.

Subsequent to the *The Unknown Internment*, further scholarship—albeit relatively little—has been published, including Lawrence DiStasi's *Una Storia Segreta: The Secret History of Italian American Evacuation and Internment during World War II* (2001) and John Eric Schmitz's *Enemies among Us: The Relocation, Internment, and Repatriation of German, Italian, and Japanese Americans during the Second World War* (2007). In the late 1990s journalist James O. Clifford used newspapers, including the *Fort Worth Star-Telegram* and the *Washington Post*, to tell the stories of the Italian American wartime relocations.

THEMES AND STYLE

The central theme of *The Unknown Internment* is one of ethnic discrimination as well as an examination of the mixed emotions of its victims, who generally identify themselves as American and exhibit love for their country despite what they endured. For example, Joe Cervetto, a window washer from San Rafael, California, was arrested after showing war movies at his window washers' association meetings; he eventually was sent to Sharp Park internment camp. Still he explains, "Well, I didn't have any hate or anything. At that time my main objective was to work and make some money. I never got involved in taking sides or anything." Alex Frediani tells how his family was forced to move to a different town in California. Though they had to leave their home and their friends, he says, "As it turned out, [relocation] was the best thing that ever happened to us.... My dad bought a home and some property.... Property after the war went sky high. So the thing worked out well."

Fox is forthright in his proclamation that *The Unknown Internment* is "frankly revisionist." He uses his fresh World War II subject matter to contradict the popular assumption that Italian Americans were not seen as a wartime threat and to note that—as with Japanese Americans—they indeed suffered relocation, internment, and other persecutions. Fox also addresses why the Italian relocation was so comparatively short-lived. The reasons, he contends, were pragmatic. Italians were thought to be economically necessary to the war effort. Furthermore, Fox notes, Italian Americans were simply too large a component of the U.S. workforce to be further excluded. The author adeptly utilizes the oral history interviews to personalize the larger contexts of his work.

The Unknown Internment is written in a style accessible to the general public rather than in a scholarly tone. In the book's preface Fox states, "There ... is a role for history, to serve as a national conscience, to give us pause, not during sunshine patriotism's heady summer days, but during the cold, dark winter of national crises." His book serves to not only inform the reader about a largely unfamiliar topic but also to reinforce the lesson that "history repeats itself." Americans, he suggests, should guard against reoccurrence of such a shameful chapter in history. Fox places the blame for such mistreatment of Italian Americans squarely on the shoulders of bickering government agencies. He writes:

> The unseemly and debilitating squabbling within the government that had characterized policy making to this point continued for several more months. This unnecessary delay ... was entirely responsible for the extended relocation period endured by the aliens, and did nothing to enhance the nation's security. Virtually unnoticed was the fact that the lives of the aliens had been turned upside down by the relocation order.

A guard tower at the Manzanar internment camp (now called the Manzanar National Historic Site) at the foot of the Sierra Nevada. Although the detention of Japanese Americans during World War II is widely recognized, fewer people know that thousands of Italian Americans were also detained. © JASON O. WATSON/ALAMY

CRITICAL DISCUSSION

Initial reaction to *The Unknown Internment* was enthusiastic and complimentary, and the work received the American Book Award for "outstanding literary achievement" in 1992. Critics and book reviewers praised Fox's book as groundbreaking. George Pozzetta, in his 1993 review for the *International Migration Review*, particularly notes the oral-history qualities of the text: "The volume admirably achieves its primary purpose of telling an interesting and little known story, an accomplishment largely achieved through the use of the prisoners' own words." In a review for the *School Library Journal*, Mike Printz draws attention to the book's larger implications: "Fox exposes this previously untold chapter in American history. This neglected episode speaks to all readers concerned with our government's commitment to libertarian ideals." Other reviewers looked to what the book showed about ethnicities in the melting pot of the United States. As Andrew Rolle writes in *California History*, "One is reminded that important aspects of America's minority history remain unexplored." In a 1993 *Western Historical Quarterly*, Philip Notarianni suggests that the work "deserves the attention of students, teachers, and anyone interested in understanding the totality of the relocation movement during World War II."

Although they are few, there have been criticisms of the work. Roger Daniels, in a 1991 review for *Pacific Historical Review*, asserts, "Although *The Unknown*

AMERICA'S INVISIBLE GULAG

Stephen Fox's interest in the little-known aspects of World War II America rests not solely with the plight of Italian Americans. In June 2000 Fox also published *America's Invisible Gulag: A Biography of German American Internment and Exclusion in World War II*. As he did with the Italian Americans in *The Unknown Internment,* Fox used extensive interviews as a basis for this book. German Americans, having generally been ignored as victims of U.S. wartime policy, were finally given some notice in another bit of Fox's groundbreaking research.

Although *America's Invisible Gulag* did not draw as much attention as *The Unknown Internment* did, this can perhaps be seen as a credit to the author. Thanks perhaps to his pioneering research in the 1980s, accounts about treatment of U.S. ethnic minorities have become more commonplace.

Internment is a pioneering treatment of an important subject, it is seriously flawed by errors of conception, methodology, and execution." Daniels faults Fox for relying too heavily upon interviewee narrative and for poor use of secondary source material. It is worthwhile to note that Fox published a revised edition of the book in 2000, changing the title to *UnCivil Liberties: Italian Americans under Siege during World War II*. In its preface Fox writes, "This edition incorporates minor factual and editing changes, but the most significant alteration is the title." He further explains, "The previous title … and some of the original content … contributed to the confusion between 'relocation' and 'internment.'"

There is little recent scholarship regarding Fox's *The Unknown Internment*. Book reviews and critiques date from time of publication, and little other scholarly work exists. Despite this, *The Unknown Internment* remains an important piece of scholarship for its pioneering examination of a previously unexplored topic.

BIBLIOGRAPHY

Sources

Daniels, Roger. Rev. of *The Unknown Internment: An Oral History of the Relocation of Italian Americans during World War II,* by Stephen Fox. *Pacific Historical Review* 60.2 (1991): 268–69. *JSTOR.* Web. 31 Jan. 2013.

Fox, Stephen. *The Unknown Internment: An Oral History of the Relocation of Italian Americans during World War II.* Boston: Twayne, 1990. Print.

Notarianni, Philip F. Rev. of *The Unknown Internment: An Oral History of the Relocation of Italian Americans during World War II,* by Stephen Fox. *Western Historical Quarterly* 24.2 (1993): 249–50. *JSTOR.* Web. 31 Jan. 2013.

Pozzetta, George E. "Italian Prisoners of War in America, 1942–1946: Captives or Allies?" Rev. of *The Unknown Internment: An Oral History of the Relocation of Italian Americans during World War II,* by Stephen Fox. *International Migration Review* 27.3 (1993): 650. *Wiley Online Library.* Web. 31 Jan. 2013.

Printz, Mike. Rev. of *The Unknown Internment: An Oral History of the Relocation of Italian Americans during World War II,* by Stephen Fox. *School Library Journal* 36.11 (1990): 154. *EBSCO Magazines & Journals.* Web. 31 Jan. 2013.

Rolle, Andrew. Rev. of *The Unknown Internment: An Oral History of the Relocation of Italian Americans during World War II,* by Stephen Fox. *California History* 70.3 (1991): 316. *California Historical Society.* Web. 31 Jan. 2013.

Further Reading

DiStasi, Lawrence, ed. *Una Storia Segreta: The Secret History of Italian American Evacuation and Internment during World War II.* Berkeley, Calif.: Heyday, 2001. Print.

Krammer, Arnold. *Undue Process: The Untold History of America's German Alien Internees.* Lanham, Md: Rowman and Littlefield, 1997. Print.

Ng, Wendy L. *Japanese American Internment during World War II: A History and Reference Guide.* Westport, Conn.: Greenwood Press, 2002. Print.

Schmitz, John Eric. *Enemies among Us: The Relocation and Repatriation of German, Italian and Japanese Americans during the Second World War.* Diss. American University, 2007. *ProQuest.* Web. 31 Jan. 2013.

Lisa Mertel

"We Have Just Begun to Not Fight"
An Oral History of Conscientious Objectors in Civilian Public Service during World War II
Heather T. Frazer, John O'Sullivan

OVERVIEW

In *"We Have Just Begun to Not Fight": An Oral History of Conscientious Objectors in Civilian Public Service during World War II* (1996), Heather T. Frazer and John O'Sullivan present transcripts of twenty interviews carried out between the late 1970s and the early to mid-1990s, primarily with conscientious objectors who were veterans of the U.S. Civilian Public Service (CPS) in World War II. One subject played a leading role in administering the service, seventeen were CPS men, and two were wives of conscientious objectors. Though diverse in their accounts of what it meant to be a conscientious objector during wartime, these testimonies yield a shared sense of social responsibility and lasting commitment to living a principled life in the face of official adversity.

The CPS was designed to allow American conscientious objectors—men eligible for military service but who refused to fight—to work for their country during wartime without having to take up arms. Many (though by no means all) of the men who entered the CPS did so for religious reasons. During World War II, there was a great stigma attached to conscientious objectors, who were commonly stereotyped as "shirkers and cowards." Frazer and O'Sullivan's book brings greater understanding to a group of men all too often neglected in U.S. military history, many of whom undertook valiant civilian work for their country. Early reviewers deemed *"We Have Just Begun to Not Fight"* a highly valuable work with a broad appeal for scholarly and popular audiences alike; it remains a unique and useful text.

HISTORICAL AND LITERARY CONTEXT

The CPS grew out of the religious concerns of the "historic peace churches"—the Mennonites, Church of the Brethren, and Religious Society of Friends (Quakers)—whose faiths rest on principles of pacifism and nonviolence. Following World War I, church leaders sought alternative ways for conscientious objectors to fulfill service obligations without disregarding their articles of faith. Launched in 1941, the CPS was a joint project between the peace churches and the Selective Service System, the branch of government that ascertained who was eligible for military conscription. However, the CPS was open to believers from outside the peace churches and even to atheists. The point was to make provision for objectors to do meaningful work while avoiding the alternatives of noncombatant duty or prison.

The histories describe a wide range of experiences for the men of the CPS: between 1941 and 1947, some twelve thousand CPS men helped fight forest fires, worked as aides in mental hospitals, and volunteered as guinea pigs for medical experiments. Because these men were conscripted without pay, compensation, medical insurance, or dependents' allowances, frustration grew when the CPS extended the original one year of service to keep pace with the war. As a result, the idealism with which these men entered the CPS sometimes flagged. Frustration, however, also had its productive side when men assigned mundane work were inspired to look for more heroic opportunities (such as "smoke jumping"—parachuting into wild areas to fight fires).

Since the 1980s, conscientious objectors have gained increasing critical attention. Frazer and O'Sullivan's book takes its place in a field partially staked out by Robert Kreider's *Sourcebook: Oral History Interviews with World War One Conscientious Objectors* (1986) and Cynthia Eller's *Conscientious Objectors and the Second World War: Moral and Religious Arguments in Support of Pacifism* (1991). More recent contributions to this growing field include James W. Tollefson's *The Strength Not to Fight: An Oral History of Conscientious Objectors of the Vietnam War* (1993) and Steven J. Taylor's *Acts of Conscience: World War II, Mental Institutions, and Religious Objectors* (2009).

As Frazer and O'Sullivan remind us, in the early twentieth century conscientious objection was not only a criminal but a capital offense. The histories of the CPS men reveal attempts to decriminalize conscientious objection, a fact relevant well beyond the context of the World War II. As Frazer and O'Sullivan put it, "although these interviews deal with events that occurred a half century ago, they retain great relevance for the post–Cold War era as the United States redefines its world role." Though the military draft is no longer in force, young men in the United States are

✥ **Key Facts**

Time Period:
Mid-20th Century

Relevant Historical Events:
Establishment of the U.S. Civilian Public Service; World War II

Nationality:
American

Keywords:
pacifism; war; conscientious objection

WAR EXPERIENCES

American film actor and conscientious objector Lew Ayres, serving as a noncombatant medic in the Philippines during World War II, treats injured Japanese prisoners of war in a field hospital, December 1944. © AP IMAGES

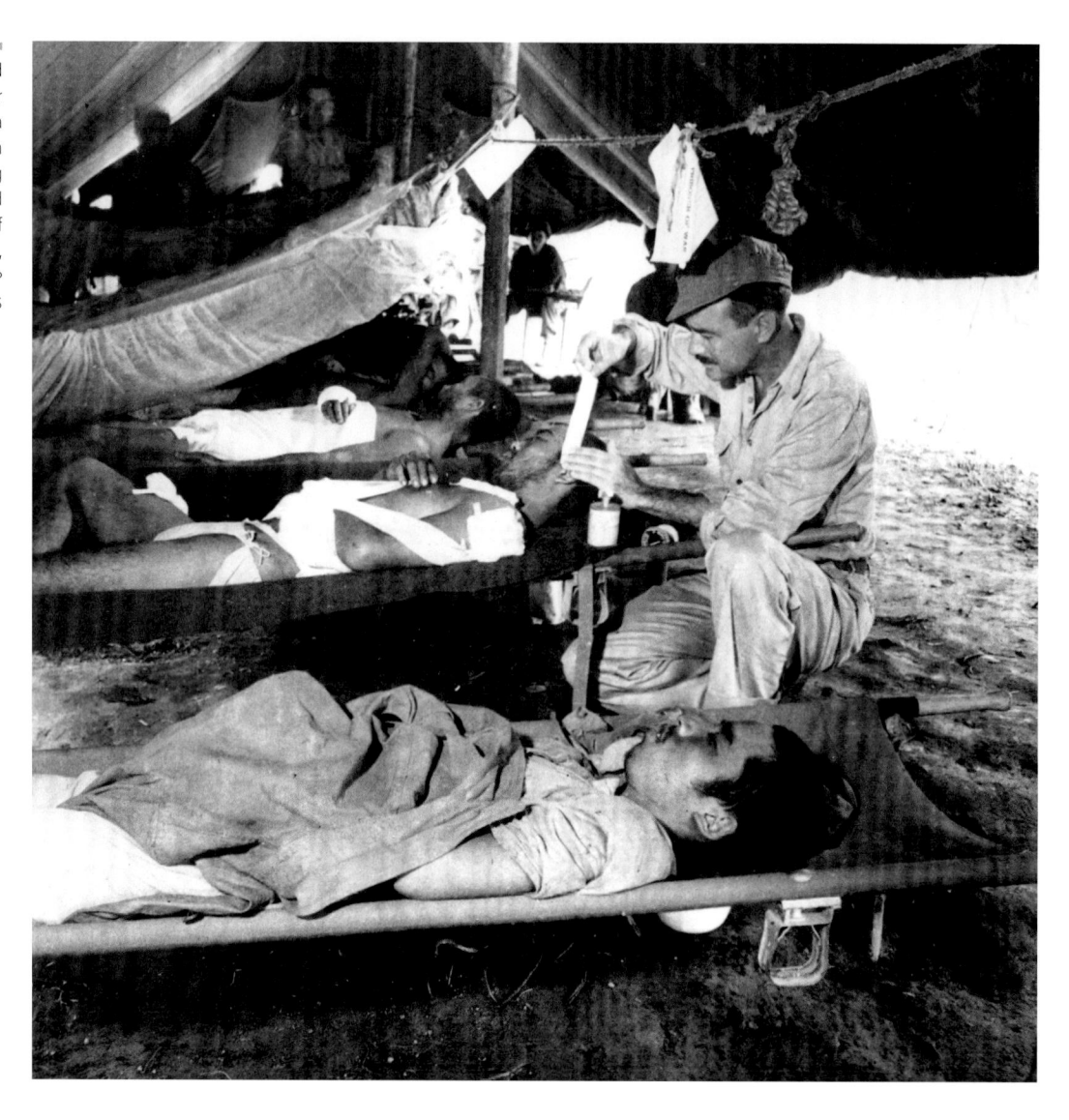

still obliged to register for Selective Service. "*We Have Just Begun to Not Fight*" marks a moment when the government conceded the right for resisters to seek alternative legal methods to serve the United States in times of national emergency.

THEMES AND STYLE

Throughout these histories, the constant theme is that of the pacifist struggling to resist taking up arms in the face of official (legal) pressures. For many, the greatest influence on their pacifist philosophy was religious upbringing. As one CPS man, Herman Will, makes clear, this did not necessarily entail "religious convictions from the Bible, I couldn't quite say that. It was mostly deep religious convictions which were embedded in my background of the family and the church really. I never was what you would call a rebellious type." Yet not all the CPS men attribute the development of their pacifism to religion. Gordon Zahn, for example, found his inspiration in popular culture: in children's stories about cowboys and Indians and war films that made the wrong impression by glorifying killing. Still others learned the more positive lessons from the political and ethical writings of Henry David Thoreau, Leo Tolstoy, and Mohandas Gandhi. The accounts range widely in the ways they express pacifism—here as a gut sentiment, there as a practical philosophy.

The authors describe their project as a "convergence of two research interests…. John O'Sullivan had written on the draft during World War II, then began examining the experiences of conscientious objectors during that war. Heather Frazer, with a background in women's history, brought a focus on the often neglected role of their wives and families." Their overall intention is to enrich our understanding of the exercise of conscience, as opposed to cowardice, in wartime, with specific attention to one project too-often overlooked in the history books. The result is a series of heavily directed interviews, with Frazer and

O'Sullivan's questions leading the speakers along particular lines of thought about the CPS and its legacy.

Excluding introduction and conclusion, the book is divided into six chapters. The first contains accounts of how the CPS was organized and managed, the second deals with the specific experiences of historic peace church members, and the third with men outside that tradition. In the fourth chapter we hear from men who left the CPS in protest (for example, after the bombing of Hiroshima) and went to jail; those in the fifth chapter pursued work beyond the mundane, volunteering, for instance, in medical experiments on the effects of starvation; the sixth and final chapter collects general reflections on the CPS experience. Each chapter contains between two and six speakers, each given his own section (except where husband and wife appear together). A small number of photographs illustrate the variety of the work experiences, showing the men in action, from teaching at the chalkboard to parachuting from an airplane.

CRITICAL DISCUSSION

Early reviewers found much to praise in *"We Have Just Begun to Not Fight"*. In a *Booklist* review, Ray Olson labeled the collection "spellbinding" and "awe inspiring." Geoffrey Smith, writing for the *Journal of American History*, commended the compilers for "bring[ing] a high degree of nuance and sophistication to the questions they ask." Edgar F. Raines Jr., historian for the U.S. Army Center of Military History starting in 1980, noted the book's broad appeal, describing a "handsome volume [that] will interest students of World War II, the peace movement, American religions, and mental health." More critically, Raines drew attention to the fact that "Frazer and O'Sullivan omit any discussion of the provenance of these interesting texts. When and where were the interviews conducted? Are they presented as transcribed?" For anyone interested in the archive, Raines's are legitimate concerns.

"We Have Just Begun to Not Fight" constitutes a powerful meditation with lasting significance. This is especially true when considering just how many American and European military personnel in recent years have jeopardized personal safety in acts of disobedience and resistance: most spectacularly in the case of U.S. army private Bradley Manning, who was charged with releasing classified documents to disclosure activists WikiLeaks, but also in the cases of Sergeant Kevin Benderman (in the United States), Malcolm Kendall-Smith (in Great Britain), and Mehmet Tarhan (in Turkey). As such, Frazer and O'Sullivan give us invaluable insight into not so much one particular world war but a certain perennial worldview worthy of continued investigation.

Although scholars have yet to discuss *"We Have Just Begun to Not Fight"* in its own right, the subject of conscientious objectors has been taken up in a number of recent studies, most notably by Lloy Kniss (*I Couldn't Fight and Other CO Stories, 1917–1960*), Edward Arnett

TWENTY-FIRST-CENTURY CONSCIENTIOUS OBJECTORS

Though the draft is no longer in operation in the United States, young men must register with the Selective Service System, which, according to the U.S. government website, participates in the "national preparedness community." This system's statutory mission is "to be prepared to provide trained and untrained personnel to the DoD [Department of Defense] in the event of a national emergency and to be prepared to implement an Alternative Service Program for registrants classified as conscientious objectors." The government recognizes objectors who refuse armed service based on religious, moral, or ethical grounds; it makes a point of excluding reasons for refusal based on "politics, expediency, or self-interest." Without the option of the Civilian Public Service program, which was terminated following the end of World War II, officially recognized conscientious objectors currently have two options: if classified 1-A-O, they serve within the armed forces in a noncombatant capacity; if classified 1-O, they fulfill their service obligation under the Alternative Service Program. Typically, the Alternative Service Program places individuals with local employers in jobs deemed significant for the health and safety of the nation—primarily in the conservation, health care, and education sectors. These provisions owe much to the peace church workers who, between the world wars, sought to protect objectors from persecution.

(*A Different Kind of War Story: A Conscientious Objector in World War II*), and Robert Cottrell (*Smokejumpers of the Civilian Public Service in World War II: Conscientious Objectors as Firefighters for the National Forest Service*). Aiming for a broader perspective, meanwhile, is Rosalie Riegle's *Doing Time for Peace: Resistance, Family, and Community*, a collection of oral histories from those who resisted from World War II to the second Iraq War. These and similar texts provide Frazer and O'Sullivan with fine critical company.

BIBLIOGRAPHY

Sources

Cottrell, Robert C. *Smokejumpers of the Civilian Public Service in World War II: Conscientious Objectors as Firefighters for the National Forest Service*. Jefferson, NC: McFarland, 2006. Print.

Frazer, Heather T., and John O'Sullivan, eds. *"We Have Just Begun to Not Fight": An Oral History of Conscientious Objectors in Civilian Public Service during World War II*. New York: Twayne, 1996.

Olson, Ray. Rev. of *"We Have Just Begun to Not Fight": An Oral History of Conscientious Objectors in the Civilian Public Service during World War II*, by Heather T. Frazer and John O'Sullivan. *Booklist* 15 Dec. 1995: 683. *Gale Literature Resource Center*. Web. 17 Jan. 2013.

Raines, Edgar F., Jr. Rev. of *"We Have Just Begun to Not Fight": An Oral History of Conscientious Objectors in the Civilian Public Service during World War II*, by Heather T. Frazer and John O'Sullivan. *Political Science Quarterly* 111.3 (1996): 560–61. *JSTOR.* Web. 17 Jan. 2013.

Smith, Geoffrey S. Rev. of *"We Have Just Begun to Not Fight": An Oral History of Conscientious Objectors in the Civilian Public Service during World War II*, by Heather T. Frazer and John O'Sullivan. *Journal of American History* 84.2 (1997): 405–35. *Proquest.* Web. 17 Jan. 2013.

Further Reading

Arnett, Edward M. *A Different Kind of War Story: A Conscientious Objector in World War II.* Bloomington, IN: Xlibris, 2012. Print.

Kniss, Lloy. *I Couldn't Fight and Other CO Stories, 1917–1960.* Ephrata, Pa. Eastern Mennonite, 2002. Print.

Kovac, Jeffrey. *Refusing War, Affirming Peace: A History of Civilian Public Service Camp #21 at Cascade Locks.* Corvallis: Oregon State University Press, 2009. Print.

Riegle, Rosalie, ed. *Doing Time for Peace: Resistance, Family, and Community.* Nashville, TN: Vanderbilt University Press, 2012. Print.

Terkel, Studs. *"The Good War": An Oral History of World War II.* New York: New Press, 1997. Print.

David Aitchison

WHAT WAS ASKED OF US
An Oral History of the Iraq War by the Soldiers Who Fought It
Trish Wood

OVERVIEW

Trish Wood's *What Was Asked of Us: An Oral History of the Iraq War by the Soldiers Who Fought It* (2006) presents the combat experiences of twenty-nine veterans serving from 2003 through 2005. Divided into four sections that cover the war from invasion to occupation, the book depicts urban warfare in up-close graphic detail. The narratives in *What Was Asked of Us* describe the difficulty of conducting combat operations against insurgents seated among—and often indistinguishable from—civilians, many of whom, while innocent, had no love for coalition forces. Comprising accounts of the war that exhibit everything from matter-of-fact acceptance to anguished remorse, the book also explores the lingering effects of combat on the troops who survive it.

Published while the Iraq War was still ongoing, *What Was Asked of Us* received mixed reviews. While some critics praised the honesty and realism of the book's narratives, others suggested Canadian-born Wood used her editorial power to emphasize the war's carnage, conveying an antiwar message in focus if not overtly in prose. Regardless of these criticisms, the book is historically important as it offers firsthand accounts of combat in Iraq. *What Was Asked of Us* has also been heralded as an opportunity to understand and better support veterans as they return to civilian life.

HISTORICAL AND LITERARY CONTEXT

The narratives in *What They Asked of Us* reflect the brutal nature of combat in Iraq. The U.S.-led action commenced with the bombing campaign of March 2003, which was quickly followed by a ground invasion resulting in the fall of Baghdad in April. Unprepared for such an early victory, coalition forces fought to secure cities, train Iraqi security forces, and begin reconstruction without a well-developed, widely communicated plan in place. Out of the chaos an Iraqi insurgency began to take shape, and attacks on U.S. forces increased through the summer and fall, particularly in Baghdad and in the western cities of Fallujah and Tikrit. Revelations that came the following April about the mistreatment of Iraqi insurgents at the Abu Ghraib prison further intensified anger against American troops. While the establishment of democracy in Iraq was marked by the first elections in January 2005, the country remained unstable, necessitating the continuing presence of occupying forces until the last of the U.S. forces pulled out of the country in December 2011.

Fighting between coalition troops and Iraqi insurgents mainly occurred in urban environments, such as the city cemetery described by marine Seth Moulton. In these environments action could quickly spiral out of control. Moulton says of the cemetery, "All of a sudden, here we're only a hundred meters in and we're already getting surrounded. There was a sense that we could be overrun at any time." In these urban environments the presence of Iraqi civilians also complicated already difficult operations. Indeed the distinction between civilians and nonuniformed insurgents was difficult to detect. The use of rocket-propelled grenades and improvised explosive devices became widespread, causing devastating injuries. Many of the "thin-skinned" Humvees and other vehicles in use by the U.S. military proved inadequate to protect troops from these hazards, leading to anger and low morale among those fighting. Troop morale was also impacted by the unpopularity of the war at home and the lack of social and occupational supports for returning veterans.

What Was Asked of Us is heir to the gritty realism of an earlier generation of combat stories from the Vietnam War. Oral histories such as Al Santoli's *Everything We Had* (1981) and Mark Baker's *Nam: The Vietnam War in the Words of the Men and Women Who Fought There* (1981) present firsthand experiences of harrowing combat and address the lasting impact of these experiences on the people who fought. *Bloods: An Oral History of the Vietnam War by Black Veterans* (1984) by Wallace Terry is also part of this tradition, although it engages more specifically with race issues within the military, a theme largely absent from *What Was Asked of Us* due to its emergence in the post–civil rights era of the early twenty-first century.

Several additional oral histories of the Iraq War followed the publication of *What Was Asked of Us*. In addition to the accounts of troops, Carl Mirra's *Soldiers and Citizens: An Oral History of Operation Iraqi Freedom from the Battlefield to the Pentagon* (2008) presents views of the war from the eyes of soldiers' loved ones, as well as some of the policy makers and pundits involved in steering and covering the war

Key Facts

Time Period:
Early 21st Century

Relevant Historical Events:
Iraq War

Nationality:
American

Keywords:
war; occupation; casualties

A marine specialist at Camp War Eagle, Iraq, 2004. American veterans of the Iraq War recount their military experiences in *What Was Asked of Us: An Oral History of the Iraq War by the Soldiers Who Fought It* by Trish Wood. © BARBARA DAVIDSON/ DALLAS MORNING NEWS/ CORBIS

effort. *Winter Soldier: Iraq and Afghanistan: Eyewitness Accounts of the Occupations,* compiled under the aegis of Iraq Veterans against the War, reprints testimony of various veterans at the Winter Soldier summit in 2008. This latter book differs from *What Was Asked of Us* in its explicitly antiwar message.

THEMES AND STYLE

The narratives in *What Was Asked of Us* focus on the horrors and the heroism of combat as well as on the painful incongruity of war experiences with the civilian life that precedes and follows them. In addition they also address the nature of the Iraq War itself, particularly the unavoidable yet devastating civilian deaths that resulted from urban combat with Iraqi insurgents. *What Was Asked of Us* is full of harrowing accounts of troops physically torn to pieces. Navy Cross recipient Justin LeHeew recalls performing a rescue in the aftermath of a friendly-fire incident in Nasiriya. "I handed Doc half a marine and said 'Put this in the back of the Humvee because marines don't leave our dead and wounded on the battlefield'; everybody comes home. Even if it's a piece of you I have a responsibility to your mom and dad to bring everything back." Infantryman Jeff Engel carries with him the image of a little girl's sandal with the foot still in it "burned and smoldered and just sitting there on the side of the road" in Diyala Province. Surgeon Earl Hecker calls the "catastrophically wounded young people" he worked on a "lost generation" and laments the fact that for many Americans the wounded are "out of sight, out of mind."

In his introduction to the book, Vietnam veteran Bobby Muller provides a compelling summary of the book's purpose: "It tells those that fought that others feel as they do, and it tells those who didn't fight what their returning family member feels, the personal toll war takes." To this end Wood focuses heavily on combat's gruesome details and the range of responses by the soldiers who witnessed them, some of whom did not feel the full impact until they returned to civilian life and had time to reflect. Like *Bloods* author Wallace Terry before her, Wood was criticized by a number of reviewers for heavy-handed editing of the interview transcripts, the practice of which has sparked a long-standing debate in oral history.

The narrative titled "It Is Gruesome to Just beyond the Level of a Horror Film" aptly describes the tone and language of *What Was Asked of Us*, which contains numerous accounts of death and devastating injuries. Throughout the text Wood intersperses recollections of Daniel Cotnoir, a marine tasked with "mortuary affairs" whose recollection of sights such as a stretcher loaded with "nine arms and ten legs and parts of another one" finds an echo in many of the other soldiers' accounts.

That these horrors, often related in the grimly dispassionate tone of those who have seen too much, further underlines the hell of war Wood is trying to convey.

CRITICAL DISCUSSION

What Was Asked of Us received a mixed reception from reviewers. Writing in the *New York Times Book Review*, Tara McKelvey calls the book "polemically edited" but also notes that "the firsthand accounts are honest, agenda-free and chilling." Kathy English's review in *Biography* was more uniformly complimentary, lauding the "emotionally powerful, post-war recollections" as an "important addition to the history of this 21st century war." In *Military Review*, Michele Miller—while expressing reservations about Wood's objectivity—affirms, "Stories appropriately titled 'I didn't pray for the Iraqis' to 'We just killed a bunch of dudes who were on our side' will appeal to most veterans."

Miller's review also touches upon the lasting value of *What Was Asked of Us*, the promotion of an understanding of "the magnitude of combat effects" on soldiers. This understanding is valuable to military tacticians and commanders, who must consider it in devising operations and leading troops. It is also valuable to civilians, who Bobby Muller describes in his introduction as "cocooned in their own worlds" and unaware of the trauma weighing on the hearts of veterans returning from fighting thousands of miles away. For these veterans, the book also offers a record of common experiences that are notoriously difficult to discuss, but the sharing of them may, as Miller's review suggests, "help our combat veterans achieve catharsis."

The firsthand accounts in *What Was Asked of Us* have been used to study posttraumatic recovery in veterans of the Iraq War. In "Posttraumatic Growth Themes: An Analysis of Oral Histories of OIF Service Members and Veterans", scholar Sesali Storm Thrasher analyzes eight of the narratives in Wood's book for ways in which combat experiences promoted personal growth. While acknowledging the small sample size, Thrasher concludes that many troops do see some benefits from combat, although "the presence of growth does not necessarily signal an end to psychological wounds accompanied by traumatic experiences."

BIBLIOGRAPHY

Sources

English, Kathy. Rev. of *What Was Asked of Us: An Oral History of the Iraq War by the Soldiers Who Fought It*, comp. Trish Wood. *Biography* 30.2 (2007): 307. Literature Resource Center. Web. 29 Jan. 2013.

McKelvey, Tara. Rev. of *What Was Asked of Us: An Oral History of the Iraq War by the Soldiers Who Fought It*, comp. Trish Wood. *New York Times Book Review* 4 Feb. 2007: 19+. Web. 29 Jan. 2013.

Miller, Michele. Rev. of *What Was Asked of Us: An Oral History of the Iraq War by the Soldiers Who Fought It*, comp. Trish Wood. *Military Review* 87.4 (2007). Questia. Web. 30 Jan. 2013.

IMPROVISED EXPLOSIVE DEVICES

The use of improvised explosive devices (IEDs) has been traced back to World War II, but the devices have been more typically used in conflicts involving insurgent groups, such as the Mujahidin who waged war against the Soviet Union in Afghanistan during the 1980s. IED design and construction evolved in Afghanistan, and the devices used against coalition troops following the country's invasion in 2001 often incorporated cell phones to detonate the explosives. The devices were easy to bury in the country's unpaved roads and were responsible for numerous deaths and injuries.

IEDs were also a significant factor in Iraq, as evidenced by the stories in *What Was Asked of Us*. While harder to hide on Iraq's mostly paved roadways, the devices were a constant threat and complicated tactical operations for troops, as convoys would often languish as bomb-clearing teams completed painstaking searches in advance of troop movements. In addition, troops protested the lack of sufficient armor on the Humvees used extensively in Iraq. According to Mathew Winn, a marine who served in Ramadi, "all the guys that have been wounded or killed from Humvees without armor would have been OK if we'd only had the right gear."

Muller, Bobby. Introduction. *What Was Asked of Us: An Oral History of the Iraq War by the Soldiers Who Fought It*, comp. Trish Wood. New York: Little, Brown, 2006. xiii–xviii. Print.

Thrasher, Sesali Storm. "Posttraumatic Growth Themes: An Analysis of Oral Histories of OIF Service Members and Veterans." *McNair Scholars Journal* 13 (2011): 199–214. Web. 31 Jan. 2013.

Wood, Trish, comp. *What Was Asked of Us: An Oral History of the Iraq War by the Soldiers Who Fought It*. New York: Little, Brown, 2006. Print.

Further Reading

Ferrari, Michelle, comp., and James Tobin, commentator. *Reporting America at War: An Oral History.* New York: Hyperion, 2003. Print.

Filkins, Dexter. *The Forever War.* New York: Knopf, 2008. Print.

Iraq Veterans against the War, and Aaron Glantz. *Winter Soldier: Iraq and Afghanistan: Eyewitness Accounts of the Occupations.* Chicago: Haymarket, 2008. Print.

Keegan, John. *The Iraq War.* New York: Knopf, 2004. Print.

Kennedy, Kelly. *They Fought for Each Other: The Triumph and Tragedy of the Hardest Hit Unit in Iraq.* New York: St. Martin's Press, 2010. Print.

Mirra, Carl. *Soldiers and Citizens: An Oral History of Operation Iraqi Freedom from the Battlefield to the Pentagon.* Basingstoke, UK: Palgrave, 2008. Print.

Santoli, Al. *Everything We Had: An Oral History of the Vietnam War.* New York: Random House, 1981. Print.

Daisy Gard

THE WORLD AT WAR
Richard Holmes

✥ Key Facts

Time Period:
Mid-20th Century

Relevant Historical Events:
World War II

Nationality:
British

Keywords:
war; genocide; nationalism

OVERVIEW

Edited by renowned military historian Richard Holmes, *The World at War* (2007) draws on hundreds of interview transcripts to present a narrative of World War II. Holmes weaves this collection together from interviews conducted between 1971 and 1973 by the producers of the landmark British Thames Television series of the same name, which first aired in October 1973. Holmes collected more than two hundred interviewee testimonies for his book, encompassing a wealth of different perspectives on the war and ranging from civilians to high-ranking diplomats, servicemen to generals. Although the oral histories were collected at the height of the Cold War, thus restricting interviewers' access to perspectives on the Eastern Front, *The World at War* nevertheless provides a detailed, nearly comprehensive tapestry of the twentieth century's deadliest conflict.

The original 1973 television broadcast of *The World at War* was heralded as a remarkable achievement in historical television programming and as the definitive documentary of World War II. Prior to the publication of Holmes's 2007 book, however, most of the project's oral histories remained locked in an archive in London's Imperial War Museum, inaccessible due to a litany of copyright restrictions. While some critics faulted Holmes's collection as being more of a pastiche and less of a true narrative, the book nevertheless marks the opening of the archive to the public; on that account it has been a great success. Taken together, Thames Television's documentary and Holmes's *The World at War* have made a lasting contribution to the memory of World War II.

HISTORICAL AND LITERARY CONTEXT

The eyewitness accounts collected in *The World at War* chronicle all of World War II, from the rise of Nazism in Germany and militarism in Japan through the Nuremberg trials following the war's conclusion. The Treaty of Versailles—which officially concluded World War I on June 28, 1919—assigned blame for the war to Germany, and the sanctions and reparations imposed severely hindered Germany's economic recovery. This created a great deal of resentment among the German people and provided the fertile soil in which the fiercely nationalistic outlook of the Nazi Party took root. Similarly, an ethos of unjust disenfranchisement among the Japanese populace fostered the growth of militaristic nationalism. The Japanese had won decisive victories in both the Sino-Japanese War (1894–1895) and the Russo-Japanese War (1904–1905), but many Japanese felt that the Japan-Russia Treaty of Peace, mediated by the U.S. president Theodore Roosevelt, was unfairly biased against Japan.

Germany's invasion of Poland in September 1939 drew declarations of war from both Britain and France. Although the United States was actively aiding the British—providing supplies and even repairing British naval ships in U.S. ports—it did not formally declare war until Japan's devastating surprise attack on Pearl Harbor, Hawaii, on December 7, 1941. However, the country was moving toward a declaration of war prior to Pearl Harbor. In *The World at War*, interviewee John McCloy, the U.S. assistant secretary of war, declares, "I've no question that the trend was towards an intervention in the war and I'm inclined to think it would not have been far removed," even if the Japanese had not attacked.

The World at War television series, for which these oral histories were collected, was by no means the first World War II documentary. In 1949 ABC Television produced *Crusade in Europe,* and in 1952 NBC produced *Victory at Sea.* In a 2011 article for *Historical Journal of Film, Radio and Television,* historian James Chapman suggests that the most "direct antecedent of *The World at War* was the BBC's *The Great War* (1964)"—not only in for its twenty-six-episode format but more importantly for combining original war footage with oral history. A significant predecessor to Holmes's oral history was Studs Terkel's *"The Good War": An Oral History of World War II,* which won the Pulitzer Prize for nonfiction in 1985. However, the two differ significantly in scope; Terkel's work is centered on America's involvement in the war, while Holmes's—although perhaps slightly skewed toward Britain—is more global in its focus.

The television series is widely recognized as having created a new benchmark for historical documentaries. Chapman recounts historian Arthur Marwick's opinion that the series "set new standards for prodigious research and integrity of presentation." Although Holmes's 2007 book was not met with the same acclaim as its television antecedent, it is especially noteworthy for its comprehensive scale. Subsequent oral histories, such as Nicholas Best's *Five Days That Shocked the World* (2012), about the last days of the war in Europe, pale by comparison. In the introduction to *The World at War,* Holmes recalls his joy at the breadth of archival information he had at his command: "Although, at this stage in my life, I am not easily impressed, there was a real sense of excitement and discovery."

THEMES AND STYLE

As the title suggests, the work's signature theme is the breadth of World War II, not only on diplomats, politicians, and generals, but on civilians the world over. Included in the chapter "Stalingrad and the Eastern Front" are the voices of such notable military figures as Albert Speer, who was Adolf Hitler's armaments minister, and Colonel General Nikolai Lomov, who was the deputy head of operations for the Soviet Red Army. Also included are the voices of soldiers in the trenches from both sides, including Albrecht Schimpf and Private Anton Bosnik. Other oral histories in the same chapter are those from a member of the Hitler Youth, a Leningrad housewife, and a student involved in the Warsaw uprising.

Holmes explains in the introduction that he edited *The World at War* to highlight the war's impact on common people. By placing the chapters on civilian bombing and the Holocaust in the middle of the book, he emphasizes that "the signature feature of the Second World War was the literally unimaginable civilian death-toll. Our minds may not shrink from it, but they are simply unable to encompass it." His decision to do so is best illustrated by the oral histories themselves. A Red Cross worker in Cologne, Germany, during the height of the Allied raids recalls that the city "was a wall of flames.... Mothers came to me who had themselves very severe burns who were scarcely capable of life, with their children in their arms, begging for help. We saw it was pointless." Even more chilling is the story of Holocaust survivor Rivka Yoselevska: "I saw three or four rows, twelve people already killed. My little daughter asked, 'Mother, why are you wearing your Sabbath dress? They are going to kill us.' … He asked, 'Whom do I shoot first?' I didn't answer. He tore the child away from me. I heard her last cry and he shot her."

In addition to Holmes's editorial decisions regarding chapter order and length, and his short introductions to each chapter, he weaves various interviews together rather than simply quoting each interviewee's transcript one at a time, playing their perspectives off one another. Utilizing not only the initial television series interviews—and at much greater length—Holmes includes voices unheard in the original documentary, extracting 280 of the archive's 368 transcripts. As he writes in the introduction, he omitted "numerous ums and errs" while "tidying up the transcripts" and occasionally "remedied some of the more obvious translation errors." On the whole, the collection directly reflects the original transcripts housed at the Imperial War Museum.

Esteemed British author and academic Richard Holmes in 2009.
© GERAINT LEWIS/ALAMY

CRITICAL DISCUSSION

Immediately following its publication in 2007, *The World at War* enjoyed a mostly positive critical reception. In a 2007 review for *Spectator,* Philip Ziegler writes that it is "skillfully edited," and in terms of remembering World War II, the book is "as near the truth as one can get." Less laudatory was Taylor Downing's 2007 review in the *Observer.* Downing recognizes the archive as a great asset but finds fault with Holmes's collection: "the book feels made up of fragments," which "doesn't make for a good read." Furthermore, he criticizes Holmes for using only interviews collected in the early 1970s, when important historical perspectives on the war—such as the breaking of Germany's Enigma code—was not yet common knowledge but had since come to light.

Scholarship on Holmes's book is minimal, although the original *World at War* documentary series has enjoyed a long and influential legacy. In a 2008 article in *Oral History,* Steve Humphries calls the series "fantastic," saying it "set the highest production standards for oral history on television." Perhaps even more profound is what the series did for Holocaust awareness. Pulitzer and Tony Award–winning playwright Tony Kushner, in a 2001 article for *Oral History,* calls *The World at War*'s episode on the Holocaust "pathbreaking" and a "crucial turning point" in the evolution of the Holocaust as a solvent historical concept, one which was "still evolving in Britain at the time."

RICHARD HOLMES AND TELEVISION HISTORY

In addition to his many works in print, Richard Holmes was involved in the production of historical television long before he was asked to edit *The World at War*. For example, *Battlefields* (1994–2002) and *War Walks* (1996–2010) were successful BBC series written and presented by Holmes. In a 2007 letter to the *Guardian*, he salutes the original *World at War* series: "However much I resent being called a television historian, there is no denying that I am a product of the television age."

Not only did he grow up admiring *The Great War* (1964) on BBC, but upon seeing *The World at War* while in graduate school, he "was captivated at once." This familiarity with television history gave him a unique perspective as he edited *The World at War*, one that allowed him to anticipate criticism of the book. Taylor Downing, in a 2007 review in the *Observer*, calls the book a rough, nonnarrative read that relies on old, perhaps outdated interviews. However, in the introduction to *The World at War*, Holmes acknowledges both of these issues: "the great virtue of the material lay not in its narrative detail but in its impressionistic quality." Quoting historian and interviewee Noble Frankland, he writes that one should recognize that the material was "not just about the war itself, 'but how it appeared to these people in 1971–3' as well."

While most scholars hold *The World at War* documentary in high, almost peerless esteem, Chapman questions conventional wisdom, especially regarding initial reactions to the series. He points out, "the critical and popular reception of the series … were rather more mixed" than is commonly thought. Examining letters from viewers as well as published reviews, he concludes that responses ranged "from adulation to outrage" and that scholars ought to view the series' reception as "more complex … than has hitherto been acknowledged." Nonetheless, he recognizes the series as a landmark in historical television, one that "anticipated the emergence of oral history as a method of historical inquiry."

BIBLIOGRAPHY

Sources

Chapman, James. "Television and History: *The World at War*." *Historical Journal of Film, Radio and Television* 31.2 (2011): 247–75. *JSTOR*. Web. 22 Jan. 2013.

Downing, Taylor. "Witness to the Greatest War of All." Rev. of *The World at War*, by Richard Holmes. *Observer*. Guardian News and Media, 29 Sept. 2007. Web. 28 Jan. 2013.

Holmes, Richard. "Witness Programme." *Guardian*. Guardian News and Media, 9 Nov. 2007. Web. 24 Jan. 2013.

———. *The World at War*. London: Ebury, 2007. Print.

Humphries, Steve. "Oral History on Television: A Retrospective." *Oral History* 36.2 (2008): 99–106. *JSTOR*. Web. 29 Jan. 2013.

Kushner, Tony. "Oral History at the Extremes of Human Experience: Holocaust Testimony in a Museum Setting." *Oral History* 29.2 (2001): 83–94. *JSTOR*. Web. 29 Jan. 2013.

Ziegler, Philip. "And When They Ask Us How Dangerous It Was." Rev. of *The World at War*, by Richard Holmes. *Spectator*. Spectator, 16 Oct. 2007. Web. 29 Jan. 2013.

Further Reading

Cook, Haruko Taya, and Theodore F. Cook. *Japan at War: An Oral History*. New York: New Press, 1992. Print.

Frazer, Heather T., and John O'Sullivan, eds. *"We Have Just Begun to Not Fight": An Oral History of Conscientious Objectors in the Civilian Public Service during World War II*. New York: Twayne, 1996. Print.

Iacobelli, Teresa. "'A Participant's History?': The Canadian Broadcasting Corporation and the Manipulation of Oral History." *Oral History Review* 38.2 (2011): 331–48. *JSTOR*. Web. 22 Jan. 2013.

Mattheisen, Donald J. "Persuasive History: A Critical Comparison of Television's *Victory at Sea* and *The World at War*." *History Teacher* 25.2 (1992): 239–51. *JSTOR*. Web. 29 Jan. 2013.

Terkel, Studs. *"The Good War": An Oral History of World War II*. New York: Pantheon, 1984. Print.

Elliott Niblock

Witnessing History

Children of Los Alamos: An Oral History of the Town Where the Atomic Bomb Began by Katrina Mason — 239

Country of My Skull: Guilt, Sorrow, and the Limits of Forgiveness in the New South Africa by Antjie Krog — 242

The Firm: The Inside Story of the Stasi by Gary Bruce — 245

Freedom Flyers: The Tuskegee Airmen of World War II by J. Todd Moye — 248

An Ill-Fated People: Zimbabwe before and after Rhodes by Lawrence Chinyani Vambe — 251

Launching the War on Poverty: An Oral History by Michael L. Gillette — 254

Machete Season: The Killers in Rwanda Speak by Jean Hatzfeld — 257

An Oral History of Abraham Lincoln: John G. Nicolay's Interviews and Essays by Michael Burlingame — 261

The Order Has Been Carried Out: History, Memory, and Meaning of a Nazi Massacre in Rome by Alessandro Portelli — 265

Peacework: Oral Histories of Women Peace Activists by Judith Porter Adams — 268

Shattered Dreams?: An Oral History of the South African AIDS Epidemic by Gerald M. Oppenheimer and Ronald Bayer — 272

Strange Ground: Americans in Vietnam 1945–1975: An Oral History by Harry Maurer — 275

Tears before the Rain: An Oral History of the Fall of South Vietnam by Larry Engelmann — 279

Voices from Chernobyl: The Oral History of a Nuclear Disaster by Svetlana Alexievich — 282

Voices from the Whirlwind: An Oral History of the Chinese Cultural Revolution by Feng Jicai — 287

The Witch Purge of 1878: Oral and Documentary History in the Early Navajo Reservation Years by Martha Blue — 290

Witnesses to Nuremberg: An Oral History of American Participants at the War Crimes Trials by Bruce M. Stave, Michele Palmer, and Leslie Frank — 293

CHILDREN OF LOS ALAMOS
An Oral History of the Town Where the Atomic Bomb Began
Katrina Mason

OVERVIEW

In her 1995 work *Children of Los Alamos: An Oral History of the Town Where the Atomic Bomb Began,* Katrina Mason compiles interviews with more than seventy adults who, during the 1940s and 1950s, spent part of their childhoods in the New Mexico town of Los Alamos. From 1943 forward Los Alamos was a site for top-secret scientific research on the development of nuclear weaponry. Tying her interviews together with insightful explanatory narrative, Mason divides the book into two sections, one highlighting the years of the Manhattan Project, when even the existence of the town and its laboratory were government secrets, and the other centered on the postwar buildup to the Cold War. Although some interviewees were adults who worked in or around the lab, the major focus of the book is the experience of the children brought to live in the insular world of Los Alamos.

Published fifty years after the bombs produced at Los Alamos were detonated in Japan, *Children of Los Alamos* received positive notice for its child's-eye view of the beginning of the nuclear age. At a time when antinuclear activism had resulted in an increasing number of bans and moratoriums on the development and testing of nuclear weapons, readers were interested in Mason's juxtaposition of national security with the sanctuary of childhood. *Children of Los Alamos*'s focus on the families of those who made history continues to ensure its place as a groundbreaking work of autobiographical narrative.

HISTORICAL AND LITERARY CONTEXT

During the 1930s, as the first rumblings of war were felt in Europe and Asia, scientists such as American Harold Urey and Italian Enrico Fermi began studying ways to unleash the power locked inside the nucleus of the atom. Fearful that German scientists would soon create a working atomic weapon, respected physicist Albert Einstein encouraged U.S. President Franklin Roosevelt to explore the development of such a weapon. On December 6, 1941, the day before the Japanese attack on Pearl Harbor plunged the United States into war, Roosevelt established the Manhattan Project, a network of scientists and facilities with the mandate of building an atomic bomb.

In 1943 the Los Alamos Ranch School, located atop a mesa above Santa Fe, New Mexico, was chosen as the site for a top-secret laboratory where the new bomb would be designed and built. Scientists and support staff from around the nation brought their families to live in the newly constructed town, which residents called "The Hill." Others involved in the plan called Los Alamos "Project Y," as its very existence was classified information. The scientists at Los Alamos were quickly successful in their mission—on July 16, 1945, the first nuclear device was detonated at a New Mexico test site, and atomic bombs were dropped on the Japanese cities of Hiroshima on August 6 and Nagasaki on August 9, killing almost 200,000 people and contributing to the swift end of World War II. The horrifying power of the new bomb also inspired a worldwide movement against nuclear weapons. By the mid-1990s, when Mason compiled and published *Children of Los Alamos,* a number of nations, including the United States and the Soviet Union, had instituted moratoriums on the testing of nuclear devices.

In the decades after World War II, a generation stunned by the implications of nuclear weaponry began to develop a literature that explored the effects and responsibilities arising from the new technology. Works such as Paul Boyer's *By the Bomb's Early Light: American Thought and Culture at the Dawn of the Atomic Age* (1985) and Allan Winkler's *Life under a Cloud: American Anxiety about the Atom* (1993) discuss the profound societal consequences of the use of nuclear power. Michael Frayn's 1998 play *Copenhagen* explores the existential fear unleashed by the bomb through the reimagining of a 1941 meeting of physicists Niels Bohr and Werner Heisenberg.

In a climate where concern about the devastating effects of atomic weapons, and of war itself, frequently focused on damage to the bodies and psyches of children, Mason's look at the covert operation at Los Alamos through the memories of children was especially affecting. By recounting the vital trivia of childhood, the interviewees in *Children of Los Alamos* put an innocent human face on a scientific mission that was, quite literally, earth shattering.

❖ **Key Facts**

Time Period:
Mid-20th Century

Relevant Historical Events:
Manhattan Project; Cold War; bombing of Hiroshima and Nagasaki

Nationality:
American

Keywords:
atom bomb; Cold War; childhood

In *Children of Los Alamos*, Katrina Mason interviews children who grew up in that community between 1943 and the late 1950s. She talked to one of the children of physicist J. Robert Oppenheimer, his son Peter. Oppenheimer is pictured here with his son Peter and daughter Toni in 1947. © ALFRED EISENSTAEDT/TIME & LIFE PICTURES/GETTY IMAGES

THEMES AND STYLE

Contradictions form a central theme of Mason's narrative. For example, the tight military security surrounding the facility provides the children with unusual freedom to develop a significant relationship with their magnificent natural surroundings, which Mason explores in a chapter called "The Lure of the Land." At the same time the children are burdened with secrecy and restrictions that are especially galling to the teenagers. As one recalls, "For a while the big thing was to see if you could sneak off The Hill … get somebody's Daddy's car, wait until real late and sneak out of the house." Mason also uncovers a culture of unusually open interracial relations within the insular community. The isolation of Los Alamos softens mistrust among the Latinos, African Americans, Native Americans, and whites, who find themselves thrown together. "On the bus going to games," one former resident remembers, "I would sit with the Spanish guys. They would teach us to sing Spanish songs and teach us how to swear in Spanish."

In her introduction Mason suggests, "Oral history may well be the twentieth century's substitute for the written memoir." She interweaves the stories of the adult children of Los Alamos to create a collective autobiographical history of a unique moment in U.S. history. Story excerpts are carefully chosen and juxtaposed to create an emotional progression that builds empathy and connection with the reader while developing the author's themes. In her 1997 article for the *Oral History Review,* Theresa Strottman explains, "Mason respects the power of what the interviewees told her and works their quotes into a narrative that emphasizes the passion attached to their revelations."

The heart of *Children of Los Alamos* is found in these personal stories, deftly edited for dramatic impact, such as the poignantly ironic memory of the daughter of a laboratory employee who, at the age of five, understood there was an important secret at Los Alamos but could not work out what it might be. She recalls being shown ducks on a local pond: "I looked at the ducks and decided they must be the secret. … I thought 'OK, I've got it.'" In addition, Mason's own expository narrative is lyrical and lucid, as when she describes how the atmosphere at Los Alamos held subtle benefits for the children who lived there: "They glimpsed, however fleetingly and indirectly, a collective community of brilliant people working together with a mission, an intensity, an excitement and a cooperative spirit that seldom occurs in human affairs."

CRITICAL DISCUSSION

When published in 1995, *Children of Los Alamos* did not receive widespread popular notice, but it was greeted with interest by historians and scholars of oral history. Strottman calls it a "well-written book," though she does question several points of Mason's methodology, suggesting that "*Children of Los Alamos* lacks analysis of what this study contributes to the published history of Los Alamos. Also missing is any evaluation of the interviewees' experiences in relation to then contemporary national trends and themes." Strottman nonetheless concludes by saying, "While this book does not offer a definitive analysis of the material it presents, serious scholars will find it a valuable resource."

Michael Welsh, writing for the *Journal of American History,* articulates the enduring value of *Children of Los Alamos:* "The work of Katrina Mason emphasizes vivid and compelling reasons to examine the highly complex and disturbing world of the Cold War at home." As ongoing political tensions worldwide have led to increasing debate about the risks and morality of nuclear weapons, Mason's examination of the roots of nuclear technology through the ingenuous observations of children has retained its relevance.

Though *Children of Los Alamos* has not received extensive scholarly analysis in the years since its publication, it has been widely examined and referenced as primary source material for those studying World War II and the roots of the Cold War. For example, Charles Thorpe and Steven Shapin's "Who Was J. Robert Oppenheimer? Charisma and Complex Organization," a study of atomic technology pioneer Robert Oppenheimer published in the *Social Studies of Science* journal, is enlivened by a child's memory of the physicist taken from Mason's work, which describes him as "a very gentle man. He had a great smile that would melt me." Other works examining the period have also found Mason's research persuasive, such as Richard Rhodes's 2007 work *The Manhattan Project: The Birth of the Atomic Bomb in the Words of Its Creators, Eyewitnesses, and Historians.*

BIBLIOGRAPHY

Sources

"LANL History." Los Alamos National Laboratories. Web. 9 Jan. 2013.

Mason, Katrina. *Children of Los Alamos: An Oral History of the Town Where the Atomic Bomb Began.* New York: Twayne, 1995. Print.

Strottman, Theresa A. "Children of Los Alamos: An Oral History of the Town Where the Atomic Age Began." *Oral History Review* 24.1 (1997): 153+. *Literature Resource Center.* Web. 8 Jan. 2013.

Thorpe, Charles, and Steven Shapin. "Who Was J. Robert Oppenheimer? Charisma and Complex Organization." *Social Studies of Science* 30.4 (2000): 545–90. *JSTOR.* Web. 9 Jan. 2013.

Welsh, Michael. "Children of Los Alamos: An Oral History of the Town Where the Atomic Age Began." *Journal of American History* 83.2 (1996): 675. *ProQuest Research Library.* Web. 10 Jan. 2013.

Further Reading

Boyer, Paul. *By the Bomb's Early Light: American Thought and Culture at the Dawn of the Atomic Age.* New York: Pantheon, 1985. Print.

Brode, Bernice. *Tales of Los Alamos: Life on the Mesa 1943–1945.* Los Alamos, N. Mex.: Los Alamos Historical Society, 2006. Print.

Hawkins, David, Edith C. Truslow, and Ralph Carlisle Smith. *Project Y, the Los Alamos Story. Part 1: Toward Trinity. Part 2: Beyond Trinity.* Los Angeles: Tomash, 1983. Print.

Hunner, John. *Inventing Los Alamos: The Growth of an Atomic Community.* Norman: University of Oklahoma Press, 2004. Print.

Rhodes, Richard. *The Manhattan Project: The Birth of the Atomic Bomb in the Words of Its Creators, Eyewitnesses, and Historians.* New York: Black Dog and Leventhal, 2007. Print.

IN THE SHADOW OF LOS ALAMOS: SELECTED WRITINGS OF EDITH WARNER

In *Children of Los Alamos,* Katrina Mason profiles Edith Warner, a Philadelphia schoolteacher who moved to New Mexico to recuperate from illness during the early 1920s. Warner fell in love with the dramatic southwest landscape and determined to stay, taking a job as caretaker of a tiny railroad freight depot for the Los Alamos Ranch School. Her home at Otowi Bridge soon became a gathering place for students, neighbors, and the occasional tourist, including Robert Oppenheimer, who met Warner while exploring the area on vacation. When the government laboratory took over the school property, Warner's informal teahouse evolved into a restaurant, inn, and getaway for employees of the secret project. Along with providing Los Alamos workers with relief from the daily pressure of their work, Warner developed relationships with scientists who were changing the world.

At the dawn of the twenty-first century, New Mexican musician and historian Patrick Burns became interested in the vivid narratives Warner, an accomplished writer, had written about her unusual life. In 2001 he published *In the Shadow of Los Alamos: Selected Writings of Edith Warner,* which brings Warner to life through extensive excerpts from her letters, journals, essays, and uncompleted autobiography. An expanded edition was released in 2008.

Warner, Edith. *In the Shadow of Los Alamos: Selected Writings of Edith Warner.* Ed. Patrick Burns. Albuquerque: University of New Mexico Press, 2008. Print.

Winkler, Allan. *Life under a Cloud: American Anxiety about the Atom.* New York: Oxford University Press, 1993. Print.

Tina Gianoulis

COUNTRY OF MY SKULL
Guilt, Sorrow, and the Limits of Forgiveness in the New South Africa
Antjie Krog

❖ Key Facts

Time Period:
Late 20th Century

Relevant Historical Events:
End of apartheid; formation of the South African Truth and Reconciliation Commission

Nationality:
South African

Keywords:
apartheid; racism; reconciliation

OVERVIEW

Antjie Krog's *Country of My Skull: Guilt, Sorrow, and the Limits of Forgiveness in the New South Africa* (1998) is an account of the origins, operation, and potential long-range effects of the South African Truth and Reconciliation Commission (TRC), which held public hearings regarding human rights violations that had occurred during the country's apartheid era. Written self-consciously from the position of a white Afrikaner woman and exploring the nature of complicity, the text recounts Krog's personal journey covering the work of the TRC as a journalist for the state-owned South African Broadcasting Corporation (SABC) in 1996 and 1997. *Country of My Skull* was published in 1998, shortly after the hearings concluded. The text is a combination of journalistic reportage, personal memoir, poetry, and oral history in the form of reproduced direct testimony from the TRC hearings from both perpetrators and victims of the crimes of apartheid.

Country of My Skull was widely reviewed, generally positively, in the mainstream press both within South Africa and internationally. Consequently, the text enlarged Krog's standing in her homeland, where she previously had been chiefly known as a poet who worked principally in the Afrikaans language, and established her reputation as an author internationally. It remains a valuable and unique addition to the oral history genre and a vital resource in studies of postapartheid South African history and literature.

HISTORICAL AND LITERARY CONTEXT

The practices of racial discrimination and legal segregation were already long-standing in South Africa when, following its election victory of 1948, the Afrikaner-dominated National Party introduced a raft of legislative measures that formalized segregation into a system of racial apartheid (apartness). This system ensured the political, economic, and social dominance of the Afrikaner-dominated white minority over the nonwhite majority. The policy was implemented, and often brutally enforced, until apartheid ended in the early 1990s. Nelson Mandela, the leader of the antiapartheid African National Congress (ANC), was released from jail in 1990 following twenty-seven years of imprisonment, and the first democratic elections with universal suffrage were held on April 27, 1994.

As part of an initiative whose stated objective was to promote "national unity" in postapartheid South Africa, the TRC was made up of three committees responsible for gathering testimony from both victims and perpetrators of human rights violations committed after 1960; administering reparations and offering rehabilitation; and, most controversially, assessing applications for amnesty for crimes committed on both sides of the racial divide. Krog, already employed as a journalist for the SABC, was given the assignment of covering the public TRC hearings for the radio show *AM Live*. *Country of My Skull* is both an analytical and personal account of that experience.

Broadly, Krog's work can be related to that of Afrikaner artists who wrote from a position within the minority but were assured dominance through apartheid. Their writings explore the continuing legacy of the complicity of the "colonizer who-refuses" in this system. Included among these artists are André Brink and Breyten Breytenbach from a group known as the Sestigers, which challenged the severe social restrictions of Afrikaner society. More specifically, *Country of My Skull* can be read in conjunction with other nonfiction accounts of the place of Afrikaner liberals in postapartheid society, such as Rian Malan's *My Traitor's Heart* (1990).

Country of My Skull remains Krog's most-read text and was further introduced to an international audience by John Boorman's 2004 film adaptation, *In My Country*, starring Juliette Binoche and Samuel L. Jackson. The text is sometimes described as being the first part of a trilogy, followed by *A Change of Tongue* (2003) and *Begging to Be Black* (2009). Additionally, *Country of My Skull* can be considered with *There Was This Goat* (2009), which Krog wrote with Nosisi Mpolweni and Kopano Ratele and investigates the case of Notrose Nobomvu Konile, whose son was among a group that was ambushed and killed by South African apartheid forces. *Country of My Skull* remains an important historical, sociological, and literary document that depicts a seminal event in South African history and provides insights for those studying the broader phenomenon of truth commissions outside of South Africa.

THEMES AND STYLE

The major themes of *Country of My Skull* are announced in the extended title of the text: guilt, sorrow, and the limits of forgiveness. The book explores the moral questions surrounding these issues: To what extent must a confession spring from a sense of guilt? Who should be empowered to grant forgiveness? Is truth enough to facilitate the process of reconciliation? In addition, Krog examines how these themes relate to herself as a white South African.

Krog describes her motivation to write *Country of My Skull* as a need "to deal with [her] own responsibility, guilt, emotions, family, and privilege" following her work on the TRC for SABC. Although the book is not a conventional oral history, it does possess several primary elements of the genre. Specifically, it includes substantial sections of evidently largely unedited testimonies from both perpetrators and victims of apartheid. Among the testimonies included is that of Zubeida Jaffer, an ANC activist who was detained and threatened with rape and the abortion of an unborn child: "Because of the trauma of it all, I think there wasn't a day that went by when I didn't think we had to do something to bring the system to an end. It totally consumed me, I couldn't think of anything else." In instances such as this, *Country of My Skull* provides a parallel to one of the fundamental objectives of the TRC itself: to restore a voice to victims of apartheid who were systematically silenced.

The collected testimonies and confessions are surrounded by a mix of analytical and personal material that seeks to complicate rather than simplify this material. As Krog says in a 2004 interview with the *Guardian:* "I'm a poet. I distrust anything that starts with a capital letter and ends with a full stop because people don't think in full, clear sentences." In this regard, the text seems to self-consciously challenge its own tentative conclusions, with its form mirroring the political, social, and philosophical uncertainties of the "new" South Africa. In the same interview with the *Guardian,* Krog asks, "Why do we all need to sow this confusion? Is it because when we see things happening we're not sure what is true because it's a new country and we're not sufficiently long enough in it to read the codes?"

CRITICAL DISCUSSION

Upon its initial publication, *Country of My Skull* was acclaimed both inside South Africa and internationally. Writing in the South African newspaper *Mail and Guardian,* Mark Gevisser states that democracy had turned "one of [South Africa's] foremost poets, into one of its most thoughtful journalists," and he goes on to call the book "eloquent … personal and profound … original [and] rigorous." In a review in the journal *African Studies,* Gerrit Olivier describes Krog's work as "a brave and honest confrontation with the process from a highly personal point of view and occasionally in searing poetic language." The book was awarded a number of prestigious literary awards in South Africa, including the Alan Paton Prize and the Olive Schreiner Prize.

In the years following its appearance, *Country of My Skull* has been the subject of much academic criticism, which has concentrated on many of the book's individual strands of inquiry. Two articles from a special edition of *Modern Fiction Studies* in 2000 illustrate this. Mark Sanders's analysis of the text centers on the ethics of producing literature under extraordinary political circumstances. Contrastingly, Michiel Heyns discusses *Country of My Skull* within the framework of "two poles, what we might call confessional fiction on the one end and heroic romance on the other. The latter category deals with white South African complicity by declaring an exception … the white person who miraculously escapes complicity and heroically opposes the regime." Heyns sees the book as "a personal rite of passage from the relatively secure world of the liberal Afrikaner to the frightening sense of complicity with the perpetrators of the horrors recounted at the hearings."

Country of My Skull remains widely discussed, with scholars concentrating on previously neglected aspects of the text. For example, Dalglish Chew's 2012 article "Accounting for Language" in the journal *Safundi* discusses Krog's treatment of the work of the Reparation and Rehabilitation Committee and the "connection between narrative ethics and the material imperatives of economic reparations."

Archbishop Desmond Tutu, pictured here in 1985, was chairman of South Africa's postapartheid Truth and Reconciliation Commission. In *Country of My Skull*, author Antjie Krog considers the commission's findings. © HULTON ARCHIVE/GETTY IMAGES

SOUTH AFRICA'S TRUTH AND RECONCILIATION COMMISSION

South Africa's Truth and Reconciliation Commission (TRC) was established in 1995 and was made up of three separate bodies: the Human Rights Violations Committee, Amnesty Committee, and Reparation and Rehabilitation Committee. Broadly, the commission was responsible for gathering information about the atrocities committed on both sides of the racial divide under apartheid and for giving voice to previously silenced victims, assessing applications for amnesty for perpetrators of crimes, and administering reparations and promoting rehabilitation for both victims and perpetrators.

The work of the commission was based on the principles of restorative rather than retributive justice. Although this was partly a practical decision designed to build political consensus and further the commission's stated aim of "nation building," the emphasis on forgiveness also had moral, religious, and philosophical motivations. The commission was chaired by Archbishop Desmond Tutu, and, although the proceedings took place in a legally secular context, the TRC operated, in part, with a Christian attitude. Perhaps more fundamentally, however, the emphasis on forgiveness was derived from the traditional African philosophy of *ubuntu*. In his book *No Future without Forgiveness* (1999), Tutu describes this as the notion that "humanity [is] intertwined" and that "we belong in a bundle of life … a greater whole [that] is diminished when others are humiliated or diminished, when others are tortured or oppressed."

BIBLIOGRAPHY

Sources

Chew, Dalglish. "Accounting for Language: Narrative Ethics and Economic Reparations in Antjie Krog's *Country of My Skull*." *Safundi* 12.1–2 (2012): 91–114. Print.

Gevisser, Mark. "Hope in the Place of Violence." *Mail and Guardian.* Mail and Guardian, May 2008. Web. 31 Jan. 2013.

Heyns, Michiel. "The Whole Country's Truth: Confession and Narrative in Recent White South African Writing." *Modern Fiction Studies* 46.1 (2000): 42–66. Print.

Krog, Antjie. *Country of My Skull: Guilt, Sorrow, and the Limits of Forgiveness in the New South Africa.* New York: Three Rivers, 1998. Print.

———. "I Write Because I Can't Speak." Interview by Rory Carroll. *Guardian.* Guardian, 1 Jan. 2004. Web. 31 Jan. 2013.

———. "License to Lie." Interview by Charlotte Spence. *Chapter 16.* Chapter 16, 11 Nov. 2011. Web. 31 Jan. 2013.

Olivier, Gerrit. "The 'Fierce Belonging' of Antjie Krog." Rev. of *Country of My Skull: Guilt, Sorrow, and the Limits of Forgiveness in the New South Africa*, by Antjie Krog. *African Studies* 57.2 (1998): 221–28. Print.

Sanders, Mark. "Truth, Telling, Questioning: The Truth and Reconciliation Commission, Antjie Krog's *Country of My Skull*, and Literature after Apartheid." *Modern Fiction Studies* 46.1 (2000): 13–41. Print.

Further Reading

Krog, Antjie. *A Change of Tongue.* Johannesburg: Random House, 2003. Print.

———. *Begging to Be Black.* Cape Town: Random House Struik, 2009. Print.

Krog, Antjie, Nosisi Mpolweni, and Kopano Ratele. *There Was This Goat: Investigating the Truth Commission Testimony of Notrose Nobomvu Konile.* Pietermaritzburg: University of Kwazulu Natal Press, 2009. Print.

Malan, Rian. *My Traitor's Heart: A South African Exile Returns to Face His Country, His Tribe, and His Conscience.* New York: Grove, 2000. Print.

Tutu, Desmond. *No Future without Forgiveness.* New York: Doubleday, 1999. Print.

Worden, Nigel. *The Making of Modern South Africa.* London: Blackwell, 2000. Print.

Franklyn Hyde

The Firm
The Inside Story of the Stasi
Gary Bruce

OVERVIEW
The Firm: The Inside Story of the Stasi by Gary Bruce (2010) is a study of the infamous East German secret police based on interviews with former Stasi agents, East German citizens who lived through the ordeal, and information gathered from declassified documents. The principal focus of the book is on two small rural districts, Gransee and Perleberg, located north of Berlin. Bruce chose those locations primarily because of the extensive amount of now-declassified Stasi documentation about people from these two districts. *The Firm* exposes the day-to-day interactions of the watchers and the watched in a brutal totalitarian state that existed for forty years.

Initially published in 2010 to coincide with the sixtieth anniversary of the founding of the Stasi, *The Firm* was applauded in early reviews for utilizing the oral history format as a bridge between traditional archival sources and popular memory. It was also praised for its piercing look into the minds of former Stasi agents who shared insights into daily life under the repressive organization. It quickly gained a reputation as the standard in the field to which other books on the Stasi will be compared. The book is particularly relevant in terms of post-9/11 topics such as homeland security, surveillance, and privacy.

HISTORICAL AND LITERARY CONTEXT
The East German Communist Party was run by leaders who saw enemies of the state in every shadow and underneath every rock. It was because of this extreme paranoia that they founded the Stasi on February 8, 1950, initially modeled on and influenced by the Soviet KGB, the security and intelligence agency of the Soviet government from 1954 to 1991. The Stasi recruited agents carefully from the ranks of postwar idealistic communists willing to defend the cause and seek out opponents of the party. In order to do this effectively, each agent had to develop a stable of informants who could warn them of dissenters in their communities. The Stasi's goal was to know as much as possible about as many citizens as possible. By the time of its overthrow in 1989, the Stasi had more than 91,000 agents with a network of well over 270,000 informants. During that time they had managed to generate more than 111 linear miles of shelves of material documenting four million East German citizens.

The Stasi used every means possible to enforce communist rule and make life miserable for anyone disagreeing with it. Through ubiquitous surveillance, physical and psychological intimidation, blackmail, and outright threats, they were able to throw the citizenry into a constant state of angst, paranoia, and confusion. As one former Stasi official put it, "The stability of our Republic … depends on the determined and self-sacrificing efforts of the members of the district offices."

The Firm is a continuation of the oral history tradition of the Holocaust. It is the detailed recounting of both hunters and hunted in communist East Germany. Bruce's fascination with the topic goes back to his graduate school studies, when he specialized in East German resistance to the communist regime after World War II. Over a period of six years, Bruce spent a total of ten months studying thousands of documents at the Stasi archives in preparation for the interviews to come. Direct influences on his work include John Dziak's *Chekisty: A History of the KGB* (1987), William Sheridan Allen's *The Nazi Seizure of Power* (1984), and Peter Hoffmann's *History of the German Resistance: 1933–1945* (1977).

The Firm has become powerfully more relevant with the passing of time. In the context of the post-9/11 world, it presents a chilling cautionary tale of the possibilities of a government that prioritizes its own security over the privacy of its people. The U.S. Department of Homeland Security, with its complex web of monitoring and surveillance—much of it based on intricate algorithms and artificial intelligence—has the potential to be much more intrusive and effective than the Stasi ever dreamed was possible. Thanks to books such as *The Firm* and other media that have focused on the Stasi secret archives in recent years—including the 2006 Oscar winner for Best Foreign Language Film, *The Lives of Others*—people in great numbers are demanding access to both learn and expose what went on during that forty-year period.

THEMES AND STYLE
The central themes of *The Firm* include government oppression, institutional paranoia, and privacy. The interviews with former Stasi officials help reveal how the human mind can take any action or situation and rationalize it into one of benevolence. For instance,

❖ *Key Facts*

Time Period:
Mid- to Late 20th Century

Relevant Historical Events:
Formation of the Stasi; division of Germany after World War II; fall of the Soviet Empire

Nationality:
East German

Keywords:
surveillance; communism; privacy

Photo of Erich Mielke, who was the head of the Stasi from 1957 to 1989.
© PETER PROBST/ALAMY

in one interview a former Stasi junior officer matter-of-factly justifies the harsh, often deadly consequences for those attempting to escape from East Germany by explaining, "If a dentist leaves our district for the West, then thousands of people go without dental care." On their highly thorough surveillance operations, another agent ponders, "Can you imagine if East Germany were hosting the World Cup? We would have to investigate every athlete, masseur, coach, and water boy." A common attitude among the agents was not only an evident lack of remorse but also a sense of self-righteousness and even martyrdom. One former officer remarked about the attempted destruction of the case files: "It's too bad we didn't destroy all of the documents. It makes me sick today to see the difficulties that some informants run into because they worked for us." Bruce notes that most Stasi believed their role was to "guarantee peace in the country and defend against enemies."

Bruce's interest in writing *The Firm* arose as a result of his work on a previous volume on anticommunist opposition groups in East Germany. He was fascinated by the mechanics of political oppression as seen through the eyes of the Stasi, their informants, and those who were the recipients of their focus. Bruce had over the years compiled many unanswered questions about the Stasi, "their daily operations, the people who worked for the Stasi, and ultimately, their demise." With access to secret police files and interviews he conducted with fourteen former Stasi and twenty "ordinary Germans who lived … during the era of Communist rule," Bruce set out to answer those questions. In the introduction to *The Firm,* he reflects on his research: "Apart from interviews, personnel files offer one of the richest sources of information on Stasi employees[,] … family relations, disciplinary measures, background, health, and so on."

The interviews Bruce conducted illustrate a complex web of interactions in everyday life under the Stasi. The conversations describe the Stasi's methods and their rationalizations for much of what they did, as well as what they believed about their organization, how they perceived themselves, and how it has all influenced their perceptions of today's world. The information gathered from files and the three dozen interviews Bruce conducted were all in German. To translate the dialogue into English without losing the original meaning or intent, he wrote the vast majority of *The Firm* in third-person narrative, often sprinkling in sentence fragments with detailed clarifications, such as in this excerpt from an interview with a former Stasi agent discussing his interactions with informers: "'Under no circumstances will I reveal the names of my informants.' It seemed important to him that I understand that he still talked to his former informants. They were not his friends, he clarified, but they still greet each other on the street, even the ones whom he pressured into informing." Although most of the feel and intensity of the actual exchange between interviewer and interviewee is lost through this narrative method, this technique allows Bruce to place the words and recollections in precise context, therefore offering additional details not necessarily possible in a direct, word-for-word exchange.

CRITICAL DISCUSSION

Upon its publication *The Firm* received highly favorable reviews that applauded its in-depth research and revealing interviews. In *Foreign Affairs* Robert Legvold writes, "This is surely the most detailed micro-analysis of the East German security." Mari Nicholson-Preuss, writing for the *Oral History Review,* calls it "a rare glimpse into life under the watchful eye of East Germany's 90,000 secret police officers." Mary Fulbrook, in her review of the work for *History Today,* observes, "There have been few attempts to gauge just what impact the Stasi had on the everyday lives of ordinary people in places far from the major centres such as Berlin.… For this reason alone Gary Bruce's in-depth local study of two otherwise relatively insignificant districts—Perleberg and Gransee—is to be welcomed."

Since *The Firm*'s publication there has been a resurgence of interest in the Stasi. In 2012 alone, the Stasi archives received nearly ninety thousand new applications from victims who wished to have access to the records that the agency had collected about them. Although Bruce has not yet developed a significant body of work (*The Firm* is his second volume of scholarship) or had sufficient time to have it properly studied, in 2013 he was working on another book about the Stasi.

Published in 2010 (and reprinted in paperback in 2012), *The Firm* has not yet influenced many writings on this topic. The few books published on the subject since Bruce's volume have focused more on the Stasi as a subtopic of East Germany and its overall history. These books include *Remembering and Rethinking the GDR* by Anna Saunders and *Within Walls: Private Life in the German Democratic Republic* by Paul Betts. That Bruce interviewed a number of former Stasi officials and informers does a great deal to further the public's knowledge and understanding of the repressive Stasi organization. Mark McCulloch, in "The Shield and Sword of Consumption: The Police-Society Relationship in the Former East Germany," reaffirms Bruce's concerns about "the lengths that the Stasi undertook in order to 'protect the economy,' including the gathering of information about mundane aspects in the lives of East German citizens." In his review for *Times Higher Education*, Gareth Dale points out that the message of this book is that it "affords a glimpse of what may await us all if civil liberties are eroded further and ordinary citizens are encouraged to engage in mutual denunciation and surveillance."

THE STASI ARCHIVES

During late 1989 and into 1990 there was a series of uprisings in East Germany that resulted in the fall of the Berlin Wall and reunification of Germany. One of the early events that triggered the massive protests occurred when the citizenry heard that the Stasi were attempting to destroy all of their records. The people overran the Stasi offices and prevented any further destruction of evidence. With German reunification on October 3, 1990, a new government was put in place, and work began to secure all Stasi records. Of the total holdings, it is estimated that the agency managed to destroy about 5 percent of all records. Sixteen thousand bags of shredded records were recovered and are slowly being reconstructed. What remains includes 111 miles of records and more than 1.4 million photographs, the vast majority of which are still housed in the former Stasi buildings in fifteen locations around eastern Germany. Records on former Stasi members are freely available to the general public, but records on private citizens are available only to the individual about whom the file was compiled.

BIBLIOGRAPHY

Sources

Andrews, Molly. "One Hundred Miles of Lives: The Stasi Files as a People's History of East Germany." *Oral History* 26.1 (1998): 24–31. *JSTOR*. Web. 13 Jan. 2013.

Dale, Gareth. "Fear and Filing in East Germany." Rev. of *The Firm: The Inside Story of the Stasi*, by Gary Bruce. *Times Higher Education*. TSL Education, 20 Jan. 2011. Web. 13 Jan. 2013.

"Flood of Applications to View Stasi Files Not Letting Up." 3 Dec. 2012. *German Missions in the United States*. Web. 1 Feb. 2013.

Fulbrook, Mary. Rev. of *The Firm: The Inside Story of the Stasi*, by Gary Bruce. *History Today*. History Today, 23 Feb. 2011. Web. 13 Jan. 2013.

Legvold, Robert. Rev. of *The Firm: The Inside Story of the Stasi*, by Gary Bruce. *Foreign Affairs*. Council on Foreign Relations, Nov.–Dec. 2010. Web. 13 Jan. 2013.

McCulloch, Mark. "The Shield and Sword of Consumption: The Police-Society Relationship in the Former East Germany." *Past Tense: Graduate Review of History* 1 (2012): 67-83. *JSTOR*. Web. 13 Jan. 2013.

Nicholson-Preuss, Mari L. Rev. of *The Firm: The Inside Story of the Stasi*, by Gary Bruce. *Oral History Review*. Oxford University Press, Summer–Fall 2011. 418–20. Web. 13 Jan. 2013.

Rubin, Eli. Rev. of *The Firm: The Inside Story of the Stasi*, by Gary Bruce. *Central European History* 45.4 (Dec. 2012): 812–14. Web. 1 Feb. 2013.

Further Reading

Childs, David, and Richard Popplewell. *The Stasi: The East German Intelligence and Security Service.* New York: New York University Press, 1996. Print.

Cooke, Paul, and Andrew Plowman. *German Writers and the Politics of Culture: Dealing with the Stasi.* New York: Palgrave Macmillan, 2003. Print.

Funder, Anna. *Stasiland: Stories from behind the Berlin Wall.* New York: Harper Perennial, 2011. Print.

Koehler, John. *Stasi: The Untold Story of the East German Secret Police.* Boulder, Colo.: Westview, 1999. Print.

Macrakis, Kristie. *Seduced by Secrets: Inside the Stasi's Spy-Tech World.* New York: Cambridge University Press, 2008. Print.

Schmeidel, John C. *Stasi: Shield and Sword of the Party.* London: Routledge, 2008. Print.

Jim Mladenovic

Freedom Flyers

The Tuskegee Airmen of World War II

J. Todd Moye

✥ Key Facts

Time Period:
Mid-20th Century

Relevant Historical Events:
World War II; integration of the U.S. military

Nationality:
American

Keywords:
civil rights; race; integration

OVERVIEW

Written by historian J. Todd Moye, *Freedom Flyers: The Tuskegee Airmen of World War II* (2010) weaves oral histories with civil rights documents to portray the experience of the first black pilots of the U.S. Army Air Corps (AAC). Moye, the director of the Tuskegee Airmen Oral History Project for the U.S. National Park Service, collected the interviews with a small staff between the years of 2000 and 2005, working with Tuskegee Airmen Inc. to publicize the project. In the book, pilots, along with doctors, secretaries, lawyers, mechanics, and other personnel at the Tuskegee Army Airfield in Alabama, relate stories of Jim Crow–era segregation policies and their efforts to stand up to racism in the South while fighting fascism overseas.

Shortly after World War II, President Harry S Truman declared the U.S. military integrated—due in part to the endeavors of the National Association for the Advancement of Colored People (NAACP), former First Lady Eleanor Roosevelt, and the achievements of black pilots during the war. Written at a time when Moye felt many Americans took for granted their open and desegregated society, *Freedom Flyers* presents the lesser-known details of early resistance to racist government policies by the pilots and the radical black journalists, activists, and intellectuals who campaigned on their behalf. The text, along with Moye's work on the Tuskegee Airmen Oral History Project, are significant contributions to the body of literature concerning race relations in the military.

HISTORICAL AND LITERARY CONTEXT

Although the oral histories compiled in *Freedom Flyers* center on the war years, Moye also includes significant legislation and U.S. War Department reports that institutionalized discrimination. One notable document is *The Use of Negro Manpower in War* (1925), which describes a U.S. Army War College study that asserts that "the psychology of the negro is such that we may not expect to draw leadership material from his race" and "the negro is unmoral." The War Department generally accepted this biased reasoning and, as Moye writes, "provided ample justification … to apply racist policies much more broadly throughout the armed services."

By the time the United States entered World War II in December 1941, the NAACP had been demanding a desegregated military for four years. A. Philip Randolph, union leader of the Brotherhood of Sleeping Car Porters, warned in the spring of 1941 of an organized march on Washington if President Franklin Delano Roosevelt did not end discrimination in the military. Moye notes that "the administration moved quickly to compromise with Randolph," issuing Executive Order 8802, which prohibited racist hiring practices in the armed forces and defense industry but did not ban segregation. Nevertheless, as the Tuskegee program graduated the first class of African American pilots in 1940, the elite, educated black pilots experienced Jim Crow–style treatment—often for the first time. Airman Milton Henry recalls being told "whenever a white man looks at you, you don't look him in the eye. You drop your eye. And don't ever look at a white woman."

Freedom Flyers falls into the tradition of black American social histories. One of the seminal texts in the genre is Richard M. Dalfiume's *Desegregation of the U.S. Armed Forces: Fighting on Two Fronts, 1939–1953* (1969). Both Moye and Dalfiume echo the editors of the *Pittsburgh Courier*, who first argued for a "double victory" over fascism in Germany and Italy and racism in the United States during World War II.

Moye's text is significant in its scope and detail. Contextualizing the construction of the Tuskegee Army Airfield and the pilots' experience, he explores much of the history of Macon County, Alabama, beginning in 1874, and follows many of the airmen he interviewed through their civil rights experiences in the 1960s. After directing the Tuskegee Airmen Oral History Project for the National Park Service, Moye was appointed director of the Oral History Program at the University of North Texas.

THEMES AND STYLE

Freedom Flyers centers on themes of systemic oppression, black Americans' early civil rights struggles, black pilots' war achievements, and the bonds created among black people during the Jim Crow era. In the book, airman Edmund L. Wilkinson recalls, "We were glad to get overseas because we figured it couldn't be any worse over there than where we were." However, Moye notes that some participants' bitterness was outweighed by their pride in being AAC pilots and their "collective determination not to disappoint other black Americans who looked up to them." Horace Augustus Bohannon remembers that when his father came to visit him at Tuskegee, "of course on guard at the gate were a black sergeant, a black corporal, a black private. The whole military is black."

In the book, Moye seeks to expose the profound effect the Tuskegee airmen had on the social fabric of American life: "No area of American social life underwent greater permanent change as a result of the war than that of race relations, because African Americans were able to force action on the debate over" equal rights. *Freedom Flyers* reveals the tensions and bigoted culture sanctioned by the Jim Crow laws that inspired many to join the civil rights movement. Moye concludes, "It is hard to imagine how the transformations that followed could have come about without the example" the Tuskegee airmen set.

Moye notes that his use of oral history is meant "to complement, round out, or challenge the archival record, or to explore topics left out of the archival record." The official records he uses include government documents such as Executive Order 9981, which Truman finally released in 1948 and which stated, "There shall be equality of treatment and opportunity for all persons in the armed services without regard to race, color, or religion or national origin." Moye only lightly edited the oral histories themselves, usually at the level of grammar, and sent them back to the participants for approval. Regarding this process he writes, "Transcribing the spoken word into written text is much more art form than science, as is transforming transcript into narrative prose."

CRITICAL DISCUSSION

Early reviewers of *Freedom Flyers* noted the value of its intimate, informed style. P. Harvey, in a 2011 review for *Choice*, calls it "an enriching, deeply humane, and academically rigorous volume." Likewise, Colleen Mondor in a 2010 review for *Booklist*, writes, "The personal nature of the examples Moye cites make it a far deeper and richer narrative than typical WWII fare." Mondor regards the "copious endnotes and a full biography" as welcome additions to the central narrative.

Freedom Flyers has deepened understanding of discriminatory legislation through its inclusion of oral history. Historian Alan M. Osur, whose books on the subject include *Separate and Unequal: Race Relations in the AAF during World War II* (2000), writes in a 2011 review for *Journal of American History* that Moye's "use of these oral histories and his development of an excellent narrative bring clarity to a complicated story." Osur argues that the real-life effects of government policies are brought to the forefront in Moye's text: "One quickly learns … the impact of AAF racial policies on individual servicemembers." In the book, officer Alexander Jefferson sums up the experience of many of the service members: "I knew racism. … I hated it. But … I lived to be part of the fantastic system that helped to change it."

Race theorists and historians have noted Moye's ability to take the long view on the civil rights struggle and demonstrate how segregation created instability for both blacks and whites. Osur notes, "Moye does not ignore the official story"; neither does he allow it to dominate his text. Instead he carefully examines "the complete record, from the 1925 army War College study through the deactivation of the Tuskegee army airfield and the breakup of the segregated flying units after World War II." As Glenn T. Eskew writes in a 2007 *American Historical Review* article regarding Moye's *Let the People Decide* (2004), Moye's research reveals "the biracialism that developed in the aftermath of the movement to show how black and white

Actor Laurence Fishburne in the 1995 movie *The Tuskegee Airmen*.
© EVERETT COLLECTION

THE TRAIN RIDE TO TUSKEGEE

Many of the Tuskegee pilots were from the North and had little or no experience with the Jim Crow laws of the South. Although in the 1930s and early 1940s racism and discrimination were rampant, the flagrant policies of states such as Alabama brought a special humiliation. Lemuel R. Custis, one of the airmen who appears in *Freedom Flyers*, recalls crossing the Mason-Dixon Line by train and how the porters used a curtain to divide black and white patrons in the dining car: "It was the first time they pulled a curtain on the old boy.... I really then understood I was black. I just thought I was before, but I knew I was after that." He states that he could not forget "how nice the porters were to me, how they helped me survive that trip."

Such discriminatory customs and widespread white supremacist psychology often contributed to camaraderie among African Americans. Airman John Roach, a northerner, recalls that, when blacks were not in the dining car, they were required to ride in the "first car behind the coal car," where the coal smoke covered the customers. He was moved to the blacks-only car just as his train to Tuskegee passed Washington, D.C.

Mississippians joined together in common cause to move their communities forward." Moye effectively argues that black American activists worked tirelessly to expose the destructive force of discriminatory policies.

BIBLIOGRAPHY

Sources

Eskew, Glenn T. Rev. of *Let the People Decide: Black Freedom and White Resistance Movements in Sunflower County, Mississippi, 1945–1986*, by J. Todd Moye. *American Historical Review* 112.5 (2007): 1573–74. JSTOR. Web. 1 Feb. 2013.

Harvey, P. Rev. of *Freedom Flyers: The Airmen of Tuskegee in World War II*, by J. Todd Moye. *Choice* (2011): 1555. Literature Resource Center. Web. 3 Feb. 2013.

Mondor, Colleen. Rev. of *Freedom Flyers: The Airmen of Tuskegee in World War II*, by J. Todd Moye. *Booklist* 1 Feb. 2010: 19. Literature Resource Center. Web. 3 Feb. 2013.

Moye, J. Todd. *Freedom Flyers: The Tuskegee Airmen of World War II*. New York: Oxford University Press, 2010. Print.

Osur, Alan M. Rev. of *Freedom Flyers: The Tuskegee Airmen of World War II*, by J. Todd Moye. *Journal of American History* 97.4 (2011): 1161. Oxford Journals. Web. 1 Feb. 2013.

Further Reading

Dalfiume, Richard M. *Desegregation of the U.S. Armed Forces: Fighting on Two Fronts, 1939–1953*. Columbia: University of Missouri Press 1969. Print.

Hart, Philip S. *Flying Free: America's First Black Aviators*. Minneapolis: Lerner, 1992. Print.

Jefferson, Alexander, and Lewis Carlson. *Red Tail Captured, Red Tail Free: The Memoirs of a Tuskegee Airman and POW*. New York: Fordham University Press, 2005. Print.

Moye, J. Todd. *Let the People Decide: Black Freedom and White Resistance Movements in Sunflower County, Mississippi, 1945–1986*. Chapel Hill: University of North Carolina Press, 2004. Print.

Nalty, Bernard C. *Strength for the Fight: A History of Black Americans in the Military*. New York: Free Press, 1986. Print.

Percy, William Alexander. "Jim Crow and Uncle Sam: The Tuskegee Flying Units and the U.S. Army Air Forces in Europe during World War II." *Journal of Military History* 67.3 (2003): 773–810. JSTOR. Web. 23 Jan. 2013.

Scott, Lawrence P., and William M. Womack Sr. *Double V: The Civil Rights Struggle of the Tuskegee Airmen*. East Lansing: Michigan State University Press, 1998. Print.

Caitlin Moore

AN ILL-FATED PEOPLE
Zimbabwe before and after Rhodes
Lawrence Chinyani Vambe

OVERVIEW

Published in 1972, Lawrence Chinyani Vambe's *An Ill-Fated People: Zimbabwe before and after Rhodes* tells the story of the VaShawasha people of Zimbabwe, who lost their land and much of their culture when their nation was invaded by British settlers at the dawn of the twentieth century. Using a mixture of written historical record, memory, and the long oral tradition of his people, the author presents a compelling portrait of a vibrant native culture overpowered by greed and racism. Vambe, born in 1917, lived through much of this painful transition, but, more important, he had access to the memories and stories of his family and other tribal elders, which constituted a history passed down orally from generation to generation.

Released in the midst of native Africans' struggle against white minority rule in the Zimbabwean nation Great Britain had renamed Rhodesia, *An Ill-Fated People* received a positive reception as a unique document of the conflict. Though some historians noted inconsistencies in Vambe's use of written historical sources, most were enthusiastic about his innovative combination of autobiography and oral lore. This elevation of "word of mouth" history as a reliable source seemed especially appropriate in describing the ineffable loss of culture that was the result of colonization.

HISTORICAL AND LITERARY CONTEXT

The nation of Zimbabwe in southern Africa has been inhabited by a number of distinct cultures since the Stone Age. By the fifteenth century the area was dominated by the Shona people, of whom Vambe's VaShawasha were a tribe. The Shona developed a flourishing civilization based on the trade of gold and ivory. Over the next hundred years, European nations such as England, France, Holland, and Portugal began seizing African territory and resources to boost their own economies, and they also developed a worldwide African slave trade. In 1889 the British government granted South African business magnate Cecil Rhodes a royal charter to expand colonization in southern Africa. By the early 1890s the ancestral land of the Shona had been seized and renamed Rhodesia. The white settlers of Rhodes's British South Africa Company embarked upon a harsh program of subjugation, forcing indigenous Africans onto reservations and eventually appropriating 50 percent of Zimbabwean land. They also instituted a system of political and social repression similar to the apartheid system of South Africa.

The native people of Zimbabwe resisted the invasion of European colonization from the arrival of the first settlers. Early armed rebellions such as the First Chimurenga (Liberation) War in 1896–1897 were brutally quashed, and an authoritarian racist regime stifled opposition. In 1965 the white Rhodesian government angered the British motherland by issuing the Unilateral Declaration of Independence (UDI). This action provoked economic sanctions from England and ignited a new wave of black African resistance, the Second Chimurenga. By 1972, when Vambe published the autobiographical history of his people, a guerrilla war raged against the white rulers of Zimbabwe.

Even in the atmosphere of discrimination and suppression that existed in colonial Rhodesia, a literature of protest and analysis emerged. In the years surrounding the declaration of the UDI, Zimbabwean nationalists such as Ndabaningi Sithole (*African Nationalism*, 1959), Stanlake Samkange (*On Trial for My Country*, 1966), and Nathan Shamuyarira (*Crisis in Rhodesia*, 1966) spoke out about the damaging effects of colonization. Indian author Nirad C. Chaudhuri anticipated Vambe's combination of personal history and political commentary in his 1951 *Autobiography of an Unknown Indian*, as did South African writers Peter Abraham (*Tell Freedom*, 1954) and Bloke Modisane (*Blame Me on History*, 1963).

Appearing at a time of increasing political unrest, *An Ill-Fated People* became part of a massive wave of Zimbabwean dissent. In addition to Vambe's text, 1972 saw the publication of Eshmael Mlambo's *Rhodesia: The Struggle for a Birthright*. The following year Leonard T. Kapungu released *The United Nations and Economic Sanctions against Rhodesia*. Vambe continued his autobiographical history in the 1976 work *From Rhodesia to Zimbabwe*, which traces his maturation and politicization in the context of colonial society. Vambe's works, with their combination of social critique and search for traditional roots, represent an important articulation of the black African experience.

❖ **Key Facts**

Time Period:
Early to Mid-20th Century

Relevant Historical Events:
British colonization of Zimbabwe; First and Second Chimurenga Wars

Nationality:
Zimbabwean

Keywords:
colonialism; independence; racism

A sculpture by an unknown artist from the Shona of Zimbabwe; the Shonas' relationship with Europeans features in *An Ill-Fated People: Zimbabwe before and after Rhodes.* © RAY IVES/ALAMY

THEMES AND STYLE

The core focus of *An Ill-Fated People* is its account of the sophisticated culture of VaShawasha society before the arrival of European invaders and what Vambe calls "the baffling and humiliating experience of being an African in Rhodesia." By recording the oral accounts passed down to tribal elders, Vambe seeks to correct the historical record of Zimbabwe, which had been distorted under colonial rule into "a compound of mystery, myths, fantasy and distortion." His criticism is sharp for "all sorts of white men [who] were charging about the country, expecting and demanding blind obedience from black people who asked for nothing more than to be left alone to live their own lives and follow their God-given customs in peace." However, he views oppression clearly as a social issue that transcends race, saying, "I do not expect that I would behave any differently if I were trapped into a position where I was expected to uphold the domination of one group of people over another."

Vambe approaches his autobiographical history by preserving conversations with "village raconteurs, far too many to mention here, [who] looked at history with naked eyes and did not prevaricate or gild facts just because they were against them." Central to his exposition are the contrasting personalities of his angry, rebellious grandmother and his accommodating grandfather, who, despite his tolerance, finds himself jailed and tortured for failing to license his dogs. Though brought to life by Vambe's vivid narrative, these characters also become symbols of the conflict within indigenous communities. Vambe's grandmother "was nauseated … by the views held by Mizha, her husband, and her two sin-fearing daughters, who took too much account of the peculiar opinions of the interfering white clerics.… This matter was African, she said.… Why should a white man be permitted to thrust his red nose into it?"

Although the oral tradition of his people provides much of the source material for *An Ill-Fated People*, Vambe writes as a historian, in methodical, measured prose. He explores written sources for historical facts before comparing these findings to the knowledge he has gleaned from the stories of tribal elders and his own childhood memories and observations. He frequently employs irony to communicate his own political conclusions, as in the story of his grandfather's unlicensed dogs: "every one of these canine animals was a 'bandit,' in other words, untaxed for that year. … Perhaps because [the tax collector] was appalled by the very idea of black people robbing the government of its much-needed tax revenue or because he felt sorry for the dogs or for all these reasons, the trooper cursed us again angrily and loudly."

CRITICAL DISCUSSION

Published at a time of increased world awareness about unrest in Rhodesia, the work won the admiration of most critics for its sensitive portrayal of the roots of the conflict. Historian Arthur Keppel-Jones, writing in the *International Journal of African Historical Studies,* called it "both less and more than a history." While admitting that "the book can be criticized for inaccuracies" in background material, he recognized that it "is to be valued as a primary source." James Casada agreed, stating in the *Annals of the American Academy of Political and Social Science* that despite its flaws, it "is a significant work … which … bids fair to dispel the miasma of racism which has long shrouded a once-proud people."

In an early review in *Africa Today,* J. Leo Cefkin foreshadowed the legacy of Vambe's work, saying, "*An Ill-Fated People* is a volume which should be widely read … by social scientists as a first-rate case study of tribal life under European settler rule." Though Zimbabwe finally achieved independence from white minority rule in 1980, Vambe's text continues to provide important historical insights, as Adrian Roscoe points out in *The Columbia Guide to Central African Literature in*

English since 1945 (2008): "Born only twenty-seven years into white rule, Vambe enjoys unrivalled chronological reach and first-hand family evidence."

Modern scholarship has focused on *An Ill-Fated People*'s contribution to the historical record of the effects of colonialism on African culture and society. In 1988 Tony Afejuku wrote an extensive analysis in *Research in African Literatures* of the ways the work bridges the genres of autobiography and history, concluding, "Vambe's *An Ill-Fated People* is remarkable as one African autobiography which has a public aspect and a sense of history diffused within it." Indeed, the work has become an important historical document regarding the region's transition from traditional culture to occupied society to postcolonial independence. For example, Carol Summers's 1994 historical study *From Civilization to Segregation: Social Ideals and Social Control in Southern Rhodesia, 1890–1934* references Vambe's work for insights into the effects of colonial missions on native spiritual life, and Mogobe B. Ramose's 2003 essay in the *African Philosophy Reader: A Text with Readings* uses the text as an authority on the effects of conquest on indigenous populations.

BIBLIOGRAPHY

Sources

Afejuku, Tony E. "Autobiography or History? Lawrence Vambe's *An Ill-Fated People*." *Research in African Literatures* 19.4 (1988): 508–19. *JSTOR*. 7 Jan. 2013.

Casada, James A. Rev. of *An Ill-Fated People: Zimbabwe before and after Rhodes,* by Lawrence Vambe. *Annals of the American Academy of Political and Social Science* 408 (1973): 141–42. *JSTOR*. 7 Jan. 2013.

Cefkin, J. Leo. Rev. of *An Ill-Fated People: Zimbabwe before and after Rhodes,* by Lawrence Vambe. *Africa Today* 20.4 (1973): 92–93. *JSTOR*. 7 Jan. 2013.

Keppel-Jones, Arthur. Rev. of *An Ill-Fated People: Zimbabwe before and after Rhodes,* by Lawrence Vambe. *International Journal of African Historical Studies* 8.1 (1975): 142–44. *JSTOR*. 6 Jan. 2013.

Ramose, Mogobe B. "Justice and Restitution in African Political Thought." *African Philosophy Reader: A Text with Readings*. London: Routledge, 2003. 461–546. Print.

Roscoe, Adrian. *The Columbia Guide to Central African Literature in English since 1945*. New York: Columbia University Press, 2008. Print.

Vambe, Lawrence. *An Ill-Fated People: Zimbabwe before and after Rhodes*. Pittsburgh: University of Pittsburgh Press, 1972. Print.

Further Reading

Chaudhuri, Nirad C. *Autobiography of an Unknown Indian*. 1951. New York: New York Review of Books, 2001. Print.

Graham, James. *Land and Nationalism in Fictions from Southern Africa*. New York: Routledge, 2009. Print.

Summers, Carol. *From Civilization to Segregation: Social Ideals and Social Control in Southern Rhodesia, 1890–1934*. Athens: Ohio University Press, 1994. Print.

Vambe, Lawrence. *From Rhodesia to Zimbabwe*. Pittsburgh: University of Pittsburgh Press, 1976. Print.

NIRAD C. CHAUDHURI: *AUTOBIOGRAPHY OF AN UNKNOWN INDIAN*

Like Lawrence Vambe, Nirad Chaudhuri was a colonial who began to write his autobiography on the eve of independence. Chaudhuri was born in a small town in the Bengal region of India in 1897, at the height of the British Empire's dominion. The son of an upper-caste lawyer, he studied history at the University of Calcutta, failing his master's exam but retaining an interest in both history and writing. He became a government clerk and freelance writer. Though he would survive to the age of 101, Chaudhuri had already lived almost a lifetime by the late 1940s, when he decided to write down his personal history.

The resulting book, *The Autobiography of an Unknown Indian* (1951), is unusual in several ways. Autobiographies of ordinary citizens were quite uncommon in early-twentieth-century India, and it was equally rare for Bengali writers to write in English. However, as its title indicates, Chaudhuri's narrative is directed at British readers, in hopes of educating them about the complex humanity, intellect, and culture of their former colonial subjects. His pointed, idiosyncratic autobiography broke new ground as a sort of personal history of a transformative time in Indian society, couched in the life story of an individual who lived through it.

Tina Gianoulis

Launching the War on Poverty
An Oral History
Michael L. Gillette

❖ Key Facts

Time Period:
Mid-20th Century

Relevant Historical Events:
Assassination of John F. Kennedy; Vietnam War; War on Poverty

Nationality:
American

Keywords:
poverty; civil rights; legislation

OVERVIEW

Edited by Michael L. Gillette, *Launching the War on Poverty: An Oral History* (2010) details the events and lobbying work surrounding President Lyndon Baines Johnson's signature program, the War on Poverty. Implemented to halt the cycle of poverty, the program focused on education and job readiness. A revision of an earlier 1996 edition, the text includes Johnson's telephone conversations and politicians' narratives recorded by oral historian Stephen Goodell from 1969 to 1970 and by Gillette ten years later. Gillette, the former director of the Oral History Program at the Lyndon Baines Johnson Library, highlights the successes of the controversial War on Poverty, arguing that key programs such as Head Start, Job Corps, and Volunteers in Service to America (VISTA; now part of AmeriCorps) are still thriving nearly five decades after the Johnson administration initiated them.

Published shortly after the release of Johnson's telephone conversations, *Launching the War on Poverty* provides insight into the president's vision for his Great Society and his ideas concerning the role of government. As the former director of the National Youth Administration in Texas—a New Deal program—Johnson insisted that his antipoverty campaign would be "a hand up, not a handout," though his domestic policy would be overshadowed by his escalation of the Vietnam War. Critics have praised Gillette's text for providing a nuanced view of Johnson's legislative strategy and its impact on American culture and politics.

HISTORICAL AND LITERARY CONTEXT

The narratives collected in *Launching the War on Poverty* begin directly following the assassination of President John F. Kennedy and continue through the end of Johnson's term. In the fall of 1963 Kennedy gave Walter Heller, chairman of the Council of Economic Advisers, approval for an antipoverty program, and Heller relayed the project ideas to Johnson after Kennedy's death. Johnson was enthusiastic, calling it "my kind of program." Gillette writes in his introduction that the president "quickly expanded the program's scope from a limited demonstration project to a nationwide offensive." Although Johnson declared that he would "find money for it one way or another," the Vietnam War prevented him from allocating more than $1 billion to the program.

In the late 1950s the civil rights movement foregrounded the cycle of poverty and the need for empowerment of the underclasses in national consciousness. In Johnson's 1964 State of the Union address, he waged "unconditional war on poverty." To this end he created the Office of Economic Opportunity, headed by Peace Corps founder Robert Sargent Shriver Jr., which borrowed its strategy of community action from the civil rights movement. This approach, Gillette explains, "emphasized mobilizing the residents of a target neighborhood to determine the community's needs and energize its resources."

Launching the War on Poverty is situated in the tradition of presidential oral histories. Oral history programs were created in presidential libraries in the 1960s to supplement information in the presidential papers. Regina Greenwell writes in 1997 in the *Journal of American History* that the "War on Poverty interviews conducted by the Johnson Library in the late 1970s and early 1980s aimed to fill such a gap." In addition, several books have capitalized on the release of Johnson's phone conversations, including *The Presidential Recordings, Lyndon B. Johnson: The Kennedy Assassination and the Transfer of Power, January 1964* (2005), edited by Kent B. Germany and Robert David Johnson, and *The Presidential Recordings, Lyndon B. Johnson: Toward the Great Society, April 14, 1964–May 31, 1964* (2007), edited by Guian A. McKee.

Gillette's text reveals the tensions between Johnson and his advisers regarding the inclusion of community action agencies, which granted "the maximum feasible participation of residents of the areas and groups served," in the Economic Opportunity Act of 1964. As McKee notes in an essay published by *Rotunda* in 2010, this language "led to the transfer of power and resources to low-income people, many of them minorities and women" who had been traditionally marginalized in local politics. McKee's perspective regarding the War on Poverty is echoed in the books *Storming Caesars Palace: How Black Mothers Fought Their Own War on Poverty* (2005) by Annelise Orleck and *Carry It On: The War on Poverty and the Civil Rights Movement in Alabama, 1964–1972* (2008) by Susan Youngblood Ashmore.

President Lyndon Johnson signs into law the Poverty Bill (also called the Economic Opportunity Act), August 20, 1964.
© EVERETT COLLECTION INC/ALAMY

THEMES AND STYLE

The themes of *Launching the War on Poverty* center on race and class tensions and decentralized government policy. Staff member Robert Lampman recalls meeting to define poverty before creating legislation aimed at eradicating it: "people said … poverty is … a spiritual concept; or it's a participation in gov't concept.… Or people would say, well, it really has to do with race; it has to do with sort of a near caste system in the United States." The discrepancies between the needs of the rural and urban poor eventually led to the adoption of community action, which created engaged, educated communities. This watershed moment, Gillette suggests, ushered in "the dramatic transformation in race relations, the impact of the women's movement, and the broad advance of empowerment."

Gillette writes that this social progress inspired him to compile *Launching the War on Poverty*. Despite lack of project funding and the upheaval caused by war, he notes, "The poverty rate dropped precipitously from 22.4 percent in 1959 to 12.6 percent in 1970." This success may have been partially due to Johnson's skill as a publicist; the president told a reporter in 1964, "I don't know if I'll pass a single law or get a single dollar appointed, but before I'm through, no community in America will be able to ignore the poverty in its midst."

Launching the War on Poverty is structured around the contemplative and conflicting narratives of the oral histories as well as the recordings of Johnson's urgent phone calls, which "not only describe events in the narrative as it is unfolding, but are themselves significant elements of that narrative." The recordings are notable for their unassuming, deeply personal tone. For example, Johnson, when speaking with economist John Kenneth Galbraith on January 29, 1964, says he would like "the best approach we could make to this thing because it means so much to the whole country. And it's got them all stimulated and inspired." Then he ends the conversation by inquiring after Galbraith's wife, saying, "I'm feeling wonderful, and I'm looking forward to seeing you."

CRITICAL DISCUSSION

Early reviews praised Gillette's editing choices and the clarity that Johnson's telephone conversations lend to the understanding of the genesis of the War on Poverty. D. R. Turner writes in a 2011 review for *Choice* that *Launching the War on Poverty* reveals how Johnson came to regard "the 'empowerment' movement as a threat to the Democratic Party." Jeffrey Helgeson, in a 2012 article for the *Southwestern Historical Quarterly*, writes that the presidential recordings, coupled with the oral history, "provide a unique view of the best intentions, achievements, and limits of one of the farthest-reaching and most controversial flurries of federal social legislation in U.S. history." Helgeson also highlights the "influences of Texas and the South

THE TWO WARS OF PRESIDENT LYNDON B. JOHNSON

Lyndon B. Johnson (1908–1973) served as president of the United States from 1963 to 1969. During that time he simultaneously escalated the war in Vietnam and declared war on poverty. Due to the expense of the military conflict, the War on Poverty program was underfunded. In *Launching the War on Poverty*, Michael L. Gillette quotes Johnson's defense of his international policy: "I gave [the War on Poverty] $250,000,000, and I'll give them twice that much if I can get out of Vietnam. But I can't deny a soldier." Nevertheless, Robert Sargent Shriver Jr., the director of the War on Poverty and founder of the Peace Corps, threatened to resign for lack of a necessary budget.

The civil rights movement in the late 1950s and early 1960s transformed into the student and peace movements in the late 1960s. Protests against the Vietnam War and racist conditions within the United States regularly challenged the policies of Johnson's administration. Under pressure from the public, Johnson remained adamant about his decision to further operations abroad. However, he fully understood the message of the protesters and acknowledged that "these kids, long-hairs, ... saying, you know, that they want poverty instead of Vietnam."

on the making of antipoverty policy," which are clear through the narratives and the presidential recordings.

Gillette's position that the War on Poverty was successful contrasts with some trends in political theory. As Helgeson notes, "Gillette's emphasis on the enduring influence of the War on Poverty runs counter to much of the recent historiography of late twentieth-century politics, which focuses on the rise of the New Right and the concomitant collapse of liberalism." However, Gillette's text remains an accurate representation of Johnson's character and tactics, and scholars remain interested in how the War on Poverty changed the way federal and local governments provide services to citizens.

Current scholarship on *Launching the War on Poverty* addresses how gender, race, and class tensions shaped legislation. Although Johnson's community action programs drew on civil rights approaches to empowerment, he professes a focus on employing African American "boys" in rural white areas and making them "taxpayers ... instead of tax-eaters." McKee notes that the War on Poverty "emphasized the correction of cultural deficiencies within poor communities" even as the individual communities quickly "developed new programs and services that met their very real need for jobs ... and for political power." Although Gillette does not highlight the corrective aspects of the program, he notes that "even allies of the War on Poverty felt threatened by federally sponsored radicalism." For example, one of the interviewees, Donald M. Baker, noted that racial tensions in the 1960s South prompted "objections ... to having blacks have any control over their own destiny or their own economic freedom."

BIBLIOGRAPHY

Sources

Gillette, Michael L. *Launching the War on Poverty: An Oral History*. 2nd ed. New York: Oxford University Press, 2010. Print.

Greenwell, Regina. "The Oral History Collections of the Presidential Libraries" *Journal of American History* 84.2 (1997): 596–603. *JSTOR*. Web. 17 Jan 2013.

Helgeson, Jeffrey. Rev. of *Launching the War on Poverty: An Oral History*, by Michael L. Gillette. *Southwestern Historical Quarterly* 115.3 (2012): 324–25. Print.

McKee, Guian A. "Lyndon B. Johnson and the War on Poverty: Introduction to the Digital Edition." *Rotunda*. University of Virginia Press, 2010. Web. 17 Jan 2013.

Turner, D. R. Rev. of *Launching the War on Poverty: An Oral History*, by Michael L. Gillette. *Choice* Apr. 2011: 1553. *Literature Resource Center*. Web. 17 Jan. 2013.

Further Reading

Ashmore, Susan Youngblood. *Carry It On: The War on Poverty and the Civil Rights Movement in Alabama, 1964–1972*. Athens: University of Georgia Press, 2008. Print.

Johnson, Lyndon B. *The Presidential Recordings, Lyndon B. Johnson: The Kennedy Assassination and the Transfer of Power, November 1963–January 1964*. Ed. Kent B. Germany and Robert David Johnson. New York: Norton, 2005. Print.

———. *The Presidential Recordings, Lyndon B. Johnson: Toward the Great Society, February 1, 1964–May 31, 1964*. Ed. Guian A. McKee. Vol. 6. New York: Norton, 2007. Print.

Markley, Gregory M. Rev. of *Launching the War on Poverty: An Oral History*, by Michael L. Gillette. *Oral History Review* 38.2 (2011): 411–13. *Oxford Journals*. Web. 17 Jan 2013.

Orleck, Annelise. *Storming Caesars Palace: How Black Mothers Fought Their Own War on Poverty*. Boston: Beacon, 2005. Print.

Orleck, Annelise, and Lisa Gayle Hazirjian, eds. *The War on Poverty: A New Grassroots History, 1964–1980*. Athens: University of Georgia Press, 2011. Print.

Caitlin Moore

Machete Season
The Killers in Rwanda Speak
Jean Hatzfeld

OVERVIEW

Machete Season: The Killers in Rwanda Speak (2005; originally published in French as *Saison de machettes*), by foreign correspondent Jean Hatzfeld, discusses the Rwandan genocide using oral narrative perspectives of ten Hutu extremists, imprisoned for participating in the 1994 slaughter of the Tutsi people, moderate Hutus, and others. Hutus form the majority of the population in Rwanda, but until the 1960s they lived under Tutsi rule backed by European colonial support. When the Belgians pulled out of Rwanda in 1962, liberating the country, the Hutu gained political power. Extremists among them blamed the Tutsis for ethnic discrimination and indentured servitude. They circulated the idea of a "demographic democracy" that would eliminate discrimination, and in 1994 they acted on this idea by turning on their Tutsi neighbors and slaughtering them. *Machete Season* is an edited version of interviews conducted in 2004 with the Hutu men—friends from the same farming village, who had been in jail for ten years. Many books have discussed the events of the Rwandan genocide, but Hatzfeld's text is unique in that, although it is a chilling account, it humanizes the Hutu killers.

At the time *Machete Season* was released, the government was considering a legal pardon of certain Hutu prisoners, such as the elderly, and a potential release from jail. The book was well received for its portrayal of the genocide from the standpoint of the perpetrators. Critics have taken issue with Hatzfeld's methods and presentation, however. Although he states that he interviewed the prisoners individually, he organizes the information in thematic chapters that combine portions of all the interviews, thus removing the statements from their original context. In addition, Hatzfeld's decision to employ a Tutsi survivor, Innocent Rwililiza, as his translator has led to questions about the authenticity of the text. Still, *Machete Season* is often used as a primary source by historians and sociologists studying genocide and the atrocities of war.

HISTORICAL AND LITERARY CONTEXT

The genocide in Rwanda resulted from decades of resentment between two related ethnicities who were turned against each other during the nineteenth-century European colonization of Africa. The Hutus and Tutsis share a common language and religion and had lived peacefully together for centuries, the ethnic label being applied fluidly and mainly according to economic and social status. The European colonists—first Germans and then Belgians—differentiated between the two groups, preferring the wealthier Tutsi people because they were often taller and more slender, with "European" facial features such as thin lips and noses. In 1923 the League of Nations gave Belgium an official mandate to govern the country. The Belgians continued to support the Tutsi monarchy, introducing identity cards in 1933 that reinforced discrimination. Unrest led the colonial government to allow democratic elections in 1960, however, and the Hutu came into power, signaling the end of the monarchy. When the nation gained independence in 1962, many Tutsis were exiled to neighboring nations, where some formed the Rwandan Patriotic Front (RPF) and threatened to wage a civil war.

The genocide was initiated on April 6, 1994, when an airplane carrying President Juvénal Habyarimana was destroyed by a rocket. A moderate Hutu, the president had worked to limit the power of Hutu extremists who wanted to eradicate the Tutsis. His death marked the beginning of a one-hundred-day killing spree during which 800,000 to one million Tutsis and moderate Hutus were murdered, often by neighbors using machetes and other farming implements. In addition to RPF threats against Hutus who refused to participate in the killings, the Rwandan media encouraged hatred of the Tutsis by accusing them of planning for war and desiring to enslave the Hutu population. Because the United Nations (UN) refused to call the massacre a genocide, international troops in the country were not allowed to respond to the violence. After gaining control of the situation, the UN Security Council established an international criminal tribunal, located in Tanzania, which has lasted almost two decades to try the leaders responsible for organizing the genocide. The Rwandan government, reestablished after the return of the RPF forces, also conducted its own series of trials, during which hundreds of thousands of Hutus were charged with participating in the murders. Hatzfeld's book consists of interviews with a few of the many average Rwandans convicted and still imprisoned by these trials.

❖ *Key Facts*

Time Period:
Late 20th to Early 21st Centuries

Relevant Historical Events:
Assassination of Rwandan president Habyarimana; Rwandan genocide

Nationality:
Rwandan

Keywords:
genocide; colonialism; ethnic discrimination

Hutu militiamen practice marching with mock wooden rifles on the road from Goma in Zaire (now the Democratic Republic of the Congo) to Kigali, Rwanda, in 1994. *Machete Season: The Killers in Rwanda Speak* presents interviews with ten Hutus who participated in the Rwandan genocide. © PETER TURNLEY/CORBIS

Machete Season is one among many books presenting various accounts of the people involved in the Rwandan genocide. Two earlier narratives of the atrocity are *Shake Hands with the Devil* (2004), a memoir by Roméo Dallaire, the Canadian general in charge of the UN peacekeeping mission who received orders not to interfere with the massacre, and *Surviving the Slaughter: The Ordeal of a Rwandan Refugee in Zaire* (2004), by Marie Béatrice Umutesi, a firsthand account of the discrimination the Hutu in Rwanda faced after the initiation of the war tribunal and of the subsequent exile of many Hutus into neighboring nations, including Zaire (present-day Democratic Republic of the Congo).

Machete Season and the author's previous work on the Tutsi perspective of the genocide, *Life Laid Bare: The Survivors of Rwanda Speak* (2000), were widely read, inspiring the author to write *The Antelope's Strategy: Living in Rwanda after the Genocide* (2010). This oral history discusses both Tutsi and Hutu views of the pardon and release of some of the Hutu prisoners.

THEMES AND STYLE

The central themes of *Machete Season* are the ease with which the Hutus became murderers, the circumstances that led to that occurrence, and the killers' ability to simultaneously participate in and bear witness to the murder of thousands of friends and acquaintances. One interviewee explains, "At the beginning we were too fired up to think. Later on we were too used to it. In our [brainwashed] condition, it meant nothing to us to think we were busy cutting our neighbours down to the last one." Collectively, the Hutu people committed murder in part by being encouraged to treat it as farm labor. Alphonse, another participant, says that, before the genocide, "I used to pay a boy to kill the chickens behind the house—and just to avoid all that mess." Then, with an *inkota*, "a sharp blade for slaughtering cattle," Alphonse reports, he was put in the position of the hired boy: along with countless other Hutus, he was paid by the extremist party and the Rwandan military to butcher Tutsis like farm animals. Pio, a third interviewee, also compares people to livestock: "I had killed chickens but never an animal the stoutness of a man, like a goat or cow. The first person, I finished him off in a rush, not thinking anything of it, even though he was a neighbor, quite close on my hill." The casual descriptions of the murders as nothing more than hired work demonstrates how the Hutus could continue to see themselves as farmers and laborers rather than crazed killers.

Hatzfeld's purpose in composing *Machete Season* was to gain further understanding of the Rwandan genocide by exploring the points of view of the men roundly condemned as responsible for the atrocities.

His work deviates from conventional procedures of recording oral history, however. Although it is common to edit primary interviews in order to create a sense of narrative, information concerning the interview process itself generally accompanies the finished text, including an explanation of attempts to verify the stories and an appendix of questions. The translation process, although addressed by the author, is still problematic with the author's claims for authenticity. Scholar Madelaine Hron, an expert on human rights and the Rwandan genocide, discusses the issues of translation in her 2011 article "Gukora and Itsembatsemba": "The role of translation in *Machete Season* is fundamental to the interpretation of this text, but it is as problematic as Hatzfeld's editing or the killer's veracity." This complexity comes from the levels of translation that occur between the interview and the finished text. Hron explains how "the killer's statements were translated from Kinyarwanda to spoken French by Rwandan Innocent Rwililiza, then into written French by Hatzfeld, and lastly, for English readers, by Linda Coverdale."

Despite the reorganization of his interview material, Hatzfeld attempts to preserve the authentic voices of his interviewees by using their vocabulary and diction: they regularly use such words as "cutting," "pruning," "job," and "season" (such as a harvest or cull) to describe the murders they committed. Hatzfeld chose to divide the book into chapters with themes such as "The First Time," "Punishment," "Looting," and "Women," each one presenting the participants' thoughts about a specific aspect of killing. Under the heading "Pardons," for example, one prisoner claims that "in the opposite situation, I would manage to forgive my offender." Another remembers, "Many Tutsi begged to be spared before the final stroke of the machete," but "we could not have cared less about whatever they were asking or even begging for"; he therefore does not expect forgiveness.

CRITICAL DISCUSSION

Machete Season initially received praise for its view into the perspective of Rwandan Hutus. A 2005 commentator in *Kirkus Reviews* calls the book a "trove for future historians and ethnographers seeking to explain the mechanics of genocide" and an "eye-opening, sobering read for the rest of us." In a 2007 review for *African Studies Review,* Lee Ann Fujii draws attention to the "detail with which some of the killers relate the first time they killed" and their borderline "pornographic" descriptions of their work. These reviewers note the shocking bluntness of *Machete Season* and the ordinariness of the imprisoned murderers.

Hron discusses the legacy of Hatzfeld's book, stating, "*Machete Season* has become a seminal text in both popular and scholarly discourses about Rwanda as it offers significant, yet contradictory, insight into complex issues raised by the 1994 genocide." Specifically, she examines the presentation of paid killers as

HATZFELD AND THE TUTSI PERSPECTIVE

Prior to composing *Machete Season: The Killers in Rwanda Speak* in 2005, Jean Hatzfeld edited another oral history about the Rwandan genocide from the perspective of several of its Tutsi survivors. *Life Laid Bare: The Survivors of Rwanda Speak* (2007; *Dans le nu de la vie: Récits des marais rwandais,* 2000) documents the stories of fourteen Tutsi victims of violence, including that of his translator, Innocent Rwililiza. Hatzfeld explains in this book that his interview subjects asked him to record the experiences of the Hutus as well, in order to present a more complete image of the events of the 1994 genocide. Hatzfeld declined, however, wanting to focus on the stories of the Tutsis. He felt that, unlike survivors of the Holocaust or other atrocities of war, the Tutsi people lacked access to Western media sources and were otherwise not considered important members of Western society.

He nevertheless compares the experiences of the survivors, saying, "During a trip to Rwanda in the middle of the exodus, I was struck by how withdrawn the survivors were in telling their stories. I was reminded that only after a long period, when countless works by others on the Holocaust had already been published, were the survivors of the Nazi concentration camps themselves willing, and able, to be heard and read, and how crucial their stories were in trying to understand what had happened."

"ordinary" or "neighborly" citizens and examines whether this idea emerged from the participants' stories or if Hatzfeld himself imposed this concept on the text during the editing process. Hron believes *Machete Season* deserves further academic study because, although it "has been amply excerpted and cited," the book "has been minimally analyzed" by scholars.

Representing the critical trend that questions the author's editorial process, Fujii writes, "Hatzfeld, the interlocutor, is absent when the killers speak, and this absence gives a false impression of the immediate context of their words." Hron also questions the effectiveness of the process in generating a true representation of the participants' narratives, writing: "Hatzfeld's editorial role reflects the way in which most human rights testimonials are disseminated in mainstream culture today—through a Western interpreter or collaborator." Despite these reservations, *Machete Season* is received as an accurate depiction of the Hutu perspective of the Rwandan genocide.

BIBLIOGRAPHY

Sources

Fujii, Lee Ann. Rev. of *Machete Season: The Killers in Rwanda Speak*, by Jean Hatzfeld. *African Studies Review* 50.1 (2007): 155–56. JSTOR. Web. 28 Nov. 2012.

Hatzfeld, Jean. *Machete Season: The Killers in Rwanda Speak.* Trans. Linda Coverdale. New York: Farrar Straus and Giroux, 2005. Print.

Hron, Madelaine. "Gukora and Itsembatsemba: The 'Ordinary Killers' in Jean Hatzfeld's *Machete Season*." *Research in African Literatures* 42.2 (2011): 125+. *Literature Resource Center*. Web. 28 Nov. 2012.

Rev. of *Machete Season: The Killers in Rwanda Speak,* by Jean Hatzfeld. *Kirkus Reviews* 1 Apr. 2005: 399+. *Literature Resource Center.* Web. 29 Nov. 2012.

Further Reading

Dallaire, Roméo A. *Shake Hands with the Devil: The Failure of Humanity in Rwanda.* Toronto: Random House, 2003. Print.

Dauge-Roth, Alexandre. *Writing and Filming the Genocide of the Tutsis in Rwanda: Dismembering and Remembering Traumatic History.* Lanham, Md.: Lexington, 2010. Print.

Hatzfeld, Jean. *The Antelope's Strategy: Living in Rwanda after the Genocide.* Trans. Linda Coverdale. London: Serpent's Tail, 2009. Print.

———. *Life Laid Bare: The Survivors in Rwanda Speak.* Trans. Linda Coverdale. New York: Other, 2006. Print.

Totten, Samuel, and Rafiki Ubaldo, eds. *We Cannot Forget: Interviews with Survivors of the 1994 Genocide in Rwanda.* New Brunswick, N.J.: Rutgers University Press, 2011. Print.

Umutesi, Marie Béatrice. *Surviving the Slaughter: The Ordeal of a Rwandan Refugee in Zaire.* Trans. Julia Emerson. Madison: University of Wisconsin Press, 2004. Print.

Katherine Barker

An Oral History of Abraham Lincoln
John G. Nicolay's Interviews and Essays
Michael Burlingame

OVERVIEW

In *An Oral History of Abraham Lincoln: John G. Nicolay's Interviews and Essays* (1996), editor Michael Burlingame presents previously unpublished interviews conducted by Lincoln's private secretary, John G. Nicolay. Nicolay carried out the interviews during the 1870s and 1880s in preparation for writing *Abraham Lincoln: A History* (1890)—the ten-volume biography that he coauthored with John M. Hay, Lincoln's personal secretary. In addition to thirty-nine interviews, Burlingame includes two of Nicolay's essays—"Lincoln in the Campaign of 1860" and "Some Incidents in Lincoln's Journey from Springfield to Washington"—which are based on Nicolay's firsthand observations. Nicolay's research not only provides more information about Lincoln's early life and presidential career, but it also makes "for enjoyable reading, adding color and detail to the story of Lincoln and his times," claims Judith A. Rice in her essay in *Civil War History*. The personal reminiscences specifically allow Lincoln scholars and admirers to view the former president through the eyes of intimate friends and contemporary colleagues.

Upon publication of *An Oral History of Abraham Lincoln*, Burlingame was lauded for bringing to light Nicolay's lost treasure trove of Lincolnia. The reviewer from the *Journal of Southern History* noted that Burlingame's text "is important and contains as much new information on Lincoln as anyone is apt to find at this late date." Burlingame's book won the 1995 Abraham Lincoln Association Prize/Southern Illinois University Press Manuscript Prize, which provided the financial support needed to publish the book in 1996. Ten years later historians such as Martin Johnson from Miami University continued to praise the book as an "important and expertly presented collection." *An Oral History of Abraham Lincoln* was the first of what has become a sizable collection of primary source materials about Lincoln expertly unearthed and edited by Burlingame.

HISTORICAL AND LITERARY CONTEXT

The interviews presented in *An Oral History of Abraham Lincoln* reveal intimate details about Lincoln's life as a young lawyer and rising star in Illinois politics, as well as his presidential career. Born in Kentucky on February 12, 1809, Lincoln lived in Indiana for most of his childhood and adolescence. In 1830 he moved to Illinois, where he served as a militia captain in the Black Hawk War of 1832. An avid reader with an ambitious streak, Lincoln taught himself law and was admitted to the bar in 1836. He then moved to Springfield and began to practice law under John T. Stuart. In 1842 Lincoln married Stuart's cousin, Mary Todd, with whom he would have four children (only Robert Todd Lincoln survived to adulthood). It was in Springfield in the late 1850s that Lincoln first met Nicolay, who was a journalist and the assistant to the Illinois secretary of state.

Lincoln served four successive terms in the Illinois House of Representatives and a two-year term in the U.S. House of Representatives. After a brief respite from politics, he returned in 1854 to oppose the spread of slavery to the western U.S. territories. Lincoln became a major player in the newly formed Republican Party and was elected the sixteenth president of the United States in 1860. His first official act as president was to appoint Nicolay as his private secretary. Afraid of what Lincoln would do to slavery in the aftermath of his election, the southern states seceded from the Union, which ultimately led to the outbreak of the Civil War. On September 22, 1862, Lincoln made history when he issued the Emancipation Proclamation: an executive order that forever freed the slaves in states in rebellion (slaves living in non-rebellious states were not freed until much later). Shortly after being reelected and days after the end of the Civil War, Lincoln was assassinated by John Wilkes Booth while attending a play at Ford's Theatre on April 14, 1865.

An Oral History of Abraham Lincoln is part of an extensive tradition of Lincoln-related texts. Although William Dean Howells wrote Lincoln's campaign biography in 1860, Nicolay and Hay's *Abraham Lincoln: A History* was the first official biography and contained "invaluable passages based on their own personal observations in Washington," writes Burlingame. Composed between 1872 and 1890, the biography first appeared as a serial in the *Century Magazine* from 1886 to 1890 before it was published as a ten-volume book. While conducting research for the biography, Nicolay interviewed people who had known Lincoln

Key Facts

Time Period:
Mid- to Late 19th Century

Relevant Historical Events:
Civil War; Emancipation Proclamation; assassination of Lincoln

Nationality:
American

Keywords:
Civil War; assassination; abolition

WITNESSING HISTORY

John G. Nicolay, left, and John Hay, standing at right, served as secretaries to President Abraham Lincoln, center, and later conducted interviews that they used to write a ten-volume biography of the president. © CORBIS

in Springfield and in Washington, D.C. However, Nicolay and Hay used the interviews sparingly in their text because they had become "skeptical about human memory," notes Burlingame. They were equally concerned that Robert Todd Lincoln might disapprove of material that reflected "poorly on Lincoln or his wife." Thus, these oral narratives lay dormant until Burlingame unearthed the transcripts at Brown University, the Library of Congress, and the Illinois State Historical Library.

Burlingame's text belongs to a long tradition of reproducing primary source historical material. This type of material specific to Lincoln first became available with the publication of Nicolay and Hay's *Abraham Lincoln: Complete Works, Comprising His Speeches, Letters, State Papers, and Miscellaneous Writings* (1894). Their collection was superseded in 1953 by Roy Prentice Basler's *Collected Works of Abraham Lincoln*. Hay's own diaries and letters have also been published under various titles, including *Lincoln and the*

Civil War in the Diaries and Letters of John Hay (1939) and *Letters of John Hay and Extracts from Diary* (1908). In addition to *An Oral History of Abraham Lincoln*, Burlingame has edited several award-winning collections of Lincoln-related primary sources, including *Lincoln Observed: Civil War Dispatches of Noah Brooks* (1998), *At Lincoln's Side: John Hay's Civil War Correspondence and Selected Writings* (2000), and *With Lincoln in the White House: Letters, Memoranda, and Other Writings of John G. Nicolay, 1860–1865* (2000).

THEMES AND STYLE

Central to *An Oral History of Abraham Lincoln* are the intimate recollections about Lincoln's struggle with depression and his relationship to Mary Todd shared by his contemporaries, close friends, and family. For example, through an interview with Orville H. Browning—Lincoln's close friend and adviser for more than thirty-five years—Nicolay became aware that Lincoln had ended his initial engagement to Mary Todd in 1841 because he was in love with Matilda Edwards. When Lincoln was rejected by Edwards, he spiraled into a depression marked by despondency and erratic behavior. Although Lincoln and Mary reconciled in 1842, Browning also revealed that Lincoln was "constantly under great apprehension lest his wife should do something which would bring him into disgrace" due to her own bouts of depression most likely brought on by the death of three of her children. Robert Todd Lincoln also testifies to his father's struggle with despondency: "I went into my father's office … and found him in [much] distress, his head leaning upon the desk in front of him, and when he raised his head there were evidences of tears upon his face."

Burlingame is a historian who has devoted his professional career to studying the life and times of Lincoln. His interest in the president began as a freshman at Princeton University, where he attended a class on the Civil War taught by David Herbert Donald, a renowned Lincoln scholar. In *Contemporary Authors Online*, Burlingame is quoted as saying, "I write about Abraham Lincoln because I like and admire him and because, improbable as it may sound, his life story has never been told adequately before. My principal contribution to the field is my willingness to dig up new information by visiting archives and libraries that others have neglected." Burlingame suggests that the frank discussion of Lincoln's depression revealed through the interviews is "perhaps the most startling new information" brought to light in *An Oral History of Abraham Lincoln*.

Burlingame arranged Nicolay's material into two sections based on the location of the interview. The first part presents the interviews conducted in Springfield, which provide information about Lincoln's early life, including his romantic attachments, military service, and early law and political career. The second part includes the interviews that took place in Washington, which deal with Lincoln's administra-

JOHN GEORGE NICOLAY: A BIOGRAPHICAL SKETCH

John George Nicolay was born Johann Georg on February 26, 1832, in Essingen, Bavaria. In 1838 he immigrated to the United States with his parents, John Jacob and Helena Nicolay, along with his four siblings. The family frequently moved before settling in Pike County, Illinois, where John Jacob and his sons operated a flour mill. Eventually Nicolay became a journalist for the *Pike County Sucker* and the *Pittsfield Free Press*. In 1851 he became friends with his future collaborator, John Hay. In 1854 Nicolay became the owner of the *Free Press,* which led to his involvement in politics. In 1857 he became a clerk in the office of the Illinois secretary of state, Ozias M. Hatch (whose interview appears in Burlingame's book). While working for the secretary of state, he met and became a devoted admirer of Abraham Lincoln.

When Lincoln was elected president, he appointed Nicolay as his personal secretary. Nicolay urged the president-elect to add Hay to the staff. In Nicolay's biography, his daughter Helen writes, "The days of the two young men were filled with duties, many of which seemed fruitless and even puerile in view of the national crisis. But the duties had to be performed … and always there was the element of uncertainty—the strain of looking for one expecting important news." In addition to handling the president's correspondence, Nicolay and Hay were occasionally entrusted with important government tasks. After Lincoln's assassination, Nicolay served as a diplomat in Europe and marshal to the U.S. Supreme Court. He considered it his life's mission to write Lincoln's definitive biography, a task that took almost two decades.

tion, his relationship with Congress, and his behavior during the war. For each entry, Burlingame includes notes detailing the background of the interviewee, controversies that were raised, and historical context for the time period discussed in the interview. According to Johnson, Burlingame took great pains in transcribing Nicolay's notes, thus preserving the language and authentic voice of the respondents.

CRITICAL DISCUSSION

Upon publication, *An Oral History of Abraham Lincoln* was well received by scholars. Rice comments that "Burlingame's editorial work is solid" and suggests that "Lincoln scholars should find this volume useful because of the information it brings together in one place and stimulating because of the larger questions it raises concerning the use of historical evidence." The *Midwest Book Review* praised Burlingame for his "masterful job in selecting and editing these hidden treasures of first-person narratives on the life and person of Abraham Lincoln. The insights revealed … are invaluable." Although Charles B. Strozier, writing for the *Presidential Studies Quarterly,* acknowledges the usefulness of Burlingame's text, he argues that "Burlingame's only real find is Browning's assertion that Lincoln broke his engagement with Mary Todd on January 1, 1841."

Since its publication, *An Oral History of Abraham Lincoln* has become a well-respected source of oral history relating to Lincoln and his times. Burlingame was awarded an Honorable Mention for the 2001 Lincoln Prize for his five edited collections of interviews, letters, lectures, memoranda, and editorial essays by Nicolay and Hay. He relied extensively on the "reminiscence material" he had gathered through his lengthy research when writing his magnum opus, the multivolume biography of Lincoln, *Abraham Lincoln: A Life* (2008), which won the prestigious Lincoln Prize in 2010.

Johnson lauds Burlingame for rescuing Nicolay from oblivion. He notes, "Burlingame … has revealed Nicolay who can now take his rightful role among the previous few important and recognized sources for the life of Lincoln." According to Johnson, Nicolay was "overshadowed by the brilliant, handsome, and accomplished John Hay" and "faded into oblivion, known only, if at all, as the foremost keeper of the sacred flame of Lincoln's memory." Strozier criticizes Burlingame as an editor, stating, "A better editor would have contextualized [the] assertion [that Lincoln broke off his engagement] by noting at the very least how hotly contested this point is." Johnson argues that only *Herndon's Informants* (1997) "can rival Burlingame's books as contributions to Lincolnia." Edited by Douglas L. Wilson and Rodney O. Davis, *Herndon's Informants* is a collection of more than six hundred letters, interviews, and statements about Lincoln's early life.

BIBLIOGRAPHY

Sources

Burlingame, Michael. *An Oral History of Abraham Lincoln: John G. Nicolay's Interviews and Essays*. Carbondale: Southern Illinois University Press, 1996. Print.

Johnson, Martin. "Nicolay's Informants." Rev. of *An Oral History of Abraham Lincoln: John G. Nicolay's Interviews and Essays*, by Michael Burlingame. *H-CivWar*. H-Net Reviews, Sept. 2006. Web. 16 Jan 2013.

"Michael Burlingame." *Contemporary Authors Online*. Detroit: Gale, 2011. *Literature Resource Center*. Web. 17 Jan. 2013.

Nicolay, Helen. *Lincoln's Secretary: A Biography of John G. Nicolay*. New York: Longmans, Green, 1949. Print.

"Projects." Abraham Lincoln Association, 2011. Web. 4 Feb. 2013.

Rev. of *An Oral History of Abraham Lincoln: John G. Nicolay's Interviews and Essays*, by Michael Burlingame. *Midwest Book Review* (1996). Print.

Rice, Judith A. Rev. of *An Oral History of Abraham Lincoln: John G. Nicolay's Interviews and Essays*, by Michael Burlingame. *Civil War History* 43.2 (1997): 176+. *General OneFile*. Web. 17 Jan. 2013.

Strozier, Charles B. Rev. of *An Oral History of Abraham Lincoln: John G. Nicolay's Interviews and Essays*, by Michael Burlingame. *Presidential Studies Quarterly* 27.3 (1997): 601+. *General OneFile*. Web. 17 Jan. 2013.

Further Reading

Burlingame, Michael. "Nicolay and Hay: Court Historians." *Journal of the Abraham Lincoln Association*. 19.1 (1998): 1–20. Print.

Erekson, Keith A. "Method and Memory in the Midwestern 'Lincoln Inquiry': Oral Testimony and Abraham Lincoln Studies, 1865–1938." *Oral History Review* 34.2 (2007): 49–72. Print.

Neely, Mark E., Jr. "John G(eorge) Nicolay." *American Historians, 1866–1912*. Ed. Clyde Norman Wilson. Detroit: Gale Research, 1986. *Dictionary of Literary Biography*. Vol. 47. *Literature Resource Center*. Web. 17 Jan. 2013.

Nicolay, John G. *With Lincoln in the White House: Letters, Memoranda, and Other Writings of John G. Nicolay, 1860–1865*. Ed. Michael Burlingame. Carbondale: Southern Illinois University Press, 2000. Print.

Rev. of *An Oral History of Abraham Lincoln: John G. Nicolay's Interviews and Essays*, by Michael Burlingame. *Journal of Southern History* (1996). Print.

Riley, Russell L. "Presidential Oral History: The Clinton Presidential History Project." *Oral History Review* 34.2 (2007): 81–106. Print.

Schwartz, Barry, and Howard Schuman. "History, Commemoration, and Belief: Abraham Lincoln in American Memory, 1945–2001." *American Sociological Review* 70.2 (2005): 183–203. Print.

Maggie Magno

THE ORDER HAS BEEN CARRIED OUT
History, Memory, and Meaning of a Nazi Massacre in Rome
Alessandro Portelli

OVERVIEW

In *The Order Has Been Carried Out: History, Memory, and Meaning of a Nazi Massacre in Rome* (2003), professor Alessandro Portelli delves into the atrocity of the Fosse Ardeatine incident from multiple perspectives in order to not only remember history but also to memorialize the victims and to link the past with the present. Portelli interviewed more than two hundred individuals to recover the facts regarding the Fosse Ardeatine massacre, which occurred on March 24, 1944. This event saw the execution of more than three hundred Italians as retaliation for the murder of thirty-three German military police in Rome by a group of communist partisans known as the Gruppi di Azione Patriottica (GAP). The author was careful to draw upon the memories of a broad spectrum of participants—victims' relatives, neighbors, partisans, right-wing activists—in order to write a thorough account of the tragedy. The memories, however, prove inconsistent, as is generally the case when hundreds of individuals reflect on the same event. Portelli uses the narratives, including those that are factually incorrect, to illustrate both the complexity of the Fosse Ardeatine tragedy and its impact upon Italian society.

Before being translated into English by Portelli, *The Order Has Been Carried Out* was originally published in Italy in 1999 as *L'ordine è già stato eseguito. Roma, le Fosse Ardeatine, la memoria*. Unanimously hailed as an exceptional work of oral history, the Italian version was awarded the prestigious Viareggio Book Prize, while the translated edition received the 2005 Oral History Association Book Award. Both book and author continue to enjoy both respect and notoriety among scholars.

HISTORICAL AND LITERARY CONTEXT

Portelli presents a notable but often misunderstood national tragedy. To this day large numbers of Italians still believe that the Nazis posted notices asking those responsible for the murder of German soldiers to admit their guilt. Such notices never existed, and the Nazis actually executed more than three hundred random individuals in retaliation for the attack without the general public's knowledge. The event occurred during a time of sharp political division in Italy, with supporters of the fascist government standing in opposition to left-wingers, of whom much of the public was suspicious, resulting in the firmly held but incorrect belief that the "cowardly" partisans who did not come forward were equally or more to blame than the Nazis for the executions.

Although initially an ally of Germany, Italy had signed an armistice with the Allies by September 1943 and would soon join them in their fight against Germany. Military losses and a deteriorating quality of life among many Italians helped to bring about these events. From August 1943 until July 1944, Rome and northern Italy were occupied by Germany, and Italians lived in fear. As in France, an underground resistance movement developed in response to the occupation, with the GAP being among the most active. Although these partisans were regarded by many as heroes during the occupation, they were forgotten—or more dramatically, blamed by some for the Fosse Ardeatine massacre—in the years following the war. Portelli attributes this in part to the influence of the Cold War and conservative Italian governments.

The Order Has Been Carried Out is indicative of the "witnessing history" genre of oral histories. Like Svetlana Alexievich's *Voices from Chernobyl: The Oral History of a Nuclear Disaster* (1997) and Larry Engelmann's *Tears before the Rain: An Oral History of the Fall of South Vietnam* (1990), Portelli's text relies on the perspectives of witnesses to a specific, tragic event. His subject matter, however, remains unique. The Fosse Ardeatine massacre, although quite notable in Italy and commemorated yearly in Rome, is not a topic of scholarship internationally.

The Order Has Been Carried Out not only challenges some traditional assumptions about the events that occurred in Rome on March 24, 1944, but it also examines ways in which individual and collective memory can influence a society decades after an actual event. Because of his unique method of presentation, wherein he often nearly confuses the reader with multiple versions of the same event, Portelli's work is regarded as pioneering in style. Years after its publication, *The Order Has Been Carried Out* is still discussed and highly regarded in scholarly articles, and Portelli's innovative style can be seen in a notable work titled *I Can Almost See the Lights of Home: A Field Trip to*

❖ *Key Facts*

Time Period:
Mid-20th Century

Relevant Historical Events:
Fosse Ardeatine massacre; World War II; Nazi occupation of Italy

Nationality:
Italian

Keywords:
fascism; massacre; occupation

The Order Has Been Carried Out offers an oral history of the Nazi massacre of Italians in March 1944. This incident occurred in a cave now called the Fosse Ardeatine. Depicted here is the memorial therein.
© PRISMA ARCHIVO/ALAMY

Harlan County, Kentucky, an audio oral history that is a mélange of memories and music.

THEMES AND STYLE

The Order Has Been Carried Out examines both the events of the Fosse Ardeatine tragedy and the themes of grief and persistence of memory. The difference in the way the same incident persists to haunt the memory of those involved is clearly illustrated by Portelli. For example, the contrast between Liana Gigliozzi's and Claudio Fano's memories is stark. Gigliozzi remembers, "My mother told me: 'Ah, because an irresponsible person, a wretch … got up one morning, went and threw a bomb, and because of him your father died.' … This idea has been rooted in me since I was three." Fano, meanwhile, sees it this way: "The guilt for the Fosse Ardeatine falls on the Germans, not the partisans; it was an act of war, it was the partisans' duty not to turn themselves in." Portelli stresses that part of the difficulty with memory is not simply that varying recollections of one event exist but that a single individual can experience "divided memory." "Memory … is not divided only *between* different persons and alignments.… Memory divides, more painfully and dramatically, also *within* a person."

As he mentions in the introduction to his book, part of Portelli's motivation for writing *The Order Has Been Carried Out* was to generate a recollection of the Fosse Ardeatine incident that differed from the traditional versions of the event, as much of the subject is based upon misinformation and misconceptions. He writes, "I am specifically fascinated by the pervasiveness of erroneous tales, myths, legends, and silences, such as those that have been woven around these events." In order to conceive the sort of broad representation needed to examine the memories of an event that is often erroneously remembered event, Portelli was, as Betsy Brinson writes in the *Oral History Review*, particularly interested in "narratives that were not factually true." He felt that by including such narratives, he would be able to reach the heart of the matter.

Portelli uses an interesting device to memorialize the victims of the Fosse Ardeatine: an alphabetical list of victims' names that begins and ends each chapter. "The names flame every chapter as though a book too can be both scholarship and memorial," David W. Blight observes in his essay "Fossilized Lies: A Reflection on Alessandro Portelli's *The Order Has Been Carried Out*." Additionally, Portelli uses uninterrupted narratives, giving the reader a more personal perspective than could be achieved with just excerpts. Finally, he confuses the reader by alternating contradictory testimonials. As John B. Wolford writes in the *Oral History Review*, "By juxtaposing multiple voices and memories to replicate multiple realities/multiple perceptions that occur with any event, Portelli forces the confused reader to personally integrate the processes of remembering, forgetting and creating narratives."

CRITICAL DISCUSSION

The initial reception to *The Order Has Been Carried Out* was overwhelmingly positive. Wolford concludes that Portelli's book "should be required reading for anyone involved in historical inquiry," and Blight states that the author produced an "extraordinary and extensive oral history," as well as "a brilliant and haunting reminder of how we can all be part of a herd heading toward tragedy." In *History Today,* John Foot writes, "There are some books which all historians should read, no matter which period they 'specialise' in. One of these is Alessandro Portelli's *The Order Has Been Carried Out.*"

Later criticism of Portelli's research addressed the issue of potential political bias in his work. Luisa Del Giudice notes in her review of *Storie orali: Racconto, immaginazione, dialogo* that "he writes and blogs for Italian newspapers of the Left, *il Manifesto, Liberazione, l'Unità.*" Portelli has never attempted to conceal his affiliation with left-wing politics and publications and, in fact, has openly discussed his ideology in interviews. Even Del Giudice mentions Portelli's ideology more as a matter of fact than as one of potential concern in regard to his work.

There is little recent scholarship regarding *The Order Has Been Carried Out.* Nevertheless, the book is still lauded for its attention to detail and extensive research, and it shall remain notable for having earned the Oral History Association Book Award in 2005. Portelli remains of pivotal importance in the realm of oral history, as Alistair Thomson writes in his article "Four Paradigm Transformations in Oral History":

> Portelli challenged the critics of "unreliable memory" head-on by arguing that "the peculiarities of oral history"—orality, narrative form, subjectivity, the "different credibility" of memory, and the relationship between interviewer and interviewee—should be considered as strengths rather than as weaknesses, a resource rather than a problem. Portelli, perhaps the most influential writer about oral history and memory, has since demonstrated these strengths in a series of outstandingly imaginative oral history studies.

BIBLIOGRAPHY

Sources

Blight, David W. "Fossilized Lies: a Reflection on Alessandro Portelli's *The Order Has Been Carried Out.*" *Oral History Review* 32.1 (2005): 5. *Literature Resources from Gale.* Web. 3 Jan. 2013.

Brinson, Betsy. "Crossing Cultures: An Interview with Alessandro Portelli." *Oral History Review* 28.1 (2001): 87. *General OneFile.* Web. 4 Jan. 2013.

Del Giudice, Luisa. Rev. of *Storie orali: Racconto, immaginazione, dialogo,* by Alessandro Portelli. *Oral History Review* 37.2 (2010): 264–68. Web. 1 Feb. 2013.

Foot, John. "A Divided Past." *History Today* 60.6 (2010): 61. *EBSCO Publishing, MAS Ultra-School Edition.* Web. 3 Jan. 2013.

Linenthal, Edward T. "Stories and Bodies: A Personal Reflection on Alessandro Portelli's *The Order Has Been Carried Out.*" *Oral History Review* 32.1 (2005): 19. *General OneFile.* Web. 4 Jan. 2013.

THE LIFE OF ALESSANDRO PORTELLI

Alessandro Portelli was born in Rome in 1942, two years before the Fosse Ardeatine massacre he writes about in *The Order Has Been Carried Out.* His mother taught English in Italy, and it was this, along with his love of British and American rock-and-roll music, that first inspired Portelli to become interested in American culture and be an exchange student in Los Angeles in 1960. During his studies in the United States, Portelli became interested in U.S. politics and was a supporter of John F. Kennedy.

Upon returning to Rome, he became involved with the radical working-class and communist politics of the late 1960s. This was Portelli's first experience with oral history, in which he attempted to document the reality of working-class Romans, as opposed to the image embraced and promoted by the Communist and Socialist parties at the time. Portelli has enjoyed a long and prolific career as a professor, a historian, a journalist, and an activist. Some of his other interests include folk music and Appalachian American culture.

Portelli, Alessandro. *The Order Has Been Carried Out: History, Memory, and Meaning of a Nazi Massacre in Rome.* New York: Palgrave Macmillan, 2003. Print.

Pugliese, Stanislao G. Rev. of *The Order Has Been Carried Out: History, Memory and Meaning of a Nazi Massacre in Rome,* by Alessandro Portelli. *H-Italy.* H-Net Reviews, Mar. 2002. Web. 3 Jan. 2013.

Slaughter, Jane. Rev. of *The Order Has Been Carried Out: History, Memory and Meaning of a Nazi Massacre in Rome,* by Alessandro Portelli. *American Historical Review* 109.5 (2004): 1531–32. *Academic Search Premier.* Web. 2 Jan. 2013.

Thomson, Alistair. "Four Paradigm Transformations in Oral History." *Oral History Review* 34.1 (2007): 49. *Literature Resources on Gale.* Web. 1 Feb. 2013.

Wolford, John B. Rev. of *The Order Has Been Carried Out: History, Memory and Meaning of a Nazi Massacre in Rome,* by Alessandro Portelli. *Oral History Review* 31.2 (2004): 118. *General OneFile.* Web. 4 Jan. 2013.

Further Reading

American Poets on the Holocaust. *Blood to Remember.* St. Louis, Mo.: Time Being, 2007. Print.

Debenedetti, Giacomo. *October 16, 1943.* Notre Dame, IN: University of Notre Dame Press, 2001. Print.

Hamilton, Paula. "The Oral Historian as Memoirist." *Oral History Review* 32.1 (2005): 11 *General OneFile.* Web. 4 Jan. 2013.

Katz, Robert. *Death in Rome.* New York: Macmillan, 1967. Print.

Pugliese, Stanislao G. *Desperate Inscriptions: Graffiti from the Nazi Prison in Rome, 1943–1944.* Boca Raton, Fla.: Bordighera, 2002. Print.

Lisa Mertel

PEACEWORK
Oral Histories of Women Peace Activists
Judith Porter Adams

Key Facts

Time Period:
20th Century

Relevant Historical Events:
Formation of the women's peace movement; rise of feminism

Nationality:
American

Keywords:
pacifism; activism; feminism

OVERVIEW

Peacework: Oral Histories of Women Peace Activists (1991), collected and edited by activist and women's studies scholar Judith Porter Adams, documents the lives of twenty-three women who were active in the women's peace movement, primarily in the Women's International League for Peace and Freedom (WILPF), Women Strike for Peace (WSP), or both. Collected in the 1980s as part of the Women's Peace Oral History Project, the book details the experiences of women who conducted peace work from the 1920s through the 1980s. All of the women who appear in the book were at least sixty at the time of their interviews. Focusing on the impact of twentieth-century warfare on the lives of individual women, *Peacework* relates the stories of disparate women who share a strong commitment to struggle for peace and justice and who represent a rich source of practical experience as activists.

Published during the early 1990s, when oral history was becoming a popular vehicle for feminist inquiry, *Peacework* was praised for presenting the contributions of the unsung rank-and-file members of women's peace organizations, many of whom devoted significant time and energy to the cause while juggling family and other commitments. Today *Peacework* remains notable as an account of history through these individual women's eyes and as an important contribution to the growing literature on women and peace.

HISTORICAL AND LITERARY CONTEXT

The stories of the activists collected in *Peacework* reflect the birth and growth of the women's peace movement in the twentieth century, a time when women were gaining a new sense of political agency. The turn-of-the-century view that women possessed a moral sense superior to that of many men created new opportunities for women, who were otherwise largely consigned to the domestic sphere. These women campaigned for a variety of moral and social causes, including the abolition of slavery and the reform of child labor laws. Early, or first-wave, feminism was also gaining steam during this period, and many of the women who would become involved in the peace movement cut their activist teeth campaigning for women's suffrage.

WILPF, the first significant women's peace organization, was formed as the Women's International Congress in 1915 in response to the outbreak of World War I. Some of the WILPF members had been politically active for decades and had voted to establish a permanent organization to promote international peace. However, Cold War nuclear concerns gave rise to another important women's peace organization, WSP, which formed in 1961 to protest the atmospheric testing of hydrogen bombs and the potential health impact of this testing on children and future generations. Early WSP organizers favored a nonhierarchical structure, prefiguring the grassroots consciousness-raising that would characterize second-wave feminism a decade later.

Peacework is in the tradition of women's oral history in North America and Europe. Anne Witte Garland's *Women Activists: Challenging the Abuse of Power* (1988), is a predecessor of *Peacework* and provides an account of individual women and the manner in which local and global events propelled them to activism. While the narratives in these two books reflect the overlapping concerns about wars and their social and environmental consequences, Garland's book also includes the stories of women focused on social issues such as the state of education in the inner city.

As women-led peace and protest movements blossomed in countries beyond the United States and Europe, a number of oral histories appeared that documented them. Notable heirs to *Peacework* include Swanee Hunt's *This Was Not Our War: Bosnian Women Reclaiming the Peace* (2004), an oral history of twenty-six women working to reconstruct their country and promote peace following years of war. Javier Auyero's *Contentious Lives: Two Argentine Women, Two Protests, and the Quest for Recognition* (2003), while more focused on economic and anti-globalization protests, uses oral history effectively to relate recent Argentine history as witnessed by committed female activists.

THEMES AND STYLE

The narratives in *Peacework* explore the activist commitment of ordinary women faced with the devastating consequences of twentieth-century warfare and weaponry, particularly as militarization affects children and future generations. In recalling the roots of their activism, many of the women echo the sentiments of Ethel Barol Taylor, who remembered reasoning that because women are often excluded from official policy-making channels, "what we had to do was make policy outside of government and demand of government that it listen to us." In addition, many women described their peace work as a response to events that directly affected their children—for instance, the discovery of high levels of strontium in milk following nuclear testing in the 1950s. Much of their activist work was squeezed in between their household and family duties. Cora Weiss remembers, "I was forever with a baby on one hip, or both, going to meetings or demonstrations."

In her introduction to *Peacework*, Adams states that her reason for interviewing women for the book and the Women's Peace Oral History Project grew out of a wish "to preserve some of their experiences, as well as to learn from their stories." Many of the women had practical know-how based on decades of peace work, which Adams worried would be lost to new generations if not recorded. She also emphasizes that the book is an attempt to tell the stories of individual participants, not to provide a complete history of the women's peace movement, because "history becomes so much more personal when linked to the lives of real women." She expands on this notion in "Women's Peace Oral History Guidelines and Resources," presented for a workshop at the 2011 WILPF Triennial Congress, in which she states that she sought to record "the first meeting around a kitchen table; the behind-the-scenes activities to keep the branch vital and energized; stories about how women used jail time after demonstration arrests to set up study groups, song sessions, and story-telling."

The pragmatic no-nonsense tone of many of the narratives in *Peacework* mirrors the approach of the women interviewed, who had to fold their political activities into their busy daily lives. Lisa Schmidt Kalvelage, who describes herself as "a respectable housewife with six children," remembers the image she and her fellow war protestors sought to convey while picketing. "We had high heels and gloves on when we carried those picket signs. We wanted to show the news that those women are 'peaceniks' and didn't fit the radical image." While many of the narratives take a level accounting of the stresses involved in activism and the modest gains made, the women remember with affection the comradery they experienced. Esther Pollack Newell recalls the jailhouse community formed among the five hundred women imprisoned for protesting nuclear testing at the Lawrence Livermore National Laboratory. As the women departed prison, they were sent off through a tunnel of hands with the chant, "Solidarity forever, solidarity forever, our union makes us strong!"

CRITICAL DISCUSSION

Peacework, while not widely reviewed upon publication, received a generally positive response from scholars and activists. Writing in the *Oral History Review* in 1992, Evelyn Hunt calls the text "a moving example of fine oral history work." She writes, "A fine view of women's solidarity, persistence, and common sense makes this a volume to pass around, especially to younger women." More mixed was Janet Nolan's review in the *Journal of American History* in 1992 in which she praises the book for its chronicling of the long-neglected contributions made by women in the peace movement but is critical of some of Adams's editorial decisions, particularly her removal of the interview questions from the text. Arguing that oral history's interactive dimension makes it especially compelling, she asserts that "it seems misguided, to say the least, to use a presentation format that eliminates this interaction."

Two women protesting the Vietnam War in 1968. Judith Porter Adams's *Peacework: Oral Histories of Women Peace Activists* includes oral histories from various female peace activists. © HARVEY L. SILVER/CORBIS

PRIMARY SOURCE

EXCERPT FROM *PEACEWORK*

ETHEL BAROL TAYLOR

I was catapulted into the peace movement with the dropping of the bomb on Hiroshima. I was pretty apolitical up to that point. I used to get up in the morning and start polishing the furniture until I was polishing the polish. I thought, "There must be more to life than this."

I had a daughter, who was a small child at the time of the bombing of Hiroshima. When I read that the blast was so hot that in some circumstances it incinerated people and left just a shadow against a stone wall, creating instant fossils, I was numbed. I realized there were wars and there were wars, but this kind of war must never happen again.

There were others who felt as I did, and a few of us got together and talked. We formed a little group of women to study issues. I think even then, even though I was not political, I had this feeling that because women are not in positions of power and they have no role in policymaking, that maybe what we had to do was to make policy outside of government and demand of government that it listen to us.

A columnist once wrote a piece about me, and she called it "Rebel in White Gloves" because in the early days of Women Strike for Peace, women in the demonstrations, who were generally middle-class women, wore white gloves and hats. We used to do things like sit down and not move in the middle of the street, or whatever, but we would have our hats and white gloves on. I always thought that was a real protection until once we had an action, and hundreds of people went to Washington as a symbolic takeover of Congress. We walked and we came to a narrow street. The police said, "Cross this street and you get arrested." Well, I realized then that, what could they do? They're not going to electrocute me. They're not going to shoot me. It was much easier to cross that street than not to cross that street, so I crossed that street. Then we sat on the ground and waited to be arrested. We sat down, but we decided we weren't going to be yanked by our armpits, we were going to walk like ladies to the police van. We did. We got to the jail, and they opened the back door of the van. I looked out, and there was a five-foot drop to the ground. I waited for the policeman to help me down. The policeman came around and said, "Jump, sister." So I jumped into an entirely new world.

I didn't realize when I first got involved, when our government dropped the bomb on Hiroshima and Nagasaki, that this was going to be a lifetime

---

In addition to making accessible unique and overlooked voices in American history, *Peacework* serves to expand contemporary ideas about the roots of protest and peace activism in the United States. The text has been used in both peace and women's studies courses. More broadly, the Women's Peace Oral History Project, which is archived at Stanford University, has served as a model for various chapters of WILPF, members of which have begun collecting their own oral histories.

Aside from the limited analysis available in book reviews, *Peacework* has attracted little critical interest as a stand-alone text. However, the book has been accorded significance as a reference work on women peace activists, as Ilene Feinman has done in *Citizenship Rites: Feminist Soldiers and Feminist Antimilitarists* (1999), which explores the complex relationships between citizenship, soldiering, and feminism. Other works such as Harriet Hyman Alonso's *Peace as a Women's Issue: A History of the U.S. Movement for World Peace and Women's Rights* (1993) rely on primary source material such as the WSP papers and other archival collections documenting women's peace organizations.

BIBLIOGRAPHY

Sources

Adams, Judith Porter. *Peacework: Oral Histories of Women Peace Activists*. Boston: Twayne, 1991. Print.

———. "Women's Peace Oral History Guidelines and Resources." *Advancing Women as Peacemakers*. U.S. Section of WILPF, n.d. Web. 9 Feb. 2013.

Hunt, Evelyn. Rev. of *Peacework: Oral Histories of Women Peace Activists*, by Judith Porter Adams. *Oral History Review* 20.1/2 (1992): 134–36. JSTOR. Web. 9 Feb. 2013.

Nolan, Janet. Rev. of *Peacework: Oral Histories of Women Peace Activists*, by Judith Porter Adams. *Journal of American History* 78.4 (1992): 1491–92. JSTOR. Web. 9 Feb. 2013.

Further Reading

Auyero, Javier. *Contentious Lives: Two Argentine Women, Two Protests, and the Quest for Recognition*. Durham, N.C.: Duke University Press, 2003. Print.

Foster, Catherine. *Women for All Seasons: The Story of the Women's International League for Peace and Freedom*. Athens: University of Georgia Press, 1989. Print.

Garland, Anne Witte. *Women Activists: Challenging the Abuse of Power*. New York: Feminist Press, 1988. Print.

commitment. I think if I had realized it I might have thought twice, because it's a terrible business to be in.

I think most of the pressures were because of the issues, not just because I was a woman—although there were those pressures too. You can really go nuts working for something and never have a success, never see enough change. [Albert] Camus said, and I'm paraphrasing, that just because a thing is hopeless doesn't mean you don't get involved. That sounds gloomy. We have had some successes, but when I first got in, there were two bombs and they were both ours. Now there are 50,000 in the world. Someone once said, "Ethel, that's going to look lousy on your resumé." I think I developed an early anger that leaders had such contempt for the people they were supposed to be leading. That anger really has sustained me.

My anger is directed towards leaders who threaten the lives of children now and those yet unborn with their inhumane policy of nuclear weapons. We started because of children, because the scientists and doctors said that the strontium 90 and iodine 131 from the atomic tests would poison our children's milk and cause cancer. When we first organized we sent out a call throughout the streets with leaflets saying, "Take your children off milk." We sent our children's baby teeth to a lab in St. Louis to determine if strontium 90 was present. We were concerned about an epidemic, like polio before vaccines, except that polio is viral and these were man-made epidemics. Those who were then children now have children themselves.

My work in Women Strike for Peace sustains me. Outside of my family and my friends, WSP to me is the most important entity. It started out as a one-day action. We would meet every week around my dining room table to plan our "strike." There was a sugar bowl in the middle of the table for contributions toward the action. Some women stopped going to the hairdresser and did their own hair and put the money in the bowl. Some put birthday checks in. In one remarkable case, a woman who had very little money would occasionally give blood to the Red Cross and put the five dollars in the bowl. There was a wonderful outpouring of feeling and sisterhood. We were the harbingers of the women's movement—our weekly round table discussions were certainly consciousness raising. It was really an amazing experience. We never pledged solidarity, but we really were solid.

SOURCE: Adams, Judith Porter. *Peacework: Oral Histories of Women Peace Activists.* Boston: Twayne, 1991.

Hunt, Swanee. *This Was Not Our War: Bosnian Women Reclaiming the Peace.* Durham, N.C.: Duke University Press, 2004. Print.

Patterson, David. *The Search for Negotiated Peace: Women's Activism and Citizen Diplomacy in World War I.* New York: Routledge, 2008. Print.

Swerdlow, Amy. *Women Strike for Peace: Traditional Motherhood and Radical Politics in the 1960s.* Chicago: University of Chicago Press, 1993. Print.

Farnoosh Fathi

Shattered Dreams?
An Oral History of the South African AIDS Epidemic
Gerald M. Oppenheimer, Ronald Bayer

❖ Key Facts

Time Period:
Late 20th to Early 21st Centuries

Relevant Historical Events:
HIV-AIDS crisis in Africa; fall of apartheid; rise of the African National Congress

Nationality:
South African

Keywords:
HIV; AIDS; public health

OVERVIEW

Based primarily on interviews conducted from 2003 to 2005 and first published in 2007, Gerald M. Oppenheimer and Ronald Bayer's *Shattered Dreams? An Oral History of the South African AIDS Epidemic* is a poignant account of South Africa's HIV-AIDS crisis in the late twentieth and early twenty-first centuries. According to Karin Shapiro in her book review for the *Journal of the History of Medicine and Applied Science*, the form of the text is an adapted variety of oral history, in which, "in between oftentimes long block quotations, the authors intersperse their contextual analyses, highlighting the political economy of health care." Derived from interviews with nurses and doctors engaged in providing frontline health services to HIV-AIDS sufferers, *Shattered Dreams?* presents both an analytical and a dramatic and an emotional account of the origins and development of the epidemic.

Received as a significant breakthrough in discussions of the HIV-AIDS crisis in South Africa, *Shattered Dreams?* was the culmination of the work entailed in four extended visits to South Africa by Oppenheimer and Bayer, where interviews were conducted with seventy-three doctors and thirteen nurses directly engaged with the crisis. Major authorities on the subject, both Oppenheimer and Bayer are professors of Clinical Sociomedical Sciences at the Mailman School of Public Health, Columbia University. Their study, which remains an important document in studies in the history and literature of the HIV-AIDS crisis in South Africa, provides an account of the epidemic from the often unique points of view that frequently challenge the politicized perspectives of official discourse.

HISTORICAL AND LITERARY CONTEXT

A major strand in Oppenheimer and Bayer's work is, as Shapiro puts it, "the political economy of health care." As such, much of *Shattered Dreams?* is composed of a discussion of the South African HIV-AIDS crisis as it relates to the sociopolitical effects of the policy of apartheid, as well as its long-range legacies in twenty-first-century South Africa. By the 1980s apartheid—the policy of forced segregation between "Whites," "Blacks," and "Coloured" that was implemented and maintained by the National Party of South Africa since 1948—had produced a country riven by extreme socioeconomic disparities. These inequalities included the access to adequate public health care, which was rationed on an extremely asymmetrical basis.

While the text does trace the origins of the HIV-AIDS epidemic to the 1980s, the bulk of *Shattered Dreams?* focuses on the "new South Africa"—the period after the release of Nelson Mandela from prison in 1990 and the first democratic elections in 1994. Central to this is an examination of the impact of the public health policies of the African National Congress (ANC) governments of Mandela and Thabo Mbeki. This includes the acute mismanagement of the HIV-AIDS crisis by Mbeki, who publicly denied the causal link between HIV and AIDS and claimed that this link was maintained fallaciously by Western drug companies interested in marketing drugs for antiretroviral therapy (ART).

At the time of publication, *Shattered Dreams?* represented a unique text in the discourse of HIV-AIDS in South Africa. Written in the loose sense as a "history from the bottom up" in the American tradition of authors such as Studs Terkel and Howard Zinn, the text concentrates on reinstating the voices of doctors and nurses, who were until then somewhat overlooked in discussions of the crisis. It can be read profitably in conjunction with other studies of the crisis published about the same time, including Nicoli Nattrass's *The Moral Economy of AIDS in South Africa* (2004), Didier Fassin's *When Bodies Remember* (2007), and Pieter Fourie and Melissa Meyer's *The Politics of AIDS Denialism* (2010). *Shattered Dreams?* can also be compared with Oppenheimer and Bayer's earlier monograph from 2000, *AIDS Doctors: Voices from the Epidemic: An Oral History*, which has a parallel theme and style that focus on the origins and development of the HIV-AIDS crisis in the United States.

At the time of publication, the work represented a unique perspective on the HIV-AIDS crisis in South Africa. It remains an important document in the propagation of information and the formulation of strategic responses to the epidemic, which is ongoing and has complex, often unaddressed, legacies. These legacies remain central to any response to the country's social problems. Beyond this the work represents

Shattered Dreams? looks at the way the AIDS epidemic affected South Africa. Though the South African government had failed AIDS policies for many years, Nelson Mandela, who served as president from 1994 to 1999, became an AIDS activist. © AP IMAGES/ SCHALK VAN ZUYDAM

a stark warning concerning the management of public health emergencies, with important lessons to be learned regarding the relationship between politics and health care for a broader non–South African audience.

THEMES AND STYLE

Thematically, *Shattered Dreams?* provides a panorama of the epidemic, tracing its origins in the 1980s and charting its progress into the twenty-first century. Chapters include "Facing AIDS: Denial, Indifference, and Fear," "The Burden of AIDS: Treatment and Its Discontents," and "Defiance: Creating Islands of Treatment," the latter being a discussion of how clinical investigators were able to use the epidemic for research, incorporating the efforts of international aid organizations and private medical insurance firms to demonstrate the efficacy of antiretroviral treatments. Interviews with doctors and nurses in this chapter show that "such innovative efforts provided the occasion for witnessing the extraordinary power of ART [and that] these experiences only served to reinforce their commitment to fundamentally changing the government's posture on AIDS."

The stated objective of the text is to provide a human face to the crisis and to "give readers an appreciation of what it has been like to be a caregiver … but also a visceral sense of the human toll that has been exacted, a toll often difficult to grasp even as the brutal statistics that define the scope of the epidemic are recited." Writing for *Oral History Review*, W. Rickard notes that *Shattered Dreams?* "chooses the same method and focus as its American predecessor [also by Oppenheimer and Bayer], *AIDS Doctors*." The method in question is perhaps best described as a hybridized form of oral history that, rather than concentrating strictly on individual personalities, weaves multiple perspectives to form a consistently threaded narrative.

Shattered Dreams? features a mix of analytical, academic (though at all times accessible) material and pertinent direct quotation from the authors' interviewees that, though clearly edited, captures an array of real spoken language. In line with the defining impulse of oral history, the work shows a commitment to allowing its subjects to speak in their own terms. For example, James Muller of the Pietermaritzburg Metropolitan Hospital Complex describes the disparity in health care as available to the rich and the poor in postapartheid South Africa: "If you are a rich man, you get a Mercedes-Benz. If you are a poor man, you walk; you go buy a pair of shoes. … But if you're a rich man, and you've got a hell of a lot of pain in your hip, you can get it fixed. But if you are a poor man, and you have a hell of a lot of pain in your hip, you can't get it fixed. That's not fair." As is common with oral history, the text retains dialectal spelling that reflects the interviewees' diverse national and cultural backgrounds, giving the text a raw, gritty feel and adding to its authenticity as a frontline-level view of the HIV-AIDS epidemic.

THABO MBEKI AND THE AIDS CONTROVERSY

An important part of the narrative promoted by Gerald M. Oppenheimer and Ronald Bayer—that the scale of South Africa's HIV-AIDS epidemic was exacerbated by poor policy decisions made by postapartheid African National Congress (ANC) governments—focuses on the role of denialism in the crisis. The most famous example of this was the controversy surrounding comments made by Thabo Mbeki in 2000 in which the South African president publicly denied the causal link between HIV and AIDS. Under the influence of Peter Duesberg from the University of California, Berkeley, Mbeki arrived at the position that AIDS developed as a result of poverty and that the HIV-AIDS link was maintained by Western drug companies whose business it was to promote antiretroviral drugs. The result was the state itself "emerg[ing] as the most persistent obstacle to the provision of antiretrovirals to South Africans suffering from AIDS."

The effects of policies based on this denialism were catastrophic. According to P. Chigwedere in the *Journal of Acquired Immune Deficiency Syndromes,* in 2008 researchers from Harvard University estimated that "more than 330,000 lives or approximately 2.2 million person-years were lost because a feasible and timely ARV [antiretroviral] treatment program was not implemented in South Africa."

CRITICAL DISCUSSION

Although there is a dearth of formal scholarship that concentrates on *Shattered Dreams?,* critical discussion locates the book as an important document of the HIV-AIDS crisis in South Africa, written by two of the most important international authorities on the subject. More broadly the authors have been lauded for the quality of their work; for example, on the back cover of *AIDS Doctors,* Studs Terkel described Oppenheimer and Bayer as "masterful interviewers."

More generally discussion of Oppenheimer and Bayer's work has concentrated on their innovative use of the oral history form. In a review of *AIDS Doctors,* Fitzhugh Mullan describes Oppenheimer and Bayer's method as not deploying "oral history in its most common form, as a chronological narrative that gives the reader a full picture of an individual. Rather, they use multiple short excerpts to amplify and punctuate the story." This produces "a rolling and colorful chorus of voices."

Because *Shattered Dreams?* has no attendant body of formal criticism, there remains considerable scope for critics to elucidate the significance of the text. Further criticism could examine the relationship between the narrative constructed in *Shattered Dreams?* and the broader historical narrative of postapartheid South Africa, examining particularly the points at which the text could challenge official political discourse.

BIBLIOGRAPHY

Sources

Chigwedere, P., et al. "Estimating the Lost Benefits of Antiretroviral Drug Use in South Africa." *Journal of Acquired Immune Deficiency Syndromes* 49.4 (2008): 410–15. Print.

Mullan, Fitzhugh. "Angels in America." Rev. of *AIDS Doctors: Voices from the Epidemic: An Oral History,* by Gerald M. Oppenheimer and Ronald Bayer. *New York Times Book Reviews 2000: Volume 2: July–December.* Chicago: Fitzroy Dearborn, 2001. 1488–89. Print.

Oppenheimer, Gerald M., and Ronald Bayer. *Shattered Dreams? An Oral History of the South African AIDS Epidemic.* Oxford, UK: Oxford University Press, 2007. Print.

Rickard, W. Rev. of *Shattered Dreams? An Oral History of the South African AIDS Epidemic,* by Gerald M. Oppenheimer and Ronald Bayer. *Oral History Review* 35.2 (2008): 227–29. Print.

Shapiro, Karin. Rev. of *Shattered Dreams? An Oral History of the South African AIDS Epidemic,* by Gerald M. Oppenheimer and Ronald Bayer. *Journal of the History of Medicine and Applied Science* 63.398–401 (2008): n. pag. Project MUSE. Web. 28 Dec. 2012.

Further Reading

Bayer, Ronald, and Gerald M. Oppenheimer. "Scale-Ups, Scarcity, and Selections: The Experience of Doctors in South Africa." *AIDS* 12.5 (2007): S43–47. Print.

Fassin, Didier. *When Bodies Remember: Experiences and Politics of AIDS in South Africa.* Los Angeles: University of California Press, 2007. Print.

Fourie, Pieter, and Melissa Meyer. *The Politics of AIDS Denialism: South Africa's Failure to Respond.* Burlington, Vt.: Ashgate, 2010. Print.

Nattrass, Nicoli. *The Moral Economy of AIDS in South Africa.* New York: Cambridge University Press, 2004. Print.

Oppenheimer, Gerald M., and Ronald Bayer. *AIDS Doctors: Voices from the Epidemic: An Oral History.* Oxford, UK: Oxford University Press, 2000. Print.

Oppenheimer, Gerald M., Ronald Bayer, and James Colgrave. "Health and Human Rights: Old Wine in New Bottles?" *Journal of Law, Medicine & Ethics* (2002): 522–32. Print.

Youde, Jeremy R. *AIDS, South Africa, and the Politics of Knowledge.* Burlington, Vt.: Ashgate, 2007. Print.

Franklyn Hyde

Strange Ground: Americans in Vietnam 1945–1975
An Oral History
Harry Maurer

OVERVIEW

Harry Maurer's *Strange Ground: Americans in Vietnam 1945–1975: An Oral History* (1989) is a collection of sixty-two oral histories of a diverse group of civilian and military individuals who were involved in the Vietnam War. The interviews, conducted in the early 1980s, cover the span of American involvement in Vietnam from 1945 to 1975. Maurer's text addresses various subjects related to America's presence in Vietnam, including the interviewees' perceptions of mistakes made during the war and their personal memories and regrets, as well as the pacification program and nature of war. As a whole, *Strange Ground* effectively presents the wide range of emotions and opinions of the general American public regarding the tragedy of Vietnam.

Written by a self-identified draft dodger, *Strange Ground* was published fourteen years after the withdrawal of the last U.S. troops from Vietnam. Critics saw value in the personal insight into America's presence in Vietnam provided by the oral histories in the book, but they found Maurer's antiwar ideology—presented primarily in the book's introduction—problematic, warning that it potentially compromised the book's objectivity. Reviewers nevertheless praised the wide range of perspectives presented in the text, which was not limited to an antiwar perspective but presented both pro- and antiwar stances, as well as more neutral personal narratives. Emerging at a time when a plethora of other books and oral histories on Vietnam were published, *Strange Ground* did not receive the high level of acclaim of other best sellers on the subject. Nonetheless, it is still highly regarded as a valuable oral history on the war.

HISTORICAL AND LITERARY CONTEXT

The Vietnam War officially began in the mid-1950s as an attempt by the United States to prevent the spread of communism from North to South Vietnam. The government quickly lost the American public's support for the war, and throughout the 1960s there were massive antiwar protests demanding an end to what was seen as a senseless conflict. As many of the interviewees in Maurer's book acknowledge, most military personnel knew that there was no way they could win the war. This contributed to low morale, anger, and increased drug use among U.S. troops. The humiliation of the North Vietnamese Army's devastating surprise attack in 1968, known as the Tet Offensive, was a turning point, leading to the initiation of a slow process of de-escalation.

In the decades immediately following the U.S. military's withdrawal from Vietnam, discussions of the war were caustic and highly charged. It quickly became clear that the Vietnam War was the United States' most divisive military involvement since the Civil War. Accusations of cover-ups and military blunders during the war discredited and disgraced numerous military and governmental personnel and sources involved in the war. Most American troops left Vietnam by March 1973, with the last departing on April 30, 1975. By the mid- to late 1980s, the American public had essentially scorned official sources on the war and was more interested in the stories of individual Americans who had experienced the war firsthand. All of the individuals interviewed for *Strange Ground* were intimately involved in the events surrounding this war, and their stories reveal much of the devastation, mishandling of situations, and atrocities carried out in the name of democracy during the war.

Upon the publication of *Strange Ground* in 1989, several oral histories on the Vietnam War were already on the market. Maurer's book follows this literary tradition, exemplified by such books as *Everything We Had: An Oral History of the Vietnam War An Oral History of the Vietnam War* (1981), edited by Al Santoli; Wallace Terry's *Bloods: An Oral History of the Vietnam War by Black Veterans* (1984); and Kim Willenson's *The Bad War: An Oral History of the Vietnam War* (1987), among others. Some oral histories on the subject focus on specific issues. For example, *Bloods* spotlights the experience of black soldiers in the war. *Strange Ground* incorporates a diverse range of interview subjects, much like Willenson's book, although *The Bad War* more directly addresses the circumstances surrounding the failure of the war.

Strange Ground has contributed to a more nuanced understanding of individual Americans'

❖ **Key Facts**

Time Period:
Mid-20th Century

Relevant Historical Events:
Vietnam War

Nationality:
American

Keywords:
war; activism; pacification

A Vietnamese vendor and an American tourist in Hanoi, Vietnam, in a photograph taken circa 1995. The experiences of many Americans in Vietnam are captured in Harry Maurer's book *Strange Ground: Americans in Vietnam 1945–1975.* © STEVE RAYMER/CORBIS

experiences of the Vietnam War, and scholars recognize it as an important oral history on this subject. Its relative success led Maurer to embark on other oral history projects, including his 1994 *Sex: An Oral History.* The author's approach to the oral historiography of war has influenced similar books published on the Vietnam War and on America's more recent military interventions, including those in Iraq. Such books include James Tollefson's *The Strength Not to Fight: An Oral History of Conscientious Objectors of the Vietnam War* (1993), Trish Wood's *What Was Asked of Us: An Oral History of the Iraq War by the Soldiers Who Fought It* (2006), and Bill Katovsky and Timothy Carlson's *Embedded: The Media at War in Iraq: An Oral History* (2003).

THEMES AND STYLE

The central themes of *Strange Ground* include the experiences of military personnel, former prisoners of war, nurses, and diplomats, as well as their opinions regarding how the war should have been fought and what can be learned from America's experiences in Vietnam. Former combat nurse Jane Piper recalls, "I got there in March. Around July, I started to cry myself to sleep at night.... I didn't realize until I got home that I had been crying for a long time." Reflecting on the mistakes made in Vietnam, Lieutenant General William Fulton states, "I think the U.S. made one basic mistake, and that was our failure to fully integrate our operations with the Vietnamese.... One of the principles of war is unity of command. In Vietnam, it was violated, pure and simple." The oral histories present the discord and turmoil that still surround the Vietnam War decades later, especially for those who were intimately involved in the conflict.

Addressing his motivations for writing *Strange Ground,* Maurer writes in the introduction, "I took my deferment and went on with my life.... This book, in a sense, grew out of that day and that dilemma" and out of the realization that he "knew nothing of the men who fought the war, nor of the fighting itself." When conducting interviews at unemployment centers across the country in the early 1980s, he gained his first insights into the discrimination and stigma faced by Vietnam veterans and embarked on an oral history project that would present the experiences of war from diverse perspectives. As he notes in the introduction, the individuals interviewed for the book were generally chosen at random; they often were acquaintances of friends, although "in certain cases ... [he] read about specific people and undertook to find them." Although he wrote the narratives based on recorded interviews with his subjects, he allows each individual to speak for himself or herself in the book.

Maurer employs a reflective and interrogative tone in *Strange Ground.* For example, in his introduction, he attempts to draw overarching conclusions regarding the war, asserting that the United States must ask a certain question when contemplating "war on foreign soil: What will we be fighting for? Ultimately, that problem was the weak link in Vietnam, not flawed strategy or tactics.... American goals seemed either muddy or misguided." Maurer interprets the events and experiences shared by the subjects of his oral histories in order to glean some insight into the war. The interviews in the book are organized by subject, but they advance chronologically, focusing on different periods of the conflict. Maurer begins each section with a timeline of historical events related to that period, and he presents a brief biography of each subject before his or her oral history. The individuals whose narratives are shared in the book include nurses, civilian aid workers, photographers and reporters, soldiers, government officials, and high-ranking military officers. Their stints in Vietnam cover the span of the U.S. presence there, beginning before 1950 and lasting until the early 1970s.

CRITICAL DISCUSSION

Although *Strange Ground* did not receive as much critical attention as *Bloods* or *Everything We Had*, scholars praised the book for its valuable contributions to oral historiography on the Vietnam War. In a 1997 article in *Organization of American Historians: Magazine of History*, William Brinker calls *Strange Ground* "one of the most valuable oral histories of the Vietnam era," describing it as "monumental in breadth and depth." Certain scholars, such as Richard Hunt, have reservations about the large time lapse between when the events occurred and when the interviews were conducted, warning in a 1991 review in *Conflict Quarterly*, "The historian needs to handle these interviews cautiously. It would be imprudent to accept them unreservedly as accurate historical documents."

Although *Strange Ground* is frequently cited among the body of oral histories on the Vietnam War, Maurer's work has been largely overshadowed by more popular collections. Thus there is little extant scholarship that discusses the book in depth. Patrick Hagopian briefly references the book in a 1991 article for *History Workshop*, but it does not make his list of best sellers that "are widely used in school and university courses about the war." The scholarship addressing *Strange Ground* focuses primarily on its function as an oral history within the genre of Vietnam War literature. Hunt writes, "To his credit, the editor allows each person to speak in his or her voice. On the basis of their interviews, most individuals have seriously reflected on the personal meaning of their time in Vietnam and the significance of the war."

Certain scholarship on *Strange Ground*, including a 1990 review published in *Kirkus Reviews*, addresses the disturbing nature of many of the stories shared by the subjects of the oral histories: "Although nearly all the accounts are involving, by far the most powerful are those of combat—from that of the free-lance reporter recalling a napalm attack ... to that of the former Special Forces operative describing the gruesome torture of Viet Cong." Other reviewers focus on a specific group of oral histories within the book. For example, in *Officer, Nurse, Woman: The Army Nurse Corps in the Vietnam War* (2010), Kara Dixon Vuic describes the interviews of women involved in the war. She cites Piper's oral history in *Strange Ground* to illustrate how "some women, despite their vulnerability, found a new sense of power and control in their relationships with men.... Many women enjoyed being the center of attention in Vietnam, but as Jane Piper warned, 'You had to remind yourself that it wasn't going to be like that when you came home.'"

JOURNALIST AND ORAL HISTORIAN HARRY MAURER

An experienced American journalist well versed in the genre of oral history, Harry Maurer began his career as a reporter and author after graduating from Columbia University in New York in 1970. Attending college at the height of the Vietnam War, he was active in antiwar protests, especially the Columbia University protests of 1968. In the mid-1970s, following his graduation and exemption from the draft, he worked as a journalist covering national unemployment, which led to the publication of his first book of oral history, *Not Working: An Oral History of the Unemployed* (1979).

He continued his work in oral history with *Strange Ground: Americans in Vietnam 1945–1975: An Oral History* (1989) and *Sex: An Oral History* (1994). He also published *Webs of Power: International Cartels and the World Economy* in 1982 in collaboration with Kurt Rudolf Mirow. Maurer began his career as an editor at *BusinessWeek* in 1985, working as copy chief for the international edition, where he oversaw two feature sections, "International Spotlight" and "Letters From." He went on to become an editor for *Bloomberg News* in Rio de Janeiro and has also worked as a writer and editor for *BusinessWeek* magazine in New York and as a contributor to *Harper's* and the *Nation*.

BIBLIOGRAPHY

Sources

Brinker, William J. "Oral History and the Vietnam War." *Organization of American Historians: Magazine of History* 11.3 (1997): 15–19. Print.

Hagopian, Patrick. "Oral Narratives: Secondary Revision and the Memory of the Vietnam War." *History Workshop* 32 (1991): 134–50. Print.

Hunt, Richard. Rev. of *Strange Ground: Americans in Vietnam 1945–1975: An Oral History*, by Harry Maurer. *Conflict Quarterly* 11.4 (1991): 60–61. Print.

Maurer, Harry. *Strange Ground: Americans in Vietnam 1945–1975: An Oral History*. New York: Henry Holt, 1989. Print.

Rev. of *Strange Ground: Americans in Vietnam 1945–1975: An Oral History*, by Harry Maurer. *Kirkus Reviews*. Kirkus Reviews, 1990. Web. 28 Jan. 2013.

Vuic, Kara Dixon. *Officer, Nurse, Woman: The Army Nurse Corps in the Vietnam War*. Baltimore: Johns Hopkins University Press, 2010. Print.

Further Reading

Nguyen, Hien Duc. Rev. of *Strange Ground: Americans in Vietnam 1945–1975: An Oral History*, by Harry Maurer. *School Library Journal* 36.2 (1990): 122. Print.

Santoli, Al. *Everything We Had: An Oral History of the Vietnam War.* New York: Random House, 1981. Print.

Terry, Wallace. *Bloods: An Oral History of the Vietnam War by Black Veterans.* New York: Random House, 1984. Print.

Tollefson, James. *The Strength Not to Fight: An Oral History of Conscientious Objectors of the Vietnam War.* Boston: Little, Brown, 1993. Print.

Willenson, Kim. *The Bad War: An Oral History of the Vietnam War.* New York: New American Library, 1987. Print.

Wood, Trish. *What Was Asked of Us: An Oral History of the Iraq War by the Soldiers Who Fought It.* New York: Little, Brown, 2006. Print.

Katrina White

Tears before the Rain
An Oral History of the Fall of South Vietnam
Larry Engelmann

OVERVIEW

With interviews collected and edited by Larry Engelmann, *Tears before the Rain: An Oral History of the Fall of South Vietnam,* published in 1990, presents narratives of American and Vietnamese witnesses, both military and civilian, who survived the collapse of South Vietnam in the first months of 1975. While previous oral histories of the conflict in Vietnam focused on certain demographics—women, African Americans, or refugees—and related their experiences during the entire war, Engelmann's book provides a cross section of a single, definitive event as witnessed by a variety of individuals.

Tears before the Rain, unlike most of the histories of Vietnam published at the time, does not take sides in the conflict and offers no specific insights into the politics of the situation. It was published at the same time as a number of high-profile books on the subject, including a memoir by CBS correspondent Morley Safer and apologias and analyses by Central Intelligence Agency director William Colby, air force strategist Mark Clodfelter, former Secretary of State Dean Rusk, and anthropologist James M. Freeman. The book at once became required reading for anyone writing about the end of the war, and it continues to be studied today.

HISTORICAL AND LITERARY CONTEXT

From 1884 until 1954 France controlled Indochina (now Cambodia, Laos, and Vietnam). After the disastrous 1954 defeat of the French Union forces at Dienbienphu by a Viet Minh army led by General Vo Nguyen Giap, the French withdrew from the region and granted independence to Cambodia, Laos, and Vietnam. Vietnam was divided—temporarily, it was assumed—into north and south regions at the 17th parallel. When the French departed, the United States took over the job of shoring up the anticommunist government of South Vietnam. The U.S. military presence in South Vietnam grew from nine hundred advisers during the Eisenhower presidency to more than 500,000 combat troops in 1968, the last full year of the Johnson presidency, but to no avail. The corruption and incompetence of the South Vietnamese government and the superior organization and motivation of the communists led to the U.S. withdrawal from the country in 1973.

The two years between the U.S. pledge to leave Vietnam and the departure of U.S. troops on April 30, 1975, were chaotic and confusing. The South Vietnamese refused to honor the cease-fire, and the firefights they provoked continued to draw in U.S. forces. The American people and the U.S. government were distracted by Watergate, which led to the resignation of President Richard M. Nixon in 1974. In March 1975 North Vietnam launched its third full-scale invasion of South Vietnam. The South Vietnamese forces collapsed, and in a matter of weeks the North Vietnamese were forty miles from Saigon. By April 29 they were on the outskirts of the city, and the Americans and their Vietnamese allies did what they could to evacuate.

By the time of the 1990 publication of *Tears before the Rain,* oral history had become a popular literary form, chiefly through the success of Studs Terkel's *Hard Times: An Oral History of the Great Depression* (1970) and *"The Good War": An Oral History of World War II* (1984), which won the Pulitzer Prize for nonfiction. The first recollections of the Vietnam War were mostly memoirs and fictional reconstructions. Oral histories began to appear around 1980, including Al Santoli's *Everything We Had: An Oral History of the Vietnam War* (1981); Wallace Terry's *Bloods: An Oral History of the Vietnam War by Black Veterans* (1984), and Kathryn Marshall's *In the Combat Zone: An Oral History of American Women in Vietnam* (1987).

Tears before the Rain received few reviews, but all were positive. The dearth of critical attention may have been the result of the book coming near the end of a series of similar histories, which gave it less influence than if it had been among the first. It was recognized as a valuable primary source of information and anecdotes about the fall of Vietnam. Nevertheless, it is not an uplifting volume, and almost none of the interviewees appears at his or her best—most were either running for their lives or standing by helplessly while horrible things happened around them.

THEMES AND STYLE

The themes of *Tears before the Rain* are the shock and panic among Americans, the anger and desperation of their Vietnamese allies, and the triumph and

❖ *Key Facts*

Time Period:
Mid- to Late 20th Century

Relevant Historical Events:
Collapse of South Vietnam; Vietnam War

Nationality:
Vietnamese

Keywords:
war; collapse; invasion

Vietnamese refugees flee rocket attacks during the fall of Saigon, April 1975. © JACQUES PAVLOVSKY/SYGMA/CORBIS

exhaustion of the communists. "When I arrived I saw the chaos, of course," recalls ABC News reporter Ken Kashiwahara. "But I didn't sense that the country was going to fall.... I think I was sort of caught up in the optimism of it all." In less than twenty-four hours, he saw the crowds inside the U.S. embassy walls, noting, "The whole scene was like an island of one kind of insanity in a world of another kind of insanity." North Vietnamese commander Colonel Bui Tin tells of how, during the 1975 surrender of General Duong Van Minh, he asked about the general's tennis and orchids. "I surprised them," he laughs, "because I knew everything about them. Everything. And they knew nothing about me!" Engelmann also devotes considerable space to the so-called boat people, the Vietnamese who feared for their safety after the communist takeover but were too poor, or too poorly connected, to evacuate with the Americans. Instead they escaped in small, barely seaworthy boats. "Every night I cry for Vietnam," remarks one who managed to get to the United States. "I remember and I cry. In the darkness my memories turn into tears."

Engelmann has said that he began to write about Vietnam as a favor to his friends. He began talking to American and South Vietnamese veterans in 1985 and continued his research for the next five years, traveling all over the United States and Southeast Asia, interviewing "victors and vanquished, children and adults, soldiers, civilians, and politicians"—in all, more than three hundred individuals—and getting them to talk "about the last days of the war in Vietnam" and about their lives since.

Tears before the Rain comprises three sections: "Americans," "Vietnamese," and "Aftermath." Each is arranged by the speaker's role, such as "Military," "Civilians," and "Media." Engelmann provides only a short preface to the book and offers no other annotation. Except for some self-serving American officials and some rehearsed recitations by North Vietnamese victors, the narratives are notable for their lack of perspective—as if it were impossible to recall the events without dropping right back into the thick of them: "I felt a woman pulling on me from the side of the stair," recalls Jan Wollett, a flight attendant on the last USAID flight out of Da Nang. "But a man behind her grabbed her and ... stepped on her back and on her head to get up and over the railing ... Mr. Daly smashed him in the head with his pistol. I remember suddenly seeing a sheet of blood splash across everything ... and I remember thinking, 'Good.'"

CRITICAL DISCUSSION

Reviews of *Tears before the Rain* were mostly positive. However, a 1990 article for *Kirkus Reviews* notes that Engelmann devotes "an inordinate number of pages to the experiences of partisan Americans, whose memories tend to dwell on the same events again and again, and who invariably castigate US politicians and reporters for 'betraying' South Vietnam." Jonathan Mirsky, writing in the *New York Review of Books* in 1990, praises the work as "revealing," noting that "where Engelmann's book becomes valuable is in the interviews with the Vietnamese, many of them boat people, who often at great peril have made their way to the United States." In a 1991 article for *Journal of Asian Studies,* Marilyn Young observes that "as a book of documents, *Tears before the Rain* makes an important contribution to the history of the demise of ... South Vietnam; it is not itself a history of that demise."

Engelmann's refusal to pursue an agenda or to editorialize on the legion of controversies surrounding America's Vietnam experience kept the book from becoming dated. He has never been accused of putting words in his subjects' mouths, a practice that has tarnished the reputation of Wallace Terry's *Bloods: An Oral History of the Vietnam War by Black Veterans* (1984). Every account of a major incident has been checked against all other accounts—on newsreel footage, in memoirs and documents, in other oral histories—and has mainly held up.

Scholars have mined *Tears before the Rain* for its vivid illustrations of the situation on the ground. The *Vietnam War Reference Library* (2001) excerpts from Engelmann's interview with Pham Van Xinh, "a security officer with the South Vietnamese military … [who] recalls what it was like when the Communists assumed control of Da Nang." Historians working on focused monographs glean what they can from Engelmann's interviews with the major players on either side, using the book for supporting evidence and for snapshots of the chaotic reality of the moment.

BIBLIOGRAPHY

Sources

Engelmann, Larry, ed. *Tears before the Rain: An Oral History of the Fall of South Vietnam.* New York: Oxford University Press, 1990. Print.

Mirsky, Jonathan. "The War That Will Not End." Rev. of *Tears before the Rain,* ed. Larry Engelmann. *New York Review of Books.* New York Review of Books, 16 Aug. 1990. Web. 4 Jan. 2013.

Rev. of *Tears before the Rain,* ed. Larry Engelmann. *Kirkus Reviews.* Kirkus Reviews, 30 Aug. 1990. Web. 5 Jan. 2013.

Santoli, Al, ed. *Everything We Had: An Oral History of the Vietnam War.* New York: Random House, 1981. Print.

"Victory for North Vietnam (1973–75)." *Vietnam War Reference Library.* Ed. Kevin Hillstrom, Laurie Collier Hillstrom, and Diane M Sawinski. Vol. 3. Detroit: UXL, 2001. 237–39. *Gale Virtual Reference Library.* Web. 2 Jan. 2013.

Young, Marilyn B. Rev. of *Tears before the Rain,* ed. Larry Engelmann. *Journal of Asian Studies* 50.2 (1991): 452–53. Print.

Further Reading

Miller, Laura M. "The Fall of Saigon." *Dictionary of American History.* Ed. Stanley I. Kutler. 3rd ed. Vol. 9. New York: Scribner, 2003. 477–79. *Gale Virtual Reference Library.* Web. 10 Jan. 2013.

Safer, Morley. *Flashbacks: On Returning to Vietnam.* New York: Random House, 1990. Print.

ORAL HISTORY AND THE HISTORIAN

The genre of oral history has as much to do with the academic profession of history as it does with sociology, anthropology, psychology, and ethnography. To the academic historian, the narratives in Larry Engelmann's *Tears before the Rain* are documents to be treated like any other primary source: checked for authenticity, corrected for bias, and compared with other documents pertaining to the same subject. Only when their reliability has been reasonably ascertained can the information they contain be provisionally accepted as factual. Oral histories are always subject to revaluation when further research turns up information that either confirms or disproves what the subject has said.

One of the problems with oral history for the academic historian is that an oral history is always the work of two people: the subject and the interviewer. The interviewer tends to be invisible in the finished product. For example, Engelmann, after his preface, is nowhere to be found in *Tears before the Rain.* Yet the questions the interviewer asks of the subject, and how the subject feels about the interviewer, can profoundly affect the shape and content of the oral history collected. Until these problems are worked out, *Tears before the Rain* will remain, as Marilyn Young writes in *Journal of Asian Studies* in 1991, "an important contribution to … history … [but] not itself a history."

Smith, Patricia. "1975: The Fall of Saigon: Why the Vietnam War Still Matters 35 Years after It Ended." *New York Times* 5 Apr. 2010: 14–17. *General OneFile.* Web. 7 Jan. 2013.

Terkel, Studs. *"The Good War": An Oral History of World War II.* New York: Pantheon, 1984. Print.

Walker, Keith. *A Piece of My Heart: The Stories of Twenty-Six American Women Who Served in Vietnam.* Novato, Calif.: Presidio, 1985. Print.

Gerald Carpenter

VOICES FROM CHERNOBYL
The Oral History of a Nuclear Disaster
Svetlana Alexievich

✣ Key Facts

Time Period:
Late 20th Century

Relevant Historical Events:
Chernobyl nuclear reactor explosion

Nationality:
Belarusan

Keywords:
nuclear disasters; collective memory; glasnost

OVERVIEW

Originally published in Russian in 1997, *Chernobyl Prayer: Chronicle of the Future* was written by Belarusan journalist Svetlana Alexievich. Edited and translated by Keith Gessen for U.S. audiences in 2006, the book was republished as *Voices from Chernobyl: The Oral History of a Nuclear Disaster*. Featuring testimony from more than one hundred survivors, *Voices from Chernobyl* chronicles the April 26, 1986, explosion at the Chernobyl nuclear power plant in Ukraine, which killed thirty-one people and exposed tens of thousands to extremely high doses of radiation. Working in a genre she calls "documentary prose," Alexievich creatively recomposes material transcribed from interviews conducted over a three-year period. At its core *Voices from Chernobyl* comprises two lengthy soliloquies by the wives of primary and secondary responders who died, dozens of multi-paragraph monologues attributed to individual survivors, and three communal choruses voiced by soldiers, citizens, and children whose names are listed collectively before the fragmentary text of their statements.

Initially greeted with ambivalence in the former Soviet Union, *Voices from Chernobyl* was embraced by Western European audiences in the late 1990s and in the first decade of the 2000s. When it was published in the United States as *Voices from Chernobyl*, it earned the National Book Critics Circle award in time for the twentieth anniversary of the disaster. With its heavy focus on the author's native Belarus and its global perspective, *Voices from Chernobyl* helped pave the way for Alexievich's unofficial designation as "The Conscience of Belarus" in 2003. However, *Voices from Chernobyl's* greatest impact has been felt on stage and screen as segments of its text have been transformed into theatrical and film productions all over the world.

HISTORICAL AND LITERARY CONTEXT

Alexievich began conducting interviews with survivors shortly after the Soviet Union's 1991 collapse, which many historians claim was hastened by the Chernobyl tragedy. Although President Mikhail Gorbachev had introduced a policy of glasnost, or "openness," several months prior to the nuclear explosion, his government was silent about flaws that had been identified in Chernobyl's reactor design well before the events of April 26. The government also refused to speak on the source of nuclear fallout detected in Sweden just two days after the explosion, the degree to which the disaster was under control as May Day parade crowds filled irradiated streets, and the safety steps Soviet citizens could have taken during the weeks and months that followed.

Although Alexievich begins interviewing her post-Chernobyl subjects as the policy of openness became more of a reality in the former Soviet Union, she encounters one interviewee who blatantly defends the Communist Party, another who argues that the Kremlin's deceit was absolutely necessary to "prevent a panic," and yet another who says he and his fellow Belarusan countrymen are "still Stalin's people." Even the dissident Alexievich might be seen as a product of her Soviet upbringing as she continues to work in a genre that—unlike the Western oral histories gaining influence in Eastern Europe after communism's fall—seriously lacks methodological transparency.

As might be expected, Alexievich was not the only journalist to respond to the Chernobyl disaster in a subtly creative, rather than overtly critical, way. Indeed the text that many consider the first literary product to emerge from the disaster—a play titled *Sarcophagus*—was written by a science journalist named Vladimir Gubarev in only seven days just months after the accident. Although drama might have allowed Alexievich to present some of the material she collected about the tragedy to similar effect, she was already a committed practitioner of documentary prose. In *Recreation of Chernobyl Trauma in Svetlana Aleksiyevich's Chernobyl'skya Molitva* (2008), Doris Scribner explains that documentary prose involves the "aesthetic arrangement of factographic documents into a new whole" and originally developed in Soviet Russia "out of a need to reshape … experience … during a time when it was not physically safe to be honest." As a Belarusan dissident influenced by Ales Adamovich's document-based "collective novels" and Vasily Bykaw's truth-telling historical fiction, Alexievich claims that she writes in this genre not to be dishonest but in order to be more emotionally honest. The initial suppression of her first two books by the Belarusan Central Committee in 1983 may also have led her toward the genre to protect her writing from

VOICES FROM CHERNOBYL

This photograph from 1990 shows the Chernobyl reactor 4 towers in the background and contaminated heavy equipment abandoned in the foreground. © CHUCK NACKE/ALAMY

PRIMARY SOURCE

EXCERPT FROM *VOICES FROM CHERNOBYL*

MONOLOGUE ABOUT LIES AND TRUTHS

Sergei Sobolev, deputy head of the Executive Committee of the Shield of Chernobyl Association

They've written dozens of books. Fat volumes, with commentaries. But the event is still beyond any philosophical description. Someone said to me, or maybe I read it, that the problem of Chernobyl presents itself first of all as a problem of self-understanding.

That seemed right. I keep waiting for someone intelligent to explain it to me. The way they enlighten me about Stalin, Lenin, Bolshevism. Or the way they keep hammering away at their "Market! Market! Free market!" But we—we who were raised in a world without Chernobyl, now live with Chernobyl.

I'm actually a professional rocketeer, I specialize in rocket fuel. I served at Baikonur [a space launch center]. The programs, Kosmos, Interkosmos, those took up a large part of my life. It was a miraculous time! You give people the sky, the Arctic, the whole thing! You give them space! Every person in the Soviet Union went into space with Yuri Gagarin, they tore away from the earth with him. We all did! I'm still in love with him—he was a wonderful Russian man, with that wonderful smile. Even his death seemed well-rehearsed.

It was a miraculous time! For family reasons I moved to Belarus, finished my career here. When I came, I immersed myself into this Chernobylized space, it was a corrective to my sense of things. It was impossible to imagine anything like it, even though I'd always dealt with the most advanced technologies, with outer space technologies. It's hard even to explain—it doesn't fit into the imagination—it's—[*He thinks.*] You know, a second ago I thought I'd caught it, a second ago—it makes you want to philosophize. No matter who you talk to about Chernobyl, they all want to philosophize. But I'd rather tell you about my own work. What don't we do! We're building a church—a Chernobyl church, in honor of the Icon of the Mother of God, we're dedicating it to "Punishment." We collect donations, visit the sick and dying. We write chronicles. We're creating a museum. I used to think that I, with my heart in the condition it's in, wouldn't be able to work at such a job. My first instructions were: "Here is money, divide it between thirty-five families, that is, between thirty-five widows." All the men had been liquidators [clean-up workers]. So you need to be fair. But how? One widow has a little girl who's sick, another widow has two children, and a third is sick herself, and she's renting her apartment, and yet another has four children. At night I'd wake up thinking, "How do I not cheat anyone?" I thought and calculated, calculated and thought. And I couldn't do it. We ended up just giving out the money equally, according to the list.

But my real child is the museum: the Chernobyl Museum. [*He is silent.*] Sometimes I think that we'll have a funeral parlor here, not a museum. I serve on the funeral committee. This morning I haven't even taken off my coat when a woman comes in, she's crying, not even crying but yelling: "Take his medals and his certificates! Take all the benefits! Give me my husband!" She yelled a long time. And left his medals, his certificates. Well, they'll be in the museum, on display. People can look at them. But her cry, no one heard her cry but me, and when I put these certificates on display I'll remember it.

SOURCE: Alexievich, Svetlana. *Voices from Chernobyl: The Oral History of a Nuclear Disaster*. Trans. Keith Gessen. Champaign, Ill. Dalkey Archive Press, 2005. All rights reserved. Reproduced by permission.

---

censorship and to spare her subjects from censure as her career continued.

Although Alexievich chose not to present the sober voices and secular prayers of *Voices from Chernobyl* in dramatic form as Gubarev had, the book has continued to assert its relevance in the realm of theater and film. Through an Irish filmmaker's production of a short picture called *The Door* (2008), one of Alexievich's monologues from *Voices from Chernobyl* came to the attention of the Academy of Motion Picture Arts and Sciences when the film was nominated for Best Live Action Short Film in 2010.

THEMES AND STYLE

The central themes of *Voices from Chernobyl* are the incomprehensibility and absurdity of the event and its aftermath, the inevitability of comparisons between the catastrophe and war, and the everyday and eternal aspects of the disaster's effects on an essentially new Chernobyl world. Each of these themes is subtly suggested in the publicly sourced "Historical Notes" section, explicitly introduced in the semipublic "Self-Interview" portion (excluded from the American edition), and reinforced and repeated in the "Solitary Human Voice" semiprivate soliloquies, the titled monologues, and the broadly differentiated choruses at the heart of the text's three main chapters. An accounting of Nazi-versus-nuclear destruction in a historical note links Auschwitz and Chernobyl in the self-interview and deepens comparisons between World War II and the disaster throughout the soliloquies, monologues, and choruses. In addition, a historical note indicating Chernobyl's impact across international borders aligns with the self-interview's description of a continuously emerging Chernobyl world and with several subjects' evocations of a newly formed Chernobylite nation.

In a lengthy self-interview that says almost nothing practical about Alexievich's information-gathering process, she expands on the idea of a Chernobyl world as she broadly explains how she collects the "feelings, thoughts, and words" of "ordinary people" on an "ordinary day" in order to convey the "life of the soul" and to depict not the "event" of Chernobyl but the "world" it created. Thus, half-earnestly and half-ironically, she suggests how the Chernobyl of the future may be seen as a world where humans confront a higher power (be it God or the Communist Party), nature, and themselves. As the book's aesthetic ornateness and methodological opaqueness suggest, Alexievich did not originally see her book as a work of oral history, which typically requires its authors "to detail the number of interviews conducted" and "the nature of those interviews," as theorist Lynn Abrams explains in *Oral History Theory* (2010). The oral history designation, therefore, appears to have been assigned to the text by Gessen, its American translator, who makes a number of significant emendations to the original, perhaps to capitalize on the popularity of oral history.

As several critics who recognize *Voices from Chernobyl* as something other than oral history have noted, the structure, the tone, and even the language are tightly controlled by Alexievich. Although she diligently tape-recorded and transcribed her subjects' words, occasionally noted their physical actions, and left intact her interviewees' direct addresses toward her as an interviewer, it remains difficult to pinpoint where her voice ends and where those of her subjects begin. Thus, although Alexievich claims that she does not intend to force her own views on her reader, her supposedly polyphonic text often ends up mirroring the type of obfuscation the Soviets perpetrated.

CRITICAL DISCUSSION

In the former Soviet Union, reactions to Alexievich's writings in general, and to *Voices from Chernobyl* in particular, have generally focused on its genre, which her early mentor and champion Adamovich emphasizes and which Alexievich continues to highlight on the website she established in 2006. Although Adamovich associates Alexievich's writings with a subgenre he calls the "collective novel," and Alexievich describes the "chorus of human voices" she aims to make heard in the "new documentary prose" form she has created, the precise genre of *Voices from Chernobyl* remains a source of contention.

Responses in Europe and the United States during the 1990s and into the twenty-first century have focused primarily on *Voices from Chernobyl's* extraordinary, remarkable, grim, and grotesque content. But in their eagerness to celebrate Alexievich's commitment to post-Soviet transparency, critics have failed to adequately acknowledge her editorial opacity. Many overlook the creative license Alexievich takes with her subjects' stories even as they defend her against charges that she quoted witnesses out of context in *Boys in Zinc* (1991). One American reviewer expresses concern about the 2006 English translation's title not because it questionably classifies the text as an oral history but because it fails to capture the feeling of shared humanity that the raw material naturally inspires.

Academic reviewers and critics have probed deeper to consider how the form Alexievich uses inevitably affects her book's content. For instance, Paul Josephson, writing for the *Russian Review* in 2006, argues that Alexievich's practice of writing up the "stories of her respondents ... in her own style" results in a text dominated by one artistic (rather than sociological or anthropological) voice that "shapes all others." Scribner contends that Alexievich's "Self-Interview" in *Voices from Chernobyl* suggests that she considers her readers "too naïve to come to [their] own conclusions," Jennifer Tishler in *Chernobyl: The Event and Its Aftermath* (2006) maintains that "by naming this section an interview rather than a monologue," Alexievich "emphasizes the lack of a dominant, authoritative voice in the book." Like many earlier reviewers, Tishler emphasizes the polyphonic nature of Alexievich's work, but in keeping with Adamovich, she does not hesitate—as other reviewers typically have—to call *Voices from Chernobyl* a "novel" rather than "testimony."

BIBLIOGRAPHY

Sources

Abrams, Lynn. "Introduction: Turning Practice into Theory." *Oral History Theory.* New York: Routledge, 2010. Print.

Alexievich, Svetlana. *Voices from Chernobyl: The Oral History of a Nuclear Disaster.* Trans. Keith Gessen. New York: Picador, 2006. Print.

Evans, Julian. "A Conspiracy of Ignorance and Obedience." Rev. of *Voices from Chernobyl*, by Svetlana Alexievich. *Telegraph* [London]. London Telegraph, 4 July 2005. Web. 26 Jan. 2013.

Josephson, Paul. Rev. of *Voices from Chernobyl*, by Svetlana Alexievich. *Russian Review* 56.2 (2006): 352–53. *JSTOR.* Web. 26 Jan. 2013.

Scribner, Doris. *Recreation of Chernobyl Trauma in Svetlana Aleksiyevich's* Chernobyl'skya Molitva. MA thesis. University of Missouri–Columbia. 2008. Web. 26 Jan. 2013.

Tishler, Jennifer. "Identity and Meaning: Chernobyl in Literature." *Chernobyl: The Event and Its Aftermath.* Ed. Leonard Berkowitz, Norma Berkowitz, and Michael Patrick. Madison, Wis.: Goblin Fern, 2006. 88–113. Web. 26 Jan. 2013.

Further Reading

Decamous, Gabrielle. "Nuclear Activities and Modern Catastrophes: Art Faces the Radioactive Waves." *Leonardo* 44.2 (2011): 124–32. *JSTOR.* Web. 26 Jan. 2013.

Ginzburg, Lydia. *On Psychological Prose.* Trans. and ed. Judson Rosengrant. Princeton, N.J.: Princeton University Press, 1991. Print.

Lucic, Ana. "A Conversation with Svetlana Alexievich." *Dalkey Archive Press.* Dalkey Archive Press, n.d. Web. 26 Jan. 2013.

Marples, David. "Chernobyl: A Reassessment." *Eurasian Geography and Economics* 45.8 (December 2004): 588–607. Web. 26 Jan. 2013.

Meier, Andrew. "The Unforgettable Fire." Rev. of *Voices from Chernobyl,* by Svetlana Alexievich. *Nation.* Nation, 30 Mar. 2006. Web. 26 Jan. 2013.

Petrucci, Mario. "'Three Drops of Salmon Oil': The Artist and the Self in the Aftermath of Chernobyl." *Interdisciplinary Science Reviews* 31.3 (2006): 254–60. *Ingentaconnect.* Web. 26 Jan. 2013.

Toker, Leona. "Toward a Poetics of Documentary Prose: From the Perspective of Gulag Testimonies." *Poetics Today* 18.2 (1997): 187–222. *JSTOR.* Web. 26 Jan. 2013.

Katie MacNamara

Voices from the Whirlwind
An Oral History of the Chinese Cultural Revolution

Feng Jicai

OVERVIEW

In *Voices from the Whirlwind: An Oral History of the Chinese Cultural Revolution* (1991), writer and artist Feng Jicai presents oral histories from veterans and victims of China's Cultural Revolution (1966–1976). The book features English translations of fourteen Chinese transcripts originally published in Feng's 1990 *I pai ko jen ti shih nien* (One hundred people's ten years). Ranging widely in sensibilities and politics, these candid and at times heart-wrenching accounts reveal the terrible disparity between the socialist ideals of Mao Zedong's so-called Great Proletarian Cultural Revolution and the uncountable abuses, from slander to torture, carried out in that revolution's name.

Voices from the Whirlwind comes close to being a dissident work. Researched and assembled in the mid- to late 1980s, its oral histories reflect on national failings at a moment when official accounts were glossing over the actualities of the Cultural Revolution—discouraging, in particular, attempts to attribute blame either to Mao or the Communist Party. Though *Voices from the Whirlwind* was funded in part by the Chinese government, for some time Feng was unable to publish further volumes from the same project for fear they would be confiscated and banned. Early reviewers in the United States commended *Voices from the Whirlwind* for its vivid and moving narratives. Some, however, thought it conspicuously silent on the question of official culpability. Even so, the book has become something of a classic in cultural and sociological studies, a rich source document for understanding an era in Chinese and world history both exhilarating and tragic.

HISTORICAL AND LITERARY CONTEXT

In 1949, after decades of fierce political struggles for control of China, Mao led the Communist Party to victory, recasting the Republic of China as the People's Republic of China. He set about reforming the country, divesting feudal landlords of private estates, purging the scene of bourgeois and capitalist interests, and establishing people's communes. These reforms were profoundly violent, entailing public executions, labor-camp internments, and mass repressions. After an early successful five-year program to modernize China's economy by giving precedence to industrial rather than agricultural production, Mao lost some status with party leaders when a second such plan, known as the Great Leap Forward (1958–1961), failed and led to bitter famine. Some historians believe he launched the Cultural Revolution primarily as a means to purge the party of rivals and reclaim leadership.

The Cultural Revolution was a party-led initiative, primarily urging the people to purge their lives of bourgeois ideology and capitalist trappings. At the forefront were the Red Guards—paramilitary student groups who helped manufacture a cult of Mao among the people; denounced and attacked suspected "counterrevolutionaries"; and brutally destroyed homes, museums, and temples that typified old (nonsocialist) Chinese society. In spite of the explicit terrorism, many people believed wholeheartedly in Mao and the revolution. Indeed, the speakers in *Voices from the Whirlwind* attest not to anxiety over the revolution as such but to the shock of finding themselves labeled as traitors to their own dear cause.

Voices from the Whirlwind is one of a number of texts seeking fresh perspectives on the meaning and value of the Cultural Revolution. It is comparable, for example, with Chihua Wen's *The Red Mirror: Children of China's Cultural Revolution* (1995), a collection of interviews with men and women who were children during the revolution and who saw their parents disgraced, imprisoned, or "re-educated." Also comparable is James Ross's *Caught in a Tornado: A Chinese American Woman Survives the Cultural Revolution* (1994), which tells the life story of a Chinese American teacher arrested in China in 1966, charged with espionage, and imprisoned for ten years. Feng, it should be noted, published a companion volume to *Voices from the Whirlwind* in 1996, *Ten Years of Madness: Oral Histories of China's Cultural Revolution*.

Feng's fourteen oral histories are essential reading for anyone trying to make sense of mass movements and their worst excesses: above all, they refuse to reductively explain away the complex sufferings of those who both believed in the Cultural Revolution and found themselves inexplicably persecuted on account of it—individuals who continue to live scarred lives. Indeed, the burgeoning genre of what is referred to as "scar literature" or the "literature of the wounded," especially when focused on modern Chinese history, owes much to *Voices from the Whirlwind*.

Key Facts

Time Period:
Mid- to Late 20th Century

Relevant Historical Events:
Chinese Cultural Revolution

Nationality:
Chinese

Keywords:
revolution; communism; torture

Chairman Mao Zedong, circa 1949. Mao was the architect of the Chinese Cultural Revolution that subjected the Chinese people to unspeakable cruelty. © JERRY TAVIN/ EVERETT COLLECTION

THEMES AND STYLE

One constant theme throughout *Voices from the Whirlwind* is the fall from innocence to experience for people who, though often immersed in Mao's revolutionary ideals, fell prey to malicious, devious, and petty factions working for the revolution. Paramount is a reckoning of psychological costs. As one survivor puts it, "My family's ruined. My wife's dead. My son's motherless. Twenty years have gone by since the Cultural Revolution and … my mind will never be the same again." Similarly, for the doctor who killed her father at his request to save him from further punishment from the Red Guards, "even today … I still can't rid myself of thoughts of the past.… There's no escaping from my memories." Concluding her interview bluntly, saying, "I can't say anymore. Please don't ask me to go on," this woman captures the torment of not just being victimized but of living with the guilt of having been compelled in the thick of the "whirlwind" to do terrible things.

Feng has described his task in presenting these oral histories as both sacred and political: a work of memorialization providing peace of mind for those who suffered in the Cultural Revolution and a gadfly to sting the consciences of those who engineered and carried out the revolution, though not to make them repent so much as to "squirm." His intention is to bring to the surface the kinds and degrees of suffering experienced, chiefly so that future generations will understand what really happened without glossing over or sensationalizing it.

The language throughout is honest and for the most part reverent, though at times strong feelings break through in strong words. Time and again, those giving account will make sure they are not being too insensitive or too revealing by asking, "Is it okay to say that?" or "Is it okay, the way I talk?" Much is at stake for these speakers, psychologically and emotionally. As one man, whose family was persecuted because it did not have the "right class background," puts it, "you've got to get your feelings out sometime, don't you? I've been holding mine inside for ten years. It's about time I found some release and that's why I'm here." This unburdening of regret and pent-up frustration is common to most of the speakers, and it is often mixed with shame and guilt: as is the case with the doctor who killed her own father as well as the former Red Guard who at first embraced the revolution but came around to thinking finally "that I'd been cheated" and "deceived."

CRITICAL DISCUSSION

As noted, early reviewers were moved by Feng's histories, though some thought the implicit criticisms fell short of their true mark. Thus, while Steven I. Levine, in a *Library Journal* review, claims that "it is impossible not to be moved by the honesty, introspection, and pathos of these stories," Gopal Sukhu, in the *Far Eastern Economic Review,* insists that "they leave one with a sense that something has been withheld. Among all the objects of blame—the opportunists, Red Guards, Gang of Four, etc.—we never find Mao or the communist party." *New York Review of Books'* writer Jonathan Mirsky consolidates this dissatisfaction, noting, "What is disturbing about many of them is that no one seems to blame for the pain and death except the people who were directly responsible: Red Guards, brutal cadres, frightening officials, colleagues, or, of course, Lin Biao and the Gang of Four. Mao and the Party are rarely mentioned."

Though Feng was not the first collector of modern Chinese oral histories (one notable precursor was Zhang Xinxin and Sang Ye's 1987 *Chinese Lives: An Oral History of Contemporary China*), numerous works in a similar vein (some of which are detailed above) followed Feng's lead in *Voices from the Whirlwind.* The growing popularity of oral histories, along with the increasing critical attention given to the history of the Cultural Revolution, however, situate Feng's volume as a seminal work, valuable to scholar and lay reader alike.

Scholars have yet to discuss *Voices from the Whirlwind* as a subject in its own right, though the book is regularly cited as a primary source on the Cultural Revolution. Lu Xiuyuan's study of the violence uniting the masses during the revolution and Geremie Barmé's work on historicizing the revolution both usefully contextualize the difficulty Feng had in publishing in China (of the many interviews collected, he published only a fraction). More commonly Feng figures in the footnotes, as in the work of Charlene Makley ("'Speaking Bitterness': Autobiography, History, and Mnemonic

Politics on the Sino-Tibetan Frontier"), David J. Davies ("Old Zhiqing Photos: Nostalgia and the 'Spirit' of the Cultural Revolution"), and Hao Ping ("Reassessing the Starting Point of the Cultural Revolution").

BIBLIOGRAPHY

Sources

Barmé, Geremie R. "History for the Masses." *Using the Past to Serve the Present.* Ed. Jonathan Unger. Armonk, N.Y.: Sharpe, 1993. Print.

Feng Jicai. *Voices from the Whirlwind: An Oral History of the Chinese Cultural Revolution.* New York: Pantheon, 1991.

Guobin, Yang. "The Liminal Effects of Social Movements: Red Guards and the Transformation of Identity." *Sociological Forum* 15.3 (2000): 379–406. *JSTOR.* Web. 17 Jan 2013.

Levine, Steven I. Rev. of *Voices from the Whirlwind: An Oral History of the Chinese Cultural Revolution,* by Feng Jicai. *Library Journal* 116.11 (1991): 91. *EBSCOhost.* Web. 17 Jan. 2013.

Lu, Xiuyuan. "A Step toward Understanding Popular Violence in China's Cultural Revolution." *Pacific Affairs* 67.4 (1994–95): 533–63. *ProQuest.* Web. 17 Jan. 2013.

Mirsky, Jonathan. "Literature of the Wounded." Rev. of *Voices from the Whirlwind: An Oral History of the Chinese Cultural Revolution,* by Feng Jicai. *New York Review of Books.* NYREV, 5 Mar. 1992. Web. 17 Jan 2013.

Sukhu, Gopal. "The Maelstrom That Mao Built." Rev. of *Voices from the Whirlwind: An Oral History of the Chinese Cultural Revolution,* by Feng Jicai. *Far Eastern Economic Review* 155.4 (1992): 32. *ProQuest.* Web. 17 Jan. 2013.

Further Reading

Hay, Jeff, ed. *The Chinese Cultural Revolution.* Detroit: Greenhaven, 2012. Print.

Kwong, Luke S. K. "Oral History in China: A Preliminary Review." *Oral History Review* 20.1–2 (1992): 23–50. *JSTOR.* Web. 17 Jan 2013.

FENG JICAI: ARTIST, CRITIC, ACTIVIST

The son of a merchant, Feng Jicai was born in the city of Tianjin in northern China. As a young man he studied at the city's Calligraphy and Painting House, where he discovered a deep appreciation for Chinese folk art. Early in his career he worked as a painting teacher, a role he was forced to give up when the Cultural Revolution struck. During the revolution Feng and his parents were forcibly evicted from their home by Red Guards and suffered abuse on account of their wealth and class.

After Mao's death Feng began a new career as a writer, eventually authoring more than forty works, including short stories, novels, documentary nonfiction, and essays. His novel *The Three-Inch Golden Lotus* made waves with its controversial study of Chinese foot binding (the traditional practice of breaking girls' feet and wrapping them to keep them small). In this and other works, Feng spoke critically, if obliquely, about the violence in his society that the Cultural Revolution had normalized. Asking to be considered an intellectual rather than just a writer and claiming he wishes to serve his culture as much as his society, in recent years Feng has turned to activism in defending his native city's cultural heritage against careless developers.

Law, Kam-yee, ed. *The Chinese Cultural Revolution Reconsidered: Beyond Purge and Holocaust.* New York: Palgrave Macmillan, 2003. Print.

Lu, Xing. *Rhetoric of the Chinese Cultural Revolution: The Impact on Chinese Thought, Culture, and Communication.* Columbia: University of South Carolina Press, 2004. Print.

Yang, Lan. *Chinese Fiction of the Cultural Revolution.* Hong Kong: Hong Kong University Press, 1998. Print.

David Aitchison

THE WITCH PURGE OF 1878
Oral and Documentary History in the Early Navajo Reservation Years
Martha Blue

❖ **Key Facts**

Time Period:
Late 19th Century

Relevant Historical Events:
Navajo War; internment of Navajo people; witch purge of 1878

Nationality:
American

Keywords:
Native Americans; witchcraft; internment

OVERVIEW

Published 110 years after the events it documents, attorney Martha Blue's thirty-five-page monograph, *The Witch Purge of 1878: Oral and Documentary History in the Early Navajo Reservation Years* (1988), interprets letters and oral accounts primarily taken several generations after the deaths of about forty Navajos in the so-called witch purge of 1878. Blue turns to these accounts to better understand the purge from an often-elided perspective—that of the Navajo people. Additionally, she is concerned with documenting how trade and intersocietal conflict between Navajos and white Americans influenced the period under examination. Trade and the reservation system significantly impaired the traditional means by which the Navajo people regulated wealth, so a great economic disparity arose, leading to jealousy and accusations of witchcraft. That the first "witch" was killed on the door of a trading post may have been a sign to the traders to abandon the area. However, through the oral histories and letters she considers, Blue concludes that witchcraft was an integral element of the Navajo belief system and that the previous interpretations of the witch purge of 1878 as solely a political ploy are erroneous.

Working more than a century after the purge, Blue relies on oral histories collected earlier by the Doris Duke Oral History Project, the Hubbell Ethnohistory Project, anthropologist Clyde Kluckhohn, and others. Similar sources informed Blue's later work, *Indian Trader: The Life and Times of J. L. Hubbell* (2000), a full-length book centered on one of the traders involved in the events surrounding the purge.

HISTORICAL AND LITERARY CONTEXT

In *The Witch Purge of 1878*, Blue writes that the witch purge arose from societal upheavals stemming from the reservation system. Defeated by U.S. military forces in the 1863–1864 campaign, the Navajo people were interred at Bosque Redondo (also known as Fort Sumner) after being forced on a 450-mile "Long Walk," which led to many deaths. In 1868 a new treaty was negotiated between General William T. Sherman and Navajo leaders, which resulted in the Navajo returning to a reservation on their ancestral lands. However, as journalist A. Lynn Allison writes in "The Navajo Witch Purge of 1878" (2001), "The freedom to return to their homeland had come at the expense of traditional Navajo ways of balancing social inequities and rationalizing inequalities of wealth and well-being." A previously unknown disparity of wealth developed on the reservation and contributed to the events of the purge.

The witch purge coincided with the expiration of an annuity granted to the Navajo people by the treaty of 1868, a widespread drought, and an increased resentment of the white American domination of the land. Furthermore, the purge was preceded by accusations of witchcraft that developed out of a growing jealousy of the few Navajos who were thriving under the reservation system, a resentment of the system itself, and the otherwise unexplained deaths of people and livestock. Those accused of witchcraft were predominantly profiting from the new order. Blue writes that during the years after the Treaty of 1868 was signed, "witchcraft scares and purges replaced war and raiding, outer-tribal activities, as instruments for dealing with aggression and anxiety."

Anthropologists Kluckhohn's and Ruth Underhill's respective projects, the 1944 *Navajo Witchcraft* and the 1956 *The Navajos;* David Brugge's "The Navajo Witch Purge of 1878" in *Awanyu* (1977); and the Doris Duke Indian Oral History Project number among the many resources upon which Blue relied for her project. The publisher of *The Witch Purge* is known for works such as *Navajo Stories from the Long Walk Period* (1973) and for propelling an interest in Navajo oral history on the connected campus of Diné (formerly Navajo) Community College, encouraging students on the reservation to interview the community elders on the subject. *The Witch Purge* was the first text published in Navajo Community College Press's Navajo Oral History Monograph Series.

Interest in revitalizing history from multiple perspectives and sources as Blue did has fueled many projects, such as Howard Bahr's *The Navajo as Seen by the Franciscans, 1898–1921: A Sourcebook* (2004). Like Blue's monograph, Bahr's book expands from a framework that admits the subjectivity of his project's outlook. The secondary theme of *The Witch Purge,* the influence of trade on Navajo life, has also influenced later works, represented particularly in Blue's extended study of the trader J. L. Hubbell.

THEMES AND STYLE

Central to *The Witch Purge of 1878* is the idea that the perspectives of those involved in historical events are crucial to providing a complete record. Using oral and primary sources, Blue complicates the commonly held assessment that the witch purge was simply a ploy by Navajo leaders to attract the attention of white Americans and scare them. She reclaims witchcraft as part of the Navajo belief system and its resurgence part of maintaining traditional, native power. Blue writes, "An ethnohistorical analysis of the Navajo Indian Reservation's Witch Purge of 1878 chips the historical view that Navajo leaders orchestrated it as part of their political gamesmanship." Paying careful attention to the remarks of those who witnessed the purge, told in most cases through their descendants, Blue depicts how the Navajo belief system intersected with the reservation system and trade with white Americans to culminate in the massacre.

Dissatisfied that many accounts of the purge are biased, in her words, from a "selective Anglo-American perspective" and exclude the role of trade on the events, Blue was inspired to present a paper filling these voids at the Navajo Studies Conference. Here, she was approached by a representative of the Navajo Community College Press about transforming her paper into a monograph. In her work Blue uncovers the Navajo accounts of the events to provide a more nuanced "detailed chronology from a cultural perspective." Because of the length of time between her study and the events on which it centers, however, she was unable to speak to any witnesses or to collect any part of the histories she analyzes.

Blue relies on letters and interviews from those who experienced or who knew those who experienced the events, calling the latter "eye witness renditions" in reference to the way their stories became "oral traditions because they have passed from mouth to mouth for a period beyond the lifetime of the informant." Many of the interviews she refers to were summarized by interpreters or edited and reworded, while others were more literally transcribed. Blue reports that she relies on the literal translation when possible, deleting only "repetitive and non-germane remarks."

CRITICAL DISCUSSION

The Witch Purge of 1878 did not garner critical attention when it emerged; it was not reviewed in any major journal or newspaper. Edward McCombs, the former director of the Navajo Community College Press, however, reports that the monograph sold well and was popular with local schools on and off the Navajo reservation.

The Witch Purge of 1878 has been cited as a useful addition to the discussion of the events of 1878 and occasionally to works pertaining to Native American culture and witchcraft. Considered an authoritative source on the witch purge, Blue's monograph is referenced in such Navajo histories as Peter Iverson and Monty Roessel's 2002 *Diné: A History of the Navajos* and Jennifer Nez Denetdale's 2007 *Reclaiming Diné History: The Legacies of Navajo Chief Manuelito and Juanita*, as well as in works on Native Americans and witchcraft such as Jean Van Derlinder's 2004 *Journal of Ideology* article "'Wayward' Indians: The Social Construction of Native American Witchcraft" and Allison's 2001 article "The Navajo Witch Purge of 1878." The latter has been heavily cited by laypeople who are looking into the paranormal, including skin-walking and shape-shifting.

Though there has been no scholarship on the monograph itself, Blue's life continues to attract attention. One of the original lawyers hired in 1967 for the Dinébe'iiná Náhiiłna be Agha'diit'ahii-, an institution born of the civil rights movement, she has acted as legal counsel for Navajos and Hopis in the United States and worked for Micronesian Legal Services. Specializing in Indian law, she has also acted as general counsel for the Havasupai. Furthermore, she has been chair of the Arizona State Bar's Art Law Committee and has served as a board member for Native Americans for Community Action. Additionally, she has done work with the Books for Kids program, Friends of Hubbell Trading Post National Historic Site, Authors Guild, and Western Writers of America; written self-help books for artists and writers; and lectured on Navajo history, regional artists, and the welfare of Native Americans.

BIBLIOGRAPHY

Sources

Allison, A. Lynn. "The Navajo Witch Purge of 1878." *PaloVerde*. Arizona State University West, May 2001. Web. 15 Jan. 2013.

This rock features a memorial to the Long Walk of the Navajos along the Pecos River in Bosque Redondo (Fort Sumner), New Mexico. This event, which began in 1864, and the pressures therein, contributed to the Navajo witch purge of 1878. © NORTH WIND PICTURE ARCHIVES/ALAMY

MARTHA BLUE AND ROBERTA BLACKGOAT IN THE NATIVE RIGHTS MOVEMENT

Martha Blue has served Native American communities for decades. As one of the founding members of the *Dinébe'iiná Náhiił;na be Agha'diit'ahii*, a nonprofit legal services corporation established by the U.S. Congress to provide equal access to justice, she has represented many who might otherwise not have been able to afford legal counsel. In one case, Blue helped Roberta Blackgoat, a Navajo elder, win financial rights denied to her after her husband was killed changing a tire by the side of the road.

That was not Blackgoat's only experience fighting injustice: she has been instrumental in the environmental and native rights movements, winning America's Unsung Woman prize in 1994—awarded by the National Women's History Project—for her role in protecting the rights of indigenous people and their land. Blackgoat protested the abuse of the land and the federal relocation of the Navajo people from it. In *Nine Women: Portraits from the American Radical Tradition*, author Judith Nies writes that Blackgoat was recognized "for her leadership in publicizing the environmental and human rights abuses that have accompanied massive strip-mining on Black Mesa, Arizona." In part because of Blackgoat's efforts, Black Mesa was named in February 2000 by the European Parliament in a human rights resolution, which Nies reports, "cit[ed] the United States for abuses in regard to 'Native Americans in the U.S.—Dineh (Navajo).'"

"Blue, Martha." *Northern Arizona Book Festival*. Northern Arizona Book Festival, 2004. Web. 17 Jan. 2013.

Blue, Martha. *The Witch Purge of 1878: Oral and Documentary History in the Early Navajo Reservation Years*. Tsaile, Ariz.: Navajo Community College Press, 1988. Print.

———. "Re: Query about *The Witch Purge of 1878* (1988)." Message to Katherine E. Bishop. 25 Jan. 2013. E-mail.

Kluckhohn, Clyde. *Navaho Witchcraft*. Boston: Beacon, 1944. Print.

McCombs, Edward W. Telephone interview. 25 Jan. 2013.

Nies, Judith. *Nine Women: Portraits from the American Radical Tradition*. 1977. Berkeley: University of California Press, 2002. Print.

Van Delinder, Jean. "'Wayward' Indians: The Social Construction of Native American Witchcraft." *Journal of Ideology*. Louisiana State University, Shreveport, 2004. Web. 16 Jan. 2013.

Zah, Peterson, and Peter Iverson. *We Will Secure Our Future: Empowering the Navajo Nation*. Tucson: University of Arizona Press, 2012. Print.

Further Reading

Bahr, Howard M., ed. *The Navajo as Seen by the Franciscans, 1898–1921: A Sourcebook*. Lanham, Md.: Scarecrow, 2004. Print.

Blue, Martha. *Indian Trader: The Life and Times of J. L. Hubbell*. Walnut, Calif.: Kiva, 2000. Print.

———. *Little Prankster Girl: At'ééd Ádiláhí Yázhí*. Illus. Kevin Smith. Trans. Peter A. Thomas. Flagstaff, Ariz.: Salina Bookshelf, 2003. Print.

Denetdale, Jennifer Nez. *Reclaiming Diné History: The Legacies of Navajo Chief Manuelito and Juanita*. Tucson: University of Arizona Press, 2007. Print.

Iverson, Peter, and Monty Roessel, photog. *Diné: A History of the Navajos*. Albuquerque: University of New Mexico Press, 2002. Print.

Walker, William H. "Where Are the Witches of Prehistory?" *Journal of Archaeological Method and Theory* 5.3 (1998): 245–308. JSTOR. Web. 15 Jan. 2013.

Katherine Bishop

WITNESSES TO NUREMBERG
An Oral History of American Participants at the War Crimes Trials
Bruce M. Stave, Michele Palmer, Leslie Frank

OVERVIEW
Published fifty years after the famous Nuremberg trials, *Witnesses to Nuremberg: An Oral History of American Participants at the War Crimes Trials* (1998) relates the memories and impressions of eleven Americans who were present for the prosecution of former Nazi leaders following the atrocities of World War II. The book's oral histories, collected and edited by Bruce M. Stave, Michele Palmer, and Leslie Frank, are divided into five categories according to the participants' role in the trial: courtroom architect, prison/security guard, interrogator/translator, attorney, or journalist. Unlike other works about Nuremberg that concentrate on the philosophical or political implications, *Witnesses to Nuremberg* describes participants' personal experiences of the events surrounding the trials.

The book appeared in the midst of several high-profile war criminal trials conducted in the 1990s. The interviews in the book were part of a larger project by the Thomas J. Dodd Research Center of the University of Connecticut. Dodd Center staff, inspired by renewed international focus on bringing war criminals to justice, sought to reexamine the Nuremberg trials for what could be learned from eyewitnesses to the event. In all, the center conducted thirty interviews, eleven of which appear in *Witnesses to Nuremberg*. Today the book marks an important and unique contribution to Nuremberg literature.

HISTORICAL AND LITERARY CONTEXT
Staged by the Allied forces after World War II, the Nuremberg trials prosecuted leading members of Nazi Germany between 1945 and 1946 at the Palace of Justice in Nuremberg, Germany. More than twenty years earlier, after the conclusion of World War I, the Leipzig war crimes trials (1921) were held in Leipzig, Germany. Unfortunately, the trials were considered ineffective because many of the suspected criminals managed to avoid prosecution. With these trials in mind, the Allies entered Nuremberg with a sense of determination and purpose. *Witnesses to Nuremberg* captures the sense of importance felt by Americans involved in the trials.

At the end of World War II, Henry Morgenthau Jr., the U.S. secretary of the treasury, devised a plan for the denazification of Germany, which would involve executing major war criminals and the deindustrialization of Germany as a whole. His program, which became known as the Morgenthau Plan, was met with little public enthusiasm or approval. As a result, President Franklin Delano Roosevelt abandoned the plan. In 1945, when Roosevelt died, his successor, President Harry S. Truman, embarked on a series of negotiations with France, the Soviet Union, and Great Britain, which eventually led to the Nuremberg trials. The significance of the trials is reflected throughout *Witnesses to Nuremburg,* such as when a prosecutor declares the trials his "guiding light" and "the most important thing I ever did."

Witnesses to Nuremberg is part of the tradition of literature about the Nuremberg trials. More specifically, the book falls into the category of oral histories about them. Hilary Gaskin's *Eyewitnesses at Nuremberg* (1991), published just seven years before *Witnesses to Nuremberg,* is a collection of twenty-four interviews that covers the Nuremberg experience but does not focus on Americans. In 2004 Leon Goldensohn published *The Nuremberg Interviews: An American Psychiatrist's Conversations with the Defendants and Witnesses,* which contains interviews between Goldensohn, a psychiatrist for the U.S. Army, and leaders from the Nazi Party charged with war crimes. Unlike the everyday people featured in *Witnesses to Nuremberg,* the focus of Goldensohn's book is largely on the trials' well-known figures.

Witnesses to Nuremberg is an important touchstone in ongoing conversations about how to try war crimes. The trials themselves served as a model for prosecuting war criminals in the Balkan wars of the 1990s and in the genocide in Rwanda in 1994. The oral histories in *Witnesses to Nuremberg* provide fresh, human insight into the trials that now serve as the basis for how the international community deals with war crimes.

THEMES AND STYLE
The main themes of *Witnesses to Nuremberg* are the personal reactions to, daily experiences of, and atmospheric recollections of the trials. Attorney Seymour Peyser recounts an interaction with Robert Ley, a Nazi labor minister who killed himself before the trial

❖ **Key Facts**

Time Period:
Mid-20th Century

Relevant Historical Events:
Nuremberg trials; end of World War II

Nationality:
American

Keywords:
Nazism; war crimes; genocide

Witnesses to Nuremberg features interviews with Americans involved with the trials of Nazi war criminals after World War II. Pictured here is the trial of a number of defendants, including Hermann Göring and Rudolf Hess.
© UNIVERSAL HISTORY ARCHIVE/GETTY IMAGES

began: "I realized suddenly that this was a human being. This guy was breathing badly because he had a bad cold." Many of the book's interviews explore the social lives of Americans in Nuremberg. Journalist Harold Burson recalls, "There was a lot of drinking. Some of the funniest people were the Russian correspondents. Some of them spoke fair English, but one thing they could do a lot better than the Americans was they could drink more whiskey." Prison guard William H. Glenny, who was eighteen at the time of the trials, remembers an air of hostility toward Americans: "In Nuremberg, they told us not to walk out by ourselves. They did not allow us to carry guns. The tension was still there."

The purpose behind composing *Witnesses to Nuremberg* was, as Donald A. Ritchie writes in the foreword to the book, to create "a historic reckoning that the world can ill afford to forget." After the construction of Thomas J. Dodd Research Center, the University of Connecticut spent the center's inaugural year devoted to reflections on the trials, at which Thomas J. Dodd had served as a prosecutor. The eleven interviews included in *Witnesses to Nuremberg* contain edited versions of the interviewees' responses alongside the interviewers' questions. As the authors explain in the introduction to the book, they included the questions to provide "a sense of the shaping of each interview."

The oral histories in *Witnesses to Nuremberg* are significant for their frank language. Unlike more academic writing about the legal implications of the trials, the book's oral histories include eyewitnesses' personal and honest reactions to the events. Each interview begins with the interviewee's life story and background, granting a personal air and context to that person's recollections about the trials. For example, the background of prison guard Glenny illuminates his habit of asking war criminals for their autographs.

CRITICAL DISCUSSION

In his analysis of *Witnesses to Nuremberg* for *Oral History Review*, Allan A. Ryan Jr. describes the book's place in the literature about Nuremberg: "Much has been written about the law of Nuremberg, and a good deal, too, about the political and theatrical aspects of it. This volume … is the latest contribution and it is a useful one." Although Ryan praises the book for focusing more on the behind-the-scenes aspects of the trials than on "the stars of Nuremberg," he criticizes several aspects of its construction. In terms of the backgrounds of each interviewee, Ryan finds that "little of this information sheds useful light on the trials themselves." Ryan also points out several factual errors, including the misspelled names of attorney A. Frank Reel and future U.S. Supreme Court associate justice William J. Brennan Jr. (*Witnesses to Nuremberg* refers to Reel as "Riel" and Brennan as "Rennan.")

Four years after the publication of *Witnesses to Nuremberg*, Robert A. Hamilton conducted an interview for the *New York Times* with one of its authors, Stave, a history professor at the University of Connecticut. Hamilton asks Stave why he chose the form of oral history to add to the literature about Nuremberg. Stave answers, "There have been many books written about Nuremberg from the official record, but we were trying to tell the story from the perspective of the Americans who were there." These perspectives are an important addition to ongoing conversations about war crimes, which were reinvigorated by the trials of the 1990s related to the wars in the Balkans and the genocide in Rwanda.

Despite the uniqueness of the book's contribution to the literature about the Nuremberg trials, *Witnesses to Nuremberg* has not received much critical attention. Nevertheless, the book appears on reading lists related to Nuremberg and oral history. Ritchie's *Doing Oral History: A Practical Guide* (2003) and Michael Salter's "The Prosecution of Nazi War Criminals and the OSS: The Need for a New Research Agenda" (2002) both refer to *Witnesses to Nuremberg* as essential reading.

BIBLIOGRAPHY

Sources

Hamilton, Robert A. "Q&A/Bruce M. Stave; Collective Memories of Nuremberg." *New York Times*. New York Times, 14 Feb. 1999. Web. 31 Jan. 2013.

Ritchie, Donald A. *Doing Oral History: A Practical Guide*. Oxford, UK: Oxford University Press, 2003. *EBSCOhost*. Web. 31 Jan. 2013.

Ryan, Allan A., Jr. Rev. of *Witnesses to Nuremberg: An Oral History of American Participants at the War Crimes Trials*, ed. Bruce M. Stave, Michele Palmer, and Leslie Frank. *Oral History Review* 29.1 (2002): 127–30. *Literature Resource Center*. Web. 28 Jan. 2013.

Salter, Michael. "The Prosecution of Nazi War Criminals and the OSS: The Need for a New Research Agenda." *Journal of Intelligence History* 2.1 (2002): 77–119. Print.

Stave, Bruce M., Michele Palmer, and Leslie Frank. *Witnesses to Nuremberg: An Oral History of American Participants at the War Crimes Trials*. New York: Twayne, 1998. Print.

Further Reading

Blumenthal, David A., and Timothy L. H. McCormack. *Legacy of Nuremberg: Civilising Influence or Institutionalised Vengeance?* Leiden, Netherlands: Brill, 2008. *EBSCOhost*. Web. 28 Jan. 2013.

Diefendorf, Jeffry M. *In the Wake of War: The Reconstruction of German Cities after World War II*. New York: Oxford University Press, 1993. Print.

Gaskin, Hilary, ed. *Eyewitnesses at Nuremberg*. London: Arms & Armour, 1991. Print.

Gilbert, G. M. *Nuremberg Diary*. Cambridge, Mass.: Da Capo, 1995. Print.

Goldensohn, Leon. *The Nuremberg Interviews: An American Psychiatrist's Conversations with the Defendants and Witnesses*. New York: Knopf, 2004. Print.

Goldhagen, Daniel Jonah. *Hitler's Willing Executioners: Ordinary Germans and the Holocaust*. New York: Knopf, 1996. Print.

Marrus, Michael R. *The Nuremberg War Crimes Trial, 1945–46: A Documentary History*. Boston: Bedford, 1997. Print.

Taylor, Telford. *The Anatomy of the Nuremberg Trials: A Personal Memoir*. New York: Little, Brown, 1993. Print.

Tusa, Ann, and John Tusa. *The Nuremberg Trial*. New York: Skyhorse, 2010. Print.

JUDGMENT AT NUREMBERG

In *Witnesses to Nuremberg*, many of the interviewers asked what the interviewees thought of the film *Judgment at Nuremberg* (1961). Written by Abby Mann and directed by Stanley Kramer, *Judgment at Nuremberg* had several well-known actors in its cast, including Marlene Dietrich, Judy Garland, and Burt Lancaster. The film was hailed for drawing attention to the Nuremberg trials and went on to receive critical acclaim, collecting eleven Academy Award nominations. Believing in the film's social message and implications, many of the cast's stars worked for a much lower salary than usual.

The interviewees, who experienced the trials firsthand, were in a unique position to judge whether the dramatic film accurately portrayed the event. Their reactions to the film were mixed. Harry Fiss, a translator, states, "It didn't affect me one way or the other," while Joseph Maier, who served in the interrogation division, calls the film "pretty accurate." Andy Logan, a correspondent for the *New Yorker*, finds *Judgment at Nuremberg* "a ridiculous film in many respects," though perhaps recognizing the film's intentions, he allows, "it meant well."

Jen Gann

Work and Family Life

Chinese Lives: An Oral History of Contemporary China by Zhang Xinxin and Sang Ye   299

The First Agraristas: An Oral History of a Mexican Agrarian Reform Movement by Ann L. Craig   302

Grandmothers, Mothers, and Daughters: Oral Histories of Three Generations of Ethnic American Women by Corinne Azen Krause   305

Habits of Change: An Oral History of American Nuns by Carole Garibaldi Rogers   308

Hooligans or Rebels?: An Oral History of Working-Class Childhood and Youth, 1889–1939 by Stephen Humphries   311

Irish Days: Oral Histories of the Twentieth Century by Margaret Hickey   315

Left Handed, Son of Old Man Hat: A Navajo Autobiography by Left Handed and Walter Dyk   318

Let Me Speak!: Testimony of Domitila, a Woman of the Bolivian Mines by Moema Viezzer and Domitila Barrios de Chungara   322

Long Journey Home: Oral Histories of Contemporary Delaware Indians by James W. Brown and Rita T. Kohn   325

Solidarity Forever: An Oral History of the IWW by Stewart Bird, Dan Georgakas, and Deborah Shaffer   328

Soviet Baby Boomers: An Oral History of Russia's Cold War Generation by Donald J. Raleigh   331

Warlpiri Women's Voices: Our Lives, Our History by Petronella Vaarzon-Morel   334

Women in the Mines: Stories of Life and Work by Marat Moore   337

Workers of the Donbass Speak: Survival and Identity in the New Ukraine, 1989–1992 by Lewis H. Siegelbaum and Daniel J. Walkowitz   340

Working: People Talk about What They Do All Day and How They Feel about What They Do by Louis "Studs" Terkel   343

CHINESE LIVES
An Oral History of Contemporary China
Zhang Xinxin, Sang Ye

OVERVIEW

Chinese Lives: An Oral History of Contemporary China is a selection of sixty-four interviews conducted by Zhang Xinxin and Sang Ye in 1984 and translated into English by W. J. F. Jenner, Delia Davin, and others in 1987. Zhang, a writer, and Sang, a journalist, traveled throughout the People's Republic of China speaking with a diverse set of people to depict the conditions of life in the country. The subjects interviewed represent a broad and often raucous slice of Chinese life, and the vignettes reveal suffering and forbearance, the vagaries of fortune and law, and a society struggling to come to terms with shifts in ideology and rapid economic change.

Published after the tumultuous years of the Cultural Revolution, the death of Mao Zedong, the institution of the one-child policy, and land and other political and socioeconomic reforms, the interviews in *Chinese Lives* first ran as columns in the *China Daily News*, a Chinese-language newspaper based in New York. Select interviews were also published in five literary journals in China before one hundred were collected in the 1986 volume *Beijingren* (People of Beijing). Zhang and Sang's work was widely acclaimed for its frankness and authenticity. For a country obsessed with class, their far-ranging survey allowed people of varying status to have a voice. Though the interviews were conducted half a decade before the Tiananmen Square pro-democracy protests, *Chinese Lives* provides a sense of the tension between the rise of the people and the reticence of many who offered information only under the condition of anonymity.

HISTORICAL AND LITERARY CONTEXT

Chinese Lives presents the messy resolution of revolution, framed in lives fragmented by war and political reforms. After war with Japan and civil war with the Kuomintang, the Communist Party established a republic built on the common Chinese people in 1949. Marking this shift was the assignment of official socioeconomic class status, which affected entrance to universities, promotions at work, and even how much grain could be bought. The 1958 initiation of the Great Leap Forward collectivized agriculture and industrial labor, which was intended to rapidly modernize China but instead led to severe famines, millions of deaths, and economic contraction. Mao's Cultural Revolution, a movement to purge capitalist and traditional influences, was another disaster, with atrocities committed against artists and intellectuals, millions of people sent to labor camps, and the destruction of works of art and historical artifacts.

Following Mao's death in 1976, many of the measures implemented under his leadership were revised. The rise to leadership of Deng Xiaoping began a series of reforms that included the contraction of land to peasants, decreased government regulation of industry, and the establishment of Special Economic Zones. These changes generally led to a higher quality of life, represented in *Chinese Lives* by subjects such as a manager whose entrepreneurial skills turned a small building team into a flourishing construction company and a mink farmer who gleefully exclaims, "Making money's the way to glory now." Yet complications from the past still haunted many, such as the schoolteacher whose dreams of attending university were interrupted by the Cultural Revolution or the prisoner who cites his "bourgeois vanity" as the "main reason" for the rape and murder of his pregnant adolescent sister.

Chinese Lives was inspired by the work of American oral historian Studs Terkel, who, in turn, had been prompted to write his first book of oral history, *Division Street: America* (1967), by Swedish anthropologist Jan Myrdal's *Report from a Chinese Village* (1962). Like Myrdal's text, *Chinese Lives* presents sketches of ordinary Chinese people in their own words with minimal intrusion by the interviewers. Oral histories of China were few before *Chinese Lives*. In addition to Myrdal's, works in this vein include Cyrus H. Peake and Arthur L. Rosenbaum's *Chinese Missionaries Oral History Collection* (1973), Columbia University's *Chinese Oral History Project* (1974), and Kong Demao and Ke Lan's *In the Mansion of Confucius' Descendants* (1984). However, these projects are far more limited in scope than the wide-ranging mosaic of subjects Zhang and Sang present in *Chinese Lives*.

In a nation politically associated with censorship and culturally associated with reserve, *Chinese Lives* remains a vibrant and important document of the diverse lives it depicts. Sang later wrote another book of oral history, *China Candid: The People on the People's*

✣ **Key Facts**

Time Period:
Late 20th Century

Relevant Historical Events:
Death of Mao Zedong; increased economic freedom in China

Nationality:
Chinese

Keywords:
economics; communism; growth

WORK AND FAMILY LIFE

A street in Guangzhou (formerly known as Canton), China, in the 1980s. Ordinary Chinese citizens discuss their lives in the 1987 book *Chinese Lives: An Oral History of Contemporary China*, by Zhang Xinxin and Sang Ye. © ALAMY

Republic (2006), with twenty-six further interviews. Zhang continued writing novels and short stories in Chinese.

THEMES AND STYLE

While the private and political sufferings of the subjects are evident, their grit and drive reminds readers that each is a survivor of a past that has been vicious and a present that does not fully resolve the wounds of history. A woman, now sixty-four, who had been sold to a brothel at age fourteen, says, "In New China I've learned I'm equal with everyone else.... I'm fairly well-off—others haven't done as well—but we've all got our problems." A woman with bound feet explains, "Yes, feudalism did terrible things to people, but I'm still alive to tell the tale." A factory worker describes his father's suicide during the Cultural Revolution in gruesome detail, concluding, "He hardly looked human. Bones sticking out everywhere. His face, hands, feet were all gone. Doesn't bother me now." An ex-soldier waiting in line for a lottery ticket opines, "If you ask me, everything depends on luck, except the guarantee you'll go on being flat broke." A rabbit-breeder remembers his family's sacrifices during the Great Leap Forward, speaking of how his father would eat husks to save grain for his son: "Can you imagine what they taste like? I cried my eyes out. That made up my mind for me: I was going to be a man and support the family."

Zhang and Sang were influenced by 1980s-era Chinese translations of Terkel's *Working* (1974) and *American Dreams: Lost and Found* (1980). They frequently conducted interviews without a tape recorder, only making short notes. As a result, the pieces in *Chinese Lives* are not transcriptions of their subjects, nor are they presented as dialogues with the interviewers. Consistent with the background of its authors, *Chinese Lives* is both a literary and historical work.

The voices of Zhang and Sang remain relatively unheard throughout the interviews, though their faithfulness to idioms and dialects was praised by their translators, who were unable to provide an equivalent in English. Nevertheless, variations in class are evident in the voices of the speakers, as translated into English slang and polished elocution, such as the contrast between a teenage popcorn vendor who gripes, "The first thing when I got to Beijing was I had to pay a fucking fine in the station," and a retired engineer who remarks about the exclusion of Chinese from certain restaurants and hotels: "I've seen quite a lot of the world, but the only places I've come across this sort of thing are in China and the United States, where blacks aren't allowed into some places. That's the racial arrogance of some American whites. But with some of us it's self-contempt."

CRITICAL DISCUSSION

Chinese Lives was praised for its candor and its representation of ordinary people in China. A review in the *Economist* describes it as "a sensation for [its] frankness about contemporary questions (the one-child policy and the party) and ancient taboos (suicide, rape, unhappy marriages])." Stanley Oziewicz commends the interviews in his review in the *Globe & Mail* as "down-to-earth and mostly unexpurgated accounts of fragments of peoples [*sic*] lives as they are," further observing, "They have not been gussied up or toned down, as has been the case with much material from the official Chinese press." According to Judith Shapiro in the *New York Times Book Review*, the "tragic, gritty, hilarious, small-minded, glorious and nakedly revealing" stories in *Chinese Lives* reveal "a complex portrait of a people undergoing confusing, exhilarating and often uneven transformation."

The interviews in *Chinese Lives* have been translated into eight languages and have influenced other oral histories of contemporary China, including Feng Jicai's *Voices from the Whirlwind* (1991), Laifong Leung's *Morning Sun* (1994), and Zhang Kijian and Calum McLeod's *China Remembers* (1999). Tamara Jacka remarks in *China Journal* that "*Chinese Lives* … has inspired countless students of Chinese society." Mary S. Erbaugh calls *Chinese Lives* a "fascinating" model of biography and a possible tool for teaching Chinese students in *Modern Language Journal*. Meanwhile, Luke S. K. Kwong, writing for *Oral History Review*, cites it as a major text, though he also writes, "For all its merit as a window on contemporary China through the lives of its ordinary citizens, it was more the product of a literary venture than that of a historical one."

Little scholarship has been done on oral history in China. As Kwong writes, oral historians in China face the problem that they may be "no more than an ideological tool in the firm grip of a repressive State. The oral historian also has reason to query whether political control, evident in virtually every facet of life in the People's Republic, has not seriously hampered … and unduly distorted the outcome." China remains a country where freedom of expression is limited. That *Chinese Lives* comments critically on the policies and conditions of life from within China confirms its status as a valuable text.

BIBLIOGRAPHY

Sources

Erbaugh, Mary. "Taking Advantage of China's Literary Tradition in Teaching Chinese Students." *Modern Language Journal* 74.1 (1990): 15–27. Print.

Jacka, Tamara. Rev. of *Chinese Women Speak*, by Denyse Verschuur-Basse. *China Journal* 39 (1998): 163–64. Print.

Kwong, Luke S. K. "Oral History in China: A Preliminary Review." *Oral History Review* 20.1–2 (1992): 23–50. Print.

Morrison, H. Jean. "Stepping behind the Bamboo Curtain." *Oral History Association Newsletter* Fall–Winter 1974: 4–5. Print.

Oziewicz, Stanley. "Fragments of Lives as They Are." *Globe & Mail* 16 Jan. 1988: C14. Print.

Rev. of *Chinese Lives: An Oral History of Contemporary China*, by Zhang Xinxin and Sang Ye. *Economist* 23 July 1988: 77. Print.

CENSORSHIP IN CHINA

While China has maintained a stunning rate of economic growth in the early twenty-first century, the government has persisted in a regime of heavy suppression of free expression. The Communist Party openly and aggressively monitors the availability and content of media, including newspapers, online resources, television, radio, literature, film, and social media. Topics that are limited include the 1989 Tiananmen Square pro-democracy protests, the Falun Gong religious sect, human rights abuses, and ethnic independence uprisings.

The writer Liu Xiaobo, awarded a Nobel Peace Prize in 2010, was incarcerated in 2009 as a political prisoner for his involvement in human rights activism. The artist Ai Weiwei, who contributed to the design of the National Stadium for the 2008 Beijing Olympics, began demanding openness and accountability from the government following the censored reports of the 2008 Sichuan earthquake, in which countless schoolchildren died due to shoddy construction work. Despite his international fame, Ai has been arrested, attacked, and imprisoned for his public and often mischievous methods of resistance. In a regime of strict control of information, civil unrest for free speech and press has yet to catch up with the more immediate imperative of widespread economic stability. Nevertheless, there is more freedom in China now than at any previous point in the nation's history.

Shapiro, Judith. "Scenes from the Kaleidoscope." *New York Times Book Review* 18 Oct. 1987. *General OneFile*. Web. 2 Feb. 2013.

Zhang Xinxin, and Sang Ye. *Chinese Lives: An Oral History of Contemporary China*. Ed. W. J. F. Jenner and Delia Davin; trans. W. J. F. Jenner, Delia Davin, et al. New York: Pantheon, 1987. Print.

Further Reading

Feng Jicai. *Voices from the Whirlwind: An Oral History of the Chinese Cultural Revolution*. New York: Pantheon, 1991. Print.

Leung, Laifong. *Morning Sun: Interviews with Chinese Writers of the Lost Generation*. New York: Sharpe, 1994. Print.

Meyer, Mahlon. *Remembering China from Taiwan: Divided Families and Bittersweet Reunions after the Chinese Civil War*. Hong Kong: Hong Kong University Press, 2012. Print.

Sang Ye. *China Candid: The People on the People's Republic*. Ed. Geremie R. Barmé and Miriam Lang. Berkeley: University of California Press, 2006. Print.

Zhang Kijian, and Calum McLeod. *China Remembers*. Oxford, UK: Oxford University Press, 1999. Print.

Zhang Xinxin. *The Dreams of Our Generation and Selections from Beijing's People*. Trans. and ed. Edward Gunn, Donna Jung, and Patricia Farr. Ithaca, N.Y.: Cornell University Press, 1986. Print.

Irene Hsiao

The First Agraristas
An Oral History of a Mexican Agrarian Reform Movement
Ann L. Craig

❖ **Key Facts**

Time Period:
Mid-20th Century

Relevant Historical Events:
Land redistribution movement in Mexico; Mexican Revolution

Nationality:
Mexican

Keywords:
land reform; revolution; redistribution

OVERVIEW

The First Agraristas: An Oral History of a Mexican Agrarian Reform Movement (1983), collected and edited by political scientist Ann L. Craig, centers on the *agrarista*, or land redistribution movement, in the small town of Lagos de Moreno in Jalisco, Mexico, during the post revolutionary period of 1924 to 1940. Craig weaves the testimonies she collected in the mid-1970s of urban workers and campesinos (farmers) with official documents, photographs, and correspondence that outline land reform, demonstrating how the reform movement utilized legalistic means to achieve its aims.

Craig's text garnered high praise for its meticulously researched connections between peasants and urban workers and local and national officials. Published in the midst of Mexico's economic crisis of the early 1980s, the book was viewed by critics as a boon to students and scholars of land use and social movements in Mexico. In her subsequent scholarship, Craig continued to examine the cost-benefit relationship between Mexican government and the people of the country, coediting both *Popular Movements and Political Change in Mexico* (1990) and *Transforming State-Society Relations in Mexico: The National Solidarity Approach* (1994). While *The First Agraristas* did meet with some criticism for its lack of attention to the role of women in the land reform movement, Craig has renewed her focus to examine gender representation in Mexican government.

HISTORICAL AND LITERARY CONTEXT

The testimonies in *The First Agraristas* concern the period following the Mexican Revolution (1910–1920). This uprising, led by Pancho Villa in the north and land reformer Emiliano Zapata in the south, challenged the power of land barons following the reign of President Porfirio Díaz (1876–1911). Díaz had worked to consolidate much of the country's wealth in the hands of a few, entrenching landless peasants in debt during an era known as the Porfiriato. Villa, Zapata, and other militant social reformers took land and arms by force, redistributing them in the process. The fighting lasted well into the 1920s, though a new constitution was drafted in 1917 that incorporated issues of land reform and abolished the *encomienda* system that legalized the slavery of Native Americans. The 1917 constitution is still in use today, Article 27 of which states, "In order … to ensure a more equitable distribution of public wealth … necessary measures shall be taken to divide up large landed estates."

Despite the popular appeal of the revolutionary ideals, many of the key leaders were caught in personal plays for power, and a startling class divide characterized by debt peonage still existed by 1924. Pressured by local leaders, President Lázaro Cárdenas (1934–1940), a moderate, established agrarian reform via the forms of the *ejido* (land collective) and workers' cooperatives, both of which were applied for by the citizens and subject to the approval of Cárdenas's government. *The First Agraristas* portrays these bureaucratic measures as effective tools for change that can, under sympathetic governments, improve living conditions for the poor.

A unique work due to Craig's meticulous research of political relationships, *The First Agraristas* remains situated in a body of oral history scholarship. Other works in the genre include Patricia Preciado Martin's *Songs My Mother Sang to Me: An Oral History of Mexican American Women* (1992), which also explores issues of labor and social conditions. Both Craig and Martin interviewed participants who were residents of the United States and compare their experiences in the two countries. The local leaders Craig interviewed were galvanized to create social change in Mexico following their experiences as migrant workers in the United States.

By demonstrating that legal and nonviolent organizational practices were instrumental in agrarian reform, *The First Agraristas* has influenced the historiography of post revolutionary Mexico. The work also sheds light on contemporary struggles and political transitions, as well as U.S.-Mexico political relations. Having earned her doctorate in comparative politics at the Massachusetts Institute of Technology in 1978, as of 2013 Craig is professor emeritus at the University of San Diego in the international studies department.

THEMES AND STYLE

Craig's text focuses on themes of labor, land redistribution, and cooperation between a government and its people. One worker's testimony effectively reveals labor conditions and the exigency for social change: "Those granaries would be filled to the top with maize. And when they shelled the corn, 25 mulecarts with large steel wheels would leave … and we had nothing left even to purchase [basic goods] with." *The First Agraristas* illustrates how the mid-1920s organizing strategy of creating alliances between peasants and unions ameliorated the indebtedness of many campesinos; however, the text also reveals the significant amount of agency required of the peasant population to initiate applications for *ejidos* and worker collectives.

Craig's motivation in writing the book was to expose how the benefits of the land reform movement were contingent on the initiative of the people as well as on the willingness of Cárdenas's administration. Cárdenas, seen as an activist following the years of oppression that characterized the Porfiriato, was in reality creating a dominant political party, eventually called Partido Revolucionario Institucional, that would rule Mexico until the landmark elections of 2000. Craig writes that the history of land redistribution "is principally a chronicle of campesino power growing in tandem with the expansion of state power, and then declining with the consolidation of the state's power and the satisfaction of the agraristas' demands for land." The concentration of power in Mexico's modern urban centers led Craig to conclude the near impossibility of a successful campesino movement under the conditions of the day.

The First Agraristas begins with an introduction and a chapter on the geography and political history of the region, which serve to contextualize the testimonies. These are followed by a chapter that uses oral history to demonstrate the effects of the *agrarista* movement on families. Historian Vicki L. Ruiz writes in the *Oral History Review* that this section is notable because Craig "maintains that important sense of distance from her informants so that this section does not digress into a litany of life stories." Michael Kearney, in a 1986 article for *Contemporary Sociology*, notes that the coupling of qualitative and quantitative sources "reveals just how the personal backgrounds, goals, strategies, ideology, and victories of local leaders and their people have been related to the larger political and social forces that took form during the revolution."

CRITICAL DISCUSSION

Early criticism of *The First Agraristas* praised Craig's archival research and scholarship. Writing for the *American Historical Review* (1985), Merilee S. Grindle notes that Craig's "evocative study of agrarian reform" reveals how the local "pursuit of reform objectives entailed considerable risk to those involved." Heather Fowler Salamini, in a 1984 article for the *Hispanic American Historical Review*, calls it a "well-researched monograph" that unearths "important statistical data … on land tenure and values."

Portrait of Mexican president Lázaro Cárdenas. Cárdenas established agrarian reform via the forms of the *ejido* (land collective) and workers' cooperatives. © AISA/EVERETT COLLECTION

The text was acclaimed in the field of oral history for its adept portrayal of personal and political, as well as rural and urban, concerns. In 1984 Ruiz, then the director of the Institute of Oral History at the University of Texas at El Paso, wrote that "the organization and style of *The First Agraristas* should serve as a model for utilizing oral sources in academic research and writing." However, it was Ruiz who raised the critique of Craig's disparate focus on men and women, arguing that because "the family forms the basic unit of production in rural Mexican society, the absence of systematic examination of women's role in Lagos de Moreno, generally, and agraismo, particularly, seems unsettling." Ruiz notes that although Craig interviewed many campesinas, she generalized their struggle in contrast with her detailed emphasis on male urban workers.

Contemporary scholarship incorporates *The First Agraristas* into analyses of community empowerment, social movements, and public policy. Tanalis Padilla, historian and author of *Rural Resistance in the Land of Zapata: The Jaramillista Movement and the Myth of the Pax-Priísta, 1940–1962* (2008), examines how the legacy of Zapata has characterized the campesino struggle in rural southern Mexico. Padilla resurrects the text for her study of agrarian reform during the generation that followed the one studied by Craig in *The First Agraristas*. Citing growing state power as a significant factor in the changing reform movement, Padilla finds that "rather than fight for land and community autonomy, this generation sought the state support necessary to make the campesino economy viable in a rapidly modernizing nation." This includes demands for "credit, technical assistance, better prices on their products, and basic state services such as schools and hospitals."

A NEW SOCIAL MOVEMENT

As the twentieth century progressed, the Mexican government moved away from the social reforms of the *ejidos* and worker collectives established in the 1930s and 1940s. The socialist ideology presented by President Lázaro Cárdenas (1934–1940) was replaced with Western imperialism and globalization. In 1994 the North American Free Trade Agreement went into effect, lifting tax barriers for large corporations in the United States, Mexico, and Canada, thus dealing a considerable blow to the environments for workers in those countries.

That same year, the legacy of Emiliano Zapata was revived, when the Ejército Zapatista de Liberación Nacional (EZLN, or Zapatistas) took up arms against the Mexican government, demanding social equity and rights for indigenous people in Mexico. The movement, while condoning armed uprisings, shares some qualities with the agrarian reform explored by Ann L. Craig in *The First Agraristas*. The spokesperson for the Zapatistas, Subcomandante Marcos, is an urban intellectual who has identified himself with the peasants and created ties between urban and rural workers. The Zapatistas are based in the south, where Zapata's influence was the strongest, and like him, they seek revolutionary change. However, the EZLN also pursues social reform through legal channels, as did the *agraristas*.

BIBLIOGRAPHY

Sources

Craig, Ann L. *The First Agraristas: An Oral History of a Mexican Agrarian Reform Movement*. Berkeley: University of California Press, 1983. Print.

Grindle, Merilee S. Rev. of *The First Agraristas: An Oral History of a Mexican Agrarian Reform Movement*, by Ann L. Craig. *American Historical Review* 90.1 (1985): 250–51. *JSTOR*. Web. 23 Jan. 2013.

Kearney, Michael. Rev. of *The First Agraristas: An Oral History of a Mexican Agrarian Reform Movement*, by Ann L. Craig. *Contemporary Sociology* 15.2 (1986): 253–54. *JSTOR*. Web. 23 Jan. 2013.

Padilla, Tanalis. *Rural Resistance in the Land of Zapata: The Jaramillista Movement and the Myth of the Pax-Priísta, 1940–1962*. Durham, N.C.: Duke University Press, 2008. Print.

Ruiz, Vicki L. Rev. of *The First Agraristas: An Oral History of a Mexican Agrarian Reform Movement*, by Ann L. Craig. *Oral History Review* 12 (1984): 153–54. *JSTOR*. Web. 23 Jan. 2013.

Salamini, Heather Fowler. Rev. of *The First Agraristas: An Oral History of a Mexican Agrarian Reform Movement*, by Ann L. Craig. *Hispanic American Historical Review* 64.3 (1984): 576–77. *JSTOR*. Web. 23 Jan. 2013.

Further Reading

Carr, Barry. "The Mexican Communist Party and Agrarian Mobilization in the Laguna, 1920–1940: A Worker-Peasant Alliance?" *Hispanic American Historical Review* 67.3 (1987): 371–404. *JSTOR*. Web. 23 Jan. 2013.

Hall, Linda B. Rev. of *The First Agraristas: An Oral History of a Mexican Agrarian Reform Movement*, by Ann L. Craig. *Agricultural History* 59.3 (1985): 463–64. *JSTOR*. Web. 23 Jan. 2013.

Knight, Alan. "Cardenismo: Juggernaut or Jalopy?" *Journal of Latin American Studies* 26.1 (1994): 73–107. *Google Scholar*. Web. 30 Jan. 2013.

Martin, Patricia Preciado. *Songs My Mother Sang to Me: An Oral History of Mexican American Women*. Tucson: University of Arizona Press, 1992. Print.

Miller, Simon. "Revisionism in Recent Mexican Historiography." *Bulletin of Latin American Research* 4.1 (1985): 77–88. *JSTOR*. Web. 23 Jan. 2013.

Caitlin Moore

Grandmothers, Mothers, and Daughters
Oral Histories of Three Generations of Ethnic American Women
Corinne Azen Krause

OVERVIEW

Grandmothers, Mothers, and Daughters: Oral Histories of Three Generations of Ethnic American Women (1991) is an oral history by Corinne Azen Krause that focuses on six immigrant families living in the Pittsburgh, Pennsylvania, area. The text tells the stories of three generations of women trying to balance their traditional ethnic identity with assimilation into mainstream American culture. In the book, the women, who were chosen because of their upward mobility within the U.S. class structure and their success in assimilating to American culture, recall their life experiences—from the grandmothers' immigration to the United States to issues facing the daughters in the contemporary world.

Although the text provides details of an important period for European American immigrants, early critics noted that Krause fails to accurately capture the voices of the women interviewed or to provide the appropriate historical context for the work. Inspired by Krause's 1978 study of 225 American women of Jewish, Italian, and Slavic heritage for the Institute for Pluralism and Group Identity of the American Jewish Committee, *Grandmothers, Mothers, and Daughters* relies on follow-up interviews conducted in 1988–1989 with eighteen of the women from the 1978 study. Today *Grandmothers, Mothers, and Daughters* is known for its highly personal portrayal of the process of assimilation to American culture for immigrant families.

HISTORICAL AND LITERARY CONTEXT

Grandmothers, Mothers, and Daughters begins with several grandmothers' recollections of the mass immigration from eastern and southern Europe to the United States between 1820 and 1920. During this period 35 million Europeans made the United States their home; the majority were of Italian, Jewish, or Slavic heritage. This migration was initiated by a succession of events, including the end of the Napoleonic Wars and the rapid growth of industrialization that made traditional peasant life an impractical method of survival. The developing U.S. coal and steel industries provided employment and opportunity to families who could no longer support themselves in their native countries.

The oral histories in *Grandmothers, Mothers, and Daughters* document the experiences of women who immigrated to Pittsburgh, a city at the forefront of the steel industry in the early 1900s that promised employment and urban development. However, the influx of immigration caused uncertainty and inconsistency among jobs and wages, and women often had to take domestic service jobs such as waitressing and housecleaning to balance their household budgets. For subsequent generations of women, societal pressures of the nuclear family, the need to work during the world wars, and the civil and women's rights movements challenged traditional roles within the household, affecting their lives and the decisions they made for themselves and their families.

Grandmothers, Mothers, and Daughters is part of a trend in academic literature in the 1980s and 1990s that applied oral history techniques to women's perspectives of immigration in the United States. Earlier oral histories that follow this trend include Elizabeth Ewen's *Immigrant Women in the Land of Dollars: Life and Culture on the Lower East Side 1890–1925* (1985), Sydney Stahl Weinberg's *The World of Our Mothers: The Lives of Jewish Immigrant Women* (1988), and Susan A. Glenn's *Daughters of the Shtetl: Life and Labor in the Immigrant Generation* (1990).

Although *Grandmothers, Mothers, and Daughters* is the most influential work of Krause's academic career, it had little initial impact on the academic community. Today it is regarded as a useful text that documents women's experiences from the time of mass immigration during the nineteenth and twentieth centuries. Records of these experiences are valuable because they provide insights into family and cultural dynamics that might not otherwise be documented and preserve many of the experiences that would otherwise pass away with the people who experienced them. Therefore, the work's historical impact is significant despite its initial reception.

THEMES AND STYLE

One of the central themes of *Grandmothers, Mothers, and Daughters* is the effect of class, gender, and ethnicity on women's life decisions. Krause explains in her introduction, "As I listened to three generations of women talk about their lives, it became clear that

❖ *Key Facts*

Time Period:
20th Century

Relevant Historical Events:
Mass immigration from eastern and southern Europe; women's rights movement; civil rights movement

Nationality:
American

Keywords:
immigration; feminism; identity

WORK AND FAMILY LIFE

A grandmother and her granddaughters in their synagogue, 1991. © DAVID TURNLEY/CORBIS

continuity and change in behavior were affected by class as well as by gender and ethnicity. The complex interaction of all three factors—ethnicity, gender, and class—influenced women's behavior, choices, and attitudes over the generations." Members of one Slavic family, for example, describe how their economic conditions improved over the course of the interviews. The grandmother remembers, "I never had shoes on my feet until I was coming to this country." Her daughter recollects, "In those days, before my mother would go to work in the morning she would give us a nickel" for lunch, while the granddaughter had a much better life, remembering her childhood dog and horse, provided by her parents.

Krause's motivation for producing *Grandmothers, Mothers, and Daughters*—which reflects her own experience balancing her traditional Jewish heritage with her academic career—was to shed light on the story of immigrant women in U.S. history. She states that research is severely lacking in this area: "In the 1960s and 1970s, history curricula in the high schools and colleges where I taught mentioned only briefly the fact that our nation is the product of diverse cultures brought to these shores by generations of immigrants of both sexes. … I wanted to bring new knowledge of immigrant and ethnic women into the mainstream of history." However, she deviates from the conventions of oral history by substantially editing the interviews so they read as autobiographical accounts instead of transcriptions of the participants' words.

The book's straightforward, consistent style is a result of its organization. Each chapter consists of the narrative of three women from different generations of one family. The narrative is accompanied by images and editorial interruptions describing aspects of the interview process or providing context. Krause admits to heavy editing of the original interviews: "Although I have tried to capture the tone and personality of each woman, in several instances I have changed the wording slightly to clarify meaning." Some critics, including Julia Hirsch in her 1994 review in *Journal of American Ethnic History,* charge that this editing process results in a monotonous text devoid of the voices of the oral history participants: "Krause's genre, oral history, can be charged with phrases and images. But, with rare exceptions, the voices in this volume are bland." Further, Hirsch states, "Too much of her narrative is matter-of-fact, devoid of pungency and music" so that the reading audience is "hard pressed to discover the particularities of the three ethnicities: everything sounds so much alike."

CRITICAL DISCUSSION

Although early reviewers noted the valuable information Krause gathered in the interview process, they criticized *Grandmothers, Mothers, and Daughters* because it provides sufficient interpretive material to supplement the oral histories. Margaret Spratt, in a 1991 review for *Pennsylvania History,* remarks that the "life stories provide invaluable information on the struggles and resiliency of ordinary women who lived during times of tremendous change," which "will be quite useful for students of ethnic and women's history." Spratt also discusses the "serious limitations" of the volume, including the lack of "analysis of the historical setting, culture, or class." In addition, she finds the "brief chapter at the beginning of the book" is "insufficient, particularly for the reader who is unfamiliar with the literature."

Since its initial appearance, scholars have accepted Krause's oral history with some hesitation as a resource for ethnic historians, sociologists, and feminists. Writing for *Polish American Studies*, Virginia R. Mitchell states, "The book will be of use not only to women's historians, but also to those interested in industrialization, economic mobility, assimilation, and ethnic identity in America." Mitchell writes that the text "is valuable in spite of the introduction and editorial interruptions" because it "help[s] illustrate the changes of the past century in a memorable and vivid manner." In a 1992 review for *History of Education Quarterly*, Judith Raftery notes, "Krause has added a valuable study to the literature" despite noticing the text's shortcomings, including the limited scope of the study and the preference for personal memory—which is often selective—over "more reliable sources."

Critics of *Grandmothers, Mothers, and Daughters* generally point to the lack of context surrounding the personal narratives and the resulting lack of clarity. Mitchell describes the author's attempts "to draw some conclusions from these personal histories as to general truths about Italian, Jewish, and 'Slavic' culture" that ultimately "are often mere stereotypes, at times contradicted by the studies themselves." Raftery follows this trend when she states the "conclusions would be more convincing had [Krause] spent more time analysing the material within its historical context." Spratt laments, "Unfortunately, the power of the women's words is diluted by an insufficient development of context."

BIBLIOGRAPHY

Sources

Hirsch, Julia. Rev. of *Grandmothers, Mothers, and Daughters: Oral Histories of Three Generations of Ethnic Women*, by Corinne Azen Krause. *Journal of American Ethnic History* 13.4 (1994): 86–88. *JSTOR*. Web. 24 Jan 2013.

Krause, Corinne Azen. *Grandmothers, Mothers, and Daughters: Oral Histories of Three Generations of Ethnic American Women*. Boston: Twayne, 1991. Print.

Mitchell, Virginia R. Rev. of *Grandmothers, Mothers, and Daughters: Oral Histories of Three Generations of Ethnic American Women*, by Corinne Azen Krause. *Polish American Studies* 50.1 (1993): 98–99. *JSTOR*. Web. 24 Jan. 2013.

Raftery, Judith. Rev. of *Grandmothers, Mothers, and Daughters: Oral Histories of Three Generations of Ethnic American Women*, by Corinne Azen Krause. *History of Education Quarterly* 32.2 (1992): 252–54. *JSTOR*. Web. 24 Jan. 2013.

Spratt, Margaret. Rev. of *Daughters of the Shtetl: Life and Labor in the Immigrant Generation*, by Susan A. Glenn, and *Grandmothers, Mothers, and Daughters: Oral Histories of Three Generations of Ethnic American Women*, by Corinne Azen Krause. *Pennsylvania History* 58.4 (1991): 340–43. *JSTOR*. Web. 24 Jan. 2013.

Further Reading

Bailey, Chris Howard. "Precious Blood: Encountering Inter-ethnic Issues in Oral History Research, Reconstruction, and Representation." *Oral History Review* 18.2 (1990): 61–108. *JSTOR*. Web. 24 Jan. 2013.

Ewen, Elizabeth. *Immigrant Women in the Land of Dollars: Life and Culture on the Lower East Side 1890–1925*. New York: Monthly Review, 1985. Print.

Gabaccia, Donna R. "Do We Still Need Immigration History?" *Polish American Studies* 55.1 (1998): 45–68. *JSTOR*. Web. 24 Jan. 2013.

Glenn, Susan A. *Daughters of the Shtetl: Life and Labor in the Immigrant Generation*. Ithaca, N.Y.: Cornell University Press, 1990. Print.

Krause, Corinne Azen. *Grandmothers, Mothers, and Daughters: An Oral History Study of Ethnicity, Mental Health, and Continuity of Three Generations of Jewish, Italian, and Slavic-American Women*. New York: Institute on Pluralism and Group Identity of the American Jewish Committee, 1978. Print.

Sassler, Sharon. "Learning to Be an 'American Lady'?: Ethnic Variation in Daughters' Pursuits in the Early 1900s." *Gender and Society* 14.1 (2000): 184–209. *JSTOR*. Web. 24 Jan. 2013.

Weinberg, Sydney Stahl. *The World of Our Mothers: The Lives of Jewish Immigrant Women*. New York: Schocken, 1988. *Questia*. Web. 24 Jan. 2013.

THE PROMISE OF PITTSBURGH IN THE EARLY TWENTIETH CENTURY

Pittsburgh, Pennsylvania, was a promising city for immigrants who were looking for jobs in the industrial age. Companies such as Carnegie Steel (sold to U.S. Steel in 1901) and Westinghouse provided jobs and encouraged immigrant labor. In 1910 Pittsburgh was the national leader in manufactured products. The success based around the city caused immigrants to flood companies as workers, but fluctuations in wages and the availability of work created an environment that was unpredictable at best. Pittsburgh was hit hard during the Great Depression but flourished during the world wars when steel was in high demand.

Pittsburgh immigrants generally settled in neighborhoods with people of similar ethnicities, sometimes near families from the same town in the old country. These neighborhoods were more stable in Pittsburgh than in many other major cities, and they continue to exist today. However, the rigidity of these ethnic cultures, according to many studies, is slowly dissolving as immigrants assimilate into mainstream American life.

Katherine Barker

Habits of Change
An Oral History of American Nuns
Carole Garibaldi Rogers

Key Facts

Time Period:
Mid- to Late 20th Century

Relevant Historical Events:
Vatican II; declining number of American nuns; Sister Formation Conference

Nationality:
American

Keywords:
Catholicism; nuns; religion

OVERVIEW

Carole Garibaldi Rogers's 2011 book *Habits of Change: An Oral History of American Nuns* (a revised edition of a 1996 book called *Poverty, Chastity and Change*) offers the varied stories of women religious (a preferred term for many) who have served during a time of transition in the Roman Catholic Church and American society. Rogers, an oral historian who primarily writes about women and religion, states that her "choice of oral history to capture the stories of women religious who lived through these changes was deliberate" in order to "hear history in the language of the narrators." Featuring fifty-one individual narrators, Rogers's book represents a true cross section of different experiences of religious life. *Habits of Change* is organized thematically, with sections as diverse as "In the Cloister," "Two African-American Voices," and "The Decision to Leave." Taken together, the book celebrates the unique experience of being an American nun.

After interviewing these women religious in the 1990s about the changes facing the church and the dwindling numbers of nuns in the United States, Rogers speaks to them again between 2009 and 2010, by which time these issues have become only more apparent. Upon its publication, *Habits of Change* was generally received positively and was viewed as a compelling and thorough oral history of an often overlooked group. Rogers's book continues to be valuable in documenting what it has meant to be an American nun during a time of transition through the direct testimony of those who have lived it.

HISTORICAL AND LITERARY CONTEXT

The stories collected in *Habits of Change* evolve over many decades, with some narrators well into their nineties, but primarily focus on the past fifty years. When many of the interviewed nuns entered religious life, they were expected to leave their families and friends completely behind for the world of the convent, which typically had strict rules about dress and conduct. As Rogers describes it, women religious before the 1950s lived much like nuns had for centuries before, choosing a life that meant "they would never own property or manage their own money, that they would remain unmarried and celibate, and that they would follow the rules of their community as interpreted for them by their superior." In 1954, however, the Sister Formation Conference was formed to better educate women religious.

The Catholic Church changed drastically after the Second Vatican Council (Vatican II) in 1965, which not only offered a broad ecumenical revamping of Catholic theology but also introduced a series of revisions to the mass and to general practices that sought to modernize the church. Vatican II, which led to a more general openness and loosening of restrictions within the church, as well as an increasing outreach to laity, led to mixed reactions among women religious. Some women welcomed the increased freedom, while others struggled to find their place in a new church. Outside activity, such as the civil rights movement and the women's movement, began to affect religious life as well. *Habits of Change* describes the lives of women religious both before and after Vatican II, as well as the lives of women who became women religious well after its establishment.

When the first edition of her oral history was published in 1996, Rogers saw her project as a unique one. In a 1998 article, "Overlooked Narrators: What Women Religious Can Contribute to Feminist Oral History," Rogers argues that these women have been unfairly overlooked as subjects of study. Although the book was groundbreaking in being such a comprehensive study of oral history, Rogers was influenced by many earlier texts, such as Ann Patrick Ware's *Midwives of the Future: American Sisters Tell Their Story* (1985), an oral history of a smaller group of American nuns discussing similar issues, and texts by nuns themselves, such as the works of Joan Chittister.

Habits of Change was a well-regarded and influential book, setting off what Rogers calls an "explosion" of writing about women religious, including many writings by women religious themselves. One work that Rogers addresses as particularly noteworthy is the two-volume *Religious Life in a New Millennium* (2000–2001) by Sister Sandra Marie Schneiders. The decision to create a second edition reflects both the book's popularity and the continued interest both Rogers and her readers had in these women.

THEMES AND STYLE

The predominant theme of *Habits of Change,* reflected in the title, is the way women religious have adjusted to changes in religious life and society and the different paths that have opened up for these women. Many discuss the evolution of their life's work, which has expanded since the Second Vatican Council to include missionary work, jobs in the medical field, and responsibilities as pastors in parishes without priests. The hierarchical, male-dominated church is a source of ambivalence for many of the women, especially concerning the issue of women becoming priests. "Many women … are prepared and could go into seminaries, and just because they're female they cannot…. I do feel that will change in time, and it must change," Sister Germaine Fritz says, adding that many disagree with her. Rogers also interviews women who have chosen to leave the religious life. Many of the testimonies focus on the diminishing of religious life in the United States and specifically the decline and aging of the U.S. nun population. "Most of us are way over 60 … and yet we are giving 1000 percent everywhere we go," Sister Kathy Quigley comments.

Rogers wrote in a later article that she chose to write about nuns because "our understanding of public events … is enhanced by including the voices of the normally unheard" and that it was important to record their history "before it is too late." She chose to compose her text of long transcripts rather than short excerpts and commentary, writing that this method felt "most appropriate for narrators who were by and large articulate [and] who had already done the hard work of self-examination and could speak out of that life knowledge." She had her subjects reflect on three questions: "Why did you enter religious life? What were some of the crisis points or times of change in your religious life? … And finally, why are you still a religious?"

The text of *Habits of Change* is divided into thematic sections grouping certain nuns' testimonies with others. The first section, "Evolving Ministries," is separated into smaller sections dealing with vocation, including "Missionary Workers" and "In the Cloister." The second section, "Changing Attitudes," is divided into parts dealing more with church politics, such as "Encounters with Judaism" and "Structures and Fissures." The final section of oral history is titled "From the Present into the Future" and has many shorter oral histories investigating the evolving role of women religious and the church. Rogers writes short introductions to her narrators, as well as updates for the later edition.

CRITICAL DISCUSSION

Habits of Change was well received not only in the religious academic community but also in the larger mainstream academic community, although it unsurprisingly gained less attention in the latter. Many writers praised Rogers's methodology and decision to focus on overlooked narrators when the first edition of the book came out in 1996. "Rogers provides a rich collection of women's narratives which can be used both substantively and methodologically," writes Marybeth Stalp in a 1997 issue of *Review of Religious Research.* However, Stalp, like Florence Deacon in *Oral History Review* (1999), found that Rogers's organization of the book detracted from the overall effect and left the reader confused. "Unless one reads the entire text in a relatively concentrated period," Deacon opines, "the thematic arrangement might not be readily apparent."

The second edition's publication brought the text some increased attention. The new edition was noted in a 2011 edition of the American Library Association's *Booklist* as a good choice for a public library. In 2012 Ann Harrington in *Theological Studies* wrote that "most compelling in this work is the voice of the individual sister putting into words her struggles, hopes, joys, sorrows, and concerns within the context of her life as a religious sister" but added that she found it "puzzling that [Rogers] chose to publish a new edition with so few new interviews." In a 2011 book review for *America,* Katarina Schuth commented that any reader would be "informed and inspired" by the book but also wondered why "neither Rogers nor her interviewees say much about younger religious in new communities and the paths they are following."

Habits of Change is considered a valuable text within the field of religious studies but has not been heavily written about in an academic context. The book is noted in Carol Coburn's 2004 article "An Overview of the Historiography of Women Religious: A Twenty-Five-Year Retrospective" in *U.S. Catholic Historian* as part of a collection of books focusing on nuns after Vatican II. It is also mentioned as an illuminating work in Tracy E. K'Meyer's 1999 article "'I Just Felt Called …': Oral History and the Meaning of Faith in American Religious History" in the *Journal of American History* as an important work of scholarship.

Habits of Change looks at the lives of nuns in the United States, of various ages and orders. Depicted here is an American nun who has dedicated 75 years to her calling, Sister Mary Alice Chineworth, a member of the Oblate Sisters of Providence. © KATHERINE FREY/THE WASHINGTON POST VIA GETTY IMAGES

PRIMARY SOURCE

EXCERPT FROM *HABITS OF CHANGE: AN ORAL HISTORY OF AMERICAN NUNS*

SISTER BONAVENTURE BURKE

At the time of the interview, Sister Bonaventure Burke lived in Saint Bernard's Convent, a four-story brick building in Nashville, Tennessee. The grass on either side of the driveway was uncut, the parking area was empty, and several of the windows on the chapel side of the building had been replaced with plywood. The week after the interview the building was to be closed, and the few Sisters who remained were to be moved to a new retirement home on the far side of Nashville.

Unlike most other Sisters of Mercy, Sister Bonaventure, 84, wears a short black veil on all occasions. She spoke with a gentle Southern accent, and laughed gently, too, most frequently at her own expense.

. . .

The thing that hurt me, that really got to me, was the changing of the habit, putting aside the habit. I've tried to be as conservative as I can, as you can see. But many of the Sisters are out of the habit completely. All the younger Sisters are. I love the habit. I felt that it wasn't so much that it distinguished me as the fact that it was a witness. People would see me, they'd know that somebody is trying to serve God to the best of her ability. And it would make them think that someone is still trying to practice Christian values. That's why I kept it.

One day I was up in the mountains and I was sitting beside a stream with this friend of our family. Way up high on the road was a little boy with a fishing rod over his shoulder. And he yelled, "Hello, Sister." He didn't know me. I didn't know him. But I was a Sister. He had gone to a Catholic school. He was very much at ease with Sisters. And so many places I've met that. People feel at home and at ease.

And then I was in the airport in San Francisco, going to see a niece. And a strange woman said, "Oh, it's good to see a Sister of Mercy. I'm a Sister of Mercy." And I thought, "Oh. You'd never know."

SOURCE: Carole Garibaldi Rogers, *Habits of Change: An Oral History of American Nuns*. New York: Oxford University Press, 2011. By permission of Oxford University Press, USA.

BIBLIOGRAPHY

Sources

Coburn, Carol. "An Overview of the Historiography of Women Religious: A Twenty-Five-Year Retrospective." *U.S. Catholic Historian* 22.1 (2004): 1–26. *JSTOR*. Web. 29 Jan. 2013.

Deacon, Florence. "Book Reviews." *Oral History Review* 26.1 (1999): 147. *Academic Search Elite*. Web. 29 Jan. 2013.

Harrington, Ann M. Rev. of *Habits of Change: An Oral History of American Nuns*. *Theological Studies* 73.3 (2012): 699–701. *Academic Search Elite*. Web. 29 Jan. 2013.

K'Meyer, Tracy E. "'I Just Felt Called …': Oral History and the Meaning of Faith in American Religious History." *Journal of American History* 86.2 (1999): 724–33. *JSTOR*. Web. 29 Jan. 2013.

Rogers, Carole Garibaldi. "Overlooked Narrators: What Women Religious Can Contribute to Feminist Oral History." *Frontiers: A Journal of Women's Studies* 19.3 (1998): 157–70. *JSTOR*. Web. 29 Jan. 2013.

———. *Habits of Change: An Oral History of American Nuns*. New York: Oxford University Press, 2011. Print.

Schuth, Katarina. "The Sisters' Stories." *America* 205.13 (2011): 25–26. *Academic Search Elite*. Web. 29 Jan. 2013.

Stalp, Marybeth C. Rev. of *Poverty, Chastity, and Change: Lives of Contemporary American Nuns*. *Review of Religious Research* 39.2 (1997): 184. *Academic Search Elite*. Web. 29 Jan. 2013.

Further Reading

Bonavoglia, Angela. *Good Catholic Girls: How Women Are Leading the Fight to Change the Church*. New York: ReganBooks, 2005. Print.

Chittister, Joan. *In My Own Words*. Ed. Mary Lou Kownacki. Liguori Mo.: Liguori, 2008. Print.

Fiedler, Maureen E., ed. *Breaking through the Stained Glass Ceiling: Women Religious Leaders in Their Own Words*. New York: Seabury, 2010. Print.

McNamara, Jo Ann. *Sisters in Arms: Catholic Nuns through Two Millennia*. Cambridge, Mass.: Harvard University Press, 1996. Print.

Rogers, Carole Garibaldi. "God Does Not Call Only the Able-Bodied." *America* 179.8 (1998): 6–9. *Academic Search Elite*. Web. 29 Jan. 2013.

Schneiders, Sandra Marie. *Finding the Treasure: Locating Catholic Religious Life in a New Ecclesial and Cultural Context*. New York: Paulist, 2000. Print.

———. *Selling All: Commitment, Consecrated Celibacy, and Community in Catholic Religious Life*. New York: Paulist, 2001. Print.

Ware, Ann Patrick, ed. *Midwives of the Future: American Sisters Tell Their Story*. Kansas City, Mo.: Leaven, 1985. Print.

Emily Jones

Hooligans or Rebels?
An Oral History of Working-Class Childhood and Youth, 1889–1939
Stephen Humphries

OVERVIEW

Derived primarily from three oral history collections housed in Bristol, Essex, and Manchester, *Hooligans or Rebels? An Oral History of Working-Class Childhood and Youth, 1889–1939* (1981) by Stephen Humphries examines the role of the British education system in the oppression of the working-class youth. Through oral accounts, period photographs, school records, and official reports, Humphries argues that classroom disturbances and the emergence of violent youth gangs during the late nineteenth and early twentieth centuries were means of resisting prejudice and cruelty inflicted upon working-class children by middle-class authorities at school, church, and other state-run institutions. Grounding his analysis of street gangs within a broader discussion of class and ethnicity, Humphries's book offers "an alternative, class-based interpretation of its behaviour, which will situate resistance within various class formations and relationships, showing the continuity and similarity between working-class youth and parent cultures."

Upon publication, *Hooligans or Rebels?* received mixed reviews. Some critics acknowledged the valuable material Humphries brings to light regarding hooliganism and the suffering endured by working-class children at the hands of well-meaning teachers and other authority figures. Others, however, criticized the author for only presenting oral histories that supported his preconceived theory. Despite its flaws, Humphries's text is considered an influential study of hooliganism and is the "most detailed historical exploration of the culture of the British youth gang," according to Andrew Davies in his 1998 article in the *Journal of Social History*.

HISTORICAL AND LITERARY CONTEXT

The stories collected in *Hooligans or Rebels?* reflect the working class's resistance to compulsory state schooling that Humphries asserts was a type of class control. The 1870 Education Act mandated compulsory education for children between the ages of five and twelve—a law that prevented children from working as laborers, thus decreasing family income. Unhappy with overly strict teachers and brutal canings, parents and students went on strike in 1889, 1911, and 1939 to demand better conditions for students and community control over education. On a day-to-day basis, parents and children often took it upon themselves to battle school injustices through confrontations with teachers or classroom disturbances. Mary Melhuish of Bristol recalls a mother who was fined twenty pounds for hitting an overly strict teacher. In recourse, the children "snowballed" the teacher: "We ripped her wig off, rubbed her head in ice balls and threw her into this big bin and we shut the door up."

The late Victorian era also witnessed a surge in the formation of youth gangs and in juvenile use of weapons in Britain's major cities. According to Humphries, gang membership provided "an inarticulate and immediate solution to the problems of disadvantage that confronted working-class youth in all spheres of life." Most working-class teenage boys joined neighborhood gangs and frequently entered into skirmishes with rival gangs, which became known as "scuttling." Employing weapons such as knives and belts, scuttlers would engage each other in fights to display toughness, fighting prowess, and the ability to withstand pain. Gangs would seek confrontations in order to acquire honor by defeating and shaming their rivals. Davies asserts that "considerable prestige was derived from displays of prowess in 'scuttling' affrays, although … the reputations of prominent gang members carried most weight among their peers and rivals."

Hooligans or Rebels? is chiefly based on three oral history collections: the Family Life and Work Experience before 1918 Collection at the University of Essex, the Manchester Studies Collection, and the Bristol People's Oral History Project at the Avon County Reference Library—a collection that Humphries helped organize. The Manchester and Bristol collections represent speakers who lived in these cities during the period covered by the book and were interviewed during the late 1970s. The author drew heavily on the Essex collection, which was founded by sociologist Paul Thompson and oral historian Thea Vigne. The stories gathered in the Essex collection prompted Thompson to write *The Edwardians* (1975) and *The Voice of the Past: Oral History* (1978). In his review of Humphries's work in the *American Historical Review,* James Bennett notes that *The Voice of the Past* "gives a methodological discussion of oral histories that Stephen Humphries assumes without further examination [in *Hooligans or*

❖ **Key Facts**

Time Period:
Late 19th to Mid-20th Centuries

Relevant Historical Events:
1870 Education Act; working-class resistance to compulsory education; formation of working-class gangs

Nationality:
British

Keywords:
working class; education; resistance

WORK AND FAMILY LIFE

One of the Crime Prevention Photos of Juvenile Aid Bureau showing delinquents gambling. May 18, 1937. In *Hooligans or Rebels?* Stephen Humphries examines childhood delinquency in Great Britain. © CORBIS

Rebels?]." Thea Thompson's *Edwardian Childhoods* was published in the same year as *Hooligans or Rebels?* and also draws on oral histories.

Hooligans or Rebels? is among the first historical accounts of youth gangs in late Victorian society. Since its publication, several other books about this topic have been published, including Geoffrey Pearson's *Hooligan: A History of Respectable Fears* (1983), in which the author is concerned with the label "hooligan" (a term adopted by the London press) and sets out to prove that the presence of gangs is not as novel and unprecedented as the media made it appear. In *Street Violence in the Nineteenth Century* (1990), Rob Sindall further investigates the role of the press in creating fear of juvenile delinquency and crime.

THEMES AND STYLE

Central to *Hooligans or Rebels?* is Humphries's assertion that classroom disobedience, "larking about," truancy, and gang formation occurred as a means of resisting class oppression. He suggests that street-gang culture "offered working-class youth the opportunity to conquer its feelings of hunger, failure and insignificance and to assert a proud and rebellious identity through which its members could feel masters of their own destiny." Humphries also analyzes the state education system and working-class resistance to it. He asserts that the oral histories of working-class school experience "bear little or no resemblance to the rhetoric of educational providers, who have invariably celebrated the development of the compulsory state schooling system in Britain as a flower of democracy planted by a benevolent middle class." Humphries's final chapter investigates the horrific treatment of those living in state-run orphanages and reformatories, which the author interprets as "the ultimate weapon deployed by a state under the dominance of middle class values against working class youth culture."

As he states in the first chapter, Humphries wrote *Hooligans or Rebels?* in order to rewrite "the history of working-class childhood and youth largely in the words of working-class people who themselves experienced it between 1889 and 1939." Since earlier generations did not leave a written record of their stories, Humphries claims that most of what has been written about working-class culture is mere interpretation by middle-class outsiders. In the same chapter Humphries declares that his own "theoretical perspective" is similar to that of the "revisionist school of Marxist sociologists and historians who … have challenged the method and metaphor upon which the orthodox literature on youth has been based." Thus, he presents a story of class conflict and insists that juvenile delinquency is not a result of ignorance or immorality but rather an expression of "resistance" against capitalist society.

Throughout the book Humphries's voice mingles with and sometimes shouts over the reminiscences of the interviewees. Whereas the interviews "exhibit a marvelous range of feeling, philosophy and expression," the author's commentary can be "hectoring and homiletic," causing the prose to "become drained of feeling as the author assumes prepared positions," states P. J. Waller in his review for the *English Historical Review*. In *Labour History*, Margaret Barbalet lauds Humphries's constant awareness "of the need to see things not from the official and bureaucratic point of view … but from the point of view of the child." For example, in a particularly poignant reminiscence, one interviewee explains why he purposefully failed the exam that would allow him to attend secondary school: "I was fully expected to pass, but I didn't because I knew that if I passed, I couldn't go. I wanted to pass, but you see because although there was help, it wouldn't have been enough for our family."

CRITICAL DISCUSSION

Initial critical reception to *Hooligans or Rebels?* was varied. Most reviewers acknowledged its important content but criticized Humphries for trying "too hard to impose his theoretical perspective … and at times the argument seems forced," writes Diana Gittins in her analysis for *Victorian Studies*. In his 1983 review in the *British Journal of Educational Studies*, Frank Coffield claims, "There is much of value in this book: we need a stronger historical and political dimension to thinking about Education," but he disagrees with Humphries's conclusions and one-sided argument. Coffield notes, "Nowhere is the reader invited to consider alternative interpretations of, or exception to, the one and only explanation favoured by the author."

As one of the first texts on late Victorian gang activity, *Hooligans or Rebels?* is considered an important work on the subject, as well as a detailed study of the British educational system. Scholars argue, however, that Humphries's use of oral history is flawed. According to Gittins, "Humphries's book is a good illustration of the inherent problems of using oral history in research of this kind. There is a real danger of simply selecting the relevant extracts from interviews to illustrate a theory, while ignoring other parts of interviews which do not support the theory."

Although Humphries's text remains influential in the study of hooliganism, scholars question some of his assertions. Davies suggests that Humphries considerably plays down acts of violence among gang members, stating that only "a small minority" of gangs possessed weapons that were "carried largely as symbols of defiance and resistance." Davies believes that gang violence was prevalent and that "scuttling affrays were characterised by the widespread use of weapons." Scholars applaud Humphries's discussion of the school strikes staged by working-class parents and students but question the lack of oral history from teachers and officials, which makes it "impossible to see the full structure at work, not to mention an oral history view of larger social and political institutions," states Bennett. As Gittins suggests, "This book could well have been more cogent had the author drawn more extensively on oral material, thus possibly revealing more about the very complex and subtle relations between social class, different sectors of social class, and the state education system."

BIBLIOGRAPHY

Sources

Barbalet, Margaret. Rev. of *Hooligans or Rebels? An Oral History of Working-Class Childhood and Youth, 1889–1939*, by Stephen Humphries. *Labour History* 46 (1984): 169–70. *JSTOR*. Web. 23 Jan. 2013.

Bennett, James. Rev. of *Hooligans or Rebels? An Oral History of Working-Class Childhood and Youth, 1889–1939*, by Stephen Humphries. *American Historical Review* 88.1 (1983): 116–17. *JSTOR*. Web. 23 Jan. 2013.

Coffield, Frank. Rev. of *Hooligans or Rebels? An Oral History of Working-Class Childhood and Youth, 1889–1939*, by Stephen Humphries. *British Journal of Educational Studies* 31.2 (1983): 166–67. *JSTOR*. Web. 23 Jan. 2013.

Davies, Andrew. "Youth Gangs, Masculinity and Violence in Late Victorian Manchester and Salford." *Journal of Social History* 32.2 (1998): 349–69. Print.

Gittins, Diana. "Let the People Speak: Oral History in Britain." Rev. of *Hooligans or Rebels? An Oral History of Working-Class Childhood and Youth, 1889–1939*, by Stephen Humphries. *Victorian Studies* 26.4 (1983): 431–41. *JSTOR*. Web. 23 Jan. 2013.

TESTIMONY FILMS

A former lecturer in sociology at the University of Essex, Stephen Humphries later became a writer and broadcaster with a special focus in oral tradition and social history. Two years after publishing *Hooligans or Rebels?* Humphries wrote *The Handbook of Oral History: Recording Life Stories* (1983). It is a detailed guide for those wishing to execute an oral history project and includes sections on writing questionnaires, using recording equipment, interviewing subjects, and working with various groups. From 1983 to 1986 Humphries coauthored four texts chronicling London's history from 1815 to 1985, which accompanied the twenty-four-part television series titled *The Making of Modern London*.

In 1992 Humphries founded Bristol-based Testimony Films—one of Britain's most successful independent producers of life story and social history documentaries. According to the organization's website, Humphries was once called the "king of oral history" by *Broadcast Magazine* and served as the honorary vice president of the British Oral History Society. Testimony Films has produced more than one hundred documentaries, many of which have received critical acclaim and have been accompanied by books coauthored by Humphries.

Humphries, Stephen. *Hooligans or Rebels? An Oral History of Working-Class Childhood and Youth, 1889–1939.* Oxford, UK: Blackwell, 1981. Print.

Purkis, Sallie. Rev. of *Hooligans or Rebels? An Oral History of Working-Class Childhood and Youth, 1889–1939,* by Stephen Humphries. *Oral History* 11.1 (1983): 72–73. *JSTOR.* Web. 23 Jan. 2013.

Waller, P. J. Rev. of *Hooligans or Rebels? An Oral History of Working-Class Childhood and Youth, 1889–1939,* by Stephen Humphries. *English Historical Review* 99.391 (1984): 464–65. *JSTOR.* Web. 23 Jan. 2013.

Further Reading

Gordon, Pamela, and Stephen Humphries. *A Labour of Love: The Experience of Parenthood in Britain, 1900–1950.* London: Sidgwick & Jackson, 1993. Print.

Roberts, Elizabeth. *A Woman's Place: An Oral History of Working-Class Women, 1890–1940.* Oxford, UK: Blackwell, 1984. Print.

———. *Women and Families: An Oral History, 1940–1970.* Oxford, UK: Blackwell 1995. Print.

Seabrook, Jeremy. *Working-Class Childhood: An Oral History.* London: Orion, 1982. Print.

Thompson, Paul. *The Edwardians: The Remaking of British Society.* London: Weidenfeld and Nicolson, 1975. Print.

———. *The Voice of the Past: Oral History.* Oxford, UK: Oxford University Press, 1978. Print.

Thompson, Paul, and Gloria Wood. *The Nineties: Personal Recollections of the Twentieth Century.* London: BBC, 1993. Print.

Thompson, Thea. *Edwardian Childhoods.* London: Routledge, 1981. Print.

Maggie Magno

Irish Days
Oral Histories of the Twentieth Century
Margaret Hickey

Key Facts

Time Period:
20th Century

Relevant Historical Events:
Easter Uprising; Irish War of Independence; Irish civil war

Nationality:
Irish

Keywords:
colonialism; independence; civil war

OVERVIEW

First published in 2001, Margaret Hickey's *Irish Days: Oral Histories of the Twentieth Century* is a compilation of the personal recollections of elderly Irish men and women. The book features twelve principal interviewees (ten men and two women) born between 1906 and 1926, plus five additional people (four men and one woman) who contribute much briefer narratives. The stories touch upon a wide variety of topics, including the respondents' childhood experiences and schooling, their careers, Irish nationalism and its attendant conflicts, Irish sports, and other aspects of Irish culture, including folklore and poetry. Considered as a group, the stories assembled in *Irish Days* provide an intimate glimpse at Irish life during an eventful period of that country's history and serve as an enduring literary portrait of a largely vanished Irish generation.

Published when the youngest of its primary contributors was seventy-five years old, *Irish Days* was well received for its preservation and dissemination of firsthand explications of Ireland's cultural past. The country's economic shift from agriculture to information and technology in the 1980s wrought profound changes in Irish life, making the predominantly rural memories enshrined in Hickey's book especially noteworthy from a historical standpoint. A relatively unscholarly and celebrated example of Irish oral history, *Irish Days* is notable within its genre for the insight it provides into the quotidian aspects of Irish life during the twentieth century rather than focusing specifically on momentous events such as wars or violent uprisings (though these are discussed as well). The book remains significant as a wide-ranging testament to the intricacies of twentieth-century Irish life as experienced by a diffuse group of witnesses.

HISTORICAL AND LITERARY CONTEXT

During the sixteenth century, the English monarchy initiated a sixty-year campaign of imperial conquest in Ireland that culminated in 1603 with the definitive establishment of centralized English control over the entirety of Ireland. This dominion remained in place for centuries, abetted by anti-Catholic legislation that served to disenfranchise the Irish majority in favor of a small Protestant minority, whose disproportionate social and political power was referred to as the Protestant Ascendancy. This subjugation led to considerable antipathy between the Irish and the English (as well as between Catholics and Protestants), a situation not improved by the deaths of approximately a million Irish people from starvation and disease during the Great Famine of the mid-nineteenth century.

During the twentieth century the island's long history of political agitation for Irish independence culminated in the Easter Uprising of 1916, an armed insurrection that lasted a week before being suppressed by British forces. This was followed by the Irish War of Independence (1919–1921), which terminated British dominion over twenty-six of Ireland's thirty-two counties and established the Irish Free State in 1922. (The six counties of Northern Ireland voluntarily remained a part of the United Kingdom, to the ongoing chagrin of many Irish nationalists. This and other compromises in the postwar treaty negotiations precipitated a year long Irish civil war.)

Irish Days is part of the ongoing tradition of Irish oral history, as well as a broader tradition of literary and historical work devoted to showcasing aspects of Irish culture. Notable predecessors of Hickey's book within oral history include Uinseann MacEoin's *Survivors* (1980) and the work of Kevin C. Kearns, whose Dublin-specific volumes, including *Dublin Pub Life and Lore* (1996) and *Dublin Voices* (1998), represent a more specialized manifestation of the type of work Hickey performed with *Irish Days*. Likewise, Hickey's focus on the Irish storytelling tradition is prefigured by scholarly volumes such as Clodagh Brennan Harvey's *Contemporary Irish Traditional Narrative: The English Language Tradition* (1992), as well as by modern narrative collections such as *Ireland's Master Storyteller: The Collected Stories of Éamon Kelly* (1998)—Kelly also being among the interviewees of *Irish Days*.

Irish Days helped to shape modern perceptions of Irish life during the first half of the twentieth century. Mary Harney, the deputy head of Ireland's government at the time, praised the book for "pay[ing] homage to our older people and to the rich oral culture that is central to Ireland's heritage." Hickey herself has continued to contribute to Irish cultural and literary life, and further historical volumes on twentieth-century Ireland, such as Benjamin Grob-Fitzgibbon's *The Irish Experience during the Second World War: An*

Rock of Cashel, Cashel Town, County Tipperary, Munster, in the Republic of Ireland. © ROBERT HARDING WORLD IMAGERY/ALAMY

Oral History (2004), continued to appear in the ensuing years. The book remains of interest for contemporary readers for the insight it provides into Ireland's progressively distant past.

THEMES AND STYLE

A central thematic element of *Irish Days* is an emphasis on the routine day-to-day travails of relatively poor Irish families. Although the interviewees vary in their socioeconomic backgrounds, one major narrative strain is a focus on the rural, hardworking lifestyle that characterized the majority of the Irish population at the time. Vocational difficulties are a recurring motif, as in this recollection by Jim Hickey: "At that time I'd be twelve or thirteen—time for leaving school and looking for something, but there was nothing. Poverty-stricken times." Similarly, Mona Henry notes that her childhood years "were poor times" and comments on her mother's resourcefulness in making use of what little she had: "But she made do. It's amazing if you had to." Ireland's past and present political struggles inevitably play a part in the narratives. Bridget Dirrane recalls that "the Black and Tans [British security forces brought into Ireland in the 1920s who were known as Black and Tans because of their uniforms] were the scourge of Ireland at this time [the revolutionary period], creating terror every place they went"—but such concerns are only a part of the book's mosaic portrait of Irish life.

Irish Days was largely compiled for commemorative purposes, in order to provide a document of what Hickey calls "the warp and weft of the fabric of Irish life in the early decades of the twentieth century," as well as to serve as a celebration of the lives of the people involved, hence Hickey's assertion that "I hope that these oral histories will demonstrate by their truthfulness, liveliness, humor, wisdom and humanity that we should be seeking out the company of old people, not out of pity but out of self-interest. We have much to learn from them." The interviews vary in format, with most taking the form of straightforward narratives while others are dialogues between two respondents who are personally acquainted.

Central to the book's overall use of language is Hickey's conviction that "the Irish genius has its finest flowering in the word, both spoken and written." To that end, a significant portion of the text consists of the recitation of poetry (some of it written by the respondents themselves); transcriptions of song lyrics from impromptu musical performances; and—in the case of Henry—a reading of an essay she wrote about her life. Likewise, Hickey's assertion that "I imposed a rule on myself from the outset never to reinterpret or otherwise 'tidy up' the storytellers' words" demonstrates her intent to faithfully render the rhythms of her respondents' sentences. The unhurried, often circuitous anecdotal narration in many of the interviews is presented as being exemplary of the Irish storytelling tradition, hence Hickey's assertion that "before the multi-distractions of television, radio, video, computer games and more, a good story was worth eking out, with all its embellishments, every aspect of it to be explored, and little grace notes added now and again."

CRITICAL DISCUSSION

Irish Days was well received upon publication in 2001, with reviewers praising the book as a rich tribute to Ireland's past. Lucille Redmond, writing in *Books Ireland*, comments on the significant gender imbalance among interviewees, calling the book "a very male oral history" but also lauding it for having "the fascination of eavesdropping on a series of lifetimes." Likewise, a review in the Irish republican newspaper *An Phoblacht* asserts that "Hickey has done a good job in selecting the stories concerned as they are quite representative of an Ireland that was predominantly agricultural and rural, a situation now rapidly changing."

Hickey's book joined the growing body of literature devoted to commemorating Ireland's past, contributing significantly to the historical legacy of twentieth-century Ireland within the modern consciousness. The book's nonacademic approach likely gives it a greater degree of accessibility to the general reader. Sean O'Grady, writing in the *Independent*, names *Irish Days* as something he purchased for his mother on the advice of a bookstore staff member tasked with providing personal shopping recommendations, a fact indicative of the book's broad popular audience. This general-audience purview may partially account for the relatively negligible amount of scholarly interest the book has attracted.

A rare example of a scholarly text engaging with the book is Claire Lynch's 2009 study *Irish Autobiography: Stories of Self in the Narrative of a Nation*, which names *Irish Days* and Glen O'Brien's *Coming Out: Irish Gay Experiences* (2003) as "excellent examples of texts which combine the autobiographies of many to produce a text which speaks for an underrepresented group."

Lynch goes on to assert that "these texts represent the next important development in Irish autobiography; anthologies of life-writing which are a true hybrid of autobiography and biography, not simply about a group but also by it." Hickey's text is not discussed beyond these comments, however, and more sustained critical commentary on the book is virtually nonexistent in current scholarship.

BIBLIOGRAPHY

Sources

Hickey, Margaret. *Irish Days: Oral Histories of the Twentieth Century.* 2001. London: Kyle Cathie, 2004. Print.

Lynch, Claire. *Irish Autobiography: Stories of Self in the Narrative of a Nation.* New York: Peter Lang, 2009. Print.

O'Grady, Sean. "A Novel Way to Shop." *Independent* 16 Nov. 2005: 44. *ProQuest Newsstand*. Web. 27 Jan. 2013.

"The Rare Aul' Times." Rev. of *Dublin through Space and Time*, ed. Joseph Brady and Anngret Simms, and *Irish Days*, by Margaret Hickey. *An Phoblacht* 7 Feb. 2002. Web. 27 Jan. 2013.

Redmond, Lucille. "Stories Tally." Rev. of *Béaloideas* Vol. 68, ed. Séamas Ó Catháin; *Irish Days*, by Margaret Hickey; *Seaweed Memories*, by Heinrich Becker; and *Northern Lights*, ed. Séamas Ó Catháin. *Books Ireland* 248 (2002): 97–98. *JSTOR*. Web. 27 Jan. 2013.

Further Reading

Coogan, Tim Pat. *Ireland in the Twentieth Century.* London: Hutchinson, 2003. Print.

Ferriter, Diarmaid. *The Transformation of Ireland.* Woodstock, N.Y.: Overlook, 2005. Print.

Grob-Fitzgibbon, Benjamin. *The Irish Experience during the Second World War: An Oral History.* Dublin: Irish Academic, 2004. Print.

Harvey, Clodagh Brennan. *Contemporary Irish Traditional Narrative: The English Language Tradition.* Berkeley: University of California Press, 1992. Print.

DUBLIN PUB LIFE AND LORE: AN ORAL HISTORY

One of the most prolific oral historians of Irish life is Kevin C. Kearns, whose numerous compilations of oral testimony, all focused specifically on Dublin, represent one of the more sustained treatments of an individual city through oral history. *Dublin Pub Life and Lore*, first published in 1996, is representative of his general approach, demonstrating the extent to which public drinking houses have served as an epicenter of social life in Dublin (and, by extension, Ireland in general). The book is in many ways a counterpart to *Irish Days*, though its approach is both more narrowly focused and more conscientiously historical.

About a third of the book consists of a lengthy explication of the history and customs of Dublin pub life, touching on the different types of pubs, the ramifications of social class within pub life, the social roles played by publicans and staff members, and various other subjects. The rest of the book consists of edited transcriptions of oral testimony—usually fairly brief in comparison to the interviews in *Irish Days*—from publicans, bartenders, and customers. The book is an exhaustive, informative portrait of one of Dublin's more influential social institutions.

Kearns, Kevin C. *Dublin Pub Life and Lore: An Oral History.* Dublin: Gill & Macmillan, 1996. Print.

———. *Dublin Voices: An Oral Folk History.* Dublin: Gill & Macmillan, 1998. Print.

Kelly, Éamon. *Ireland's Master Storyteller: The Collected Stories of Éamon Kelly.* Dublin: Marino, 1998. Print.

MacEoin, Uinseann. *Survivors: The Story of Ireland's Struggle as Told through Some of Her Outstanding Living People.* Dublin: Argenta, 1980. Print.

James Overholtzer

LEFT HANDED, SON OF OLD MAN HAT
A Navajo Autobiography
Left Handed, Walter Dyk

❖ **Key Facts**

Time Period:
Mid- to Late 19th Century

Relevant Historical Events:
Forced relocation of Navajos to reservations; American westward expansion

Nationality:
American

Keywords:
colonialism; Native Americans; relocation

OVERVIEW

Published in various editions in 1938, 1967, 1980, and 1995, Walter Dyk's *Left Handed, Son of Old Man Hat: A Navajo Autobiography* is the oral history of a Navajo man beginning with his birth in the late 1860s and ending with his marriage twenty years later. Speaking through interpreter Philip Davis, Left Handed recounts stories of his life, family, and tribe in lively detail, which Dyk records with no added commentary. By presenting Left Handed's compelling coming-of-age story in his own words, the text broke new ground with its intimate picture of Navajo culture and traditions viewed not from the outside by conquerors or anthropologists but through the eyes of an integrated member of Native American society.

When the text was first published in 1938 under the title *Son of Old Man Hat: A Navaho Autobiography,* with Left Handed credited as author, historians and others interested in indigenous culture enthusiastically welcomed it as a fresh and realistic look at Native American life. Oliver LaFarge of the *Saturday Review* began his 1938 review of the autobiography by writing, "Here is something new and real." *Left Handed* soon became a classic ethnography. However, as scholarly investigation of the problematic nature of translated oral history became more thorough, later critics questioned the authenticity of Left Handed's voice and the validity of Dyk's research methods.

HISTORICAL AND LITERARY CONTEXT

The Navajo people, who call themselves Diné, are descended from the Athabascan group of Native Americans believed to have migrated from Asia through Alaska and Canada into the present-day southwestern United States. Established in the area by the sixteenth century, the Navajo waged territorial battles with other tribes, suffered enslavement and torture under the invading Spanish, and skirmished with newly established Mexican authorities before coming under U.S. control after the end of the Mexican War in 1848. As the largest U.S. Indian tribe both in population and in territory, the Navajos evolved a highly developed matrilineal culture based on close family ties, ceremonial religion, and traditional trades of sheepherding, silver working, weaving, and farming.

American colonizers continued the harsh policies of Spanish and Mexican rulers toward the indigenous populations. Between the late 1800s and the early 1900s, many Navajos were forced to relocate to an expanding system of reservations. In 1930 the U.S. government escalated its attack on Native American culture by forcibly removing Navajo children from their families and placing them in boarding schools, which were often run by Christian missionaries. There, the children were separated not only from their families and communities but also from their traditions, their language, and even their names. From 1932 to 1936 the government launched an attack on the Navajo economic system with the Stock Reduction Act, which mandated the slaughter of hundreds of thousands of tribal sheep, goats, and horses. The act highlighted the cultural ignorance of the U.S. government toward the Navajo nation: authorities met with groups of tribal men to explain the law, oblivious that the Navajo women owned and controlled livestock.

Although many indigenous peoples had a strong oral tradition, written literature did not become a significant part of Native American culture until the arrival of European colonists. Even after Native Americans, often educated by missionaries, began to write religious texts in English, personal narratives were uncommon. One of the first, the life story of a Massachusetts Pequot titled *A Son of the Forest: The Experiences of William Apes, A Native of the Forest, Written by Himself,* appeared in 1829. In 1920 Paul Radin helped introduce a new kind of Indian autobiography by transcribing the oral history of a Winnebago man in *Crashing Thunder.* Soon great public interest developed in the stories of Native Americans as told—at least theoretically—in their own words. Works such as *Black Elk Speaks* (1932) by John G. Neihardt and *The Autobiography of a Papago Woman* (1936) by Ruth Underhill became international best sellers.

Dyk's work in transcribing and editing Left Handed's story fit within the popular genre of American Indian life stories. However, the book's intimate focus on the universality of Left Handed's experience and its detailed and respectful insights into day-to-day Navajo family life made it uniquely interesting to scholars. In an era when many whites

Navajo Indians, including a medicine man at center, in 1938, the year *Son of Old Man Hat: A Navajo Autobiography* was published. © AP IMAGES

questioned the humanity of indigenous people, *Left Handed* was not only educational but also a progressive statement.

THEMES AND STYLE

A major focus of Dyk's oral history is self-development and the process of coming of age. Chapter headings such as "Jealousies and Quarrels," "How They Find You've Been with a Woman and What to Do about It," and "He Loses a Horse and a Girl but Is Consoled" reinforce the connection of the narrative to other coming-of-age stories and to the reader's own experience. Left Handed's youthful curiosity about sex is recognizable to any modern reader: "When I went out herding and saw a billy goat or a ram get on a goat or a sheep I used to think, 'A man must do just the same thing to a woman.'" Vivid details of Navajo cultural life form another theme, captured by such subtle details as, "My father used to go out and sing when he walked about in the corral … so that if it got too cold the sheep wouldn't freeze…. This song is called the Owl Song, because the owl can stand anything."

In his introduction Dyk articulates one of the important motives behind the publication of Left Handed's story: the presentation of the Navajo as a complete human being. Dyk writes, "May this narrative of his life help allay once and for all that strange and monstrous apparition, the 'Primitive Mind.'" Although he was successful in conveying Left Handed's thoughtful nature and sharp wit, many questions remain about the methodology of the oral history. Recording the recollections of a Navajo speaking his native language posed special problems. Dyk's narrative does not make clear distinctions between the voice of Left Handed and the possibly intrusive voice of the translator. Equally confusing is the author accreditation in the various editions: the 1938 edition lists Left Handed as author, adding "recorded by Walter Dyk," while the 1967 edition lists Dyk as author and Left Handed as subject. A second volume of the Navajo's recollections, published by Dyk's wife in 1980 after his death, credits Walter and Ruth Dyk as authors.

The narrative style of *Left Handed* is engaging and lyrical, evincing both simplicity and shrewdness. The first line demonstrates Left Handed's bond with the natural world: "I was born when the cottonwood leaves were about the size of my thumbnail." Homely details confer a sense of reality that brings descriptions to life: "As soon as I unpacked and turned (the horse) loose he dropped to the ground and rolled around, bathing himself in the sand…. I wasn't hungry, so I just sat there against my load, looking at the horse eating grass."

LIFE LIVED LIKE A STORY

For many non–Native American historians and anthropologists, understanding the rhythm and idiom of American Indian storytelling can be challenging. Cultural differences of expression have sometimes caused well-meaning recorders to edit out significant parts of American Indian narratives as simple repetition or digression—as in the case of some of Left Handed's stories. In 1990 anthropologist Julie Cruikshank attempted to bridge this gap with her book *Life Lived Like a Story: Life Stories of Three Yukon Native Elders.*

Written in collaboration with Angela Sidney, Kitty Smith, and Annie Ned—three Native Canadian women of Athabascan and Tlingit heritage—*Life Lived Like a Story* is an attempt to record the women's life stories. Cruikshank was at first disconcerted to find her subjects repeatedly diverging into storytelling and myth. She soon realized, however, that in Native American culture, these stories represented a legitimate and fundamental part of personal autobiography. Consequently, Cruikshank worked to weave Sidney's, Smith's, and Ned's personal recollections with the folktales, oral history, and myths they told her in order to create a more complete and culturally sensitive picture of the women's lives as part of their tribal history and tradition.

CRITICAL DISCUSSION

An innovative entry in the genre of American Indian autobiography, *Left Handed* received a warm reception from critics upon its release in 1938. Leland Wyman praised the book's scope in a 1939 review for *American Anthropologist:* "This story offers the most considerable body of ... concrete data yet published." W. C. Bennett, reviewing the book for *American Sociological Review* in 1939, noted the "universality of the narrative which is one of its fascinations. This is the story of a human being with his changing interests, fears, desires, reactions." Bennett also remarked on the jarring incongruities of language: "Dr. Dyk's translations slap at the reader." Reviewing the second volume of Left Handed's story, Richard Drinnon in a 1982 article for *Winterthur Portfolio* praised the writing style, which he characterized as "slow, dreamy narrative [that] piled detail upon detail." However, Drinnon questioned the authenticity of Left Handed's voice as storyteller, asserting that Davis, the uncredited interpreter, may have been responsible for much of the tone and wording of the narrative.

Dyk and Left Handed played a large part in introducing the genre of narrated American Indian autobiography in the 1930s. In a 1998 article in the *Journal of American Ethnic History,* Pauline Strong wrote, "Whether self-authored or narrated to intermediaries ... Native American autobiographies have long been valued by scholars, teachers, and students for their seemingly immediate evocation of lived experience." The frequent republication of Left Handed's autobiography attests to the narrative's continuing value as a source of authoritative information on Navajo culture and family life and as an example of the problems of narrated autobiography.

Much of the modern study of *Left Handed* revolves around exploring these contradictions. In a 1999 article in *Mosaic,* Susan B. Brill de Ramirez asserted that Dyk's recording method did not take into account the ways that the American Indian storytelling tradition could subvert scientific objectivity. Brill de Ramirez views the narrative as the "Navajo storyteller's commentary on the colonization of Navajo (and other Native) people's lives, cultures, traditions, and stories." Writing for the *International Review of Social Research* in 2012, Sam Pack examined the second volume of Left Handed's story in light of the ways European literary bias can unintentionally corrupt the narrative. For example, Pack observed, "Although repetition disturbs the Western ear, for many indigenous peoples, repetition serves as a rhetorical feature in oral narrative."

BIBLIOGRAPHY

Sources

Bennett, W. C. Rev. of *Son of Old Man Hat: A Navaho Autobiography,* by Left Handed and Walter Dyk. *American Sociological Review* 4.3 (1939): 446. *JSTOR.* Web. 21 Jan. 2013.

Brill de Ramirez, Susan B. "The Resistance of American Indian Autobiographies to Ethnographic Colonization." *Mosaic* 32.2 (1999): 59–73. *ProQuest.* Web. 21 Jan. 2013.

Cruikshank, Julie. *Life Lived Like a Story: Life Stories of Three Yukon Native Elders.* Lincoln: University of Nebraska Press, 1990. Print.

Drinnon, Richard. Rev. of *Left Handed, Son of Old Man Hat: A Navajo Autobiography,* by Walter Dyk and Ruth Dyk. *Winterthur Portfolio* 171.2–3 (1982): 164–66. *JSTOR.* Web. 21 Jan. 2013.

LaFarge, Oliver. Rev. of *Son of Old Man Hat: A Navaho Autobiography,* by Left Handed and Walter Dyk. *Saturday Review* 24 Dec. 1938: 6. *UNZ.* Web. 21 Jan. 2013.

Left Handed, and Walter Dyk. *Left Handed, Son of Old Man Hat: A Navajo Autobiography.* Lincoln: University of Nebraska Press, 1995. Print.

Pack, Sam. "Towards a Reflexive Ethnography: (Re-)inserting the Producer and Process into the Research Equation." *International Review of Social Research* 2.3 (2012): 43–58. *IRSR.* Web. 22 Jan. 2013.

Strong, Pauline Turner. "*Left Handed, Son of Old Man Hat: A Navajo Autobiography.*" *Journal of American Ethnic History* 17.3 (1998): 99–104. *General Reference Center GOLD.* Web. 19 Jan. 2013.

Wyman, Leland C. Rev. of *Son of Old Man Hat A Navaho Autobiography,* by Left Handed and Walter Dyk. *American Anthropologist* 41.2 (1939): 309–10. *JSTOR.* Web. 21 Jan. 2013.

Further Reading

Eggan, Fred, and Michael Silverstein. "Walter Dyk: 1899–1972." *American Anthropologist* 76 (1974): 86–87. Print.

Krupat, Arnold, ed. *Native American Autobiography: An Anthology.* Madison: University of Wisconsin Press, 1994. Print.

Rios, Theodore, and Kathleen Mullen Sands. *Telling a Good One: The Process of a Native American Collaborative Biography.* Lincoln: University of Nebraska Press, 2000. Print.

Sarris, Greg. *Keeping Slug Woman Alive: A Holistic Approach to American Indian Texts.* Berkeley: University of California Press, 1993. Print.

Sellers, Stephanie A. *Native American Autobiography Redefined.* New York: Peter Lang, 2006. Print.

Wong, Hertha D. "Preliterate Native American Autobiography: Forms of Personal Narrative." *MELUS* 14.1 (1987): 17–32. *JSTOR.* Web. 22 Jan. 2013.

Tina Gianoulis

LET ME SPEAK!
Testimony of Domitila, a Woman of the Bolivian Mines
Moema Viezzer, Domitila Barrios de Chungara

✧ Key Facts

Time Period:
Mid-20th Century

Relevant Historical Events:
Repression of tin miners' rights; Bolivian political upheaval

Nationality:
Bolivian

Keywords:
labor rights; unionism; women's writing

OVERVIEW

Collected by journalist Moema Viezzer, *Let Me Speak!: Testimony of Domitila, a Woman of the Bolivian Mines* (1977, 1978) is a series of interviews, speeches, and letters that recount Domitila Barrios de Chungara's evolution from a miner's wife to a powerful political organizer during the 1950s, 1960s, and 1970s. Rooted in personal anecdotes, Barrios de Chungara's narrative sheds light on Bolivian miners' harsh and unfair working conditions and the myriad ways in which these circumstances deleteriously affected miners' wives, children, and larger communities. Although Barrios de Chungara relies heavily on personal experience, her narrative moves beyond autobiography: she repeatedly reminds readers that she is speaking out for her community, as well as working-class people in general.

While *Let Me Speak!* makes a forceful argument against the exploitation of workers by both the Bolivian government and large corporations, reviewers immediately praised the oral history for capturing an unstudied area of Bolivian class struggles: the nuanced and complicated role of women activists. Although Barrios de Chungara did not consider herself to be a feminist per se, *Let Me Speak!* encouraged women to become involved with political and social movements. The oral history was inspired by Barrios de Chungara's testimony at the 1975 International Women's Year Tribunal, sponsored by the United Nations in Mexico City. Published first in Spanish in 1977 as *Si me permiten hablar*, the English translation appeared a year later. *Let Me Speak!* remains a foundational text in the emerging genre of the testimonial.

HISTORICAL AND LITERARY CONTEXT

Throughout the period of Barrios de Chungara's narrative, tin miners' working conditions in Bolivia were, by all accounts, dangerous and loathsome. Barrios de Chungara lived in a company-owned shack in Siglo XX, a town run by the mining company. Although the heightened demand for tin during World War II had alerted the international community to the abhorrent conditions in the mines, workers' wages and rights did not improve much. This was not, however, for lack of effort, as Bolivia was home to strong, fiercely independent unions. Throughout the 1950s and 1960s the Bolivian government underwent extreme political changes, marked by authoritarianism, quick successions of leaders (often elbowed out of power by military or political pressure), and 1967's guerrilla uprising.

In this heated political environment, Barrios de Chungara became increasingly involved in Siglo XX's Housewives Committee, a union of tin miners' spouses that supported comprehensive workers' rights. By the late 1960s she held a leadership position within the organization. This caused significant personal stresses: her husband lost his job due to her political activities, she was brutalized by both her husband and police for her outspokenness and organizing, and she spent considerable time away from her family—in jail and then temporary exile. Indeed, much of *Let Me Speak!* details how a woman's choice to work for a union intimately affects family dynamics, especially in a Bolivian society rooted in patriarchal gender roles.

Let Me Speak! is considered a *testimonio*, an oral history told in a straightforward, candid tone. Perhaps the most famous text in this genre, which is also associated with Latin America, is *I, Rigoberta Menchú: An Indian Woman in Guatemala* (1984), edited by Elisabeth Burgos-Debray. *Testimonios*, although narrated by one speaker, are transcriptions of oral history intended to speak for the collective—often a historically exploited people. Upon its publication, Barrios de Chungara's narrative joined a bevy of other *testimonios* also concerned with women's rights, political experiences, and daily lives in Latin America, such as *Child of the Dark: The Diary of Carolina Maria de Jesus* (1962).

Let Me Speak! has emerged as one of the most recognized and discussed *testimonios* about working-class women's experience in Latin America and has been translated widely. After the publication of *Let Me Speak!* Barrios de Chungara continued to fight against oppression in Bolivia, becoming nationally known for leading a successful hunger strike against General Hugo Bánzer's dictatorship in 1979. Inspired by her attendance at the second International Women's Conference in 1980, Barrios de Chungara published *Here Too, Domitila* (*Aquí también, Domitila!,* 1985) with David Acebey, in which she discusses her conversations about equality and women's rights with conference attendees.

THEMES AND STYLE

The major topics addressed in *Let Me Speak!* include the mistreatment of miners and mining communities,

Worker at a mine in Potosí, Bolivia. © PHOTO MERE LATIN/ALAMY

arguments for women's involvement in political organizing, and an exploration of working-class women's daily lives in Bolivia. Barrios de Chungara argues that women's domestic chores—cooking, cleaning, washing clothes—is actual work, just like a man's job in the mines. She observes that "in spite of everything [women] do, there's still the idea that … women don't contribute economically to the home." *Let Me Speak!* actively challenges this ingrained paradigm and claims that women should be able to fully "participate in the struggle of the working class." Even though the home is a private space, it is still, she points out, "part of the whole system of exploitation." Throughout the text, Barrios de Chungara's feminist leanings are evident.

Barrios de Chungara's primary objective for producing her oral history was to educate and inspire Bolivian mining communities and working people in general. On the opening page she proclaims, "I want [this book] to reach the poorest people, the people who don't have any money, but who need some orientation." Barrios de Chungara also wanted her story to serve as an educational tool, helping future organizers avoid "the mistakes we've committed in the past." She writes that her desire is not to share her own unique life history but to speak for a movement larger than herself: "I don't want anyone at any moment to interpret the story I'm about to tell as something that is only personal."

Barrios de Chungara relies on a straightforward, linear narrative to share her ideas about Bolivian politics and workers' and women's rights. On the whole, the tone is conversational, as the natural rhythms of everyday speech are preserved. Viezzer, Barrios de Chungara's collaborator, notes in the introduction that the text is an amalgamation of "discussions, conversations, and dialogues" with all kinds of people—from scholars to miners to televisions crews. As a result, writes Viezzer, "there are a variety of [rhetorical] styles in this book." The two collaborators believed it was important to maintain Barrios de Chungara's distinctive language, which was rich with what Viezzer terms "her expressions, her localisms, and her grammatical constructions, marked, at times, by the Quechua language." Two chapters, "Her People" and "Her Life," make up the bulk of the text. In "Her People," Barrios de Chungara provides information about mine life, including details about the daily routines of miners' wives and workers' organizations. "Her Life," the largest section of the narrative, focuses on Barrios de Chungara's life history, with special attention paid to her political activities.

CRITICAL DISCUSSION

Let Me Speak! received a warm critical reception upon its publication. Writing for *Latin American Perspectives,* Norma Chinchilla noted that Barrios de Chungara's narrative is a "rich and fascinating contribution to books, tapes, and films about the lives of working-class women organizers." In particular, Chinchilla praised Barrios de Chungara's discussion of the complex challenges facing politically active Bolivian women. In a review for the *Hispanic American Historical Review,* Asunción Lavrin echoed Chinchilla's sentiments, writing that "[*Let Me Speak!*] brings special understanding to the problems of mine women at home and in society at large." Although many scholars lauded the work for its simple narrative

"HOW A MINER'S WIFE SPENDS HER DAY"

One of the most valuable components of *Let Me Speak!* is Domitila Barrios de Chungara's exploration of the daily lives of miners' wives in a section titled "How a Miner's Wife Spends Her Day." Scholars have praised the book for shedding light on this aspect of Bolivian society. Barrios de Chungara notes that miners' shifts are always changing and that housewives must adapt their schedules so they can prepare meals for their *compañeros*, or husbands. Because a mine worker's wages do not cover a mining family's expenses, Barrios de Chungara supplemented her family's income by preparing Bolivian pies called *salteñas*, which she sold every morning on the streets. The afternoons were spent washing clothes. "There are no laundries," Barrios de Chungara writes. "We use troughs and have to go get the water from the pump." Food was purchased from the company store, where the prices were high and the lines long. When Barrios de Chungara was especially busy, her children helped her sell *salteñas* and wait in line at the store, which could be dangerous during meat shortages because kids were occasionally killed in the "terrible crush" of bodies. Such work, Barrios de Chungara argues, is "unpaid work that [wives and children] are doing for the boss."

style, William Roseberry observed in *American Anthropologist* that such a linear approach prevents adequate "reflective analysis."

Let Me Speak! has become a vital text for scholars studying Latin American class struggles, particularly the roles of women in them. In an article for *Women's Studies Quarterly*, Amy Lind writes that Barrios de Chungara's "testimony has been used in women's studies classrooms throughout the United States." Although *Let Me Speak!* continues to be researched and discussed, the lives of Bolivian miners and their families have scarcely improved since its publication. Moreover, according to Lind, Barrios de Chungara's fight for social justice has largely been "forgotten by the Western press and feminists." Despite Barrios de Chungara's desire for *Let Me Speak!* to serve as a manual for her people, there has been little investigation in English-speaking literature as to whether the text has actually been used for such a purpose.

Barrios de Chungara's narrative has been included in recent scholarly discussions about Latin American *testimonios*, particularly those authored by people who have experienced the effects of colonialism firsthand. Georg M. Gugelberger and Michael Kearney write in *Latin American Perspectives* that testimonials such Barrios de Chungara's pivot leverage away from traditional centers of colonial power, allowing "subaltern peoples at the periphery or the margin of the colonial situation" to speak out from their distinctive—often overlooked—point of view. Writing for the *NWSA Journal*, Shari Stone-Mediatore elaborates on Gugelberger and Kearney's thesis, contending that *Let Me Speak!* offers oppressed people the opportunity to "recast history itself."

BIBLIOGRAPHY

Sources

Barrios de Chungara, Domitila, and Moema Viezzer. *Let Me Speak! Testimony of Domitila, a Woman of the Bolivian Mines.* Trans. Victoria Ortiz. New York: Monthly Review, 1978. Print.

Chinchilla, Norma. "Working-Class Feminism: Domitila and the Housewives Committee." *Latin American Perspectives* 6.3 (1979): 87–92. JSTOR. Web. 30 Dec. 2012.

Gugelberger, Georg M., and Michael Kearney. "Voices for the Voiceless: Testimonial Literature in Latin America." *Latin American Perspectives* 18.3 (1991): 3–14. JSTOR. Web. 1 Jan. 2013.

Lavrin, Asunción. Rev. of *Let Me Speak! Testimony of Domitila, a Woman of the Bolivian Mines*, by Domitila Barrios de Chungara and Moema Viezzer. *Hispanic American Historical Review* Feb. 1980: 160. JSTOR. Web. 30 Dec. 2012.

Lind, Amy. "Feminist Post-Development Thought: 'Women in Development' and the Gendered Paradoxes of Survival in Bolivia." *Women's Studies Quarterly* 31.3–4 (2003): 227–46. JSTOR. Web. 31 Dec. 2012.

Roseberry, William. Rev. of *Let Me Speak! Testimony of Domitila, a Woman of the Bolivian Mines*, by Domitila Barrios de Chungara and Moema Viezzer. *American Anthropologist* Mar. 1980: 209. JSTOR. Web. 30 Dec. 2012.

Stone-Mediatore, Shari. "Challenging Academic Norms: An Epistemology for Feminist and Multicultural Classrooms." *NWSA Journal* 19.2 (2007): 55–77. Project MUSE. Web. 1 Jan. 2013.

Further Reading

Barrios de Chungara, Domitila, and David Acebey. *Aquí También, Domitila!: Testimonios.* Mexico City: Siglo Veintiuno Editores, 1985. Print.

Carey-Webb, Allen. "Auto/Biography of the Oppressed: The Power of Testimonial." *English Journal* 80.4 (1991): 44–47. Web. 1 Jan. 2013.

Gugelberger, Georg M., ed. *The Real Thing: Testimonial Discourse and Latin America.* Durham, N.C.: Duke University Press, 1996. Print.

Jesus, Carolina Maria de. *Child of the Dark: The Diary of Carolina Maria de Jesus.* Trans. David St. Clair. New York: Dutton, 1962. Print.

Lewis, Oscar, Ruth M. Lewis, and Susan M. Rigdon. *Living the Revolution: An Oral History of Contemporary Cuba.* Urbana: University of Illinois Press, 1977–78. Print.

Menchú, Rigoberta. *I, Rigoberta Menchú: An Indian Woman in Guatemala.* Ed. Elisabeth Burgos-Debray. London: Verso, 1984. Print.

Viezzer, Moema. "El Comite de Amas de Casa de Siglo XX: An Organizational Experience of Bolivian Women." Trans. James Dietz and Paula Tuchman. *Latin American Perspectives* 6.3 (1979): 80–86. Web. 1 Jan. 2013.

Claire Skinner

LONG JOURNEY HOME
Oral Histories of Contemporary Delaware Indians
James W. Brown, Rita T. Kohn

OVERVIEW

Long Journey Home: Oral Histories of Contemporary Delaware Indians (2008), edited by James W. Brown and Rita T. Kohn, is a richly illustrated collection of firsthand reflections on the tribal experiences of descendants of the White River (Indiana) Delawares from the late nineteenth to the early twenty-first century. The book comprises testimonies from four distinct archival projects undertaken in 1936, 1968, 1995, and 1998–2004, the last overseen by Brown and Kohn. The constant theme throughout the otherwise diverse accounts is how these Delawares have managed to keep their cultural heritage alive in spite of the successive forced removals that led them from their original homelands in the east to their present home in and around Bartlesville, Oklahoma.

Long Journey Home complements the work of groups within Oklahoma's Delaware community intent on preserving and raising awareness (both inside and outside the community) of traditional Delaware culture. The contemporary interviews made between 1998 and 2004, in particular, reveal a present-day generation struggling to reconnect with an interrupted heritage. The book was released to critical acclaim, though some reviewers were not wholly satisfied with the editors' methods of selection (almost all the interviewees belong to a single genealogical line) and organization (the histories are repetitive). Brown and Kohn nevertheless make a significant contribution to a more nuanced understanding of U.S. history, revealing the lives and accomplishments of a people all too often neglected in major accounts.

HISTORICAL AND LITERARY CONTEXT

The earliest of the oral histories collected in *Long Journey Home* come from Delaware men and women who were born in the 1850s, 1860s, and 1870s and were primarily concerned with telling how they came as children with their families to Indian Territory (western lands designated by the U.S. government for settlement by Native Americans forced to give up their eastern homelands for European settlers). In these and later histories, the stories dwell heavily on home, school, and work life, making intimate reflections of mostly personal significance and revealing broader implications of Native American communities at the mercy of an aggressively encroaching white culture.

As Deborah Nichols-Ledermann and James A. Rementer make clear in their introduction to *Long Journey Home*, the history of the Delawares is one of long suffering. Originally a scattered people, they lived in discrete but networked communities across the region now comprising southeastern New York, eastern Pennsylvania, northern Delaware, and New Jersey. The oral histories begin at a relatively late moment in the tribe's westward migration over two centuries from Pennsylvania through Ohio, Missouri, and Kansas, with recollections of coming from Kansas to Oklahoma in the early to mid-nineteenth century. From the early accounts to those of the present day, the Native Americans interviewed seek to recuperate traditions lost as they were compelled, for one reason or another, to deviate from the traditional ways.

The book grew out of an earlier "pan–Great Lakes" project by Kohn and William Lynwood Montell, documented in their 1997 *Always a People: Oral Histories of Contemporary Woodland Indians*. Originally intent on showing the shared experiences of a number of Native American woodland nations, Kohn decided that, of the eleven tribes studied, the Delawares merited more attention. While researching *Long Journey Home*, Brown and Kohn also filmed the interviewees to produce an Emmy Award–winning documentary released in 2003, *Long Journey Home: The Delawares of Indiana*. Taken together, these works reveal a broad and ongoing commitment to publicizing the legacies of Native Americans in the United States and a more specific interest in bringing to the fore the much overlooked story of the Delawares.

Long Journey Home makes strong statements about the plight of not just the Delawares but also all indigenous peoples in the United States compelled at one time or another to give up traditional ways of life. Importantly, the contemporary Delawares who speak in these histories refuse to consider themselves mere victims of U.S. progress. Rather, they reveal themselves to be accomplished community builders, proactive in educating and uplifting their people and committed to preserving everything valuable in their culture under threat. Published in an era still given to the excesses of racism and ethno-nationalism, Brown

❖ **Key Facts**

Time Period:
Late 19th to Early 21st Centuries

Relevant Historical Events:
Continued forced relocation of the Delaware

Nationality:
American

Keywords:
Native Americans; relocation; civil rights

Lenape Indians Anigia Gltodi Aniwaya, right, and Patricia Harbach, left, dance at a tribal gathering to raise awareness about the dangers of nuclear irradiated foods on November 23, 2003, in Milford Square, Pennsylvania. *Long Journey Home* compiles oral histories of the Lenape, also known as the Delaware Indians. © AP IMAGES/BRADLEY C BOWER

and Kohn's book offers a mighty example of a people who, in spite of their suffering, are working hard to remember who they are.

THEMES AND STYLE

The dominant themes in *Long Journey Home* deal with the value of tribal identity and community bonds in a world offering more and more scope for deviating from the traditional ways of life. In many of the contemporary interviews, modern Delawares reforge their connections with their elders; think ahead for the sake of the upcoming generations; and come to a strong sense of who they are through powwows, dances, storytelling, traditional dress revivals, and efforts to keep the native language alive. Such is the case for tribal council member Paula Martin Pechonick, who re-creates traditional clothes for tribal gatherings and historical reconstructions, as well as for former Assistant Chief Michael Pace. A member of the Cultural Preservation Committee, Pace's mission is to give modern Delawares "a little better access to their own history," offering "an avenue so that they may come and learn a little bit more about their own culture."

In their opening remarks, Brown and Kohn describe *Long Journey Home* as a kind of catalyst for further investigations into the larger Delaware story: "We hoped to inspire others to undertake their own books to give voice and visibility to other groups of Delawares whose tribal centers are in Canada and other parts of the United States." At the level of the text, they claim to make similar demands on the reader: making "no attempt to censor or explicate" the collected histories, they organize the speakers alphabetically and so leave the readers to be "active participants, picking up points and making connections on their own." In both instances, the book figures not as the last word on the subject but rather as a leaping off point for others to make new and further discoveries. In this sense, Brown and Kohn claim that their "book represents communion between teller and listener in the tradition of oral transmittal."

Long Journey Home opens with Rementer and Nichols-Ledermann's historical overview of the Delaware nation. The oral histories follow in four sections. The first transcribes ten interviews recorded in 1937–38 as part of the Works Progress Administration's Indian-Pioneer History of Oklahoma project. The second section presents three interviews recorded in 1968, the third offers two from 1995, and the fourth provides thirty-one undertaken specifically for *Long Journey Home*. The book concludes with a transcription of a roundtable discussion of the Lenape (Delaware) Program at Conner Prairie Living History Museum in Fishers, Indiana, a museum used by several of the interviewees to consolidate their historical awareness of their community. The heavy use of color photographs throughout, as Marshall Joseph Becker noted in his review for the *American Indian Culture and Research Journal*, gives the work a "picture-book quality."

CRITICAL DISCUSSION

Most reviewers gave *Long Journey Home* a warm reception upon its publication. Brice Obermeyer, in his 2008 analysis for the *Journal of Folklore Research Reviews*, called it "an attractive, wonderfully illustrated and accessible book," one making "an important contribution to the literature on the Eastern Delaware." L. M. Hauptman, writing in 2008 for *Choice*, similarly thought it a "valuable collection … nicely illustrated and carefully edited," while Dawn Marsh's *Ohio History* review from 2009 described it as "a tantalizing sampling of Indian oral histories." Not all reviewers, however, looked favorably upon Brown and Kohn's editing. Alex T. Primm in his 2010 article in the *Oral History Review*, for instance, complained that "much material is repeated" while "seemingly trivial events obscure the bigger picture."

Long Journey Home was a timely publication, signaling renewed interest in the history of the Delaware Indians. The following year two further studies were published: Obermeyer's *Delaware Tribe in a Cherokee Nation* and Gunlög Maria Fur's *A Nation of Women: Gender and Colonial Encounters among the Delaware Indians*. In 2012 two more notable works appeared: *Contested Territories: Native Americans and Nonnatives in the Lower Great Lakes, 1700–1850*, edited by Charles Beatty-Medina and Melissa Rinehart, and *On Records: Delaware Indians, Colonists, and the Media of History and Memory*, by Andrew Newman. *Long Journey Home* thus finds itself among a growing scholarship on the Delaware people, their land, and their culture.

Long Journey Home has not yet been discussed as a work in its own right. One of the few scholars to make extensive reference to it is coeditor Brown in an article on race, ethnicity, and stereotypes. In "The Lenape: Cultural Survival or Assimilation?" Brown interprets selected oral histories from *Long Journey Home* in order to dispel damaging stereotypes of Native American: his point is that, despite popular misconceptions, native cultures are rich and thriving, and, consequently, media images should reflect Native Americans in all their complexity.

BIBLIOGRAPHY

Sources

Becker, Marshall Joseph. Rev. of *Long Journey Home: Oral Histories of Contemporary Delaware Indians*, ed. James W. Brown and Rita T. Kohn. *American Indian Culture and Research Journal* 32.3 (2008): 192–95. *WilsonWeb*. Web. 9 Jan. 2013.

Brown, James W. "The Lenape: Cultural Survival or Assimilation?" *Images That Injure: Pictorial Stereotypes in the Media*. 3rd ed. Ed. Susan Dente Ross and Martin Lester. Santa Barbara, Calif.: Praeger, 2011. Print.

Brown, James W., and Rita T. Kohn, eds. *Long Journey Home: Oral Histories of Contemporary Delaware Indians*. Bloomington: Indiana University Press, 2008. Print.

Hauptmann, L. M. Rev. of *Long Journey Home: Oral Histories of Contemporary Delaware Indians*, ed. James W. Brown and Rita T. Kohn. *Choice* 45.12 (2008): 2222. *ProQuest Research Library*. Web. 9 Jan. 2013.

Marsh, Dawn. Rev. of *Long Journey Home: Oral Histories of Contemporary Delaware Indians*, ed. James W. Brown and Rita T. Kohn. *Ohio History* 116 (2009): 131–32. *Project MUSE*. Web. 9 Jan. 2013.

Obermeyer, Brice. Rev. of *Long Journey Home: Oral Histories of Contemporary Delaware Indians*, ed. James W. Brown and Rita T. Kohn. *Journal of Folklore Research Reviews* (2008). *IUScholarWorks Journals*. Web. 9 Jan. 2013.

Primm, Alex T. Rev. of *Long Journey Home: Oral Histories of Contemporary Delaware Indians*, ed. James W. Brown and Rita T. Kohn. *Oral History Review* 37.1 (2010): 131–33. *Project MUSE*. Web. 9 Jan. 2013.

Further Reading

Beatty-Medina, Charles, and Melissa Rinehart, eds. *Contested Territories: Native Americans and Non-natives in the Lower Great Lakes, 1700–1850*. East Lansing: Michigan State University Press, 2012. Print.

Bierhorst, John. *The White Deer & Other Stories Told by the Lenape*. New York: Morrow, 1995. Print.

Fur, Gunlög Maria. *A Nation of Women: Gender and Colonial Encounters among the Delaware Indians*. Philadelphia: University of Pennsylvania Press, 2009. Print.

A BRIEF HISTORY OF THE DELAWARE INDIANS

The native peoples now generally known as Delaware Indians were originally known as Lenape (len-NAH-pay), an Algonquin word that translates in the singular as "common person" and in the plural as "common people," or sometimes just "the people." They came to be known as the Delaware Indians for their proximity to the Delaware River, which had been named after the governor of the colony at Jamestown, Virginia, Lord De La Warr. On September 17, 1778, they were the first Indian nation to sign a treaty with the U.S. government, a fact that did not prevent their numerous forced removals.

According to the Delaware Tribe's official website, their westward migration began with the so-called Walking Purchase of 1737. William Penn's sons (then the proprietors of Pennsylvania) duped the Lenape into parting with their land by falsely claiming that their ancestors had promised to sell the land to the Penns—"as much as could be covered in a day-and-a-half's walk." Assuming the walk would be carried out in good conscience, the Lenape agreed to let the area be walked off, only to discover that the Penns had hired three of Pennsylvania's fastest runners, one of whom managed to cover fifty-five miles. Thus began the long and painful history of displacement for the Delawares.

Kohn, Rita T., and William Lynwood Montell. *Always a People: Oral Histories of Contemporary Woodland Indians*. Bloomington: Indiana University Press, 1997. Print.

Kraft, Herbert C. *The Lenape-Delaware Indian Heritage: 10,000 BC to AD 2000*. Stanhope, N.J.: Lenape, 2001. Print.

Long Journey Home: The Delawares of Indiana. Dir. Michael Atwood. Cinema Guild, 2004. DVD.

Newman, Andrew. *On Records: Delaware Indians, Colonists, and the Media of History and Memory*. Lincoln: University of Nebraska Press, 2012. Print.

Obermeyer, Brice. *Delaware Tribe in a Cherokee Nation*. Lincoln: University of Nebraska Press, 2009. Print.

David Aitchison

Solidarity Forever
An Oral History of the IWW
Stewart Bird, Dan Georgakas, Deborah Shaffer

❖ Key Facts

Time Period:
20th Century

Relevant Historical Events:
Formation of the IWW; increased corporatism in the United States

Nationality:
American

Keywords:
labor; unionism; corporatism

OVERVIEW

In *Solidarity Forever: An Oral History of the IWW* (1985), Stewart Bird, Dan Georgakas, and Deborah Shaffer collect testimonies from veterans of the Industrial Workers of the World (IWW), the so-called one big union that formed in 1905 with the goal of abolishing the capitalist wage system. The book primarily includes edited transcripts of interviews filmed by Bird and Shaffer in the 1970s, many of which first appeared in their acclaimed 1979 documentary, *The Wobblies* (the nickname given to IWW members). The interviewees reflect mostly on episodes from the 1910s and 1920s, when the IWW peaked in popularity and notoriety before faltering under the onslaught of state and federal antiunion forces. Though diverse, these frank histories evince a shared faith in the revolutionary-democratic principles expressed by the IWW in its heyday.

Begun in the 1970s and published in the 1980s, *Solidarity Forever* was produced in an era drastically different from the one described in the book's oral histories. More than anything, a workers' revolution no longer seemed feasible: capitalism had proved itself robust, compelling many if not most working-class families to join the ranks of the middle classes following the United States' boom after World War II. The IWW, active throughout the century, never regained the influence it wielded in earlier decades. Bird and his coauthors sought to remind readers of the union's enduring relevance at a time when, despite national prosperity, class disparities were in fact growing. Like *The Wobblies*, *Solidarity Forever* was released to critical acclaim, and it remains a classic labor text.

HISTORICAL AND LITERARY CONTEXT

The American Federation of Labor (AFL), a trades union association, was formed in 1886. The IWW was formed by union activists who believed that the AFL perpetuated hierarchies between skilled and unskilled workers and had obstructed the working classes in the fight for better conditions. The oral histories recorded in *Solidarity Forever* document the lasting impressions of the IWW on its members, who ranged from northeastern longshoremen and textile workers to lumberjacks, grain harvesters, and hard rock miners. Though many of the accounts deal with day-to-day occurrences of working life, much attention is given to momentous events involving the IWW, such as the strikes in Lawrence, Massachusetts, and Paterson, New Jersey, and the general strike of 1917.

These oral histories deal with a troubled period in U.S. history: a time when corporate giants including U.S. Steel and Standard Oil were ever seeking to increase profits. Typically this meant speeding up production while cutting labor costs, exemplified in the adoption of time-and-motion studies and the introduction of assembly lines. The pursuit of efficiency, however, often led to dismal and even deadly conditions for working men and women, whose complaints were often silenced by the managers and owners of industry. The IWW set out to organize workers at the mercy of the corporations, especially unskilled and migrant workers traditionally neglected by other unions. In *Solidarity Forever* former IWW members and organizers give testimony to the rigors of working-class life and the bitter battles fought for shorter hours and better pay.

While *The Wobblies* gives a more apparent sense of these eighty- and ninety-year-old veterans, the book—as Georgakas's introduction makes clear—provides "longer oral histories from IWWs featured in the film, interviews not included in the film, additional photographic documentation of the IWW, and the kind of statistical and historical detailing that is awkward in cinema." For its insights into the hardships of working-class life, *Solidarity Forever* is also comparable with Marat Moore's 1996 *Women in the Mines: Stories of Life and Work,* whose early chapters similarly discuss the often-bloody confrontations between labor and capital.

With *Solidarity Forever* Bird, Shaffer, and Georgakas make a significant contribution not only to U.S. labor studies but also to a broader history of radicalism in the United States. Produced at a time when researchers in radical studies were increasingly interested in identity politics rather than economic inequalities, the book refuses to give up "class" as a keyword for critical inquiry. Bearing in mind that scholarly conversations have returned recently to the language of class disparity—following the democratic uprisings around the globe and the spate of "Occupy" actions throughout the world—the text provides a vital link between the grassroots revolutionary movements of the early twentieth and early twenty-first centuries.

THEMES AND STYLE

The book's overarching theme is the impact of the IWW, in terms of organization and ethos, on the hearts and minds of ordinary working people. As one migrant worker, Jack Miller, tells it:

> If it had not been for my contact with the IWW and what I gained from them, I would have probably become a criminal.... Through the IWW I began to consider how man had risen from the beastly stage through the ages. I could see a future that I could be part of creating. I began to see how you contribute to my wellbeing and I to yours. I saw what love was in the finest sense.

Miller and others like him attest to a spirit of social responsibility and attachments inspired by the IWW that run deeper than mere political or dogmatic affiliation.

Solidarity Forever was meant to rouse a new generation of Americans to the possibilities of a working class mobilized to combat the ills of capitalism. More broadly, as Georgakas explains it, "Americans interested in social justice can profit greatly by examining the IWW for a way of being that might once again inspire the American imagination." Bird, Shaffer, and Georgakas supplement the veterans' testimonies with photographs of workers, organizers, and strikers, along with facsimiles of IWW cartoons and posters; these illustrations serve to persuade readers that the activism informing these oral histories had, and still has, substance enough to challenge the capitalist order of things.

The book opens with an essay by Georgakas charting the beginnings of the IWW and the union's continuing significance for contemporary social movements seeking radical change. It proceeds with twenty-eight oral interviews, each contextualized by Georgakas and clustered in sections with titles such as "Women in Textiles," "Timberbeasts," "Hard Rock Mining," and "Civil Liberties for All." The book closes with a transcription of Ralph Chaplin's classic "Solidarity Forever," a song still sung at union protests and rallies across the United States and around the world. The veterans' voices throughout are presented in vernaculars ranging from plain spoken to eloquent; for example, textile worker Irma Lombardi opines that "the unions have changed. Bad people have infiltrated them." On the other hand, IWW member (and later first American Civil Liberties Union director) Roger Baldwin makes a more consciously historical claim: "The IWW was involved in one of the greatest historic trials of free speech in the history of the United States."

CRITICAL DISCUSSION

On release, the book received much praise. In the *Wisconsin Magazine of History,* John R. Salter Jr. described it as "a unique addition to the first-rate works on the only indigenously revolutionary movement in the United States since the 1770's." Mark McColloch spelled out the book's broad appeal in a *Journal of American History* review: "Students of labor history and civil liberties, as well as those who are attracted by the ideals and behavior of the Wobblies, will certainly wish to read this book." Attesting to the intimate quality of the collected testimonies, Ronald L. Filippelli stated in the *Library Journal:* "Anyone interested in the American revolutionary heritage will cherish this [book]" and "savor the memories of these humane, intelligent, and inspiring survivors of one of America's great radical movements."

As the above reviewers make clear, *Solidarity Forever* is a rich resource for students of U.S. history, bearing witness as it does to the IWW's struggles for not only radical change but also basic constitutional freedoms. The recollections of these miners, lumberjacks, longshoremen, and millworkers count among the last living testimonies to a formative period in modern U.S. history.

Scholars are yet to discuss *Solidarity Forever* as a work in its own right; it figures, rather, as a source document, cited to support larger historical claims about the period. For example, Hester Furey, writing in the *Journal of the Midwest Modern Language Association,* cites the contribution by labor organizer and folk singer Bruce "Utah" Phillips to support her argument on the interrelations between IWW songs and modernist poetry. "By our standards of authorial behavior and literary ownership," she observes, "IWW songwriters ... displayed an alarming disregard for maintenance of property boundaries, 'borrowing' tunes, or, as Utah Phillips forthrightly says, stealing them." More commonly *Solidarity Forever* figures only in footnotes—as in the work of Anton Rosenthal ("Radical Border Crossers: The Industrial Workers of the World and Their Press in Latin America") and Samuel Schrager ("Migratory Lumberjack: A Portrait of Michigan Bill Stowell").

During an Industrial Workers of the World (IWW) rally in Union Square in New York City in the early twentieth century, a participant wears a hat card reading, "Bread or Revolution." *Solidarity Forever* offers a history of the IWW from its inception, including such events. © EVERETT COLLECTION INC/ALAMY

COMIC BOOKS AS HISTORY BOOKS

In 2005 Paul Buhle and Nicole Schulman celebrated the centenary of the founding of the IWW by coediting *Wobblies!: A Graphic History of the Industrial Workers of the World*. Three years later Buhle edited a similar history, this time dealing with the New Left generation, *Students for a Democratic Society: A Graphic History,* written by Harvey Pekar and illustrated by Gary Dumm. Also in 2008, Buhle edited a historical biography of the Argentine revolutionary Che Guevara, *Che: A Graphic Biography,* by Spain Rodriguez, and in 2009 he edited *Studs Terkel's Working: A Graphic Adaptation,* a reworking of a labor classic, again featuring the work of Pekar.

These ventures in history telling through the comic-book medium reveal a commitment to reaching out to nontraditional audiences. Many of the writers and artists collaborating in these works are—like Pekar, who made his name with the autobiographical *American Splendor* (begun in 1976)—veterans of the underground comics scene. As such, while ostensibly appealing to younger readers, they tap into the nostalgia of a much older generation of counterculture readers. These and similar works offer pithy and dramatic introductions to, and interpretations of, leftist political movements in the United States.

BIBLIOGRAPHY

Sources

Bird, Stewart, Dan Georgakas, and Deborah Shaffer, comps. *Solidarity Forever: An Oral History of the IWW.* Chicago: Lake View, 1985. Print.

Filippelli, Ronald L. Rev. of *Solidarity Forever: An Oral History of the IWW,* by Stewart Bird, Dan Georgakas, and Deborah Shaffer. *Library Journal* 110 (1985): 93. EBSCOhost. Web. 9 Jan. 2013.

Furey, Hester L. "IWW Songs as Modernist Poetry." *Journal of the Midwest Modern Language Association* 34.2 (2001): 51–72. JSTOR. Web. 9 Jan. 2013.

McColloch, Mark. Rev. of *Solidarity Forever: An Oral History of the IWW,* by Stewart Bird, Dan Georgakas, and Deborah Shaffer. *Journal of American History* 73.1 (1986): 227. JSTOR. Web. 9 Jan. 2013.

Salter, John R., Jr. Rev. of *Solidarity Forever: An Oral History of the IWW,* by Stewart Bird, Dan Georgakas, and Deborah Shaffer. *Wisconsin Magazine of History* 70.3 (1987): 225–26. JSTOR. Web. 9 Jan. 2013.

Further Reading

Buhle, Paul, and Nicole Schulman. *Wobblies!: A Graphic History of the Industrial Workers of the World.* New York: Verso, 2005. Print.

Cortez, Carlos. *Where Are the Voices? and Other Wobbly Poems.* Chicago: C. H. Kerr, 1997. Print.

McCarthy, Timothy Patrick, and John McMillian, eds. *The Radical Reader: A Documentary History of the American Radical Tradition.* New York: New Press, 2003. Print.

Rosenthal, Anton. "Radical Border Crossers: The Industrial Workers of the World and Their Press in Latin America." *Estudios Interdisciplinarios de América Latina y el Caribe* 22.2 (2012): n. pag. Tel Aviv U. Web. 9 Jan. 2013.

Salerno, Salvatore. *Red November, Black November: Culture and Community in the Industrial Workers of the World.* Albany: State University of New York Press, 1989. Print.

Schrager, Samuel. "Migratory Lumberjack: A Portrait of Michigan Bill Stowell." *Forest & Conservation History* 35.1 (1991): 4–15. JSTOR. Web. 9 Jan. 2013.

David Aitchison

Soviet Baby Boomers
An Oral History of Russia's Cold War Generation
Donald J. Raleigh

OVERVIEW

In *Soviet Baby Boomers: An Oral History of Russia's Cold War Generation* (2012), Donald J. Raleigh offers what he calls a "composite narrative" of biography and history, weaving together the life stories of sixty Russians to make sense of the much larger fate of Russia in the late twentieth century. His subjects are men and women born after World War II who graduated in 1967 from two elite schools: one in Moscow, the other in the provincial city of Saratov. Drawing on interviews with these baby boomers (children born when the national birthrate increased dramatically), Raleigh traces the nation's trajectory leading up to and beyond the collapse of the Soviet Empire.

Raleigh claims that these oral histories provide new insights into post-1945 Soviet history, with his subjects now speaking openly about growing up in Russia in ways they never did before the dissolution of the Soviet Union in 1991. That is, since the Soviet state had a reputation for manufacturing fictions of national progress, as well as a long history of silencing its critics, what survives in official records and public discourse is often at odds with actual experiences. Interviewed between 2001 and 2008, Raleigh's subjects tell a more nuanced story, attentive to the vicissitudes of life under the communist leadership of, among others, Nikita Khrushchev (1953–1964), Leonid Brezhnev (1964–1982), and Mikhail Gorbachev (1985–1991). Released to critical acclaim, Raleigh's book promises to have lasting significance for studies of Soviet and post-Soviet Russia.

HISTORICAL AND LITERARY CONTEXT

The Soviet Union (1922–1991) emerged in the aftermath of the Bolshevik Revolution of 1917, which put an end to czarist rule in Russia and, under the leadership of Vladimir Lenin, cleared the ground for massive political, economic, and industrial reforms in the name of socialism. A union of fifteen republics, it was governed by the single-party rule of the Communist Party. After Lenin's death in 1924, Joseph Stalin rose to prominence and ultimately assumed sole leadership of the Soviet Union. Stalin is chiefly remembered for a ruthless authoritarian regime consolidated by criminalizing, incarcerating, and executing millions of people. Raleigh's baby boomers, born in 1949 and 1950, were children just when that regime was at an end, when new freedoms and prosperity under Khrushchev were in the offing.

Raleigh began research on *Soviet Baby Boomers* a decade after the Soviet Union's dissolution, at a moment when he could look back on the transformation of Soviet Russia since midcentury: from totalitarian communist state, through the period of "de-Stalinization" inaugurated by Khrushchev, to the beginnings of a more open consumer society broached by Gorbachev's policies of perestroika (political and economic reform) and glasnost (governmental practice made more transparent). Raleigh expected his subjects, through their unique life stories, to capture collectively what it meant to "live Soviet" in those decades.

Soviet Baby Boomers expands on Raleigh's earlier *Russia's Sputnik Generation: Soviet Baby Boomers Talk about Their Lives* (2006), another work relying on oral history, albeit more conventionally. Rather than synthesizing his subjects' accounts as he does in the later book, in *Russia's Sputnik Generation* Raleigh provides discrete transcripts of eight interviews. Both these texts can be compared to *Living through the Soviet System* (2005), in which editors Daniel Bertaux, Paul Thompson, and Anna Rotkirch present life stories and family histories of everyday Soviet Russia told in the freer spirit of glasnost. More recently, Jehanne M. Gheith and Katherine R. Jolluck's *Gulag Voices: Oral Histories of Soviet Incarceration and Exile* (2011) seeks out the darker testimonies of Russia's survivors of the Gulag (Stalin's system of forced labor camps).

Soviet Baby Boomers makes a substantial contribution to Soviet studies. Raleigh's interviewees are, of course, not representative of a broad social spectrum: they constitute, rather, a privileged class, graduates of schools that targeted children of party officials and intelligentsia. But it is precisely as urban professionals that they offer insights into the desires and achievements of a generation often neglected in Soviet histories. Growing up deeply invested in the "Soviet dream," these speakers bring a fresh understanding of Russian failings and, perhaps more importantly, achievements. Published in an era still mindful of the Cold War divide, Raleigh's book has much to teach about a society often mistakenly considered to be at complete odds with that of the United States.

❖ *Key Facts*

Time Period:
Mid- to Late 20th Century

Relevant Historical Events:
Decline and collapse of the Soviet Union; "de-Stalinization"

Nationality:
Russian

Keywords:
communism; Cold War; Soviet Union

WORK AND FAMILY LIFE

Soviet Baby Boomers looks at how growing up after the death of Soviet leader Joseph Stalin, depicted here, affected students who graduated from elite educational institutions in 1967. © LEBRECHT MUSIC AND ARTS PHOTO LIBRARY/ALAMY

THEMES AND STYLE

One central theme of *Soviet Baby Boomers* is the function of oral history as a means of remembering elements of the past that state propaganda urged people to forget. As Irina Vizgalova's father cautioned her, "don't poke your nose in politics, because they're good at rewriting our history." Raleigh's response is not to indict the rewriting of history as such but to insist on the capacity to rewrite it—in his case, by appealing not to public but to private realms of discourse, especially those generated within the family, providing alternative accounts. Just as pertinent is how Soviet prosperity encouraged the parents of these baby boomers to seek private family spaces, fostering values that would in time conflict greatly with the collective principles of state communism.

Raleigh writes in order to "throw light on a critical generation of people who had remained largely faceless and ignored up until now.... I explore the margins among the political, the personal, and the professional ... to grasp what it means to 'live Soviet' during the Cold War."

In doing so, he deploys the methodology of oral history strategically, drawing on a period when, after decades of state-sponsored repression and censorship, "citizens began to talk openly about their past." He makes it clear, however, that he is interested in the individual life story only to the extent that it helps him understand "the fate of the Soviet Union."

Between his introduction and conclusion, Raleigh divides his book into seven chapters, which are arranged in roughly chronological order: the first begins with recollections of family difficulties in the revolutionary period because of class profiling, and the last arrives at the economic hardships of the post-Soviet 1990s. His prose is well-crafted, his arguments dialectical (that is, he reveals how certain elements generate the forces that in time come to challenge and overthrow those elements that produced them). "The Baby Boomers came of age at the zenith of Soviet socialism," he writes, "only to see the system crumble some three decades later. Ironically, much of this had to do with the Soviet system's very success at effecting social change, whose byproducts included rapid urbanization and a rise in the number of educated professionals." Here, and elsewhere, Raleigh is thinking deeply about social transformation in ways that insist that the reader finds continuities rather than stark contrasts between eras and regimes. Soviet communism, he notes, made its own demise possible, primarily by instilling in a generation of Russians values that would not be satisfied with the impoverished solutions of the Soviet state.

CRITICAL DISCUSSION

Upon its release, *Soviet Baby Boomers* received much praise. K. C. O'Connor, writing for *Choice,* thought it should be "required reading for anyone interested in understanding changing Soviet attitudes during the era of late socialism." In the *Slavic Review,* Juliane Fürst commended Raleigh for providing "the first full-blown Soviet oral history study by a western scholar that relies exclusively on interviews as primary sources and applies a strict oral history methodology to the selection and analysis of its sixty interviews." Like Robert Legvold's review in *Foreign Affairs,* Fürst found Raleigh's work "fascinating." Mark Edele, in a *Region* review, similarly saw much to praise, though he questioned Raleigh's interview pool. "The focus on the elite," as he saw it, "somewhat blunts the analytical possibilities of Raleigh's study."

Soviet Baby Boomers has much to say about the transformations and upheavals in the last four decades of the Soviet Union. As a "composite narrative" of biography and history, it embeds its oral histories in a more conventional historical synthesis, making for a many-voiced text, albeit one guided firmly by Raleigh. The resulting narrative is unique and compelling, a model work of history sure to be copied in years to come.

Published in 2012, *Soviet Baby Boomers* is too new to be the subject of scholarship beyond reviews. However, it is probable that the narrative will be taken up in much the same way as Raleigh's *Russia's Sputnik Generation,* a work cited regularly in various studies of late twentieth-century Russian society. Anna Paretskaya in *Sociological Theory* (2010), for example, referenced Raleigh's baby boomers to show that a discourse of "postcollectivism" generated by the Communist Party compelled individuals to fashion identities more in keeping with capitalist values. Meanwhile, discussing "myth-making" in Soviet space-program propaganda, Slava Gerovitch in the *Russian Review* (2011) called on Raleigh's interviewees to corroborate "the formative role of the key events of the Space Age" on their lives. Finally, Peter J. Schmelz, tracing "nuclear themes" in Russian culture in a 2009 article, quoted one baby boomer who testifies to fearing the United States on account of the Cuban missile crisis (when the United States and the Soviet Union came close to nuclear war in 1962). Written in the same vein as *Russia's Sputnik Generation*, *Soviet Baby Boomers* offers a similar wealth of testimonies sure to prove invaluable to future historians.

BIBLIOGRAPHY

Sources

Edele, Mark. Rev. of *Soviet Baby Boomers: An Oral History of Russia's Cold War Generation*, by Donald J. Raleigh. *Region: Regional Studies of Russia, Eastern Europe, and Central Asia* 1.2 (2012): 315–17. Project Muse. Web. 27 Jan. 2013.

Fürst, Juliane. Rev. of *Soviet Baby Boomers: An Oral History of Russia's Cold War Generation*, by Donald J. Raleigh. *Slavic Review* 71.4 (2012): 955–56. JSTOR. Web. 27 Jan. 2013.

Gerovitch, Slava. "The Creation of Soviet Space History Myths." *Russian Review* 70 (2011): 460–84. Wiley. Web. 27 Jan. 2013.

Legvold, Robert. Rev. of *Soviet Baby Boomers: An Oral History of Russia's Cold War Generation*, by Donald J. Raleigh. *Foreign Affairs* 91.1 (2012): 199–200. Proquest. Web. 27 Jan. 2013.

O'Connor, K. C. Rev. of *Soviet Baby Boomers: An Oral History of Russia's Cold War Generation*, by Donald J. Raleigh. *Choice* (2012): 1944. Proquest. Web. 27 Jan. 2013.

Paretskaya, Anna. "The Soviet Communist Party and the Other Spirit of Capitalism." *Sociological Theory* 28.4 (2010): 377–401. JSTOR. Web. 27 Jan. 2013.

Schmelz, Peter J. "Alfred Schnittke's *Nagasaki*: Soviet Nuclear Culture, Radio Moscow, and the Global Cold War." *Journal of the American Musicological Society* 62.2 (2009): 413–74. JSTOR. Web. 27 Jan. 2013.

Further Reading

Diuk, Nadia. *The Next Generation in Russia, Ukraine, and Azerbaijan: Youth, Politics, Identity, and Change.* Lanham, Md.: Rowman and Littlefield, 2012. Print.

Kotkin, Stephen. *Uncivil Society: 1989 and the Implosion of the Communist Establishment.* New York: Modern Library, 2009. Print.

GLASNOST: DEATH KNELL FOR THE SOVIET UNION

When Mikhail Gorbachev announced his policy of glasnost—a word commonly translated as "openness"—he was, in many ways, continuing the work begun by Nikita Khrushchev some forty years previously. Just as Khrushchev in the 1950s publicly disclosed Joseph Stalin's betrayal of the revolution and the corruption of the Soviet bureaucracy, Gorbachev in the 1980s sought to curtail the abuses of power within the Communist Party and the Soviet government. Releasing information previously suppressed, and opening decision making to scrutiny and debate, Gorbachev inspired unprecedented levels of freedom of expression in the Soviet Union. Such openness, he hoped, would inform the renovation of Soviet society. Unwittingly, however, he sowed the seeds of social revolution. With the media freed from party control, with increased traffic in ideas and cultural work between the East and West, and with the dramatic disclosures of formerly celebrated Soviet history as stained in blood, people began to lose faith in the Soviet system. Writers and journalists exercised their newfound freedoms with penetrating critiques of the Soviet Union and its leadership, clearing the way for calls to dissolve the union and restore independence to its member republics.

My Perestroika. Dir. Robin Hessman. Red Square, 2010. Film.

Popov, G. K. *Mikhail Gorbachev's Perestroika: The Departure from Socialism.* Clifton, NJ: OS Enterprises, 2012. Print.

Sinyavski, Andrei. *The Russian Intelligentsia.* New York: Columbia University Press, 1997. Print.

Smith, Mark B. *Property of Communists: The Urban Housing Program from Stalin to Khrushchev.* DeKalb: Northern Illinois University Press, 2010. Print.

Spufford, Francis. *Red Plenty.* London: Faber, 2007. Print.

Traill, Kim. *Red Square Blues: A Beginner's Guide to the Decline and Fall of the Soviet Union.* Pymble, Australia: Harper, 2009. Print.

Yurchak, Alexei. *Everything Was Forever, until It Was No More: The Last Soviet Generation.* Princeton, N.J.: Princeton University Press, 2005. Print.

David Aitchison

Warlpiri Women's Voices
Our Lives, Our History
Petronella Vaarzon-Morel

✢ **Key Facts**

Time Period:
Early to Mid-20th Century

Relevant Historical Events:
European settlement of the Central Desert; eviction of Warlpiri families

Nationality:
Australian

Keywords:
settlement; land rights; women's rights

OVERVIEW

Warlpiri Women's Voices: Our Lives, Our History (1995) is a collaboration between anthropologist Petronella Vaarzon-Morel and a group of Warlpiri women from Willowra in Australia's Northern Territory. Combining personal experience and received oral history, the stories deal with Warlpiri daily life from the period before Europeans arrived in Australia through the government creation of Aboriginal settlements after World War II. The nine women interviewed, all from the Lander River region, ranged in age from their mid-fifties to their mid-eighties. Each story is told by a woman who witnessed the events or knew someone who was there. Taken as a whole, the stories reflect the ongoing relationship between the Warlpiri and the land.

In 1987 the Institute for Aboriginal Development (IAD) asked Vaarzon-Morel to submit a proposal to the United Nations Educational, Scientific and Cultural Organization (UNESCO) for a study on the impact of social and economic change on Aboriginal women. With the support of the Willowra Community Council, Vaarzon-Morel, who had worked with the community for many years both as a teacher and as their researcher for the Willowra Land Claim, made the unusual decision to submit the proposal in conjunction with the senior women interviewed in the project. The work filled a need for local history from an Aboriginal viewpoint. Almost ten years later, continuing demand for copies of the original IAD report led Vaarzon-Morel and her coresearchers to publish the transcribed and translated narratives in book form with the hope of reaching a wider audience.

HISTORICAL AND LITERARY CONTEXT

Warlpiri Women's Voices traces the Warlpiri experience of what Ute Eickelcamp describes as "Aboriginal dispossession, displacement, and discrimination." In the early twentieth century, Europeans settled in the central desert, establishing mining camps and cattle stations that gradually disrupted both the region's ecology and the traditional Warlpiri relationship to the land. European settlement led to violent clashes over land and, more importantly, water use. Over time, the Warlpiri families were systematically evicted from their ancestral territories. By 1955 two-thirds of the Warlpiri lived on government settlements. In the late 1950s, Australia's Aboriginal peoples were declared wards of the government and placed under the "protection" of the newly formed Department of Welfare with the goal of assimilating them into Australian society.

Relocation to government settlements represented more than an economic change for the Warlpiri. The Warlpiri relationship to specific tracts of land includes ritual and mythological elements that are embodied in stories, songs, and ceremonies. The right of individuals to tell these stories is based on the chain of authority linking them to their ancestors, to the ancient time of creation known as Jukurrpa (Dreamings), and to the land itself. Knowledge of these traditions is so strongly linked to specific places that knowledge of them served as virtual property deeds when land claims went to court under the 1976 Aboriginal Land Rights Act. This tightly knit link between individual, community, land, and story is clear in *Warlpiri Women's Voices*. The women whose stories are included in *Warlpiri Women's Voices* were recognized by their community "as having the authority to talk for the land and the historical events that have taken place on it."

Warlpiri Women's Voices is the third volume in an oral history series published by the IAD and part of a vibrant movement among Aboriginal peoples in the 1980s and 1990s known as "life-writing." Described by Gillian Weiss as "a means by which they can give voice to their own stories, take possession of their own past," life-writing became an important medium of expression within Aboriginal communities, allowing them to retell their experience of invasion, displacement, and resettlement using both individual and community memories.

Like other oral history projects in the 1980s, the original purpose of the collection of stories that became *Warlpiri Women's Voices* was to fill what Eickelcamp identifies as a widespread need to "connect the younger generation with the past and serve as educational resources of Indigenous Studies in Aboriginal schools." The Warlpiri narratives and their English translations were successfully used as texts in the Willowra School, and they were later adopted by the IAD for use as course material in adult education courses. The materials reached a wider Australian audience with their republication in the 1990s.

A 2012 Sydney, Australia, performance by the Australian Aboriginal Bangarra Dance Theatre, a dance troupe that combines traditional stories and contemporary styles. Warlpiri Aboriginal women discuss their history in *Warlpiri Women's Voices*, edited by Petronella Vaarzon-Morel. © AP IMAGES/RICK RYCROFT

THEMES AND STYLE

Grace Koch, editor of a related collection of Warlpiri oral history, sums up the central themes of *Warlpiri Women's Voices* as "powerful assertions of the importance of the land and of passing on traditional knowledge to care for it properly." Rosie Nungarrayi establishes those themes in the first section of the book, telling of the "olden times" when "we walked around hunting, catching goannas, gathering berries, and digging for yams.… No whiteman's flour—only food from the land." Later stories recount violence suffered by the Warlpiri at the hands of the Europeans, changes in their lives as they moved to the government settlements, and the strategies they used to maintain their relationship to the land and their culture.

In her introduction, Vaarzon-Morel states that the purpose of the project was to "document women's knowledge about the past and their perceptions of change." The women involved in the project were conscious that the next generations were less rooted in the Warlpiri oral tradition; they wanted their history recorded for their children "and those who followed." Linguist and anthropologist Michele Grossman points out that *Warlpiri Women's Voices* is unusual in that the narrators were "active agents in the production and management both of text-as-social relations and the text-as-cultural-artifact." The senior women chose two local literacy instructors, Georgina Napangardi and Janet Nakamarra Long, to help Vaarzon-Morel to record the oral histories. Once recorded, the Warlpiri women themselves translated the narratives using a collective process of discussion and retelling. When the collection was prepared for publication in its current format, almost ten years later, Vaarzon-Morel compiled and edited the texts and wrote introductions that provide a historical context for the accounts.

Although many of the stories in this collection are modern in content, they were told in a style similar to that used by the women when they told traditional stories, including the use of intonation, facial expressions, body language, and Warlpiri sign language—elements that the collectors were unable to capture on tape. The women themselves chose the topics for the stories and the manner in which they are organized. The stories are presented in three sections organized in roughly chronological order: "Following the tracks of our ancestors," which deals with traditional Warlpiri life; "Olden Time: the first white men," which tells stories from the early period of European occupation; and "Changes," which deals with the period following World War II. Most of the stories were told in Warlpiri, which was subsequently translated into standard English. In one case, the narrator chose to speak in Aboriginal English. Both Warlpiri and English texts are included in the collection.

CRITICAL DISCUSSION

The initial reaction to the 1987 report that became *Warlpiri Women's Voices* came within the Warlpiri community itself. The transcribed and translated narratives were read to small groups, occasionally retranslated into Warlpiri for listeners who had little English. Listeners entered into a dialogue with the texts as if they were a traditional storytelling performance—some using Warlpiri sign language to sign the stories as they were

PRIMARY SOURCE

EXCERPT FROM *WARLPIRI WOMEN'S VOICES*

MOLLY NUNGARRAYI

In the olden days they looked after each other, in the olden time. Poor things, the old people—grandmothers, grandfathers, fathers and mothers—used to look after each other. They didn't rubbish each other. Our daughters looked after us also. The people looked after a kinsman until he grew older and older and became sick and tired and passed away. Then they buried him. All the deceased's relatives did this, women and men. They used to get firewood for the old people and make windbreaks and humpies in case it rained. The younger ones kept on looking after those poor old things, because the old ones once got food for them and took care of them. The old men fed us young ones from the time that they were single until they were married.

When grandma was sick her husband found bush medicine for her. When there were bad colds everyone got them—even the old ones. The old man made bush medicine for them and made them better. When everyone was healthy again the husband went off hunting, and the mother and daughter looked for goannas, yams and seeds.

When we were sick they gathered medicine from the bush and used it to cure our sickness. When we had colds they rubbed us with this bush medicine and put the plant in our nose so that we could inhale it. There was no whitefella medicine. They used to rub the medicine everywhere, all over our bodies. The next morning the person used to wake up feeling good and well. That's how they made us better, with bush medicine. Before whitefella medicine or motorcars.

SOURCE: Vaarzon-Morel, Petronella, ed. *Warlpiri Women's Voices: Our Lives, Our History*. Alice Springs, Australia: IAD Press, 1995. All rights reserved. Reproduced by permission.

read. Copies of the transcribed tapes that were given to the Willowra School were read until the copies fell apart.

At the time of the initial report, published Aboriginal history was rare, and the transcribed narratives became a standard text in Aboriginal studies courses at the IAD at Alice Springs. When the revised version was published in 1995, it received only two reviews, by Grace Koch and Jo Lampert, and both praised the work as an important addition to Aboriginal studies courses and school libraries.

Today *Warlpiri Women's Voices* is primarily used as source material for scholarly work in Aboriginal studies rather than the subject of scholarship in and of itself. Narratives from the collection are quoted in articles on subjects as diverse as initiation journeys, the development of an Aboriginal health-care system, and desert land management. Despite the growth of interest in textual representation by indigenous peoples in both Australia and North America, *Warlpiri Women's Voices* has received almost no scholarly interest. The lone exception is Grossman, who has looked at the work both in terms of cross-cultural and cross-generational "collaborative textual and editorial practices" and "indigenous agency" and Penny Summerfield's concept of subjective "dis/composure."

BIBLIOGRAPHY

Sources

Eickelcamp, Ute. "Children and Youth in Aboriginal Australia: An Overview of the Literature." *Anthropological Forum* 20.2 (2010): 147–66. *Taylor Francis Online*. Web. 8 Jan. 2013.

Grossman, Michele. "Xen(ography) and the Art of Representing Otherwise: Australian Indigenous Life-Writing and the Vernacular Text." *Postcolonial Studies* 8.3 (2005): 277–301. Print.

Grossman, Michele, Renée Hulan, and Renate Eigenbrod. "Fighting with Our Tongues, Fighting for Our Lives: Talk Text and Amodernity in *Warlpiri Women's Voices: Our Lives, Our History*." *Aboriginal Oral Traditions: Theory, Practice, Ethics*. Ed. Renate Eigenbrod and Renée Hulan. Black Point, Canada: Fernwood, 2008. Print.

Koch, Grace. Rev. of *Warlpiri Women's Voices: Our Lives, Our History*, ed. Petronella Vaarzon-Morel. *Australian Aboriginal Studies* Fall 1998: 82–83. Print.

Lampert, Jo. Rev. of *Warlpiri Women's Voices: Our Lives, Our History*, ed. Petronella Vaarzon-Morel. *Australian Journal of Indigenous Education* 24.1 (1996): 43–44. Print.

Vaarzon-Morel, Petronella, ed. *Warlpiri Women's Voices: Our Lives, Our History*. Alice Springs, Australia: IAD, 1995. Print.

Weiss, Gillian, ed. *Trying to Get It Back: Indigenous Women, Education, and Culture*. Waterloo, Canada: Wilfred Laurier University Press, 2000. Print.

Further Reading

Bell, Diane. *Daughters of the Dreaming*. Melbourne: Allen and Unwin, 1983. Print.

Brewster, Anne. *Literary Formations: Post-Colonialism, Nationalism, Globalism*. Carlton, Australia Melbourne University Press, 1995. Print.

Hulan, Renée, and Regnate Eigenbrod. *Aboriginal Oral Traditions: Theory, Practice, Ethics*. Halifax: Fernwood, 2008. Print.

Meggitt, M. J. *Desert People: A Study of the Walbiri Aborigines of Central Australia*. Chicago: University of Chicago Press, 1965. Print.

Muecke, Stephen. *Textual Spaces: Aboriginality and Cultural Studies*. Kensington, Australia: New South Wales University Press, 1992. Print.

Napaljarri, Peggy Rockman, and Lee Cataldi, collectors and trans. *Warlpiri Dreamings and Histories (Yimikirli)*. San Francisco: Harper Collins, 1994. Print.

Read, Peter, and Jay Read. *Long Time, Olden Time: Aboriginal Accounts of Northern Territory History*. Alice Springs, Australia: Institute for Aboriginal Development Publications, 1991. Print.

Reynolds, Henry. *The Other Side of the Frontier: Aboriginal Resistance to the European Invasion of Australia*. Sydney: University of New South Wales Press, 2006. Print.

Pamela Toler

Women in the Mines
Stories of Life and Work
Marat Moore

OVERVIEW

Women in the Mines: Stories of Life and Work (1996) by Marat Moore is an oral history of the life and trials of women coal miners in the United States. The twenty-four memoirs selected for the book come from a series of interviews Moore conducted in the 1980s and 1990s about the experiences of female miners between the early twentieth century and the time of the interviews. The stories reflect Moore's experience as a coal miner and as an active member of the United Mine Workers of America (UMWA) and the Coal Employment Project (CEP), a nonprofit organization designed to support women miners. Through the memoirs, she covers such topics as workplace discrimination, union involvement, and the sense of camaraderie among work crews.

The book appeared in May 1996, shortly after Moore won a sexual discrimination lawsuit against the UMWA. After losing her job with the union without notice or due cause, she discovered that a man with fewer qualifications had been selected to replace her before she was fired. The release of *Women in the Mines* shortly after this victory suggested that the book would be an overtly feminist text promoting theoretical discussions of sexual equality within the workplace. However, the book received positive reviews for its surprisingly balanced presentation of the benefits and hardships of women working in coal mines. The text takes a moderate feminist position that praises men for their acceptance of women as miners but questions the misogynistic policies that persist in the industry. Due to the sophistication of Moore's text, *Women in the Mines* continues to be an influential primary source for scholars studying the sociological impact of women in nontraditional professions.

HISTORICAL AND LITERARY CONTEXT

Records of women working in coal mines date back to thirteenth-century Europe. In 1842 an investigatory commission persuaded the British Parliament to ban women and children from working underground for health reasons. Belgium also officially stated that women were not physically able to work underground and subsequently banned them from many coal mines. During the 1920s advancements in technology significantly reduced the number of mining jobs, and newly developing international labor laws pushed for a ban on employing women in mines. However, the world wars reversed this trend in the United States as economic pressures forced companies to hire women for mining operations. Further mechanization of the mining process reduced the number of jobs available to women, resulting in continued resistance to women working in the mines.

In 1973 a federal mandate allowed women to seek higher-wage jobs in the coal mining industry, causing an influx of women into mining jobs. These women often faced sexual harassment, blatant misogyny, community opposition from women and men, and lack of support from union representatives. *Women in the Mines* represents a cross section of female miners who worked underground before, during, and after this time of change. In the stories, the women discuss how their experiences changed them on a personal level and altered the way women miners are perceived within the union and trade.

Women in the Mines is one of numerous books released in the mid-1990s about the experience of women in mining from the perspective of female miners or miners' wives. Carol A. B. Giesen's *Coal Miners' Wives: Portraits of Endurance* (1995) is an oral history about the experiences of women struggling with the dangers of mining and injuries facing their husbands and other family members due to unsafe work environments. In 1996 Brigid O'Farrell and Joyce L. Kornbluh released *Rocking the Boat: Union Women's Voices, 1915–1975,* which discusses the modern history of women in unionized environments, including the UMWA. That same year Randall Norris and photographer Jean-Philippe Cyprès released *Women of Coal* (1996), an oral history about the stereotypes facing female miners in the Appalachian region.

After the publication of *Women in the Mines,* researchers continued to release studies on women in mining. In 1997 Sally Springmeyer Zanjani published *A Mine of Her Own: Women Prospectors in the American West, 1850–1950,* which largely focuses on mining in Nevada and Alaska. Also that year, Mary Murphy released *Mining Cultures: Men, Women, and Leisure in Butte, 1914–41* (1997), which discusses the lives of families in a mining town and women's journey toward equality within the mines.

❖ Key Facts

Time Period:
20th Century

Relevant Historical Events:
Increased opportunity for women in mining; formation of the Coal Employment Project

Nationality:
American

Keywords:
mining; unionism; labor

Female coal miner, Colorado. Marat Moore drew upon her work in coal mines for *Women in the Mines: Stories of Life and Work*. © TYLER STABLEFORD/STONE/ GETTY IMAGES

THEMES AND STYLE

The central theme of *Women in the Mines* is the presentation of women miners as average people trying to make enough money to support their families—not as extreme feminists striving to prove their equality for academic principles. Moore states in her introduction, "By crossing mine portals into a high-wage, virtually all-male occupation, women expanded the horizons of non-traditional work in the wake of affirmative action mandates." The interview participants discuss the necessity of their decision to enter the mines. Elizabeth Zofchak Stevens recalls, "It was Depression time.... My father took me to work in the mine dressed up like a boy.... It made me feel good to know I could help the family." Likewise, Patricia Brown gives up her career as a preschool teacher for the wages of a coal miner: "Before, I was making $7,000 a year. Now I make $19,000." Brown explains her choice: "I went underground in 1980 because I wanted a better life for my children. I wanted them to go to college."

Moore's motivations for producing *Women in the Mines* stem from her experience as a coal miner and her desire to record the stories of female miners for future generations of women in male-dominated professions. To present a more complete picture of women working in coal mines, she documents the progression of women's rights within trade unions. In the preface, she writes, "Their story is part of a larger history of social upheaval created by the broad entry of women into the workforce of the United States in the last several decades."

The structure of *Women in the Mines* allows the interview participants to discuss their stories with minimal interference from the interviewer. Each woman has her own chapter, which begins with photographs and a brief biography. They tell their stories with minimal contextual interjection, separated by italics, from Moore. The chapters are organized into two chronological sections: "The Women before Us," which covers the first half of the twentieth century, and "The New Miners," which discusses modern mining issues such as unionization and legislation against discrimination. In each of the chapters, Moore maintains the voice of the speakers by recording their diction and grammar. Ethel Day Smith, for example, recalls how her father, "Daddy," paid no mind to her being a girl in the mines, while her mother was less enthusiastic: "My mother was kind of scary about us going in. Mother said many a time she would rather be in the mine than her children."

CRITICAL DISCUSSION

Women in the Mines received positive criticism for Moore's approach to oral history and her success in compiling interviews that both stand alone and function as a whole to create an overall account of the benefits and hardships of coal mining for women. Dana Frank, in her 1996 review for *Women's Review of Books,* calls the text "a fascinating window into the struggles of twenty-four women coal miners." Frank is particularly interested in the portrayal of the women themselves, who "didn't go after their jobs out of any abstract feminist principles or conscious desire to break down gender roles" but were drawn to "the lucrative stability of coal mining" versus "the meagerly paid irregularity of traditional women's employment."

Since its initial appearance, *Women in the Mines* has been lauded for accurately presenting the struggles of women miners without suffocating the text with academic analysis or overtly feminist propaganda. Professor Suzanne E. Tallichet's 1999 review for *NWSA Journal* praises Moore's "sophisticated brand of feminism" in which "men *in toto* are not the enemy; but those who unfairly assert patriarchal privilege in the forms of domestic violence, company control, sexual harassment, and opposition within the union 'family' are a threat to women's economic independence and, ultimately, their dignity." Tallichet suggests, "Academics would do well to emulate this work and its resulting authenticity."

Scholarship on *Women in the Mines* generally praises the author for compiling a beneficial resource for academics in many disciplines. In a 1998 review in *Labour,* Tom Johnson observes that the book "is one of a kind, in which coal miners and coalfield activists tell their stories, in their own voices, without the varnish (or interference) of academics or journalists." Tallichet notes, "By making the connection between private life experiences and public historical events, Moore has accomplished a primary sociological task, exposing the rich interaction between individuals and their participation in social institutions." Katharine Aiken in a 1999 article for *Oral History Review* compares *Women in the Mines* with other oral histories about women miners released in the 1990s: "Moore brings a different perspective to her *Women in the Mines*, as she worked as an underground miner herself" and was heavily involved with the UMWA and CEP. According to Aiken, this involvement adds to the authenticity of the work: "As an active participant in the Coal Employment Project, Marat was able to comment in depth on that organization's activities and interview other activists as well."

BIBLIOGRAPHY

Sources

Aiken, Katharine. Rev. of *Women in the Mines: Stories of Life and Work*, by Marat Moore. *Oral History Review* 26.1 (1999): 119. *Literature Resource Center*. Web. 17 Jan. 2013.

Frank, Dana. Rev. of *Women in the Mines: Stories of Life and Work*, by Marat Moore. *Women's Review of Books* Oct. 1996: 17. *Literature Resource Center*. Web. 17 Jan. 2013.

Johnson, Tom. Rev. of *Women in the Mines: Stories of Life and Work*, by Marat Moore. *Labour/Le Travail* 41 (1998): 299–300. Web. 17 Jan. 2013.

Moore, Marat. *Women in the Mines: Stories of Life and Work.* Twayne's Oral History Series 20. New York: Twayne, 1996. Print.

Tallichet, Suzanne E. Rev. of *Women in the Mines: Stories of Life and Work*, by Marat Moore. *NWSA Journal* 11.3 (1999): 202. *Literature Resource Center*. Web. 17 Jan. 2013.

Further Reading

Giesen, Carol A. B. *Coal Miners' Wives: Portraits of Endurance.* Lexington: University Press of Kentucky, 1995. Print.

Murphy, Mary. *Mining Cultures: Men, Women, and Leisure in Butte, 1914–41.* Urbana: University of Illinois Press, 1997. Print.

WOMEN HELPING WOMEN: THE COAL EMPLOYMENT PROJECT

Several laws and social advances facilitated the hiring of women by coal mining companies, including the 1963 Equal Pay Act, which classified women as a social class that deserved protection from job discrimination, and the 1964 Civil Rights Act. Perhaps the greatest source of support for female miners was a nonprofit women's organization founded by Betty Jean Hall: the Coal Employment Project (CEP). Hall, a lawyer, was working on a gender discrimination case for a group of Appalachian activists who had been denied work in a coal mine when she discovered U.S. Executive Order 11246, a directive passed in 1965 that banned all forms of gender discrimination within companies that held federal contracts, which included coal mining companies.

Hall's involvement in the lawsuit inspired her to establish CEP in 1977 in order to support female miners in their efforts to secure jobs, combat gender discrimination and sexual harassment, and educate themselves and their employers about women's rights in the workplace. The organization has been involved in activism alongside and in opposition to the United Mine Workers of America and remains active, publishing a regular newsletter and hosting conferences about issues facing miners with special workshops dedicated to sexual harassment and workplace safety.

Norris, Randall, and Jean-Philippe Cyprès. *Women of Coal.* Lexington: University Press of Kentucky, 1996. Print.

O'Farrell, Brigid, and Joyce L. Kornbluh, eds. *Rocking the Boat: Union Women's Voices, 1915–1975.* New Brunswick, N.J.: Rutgers University Press, 1996. Print.

Zanjani, Sally Springmeyer. *A Mine of Her Own: Women Prospectors in the American West, 1850–1950.* Lincoln: University of Nebraska Press, 1997. Print.

Katherine Barker

Workers of the Donbass Speak
Survival and Identity in the New Ukraine, 1989–1992
Lewis H. Siegelbaum, Daniel J. Walkowitz

❖ Key Facts

Time Period:
Late 20th Century

Relevant Historical Events:
Achievement of Ukrainian independence; fall of the Soviet Union; introduction of a market economy to Ukraine

Nationality:
Ukrainian

Keywords:
capitalism; communism; mining

OVERVIEW

Collected and edited by historians Lewis H. Siegelbaum and Daniel J. Walkowitz, *Workers of the Donbass Speak: Survival and Identity in the New Ukraine, 1989–1992* (1995) uses interviews to chronicle the changes within the mining community of eastern Ukraine after the country's 1991 declaration of independence from the Soviet Union. Originally conceived as a film project to be compared and contrasted to filmed interviews with steelworkers in Pittsburgh, the book is composed of interviews conducted throughout three trips to Ukraine the editors took in 1989, 1991, and 1992. Unlike many historical analyses of this period in Ukraine, the oral histories in *Workers of the Donbass Speak* allow members of the working class to tell their own stories.

Because the oral histories recorded in *Workers of the Donbass Speak* straddle the 1991 collapse of the Soviet Union, they can be taken as immediate evidence of the changes that occurred in the mining industry as felt by the workers. Unlike the years of Soviet-controlled communication with the Western world, in the late 1980s and early 1990s new freedoms allowed the subjects to speak on the record in frank terms about the effect of the late Soviet and immediate post-Soviet eras on the Ukrainian working class.

HISTORICAL AND LITERARY CONTEXT

The Donbass region of eastern Ukraine runs along the Don River basin and was an important area of coal mining vital to the Soviet economy for decades. As a result, this region was heavily affected by the shift from Soviet rule to independence. The interviews collected in *Workers of the Donbass Speak* showcase both old and new attitudes toward the Soviet regime. The first section of the book contains interviews with seven retired workers, all of whom grew up during Joseph Stalin's rule (circa 1922–1953). The retired workers express nostalgia for the stability of the past and apprehension for the unknowns of the present. Although the working conditions for miners were worse and miners suffered more injuries when Ukraine was under Soviet rule, the retired miners note that during that time prices were lower and that workers made sacrifices with a sense of pride and honor they feel does not exist among post-Soviet miners.

When, in the summer of 1989, Siegelbaum and Walkowitz arrived in Donetsk, Ukraine, to conduct interviews, they found that their subjects had much to say. By chance, their visit coincided with a union-wide miners' strike. In fact, Siegelbaum and Walkowitz ended up assisting in spreading the strike's slogan: "Perestroika from below." When the Soviet Union collapsed at the end of 1991, however, the miners faced new challenges, such as an unstable market economy and the communist pasts of their newly nationalist governmental officials. Rather than finding themselves in power after they worked toward communism's fall, the Ukrainian miners found that the political power of the elites had simply changed locations—from Moscow to Kiev, the capital of Ukraine.

According to the authors themselves, *Workers of the Donbass Speak* "originated in Pittsburgh, where a laid-off steelworker, Larry Evans, had produced a series of programs for local cable television based on interviews with his former workmates, many of whom had been prematurely 'retired' by mill closings." Intending to make an accompanying film of interviews with Ukrainian miners, Siegelbaum and Walkowitz traveled to Donetsk. The interviews from this first visit (some of which also appear in *Workers of the Donbass Speak*) are compiled in a one-hour documentary, *Perestroika from Below*, which was produced by Walkowitz and Barbara Abrash in collaboration with Siegelbaum.

An early contribution to the field of post-Soviet studies, *Workers of the Donbass Speak* retains its importance by intimately charting the political, cultural, and economic climates as demonstrated by the oral histories of Ukrainian miners. The oral histories found within *Workers of the Donbass Speak* serve as an excellent example of allowing history to be dictated not only by those in highly educated circles but also by members of the working class.

THEMES AND STYLE

The central themes of *Workers of the Donbass Speak* are the effects of the transition from Soviet rule to an independent Ukraine, current and past labor politics, and the self-expression of the working class. In the first section of the book, a miner states that in the past, "the union was more concerned with pleasing our higher authorities" than with the concerns of the

Ukraine coal miners in a pit cage come to the surface at Sots Donbass mine, in the eastern Ukrainian city of Donetsk, the coal capital of the Donbass. © MIKE GOLDWATER/ALAMY

miners. Despite this feeling, some of the older miners declare their nostalgia for the past. In one interview a retired steelworker acknowledges the current mixed feelings about the communist rule of Stalin but also maintains that in his generation "people connected his name with the annual reduction of prices for food and industrial goods. He meant a lot to us." In another interview a retired mining engineer comments on the political shifts as reflected in the ability to conduct the interview itself: "Who could imagine that I would have Americans in my place and talk with them? It was impossible under Stalin. You are the same people as we are."

As expressed by Walkowitz and Siegelbaum in the introduction, *Workers of the Donbass Speak* "presents the struggles and transformations of the years 1989–93 not through the carefully crafted and modulated words of politicians and intellectuals, but in the often rough, earnest cadences of working men and women in the eastern Ukrainian industrial city of Donetsk." Videotaped and conducted in Russian (the Donbass region of east Ukraine is a heavily Russian-speaking area), the original interviews were then taken to Moscow and New York, where they were transcribed and translated. According to Walkowitz and Siegelbaum, the interviews included in the book represent only about 10 percent of those actually conducted. The original interviews, including full sets of videotaped interviews and complete copies of the English and Russian versions, are archived at the University of Pittsburgh Library and the Institute for the Study of Employment in Moscow.

Workers of the Donbass Speak is split into three sections, each section representing a separate time and group of interviews. Interspersed between these interviews are analytical essays of the interview material by Siegelbaum, Walkowitz, and political historian Stephen Crowley. The interviews themselves contain plainspoken dialogue and lack the elevated, calculated language that the editors sought to avoid by concentrating most of the book's content on interviews with members of the working class. The essays, on the other hand, are written in a more academic tone and style. In their introduction, the editors make a point of not overstating the essays' importance, declaring them simply "examples of how scholars with different kinds of disciplinary training and expertise integrate the interview material with other kinds of data to identify patterns of attitudes and behavior."

CRITICAL DISCUSSION

Perhaps because of the then-recent nature of many of the events covered in *Workers of the Donbass Speak*, the initial reaction from critics focused mostly on the politics within the book as well as the perceived politics of its editors. In his 1996 review for *Labor History* Stephen Kotkin notes that "an entire industry seems to be slowly dying. Siegelbaum and Walkowitz express much sympathy, and a stronger sense of betrayal—directed at history itself—than their struggling proletarian subjects." Paul Flenley's 1998 review for *Labour History Review* also concentrates more on the book's political achievements than its literary value, noting

PITTSBURGH AND DONETSK: SISTER CITIES

Although the interviews within *Workers of the Donbass Speak* seek to tell the story of the Ukrainian mining community, the book also contains an analysis comparing the working class of post-Soviet Ukraine to that of the working class of de industrialized Pittsburgh. In his essay accompanying the third section of *Workers of the Donbass Speak*, Walkowitz sums up his comparative analysis of the two cities, noting that "images of American culture, stretching from Disneyland to Pittsburgh, fuel the social and political imagination" and calling Donetsk "the other Pittsburgh." Meanwhile, in the actual Pittsburgh, Larry Evans, the original inspiration for the interviews conducted by Siegelbaum and Walkowitz, continued his activism connected to the steel industry. Even before beginning the film project that would go on to inspire Siegelbaum and Walkowitz to give a voice to the miners in Donetsk, Evans organized the publication of the *Mill Hunk Herald*, a quarterly magazine. The *Mill Hunk Herald*, aimed at steelworkers as well as other members of the working class, had the unusual structure of letting its writers dictate its content and allowed its readers to vote on the format, price, and advertising policies. After the *Mill Hunk Herald* Evans went on to organize the *Northside Chronicle,* another publication focusing on the survival of the Pittsburgh community. Though their cities are across the world from one another, the working class of Donetsk and Pittsburgh have been given a voice by these interviews, films, and publications.

that "*Workers of the Donbass Speak* provides us with the opportunity to look at developments from below."

In the years after editing and collecting interviews for *Workers of the Donbass Speak,* both Siegelbaum and Walkowitz have gone on to publish more titles about similar subjects. Siegelbaum, a professor at Michigan State University, is also the editor of *Borders of Socialism: Private Spheres of Soviet Russia* (2006) and the author of *The Faustian Bargain of the Soviet Automobile* (2008) and *Cars for Comrades: The Life of the Soviet Automobile* (2008). Walkowitz, a professor at New York University, is the author of *Working with Class: Social Workers and the Politics of Middle-Class Identity* (1999). The legacy of *Workers of the Donbass Speak* exists within the continued and committed historical study of its editors.

Despite its position as an early contribution to the field of post-Soviet studies, *Workers of the Donbass Speak* has not been the recipient of more recent critical attention. Like the reviews focusing solely on *Workers of the Donbass Speak,* Michael Burawoy's 1997 analytical essay for the *American Journal of Sociology,* "The Soviet Dissent into Capitalism," concentrates on the book's politics by comparing it to the politics of other books about post-Soviet economies published in the same year. In summing up the merit of *Workers of the Donbass Speak,* Burawoy concludes that Siegelbaum and Walkowitz "describe the tragedy that has befallen the miners of the Donbass, their struggles for survival, and the identities they seek to forge, but they offer no solutions."

BIBLIOGRAPHY

Sources

Burawoy, Michael. "The Soviet Descent into Capitalism." *American Journal of Sociology* 102.5 (1997): 1430–44. JSTOR. Web. 14 Jan. 2013.

Flenley, Paul. Rev. of *Workers of the Donbass Speak: Survival and Identity in the New Ukraine, 1989–1992,* ed. Lewis. H. Siegelbaum and Daniel J. Walkowitz. *Labour History Review* 63.2 (1998): 241–43. *Academic Search Premier.* Web. 14 Jan. 2013.

Kotkin, Stephen. Rev. of *Workers of the Donbass Speak: Survival and Identity in the New Ukraine, 1989–1992,* ed. Lewis H. Siegelbaum and Daniel J. Walkowitz. *Labor History* 37.1 (1996): 145. *British Library Document Supply Centre Inside Serials & Conference Proceedings.* Web. 14 Jan. 2013.

Siegelbaum, Lewis H., and Daniel J. Walkowitz, eds. *Workers of the Donbass Speak: Survival and Identity in the New Ukraine, 1989–1992.* Albany: State University of New York Press, 1995. Print.

Further Reading

Aslund, Anders. *How Russia Became a Market Economy.* Washington, D.C.: Brookings Institution, 1995. Print.

Clarke, Simon, ed. *Management and Industry in Russia: Formal and Informal Relations in the Period of Transition.* Brookfield, Vt.: Ashgate, 1995. Print.

Filtzer, Donald A., et al., eds. *A Dream Deferred: New Studies in Russian and Soviet Labour History.* New York: Peter Lang, 2008. Print.

Siegelbaum, Lewis H., ed. *Borders of Socialism: Private Spheres of Soviet Russia.* New York: Palgrave Macmillan, 2006. Print.

———. *Cars for Comrades: The Life of the Soviet Automobile.* Ithaca, N.Y.: Cornell University Press, 2008. Print.

———. *The Faustian Bargain of the Soviet Automobile.* Trondheim: Norwegian University of Science and Technology, 2008. Print.

Siegelbaum, Lewis H., and Andrei Sokolov, eds. *Stalinism as a Way of Life: A Narrative in Documents.* New Haven, Conn.: Yale University Press, 2000. Print.

Walkowitz, Daniel J. *Working with Class: Social Workers and the Politics of Middle-Class Identity.* Chapel Hill: University of North Carolina Press, 1999. Print.

Jen Gann

WORKING

People Talk about What They Do All Day and How They Feel about What They Do

Louis "Studs" Terkel

OVERVIEW

Collected and edited by oral historian Louis "Studs" Terkel, *Working: People Talk about What They Do All Day and How They Feel about What They Do* (1974) presents firsthand accounts of the occupational experiences of ordinary Americans working in a variety of fields. Terkel, an experienced radio broadcaster, used his considerable skills as an interviewer to examine the causes of widespread malaise in the workplace. Quoting interviewee Nora Watson, he summarizes the theme of the narratives in his book: "I think most people are looking for a calling, not a job. Most of us, like the assembly line worker, have jobs that are too small for our spirit. Jobs are not big enough for people."

Working was published during a period of increased public awareness of the personal and social consequences of poor working conditions and unsatisfying work. Widely read and well reviewed by critics, *Working* was cheered as an expression of real voices plainly expressing the alienation felt by many forced to pass the lion's share of their waking hours in essentially meaningless activity. Notable as a historic record of the American worker in the second half of the twentieth century, the book, as part of Terkel's broader body of work, is also credited with popularizing the oral history genre.

HISTORICAL AND LITERARY CONTEXT

As the dust settled from World War II, the United States entered an unprecedented period of economic growth. National income nearly doubled in the 1950s, and again in the 1960s. The middle class had more disposable income than ever, and demand for goods and services rose. The labor pool also increased during this time as baby boomers, born between 1946 and 1964, came of age and an increasing number of women entered the workforce. In addition, secondary education was now compulsory, as children were no longer needed for farm labor. This increase in average educational attainment brought with it a shift in expectations about work. Moreover, the tumult of the civil rights and antiwar movements of the 1960s introduced a strain of thought into the public consciousness, which, if not overtly antiauthoritarian, was typified by a need to question the methods and purpose of established institutions such as work.

Working reflects these economic and social changes, as well as the changing nature of work itself, particularly as automation spread across industries. In 1971 General Motors began production of the Chevrolet Vega at its Lordstown, Ohio, facility. Workers expected to keep pace with a new one-hundred-cars-an-hour assembly line began to sabotage the cars and eventually launched a twenty-two-day strike, which is estimated to have cost the company $150 million. In important ways, these workers became emblematic of job dissatisfaction across the country. A growing awareness of this dissatisfaction, in turn, prompted a study by the U.S. Department of Health, Education, and Welfare, the findings of which were released in the 1973 *Work in America* report. The report confirmed the general sense that American workers felt alienated from an institution that many looked to for a source of meaning and status.

Terkel had produced several previous oral histories dealing with the social and economic concerns of everyday American citizens. *Division Street: America* (1967) presents the stories of a cross section of Chicagoans, discussing the trials and joys of daily life in their home city. *Division Street* was criticized by some as minimizing the darker aspects of people's lives, a charge Terkel largely avoided in his next history. *Hard Times: An Oral History of the Great Depression* (1970) hearkens back to the United States of the 1930s, comprising memories of the Depression from people of various classes.

Working was made into a Broadway musical that ran in 1978, and was later adapted for television, appearing in 1982 as part of the PBS *American Playhouse* series. Terkel's interest in preserving American experiences through oral history continued, and in 1984 he published *"The Good War": An Oral History of World War II*, which won the Pulitzer Prize for nonfiction. *Gig: Americans Talk about Their Jobs* (2000), compiled by John and Marisa Bowe, who credit *Working* as their model, brings Terkel's concept to bear on a new generation of workers facing twenty-first-century challenges.

❖ *Key Facts*

Time Period:
Mid- to Late 20th Century

Relevant Historical Events:
Post–World War II prosperity; baby boom; increased worker disaffection

Nationality:
American

Keywords:
labor; prosperity; disaffection

WORK AND FAMILY LIFE

Pulitzer Prize–winning author Studs Terkel talks with a taxi driver in Chicago in April 1978. © STEVE RAYMER/NATIONAL GEOGRAPHIC STOCK

THEMES AND STYLE

Central to *Working* is an almost universal search for meaning and a living in one's work. Both blue- and white-collar workers express a desire to take pride in their work and to be accorded respect. In these narratives, dissatisfaction results when job conditions prevent one or both of these things. Flight attendant Terry Mason laments, "They call us professional people, but they talk to us as very young … even though you've been flying twenty years they check you and say that's a no-no." Stonemason Carl Murray Bates remembers the previous generation who "knew their trade" and strove for smooth perfection. Comparing his era to the past he comments, "It's harder now … you have no way to use your tools … no way to use a level or a plumb." Still, Bates also takes pleasure in driving through towns to see the work he has done, calling it "immortality."

Terkel describes his job as an oral historian as "prospecting" and his gold, "the extraordinary dreams of ordinary people," which he seeks to record and share. As is common in oral histories, the questions posed in the interviews have been largely edited out of the narratives, which read as monologues. The narrative flow, however, suggests that Terkel, who is often praised for his listening ear, encouraged free association as perhaps the best means of procuring insights. Indeed he notes that on occasion, when he played back the interview tapes, his interviewee "murmured, 'I never realized I felt that way.'"

The language in *Working* reflects the diversity of backgrounds and personalities of its subjects, underlining the book's representation of the people of America. The book includes the down-home twang of farm woman Katherine Haynes, a self-described "flat old hillbilly"; the urban repartee of car hiker Alfred "Lovin' Al the Wizard" Pommelier; and the zany sales speak of car dealer Johnny Bosworth, who opines, "If you hit a person's logic you've got 'im. Unless you've got a ding-aling." Preserving the language of the various workers as they discuss their lives and work in some sense demonstrates Terkel taking pride in his own craft.

CRITICAL DISCUSSION

Working was heralded as timely and important when published, garnering mostly positive reviews. Typical was Marshall Berman's 1974 piece in the *New York Times*, which lauded the book as "full of luminous moments" and possessing "a very special electricity and emotional power." Berman's praise is slightly tempered by his suggestion that Terkel could have used a finer focus to give "some sort of structure and coherence to the marvelous material."

Working was studied extensively in high schools as a piece of literature and as a source of information about particular occupations and the inner lives of those who practiced them. In a 1976 review in the *English Journal,* educator Thomas Smith notes its utility "as a model in developing a communication skill that is too often neglected in the English classroom—the personal interview." Use of the text in high schools was not without controversy, however, as some parents and administrators objected to the profanity in several of the narratives. Although much of the career-related material in *Working* is now outdated, the book continues to be regarded as a valuable record of social and economic conditions in the United States in the mid- to late twentieth century and is often included in American studies curricula. Terkel is also widely credited with popularizing oral history and paving the way for such contemporary projects as StoryCorps.

In the decades since it appeared, scholars have analyzed Terkel's methods as an oral historian in *Working*. In a 1976 article in *Journal of General Education,* Dorothy Deering responds to what she characterizes as criticism of Terkel's nonscientific methods of sampling and lack of critical analysis: "The primary value of Terkel's book is the direct access it provides to the dynamic voices of American men and women who are capable of speaking for themselves and in the process composing the history of our era." In *Doing Oral History* (2003), Donald Ritchie explores the qualities that have made Terkel an exceptionally successful interviewer. Quoting Terkel, Ritchie concludes, "For Studs Terkel, the trick to interviewing successfully is 'engaging in conversation, having a cup of coffee.'"

BIBLIOGRAPHY

Sources

Berman, Marshall. "Everybody Who's Nobody and the Nobody Who's Everybody" Rev. of *Working: People Talk about What They Do All Day and How They Feel about What They Do,* by Studs Terkel. *New York Times.* New York Times, 24 Mar. 1974. Web. 31 Jan. 2013.

Bowe, John, and Marisa Bowe, eds. *Gig: Americans Talk about Their Jobs.* New York: Three Rivers, 2001. Print.

Deering, Dorothy. "Egalitarian History in Studs Terkel's *Working.*" *Journal of General Education* 28.2 (1976): 103–13. *JSTOR.* Web. 31 Jan. 2013.

Ritchie, Donald. *Doing Oral History: A Practical Guide.* Oxford, UK: Oxford University Press, 2003. Print.

GIG: AMERICANS TALK ABOUT THEIR JOBS

Edited by John and Marisa Bowe, *Gig: Americans Talk about Their Jobs* is something of a twenty-first century update to Terkel's *Working: People Talk about What They Do All Day and How They Feel about What They Do* by self-proclaimed fans of Studs Terkel. Comprising 120 narratives, *Gig* describes a variety of new professions, including Wal-Mart greeter, food stylist, art mover, corporate headhunter, and long-haul trucker. *Gig* also includes a few narratives by celebrities, including film producer Jerry Bruckheimer and model Heidi Klum.

Gig began its life as the column "Work" in the Webzine *Word*. The content of the book includes previously published interviews and new material collected throughout the country. Like Terkel, the editors of *Gig* profess a desire to let the stories of the individuals they interviewed speak for themselves. Many of the workers interviewed for *Gig,* like those in *Working,* search for meaning in their work. Steelworker Denise Barber says, "This job is no more meaningful than any other job except it means something to me." Echoing the words of Terkel's steelworker Mike Lefevre, who considers himself "a dying breed," Barber encourages her children to go to college rather than follow her into the mill. "Jobs like this are disappearing," she says. "The best real ones are going to be gone."

Smith, Thomas. Rev. of *Working: People Talk about What They Do All Day and How They Feel about What They Do,* by Studs Terkel. *English Journal* 65.1 (1976): 69–70. *JSTOR.* Web. 31 Jan. 2013.

Terkel, Studs. *Working: People Talk about What They Do All Day and How They Feel about What They Do.* New York: Pantheon, 1974. Print.

Further Reading

Abrams, Lynn. *Oral History Theory.* New York: Routledge, 2010. Print.

Isay, David, ed. *Listening Is an Act of Love: A Celebration of American Life from the StoryCorps Project.* New York: Penguin, 2007. Print.

Terkel, Studs. *Division Street: America.* New York: Avon, 1967. Print.

———. *"The Good War": An Oral History of World War II.* New York: Pantheon, 1984. Print.

———. *Hard Times: An Oral History of the Great Depression.* New York: Pantheon, 1970. Print.

Daisy Gard

Subject Index

Italic page numbers indicate illustrations. **Bold** page numbers and titles refer to main articles.

A

AAC. *See* Army Air Corps
Aaron, Daniel, **2:**271
Abandoned Baobab, The (Bugul), **1:61–64**
Abandonment, Bugul (Ken) on experience of, **1:**61–62
a/b: Auto/Biography Studies (journal), **1:**246
Abbey, Edward, *Desert Solitaire*, **1:**234
Abbey Theatre (Dublin), **2:**126, 128
Abbott, Lyman, **1:**52
Abdel-Fattah, Randa, *Does My Head Look Big in This?*, **1:**41–42
Abdo, Diya M., **3:**49
Abdul Hamid (Ottoman sultan), **2:**106
"Able-bodied," social construction of concept, **1:**8
Abolition, of slavery
    in Britain and British colonies, **1:**34, 81, 111, **3:**23
    in Cuba, **3:**7
    in U.S., **1:**33, 50
Abolitionist movement
    Adams (John Quincy) in, **2:**70
    in Britain, **1:**81–83, 111, **3:**23
    Douglass (Frederick) in, **1:**33
    Equiano (Olaudah) in, **1:**81–83
    Grimké (Charlotte Forten) in, **2:**29
    Higginson (Thomas Wentworth) in, **2:**238
    Jacobs (Harriet A.) in, **1:**142
    James (Henry) in, **2:**113
    Kemble (Fanny) in, **2:**335
    origins and rise of, **1:**142
    Prince (Mary) in, **3:**23, 25
    Ruete's (Emily) critique of, **1:**92
    "tragic mulatto" tradition in literature of, **1:**72
    in U.S. South vs. North, **1:**33
    Wheatley (Phillis) invoked in, **2:**45
Abootalebi, Ali R., **3:**220
Aboriginal Land Rights Act of 1976 (Australia), **3:**334
Aborigines, Australian
    Unaipon (David) on life as, **1:**149–151
    women, oral histories of, **3:**334–336
Aborigines' Friends' Association (AFA), **1:**149, 150, 151
Aborigines' Progressive Association, **1:**150
Abortion, in *A Mountainous Journey* (Tuqan), **1:**226, 227
About, Edmund, *Germaine*, **2:**115
Abouzeid, Leila, **3:**49
Abraham, Peter, **3:**251
Abraham Lincoln: A History (Nicolay and Hay), **3:**261–262
Abraham Lincoln: A Life (Burlingame), **3:**264
Abraham Lincoln: Complete Works (Nicolay and Hay), **3:**262
Abrams, Lynn
    A History of Everyday Life in Twentieth Century Scotland, **3:**173, 175
    Myth and Materiality in a Woman's World, **3:**175
    Oral History Theory, **3:173–175**, 179, 181, 285
    on *Women and Families* (Roberts), **3:**146
Abrash, Barbara, **3:**340
Abudi, Dalya, **1:**227
Abu Ghraib prison (Iraq), **3:**231
Account of Corsica (Boswell), **2:**328
Acculturation, in U.S., **1:**15–17. *See also* Assimilation
Accuracy. *See* Truth
Acebey, David, **3:**322
Achebe, Chinua, **1:**214
Acheson, Katherine O., **2:**64
Acker, Kathy, **1:**249
Acting career, of Kemble (Fanny), **2:**335–337
Actions, in identity, Rousseau (Jean-Jacques) on, **1:**200, 201
Acton, Carol, **2:**260, 261
Acts and Monuments, The (Day), **2:**97
Acts of Conscience (Taylor), **3:**227
Adamovich, Ales, **3:**282, 285
Adams, Abigail, **2:87**
    Adams's (John) correspondence with, **2:**316
    family of, **1:**133, **2:**69
    Letters of Mrs. Adams, **2:**87, 89
    "Letter to Her Daughter from the New White House," **2:87–90**

347

SUBJECT INDEX

Adams, Ansel, **3:**102
Adams, Charles Francis, **1:**132, **2:**69, 87, 89
Adams, Henry
  The Education of Henry Adams, **1:**15, **132–134,** 180
  Mont-Saint-Michel and Chartres, **1:**132
Adams, John, **1:**132, **2:**69, 87, 316
Adams, John Quincy, **2:**70
  The Diary of John Quincy Adams, **2:69–71**
  family of, **1:**132, *133*
  Kemble's (Fanny) friendship with, **2:**335
Adams, Judith Porter, *Peacework,* **3:268–271**
Adams, Lauren, **2:**296
Adams, Marian, **1:**133
Adams, Percy, **2:**206
Adams, Timothy, **1:**124
Adams, Timothy Dow, **1:**165
Adler, Nanci, **3:**19
Adolescents
  as audience for *Go Ask Alice* (anonymous), **2:**294–296
  as audience for *Red Scarf Girl* (Jiang), **1:**161, 162
  drug use by, **2:**294–296
Adopted Territory (Kim), **1:**102–103
Adoption
  interracial/intercultural, **1:**102–104
  tradition of memoirs of, **1:**102
Adventures of Huckleberry Finn (Twain), **1:**146, 147–148
Advice
  in *The Autobiography of Ben Franklin* (Franklin), **1:**179
  in *Letters to a Young Poet* (Rilke), **2:**149–150
  in *Walden* (Thoreau), **1:**234
Aesthetics, Ruskin's (John) writings on, **1:**264
AFA. *See* Aborigines' Friends' Association
Afejuku, Tony, **3:**253
Affirmative action, in U.S.
  establishment and purpose of, **1:**15

Rodriguez's (Richard) critique of, **1:**15, 16
  state bans on, **3:**20
Afghanistan
  Ahmedi (Farah) on life in, **1:**40–42
  Soviet war in, **1:**40, **3:**233
  Taliban in, rise of, **1:**40
  U.S. war in, **1:**42, **3:**207, 233
AFL. *See* American Federation of Labor
Africa. *See also specific countries*
  autobiographical tradition of, **1:**64
  borders in, establishment of, **1:**114
  colonial (*See* Africa, colonialism in)
  feminist autobiographies from, **1:**64
  Haley's (Alex) travels in, **1:**262
  idealization of, by Laye (Camara), **1:**130
  négritude movement in, **1:**61
  non–Africans' collaboration with authors of, **1:**64
  oral traditions of, **1:**64, **2:**242
  trauma literature of, **1:**313–314
  trickster stories of, **2:**3
Africa, colonialism in. *See also specific countries*
  Bugul (Ken) on legacy of, **1:**61–64
  cultural impacts of, **3:**141
  end of, **1:**3, 61
  in interior of continent, **3:**37
  Lessing (Doris) on experience of, **1:**167–169
  Nigerian Civil War and, **1:**215
  origins of, **1:**61, **3:**141, 251
Africa, Thomas W., **1:**221
African, The (Courlander), **1:**262
African American(s)
  citizenship for, **1:**50, **2:**38, 238
  in Civil War regiments, **2:238–240,** *239*
  communism among, **1:**3–5
  discrimination against (*See* Civil rights movement; Racism)
  family life of, **1:**273–275
  folklore of, **1:**9
  genealogy of, **1:**261–263
  in Great Depression, **3:**99
  Great Migration of, **1:**50, 52, 84, 273, **3:**99

in interracial relationships, **1:**72–74
  Islam among, **1:**186–188
  lynchings of, **1:**18, 50
  masking tradition of, **1:**144
  in Reconstruction era, **1:**50
  as slaves (*See* Slave(s))
  in theater, rise of, **1:**273
  in Vietnam War, **3:**199–201
  voting rights for, **1:**50, **2:**238
  women (*See* African American women)
  in World War II, **3:**248–250
African American autobiographical writing. *See also* Slave narratives; *specific works and writers*
  by Angelou (Maya), **1:**18–20
  by Du Bois (W. E. B.), **1:**3–5
  by Grimké (Charlotte Forten), **2:**29–31
  by Haley (Alex), **1:**261–263
  by Hansberry (Lorraine), **1:**273–275
  by hooks (bell), **1:**249–251
  by Hurston (Zora Neale), **1:**9–11
  by King (Martin Luther, Jr.), **2:**32–34
  by Lorde (Audre), **2:**3–5
  by Malcolm X, **1:**186–188
  by McBride (James), **1:**72–74
  by McKay (Claude), **1:**84–86
  by Obama (Barack), **1:**78–80
  by Parks (Rosa), **1:**37–39
  as staple of African American literature, **1:**37
  tradition of, **3:**23–24
  by Wheatley (Phillis), **2:**44–46
  by Wright (Richard), **1:**122–124
African American identity. *See also* Multicultural and multiracial identities
  vs. feminist identity, of women, **2:**3
  Haley (Alex) on, **1:**261–263
  Obama (Barack) on, **1:**78–80
African American oral histories
  of civil rights movement, **3:**44–46, 99–101
  of Coe Ridge colony, **3:**90–92
  of Detroit, **3:**99–101

of higher education at white colleges, **3:**20–22

of Tuskegee Airmen, **3:**248–250

of Vietnam War veterans, **3:**199–201

African American Review (journal), **1:**250, **2:**5

African American women

Angelou (Maya) on lives of, **1:**18–19

in feminism, **1:**249, 250, **2:**3, 5

feminist vs. black identity of, **2:**3

hooks (bell) on lives of, **1:**249–250

as slaves, Jacobs (Harriet A.) on lives of, **1:**34, 35

African National Congress (ANC)

AIDS epidemic and, **3:**272, 274

establishment of, **2:**241

Luthuli (Albert) in, **1:**24, 25

Mandela (Nelson) in, **1:**27, 28, 29, **3:**242

Plaatje (Solomon Tshekisho) in, **2:**241

Africans in America (television miniseries), **3:**45

African Studies (journal), **3:**243

African Studies Review (journal), **3:**259

Africa Remembered (Curtin), **3:**141

Africa Today (journal), **1:**25, 115, **3:**142, 252

Afrikaners, **1:**27, **2:**241, **3:**242

Afro-American Studies (journal), **1:**187

Age (journal), **1:**48

Agenda (journal), **1:**39

Age of Illusion, The (Blythe), **3:**61

Agnew, Christopher S., **3:**126

Agosín, Marjorie

Always from Somewhere Else, **1:**75

A Cross and a Star, **1:**75–77, 99

Uncertain Travelers, **1:**75

Agrarian ideology, **2:**215

Agrarian reform movement, in Mexico, **3:**302–304

Agrarista movement, **3:**302–304

Agriculture, in England, oral histories of life in, **3:**59–61, 63–65

AHA Foundation, **1:**209

Ahimsa, **1:**243, 244

Ahmedi, Farah, *The Story of My Life,* **1:40–42,** 41

Ahn Doo-hee, **1:**322

AIDS

emergence of, **3:**85

in South Africa, **1:**29, **3:**272–274

in U.S., **3:**85

AIDS Doctors (Oppenheimer and Bayer), **3:**272, 273, 274

Aiken, Katharine, **3:**339

AIM. *See* American Indian Movement

Ain't I a Woman (hooks), **1:**250

Airline industry, arbitration in, **3:154**

Ai Weiwei, **3:**301

Akazawa, Dennis, **3:**85

Akenfield: Portrait of an English Village (Blythe), **3:59–62**

Akharbach, Latifa, *Femmes et Politique,* **3:**47

Akhtar, Aasim Sajjad, **3:**178

Akiga's Story (East), **3:**141

Akiyama, Itsu, **3:**81

Alabama, Montgomery bus boycott in, **1:**20, 37, 38, 39, **2:**32, **3:**44, 45

Alan Paton Prize, for *Country of My Skull* (Krog), **3:**243

Albert (prince consort), **2:**209, 210

Alberti, Rafael, **1:**222

Alcatraz Island (San Francisco), AIM occupation of, **1:**54

Alcohol

in Appalachia, **3:**90, 91

in Idaho, **3:**95

Alcott, Amos Bronson, **1:**235

Alcott, Louisa May, **2:**223

Alexander, Elizabeth, **2:**4

Alexander, Harriet, **2:**340

Alexander, John, **1:**150, 151

Alexander, Margaret Walker, *Jubilee,* **1:**262

Alexander II (tsar of Russia), **1:**193, 195

Alexander the Great, **1:**105, 218

Alexandra Feodorovna, *The Last Diary of Tsaritsa Alexandra,* **2:84–86,** 85

Alexievich, Svetlana

Boys in Zinc, **3:**285

Voices from Chernobyl, **3:**265, **282–286**

Alexis, Phil, **3:**108

Alexius Comnenus, **1:**285

Alger, Derek, **1:**297

Algeria

Amrouche (Fadhma Aïth Mansour) on life in, **1:**93–95

Feraoun (Mouloud) on life in, **2:**262–264

French colonial rule of, **1:**93–94, **2:**262–264

postcolonial, challenges facing, **2:**262

War of Independence in, **1:**93, **2:**262–264, *263*

Algerian War of Independence (1954–1962), **1:**93, **2:**262–264, *263*

Ali, Muhammad, **3:**44

Alienation

of Agosín (Marjorie), **1:**75

of American workers, **3:**343

of Amrouche (Fadhma Aïth Mansour), **1:**93–94

of Bugul (Ken), **1:**61–62

of Conrad (Joseph), **2:**192, 193

of Kim (Elizabeth), **1:**103

of Laye (Camara), **1:**128, 129

of Obama (Barack), **1:**78

of Ruete (Emily), **1:**90

of Santiago (Esmeralda), **1:**108–110

Alien Land Law of 1913 (California), **3:**195

ALIS. *See* Association du Locked-in Syndrome

All Change Here (Mitchison), **2:**235

Allen, Brooke, **2:**73

Allen, Harley, **3:**159

Allen, Hope Emily, **1:**191

Allen, Prudence, **2:**162

Allen, Roger, **1:**137

Allen, William Sheridan, *The Nazi Seizure of Power,* **3:**245

Allende, Isabel, **1:**76

Paula, **1:**222

Allende, Salvador, **1:**222, *223*

All God's Dangers (Rosengarten), **3:**73, 179

Allison, A. Lynn, **3:**290

Allison, Fred H., **3:**211

SUBJECT INDEX

Almayer's Folly (Conrad), **2:**192
Almost a Woman (Santiago), **1:**108, 109
Along Freedom Road (Cecelski), **3:**21
Along This Way (Johnson), **1:**13, 84, 122
Alonso, Harriet Hyman, **3:**270
'Alqam, Nabil, **2:**106
Alta California, oral histories of, **3:**114–116, *115*
Alter, Robert, **1:**272
Alternative Service Program, **3:**229
Alvarez, Julia, *How the Garcia Girls Lost Their Accents,* **1:**108
Alvarez-Borland, Isabel, **1:**297
Always a People (Kohn and Montell), **3:107–109,** 325
Always from Somewhere Else (Agosín), **1:**75
Al-Windawi, Mouayad, **2:**276
Al-Windawi, Thura, *Thura's Diary,* **2:275–277**
Amado, Jorge, **2:**8
Amador, José María, **3:**114–116
Amalric, Mathieu, **1:**7
Amanpour, Christiane, **2:**278
Ambrose, **1:**196, 197
Amerasian Immigration Act of 1982 (U.S.), **1:**170
America (journal), **2:**56, **3:**46, 309
America, Columbus's (Christopher) discovery of, **2:**201–203
American Anthropologist (journal), **3:**81, 142, 168, 320, 324
American Anti-Slavery Society, **1:**33, 142
American Arbitration Association, **3:**154
American autobiographical writing. *See also* African American(s); Asian American(s); Native American(s); *specific works and writers*
    by Adams (Abigail), **2:**87–90
    by Adams (Henry), **1:**132–134
    by Adams (John Quincy), **2:**69–71
    by Bechdel (Alison), **1:**139–141
    by Buck (Lucy), **2:**271–273
    by Carver (Jonathan), **2:**205–207
    by Chesnut (Mary Boykin Miller), **2:**250–252

    by Condict (Jemima), **2:**78–80
    by Conroy (Frank), **1:**164–166
    by Crèvecoeur (Michel-Guillaume Saint-Jean de), **2:**213–215
    by Dillard (Annie), **1:**279–281
    by Emerson (Ralph Waldo), **2:**139–141
    by Franklin (Benjamin), **1:**179–182
    by Gellhorn (Martha), **2:**101–103
    by Hawthorne (Nathaniel), **2:**223–225
    by Higginson (Thomas Wentworth), **2:**238–240
    by Houston (James D.), **1:**299–301
    by James (Henry), **2:**113–115
    by Jefferson (Thomas), **2:**316–318
    by Keller (Helen), **1:**43–46
    by Lee (Robert E.), **2:**38–40
    by McCarthy (Mary), **1:**258–260
    by McCourt (Frank), **1:**119–121
    by Medina (Pablo), **1:**296–298
    by Moore (Molly), **2:**278–280
    by Nabokov (Vladimir), **1:**270–272
    by Nin (Anaïs), **2:**123–125
    by O'Connor (Flannery), **2:**129–131
    by Olney (James), **1:**246–248
    by Plath (Sylvia), **2:**47–49
    by Poe (Edgar Allan), **2:**41–43
    by Rodriguez (Richard), **1:**15–17
    by Rowlandson (Mary), **1:**325–328
    by Santiago (Esmeralda), **1:**108–110
    by Sinor (Jennifer), **2:**163–165
    by Stanton (Elizabeth Cady), **1:**12–14
    by Stein (Gertrude), **1:**332–334
    by Stewart (Elinore Pruitt), **2:**91–93
    by Stone (Kate), **2:**244–246
    by Styron (William), **1:**204–206
    by Thoreau (Henry David), **1:**233–236
    by Twain (Mark), **1:**146–148
    by Ulrich (Laurel Thatcher), **2:**331–333

    by Wiesel (Elie), **1:**318–320
    by Williams (Tennessee), **2:**152–154
    by Wolff (Tobias), **1:**47–49
American Book Award
    for *Lakota Woman* (Brave Bird), **1:**23
    for *Sophie's Choice* (Styron), **1:**204
    for *The Unknown Internment* (Fox), **3:**225
American Cancer Society, **2:**3–4
American Childhood, An (Dillard), **1:**279
American Civil War (1861–1865)
    African American soldiers in, **2:**238–240, *239*
    Buck (Lucy) on life in South during, **2:**271–273
    Chesnut (Mary Boykin Miller) on life in South during, **2:**250–252
    conscientious objectors in, **3:**223
    diaries kept during, **2:**244, 271
    Douglass (Frederick) in, **1:**33
    Lee (Robert E.) in, **2:**38, 39–40
    Lincoln (Abraham) in, **3:**261
    slavery as issue in, **1:**50, **2:**38, 250
    start of, **2:**250, **3:**261
    Stone (Kate) on life in South during, **2:**244–246
American Dream
    Franklin (Benjamin) and, **1:**180
    Hispanic Americans' pursuit of, **3:**121, 122
    homesteading and, **2:**91
    Siv (Sichan) on, **1:**306, 307, 308
American Dreams (Terkel), **3:**300
American Ethnologist (journal), **3:**142
American Experience, The (television show), **3:**45
American Federation of Labor (AFL), **3:**328
American Historical Review (journal)
    on *Doña María's Story* (James), **3:**75
    on *The First Agraristas* (Craig), **3:**303
    on *Freedom Flyers* (Moye), **3:**249
    on *Hooligans or Rebels?* (Humphries), **3:**311

on *Survivors* (Miller and Miller), **3:**42

on *The Voice of the Past* (Thompson), **3:**188

on *Women in the Chinese Enlightenment* (Wang), **3:**148

American Indian Movement (AIM)
Brave Bird (Mary) in, **1:**21–23
FBI in conflicts with, **1:**96
occupation of Alcatraz by, **1:**54
occupation of Wounded Knee by, **1:**21, 22–23, 96
origins of, **1:**21, 54
Peltier (Leonard) in, **1:**96–98

American Indians. *See* Native American(s)

American Journal of Sociology, **3:**342

American Leaders in Nursing (Safeir), **3:**170

American Literary History (journal), **1:**173, **2:**4

American literature
disability studies on, **1:**8
realism in, rise of, **2:**240

American Mercury (journal), **2:**184

American Music (journal), **3:**133

American Notes (Dickens), **1:**43, 146, **2:**223

American oral histories. *See also* African American oral histories; Native American oral histories
of anarchists, **3:**3–5
of Appalachians, **3:**66–69, 86–89, 90–92
of coal miners, **3:**66–69, 96–98, 337–339
of colonial Californians, **3:**114–116
of draft resisters, **3:**221–223
of gay Asian Americans, **3:**83–85
on Great Depression, **3:**161–163
of Hispanic Americans, **3:**121–123, 131–133
of Idaho homesteaders, **3:**93–95
of Iraq War veterans, **3:**231–233
of Italian Americans, **3:**224–226
of IWW members, **3:**328–330
of Japanese American internees, **3:**80–81, 102–104, 195–198

of Japanese immigrants, first-generation, **3:**80–82
of Japanese war brides, **3:**127–130, *128*
of Jewish Americans, **3:**118–120
of labor arbitrators, **3:**153–155
of Lincoln (Abraham), **3:**261–264
of Los Alamos residents, **3:**239–241
of Mexican Americans, **3:**131–134
of nuns, **3:**308–310
of Nuremberg trial participants, **3:**293–295
origins of field, **3:**186
of Owens Valley residents, **3:**102–104
recognition of value of, **3:**20, 90
of teachers, **3:**77–79
of Tuskegee Airmen, **3:**248–250
on Vietnam War, **3:**199–201, 209–211, 221–223, 275–277
on war on poverty, **3:**254–256
of women coal miners, **3:**337–339
of women immigrants, **3:**305–307, *306*
of women peace activists, **3:**268–271
on workers' experiences, **3:**343–345
on World War II, **3:**202–204, 212–214, 224–226, 248–250

American Prospect (magazine), **1:**209

American Quarterly, **1:**71

American Revolutionary War (1775–1783)
Adams (John Quincy) on, **2:**69
autobiographies of era of, **1:**179–180
Condict (Jemima) on life during, **2:**78–80
conscientious objectors in, **3:**223
Crèvecoeur (Michel-Guillaume Saint-Jean de) on, **2:**213, 214
end of, **2:**69
Franklin (Benjamin) on, **1:**179
socioeconomic role of women after, **2:**331–332
start of, **2:**69
Wheatley's (Phillis) views on, **2:**44, 45

American Scholar (journal), **1:**280

"American Scholar, The" (Emerson), **1:**180

American Slave, The (Rawick), **1:**35

American Slavery as It Is (Weld), **1:**33, 142

American Sociological Review (journal), **3:**320

American Spectator (magazine), **1:**307

American Splendor (Pekar), **1:**139, **3:**330

American Studies (journal), **1:**35

American Theater (journal), **3:**213

American Transcendental Quarterly, **2:**141

American Woman Suffrage Association, **1:**12

American women. *See also* African American women
as coal miners, oral histories of, **3:**337–339
colonial, autobiographical writing by, **2:**78–79
education of, in eighteenth century, **2:**316–318
gender roles of, eighteenth-century, **2:**316
gender roles of, twentieth-century, **2:**47
as immigrants, oral histories of, **3:**305–307
Mexican American, oral histories of, **3:**131–133
as nuns, oral histories of, **3:**308–310
after Revolutionary War, socioeconomic role of, **2:**331–332
as teachers, oral histories of, **3:**77–79
in women's rights movement, **1:**12–14, **2:**47

Americas (journal), **3:**116

America's Invisible Gulags (Fox), **3:**226

AmeriCorps, **3:**254

Amerika (Kafka), **2:**120

Améry, Jean, **1:**318

Amidist Buddhism, **2:**59

Amistad (film), **2:**71

Amistad case, **2:**70, 71

Amman, John, *Black Man's Grave*, **1**:312

Ammonds, Edith, **2**:91

Ammonds, Ida Mary, **2**:91

Among You Taking Notes (Mitchison), **2**:235–237

'Amr, Sa'di, **2**:104

'Amr, Sāmī, *A Young Palestinian's Diary*, **2**:104–106

Amritsar (India), massacre of 1919 in, **1**:242, 289

Amrouche, Fadhma Aïth Mansour, *My Life Story*, **1**:93–95

Amrouche, Jean, **1**:93, 94, 95

Amrouche, Taos (Mary-Louise), **1**:94
- *Jacinthe Noir*, **1**:93
- in *My Life Story* (Amrouche), **1**:93, 94, 95

Analytical Review (journal), **1**:82

Anarchism, in U.S., **3**:3–5

Anarchist Voices (Avrich), **3**:3–6

ANC. *See* African National Congress

An Ch'ang-ho, **1**:324

Andersen, Hans Christian, **2**:166

Andersen, Hendrik C., **2**:115

Anderson, Helen, **2**:60

Anderson, John Lee, **2**:220

Anderson, John Q., **2**:244

Anderson, Nan, **3**:92

Anderson, Stuart, **3**:170, 171

Anderson, Thomas P., **3**:207

Anderson, W. E. K., **2**:310, 311

And Justice for All (Tateishi), **3**:195–198, 224

Andonian, Aram, *The Memoirs of Naim Bey*, **3**:40

Andreas, Friedrich, **2**:151

Andreas-Salomé, Lou, **2**:149, 151

Andrew, Donna T., **2**:330

Angela's Ashes (McCourt), **1**:119–121

Angelico, Fra, **1**:197

Angelou, Maya, **1**:19
- *I Know Why the Caged Bird Sings*, **1**:18–20, 249
- "On the Pulse of the Morning," **1**:20
- *A Song Flung Up to Heaven*, **1**:18
- in tradition of Prince (Mary), **3**:24
- Wolff (Tobias) compared to, **1**:47

Anglia (journal), **1**:121

Anglicanism
- *Book of Common Prayer* in, **2**:98
- Edward VI in, **2**:97–99
- in English Civil War, **2**:26, 72, 256
- establishment of, **2**:72
- Methodism's rise and, **2**:195
- vs. Puritanism, **2**:26, 27
- rise of, **2**:97–98
- in slavery, **3**:23
- Wesley (John) in, **2**:195–196
- Woodforde (James) as clergyman in, **2**:287–289, *288*

Anglo–Boer War (1899–1902), **2**:241–243, *242*

Anglo–German Agreement (1890), **1**:114

Anglo-Iranian Oil Company, **3**:218

Anglorum Speculum, **2**:63–64

Angoff, Charles, **2**:184–185

Animal Farm (Orwell), **2**:117, *118*

Anisfield-Wolf Book Award
- for *The Autobiography of Malcolm X* (Malcolm X), **1**:186
- for *The Color of Water* (McBride), **1**:73
- for *Dust Tracks on a Road* (Hurston), **1**:9
- for *Maasai* (Beckwith and Saitoti), **1**:114

Aniwaya, Anigia Gltodi, **3**:326

Anna Karenina (Tolstoy), **1**:193

Annals of Ballitore, The (Leadbeater), **2**:157–159

Annals of the American Academy of Political and Social Science, **1**:291, **2**:7, 17, **3**:252

Anna of the Five Towns (Bennett), **2**:136

Anne Frank: The Diary of a Young Girl (Frank). *See Diary of Anne Frank, The* (Frank)

Anne of Denmark, **2**:62

Annie's Baby (Sparks), **2**:294

An Phoblacht (newspaper), **3**:316

Ansary, Tamim, **1**:40

Anselment, Raymond, **2**:258

Antelope's Strategy, The (Hatzfeld), **3**:258

Anthony, Joseph, **2**:261

Anthony, Susan B., **1**:12, 13

Anthropology
- in Africa, rise of, **3**:37
- Hurston's (Zora Neale) work in, **1**:9, 11
- Underhill's (Ruth) success in, **1**:70
- *The Worlds of a Maasai Warrior* (Saitoti) in, **1**:115

Antiautobiography
- *Autobiography: Essays Theoretical and Critical* (Olney) on, **1**:246, 247
- *Roland Barthes* (Barthes) as, **1**:268–269

Anticolonialism
- of Gandhi (Mohandas), **1**:242–244, 289
- of Nehru (Jawaharlal), **1**:289–291

Anti-Confucianism, **3**:124, 126

Antimiscegenation laws, U.S., **1**:72

Antioch Review (journal), **1**:124, **2**:221

Antiquarianism, **2**:177, 179

Antiretroviral therapy (ART), **3**:272, 273, 274

Anti-Semitism. *See also* Holocaust
- in Chile, Agosín (Marjorie) on, **1**:75
- in Germany, of Hitler (Adolf), **1**:31–32
- in Germany, Stein (Gertrude) on, **1**:333
- in Great Depression, **3**:118

Antiwar views. *See also* Pacifism; Peace activists
- of Sassoon (Siegfried), **2**:247, 248
- in *Strange Ground* (Maurer), **3**:275
- during Vietnam War, **3**:221, 222, 275, 277

Antoon, Sinan, **1**:255, 257

Antwerp (Belgium), Cavendish's (Margaret) exile in, **1**:229

ANZAC. *See* Australian and New Zealand Army Corp

"ANZAC Memories" (Thomson), **3**:177, 178

Anzaldúa, Gloria, *Borderlands/The Fontera*, **1**:56

Apache, Geronimo on, **1:**302–304
Apartheid, South African
    AIDS epidemic and, **3:**272
    end of, **1:**25, **3:**242
    establishment of, **1:**24, 27, **3:**242
    Luthuli (Albert) on, **1:**24–26
    Mandela (Nelson) on, **1:**27–29
    Truth and Reconciliation Commission on, **3:**242–244
Apess, William, *A Son of the Forest,* **1:**56, **3:**318
A/PLG. *See* Asian Pacific Lesbians and Gays
Apologia Pro Vita Sua (Newman), **1:**65
Appalachian Journal, **3:**92
Appalachian oral histories
    of African Americans of Coe Ridge, **3:**90–92
    of coal miners, **3:**66–69, 86, 87, *87, 91,* 96–98
    on culture, **3:**86–89
Appalachian Oral History Project, **3:**86–88
Appalachian stereotypes, **3:**68, 86, 96
Applegate, Wash, **3:**95
Apted, Michael, **3:**53
Aptheker, Herbert, **1:**3, 4
Apuleius of Madaura, *The Golden Ass,* **1:**198
Aquash, Mi'kmaq Anna Mae, **1:**98
Arab, Si Abderrahmane, **2:**262
Arab(s), racial profiling of, **3:**195, 197
Arabic autobiographical writing. *See also specific works and writers*
    by Al-Windawi (Thura), **2:**275–277
    by 'Amr (Sāmī), **2:**104–106
    by Darwish (Mahmoud), **1:**255–257
    by Ghazzawi ('Izzat), **2:**50–52
    by Hussein (Taha), **1:**135–137
    by Ruete (Emily), **1:**90–92
    tradition of, **1:**135–136, 137, 285, **2:**50
    by Tuqan (Fadwa), **1:**225–227
    by Usāmah ibn Munqidh, **1:**285–288
    by women, rise of, **1:**225–226

Arab–Israeli War (1967), **1:**225
Arab Revolt (1936–1939), **1:**227, **2:**104
Arab slavery, **1:**90, 92
Arab Studies Journal, **1:**287
Arab-Syrian Gentleman and Warrior in the Period of the Crusades, An (Usamah), **1:**285–288
Arafat, Yasser, **2:**50
Aragon, Louis, **2:**52
Arbitration, labor
    vs. mediation, **3:**155
    oral histories on development of, **3:**153–155
Arcadia (Stoppard), **2:**145
Archambault, Paul, **1:**183, 184
Archdiocese of Guatemala, **1:**99
Archer, W. H., **2:**191
Arctic (journal), **3:**139
Arctic Dreams (Lopez), **1:**279
Arden, Jane, **2:**109
ARENA. *See* National Republican Alliance
Arendt, Hannah, **2:**22, 121
Arethas of Caesarea, **1:**220
Are You My Mother? (Bechdel), **1:**140, 141
Argentina
    coup of 1943 in, **2:**220, **3:**73
    Guevara (Ernesto "Che") in, **2:**220–222
    Jews in, **1:**75
    labor movement in, oral histories of, **3:**73–75
    Peronism in, **3:**73–75
Arias, Arturo, **3:**165
Ariel (Plath), **2:**47
Aristocracy
    Chinese, **3:**124, 125
    French, **2:**306–307
    Japanese, **2:**297
Aristotle, **2:**96
Arizona
    coal mining in, **3:**11, 292
    Mexican American women in, oral histories of, **3:**131–133
    Navajo–Hopi land dispute in, oral histories of, **3:**10–12

Arizona Quarterly, **1:**281, **3:**201
Arkansas, Angelou (Maya) on life in, **1:**18
Arkansas Historical Quarterly, **3:**197
Arkin, Mark, **2:**337
Armed Forces & Society (journal), **3:**207
Armenian genocide, oral histories of, **3:**40–42, *41*
Armitage, Susan, **3:**191–192
Armstrong, Liahna, **2:**163, 164
Army Air Corps (AAC), U.S., Tuskegee Airmen in, **3:**248–250
Army Life in a Black Regiment (Higginson), **2:**238–240
Arnett, Edward, **3:**229
Arnold, Matthew, **1:**181, **2:**147
Arntzen, Sonja, **2:**297, 298, 299
Arranged marriage
    in China, **1:**153, 154, 338, 339, **2:**170
    in Montenegro, **3:**136, 137
ART. *See* Antiretroviral therapy
Art, of Bashkirtseff (Marie), **2:**306, *307,* 308
Art criticism, by Ruskin (John), **1:**264, 265
Arthur, Chester, **3:**10
Arthur, Emry, **3:**159
Arthur Ruppin (Ruppin), **2:**104
Arvin, Newton, **2:**114–115
Asa-Asa, Louis, **3:**24
Ascham, Roger, **2:**99
Ascherson, Neal, **2:**102
Ashkenazic Jews, **3:**118, 119
Ashmore, Susan Youngblood, *Carry It On,* **3:**254
Ashton, Susanna, **1:**52
Asia, Polo's (Marco) travels in, **1:**105–107. *See also* Southeast Asia; *specific countries*
Asian Affairs (journal), **1:**307
Asian American(s). *See also* Japanese American(s)
    gay, oral histories of, **3:**83–85, *84*
    racism against, **1:**103, 171
    stereotypes of, **1:**173, 174

SUBJECT INDEX

Asian American autobiographical writing. *See also specific works and writers*
    by Hayslip (Le Ly), **1:**335–337
    by Houston (Jeanne Wakatsuki), **1:**299–301
    by Kim (Elizabeth), **1:**102–104
    by Kingston (Maxine Hong), **1:**173–175
    by Min (Anchee), **1:**158–160
    by Nguyen (Kien), **1:**170–172
    by Siv (Sichan), **1:**306–308
    by Uchida (Yoshiko), **1:**309–311

Asian Pacific Lesbians and Gays (A/PLG), **3:**83, 84, 85
Asian Review of Books, **3:**16
Asian Studies Review (journal), **3:**148
As I Crossed a Bridge of Dreams (Sarashina), **2:189–191**, 290–291
Asisara, Lorenzo, **3:**114–116
Ask the Fellows Who Cut the Hay (Evans), **3:**59, **63–65**
Asleson, David, *Up the Swiftwater,* **3:**93
Assassination
    of Kennedy (John F.), **3:**254
    of Kim Ku, **1:**322
    of King (Martin Luther, Jr.), **1:**20
    of Lincoln (Abraham), **2:**246, **3:**261
    of Malcolm X, **1:**186, 188
Assimilation, in Australia, of Aborigines, **1:**149, 151, **3:**334
Assimilation, in U.S.
    of Japanese war brides, **3:**127
    of Native Americans, **3:**109
    oral histories of, **3:**305–307
    of refugees, **1:**307
    Rodriguez (Richard) on experience of, **1:**15–17
    Santiago (Esmeralda) on experience of, **1:**108
Association du Locked-in Syndrome (ALIS), **1:**7
Astell, Mary, *A Serious Proposal to the Ladies,* **2:**35
"As-told-to" accounts, of Native Americans, **1:**56
Atheism, of Darwin (Charles), **1:**65–67
Atlanta Compromise Address (Washington), **1:**50

Atlantic (magazine), **2:**335, **3:**61
Atlantic Monthly (magazine)
    Army Life in a Black Regiment (Higginson) in, **2:**238, 239–240
    Hawthorne's (Nathaniel) letters in, **2:**224
    Letters of a Woman Homesteader (Stewart) in, **2:**91, 92
    "Life in the Sea Islands" (Grimké) in, **2:**31
    Life on the Mississippi (Twain) in, **1:**146, 147
    on *The Story of My Life* (Keller), **1:**44
Atlantis (journal), **2:**131
Atom Boy (Osamu), **1:**293
Atomic weapons. *See* Nuclear weapons
At the Edge of the Abyss (Koker), **2:**253
"At the Home of Frederick Douglass" (Grimké), **2:**29
Audacity of Hope, The (Obama), **1:**78, 80
Auden, W. H., **1:**125, 276, **2:**147, 150
Audience
    adolescent, of *Go Ask Alice* (anonymous), **2:**294
    adolescent, of *Red Scarf Girl* (Jiang), **1:**161, 162
    authors' pact with, Lejeune (Philippe) on, **1:**239–240, **2:**174
    construction of memoirs to appeal to, **1:**164
    of *De Profundis* (Wilde), **2:**10
    European, of *Letters from an American Farmer* (Crèvecoeur), **2:**213, 214
    European, of *The Autobiography of Ben Franklin* (Franklin), **1:**181
    of letters, **2:**217
    white (*See* White audience)
    of *The Woman Warrior* (Kingston), **1:**174, 175
Audio adaptations, of *Dreams from My Father* (Obama), **1:**80
Augustine (saint), **1:197**
    City of God, **1:**198
    Confessions, **1:**183, 193, **196–199**, 201
    Dialogues, **1:**186

An Interrupted Life (Hillesum) on, **2:**22, 24
    Malcolm X compared to, **1:**186, 188
    Olney (James) on, **1:**248
    Retractions, **1:**196, 198
    Soliloquies, **1:**196
    Teresa of Ávila influenced by, **1:**211
Augustus (Roman emperor), **1:**218, 220
"Auld Robin Gray" (Barnard), **2:**217, 218
Auschwitz and After (Delbo), **3:**34
Auschwitz concentration camp, **1:**318–320, **2:**22, **3:35**, 51
Ausgabe, Kritische, **2:**120
Auslander, Shalom, **2:**255
Aus Meinem Leben (Goethe). *See Truth and Fiction Relating to My Life* (Goethe)
Austen, Jane, **2:**133, 287, 289, 312
Auster, Paul, *The Invention of Loneliness,* **1:**279
Austin, Kelly, **1:**223
Australasian Journal of American Studies, **2:**30
Australia
    Aborigines of, **1:**149–151, **3:**334–336
    British colonial rule of, **1:**149
    Unaipon (David) on life in, **1:**149–151
    Vietnamese refugees in, **1:**337
    Warlpiri people of, oral histories of, **3:**334–336
    in World War I, **3:**177
Australian and New Zealand Army Corp (ANZAC), **3:**177
Australian Journal of French Studies, **2:**81
Australian Journal of International Affairs, **3:**207
Austria
    Jewish immigration to China from, **3:**14–16
    Satrapi (Marjane) in, **1:**155, 156
Authenticity. *See also* Truth
    of *Black Boy* (Wright), **1:**124

of *Memories of a Catholic Girlhood* (McCarthy), **1:**260

of *The Sovereignty and Goodness of God* (Rowlandson), **1:**326

of *A Woman in Berlin* (anonymous), **2:**282

Author(s)

autobiography's relationship to, Barthes (Roland) on, **1:**267–268

in pact with audience, Lejeune (Philippe) on, **1:**239–240, **2:**174

Authority, shared, in oral histories, **3:**179–181, 190

Authorship

of *Chona* (Chona and Underhill), **1:**69

of *Go Ask Alice* (anonymous), **2:**294

of *Incidents in the Life of a Slave Girl* (Jacobs), **1:**144

of *Journal of the First Voyage to America* (Columbus), **2:**201, 203

of *Left Handed, Son of Old Man Hat* (Dyk), **3:**318, 319, 320

meaning of, Barthes (Roland) on, **1:**267–269

of *Mein Kampf* (Hitler), **1:**30, 32

of oral histories, **3:**179

of slave narratives, **1:**82–83

Autobiographical Pact, The (Lejeune), **1:239–241**

Autobiographical studies

Barthes (Roland) in, **1:**267–269

D'Israeli (Isaac) in, **2:**177–179

Lejeune (Philippe) in, **1:**239–240, **2:**174–175

Olney (James) in, **1:**246–248

origins and rise of, **1:**239–240, 246–248, **2:**174

Autobiography. *See also specific types and works*

author's relationship to, Barthes (Roland) on, **1:**267–268

definition of, **1:**239

literary criticism as form of, **1:**247

vs. memoir, **1:**248, 279

origins and rise of, **1:**239, 246

rules for genre of, **1:**239, 246

Autobiography (Mill), **2:**16

Autobiography (Oliphant), **2:**335

Autobiography (Thornton), **1:**230

Autobiography, 1743–1790 (Jefferson), **1:**179, **2:**69

Autobiography, An, or The Story of My Experiments with Truth (Gandhi), **1:24, 242–245**

Autobiography, An, with Musings on Recent Events in India (Nehru), **1:289–292**

Autobiography and Postmodernism (journal), **1:**167

Autobiography: Essays Theoretical and Critical (Olney), **1:246–248,** *247*

Autobiography in France (Lejeune), **1:**239, **2:**174

Autobiography of a Chinese Woman (Chao), **1:**338

Autobiography of Alice B. Toklas, The (Stein), **1:**332, 334

Autobiography of an Unknown Indian (Chaudhuri), **3:**251, 253

Autobiography of a Papago Woman, The (Underhill), **3:**318

Autobiography of a Runaway Slave (Barnet and Montejo). *See Biography of a Runaway Slave* (Barnet and Montejo)

Autobiography of a Schizophrenic Girl, The (Sechehaye), **1:**164

Autobiography of a Slave, The (Manzano), **3:**7

Autobiography of Ben Franklin, The (Franklin), **1:179–182, 2:213**

Autobiography of Benjamin Rush (Rush), **1:179–180**

Autobiography of Charles Darwin, The (Darwin), **1:65–68**

Autobiography of Giambattista Vico, The (Vico), **1:183–185**

Autobiography of H.I.H. Soraya, The (Esfandiary), **3:**218

Autobiography of Malcolm X, The (Malcolm X), **1:78, 186–188, 3:44**

Autobiography of W. E. B. Du Bois, The (Du Bois), **1:3–5,** 18

Autobiography of William Butler Yeats, The (Yeats), **2:**127–128

Autoethnography

Dust Tracks on a Road (Hurston) as, **1:**11

Memoirs of an Arabian Princess from Zanzibar (Ruete) as, **1:**91

The Way to Rainy Mountain (Momaday) as, **1:**55

Automobile industry

automation of, **3:**343

in Detroit, **3:**99, 100, 101

Auyero, Javier, *Contentious Lives,* **3:**268

Avant-garde memoirs

Bone Black (hooks) as, **1:**249

The Diary of Anaïs Nin (Nin) as, **2:**123

Stop-Time (Conroy) as, **1:**164

Avary, Myrta Lockett, **2:**250, 251

Aventure ambiguë, L' (Kane), **1:**61

Avery, Genevieve, **3:**94

Avery, Oral, **3:**94

Aviation, U.S.

naval, oral histories of, **3:**202–204

Tuskegee Airmen in, oral histories of, **3:**248–250

Avrich, Karen, **3:**3

Avrich, Paul

Anarchist Voices, **3:3–6**

Sasha and Emma, **3:**3

Awards, book. *See also* Nobel prizes

for *Abraham Lincoln: A Life* (Burlingame), **3:**264

for *Akenfield* (Blythe), **3:**59

for *Angela's Ashes* (McCourt), **1:**120

for *The Audacity of Hope* (Obama), **1:**80

for *The Autobiography of Malcolm X* (Malcolm X), **1:**186

for *The Barracks Thief* (Wolff), **1:**47

for *The Cancer Journals* (Lorde), **2:**5

for *The Color of Water* (McBride), **1:**73

for *The Confessions of Nat Turner* (Styron), **1:**204

for *Country of My Skull* (Krog), **3:**243

for *The Dark Child* (Laye), **1:**128

for *Dreams from My Father* (Obama), **1:**80

for *Dust Tracks on a Road* (Hurston), **1:**9

for *The Education of Henry Adams* (Adams), **1:**132, 134

SUBJECT INDEX

Awards, book, *continued*
    for "The Good War" (Terkel), **3:**161, 212, 234, 279, 343
    for *House Made of Dawn* (Momaday), **1:**54
    for *The Invisible Thread* (Uchida), **1:**309–310
    for *Lakota Woman* (Brave Bird), **1:**23
    for *Letters Underway* (Ghazzawi), **2:**50
    for *A Long Way Gone* (Beah), **1:**313
    for *Maasai* (Beckwith and Saitoti), **1:**114
    for *Memory and Narrative* (Olney), **1:**248
    for *An Oral History of Abraham Lincoln* (Burlingame), **3:**261
    for *The Order Has Been Carried Out* (Portelli), **3:**265, 267
    for *Pilgrim at Tinker Creek* (Dillard), **1:**279
    for *Red Scarf Girl* (Jiang), **1:**161
    for *Riwan ou le chemin de sable* (Bugul), **1:**64
    for *Roots* (Haley), **1:**261
    for *Sophie's Choice* (Styron), **1:**204
    for *Thura's Diary* (Al-Windawi), **2:**275
    for *The Unknown Internment* (Fox), **3:**225
    for *Voices from Chernobyl* (Alexievich), **3:**282
    for *Wild Swans* (Chang), **1:**159
    for *The Woman Warrior* (Kingston), **1:**173
Axelrod, Steven Gould, **2:**48–49
Axford, Roger W., *Too Long Been Silent*, **3:**196
Ayres, Lew, **3:228**
Ayyam, al- (Hussein). *See Egyptian Childhood, An* (Hussein)
Ayyam al-'Arab, **1:**137
Azuma, Eiichiro, **3:**82

B

B., David, *Epileptic*, **1:**155
Baath party (Iraq), **2:**275, 276

Baba of Karo (Smith), **3:**141
Baby boomers
    drug use by, **2:**294
    Mexican American, **3:**133
    Soviet, oral histories of, **3:**331–333
    in workforce, **3:**343
Baby Doll (film), **2:**152
Back Bay Banner (periodical), **1:**274
Back in the World (Wolff), **1:**47
Bacon, Francis, **2:**66
Badenhausen, Richard, **1:**331
Baden-Powell, Robert, **2:**243
Bad War, The (Willenson), **3:**275
Baer, Allison, **1:**41–42
Baer, Elizabeth, **2:**271, 272, 273
Baer, Elizabeth R., **3:**36
Baez, Joan, **3:**159
Bagehot, Walter, **2:**35, 36
Baggett, Paul, "Caught between Homes," **1:**113
Baghdad (Iraq)
    in Iraq War, **2:**275–276, **3:**231
    Jewish immigration to China from, **3:**16
Baghdad Burning (Riverbend), **2:**275
Baghdad Burning II (Riverbend), **2:**275
Bagnold, Enid
    Brittain (Vera) compared to, **1:**329, **2:**259
    The Chalk Garden, **2:**259, 261
    The Chinese Prime Minister, **2:**261
    A Diary without Dates, **1:**329, **2:**259–261
    The Happy Foreigner, **2:**259
    National Velvet, **2:**259, 260, 261
    Sassoon (Siegfried) compared to, **2:**247
Bahr, Howard, *The Navajo as Seen by the Franciscans*, **3:**290
Bailer, Kermit G., **3:**100
Bailey, Kevin, **3:187**
Bailey, Peter J., **1:**48
Baillie, F. D., **2:**241
Bai Wei, *Tragic Life*, **1:**338
Baker, Alison, *Voices of Resistance*, **3:47–49**
Baker, Donald M., **3:**256
Baker, Felicity, **1:**202

Baker, Godfrey Evan, **2:**229
Baker, Ida, **2:**133
Baker, James T., **3:**162
Baker, Mark, *Nam*, **3:**199, 209, 210, 221, 231
Baker, Simon, **1:**126
Baker, William Massing, **2:**229
Bakgatla tribe, **2:**237
Bakhtiar, Shapour, **3:**220
Bakunin, Mikhail, **2:**120
Balaban, John, **3:**222
Balch, J. S., **1:**85
Baldick, Robert, **2:**81, 83
Baldwin, James
    Go Tell It on the Mountain, **1:**167, 261
    Notes of a Native Son, **1:**79–80
    on *To Be Young, Gifted and Black* (Hansberry), **1:**274
    Wright's (Richard) influence on, **1:**122, 124
Baldwin, Roger, **3:**329
Baldwin, William, **2:**99
Balkan Wars (1912–1913), **3:**135, 293, 294
Ball, Dewi Ioan, *Fighting Words*, **1:**97
Ballad of Reading Gaol, The (Wilde), **2:**9
Ballantyne, James, **2:**310
Ballard, Ephraim, **2:**333
Ballard, George, **1:**231
Ballard, Martha, **2:**331–333
Ballard, Molly, **3:**92
Ballent, Anahi, **3:**75
Ballet, inspired by Unaipon (David), **1:**149
Bampfield, Joseph, **1:**315, 316
Bancroft, Hubert H., **3:**114, 116
Banerjee, A., **2:**153
Bangarra Dance Theatre, **3:335**
Bangladesh, establishment of, **1:**87
Banjo (McKay), **1:**86
Banks, Ann, *First Person America*, **3:**161
Banks, Dennis, **1:**23
Banta, Martha, **2:**115
Bánzer, Hugo, **3:**322
Baobab fou, Le (Bugul). *See Abandoned Baobab, The* (Bugul)
Barbalet, Margaret, **3:**313

Barber, Denise, **3**:345
Barberini, Francesco, **1**:220
Barefoot Gen (Nakazawa), **1:293–295**
Barker, Eileen, **3**:41
Barker, Pat, **2**:248
Barlow, Joel, **2**:109
Barlow, Nora, **1**:67
Barmé, Geremie, **3**:288
Barnard, Anne, **2:218**
    "Auld Robin Gray," **2**:217, 218
    Journal of a Tour into the Interior, **2**:217, 218
    The Letters of Lady Anne Barnard to Henry Dundas, **2:217–219**
Barnes, Djuna, **1**:333
Barnes, Steven A., **3**:19
Barnet, Miguel, *Biography of a Runaway Slave*, **3:7**, 7–9
Barnouw, Dagmar, **1**:248
Barracks Thief, The (Wolff), **1**:47
Barre, Mohamed Siad, **1**:207
Barrel of a Pen (Ngũgĩ), **2**:12
Barrett, S. M., *Geronimo: His Own Story*, **1:302–305**
Barrio Boy (Galarza), **1**:15
Barrios de Chungara, Domitila
    Here Too, Domitila, **3**:322
    Let Me Speak!, **3**:74, **114–115**, **322–324**
Barry, Tom, *Guerilla Days in Ireland*, **3**:27
Barth, Karl, **2**:167
Barthes, Roland, **1:268**
    "The Death of the Author," **1**:267, 269
    Michelet par lui-même, **1**:267
    Roland Barthes, **1**:249, **267–269**
Bartlett, Rosamund, **1**:194, 195
Bashkirtseff, Marie
    The Journal of Marie Bashkirtseff, **2:306–308**
    The Last Confessions of Marie Bashkirtseff, **2**:306
    paintings of, **2**:306, *307,* 308
Baskin, John, *New Burlington*, **3**:86
Basler, Roy Prentice, *Collected Works of Abraham Lincoln*, **3**:262
Bass, Jonathan S., **2**:33–34
Bastien-Lepage, Jules, **2**:306

Bataille, Gretchen, **1**:23
Batchelor, Joy, **2:118**
Bates, Carl Murray, **3**:344
Bates, Edwin Morris, **2**:317
Batista, Ernesto, **2**:222
Batista, Fulgencio, **1**:296, *297*
Battlefields (television series), **3**:236
Battle of Valle Giula, The (Portelli), **3**:97, 157
Bauby, Jean-Dominique, *The Diving Bell and the Butterfly*, **1:6–8**
Baum, Geraldine, **2**:339
Baum, Oskar, **2**:120
Baum, Willa, **3**:188
Bauman, Janine, **3**:51
Baumel, Judith, *Double Jeopardy*, **3**:35
Baumgartner, Barbara, **3**:24–25
Bautista, Paul, **3**:85
Bawer, Bruce, **1**:280
Bayer, Ronald
    AIDS Doctors, **3**:272, 273, 274
    Shattered Dreams?, **3:272–274**
Beagle, H.M.S., **1**:65, 66
Beah, Ishmael, *A Long Way Gone*, **1:312–314**, *313*
Beamon, Mike, **3**:211
Bean, Thomas W., **2**:276
Bearden, Russell, **3**:197
Beatrice (princess), **2**:210
Beatty-Medina, Charles, *Contested Territories*, **3**:326
Beauchamp, Kathleen Mansfield. *See* Mansfield, Katherine
Beauchamp, Leslie, **2**:133, 135
Beaudry, Catherine, **1**:202
Bechdel, Alison
    Are You My Mother?, **1**:140, 141
    Dykes to Watch Out For, **1**:139, 141
    Fun Home, **1:139–141**, *140*
Bechdel, Bruce, **1**:139, 140
Bechdel test, **1**:141
Becker, Marshall Joseph, **3**:109
Beckham, Edward, **2**:27
Beckwith, Carol, *Maasai*, **1**:114
Becoming Madame Mao (Min), **1**:159
Bede, **3**:186
Bedoukian, Kerop, *The Urchin*, **3**:40
Beebe, Rose Marie

The History of Alta California, **3**:115
Testimonios, **3**:116
Beer and Revolution (Goyens), **3**:5
Beerbohm, Max, **1**:253, **2**:289
Beer brewing, in English villages, **3**:64
Beer Hall Putsch (1923), **1**:30
Beevor, Anthony, **2**:281, 282
Begging to Be Black (Krog), **3**:242
Begin, Menachem, **1**:225
Behar, Ruth
    on *Songs My Mother Sang to Me* (Preciado Martin), **3**:133
    Traveling Heavy, **1**:297
Behind the Burqa (Yasgur), **1**:40
Behind the Scenes (Keckley), **1**:52
Behn, Aphra, **1**:315, **2**:324
Beier, Lucinda McCray, *For Their Own Good*, **3**:144–145
Beik, Mildred Allen, **3**:67, 68, 95
Beineix, Jacques, **1**:6, 7
Beirne, Paul, **1**:324
Belarus
    censorship in, **3**:282–284
    Chernobyl nuclear disaster and, **3**:282–284
Belgium
    Bugul's (Ken) experience as African in, **1**:61–62
    Cavendish's (Margaret) exile in, **1**:229
    Congo as colony of, **2**:192–194
    Rwanda as colony of, **3**:257
    women miners in, **3**:337
Bell, Angelica, **2**:268
Bell, Anne Olivier, **2**:181–182
Bell, Clive, **2**:268
Bell, Ian, **1**:202
Bell, Vanessa, **2**:268
Bellanca, Mary Ellen, **2**:301
Belles Lettres (journal), **1**:280
Bell Jar, The (Plath), **2**:47
Bells of Nagasaki, The (Nagai), **1**:293
Beloved Land (Preciado Martin), **3**:131
Beltrán, Alberto, **3**:167
Benally, Malcolm D., *Bitter Water*, **3:10–13**
Benderman, Kevin, **3**:229

SUBJECT INDEX

Benét, William Rose, **2:**185
Bengal
    British colonial rule of, **2:**328, **3:**253
    Mahomet (Dean) in, **2:**229–231
    religious riots of 1946 in, **1:**244
Bengali Girls Don't (Sherman), **1:**312
Bennett, Andrew, **2:**134
Bennett, Arnold, **2:137**
    Anna of the Five Towns, **2:**136
    Clayhanger trilogy, **2:**136, 137
    Hilda Lessways, **2:**138
    The Journals of Arnold Bennett, **2:136–138**
    Letters of Arnold Bennett, **2:**138
    A Man from the North, **2:**136
    The Old Wives' Tale, **2:**136
    Woolf (Virginia) on novels of, **2:**137, 138
Bennett, James, **3:**311–312, 313
Bennett, John, *Uqalurait*, **3:**107, **138–140**
Bennett, W. C., **3:**320
Bennett, Yvonne, **1:**331
Bentham, Jeremy, **2:**177
Benyon, Hew, **3:**54
Berber Academy, **1:**93
Berber culture
    in Morocco, **3:**47
    preservation of, **1:**93–95
Berber Dahir, **3:**47
Beresford, John, **2:**287
Bergen, Doris, **2:**24
Bergen-Belsen concentration camp, **2:**253, **3:**51
Bergin, Thomas Goddard, **1:**183, 184, 185
Bergreen, Laurence, **2:**203
Berisso (Argentina), oral history of life in, **3:**73–75
Berkeljon, Sara, **1:**207
Berkowitz, Leah, **2:**273
Berlin (Germany)
    Soviet occupation of, **2:**281–282
    Spandau prison in, **2:**54–56, 55
Berlin, Isaiah, **1:**185
Berlin Wall, fall of, **3:**247
Berman, Marshall, **3:**344–345

Bermuda, oral histories of slavery in, **3:**23, 23–25
Bernard, Gretchen Dobrott, **2:**131
Berne, Suzanne, **1:**280
Bernstein, Gail Eiseman, **3:**119
Bernstein, Irving, **3:**154
Berridge, Virginia, **3:**170, 171
Bertaux, Daniel, *Living through the Soviet System*, **3:**331
Bertraux-Wiame, Isabelle, **3:**188
Best, Nicholas, *Five Days That Shocked the World*, **3:**235
Beston, John, **1:**150–151
Beti, Mongo, **1:**130
Betts, Paul, **3:**247
Between Management and Labor (Friedman), **3:153–156,** 157
Bevan, Nye, **2:**235
Beverley, John, **3:**74
Beyond Manzanar (Houston), **1:**299
Bhabha, Homi, **1:**87
BIA. *See* Bureau of Indian Affairs
Biafran War, **1:**312
Biblical references
    in *Confessions* (Augustine), **1:**196
    in *An Interrupted Life* (Hillesum), **2:**22
    in *Jemima Condict* (Condict), **2:**79
    in *The Sovereignty and Goodness of God* (Rowlandson), **1:**326
    in *The Story of My Life* (Keller), **1:**44
Bicknell, Alexander, **2:**207
Biddle, Francis, **3:**224
Biel, Steven, **3:**4, 5
Bierce, Ambrose, **2:**240
Bigelow, John, **1:**179, 181
Biggs, Henry, **3:**99
Big Sea, The (Hughes), **1:**84, 122
Big Woods (Faulkner), **2:**215
Bilbo, Theodore, **1:**123
Bildungsroman, **1:**30, **2:**221
Bilingual education, in U.S., **1:**15–17
Bilingual Education Act of 1968 (U.S.), **1:**17
Billington, Ray Allen, **2:**29
Bingham, Caleb, *The Columbian Orator*, **1:**33–34
Binoche, Juliette, **3:**242

Biographies, origins and rise of, **2:**177, 178
Biography (journal), **1:**205, 290, **2:**77, 175, **3:**73, 233
Biography of a Runaway Slave (Barnet and Montejo), **3:7–9**
Biomythography, *Zami* (Lorde) as, **1:**9, 39, 249
Bioy Casares, Adolfo, *Rest for Travelers*, **1:**223
Biracial individuals. *See* Multiracial individuals
Bird, Stewart, *Solidarity Forever*, **3:328–330**
Bird by Bird (Lamott), **1:**280
Birley, Anthony, **1:**220
Birmingham News (newspaper), **2:**32
Birrell, Augustine, **2:**126
Bishop, Elizabeth, **2:**129
Bisisu, Mu'in, **2:**52
    Palestinian Notebooks, **2:**50
Bisky, Jens, **2:**281
Bismarck, Otto von, **1:**90
Bitsui, Roman, **3:**12
Bitter Water (Benally), **3:10–13**
Black (color), hooks (bell) on meanings of, **1:**250
Black Americans. *See* African American(s)
Black Bolshevik (Haywood), **1:**4
Black Boy (Wright), **1:122–124**
Black Chronicle, The (Hampton), **3:**44
Black Collegian (journal), **1:**250
Black Cuban, Black American (Grillo), **1:**296
Black Elk, Benjamin, **3:**110
Black Elk, Nicolas, *Black Elk Speaks*, **1:**21, 56, 302, **3:110–113,** *111*, 318
Black Elk Speaks (Black Elk and Neihardt), **1:**21, 56, 302, **3:110–113,** 318
Blackest Page in Modern History, The (Gibbons), **3:**40
Black Flame trilogy (Du Bois), **1:**5
Blackgoat, Roberta, **3:**292
Black Hawk, **1:**302
Black Hawk War (1832), **1:**302
"Black History, Oral History, and Genealogy" (Haley), **3:**186

Black identity. *See* African American identity
Black Man's Grave (Stewart and Amman), **1**:312
Black Mesa (Arizona)
    coal mining on, **3**:10, 292
    Navajo–Hopi land dispute in, oral histories of, **3**:10–12
Black Muslims, **1**:186, 188
Black nationalism
    of Du Bois (W. E. B.), **1**:4
    of Malcolm X, **1**:78
    Obama's (Barack) rejection of, **1**:78, 79
Black Panthers, **3**:200
Black Power movement, **1**:21
Blacks at Harvard (Sollors et al.), **3**:21
Black Unicorn, The (Lorde), **2**:4
Blackwood's Edinburgh Magazine, **3**:25
Blackwood's Magazine, **1**:316
Black Words, White Page (Shoemaker), **1**:150, 151
Black Worker in the Deep South (Hudson), **1**:3
Blaeser, Kimberly, **1**:56
Blair, Dorothy S., **1**:93, 94, 95
Blair, Hugh, **2**:109
Blair, Walter, **1**:148
Blake, Debra J., **3**:132, 133
Blake, Lillie Devereux, **2**:89
Blalock, Lucy Sadie Parks, **3**:108
Blaxhall (England), oral histories of life in, **3**:63–65
Blayney, Michael, **1**:262
Blessed by Thunder (Fernández Barrios), **1**:296
Blight, David W., **3**:266–267
Blindness
    of Hussein (Taha), **1**:135, 136, 137
    Keller (Helen) on experience of, **1**:43–46
Blithedale Romance, The (Hawthorne), **2**:225
Blixen, Karen, **2**:12
Blood, George, **2**:110
Blood Diamond (film), **1**:312
Blood Meridian (McCarthy), **1**:304

Blood of Spain (Fraser), **3**:176
Bloods: An Oral History of the Vietnam War by Black Veterans (Terry), **3**:199–201
    Everything We Had (Santoli) vs., **3**:210
    Strange Ground (Maurer) vs., **3**:275
    The Strength Not to Fight (Tollefson) vs., **3**:221
    Tears before the Rain (Engelmann) vs., **3**:279, 280
    What Was Asked of Us (Wood) vs., **3**:231, 232
Bloody Harlan (Taylor), **3**:96
Bloom, David, **2**:237
Bloom, Harold, **2**:139
Bloomsbury group, **2**:133, 180, 268–269
Blue, Martha
    Indian Trader, **3**:290, 291
    The Witch Purge of 1878, **3**:290–292
Blue Genes (Lukas), **1**:204–205
Blue Octavo Notebooks, The (Kafka), **2**:122
Blue Peter (periodical), **2**:193
Bluest Eye, The (Morrison), **1**:19, 175
Bluett, Thomas, *Some Memories of the Life of Job*, **3**:141
Blumenfeld, Yorick, **3**:61
Blunden, Edmund, *Undertones of War*, **1**:329
Blythe, Ronald
    The Age of Illusion, **3**:61
    Akenfield, **3**:59–62
    on *A Country Parson* (Woodforde), **2**:288, 289
    A Treasonable Growth, **3**:61
    The View in Winter, **3**:60
Boarding schools
    experimental, Conroy (Frank) on, **1**:164
    Native Americans at, **3**:109, 318
Boas, Franz, **1**:9, 11
Boat people, Vietnamese, **3**:280
Boccaccio, Giovanni, *Decameron*, **1**:229
Body(ies)
    able, social construction of, **1**:8

    of black women, **1**:18
    in identity, Rousseau (Jean-Jacques) on, **1**:200, 201
    meatiness of, Suleri (Sara) on, **1**:89
Body and Soul (Conroy), **1**:166
"Body Talk" (Spitzack), **3**:190
Boehmer, Elleke, **2**:241–242, 243
Boer War, Second. *See* Anglo–Boer War
Boer War, The (Churchill), **2**:241
Boer War Diary of Sol Plaatje, The (Plaatje), **2**:241–243
Boethius, *Consolation of Philosophy*, **2**:14
Bogart, Barbara Allen, *From Memory to History*, **3**:90
Boggs, Grace Lee, **3**:101
Boggs, James, **3**:99
Bohannon, Horace Augustus, **3**:249
Bohr, Niels, **3**:239
Bolívar, Antonio, **3**:169
Bolivia, oral histories of working-class women in, **3**:322–324, *323*
Bolshevik Revolution (1917), **2**:84, **3**:331
Bolshevism, **1**:270, 271
BOMB (magazine), **1**:48
Bone Black (hooks), **1**:249–251
Bonhoeffer, Dietrich, **2**:22
BookBrowse, **1**:159
Booklist (magazine)
    on *Freedom Flyers* (Moye), **3**:249
    on *Habits of Change* (Rogers), **3**:309
    on *Into the Jet Age* (Wooldridge), **3**:203
    on *Between Management and Labor* (Friedman), **3**:155
    on *Prison Writings* (Peltier), **1**:97
    on *Red Scarf Girl* (Jiang), **1**:162
    on *Ten Thousand Sorrows* (Kim), **1**:104
    on *Thura's Diary* (Al-Windawi), **2**:276
    on *Untold Tales, Unsung Heroes* (Moon), **3**:100
    on "We Have Just Begun to Not Fight" (Frazer and O'Sullivan), **3**:229
    on *Zlata's Diary* (Filipovic), **2**:339

Bookman (journal), **2:**194

Book of Common Prayer, **2:**98

Book of Margery Kempe, The (Kempe), **1:189–192,** 211, **2:**226

Book of Memories, The (Shua), **1:**75

Book of My Mother (Cohen), **1:**99

Book of the City of Ladies, The (Christine), **2:**162

Books Abroad (magazine), **2:**17

Books & Culture (journal), **3:**68

Books Ireland (journal), **2:**159, **3:**316

Boomer, Walter E., **2:**278–279, 280

Boorman, John, **3:**68, 242

Booth, Alison, **2:**210–211, 337

Booth, John Wilkes, **3:**261

Bootlegging. *See* Moonshine

Bootstrap, Operation, **1:**108

Borden, Mary, *The Forbidden Zone,* **2:**259

Borderlands literature, *When I Was Puerto Rican* (Santiago) as, **1:**109

Borderlands/The Fontera (Anzaldúa), **1:**56

Bordin, Guy, **3:**139–140

Boren, Mark Edelman, **2:**114

Borges, Jorge Luis, **1:**224

Bornat, Joanna
    on *Daring Hearts* (Brighton Ourstory), **3:**72
    Oral History, Health and Welfare, **3:170–172**

Born on the Fourth of July (Kovic), **1:**335, **3:**209

Borowski, Tadeusz, **1:**318

Bosnia, Filipovic (Zlata) on life in, **2:**338–340

Bosnian War (1992–1995), **2:**338–339

Bosnik, Anton, **3:**235

Bosque Redondo Reservation, **3:**10, 290, *291*

Bostdorff, Denise M., **2:**33

Bostock, Lisa, **3:**171

Boston College, **3:**29

Boston Globe (newspaper), **1:**16, 72

Bostonians, The (James), **2:**113

Boston Irish Reporter, **3:**29

Boston Tea Party, **2:**79

Bostridge, Mark, **1:**330, **2:**269

Boswell, James, **2:329**
    Account of Corsica, **2:**328
    The Journal of a Tour to the Hebrides, **2:**328
    Life of Samuel Johnson, **2:**177, 195, 309, 328, 329–330
    London Journal, **2:328–330**
    Woodforde (James) compared to, **2:**287, 288

Bosworth, Johnny, **3:**344

Botswana, Mitchison's (Naomi) visits to, **2:**237

Bottrall, Margaret, **1:**316

Bouhaddou, Saadia, **3:**48

Boundary 2 (journal), **2:**128

Bourgeacq, Jacques, **1:**128

Bourne, Edward, **2:**206

Boutcher, Warren, **2:**256

Bow, Leslie, **1:**337

Bowden, George, **2:**135

Bowe, John, *Gig,* **3:**343, 345

Bowe, Marisa, *Gig,* **3:**343, 345

Bowen, Elizabeth, **2:**101, 181
    The Death of the Heart, **2:**133

Bowker, Gordon, **2:**118

Bowring, Richard, **2:**290, 291, 292

Boyd, Belle, **2:**273

Boyer, Paul, *By the Bomb's Early Light,* **3:**239

Boyle, Kevin, **3:**101

Boyle, Robert, **2:**65

Boyle, Tony, **3:**98

Boy scouts, **1:**47, 48

Boys in Zinc (Alexievich), **3:**285

Boys' Life (magazine), **1:**47

Boys Will Be Boys (Suleri), **1:**88

Boyyd, Nan Alamilla, **3:**85

Bracken, John, **2:63**

Bradbury, Malcolm, **1:**280

Bradford, Clare, **1:**41

Bradford, Gamaliel, **2:**39, 314

Bradley, David, *Dissent,* **1:**80

Bradley, Ed, **3:**200

Bradley, William A., **1:**86

Bradstreet, Anne, **1:**315

Bragg, Melvyn, *Speak for England,* **3:**144

Brahms, Johannes, **1:**206

Brainwashing, in Cultural Revolution, **1:**161, 162

Branch, Michael P., **2:**214, 215

Braudel, Fernand, **3:**159

Brave Bird, Mary
    Lakota Woman, **1:21–23**
    Ohitika Woman, **1:**21, 23

Bravman, Bill, **3:**142

Brawne, Fanny, **2:**147

Braxton, Joanne, **1:**19

Braxton, Joanne M., **2:**31

Bray, William, **2:**65

Brazell, Karen, **2:**59, 60

Brazil
    de Jesus (Carolina Maria) on experience of poverty in, **2:**6–8
    Jews in, **1:**75

Breast cancer, Lorde's (Audre) battle with, **2:**3–5

Brée, Germaine, **1:**246, 247

Breen, Joe, **1:120**

Breidenbach, Bernhard von, *Peregrinationes in Montem Zion,* **2:**227

Brennan, William J., Jr., **3:**294

Brenner, Rachel, **2:**24

Brent, Jonathan, **2:**85–86

Breslau, Louise, **2:**306

Bressler, Leo A., **1:**235

Brewsie and Willie (Stein), **1:**333

Brewton, Vince, **1:**35

Breytenbach, Breyten, **3:**242

Brezhnev, Leonid, **3:**331

Bride of Lammermoor, The (Scott), **2:**209

Bridge, Horatio, **2:**223

Bridgman, Laura, **1:**43

Brief History of the War with the Indians in New England, A (Mather), **1:**325

Briggs, Anthony, **1:**195

Briggs, Asa, **3:**64

Briggs, Julia, **2:**182

Briggs, Kate, **2:**182

Briggsoth, Jean L., *Never in Anger,* **3:**138

Brighton (England), oral histories of gay life in, **3:**70–72, *71*

Brighton Gay Switchboard, **3:**72

Brighton Ourstory, *Daring Hearts,* **3**:70–72

Brigido-Corachán, Anna, **1**:56

Brill de Ramirez, Susan B., **3**:320

Brink, André, **1**:27, **3**:242

Brinker, William, **3**:277

Brinkman, Antoinette, **1**:103

Brinnin, John Malcolm, **1**:332–333

Brinson, Betsy, **3**:159, 266

Brissman, Barry, **1**:338, 339

Brissman, Lily Chia, **1**:338, 339

Bristol (England), oral histories of working-class youth in, **3**:311–313, *312*

Britain. *See also* England; Ireland; Scotland; Wales
 abolitionist movement in, **1**:81–83, 111, **3**:23
 abolition of slavery in, **1**:34, 81, 111, **3**:23
 African Britons in, **1**:81–82
 censorship of Irish history in, **3**:27, 28, 29
 class in (*See* Social class)
 education in, **2**:136, 320, **3**:311–313
 empire of (*See* British Empire)
 establishment of Great Britain (1707), **2**:328
 Franklin (Benjamin) in, **1**:179
 Great Depression in, **3**:53
 health-care industry of, **3**:170–172
 homosexuality in, ban on, **2**:9, 183, **3**:70
 industrialization of, **2**:16, 146, 300, **3**:59, 63
 Iranian relations with, **3**:218
 Irish Rebellion (1798) against, **2**:157, *158,* 159
 in Israel's establishment, **1**:225
 letter writing in, **2**:146, 217
 literacy in, rise of, **2**:136, 146, 320
 lost generation of, **1**:329
 Mahomet's (Dean) influence on culture of, **2**:230, 231
 Mass Observation Project in, **2**:235, 236, 237, 265, 266, 267
 nature writing in, golden age of, **2**:300
 Palestine under, **2**:104–106, **3**:14
 racism in, **2**:230
 religion in (*See* British religion)
 slave trade in, **1**:34, 81, 111
 social history of, Webb (Beatrice) on, **2**:16–18
 travel narratives in, popularity of, **2**:229
 Victorian (*See* Victorian era)
 wars of (*See specific wars*)
 women's rights movement in, **1**:329, 331, **2**:109

British Critic (journal), **2**:179

British Empire
 abolition of slavery in, **1**:34, 81, 111, **3**:23
 African countries in, **1**:167
 Australia in, **1**:149
 Egypt in, **1**:135
 during French Revolution, **2**:217, 218, 219
 India in (*See* India, British)
 Jamaica in, **1**:111
 Kenya in, **2**:12, **3**:141–143
 Nigeria in, **1**:214
 racism against people of color from, **2**:230
 Seven Years' War in expansion of, **2**:328
 South Africa in, **2**:217–219, 241–243
 Victorian era expansion of, **2**:16
 Zimbabwe (Rhodesia) in, **1**:167, **3**:251–253

British Journal of Aesthetics, **2**:128

British Journal of Education Studies, **3**:313

British Mandate for Palestine, **2**:104–106

British Medical Journal, **1**:6, 7–8

British monarchy. *See also* English Civil War; *specific rulers*
 in Renaissance, **2**:97–99
 Slingsby (Henry) on loyalty to, **2**:256–258

British Museum, **2**:183

British oral histories. *See also* English oral histories; Irish oral histories
 on health-care industry, **3**:170–172
 origins of field, **3**:186
 recognition of value of, **3**:64
 on World War II, **3**:234–236

British Petroleum, **3**:218

British religion. *See also* Anglicanism
 Catholicism, decline of, **2**:97, 99, 226
 Christianity, arrival of, **1**:189
 Great Awakening in, **2**:197
 Methodism, **2**:195–196
 Puritanism, **2**:72, 74
 Quakerism, **2**:26–28, 157–159

British women. *See* English women

Brittain, Vera, **1**:330
 Bagnold (Enid) compared to, **1**:329, **2**:259
 Mitchison (Naomi) compared to, **2**:235
 Sassoon (Siegfried) compared to, **2**:247
 Testament of Experience, **1**:330
 Testament of Friendship, **1**:330, 331
 Testament of Youth, **1**:329–331, **2**:247–248, 259, 269, **3**:176

Brittain, Victoria, **2**:14

Brod, Max, **2**:120, 121, 122

Brokenburn (Stone), **2**:244–246

Brooke, James, **2**:12

Brook Farm (utopian community), **1**:14, 235

Brookfield strike of 1970s, **3**:96

Brooklyn Historical Society, **3**:180

Brooks, Max, **3**:212

Brooks, Pam, **1**:39

Brooks, Van Wyck, **1**:134

Brothers: Black Soldiers in the Nam (Goff et al.), **3**:199

Broussard, Allen, **3**:21

Brown, C. G., **3**:173

Brown, Hume, **2**:309

Brown, James W., *Long Journey Home,* **3**:107, **325–327**

Brown, Jennifer S. H., **3**:109

Brown, John (abolitionist), **1**:33, **2**:29, 238

Brown, John (servant), **2**:209

Brown, Joseph Epes, **3:**111
Brown, Patricia, **3:**338
Brown, William Wells
    Clotel, **1:**72
    Narrative, **1:**50
    The Negro in the American Rebellion, **2:**238
Browne, Janet, **1:**66, 67
Browne, Thomas, **2:**65, 67
Browning, Elizabeth Barrett, **2:**29
Browning, Orville H., **3:**263–264
Browning, Robert, **1:**264, 265
Brownmiller, Susan, **2:**283
Brown v. Board of Education, **1:**122, 249, **3:**44
Bruce, Edward Caledon, **2:**39
Bruce, Gary, *The Firm*, **3:245–247**
Bruckheimer, Jerry, **3:**345
Brugge, David M.
    The Navajo-Hopi Land Dispute, **3:**10
    "The Navajo Witch Purge of 1878," **3:**290
Bruner, Charlotte H., *Unwinding Threads*, **1:**94
Bruss, Elizabeth W., **1:**246
Bry, Theodor de, **2:**202
Bryant, Emma Spaulding, **2:**252
Bryant, Harold, **3:**201
Bryant, John Emory, **2:**252
Brydges, Samuel Egerton, **1:**231
Bryson, David, **3:**65
Buch, H. C., *Sansibar Blues*, **1:**92
Buchanan, John, **3:**177–178
Buchenwald concentration camp, **3:**51
Buck, Lucy
    Sad Earth, Sweet Heaven, **2:**271, 273
    Shadows on My Heart, **2:38, 271–274**
Buck, Neville, **2:**271
Buck, Pearl S., *The Good Earth*, **1:**159
Budberg, Moura, **1:**254
Buddhism, in Japan
    Murasaki Shikibu on, **2:**290, 291
    Nijo (Lady) as nun in, **2:**59, 60
    rise of, **2:**59, 61, 189
Buel, Joy Day, **2:**332

Buel, Richard, **2:**332
Buell, Lawrence, **1:**236
Bueno, Eva Paulino, **2:**8
Bueno, Fernanda, **2:**222
Buergenthal, Thomas, *A Lucky Child*, **1:**312
Buff, Truman, **3:**103
Buggery Act of 1533 (England), **3:**70
Bugul, Ken, **1:62**
    The Abandoned Baobab, **1:61–64**
    Cendres et braises, **1:**61
    Riwan ou le chemin de sable, **1:**61, 64
Buhari, Muhammadu, **1:**216
Buhle, Paul, **3:**159, 181, 330
Bui Tin, **3:**280
Bulletin of the School of Oriental Studies, **1:**137, 287
Bundeson, Lynne, **1:**336
Bunin, Ivan, **1:**270
Bunyan, John, *Grace Abounding to the Chief of Sinners*, **2:**26
Burawoy, Michael, **3:**342
Burde, Edgar, **1:**147
Bureau of Indian Affairs (BIA), U.S., **1:**69
Burgos-Debray, Elisabeth, **3:**114, 164, 165, 322
Burgunder, Rose, **1:**206
Burke, Bonaventure, **3:**310
Burke, Edmund, **1:**88, **2:**157, 158, 217
Burke, Peter, **1:**185
Burkett, B. G., **3:**201, 211
Burlingame, Michael
    Abraham Lincoln: A Life, **3:**264
    An Oral History of Abraham Lincoln, **3:261–264**
Burma, British colonial rule of, **2:**119
Burmese Days (Orwell), **2:**119
Burnett, Richard, **3:**159
Burney, Charles, **2:**312
Burney, Edward Francis, **2:**313
Burney, Fanny, **2:313**
    Diary and Letters of Madame D'Arblay, **2:**312, 314
    Evelina, **2:**312–313, 314
    Letters and Journals of Fanny Burney, **2:312–315**

    The Memoirs of Dr. Burney, **2:**312, 313
    Pope (Alexander) and, **2:**217
Burns, Anthony, **2:**29
Burns, Harry, **3:**95
Burns, Patrick, **3:**241
Burns, Robert, **2:**328
Burqas, **1:**40
Burr, Aaron, *The Private Journal of Aaron Burr*, **2:**88
Burr, Anna Robeson, **1:**246
Burroughs, Carolyn, **2:**337
Burroughs, John, **2:**141
Burson, Harold, **3:**294
Burst of Light, A (Lorde), **2:**3
Burton, Robert, **2:**177
Burton, Vicki Tolar, **2:**196
Buruma, Ian, *Murder in Amsterdam*, **1:**209
Bush, George H. W., **1:**300, **2:**278
Bush, George W., **1:**306, **2:**275
Bush, Laura, **1:**41
BusinessWeek (magazine), **3:**277
Butcher, Tim, *Chasing the Devil*, **1:**312
Bute, Lord, **2:**328
Butler, Dino, **1:**96
Butler, George E., **1:**206
Butler, Pierce Mease, **2:**335, 337
Butler, Samuel, **1:**218–219
Butor, Michel, **1:240**
Byatt, A. S., **1:**168
    Possession, **2:**77
Bykaw, Vasily, **3:**282
Byodoin Temple (Kyoto), **2:**298
Byrd, Jim, **3:**87
Byrd, Richard, **2:**280
Byron, George Gordon Noel, **2:144**
    Camino Real (Williams) on, **2:**154
    The Journal of Sir Walter Scott (Scott) on, **2:**309
    Kemble's (Fanny) friendship with, **2:**335
    Letters and Journals of Lord Byron, **2:143–145,** 309
    The Letters of John Keats (Keats) on, **2:**146
By the Bomb's Early Light (Boyer), **3:**239

C

Cadle, Tillman, **3:**158
Cady, Daniel, **1:**13
Caesar, Julius, **1:**218, 220
Caillouet, Ruth R., **1:**40–41, 42
Cain, William E., **1:**4–5
Caine, Barbara, **2:**17
Cairnie, Julie, **1:**169
Caldas (destroyer), **3:**183, 185
California
    affirmative action in, **3:**20
    African Americans in higher education in, **3:**20
    colonial, oral histories of, **3:**114–116
    gay Asian Americans in, oral histories of, **3:**83–85
    Gold Rush in, **3:**114
    immigrant land ownership in, restrictions on, **3:**195
    Italian American relocation in, **3:**224
    Japanese American internment in, **1:**299–301, **3:**102–104, 197
    missions of, **3:**114–116
    Owens Valley region of, oral histories of, **3:**102–104
    statehood for, **3:**114
California History (journal), **3:**225
California State University at Fullerton, Japanese American Oral History Project at, **3:**80, 102, 195
Californios
    definition of, **3:**114
    oral histories of, **3:**114–116
Californio Voices (Savage), **3:114–117,** 121
Calked Boots and Other Northwest Writings (Russell), **3:**93
Call, M. S., **1:**32
Callaloo (journal), **1:**5, 251, **3:**24
Callow, Simon, **2:**154
Calvino, Italo, *Invisible Cities,* **1:**105
Cambodia, under Khmer Rouge, Siv (Sichan) on life in, **1:**306–308
Cambodian Americans, Siv (Sichan) on experience of, **1:**306–308
Camden Society, **2:**226, 228

Cameron, David, **2:**261
Cameron, Samantha, **2:**261
Camino Real (Williams), **2:**154
Camp and Community (Garrett and Larson), **3:**102, 103–104
Campbell, John Angus, **1:**67
Campesinos, **3:**302–303
Camus, Albert
    Feraoun's (Mouloud) friendship with, **2:**262
    The Myth of Sisyphus, **1:**204
    Styron (William) influenced by, **1:**204, 205
    Wright's (Richard) friendship with, **1:**124
Canada
    oral histories of Inuits in, **3:**138–140, *139*
    U.S. draft evasion in, **3:**221
Canadian Book Review Annual, **3:**140
Canadian Journal of History, **2:**330, **3:**29
Canadian Literature (journal), **1:**103, **2:**175
Canadian Review of American Studies (journal), **1:**157
Cancer, Lorde's (Audre) battle with, **2:**3–5
Cancer Journals, The (Lorde), **2:3–5**
Cancian, Frank, **3:**168
Candor. *See also* Truth
    in *The Long Walk to Freedom* (Mandela), **1:**29
Caninius Rufus, **2:**95, 96
Canterbury Tales (Chaucer), **1:**191, 229
Canto general (Neruda), **1:**223
Cape of Good Hope, **2:**198, 199, 217, 218
Capitalism
    IWW's opposition to, **3:**328, 329
    working class in, **3:**53
Capital punishment. *See* Execution
Capital Times (newspaper), **2:**276
Capitulations of Santa Fé, **2:**201
Capote, Truman, **2:**152
Captivity narratives, **1:**81, 325–326
Caputo, John D., **2:**167
Caputo, Philip, *A Rumor of War,* **3:**209
Carboni, Sante, **3:**158

Cardanus, Hieronymus, **2:**98–99
Cárdenas, Lázaro, **3:**302, 303, *303,* 304
Carey, John, **2:**138
Caribbean autobiographical writing
    by McKay (Claude), **1:**84–86
    by Medina (Pablo), **1:**296–298
    by Santiago (Esmeralda), **1:**108–110
    by Seacole (Mary), **1:**111–113
Carlisle, Elizabeth Pendergast, **2:**332
Carlo Tresca (Pernicone), **3:**5
Carlson, Timothy, *Embedded,* **3:**276
Carlyle, Thomas, **2:**139–140, 144, 196, 310, 321
Carmelite religious order, **1:**211, 212
Carmody, Deidre, **1:**262
Carnegie, Andrew, **1:**52
Carranza, Venustiano, **3:**167
Carrera, Elena, **1:**213
Carretta, Vincent, **1:**82, 83, **2:**46
Carrier Warfare in the Pacific (Wooldridge), **3:202–204**
Carril, Delia del, **1:**223
Carrington, Dora, **2:**269
Carry It On (Ashmore), **3:**254
Carter, Jimmy, **1:**311, **3:**221
Carter, John, **1:**18
Carter, Ross S., *Those Devils in Baggy Pants,* **3:**212
Carter, Steven, **1:**274
Cartesian rationalism, **1:**183, 184
Carver, Jonathan
    The Journals of Jonathan Carver and Related Documents, **2:205–208**
    Travels through the Interior Parts of North America, **2:**205
Cary, Max, **1:**218, **2:**94, 95–96
Casada, James, **3:**252
Casaubon, Méric, **1:**220
Casey-Leininger, Charles F., **3:**100
Cash, Jean W., **2:**131
Caspar, C., **1:**31, 32
Cassius Dio, *Historia Romana,* **1:**220
Cast a Cold Eye (McCarthy), **1:**258
Castellanos, Miguel, **3:**206
Castle, The (Kafka), **2:**120
Castro, Fidel, **1:**296, 298, **2:**222, 280

Cat(s)
  in *A Country Parson* (Woodforde), **2:**289
  Lessing (Doris) on, **1:**169
Catherine of Siena (saint), **1:**189
Catholicism. *See also* Christian autobiographical writing
  Augustine in, **1:**196–198
  Boswell's (James) conversion to, **2:**329
  Counter-Reformation in, **1:**211
  in England, decline of, **2:**97, 99, 226
  in Ireland, **1:**119–120
  of McCarthy (Mary), **1:**259
  of Mexican American women, **3:**132
  nuns in, oral histories of, **3:**308–310
  of O'Connor (Flannery), **2:**129, 130
  Teresa of Ávila in, **1:**211–213
  Vatican II in, **3:**308, 309
  Williams's (Tennessee) conversion to, **2:**152
Catlett, Elizabeth, **2:45**
Catliln, George, **1:**330
Caton, William, **2:**26
Caton-Jones, Michael, **1:**47, 49
Catt, Carrie Chapman, **1:**12
Caucasia (Senna), **1:**72, 74
Caudill, Harry, *Night Comes to the Cumberlands*, **3:**66
"Caught between Homes" (Baggett), **1:**113
Caught in a Tornado (Ross), **3:**287
Cavell, Stanley, **1:**236
Cavendish, Margaret, **1:230**
  Clifford (Anne) compared to, **2:**62
  A Description of the New World, **1:**231
  Nature's Pictures Drawn by Fancy's Pencil to the Life, **1:**229, 231
  Osborne (Dorothy) compared to, **2:**324
  A True Relation of My Birth, Breeding, and Life, **1:229–232**
Cavendish, William, **1:**229
Cavett, Dick, **1:**260

CCP. *See* Chinese Communist Party
CDC. *See* Centers for Disease Control and Prevention
Cecelski, David, *Along Freedom Road*, **3:**21
Cecil, David, **2:**268
Cefkin, J. Leo, **3:**252
Cellini, Benvenuto, **1:**239
Cendrata, Lodovico, **2:**160
Cendres et braises (Bugul), **1:**61
Censorship
  in Belarus, **3:**282–284
  in Britain, **3:**27, 28, 29
  in China, **3:**287, 301
  in Kenya, **2:**14
  in Mexico, **3:**31, 32
  in Russia, **1:**193, 194
  in U.S., **1:**20, **2:**123, **3:**201
Centenary Edition of the Works of Nathaniel Hawthorne, The (Hawthorne), **2:**223
Centers for Disease Control and Prevention (CDC), U.S., **3:**85
Central Intelligence Agency (CIA), U.S., **1:**298, **3:**164
Century Magazine, **3:**261
CEP. *See* Coal Employment Project
Cereta, Laura, *Collected Letters of a Renaissance Feminist*, **2:160–162**
Cerro Gordo (California), **3:**103
Cervantes, Lorna Dee, **3:**133
Cervetto, Joe, **3:**225
Césaire, Aimé, **1:**61
Cha, Theresa Hak Kyung, *Dictee*, **1:**102
Chadwick, Owen, **1:**239
Chai, May-Lee, **1:**307–308
Chalk Garden, The (Bagnold), **2:**259, 261
Challener, Daniel D., **1:**48
Challenger, Melanie, **2:**338
Chalmers, Martin, **2:**304
Chamberlain, John, **1:**32
Chamberlain, Joseph, **2:**17
Chamberlain, Mary
  Fenwomen, **3:**61
  on *Women's Words* (Gluck and Patai), **3:**191
Chamberlain, Neville, **2:**265

Chamberlain, Samuel, *My Confessions*, **1:**304
Chamosa, Oscar, **3:**74, 75
Champagne, Roland, **1:**268, **2:**175
Chamula (Mexico), oral histories of indigenous people of, **3:**167–169
Chander, Manu, **1:**256, 257
Chandler, Sally, **3:**188
Chang, Gordon, **3:**81
Chang, Iris, **2:**19, 20
Chang, Jung, *Wild Swans*, **1:**158–159
Change of Tongue, A (Krog), **3:**242
Channing, Ellery, **2:**139
Chanthaphavong, Samaya L. S., **2:**299
Chao, Buwei Yang, *Autobiography of a Chinese Woman*, **1:**338
Chapelle, Dickey, *What's a Woman Doing Here?*, **2:**280
Chaplin, Charlie, **2:**183
Chaplin, Ralph, **3:**329
Chapman, James, **3:**234, 236
Chapman, Jedediah, **2:**79
Chapman, Maria Weston, *The Liberty Bell*, **1:**142
Character of England, A (Evelyn), **2:**65
Chardin, Jean-Baptiste-Siméon, **2:**110
Charles I (king of England)
  Eikon Basilike, **2:**256, 258
  in English Civil War, **1:**315, 317, **2:**26, 65, 72, 178, 256, 257, *257*
Charles II (king of England), **1:316**
  Evelyn (John) and, **2:**65
  Halkett (Anne), **1:**315, 316
  restoration of, **1:**315, **2:**26, 65, 72, 256, 258
Charlevoix, Pierre-François-Xavier de, *Journal of a Voyage to North-America*, **2:**205
Chasing the Devil (Butcher), **1:**312
Chatterjee, Partha, **1:**291
Chaucer, Geoffrey
  Canterbury Tales, **1:**191, 229
  The Letters of John Keats (Keats) on, **2:**146
Chaudhuri, Nirad C., *Autobiography of an Unknown Indian*, **3:**251, 253
Chavez, Cesar, **3:**133
Che: A Graphic Biography (Buhle and Rodriguez), **3:**330

Cheke, John, **2:**97
Chekhov, Anton, **1:**47, **2:**133
Chekisty (Dziak), **3:**245
Chen, Joan, **1:**158
Chen, Paul, **3:**84
Cheney, Anne, **1:**274, 275
Cheney, Dick, **2:**278
Cheng, Nien, **1:**159
Cheng Yu-hsiu (Madame Wei), **1:153**
    A Girl from China, **1:**152, 154
    My Revolutionary Years, **1:152–154**
Cherie (Goncourt), **2:**308
Chernobyl nuclear disaster (1986), **3:**282–285, *283*
Chertkov, Vladimir, **1:**195
Chesnut, Mary Boykin Miller
    A Diary from Dixie, **2:250–252**
    Mary Chesnut's Civil War, **2:**250, 251, 271
    The Private Mary Chesnut, **2:**250
    Stone (Kate) compared to, **2:**244, 246
Chew, Daglish, **3:**243
Chiang Kai-sheck, **1:**338
Chiapas (Mexico), oral histories of indigenous people of, **3:**167–169, *168*
Chiarello, Barbara, **2:**255
Chicago (Illinois)
    Hansberry (Lorraine) on life in, **1:**273, 275
    Haymarket Riot in, **3:**4
    race riots in, **3:**45
    Wright's (Richard) move to, **1:**122
Chicago Daily Tribune (newspaper), **2:**89
Chicago Renaissance, **1:**273
Chicago Sun-Times (newspaper), **1:**40, 41
Chicago Tribune (newspaper), **1:**23, 40, 41, **2:**121
Chicana women, oral histories of, **3:**131–133, *132*
Chicano, use of term, **3:**133
Chicano movement, **3:**133
Chicano studies, rise of, **3:**131–133
Chicken with Plums (Satrapi), **1:**155–156
Chigwedere, P., **3:**274
Child, Lydia Maria, **1:**142, 144

Childhood
    in Arabic autobiographies, **1:**135, 136
    idealization of, **1:**128
    treatment of, in memoirs, **1:**47
    during wartime, memoirs of, **1:**312–314
Child in the House, The (Pater), **1:**276
Child of the Dark (de Jesus), **2:6–8,** **3:**164, 322
Children
    of British working class, **3:**53–54, *54*, 311–313, *312*
    as casualties of Holocaust, **3:**36
    Cuban, immigration of, **1:**298
    interracial adoption of, **1:**102–104
    of Los Alamos, oral histories of, **3:**239–241
    as soldiers in Sierra Leone, **1:**312–314
Children of Los Alamos (Mason), **3:239–241**
Children of Sanchez (Lewis), **3:**31
Children's of Cambodia's Killing Fields (Pran), **1:**306
Childress, Lee, **3:**209
Child's Christmas in Wales, A (Thomas), **1:125–127**
Chile
    Agosín (Marjorie) on experience of Jews in, **1:**75–77
    autobiographical tradition of, **1:**222
    German immigration to, **1:**75, 77
    mass disappearances in, **1:**75
    military coup of 1973 in, **1:**222
    Neruda (Pablo) on life in, **1:**222–224
Chimurenga (Liberation) War, First (1896–1897), **3:**251
Chimurenga (Liberation) War, Second, **3:**251
Chin, Frank, **1:**175
China. *See also* Chinese autobiographical writing; Chinese oral histories
    arranged marriage in, **1:**153, 154, 338, 339, **2:**170
    censorship in, **3:**287, 301
    Confucianism in, **3:**124–126

    Cultural Revolution in (*See* Cultural Revolution)
    Du Bois (W. E. B.) and, **1:**3, 4
    dynastic rule of, end of, **3:**124, 126, 147
    establishment of republic, **2:**170, **3:**124, 126, 147, 299
    feminism in, rise of, **3:**147–149
    folklore of, **1:**173, 174
    foot binding in, **1:**338, **3:**147, 289
    Gandhi's (Mohandas) influence on protests in, **1:**242
    gender roles in, **1:**153, 158, 160, 338, **3:**147–149
    Great Leap Forward in, **3:**287, 299, 300
    Japanese invasion of (1931), **3:**215
    Japanese relations with, **1:**340, **3:**149
    Japan influenced by, in Heian period, **2:**189
    Jewish refugees in, oral histories of, **3:**14–16
    Kingston (Maxine Hong) on culture of, **1:**173–175
    Korean Provisional Government in, **1:**322, 324
    Long March in, **1:**338
    May Fourth Movement in, **1:**338, **3:**126, 147–149
    Nanking Massacre in, **1:**340, **2:**19–21
    Northern Expedition in, **1:**338
    Polo's (Marco) travels in, **1:**105, 106, 107
    Rabe (John) in, **2:**19–21
    Revolution of 1911–1912 in, **2:**170
    in Sino–Japanese Wars, **1:**322, 339, 340
    women of (*See* Chinese women)
    during World War II, **1:**152, 153, **3:**14–16
China Candid (Sang), **3:**299–300
China Daily News (newspaper), **3:**299
China Journal, **1:**339, **3:**149, 301
China Men (Kingston), **1:**173
China Remembers (Zhang and McLeod), **3:**301
Chinchilla, Norma, **3:**323

SUBJECT INDEX

Chinese American(s)
- Kingston (Maxine Hong) on experience of, **1:**173–175
- Min (Anchee) on experience of, **1:**158–160
- stereotypes of, **1:**173, 174

Chinese autobiographical writing. *See also specific works and writers*
- by Cheng Yu-hsiu (Madame Wei), **1:**152–154
- expatriate, tradition of, **1:**158–159
- by Jiang (Ji-li), **1:**161–163
- by Lu Xun and Xu Guangping, **2:**170–172
- by Min (Anchee), **1:**158–160
- by women, rise of, **1:**152–153, 159, 338
- by Xie Bingying, **1:**338–340

Chinese Civil War (1927–1950), **3:**126

Chinese Communist Party (CCP). *See also* Cultural Revolution
- censorship by, **3:**301
- Cheng Yu-hsiu on, **1:**152
- Jiang (Ji-li) on, **1:**161, 162
- in liberation of women, **3:**147, 148
- Lu Xun and, **2:**170, 172
- oppression under, **1:**338
- origins and rise of, **2:**170, **3:**287

Chinese language
- Japanese writers' use of, **2:**290, 292
- in *The Woman Warrior* (Kingston), **1:**173, 174

Chinese Lives (Zhang and Sang), **3:288, 299–301**

Chinese Missionaries Oral History Collection (Peake and Rosenbaum), **3:**299

Chinese oral histories
- on Cultural Revolution, **3:**287–289, 299–300
- of descendants of Confucius, **3:**124–126
- government influence on, **3:**301
- on life in late twentieth century, **3:**299–301, *300*
- of women in May Fourth Movement, **3:**147–149

Chinese Oral History Project (Columbia University), **3:**299

Chinese Prime Minister, The (Bagnold), **2:**261

Chinese Revolution (1911–1912), **2:**170

Chinese women
- in arranged marriages, **1:**153, 154, 338, 339, **2:**170
- autobiographies by, rise of, **1:**152–153, 159, 338
- feminism among, rise of, **3:**147–149
- foot binding of, **1:**338, **3:**147, 289
- gender roles of, **1:**153, 158, 160, 338, **3:**147–149
- in May Fourth Movement, oral histories of, **3:**147–149
- in military, **1:**338–340
- stereotypes of, **1:**173, **3:**147
- traditional treatment of, **3:**147
- in World War II, Cheng Yu-hsiu on, **1:**152–154
- Xie Bingying of lives of, **1:**338–340

Chineworth, Mary Alice, **3:309**
Ch'ing, Ai, **1:**222
Chinweizu, **1:**115
Chiricahua Apache, Geronimo on, **1:**302–304
Chisholm, Anne, **2:**269
Chittister, Joan, **3:**308
Choi, Samuel, **2:**314
Choi, Young Back, **1:**323
Choice (journal), **3:**19, 249, 255, 326, 332
Chona (Chona and Underhill), **1:69–71**
Chona, Maria, *Chona*, **1:**69–71
Chrisman, Laura, **2:**242

Christian autobiographical writing. *See also specific works and writers*
- by Augustine, **1:**196–198
- by Fox (George), **2:**26–28
- by Guylforde (Richarde), **2:**226–228
- by Kempe (Margery), **1:**189–191
- by Kierkegaard (Søren), **2:**166
- by Rowlandson (Mary), **1:**325–328
- by Teresa of Ávila, **1:**211–213
- by Tolstoy (Leo), **1:**193–195
- tradition of, **2:**166
- by Wesley (John), **2:**195–197

Christian Gauss Award, for *Memory and Narrative* (Olney), **1:**248
Christian Herald (periodical), **3:**110

Christianity. *See also specific denominations*
- in Crusades, **1:**285–288
- early history of, **1:**196
- in England, arrival of, **1:**189
- fundamentalist, **1:**102, 103
- Great Awakening in, **1:**179, **2:**197
- hostility between Islam and, after Crusades, **2:**226
- Kim Ku influenced by, **1:**322
- *The Letters of the Younger Pliny* (Pliny) in, **2:**94
- Marcus Aurelius on, **1:**220
- pilgrimages to Jerusalem in, **2:**226–228
- Protestant Reformation in, **1:**211
- slavery and, **1:**34, 144, **2:**44, 46
- Wells's (H. G.) rejection of, **1:**252–253

Christianity, conversion to
- by Africans, **1:**64
- by Australian Aborigines, **1:**149, 151
- by Equiano (Olaudah), **1:**82
- by Native Americans, **1:**56, **2:**46, **3:**114, 115

Christie, Agatha, **2:**259
Christine de Pisan, **2:**160, 162
- *The Book of the City of Ladies*, **2:**162

Christmas, Thomas (Dylan) on, **1:**125–126, *126*
Christopher, Neil, *Ilagiinniq*, **3:**138
Christopher Award, for *Thura's Diary* (Al-Windawi), **2:**275
Chronology, lack of. *See* Nonchronological order
Church, Thomas, **2:**196
Churches, origins of abolitionist movement in, **1:**142
Churchill, Caryl, *Top Girls*, **2:60**
Churchill, Ward, *Struggle for the Land*, **3:**10
Churchill, Winston
- *The Boer War*, **2:**241
- *Nella Last's War* (Last) on, **2:**265

Church of England. *See* Anglicanism
Church of the Brethren, **3:**223, 227
Chute, Hillary, **1:**157
CIA. *See* Central Intelligence Agency
Ciberletras (journal), **1:**77
Cicero, Marcus Tullius, **2:**94, 95
    Hortensius, **1:**196, 198
Cichy, Rose M., **3:**35
Cienfuegos, Camilo, **2:**222
Cimarróns, **3:**7
Circumcision
    female, Hirsi Ali (Ayaan) on, **1:**207
    male, Perera (Victor) on, **1:**99, 100
Cisneros, Sandra, *The House on Mango Street,* **1:**108
Citizen 13660 (Okubo), **1:**299
Citizenship, Australian, for Aborigines, **1:**149
Citizenship, U.S.
    for African Americans, **1:**50, **2:**38, 238
    for Japanese immigrants, **1:**309
    for Puerto Ricans, **1:**108
Citoyenne, La (newspaper), **2:**306
City College (New York City), **1:**249, 251
City of God (Augustine), **1:**198
Civil disobedience
    in India, by Gandhi (Mohandas), **1:**242, **2:**32
    in Palestinian intifada, first, **2:**50
    in U.S. civil rights movement, **2:**32–33, **3:**101
Civilian Public Service (CPS), U.S., **3:**227–229
Civilians
    in Iraq War, **2:**275, **3:**231, 232
    in Vietnam War, **1:**335–337
    in World War II, **1:**332–333, **3:**235
"Civilized" mind, theories of, **3:**37
Civil Liberties Act of 1988 (U.S.), **1:**311, **3:**197
Civil rights
    for African Americans (*See* Civil rights movement)
    for gays and lesbians, **3:**70, 72, 83–84
    for Native Americans, **1:**21, **3:**291, 292
    in Reconstruction era, **1:**50
Civil Rights Act of 1964 (U.S.), **1:**20, **3:**339
Civil rights movement, U.S.
    Angelou (Maya) in, **1:**18, 20
    civil disobedience in, **2:**32–33, **3:**101
    debate over approach to, **1:**186
    in Detroit, **3:**99–101
    disability studies and, **1:**8
    Du Bois (W. E. B.) in, **1:**3–4
    Gandhi's (Mohandas) influence on, **1:**242
    gradualist approach to, **2:**32–33
    Hansberry (Lorraine) in, **1:**273–275
    Jewish support for, **3:**118
    King (Martin Luther, Jr.) in, **2:**32–34
    Malcolm X in, **1:**186
    Montgomery bus boycott in, **1:**20, 37, 38, 39, **2:**32, **3:**44, 45
    oral histories of, **3:**44–46, 99–101
    origins and development of, **3:**44
    Parks (Rosa) in, **1:**37–39, **3:**101
    SCLC in, **1:**18, 20
    Vietnam War and, **3:**199, 200
    war on poverty and, **3:**254, 256
Civil war(s). *See specific countries*
Civil War Diary of Sarah Morgan, The (Morgan), **2:**271
Civil War History (journal), **2:**240, **3:**261
Cixous, Hélène, **1:**250, **2:**124
Clair, William, **2:**144
Clarissa (Richardson), **2:**301
Clark, Gillian, **1:**197, 198
Clark, John Pepper, **1:**214
Clark, Mary Higgins, **1:**40
Clarkson, Thomas, **1:**81, 83, **2:**75
Clary-Lemon, Jennifer, **3:**175
Clasby, Nancy, **1:**188
Class. *See* Social class
Classic Slave Narratives, The (Gates), **1:**82, 83
Clayhanger trilogy (Bennett), **2:**136, 137
Clayton, Frances, **1:**39
Clemens, Samuel Langhorne. *See* Twain, Mark
Clemm, Maria, **2:**41–43
Clifford, Anne, **2:**63
    The Diaries of Lady Anne Clifford, **2:**62–64
    "Knole Diary," **2:**62, 64
Clifford, D. J. H., **2:**62, 64
Clifford, Geraldine Jonçich, **3:**77
Clifford, James O., **3:**224
Cline, David, **3:**97, 98
Clinton, Bill, **1:**20, 219, **3:**166, 221
Clio (journal), **1:**272
Clive, Robert, **2:**178
Clodfelter, Mark, **3:**279
Clotel (Brown), **1:**72
Cloud Cuckoo Land (Mitchison), **2:**237
Clubbe, John, **2:**144, 145
Clybourne Park (Norris), **1:**273
Coal Employment Project (CEP), **3:**337, 339
Coal Hollow (Light and Light), **3:**66–69
Coal Miners' Wives (Giesen), **3:**337
Coal mining
    in Arizona, on Native American lands, **3:**10, *11,* 292
    in Kentucky, oral histories of, **3:**86–87, 96–98, *97,* 157
    in Ukraine, oral histories of, **3:**340–342
    in West Virginia, oral histories of, **3:**66–69, *67,* 91
    women in, oral histories of, **3:**337–339, *338*
Coburn, Carol, **3:**309
Codrescu, Andrei, **1:**167
Coe, Calvin, **3:**92
Coe, Joe, **3:**92
Coe, John, **3:**90
Coe, Little John, **3:**92
Coe, Samuel S., **3:**90
Coeckelbergh, Mark, **2:**168
Coe Ridge (Kentucky), oral histories of life in, **3:**90–92
Coetzee, J. M., **1:**27
Coeur d'Alene (Idaho), oral histories of life in, **3:**93, 95

SUBJECT INDEX

Coffee, **1:**257
Coffield, Frank, **3:**313
Cohen, Albert, *Book of My Mother,* **1:**99
Cohen, Eliot, **2:**279, 280
Cohen, Jacob, **3:**103
Cohen, J. M., **2:**203
Cohen, Joshua, **1:**255–256
Cohen, Lucy, **3:**122
Colaiaco, James A., **2:**33
Colby, Clara, **1:**12
Colby, William, **3:**279
Cold War
    Du Bois (W. E. B.) and, **1:**3
    Salvadoran Civil War in, **3:**205
    Soviet oral histories of, **3:**331–333
    in *This Boy's Life* (Wolff), **1:**47
    women's peace movement during, **3:**268
Cole, Lori E., **3:**191
Cole, Margaret I., **2:**16, 172
Coleman, Emily Holmes, **1:**127
Coler, Jack, **1:**96
Coleridge, Samuel Taylor
    Byron (George Gordon Noel) compared to, **2:**143
    Journals of Ralph Waldo Emerson (Emerson) on, **2:**141
    Literary Fund and, **2:**207
    The Rime of the Ancient Mariner, **3:**183
    Robinson (Henry Crabb) and, **2:**75
    Wordsworth (Dorothy) influenced by, **2:**300
Coleridge, Sara, *Memoirs and Letters of Sara Coleridge,* **2:**16
Collected Letters (Poe), **2:**41
Collected Letters of a Renaissance Feminist (Cereta), **2:160–162**
Collected Letters of Mary Wollstonecraft, The (Wollstonecraft), **2:109–112**
Collected Works of Abraham Lincoln (Basler), **3:**262
Collected Works of W. B. Yeats, The (Yeats), **2:**126, 128
Collective bargaining, arbitration in, **3:**153
Collective living, Stanton (Elizabeth Cady) on, **1:**14

Collective narratives, of Native Americans, **1:**54
Collective novels, **3:**282, 285
College Literature (journal), **1:**98, 141, 160, **2:**260, 261
Colleges, white, African Americans at, **3:**20–22
Collier's (magazine), **2:**103
Collingwood, Luke, **1:**83
Collins, Anne, *Divine Songs and Meditacions,* **1:**229
Collins, Michael, **3:**27
Collister, Peter, **2:**307
Colombia
    coup of 1953 in, **3:**183, 185
    oral history of shipwrecked sailor from, **3:**183–185, *184*
Colonialism. *See also* Africa, colonialism in; *specific countries*
    Fanon (Frantz) on violent resistance to, **1:**244, **2:**262
    Gandhi's (Mohandas) nonviolent resistance to, **1:**242–244
    Las Casas's (Bartolomé de) critique of, **2:**201, 202, 203
    Orwell's (George) critique of, **2:**119
Color
    hooks (bell) on meanings of, **1:**250
    Nabokov's (Vladimir) perception of, **1:**272
Colorado River, **1:**69
Color-graphemic synethesia, **1:**272
Color of Water, The (McBride), **1:72–74**
Color Purple, The (Walker), **1:**18, 175
Columbian Orator, The (Bingham), **1:**33–34
Columbia University
    Chinese Oral History Project, **3:**299
    Maurer (Harry) at, **3:**277
    Obama (Barack) at, **1:**78
Columbus, Christopher, **2:202**
    Gama (Vasco da) compared to, **2:**200
    Journal of the First Voyage to America, **2:201–204,** 205
    in Puerto Rico, **1:**108
Columbus, Ferdinand, **2:**203

Comaneci, Nadia, *Letters to a Young Gymnast,* **2:**150
Comaroff, John, **2:**241
Comerford, Linda Brill, **1:**162
Comerford, Maire, **3:**29
Comics
    autobiographical, **1:**139–140, 155–157
    gay- and lesbian-themed, **1:**139, 141
    Japanese, **1:**293–294
    on labor movement, **3:**330
Coming-of-age
    in *Angela's Ashes* (McCourt), **1:**119–121
    in *Black Boy* (Wright), **1:**122–124
    in *Bone Black* (hooks), **1:**249
    in *A Child's Christmas in Wales* (Thomas), **1:**125–127
    in *Chona* (Chona and Underhill), **1:**69
    in *The Dark Child* (Laye), **1:**128
    in *Dust Tracks on a Road* (Hurston), **1:**9
    in *The Education of Henry Adams* (Adams), **1:**132–134
    in *An Egyptian Childhood* (Hussein), **1:**136
    in *Fun Home* (Bechdel), **1:**139
    in *Incidents in the Life of a Slave Girl* (Jacobs), **1:**144
    in *Left Handed, Son of Old Man Hat* (Dyk), **3:**318, 319
    in *Life on the Mississippi* (Twain), **1:**146
    in *My Life Story* (Unaipon), **1:**149–151
    in *My Revolutionary Years* (Cheng), **1:**152–154
    in *Under My Skin* (Lessing), **1:**167–169
    in *Persepolis* (Satrapi), **1:**155–157
    in *Red Azalea* (Min), **1:**158–160
    in *Red Scarf Girl* (Jiang), **1:**161–163
    in *Stop-Time* (Conroy), **1:**164, 165
    in *The Unwanted* (Nguyen), **1:**170–172
    in *The Woman Warrior* (Kingston), **1:**174, 175

Coming of Age in Mississippi (Moody), **1:**37
Comitini, Patricia, **2:**301
Committee for Effecting Abolition of the Slave Trade, **1:**81
Committee for Peasant Unity, **3:**166
Commonplace books, **2:**140
Communication Studies (journal), **1:**14
Communism
    in Cambodia, under Khmer Rouge, **1:**306
    in Cuba, establishment of, **1:**296
    Du Bois's (W. E. B.) support for, **1:**3–5
    in East Germany, oppression under, **3:**245–246
    in India, Nehru's (Jawaharlal) advocacy for, **1:**289
    McKay's (Claude) support for, **1:**84, 85
    in Russia, establishment of, **1:**270
    U.S. containment policy on, **3:**205
    in Vietnam, postwar, **1:**170, 171
Communist Party, Chilean, **1:**222
Communist Party, Chinese. *See* Chinese Communist Party
Communist Party, East German, **3:**245
Communist Party, South African, **1:**27
Communist Party, U.S., **1:**3, 4, 122, 123
Community, sense of, among gay Asian Americans, **3:**83–85
Comparatist (journal), **1:**223
Comparative Literature Studies (journal), **1:**277
Comparative Studies of Society and History (journal), **3:**96
Complete Notebooks of Henry James, The (James), **2:113–116**
Complete Works of George Orwell (Orwell), **2:**117, 118
Computers and the Humanities (journal), **2:**203
Conan Doyle, Arthur
    The Great Boer War, **2:**241
    Partridge (Frances) and, **2:**269
Concentration camps. *See* Holocaust concentration camps
Conclusive Evidence (Nabokov). *See Speak, Memory* (Nabokov)

Concubines, in Japan, **2:**299
Condict, Jemima, *Jemima Condict*, **2:78–80**
Coney, Juliet, **2:**91, 92
Confederacy. *See* American Civil War
Confession, A (Tolstoy), **1:193–195,** 270
Confessions (Augustine), **1:196–199**
    The Autobiography of Giambattista Vico (Vico) vs., **1:**183
    The Autobiography of Malcolm X (Malcolm X) vs., **1:**186
    Confessions (Rousseau) influenced by, **1:**197, 201
    A Confession (Tolstoy) vs., **1:**193
    as first autobiography, **1:**196
    Teresa of Ávila influenced by, **1:**211
Confessions (Rousseau), **1:**193, 197, **200–203,** 276
Confessions of Lady Nijō (Nijō), **2:59–61**
Confessions of Nat Turner, The (Styron), **1:**204, 206
Confidence (James), **2:**114
Confieso que he vivido (Neruda). *See Memoirs* (Neruda)
Conflict Quarterly, **3:**277
Confluencia (journal), **1:**109
Confucianism, **3:**124–126
    gender roles in, **3:**147
    Kim Ku influenced by, **1:**322
    Kong Decheng on, **3:**124–126
    movements against, **3:**124, 126
    rituals of, **3:**124, 125
Confucius, **3:**125
    descendants of, **3:**124–126
Congo
    Belgian colonial rule of, **2:**192–194, *193*
    Conrad's (Joseph) travels in, **2:**192–194
Congo Diary, The (Conrad), **2:192–194**
Congress, Continental, **2:**69
Congress, U.S.
    gag rule on slavery in, **2:**70
    House Un-American Activities Committee of, **2:**152

    and water resources on reservations, **1:**69
Congress of Racial Equality, **2:**32
Congress Party (India), **1:**242, 289, 290, 291
Connally, John B., **3:**202, 203
Connecticut Gazette (newspaper), **2:**44
Conner, John, **2:**295
Conner, Valerie Jean, *The National War Labor Board*, **3:**153–154
Connolly, Cyril, **2:**235
Conquered, The (Mitchison), **2:**237
Conquest, Robert, **3:**19
Conrad, Joseph
    Almayer's Folly, **2:**192
    The Congo Diary, **2:192–194**
    Dogs Bark, **1:**166
    Heart of Darkness, **2:**192–193, 194
    Last Essays, **2:**193, 194
    Literary Fund and, **2:**207
    "An Outpost of Progress," **2:**192, 194
    "Up-river Book," **2:**194
Conrad, Peter, **2:**153–154
Conroy, Frank, **1:165**
    Body and Soul, **1:**166
    Stop-Time, **1:164–166,** 270
Conscientious objectors (COs)
    in Vietnam War, **3:**221–223, *222*
    in World War II, **2:**268–269, **3:**223, 227–229
Conscientious Objectors and the Second World War (Eller), **3:**227
Consciousness
    double, Obama (Barack) on, **1:**79
    in locked-in syndrome, **1:**6
    racial, Du Bois (W. E. B.) in advancement of, **1:**4
Consolation of Philosophy (Boethius), **2:**14
Constantine (Roman emperor), **1:**196
Constitution, Mexican, **3:**302
Constitutional amendments, U.S.
    Fifteenth, **1:**50, **2:**238
    Fourteenth, **1:**50
    Nineteenth, **1:**13
    Thirteenth, **1:**50

SUBJECT INDEX

Consumerism, rise of, before Great Depression, **3:**161
Containment policy, U.S., **3:**205
Conteh-Morgan, John D., **1:**129, 130
Contemporary Irish Traditional Narrative (Harvey), **3:**315
Contemporary Jewish Record (magazine), **1:**333
Contemporary Literary Criticism (journal), **1:**159
Contemporary Literature (journal), **1:**47, 48, 49
Contemporary Sociology (journal), **3:**303
Contentious Lives (Auyero), **3:**268
Contested Territories (Beatty-Medina and Rinehart), **3:**326
Continental Congress, **2:**69
Controlled Substances Act of 1970 (U.S.), **2:**294
Conversation in Religion & Theology (journal), **2:**195
Conversations with Myself (Mandela), **1:**27–28
Cony, Daniel, **2:**331, 332
Cook, E. T., **1:**265
Cook, Haruko Taya, *Japan at War*, **3:**215–217
Cook, Theodore F., *Japan at War*, **3:**215–217
Cooper, Ilene, **1:**162
Cooper, James Fenimore, *Last of the Mohicans*, **1:**56
Cooper, Laura, **3:**155
Coox, Alvin, **3:**216
Copenhagen (Frayn), **3:**239
Corcoran, Patrick, **1:**62
Corngold, Stanley, **2:**122
Corn King and the Spring Queen, The (Mitchison), **2:**237
Cornwell, Jocelyn, *Hard-Earned Lives*, **3:**170
Corr, Edwin G., **3:**205, 206
Correspondence. *See* Letter(s)
Corrigan, Felicitas, **2:**248
Corrigan, Philip, **3:**54
Corsini, Lorenzo, **1:**185
Cortizas, Nancy, **3:**122
Cory, Arthur M., **2:**141
COs. *See* Conscientious objectors

Costa, Richard, **1:**253
Costantino, Manuela, **1:**157
Cotnoir, Daniel, **3:**232
Cottage Dialogues among the Irish Peasantry (Leadbeater), **2:**157
Cottage Diaries, The (Leadbeater), **2:**157
Cottegnies, Line, **1:**231
Cottrell, Robert, **3:**229
Coulson, Robert, *Family Mediation*, **3:**154
Counterinsurgency, in Salvadoran Civil War, **3:**205, 206
Counter-Reformation, **1:**211
Count of Monte Christo, The (Dumas), **1:**6
Country of My Skull (Krog), **3:**242–244
Country Parson, A (Woodforde), **2:**287–289
Country Voices (Masumoto), **3:**224
Couple of Blaguards, A (McCourt), **1:**119
Courlander, Harold, *The African*, **1:**262
Courtney, Roger, *Palestinian Policeman*, **2:**104
Courts. *See* Judicial system; Supreme Court
Couser, G. Thomas, **2:**251
Coustillas, Pierre, **2:**320, 321
Coverdale, Linda, **3:**259
Coward, Noël, *The Noël Coward Diaries*, **2:**152
Cox, James M., **1:**246, 247
Cox, Virginia, **2:**161
CPS. *See* Civilian Public Service
Crabbe, George, **2:**158
Craig, Ann L.
  The First Agraristas, **3:**167, 302–304
  Popular Movements and Political Change in Mexico, **3:**302
  Transforming State-Society Relations in Mexico, **3:**302
Crane, Hart, **2:**152
Crane, Stephen, **2:**240
Crangle, Sara, **2:**325–326
Cranmer, Thomas, **2:**97, 98
Cranston, Edwin A., **2:**190

Crapanzano, Vincent, *Tuhami*, **3:**47
Crashing Thunder (Radin), **3:**318
Crawford, Julie, **2:**63
Crawford, Miki Ward, *Japanese War Brides in America*, **3:**127–130
Creation stories
  Apache, **1:**302
  Kiowa, **1:**54, 55
Creswell, John, **1:**280–281
Crèvecoeur, Michel-Guillaume Saint-Jean de, *Letters from an American Farmer*, **2:**213–216
Crick, Francis, **3:**37
Crimean War (1853–1856), **1:**111–113
Criminal activity. *See* Hate crimes; War crimes
Crisis (journal), **1:**4
Crisp, Samuel, **2:**312–313
Critical Review (newspaper), **2:**206
Criticism. *See* Literary criticism
Criticism (journal), **1:**188, 260, **2:**8
Critique (journal), **1:**165, 166
Critofari, Rita, **1:**40
Croker, John, **2:**314
Cromwell, Oliver, **1:**315, **2:**26, 65, 72, 178, 256
Cross and a Star, A (Agosín), **1:**75–77, 99
Cross and the Pear Tree, The (Perera), **1:**99
Cross-cultural adoption, Kim (Elizabeth) on, **1:**102–104
Cross-cultural autobiographies
  The Abandoned Baobab (Bugul), **1:**61–64
  Chona (Chona and Underhill), **1:**69–71
  The Color of Water (McBride), **1:**72–74
  A Cross and a Star (Agosín), **1:**75–77
  The Dark Child (Laye), **1:**128–130
  Dreams from My Father (Obama), **1:**78–80
  Infidel (Hirsi Ali), **1:**207–209
  The Interesting Narrative of the Life of Olaudah Equiano (Equiano), **1:**81–83
  A Long Way from Home (McKay), **1:**84–86

Meatless Days (Suleri), **1:**87–89

Memoirs of an Arabian Princess from Zanzibar (Ruete), **1:**90–92

My Life Story (Amrouche), **1:**93–95

Prison Writings (Peltier), **1:**96–97

Rites: A Guatemalan Boyhood (Perera), **1:**99–101

Ten Thousand Sorrows (Kim), **1:**102–104

The Travels of Marco Polo (Polo), **1:**105–107

When I Was Puerto Rican (Santiago), **1:**108–110

The Woman Warrior (Kingston), **1:**173–175

The Wonderful Adventures of Mrs. Seacole (Seacole), **1:**111–113

The Worlds of a Maasai Warrior (Saitoti), **1:**114–116

Cross-cultural families. *See* Multicultural families

Cross-cultural identity. *See* Multicultural and multiracial identities

Crothers, A. Glenn, **3:**192

Crow, Liz, **1:**45

Crow Dog, Leonard, **1:**21

Crow Dog, Mary. *See* Brave Bird, Mary

Crowell, Sandra, *Up the Swiftwater*, **3:**93

Crowley, Stephen, **3:**341

Cruikshank, Julie, *Life Lived Like a Story*, **3:**320

Crusade in Europe (television show), **3:**234

Crusades, **1:**285–288, **2:**226

Cruse, Howard, *Stuck Rubber Baby*, **1:**139

Cruzeiro Internacional, O (magazine), **1:**222

Cry, the Beloved Country (Paton), **1:**27

Cuba
    immigration to U.S. from, **1:**296–298
    Medina (Pablo) on life in, **1:**296–297
    Motorcycle Diaries (Guevara) in, **2:**220
    Revolution in (*See* Cuban Revolution)
    runaway slaves in, oral histories of, **3:**7–9
    War of Independence in, **3:**7

Cuban American(s)
    autobiographical tradition of, **1:**296–297
    Medina (Pablo) on life as, **1:**296–298

Cuban identity, **1:**296–297

Cuban Revolution, **1:**296
    Chapelle's (Dickey) reporting on, **2:**280
    end of, **2:**222
    Guevara (Ernesto "Che") in, **2:**220, 221, 222

Cuban War of Independence (1895–1898), **3:**7

Cubilié, Anne, **3:**35

Cugoana, Ottobah, *Thoughts and Sentiments on the Evil and Wicked Traffic of the Slavery and Commerce of the Human Species*, **1:**81

Culman, Ernest, **3:**15

Cultural identity. *See also* Multicultural and multiracial identities
    of Korean American adoptees, **1:**102–103

Cultural Revolution (1966–1976)
    Cheng Yu-hsiu on, **1:**153
    Confucianism's rebirth after, **3:**124
    Jiang (Ji-li) on, **1:**161–162
    Kong Demao in, **3:**124–125
    Min (Anchee) on, **1:**158–160
    oral histories of, **3:**287–289, 299–300
    policies of, **3:**287, 299
    start of, **3:**287

Cultural studies, rise of, **1:**15

Cultural transmission, by Native Americans, **3:**107–109, 325–326

Culture. *See* Popular culture; *specific cultures*

Cumming, L. M., **1:**316

Cunningham, Valentine, **3:**59–60

Cuppy, Will, **2:**193–194

Curiosities of Literature (D'Israeli), **2:**177

Curious Journey (film), **3:**27, 28

Curious Journey (Griffith and O'Grady). *See Ireland's Unfinished Revolution* (Griffith and O'Grady)

Curnutt, Kirk, **1:**333

Curriculum Vitae (Klemperer), **2:**304, 305

Currie, Ruth Douglas, **2:**252

Curtin, Philip D., *Africa Remembered*, **3:**141

Curtis, Anthony, **2:**185

Custer, George, **3:**110

Custer Died for Our Sins (Deloria), **1:**54

Custis, Lemuel R., **3:**250

Cvetkovich, Ann, **1:**141

Cyprès, Jean-Philippe, *Women of Coal*, **3:**337

Czechoslovakia
    Kafka (Franz) on life in, **2:**120–122
    Prague Spring in, **3:**33

D

Daedalus (journal), **2:**122

Dahlgren, Dorothy, *In All the West No Place Like This*, **3:**93

Daily Arkansas Gazette (newspaper), **1:**147

Daily Show, The (television show), **1:**312

Daisy Miller (James), **1:**133, **2:**114

Daklugie, Asa, **1:**302

Dakota Territory, homesteaders in, **2:**163–164

Dalai Lama, **1:**96

Dale, Gareth, **3:**247

Dale, Stephen, **2:**231

Dalfiume, Richard M., *Desegregation of the U.S. Armed Forces*, **3:**248

Dallaire, Roméo, *Shake Hands with the Devil*, **3:**258

Dallaway, James, **2:**36

Dalrymple, William, **2:**231

Daly, Jane, **2:**229

Daly, Leo, **2:**159

Daly, Mary, *Gyn/Ecology*, **2:**3, 5

Dana, Richard Henry, *Two Years before the Mast*, **1:**234

Dancing, by teachers, ban on, **3:**78
Daniel, Samuel, **2:**62, 63, 256
Daniels, Roger, **3:**225–226
Danish autobiographical writing, by Kierkegaard (Søren), **2:**166–169
Danish national identity, **2:**166
Dantas, Audálio, **2:**6, 7
Dardis, Kimiko, **3:**128
Daring Hearts (Brighton Ourstory), **3:**70–72
Dark Child, The (Laye), **1:**128–131
Darkness Visible (Styron), **1:**204–206
Darkwater (Du Bois), **1:**3
Darley, Gillian, **2:**67
Darry, Walt, **3:**95
Darwaza, Muhammad 'Izzat, **2:**104
Darwin, Charles, **1:**66
    The Autobiography of Charles Darwin, **1:**65–68
    The Descent of Man, **1:**65
    Journal and Remarks 1832–1835, **1:**65
    London and the Life (Gissing) on, **2:**321
    On the Origin of Species, **1:**65
Darwin, Emma, **1:**65
Darwish, Mahmoud, **1:**256
    In the Presence of Absence, **1:**255–257
    Journal of an Ordinary Grief, **1:**255
    Letters Underway (Ghazzawi) on, **2:**50
    Memory for Forgetfulness, **1:**255, 257, **2:**50
Das, Kamala, *My Life*, **1:**87
Dash, G. A., *Oral History Project*, **3:**153
Dashkova, Ekaterina, *Memoirs of the Princess Daschkaw*, **2:**306
Daudet, Edmond, **2:**83
Daugherty, Rae, **3:**108
Daughter of Isis, A (Saadawi), **1:**226
Daughters of the Shtetl (Glenn), **3:**305
David, Deidre, **2:**336
Davidson, Gordon W., **2:**92
Davidson, Thomas, **2:**16
Davies, Andrew, **3:**311, 313
Davies, Catherine, **3:**73, 75
Davies, David J., **3:**289

Davin, Delia, **3:**299
Davis, Angela, *Modern Motherhood*, **3:**145
Davis, Ann Marie, **3:**128–129
Davis, Jefferson, **2:**250, *251*
Davis, Margaret H., **1:**327
Davis, Philip, **3:**318, 320
Davis, Rocío G., **1:**172, 311
Davis, Rodney O., *Herndon's Informants*, **3:**264
Davis, Susan Schaefer, **3:**48
Davis, Thulani, **1:**250
Davis, Varina, **2:**250, 251
Davison, Peter, **2:**117, 118–119
Dawes Act of 1887 (U.S.), **3:**107
Dawkins, Richard, **1:**209
Dawn (Wiesel), **1:**319
Dawson, Sarah Morgan, **2:**244, 246
Day (Wiesel), **1:**319
Day, John, *The Acts and Monuments*, **2:**97
Dayal, Samir, **1:**88–89
Daybooks, **2:**333
Days of Decision (Gioglio), **3:**221
Deacon, Florence, **3:**309
Deaf-blindness, **1:**43–46
Dean, Bradley P., **1:**235
Death
    in *The Congo Diary* (Conrad), **2:**193
    in *In the Presence of Absence* (Darwish), **1:**255–257
Death of Luigi Trastulli and Other Stories, The (Portelli), **3:**96, 157–160
Death of Synge, The (Yeats), **2:**126, 127
"Death of the Author, The" (Barthes), **1:**267, 269
Death of the Heart, The (Bowen), **2:**133
Death penalty. *See* Execution
Death threats
    against Hirsi Ali (Ayaan), **1:**207
    against Rushdie (Salman), **1:**155
De Beer, Esmond S., **2:**65, 66
DeBlasio, Donna M., **3:**97
Decameron (Boccaccio), **1:**229
Declaration of Sentiments, The, **1:**12
Decolonising the Mind (Ngũgĩ), **2:**13

De Costa, Denise, **2:**24
Deering, Dorothy, **3:**345
Deffand, La Marquise du, **2:**268
Defoe, Daniel, **1:**92
    Journal of the Plague Year, **2:**174
    Robinson Crusoe, **3:**183
De Forest, William, *Miss Ravenel's Conversion*, **2:**240
Degen, Bill, **3:**94
Degler, Carl N., **2:**333
De Interpretatione (Demetrius), **2:**94
De Jesus, Carolina Maria, *Child of the Dark*, **2:**6–8, **3:**164, 322
De Klerk, Frederik Willem, **1:**27
Delaney, Lucy, *From the Darkness Cometh the Light*, **2:**250
Delaney, William, **2:**278, 279
Delaware Indians, oral histories of, **3:**107–109
Delaware Tribe in a Cherokee Nation (Obermeyer), **3:**326
Delbo, Charlotte, *Auschwitz and After*, **3:**34
Deleuze, Gilles, **2:**122
Del Giudice, Luisa, **3:**267
Deliverance (film), **3:**68
Deliverance (silent film), **1:44**
Dell'antichissima sapienza italica (Vico), **1:**183
Deloria, Vine, Jr., **3:**111
    Custer Died for Our Sins, **1:**54
Delta Airlines, **3:154**
Demetrius, *De Interpretatione*, **2:**94
Democracy, Du Bois (W. E. B.) on, **1:**4, 5
Democratic National Convention of 2004, **1:**78
Denetdale, Jennifer Nez, **3:**10, 12, 291
Deng Xiaoping, **3:**299
Denial
    as final phase of genocide, **3:**42
    of HIV-AIDS link, **3:**274
    of Holocaust, **3:**50
De Niro, Robert, **1:**47, 49
Denmark
    Kierkegaard (Søren) in, **2:**166–169
    national identity of, **2:**166
Denton, Kirk A., **2:**172

Depression (economic). *See* Great Depression
Depression (mood)
   Lincoln's (Abraham) struggle with, **3:**263
   rise of memoirs of, **1:**204–205
   Styron (William) on battle with, **1:**204–205
De Profundis (Wilde), **2:**9–11
De Quincey, Thomas, **2:**67, 140
Dernière impression, La (Haddad), **2:**262
Derounian-Stodola, Kathryn Zabelle, **1:**326, 327
Derrida, Jacques, **2:**167
Desai, Anita, *In Custody,* **1:**87
Descartes, René, *Discourse on the Method,* **1:**183, 184
Descent of Man, The (Darwin), **1:**65
Description of the New World, A (Cavendish), **1:**231
Desegregation of the U.S. Armed Forces (Dalfiume), **3:**248
Desert Exile (Uchida), **1:**309
Desert Solitaire (Abbey), **1:**234
Desert Storm, Operation. *See* Gulf War
Desmond, Adrian, **1:**67
Des Pres, Terrence, **2:**24
Destruction and Reconstruction (Taylor), **2:**250
Detained (Ngũgĩ), **1:**215, **2:**12–15
De Tilène au Plateau (Diallo), **1:**64
Detroit (Michigan)
   civil rights movement in, oral histories of, **3:**99–101
   migration of African Americans to, **3:**99
   race riots in, **3:**99, 100, *100,* 101
Detroit Lives (Mast), **3:**99
Detroit Summer, **3:**101
Detroit Urban League, **3:**99, 101
Detroit WestSiders, **3:**99
Deutschmann, David, **2:**220
De Valera, Eamon, **3:**27
De Veaux, Alexis, **2:**5
Dever, Carolyn, **1:**67
Devil on the Cross (Ngũgĩ), **2:**12, 13
Devil That Danced on the Water, The (Forna), **1:**312

DeVore, Irven, **3:**37
DeVoto, Bernard, **1:**148
DeWitt, John L., **3:**224
Dial (magazine), **1:**52, 233, **2:**92
Diallo, Bakary, *Force-Bonté,* **1:**61
Diallo, Nafissatou, *De Tilène au Plateau,* **1:**64
Dialogue and Armed Conflict (Roett and Smyth), **3:**205
Dialogues (Augustine), **1:**186
Dialogues (Rousseau), **1:**200
Diamonds, of Sierra Leone, **1:**312
Diaoyu/Senkaku (islands), **1:**340
Diaries. *See also specific works and writers*
   of American Civil War, **2:**244, 271
   British, in Mass Observation Project, **2:**235, 237
   D'Israeli (Isaac) on study of, **2:**177–179
   fictional, **2:**174
   Lejeune (Philippe) on study of, **2:**174–176
   posthumous publication of, **2:**174
   privacy as defining characteristic of, **2:**174
   rise in popularity of, **2:**65, 66, 120, 174, 177
   as source for biographies, **2:**177, 178
Diaries, 1915–1918 (Sassoon), **2:**247–249
Diaries, 1931–1949 (Orwell), **2:**117–119
Diaries of Beatrice Webb (Webb), **2:**16–18
Diaries of Franz Kafka, The (Kafka), **2:**120–122
Diaries of Lady Anne Clifford, The (Clifford), **2:**62–64
Diário da Noite (newspaper), **2:**6
Diary, Reminiscences and Correspondence of Henry Crabb Robinson (Robinson), **2:**75–77
Diary and Letters of Madame D'Arblay (Burney), **2:**312, 314
Diary from Dixie, A (Chesnut), **2:**250–252

Diary of a Madman (Gogol), **2:**174
Diary of Anaïs Nin, The (Nin), **2:**123–125
Diary of Anne Frank, The (Frank), **2:**253–255, *254*
   An Interrupted Life (Hillesum) vs., **2:**22
   Night (Wiesel) vs., **1:**320
   Red Scarf Girl (Jiang) inspired by, **1:**161
   Thura's Diary (Al-Windawi) vs., **2:**275, 277
   A Woman in Berlin (anonymous) vs., **2:**281
   A Woman Soldier's Own Story (Xie) vs., **1:**340
   Zlata's Diary (Filipovic) vs., **2:**338, 339, 340
Diary of a Nobody, The (Grossmith and Grossmith), **2:**174
Diary of John Evelyn, The (Evelyn), **2:**65–68, *72,* 328
Diary of John Quincy Adams, The (Adams), **2:**69–71
Diary of Khalil al-Sakakini, The (Sakakini), **2:**104, 106
Diary of Lady Murasaki, The (Murasaki), **2:**59, **290–293**
Diary of Robert Hooke, The (Hooke), **2:**72
Diary of Samuel Pepys, The (Pepys), **2:**72–74
   The Diary of John Evelyn (Evelyn) vs., **2:**65, 66, 72
   posthumous publication of, **2:**174, 328
   Scott (Walter) influenced by, **2:**309
Diary of Sir Henry Slingsby, The (Slingsby), **2:**256–258
Diary of Virginia Woolf, The (Woolf), **2:**133, 163, 180–182
Diary without Dates, A (Bagnold), **1:**329, **2:**259–261
Diary with Reminiscences of the War and Refugee Life in the Shenandoah Valley, A (McDonald), **2:**271
Dias, Bartolomeu, **2:**198, 199, 200
Díaz, Porfirio, **3:**167, 302, 303
Dib, Mohammed, **2:**262
DiCaprio, Leonardo, **1:**47, 49

SUBJECT INDEX

Dickens, Charles
   American Notes, **1:**43, 146, **2:**223
   Crèvecoeur (Michel-Guillaume Saint-Jean de) and, **2:**214
   The Diaries of Franz Kafka (Kafka) on, **2:**120
   Emerson (Ralph Waldo) and, **2:**140
   Goethe's (Johann Wolfgang von) influence on, **1:**276
   Journal of Katherine Mansfield (Mansfield) on, **2:**133
   London and the Life (Gissing) on, **2:**321
Dickey, Roland, **1:**56
Dickinson, Emily, **2:**238
Dictators, Latin American right-wing, rise of, **3:**185
Dictee (Cha), **1:**102
Didion, Joan, *Slouching towards Bethlehem,* **1:**88
Diet, of Gandhi (Mohandas), **1:**243. *See also* Food
Dieterich-Ward, Allen, **3:**96, 98
Dietrich, Marlene, **3:**295
Different Voices (Rittner and Roth), **3:**34
Dillard, Annie, **1:**280
   An American Childhood, **1:**279
   Living by Fiction, **1:**279
   Pilgrim at Tinker Creek, **1:**279
   Teaching a Stone to Talk, **1:**279
   The Writing Life, **1:**168, **279–281**
Dillard, Ernest, **3:**99–100
Diné. *See* Navajo
Di Porcía, Gian Artico, **1:**183, 184
Direct action, in civil rights movement, **2:**32–34
Dirrane, Bridget, **3:**316
Dirty Realism movement, **1:**48
Disabilities, people with
   Bauby (Jean-Dominique) on experience of, **1:**6–8
   education of, **1:**43, 44–45
   Keller (Helen) on experience of, **1:**43–46
   social construction of "able body" and, **1:**8
Disability & Society (journal), **1:**45

Disability literature, *The Diving Bell and the Butterfly* (Bauby) as, **1:**8
Disability studies, **1:**8, 41
Disability Studies Quarterly, **1:**41
"Disabled" (Owen), **1:**8
Disappearances, mass
   in Chile, **1:**75
   in Guatemala, **1:**99
Discourse on the Method (Descartes), **1:**183, 184
Discovery of India, The (Nehru), **1:**290, 291
Disease. *See specific diseases*
Dispatches (Herr), **1:**259, **3:**209
D'Israeli, Benjamin, **2:**177, 179
D'Israeli, Isaac
   Curiosities of Literature, **2:**177
   Miscellanies, **2:**177
   "Some Observations on Diaries, Self-Biography, and Self-Characters," **2:177–179**
Dissent (Bradley), **1:**80
DiStasi, Lawrence, *Una Storia Segreta,* **3:**224
Diurnal texts, **2:**163, 164
Divers Voyages Touching the Discoverie of America (Hakluyt), **2:**229
Divine Songs and Meditacions (Collins), **1:**229
Divine visions, of Teresa of Ávila, **1:**211, 212
Divine will, Usāmah ibn Munqidh on, **1:**285, 286
Diving Bell and the Butterfly, The (Bauby), **1:6–8**
Diving Bell and the Butterfly, The (film), **1:**6, 7
Division Street (Terkel), **3:**161, 299, 343
Divorce, in Heian period of Japan, **2:**299
Djebar, Assia, **1:**93
   Women of Algiers in Their Apartment, **1:**207
Do, Anh, *The Happiest Refugee,* **1:**337
Dobe region (Africa), oral histories of !Kung people of, **3:**37–38
Documentary films. *See also specific films*

   on Ballard (Martha), **2:**331
   on Delaware Indians, **3:**325
   on Holocaust, **3:**50, 52
   on Irish independence movement, **3:**27, 28
   on IWW, **3:**328
   on Navajo-Hopi land dispute, **3:**10, 11, 12
   on Peltier (Leonard), **1:**96
   on Saitoti (Tepilit Ole), **1:**114
   on Ukrainian coal miners, **3:**340
   on World War II, **3:**234
Documentary prose, in *Voices from Chernobyl* (Alexievich), **3:**282, 285
Dodd, Thomas J., **3:**294
Dodd, William E., **2:**251
Does My Head Look Big in This? (Abdel-Fattah), **1:**41–42
Dogs, in *A Country Parson* (Woodforde), **2:**288, 289
Dogs Bark (Conrad), **1:**166
Doi, Kochi, **2:**190, 290, 292
Doing Oral History (Ritchie), **3:**186, 294, 345
Doing Time for Peace (Riegle), **3:**229
Domesticity
   Stanton (Elizabeth Cady) on, **1:**13, 14
   Wordsworth (Dorothy) on, **2:**300, 301
Domestic Manners of the Americans (Trollope), **2:**223
Domestic violence
   in Islam, Hirsi Ali (Ayaan) on, **1:**207–209
   Malcolm X on experience of, **1:**187
   Wolff (Tobias) on experience of, **1:**47–49
Domingo, Jesús, **3:**169
Domingues, Francisco, **2:**200
Donald, David Herbert, **3:**263
Doña María's Story (James), **3:73–76**
Donbass region (Ukraine), oral histories of miners in, **3:**340–342
Donne, John, **2:**62
Donovan, Frances R., *The Schoolma'am,* **3:**77
Doody, Margret Anne, **2:**314

Doolittle, Hilda. *See* H.D.
Door, The (film), **3:**284
Dore, Elizabeth, **3:**75
Dorfman, Ariel, *Heading South, Looking North,* **1:**75
Doris Duke Indian Oral History Project, **3:**290
Doss, Helen, *The Family Nobody Wanted,* **1:**102
Dostoyevsky, Fyodor, **2:**22, 120, 133, 183, 184
Double consciousness, Obama (Barack) on, **1:**79
Double Jeopardy (Baumel), **3:**35
Dougherty, Jack, **3:**22
Dougherty, Jane Elizabeth, **1:**263
Douglas, Alfred, **2:**9–10
Douglas, David, **2:**309, 310
Douglass, Frederick, **1:**34. *See also Narrative of the Life of Frederick Douglass* (Douglass)
    Grimké (Charlotte Forten) influenced by, **2:**29
    Life and Times of Frederick Douglass, **1:**34
    My Bondage and My Freedom, **1:**34
    "Self-Made Men," **1:**180
    "What, to the Slave, Is the Fourth of July?," **1:**79
Dove Cottage (Grasmere), **2:**300, *301*
Down Came the Rain (Shields), **1:**204
Downing, Taylor, **3:**235, 236
Down These Mean Streets (Thomas), **1:**109
Draft, U.S. military, **3:**221–223
Drake, Barbara, **2:**172
Drake, Betsy, **2:**102
Dreaming of Sheep in Navajo Country (Weisiger), **3:**10
Dream of Africa, A (Laye), **1:**129
Dreams from My Father (Obama), **1:78–80**
Dreams of Trespass (Mernissi), **1:**226, 227
Dred Scott decision, **2:**38
Dreiser, Theodore, **1:**273, **2:**136
    Harlan Miners Speak, **3:**96
Drew, Bettina, **2:**338, 339, 340
Drinnon, Richard, **3:**320

Drugs
    adolescent use of, *Go Ask Alice* (anonymous) on, **2:**294–296
    in culture of 1960s, **2:**294
    U.S. war on, **2:**294
    Williams's (Tennessee) struggle with addiction to, **2:**152
Drummond, Henry, **1:**150
Dryden, John, **1:**90
D'Souza, Dinesh, **3:**166
Dube, John, **2:**241
Duberman, Martin, **1:**4
Dublin (Ireland)
    Abbey Theatre of, **2:**126, 128
    oral histories of life in, **3:**315, 317
Dublin Pub Life and Lore (Kearns), **3:**315, 317
Dublin Voices (Kearns), **3:**315
Du Bois, W. E. B., **1:**4
    The Autobiography of W. E. B. Du Bois, **1:3–5**, 18
    on *Black Boy* (Wright), **1:**123
    Black Flame trilogy, **1:**5
    Darkwater, **1:**3
    Dusk of Dawn, **1:**3, 4
    on *Home to Harlem* (McKay), **1:**84
    The Souls of Black Folk, **1:**4, 51
    The Study of the Negro Problem, **1:**50
    on *Up from Slavery* (Washington), **1:**51, 52
    and Washington (Booker T.), debate between, **1:**186
Dudley, David L., **1:**4
Duesberg, Peter, **3:**274
Duffey, Carolyn, **1:**93, 94
Dumas, Alexandre, *The Count of Monte Christo,* **1:**6
Dumm, Gary, *Students for a Democratic Society,* **3:**330
Dunbar, Paul Laurence, "Sympathy," **1:**50
Duncan, Isadora, **1:**85
Duncan, Patti, **1:**159
Duncan, Robert, **2:**123
Dundas, Henry, **2:**217–219
Dunham, Ann, **1:**78
Dunham, Janice, **1:**97

Dunmore, Helen, **1:**195
Dunn, Oliver, **2:**203
Dunnaway, Jen, **3:**201
Dunton, John, **2:**195
Duong Thu Huong, *Paradise of the Blind,* **1:**335
Duong Van Minh, **3:**280
Durham University Journal, **2:**185
Durrell, Lawrence, **2:**123
Duryea, Lyman C., **3:**206
Dusk of Dawn (Du Bois), **1:**3, 4
Dustan, Hannah, **1:**326, 328
Duston, Troy, **3:**20
Dust Tracks on a Road (Hurston), **1:9–11,** 18, 122
Dutch autobiographical writing
    by Hillesum (Etty), **2:**22–24
    by Hirsi Ali (Ayaan), **1:**207–209
Dyer, Geoff, **2:**81
Dyer, Reginald, **1:**289
Dyk, Ruth, **3:**319
Dyk, Walter, *Left Handed, Son of Old Man Hat,* **3:318–321**
Dykes to Watch Out For (Bechdel), **1:**139, 141
Dylan, Bob, **3:**159
Dziak, John, *Chekisty,* **3:**245

E

Eaglestone, Robert, **1:**313–314
Eakin, Paul John, **1:**188, 246
Early American Literature (journal), **1:**327
Earthquakes
    in China, **3:**301
    in Iran, **3:**220
East, Rupert, *Akiga's Story,* **3:**141
East Anglia (England), oral histories of village life in, **3:**59–61, *60*
Eastern California Museum (ECM), **3:**102
Easter Uprising of 1916 (Ireland), **3:**27, *28,* 315
East Germany, oral histories of Stasi in, **3:**245–247
East India Company, **2:**229–231
East of the Mediterranean (Munif), **2:**50

Easton, Celia A., **2**:289
East West Exchange, **1**:163
Eberstadt, Fernanda, **1**:156–157
Ecce Homo (Nietzsche), **1**:183
Echeverría, Luis, **3**:32
Eclectic Review (journal), **2**:178–179
ECM. *See* Eastern California Museum
Eco-criticism, **1**:279
Economic disparity
  industrialization in rise of, **2**:300
  among Native Americans, **3**:290
  in oral histories, **3**:190
Economic opportunity, for blacks in Reconstruction era, **1**:50
Economic Opportunity Act of 1964 (U.S.), **3**:254, *255*
Economic problems. *See* Finances, personal
Economic racism, **1**:4
Economics, of cancer, **2**:3–4, 5
Economist, The (weekly), **1**:126, **3**:300–301
Economy
  Britain, working class in, **3**:53
  Chinese, as socialist market, **1**:158
  German, after World War I, **1**:30, **3**:234
  Mexican, indigenous people in, **3**:168
Economy, U.S. *See also* Great Depression
  prosperity in, before Great Depression, **3**:161
  slavery in, **1**:33
  women in post-revolutionary, **2**:331–332
  after World War II, **3**:343
Écriture artiste, **2**:81, 83
Écriture féminine, **1**:250, **2**:124
Edel, Leon, **2**:113, 115
Edele, Mark, **3**:332
Edelstein, Tilden, **2**:239, 240
Edgeworth, Maria, **2**:157
Edinburgh Review (journal), **2**:35, 36, 73, 314
Editor & Publisher (magazine), **2**:279

Education
  Arab, poetry in, **1**:287
  in Britain, **2**:136, 320, **3**:311–313
  of children with disabilities, **1**:43, 44–45
  French, in Algeria, **1**:93, 94, **2**:262–263
  Islamic, in Egypt, **1**:135
  self-, Franklin (Benjamin) on, **1**:179, 180
  of women (*See* Education, of women)
Education, in U.S.
  Adams's (Henry) critique of, **1**:132–134
  affirmative action in, **1**:15
  of African Americans, at white colleges, **3**:20–22
  of African Americans, in Reconstruction, **1**:51
  anarchists' critique of, **3**:5
  bilingual, **1**:15–17
  at experimental boarding schools, **1**:164
  of Native Americans, at boarding schools, **3**:109, 318
  oral histories of teachers in, **3**:77–79
  racial quotas in, **3**:20
  Rodriguez (Richard) on, **1**:15–16
  school desegregation in, **1**:122, 249, **3**:44
  secondary, as compulsory, **3**:343
  of slaves, in preparation for emancipation, **2**:29–31, *30*
Education, of women
  in eighteenth-century Europe, **2**:35–36
  in eighteenth-century U.S., **2**:316–318
  in fifteenth-century Europe, **2**:160–161
  in Morocco, **3**:49
Education Act of 1870 (Britain), **3**:311
Educational Studies (journal), **3**:78
Education of Henry Adams, The (Adams), **1**:15, **132–134**, 180
Edwardian Childhoods (Thompson), **3**:312

Edwardians, The (Thompson), **3**:176, 186, 311
Edwards, Beatrice, *Places of Origin*, **3**:205
Edwards, Jonathan, **2**:197
Edwards, Louise, **3**:148–149
Edwards, Matilda, **3**:263
Edwards, Reginald, **3**:201
Edward VI (king of England), *The Literary Remains of Edward VI*, **2:97–100**, *98*
Edward VII (king of Great Britain), **2**:210
Edward VIII (king of Great Britain), **2**:235
Egan, Susanna, **1**:248
Eggers, Dave, *Voice of Witness*, **3**:161
Eglington, Lord, **2**:329
Egocentrism, Soyinka (Wole) accused of, **1**:216
Egotism, Romantic, **2**:177, 179
Egypt
  autobiographical tradition of, **1**:136
  British colonial rule of, **1**:135
  Hussein (Taha) on life in, **1**:135–137
  independence of (1922), **1**:135
  Islamic education in, **1**:135
  Revolution of 1919 in, **1**:135
  Revolution of 1952 in, **1**:135
  Usāmah ibn Munqidh on history of, **1**:285
Egyptian Childhood, An (Hussein), **1:135–138**
Eickelcamp, Ute, **3**:334
Eighteen Poems (Thomas), **1**:125
Eighteenth-Century Studies (journal), **1**:327
8 mars (journal), **3**:47
Eighty Years and More, Reminiscences 1815–1897 (Stanton), **1:12–14**
Eikon Basilike (Charles I), **2**:256, 258
Einstein, Albert, **3**:239
Eire, Carlos, *Waiting for Snow in Havana*, **1**:296–297
Eire-Ireland (journal), **2**:308
Ejército Zapatista de Liberación Nacional (EZLN), **3**:304

Ejido (land collective), **3:**302–304
Elaine Massacre (1919), **1:**18
Elementary Education Act of 1870 (Britain), **2:**136, 320
Elena, Eduardo, **3:**75
El Fassi, Malika, **3:**48
Elfenbein, Andrew, **2:**144, 145
ELH (journal), **2:**64
Eli (Sachs), **2:**255
Eliach, Yaffa, **3:**34
   Holocaust Oral History Manual, **3:**35
Eliot, T. S., **2:**147, 180
Elizabeth Cady Stanton as Revealed in Her Letters, Diary and Reminiscences (Stanton and Stanton), **1:**13
Elizabeth I (queen of England), **2:**62, 72, 99
Elle (magazine), **1:**6
Eller, Cynthia, *Conscientious Objectors and the Second World War,* **3:**227
Ellipses, Bagnold's (Enid) use of, **2:**260
Ellis, Henry, **2:**226
Ellis, Russ, **3:**21, 22
Ellison, Ralph, **1:**122, 124
Ellman, Richard, **2:**10
Ellwood, Thomas, **2:**26
Elman, Richard, **1:**100
Elon, Amos, **2:**304
El Salvador, oral histories of civil war in, **3:**205–208, *206*
El Salvador at War (Manwaring and Prisk), **3:205–208**
El Salvador: Testament of Terror (Fish and Sganga), **3:**206
Eltis, David, **1:**263
Eluard, Paul, **2:**52
Éluard, Paul, **1:**222
Emancipation Act of 1834 (Britain), **1:**111
Emancipation Proclamation of 1863 (U.S.), **1:**50, **3:**261
Embedded journalism, **2:**278–280
Embedded: The Media at War in Iraq (Katovsky and Carlson), **3:**276
Embroideries (Satrapi), **1:**155
Emergence of a UAW Local, The (Friedlander), **3:**153
Emerson, Everett, **2:**214

Emerson, Gloria, **2:**278
Emerson, Ralph Waldo, **2:140**
   "The American Scholar," **1:**180
   Dillard (Annie) influenced by, **1:**279
   Hawthorne (Nathaniel) and, **2:**139, 223
   James's (Henry) friendship with, **2:**113
   Journals of Ralph Waldo Emerson, **2:139–142**
   "Nature," **2:**141
   Robinson's (Henry Crabb) friendship with, **2:**75
   "Self-Reliance," **1:**180
   Thoreau (Henry David) and, **1:**233, **2:**139, 140
Emigration. *See* Immigration
Emms, Stephen, **2:**154
Emotions
   of Christmas, Thomas (Dylan) on, **1:**125–126
   in *The Diary of John Quincy Adams* (Adams), **2:**70
   in "Letter to Maria Clemm" (Poe), **2:**41–43
   in Stoicism, **1:**218
Empathy, in feminist oral history, **3:**190
Enahoro, Peter, **1:**215–216
Encomienda system, **2:**202, **3:**302
En 18 (Goncourt and Goncourt), **2:**82
Enemies among Us (Schmitz), **3:**224
"Enemy aliens," U.S. treatment of, **3:**224
Enfance (Sarraute), **1:**268
Enfant Noir, L' (Laye). *See Dark Child, The* (Laye)
Engel, Jeff, **3:**232
Engelmann, Larry, *Tears before the Rain,* **3:**210, 265, **279–281**
Engendering the Chinese Revolution (Gilmartin), **3:**147
Enger, Leif, **1:**281
   Peace Like a River, **1:**281
England. *See also* Britain; English autobiographical writing; English oral histories
   agriculture in, **3:**59–61, 63–65

   Bloomsbury group in, **2:**133, 180, 268–269
   Catholicism in, decline of, **2:**97, 99, 226
   Christianity in, arrival of, **1:**189
   homosexuality in, **3:**70–72
   Irish conquest by, **3:**315
   Lessing's (Doris) move to, **1:**167
   Mansfield's (Katherine) travels in, **2:**133, 135
   Victorian (*See* Victorian era)
   women of (*See* English women)
Engle, Paul, **2:**121
English, Kathy, **3:**233
English autobiographical writing. *See also specific works and writers*
   by Bagnold (Enid), **2:**259–261
   by Barnard (Anne), **2:**217–219
   by Bennett (Arnold), **2:**136–138
   by Brittain (Vera), **1:**329–331
   by Burney (Fanny), **2:**312–314
   by Byron (George Gordon Noel), **2:**143–145
   by Cavendish (Margaret), **1:**229–231
   by Clifford (Anne), **2:**62–64
   by Conrad (Joseph), **2:**192–194
   by Darwin (Charles), **1:**65–67
   by D'Israeli (Isaac), **2:**177–179
   by Edward VI, **2:**97–99
   by Equiano (Olaudah), **1:**81–83
   by Evelyn (John), **2:**65–67
   by Fox (George), **2:**26–28
   by Gissing (George), **2:**320–322
   by Guylforde (Richarde), **2:**226–228
   by Halkett (Anne), **1:**315–317
   by Keats (John), **2:**146–148
   by Kemble (Fanny), **2:**335–337
   by Kempe (Margery), **1:**189–191
   by Last (Nella), **2:**265–267
   by Lessing (Doris), **1:**167–169
   by Maugham (W. Somerset), **2:**183–185
   by Montagu (Mary Wortley), **2:**35–37
   by Orwell (George), **2:**117–119
   by Partridge (Frances), **2:**268–270

English autobiographical writing, *continued*
- by Pepys (Samuel), **2**:72–74
- by Robinson (Henry Crabb), **2**:75–77
- in Romantic era, surge of, **2**:16
- by Ruskin (John), **1**:264–266
- by Sassoon (Siegfried), **2**:247–249
- by Slingsby (Henry), **2**:256–258
- by Victoria, **2**:209–211
- in Victorian era, traits of, **1**:65, 67
- by Webb (Beatrice), **2**:16–18
- by Wells (H. G.), **1**:252–254
- by Wesley (John), **2**:195–197
- by Wilde (Oscar), **2**:9–11
- by Wollstonecraft (Mary), **2**:109–111
- by Woodforde (James), **2**:287–289
- by Woolf (Virginia), **2**:180–182
- by Wordsworth (Dorothy), **2**:300–302

English Civil War (1642–1651)
- Anglicanism in, **2**:26, 72, 256
- Cavendish (Margaret) on life during, **1**:229, 231
- Evelyn (John) on life during, **2**:65
- Halkett (Anne) on life during, **1**:315–317
- Osborne (Dorothy) on life during, **2**:324
- Slingsby (Henry) in, **2**:256–258

English Historical Review (journal), **2**:17–18, **3**:313
English in Africa (journal), **2**:218
English Journal, **1**:16, 42, 253, **2**:254, **3**:345

English language
- *The Book of Margery Kempe* (Kempe) as first autobiography in, **1**:189
- in Puerto Rico, **1**:109
- in U.S. education, **1**:15, 16, 17

English Literature in Transition (journal), **2**:10

English oral histories
- of gays and lesbians, **3**:70–72
- of village life, **3**:59–61, 63–65
- of working-class women, **3**:144–146
- of working-class youth, **3**:311–313, *312*

English Studies in Canada (journal), **1**:169

English women
- eighteenth-century, Montagu (Mary Wortley) on opportunities for, **2**:35
- land inheritance by, Clifford (Anne) on, **2**:62–63, 64
- medieval, Kempe (Margery) on, **1**:189–191
- seventeenth-century, Clifford (Anne) on, **2**:62–64
- Victorian, Webb (Beatrice) on, **2**:16–18
- in workforce, entry of, **2**:266, **3**:145
- working-class, oral histories of, **3**:144–146
- in World War I, **1**:329–331, **2**:259

"Enigma of Arrival, The" (Paquet), **1**:112–113

Enlightenment
- Goethe (Johann Wolfgang von) in, **1**:276
- Jefferson (Thomas) in, **2**:316
- Scottish contributions to, **2**:328
- Wollstonecraft (Mary) in, **2**:109

Enneads (Plotinus), **1**:196
Enright, Pat, **3**:159
Entrepreneurs, Hispanic American, oral histories of, **3**:121–123
Entrepreneurs in Cultural Context (Greenfield), **3**:121
Environmental costs, of coal mining, **3**:66, 67, 86
Environmental factors, in cancer, **2**:3
Enzensberger, Hans Magnus, **2**:282
Enzer, Hyman A., **2**:254
Epictetus, **2**:96
Epileptic (David B.), **1**:155
Epistulae familiares (Cereta). *See Collected Letters of a Renaissance Feminist* (Cereta)
Eppes, Elizabeth, **2**:316
Epstein, Joseph, **2**:185
Equal Accommodations Act of 1938 (Michigan), **3**:99
Equality. *See* Gender equality; Racial equality; Social equality
Equal Pay Act of 1963 (U.S.), **3**:339

Equiano, Olaudah, **1**:82
- *The Interesting Narrative of the Life of Olaudah Equiano*, **1**:34, 81–83, 142, **3**:23
- Wheatley (Phillis) compared to, **1**:81, **2**:44

Erasmus, Desiderius, **1**:196, **2**:98
Erbaugh, Mary S., **3**:301
Erdoes, Erich, **1**:23
Erdoes, Richard, **1**:21, 23
Ergas, Yasmine, **2**:23, 24
Escalante Fontaneda, Hernando de, **1**:325
Esfandiary, Soraya, *The Autobiography of H.I.H. Soraya*, **3**:218
Eskew, Glenn T., **3**:249–250
Eskimo, The (Weyer), **3**:138
Espada, Martin, **1**:109
Espectador, El (newspaper), **3**:183, 184, 185
Espionage, by Maugham (W. Somerset), **2**:183
Essais (Montaigne), **2**:72
Essay on the Principles of Population (Malthus), **1**:65
Essay to Revive the Antient Education of Gentlewomen, An (Makin), **2**:35
Essex (England), oral histories of working-class youth in, **3**:311–313, *312*
Estrangement (Yeats), **2**:126–128
Ethnic discrimination. *See* Anti-Semitism; Racism
Ethnic identity, assimilation and oral histories of, **3**:305
- Rodriguez (Richard) on, **1**:15–17
- Santiago (Esmeralda) on, **1**:108
Ethnicity, in *Dust Tracks on a Road* (Hurston), **1**:11
Ethnographic autobiography, Native American, **1**:69–70

Ethnography
- in *Doña María's Story* (James), **3**:73
- in *Juan the Chamula* (Pozas), **3**:167, 168
- in *Nisa* (Shostak), **3**:37–38

Ethnology (journal), **1**:115
Etter-Lewis, Gwendolyn, **3**:191
- *My Soul Is My Own*, **3**:21

Europe. *See also specific countries*
   The Autobiography of Ben Franklin (Franklin) in, **1:**181
   Bugul's (Ken) experience as African in, **1:**61–62
   colonies of (*See* Colonialism)
   gender roles in, eighteenth-century, **2:**35–37
   gender roles in, Renaissance, **2:**160–162
   instability in interwar period of, **1:**329
   James's (Henry) time in, **2:**113, 114
   Letters from an American Farmer (Crèvecoeur) in, **2:**213, 214
   querelle de femmes in early modern, **2:**160
   Ruete's (Emily) experience as African in, **1:**90–92
   student movements of 1968 in, **3:**33
   travel narratives of, **1:**90–91
   women of, vs. Muslim women, **1:**90
European Journal of American Studies, **1:**78
European Parliament, **3:**292
European Romantic Review (journal), **2:**301
Eusebius, **2:**94
Eustics, Ida Elrod, **1:10**
Evans, Elizabeth, **2:**78, 79, 80
Evans, George Ewart, *Ask the Fellows Who Cut the Hay,* **3:**59, **63–65**
Evans, Larry, **3:**340, 342
Evelina (Burney), **2:**312–313, 314
Evelyn, John, **2:**66
   Boswell (James) compared to, **2:**328
   A Character of England, **2:**65
   The Diary of John Evelyn, **2:**65–68, 72, 328
   Fumifugium, **2:**65
   Pepys (Samuel) compared to, **2:**65, 66, 72
   Sculptura, **2:**65
   Woodforde (James) compared to, **2:**287
Evelyn, Mary, **1:**229

Everybody's Autobiography (Stein), **1:**332
Everything We Had (Santoli), **3:**199, 201, **209–211**, 231, 275, 279
Evil spirits, *The Diary of Lady Murasaki* (Murasaki) on, **2:**292
Evolution, **1:**65–67
Ewen, Elizabeth, *Immigrant Women in the Land of Dollars,* **3:**305
Examiner (newspaper), **2:**146
Execution
   of Alexandra Feodorovna, **2:**84
   of Charles I, **2:**26, 65, 72, 178, 256, 257, *257*
   of Nazi war criminals, **2:**56
   of Slingsby (Henry), **2:**256, 257
Executive Order 8802, U.S., **3:**44, 248
Executive Order 9066, U.S., **1:**299, 311, **3:**104, 195, 224
Executive Order 9981, U.S., **3:**199, 249
Executive Order 11246, U.S., **3:**339
Exile
   Cavendish (Margaret) in, **1:**229
   Cubans in, **1:**296–297
   Darwish (Mahmoud) in, **1:**255
   Iranians in, **3:**218
   Jews in, **1:**75
   Laye (Camara) in, **1:**130
   Luthuli (Albert) in, **1:**24
   Nabokov (Vladimir) in, **1:**270
   Soyinka (Wole) in, **1:**214
Exiled Memories (Medina), **1:296–298**
Existentialism, Wiesel (Elie) influenced by, **1:**318
Exodus to Shanghai (Hochstadt), **3:14–16**
Experiment in Autobiography, An (Wells), **1:252–254**
Exploration, global
   by Columbus (Christopher), **2:**201–203
   by Gama (Vasco da), **2:**198–200
   tradition of narratives of, **2:**198–199
Exploration, of U.S. West, by Carver (Jonathan), **2:**205–207. *See also* Westward expansion
Expression, freedom of
   in China, **3:**301

   in South Africa, **1:**29
   in Soviet Union, **3:**333
Extraordinary Work of Ordinary Writing, The (Sinor), **2:163–165**
Extrapolation (journal), **1:**253
Extremist Islam. *See* Fundamentalist Islam
Eyes on the Prize (television series), **2:**34, **3:**44, 45, 46
Eyewitnesses at Nuremberg (Gaskin), **3:**293
EZLN. *See* Ejército Zapatista de Liberación Nacional

F

Fabian Society, **2:**16, 172, 235
Face of War, The (Gellhorn), **2:**102
Faces in a Mirror (Pahlavi), **3:**218
Fachinger, Petra, **1:**17
Faderman, Lillian, *Gay L.A.,* **3:**83–84
Fadiman, Jeffrey A.
   The Moment of Conquest, **3:**141
   An Oral History of Tribal Warfare, **3:**141
   South Africa's "Black" Market, **3:**142
   When We Began, There Were Witchmen, **3:141–143**
Faery, Rebecca Blevins, **1:**325–326
Faith. *See* Religious faith
Falk, Stanley, **3:**216
Fallen Leaves (Nguyen), **1:**335
Falling Leaves (Yen Mah), **1:**159
Fall of the Shah (Hoveyda), **3:**218
Familiar letters, **2:**217
Family(ies)
   African American, Hansberry's (Lorraine) depiction of, **1:**273–275
   Chinese, Cheng Yu-hsiu on, **1:**153
   dysfunctional, of Bechdel (Alison), **1:**139–140
   English working-class, oral histories of, **3:**144–146
   instability in, Wolff (Tobias) on, **1:**47–49
   multicultural (*See* Multicultural families)

Family Letters of Thomas Jefferson, The (Jefferson), **2:**317
Family Mediation (Coulson), **3:**154
Family Nobody Wanted, The (Doss), **1:**102
Famine
    in China, **3:**287, 299, 300
    in Ireland, **3:**27, 315
    in Ukraine, **3:**19
Fano, Claudio, **3:**266
Fanon, Frantz
    Feraoun (Mouloud) compared to, **2:**262, 263, 264
    Gandhi (Mohandas) compared to, **1:**244
    The Wretched of the Earth, **1:**207, **2:**263
Fanshawe, Ann, *Memoirs,* **1:**229–230, 315, 316, 317
Fanshawe, Richard, **1:**317
Farabundo Marti National Liberation Front (FMLN), **3:**205
Faragher, John Mack, **2:**91, 92
Farah, Nurrudin, *Sweet and Sour Milk,* **1:**207
Färberböck, Max, **2:**281
Fard, W. D., **1:**188
Far Eastern Economic Review (journal), **3:**288
Farewell to Arms, A (Hemingway), **2:**259
Farewell to Manzanar (Houston and Houston), **1:299–301,** 309
Farmanfarmian, Abolbashar, **3:**220
Farmer, James, *Lay Bare the Heart,* **3:**44
Farmer-Kaiser, Mary, **2:**246
Farming. *See* Agriculture
Farming the Home Place (Matsumoto), **3:**80
Farral, Fred, **3:**177
Farrison, Edward, **1:**11
Fassin, Didier, *When Bodies Remember,* **3:**272
Fast Horse, Lizzy, **1:**22
Father's Law, A (Wright), **1:**124
"Father's Legacy, A" (Slingsby), **2:**256, 257, 258
Fatwa, against Rushdie (Salman), **1:**155

Faulkner, William, **1:**123, **2:**152
    Big Woods, **2:**215
Faunce, William, **1:**220
Fausel, Nettie, **3:**103
Faust, Drew Gilpin, **2:**246, 271, 272
Faustine, La (Goncourt), **2:**308
Favelas (shantytowns), **2:**6–8, *7*
Fay, Frank, **2:**128
Fay, Willie, **2:**128
Fayer, Steve, *Voices of Freedom,* **3:44–46**
FBI. *See* Federal Bureau of Investigation
FDR. *See* Revolutionary Democratic Front
February Revolution (1917), **2:**84
Fedele, Cassandra, **2:**160
Federal Bureau of Investigation (FBI), **1:**96–98, **3:**224
Federal Writers' Project (FWP), **3:**22, 86, 161, 173, 179
Feinesser, Bronislawa, **3:**35
Feinman, Ilene, **3:**270
Felber, Lynette, **2:**124
Fellman, Michael, **2:**39
Fellows, Jay, **1:**266
Female circumcision, Hirsi Ali (Ayaan) on, **1:**207
Female Peronist Party (Argentina), **3:**75
Feminine writing style, vs. masculine writing style, **1:**250
Feminism
    black perspective in, need for, **1:**249, 250, **2:**3, 5
    in China, rise of, **3:**147–149
    in field of history, **3:**176, 177
    in field of oral history, **3:**190–192
    first-wave, **3:**268
    global rise of, **3:**37
    and interest in women's autobiographies, **1:**37
    in peace movement, **3:**268
    second-wave, **3:**268
    of *Walden* (Thoreau), **1:**236
    during World War II, Mitchison (Naomi) on, **2:**235–236
Feminist autobiographical writing
    The Abandoned Baobab (Bugul) as, **1:**64
    Bone Black (hooks) as, **1:**249–250

    Child of the Dark (de Jesus) as, **2:**6
    Collected Letters of a Renaissance Feminist (Cereta) as, **2:**160–162
    The Collected Letters of Mary Wollstonecraft (Wollstonecraft) as, **2:**109–111
    Diaries of Beatrice Webb (Webb) as, **2:**16, 18
    The Diaries of Lady Anne Clifford (Clifford) as, **2:**64
    The Diary of Anaïs Nin (Nin) as, **2:**124
    The Journal of Marie Bashkirtseff (Bashkirtseff) as, **2:**306
    Let Me Speak! (Viezzer and Barrios de Chungara) as, **3:**322–323
    Letters and Journals of Fanny Burney (Burney) as, **2:**313–314
    Letters of a Woman Homesteader (Stewart) as, **2:**91
    The Letters of Lady Anne Barnard to Henry Dundas (Barnard) as, **2:**218
    "Letter to Her Daughter" (Montagu) as, **2:**35–37
    Meatless Days (Suleri) as, **1:**88–89
    A Mountainous Journey (Tuqan) as, **1:**225, 227
    tradition of, **1:**249
    Women in the Mines (Moore) as, **3:**337, 338
Feminist science fiction, **2:**237
Feminist Studies (journal), **1:**113
Femme d'Afrique (Kéita), **1:**64
Femmes et Politique (Akharbach and Rerhaye), **3:**47
Feng Jicai
    Let One Hundred Flowers Bloom, **1:**161
    Ten Years of Madness, **3:**287
    The Three-Inch Golden Lotus, **3:**289
    Voices from the Whirlwind, **3:287–289,** 301
Fenwomen (Chamberlain), **3:**61
Feraoun, Mouloud
    Journal, 1955–1962, **2:262–264**
    The Poor Man's Son, **2:**262, 263, 264
Ferdinand (king of Spain), **2:**201
Ferman, Claudia, **3:**166

Fermi, Enrico, **3:**239
Fernández-Armesto, Felipe, **2:**200
Fernández Barrios, Flor, *Blessed by Thunder,* **1:**296
Ferrari, Christine, **2:**30
Ferrie, Pauline, **3:**29
Ferris, Ina, **2:**179
Ferris, Jean Leon Gerome, **1:180**
Fest, Joachim, **2:**55, 56
Feudalism, in China, **3:**124
Fiction
    in collective novels, **3:**282, 285
    in *An Egyptian Childhood* (Hussein), **1:**136
    in *Go Ask Alice* (anonymous), **2:**294
    in novels of manners, **2:**312
    science, **1:**231, **2:**237
    in *Stop-Time* (Conroy), **1:**164, 165
    transcendental, **1:**281
    in *Truth and Fiction Relating to My Life* (Goethe), **1:**276
Fictional diaries, **2:**174
Fielding, Henry, **2:**328
Fields, James T., **2:**224
Fierce Attachments (Gornick), **1:**279
Fifteenth Amendment, **1:**50, **2:**238
Fifth Column, The (Hemingway), **2:**102
Fighting Words (Ball and Porter), **1:**97
Filipovic, Alica, **2:**338
Filipovic, Malik, **2:**338
Filipovic, Zlata, *Zlata's Diary,* **2:**275, **338–340**, *339*
Filippelli, Ronald L., **3:**329
Film adaptations. *See also* Documentary films; *specific films*
    of *Akenfield* (Blythe), **3:**59
    of *Angela's Ashes* (McCourt), **1:**120, *120*
    of *The Autobiography of Malcolm X* (Malcolm X), **1:**186
    of *Country of My Skull* (Krog), **3:**242
    of *The Diary of Anne Frank* (Frank), **2:**253, 254
    of *The Diving Bell and the Butterfly* (Bauby), **1:**6, 7, *7*
    of *An Egyptian Childhood* (Hussein), **1:**137
    of *Farewell to Manzanar* (Houston and Houston), **1:**299
    of *Geronimo* (Geronimo and Barrett), **1:**304
    of *The Good Man of Nanking* (Rabe), **2:**19
    of *Letters of a Woman Homesteader* (Stewart), **2:**91
    of *Motorcycle Diaries* (Guevara), **2:**220
    of *National Velvet* (Bagnold), **2:**261
    of *Native Son* (Wright), **1:**124
    of *Persepolis* (Satrapi), **1:**156, 157
    of *The Story of My Life* (Keller), **1:44**
    of *This Boy's Life* (Wolff), **1:**47, 49
    of *When Heaven and Earth Changed Places* (Hayslip), **1:**335, 336
    of Williams's (Tennessee) plays, **2:**152
    of *A Woman in Berlin* (anonymous), **2:**281
Finances, personal
    Poe's (Edgar Allan) preoccupation with, **2:**41–42
    Scott's (Walter) trouble with, **2:**309, 310
Finley, C. Stephen, **1:**265–266
Finn, Margot, **2:**289, 322
Finnegans Wake (Joyce), **1:**185
Firestone, Jennifer, **2:**150
Firestone, Shulamith, **3:**37
Firm, The (Bruce), **3:245–247**
First Agraristas, The (Craig), **3:167, 302–304**
First Household under Heaven, The (Meng), **3:**125
First Nations people. *See* Native American(s)
First Person America (Banks), **3:**161
First South Carolina Volunteers, **2:**238–240
First They Killed My Father (Ung), **1:**306
First Well, The (Jabra), **1:**136
Fisch, Max Harold, **1:**183, 184, 185
Fish, Joe, *El Salvador,* **3:**206
Fishburne, Laurence, **3:**249
Fishel, John T., *Uncomfortable Wars Revisited,* **3:**207
Fisher, Michael H., **2:**231
Fish in the Water, A (Vargas Llosa), **1:**168
Fishkin, Shelley Fisher, **1:**173
Fiss, Harry, **3:**295
FitzGerald, Edward, **2:**196
Fitzgerald, F. Scott, **1:**140
    The Great Gatsby, **1:**47
Fitzgerald, Robert, **2:**129, 131
Fitzgerald, Sally, **2:**129, 131
Fitzpatrick, David, *Politics and Irish Life,* **3:**27
Five Days That Shocked the World (Best), **3:**235
Flanagan, John Richard, **1:**154
Flaubert, Gustave, **2:**120, 268
    Letters, **2:**268
    Sentimental Education, **1:**128
Flaxman, John, **2:**77
Fleche, Andre, **2:**240
Fleishmann, Ulrich, **3:**8
Flenley, Paul, **3:**341–342
FLN. *See* National Liberation Front
Floating nation, Puerto Rico as, **1:**108
Florida, U.S. annexation of, **2:**69
Florio, John, **2:**256
Flu pandemic of 1918, **1:**258
Flynn, Sarah, **3:**44
FMLN. *See* Farabundo Marti National Liberation Front
Folklore
    African American, **1:**9
    Chinese, **1:**173, 174
Folk music, **3:**96, 157, 159
Follain, John, **1:**40
Fones-Wolf, Ken, **3:**97–98
Food
    in *A Country Parson* (Woodforde), **2:**288, 289
    diet of Gandhi (Mohandas), **1:**243
    in *Meatless Days* (Suleri), **1:**87, 88–89
    in *When I Was Puerto Rican* (Santiago), **1:**109
Foot, John, **3:**267
Foot binding, **1:**338, **3:**147, 289

SUBJECT INDEX

Forbes, Andrew, **3:**102
Forbes, Shannon, **1:**121
Forbidden Zone, The (Borden), **2:**259
Force-Bonté (Diallo), **1:**61
Forced labor
　in China, **1:**158
　in Soviet Union (*See* Gulag system)
Ford, Gerald, **1:**311, **3:**221
Ford, Henry
　The International Jew, **1:**30, 32
　My Life and Work, **1:**30
Forefathers' Eve (Mickiewicz), **2:**192
Foreign Affairs (journal), **2:**279, **3:**246, 332
Forgiveness, in Truth and Reconciliation Commission, **3:**243, 244
Forna, Aminatta, *The Devil That Danced on the Water,* **1:**312
Forrester, Michael, *Tsuchino,* **3:**127–128
Fors Clavigera (Ruskin), **1:**264
Forster, E. M., **2:**180, 235
Forten, James, **2:**29
Forten, Richard, **2:**29
For Their Own Good (Beier), **3:**144–145
For Those Who Come After (Krupat), **1:**71
Fortnightly Review (magazine), **2:**82–83
For Whom the Bell Tolls (Hemingway), **2:**101
Fosse Ardeatine massacre (1944), oral histories of, **3:**265–267, *266*
Fossey, Diane, **3:**37
Foster, David, **2:**10
Foster, David William, **1:**17
Foster, Ollie, **3:**100
Foundation Act of 1934 (Britain), **1:**149
Fourie, Pieter, *The Politics of AIDS Denialism,* **3:**272
Fourteen Points (Wilson), **3:**29
Fourteenth Amendment, **1:**50
Fox, George, *Journal of George Fox,* **2:**26–28, *27*
Fox, Margaret, **2:**26
Fox, Stephen
　America's Invisible Gulags, **3:**226
　UnCivil Liberties, **3:**226

The Unknown Internment, **3:**215, **224–226**
Foxe, John, **2:**97, 98–99
Foy, Harriet D., **1:**10
France. *See also* French autobiographical writing
　Algeria as colony of, **1:**93–94, **2:**262–264
　Bashkirtseff (Marie) as immigrant in, **2:**306–308
　cultural decadence of, **2:**306–307
　Franklin (Benjamin) as ambassador to, **1:**179, *180*
　in French and Indian War, **2:**205
　Guinea as colony of, **1:**128, 129, 130
　Indochina as colony of, **3:**279
　Jefferson (Thomas) as diplomat in, **2:**316, 317–318
　Laye's (Camara) education in, **1:**128–129
　letter writing in, **2:**217
　literary critical theories of, **1:**239
　locked-in syndrome in literature of, **1:**6
　Morocco as protectorate of, **3:**47
　Nin's (Anaïs) life in, **2:**123
　Revolution in (*See* French Revolution)
　Senegal as colony of, **1:**61
　student movements of 1968 in, **3:**33
　Vietnam under, **1:**335, **3:**279
　Wollstonecraft's (Mary) travels in, **2:**109
　women's rights movement in, **2:**306
　in World War II, German occupation of, **1:**332–334
　Wright's (Richard) move to, **1:**124
France, Peter, **1:**201
Francis, Charles E., *The Tuskegee Airmen,* **3:**212
Francophone literature
　of Algeria, **2:**262, 264
　of Senegal, **1:**61
Frank, Anne, *The Diary of Anne Frank,* **2:253–255,** *254*
　An Interrupted Life (Hillesum) vs., **2:**22

Night (Wiesel) vs., **1:**320
Red Scarf Girl (Jiang) inspired by, **1:**161
Thura's Diary (Al-Windawi) vs., **2:**275, 277
A Woman in Berlin (anonymous) vs., **2:**281
A Woman Soldier's Own Story (Xie) vs., **1:**340
Zlata's Diary (Filipovic) vs., **2:**338, 339, 340
Frank, Dana, **3:**338
Frank, Leslie, *Witnesses to Nuremberg,* **3:293–295**
Frank, Margot, **2:**253, 255
Frank, Otto, **2:**253, 254, 255
Franklin, Aretha, **1:**274–275
Franklin, Benjamin, **1:180**
　The Autobiography of Ben Franklin, **1:179–182, 2:**213
　Poor Richard's Almanac, **2:**88
　Shadows on My Heart (Buck) on, **2:**271
Franklin, Ruth, **1:**320
Franklin, USS, **3:203**
Franklin, William, **1:**179
Franklin, William Temple, **1:**179
Franks, in Crusades, **1:**285–288
Franz Sternbalds Wanderungen (Tieck), **1:**276
Fraser, Roland, *Blood of Spain,* **3:**176
Frasher, Burton, **3:**102
Frayn, Michael, *Copenhagen,* **3:**239
Frazer, Heather T., *"We Have Just Begun to Not Fight",* **3:227–230**
Frederick II (king of Prussia), **1:**276
Frederick the Great, "Le Stoicien," **1:**218
Frediani, Alex, **3:**225
Fredrickson, George, **2:**240
Freedom
　of expression (*See* Expression)
　Mandela's (Nelson) conception of, **1:**28
　mental, in locked-in syndrome, **1:**6–7
　moral imperative of, Soyinka (Wole) on, **1:**215
　value of, Jacobs (Harriet A.) on, **1:**143–145

Freedom (newspaper), **1:**273
Freedom Charter of 1955 (South Africa), **1:**24, 25
Freedom Flyers (Moye), **3:**99, **248–250**
Freedom Writers Diary, The (Gruwell), **2:**338, 339, 340
Freeman, James M., **3:**279
Freemont boarding school, **1:**164
Free schools, **3:**5
Free will, Augustine on, **1:**196, 198
French Americans, **2:**213–215
French and Indian War (1754–1763), **2:**205, 213
French autobiographical writing. *See also specific works and writers*
    by Barthes (Roland), **1:**267–269
    by Bauby (Jean-Dominique), **1:**6–8
    by Goncourt (Edmond de and Jules de), **2:**81–83
    by Lejeune (Philippe), **1:**239–240, **2:**174–176
    by Rousseau (Jean-Jacques), **1:**200–202
French education, in Algeria, **1:**93, 94, **2:**262–263
French Review (journal), **1:**128
French Revolution (1789–1799)
    Armenian nationalists influenced by, **3:**40
    British Empire during, Barnard (Anne) on, **2:**217, 218, 219
    British views on, **2:**309
    Enlightenment ideas in, **2:**109
    Goethe (Johann Wolfgang von) and, **1:**276
    U.S. anarchists influenced by, **3:**3
French Studies (journal), **2:**307
Frere, Bartie, **1:**91
Freud, Sigmund
    Andreas-Salomé (Lou) and, **2:**151
    on Augustine, **1:**197
    Barthes's (Roland) use of ideas of, **1:**267
    Bloomsbury group's discussions of, **2:**268
    and Darwin's (Charles) motivations, **1:**67

    and diaries, rise of, **2:**120
    The Origin and Development of Psychoanalysis, **2:**175
Frey, James, *A Million Little Pieces*, **1:**313, **2:**296
Friedan, Betty, **3:**37
Friedlander, Peter, **3:**174
    The Emergence of a UAW Local, **3:**153
Friedman, Clara, *Between Management and Labor*, **3:153–156,** 157
Frisbie, Charlotte, **3:**12
Frisch, Michael
    in field of oral history, **3:**173, 174
    on *Hard Times* (Terkel), **3:**162
    "Oral History and the Digital Revolution," **3:**181
    Portraits in Steel, **3:**181
    A Shared Authority, **3:**173, **179–182,** 190, 192
Fritz, Germaine, **3:**309
From Baghdad to Brooklyn (Marshall), **3:**120
From Behind the Veil (Stepto), **1:**35
From Memory to History (Montell and Bogart), **3:**90
Frommer, Harvey
    Growing Up Jewish in America, **3:118–120**
    It Happened in Brooklyn, **3:**118
Frommer, Myrna Katz
    Growing Up Jewish in America, **3:118–120**
    It Happened in Brooklyn, **3:**118
From Rhodesia to Zimbabwe (Vambe), **3:**251
From the Darkness Cometh the Light (Delaney), **2:**250
Fronto, Marcus Cornelius, **1:**220
Fruitlands (utopian community), **1:**235
Fry, Amelia, **3:**188
Frye, Northrop, **1:**276
Fuchs, Esther, *Women and the Holocaust*, **3:**35
Fugitive Slave Act of 1850 (U.S.), **2:**29
Fugitive slaves
    in abolitionist movement, **1:**142
    oral histories of, **3:**7–9
    return of, **2:**29

Fujii, Lee Ann, **3:**259
Fujiwara no Kintō, **2:**189
Fujiwara no Michinaga, **2:**290, 292
Fujiwara Takayoshi, **2:291**
Fujiwara Teika, **2:**189
Fulbrook, Mary, **3:**246
Fulkerson, Richard, **2:**33
Fuller, Margaret, **2:**139
Fuller, William Robertson, **2:**241
Fullerton, Morton, **2:**113, 115
Fulton, William, **3:**276
Fumifugium (Evelyn), **2:**65
Fundamentalist Christianity, **1:**102, 103
Fundamentalist Islam, **1:**156, 208
Fun Home (Bechdel), **1:139–141**
Fur, Gunlög Maria, *A Nation of Women*, **3:**326
Furey, Hester, **3:**329
Fürst, Juliane, **3:**332
Furuseth, Owen, **3:**123
Fussell, Paul, **3:**61
FWP. *See* Federal Writers' Project

G

Gaelic League, **3:**27
Gaitán Ayala, Jorge Eliécer, **3:**185
Gaither, Frances, **2:**30
Galarza, Ernesto, *Barrio Boy*, **1:**15
Galaty, John, **1:**114, 115, **3:**142
Galbraith, John Kenneth, **3:**255
Galloway, Grace Growdon, **2:**79
Galsworthy, John, **2:**136
Galvin, John, **3:**206
Gama, Vasco da, *A Journal of the First Voyage of Vasco da Gama*, **2:198–200,** *199,* 201
Gandhi, Mohandas, **1:243**
    An Autobiography, **1:**24, **242–245**
    civil disobedience by, **1:**242, **2:**32
    conscientious objectors influenced by, **3:**228
    Hind Swaraj, **1:**289
    Luthuli (Albert) influenced by, **1:**24
    Nehru's (Jawaharlal) relationship with, **1:**289–290, 291

SUBJECT INDEX

Gandhi, Rajiv, **1:290**
Gangs, British youth, **3:**311–313
Gao, Anhua, *To the Edge of the Sky*, **1:**159
Gao Xingjian, **1:**159
GAP. *See* Gruppi di Azione Patriottica
Garceau, Dee, **2:**91, 92–93
García Lorca, Federico, **1:**222
García Márquez, Gabriel, *The Story of a Shipwrecked Sailor*, **3:183–185**
Gardiner, Samuel Rawson, **1:**316
Garff, Joakim, **2:**167–168
Garland, Anne Witte, *Women Activists*, **3:**268
Garland, Judy, **3:**295
Garnett, Anne, **2:**235
Garnett, Constance, **2:**268
Garrett, Daniel, **1:**256, 257
Garrett, Jessie, *Camp and Community*, **3:**102, 103–104
Garrison, William Lloyd, **1:**33, **2:**29
Garvey, Marcus, **1:**52, 84, 186, 187
Gary Convention of 1972, **3:**45
Gaskell, Elizabeth, **2:**143
Gaskin, Hilary, *Eyewitnesses at Nuremberg*, **3:**293
Gass, William H., **2:**149, 150
Gataker, Thomas, **1:**220
Gates, Henry Louis, Jr.
   The Classic Slave Narratives, **1:**82, 83
   In Search of Our Roots, **1:**263
   "Remembrance of Things Pakistani," **1:**88
   on Wheatley (Phillis), **2:**46
Gatten, Aileen, **2:**290, 292
Gatti, Tom, **1:**141
Gaulle, Charles de, **2:**262
Gay, Peter, **2:**304
Gay Caucus Book of the Year award, for *The Cancer Journals* (Lorde), **2:**5
Gay L.A. (Faderman and Timmons), **3:**83–84
Gay Liberation Front, **3:**72
Gay men. *See* Homosexuality
Gay rights movement, rise of
   in Britain, **3:**70, 72
   in U.S., **3:**83–84

Gay subculture, of Harlem Renaissance, **1:**84
Gay themes
   in comics, **1:**139, 141
   in *Hunger of Memory* (Rodriguez), **1:**17
Geertz, Clifford, **3:**74
Gehen-Bleiben (play), **2:**304
Geiger, H. Jack, **1:**73
Gelb, Norman, **2:**206
Gelles, Edith, **2:**89, 90
Gellhorn, Martha, **2:102**
   The Face of War, **2:**102
   Moore (Molly) and, **2:**278
   Selected Letters of Martha Gellhorn, **2:101–103**
   The Trouble I've Seen, **2:**101
Gellhorn, Walter, **3:**154, 155
Gender, in writing styles, **1:**250
Gender & History (journal), **3:**175
Gender discrimination, in coal mining, **3:**337, 339
Gender equality
   in Heian period of Japan, lack of, **2:**299
   Stanton (Elizabeth Cady) on, **1:**12, 13
Gender roles
   in Britain, **3:**144–146
   in China, **1:**153, 158, 160, 338, **3:**147–149
   in Europe, eighteenth-century, **2:**35–37
   in Europe, Renaissance, **2:**160–162
   in Iran, **1:**155
   in Ireland, **2:**157
   in Japan, **2:**60–61
   in Kenya, **3:**143
   in Montenegro, **3:**135, 136, 137
   in U.S., eighteenth-century, **2:**316
   in U.S., twentieth-century, **2:**47
   in World War I, **1:**331
Gender studies
   Red Azalea (Min) in, **1:**158, 160
   The Sovereignty and Goodness of God (Rowlandson) in, **1:**327
Genealogy, of Haley (Alex), **1:**261–263

General Allotment Act of 1887 (U.S.), **3:**107
General Magazine and Impartial Review, **1:**82
General Motors, **3:**343
Geneva Convention on the Laws and Custom of War (1949), **2:**56
Genghis Khan, **1:**105, 107
Genocide
   Armenian, **3:**40–42, *41*
   in Cambodia, **1:**306
   denial as final stage of, **3:**42
   in Guatemala, **3:**164
   in Nazi Germany (*See* Holocaust)
   in Rwanda, **1:**312, **3:**257–259, 293, 294
   in Ukraine, **3:**19
Genre (journal), **1:**248
"Gentlemen's Agreement" of 1907, **3:**80
Georgakas, Dan, *Solidarity Forever*, **3:328–330**
George, Keller, **3:**109
George, Susanne K., **2:**91–92, 93
George III (king of England), **2:**69, 328
Georgia, colonial, Wesley's (John) mission to, **2:**195, 196
Georgia Historical Quarterly, **1:**38
Georgia Review (journal), **1:**109
Georgia Weekly Telegraph (newspaper), **2:**38, 39
Gerardi, Juan, **1:**99
Géricault, Théodore, **2:144**
Gerlin, Valeria Mikhailovna, **3:**18
Germaine (About), **2:**115
German Americans, relocation in World War II, **3:**224, 226
German autobiographical writing. *See also specific works and writers*
   by Goethe (Johann Wolfgang von), **1:**276–278
   by Hitler (Adolf), **1:**30–32
   by Klemperer (Victor), **2:**303–305
   by Rabe (John), **2:**19–21
   by Rilke (Rainer Maria), **2:**149–151
   by Speer (Albert), **2:**54–56

German language, Nazi use of, **2:**303, 304, 305
German Romanticism, **2:**76
Germany. *See also* German autobiographical writing
    bildungsroman genre in, **1:**30
    economy of, **1:**30
    emigration to Chile from, **1:**75, 77
    Great Awakening in, **2:**197
    Künstler-Roman genre in, **1:**276
    nationalism in, **1:**30–32, 329, **2:**120, **3:**234
    Nazi (*See* Nazi Germany)
    reunification of, **3:**247
    Robinson's (Henry Crabb) travels in, **2:**75, 77
    Ruete's (Emily) move from Zanzibar to, **1:**90
    Stasi in, oral histories of, **3:**245–247
    student movements of 1968 in, **3:**33
    wars of (*See* specific wars)
Germany, Kent B., **3:**254
Geronimo (film), **1:**304
Geronimo, *Geronimo: His Own Story*, **1:**302–305, *303*
Geronimo: An American Legend (film), **1:**304
Geronimo: His Own Story (Geronimo and Barrett), **1:302–305**
Gerovitch, Slava, **3:**333
Gesner, Andreas, **1:**220
Gessen, Keith, **3:**282, 285
Getty, Serena, **2:**54–55
Gevisser, Mark, **3:**243
Gewen, Barry, **3:**213
Ghana (Nkrumah), **1:**290, **2:**12, 13
Ghana, Du Bois (W. E. B.) and, **1:**3, 4
Gharagozlou, Mary, **3:**220
Ghazzawi, 'Izzat
    Letters Underway, **2:50–53**
    The Woman Prisoner, **2:**50
Ghazzawi, Rami, **2:**50
Gheith, Jehanne M., *Gulag Voices*, **3:17–19**, 331
Ghent, Treaty of, **2:**69
Ghost Dance, **3:**110

Ghost masks, Chinese, **1:174**
Gibb, H. A. R., **1:**137, 287
Gibbon, Edward, **1:**198, **2:**37, 328
Gibbons, Herbert Adams, *The Blackest Page in Modern History*, **3:**40
Gibson, Marion, **1:**337
Gibson, Roy, **2:**95, 96
Gibson, William (playwright), **1:**43–44
Gibson, William Ford (novelist), **2:**145
Gide, André, **1:**278
    Log-book of the Coiners, **2:**180, 182
Giesen, Carol A. B., *Coal Miners' Wives*, **3:**337
Gig (Bowe and Bowe), **3:**343, 345
Gigliozzi, Liana, **3:**266
Gikandi, Simon, **2:**14
Gikuyu language, **2:**12, 13, 14
Gilbert, Sandra M., **2:**237
Gillette, Michael L., *Launching the War on Poverty*, **3:254–256**
Gillray, James, **2:**158
Gilman, Charlotte Perkins, **1:**14, **2:**324
Gilman, Richard, **2:**131
Gilmartin, Christina, **3:**149
Gilmartin, Elizabeth Kelley, *Engendering the Chinese Revolution*, **3:**147
Giltrow, Janet, **2:**207
Ginther, Ronald Debs, **3:162**
Gioglio, Gerald P., *Days of Decision*, **3:**221
Girl from China, A (Cheng), **1:**152, 154
Girl in the Tangerine Scarf, The (Kahf), **1:**41–42
Girl Rebel (Xie), **1:**338
Girl with the White Flag, The (Higa), **1:**153
Gissing, George
    London and the Life of Literature in Late Victorian England, **2:320–323**
    New Grub Street, **2:**320, 321, 322
Gittins, Diana, **3:**313
Gladiator (film), **1:**219
Gladstone, W. E., **2:**307
Glasgow, Jacqueline N., **1:**41–42, 311
Glasnost, **3:**282, 331, 333
Glass Menagerie, The (Williams), **2:**152

Glazier, Jack, **3:**141
Glenarvon (Lamb), **2:**145
Glendinning, Victoria, **1:**205
Glenn, Susan A., *Daughters of the Shtetl*, **3:**305
Glenny, William H., **3:**294
Globe & Mail (newspaper), **3:**119–120, 301
GLQ: A Journal of Lesbian and Gay Studies, **3:**72
Gluck, Sherna Berger
    Rosie the Riveter Revisited, **3:**224
    Women's Words, **3:190–192**
Go Ask Alice (anonymous), **2:294–296**
God, will of, Usāmah ibn Munqidh on, **1:**285, 286
Go-Daigo (Japanese emperor), **2:**61
Goddard, James Stanley, **2:**205, 207
God of Small Things, The (Roy), **1:**87
Godolphin, Margaret, **2:**66
Godwin, William, **2:**76, 109, 111
    Memoir, **2:**109
Goethe, Johann Wolfgang von, **1:**277
    Kafka (Franz) influenced by, **2:**120
    Kierkegaard's (Søren) critique of, **2:**166
    The Sorrows of Young Werther, **1:**276, 277, 339, **2:**166
    Styron (William) compared to, **1:**206
    Truth and Fiction Relating to My Life, **1:276–278**
    Wilhelm Meister's Apprenticeship, **1:**30
Goff, Stanley, *Brothers*, **3:**199
GoFukakusa (Japanese emperor), **2:**59, 60, 61
Gogh, Theo van, **1:**207, 209
Gogol, Nikolay, **2:**172
    Diary of a Madman, **2:**174
Going after Cacciato (O'Brien), **1:**335
Golb, Joel, **1:**32
Goldberg, Lina, **2:**295
Golden Ass, The (Apuleius), **1:**198
Goldenberg, Myrna, **3:**36
Golden Bones (Siv), **1:306–308**
Golden Book of the Emperor Marcus Aurelius (Guevara), **1:**218

SUBJECT INDEX

Goldensohn, Leon, *The Nuremberg Interviews,* **3:**293
Goldhagen, Daniel, **2:**304–305
Goldman, Emma, *Living My Life,* **3:**3
Gold Rush, California, **3:**114
Goldzwig, Steven R., **2:**33
Gomaa, Sally, **1:**144
Gomez, Iris, *Try to Remember,* **1:**108
Gómez, Laureano, **3:**183, 185
Gomez, Maximo, **3:**7
Goncourt, Edmond de
    Bashkirtseff (Marie) influenced by, **2:**306, 307–308
    Cherie, **2:**308
    En 18, **2:**82
    La Faustine, **2:**308
    Journal des Goncourt, **2:**81–83
Goncourt, Jules de
    En 18, **2:**82
    Journal des Goncourt, **2:**81–83
Gonne, Maud, **2:**127
Goodall, Jane, **3:**37
Goodbye to All That (Graves), **1:**329
Good Earth, The (Buck), **1:**159
Goodell, Stephen, **3:**254
Goodfriend, Joyce D., **2:**79
Good Housekeeping (magazine), **1:**154
"Good Man Is Hard to Find, A" (O'Connor), **2:**130
Good Man of Nanking, The (Rabe), **2:19–21**
Good Morning America (television show), **1:**40, 41
Goodrich, Chris, **1:**29, **3:**222
Goodrich, Frances, **2:**253
"Good War, The" (Terkel), **3:212–214**
    Bloods (Terry) vs., **3:**199
    Carrier Warfare in the Pacific (Wooldridge) vs., **3:**202
    Pulitzer Prize won by, **3:**161, 212, 234, 279, 343
    in rise of oral history, **3:**279
    The World at War (Holmes) vs., **3:**234
Goodwin, Jason, **1:**107
Good Wives (Ulrich), **2:**331–332
Goolagong, Evonne, **1:**149
Gorbachev, Mikhail, **3:**17, 282, 331, 333

Gordimer, Nadine, **1:**27
Gordon, Andrew, **3:**216
Gordon, Ann D., **1:**13
Gordon, Caroline, **2:**129
Gordon, Eleanor, **3:**175
Gordon, Ian, **2:**134
Gordon, Mary McDougall, **2:**79
Göring, Hermann, **3:294**
Gorky, Maxim, **1:**254
Gornick, Vivian, *Fierce Attachments,* **1:**279
Gorra, Michael, **1:**88
Gossamer Years, The (Michitsuna), **2:189, 290, 297–299**
Gossen, Gary H., *Telling Maya Tales,* **3:**167
Go Tell It on the Mountain (Baldwin), **1:**167, 261
Gotlieb, Howard, **2:**101
Gottesmann, Christoph, **2:**282
Gougeon, Len, **2:**141
Gowon, Yakubu, **1:**214, 215, 216
Goyens, Tom, *Beer and Revolution,* **3:**5
Goyette, Gabriele, **1:10**
Graburn, Nelson, **3:**140
Grace Abounding to the Chief of Sinners (Bunyan), **2:**26
Graden, Dale, **3:**8
Graham, Elspeth, **1:**231
Graham, John, **1:**98
Grammy Award, for Obama's (Barack) audio adaptations, **1:**80
Granado, Alberto, **2:**220
Grandmothers, Mothers, and Daughters (Krause), **3:305–307**
Grand Prix Littéraire d'Afrique Noir, for *Riwan ou le chemin de sable* (Bugul), **1:**64
Grant, Duncan, **2:**268
Graphic autobiographies
    Barefoot Gen (Nakazawa), **1:**293–295
    Fun Home (Bechdel), **1:**139–141
    Persepolis (Satrapi), **1:**155–157
Grasmere (England), Dove Cottage in, **2:**300, *301*
Grasmere Journals (Wordsworth), **2:16, 300–302**
Grass Is Singing, The (Lessing), **1:**169

Graulich, Melody, **2:**91, 92
Graves, Phyllis, **1:**311
Graves, Robert, **2:**248
    Goodbye to All That, **1:**329
Gray, Doris H., *Muslim Women on the Move,* **3:**48
Gray, Francine du Plessix, **2:**102
Gray, Rockwell, **1:**247
Gray, Thomas, **2:**146
Greasley, Philip, **3:**213
Great Awakening, **1:**179, **2:**197
Great Boer War, The (Conan Doyle), **2:**241
Great Britain. *See* Britain
Great Depression
    African Americans during, **3:**99
    in Appalachia, **3:**96
    in Britain, **3:**53
    end of, **3:**161
    global impact of, **3:**212
    in Harlem, **1:**84
    in Idaho, **3:**93, 94
    Jews during, **3:**118
    Native Americans during, **1:**69
    New Deal in, **3:**161 (*See also* Federal Writers' Project)
    oral histories of, **3:**86, 161–163, *162*
    start of, **3:**161, 212
    unemployment in, **3:**161, 212
Great Exodus (1879), **1:**50
Great Famine (Ireland), **3:**315
Great Famine of 1932–1933 (Ukraine), **3:**19
Great Gatsby, The (Fitzgerald), **1:**47
Great Lakes Review, **3:**213
Great Leap Forward, **3:**287, 299, 300
"Great Men" project, of Nevins (Allan), **3:**161, 173, 179, 181, 186
Great Migration, **1:**50, 52, 84, 273, **3:**99
Great Plains Quarterly, **2:**164
Great Proletarian Cultural Revolution. *See* Cultural Revolution
Great Reforms (Russia), **1:**193
Great Society, **3:**254
"Great Wall of China, The" (Kafka), **2:**120

Great War, The (television series), **3:**234, 236
Greece, ancient
    letter writing in, **2:**94
    slavery in, **2:**96
Green, Anna, **3:**175
Green, John, **2:**276
Green, Maia, **3:**142
Green, Roland, **3:**203
Greenberg, Jack, **1:**38
Greenberg, Martin, **2:**121
Greenberger, Evelyn B., **2:**141
Greene, Graham, **2:**130, 136, 152
    A Sort of Life, **1:**47
Greene, Janet Wells, **3:**97
Greenfield, Sidney, *Entrepreneurs in Cultural Context,* **3:**121
Greenwell, Regina, **3:**254
Greer, Germaine, **3:**37
Gregory, Horace, **2:**121
Gregory, Lady, **2:**126, 128
Grele, Ronald J., **3:**45, 51, 52, 174
Grewal, Inderpal, **1:**88–89
Grey, Jane, **2:**99
Grice, Helena, **1:**160
Griffith, Andy, **2:**295
Griffith, Elisabeth, **1:**13–14
Griffith, Julia, *The Liberty Bell,* **1:**142
Griffith, Kenneth, *Ireland's Unfinished Revolution,* **3:**27–30
Grillo, Evelio, *Black Cuban, Black American,* **1:**296
Grimes, Tom, *Mentor,* **1:**164
Grimes, William, **1:**209
Grimké, Angelina, **2:**31
Grimké, Angelina Weld, **2:**31
Grimké, Charlotte Forten
    "At the Home of Frederick Douglass," **2:**29
    The Extraordinary Work of Ordinary Writing (Sinor) compared to, **2:**163
    Higginson (Thomas Wentworth) and, **2:**29, 238
    The Journals of Charlotte Forten Grimké, **2:**29–31
    "Life in the Sea Islands," **2:**31
Grimké, Francis, **2:**31

Grimké, Sarah, **2:**31
Grindle, Merilee S., **3:**303
Griswold, Rufus W., **2:**41
Grob-Fitzgibbon, Benjamin, *The Irish Experience during the Second World War,* **3:**315–316
Gronniosaw, James Albert Ukawsaw, **1:**81, **2:**44
Grose, John Henry, *Voyage to the East Indies,* **2:**229
Gross, Robert, **1:**19
Grossman, Michele, **3:**335, 336
Grossmith brothers, *The Diary of a Nobody,* **2:**174
Grotius, Hugo, **2:**177
Group, The (McCarthy), **1:**258
Group Areas Act of 1950 (South Africa), **1:**24
Growing Up Jewish in America (Frommer and Frommer), **3:118–120**
Grundtvig, N. F. S., **2:**166
Gruppi di Azione Patriottica (GAP), **3:**265
Gruwell, Erin, *The Freedom Writers Diary,* **2:**338, 339, 340
Gu, Ming Dong, **2:**172
Guajardo, Paul, **1:**16
Guardian (newspaper), **1:**330, **2:**133, 154, **3:**243
Guardian of the Word, The (Laye), **1:**129
Guatemala
    Civil War of, **1:**99, **3:**164, 165–166
    human rights abuses in, **1:**99, 100, **3:**164–166
    indigenous populations of, massacres of, **1:**99, **3:**164
    indigenous populations of, oral histories of, **3:**164–166
    Perera (Victor) on life in, **1:**99–101
"Guatemala: Always La Violencia" (Perera), **1:**99
Guatemalan Civil War (1960–1996), **1:**99, **3:**164, 165–166
Guatemala: Never Again! (Archdiocese of Guatemala), **1:**99
Guattari, Félix, **2:**122
Guavas, **1:**109

Gubar, Susan, **2:**237
Gubarev, Vladimir, *Sarcophagus,* **3:**282, 284
Guerilla Days in Ireland (Barry), **3:**27
Guérin, Daniel, *No Gods, No Masters,* **3:**3
Guérin, Eugénie de, **2:**306
Guevara, Antonio, *Golden Book of the Emperor Marcus Aurelius,* **1:**218
Guevara, Ernesto "Che," **2:**221
    Che: A Graphic Biography (Buhle and Rodriguez) on, **3:**330
    Motorcycle Diaries, **1:**223, **2:220–222**
Guggenheim, Peggy, **2:**152
Guglielmo, Jennifer, *Living the Revolution,* **3:**5
Guiler, Hugh Parker, **2:**123
Guilt, in *Country of My Skull* (Krog), **3:**243
Guinea
    French colonial rule of, **1:**128, 129, 130
    independence of (1958), **1:**130
    Laye (Camara) on life in, **1:**128–130, *129*
Guisson, Lorraine, *Image du monde,* **1:**105
Guiteras-Holmes, Calixta, *Perils of the Soul,* **3:**167
Gulag Archipelago, The (Solzhenitsyn), **1:**201, **3:**17
Gulag system, oral histories of, **3:**17–19, *18*
Gulag Voices (Gheith and Jolluck), **3:17–19,** 331
Gulf War (1991), **2:**275, 278–280, *279*
Gulliford, Andrew, **3:**77
Gundy, Jeff, **1:**109
Gunning, Sarah Ogan, **3:**159
Gurewitsch, Brana
    Holocaust Oral History Manual, **3:**35
    Mothers, Sisters, Resisters, **3:34–36**
Gusdorf, George, **1:**246, 248
Gustavson, Andrea, **3:**162–163, 213
Guy, Josephine M., **2:**10
Guy Domville (James), **2:**114
Guylforde, John, **2:**228

Guylforde, Richarde, *The Pylgrymage of Sir Richarde Guylforde,* **2:226–228**

Gyn/Ecology (Daly), **2:**3, 5

H

Ha, Quan Manh, **1:**307

Habit of Being, The (O'Connor), **2:129–132**

Habits of Change (Rogers), **3:308–310**

Habits of mind, Darwin (Charles) on, **1:**65–67

Habyarimana, Juvénal, **3:**257

Hachicho, Mohamad Ali, **2:**227, 228

Hachiya, Michihiko, *Hiroshima Diary,* **1:**293

Hackett, Albert, **2:**253

Haddad, Malek, *La Dernière impression,* **2:**262

Hadot, Pierre, **1:**221

Hagiographies
  The Autobiography of Malcolm X (Malcolm X) as, **1:**186, 188
  and *The Book of Margery Kempe* (Kempe), **1:**189, 190, 191

Hagood, Taylor, **1:**8

Hagopian, Patrick, **3:**201, 209, 211, 277

Haizlip, Shirlee, *The Sweeter the Juice,* **1:**73

Hakakian, Roya, *Journey to the Land of No,* **1:**155

Hakluyt, Richard, **2:**199
  Divers Voyages Touching the Discoverie of America, **2:**229
  The Principle Navigations, Voiages, Traffiques and Discoveries of the English Nation, **2:**229

Hakluyt Society, **2:**198, 199

Halas, John, **2:**118

Hale, Sondra, **3:**48–49, 191

Halevy, Irving, **3:**154–155

Haley, Alex, **1:**262
  "Black History, Oral History, and Genealogy," **3:**186
  "My Furthest-Back Person—'The African,'" **1:261–263**
  Roots, **1:**18, 78, 261–263
  in writing of *The Autobiography of Malcolm X,* **1:**78, 186, 187, **3:**44

Halkett, Anne, *The Memoirs of Lady Anne Halkett,* **1:**230, **315–317**

Halkett, James, **1:**315

Hall, Betty Jean, **3:**339

Hall, Joan Wylie, **2:**153

Hall, Peter, **3:**59

Halperin, John, **2:**322

Halpern, Frida, **1:**76

Halsband, Robert, **2:**36

Hamdani, Abu Firas al-, **2:**52

Hamilton, J. Angus, *The Siege of Mafeking,* **2:**241

Hamilton, Paula, **3:**188

Hamilton, Robert A., **3:**294

Hamilton, William, **2:**196

Hamlet (Shakespeare), **1:**277

Hammon, Britton, **2:**44

Hammon, Jupiter, **2:**44

Hampton, Henry
  The Black Chronicle, **3:**44
  in *Eyes on the Prize* (television series), **2:**34
  Voices of Freedom, **3:44–46**

Hamsun, Knut, **2:**120

Handbook of Oral History, The (Humphries), **3:**313

Handley, George B., **1:**223–224

Han dynasty, Confucianism in, **3:**124

Hansberry, Lorraine, **1:**274
  A Raisin in the Sun, **1:**273, 274, 275
  The Sign in Sidney Brustein's Window, **1:**274
  To Be Young, Gifted and Black, **1:273–275**

Hansen, Arthur A., **3:**80–81, 197
  Japanese American World War II Evacuation Oral History Project, **3:**215
  Voices Long Silent, **3:**195

Han Yong Un, **1:**322

Hao Ping, **3:**289

Happiest Refugee, The (Do), **1:**337

Happy Foreigner, The (Bagnold), **2:**259

Haralson, Eric, **2:**115

Harbach, Patricia, **3:**326

Harbord, Gordon, **2:**249

Hardack, Richard, **1:**281

Hard-Earned Lives (Cornwell), **3:**170

Harder Journey, The (Tuqan), **1:**226

Hardships and Happy Times (Russell), **3:**93

Hard Times: An Oral History of the Great Depression (Terkel), **3:161–163,** 179, **199,** 212, 279, 343

Hardy, Thomas, **2:**136–137, 180, 181, 321

Harem Years (Shaarawi), **1:**225–226

Harlan, Louis R., **1:**52

Harlan County (Kentucky)
  oral histories of coal miners in, **3:**96–98, 157
  oral histories of working class in, **3:**157–159

Harlan County, USA (documentary), **3:**98

Harlan Miners Speak (Dreiser), **3:**96

Harlem, in Great Depression, **1:**84

"Harlem" (Hughes), **1:**275

Harlem: Negro Metropolis (McKay), **1:**85

Harlem Renaissance
  autobiographies of participants in, **1:**3
  vs. Chicago Renaissance, **1:**273
  Du Bois (W. E. B.) in, **1:**3
  gay subculture of, **1:**84
  Hurston (Zora Neale) in, **1:**9
  McKay (Claude) in, **1:**84–86
  origins of, **1:**84

Harling, Sean, **3:**28

Harman, Claire, **2:**313–314

Harney, Mary, **3:**315

Harper, Frances Ellen Watkins, *Iola Leroy,* **1:**143

Harper, Helen, **1:**162, **2:**276

Harries, Meirion, *Soldiers of the Sun,* **3:**215

Harries, Susie, *Soldiers of the Sun,* **3:**215

Harrington, Ann, **3:**309

Harris, Frank, **2:**261

Harris, Lillian Craig, **3:**126

Harrison, Thomas, **2:**235

Harrold, Charles, **2:**76

Hart, Frederick, **3:200**

Hart-Davis, Rupert, **2:**247, 248

Hartle, Ann, **1**:202
Harvard Book Review, **1**:48, 280
Harvard Iranian Oral History Project (HIOHP), **3**:218–220
Harvey, Clodagh Brennan, *Contemporary Irish Traditional Narrative,* **3**:315
Harvey, P., **3**:249
Harwood, Ronald, **1**:6
Haskins, Jim, *Rosa Parks: My Story,* **1**:37–39
Hassan, Kenja, **3**:12
Hastings, Selina, **2**:185
Hatch, Ozias M., **3**:263
Hatcher, Richard, **3**:45
Hate crimes, against gay men and lesbians, **1**:139
Hathaway, Donny, **1**:274
Hatherell, William, **2**:260
Hattin, Battle of (1187), **1**:286
Hatzfeld, Jean
  The Antelope's Strategy, **3**:258
  Life Laid Bare, **3**:258, 259
  Machete Season, **1**:312, **3**:257–260
Hauptman, L. M., **3**:326
Hausa people, **1**:214
Haushofer, Karl, **1**:32
Haviland, John B., **3**:169
Hawaii. *See* Pearl Harbor
Hawkesworth, E. C., **3**:135, 136, 137
Hawthorne, Julian, **2**:224
Hawthorne, Nathaniel
  The Blithedale Romance, **2**:225
  The Centenary Edition of the Works of Nathaniel Hawthorne, **2**:223
  Emerson (Ralph Waldo) and, **2**:139, 223
  The House of the Seven Gables, **2**:223–224
  James (Henry) and, **2**:113, 114, 115
  lost notebook of, **2**:224, 225
  The Love Letters of Nathaniel Hawthorne, **2**:225
  The Marble Faun, **2**:224, 225
  Notebooks and Letters, **2**:113, 223–225
  Robinson (Henry Crabb) compared to, **2**:75
  The Scarlet Letter, **2**:223–224

Hawthorne, Sophia Peabody, **2**:223, 224, 225
Haxton, Frederick Gerald, **2**:183
Hay, John M., **3**:262
  Abraham Lincoln: A History, **3**:261–262
  Abraham Lincoln: Complete Works, **3**:262
  Letters of John Hay, **3**:263
  Lincoln and the Civil War Diaries and Letters of John Hay, **3**:262–263
Haydon, Benjamin, **2**:146
Hayes, Thomas, **1**:216
Hayls, John, **2**:73
Haymarket Riot (1886), **3**:4
Haynes, Katherine, **3**:344
Hays, Mary, **2**:109, 110
Hays, Megan, **3**:136–137
Hays, Rusel Everett, **3**:185
Hayslip, Le Ly, **1**:336
  When Heaven and Earth Changed Places, **1**:170–171, 335–337
  Woman of Peace, **1**:335
Haywood, Harry, *Black Bolshevik,* **1**:4
Hazlitt, William, **2**:146
H.D. (Hilda Doolittle), **2**:123
Heading South, Looking North (Dorfman), **1**:75
Head of the Class (Morris), **3**:20–22
Head Start program, **3**:254
Healey, Mark, **3**:74
Health-care industry
  British, oral histories of, **3**:170–172
  South African, oral histories of, **3**:272–274
Health problems. *See also specific types*
  of Bauby (Jean-Dominique), **1**:6–8
  of Mansfield (Katherine), **2**:133, 134
  of Styron (William), **1**:204–205
Healy, George Peter Alexander, **2**:70
Heartland (film), **2**:91
Heart of Darkness (Conrad), **2**:192–193, 194
Heaven and Earth (film), **1**:335, *336*
Hecker, Earl, **3**:232

Heflin, Ruth J., **3**:112
Hegel, Georg Wilhelm Friedrich, **2**:166
Heian period (Japan)
  Michitsuna No Haha on life in, **2**:297–299
  Murasaki Shikibu on life in, **2**:290–292
  Nijo (Lady) on life in, **2**:60, 61
  Sarashina (Lady) on life in, **2**:189–191
Heilman, Anna, **3**:35
Heinemann Award, for *Akenfield* (Blythe), **3**:59
Heisenberg, Werner, **3**:239
Helfand, Judy, **1**:336
Helgeson, Jeffrey, **3**:255–256
Hélias, Pierre Jakez, *The Horse of Pride,* **3**:61
Heline, Oscar, **3**:162
Heller, Walter, **3**:254
Hellman, Lillian, **1**:260
Helms, Jessie, **2**:5
Helsinger, Elizabeth K., **1**:264, 265, 266
Helstern, Linda Lizut, **3**:12
Hemenway, Robert, **1**:9
Hemingway, Ernest
  A Farewell to Arms, **2**:259
  The Fifth Column, **2**:102
  For Whom the Bell Tolls, **2**:101
  Gellhorn's (Martha) marriage to, **2**:101, 102
  Notebooks (Williams) on, **2**:152
  The Sun Also Rises, **2**:259
  Wolff (Tobias) influenced by, **1**:47
Hemlow, Joyce, **2**:314
Henderson, John, **2**:96
Henderson, Thelton, **3**:20
Hendricks, Cecilia Hennel, **2**:91
Henige, David, **2**:203
Hennepin, Louis, *A New Discovery of a Vast Country in America,* **2**:205
Henrietta Maria (queen of England), **1**:229
Henry, Milton, **3**:248
Henry, Mona, **3**:316
Henry the Navigator, **2**:198
Henry VII (king of England), **2**:226, 228

SUBJECT INDEX

Henry VIII (king of England), **2:**72, 97, 226
Hensher, Philip, **2:**153
Hentges, Frank, **3:**162
Hentges, Rome, **3:**162
Henze, Hans Werner, **3:**7
Hepburn, James, **2:**138
Hepburn, Katharine, **2:**261
Here I Stand (Robeson), **1:**37
Here's to You, Jesus (Poniatowska), **3:**32
Heresy, Teresa of Ávila and, **1:**211, 212
Here Too, Domitila (Barrios de Chungara), **3:**322
Herman, David, **2:**128
Hermione, Countess of Ranfurly, **2:**235
Herndon, Angelo, **1:**85
Herndon's Informants (Wilson and Davis), **3:**264
Herodotus, **3:**186
Herr, Michael, *Dispatches,* **1:**259, **3:**209
Herrera, Spencer, **1:**17
Herron, L. E., **1:**52
Hershatter, Gail, **1:**340
Herzen, Alexander, **1:**270, **2:**120
Hess, Rudolph, **1:**32, **3:**294
Hester, Elizabeth, **2:**130–131
H-Ethnic (journal), **3:**8
Hevener, John W., *Which Side Are You On?,* **3:**96
Hewitt, David, **2:**311
Hewitt, Martin, **2:**66, 67
Heyerdahl, Marian, **1:**339
Heylin, Peter, **2:**99
Heyns, Michiel, **3:**243
Heywood, Christopher, **2:**242
Heywood, Thomas, **2:**162
H. G. Wells in Love (Wells), **1:**252, 253, 254
Hibakusha literature, **1:**293
Hibberd, Dominic, **2:**248, 249
Hibbert, Christopher, **2:**210
Hickey, Jim, **3:**316
Hickey, Margaret, *Irish Days,* **3:**315–317
Higa, Tomiko, *The Girl with the White Flag,* **1:**153
Higgins, Marguerite, **2:**278

Higginson, Thomas Wentworth
  Army Life in a Black Regiment, **2:**238–240
  Grimké (Charlotte Forten) and, **2:**29, 238
Hijuelos, Oscar, *Thoughts without Cigarettes,* **1:**75
Hikmet, Nazim, **2:**51
Hilda Lessways (Bennett), **2:**138
Hill, Joan, **3:**68
Hill, W. Nick, **3:**7, 8
"Hillbilly" culture, **3:**86
Hill Country Teacher (Manning), **3:77–79**
Hillenbrand, Carole, **1:**286, 287
Hillers, Marta, **2:**281
Hillesum, Etty
  An Interrupted Life, **2:22–25**
  The Letters and Diaries of Etty Hillesum, **2:**253
Him, Chanrithy, *When Broken Glass Floats,* **1:**306
Hinds, Hilary, **2:**27
Hind Swaraj (Gandhi), **1:**289
Hinduism, **1:**242, 244
Hindus, Maurice, **1:**271
Hinnant, Charles, **2:**329–330
Hinton, Deane, **3:**206
Hinton, James, **2:**267
Hintz, Carrie, **2:**326
HIOHP. *See* Harvard Iranian Oral History Project
Hipp, Daniel, **2:**249
Hirohito (emperor of Japan), **3:**215
Hiroshima (Japan), U.S. nuclear bombing of, **1:**293–294, **3:**239
Hiroshima Diary (Hachiya), **1:**293
Hiroshima: The Autobiography of Barefoot Gen (Nakazawa), **1:**293, 295
Hirsch, Jerrold, **3:**22, 192
Hirsch, Julia, **3:**306
Hirsi Ali, Ayaan, **1:**208
  Infidel, **1:207–210**
  Nomad, **1:**209
Hispanic-American Entrepreneur, The (Owsley), **3:121–123**
Hispanic American Historical Review (journal), **2:**7, **3:**122, 303, 323

Hispanic and Latino Americans
  as entrepreneurs, oral histories of, **3:**121–123
  Medina (Pablo) on experience of, **1:**296–298
  Santiago (Esmeralda) on experience of, **1:**108–110
  in South, **3:**123
  women, oral histories of, **3:**131–133
Historia Augusta, **1:**220
Historian (journal), **2:**231
Historia Romana (Cassius Dio), **1:**220
Historical Clarifications Commission, UN, **3:**166
Historical Journal of Film, Radio and Television, **3:**234
Historie de ma vie (Amrouche). *See My Life Story* (Amrouche)
History, field of. *See also* Oral histories
  Popular Memory Group's critique of, **3:**176–178
  role of oral histories in, **3:**281
History (journal), **2:**206, **3:**145
History and Theory (journal), **1:**26
History in Africa (journal), **1:**25
History of Alta California, The (Osio et al.), **3:**115
History of Education Quarterly, **3:**307
History of Everyday Life in Twentieth Century Scotland, A (Abrams), **3:**173, 175
History of Indies (Las Casas), **2:**201
History of Mary Prince, The (Prince), **1:**111, 113, **3:23–26**
History of the German Resistance (Hoffmann), **3:**245
History of Woman Suffrage (Stanton et al.), **1:**12
History Today (journal), **2:**200, **3:**246, 267
History Workshop Journal, **3:**54, 146, 173, 176, 209, 277
Hitchcott, Nicki, **1:**64
Hitchens, Christopher
  on Guevara (Ernesto "Che"), **2:**222
  on *Infidel* (Hirsi Ali), **1:**209
  Letters to a Young Contrarian, **2:**150
  on Orwell (George), **2:**117, 118, 119

Hitler, Adolf, **1:**31. *See also* Holocaust; Nazi Germany
    Chilean support for, **1:**75
    fall of Berlin and, **2:**281
    Final Solution of, **1:**318
    Mein Kampf, **1:**30–32
    Nella Last's War (Last) on, **2:**265
    Rabe's (John) letter on Nanking Massacre to, **2:**19, 21
    rise to power, **3:**14
    Speer's (Albert) relationship with, **2:**54, 55, 56
    Stein (Gertrude) on, **1:**332
    suicide of, **2:**281
Hitti, Philip K., **1:**287
HIV. *See* AIDS
Hoak, Dale, **2:**98, 99
Hobart, Mary, **2:**331
Hobbs, Nancy, **1:**38
Hobsbawm, Eric J., **2:**18
Hoby, Margaret, **2:**62
Hochstadt, Steve, *Exodus to Shanghai,* **3:**14–16
Hodgson, Dorothy L., **1:**115–116
Hoess, Rudolph, *My Soul,* **2:**54
Ho Feng-Shan, **3:**14
Hoffaman, Abraham, *Vision or Villainy,* **3:**102
Hoffe, Esther, **2:**122
Hoffman, Abbie, **1:**205
Hoffman, Michael J., **1:**333
Hoffman, Nancy, *Woman's "True" Profession,* **3:**77
Hoffmann, Peter, *History of the German Resistance,* **3:**245
Hofstadter, Richard, **1:**134
Hogarth Press, **2:**268
Hoggart, Richard
    The Uses of Literacy, **1:**16
    The Worst of Times, **3:**53
Holcomb, Gary Edward, **1:**85
Holden, Philip, **1:**290, 291
Holland. *See* Netherlands
Holland, Tom, **2:**145
Hollander, Tom, **2:**10
Holler, Clyde, **3:**112
Holmes, Amy J., **2:**244
Holmes, Henry Bry, **2:**245, 246

Holmes, Oliver Wendell, Jr., **1:**134
Holmes, Richard, *The World at War,* **3:**234–236, *235*
Holmes, Stephen, **1:**209
Holocaust
    denial of, **3:**50
    goal of, **3:**50
    Jewish immigration to escape, **1:**75, 76, **3:**14–16
    memorials to, **1:**319, **3:**51
    Nuremberg Laws in, **2:**253, **3:**14
    origins of, **3:**14, 34, 50
    rape in, **2:**283
    targets of, **3:**36, 50
    women survivors of, **3:**34–36
Holocaust autobiographies
    by Frank (Anne), **2:**253–255
    by Hillesum (Etty), **2:**22–24, 253
    by Klemperer (Victor), **2:**303–305
    by Nazis, **2:**54–56
    rise of, **1:**318
    by Wiesel (Elie), **1:**318–320
Holocaust concentration camps
    Auschwitz, **1:**318–320, **2:**22, **3:**35, 51
    Bergen-Belsen, **2:**253, **3:**51
    Buchenwald, **3:**51
    Mauthausen, **3:**51
    Westerbork, **2:**22–24, 253
Holocaust oral histories
    of American survivors and witnesses, **3:**50–52
    of Jewish refugees in China, **3:**14–16
    rise of, **3:**15, 34, 50
    of women survivors, **3:**34–36
    in *The World at War* (Holmes), **3:**235
Holocaust Oral History Manual (Gurewitsch and Eliach), **3:**35
Holoch, Adele, **2:**13
Holroyd, Michael, **2:**269
Holtby, Winifred, **1:**330, 331
    South Riding, **1:**331
Holton, Woody, **2:**90
Holy Club, **2:**195, 197
Holy Land, Guylforde's (Richarde) pilgrimage to, **2:**226–228

Homans, Margaret, **2:**211
Home Elsewhere, A (Stepto), **1:**80
Home Front, The (Satterfield), **3:**202
Homeland Security Department, U.S., **3:**245
Homes, A. M., **1:**48
Homestead Act of 1862 (U.S.), **2:**163, 165
Homesteading
    oral histories of, **3:**93–95
    Ray (Annie) on experience of, **2:**163–164
    Stewart (Elinore Pruitt) on experience of, **2:**91–93, *92*
Home to Harlem (McKay), **1:**84, 86
Homoeroticism
    in James's (Henry) novels, **2:**115
    in Marcus Aurelius's letters, **1:**220
    in *Red Azalea* (Min), **1:**160
Homosexuality
    of Bechdel (Alison), **1:**139, 140
    in Britain, legal ban on, **2:**9, 183, **3:**70
    in Britain, oral histories of, **3:**70–72
    Byron (George Gordon Noel) and, **2:**144
    Chinese persecution of, **1:**158
    in *Fun Home* (Bechdel), **1:**139–141
    gay rights movement, **3:**70, 72, 83–84
    in Harlem Renaissance, **1:**84
    in *Hunger of Memory* (Rodriguez), **1:**17
    James (Henry) and, **2:**115
    in *A Long Way from Home* (McKay), **1:**85
    of Lorde (Audre), **1:**39, **2:**3, 5
    of Maugham (W. Somerset), **2:**183, 185
    of McKay (Claude), **1:**84
    of Sassoon (Siegfried), **2:**247, 248
    in U.S., oral histories of, **3:**83–85
    U.S. attitudes toward, evolution of, **1:**139
    in U.S. military, **1:**139
    of Wilde (Oscar), **2:**9–10
    of Williams (Tennessee), **2:**152

Hong, Christina, **1:**294
Hood River Issei, The (Tamura), **3:**80–82
Hooke, Robert, *The Diary of Robert Hooke,* **2:**72
hooks, bell, **1:**250
    Ain't I a Woman, **1:**250
    Bone Black, **1:**249–251
    Wounds of Passion, **1:**250, 251
Hooligan: A History of Respectable Fears (Pearson), **3:**312
Hooligans or Rebels? (Humphries), **3:**144, 311–314
Hooper, Charles, **1:**24
Hooper, Finley, **2:**96
Hooper, Sheila, **1:**24
Hooten, Elizabeth, **2:**26
Hope against Hope (Mandlestam), **1:**271
Hopi, in land dispute with Navajo, oral histories of, **3:**10–12
Hopkins, Anthony, **2:**71
Hopkins, Gerard Manley, **2:**147
Hopkinson, Amanda, **2:**221
Hopkinson, Francis, **2:**316
Hopkinson, Mrs. Thomas, **2:**316, 317
Horacek, Parson, **2:**149
Horn, Eva, **1:**32
Horn Book Magazine, **1:**162
Horniman, Annie, **2:**128
Horowitz, David, **3:**165
Horse of Pride, The (Hélias), **3:**61
Hortensius (Cicero), **1:**196, 198
Horwitz, Tony, **1:**280
Hosbawm, Eric, **3:**186
Hoskins, Katherine, **2:**115
Hospicio é Deus (Lopes Cançado), **2:**6
Hosseini, Khaled, *The Kite Runner,* **1:**40
Houlbrook, Matt, **3:**72
House Arrest (film), **1:**6, 7
Households, isolated vs. collective, Stanton (Elizabeth Cady) on, **1:**14
House Made of Dawn (Momaday), **1:**54
House of Confucius, The (Kong). See *In the Mansion of Confucius' Descendants* (Kong)

House of Representatives, U.S., gag rule on slavery in, **2:**70
House of Si Abd Allah, The (Munson), **3:**47
House of the Seven Gables, The (Hawthorne), **2:**223–224
House on Mango Street, The (Cisneros), **1:**108
House Un-American Activities Committee (HUAC), **2:**152
Housewife, 49 (television show), **2:**265
Houston, James D., *Farewell to Manzanar,* **1:**299–301
Houston, Jeanne Wakatsuki, **1:**300
    Beyond Manzanar, **1:**299
    Farewell to Manzanar, **1:**299–301, 309
    The Legend of Fire Horse Woman, **1:**299
Houston Chronicle (newspaper), **2:**85
Hoveyda, Abbas, **3:**218
Hoveyda, Fereydoun, *Fall of the Shah,* **3:**218
Howard, Maureen, **2:**48
Howard, Neil, **1:**244
Howard-Stepney, Marged, **1:**127
Howe, Barbara, **3:**68
Howe, Florence, *With Wings,* **1:**8
Howe, Lawrence, **1:**146, 147, 148
Howells, William Dean, **1:**146, **2:**239–240, **3:**261
Hower, Edward, **1:**23
How I Grew (McCarthy), **1:**258
Howkins, Alun, **3:**64–65
How the Garcia Girls Lost Their Accents (Alvarez), **1:**108
Hron, Madelaine, **3:**259
HUAC. See House Un-American Activities Committee
Huang Dinghui, **3:**148
Hubbell, J. L., **3:**290, 291
Hudson, Derek, **2:**77
Hudson, Hosea
    Black Worker in the Deep South, **1:**3
    The Narrative of Hosea Hudson, **1:**3–4
Hudson Review (journal), **1:**165, 168, **2:**115
Hughes, Barbara, **2:**159

Hughes, Langston
    The Big Sea, **1:**84, 122
    "Harlem," **1:**275
    I Wonder as I Wander, **1:**37
    Mulatto, **1:**72
Hughes, Ted, **2:**47, 48, 49
Human body. See Body
Humanism
    Cereta (Laura) in, **2:**160, 161
    Kierkegaard's (Søren) critique of, **2:**166, 167
Human rights
    "Letter from the Birmingham Jail" (King) as argument for, **2:**32
    universal, development of concept, **2:**316
Human rights abuses. See also Genocide
    in Cambodia, **1:**306
    in China, **1:**158, 161
    in Guatemala, **1:**99, 100, **3:**164–166
    in Iran, **1:**155
    in Iraq, **2:**275
    in Nazi Germany (See Holocaust)
    in Nigeria, **1:**214, 215, 216
    in Sierra Leone, **1:**312
    in South Africa, **3:**242
    in Ukraine, **3:**19
    in Vietnam, **1:**171, 172
Hume, David, **2:**328
Humor
    in *Angela's Ashes* (McCourt), **1:**119
    in *The Autobiography of Ben Franklin* (Franklin), **1:**181
    in *Confessions of Lady Nijo* (Nijo), **2:**60
    in *The Diary of Anne Frank* (Frank), **2:**253–254, 255
    in *Journals of Ralph Waldo Emerson* (Emerson), **2:**141
    in "Letter to Her Daughter from the New White House" (Adams), **2:**87
    in *Life on the Mississippi* (Twain), **1:**147
    in *Praeterita* (Ruskin), **1:**265
    in *Prison Writings* (Peltier), **1:**97

in *Selected Letters of Martha Gellhorn* (Gellhorn), **2:**102

in *Up from Slavery* (Washington), **1:**51–52

in *A Woman in Berlin* (anonymous), **2:**282

Humphrey, Carol Sue, **2:**318

Humphries, Stephen

The Handbook of Oral History, **3:**313

Hooligans or Rebels?, **3:**144, 311–314

on *The World at War* (Holmes), **3:**235

Hunger of Memory (Rodriguez), **1:**15–17, 47

Hunsaker, Steven V., **1:**100

Hunt, Evelyn, **3:**269

Hunt, Leigh, **2:**143, 144, 146

Hunt, Richard, **3:**277

Hunt, Swanee, *This Was Not Our War,* **3:**268

Huntington, Countess of, **2:**44, 46

Huntsman, Jeffrey, **1:**56

Hurst, Fannie, **1:**10

Imitation of Life, **1:**72

Hurston, Zora Neale

Angelou (Maya) inspired by, **1:**18

Dust Tracks on a Road, **1:**9–11, 18, 122

Mules and Men, **1:**9

Polk County, **1:**10

Seraph on the Suwanee, **1:**9

Tell My Horse, **1:**9, 11

Their Eyes Were Watching God, **1:**11

in tradition of Prince (Mary), **3:**24

Hurvitz, Yair, **2:**50

Husain, Adnan, **1:**287–288

Husayn, Taha. *See* Hussein, Taha

Hussain, Soofia, **3:**81

Hussein, Saddam, **2:**275, 276, 278, 279

Hussein, Taha, *An Egyptian Childhood,* **1:**135–138

Hutchinson, Mary, **2:**300

Hutchisson, James M., **2:**42

Hutu people, **3:**257–259, *258*

Huxley, Elspeth, **2:**12

Huxley, Thomas, **1:**67

Huynh, Jade Ngoc Quang, *South Wind Changing,* **1:**171

Hyde-Lees, Georgie, **2:**126

Hypocrisy

in American Revolution, **2:**44, 45

in European culture, **1:**90

in slavery, **1:**34, 144, **2:**44, 45, 46

I

I, Rigoberta Menchú (Menchú), **3:**164–166

Californio Voices (Savage) vs., **3:**114

Child of the Dark (de Jesus) vs., **2:**8

Doña María's Story (James) vs., **3:**73–74

Let Me Speak! (Viezzer and Barrios de Chungara) vs., **3:**322

Rites: A Guatemalan Boyhood (Perera) vs., **1:**99

Women's Words (Gluck and Patai) on, **3:**191

IAD. *See* Institute for Aboriginal Development

I Am Rosa Parks (Parks), **1:**38

Ibn Asakir, **1:**287

Ibrahim, Christy Thompson, **1:**8

I Can Almost See the Lights of Home (Portelli), **3:**265–266

Ichijō (emperor of Japan), **2:**290, 291, 292

Ida (Stein), **1:**332

Idaho, oral histories of life in, **3:**93–95, *94*

Idealization

of Africa, by Laye (Camara), **1:**130

of childhood, by Laye (Camara), **1:**128

of colonial America, by Crèvecoeur (Michel-Guillaume Saint-Jean de), **2:**213–215

Identity. *See also* Ethnic identity; Multicultural and multiracial identities; National identity; *specific groups*

divided nature of, Rousseau (Jean-Jacques) on, **1:**200–202

language in, role of, **1:**15–17, **3:**108, 109

postcolonial, **1:**87–89

Identity formation

in *Angela's Ashes* (McCourt), **1:**121

in *Dust Tracks on a Road* (Hurston), **1:**11

of Irish immigrants, **1:**121

in *Journal, 1955–1962* (Feraoun), **2:**262–263

in *The Journals of Charlotte Forten Grimké* (Grimké), **2:**31

in *Praeterita* (Ruskin), **1:**265

in *Wars I Have Seen* (Stein), **1:**333–334

Identity politics

Columbus's (Christopher) legacy and, **2:**203

cultural studies and, **1:**15

disability studies and, **1:**8

Rodriguez's (Richard) critique of, **1:**15–16

IEDs. *See* Improvised explosive devices

If This Is a Man (Levi), **1:**318

"If We Must Die" (McKay), **1:**84

Igbo people, **1:**214, 215

Ignatius of Loyola (saint), **1:**211

"I Have a Dream" (King), **1:**79, **2:**32

I Know Why the Caged Bird Sings (Angelou), **1:**18–20, 249

Ilagiinniq (Tulugarjuk and Christopher), **3:**138

Ill-Fated People, An (Vambe), **3:**251–253

Illinois, Lincoln's (Abraham) life and career in, **3:**261, 263. *See also* Chicago

Illness. *See* Health problems

Illustrated Times of London, **1:**112

Imad al-Din al-Katib al-Isfahani, *The Syrian Thunderbolt,* **1:**286

Image du monde (Guisson), **1:**105

Images and Conversations (Preciado Martin), **3:**121

Imitation of Life (Hurst), **1:**72

Imlay, Gilbert, **2:**111

Immigrant Women in the Land of Dollars (Ewen), **3:**305

SUBJECT INDEX

Immigration
- to Australia, from Vietnam, **1**:337
- to Chile, from Germany, **1**:75, 77
- to France, by Bashkirtseff (Marie), **2**:306–308
- from Ireland, **1**:119
- to Ireland, by Mahomet (Dean), **2**:229
- Jewish (*See* Jewish immigration)

Immigration, to U.S.
- by Agosín (Marjorie), **1**:75
- by Ahmedi (Farah), **1**:40, 41
- by Cheng Yu-hsiu, **1**:152
- Cuban, **1**:296–298
- by Hayslip (Le Ly), **1**:335
- Japanese, **1**:309, **3**:80–82, 127–129, 195
- Jewish, **3**:14, 118, 120
- Latin American, **1**:108–110, **3**:121
- by Medina (Pablo), **1**:296, 297
- by Min (Anchee), **1**:158
- by Nabokov (Vladimir), **1**:270
- by Nguyen (Kien), **1**:170, 171
- oral histories of, **3**:80–82, 305–307
- by Santiago (Esmeralda), **1**:108–110
- by Siv (Sichan), **1**:306, 307
- Southeast Asian, **1**:170, 171, 306–307, 337
- by Suleri (Sara), **1**:87
- after Vietnam War, **1**:170, 171, 337

Immigration Act of 1924 (U.S.), **3**:80, 127, 195

Immigration Act of 1982, Amerasian (U.S.), **1**:170

Immigration and Nationality Act of 1952 (U.S.), **3**:127

Immigration Reform and Control Act of 1986 (U.S.), **3**:121

Impeachment, of Johnson (Andrew), **1**:5

Imprisonment
- of Fox (George), **2**:26
- of Gandhi (Mohandas), **1**:242
- of Ghazzawi ('Izzat), **2**:50
- of Khomeini (Ruhollah), **3**:218, 219
- of Kong Demao, **3**:124
- of Mandela (Nelson), **1**:24, 27–29, **3**:242
- of Nehru (Jawaharlal), **1**:289, 290, 291
- of Ngũgĩ wa Thiong'o, **2**:12–14, *13*
- of Peltier (Leonard), **1**:96–98
- of Polo (Marco), **1**:105
- in Soviet Gulag system, oral histories of, **3**:17–19
- of Soyinka (Wole), **1**:214–216
- of Speer (Albert), **2**:54–56
- of Wilde (Oscar), **2**:9–10

Improvised explosive devices (IEDs), **3**:233

Inada, Lawson Fusao, *Only What We Could Carry*, **3**:80

In All the West No Place Like This (Kincaid and Dahlgren), **3**:93

Incarceration. *See* Imprisonment

Incest, Nin's (Anaïs) experience of, **2**:124

Incident at Oglala (documentary), **1**:96

Incidents in the Life of a Slave Girl (Jacobs), **1**:142–145
- autobiographies inspired by, **1**:18
- *A Diary from Dixie* (Chesnut) vs., **2**:250
- Equiano's (Olaudah) influence on, **1**:83
- *The Journals of Charlotte Forten Grimké* (Grimké) vs., **2**:29
- *Narrative of the Life of Frederick Douglass* (Douglass) vs., **1**:34, 35, 142, 143

In Country (Mason), **1**:335

In Custody (Desai), **1**:87

Independent (newspaper), **2**:239, 269, 276, **3**:316

Indexicality, **2**:267

India
- British partition of (1947), **1**:87, 244
- food of, in Britain, **2**:230, 231
- Gama's (Vasco da) first voyage to, **2**:198–200
- under Mogul Empire, **2**:229
- nationalism in, **1**:289–290

India, British colonial rule of
- Chaudhuri (Nirad C.) on life under, **3**:253
- East India Company in, **2**:229
- end of (1947), **1**:87, 244
- establishment of, **2**:229, 328
- Gandhi (Mohandas) in movement against, **1**:242–244, 289–290
- legacy of, **1**:87–89
- Mahomet (Dean) on culture of, **2**:229–231
- Nehru (Jawaharlal) in movement against, **1**:289–291

Indiana Magazine of History, **3**:109

Indian nationalism, **1**:289–290

Indian Removal Act of 1830 (U.S.), **1**:302, **3**:107

Indian Reorganization Act of 1934 (U.S.), **3**:107

Indian Territory, **3**:325

Indian Trader (Blue), **3**:290, 291

Indigenous people. *See also specific countries and groups*
- Columbus's (Christopher) encounters with, **2**:201, 202, *202*
- Gama's (Vasco da) encounters with, **2**:199

Individual actions, in identity, Rousseau (Jean-Jacques) on, **1**:200, 201

Individuals
- authors as, Lejeune (Philippe) on value of, **1**:239
- in Romantic era, focus on, **2**:16
- "self-made," **1**:180

Indochina, French colonial rule of, **3**:279

Indochinese Refugees (Scott), **1**:335

Indoctrination, in Cultural Revolution, **1**:159, 161, 162

Indonesia, Obama (Barack) in, **1**:78

Industrialization
- in Argentina, **3**:73
- and international labor movement, **3**:157
- in Soviet Union, **3**:17
- of U.S., Thoreau (Henry David) on, **1**:233

Industrialization, in Britain
- of agriculture, **3**:59, 63

in concepts of progress, **2:**146
economic inequality in, **2:**300
social inequality in, **2:**16
Industrial Revolution, Second
Adams (Henry) on, **1:**132, 134
Twain (Mark) and, **1:**146
Industrial Workers of the World (IWW), **3:**329
establishment of, **3:**328
oral histories of, **3:**328–330
working conditions improved by, **3:**93
Infidel (Hirsi Ali), **1:207–210**
Influenza pandemic of 1918, **1:**258
Ingle, H. Larry, **2:**26, 28
Inheritance law, English, women in, **2:**62–63, 64
In Her Own Words (Morantz), **3:**170
In Light of India (Paz), **1:**222–223
Inman, Henry, **2:336**
In My Country (film), **3:**242
Innocence, loss of
in *The Dark Child* (Laye), **1:**129
in *Incidents in the Life of a Slave Girl* (Jacobs), **1:**144
Innocents Abroad, The (Twain), **1:**146
Innovations, in autobiographical writing
of Cavendish (Margaret), **1:**230, 231
of Conroy (Frank), **1:**165
of Hussein (Taha), **1:**135–136
of Kingston (Maxine Hong), **1:**173
of Pepys (Samuel), **2:**72
of Rousseau (Jean-Jacques), **1:**200–202
of Stein (Gertrude), **1:**332, 333, 334
In Pharaoh's Army (Wolff), **1:**47
In Search of Lost Time (Proust), **1:**265, 270
In Search of Our Roots (Gates), **1:**263
Inside the Third Reich (Speer), **2:**54
In Sierra Leone (Jackson), **1:**312
Institute for Aboriginal Development (IAD), **3:**334, 336
Insurgencies
in Iraq War, **3:**231, 232, 233

in Salvadoran Civil War, **3:**205, 206, 207
Insurrection Act of 1796 (Britain), **2:**159
Intellectual development, in *The Autobiography of Giambattista Vico* (Vico), **1:**183–185
Intellectual Memoirs (McCarthy), **1:**258
Intercultural adoption, Kim (Elizabeth) on, **1:**102–104
Interesting Narrative of the Life of Olaudah Equiano, The (Equiano), **1:34, 81–83,** 142, **3:**23
Interior, U.S. Department of, **3:**11
Interior Castle (Teresa of Ávila), **1:**212
International Affairs (journal), **1:**25, 291
International Court of Justice, **1:**306
International Jew, The (Ford), **1:**30, 32
International Journal of African Historical Studies, **3:**142, 252
International Journal of Middle East Studies, **3:**220
International Law Commission, UN, **2:**56
International Migration Review (journal), **3:**81, 225
International Review (journal), **2:**70
International Review of Social Research (journal), **3:**320
International Women's Conference, **3:**322
International Women's Year Tribunal, **3:**322
International Workingmen's Association, **3:**3
Internment. *See* Japanese American internment
Interpreter of Maladies (Lahiri), **1:**87
Interpreting the Self (Reynolds), **1:**136, 137, 286, 287
Interracial adoption, Kim (Elizabeth) on, **1:**102–104
Interracial relationships
in Appalachia, **3:**92
in Korean War, **1:**102
McBride (James) on, **1:**72–74
U.S. attitudes toward, **1:**72–74
in U.S. postwar occupation of Japan, **3:**127–129

U.S. Supreme Court on, **1:**72, 78
Vietnamese attitudes toward, **1:**170, 171
in Vietnam War, **1:**170
Interrupted Life, An (Hillesum), **2:22–25**
Intertexts (journal), **3:**116
"Interviewing Women" (Oakley), **3:**190
Interviews. *See* Oral histories
In the Cities of the South (Seabrook), **3:**54
In the Combat Zone (Marshall), **3:**221, 279
In the Garden of North American Martyrs (Wolff), **1:**47
In the Mansion of Confucius' Descendants (Kong and Ke), **3:124–126,** 299
In the Presence of Absence (Darwish), **1:255–257**
Intifada, first, **1:**225, **2:**50–52
Into the Jet Age (Wooldridge), **3:**203
Introspection, Ruskin's (John) fear of, **1:**265, 266
Inuits, oral histories of, **3:**138–140, 139
Inuktitut language, **3:**138, 139–140
Invention of Loneliness, The (Auster), **1:**279
Investigation of Dogmatic Theology (Tolstoy), **1:**194
Invisible Cities (Calvino), **1:**105
Invisible Soldier, The (Motley), **3:**212
Invisible Thread, The (Uchida), **1:309–311**
Iola Leroy (Harper), **1:**143
Iowa, labor movement in, **3:**153
Iran
coup of 1953 in, **3:**218
in Iran–Iraq War, **3:**219
Islam in, **1:**155, 156
oral histories of political history of, **3:**218–220
Revolution of 1979 in, **1:**155, 157, **3:**218, 220
Satrapi (Marjane) on life in, **1:**155–157
uprising of 1963 in, **3:**218, 219
White Revolution in, **3:**218
women's rights in, **3:**218

Iranian Studies (journal), **3:**219
Iran–Iraq War (1980–1988), **1:**155, 157
Iraq. *See also* Iraq War
    in Gulf War, **2:**275, 278–280
    in Iran–Iraq War, **1:**155, 157
IraqGirl: Diary of a Teenage Girl in Iraq, **2:**275
Iraq Veterans against the War, **3:**232
Iraq War (2003–2011), **2:276**
    Al-Windawi (Thura) on experience of, **2:**275–276
    embedded journalists in, **2:**278, 280
    vs. Salvadoran Civil War, **3:**207
    U.S. veterans of, oral histories of, **3:**231–233, *232*
Ireland
    Catholicism in, **1:**119–120
    Civil War in, **3:**27, 315
    Easter Uprising in, **3:**27, 315
    English conquest of, **3:**315
    famine in, **3:**27, 315
    gender roles in, **2:**157
    independence movement in, **3:**27–29
    independence of (1922), **1:**119, **3:**315
    Leadbeater (Mary) on life in, **2:**157–159
    Mahomet's (Dean) move to, **2:**229
    McCourt (Frank) on life in, **1:**119–121
    nationalism in, **1:**119, **2:**127, 128, **3:**315
    oral histories of, **3:**27–29, 315–317
    oral traditions of, **1:**121
    poverty in, **1:**119–121
    Quakerism in, **2:**157–159
    Rebellion of 1798 in, **2:**157, *158,* 159
    War of Independence in, **3:**27–29, 315
    Yeats (William Butler) on life in, **2:**126–128
Ireland's Unfinished Revolution (Griffith and O'Grady), **3:27–30**
Irele, Abiola, **1:**130

Irish Americans, McCourt (Frank) on experience of, **1:**119–121
Irish autobiographical writing
    by Leadbeater (Mary), **2:**157–159
    rise in popularity of, **1:**119, 120
    tradition of, **1:**119, 121
    by Yeats (William Butler), **2:**126–128
Irish Civil War (1922–1923), **3:**27, 315
Irish Days (Hickey), **3:315–317**
Irish Experience during the Second World War, The (Grob-Fitzgibbon), **3:**315–316
Irish identity, **1:**121
Irish nationalism, **1:**119, **2:**127, 128, **3:**315
Irish National Theatre Society, **2:**128
Irish oral histories
    on life in twentieth century, **3:**315–317
    on War of Independence, **3:**27–29
Irish Rebellion (1798), **2:**157, *158,* 159
Irish Republican Brotherhood, **3:**27
Irish University Review (journal), **1:**121
Irish Voice (newspaper), **3:**29
Irish War of Independence (1919–1921), **3:**27–29, 315
Irizarry, Estelle, **2:**203
Irvine, Weldon, **1:**274
Isabella of Castille, **2:**201
Isani, Mukhtar Ali, **2:**45
Isay, David, **3:174**
Isca, Valerio, **3:**5
Isham, Ralph Hayward, **2:**330
Isherwood, Christopher, *The World in the Evening,* **2:**152
Islam. *See also* Muslim *entries*
    fundamentalist, **1:**156, 208
    Hirsi Ali's (Ayaan) critique of, **1:**207–209
    in Iran, **1:**155, 156
    Malcolm X's conversion to, **1:**186–188
    violence against women in, **1:**207–209
Islamic education, in Egypt, **1:**135
Isocrates, *To Nicocles,* **2:**94

Isolation
    of households, Stanton (Elizabeth Cady) on, **1:**14
    personal, Hawthorne (Nathaniel) on, **2:**223, 224
Israel
    establishment of (1948), **1:**225, 255, **2:**104, **3:**118
    Palestinian territories occupied by, **1:**225, **2:**50, *51*
Israeli–Palestinian conflict, **1:**225, 255, 257, **2:**50–52
Issei, **3:**80–82
Italian Americans, relocation during World War II, oral histories of, **3:**224–226
Italian autobiographical writing
    by Cereta (Laura), **2:**160–162
    by Polo (Marco), **1:**105–107
    by Vico (Giambattista), **1:**183–185
Italian oral histories
    on Fosse Ardeatine massacre, **3:**265–267
    on working class, **3:**157–159
Italian Quattrocento, **2:**160
Italy. *See also* Italian autobiographical writing
    education of women in, **2:**160–161
    Fosse Ardeatine massacre in, **3:**265–267
    labor movement in, **3:**157–159, *158*
    Montagu's (Mary Wortley) move to, **2:**35
    Nazi occupation of, **3:**265–267
    Renaissance, women in, **2:**160–162
    working class in, **3:**157–159
It Happened in Brooklyn (Frommer and Frommer), **3:**118
It Happened to Nancy (Sparks), **2:**294
Iverson, Peter, **3:**291
Iwakoshi, Miyo, **3:**82
I Will Bear Witness (Klemperer), **2:303–305**
I Will Marry When I Want (Ngũgĩ), **2:**12
I Wonder as I Wander (Hughes), **1:**37
IWW. *See* Industrial Workers of the World
Izumi Shikibu, **2:**189, 190, 290

J

Jabra, Jabra Ibrahim, *The First Well*, **1**:136
Jacinthe Noir (Amrouche), **1**:93
Jack, Peter Monro, **2**:149
Jacka, Tamara, **3**:301
Jackson, Andrew, **1**:302, **2**:335
Jackson, Anna, **2**:134, 135
Jackson, Ernest, **2**:263
Jackson, Jamie Smith, **2:295**
Jackson, Michael, *In Sierra Leone*, **1**:312
Jackson, Molly, **3**:157
Jackson, Samuel L., **3**:242
Jackson, Timothy P., **2**:24
Jackson-Schebetta, Lisa, **2**:102
JACL. *See* Japanese American Citizens League
Jacobs, Harriet A., *Incidents in the Life of a Slave Girl*, **1:142–145**, *143*
  autobiographies inspired by, **1**:18
  A Diary from Dixie (Chesnut) vs., **2**:250
  Equiano's (Olaudah) influence on, **1**:83
  The Journals of Charlotte Forten Grimké (Grimké) vs., **2**:29
  Narrative of the Life of Frederick Douglass (Douglass) vs., **1**:34, 35, 142, 143
Jacobsen, Jens Peter, **2**:149
Jacob's Room (Woolf), **2**:138
Jaffer, Zubeida, **3**:243
Jamaica
  English colonial rule of, **1**:111
  McKay's (Claude) youth in, **1**:84, 85
  slavery in, **1**:111
Jamaican autobiographical writing
  by McKay (Claude), **1**:84–86
  by Seacole (Mary), **1**:111–113
James, Alice, **2**:113
James, Daniel, *Doña María's Story*, **3:73–76**
James, Henry, **2:114**
  Adams (Henry) influenced by, **1**:132–133
  The Bostonians, **2**:113
  The Complete Notebooks of Henry James, **2:113–116**
  Confidence, **2**:114
  Daisy Miller, **1**:133, **2**:114
  Gellhorn (Martha) on, **2**:101
  Guy Domville, **2**:114
  on *Journal des Goncourt* (Goncourt and Goncourt), **2**:82–83
  Kemble's (Fanny) friendship with, **2**:335, 336
  The Notebooks of Henry James, **2**:113, 114, 115
  The Portrait of a Lady, **1**:133, **2**:113
  Roderick Hudson, **2**:114
  The Spoils of Poynton, **2**:115
  Wells's (H. G.) letters to, **1**:252, 253
  The Wings of the Dove, **2**:113, 115
James, William, **1**:197, **2**:113
James I (king of England), **1**:316, **2**:62
James II (king of England), **1**:315
Jameson, Anna, **2**:335
Jamison, Kay Redfield, *An Unquiet Mind*, **1**:204
Japan. *See also* Japanese autobiographical writing
  Buddhism in (*See* Buddhism)
  China invaded by (1931), **3**:215
  Chinese relations with, **1**:340, **3**:149
  gender roles in, **2**:60–61
  Heian period in (*See* Heian period)
  hibakusha literature of, **1**:293
  immigration to U.S. from, **1**:309, **3**:80–82, 127–129, 195
  Kamakura period in, **2**:59–61
  Korea under rule of, **1**:322–324
  marriage in, **2**:297–299
  Mongol invasions of, **2**:59
  in Nanking Massacre, **1**:340, **2**:19–21
  Nara period in, **2**:189
  nationalism in, **3**:234
  in Russo–Japanese War, **1**:322, **3**:234
  in Sino–Japanese Wars, **1**:322, 339, 340, **3**:234
  in World War II, oral histories of, **3**:127–129, 215–217 (*See also* World War II)
Japan at War (Cook and Cook), **3:215–217**
Japanese, Nazis & Jews (Kranzler), **3**:15
Japanese American(s)
  autobiographical tradition of, **1**:299, 309
  first-generation, oral histories of, **3**:80–82
  Houston (Jeanne Wakatsuki) on experience of, **1**:299–301
  internment of (*See* Japanese American internment)
  Japanese war brides, oral histories of, **3**:127–129, *128*
  racism against, **1**:309, **3**:81, 82, 127, 195
  Uchida (Yoshiko) on experience of, **1**:309–311
Japanese American Citizens League (JACL), **3**:197
Japanese American internment, **1:310, 3:196**
  establishment of policy, **1**:299, 311, **3**:104, 195
  Houston (Jeanne Wakatsuki) on experience of, **1**:299–301
  Italian American relocation and, **3**:224
  at Manzanar, **1**:299–301, **3**:102–104, 197, *225*
  oral histories of, **3**:80–81, 102–104, 195–197
  reparations for, **3**:195, 197
  Uchida (Yoshiko) on experience of, **1**:309–311
Japanese American Oral History Project, **3**:80, 102, 195
Japanese American World War II Evacuation Oral History Project (Hansen), **3**:215
Japanese autobiographical writing. *See also specific works and writers*
  by Michitsuna No Haha, **2**:297–299
  by Murasaki Shikibu, **2**:290–292
  by Nakazawa (Keiji), **1**:293–295
  by Nijo (Lady), **2**:59–61
  by Sarashina (Lady), **2**:189–191
  by women, tradition of, **2**:59, 60

SUBJECT INDEX

Japanese War Brides in America (Crawford et al.), **3:127–130**
Japan-Russia Treaty of Peace, **3**:234
Jarrell, Randall, **1**:205
Jaspers, Karl, **2**:167
Jawhariyyeh, Wasif, **2**:104
Jay's Journal (Sparks), **2**:294
Jayyusi, Salma Khadra, **1**:225, 227
Jazz
 and *Stop-Time* (Conroy), **1**:165, 166
 Terkel's (Louis "Studs") writing style compared to, **3**:214
Jefferson, Alexander, **3**:249
Jefferson, Lucy, **2**:316
Jefferson, Martha, **2**:316–318
Jefferson, Mary, **2**:316
Jefferson, Thomas, **2:317**
 Autobiography, 1743–1790, **1**:179, **2**:69
 on coal in Appalachia, **3**:86
 Crèvecoeur (Michel-Guillaume Saint-Jean de) and, **2**:213, 215
 The Family Letters of Thomas Jefferson, **2**:317
 Letters from Jefferson to His Daughter, **2**:38, **316–319**
 Notes on the State of Virginia, **2**:45, 215
 on Wheatley's (Phillis) poetry, **2**:45
Jeffrey, Francis, **2**:35, 36, 73
Jelinek, Estelle, **1**:246
Jelmek, Estelle C., **1**:14
Jemima Condict (Condict), **2:78–80**
Jemison, Mary, **1**:326
Jenner, W. J. F., **3**:299
Jennings, Humphrey, **2**:235
Jeon, Miseli, **1**:103, 104
Jerome, **2**:94
Jerusalem, **2:227**
 under British Mandate, 'Amr (Sāmī) on, **2**:104, 105, *105*
 Guylforde's (Richarde) pilgrimage to, **2**:226–228
 secular education in, **2**:106
Jessee, Erin, **3**:180
Jesus, Carolina Maria de. *See* De Jesus, Carolina Maria

Jew(s)
 anarchism among, **3**:3
 in Chile, **1**:75–77
 in Guatemala, **1**:99–100
 in interracial relationships, **1**:72–74
 prejudice against (*See* Anti-Semitism)
 The Protocols of the Elder of Zion on conspiracy of, **1**:32
 in World War II (*See* Holocaust)
Jewel of the Desert (Taylor), **3**:80
Jewish American Committee, **3**:118
Jewish autobiographical writing. *See also specific works and writers*
 by Agosín (Marjorie), **1**:75–77
 by D'Israeli (Isaac), **2**:177, 179
 by Frank (Anne), **2**:253–255
 by Hillesum (Etty), **2**:22–24
 by Kafka (Franz), **2**:120–122
 by Klemperer (Victor), **2**:303–305
 by Perera (Victor), **1**:99–101
 by Stein (Gertrude), **1**:332, 333
 by Wiesel (Elie), **1**:318–320
Jewish Community of North Minneapolis, The (Lewin), **3**:50
Jewish identity
 of Jewish Americans, **3**:119
 of Jewish refugees, **1**:75–77
Jewish immigration
 to China, **3**:14–16
 to Latin America, **1**:75, 76, *76*
 to Palestine, **2**:105, **3**:14
 to U.S., **3**:14, 118, 120
Jewish oral histories. *See also* Holocaust oral histories
 of anarchists, **3**:3
 of U.S. life, **3**:118–120
Jewish Social Studies (journal), **1**:31
Jeyifo, Biodun, **1**:215, 216
Jiang, Ji-li
 Magical Monkey King, **1**:163
 Red Scarf Girl, **1**:153, 154, 159, **161–163**
Jiang Quing, **1**:158
Jiang Zemin, **1**:158
Jim Crow laws. *See* Racial segregation

Job Corps, **3**:254
Johansen, Bruce, **1**:97
John, Augustus Edwin, **2:127**
John II (king of Portugal), **2**:198
John of the Cross (saint), **1**:211
Johnson, Andrew, **1**:5
Johnson, Arvid, **3**:94
Johnson, Charles, **1**:10
Johnson, David, **2**:219, **3**:143
Johnson, E. D. H., **2**:300
Johnson, James Weldon, *Along This Way*, **1**:13, 84, 122
Johnson, Josephine, **2**:152
Johnson, Kendall, **1**:54, **2**:115
Johnson, Lyndon Baines, **3**:254–256, *255*
Johnson, Martin, **3**:261, 264
Johnson, Pamela Hansford, **1**:127
Johnson, Penny, **1**:226
Johnson, Richard, *Making History*, **3**:176, 177
Johnson, Robert David, **3**:254
Johnson, Samuel
 on *Evelina* (Burney), **2**:313
 letters of, **2**:217
 Life of Samuel Johnson (Boswell) on, **2**:177, 195, 309, 328, 329–330
 on *Turkish Embassy Letters* (Montagu), **2**:37
Johnson, Tom, **3**:200, 338
Johnsrud, Harold, **1**:258
Jolluck, Katherine R., *Gulag Voices*, **3:17–19**, 331
Jolote, Juan Pérez, **3**:167–169
Jones, Bob, **3**:5
Jones, Catherine, **2**:311
Jones, Edward P., **1**:122
Jones, John Paul, **1:180**
Jones, J. William, **2**:38, 39
Jones, Lu Ann, **3**:135–136, 137
Jones, Roderick, **2**:261
Jörgensen, Beth Ellen, **3**:31, 32
Josephson, Paul, **3**:285
Journal(s). *See also specific works and writers*
 Lejeune (Philippe) on study of, **2**:174–175

rise in popularity of, in England, **2:**177

of ships' captains, Spanish law on, **2:**201

as source for biographies, **2:**177, 178

Journal, 1955–1962 (Feraoun), **2:262–264**

Journal and Remarks 1832–1835 (Darwin), **1:**65

Journal des Goncourt (Goncourt and Goncourt), **2:81–83**

Journal for Early Modern Cultural Studies, **2:**199

Journal for the Scientific Study of Religion, **3:**41

Journalism

African Americans in, **3:**199–200

Gellhorn's (Martha) career in, **2:**101–102

on hooliganism in Britain, **3:**312

literary, in Enlightenment England, **2:**328

Moore's (Molly) career in, **2:**278–280

Orwell's (George) work in, **2:**117

Journal of Acquired Immune Deficiency Syndromes, **3:**274

Journal of Adolescent & Adult Literacy, **1:**41, 162, **2:**276

Journal of American Ethnic History, **3:**5, 81, 306, 320

Journal of American Folklore, **3:**88, 91, 109

Journal of American History

on *And Justice for All* (Tateishi), **3:**197

on *Bloods* (Terry), **3:**201

on *Brokenburn* (Stone), **2:**246

on *Children of Los Alamos* (Mason), **3:**240

on *The Death of Luigi Trastulli* (Portelli), **3:**159

on *Freedom Flyers* (Moye), **3:**249

on *Habits of Change* (Rogers), **3:**309

on *Head of the Class* (Morris), **3:**22

on *Hill Country Teacher* (Manning), **3:**77

on *The Hispanic-American Entrepreneur* (Owsley), **3:**122

on *The Hood River Issei* (Tamura), **3:**80

on *Launching the War on Poverty* (Gillette), **3:**254

on *A Midwife's Tale* (Ulrich), **2:**333

on *Our Appalachia* (Shackelford and Weinberg), **3:**87

on *Peacework* (Adams), **3:**269

on *A Shared Authority* (Frisch), **3:**181

on *Solidarity Forever* (Bird et al.), **3:**329

on *They Say in Harlan County* (Portelli), **3:**98

on *"We Have Just Begun to Not Fight"* (Frazer and O'Sullivan), **3:**229

Journal of American Studies, **3:**5, 163, 213

Journal of an Ordinary Grief (Darwish), **1:**255

Journal of Appalachian Studies, **3:**68

Journal of Arabic and Islamic Studies, **1:**255

Journal of a Residence in America (Kemble), **2:**335, 336

Journal of a Residence on a Georgian Plantation (Kemble), **2:**335, 336, 337

Journal of Asian American Studies, **3:**84, 85

Journal of Asian and African Studies, **3:**148

Journal of Asian Studies, **3:**148, 280, 281

Journal of a Tour into the Interior (Barnard), **2:**217, 218

Journal of a Tour to the Hebrides, The (Boswell), **2:**328

Journal of a Voyage to North-America (Charlevoix), **2:**205

Journal of Black Studies, **1:**5, 188

Journal of Canadian Studies, **3:**181

Journal of Commonwealth Literature, **1:**88

Journal of Conflict Studies, **3:**207

Journal of Contemporary History, **3:**35

Journal of English Studies, **1:**251

Journal of Family History, **2:**91, **3:**126

Journal of Folklore Research Reviews, **3:**12, 326

Journal of General Education, **3:**345

Journal of George Fox (Fox), **2:26–28**

Journal of Ideology, **3:**291

Journal of Japanese Studies, **2:**60, **3:**216

Journal of John Woolman, The (Woolman), **2:**213

Journal of Jules Renard, The (Renard), **2:**183

Journal of Katherine Mansfield (Mansfield), **2:133–135**

Journal of Literary Studies, **1:**29

Journal of Madam Knight, The (Knight), **2:**78

Journal of Magellan's Voyage (Pigafetta), **2:**201

Journal of Marie Bashkirtseff, The (Bashkirtseff), **2:306–308**

Journal of Military History, **3:**116, 216

Journal of Modern African Studies, **1:**26

Journal of Modern History, **3:**19

Journal of Modern Literature, **1:**17, **2:**122, 269

Journal of Narrative Theory, **1:**121

Journal of Negro History, **1:**11, **2:**45

Journal of New Zealand Literature, **2:**134

Journal of Pan African Studies, **1:**244

Journal of Sir Walter Scott, The (Scott), **2:**67, **309–311**

Journal of Social and Clinical Psychology, **1:**205

Journal of Social Archaeology, **3:**116

Journal of Social History, **3:**75, 145, 311

Journal of Southeast Asian American Education and Advancement, **1:**307

Journal of Southern History, **3:**78, 91, 96, 261

Journal of the American Oriental Society, **1:**287

Journal of the First Voyage of Vasco da Gama, A (Author Unknown), **2:198–200,** 201

Journal of the First Voyage to America (Columbus), **2:201–204,** 205

Journal of the History of Medicine and Applied Science, **3:**272

Journal of the History of Sexuality, **3:**84

Journal of the Midwest Modern Language Association, **3:**329

Journal of the Plague Year (Defoe), **2:**174

SUBJECT INDEX

Journal of the Royal Anthropological Institute, **3:**142

Journal of Women's History, **3:**136

Journals of Arnold Bennett, The (Bennett), **2:136–138**

Journals of Charlotte Forten Grimké, The (Grimké), **2:29–31**

Journals of John Wesley (Wesley), **2:195–197**

Journals of Jonathan Carver and Related Documents, The (Carver), **2:205–208**

Journals of Ralph Waldo Emerson (Emerson), **2:139–142**

Journals of Søren Kierkegaard (Kierkegaard), **2:166–169**

Journey of Tai-me, The (Momaday), **1:**54

Journey's End (Sherriff), **1:**329

Journey to the Land of No (Hakakian), **1:**155

Jouvenel, Bertrand de, **2:**102

Joyce, James
  Conroy (Frank) influenced by, **1:**164
  Evelyn's (John) influence on, **2:**67
  Finnegans Wake, **1:**185
  Goethe's (Johann Wolfgang von) influence on, **1:**276
  Literary Fund and, **2:**207
  Portrait of the Artist as a Young Man, **1:**276, **2:**126
  Thomas (Dylan) influenced by, **1:**125
  Ulysses, **1:**146, **2:**67, 180
  Vico's (Giambattista) influence on, **1:**185
  Woolf's (Virginia) critique of, **2:**180

Joye, Harlon, *Living Atlanta,* **3:**44

Juan Pérez Jolote (Pozas). *See Juan the Chamula* (Pozas)

Juan the Chamula (Pozas), **3:167–169**

Jubilee (Alexander), **1:**262

Judaism. *See* Jew(s)

Judas Kiss, The (play), **2:**10

Judgment at Nuremberg (film), **3:**295

Judicial system, U.S. *See also* Supreme Court
  racism of, in Peltier's (Leonard) trial, **1:**96

Judy Lopez Memorial Award for Children's Literature, for *Red Scarf Girl* (Jiang), **1:**161

Julian (Roman emperor), **1:**220

Julian of Eclanum, **1:**198

Julian of Norwich, **1:**189
  Showings, **1:**211

Jung, Carl, **1:**252, **3:**111

Junod, Violaine, **1:**25

Justice Department, U.S., **3:**224

K

Kabyle culture, preservation of, **1:**93–95

Kadi, Joanna, **1:**227

Kafka, Franz, **2:**121
  Amerika, **2:**120
  The Blue Octavo Notebooks, **2:**122
  The Castle, **2:**120
  The Diaries of Franz Kafka, **2:120–122**
  "The Great Wall of China," **2:**120
  The Trial, **2:**120, 121–122

Kagan, Richard C., **1:**172

Kagero Diary, The (Michitsuna). *See Gossamer Years, The* (Michitsuna)

Kahf, Mohja, *The Girl in the Tangerine Scarf,* **1:**41–42

Kahn, Ava, **3:**51–52

Kahn-Levitt, Laurie, **2:**331

Kakutani, Michiko, **1:**79, 120, **3:**183, 184, 185, 201

Kalvelage, Lisa Schmidt, **3:**269

Kamakura period (Japan), Nijo (Lady) on life in, **2:**59–61

Kameyama (Japanese emperor), **2:**59

Kana writing, **2:**290, 292

Kandinsky, Wassily, **1:**272

Kane, Cheikh Hamidou, *L'Aventure ambiguë,* **1:**61

Kanon, Joseph, **2:**282

KANU. *See* Kenya African National Union

Kaori Hayashi, Katie, *Japanese War Brides in America,* **3:127–130**

Kaplan, Morris, **3:**72

Kappus, Franz Xaver, **2:**149–150

Kapungu, Leonard T., *The United Nations and Economic Sanctions against Rhodesia,* **3:**251

Karkabi, Barbara, **2:**85

Karlsen, Carol F., **2:**333

Karr, Mary, **1:**40, 251, 259–260

Karush, Matthew, **3:**74, 75

Kashiwahara, Ken, **3:**280

Kashmir, dispute over, **1:**87

Katherine Mansfield Notebooks, The (Mansfield), **2:**133, 134

Katovsky, Bill, *Embedded,* **3:**276

Katz, Kimberly, **2:**104, 105, 106

Kaunda, Kenneth, *Zambia Must Be Free,* **1:**290

Kazan, Elia, **2:**152

Kazin, Alfred, **1:**320, **2:**47

Kearney, Michael, **3:**303

Kearns, Judith, **1:**316

Kearns, Kevin C.
  Dublin Pub Life and Lore, **3:**315, 317
  Dublin Voices, **3:**315

Keats, George, **2:**147

Keats, John, **2:**147
  The Letters of John Keats, **2:146–148**
  Life, Letters, and Literary Remains, **2:**146
  Selected Letters, **2:**146

Keckley, Elizabeth Hobbes, *Behind the Scenes,* **1:**52

Keenan, Edward N., **3:**219

Keene, Donald, **2:**191

Kehagia, Angie, **2:**124–125

Kéita, Aoua, *Femme d'Afrique,* **1:**64

Keitel, Wilhelm, **2:**54

Ke Lan, *In the Mansion of Confucius' Descendants,* **3:124–126**, 299

Keller, Bill, **1:**28, 29

Keller, Helen, **1:**44
  Midstream, **1:**44
  "My Life," **1:**43
  The Story of My Life, **1:43–46**
  The World I Live In, **1:**44, 45

Kellerman, Stewart, **1:**100

Kelley, James E., Jr., **2:**203
Kelly, Debra, **2:**263–264
Kelly, Éamon, **3:**315
Kelly, Orrin, **3:**162
Kelly, Sheldon, **1:**307
Kemble, Charles, **2:**335
Kemble, Fanny, **2:336**
    Journal of a Residence in America, **2:**335, 336
    Journal of a Residence on a Georgian Plantation, **2:**335, 336, 337
    "An Old Woman's Gossip," **2:**335
    Records of a Girlhood, **2:335–337**
    A Year of Consolation, **2:**336
Kemp, Lysander, **3:**167, 168
Kempe, Margery, *The Book of Margery Kempe,* **1:189–192,** 211, **2:**226
Kendall-Smith, Malcolm, **3:**229
Kennedy, John F., **2:**32, **3:**254
Kennedy, Randall, *Blacks at Harvard,* **3:**21
Kentucky
    coal mining in, oral histories of, **3:**86–87, 96–98, *97,* 157
    Coe Ridge community in, oral histories of, **3:**90–92
    school desegregation in, **1:**249
    working class in, oral histories of, **3:**157–159
Kenya
    borders of, establishment of, **1:**114
    British colonial rule of, **2:**12, **3:**141–143
    independence of (1963), **2:**12, **3:**141
    Mau Mau rebellion in, **2:**12
    Meru people of, oral histories of, **3:**141–143, *142*
    Ngũgĩ wa Thiong'o on life in, **2:**12–14
    Obama's (Barack) visits to, **1:**78, 79
Kenya African National Union (KANU), **2:**12
Kenyatta, Jomu, **2:**12
Keppel-Jones, Arthur, **3:**252
Keppler, Joseph, **1:**147
Kermode, Frank, **1:**268, 269
Kerouac, Jack, *On the Road,* **1:**234
Kerr, Walter, **2:**154

Kertész, Imre, **1:**318
Kesselman, Wendy, **2:**253
Kessler, Lauren, *Stubborn Twig,* **3:**80
Keynes, John Maynard, **2:**180
Keyser, Katherine, **1:**258
KGB, Stasi modeled on, **3:**245
Khalid, Robina Josephine, **2:**5
Khalifat movement, **1:**244
Khan, Shahnaz, **1:**88
Khashan, 'Abd al-Karim, **2:**52
Khmer Rouge, **1:**306–308
Khomeini, Ruhollah, **1:**155, **3:**218, 219
Khrushchev, Nikita, **3:**331, 333
Kidder, Annemarie S., **2:**149
Kiehr, Kathy, **3:187**
Kierkegaard, Søren, *Journals of Søren Kierkegaard,* **2:166–169,** *167*
Kihn, W. Langdon, **1:55**
Kikumura, Akemi, **1:**300
Kilani, Sami, *Three Minus One,* **2:**52
Kilinc, Ibrahim, **3:**219
Killam, Douglas, **2:**14
Kilvert, Francis, **2:**287, 288
Kim, Eleana J., *Adopted Territory,* **1:**102–103
Kim, Elizabeth, *Ten Thousand Sorrows,* **1:102–104,** *103*
Kim, Richard E., *Lost Names,* **1:**102
Kim Gu. *See* Kim Ku
Kim Ku, *Paekpom Ilchi,* **1:322–324,** *323*
Kimura, Saeko, **2:**61
Kincaid, Jamaica, **1:**111
Kincaid, Simone Carbonneau, *In All the West No Place Like This,* **3:**93
Kindersley, Jemima, *Letters from the Island of Teneriffe,* **2:**229
King, Adele, **1:**128, 130
King, Clarence, **1:**132
King, Florence, **2:**331
King, Martin Luther, Jr., **2:33**
    assassination of, **1:**20
    Gandhi's (Mohandas) influence on, **1:**242
    "I Have a Dream," **1:**79, **2:**32
    "Letter from the Birmingham Jail," **2:32–34**

    vs. Malcolm X, approaches of, **1:**186
    national holiday celebrating, **1:**37, **2:**33
    in SCLC, **1:**20, **2:**32, 34
    Voices of Freedom (Hampton and Fayer) on, **3:**44
King, Mary Elizabeth, **2:**52
King, Peter, **2:**24
King, R. W., **2:**76–77
King Lear (Shakespeare), **2:**147
King Philip's War (1675–1676), **1:**325–328, *326*
Kingsley, Mary, *Travels in West Africa,* **2:**335
Kingston, Maxine Hong
    China Men, **1:**173
    Tripmaster Monkey, **1:**173
    The Woman Warrior, **1:**75, 100, **173–176**
Kinnell, Galway, **2:**150
Kinsington (London), **2:321**
Kiowa Tribe, Momaday (N. Scott) on history of, **1:**54–56
Kipling, Rudyard, **1:**88, **2:**192
Kirkus Reviews (magazine)
    on *Bone Black* (hooks), **1:**250
    on *Golden Bones* (Siv), **1:**307
    on *Growing Up Jewish in America* (Frommer and Frommer), **3:**119
    on *Machete Season* (Hatzfeld), **3:**259
    on *Spandau* (Speer), **2:**56
    on *Strange Ground* (Maurer), **3:**277
    on *The Strength Not to Fight* (Tollefson), **3:**222
    on *Tears before the Rain* (Engelmann), **3:**280
    on *The Unwanted* (Nguyen), **1:**172
Kirsch, Jonathan, **2:**279, **3:**45
Kitab al-I'tibar (Usamah). *See Arab-Syrian Gentleman and Warrior in the Period of the Crusades, An* (Usamah)
Kite Runner, The (Hosseini), **1:**40
Ki Tsurayuki, **2:**191
Klæstrup, Peter, **2:167**
Klaus, Ida, **3:**155
Klee, Paul, **2:**120

SUBJECT INDEX

Kleege, Georgina, **1**:45
Klein, Josephine, *Samples from English Culture,* **3**:144
Klemperer, Eva, **2**:303, 305
Klemperer, Victor
    Curriculum Vitae, **2**:304, 305
    I Will Bear Witness, **2**:303–305
    The Lesser Evil, **2**:304
    Lingua Tertii Imperii (LTI), **2**:304, 305
Klinkhammer, Stephen, **3**:209
Klotter, James C., **3**:88
Kluckhohn, Clyde, **3**:290
Klum, Heidi, **3**:345
K'Meyer, Tracy E., **3**:192, 309
Knight, Sarah Kemble, *The Journal of Madam Knight,* **2**:78
Knight, William Angus, **2**:300
Kniss, Lloy, **3**:229
"Knole Diary" (Clifford), **2**:62, 64
Knoll, Kristina R., **1**:41
Ko, Dorothy, **3**:147
Koch, Grace, **3**:335, 336
Koch, John T., **3**:29
Koegel, John, **3**:133
Kohbieter, Gérard, **3**:15
Kohn, Alfred, **3**:15
Kohn, Hans, **1**:291
Kohn, Rita T.
    Always a People, **3**:107–109, 325
    Long Journey Home, **3**:107, 325–327
Koker, David, *At the Edge of the Abyss,* **2**:253
Kong Decheng, **3**:124
Kong Demao, *In the Mansion of Confucius' Descendants,* **3**:124–126, 299
Konile, Notrose Nobomvu, **3**:242
Konner, Melvin, **3**:37
Konrad Wallenrod (Mickiewicz), **2**:192
Koppedrayer, Kay, **1**:244
Kopple, Barbara, **3**:98
Korea
    division of (1945), **1**:322
    independence movement in, **1**:322–324
    interracial children in, **1**:102

Japanese imperialist rule of, **1**:322–324
    Kim Ku on life in, **1**:322–324
Korea Herald (newspaper), **1**:103
Korean Americans, Kim (Elizabeth) on experience of, **1**:102–104
Korean Provisional Government (KPG), **1**:322–324
Korean War (1950–1953), **1**:102, **3**:199
Korg, Jacob, **1**:126, **2**:322
Kornbluh, Joyce L., *Rocking the Boat,* **3**:337
Kostopulos-Cooperman, Celeste, **1**:77
Kotkin, Stephen, **3**:341
Kotze, Annemare, **1**:198
Kovic, Ron, *Born on the Fourth of July,* **1**:335, **3**:209
Kovner, Sarah, *Occupying Power,* **3**:128
Kozol, Jonathon, *Letters to a Young Teacher,* **2**:150
KPG. *See* Korean Provisional Government
Kramer, Jane, **1**:175
Kramer, Samuel, **2**:94
Kramer, Stanley, **3**:295
Kramskoy, Nicholas, **1**:194
Kranzler, David, *Japanese, Nazis & Jews,* **3**:15
Krapf, Ludwig, **1**:115
Krause, Corinne Azen, *Grandmothers, Mothers, and Daughters,* **3**:305–307
Kreider, Robert, *Sourcebook,* **3**:227
Kresh, Joseph, **2**:121
Kristof, Nicholas, **1**:209
Krog, Antjie
    Begging to Be Black, **3**:242
    A Change of Tongue, **3**:242
    Country of My Skull, **3**:242–244
    There Was This Goat, **3**:242
Kropotkin, Peter, **2**:120
Krowl, Michelle, **2**:273
Krupat, Arnold, *For Those Who Come After,* **1**:71
Kruse, Horst, **1**:146, 147
Kublai Khan, **1**:105, 106, 107
Kuhn, Clifford, *Living Atlanta,* **3**:44
Kukis, Mark, **3**:212

Ku Klux Klan, **1**:186–187
Kumashiro, Kevin, *Restoried Selves,* **3**:83
!Kung people, oral histories of, **3**:37–38
Kunin, Aaron, **2**:64
Künstler, Mort, **2**:273
Künstler-Roman, **1**:276
Kushner, Tony, **3**:235
Kusmer, Kenneth, **3**:87–88
Kuwait, in Gulf War (1991), **2**:278–280
Kwong, Luke S. K., **3**:301
Kyalanova, Irina, **1**:314
Kyoto (Japan), **2**:59, 61, 189, 290, 297, *298*

L

Labor, forced
    in China, **1**:158
    in Soviet Union (*See* Gulag system)
Labor arbitration, oral histories of, **3**:153–155
Labor History (journal), **3**:341
Labor movement, oral histories of
    arbitration in, **3**:153–155
    in Argentina, **3**:73–75
    in Bolivia, **3**:322–324
    in Idaho, **3**:93
    in Iowa, **3**:153
    in Italy, **3**:157–159, *158*
    by IWW members, **3**:328–330
    in Kentucky, **3**:96–98, 157–159
    in Michigan, **3**:99, 101
    tradition of, **3**:153, 157
Labor Party (Argentina), **3**:73
Labor strikes
    by coal miners, **3**:96–98
    by IWW, **3**:328
Labor Studies Journal, **3**:68
Labour (journal), **3**:338
Labour History (journal), **3**:177, 313
Labour History Review (journal), **3**:64, 341
Labour Party (Britain), **2**:16
Lacan, Jacques, **1**:267, **3**:188
Ladies' Home Journal, **1**:43

Ladjevardi, Habib
- *Memoirs of Fatemeh Pakravan,* **3:**218–220
- *Memoirs of Prince Hamid Kadjar,* **3:**219
- *Memoirs of Shapour Bakhtiar,* **3:**220

Lady Murasaki Shu (Murasaki), **2:**291

LaFarge, Oliver, **3:**318

Laffont, Robert, **2:**338

La Forte, Robert S., *Remembering Pearl Harbor,* **3:**202

Lagos de Moreno (Mexico), land redistribution movement in, **3:**302–303

Lahiri, Jhumpa, *Interpreter of Maladies,* **1:**87

Lahontan, Baron de, *New Voyages to North-America,* **2:**205

Lakota Sioux
- Black Elk on life as, **3:**110–113
- Brave Bird (Mary) on life as, **1:**21–23, 22

Lakota Woman (Brave Bird), **1:21–23**

Lalla Aicha (princess of Morocco), **3:**49

Lamb, Caroline, **2:**143, 145
- *Glenarvon,* **2:**145

Lamb, Charles, **2:**75

Lamb, Mary Ellen, **2:**64

Lame Deer, **1:**23

Lamentation of a Sinner (Parr), **2:**97

Lamott, Anne, *Bird by Bird,* **1:**280

Lampert, Jo, **3:**336

Lampkins, Robert, **3:**87

Lampman, Robert, **3:**255

La Navidad, **2:**203

Lancashire (England), **3:**64

Lancaster, Burt, **3:**295

Land
- of Australian Aborigines, **1:**149, **3:**334–335
- British, inheritance by women, **2:**62–63, 64
- of Maasai people, **1:**114
- Mexican, redistribution of, **3:**302–304
- of Native Americans, **1:**302, **3:**10–12, 110
- U.S., restrictions on immigrant ownership of, **3:**195
- of VaShawasha people, **3:**251

Landlord's Friend, The (Leadbeater), **2:**157

Land Ordinance of 1785 (U.S.), **2:**163

Land redistribution movement, in Mexico, **3:**302–304

Lane, Charles, **1:**235

Lane, James B., **3:**161

Langbauer, Laurie, **2:**209, 211

Langer, Lawrence, **2:**24

Langford, Rachel, **2:**174

Langhamer, Claire, **3:**146

Language(s)
- acquisition of, by Keller (Helen), **1:**44
- in identity, **1:**15–17, **3:**108, 109
- power of, Momaday (N. Scott) on, **1:**55
- in U.S. education, **1:**15, 16

Language of Blood, The (Trenka), **1:**102

La Niña (ship), **2:**203

Lanzmann, Claude, **3:**50, 52

La Pinta (ship), **2:**203

Larcius Macedo, **2:**96

Larg, D. G., **2:**77

Larner, John, **1:**107

Larson, Charles R., **1:**129

Larson, Ronald, *Camp and Community,* **3:**102, 103–104

Larson, Wendy, **3:**148

La Salle, Robert de, **1:**146–147

Las Casas, Bartolomé de
- *History of Indies,* **2:**201
- *Journal of the First Voyage to America* (Columbus) assembled by, **2:**201–203, 205
- *A Short Account of the Destruction of the Indies,* **2:**201

Lassner, Phyllis, **2:**269

Last, Clifford, **2:**265, 266

Last, Nella
- Mitchison (Naomi) compared to, **2:**235
- *Nella Last's Peace,* **2:**265
- *Nella Last's War,* **2:265–267**

Last, William, **2:**265

Last Confessions of Marie Bashkirtseff, The (Bashkirtseff), **2:**306

Last Diary of Tsaritsa Alexandra, The (Alexandra), **2:84–86**

Last Essays (Conrad), **2:**193, 194

Last Maasai Warrior, The (Meikuaya and Ntirkana), **1:**114

Last Man, The (Shelley), **2:**145

Last of the Mohicans (Cooper), **1:**56

"Late Benjamin Franklin, The" (Twain), **1:**181–182

Latimer, Hugh, **2:**97

Latin America. *See also specific countries*
- Agosín (Marjorie) on experience of Jews in, **1:**75–77
- autobiographical tradition of, **1:**222–223
- culture of, in U.S. culture, **1:**109
- Guevara's (Ernesto "Che") journey through, **2:**220–222
- immigration to U.S. from, **1:**108–110, **3:**121
- Perera (Victor) on experience of Jews in, **1:**99–100
- poverty in, **2:**220–221
- right-wing dictators in, rise of, **3:**185
- testimonios of (*See* Testimonios)

Latin American Perspectives (journal), **3:**323

Latino Americans. *See* Hispanic and Latino Americans

Lau, Peter, **3:**22

Launching the War on Poverty (Gillette), **3:254–256**

La Viers, Henry, **3:**87

Lavrin, Asunción, **3:**323

Law and Literature (journal), **1:**314

Lawlor, Bruce, **3:**210

Law of Flight (Guatemala), **1:**101

Lawrence, D. H., **2:**123, 136, 152, 207, 213

Lawtoo, Nidesh, **1:**16–17

Lay Bare the Heart (Farmer), **3:**44

Laye, Camara
- *The Dark Child,* **1:**128–131
- *A Dream of Africa,* **1:**129
- *The Guardian of the Word,* **1:**129
- *The Radiance of the King,* **1:**128

Lazraq, Zhor, **3:**48
Leadbeater, Betsy, **2:**157–158
Leadbeater, Lydia, **2:**158
Leadbeater, Mary
    The Annals of Ballitore, **2:**157–159
    Cottage Dialogues among the Irish Peasantry, **2:**157
    The Cottage Diaries, **2:**157
    The Landlord's Friend, **2:**157
    Tales for Cottagers, **2:**157
Leadbeater, William, **2:**157
Leading the Way (Santoli), **3:**210
League of Nations, **3:**257
League of Nations Union, **1:**329
Lears, Jackson, **1:**134
Leaves from the Journal of Our Life in the Highlands (Victoria), **2:209–212**
"Leaves of Memory" (Unaipon), **1:**149
Lebovitz, Hal, **1:**247
Lecar, Mike, **3:**119
Ledoux, Charles Alexandre Picard, **2:**184
Ledy, Cheik, **1:**28
Lee, Chong-Sik, **1:**323
Lee, Ellen, *Once They Hear My Name,* **1:**102
Lee, Felicia R., **1:**74
Lee, Hannah, **3:**16
Lee, Hermione, **2:**133, 134
Lee, Jennie, **2:**235
Lee, Joan Faung Jean, *Oral Histories of First to Fourth Generation Americans,* **3:**83
Lee, Jongsoo, **1:**322
Lee, Leo Ou-Fan, **2:**172
Lee, Margaret Juhae, **1:**103
Lee, Mary, **2:**38
Lee, Maryat, **2:**129, 131
Lee, Mary Custis, **2:**40
Lee, Richard, **3:**37
Lee, Robert E., **2:**39
    Buck (Lucy) and, **2:**273
    "Letter to His Son," **2:38–40**
Lee, Susan Savage, **2:**153
Lee Kuan Yew, *The Singapore Story,* **1:**290

Leepson, Marc, **3:**211
Leeson, David, **3:**29
Lefevre, Mike, **3:**345
Left Handed, *Left Handed, Son of Old Man Hat,* **3:318–321**
Left Handed, Son of Old Man Hat (Left Handed and Dyk), **3:318–321**
Legacy (journal), **2:**29
Legend of Fire Horse Woman, The (Houston), **1:**299
Legislation. *See specific laws*
Legvold, Robert, **3:**246, 332
LeHeew, Justin, **3:**232
Lehmann-Haupt, Christopher, **1:**48
Leibniz, Gottfried Wilhelm, **1:**183
Leigh, Augusta, **2:**143
Leighton, Frederic, **2:**335
Leighton, Roland, **1:**329, 330
Leipzig war crimes trials (1921), **3:**293
Leiris, Michel, **1:**247
Lejeune, Philippe
    The Autobiographical Pact, **1:239–241**
    Autobiography in France, **1:**239, **2:**174
    Me Too, **2:**174
    On Diary, **2:**174, 175
    "Practice of the Private Journal," **2:174–176**
Lenape. *See* Delaware Indians
L'Enfant, Pierre, **2:**87
Lenin, Vladimir, **1:**270, **3:**331
Lenta, Margaret, **2:**218
Lenz, Peter, **1:**121
Leonard, Karen, **3:**81
Leon Montiel, Livia, **3:**131
Leopold II (king of Belgium), **2:**192
Leppmann, Wolfgang, **2:**149
Lesbians. *See* Homosexuality
Lesinska, Zofia, **1:**333
Lesser Evil, The (Klemperer), **2:**304
Lessing, Doris, **1:168**
    The Grass Is Singing, **1:**169
    Memoirs of a Survivor, **1:**167
    Under My Skin, **1:167–169**
    Walking in the Shade, **1:**167
Le Sueur, James, **2:**263, 264

Let Me Speak! (Viezzer and Barrios de Chungara), **3:**74, 114–115, **322–324**
Let My People Go (Luthuli), **1:24–26**
Let One Hundred Flowers Bloom (Feng), **1:**161
Letter(s), writing of. *See also specific works and writers*
    in Britain, art of, **2:**146, 217
    consideration of audience in, **2:**217
    early history of, **2:**94
    in France, **2:**217
    manuals on, **2:**217
    in U.S., as social convention, **2:**223
"Letter from the Birmingham Jail" (King), **2:32–34**
Letters and Diaries of Etty Hillesum, The (Hillesum), **2:**253
Letters and Journals of Fanny Burney (Burney), **2:312–315**
Letters and Journals of Lord Byron (Byron), **2:143–145,** 309
Letters between Two (Lu and Xu), **2:170–173**
Letters from an American Farmer (Crèvecoeur), **2:213–216**
Letters from Jefferson to His Daughter (Jefferson), **2:**38, **316–319**
Letters from the Island of Teneriffe (Kindersley), **2:**229
Letters Home (Plath), **2:47–49**
Letters of Arnold Bennett (Bennett), **2:**138
Letters of a Woman Homesteader (Stewart), **2:91–93**
Letters of John Hay (Hay), **3:**263
Letters of John Keats, The (Keats), **2:146–148**
Letters of Lady Anne Barnard to Henry Dundas, The (Barnard), **2:217–219**
Letters of Mrs. Adams (Adams), **2:**87, 89
Letters of Rainer Maria Rilke (Rilke), **2:**150
Letters of Sidney and Beatrice Webb, The (Webb and Webb), **2:**172
Letters of the Younger Pliny, The (Pliny), **2:94–96**

Letters on an Elk Hunt (Stewart), **2**:91

Letters on God and Letters to a Young Woman (Rilke), **2**:149

Letters to a Young Contrarian (Hitchens), **2**:150

Letters to a Young Gymnast (Comaneci), **2**:150

Letters to a Young Novelist (Vargas Llosa), **2**:150

Letters to a Young Poet (Rilke), **2**:149–151

Letters to a Young Teacher (Kozol), **2**:150

Letters Underway (Ghazzawi), **2**:50–53

Letters Written during a Short Residence in Sweden, Norway, and Denmark (Wollstonecraft), **2**:111

"**Letter to Her Daughter**" (Montagu), **2**:35–37

"**Letter to Her Daughter from the New White House**" (Adams), **2**:87–90

"Letter to His Daughter" (Jefferson), **2**:38

"**Letter to His Son**" (Lee), **2**:38–40

"**Letter to Maria Clemm**" (Poe), **2**:41–43

"**Letter to the Reverend Samson Occom**" (Wheatley), **2**:44–46

Let the People Decide (Moye), **3**:249

Lettsom, John Coakley, **2**:207

Leung, Laifong, *Morning Sun,* **3**:301

Levi, Primo
    If This Is a Man, **1**:318
    suicide of, **1**:204, 205

Levin, Meyer, **2**:253

Levin, Susan M., **2**:301

Levine, Robert, **2**:7–8

Levine, Steven, **1**:339, **3**:288

Lévi-Strauss, Claude, *Tristes Tropiques,* **3**:37

Levy, Eric P., **1**:121

Lewalski, Barbara, **2**:64

Lewin, Recha, **3**:50

Lewin, Rhoda
    The Jewish Community of North Minneapolis, **3**:50
    Witnesses to the Holocaust, **3**:50–52

Lewis, Jane, **2**:18

Lewis, Oscar
    Children of Sanchez, **3**:31
    Pedro Martinez, **3**:31

Lewis, R. W. B., **1**:235

Lewy, Guenter, **3**:42

Ley, Robert, **3**:293–294

Ley de Fuga (Guatemala), **1**:101

Liberalism, in Russia, rise of, **1**:193

Liberator (newspaper), **1**:33, 35, **2**:29, 31, 45

Liberty Bell, The (Chapman and Griffith), **1**:142

Libowitz, Richard, **1**:320

Library Journal
    on *Exiled Memories* (Medina), **1**:297
    on *Mothers, Sisters, Resisters* (Gurewitsch), **3**:35
    on *Prison Writings* (Peltier), **1**:97
    on *Solidarity Forever* (Bird et al.), **3**:329
    on *Ten Thousand Sorrows* (Kim), **1**:103
    on *Voices from the Whirlwind* (Feng), **3**:288
    on *A Woman at War* (Moore), **2**:279
    on *A Woman Soldier's Own Story* (Xie), **1**:339
    on *The Woman Warrior* (Kingston), **1**:175

Lieberman, Thorney, **3**:66

Liédet, Loyset, **1**:286

Lie Down in Darkness (Styron), **1**:204, 206

Life (magazine), **1**:304, **3**:61

Life, Letters, and Literary Remains (Keats), **2**:146

Life, The (Teresa of Ávila), **1**:211–213

Life and Times of Frederick Douglass (Douglass), **1**:34

Life for Africa, A (Mitchison), **2**:237

"Life in the Sea Islands" (Grimké), **2**:31

Life Laid Bare (Hatzfeld), **3**:258, 259

Life Lived Like a Story (Cruikshank), **3**:320

Life of Samuel Johnson (Boswell), **2**:177, 195, 309, 328, 329–330

Life on the Mississippi (Twain), **1**:146–148

Life under a Cloud (Winkler), **3**:239

Life-writing movement, of Aborigines, **3**:334

Lifton, Betty Jean, *Twice Born,* **1**:102

"Ligeia" (Poe), **3**:38

Light, Kenneth
    Coal Hollow, **3**:66–69
    Valley of Shadows and Dreams, **3**:67

Light, Melanie
    Coal Hollow, **3**:66–69
    Valley of Shadows and Dreams, **3**:67

Light, Steve, **1**:251

Likud party (Israel), **1**:225, **2**:52

Lincoln, Abraham, **3**:262
    and African American soldiers, **2**:240
    assassination of, **2**:246, **3**:261
    election of, **2**:38, 250
    Emancipation Proclamation of, **1**:50, **3**:261
    Homestead Act under, **2**:164
    oral history of life of, **3**:261–264
    views on slavery, **2**:38

Lincoln, Kenneth, **1**:54

Lincoln, Mary Todd, **1**:52, **3**:261, 263, 264

Lincoln, Robert Todd, **3**:261, 262, 263

Lincoln and the Civil War Diaries and Letters of John Hay (Hay), **3**:262–263

Lincoln Prize, for *Abraham Lincoln: A Life* (Burlingame), **3**:264

Linderman, Frank, *Pretty-Shield,* **1**:70

Lindstrom, Naomi, **1**:76

Lingua Tertii Imperii (LTI) (Klemperer), **2**:304, 305

Linguistic autobiographies, *Hunger of Memory* (Rodriguez) as, **1**:17

Linneaus, Carl, **2**:300

Linton, Sherri LaVie, **1**:10

Lin Yutang, **1**:338

Lionnet, Françoise, **1**:11

Lipsitz, George, **3**:191

LIS Organization, **1**:7

Liszt, Franz, **1**:272

Literacy
- in Britain, rise of, **2:**136, 146, 320
- in Middle Ages, **1:**189
- in *Narrative of the Life of Frederick Douglass* (Douglass), **1:**35
- and slave narratives, **1:**35

Literary autobiographies. *See also specific works and writers*
- Lejeune (Philippe) on study of, **2:**174
- religious struggle in, **2:**26
- self as topic in, **1:**167

Literary criticism
- Bennett's (Arnold) career in, **2:**136
- disability studies in, **1:**8
- as form of autobiography, **1:**247
- French theories in, **1:**239
- by Hawthorne (Nathaniel), **2:**223–224
- Hussein's (Taha) career in, **1:**135
- by Maugham (W. Somerset), **2:**183
- poststructuralism in, **1:**267
- structuralism in, **1:**239, 267
- by Woolf (Virginia), **2:**137, 138, 180

Literary Fund, **2:**207

Literary references
- in *De Profundis* (Wilde), **2:**9
- in *Fun Home* (Bechdel), **1:**140, 141
- in *Walden* (Thoreau), **1:**235

Literary Remains of Edward VI, The (Edward VI), **2:97–100**

Literary Review (journal), **1:**256

Literary theory, Barthes's (Roland) work in, **1:**267

Literature and Medicine (journal), **1:**7, 8

Lithuania, Jewish immigration to China from, **3:**16

Little Big Horn, Battle of (1876), **3:**110

Litz, Alyce, **1:**40

Liu Xiaobo, **3:**301

Lives of Others, The (film), **3:**245

Living Atlanta (Kuhn et al.), **3:**44

Living by Fiction (Dillard), **1:**279

Living My Life (Goldman), **3:**3

Living the Revolution (Guglielmo), **3:**5

Living through the Soviet System (Bertaux et al.), **3:**331

Lloréns Torres, Luis, **1:**108

Lloyd, Constance, **2:**9

Lloyd's Evening Post, **2:**196

Lobato, Mirta Zaida, **3:**74, 75

Locke, Alain, **1:**84, 85

Locke, John, **2:**140

Locked-in syndrome, **1:**6–8

Lockhart, John Gibson, **2:**143, 144
- *Memoirs of the Life of Sir Walter Scott*, **2:**309, 310

Lockhart, Sophia Scott, **2:**309

Loftis, John, **1:**316

Logan, Andy, **3:**295

Log-book of the Coiners (Gide), **2:**180, 182

Logging industry, in Idaho, **3:**93

Loisel, Clary, **3:**33

Lomax, Alan, **1:**9

Lomax, Dana Teen, **2:**150

Lombardi, Irma, **3:**329

Lomov, Nikolai, **3:**235

London (England)
- Boswell's (James) move to, **2:**328
- Great Fire of, **2:**73
- Kinsington district in, **2:321**
- literary journalism in, **2:**328

London and the Life of Literature in Late Victorian England (Gissing), **2:320–323**

London Journal (Boswell), **2:328–330**

London Review of Books, **2:**14

London School of Economics and Political Science, **2:**16, 172

Long, Huey, **1:**5

Long, Janet Nakamarra, **3:**107, 335

Long, Judith, **2:**92

Long, Lisa, **2:**29, 31

Longfellow, Henry Wadsworth, **2:**223

Long Journey Home (Brown and Kohn), **3:**107, **325–327**

Long Journey Home (documentary), **3:**325

Long March, **1:**338

Long Walk to Freedom, The (Mandela), **1:25, 27–29**, 96, 290

Long Way from Home, A (McKay), **1:84–86**

Long Way Gone, A (Beah), **1:312–314**

Looking Cloud, Arlo, **1:**98

Look up for Yes (Tavalaro), **1:**6

Lopes Cançado, Maura, *Hospicio é Deus*, **2:**6

Lopez, Barry, *Arctic Dreams*, **1:**279

Lorde, Audre, **2:**4
- *The Black Unicorn*, **2:**4
- *A Burst of Light*, **2:**3
- *The Cancer Journals*, **2:3–5**
- hooks (bell) compared to, **1:**249, 251
- Hurston's (Zora Neale) influence on, **1:**9
- in tradition of Prince (Mary), **3:**24
- *Zami*, **1:**9, 37, 39, 249, **2:**5

Lorifo, Marie, **1:**128

Lori-Parks, Suzan, **1:**273

Lort, Michael, **2:**313

Los Alamos (New Mexico), oral histories of, **3:**239–241

Los Angeles (California)
- gay Asian Americans in, **3:**83–85
- water resources for, **3:**102, 103

Los Angeles Times (newspaper)
- on *Barefoot Gen* (Nakazawa), **1:**294
- on *Diaries, 1931–1949* (Orwell), **2:**118
- on *A Diary without Dates* (Bagnold), **2:**260
- on *Farewell to Manzanar* (Houston and Houston), **1:**299, 300
- on *The Long Walk to Freedom* (Mandela), **1:**29
- on *The Strength Not to Fight* (Tollefson), **3:**222
- on *Voices of Freedom* (Hampton and Fayer), **3:**45
- on *When Heaven and Earth Changed Places* (Hayslip), **1:**336
- on *When I Was Puerto Rican* (Santiago), **1:**109
- on *A Woman at War* (Moore), **2:**279
- on *Zlata's Diary* (Filipovic), **2:**339

Lost-Found Nation of Islam. *See* Black Muslims

Lost generation, **1:**329

Lost Names (Kim), **1:**102

Lost Years (Vu), **1:**170

Lotte in Weimar (Mann), **1:**277
Louisiana
    during Civil War, Stone (Kate) on life in, **2:**244–246, *245*
    Hispanic American entrepreneurs in, oral histories of, **3:**121–123
    U.S. purchase of, **2:**69
Louis XVI (king of France), **2:**213
Love Carried Me Home (Miller), **3:**35
Lovejoy, David, **2:**27
Love Letters of Dorothy Osborne to Sir William Temple, The (Osborne), **2:324–327**
Love Letters of Dylan Thomas, The (Thomas), **1:**127
Love Letters of Nathaniel Hawthorne, The (Hawthorne), **2:**225
Lovesey, Oliver, **1:**88, 215, 216
Loving v. Virginia, **1:**72, 78
Lowell, Amy, **2:**190, 292
Lowell, James Russell, **1:**235
Lowell, Robert, **2:**129
Lowenthal, Cynthia, **2:**36, 37
"Low-intensity" conflicts, **3:**207
Loyalty
    in Japanese American internment, **3:**196
    to monarchy, Slingsby (Henry) on, **2:**256–258
Lozano, Connie, **3:**103
LSD, **2:**295
Lucas, E. V., **2:**10
Lucassen, Jan, **3:**75
Lucky Child, A (Buergenthal), **1:**312
Lugo, Catherine, **3:**88
Luis, Keridwen, **3:**38
Luis, William, **3:**8
Lukas, Christopher, *Blue Genes,* **1:**204–205
Lu Lihua, **3:**148
Luna, Rachael, **3:**78
Luongo, Katherine, **3:**143
Lupus, **2:**129
Luscombe, Belinda, **1:**312, 314
Luthuli, Albert, **1:**24
    Let My People Go, **1:**24–26
    "Our Struggles for Progress," **1:**25
    "We Don't Want Crumbs," **1:**25

Lu Xiuyuan, **3:**288
Lu Xun, *Letters between Two,* **2:170–173,** *171*
Ly, Monirith, **1:**307
Lydgate, John, **1:190**
Lydston, Stub, **3:**103
Lyell, Charles, *Principles of Geology,* **1:**65
Lynch, Claire, **3:**316–317
Lynchings, **1:**18, 50
Lynd, Alice, *Rank and File,* **3:**179
Lynd, Staughton, *Rank and File,* **3:**179
Lynn, Kenneth, **2:**251
Lyon, Isabel Van Kleek, **1:**148

M

Maalouf, Amin, **1:**286
Maasai (Beckwith and Saitoti), **1:**114
Maasai people, Saitoti (Tepilit Ole) on experience of, **1:**114–116, *115*
Maathai, Wangari, *Unbound,* **1:**114
Macaulay, Thomas Babington, **2:**144, 314, 329
MacCarthy, Desmond, **2:**268
MacCarthy, Molly, **2:**268
MacDonald, John, **3:**139
MacDonald, Ramsay, **2:**17
MacEoin, Uinseann, *Survivors,* **3:**27, 315
Machete Season (Hatzfeld), **1:**312, **3:257–260**
MacKenzie, Jeanne, **2:**16, 17
MacKenzie, Norman, **2:**16, 17, 172
MacLane, Mary, **2:**306
MacLennan, Birdie, **1:**280
Macqueen, James, **3:**25
Macy, John, **1:**43
Maddocks, Melvin, **3:**61
Maddy-Weitzman, Bruce, **3:**49
Madero, Francisco, **3:**167
Madge, Charles, **2:**235
Madison, James, **2:**316
Madison, R. D., **2:**240
Madmen and Specialists (Soyinka), **1:**214
Madsen, Kim, **3:**174–175
Mafeking, siege of (1899–1900), **2:**241–243

Magan, Hirsi, **1:**207
Magellan, Ferdinand, **2:**201
Magical Monkey King (Jiang), **1:**163
Mahomet, Dean, *The Travels of Dean Mahomet,* **2:229–232**
Mahoney, Dennis F., **1:**277, 278
Mai, Angelo, **1:**220
Maid's Daughter, The (Romero), **1:**108
Maier, Joseph, **3:**295
Mail and Guardian (newspaper), **3:**243
Mailer, Norman, **1:**165
Maitland, Sarah, **1:**280
Makin, Bathsua, *An Essay to Revive the Antient Education of Gentlewomen,* **2:**35
Making History (Johnson et al.), **3:**176, 177
Making of a Gay Asian Community, The (Wat), **3:83–85**
Making of Modern London, The (television series), **3:**313
Makley, Charlene, **3:**288–289
Malan, Daniel François, **1:**27
Malan, Rian, *My Traitor's Heart,* **3:**242
Malcolmson, Patricia, **2:**265
Malcolmson, Robert, **2:**265
Malcolm X, *The Autobiography of Malcolm X,* **1:**78, **186–188,** *187,* **3:**44
Malik ibn al-Rayb, **1:**255
Malingre, Rose, **2:**83
Malinke people, **1:**128, 130
Mallon, Thomas, **1:**7
Malone, Edmond, **2:**330
Malthus, Thomas, *Essay on the Principles of Population,* **1:**65
Malti-Douglas, Fedwa, **1:**92, 137, 227
Mammeri, Mouloud, **2:**262
Man (journal), **3:**168
Manalansan, Martin F., IV, **3:**83, 84, 85
Manar, Al- (journal), **1:**135
Manchester (England), oral histories of working-class youth in, **3:**311–313, *312*
Manchu dynasty, **1:**152, 153
Manchurian Incident (1931), **3:**215
Mandel, Barrett John, **1:**187, 246, 247
Mandel, Naomi, **1:**320

SUBJECT INDEX

Mandela, Nelson, **1:**28
 AIDS epidemic and, **3:**272, *273*
 Conversations with Myself, **1:**27–28
 imprisonment of, **1:**24, 27–29, **3:**242
 The Long Walk to Freedom, **1:**25, **27–29,** 96, 290
Mandela, Winnie, **1:**28, 29
Mandeville, John, *The Travels of Sir John Mandeville,* **2:**198, 227
Man Died, The (Soyinka), **1:214–217,** **2:**12, 14
Mandlestam, Nadezhda, *Hope against Hope,* **1:**271
Man from the North, A (Bennett), **2:**136
Manga (Japanese comics), **1:**293
Manhattan Project, oral histories of, **3:**239–240
Manichaeans, **1:**196
Manji, Irshad, *The Trouble with Islam Today,* **1:**207
Mann, Abby, **3:**295
Mann, Thomas, *Lotte in Weimar,* **1:**277
Manning, Bradley, **3:**229
Manning, Diane, *Hill Country Teacher,* **3:77–79**
"Man of Constant Sorrow" (song), **3:**159
Man of the Serengeti (documentary), **1:**114
Mansart Builds a School (Du Bois), **1:**5
Mansfield, Katherine, **2:**134
 Bashkirtseff's (Marie) influence on, **2:**306
 Journal of Katherine Mansfield, **2:133–135**
 The Katherine Mansfield Notebooks, **2:**133, 134
 Partridge (Frances) compared to, **2:**269
 Scrapbook of Katherine Mansfield, **2:**134
 A Writer's Diary (Woolf) on, **2:**180
Mansfield decision (1789, Britain), **1:**81, 83, **3:**23
Mantel, Hilary, **1:**169
Manter, Lisa, **1:**191
Manuel I (king of Portugal), **2:**198, 199

Manwaring, Max G.
 El Salvador at War, **3:205–208**
 Small Wars & Insurgencies, **3:**206
 Uncomfortable Wars, **3:**207
 Uncomfortable Wars Revisited, **3:**207
Manzanar (Wehrey), **3:**102
Manzanar internment camp (California), **1:**299–301, **3:**102–104, 197, *225*
Manzano, Juan Francisco, *The Autobiography of a Slave,* **3:**7
Mao Zedong, **1:**158, **3:**288. See also Cultural Revolution
 death of, **3:**299
 in Long March, **1:**338
 Lu Xun and, **2:**170
 rise to power, **3:**287
Mapes, Elizabeth A., **2:**254
Mara, Michael, **2:**61
Marble Faun, The (Hawthorne), **2:**224, 225
Marcello, Ronald E., *Remembering Pearl Harbor,* **3:**202
Marchand, Leslie A., **2:**144
Marchesi, Ilaria, **2:**96
March 1 Movement (Korea), **1:**324
March on Washington (1963), **1:**20
Marcus, Eric, *The Struggle for Gay and Lesbian Equal Rights,* **3:**83
Marcus, Jane, **2:**17
Marcus Aurelius, *The Meditations of the Emperor Marcus Aurelius Antoninus,* **1:218–221,** *219*
Marek, Kurt, **2:**282
Margaret (princess), **2:**152
Marie, Adrien, **2:**82
Marijuana, **2:**295
Maritime literature, tradition of, **3:**183
Mark, Thomas, **2:**126
Mark Twain Project, **1:**148
Marquette, Jacques, **1:**146–147
Marrant, John, **1:**81
Marriage
 arranged, in China, **1:**153, 154, 338, 339, **2:**170
 arranged, in Montenegro, **3:**136, 137
 in eighteenth century, limitations of, **2:**35, 36

 forced, **1:**209
 in Heian period of Japan, **2:**297–299
 interracial (See Interracial relationships)
 Osborne's (Dorothy) ideas about, **2:**324–325
 Pepys's (Samuel) depiction of, accuracy of, **2:**73
 same-sex, **1:**139
 of women teachers in U.S., ban on, **3:**78, 79
Marse Chan (Page), **2:**250
Marsh, Dawn, **3:**326
Marshall, Dick, **1:**98
Marshall, Jack, *From Baghdad to Brooklyn,* **3:**120
Marshall, Joanna, **1:**109
Marshall, Kathryn, *In the Combat Zone,* **3:**221, 279
Martin, Isabella, **2:**250, 251
Martin, Keavy, *Stories in a New Skin,* **3:**138
Martin, Ramela, *Out of Darkness,* **3:**40
Martin, Tera, **1:**174
Martineau, Harriet, **2:**29, 335
Martone, Michael, **1:**48
Martyn, Edward, **2:**128
Marwick, Arthur, **3:**234
Marxism
 in Cultural Revolution, **1:**161
 of Guevara (Ernesto "Che"), **2:**220
Mary Chesnut's Civil War (Chesnut), **2:**250, 251, 271
Mary I (queen of England), **2:**98, 99
Mary II (queen of England), **2:**324, *325*
Maryland, interracial marriage in, **1:**72
Masculine writing style, vs. feminine writing style, **1:**250
Masculinity, in *Journal of George Fox* (Fox), **2:**27
Masking, African American tradition of, **1:**144
Masks, Chinese ghost, **1:**174
Mason, Bobbie Ann, *In Country,* **1:**335
Mason, Katrina, *Children of Los Alamos,* **3:239–241**
Mason, Keith, **2:**206

Mason, Mary, **1:**246

Mason, Terry, **3:**344

Massacre in Mexico (Poniatowska), **3:**31–33

Massey, Mary Elizabeth, **2:**246

Mass Observation Project, **2:**235, 236, 237, 265, 266, 267

Masson, David, **2:**310–311

Masson, Madeleine, **2:**218

Mast, Robert, *Detroit Lives,* **3:**99

Mastectomies, **2:**3

Masumoto, David Mas, *Country Voices,* **3:**224

Matagari (Ngũgĩ), **2:**14

Mather, Cotton, **1:**326, 328

Mather, Increase, **1:**325, 326

    A Brief History of the War with the Indians in New England, **1:**325

Matrilineal culture, of Navajo, **3:**318

Matsumoto, Valerie, *Farming the Home Place,* **3:**80

Mattachine Society, **3:**83

Matthews, William, **2:**65

Matthiessen, F. O., **1:**235, **2:**113, 114, 115

Maturation, Conroy (Frank) on experience of, **1:**164

Maugham, Robin, **2:**185

Maugham, W. Somerset, **2:**184

    Bennett (Arnold) compared to, **2:**136

    The Razor's Edge, **2:**185

    The Summing Up, **2:**183

    A Writer's Notebook, **2:**183–185

Mau Mau rebellion, **2:**12

Maunsell, Jerome, **2:**122

Maupassant, Guy de, **2:**113, 183, 306

Maurer, Harry

    Not Working, **3:**277

    Sex: An Oral History, **3:**276, 277

    Strange Ground, **3:**275–278

    Webs of Power, **3:**277

Mauriac, François, **1:**318, **2:**130

Maus (Spiegelman), **1:**139, 141, 156, 293

Mauthausen concentration camp, **3:**51

Mawer, William, **1:**67

"Mawtini" (Tuqan), **1:**227

Mayans, **3:**166, 167

Mayer, Henry, **3:**45

May Fourth (New Culture) Movement (China), **1:**338, **3:**126, 147–149, *148*

Mayo, John, **3:**87

M'Baye, Mariétou. *See* Bugul, Ken

Mbeki, Thabo, **1:**29, **3:**272, 274

McBride, James, *The Color of Water,* **1:**72–74, *73*

McBride, Ruth, **1:**72–74

McCabe, Dabney, **2:**39

McCann, Justin, **1:**191

McCarthy, Cormac, *Blood Meridian,* **1:**304

McCarthy, Justin, **3:**42

McCarthy, Kevin, **1:**259

McCarthy, Mary, **1:**259

    Cast a Cold Eye, **1:**258

    The Group, **1:**258

    How I Grew, **1:**258

    Intellectual Memoirs, **1:**258

    Memories of a Catholic Girlhood, **1:**258–260

McCloy, John, **3:**234

McColloch, Mark, **3:**329

McCombs, Edward, **3:**291

McCourt, Angela, **1:**120

McCourt, Frank

    Angela's Ashes, **1:**119–121

    A Couple of Blaguards, **1:**119

    Teacher Man, **1:**119

    'Tis, **1:**119

McCourt, Malachy, **1:**119

McCulloch, Mark, **3:**247

McDonald, Cornelia Peake, *A Diary with Reminiscences of the War and Refugee Life in the Shenandoah Valley,* **2:**271

McDonald, F. W., **2:**196

McDonough, A. R., **2:**336

McDougall, Bonnie S., **2:**171, 172

McElroy, John Harmon, **2:**214, 215

McGill, Robert, **2:**131

McKay, Claude, **1:**85

    Banjo, **1:**86

    Harlem: Negro Metropolis, **1:**85

    Home to Harlem, **1:**84, 86

    "If We Must Die," **1:**84

    A Long Way from Home, **1:**84–86

McKay, Nellie, **1:**10, 11

McKee, Guian A., **3:**254, 256

McKelvey, Tara, **3:**233

McKenzie, Barbara, **1:**260

McKinney, Gordon B., **3:**92

McLean, Norman, *A River Runs through It,* **1:**281

McLeod, Calum, *China Remembers,* **3:**301

McLynn, Frank, **1:**220

McNeil, Linda, **3:**78

McNeill, Laurie, **2:**175

McPherson, Dolly, **1:**20

McPherson, Robert S., **3:**12

    Navajo Land, Navajo Culture, **3:**10

Mead, Margaret, **1:**9

Meatless Days (Suleri), **1:**87–89

Meatpacking industry, in Argentina, **3:**73–75

Medeiros-Lichem, María Teresa, **3:**32

Media coverage. *See* Journalism; War correspondents

Mediation, vs. arbitration, **3:**155

Medical conditions. *See* Health problems; *specific conditions*

Medicine

    British, oral histories of, **3:**170–172

    midwifery in, **2:**331–333, *332*

    technological advances in, **3:**170

Medieval era. *See* Middle Ages

Medina, Pablo

    Exiled Memories, **1:**296–298

    Pork Rind and Cuban Songs, **1:**296

Meditations of the Emperor Marcus Aurelius Antoninus, The (Marcus Aurelius), **1:**218–221

Medwick, Cathleen, **1:**212

Mee, Jon, **2:**146, 147

Meikuaya, Wilson, *The Last Maasai Warrior,* **1:**114

Meinecke, Friedrich, **1:**185

Mein Kampf (Hitler), **1:**30–32

Melancholy, in *Confessions of Lady Nijo* (Nijo), **2:**60

Melhuish, Mary, **3:**311

Melman, Billie, **1:**91

MELUS (journal), **1:**17, 71, 109, 175

Melville, Herman, **1:**277, **2:**215, 223, 224

    Moby Dick, **2:**224

Memmott, Carol, **1:**172

Memoir. *See also specific works and writers*

    vs. autobiography, **1:**248, 279

    construction of, to appeal to audience, **1:**164

Memoir (Godwin), **2:**109

Memoir Club, **2:**182

Memoirs (Fanshawe), **1:**229–230, 315, 316, 317

Memoirs (Neruda), 1:222–224

Memoirs (Scott), **2:**309

Memoirs (Williams), **2:**152, 153

Memoirs and Letters of Sara Coleridge (Coleridge), **2:**16

Memoirs of a Fox-Hunting Man (Sassoon), **1:**329, **2:**247

Memoirs of an Arabian Princess from Zanzibar (Ruete), **1:90–92**

Memoirs of a Spacewoman (Mitchison), **2:**237

Memoirs of a Survivor (Lessing), **1:**167

Memoirs of Dr. Burney, The (Burney), **2:**312, 313

Memoirs of Fatemeh Pakravan (Ladjevardi), **3:218–220**

Memoirs of Lady Anne Halkett, The (Halkett), **1:**230, **315–317**

Memoirs of Naim Bey, The (Andonian), **3:**40

Memoirs of Prince Hamid Kadjar (Ladjevardi), **3:**219

Memoirs of Shapour Bakhtiar (Ladjevardi), **3:**220

Memoirs of the Life of Sir Walter Scott (Lockhart), **2:**309, 310

Memoirs of the Princess Daschkaw (Dashkova), **2:**306

Memorial de isla negra (Neruda), **1:**223

Memories of a Catholic Girlhood (McCarthy), **1:258–260**

Memory(ies)

    of Christmas, Thomas (Dylan) on, **1:**125–126

    enigmatic nature of, Suleri (Sara) on, **1:**87, 88

    fluid nature of, Agosín (Marjorie) on, **1:**75–76

    in locked-in syndrome, Bauby (Jean-Dominique) on, **1:**6–7

    in oral history field, **3:**176–178, 186

    of survivors of Armenian genocide, reliability of, **3:**42

    and time, Conroy (Frank) on, **1:**164, 165, 166

    and time, Nabokov (Vladimir) on, **1:**271, 272

    of witnesses, Portelli (Alessandro) on, **3:**265, 266

Memory and Narrative (Olney), **1:**246, 248

Memory for Forgetfulness (Darwish), **1:**255, 257, **2:**50

Memory Studies (journal), **3:**98

Menchú, Rigoberta, *I, Rigoberta Menchú,* **3:164–166,** *165*

    Californio Voices (Savage) vs., **3:**114

    Child of the Dark (de Jesus) vs., **2:**8

    Doña María's Story (James) vs., **3:**73–74

    Let Me Speak! (Viezzer and Barrios de Chungara) vs., **3:**322

    Rites: A Guatemalan Boyhood (Perera) vs., **1:**99

    Women's Words (Gluck and Patai) on, **3:**191

Mencken, H. L., **2:**137

Mendibil, Claude, **1:**6, 7

Meng Jixin, *The First Household under Heaven,* **3:**125

Mennonites, **3:**223, 227

Mental freedom, in locked-in syndrome, **1:**6–7

Mental illness

    of Ruskin (John), **1:**264

    Styron (William) on struggle with, **1:**204–205

Mentor (Grimes), **1:**164

Merchant, G. W., **1:**67

Mercier, Laurie, **3:**81

Meredith, George, **2:**320

Merlo, Frank, **2:**153

Mernissi, Fatima, *Dreams of Trespass,* **1:**226, 227

Mersky, Peter, **3:**203

Meru people, oral histories of, **3:**141–143, *142*

Meschia, Karen, **2:**237

Mesopotamia, letter writing in, **2:**94

Messerschmidt, J. W., **2:**282

Metacomet, **1:**325

Metaphors of Self (Olney), **1:**246

Meth, Rose, **3:**35

Methodism, **2:**195–196

Me Too (Lejeune), **2:**174

Mexican Americans

    Rodriguez (Richard) on experience of, **1:**15–17

    women, oral histories of, **3:**131–134, *132*

Mexican-American War (1846–1848), **1:**304

Mexican Indians, oral histories of, **3:**167–169

Mexican oral histories

    on agrarian reform movement, **3:**302–304

    of indigenous people, **3:**167–169

    on Tlatelolco massacre of 1968, **3:**31–33

Mexican Revolution (1910–1920), **3:**167, 302

Mexico

    agrarian reform movement in, **3:**302–304

    California as colony of, **3:**114

    constitution of, **3:**302

    indigenous people of, **3:**167–169, 304

    Revolution of 1910–1920 in, **3:**167, 302

    Tlatelolco massacre of 1968 in, **3:**31–33

Meyer, Melissa, *The Politics of AIDS Denialism,* **3:**272

Meyers, Gladys Peterson, **3:**78

MFS Modern Fiction Studies (journal), **1:**85

Mhudi (Plaatje), **2:**241, 243

Michaels, Walter Benn, *The Trouble with Diversity,* **1:**16

Michelet, Jules, **1**:267
Michelet par lui-même (Barthes), **1**:267
Michigan. *See* Detroit
Michigan Equal Accommodations Act of 1938, **3**:99
Michigan Historical Review (journal), **2**:207, **3**:100
Michilimackinac, Fort, **2**:205–207, *206*
Michi's Memories (Tamura), **3**:127
Michitsuna No Haha, *The Gossamer Years,* **2**:189, 290, **297–299**
Mickiewicz, Adam
    Forefathers' Eve, **2**:192
    Konrad Wallenrod, **2**:192
Middle Ages
    Christianity in, **1**:189
    Confessions (Augustine) in, **1**:198
    Kempe (Margery) on life in, **1**:189–191
    literacy in, **1**:189
    pilgrimages in, **1:190,** 191, **2**:226
Middle class, English
    expansion of, **2**:177
    Last (Nella) on life of, **2**:265
    Pepys (Samuel) on life of, **2**:72
    Victoria and, **2**:209, 211
    Woodforde (James) on life of, **2**:287–288
Middle East Journal, **1**:209, **3**:49, 219
Middle East Report, **1**:209
Middle East Studies Association Bulletin, **3**:48, 220
Middle Passage, **1**:82, 83
Midgley, Peter, **2**:242
Midnight's Children (Rushdie), **1**:87
Midstream (Keller), **1**:44
Midwest Book Review, **3**:263
Midwifery, **2**:331–333, *332*
Midwife's Tale, A (Ulrich), **2:331–334**
Midwives of the Future (Ware), **3**:308
Mieder, Wolfgang, **2**:305
Mielke, Erich, **3:246**
Migration, of African Americans within U.S., **1**:50, 52, 84, 273. *See also* Immigration
Mihailovic, Draza, **3**:135
Milani, Abbas, *The Persian Sphinx,* **3**:218, 219
Milani, Farzaneh, **1**:209

Milburn, Clara, **2**:235
    Mrs. Milburn's Diary, **2**:265
Mildmay, Grace, **1**:229
Miles, Jack, **2**:339
Miles, Nelson, **1**:303
Milich, Zorka, *A Stranger's Supper,* **3:135–137**
Military, Australian, in World War I, **3**:177
Military, Chinese, women in, **1**:338–340
Military, Colombian, **3**:183–185
Military, U.S. *See also* Veterans; *specific wars*
    African Americans in, **2**:238–240, **3**:199–201, 248–250
    desegregation of, **3**:199, 248, 249
    draft in, **3**:221–223
    homosexuality in, **1**:139
    Japanese Americans in, **3**:196
    Japanese war brides and, **3**:127–129, *128*
    journalists embedded with, **2**:278–280
    Korean American children of, **1**:102
    racism in, **3**:44, 199–201, 248–250
    slaves as soldiers in, **2**:238–240
    Styron (William) in, **1**:206
    Vietnamese American children of, **1**:170
    Wolff (Tobias) in, **1**:47
Military Review (journal), **3**:233
Militia groups, in Scotland, **2**:309
Mill, James, **2**:177
Mill, John Stuart, *Autobiography,* **2**:16
Millay, Edna St. Vincent, **1**:258
Miller, Anita, **2**:138
Miller, Donald E., *Survivors,* **3:40–43,** 50
Miller, Henry, **2**:123, 124
    Tropic of Cancer, **2**:123
Miller, Jack, **3**:329
Miller, Joy E., *Love Carried Me Home,* **3**:35
Miller, June, **2**:124
Miller, Lorna Touryan, *Survivors,* **3:40–43,** 50

Miller, Michele, **3**:233
Miller, William Lee, **2**:71
Millett, Kate, **3**:37
Mill Hunk Herald (magazine), **3**:342
Milligan, Don, **3**:71–72
Million Little Pieces, A (Frey), **1**:313, **2**:296
Milosz, Czeslaw, **1**:255
Milton, John, **2**:140, 146
Min, Anchee
    Becoming Madame Mao, **1**:159
    Pearl of China, **1**:159
    Red Azalea, **1:158–160**
Minamoto no Rinshi, **2**:290, 292
Minamoto no Yoritomo, **2**:61
Minear, Richard, **1**:295
Mine of Her Own, A (Zanjani), **3**:337
Mining. *See also* Coal mining
    in Bolivia, oral histories of, **3**:322–324
    prohibitions on women in, **3**:337
    in Ukraine, oral histories of, **3**:340–342
Mining Cultures (Murphy), **3**:337
Minneapolis Star Tribune (newspaper), **1**:172
Minnesota History (journal), **3**:51
Minorities Research Group, **3**:70
Minority groups. *See* Assimilation; *specific groups*
Minority Report to the Commission of the Poor Law (Webb), **2**:16
Minus, Ed, **2**:269
Miracle Worker, The (teleplay), **1**:44, 45
Miranda, Deborah A., **3**:116
Mirollo, James V., **1**:213
Mirow, Kurt Rudolf, *Webs of Power,* **3**:277
Mirra, Carl, *Soldiers and Citizens,* **3**:231–232
Mirsky, Jonathan, **3**:280, 288
Miscellanies (D'Israeli), **2**:177
Misery memoirs, *Angela's Ashes* (McCourt) as, **1**:120–121
Missing Pages (Terry), **3**:199–200
Missionary work
    in colonial California, **3**:114–116
    in Great Awakening, **2**:197
    of Wesley (John), **2**:195–196

Mississippi Quarterly, **1**:35, 38, **2**:42

Mississippi River, Twain (Mark) on, **1**:146–147

Mississippi Valley Historical Review (journal), **2**:92

Missouri Compromise (1820), **1**:33

Miss Ravenel's Conversion (De Forest), **2**:240

Mistral, Gabriela, **1**:222, 223

Mitchell, Stephen, **2**:149

Mitchell, Virginia R., **3**:307

Mitchison, Clemency, **2**:235, 236

Mitchison, Naomi, *Among You Taking Notes,* **2**:235–237, *236*

Mitford, John, **2**:143

Mitford, Mary Russell, *Our Village,* **3**:59

Mitson, Betty E., *Voices Long Silent,* **3**:195

Mittler, Barbara, **3**:148

Miyata Waichirō, **2**:191

MK. *See* Umkhonto we Sizwe

Mkhize, Sibongiseni, **1**:26

Mlambo, Eshmael, *Rhodesia,* **3**:251

MLN (journal), **3**:8

Moby Dick (Melville), **2**:224

Mock autobiographies, *Stop-Time* (Conroy) as, **1**:164, 165

Modern Asia Studies (journal), **2**:198, 200

Modern Drama (journal), **2**:102

Modern Fiction Studies (journal), **3**:74, 243

Modernism

Bagnold (Enid) in, **2**:261

Bennett (Arnold) in, **2**:136, 138

Brittain (Vera) in, **1**:330

Lu Xun in, **2**:172

Nin (Anaïs) in, **2**:123

origins and rise of, **2**:180

Stein (Gertrude) in, **1**:332, 333, 334

vs. traditionalism, Woolf (Virginia) on, **2**:138

Woolf (Virginia) in, **2**:180

Modernization

in Iran, rise of, **3**:218

in Russia, rise of, **1**:193

in U.S., Thoreau's (Henry David) critique of, **1**:233

Modern Judaism (journal), **1**:320

Modern Language Journal, **3**:301

Modern Motherhood (Davis), **3**:145

Modern Painters (Ruskin), **1**:264

Modern Philology (journal), **1**:247, 248, 264

Modern schools, **3**:5

Modisane, Bloke, **3**:251

Modkad, Jessica, **1**:209

Mogul Empire, **2**:229, *230*

Mohammed Reza Pahlavi (shah of Iran), **1**:155, **3**:218, *219*

The Shah's Story, **3**:218

Mohammed V (sultan of Morocco), **3**:47, 49

Mohegan tribe, **1**:56, **2**:44, 46

Mohr, Nicholasa, **1**:108

Moi, Daniel arap, **2**:12, 14

Moira, Fran, **2**:4

Momaday, Al, **1**:54, *55*

Momaday, N. Scott

House Made of Dawn, **1**:54

The Journey of Tai-me, **1**:54

The Names: A Memoir, **1**:54

The Way to Rainy Mountain, **1**:54–57, *55*

Moment of Conquest, The (Fadiman), **3**:141

Moments of Being (Woolf), **1**:249, **2**:182

Momoh, Joseph, **1**:312

Monaghan, Patricia, **1**:97

Monarchy. *See* British monarchy

Monasticism

Teresa of Ávila on, **1**:211–213

in U.S., oral histories of, **3**:308–310

Mondor, Colleen, **3**:249

Money. *See* Finances

Möngke Khan, **1**:107

Mongol Empire, **1**:105–107, **2**:59

Monroe, Ed, **1**:335

Montagu, Edward Wortley, **2**:35

Montagu, Mary Wortley, **2**:36

audience of letters of, **2**:217

"Letter to Her Daughter," **2**:35–37

Ruete (Emily) compared to, **1**:90

Turkish Embassy Letters, **2**:35, 37

Montaigne, Michel de, **2**:62, 256, 257

Essais, **2**:72

Monteiro, Anthony, **1**:5

Montejo, Esteban, *Biography of a Runaway Slave,* **3**:7–9

Montell, William Lynwood

Always a People, **3**:107–109, 325

From Memory to History, **3**:90

The Saga of Coe Ridge, **3**:90–92

Montenegro, oral histories of women of, **3**:135–137, *136*

Montgomery, James A., **1**:287

Montgomery bus boycott (1955), **1**:20, 37, 38, 39, **2**:32, **3**:44, 45

Monthly Review (journal), **1**:82

Montoya, Maria, **3**:133

Mont-Saint-Michel and Chartres (Adams), **1**:132

Moody, Anne, *Coming of Age in Mississippi,* **1**:37

Moon, Elaine Latzman, *Untold Tales, Unsung Heroes,* **3**:99–101

Moon, in Japanese poetry, **2**:191

Mooney, Christopher Gerald, **1**:150

Moonshine

in Appalachia, **3**:90, 91

in Idaho, **3**:95

Moore, Dorothy, **2**:333

Moore, Elijah, **2**:333

Moore, G. E., **2**:268

Moore, Gerald, **1**:128, 129

Moore, James, **1**:67

Moore, Kofoworola Aina, **1**:64

Moore, Marat, *Women in the Mines,* **3**:157, 328, **337–339**

Moore, Molly, *A Woman at War,* **2**:278–280

Moore, Thomas, **2**:143, 144

Moorehead, Caroline, **2**:101, 102

Moorhead-Rosenberg, Florence, **1**:77

Moosa, Matti, **1**:137

Moral Economy of AIDS in South Africa, The (Nattrass), **3**:272

Morality

Conrad's (Joseph) concern with, **2**:192, 193

Neruda (Pablo) on poetry and, **1**:223

Morantz, Regina, *In Her Own Words,* **3:**170

Mora-Torres, Gregorio, **3:**114, 115, 116

Moravians, **2:**196, 197

More Leaves from the Journal of Our Life in the Highlands (Victoria), **2:**209

Morello, Ruth, **2:**95, 96

Moreno Franglinal, Manuel, *The Sugarmill,* **3:**7

Morgan, Sarah, *The Civil War Diary of Sarah Morgan,* **2:**271

Morgan, Ted, **2:**56

Morgan, Winifred, **1:**35

Morgenthau, Henry, Jr., **3:**293

Morgenthau Plan, **3:**293

Morley, Christopher, **2:**330

Morley, Edith, **2:**77

Mormino, Gary R., **3:**191

Morning Sun (Leung), **3:**301

Moroccan Soul, The (Segalla), **3:**48

Morocco, oral histories of women in independence movement of, **3:**47–49, *48*

Morris, Gabrielle, *Head of the Class,* **3:20–22**

Morris, Ivan, **2:**190

Morris, John N., **1:**247

Morris, Margaret Hill, **2:**80

Morrison, Toni, *The Bluest Eye,* **1:**19, 175

Morse, Richard M., **2:**7

Mort, John, **3:**100

Mortensen, Peter, **2:**163, 164, 165

Mortimer, Mildred, **1:**62

Mortimer, Raymond, **2:**268

Mosaic (journal), **1:**110, **3:**320

Mosby, John Singleton, *War Reminiscences,* **2:**250

Moss, William W., **3:**125–126, 213

Mossadegh, Mohammad, **3:**218, 219

Mostow, Joshua, **2:**292

Mother and Son (Seabrook), **3:**55

Mother-daughter relationships
in *A Mountainous Journey* (Tuqan), **1:**226, 227
in Plath's (Sylvia) writings, **2:**47–49

in *Ten Thousand Sorrows* (Kim), **1:**102–104

Motherhood
Jacobs (Harriet A.) on, **1:**142
Stanton (Elizabeth Cady) on, **1:**13

Mothers, Sisters, Resisters (Gurewitsch), **3:34–36**

Motley, Mary Penick, *The Invisible Soldier,* **3:**212

Motoori Norinaga, **2:**190

Motorcycle Diaries (Guevara), **1:**223, **2:220–222**

Motsa, Zodwa, **1:**29

Mouffe, Barbara S., **2:**224

Moujahide, Ghalia, **3:**48

Moulton, Seth, **3:**231

Mountain, Carolyn, **3:**122, 123

Mountainous Journey, A (Tuqan), **1:225–228**

Mount Holyoke College, **1:**109

Mount Kenya, oral histories of Meru people of, **3:**141–143

Mount Vesuvius, eruption of, **2:**94, 95

Mourão, Manuela, **2:**199, 200

Movies. *See* Film adaptations; *specific movies*

Moving Out (Spence), **2:**163

Moya, Jose C., **3:**75

Moye, J. Todd
Freedom Flyers, **3:**99, **248–250**
Let the People Decide, **3:**249

Mpolweni, Nosisi, *There Was This Goat,* **3:**242

Mrs. Milburn's Diary (Milburn), **2:**265

Mrs. Miniver (film), **2:**265

Ms. magazine, **1:**11

Mudimbe-Boyi, Elisabeth, **1:**64

Muecke, Stephen, **1:**151

Muhammad, Elijah, **1:**186, 188

Muhlen, Norbert, **2:**56

Muhlenfeld, Elisabeth, **2:**250, 251

Mu'in al-Din Unur, **1:**285

Muir, John (naturalist), **1:**234

Muir, John (Vietnam veteran), **3:**209

Mujahidin, **3:**233

Mulan (legendary figure), **1:**152, 153, 340

Mulatto (Hughes), **1:**72

Mulattos
Jewish–black, **1:**74
as "tragic," in literary tradition, **1:**72

Mules and Men (Hurston), **1:**9

Mulford, Jeremy, **2:**266

Mullan, Fitzhugh, **3:**274

Muller, Bobby, **3:**232, 233

Muller, James, **3:**273

Mullin, Janet E., **2:**289

Mullins, Emer, **3:**29

Multicultural and multiracial identities
Kim (Elizabeth) on, **1:**102–103
Kingston (Maxine Hong) on, **1:**173–175
McBride (James) on, **1:**72–74
Nguyen (Kien) on, **1:**170
Obama (Barack) on, **1:**78–80
Santiago (Esmeralda) on, **1:**108–110
Suleri (Sara) on, **1:**87–88
"tragic mulatto" tradition and, **1:**72

Multicultural Autobiography (Payne), **1:**247–248

Multicultural families
Kim (Elizabeth) on, **1:**102–103
McBride (James) on, **1:**72–74
Obama (Barack) on, **1:**78–80
Suleri (Sara) on, **1:**87–88

Multiculturalism
academic debate over, **1:**16
and Columbus's (Christopher) legacy, **2:**203

Multicultural literary studies, *The Story of My Life* (Ahmedi) in, **1:**40–42

Multiracial individuals, racism against
in Korea, **1:**102
in Vietnam, **1:**170, 171

Multiracial literature, rise of, **1:**73–74

Munck, Ronnie, **3:**29

Munif, Abdelrahman, *East of the Mediterranean,* **2:**50

Munns, Jessica, **2:**67

Munson, Henry, Jr., *The House of Si Abd Allah,* **3:**47

Murao, Helen, **3:**197

SUBJECT INDEX

Murasaki Shikibu, **2:190**
 The Diary of Lady Murasaki, **2:**59, **290–293**
 Lady Murasaki Shu, **2:**291
 Michitsuna No Haha in family of, **2:**297
 The Tale of Genji, **2:**59, 60, 189, 190, 290–292, *291*
Murder in Amsterdam (Buruma), **1:**209
Murdock, Kenneth B., **2:**113, 114, 115
Murphy, Caryle, **2:**278
Murphy, Mary, **2:**17
 Mining Cultures, **3:**337
Murray, Albert, *The Omni-Americans,* **1:**124
Murray, John, **2:**143
Murry, John Middleton, **2:**133, 134, 135
Museum of North Idaho, **3:**93, 95
Music
 Conroy (Frank) on, **1:**166
 folk music revival of 1960s, **3:**96
 in Japanese American internment camps, **3:**104
 of labor movement, **3:**329
 of Mexican American women, **3:**131–133
 of working class, **3:**157, 159
Muslim(s)
 African American, **1:**186–188
 in conflict with Christians, after Crusades, **2:**226
 in conflict with Hindus, in India, **1:**244
 of India, **1:**244, **2:**230
 Malinke people as, **1:**128
 racial profiling of, in U.S., **3:**195, 197
 slavery in countries of, **1:**90, 92
Muslim autobiographical writing. *See also specific works and writers*
 by Ahmedi (Farah), **1:**40–42
 by Hirsi Ali (Ayaan), **1:**207–209
 by Laye (Camara), **1:**128–130
 by Malcolm X, **1:**186–188
 by Usāmah ibn Munqidh, **1:**285–288
Muslim women
 Ahmedi (Farah) on experience of, **1:**40–42

 circumcision of, **1:**207
 vs. European women, roles of, **1:**90
 Hirsi Ali (Ayaan) on mistreatment of, **1:**207–209
 Ruete (Emily) on rights and roles of, **1:**90–92
 Western biases in narratives depicting, **1:**40, 41
 Western misconceptions about, **1:**90, 91
Muslim Women on the Move (Gray), **3:**48
My Apprenticeship (Webb), **2:**17
My Bondage and My Freedom (Douglass), **1:**34
My Brother Ibrahim (Tuqan), **1:**227
My Confessions (Chamberlain), **1:**304
Myers, Brian, **1:**103
Myers, Constance, **3:**87
Myerson, Joel, **2:**224, 225
My Forty Year Fight for Korea (Yim), **1:**323
"My Furthest-Back Person— 'The African'" (Haley), **1:261–263**
My Life (Das), **1:**87
"My Life" (Keller), **1:**43
My Life and Work (Ford), **1:**30
My Life Story (Amrouche), **1:93–95**
My Life Story (Unaipon), **1:149–151**
Myrdal, Jan, *Report from a Chinese Village,* **3:**299
My Revolutionary Years (Cheng), **1:152–154**
My Soul (Hoess), **2:**54
My Soul Is My Own (Etter-Lewis), **3:**21
Mystery and Manners (O'Connor), **2:**131
Mysticism
 of Kempe (Margery), **1:**189–191
 of Teresa of Ávila, **1:**211–213
Myth and Materiality in a Woman's World (Abrams), **3:**175
Myth of Sisyphus, The (Camus), **1:**204
Mythology
 of Aborigines, **1:**149
 of Kiowas, **1:**54–56
 of Navajo, **3:**320

Myths and Legends of the Australian Aboriginals (Unaipon), **1:**149
My Traitor's Heart (Malan), **3:**242

N

NAACP. *See* National Association for the Advancement of Colored People
Nablus (West Bank), **1:**225, *226*
Nabokov, Vladimir, **1:**271
 Speak, Memory, **1:**249, 270
 Speak, Memory: An Autobiography Revisited, **1:**270–272
Nadeau, Remi, *The Water Seekers,* **3:**102
Nafisi, Azar, *Reading Lolita in Tehran,* **1:**155, 157, 209
NAFTA. *See* North American Free Trade Agreement
Nagai, Takashi
 The Bells of Nagasaki, **1:**293
 We of Nagasaki, **1:**293
Nagasaki (Japan), U.S. nuclear bombing of, **3:**239
Nagel, Paul C., **2:**71
Naghibi, Nima, **1:**157
Naipaul, V. S., **1:**88
Najder, Zdzisław, **2:**192
Nakazawa, Keiji, **1:**294
 Barefoot Gen, **1:293–295**
 Hiroshima, **1:**293, 295
Nam (Baker), **3:**199, 209, 210, 221, 231
Names, of slaves, **1:**52
Names, The: A Memoir (Momaday), **1:**54
Nanking (Nanjing) Massacre (1937)
 Rabe's (John) account of, **2:**19–21
 Sino–Japanese relations after, **1:**340
Napangardi, Georgina, **3:**107, 335
Napoleon (Scott), **2:**310
Napoléon Bonaparte, **1:**276, **2:**217
Napoleonic wars, **1:**276
Napoleon III, **2:**82
Narain, Mona, **2:**231
Nara period (Japan), **2:**189
Narrative (Brown), **1:**50
Narrative (journal), **1:**164, 165

Narrative of Hosea Hudson, The (Hudson), **1:**3–4

Narrative of Sojourner Truth (Truth), **1:**37

Narrative of the Life and Travels of Mrs. Nancy Prince (Prince), **3:**24

Narrative of the Life of Frederick Douglass (Douglass), 1:33–36

    Eighty Years and More (Stanton) vs., **1:**12

    Equiano's (Olaudah) influence on, **1:**82–83

    Incidents in the Life of a Slave Girl (Jacobs) vs., **1:**34, 35, 142, 143

    Up from Slavery (Washington) vs., **1:**50

Narrative point of view (perspective)

    in *The Autobiography of Giambattista Vico* (Vico), **1:**184

    in *Bone Black* (hooks), **1:**249, 250, 251

    in *A Cross and a Star* (Agosín), **1:**76

    in *The Woman Warrior* (Kingston), **1:**173

    in *The Writing Life* (Dillard), **1:**280, 281

Narrative voice

    of *Angela's Ashes* (McCourt), **1:**120

    of *The Autobiography of Malcolm X* (Malcolm X), **1:**187

    of *Bone Black* (hooks), **1:**250

    of *The Color of Water* (McBride), **1:**73

    of *A Cross and a Star* (Agosín), **1:**76

    of *The Education of Henry Adams* (Adams), **1:**133

    of *An Egyptian Childhood* (Hussein), **1:**136

    of *Go Ask Alice* (anonymous), **2:**295

    of *I Know Why the Caged Bird Sings* (Angelou), **1:**18, 19

    of *Lakota Woman* (Brave Bird), **1:**23

    of *My Revolutionary Years* (Cheng), **1:**153

    of *Nella Last's War* (Last), **2:**266

    of *Paekpom Ilchi* (Kim), **1:**323

    of *Red Scarf Girl* (Jiang), **1:**161, 162

    of *Ten Thousand Sorrows* (Kim), **1:**103

    of *When Heaven and Earth Changed Places* (Hayslip), **1:**336

    of *The Woman Warrior* (Kingston), **1:**173

    of *The Writing Life* (Dillard), **1:**281

Nasar, Sylvia, **2:**18

Nash, Charles Elventon, *The History of Augusta*, **2:**331, 333

Nash, Christine, **3:**61

Nash, John, **3:**61

Nash, Philip Tajitsu, **3:**197

Nassiri, Nematollah, **3:**219

Nation (magazine), **1:**100, 103, 258, **2:**92, 102

Nation, Michael, **3:**211

National Academy of Arbitrators, **3:**153

National American Women's Suffrage Association (NAWSA), **1:**12, 13

National Anti-Slavery Standard (newspaper), **1:**144

National Association for the Advancement of Colored People (NAACP)

    on anti-lynching legislation, **1:**18

    in civil rights movement, **3:**44

    Du Bois (W. E. B.) in, **1:**4

    establishment of, **3:**44

    in military desegregation, **3:**248

National Book Award, for *Roots* (Haley), **1:**261

National Book Critics Circle Award

    for *Voices from Chernobyl* (Alexievich), **3:**282

    for *The Woman Warrior* (Kingston), **1:**173

National Geographic, **1:**114

National Health Service (Britain), **3:**170

National identity

    Danish, **2:**166

    Portuguese, **2:**199–200

Nationalism

    Armenian, **3:**40

    black, **1:**4, 78, 79

    British, **2:**219

    Chinese, **2:**170

    German, **1:**30–32, 329, **2:**120, **3:**234

    Indian, **1:**289–290

    Irish, **1:**119, **2:**127, 128, **3:**315

    Japanese, **3:**234

    Moroccan, **3:**47–49

    Palestinian, **1:**225, 227

    Puerto Rican, **1:**108

Nationalist Party (China), **1:**338

Nationalization

    in Cuba, **1:**296

    in Iran, **3:**218

National Liberation Front (FLN) (Algeria), **2:**262

National Party (South Africa), **1:**24, 27, **3:**242

National Republican Alliance (ARENA), **3:**205

National Savings Movement (Britain), **3:145**

National security, U.S.

    East German Stasi and, **3:**245

    racism and, **3:**195, 197

National Socialist German Workers' Party, **1:**30. See also Nazi Germany

National Velvet (Bagnold), **2:**259, 260, 261

National War Labor Board, The (Conner), **3:**153–154

National War Labor Board (NWLB), U.S., **3:**153–154

National Woman Suffrage Association, **1:**12

Nation of Islam. See Black Muslims

Nation of Women, A (Fur), **3:**326

Native American(s)

    in AIM (*See* American Indian Movement)

    Carver's (Jonathan) encounters with, **2:**205, 206, 207

    civil rights of, **1:**21, **3:**291, 292

    Columbus's (Christopher) encounters with, **2:**202

    conversion to Christianity, **1:**56, **2:**46, **3:**114, 115

    cultural transmission by, **3:**107–109, 325–326

    education of, at boarding schools, **3:**109, 318

Native American(s), *continued*
- forced removal of, **1:**302, **3:**290, *291,* 318, 325, 327
- in King Philip's War, **1:**325–328, *326*
- oral traditions of, **1:**21, 54, 55, 96, 302, 304, **3:**138
- in Pan-Indian movement, **1:**54
- racism against, **1:**96
- religion of, **3:**110–112
- U.S. treaties with, **1:**69, **3:**107, 110, 290, 327
- U.S. wars with, **1:**302–304, **3:**110

Native American autobiographical writing. *See also specific works and writers*
- by Brave Bird (Mary), **1:**21–23
- by Chona (Maria), **1:**69–71
- in collective narratives vs. autobiographies, **1:**54
- by Geronimo, **1:**302–304
- by Momaday (N. Scott), **1:**54–56
- non–Native writers' collaboration in, **1:**21, 23, 56, 69–70
- by Peltier (Leonard), **1:**96–98
- rise of, **1:**54
- tradition of, **1:**54, 56, **3:**110, 318, 320

Native American identity
- language in, **3:**108, 109
- search for, **1:**22, 55, 56

Native American oral histories
- from Alta California, **3:**114–116, *115*
- of Black Elk, **3:**110–113
- of Delaware Indians, **3:**107–109
- of Inuits, **3:**138–140
- of Left Handed, **3:**318–320
- of Navajo, **3:**10–12, 290–292, 318–320
- from Owens Valley (California), **3:**102, 103
- of Woodland Indians, **3:**107–109

Native American renaissance, **1:**54

Native American reservations
- Brave Bird (Mary) on life on, **1:**21
- Chona (Maria) on life on, **1:**69
- economic disparities in, **3:**290
- establishment of system of, **1:**69, 302, **3:**318

Geronimo on life on, **1:**302
Navajo, **3:**10–12, 290–291, 318
Navajo–Hope land dispute in, **3:**10–12
Peltier (Leonard) on life on, **1:**96
social change in, **3:**290
water resources of, **1:**69, **3:**11

Native Land Act of 1913 (South Africa), **2:**241

Native Life in South Africa (Plaatje), **2:**241, 242, 243

Native Son (Wright), **1:**122, 123, 273

NATO, demonstrations against, **3:**157, 158

Nattrass, Nicoli, *The Moral Economy of AIDS in South Africa,* **3:**272

Natural History (journal), **3:**38

Naturalistic diction, in *Notebooks and Letters* (Hawthorne), **2:**224

Natural philosophy, **2:**300

Natural selection, **1:**65

Natural Theology (Paley), **1:**65

Natural world
- British writing on, golden age of, **2:**300
- Dillard's (Annie) essays on, **1:**279
- Neruda's (Pablo) love of, **1:**223–224
- Thoreau (Henry David) on, **1:**233–236
- in transcendental fiction, **1:**281
- Wordsworth's (Dorothy) descriptions of, **2:**300–302

"Nature" (Emerson), **2:**141

Nature's Pictures Drawn by Fancy's Pencil to the Life (Cavendish), **1:**229, 231

Naudowessee tribe, **2:**206

Navajivan (journal), **1:**242

Navajo, **3:**319
- in land dispute with Hopi, oral histories of, **3:**10–12
- Left Handed on life of, oral history of, **3:**318–320
- "Long Walk" of, **3:**290, *291*
- matrilineal culture of, **3:**318
- origins of, **3:**318
- witch purge of 1878 among, oral histories of, **3:**290–292

Navajo as Seen by the Franciscans, The (Bahr), **3:**290

Navajo-Hopi Land Dispute, The (Brugge), **3:**10

Navajo-Hopi Settlement Act of 1974 (U.S.), **3:**10

Navajo Land, Navajo Culture (McPherson), **3:**10

Navajo language, **3:**11, 12

Navajos, The (Underhill), **3:**290

Navajo Times (newspaper), **3:**12

"Navajo Witch Purge of 1878, The" (Brugge), **3:**290

Naval Aviation News, **3:**203

Navarrete, Martín Fernández de, **2:**201

Navy, Colombian, **3:**183–185

Navy, U.S., in World War II, oral histories of, **3:**202–204, *203*

NAWSA. *See* National American Women's Suffrage Association

Naylor, James, **2:**26

Naylor, Phillip, **2:**263

Nazi Germany. *See also* Holocaust
- autobiographies written after end of, **2:**54
- bombardment of Britain by, **2:**265, 269, 270
- Chilean support for, **1:**75
- establishment of, **3:**14
- extent of conquest by, **3:**14
- fall of, **2:**281–282
- Fosse Ardeatine massacre by, **3:**265–267
- France occupied by, **1:**332–334
- Italy occupied by, **3:**265–267
- Klemperer (Victor) on rise of, **2:**303–305
- Nanking Massacre and, **2:**19, 20, 21
- Netherlands occupied by, **2:**22–24, 253–255
- Speer's (Albert) role in, **2:**54–56
- war crimes of, **1:**77, **2:**54–56, **3:**293–295

Nazi Seizure of Power, The (Allen), **3:**245

NCR Book Award, for *Wild Swans* (Chang), **1:**159

Neal, R. S., **3:**178

Ned, Annie, **3:**320

Nedjma (Yacine), **2:**262

Neeson, Liam, **2:**10
Negative capability, **2:**146, 147
Négritude movement, **1:**61, 128
Negro in the American Rebellion, The (Brown), **2:**238
Nehru, Jawaharlal, **1:290**
   An Autobiography, with Musings on Recent Events in India, **1:289–292**
   The Discovery of India, **1:**290, 291
   Whither India?, **1:**290
Neihardt, John G., *Black Elk Speaks,* **1:**21, 56, 302, **3:110–113,** 318
Neilson, William Allan, **1:**44–45
Nella Last's Peace (Last), **2:**265
Nella Last's War (Last), **2:265–267**
Nelson, Edward, **3:**51
Nelson, Truman, **1:**4
Nemiroff, Robert, **1:**273, 274, 275
Neoliberalism, in Argentina, rise of, **3:**74
Neoplatonism, of Augustine, **1:**196, 197
Neruda, Pablo
   Canto general, **1:**223
   Memoirs, **1:222–224**
   Memorial de isla negra, **1:**223
Nesbitt, Gussie, **3:**45
Netherlands
   colonialism of, Barnard's (Anne) critique of, **2:**218
   Hillesum (Etty) on life in, **2:**22–24
   Hirsi Ali (Ayaan) on life in, **1:**207–209
   Nazi occupation of, **2:**22–24, 253–255
Neubauer, Carol, **1:**18
Never in Anger (Briggsoth), **3:**138
Nevins, Allan
   on *The Diary of John Quincy Adams* (Adams), **2:**70
   "Great Men" project of, **3:**161, 173, 179, 181, 186
   influence on oral history field, **3:**37, 173
New Age (journal), **1:**25
New Burlington (Baskin), **3:**86
New Challenge (journal), **1:**85
New Criterion (journal), **2:**73, 185, 337

New Culture Movement. *See* May Fourth Movement
New Deal, **3:**161. *See also* Federal Writers' Project
New Discovery of a Vast Country in America, A (Hennepin), **2:**205
Newell, Esther Pollack, **3:**269
New England Quarterly, **2:**114
New German Critique (journal), **1:**32
New Grub Street (Gissing), **2:**320, 321, 322
New Harmony (utopian community), **1:**14
Newman, Andrew, *On Records,* **3:**326
Newman, John Henry, *Apologia Pro Vita Sua,* **1:**65
New Mexico
   Bosque Redondo Reservation in, **3:**10, 290, *291*
   oral histories of development of atom bomb in, **3:**239–241
New Negro movement, **1:**84. *See also* Harlem Renaissance
New Orleans (Louisiana), oral histories of Hispanic American entrepreneurs in, **3:**121–123, *122*
New Republic (magazine), **1:**4, 258, **2:**150, 340, **3:**61
New Science (Vico), **1:**183, 184, 185
New Statesman (journal), **3:**59
New Statesman & Society (journal), **2:**221
Newsweek (magazine), **1:**19
New Voyages to North-America (Lahontan), **2:**205
New War Diary (Xie), **1:**339–340
New West Indian Guide (journal), **3:**7, 8
New Woman, **2:**259
New World, Columbus's (Christopher) discovery of, **2:**201–203
New York (state), interracial marriage in, **1:**72
New York City. *See also* Harlem Renaissance
   African American migration to, **1:**84
   City College in, **1:**249, 251
   in Great Depression, **1:**84
   Hansberry (Lorraine) on life in, **1:**273

   Jews living in, **3:**118, 119, *119,* 120
New York Daily Tribune (newspaper), **1:**142
New Yorker (magazine), **1:**258, 270, 300
New York Intellectuals, **1:**258
New York Post (newspaper), **3:**165
New York Review of Books, **1:**7, 79, **3:**60, 165, 280, 288
New York Times (newspaper)
   on *The Abandoned Baobab* (Bugul), **1:**62–63
   on *Along This Way* (Johnson), **1:**84
   on *Angela's Ashes* (McCourt), **1:**120
   on *Bloods* (Terry), **3:**201
   on *Bone Black* (hooks), **1:**250
   on *The Color of Water* (McBride), **1:**73, 74
   on *Diaries of Beatrice Webb* (Webb), **2:**17
   on *The Diaries of Franz Kafka* (Kafka), **2:**121
   on *A Diary from Dixie* (Chesnut), **2:**251
   on *The Diary of Anne Frank* (Frank), **2:**253
   on *The Diary of John Quincy Adams* (Adams), **2:**70
   on *The Diary of Samuel Pepys* (Pepys), **2:**73
   on *Dreams from My Father* (Obama), **1:**79
   on *Everything We Had* (Santoli), **3:**211
   on *Geronimo* (Geronimo and Barrett), **1:**304
   on *Hard Times* (Terkel), **3:**162
   on *Hunger of Memory* (Rodriguez), **1:**16
   on *Infidel* (Hirsi Ali), **1:**209
   on *Letters to a Young Poet* (Rilke), **2:**149
   on Levi's (Primo) suicide, **1:**204, 205
   on *London and the Life* (Gissing), **2:**322
   on *The Long Walk to Freedom* (Mandela), **1:**28, 29
   on *Mein Kampf* (Hitler), **1:**32

SUBJECT INDEX

New York Times (newspaper), **continued**
    on *Memoirs* (Neruda), **1:**223
    on *Memories of a Catholic Girlhood* (McCarthy), **1:**259
    on *Motorcycle Diaries* (Guevara), **2:**220
    "My Furthest-Back Person— 'The African'" (Haley) in, **1:**261
    on *Our Appalachia* (Shackelford and Weinberg), **3:**87
    on *Persepolis* (Satrapi), **1:**156–157
    on *Red Azalea* (Min), **1:**158
    on *Rites: A Guatemalan Boyhood* (Perera), **1:**100
    on *Roots* (Haley), **1:**262
    on *Rosa Parks: My Story* (Parks and Haskins), **1:**38
    on *Selected Letters of Martha Gellhorn* (Gellhorn), **2:**102
    on *Shoah* (film), **3:**52
    on *Speak, Memory* (Nabokov), **1:**271
    on *The Story of a Shipwrecked Sailor* (García Márquez), **3:**183
    on *This Boy's Life* (Wolff), **1:**48
    on *Up from Slavery* (Washington), **1:**52
    on *When Heaven and Earth Changed Places* (Hayslip), **1:**336
    on *Witnesses to Nuremberg* (Stave et al.), **3:**294
    on *A Woman in Berlin* (anonymous), **2:**282
    on *The Woman Warrior* (Kingston), **1:**175
    on *Working* (Terkel), **3:**344
    on *The Writing Life* (Dillard), **1:**280
New York Times Book Review
    on *Chinese Lives* (Zhang and Sang), **3:**301
    on *Darkness Visible* (Styron), **1:**205
    on *A Diary without Dates* (Bagnold), **2:**260
    on *Dust Tracks on a Road* (Hurston), **1:**10–11
    on *Farewell to Manzanar* (Houston and Houston), **1:**300
    on *Fun Home* (Bechdel), **1:**141
    on *The Good Man of Nanking* (Rabe), **2:**20
    on *"The Good War"* (Terkel), **3:**213
    on *The Habit of Being* (O'Connor), **2:**131
    on *The Journals of Charlotte Forten Grimké* (Grimké), **2:**30
    on *Letters Home* (Plath), **2:**48
    on *A Midwife's Tale* (Ulrich), **2:**333
    on *The Travels of Dean Mahomet* (Mahomet), **2:**231
    on *Voices of Freedom* (Hampton and Fayer), **3:**45
    on *What Was Asked of Us* (Wood), **3:**233
    on *A Writer's Diary* (Woolf), **2:**181
    on *Zlata's Diary* (Filipovic), **2:**339
New York Times Magazine, **1:**99
New Zealand, Mansfield (Katherine) on life in, **2:**133–135
Next Year in Cuba (Pérez Firmat), **1:**296
Ng, Wendy, **3:**81
Ngarrindjeri people, **1:**149, 151
Ngor, Haing, *Survival in the Killing Fields,* **1:**306
Ngũgĩ wa Mirii, **2:**12
Ngũgĩ wa Thiong'o
    Barrel of a Pen, **2:**12
    Decolonising the Mind, **2:**13
    Detained: A Writer's Prison Diary, **1:**215, **2:**12–15
    Devil on the Cross, **2:**12, 13
    I Will Marry When I Want, **2:**12
    Matagari, **2:**14
    Petals of Blood, **2:**12
Nguyen, Kien, *The Unwanted,* **1:**170–172
Nguyen, Nathalie Huynh Chau, **1:**172
Nguyen, Viet Thanh, **1:**336–337
Nguyen Thi Thu Lam, *Fallen Leaves,* **1:**335
Nicene Creed, **1:**196
Nicholas II (tsar of Russia), **1:**270, **2:**84, 85
Nichols, John Gough, **1:**316, **2:**97, 99
Nichols, Julie, **2:**164
Nichols, Madaline W., **2:**7
Nichols, Martha, **1:**251
Nichols-Ledermann, Deborah, **3:**325, 326
Nicholson-Preuss, Mari, **3:**246

Nicolay, Helen, **3:**263
Nicolay, Helena, **3:**263
Nicolay, John G., **3:262**
    Abraham Lincoln: A History, **3:**261–262
    Abraham Lincoln: Complete Works, **3:**262
    in *An Oral History of Abraham Lincoln* (Burlingame), **3:**261–264
Nicolay, John Jacob, **3:**263
Nies, Judith, **3:**292
Nietzsche, Friedrich
    Andreas-Salomé (Lou) and, **2:**151
    Ecce Homo, **1:**183
    Vico (Giambattista) compared to, **1:**183, 184–185
Nigeria
    Civil War of, **1:**214–216
    Equiano (Olaudah) in, **1:**81–83
    independence of (1960), **1:**214
    postcolonial governments of, **1:**214–216
    Soyinka (Wole) on life in, **1:**214–216
Nigerian Civil War (1967–1970), **1:**214–216
Night (Wiesel), **1:318–321**
Night Comes to the Cumberlands (Caudill), **3:**66
Nightingale, Florence, **1:**111, 112, 113
Nijo, Lady, *Confessions of Lady Nijo,* **2:59–61**
Nikki genre, **2:**191
Nilsen, Alleen Pace, **2:**294, 295
Nin, Anaïs, **2:**124
    Bashkirtseff's (Marie) influence on, **2:**306
    The Diary of Anaïs Nin, **2:123–125**
    The Extraordinary Work of Ordinary Writing (Sinor) compared to, **2:**163
Nineteen Eighty-Four (Orwell), **2:**117, 118, 255
Nineteenth Amendment, **1:**13
Nineteenth Century (journal), **2:**307
Ninety-Four Years of a Floating Life (Su), **1:**338

Nisa: The Life and Words of a !Kung Woman (Shostak), **3:37–39**
Nisei Daughter (Sone), **1:**299, 309
Nisei Soldiers Break Their Silence (Tamura), **3:**80
Nixon, Richard, **1:**21, **2:**294, **3:**279
Nkrumah, Kwame, **1:**4
    Ghana, **1:**290, **2:**12, 13
Nobel prizes
    to Buck (Pearl S.), **1:**159
    to García Márquez (Gabriel), **3:**183
    to King (Martin Luther, Jr.), **2:**32
    to Lessing (Doris), **1:**168
    to Luthuli (Albert), **1:**25
    to Maathai (Wangari), **1:**114
    to Mandela (Nelson), **1:**29
    to Menchú (Rigoberta), **3:**164, 165, 166
    to Mistral (Gabriela), **1:**222
    to Neruda (Pablo), **1:**222
    to Soyinka (Wole), **1:**214
    to Wiesel (Elie), **1:**320
Noche de Tlatelolco, La (Poniatowska). See *Massacre in Mexico* (Poniatowska)
Noël Coward Diaries, The (Coward), **2:**152
No Future without Forgiveness (Tutu), **3:**244
No Gods, No Masters (Guérin), **3:**3
Nolan, Janet, **3:**269
Nomad (Hirsi Ali), **1:**209
Nominalism, **1:**239
Nomura, Mary, **3:**104
Nonchronological order
    in *The Dark Child* (Laye), **1:**129
    in *Stop-Time* (Conroy), **1:**164, 165
Nonfiction essays, tradition of, **1:**279
No-No Boy (Okada), **1:**309
Nonviolent movements
    in India, Gandhi (Mohandas) in, **1:**242–244, 289–290
    in South Africa, against apartheid, **1:**24–26
    in U.S., King (Martin Luther, Jr.) in, **2:**32–34
Noonan, Lucille Brody, **3:**119
Norma Rae (film), **3:**98

Norrell, Robert J., **1:**38, 52
Norris, Bruce, *Clybourne Park,* **1:**273
Norris, Leslie, **1:**126
Norris, Randall, *Women of Coal,* **3:**337
North, James W., **2:**333
North, U.S.
    abolitionism in, **1:**33
    in Civil War (See American Civil War)
    Great Migration to, **1:**50, 52, 84, 273, **3:**99
    racial segregation in, **3:**250
    racism in, **1:**122
North American Free Trade Agreement (NAFTA), **3:**304
North American Review (journal), **1:**132, 134, 148, 202, **2:**89, 336
North Carolina, oral histories of coal mining in, **3:**86–87
Northern Expedition, **1:**338
Northern Ireland
    conflict over, **3:**27
    establishment of, **1:**119
North Fork of the Coeur d'Alene River (Russell), **3:**93
North Korea, establishment of (1945), **1:**322
Northside Chronicle, **3:**342
Northup, Solomon, *Twelve Years a Slave,* **1:**50
North Vietnam, establishment of (1954), **1:**335, **3:**279. See also Vietnam War
Norton, M. D. Herter, **2:**149
Norton, W. W., **2:**150
Nostalgia
    for Christmas, Thomas (Dylan) on, **1:**125, 126
    for English rural landscapes, **3:**63
    of Ukrainian miners, **3:**340, 341
Notarianni, Philip, **3:**225
Notebooks (Williams), **2:152–154**
Notebooks and *Letters* (Hawthorne), **2:113, 223–225**
Notebooks of Henry James, The (James), **2:**113, 114, 115
Notes of a Native Son (Baldwin), **1:**79–80

Notes on the State of Virginia (Jefferson), **2:**45, 215
Not Working (Maurer), **3:**277
Novel(s). See also Fiction
    collective, **3:**282, 285
    of manners, **2:**312
Ntirkana, Jackson, *The Last Maasai Warrior,* **1:**114
Nuclear disaster, Chernobyl, **3:**282–285
Nuclear weapons
    movement against, **3:**239, 268, 269
    Pakistani, **1:**87
    U.S. development of, oral histories of, **3:**239–241
    U.S. use of, in World War II, **1:**293–294
Nunavut (Canada), oral histories of Inuits in, **3:**138–140, *139*
Nungarrayi, Molly, **3:**336
Nungarrayi, Rosie, **3:**335
Nuns, American, oral histories of, **3:**308–310
Nuremberg Interviews, The (Goldensohn), **3:**293
Nuremberg Laws of 1935 (Germany), **2:**253, **3:**14
Nuremberg Rallies, **1:**31
Nuremberg trials (1945–1946), **3:**294
    critics of, **2:**56
    oral histories of, **3:**293–295
    outcome of, **2:**56
    Speer (Albert) in, **2:**54, 56
Nursing
    in Crimean War, **1:**111–113
    in World War I, **1:**329, 330, **2:**259–261, *260*
NWLB. See National War Labor Board
NWSA Journal, **3:**338

O

OAH Magazine of History, **3:**101
Oakley, Ann
    "Interviewing Women," **3:**190
    The Sociology of Housework, **3:**144

SUBJECT INDEX

Obama, Barack, **1:**79
    The Audacity of Hope, **1:**78, 80
    Dreams from My Father, **1:**78–80
    King's (Martin Luther, Jr.) influence on, **2:**33
Obama, Barack, Sr., **1:**78, 79, 80
Obama, Sasha, **1:**79
Obermeyer, Brice, *Delaware Tribe in a Cherokee Nation,* **3:**326
O'Brien, Glen, **3:**316
O'Brien, Tim, **3:**201
    Going after Cacciato, **1:**335
O Brother Where Art Thou (film), **3:**159
Observer (newspaper), **1:**80, **2:**153, **3:**235, 236
O'Casey, Sean, **1:**119, **3:**27
    The Silver Tassie, **1:**329
Ocasio-Melendez, Marcial, **3:**122
Occom, Samson
    "A Short Narrative of My Life," **1:**56
    Wheatley's (Phillis) letter to, **2:**44–46
Occupying Power (Kovner), **3:**128
"Occupy" movement, **3:**328
O'Connor, Flannery, **2:**130
    "A Good Man Is Hard to Find," **2:**130
    The Habit of Being, **2:**129–132
    Mystery and Manners, **2:**131
O'Connor, Frank, **1:**119
O'Connor, K. C., **3:**19, 332
October Revolution (1917), **1:**270
O'Donnell, James, **1:**197, 198
O'Faolain, Sean, **1:**119
O'Faolin, Nuala, **1:**119
O'Farrell, Brigid, *Rocking the Boat,* **3:**337
Ofer, Dalia, **3:**35
Offences Against the Person Act of 1861 (Britain), **3:**70
Off Our Backs (magazine), **1:**336, **2:**4
Oglala Sioux. *See* Lakota Sioux
O'Grady, Sean, **3:**316
O'Grady, Timothy, *Ireland's Unfinished Revolution,* **3:**27–30
Ogun (deity), **1:**216
O'Hara, Daniel, **2:**128

O'Hara, John, **2:**137
Ohio History (journal), **3:**326
Ohitika Woman (Brave Bird), **1:**21, 23
Oil industry, in Iran, **3:**218
Okada, John, *No-No Boy,* **1:**309
Okigbo, Christopher, **1:**214
Okihiro, Gary Y., **3:**197
Oklahoma, forced relocation of Delaware Indians to, **3:**325
Okubo, Miné, *Citizen 13660,* **1:**299
"Old Times on the Mississippi" (Twain), **1:**146
Old Wives' Tale, The (Bennett), **2:**136
"Old Woman's Gossip, An" (Kemble), **2:**335
Oliphant, Margaret, **2:**210
    Autobiography, **2:**335
Olive Schreiner Prize, for *Country of My Skull* (Krog), **3:**243
Olivier, Gerrit, **3:**243
Olivieri, Giovanni, **2:**160
Olney, James
    Autobiography: Essays Theoretical and Critical, **1:**246–248, *247*
    Memory and Narrative, **1:**246, 248
    Metaphors of Self, **1:**246
    Tell Me Africa, **1:**246
Olschki, Leonardo, **1:**105, 107
Olson, Ray, **3:**229
Olympica, Nazaria, **2:**160, 161
Olympics, **1:**158, **3:**32
O'Malley, Andrew, **1:**157
O'Malley, Ernie, *The Singing Flame,* **3:**27
Ombudsman, origin of term, **3:**154
Omni-Americans, The (Murray), **1:**124
Omori, Annie Shepley, **2:**190, 290, 292
O'Nan, Stewart, **3:**211
"On Being Brought from Africa to America" (Wheatley), **2:**46
Once They Hear My Name (Lee et al.), **1:**102
Ondaatje, Michael, *Running in the Family,* **1:**88
On Diary (Lejeune), **2:**174, 175
One Day in the Life of Ivan Denisovich (Solzhenitsyn), **3:**17
O'Neill, Eugene, **2:**152

O'Neill, Kevin, **2:**159
O'Neill, Michael, **3:**55
Only What We Could Carry (Inada), **3:**80
Ono Kazuko, **3:**149
On Records (Newman), **3:**326
On the Origin of Species (Darwin), **1:**65
"On the Pulse of the Morning" (Angelou), **1:**20
On the Road (Kerouac), **1:**234
Opequon, Battle of (1862), **2:**272
Operas, Chinese, **1:**159
Operation Bootstrap, **1:**108
Operation Desert Storm. *See* Gulf War
Operation Pedro Pan, **1:**298
Opium, Marcus Aurelius and, **1:**221
Oppenheimer, Gerald M.
    AIDS Doctors, **3:**272, 273, 274
    Shattered Dreams?, **3:**272–274
Oppenheimer, J. Robert, **3:**240, *240,* 241
Oppenheimer, Peter, **3:**240
Oppenheimer, Toni, **3:**240
Opper, Frederick, **3:**4
Oppression
    communist, in China, **1:**338
    of indigenous people of Guatemala, **3:**164–166
    political, in East Germany, **3:**245–246
    racial, Angelou (Maya) on, **1:**18
Oral American Historians Magazine, **3:**21
Oral contraceptives, **3:**170, *171*
Oral histories. *See also specific works and writers*
    Abrams (Lynn) on theory of, **3:**173–175
    audio vs. print recording of, **3:**65
    class differences in collection of, **3:**177
    definitions of, **3:**97, 158, 285
    economic disparities in collection of, **3:**190
    evaluation of reliability of, **3:**281
    four forms of, **3:**174
    Frisch (Michael) on shared authority in, **3:**179–181, 190

guidelines for collecting, **3:**187–188, 313

internationalization of, **3:**129

motivations for collecting, **3:**135

origins and development of field, **3:**37, 157, 173, 179–181, 186

Popular Memory Group on need for, **3:**176–178

Portelli (Alessandro) in field of, **3:**159, 173, 267

as primary sources in field of history, **3:**281

recognition of value of, **3:**20, 64, 90, 173, 186

as social change agent, **3:**86, 186, 187

subjectivity in, **3:**162, 173, 186

technological advances in, **3:**181

Thompson (Paul) on value of, **3:**186–189, 209

of women, feminist approach to, **3:**190–192

Oral Histories of First to Fourth Generation Americans (Lee), **3:**83

Oral History (journal)

"ANZAC Memories" (Thomson) in, **3:**177, 178

on *Daring Hearts* (Brighton Ourstory), **3:**72

on *The Death of Luigi Trastulli* (Portelli), **3:**159

on *Ireland's Unfinished Revolution* (Griffith and O'Grady), **3:**29

"popular memory" issue of, **3:**177, 178

on *The Voice of the Past* (Thompson), **3:**188

on *Women's Words* (Gluck and Patai), **3:**192

on *Working-Class Childhood* (Seabrook), **3:**54

on *The World at War* (Holmes), **3:**235

Oral History, Health and Welfare (Bornat et al.), **3:170–172**

"Oral History and the Digital Revolution" (Frisch), **3:**181

Oral History Association Book Award, for *The Order Has Been Carried Out* (Portelli), **3:**265, 267

Oral History of Abraham Lincoln, An (Burlingame), **3:261–264**

Oral History of Tribal Warfare, An (Fadiman), **3:**141

Oral History Project: The Early Days of Labor Arbitration (Dash), **3:**153

Oral History Reader, The (Perks and Thomson), **3:**173, 178, 179, 181

Oral History Review (journal)

on *Always a People* (Kohn and Montell), **3:**109

on *And Justice for All* (Tateishi), **3:**197

on *Children of Los Alamos* (Mason), **3:**240

on *Chinese Lives* (Zhang and Sang), **3:**301

on *Coal Hollow* (Light and Light), **3:**67

on *The Death of Luigi Trastulli* (Portelli), **3:**159

on *El Salvador at War* (Manwaring and Prisk), **3:**207

on *Everything We Had* (Santoli), **3:**210, 211

on *The Firm* (Bruce), **3:**246

on *The First Agraristas* (Craig), **3:**303

on *"The Good War"* (Terkel), **3:**213

on *Habits of Change* (Rogers), **3:**309

on *The Hispanic-American Entrepreneur* (Owsley), **3:**122

on *In the Mansion of Confucius' Descendants* (Kong and Ke), **3:**125

on *Japan at War* (Cook and Cook), **3:**216

on *Japanese War Brides in America* (Crawford et al.), **3:**128, 129

on *Long Journey Home* (Brown and Kohn), **3:**326

on *Oral History Theory* (Abrams), **3:**174

on *The Order Has Been Carried Out* (Portelli), **3:**266

on *Peacework* (Adams), **3:**269

on *A Shared Authority* (Frisch), **3:**179, 180, 181

on *Shattered Dreams?* (Oppenheimer and Bayer), **3:**273

on *The Strength Not to Fight* (Tollefson), **3:**223

on *Survivors* (Miller and Miller), **3:**41

on *Swiftwater People* (Russell), **3:**95

on *They Say in Harlan County* (Portelli), **3:**97

Thomson (Alistair) in, **3:**135

on *The Voice of the Past* (Thompson), **3:**188

on *Voices from this Long Brown Land* (Wehrey), **3:**103

on *Witnesses to Nuremberg* (Stave et al.), **3:**294

on *Witnesses to the Holocaust* (Lewin), **3:**51

on *Women in the Mines* (Moore), **3:**339

on *Women's Words* (Gluck and Patai), **3:**191

Oral History Society, **3:**65, 170, 172

Oral History Society (journal), **3:**5

Oral History Theory (Abrams), **3:173–175**, 179, 181, 285

Oral traditions

African, **1:**64, **2:**242

African American, **1:**262

Irish, **1:**121

Kabyle, **1:**93

Native American, **1:**21, 54, 55, 96, 302, 304, **3:**138

VaShawasha, **3:**251, 252

Welsh, **1:**125

Oratorical autobiography, *Eighty Years and More* (Stanton) as, **1:**14

Ordeal of Mansart, The (Du Bois), **1:**5

Order Has Been Carried Out, The (Portelli), **3:**158, **265–267**

Oregon, Japanese immigrants in, **3:**80–82, *81*

Oregon Historical Quarterly, **3:**82

Oregon Trail, The (Parkman), **1:**234

Oregon Treaty (1846), **2:**69

Organisation de l'Armee Secrete, **2:**262

Organization of American Historians: Magazine of History, **3:**277

Oriental Observer (periodical), **1:**277

Origin and Development of Psychoanalysis, The (Freud), **2:**175

SUBJECT INDEX

Origin myths. *See* Creation stories
Orlando (Woolf), **1:**173, **2:**64, 181
Orleck, Annelise, *Storming Caesars Palace,* **3:**254
Orphans
    of influenza pandemic, **1:**258
    Kim (Elizabeth) as, **1:**102
    Korean, **1:**102
    McCarthy (Mary) as, **1:**259
Orthodox Jews, **3:**16
Orwell, George
    Animal Farm, **2:**117, *118*
    on *An Autobiography* (Gandhi), **1:**244
    Burmese Days, **2:**119
    Complete Works of George Orwell, **2:**117, 118
    Conroy (Frank) influenced by, **1:**164
    Diaries, 1931–1949, **2:117–119**
    Nineteen Eighty-Four, **2:**117, 118, 255
    The Road to Wigan Pier, **2:**117, **3:**66
Osamu, Tezuka, *Atom Boy,* **1:**293
Osborne, Dorothy, *The Love Letters of Dorothy Osborne to Sir William Temple,* **2:324–327**
Osio, Antonio María, *The History of Alta California,* **3:**115
Oslo Accords (1993), **2:**50, 52
Osorio, Arana, **1:**99
Osterud, Nancy Gray, **3:**135–136, 137
O'Sullivan, John, *"We Have Just Begun to Not Fight",* **3:227–230**
Osur, Alan M., **3:**249
Ota, Shelley, *Upon Their Shoulders,* **1:**309
Otero Silva, Miguel, **1:**222
O'Toole, Sean, **2:**115
Ottoman Empire
    in Armenian genocide, **3:**40–42
    in Crimean War, **1:**113
    Jewish immigration to China from, **3:**16
    Young Turk Revolution in, **2:**106
Ottway, Sheila, **1:**316–317
Ou, Li, **2:**147

Our Appalachia (Shackelford and Weinberg), **3:**66, **86–89**
Our Nig (Wilson), **1:**142
Our Partnership (Webb), **2:**17, 172
OurStory Scotland, **3:**70
"Our Struggles for Progress" (Luthuli), **1:**25
Our Village (Mitford), **3:**59
Outlook (journal), **1:**50, 51, **3:**119
Out of Darkness (Martin), **3:**40
"Outpost of Progress, An" (Conrad), **2:**192, 194
Outsider literature, *The Cancer Journals* (Lorde) as, **2:**3
Overboe, James, **1:**8
Overland Monthly and Out West Magazine, **2:**127
Owen, Robert Dale, **1:**14
Owen, Wilfred
    "Disabled," **1:**8
    Sassoon (Siegfried) and, **2:**247, 248
Owens Valley, The (Wehrey), **3:**102
Owens Valley (California), oral histories of, **3:**102–104, *103*
Owsley, Beatrice Rodriguez, *The Hispanic-American Entrepreneur,* **3:121–123**
Oxford University, **2:**287
Ozersky, Josh, **1:**188
Oziewicz, Stanley, **3:**301

P

PAC. *See* Pan African Congress
Pace, Michael, **3:**326
Pacheco, José Emilio, **3:**31, 32
Pacific Coast Philology (journal), **1:**93
Pacific Historical Review (journal), **3:**148, 225
Pacific Review (journal), **3:**126
Pacifism. *See also* Conscientious objectors
    of Brittain (Vera), **1:**329–331, **2:**269
    of Kingston (Maxine Hong), **1:**175
    of Partridge (Frances), **2:**268–269

Pacifist's War, A (Partridge), **2:268–270**
Pack, Sam, **3:**320
Packer, George, **2:**322
Pacte autobiographique, Le (Lejeune). *See Autobiographical Pact, The* (Lejeune)
Paderni, Paola, **3:**149
Padilla, Herberto, *Self-Portrait of the Other,* **1:**296
Padilla, Tanalis, **3:**303
Paekpom Ilchi (Kim), **1:322–324**
Page, Thomas Nelson, *Marse Chan,* **2:**250
Pahlavi, Ashraf, *Faces in a Mirror,* **3:**218
Paige, Leroy "Satchel," **1:**247
Paine, Albert Bigelow, **1:**148
Painter, Nell Irvin, **1:**3–4
Paintings, by Bashkirtseff (Marie), **2:**306, *307,* 308
Paiute tribe, **3:**102, 103
Pakistan
    Ahmedi's (Farah) escape from Afghanistan to, **1:**40, 41
    establishment of (1947), **1:**87, 244
    legacy of colonialism in, **1:**87–89
    Suleri (Sara) on life in, **1:**87–89
    U.S. relations with, **1:**87
Pakravan, Fatemeh, *Memoirs of Fatemeh Pakravan,* **3:**218–220
Pakravan, Hassan, **3:**218–220
Pakravan, Saïdeh, **3:**218
Palestine, under British Mandate
    'Amr (Sāmī) on life in, **2:**104–106
    Jewish immigration to, **2:**105, **3:**14
Palestine Broadcasting Service (PBS), **1:**227
Palestine-Israel Journal of Politics, Economics, and Culture, **2:**50
Palestine Liberation Organization (PLO), **2:**50
Palestinian autobiographical writing. *See also specific works and writers*
    by 'Amr (Sāmī), **2:**104–106
    by Darwish (Mahmoud), **1:**255–257
    by Ghazzawi ('Izzat), **2:**50–52
    tradition of, **1:**225–226, **2:**50, 104
    by Tuqan (Fadwa), **1:**225–227

Palestinian–Israeli conflict. *See* Israeli–Palestinian conflict
Palestinian nationalism, **1:**225, 227
Palestinian Notebooks (Bisisu), **2:**50
Palestinian Policeman (Courtney), **2:**104
Palestinian statehood, calls for, **2:**50, 52
Palestinian territories, Israeli occupation of, **1:**225, **2:**50, *51*
Paley, William, *Natural Theology,* **1:**65
Pall Mall Gazette (newspaper), **2:**83
Palmer, Michele, *Witnesses to Nuremberg,* **3:293–295**
Pan African Congress (PAC), **1:**25
Pan-Indian movement, **1:**54
Papago culture, Chona (Maria) on life in, **1:69,** 69–71
Paquet, Sandra, "The Enigma of Arrival," **1:**112–113
Paradise of the Blind (Duong), **1:**335
Paradox, in *In the Presence of Absence* (Darwish), **1:**255, 256
Paranoia, in East Germany, **3:**245
Paretskaya, Anna, **3:**332
Paris (France)
  American expatriates in, **2:**101
  Gellhorn (Martha) in, **2:**101
  nineteenth-century, Goncourts (Jules and Edmond de) on life in, **2:**81–83
  Wright's (Richard) move to, **1:**124
Paris, Treaty of (1783), **2:**69
Paris Commune of 1871, **3:**3
Paris France (Stein), **1:**332
Park, Eugene, **1:**324
Parker, Dorothy, **1:**258, **2:**133, 134
Parker, John, **2:**205, 206, 207
Parkins, Ilya, **1:**331
Parkman, Francis, **1:**146
  The Oregon Trail, **1:**234
Parks, Rosa, **1:38, 3:45**
  and civil rights movement in Detroit, **3:**101
  I Am Rosa Parks, **1:**38
  Quiet Strength, **1:**38
  Rosa Parks: My Story, **1:**19, **37–39**

Parliament, British
  in English Civil War (*See* English Civil War)
  on women miners, **3:**337
Parliament, European, **3:**292
Parr, Joy, **3:**181
Parr, Katherine, **2:**97, 99
  Lamentation of a Sinner, **2:**97
Parrington, Vernon, **2:**213
Parry, David, **1:**183, 184–185
Parry, Edward Abbott, **2:**324, 325
Parsons, Daniel, **2:**256, 257–258
Parsons, Neil, **2:**241
Partido Independiente de Color (PIC), **3:**8
Partido Revolucionario Institucional, **3:**303
Partisan Review (journal), **1:**258, 272
Partridge, Frances, *A Pacifist's War,* **2:268–270,** *269*
Partridge, Ralph, **2:**268, 269
Pascal, Blaise, *Pensées,* **1:**218
Pascal, Roy, **1:**246
Passerini, Luisa, **3:**74, 159, 173
"Passing"
  as black, **1:**74
  as white, **1:**72
Pass Laws Act of 1952 (South Africa), **1:**24, 25
Patai, Daphne, *Women's Words,* **3:190–192**
Pater, Walter, **1:**264, **2:**183, 184
  The Child in the House, **1:**276
Patmore, Coventry, **2:**147
Paton, Alan, *Cry, the Beloved Country,* **1:**27
Patriarchy
  Italian Renaissance, **2:**160
  in Montenegro, **3:**135, 136, 137
  Palestinian, Tuqan's (Fadwa) critique of, **1:**226, 227
Patriotism. *See also* Nationalism
  British, of Barnard (Anne), **2:**217, 218, 219
Patterson, David, **2:**24
Paul, Moses, **2:**46
Paula (Allende), **1:**222
Payn, Graham, **2:**152

Payne, Ethel, **3:**199–200
Payne, James Robert, *Multicultural Autobiography,* **1:**247–248
Paz, Octavio, **3:**32
  In Light of India, **1:**222–223
PBS. *See* Palestine Broadcasting Service
Peabody Western Coal Company, **3:**11
Peace activists, women, oral histories of, **3:**268–271
Peace Like a River (Enger), **1:**281
Peacework (Adams), **3:268–271**
Peacocks Fly to the Southeast, The, **1:**338
Peake, Cyrus H., *Chinese Missionaries Oral History Collection,* **3:**299
Pearce, Jenny, *Promised Land,* **3:**205–206
Pearl Harbor, Japanese bombing of, **1:**299, 300, 309, **3:**195, 202, 212, 215, 234
Pearlman, Elihu, **2:**73
Pearl of China (Min), **1:**159
Pearse, Patrick, **3:**27
Pearson, Geoffrey, *Hooligan,* **3:**312
Pechonick, Paula Martin, **3:**326
Peckard, Peter, **1:**83
Pedersen, David, **3:**207
Pedro Martinez (Lewis), **3:**31
Pedro Pan, Operation, **1:**298
Peer pressure, *Go Ask Alice* (anonymous) on, **2:**295
Pekar, Harvey
  American Splendor, **1:**139, **3:**330
  Students for a Democratic Society, **3:**330
  Studs Turkel's Working, **3:**330
Pelagius, **1:**196, 198
Peled-Elhanan, Nurit, **2:**50–51
Peltier, Leonard, *Prison Writings,* **1:96–98,** *97*
PEN/Faulkner Award, for *The Barracks Thief* (Wolff), **1:**47
Penn, William, **2:**26, **3:**327
Pennsylvania
  Ukraine compared to, **3:**340, 342
  women immigrants in, oral histories of, **3:**305–307
Pennsylvania History (journal), **2:**79, **3:**191, 306

SUBJECT INDEX

Pensées (Pascal), **1:**218
Pepys, Samuel, **2:73**
    Boswell (James) compared to, **2:**328
    The Diary of Samuel Pepys, **2:72–74,** 174, 309, 328
    Evelyn (John) compared to, **2:**65, 66, 72
    on *A True Relation of My Birth, Breeding, and Life* (Cavendish), **1:**230
Percy, Walker, **2:**129
Peregrinationes in Montem Zion (Breidenbach), **2:**227
Perera, Victor
    The Cross and the Pear Tree, **1:**99
    "Guatemala: Always La Violencia," **1:**99
    Rites: A Guatemalan Boyhood, **1:**75, **99–101**
    Unfinished Conquest, **1:**99
Perestroika, **3:**17, 331
Perestroika from Below (documentary), **3:**340
Pérez Firmat, Gustavo, *Next Year in Cuba,* **1:**296
Pérez Rosales, Vicente, *Recuerdos del pasado,* **1:**222
Perils of the Soul (Guiteras-Holmes), **3:**167
Perissinotto, Giorgio, **3:**116
Perkins, Charlie, **1:**149
Perks, Robert
    Oral History, Health and Welfare, **3:170–172**
    The Oral History Reader, **3:**173, 178, 179, 181
Perlman, Itzhak, **1:**272
Perloff, Marjorie, **2:**150
Pernicone, Nunzio, *Carlo Tresca,* **3:**5
Perón, Eva, **3:**73, *74,* 75
Perón, Juan, **2:**220, **3:**73, 75
Peronism, **3:**73–75
Perrucci, Robert, **3:**207
Perry, Lorry, **2:**175
Perry, Yaakov, **1:**17
Persecution, of Jews. See Holocaust
Persepolis (Satrapi), **1:**139, 141, **155–157,** *156,* 293

Persia
    Lessing (Doris) on life in, **1:**167
    Polo's (Marco) travels in, **1:**106, 107
Persian Gulf War (1991). See Gulf War
Persian Sphinx, The (Milani), **3:**218, 219
Persona, Wells (H. G.) on, **1:**252
Personal finances. See Finances
Personalist Forum (journal), **1:**183
Personality and Individual Differences (journal), **2:**124
Perspective. See Narrative point of view
Petals of Blood (Ngũgĩ), **2:**12
Peters, H. F., **2:**150
Peterson, Andrea, **1:**331
Petilianus, **1:**196
Peyser, Seymour, **3:**293–294
Phaler, Karl, **3:**209
Pham Thanh Cong, **1:336**
Pham Van Xinh, **3:**281
Phelps, Elizabeth Porter, **2:**332
Philadelphia Inquirer (newspaper), **3:**222
Philadelphia Jewish Voice (journal), **3:**16
Philippi, Bernardo, **1:**77
Phillips, Bruce "Utah," **3:**329
Phillips, Richard, **2:**35
Phillips, Wendell, **1:**33
Phillpotts, Eden, **2:**137
Philosophical autobiographies
    The Autobiography of Giambattista Vico (Vico) as, **1:**183–185
    Confessions (Rousseau) as, **1:**200–202
    Journals of Søren Kierkegaard (Kierkegaard) as, **2:**166–168
    Meditations (Marcus Aurelius) as, **1:**218–221
    tradition of, **1:**183–184
Philosophy, natural, **2:**300
Philosophy and Social Criticism (journal), **2:**168
Philosophy East and West (journal), **3:**148
Photography
    in *Coal Hollow* (Light and Light), **3:**66, 67

    in *Long Journey Home* (Brown and Kohn), **3:**326
    in oral history field, **3:**181
    in *Solidarity Forever* (Bird et al.), **3:**329
Phylon (journal), **2:**33
PIC. See Partido Independiente de Color
Picasso, Pablo, **1:**332
Picture of Dorian Gray, The (Wilde), **2:**9
Pierce, Franklin, **2:**223
Piercy, Marge, **2:**4
Pif Magazine, **1:**297
Pigafetta, Antonio, *Journal of Magellan's Voyage,* **2:**201
Pignalosa, Giovanni, **3:**159
Pilgrimages
    of Guylforde (Richarde), **2:**226–228
    in Middle Ages, **1:190,** 191, **2:**226
    tradition of narratives of, **2:**198–199, 226
Pilgrim at Tinker Creek (Dillard), **1:**279
Pillow Book, The (Sei), **2:**59, 189, 190, 290
Pine, Frank Woodworth, **1:**181
Pine Ridge Reservation (South Dakota)
    AIM occupation of Wounded Knee at, **1:**21, 22–23, 96
    Peltier (Leonard) in shootout at, **1:**96
Pini, Robert, **1:**115
Pinochet, Augusto, **1:**75, 77, 222, **3:**185
Piper, Jane, **3:**276, 277
Pipino, Francesco, **1:**107
Pitt, William, the Elder, **2:**328
Pitt, William, the Younger, **2:**217
Pitt-Rivers, Julian, **3:**168, 169
Pittsburgh (Pennsylvania)
    Ukraine compared to, **3:**340, 342
    women immigrants in, oral histories of, **3:**305–307
Pittsburgh Courier (newspaper), **3:**248
Pittsfield Free Press, **3:**263
Plaatje, Solomon Tshekisho
    The Boer War Diary of Sol Plaatje, **2:241–243**

Mhudi, **2:**241, 243

Native Life in South Africa, **2:**241, 242, 243

Places of Origin (Edwards and Siebentritt), **3:**205

Plagiarism. *See also* Authorship

    Carver (Jonathan) accused of, **2:**205, 206, 207

    Cereta (Laura) accused of, **2:**160

    by Mahomet (Dean), **2:**229

Plain, Gill, **2:**237

Plassey, Battle of (1757), **2:**229

Plath, Aurelia Schober, **2:**47–49

Plath, Sylvia, **2:**48

    Ariel, **2:**47

    The Bell Jar, **2:**47

    Letters Home, **2:**47–49

    The Unabridged Journals of Sylvia Plath, **2:**49

Plath, Warren, **2:**47

Plato, *Seventh Letter,* **2:**94

Plessy v. Ferguson, **1:**37, 50, 122

Pliny the Elder, **2:**94, 96

Pliny the Younger, *The Letters of the Younger Pliny,* **2:94–96,** 95

PLO. *See* Palestine Liberation Organization

Plöckinger, Othmar, **1:**32

Plotinus, *Enneads,* **1:**196

Plum, Fred, **1:**6

Plumstead, A. W., **2:**215

Plunka, Gene A., **2:**255

PMLA (journal), **1:**147, **2:**63

Poddar, Prem, **3:**143

Poe, Edgar Allan, **2:**42

    Collected Letters, **2:**41

    "Letter to Maria Clemm," **2:41–43**

    "Ligeia," **3:**38

Poe, Neilson, **2:**41–42

Poe, Virginia Clemm, **2:**41–43

Poems on Various Subjects (Wheatley), **2:**44

Poetic style

    of *Black Boy* (Wright), **1:**123

    of *Child of the Dark* (de Jesus), **2:**6, 7

    of *A Cross and a Star* (Agosín), **1:**76

    of *The Dark Child* (Laye), **1:**128, 129

    of *The Journals of Charlotte Forten Grimké* (Grimké), **2:**30

    of *Memoirs* (Neruda), **1:**223

    of *A Mountainous Journey* (Tuqan), **1:**227

    of *Narrative of the Life of Frederick Douglass* (Douglass), **1:**35

    of *The Way to Rainy Mountain* (Momaday), **1:**55

    of *The Writing Life* (Dillard), **1:**280

Poetique (journal), **2:**174

Poetry. *See also specific poets*

    in *Confessions of Lady Nijo* (Nijo), **2:**59, 60

    Japanese *waka,* **2:**189, 191, 292

    in *Letters Underway* (Ghazzawi), **2:**51–52

    in medieval Arab education, **1:**287

    on racism, effects of, **1:**50

    Romantic, **2:**143, 146

    social role of, Neruda (Pablo) on, **1:**222, 223

    in *Ten Thousand Sorrows* (Kim), **1:**103

    in *When I Was Puerto Rican* (Santiago), **1:**108

Point of view. *See* Narrative point of view

Pokagon, Simon, *Queen of the Woods,* **3:**110

Poland

    Jewish immigration to China from, **3:**16

    Russian occupation of, **2:**192

Police, East German. *See* Stasi

Polish American Studies (journal), **3:**307

Polish autobiographical writing, by Conrad (Joseph), **2:**192–194

Politeness, in letter writing, **2:**217

Political activism

    of Douglass (Frederick), **1:**34, 35

    of Kingston (Maxine Hong), **1:**175

    of Soyinka (Wole), **1:**214

Political autobiography, *Dreams from My Father* (Obama) as, **1:**78–80

Political development

    of Guevara (Ernesto "Che"), **2:**220–222

    of Lu Xun, **2:**170–172

Political parties. *See specific parties*

Politics and Irish Life (Fitzpatrick), **3:**27

Politics of AIDS Denialism, The (Fourie and Meyer), **3:**272

Polk County (Hurston), **1:**10

Pollard, Edward, **2:**39

Pollin, Burton R., **2:**41, 42

Pollitt, Katha, **2:**124

Polner, Murray, **3:**16

Polo, Marco, *The Travels of Marco Polo,* **1:105–107,** 106, **2:**198, 201

Pol Pot, **1:**306

Pommelier, Alfred, **3:**344

Pompeii, destruction of, **2:**94, 95

Poniatowska, Elena, **3:**32

    Here's to You, Jesus, **3:**32

    Massacre in Mexico, **3:**31–33

Poole, Elijah. *See* Muhammad, Elijah

Pooley, William V., **2:**92

Poor Bear, Myrtle, **1:**97

Poore, Charles, **1:**259

Poor Man's Son, The (Feraoun), **2:**262, 263, 264

Poor Richard's Almanac (Franklin), **2:**88

Pope, Alexander, **2:**146, 217, 328

Popkin, Jeremy D., **2:**174, 175

Popular culture

    Boswell (James) in, **2:**328

    Byron (George Gordon Noel) in, **2:**145

    Darwin (Charles) in, **1:**67

    Guevara (Ernesto "Che") in, **2:**221

Popular Memory Group, "Popular Memory: Theory, Politics, Method," **3:176–178**

"Popular Memory: Theory, Politics, Method" (Popular Memory Group), **3:176–178**

Popular Movements and Political Change in Mexico (Craig), **3:**302

Pork Rind and Cuban Songs (Medina), **1:**296

Porte, Joel, **2:**140

Portelli, Alessandro
 The Battle of Valle Giula, **3:**97, 157
 The Death of Luigi Trastulli, **3:**96, **157–160**
 in field of oral history, **3:**159, 173
 I Can Almost See the Lights of Home, **3:**265–266
 The Order Has Been Carried Out, **3:**158, **265–267**
 They Say in Harlan County, **3:**87, **96–98,** 158
Porter, Jay, *Fighting Words,* **1:**97
Porter, Katherine Anne, **2:**152
Porter, Tracey, *Treasures in the Dust,* **1:**161
Porterfield, Amanda, **3:**112
Portrait of a Lady, The (James), **1:**133, **2:**113
Portrait of the Artist as a Young Man (Joyce), **1:**276, **2:**126
Portraits in Steel (Frisch), **3:**181
Port Royal Experiment, **2:**29–31
Portugal
 colonial power of, origins of, **2:**198
 Gama's (Vasco da) exploration for, **2:**198–200
 national identity of, **2:**199–200
Portuguese Studies (journal), **2:**200
Positions Asia Critique (journal), **1:**336
Positions: East Asia Cultures Critique (journal), **2:**292
Posner, Jerome B., **1:**6
Possession (Byatt), **2:**77
Postcolonial identity, **1:**87–89
Postcolonialism
 in *Meatless Days* (Suleri), **1:**87–89
 Orwell (George) in, **2:**119
Postcolonial studies
 The Boer War Diary of Sol Plaatje (Plaatje) in, **2:**243
 The Letters of Lady Anne Barnard to Henry Dundas (Barnard) in, **2:**218–219
 Memoirs of an Arabian Princess from Zanzibar (Ruete) in, **1:**90–91
 My Life Story (Amrouche) in, **1:**94
 The Unwanted (Nguyen) in, **1:**172
 The Wonderful Adventures of Mrs. Seacole (Seacole) in, **1:**112

Postman, Neil, **3:**119
Postmodern, origins of term, **1:**167
Postmodern autobiography
 Dreams from My Father (Obama) as, **1:**79
 Meatless Days (Suleri) as, **1:**87–89
 Under My Skin (Lessing) as, **1:**167–169
 The Woman Warrior (Kingston) as, **1:**173, 174
Postmodernism
 Kierkegaard's (Søren) influence on, **2:**167
 origins and rise of, **1:**167
 self in, **1:**167
 truth in, **1:**168
Poststructuralism, **1:**267
Potawatomi tribe, **3:**110
Potter, Hillary, **3:**122
Potter, Martha Beatrice. *See* Webb, Beatrice
Potter, Tiffany, **1:**327–328
Pottle, Frederick, **2:**328
Pound, Ezra, **2:**126
Poverty
 difficulty of defining, **3:**255
 primary, **3:**53
Poverty, in Britain
 in English villages, **3:**59
 McCourt (Frank) on, **1:**119–121
 in Victorian era, **2:**16
 among working class, **3:**53
Poverty, in Latin America
 in Brazil, de Jesus (Carolina Maria) on, **2:**6–8
 in Guatemala, Menchú (Rigoberta) on, **3:**164–165
 Guevara (Ernesto "Che") on, **2:**220–221
Poverty, in U.S.
 among coal miners, **3:**66, 67
 war on, oral histories of, **3:**254–256
 Wright (Richard) on, **1:**122
Powell, Enoch, **3:**186
Powell, Malea, **3:**109
Powers, Lyall H., **2:**113, 115
Powers, William, **3:**111–112

Powwows, **3:**108
Pozas, Ricardo, *Juan the Chamula,* **3:167–169**
Pozzetta, George, **3:**225
"Practice of the Private Journal" (Lejeune), **2:174–176**
Praeterita (Ruskin), **1:264–266**
Pragmatism, of Washington (Booker T.), **1:**51, 52
Prague (Czechoslovakia), Kafka (Franz) on life in, **2:**120–122
Prague Spring (1968), **3:**33
Pran, Dith, *Children's of Cambodia's Killing Fields,* **1:**306
Pratt, Mary Louise, **3:**166
Pratt, Richard Henry, **3:**109
Preciado Martin, Patricia
 Beloved Land, **3:**131
 Images and Conversations, **3:**121
 Songs My Mother Sang to Me, **3:131–134,** 302
Preece, Harold, **1:**10
Prejudice. *See also* Anti-Semitism; Racism
 against homosexuality, **1:**139
Prelude, The (Wordsworth), **1:**201, 264, **2:**302
Prendergast, Christopher, **1:**268–269
Prescott, Orville, **1:**271
Presidential elections, U.S.
 of 1860, **3:**261
 of 1992, **3:**221
Presidential oral histories
 of Johnson (Lyndon Baines), **3:**254–256
 of Lincoln (Abraham), **3:**261–264
 tradition of, **3:**254
Presidential Studies Quarterly, **2:**33, **3:**263
Presidios, of California, **3:**114–116
Press coverage. *See* Journalism; War correspondents
Prester John's Letter on the Wonders of India, **1:**105
Pretty-Shield (Linderman), **1:**70
Pride, cultural, of Woodland Indians, **3:**108, 109
Priestley, J. B., **2:**137
Primary poverty, **3:**53

"Primitive" mind, theories of, **3**:37
Primm, Alex T., **3**:326
Prince, Mary, *The History of Mary Prince,* **1**:111, 113, **3**:23–26
Prince, Nancy, *Narrative of the Life and Travels of Mrs. Nancy Prince,* **3**:24
Principle Navigations, Voiages, Traffiques and Discoveries of the English Nation, The (Hakluyt), **2**:229
Principles of Geology (Lyell), **1**:65
Pringle, Thomas, **3**:23, 24–25
Printz, Mike, **3**:225
Prisk, Court, *El Salvador at War,* **3:205–208**
Prison. *See* Imprisonment
Prison narratives, Arabic tradition of, **2**:50. *See also specific works*
Prison Writings (Peltier), **1:96–98**
Pritchard, William, **1**:168
Pritchett, V. S., **3**:60
Privacy
    of diaries, as defining characteristic, **2**:174
    under East German Stasi, **3**:245
    James's (Henry) concern with, **2**:114, 115
    of Kierkegaard (Søren), violation of, **2**:166, 167
    in *Letters between Two* (Lu and Xu), **2**:171
    Maugham's (W. Somerset) concern with, **2**:183, 185
Private Journal of Aaron Burr, The (Burr), **2**:88
Private Mary Chesnut, The (Chesnut), **2**:250
Prix Européen de l'Essai Charles Veillon, Le, for *The Dark Child* (Laye), **1**:128
Prix Goncourt, establishment of, **2**:82
Profiling, racial, **3**:195, 197
Progoff, Ira, **2**:123
Progress
    industrialization in Keats's (John) concept of, **2**:146
    national, Emerson (Ralph Waldo) on, **2**:139, 140
Prohibition, in Idaho, **3**:95

Prohibition of Mixed Marriages Act of 1949 (South Africa), **1**:27
Project Gen, **1**:294
Proletarian Cultural Revolution. *See* Cultural Revolution
Promised Land (Pearce), **3**:205–206
Propaganda
    British, in World War II, **2**:270
    in Cultural Revolution of China, **1**:158, 159, *162*
    Orwell (George) on, **2**:117, 118
    Soviet, in World War II, **2**:282
    in Vietnam, **1**:171
Proposition 209 (California), **3**:20
Prose, Francine, **2**:231, 339, 340
Protection of State Information Bill (South Africa), **1**:29
Protestantism. *See also specific types*
    origins of, **1**:211
    rise of, in England, **2**:97–99
Protestant Reformation, **1**:211, **2**:72, 166
Protocols of the Elder of Zion, The, **1**:32
Proust, Marcel
    In Search of Lost Time, **1**:265, 270
    and *Speak, Memory* (Nabokov), **1**:272
Prouty, Olive Higgins, **2**:47
Psalms, book of, **1**:196, 198
Pseudonyms
    Bugul (Ken) as, **1**:61, 62
    Twain (Mark) as, **1**:146, 147
Psychoanalysis
    Nin's (Anaïs) experience with, **2**:123
    and rise of diaries, **2**:120
Public Historian (journal), **3**:68, 97
Publishers Weekly
    on *Barefoot Gen* (Nakazawa), **1**:294
    on *Bone Black* (hooks), **1**:250
    on *Carrier Warfare in the Pacific* (Wooldridge), **3**:203
    on *Growing Up Jewish in America* (Frommer and Frommer), **3**:119
    on *In the Cities of the South* (Seabrook), **3**:54

    on *Red Scarf Girl* (Jiang), **1**:161, 162
    on *A Stranger's Supper* (Milich), **3**:136
    on *A Woman at War* (Moore), **2**:279
    on *Zlata's Diary* (Filipovic), **2**:339
Puck (magazine), **3**:4
Puerto Rico
    Santiago (Esmeralda) on life in, **1**:108–110
    Spanish colonial rule of, **1**:108
    as U.S. territory, **1**:108
Pulitzer Prize
    for *Angela's Ashes* (McCourt), **1**:120
    for *The Confessions of Nat Turner* (Styron), **1**:204
    for *The Education of Henry Adams* (Adams), **1**:132, 134
    for "*The Good War*" (Terkel), **3**:161, 212, 234, 279, 343
    for *House Made of Dawn* (Momaday), **1**:54
    for *Maus* (Spiegelman), **1**:293
    for *A Midwife's Tale* (Ulrich), **2**:331
    for *Pilgrim at Tinker Creek* (Dillard), **1**:279
    for *Roots* (Haley), **1**:261
Puritanism
    in Britain, **2**:72, 74
    in U.S., **1**:325–327
Purves, Bill, **3**:16
Pushkin, Aleksandr, **2**:143
Pylgrymage of Sir Richarde Guylforde, The (Guylforde), **2:226–228**
Pynson, Richard, **2**:227

Q

Qa'ida, al-, **2**:275
Qasim, Samih al-, **1**:225
Qawuqji, Fawzi al-, **2**:104
Qing dynasty (China), **3**:147
Qiu Jin, **1**:152
Quade, Penelope, **1**:253
Quadriplegia, **1**:6–8

SUBJECT INDEX

Quakerism
- conscientious objection in, **3**:223, 227
- of Fox (George), **2**:26–28
- of Leadbeater (Mary), **2**:157–159
- origins of, **2**:26–28, 157
- persecution of, **2**:26–28
- women's role in, **2**:28, 157

Quan, Adan, **2**:221
Quarterly Journal of Speech, **2**:33
Quarterly Review, **2**:309, 314
Queen of the Woods (Pokagon), **3**:110
Queer studies
- *Daring Hearts* (Brighton Ourstory) in, **3**:70
- *Fun Home* (Bechdel) in, **1**:141
- *Hunger of Memory* (Rodriguez) in, **1**:17
- *A Long Way from Home* (McKay) in, **1**:85

Querelle de femmes, **2**:160
Quiche tribe, **3**:164, 165
Quiet Strength (Parks), **1**:38
Quigley, Kathy, **3**:309
Quinn, Arthur Hobson, **2**:42
Quintilian, **2**:95
Quintus, **2**:94
Quinzaine litteraire (journal), **1**:267
Quite Early One Morning (Thomas), **1**:125
Quit India movement, **1**:291
Qur'an, Hussein's (Taha) study of, **1**:135, 136

R

Rabe, John, *The Good Man of Nanking,* **2**:19–21, *20*
Rabelais, Kevin, **1**:48
Rabin, Yitzhak, **2**:50
Rabinowitz, Dorothy, **1**:300
Race
- development of concept of, **2**:200
- in education, Rodriguez (Richard) on, **1**:15–16
- sociology of, Du Bois (W. E. B.) on, **1**:5

Race relations, in U.S.
- Du Bois (W. E. B.) on, **1**:3–5
- Hurston (Zora Neale) on, **1**:9
- in military, in Vietnam War era, **3**:199–201
- in Reconstruction era, **1**:50–52
- Washington (Booker T.) on, **1**:50–52

Race riots
- in Chicago, **3**:45
- in Detroit, **3**:99, 100, *100,* 101

Racial consciousness, Du Bois (W. E. B.) in advancement of, **1**:4
Racial equality
- Communist Party on, **1**:84
- Washington (Booker T.) on, **1**:50, 51

Racial identity. *See* African American identity; Multicultural and multiracial identities
Racial oppression, Angelou (Maya) on, **1**:18
Racial profiling, of Arab and Muslim Americans, **3**:195, 197
Racial purity
- in Korea, **1**:102
- in Vietnam, **1**:170

Racial quotas, in U.S. higher education, **3**:20
Racial segregation, in South Africa. *See* Apartheid
Racial segregation, in U.S.
- *de jure* vs. *de facto,* **3**:20
- in Detroit, oral histories of, **3**:99–100
- in higher education, **3**:20
- hooks (bell) on end of, **1**:249
- institutionalization of, **1**:37, 50, 122, **3**:44
- in military, end of, **3**:199, 248, 249
- in North vs. South, **3**:250
- Parks (Rosa) on experience of, **1**:37–39
- in schools, end of, **1**:122, 249, **3**:44
- Supreme Court on, **1**:37, 50, 122, 249, **3**:44
- Wright (Richard) on experience of, **1**:122–124, *123*

Racial tropes, in *Dreams from My Father* (Obama), **1**:80
Racism
- in Australia, against Aborigines, **1**:149
- in Britain, **2**:230
- in Chile, against Jews, **1**:75–77
- in Korea, against multiracial individuals, **1**:102
- in South Africa, under apartheid, **1**:24–26, 27–29
- in Vietnam, against multiracial individuals, **1**:170, 171

Racism, in U.S.
- Angelou (Maya) on experience of, **1**:18–19
- Du Bois (W. E. B.) on pervasiveness of, **1**:3–5
- gradualist approach to, King (Martin Luther, Jr.) on, **2**:32–33
- Hansberry (Lorraine) on experience of, **1**:273
- in higher education, oral histories of, **3**:20–22
- hooks (bell) on experience of, **1**:249–250
- against Italian Americans, **3**:224–226
- against Japanese Americans, **1**:309, **3**:81, 82, 127, 195
- against Korean Americans, **1**:103
- Malcolm X on experience of, **1**:186–187
- in military, **3**:44, 199–201, 248–250
- in national security policy, **3**:195, 197
- against Native Americans, **1**:96
- in North vs. South, **1**:122
- Parks (Rosa) on experience of, **1**:37–39
- in Peltier's (Leonard) trial, **1**:96
- in Reconstruction era, **1**:50
- against Vietnamese Americans, **1**:171
- Wright (Richard) on experience of, **1**:122–124

Radar, development of, **3**:202
Radcliffe College, **1**:43
Radhakrishnan, S., **1**:244

Radiance of the King, The (Laye), **1:**128
Radicalism, in U.S., history of, **3:**328–329
Radin, Paul, *Crashing Thunder*, **3:**318
Radio broadcasts, of Thomas (Dylan), **1:**125, 126
Raftery, Judith, **3:**307
Rahv, Philip, **1:**260
Railroads, U.S.
    expansion of, **1:**233
    racial segregation in, **3:**250
Rainbow, Edward, **2:**63
Raines, Edgar F., Jr., **3:**229
Raisin in the Sun, A (Hansberry), **1:**273, 274, 275
Rak, Julie, **1:**248, **2:**174, 175
Raleigh, Donald J.
    Russia's Sputnik Generation, **3:**331, 332, 333
    Soviet Baby Boomers, **3:331–333**
Ramey, Delphia, **3:**87
Ramose, Mogobe B., **3:**253
Ramsdell, Lea, **1:**17
Ramsey, Roger, **1:**165
Ramsland, John, **1:**150
Ranching, in U.S. West, **2:**91–93
Rancour-Laferriere, Daniel, **1:**195
Randolph, A. Philip, **3:**248
Rank, Otto, **2:**123
Rank and File: Histories of Working Class Organizers (Lynd and Lynd), **3:**179
Raoul, Valerie, **1:**7, **2:**307
Rape
    in *I Know Why the Caged Bird Sings* (Angelou), **1:**18, 19
    in *A Woman in Berlin* (anonymous), **2:**281–282
    in World War II, **2:**281–283
Raphael, Jody, **2:**282
Rappaport, Helen, **2:**210
Rasputin, Grigori, **2:**85, 86
Ratele, Kopano, *There Was This Goat*, **3:**242
Rationalism
    Cartesian, **1:**183, 184
    Kierkegaard's (Søren) critique of, **2:**166, 167
Rauff, Walter, **1:**77

Rauwerda, A. M., **3:**25
Ravel, Maurice, **2:**137
Ravenstein, Ernest, **2:**199
Rawick, George P., *The American Slave*, **1:**35
Rawlings, Claude, **1:**166
Ray, Annie, **2:**163–165
Ray, Charles, **2:**163, 164
Ray, Sangeeta, **1:**88
Raynaud, Claudine, **1:**9, 11
Rayson, Ann, **1:**300–301
Razor's Edge, The (Maugham), **2:**185
Read, Florence, **1:**4
Read, J., *Speaking Our Minds*, **3:**170
Reading Lolita in Tehran (Nafisi), **1:**155, 157, 209
Reagan, Ronald, **1:**37, 311, **2:**32–33
Realism
    in American literature, rise of, **2:**240
    in depictions of war, **2:**240
Recession, agricultural, in Britain, **3:**59, 61
Reconstruction era, **1:**50–52, **2:**238, 252
Records of a Girlhood (Kemble), **2:335–337**
Recuerdos del pasado (Pérez Rosales), **1:**222
Red Air Fighter, The (Richthofen), **1:**30
Red Azalea (Min), **1:158–160**
Red Buffalo (journal), **3:**162, 179
Redford, Rachel, **1:**80
Red Guards (China), **1:**158, 161, **3:**287, 288, 289
Red Lantern, The (opera), **1:**159
Redman, Ben Ray, **1:**333
Red Man's Religion (Underhill), **1:**70
Red Mirror, The (Wen), **3:**287
Redmond, Lucille, **2:**159, **3:**316
Red Power movement, **1:**21
Red Scarf Girl (Jiang), **1:**153, 154, 159, **161–163**
Reed, Matt, **1:**272
Reel, A. Frank, **3:**294
Reese, Florence, **3:**98
Reeves, Amber, **1:**254
Reeves, Ambrose, **1:**25

Reformation. *See* Protestant Reformation
Refugees
    Jewish, **1:**75–77, **3:**14–16
    Southeast Asian, **1:**306–307, 337
Regard, Frédéric, **1:**240
Regents of the University of California v. Bakke, **3:**20
Region (journal), **3:**332
Reich-Ranicki, Marcel, **2:**304
Reidy, Joseph, **3:**200–201
Reitell, Elizabeth, **1:**127
Relief of Mafeking, The (Young), **2:**241
Religion. *See also* specific religions
    in abolitionist movement, **1:**142
    in conscientious objection, **3:**221, 223, 227, 228
    theological certainty in, Robinson (Henry Crabb) on, **2:**76
    tradition of autobiographies of, **1:**193, 211
    women's roles in, Stanton (Elizabeth Cady) on, **1:**12
Religious faith
    Darwin's (Charles) loss of, **1:**65–67
    struggles with, in literary autobiographies, **2:**26
    Wiesel's (Elie) loss of, **1:**319–320
Religious Life in a New Millennium (Schneiders), **3:**308
Relocation law (Public Law 93–531), **3:**11
Remembering Pearl Harbor (La Forte and Marcello), **3:**202
Remembrance
    Clifford (Anne) on, **2:**62, 63
    Wiesel (Elie) on, **1:**318
"Remembrance of Things Pakistani" (Gates), **1:**88
Rementer, James A., **3:**325, 326
Remini, Robert V., **2:**71
Renaissance
    English monarchy in, **2:**97–99
    origins of autobiography in, **1:**239
    rise of diaries in, **2:**120
    women's role in, **2:**160–162
Renard, Jules, *The Journal of Jules Renard*, **2:**183

Reparations
    for Japanese American internment, **3:**195, 197
    for World War I, **1:**30
Reporter (journal), **1:**320
Report from a Chinese Village (Myrdal), **3:**299
Report of the Departmental Committee on Homosexual Offences and Prostitution (1957), **3:**70
Rerhaye, Narjis, *Femmes et Politique,* **3:**47
Research in African Literatures (journal), **1:**215, **2:**14, 263, **3:**253
Reservations. *See* Native American reservations
"Resistance to Civil Government" (Thoreau), **1:**242
Rest for Travelers (Bioy Casares), **1:**223
Restoration (England), **2:**65, 72, 73
Restoration and 18th Century Theatre Research (journal), **2:**337
Restoried Selves (Kumashiro), **3:**83
Retractions (Augustine), **1:**196, 198
Return to Nisa (Shostak), **3:**38
Reuss, Richard A., **3:**91
Revelli, Nuto, *The World of the Defeated,* **3:**61
Reverdy, Pierre, **1:**223
Reveries of the Solitary Walker (Rousseau), **1:**200
Reveries over Childhood and Youth (Yeats), **2:**126, 127
Review of Contemporary Fiction (journal), **1:**256
Review of English Studies (journal), **2:**77
Review of Religious Research (journal), **3:**309
Reviews in American History (journal), **3:**4, 87, 116
Revolutionary Democratic Front (FDR), **3:**205
Revolutionary United Front (RUF), **1:**312
Revolutionary War, American. *See* American Revolutionary War
Revoyr, Nina, *Southland,* **1:**309
Reynolds, Dwight F., *Interpreting the Self,* **1:**136, 137, 286, 287
Reynolds, Harriet, **2:**224

Reynolds, J., *Speaking Our Minds,* **3:**170
Reynolds, John Hamilton, **2:**146
Reynolds, William James, **2:**224
Rhee, Syngman, **1:**323, 324
Rhetoric, of Augustine, **1:**198
Rhetoric of English India, The (Suleri), **1:**87–88
Rhetoric Review (journal), **2:**30
Rhodes, Cecil, **1:**218, **3:**251
Rhodes, James, **1:**297
Rhodes, Richard, **3:**162, 241
Rhodesia
    British colonial rule of, **1:**167, **3:**251–253
    Lessing (Doris) on life in, **1:**167
Rhodesia (Mlambo), **3:**251
Rhys, Jean, **1:**111
Ribière, Mireille, **1:**269
Rice, Howard C., **2:**215
Rice, Judith A., **3:**261, 263
Rice, Julian, **1:**23
Rice bars, **3:**83, 84
Rich, Adrienne, **2:**3
Rich, Elizabeth, **1:**98
Richard III (king of England), **2:**228
Richards, Cynthia D., **2:**111
Richardson, Bob, **1:**279–280
Richardson, Dorothy, **2:**123
Richardson, Jonathan, **2:**36
Richardson, Karl Spence, **2:**163
Richardson, Robert D., **2:**141
Richardson, Samuel, **2:**328
    Clarissa, **2:**301
Richardson, Sue, **2:**271
Richlin, Amy, **1:**220
Richthofen, Manfred von, *The Red Air Fighter,* **1:**30
Rick, Dorothy, **3:**5
Rickard, W., **3:**273
Ricosti, Neide, **2:**8
Rida, Rashid, **1:**136
Ridley, Glynis, **2:**67
Rieff, Davic, **2:**340
Riegle, Rosalie, *Doing Time for Peace,* **3:**229
Riesco, Laura, **1:**76

Rife, Flora, **3:**87
Rigaur, Gerd, **2:304**
Rightist movements, Hitler's (Adolf) influence on, **1:**30, 32
Right-wing dictators, Latin American, rise of, **3:**185
Rigney, Anne, **2:**311
Rilke, Rainer Maria, **2:150**
    An Interrupted Life (Hillesum) on, **2:**22
    Letters of Rainer Maria Rilke, **2:**150
    Letters on God and Letters to a Young Woman, **2:**149
    Letters to a Young Poet, **2:149–151**
    Notebooks (Williams) on, **2:**152
Rilke, Ruth, **2:**149
Rime of the Ancient Mariner, The (Coleridge), **3:**183
Rinehart, Melissa, *Contested Territories,* **3:**326
Ringelheim, Joan, **3:**35–36
Ripley, George, **1:**235
Ripley, Sophia, **1:**235
Ritchie, Donald
    on *Between Management and Labor* (Friedman), **3:**155
    Doing Oral History, **3:**186, 294, 345
    on *Head of the Class* (Morris), **3:**21
    on *Witnesses to Nuremberg* (Stave et al.), **3:**294
Rites: A Guatemalan Boyhood (Perera), **1:**75, **99–101**
Ritter, Evelyn J., **3:**107
Rittner, Carol, *Different Voices,* **3:**34
Ritts, Morton, **3:**120
Ritualism, Chinese, **3:**124, 125
Rivas, Gladys C., **3:**207
Rive, Richard, *Writing Black,* **1:**25
Rivera, José, **2:**220
Riverbend
    Baghdad Burning, **2:**275
    Baghdad Burning II, **2:**275
River Runs through It, A (McLean), **1:**281
Rivers, W. H. R., **2:**248
Riwan ou le chemin de sable (Bugul), **1:**61, 64

Roach, John, **3**:250

Road to Wigan Pier, The (Orwell), **2**:117, **3**:66

Robbins, Amy Catherine, **1**:254

Roberts, Adam, **2**:33

Roberts, David, **1**:302, 304

Roberts, Elizabeth
in *Oral History, Health and Welfare* (Bornat et al.), **3**:171
in origins of oral history, **3**:64
A Woman's Place, **3**:144, 145, 146
Women and Families, **3**:144–146

Roberts, Nesta, **3**:54

Roberts, Rosemary, **3**:124, 125

Roberts, Sasha, **2**:325

Robeson, Paul, **1**:273
Here I Stand, **1**:37

Robideau, Bob, **1**:96

Robin, Diana, **2**:160

Robinson, A. M. Lewin, **2**:217

Robinson, Amy, **1**:113

Robinson, Henry Crabb, *Diary, Reminiscences and Correspondence of Henry Crabb Robinson*, **2**:75–77

Robinson, Jo Ann Gibson, **1**:37

Robinson, Jo Ann O., **3**:223

Robinson Crusoe (Defoe), **3**:183

Robles, Emmanuel, **2**:262, 263

Rock Burst (Russell), **3**:93, 95

Rocking the Boat (O'Farrell and Kornbluh), **3**:337

Rocky Mountain Review (journal), **2**:153

Roderick Hudson (James), **2**:114

Rodier, Katharine, **2**:31

Rodin, Auguste, **2**:149

Rodina, Nina Ivanovna, **3**:18

Rodríguez, Andrés, **2**:146, 147

Rodriguez, Richard, *Hunger of Memory*, **1**:15–17, 47

Rodriguez, Spain, *Che: A Graphic Biography*, **3**:330

Roessel, Monty, **3**:291

Roett, Riordan, *Dialogue and Armed Conflict*, **3**:205

Rogers, Byron, **2**:102

Rogers, Carole Garibaldi, *Habits of Change*, **3**:308–310

Rogers, Katharine, **2**:37

Rogers, Robert, **2**:205, 207

Rogers, Seth, **2**:31

Rogovin, Milton, **3**:181

Rohlmann, Monika, **3**:140

Rohrbach, Augusta, **2**:252

Rohter, Larry, **2**:220

Rojas Pinilla, Gustavo, **3**:183, 184, 185

Roland Barthes (Barthes), **1**:249, **267–269**

Roldán, María, **3**:73–75

Rolle, Andrew, **3**:225

Rollins, Edwin, **1**:39

Roman autobiographical writing
by Augustine, **1**:196–198
by Marcus Aurelius, **1**:218–221
by Pliny the Younger, **2**:94–96

Roman Empire, under Marcus Aurelius, **1**:218–221

Romanov dynasty (Russia), **2**:84–86

Romanticism
Byron (George Gordon Noel) in, **2**:143
D'Israeli's (Isaac) influence on, **2**:179
egotism in, **2**:177, 179
German, **2**:76
Keats (John) in, **2**:146
surge of autobiographies in era of, **2**:16, 177

Romantic relationships
in *An Interrupted Life* (Hillesum), **2**:22, 24
of Wells (H. G.), **1**:252, 253, 254

Romantic Review (journal), **2**:175

Rome, ancient
under Marcus Aurelius, **1**:218–221
Pliny the Younger on history of, **2**:94–96
slavery in, **2**:96

Rome (Italy), Fosse Ardeatine massacre in, **3**:265–267

Romero, Mary, *The Maid's Daughter*, **1**:108

Rooke, Tetz, **1**:255, 256, 257

Roosevelt, Eleanor, **2**:101, 103, 254, **3**:248

Roosevelt, Franklin D.
African American votes for, **3**:44
Great Depression and, **3**:161, 212
Italian American relocation under, **3**:224–226
Japanese American internment under, **1**:299, 309, 311, **3**:104, 195
labor arbitration under, **3**:153
Manhattan Project under, **3**:239
on Morgenthau Plan, **3**:293
racism in military under, **3**:44, 248

Roosevelt, Kermit, **2**:220

Roosevelt, Theodore
Geronimo and, **1**:302, 304
in Japan-Russia Treaty of Peace, **3**:234
Through the Brazilian Wilderness, **2**:220

Roots (Haley), **1**:18, 78, 261–263

Roque Ramirez, Horatio, **3**:85

Rosa Parks: My Story (Parks and Haskins), **1**:19, **37–39**

Roscoe, Adrian, **3**:252–253

Rose, Ellen Cronon, **1**:169

Rose, Jacqueline, **2**:49

Rose, Mary Beth, **1**:231

Rose, Michael E., **3**:145

Roseberry, William, **3**:324

Rose Hill (Wolcott), **3**:86

Roseman, Mark, **3**:35

Rosen, Edgar, **2**:17

Rosenbaum, Arthur L., *Chinese Missionaries Oral History Collection*, **3**:299

Rosenfeld, Maya, **2**:52

Rosengarten, Theodore, *All God's Dangers*, **3**:73, 179

Rosenthal, Anton, **3**:329

Rosenwald, Lawrence Alan, **2**:140, 141

Rosianus Geminus, **2**:96

Rosie the Riveter Revisited (Gluck), **3**:224

Ross, David, **3**:209, 210

Ross, Ellen, **3**:145

Ross, James, *Caught in a Tornado*, **3**:287

Ross, Robert, **2**:9, 10

Ross, Sarah Gwyneth, **2**:160

SUBJECT INDEX

Roth, John, *Different Voices,* **3:**34
Rothchild, Sylvia, *Voices of the Holocaust,* **3:**50
Rotkirch, Anna, *Living through the Soviet System,* **3:**331
Roughing It (Twain), **1:**146
Rouse, David, **3:**155
Rousseau, Jean-Jacques, **1:201**
    Boswell (James) and, **2:**329
    Confessions, **1:**193, 197, **200–203,** 276
    Dialogues, **1:**200
    Laye (Camara) compared to, on childhood, **1:**128
    Olney (James) on, **1:**248
    Reveries of the Solitary Walker, **1:**200
    U.S. anarchists influenced by, **3:**3
Rowe, John Carlos, **1:**133, 134
Rowlandson, Mary, *The Sovereignty and Goodness of God,* **1:**81, **325–328,** **3:**24
Rowlatt Acts of 1919 (Britain), **1:**242, 289
Rowley, Hazel, **1:**124
Rowley, Susan, *Uqalurait,* **3:**107, **138–140**
Rowntree, Seebohm, **3:**53
Roy, Arundhati, *The God of Small Things,* **1:**87
Royal Literary Fund, **2:**207
Royal Society, **2:**65
RPF. *See* Rwandan Patriotic Front
Ruark, Robert, **2:**12
Ruch, Barbara, **2:**61
Rudnytsky, P., **1:**247
Ruete, Emily, *Memoirs of an Arabian Princess from Zanzibar,* **1:90–92**
Ruete, Rudolph Heinrich, **1:**90
RUF. *See* Revolutionary United Front
Ruiz, Vicki L., **3:**303
Rule and Exercises of Holy Living and Dying (Taylor), **2:**195
"Rule of taste," **2:**189
Rumor of War, A (Caputo), **3:**209
Running in the Family (Ondaatje), **1:**88
Rupert, Harry Cramer, **2:**93
Ruppin, Arthur, *Arthur Ruppin,* **2:**104

Rural England
    depopulation of, **3:**59
    oral histories of life in, **3:**59–61, 63–65
Rural Ireland, oral histories of life in, **3:**315–317, *316*
Rural women, tradition of oral histories of, **3:**135–136
Rush, Benjamin, *Autobiography of Benjamin Rush,* **1:**179–180
Rush, Norman, **1:**63
Rushdie, Salman
    fatwa against, **1:**155
    on *Infidel* (Hirsi Ali), **1:**207
    Midnight's Children, **1:**87
    Shame, **1:**87
    Suleri (Sue) and, **1:**88
Rusk, Dean, **3:**279
Ruskin, John, **1:265**
    Fors Clavigera, **1:**264
    Modern Painters, **1:**264
    Praeterita, **1:264–266**
    Unto This Last, **1:**242
    The Works of John Ruskin, **1:**265
Ruskin, John James, **1:**264
Ruskin, Margaret (Cock), **1:**264
Russell, Bert
    Calked Boots and Other Northwest Writings, **3:**93
    Hardships and Happy Times, **3:**93
    North Fork of the Coeur d'Alene River, **3:**93
    Rock Burst, **3:**93, 95
    The Sawdust Dream, **3:**93
    Swiftwater People, **3:93–95**
Russell, George, **2:**126, 128
Russell, Marie, **3:**93, 95
Russia. *See also* Soviet Union
    Alexandra Feodorovna on life in, **2:**84–86
    autobiographical tradition of, **1:**270
    Bolshevik Revolution in, **2:**84, **3:**331
    censorship in, **1:**193, 194
    communism in, establishment of, **1:**270
    February Revolution in, **2:**84

    Great Reforms in, **1:**193
    Jewish immigration to China from, **3:**16
    liberalism in, rise of, **1:**193
    Maugham's (W. Somerset) travels in, **2:**183, 184
    Nabokov (Vladimir) on life in, **1:**270–272
    October Revolution in, **1:**270
    Poland occupied by, **2:**192
    Revolution of 1917 in, **1:**270
    Romanov dynasty in, end of, **2:**84–86
    in Russo–Japanese War, **1:**322
    Tolstoy (Leo) on life in, **1:**193–195
Russian Americans, Nabokov (Vladimir) as, **1:**270–272
Russian Orthodox Church, **1:**193, 194
Russian Review (journal), **3:**285, 333
Russian Revolution (1917), **1:**270
Russian Thought (journal), **1:**194
Russia's Sputnik Generation (Raleigh), **3:**331, 332, 333
Russo–Japanese War (1904–1905), **1:**322, **3:**234
Rustichiello of Pisa, **1:**105, **2:**201
Rustin, Bayard, **1:**20
Rutherford, R. B., **1:**220
Rwanda, Belgian colonial rule of, **3:**257
Rwandan genocide
    oral histories of, **1:**312, **3:**257–259
    war crimes trials after, **3:**293, 294
Rwandan Patriotic Front (RPF), **3:**257
Rwililiza, Innocent, **3:**257, 259
Ryan, Allan A., Jr., **3:**294
Ryan, Hugh, **1:**168
Ryerson, Richard Alan, **2:**90

S

Saadawi, Nawal El, *A Daughter of Isis,* **1:**226
Sabbagh, Suha, **1:**94
SABC. *See* South African Broadcasting Corporation
Sabor, Peter, **2:**314
Sachs, Nelly, *Eli,* **2:**255

Sackville, Margaret, **2:**64
Sackville-West, Vita, **2:**62, 64, 181
SACP. *See* South African Communist Party
Sad Earth, Sweet Heaven (Buck), **2:**271, 273
Sadler, Thomas, **2:**75, 77
Saemann, Karyn, **2:**276
Safeir, Gwendolen, *American Leaders in Nursing,* **3:**170
Safer, Morley, **3:**279
Safundi (journal), **3:**243
Saga of Coe Ridge, The (Montell), **3:90–92**
Sago mine disaster of 2006 (West Virginia), **3:**66, 67
Saigon, fall of, **3:**209, 279, *280*
Saints. *See also* specific saints
　　lives of (*See* Hagiographies)
　　relics of, **2:**226
Saint-Simon, Duc de, **2:**174
Saitoti, Tepilit Ole
　　Maasai, **1:**114
　　The Worlds of a Maasai Warrior, **1:114–116**
Sajdi, Dana, **1:**287
Sakakini, Khalil al-, *The Diary of Khalil al-Sakakini,* **2:**104, 106
Saladin, **1:**285–286, *286*
Salama, Gwen, **3:**45
Salamini, Heather Fowler, **3:**303
Salazar, Claudia, **3:**191
Sale, Roger, **1:**165
Salemi, Esmail, **3:**218
Saliba, Sue, *Watching Seagulls,* **1:**161
Salisbury, Richard, **3:**207
Salles, Walter, **2:**220
Salm, Arthur, **3:**67
Salmagundi (journal), **1:**247
Salme, Sayyida. *See* Ruete, Emily
Salomé (Wilde), **2:**183
Salter, Andrea, **2:**267
Salter, John R., Jr., **3:**329
Salter, Michael, **3:**294
Salt Lake Tribune (newspaper), **1:**38
Salvadoran Civil War, oral histories of, **3:**205–208, *206*
Same-sex marriage, **1:**139

Samkange, Stanlake, **3:**251
Samples from English Culture (Klein), **3:**144
Sampson, Anthony, **1:**27
Samway, Patrick H., **3:**45–46
Sánchez, Rosaura, **3:**114, 116
　　Telling Identities, **3:**115, 121–122
Sancho, Ignatius, **1:**81, **2:**44
Sand, Georges, **2:**82
Sanders, Mark, **1:**314, **3:**243
Sanders, Robert, *Brothers,* **3:**199
Sanders, Valerie, **2:**336
San Diego Union-Tribune (newspaper), **3:**67
Sandos, James A., **3:**116
Sands, Kathleen M., **1:**70, 71
Sandul, Paul, **3:**188
Sang Ye
　　China Candid, **3:**299–300
　　Chinese Lives, **3:**288, **299–301**
Sansibar Blues (Buch), **1:**92
Sansom, George, **2:**189
Santa Fe, USS, **3:203**
Santa María (ship), **2:**203
Santiago, Esmeralda
　　Almost a Woman, **1:**108, 109
　　The Turkish Lover, **1:**108
　　When I Was Puerto Rican, **1:108–110**
Santoli, Al
　　Everything We Had, **3:**199, 201, **209–211,** 231, 275, 279
　　Leading the Way, **3:**210
　　To Bear Any Burden, **3:**210
Santoni, Pedro, **3:**116
Santrouschitz, Hermine, **2:**253
Sao Paulo (Brazil), de Jesus (Carolina Maria) on favelas of, **2:**6–8
Sapia, Yvonne, **1:**109
Sarajevo (Bosnia), Bosnian War in, **2:**338–340
Sarashina, Lady
　　As I Crossed a Bridge of Dreams, **2:189–191,** 290–291
　　Michitsuna No Haha as aunt of, **2:**297
Sarashina Diary. See As I Crossed a Bridge of Dreams

Sarcasm, in *The Education of Henry Adams* (Adams), **1:**132, 133
Sarcophagus (Gubarev), **3:**282, 284
Sargent, John Singer, **2:**114
Saro-Wiwa, Ken, **1:**214
　　Sozaboy, **1:**312
Sarra, Edith, **2:**191, 299
Sarraute, Nathalie, *Enfance,* **1:**268
Sartre, Jean-Paul, **1:**124, 318, **2:**152, 167
Sasha and Emma (Avrich), **3:**3
Sassoon, Siegfried, **2:247**
　　on *A Country Parson* (Woodforde), **2:**287, 289
　　Diaries, 1915–1918, **2:247–249**
　　Memoirs of a Fox-Hunting Man, **1:**329, **2:**247
　　Orwell (George) compared to, **2:**117
　　Sherston's Progress, **2:**247
Satire, in "Letter to the Reverend Samson Occom" (Wheatley), **2:**44, 45
Satirist, The (newspaper), **1:**277
Satrapi, Marjane
　　Chicken with Plums, **1:**155–156
　　Embroideries, **1:**155
　　Persepolis, **1:**139, 141, **155–157,** *156,* 293
Sattelmeyer, Robert, **1:**235
Satterfield, Archie, *The Home Front,* **3:**202
Saturday Evening Post (magazine), **2:**250
Saturday Review (magazine), **1:**271, **2:**185, **3:**318
Saturday Review of Literature (magazine), **1:**333
Saturday Review/World (magazine), **1:**300
Satyagraha, **1:**242
Saudi Arabia, in Gulf War, **2:**278, 279
Saunders, Anna, **3:**247
Saunders, Keith B., **1:**149
Saunders, Loraine, **2:**118–119
Saussure, Ferdinand de, **1:**267
Savage, Priscilla, **3:**64
Savage, Thomas, *Californio Voices,* **3:114–117,** 121

SAVAK, **3:**219
Savicheva, Tanya, **2:**277
Savin, Ada, **1:**100
Savoye, Jeffrey A., **2:**41
Sawdust Dream, The (Russell), **3:**93
Saxton, Marsha, *With Wings,* **1:**8
Sayigh, Mai, *The Siege,* **1:**226
Sayre, Robert, **2:**207
Scalp hunters, **1:**304
Scammell, G. V., **2:**198, 200
Scandinavia, Wollstonecraft's (Mary) travels in, **2:**111
Scaphandre et le papillon, Le (Bauby). *See Diving Bell and the Butterfly, The* (Bauby)
Scarlet Letter, The (Hawthorne), **2:**223–224
Scar literature, *Voices from the Whirlwind* (Feng) as, **3:**287
Schaefer, Paul, **1:**77
Schapera, Isaac, **2:**242
Scharnhorst, Gary, **1:**235
Schayegh, Cyrus, **3:**220
Schiller, Friedrich, **1:**277
Schimpf, Albrecht, **3:**235
Schmelz, Peter J., **3:**333
Schmidt, Matthias, **2:**54
Schmidt, Rob, **3:**68
Schmitz, John Eric, *Enemies among Us,* **3:**224
Schnabel, Julian, **1:**6
Schneider, Karen, **2:**269
Schneiders, Sandra Marie, *Religious Life in a New Millennium,* **3:**308
Schoeneman, Katherine A., **1:**205
Schoeneman, Thomas J., **1:**205
Schonbrun, Eva, **3:**35
School Library Journal, **1:**311, **3:**45, 225
Schoolma'am, The (Donovan), **3:**77
Schools. *See* Education
Schopenhauer, Arthur, **1:**193, 194
The World as Will and Representation, **1:**193
Schrager, Samuel, **3:**329
Schreiber, Harry, **3:**21
Schubnell, Matthias, **1:**56
Schulkind, Jeanne, **2:**182
Schulman, Nicole, *Wobblies!,* **3:**330

Schuth, Katarina, **3:**309
Schwanitz, Wolfgang, **1:**209
Schwartz, Matthew, **2:**96
Schwarz-Bart, Simone, *Ti Jean L'Horizon,* **1:**64
Schwarzkopf, Norman, **2:**279
Scibetta, Barbara, *War Brides of World War II,* **3:**127
Science, Darwin (Charles) on success in, **1:**65–67
Science and Engineering Ethics (journal), **2:**168
Science fiction
    by Cavendish (Margaret), **1:**231
    feminist, **2:**237
SCLC. *See* Southern Christian Leadership Conference
Scotland. *See also* Scottish autobiographical writing
    in Enlightenment, contributions of, **2:**328
    in establishment of Great Britain, **2:**328
    militia groups in, **2:**309
    oral histories of life in, **3:**173, 175
    Victoria's visits to Highlands of, **2:**209–211
    during World War II, Mitchison (Naomi) on life in, **2:**235–237
Scott, David, **2:**258
Scott, Joanna C., *Indochinese Refugees,* **1:**335
Scott, Margaret, **2:**133, 134
Scott, Rebecca, **3:**68
Scott, Shaunna L., *Two Sides to Everything,* **3:**96
Scott, Walter, **2:310**
    "Auld Robin Gray" (Barnard) and, **2:**217
    The Bride of Lammermoor, **2:**209
    The Journal of Sir Walter Scott, **2:**67, **309–311**
    Kemble's (Fanny) friendship with, **2:**335
    Memoirs, **2:**309
    Napoleon, **2:**310
    Shadows on My Heart (Buck) on, **2:**271
    Waverly, **2:**309

Scottish autobiographical writing
    by Boswell (James), **2:**328–330
    by Mitchison (Naomi), **2:**235–237
    by Scott (Walter), **2:**309–311
Scottish Geographical Magazine, **2:**198
Scottish Historical Review (journal), **2:**236, 288–289, **3:**146
Scott-Moncrieff, G., **2:**329
Scrapbook of Katherine Mansfield (Mansfield), **2:**134
Scribner, Charles, **2:**101
Scribner, Doris, **3:**282, 285
Scribner's Monthly, **2:**114
Scrots, Guillaume, **2:98**
Sculptura (Evelyn), **2:**65
Seabrook, Jeremy
    In the Cities of the South, **3:**54
    Mother and Son, **3:**55
    Unemployment, **3:**54
    The Unprivileged, **3:**55
    Working-Class Childhood, **3:**53–55
Seacole, Mary, *The Wonderful Adventures of Mrs. Seacole in Many Lands,* **1:111–113,** *112*
Seaman, Donna, **1:**104, **2:**339
Season of Anomy (Soyinka), **1:**214
Seaver, Paul S., **2:**74
Secession, Lee's (Robert E.) views on, **2:**38, 39
Sechehaye, Marguerite, *The Autobiography of a Schizophrenic Girl,* **1:**164
Second Common Reader (Woolf), **2:**289
Secundinus, **1:**196
Sedgwick, Ellery, **2:**91
See, Lisa, **1:**159
Seeger v. United States, **3:**223
Seelig, Sharon, **1:**317
Seelig, Sharon Cadman, **2:**64
Segalla, Spencer D., *The Moroccan Soul,* **3:**48
Segregation. *See* Racial segregation; Sexual segregation
Seidensticker, Edward, **2:**297, 298, 299
Seidler, Ned M., **1:66**

Sei Shōnagon
- *The Diary of Lady Murasaki* (Murasaki) on, **2**:290, 291
- Michitsuna No Haha in family of, **2**:297
- *The Pillow Book,* **2**:59, 189, 190, 290

Seitz, James, **1**:268
Selected Autobiographies by Women Writers (Xie), **1**:340
Selected Letters (Keats), **2**:146
Selected Letters of Martha Gellhorn (Gellhorn), **2**:101–103
Selective Service, U.S., **3**:221, 227, 229
Self. *See also* Identity
- Hurston's (Zora Neale) views on, **1**:9, 10
- in identity, Rousseau (Jean-Jacques) on, **1**:200–202
- importance in society, and rise of autobiographies, **1**:246
- Lessing (Doris) on nature of, **1**:167, 168
- Native American vs. Western conceptions of, **1**:56
- in postmodernism, **1**:167

Self-actualization, in *Ten Thousand Sorrows* (Kim), **1**:103
Self-doubt, of Hawthorne (Nathaniel), **2**:223–224
Self-education, Franklin (Benjamin) on, **1**:179, 180
Self-elegy, of Darwish (Mahmoud), **1**:255–257
Self-Help (Smiles), **2**:310
Self-help books, *The Autobiography of Ben Franklin* (Franklin) as precursor to, **1**:182
Self-knowledge, Styron's (William) struggle for, **1**:204
"Self-made" individuals, Franklin (Benjamin) and, **1**:180
"Self-Made Men" (Douglass), **1**:180
Self-Portrait of the Other (Padilla), **1**:296
"Self-Reliance" (Emerson), **1**:180
Selkirk, Andrew, **3**:183
Sellin, Eric, **1**:128, **2**:263
Selochan, Viberto, **3**:207
Selznick, Irene Mayer, **2**:261
Seme, Pixley ka Isaka, **2**:241

Semiology, **1**:267
Sending My Heart Back across the Years (Wong), **1**:56
Seneca, **2**:94, 96
Seneca Falls Convention (1848), **1**:12
Senegal
- Bugul (Ken) on life in, **1**:61–64
- French colonial rule of, **1**:61
- independence of (1960), **1**:61

Senesh, Hannah, **2**:22
Senghor, Léopold-Sédar, **1**:61, 128
Senkaku/Diaoyu (islands), **1**:340
Senkewicz, Robert M.
- *The History of Alta California,* **3**:115
- *Testimonios,* **3**:116

Senna, Danzy, *Caucasia,* **1**:72, 74
Sentimental Education (Flaubert), **1**:128
"Separate but equal" doctrine
- end of, **3**:44
- establishment of, **1**:37, 50

Sephardic Jews
- in Guatemala, **1**:99–100
- immigration to U.S., **3**:118, 120

September 11, 2001, terrorist attacks
- East German Stasi and, **3**:245
- Hirsi Ali (Ayaan) on aftermath of, **1**:207
- national security after, **3**:195, 197, 245
- racial profiling after, **3**:195, 197
- *The Story of My Life* (Ahmedi) after, **1**:40
- U.S.-led invasion of Iraq after, **2**:275

Septicus Clarus, **2**:95
Seraph on the Suwanee (Hurston), **1**:9
Serbs, in Bosnian War, **2**:338
Serengeti National Park, **1**:114
Serious Proposal to the Ladies, A (Astell), **2**:35
Serrano, Jorge, **1**:99
Sestigers, **3**:242
Seton, William, **2**:213
Set This House on Fire (Styron), **1**:206
Seutonius Tranquillus, **2**:94
Seventh Letter (Plato), **2**:94

Seven Years' War (1754–1763), **1**:276, **2**:205, 328
Sévigné, Madame de, **2**:35
Sewanee Review (journal), **1**:165, **2**:76, 153, 269
Seward, Anna, **2**:217
Sex: An Oral History (Maurer), **3**:276, 277
Sexual activity
- adolescent, *Go Ask Alice* (anonymous) on, **2**:294
- in *The Diary of Anaïs Nin* (Nin), **2**:123
- in Japan, in Kamakura period, **2**:60–61
- in *Nisa* (Shostak), **3**:37, 38

Sexual discrimination
- in China, **3**:148
- in coal mining, **3**:337, 339

Sexuality, of African American women
- Angelou (Maya) on, **1**:18
- hooks (bell) on, **1**:250
- Jacobs (Harriet A.) on, **1**:143–144

Sexual orientation. *See* Homosexuality
Sexual segregation, among Meru people, **3**:143
Sexual violence, in Guatemala, **1**:100. *See also* Rape
Sforza, Ascanio Maria, **2**:160, 161
Sganga, Cristina, *El Salvador,* **3**:206
Shaarawi, Huda, **1**:136
- *Harem Years,* **1**:225–226

Shackelford, Laurel, *Our Appalachia,* **3**:66, **86–89**
Shackleton, Abraham, **2**:157
Shackleton, Elizabeth, **2**:157
Shackleton, Richard, **2**:157
Shadows on My Heart (Buck), **2**:38, **271–274**
Shaffer, Deborah, *Solidarity Forever,* **3**:328–330
Shah, Saira, *The Storyteller's Daughter,* **1**:40
Shah's Story, The (Mohammed Reza), **3**:218
Shaka (Zulu leader), **1**:25
Shake Hands with the Devil (Dallaire), **3**:258

Shakespeare, William
    Hamlet, **1:**277
    Journal of Katherine Mansfield (Mansfield) on, **2:**133
    Journals of Ralph Waldo Emerson (Emerson) on, **2:**140
    Kemble's (Fanny) performances of, **2:**337
    King Lear, **2:**147
    The Letters of John Keats (Keats) on, **2:**146
    pilgrimage narratives used by, **2:**226
    Two Gentlemen of Verona, **2:**226, 228
Shame (Rushdie), **1:**87
Shamuyarira, Nathan, **3:**251
Shanghai (China), oral histories of Jewish refugees in, **3:**14–16, *15*
Shapin, Steven, **3:**240
Shapiro, Judith, **3:**301
Shapiro, Karin, **3:**272
Shapiro, Stephen A., **1:**277–278
Shared Authority, A (Frisch), **3:**173, **179–182,** 190, 192
Sharma, Govind, **2:**14
Sharp, Granville, **1:**83
Shattered Dreams? (Oppenheimer and Bayer), **3:**272–274
Shaw, George Bernard, **1:**84, **2:**16, 17, 128
Shaw, Nate, **3:**73
Shawqi, Ahmad, *al-Shawqiyyat*, **1:**135–136
Shawqiyyat, al- (Shawqi), **1:**135–136
Sheard, S., **3:**171
Shelley, Mary, *The Last Man*, **2:**145
Shelley, Percy Bysshe, **2:**143, 145, 146, 154
Shell shock, **2:**247, 248
Shepard, Alex, **3:**175
Shepard, Matthew, **1:**139
Sheridan, Dorothy, **2:**236
Sheridan, Richard Brinsley, **1:**34, **2:**217
Sherman, Beatrice, **1:**10–11
Sherman, L. A., *Bengali Girls Don't*, **1:**312
Sherman, William T., **3:**290
Sherriff, R. C., *Journey's End*, **1:**329

Sherry, Norman, **2:**194
Sherston's Progress (Sassoon), **2:**247
Sherwin-White, A. N., **2:**95
Shi, Shumei, **2:**172
Shields, Brooke, *Down Came the Rain*, **1:**204
Shinoda, Paul, **3:**196
Shipler, David, **1:**336
Shirane, Haruo, **2:**59
Shirinian, Lorne, **3:**42
Shizuo, Tanisuga, **3:**216
Shoah (film), **3:**50, 52
Shockley, Evelyn, **1:**250
Shoemaker, Adam, *Black Words, White Page*, **1:**150, 151
Shona people, **3:**251, *252*
Shopes, Linda, **3:**98, 181
Short, John, **2:**167
Short, William, **2:**213
Short Account of the Destruction of the Indies, A (Las Casas), **2:**201
"Short Narrative of My Life, A" (Occom), **1:**56
Shōshi (empress of Japan), **2:**290, 291, 292
Shostak, Marjorie
    Nisa, **3:37–39**
    Return to Nisa, **3:**38
Showings (Julian of Norwich), **1:**211
Shrader, Charles R., **3:**210
Shrier, Helene, **3:**119, 120
Shriver, Robert Sargent, Jr., **3:**254, 256
Shua, María, *The Book of Memories*, **1:**75
Shukert, Elfrieda, *War Brides of World War II*, **3:**127
Shumaker, Wayne, **1:**246
Shuman, Amy, **3:**159
Shupe, Kevin, **1:**304
Shuttle in the Crypt, A (Soyinka), **1:**214
Sidney, Angela, **3:**320
Siebentritt, Gretta Tovar, *Places of Origin*, **3:**205
Siege, The (Sayigh), **1:**226
Siegelbaum, Lewis H., *Workers of the Donbass Speak*, **3:**157, **340–342**
Siege of Mafeking, The (Hamilton), **2:**241

Siemens, **2:**19
Sierra Eye (magazine), **1:**313
Sierra Leone
    Beah (Ishmael) on life in, **1:**312–314
    civil war of, **1:**312–314
Siglo XX (Bolivia), **3:**322
Siglo XX Housewives Committee, **3:**322
Sign in Sidney Brustein's Window, The (Hansberry), **1:**274
Sign language, Warlpiri, **3:**335–336
Signs (journal), **1:**88
Silver Tassie, The (O'Casey), **1:**329
Silvester, Christopher, **2:**276
Sim, Lorraine, **2:**269
Simmons, Allan H., **2:**194
Simms, Laura, **1:**314
Simone, Nina, **1:**274
Simplicity, Thoreau's (Henry David) advocacy of, **1:**233, 234
Simpson, Carol Chung, **3:**127
Simpson, Wallis, **2:**235
Sin, struggle with
    Augustine on, **1:**196–198
    Kempe (Margery) on, **1:**189, 190
Sindall, Rob, *Street Violence in the Nineteenth Century*, **3:**312
Singapore, Neruda (Pablo) in, **1:**224
Singapore Story, The (Lee), **1:**290
Singh, Ajay, **1:**299, 300
Singh, Amar, **2:**231
Singh, Amardeep, **2:**231
Singh, Nikky-Guninder Kaur, **2:**185
Singing Flame, The (O'Malley), **3:**27
Singing for Power (Underhill), **1:**70
Singletary, Otis A., **2:**245
Sino–Japanese War, First (1894–1895), **1:**322, 340, **3:**234
Sino–Japanese War, Second (1937–1945), **1:**339, 340
Sino-Judaic Institute, **3:**16
Sinor, Jennifer, *The Extraordinary Work of Ordinary Writing*, **2:163–165**
Sioux. *See* Lakota Sioux
Sisterhood, in oral history field, **3:**190
Sithole, Jabulani, **1:**26
Sithole, Ndabaningi, **3:**251

SUBJECT INDEX

Siv, Sichan, *Golden Bones,* **1**:306–308, *307*
Skenazy, Paul, **1**:174
Skin color, hooks (bell) on meanings of, **1**:250
Skinner, B. F., **1**:234
Skinner, John, **1**:190, 191
Skousen, Mark, **1**:182
Slade, Carole, **1**:213
Slantchev, Brantislav, **2**:299
Slave(s)
    as Civil War soldiers, **2**:238–240
    education of, in preparation for emancipation, **2**:29–31, *30*
    former, oral histories of, **3**:23–25
    genealogy of, **1**:261–263
    Jacobs (Harriet A.) on families of, **1**:142–143
    naming of, **1**:52
    rebellions by, **2**:238
    runaway, oral histories of, **3**:7–9
    separation of families of, **1**:261, 262
Slave narratives. *See also specific works and writers*
    authorship of, **1**:82–83
    Behind the Scenes (Keckley) as, **1**:52
    A Diary from Dixie (Chesnut) compared to, **2**:250
    Incidents in the Life of a Slave Girl (Jacobs) as, **1**:18, 34, 35, 142–145
    The Interesting Narrative of the Life of Olaudah Equiano (Equiano) as, **1**:34, 81–83, 142
    The Journals of Charlotte Forten Grimké (Grimké) vs., **2**:29
    modern autobiographies inspired by, **1**:18, 37
    Narrative (Brown) as, **1**:50
    Narrative of the Life of Frederick Douglass (Douglass) as, **1**:33–35
    Twelve Years a Slave (Northup) as, **1**:50
    Up from Slavery (Washington) as, **1**:50–52
    WPA collection of, **1**:35
Slave owners
    effects of slavery on, Douglass (Frederick) on, **1**:34

    naming of slaves by, Washington (Booker T.) on, **1**:52
    power of, Jacobs (Harriet A.) on, **1**:142
Slavery. *See also* Abolitionist movement
    Adams (John Quincy) on debate over, **2**:69, 70, 71
    in ancient Greece and Rome, **2**:96
    Arab vs. Western institution of, **1**:90, 92
    in Bermuda, oral histories of, **3**:23–25
    British abolition of, **1**:81, **3**:23
    Chesnut (Mary Boykin Miller) on, **2**:251
    Christianity and, **1**:34, 144, **2**:44, 46
    as Civil War issue, **1**:50, **2**:38, 250
    in Cuba, oral histories of, **3**:7–9
    Cuban abolition of, **3**:7
    Douglass's (Frederick) critique of, **1**:33–35
    Equiano's (Olaudah) critique of, **1**:81–83
    Jacobs's (Harriet A.) critique of, **1**:142–145
    in Jamaica, **1**:111
    Kemble's (Fanny) critique of, **2**:335
    Lincoln's (Abraham) views on, **2**:38
    Ruete (Emily) on, **1**:90, 92
    Stone (Kate) on, **2**:245
    U.S. abolition of, **1**:50
    Wheatley's (Phillis) critique of, **2**:44–46
Slave trade
    British abolition of, **1**:34, 111, **3**:23
    British debate over, **1**:81
    Equiano's (Olaudah) critique of, **1**:81–83
    increase in access to records of, **1**:263
    U.S. abolition of, **1**:33
Slavic Review (journal), **3**:332
Slavonic and East European Studies (journal), **3**:135
Sleeper, Jim, **3**:119

Slingsby, Henry
    The Diary of Sir Henry Slingsby, **2**:256–258
    "A Father's Legacy," **2**:256, 257, 258
Slouching towards Bethlehem (Didion), **1**:88
Small, Ian, **2**:9, 10
Small, Meredith, **3**:38
Small Talk (Mitchison), **2**:235
Small War (1895–1898), **3**:7. *See also* Spanish–American War
Small Wars & Insurgencies (Manwaring), **3**:206
Smiles, Samuel, **1**:65
    Self-Help, **2**:310
Smith, Abigail Adams, **2**:87–90
Smith, Adam, **2**:328
    Wealth of Nations, **2**:200
Smith, Angela K., **2**:18, 261
Smith, Betty, **2**:251
Smith, Bruce, **3**:177–178
Smith, Charlotte, **2**:300
Smith, Clark, *Brothers,* **3**:199
Smith, David Lee, **3**:108
Smith, Donald, **2**:236
Smith, Ethel Day, **3**:338
Smith, Gail K., **2**:331
Smith, Gayle, **3**:210
Smith, Geoffrey, **3**:229
Smith, Graham, **3**:171
Smith, Heather, **3**:123
Smith, John (captain), **1**:218
Smith, Joseph, **2**:178
Smith, Kitty, **3**:320
Smith, Mary F., *Baba of Karo,* **3**:141
Smith, Nadia Clare, **2**:308
Smith, Sidonie, **1**:246
Smith, Stevie, **2**:235
Smith, Thomas, **3**:345
Smith, W. Ramsay, **1**:149
Smith College, **2**:47
Smollett, Tobias, **2**:37, 328
Smyth, Frank, *Dialogue and Armed Conflict,* **3**:205
Snodgrass, Mary Ellen, **1**:301
Snow, C. B., **1**:149

THE LITERATURE OF AUTOBIOGRAPHICAL NARRATIVE ✣ VOLUME 3 ✣ ORAL HISTORIES   437

Snow, Edward, **2:**150, 151
Snow, William, **2:**39
Sobukwe, Robert, **1:**25
Social change
    in Appalachia, **3:**86
    in English villages, **3:**59–61, 63–64
    in English working class, **3:**53, 144
    on Native American reservations, **3:**290
    oral histories as agent for, **3:**86, 186, 187
Social class divisions. *See also* Middle class; Working class
    in Brazil, **2:**6, 7
    in Britain, **1:**252–253, **2:**259
    in China, **1:**338, **3:**299
    in collection of oral histories, **3:**177
    in India, **1:**244, 289
    in Ireland, **1:**119–120
    in U.S., **3:**328
Social construction, of "able-bodied," **1:**8
Social equality
    in Britain, in Victorian era, **1:**252, **2:**16
    in U.S., affirmative action and, **1:**15, 16
Social History (journal), **3:**149, 176, 178
Socialism
    in field of history, **3:**176, 177
    in India, Nehru's (Jawaharlal) advocacy of, **1:**289, 290, 291
    in labor movement, **3:**157
    in *The Voice of the Past* (Thompson), **3:**186, 188
    during World War II, Mitchison (Naomi) on, **2:**235
Socialist market economy, of China, **1:**158
Social mobility, in Britain, **1:**252–253
Social reform
    in Brazil, **2:**6
    in Britain, **1:**264, 329, **2:**16
Social Studies of Science (journal), **3:**240
Social welfare, in Britain, oral histories of, **3:**170–172

Society
    poetry in, Neruda (Pablo) on, **1:**222, 223
    self in, and rise of autobiographies, **1:**246
Society of Friends. *See* Quakerism
Society of United Irishmen, **2:**159
Sociological Theory (journal), **3:**332
Sociology
    of race, Du Bois (W. E. B.) on, **1:**5
    Webb's (Beatrice) career in, **2:**16, 17
Sociology of Housework, The (Oakley), **3:**144
Soetoro, Lolo, **1:**78
Soldiers and Citizens (Mirra), **3:**231–232
Soldiers of the Sun (Harries and Harries), **3:**215
Solidarity and Survival (Stromquist), **3:**153
Solidarity Forever (Bird et al.), **3:328–330**
"Solidarity Forever" (song), **3:**329
Soliloquies (Augustine), **1:**196
Solimena, Francesco, **1:184**
Sollors, Werner, *Blacks at Harvard,* **3:**21
Solomon, Charles, **1:**294
Solomon, Martha, **1:**14
Solotaroff-Enzer, Sandra, **2:**254
Solzhenitsyn, Aleksandr
    The Gulag Archipelago, **1:**201, **3:**17
    One Day in the Life of Ivan Denisovich, **3:**17
Somalia
    Hirsi Ali (Ayaan) on life in, **1:**207–209
    interpretation of Islam in, **1:**207
    women in, treatment of, **1:**207
Somali Salvation Democratic Front, **1:**207
Some Memories of the Life of Job (Bluett), **3:**141
"Some Observations on Diaries, Self-Biography, and Self-Characters" (D'Israeli), **2:177–179**
Somerson, Wendy, **1:**160
Sommer, Barbara, **3:**109
Somoza Debayle, Anastasio, **3:**185

Sone, Monica, *Nisei Daughter,* **1:**299, 309
Song Flung Up to Heaven, A (Angelou), **1:**18
Songs My Mother Sang to Me (Preciado Martin), **3:131–134,** 302
Son of Old Man Hat (Left Handed and Dyk). *See Left Handed, Son of Old Man Hat* (Left Handed and Dyk)
Son of the Forest, A (Apess), **1:**56, **3:**318
Sontag, Susan, **2:**122
Sophie's Choice (Styron), **1:**204, 206, **3:**36
Sorghaghtani Beki, **1:**107
Sorin, Gerald, **3:**5
Sorrel, Lorraine, **2:**4
Sorrows of Young Werther, The (Goethe), **1:**276, 277, 339, **2:**166
Sort of Life, A (Greene), **1:**47
Soul, Augustine on, **1:**196
Souls of Black Folk, The (Du Bois), **1:**4, 51
Sourcebook (Kreider), **3:**227
South, U.S.
    abolitionism in, **1:**33
    Angelou (Maya) on life in, **1:**18–20
    in Civil War (*See* American Civil War)
    Great Migration out of, **1:**50, 52, 84, 273, **3:**99
    Latino Americans in, **3:**123
    lynchings in, **1:**18, 50
    racial segregation in, vs. North, **3:**250
    racism in, vs. North, **1:**122
    Reconstruction era in, **1:**50–52, **2:**238, 252
    slavery in economy of, **1:**33
    Wright (Richard) on life in, **1:**122–124
South Africa. *See also* South African autobiographical writing
    AIDS in, **1:**29, **3:**272–274
    Anglo–Boer War in, **2:**241–243
    apartheid in (*See* Apartheid)
    British colonial rule of, Barnard (Anne) on life under, **2:**217–219
    British colonial rule of, establishment of, **2:**241–243

freedom of expression in, **1:**29
Truth and Reconciliation Commission of, **3:**242–244
unification of (1910), **2:**241, 242
South African autobiographical writing. *See also specific works and writers*
by Lessing (Doris), **1:**167–169
by Luthuli (Albert), **1:**24–26
by Mandela (Nelson), **1:**27–29
by Plaatje (Solomon Tshekisho), **2:**241–243
South African Broadcasting Corporation (SABC), **3:**242
South African Communist Party (SACP), **1:**27
South African Native National Congress, **2:**241
South African oral histories
on AIDS epidemic, **3:**272–274
on Truth and Reconciliation Commission, **3:**242–244
South African War. *See* Anglo–Boer War
South Africa's "Black" Market (Fadiman), **3:**142
South Carolina, during Civil War, Chesnut (Mary Boykin Miller) on, **2:**250–252
South Central Review (journal), **2:**255
South Dakota. *See* Pine Ridge Reservation; Wounded Knee
Southeast Asia. *See also specific countries*
immigration to U.S. from, **1:**170, 171, 306
refugees from, **1:**306–307, 337
Southeast Review of Asian Studies (journal), **1:**307
Southern Christian Leadership Conference (SCLC)
Angelou (Maya) in, **1:**18, 20
establishment of, **1:**20
King (Martin Luther, Jr.) in, **1:**20, **2:**32, 34
Southern Command, U.S., **3:**205, 207
Southern Horrors (Wells), **1:**50
Southern Literary Journal, **2:**131
Southern Literary Messenger (magazine), **2:**41
Southern Manifesto (1956), **1:**249

Southern Workman (journal), **1:**52
Southey, Robert, **2:**66–67, 196
South Korea
establishment of (1945), **1:**322
Kim Ku on life in, **1:**322–324
Southland (Revoyr), **1:**309
South Riding (Holtby), **1:**331
South Vietnam. *See also* Vietnam War
establishment of (1954), **1:**335, **3:**279
fall of, oral histories of, **3:**279–281
U.S. military involvement in, origins of, **3:**279
Southwestern American Literature (journal), **3:**12
Southwestern Historical Quarterly, **2:**245, **3:**255
South Wind Changing (Huynh), **1:**171
Sovereignty and Goodness of God, The (Rowlandson), **1:**81, **325–328**, **3:**24
Soviet Baby Boomers (Raleigh), **3:331–333**
Soviet Union. *See also* Russia
Afghan war with, **1:**40, **3:**233
baby boomers of, oral histories of, **3:**331–333
Berlin occupied by, **2:**281–282
Chernobyl nuclear disaster in, **3:**282–285
collapse of, **3:**282, 331, 333, 340
Du Bois (W. E. B.) and, **1:**3, 4
establishment of, **3:**331
glasnost in, **3:**282, 331, 333
Gulag system in, oral histories of, **3:**17–19
industrialization in, **3:**17
KGB of, Stasi modeled on, **3:**245
McKay's (Claude) reception in, **1:**84, 85
perestroika in, **3:**17, 331
Sowden, Benjamin, **2:**37
Soyinka, Wole, **1:**215
Madmen and Specialists, **1:**214
***The Man Died*, 1:214–217, 2:**12, 14
Season of Anomy, **1:**214
A Shuttle in the Crypt, **1:**214
Sozaboy (Saro-Wiwa), **1:**312
Spacks, Patricia Meyer, **2:**35

Spain
California as colony of, **3:**114
colonial power of, origins of, **2:**201, 202
Columbus's (Christopher) exploration for, **2:**201–203
in Cuban War of Independence, **3:**7
Morocco as protectorate of, **3:**47
Puerto Rico as colony of, **1:**108
in Ten Years' War, **3:**7
Teresa of Ávila in, **1:**211–213
Spandau (Speer), **2:54–56**
Spandau prison (Berlin), **2:**54–56, 55
Spanish–American War (1898), **1:**108, 332, **3:**7
Spanish Civil War (1936–1939)
Gellhorn's (Martha) reporting on, **2:**101–103
Guevara (Ernesto "Che") influenced by, **2:**220
Neruda's (Pablo) experience in, **1:**222
Spanish Inquisition, **1:**211
Spanish language
in identity, **1:**15–17
in Puerto Rico, **1:**109
in U.S. education, **1:**15, 16, 17
Spared Angola (Suárez), **1:**296
Sparks, Beatrice
Annie's Baby, **2:**294
as author of *Go Ask Alice* (anonymous), **2:**294–296
It Happened to Nancy, **2:**294
Jay's Journal, **2:**294
Spartacus (magazine), **3:**70
Speak, Memory (Nabokov), **1:**249, 270
Speak, Memory: An Autobiography Revisited (Nabokov), **1:270–272**
Speak for England (Bragg), **3:**144
Speaking Our Minds (Read and Reynolds), **3:**170
Spear, Thomas, **3:**143
Spectator (magazine), **2:**102, 231, 328, **3:**59, 235
Spector, Scott, **2:**122
Speer, Albert
Inside the Third Reich, **2:**54
***Spandau*, 2:54–56**
in *The World at War* (Holmes), **3:**235

Spence, Polly, *Moving Out,* **2:**163
Spencer, Terence, **2:**228
Spender, Stephen, **2:236**
Spengemann, William, **1:**246
Spenser, Edmund, **2:**62, 146
Spiegelman, Art
    Maus, **1:**139, 141, 156, 293
    Nakazawa's (Keiji) influence on, **1:**293, 294
Spielberg, Steven, **2:**71
Spier, Julius, **2:**22
Spion Kop, Battle of (1900), **2:242**
Spiritual fulfillment, Wells (H. G.) on, **1:**252
Spiritual suffering, Peltier (Leonard) on, **1:**96, 97
Spitzack, Carole J., "Body Talk," **3:**190
Spivak, Gayatri Chakravorty, **1:**87
Spoils of Poynton, The (James), **2:**115
Spokesman Review (newspaper), **3:**95
Spratt, Margaret, **3:**306–307
Sprinkler, Michael, **1:**246, 247
Stacey, Judith, **3:**191
Staël, Madame de, **2:**75–76
Staempfle, Bernhard, **1:**32
Stalin, Joseph, **3:**332
    Gulag system under, **3:**17, 18, 19
    Khrushchev (Nikita) on, **3:**333
    oral histories about life under, **3:**340, 341
    rise to power, **3:**331
Stalingrad, Battle of (1942–1943), **2:**281
Stallings, Selona, **1:**205
Stallworthy, John, **2:**248
Stalp, Marybeth, **3:**309
Stanford University, **1:**15, *16*
Stanton, Elizabeth Cady, **1:13**
    Eighty Years and More, **1:12–14**
    History of Woman Suffrage, **1:**12
    The Woman's Bible, **1:**12, 13
Stanton, Harriot, **1:**13
Stanton, Henry, **1:**13
Stanton, Theodore, **1:**13
Staples, Suzanne Fisher, **1:**41
Starfield, Jane, **2:**242
Stark, Arthur, **3:**155
Starr, Louis M., **3:**186, 188

Starr, Roger, **3:**61
Stasi, oral histories of, **3:**245–247
Staten, Henry, **1:**16–17
Staub, Michael E., **1:**71
Stavanger International Prize for Freedom of Expression, for *Letters Underway* (Ghazzawi), **2:**50
Stave, Bruce M., *Witnesses to Nuremberg,* **3:293–295**
St. Clair, David, **2:**6
Steel Shavings (magazine), **3:**161
Steelworkers Trilogy, **3:**153
Steer, George, **2:**101
Steffen-Fluhr, Nancy, **1:**253
Stein, Daniel, **1:**78
Stein, Emmanuel, **3:**154
Stein, Gertrude
    The Autobiography of Alice B. Toklas, **1:**332, 334
    Brewsie and Willie, **1:**333
    Everybody's Autobiography, **1:**332
    Ida, **1:**332
    Paris France, **1:**332
    Wars I Have Seen, **1:332–334**
    Wright's (Richard) friendship with, **1:**124
Steinhoff, Johannes, *Voices from the Third Reich,* **3:**215
Stelzig, Eugene, **2:**77
Stengel, Richard, **1:**28
Stephens, Gregory, **1:**109
Stepto, Robert B.
    From Behind the Veil, **1:**35
    A Home Elsewhere, **1:**80
Stereotypes
    of Appalachian culture, **3:**68, 86, 96
    of Chinese Americans, **1:**173, 174
    of Chinese women, **1:**173, **3:**147
    of Japanese war brides, **3:**128
    of Japan in World War II, **3:**215
    of Mexican Americans, **3:**131, 133
Sterling, Bruce, **2:**145
Sterne, Laurence, **2:**328
Stevens, Ayako, **3:**128
Stevens, Elizabeth Zofchak, **3:**338
Stevenson, Adlai, **2:**101
Stevenson, Brenda, **2:**29, 30, 31

Stevenson, Robert Louis, **2:**73
Stewart, Clyde, **2:**91
Stewart, Elinore Pruitt
    Letters of a Woman Homesteader, **2:91–93**
    Letters on an Elk Hunt, **2:**91
Stewart, Gary, *Black Man's Grave,* **1:**312
Stewart, Henry C., **1:**8
Stewart, Jon, **1:**312
Stewart, Randall, **2:**225
Stille, Alexander, **3:**159
Still Ready (film), **3:**48
Stizia, Lorraine, **3:**192
St. John, J. Hector. *See* Crèvecoeur, Michel-Guillaume Saint-Jean de
St. Louis Globe-Democrat (newspaper), **1:**147
St. Louis Post Dispatch (newspaper), **1:**85, 299
Stock, Brian, **1:**198
Stock market, U.S., 1929 crash of, **3:**161, 212
Stock Reduction Act (U.S.), **3:**318
"Stoicien, Le" (Frederick the Great), **1:**218
Stoicism, **1:**218–221
Stoll, David, **3:**164, 165, 166
Stone, Albert E., **2:**213, 214
Stone, Harlan Fiske, **2:**56
Stone, Kate, *Brokenburn,* **2:244–246**
Stone, Norman, **2:**85
Stone, Oliver, **1:**335, *336*
Stone, William, **2:**244, 246
Stoppard, Tom, *Arcadia,* **2:**145
Stop-Time (Conroy), **1:164–166,** 270
Stories in a New Skin (Martin), **3:**138
Storming Caesars Palace (Orleck), **3:**254
StoryCorps, **3:174,** 345
Story of a Shipwrecked Sailor, The (García Márquez), **3:183–185**
Story of My Life, The: An Afghan Girl on the Other Side of the Sky (Ahmedi), **1:40–42**
Story of My Life, The: Helen Keller (Keller), **1:43–46**
Story of My Life and Work, The (Washington), **1:**37
Storyteller's Daughter, The (Shah), **1:**40

Storytelling traditions
- German, **1:**30
- Irish, **3:**315
- Native American, **1:**21, 22, 55, 302, 304, **3:**320

Stowe, Harriet Beecher, **2:**143
- *Uncle Tom's Cabin*, **1:**33, 144

Strachey, Alix, **2:**268
Strachey, James, **2:**268
Strachey, Julia, **2:**268
Strachey, Lionel, **1:**90, 91
Strachey, Lytton, **2:**268
Strange Ground (Maurer), **3:275–278**
Stranger's Supper, A (Milich), **3:135–137**
Strata (journal), **3:**174
Stream-of-consciousness
- *A Diary without Dates* (Bagnold) compared to, **2:**260
- *Life on the Mississippi* (Twain) as precursor to, **1:**146
- in *The Man Died* (Soyinka), **1:**216
- in *Memoirs* (Neruda), **1:**223
- in *The Woman Warrior* (Kingston), **1:**174

Street, Brian, **2:**237
Streetcar Named Desire, A (film), **2:**152
Streetcar Named Desire, A (Williams), **2:**152
Street Violence in the Nineteenth Century (Sindall), **3:**312
Strength Not to Fight, The (Tollefson), **3:221–223**, 227, 276
Strickland, Susanna, **3:**23, 24, 25
Strikes. *See* Labor strikes
Strindberg, August, **2:**120
Strobel, Larry, *When the Mill Whistle Blew*, **3:**93
Stromquist, Shelton, *Solidarity and Survival*, **3:**153
Strong, Pauline, **3:**320
Strottman, Theresa, **3:**240
Strozier, Charles B., **3:**263–264
Structuralism, **1:**239, 267
Struggle for Gay and Lesbian Equal Rights, The (Marcus), **3:**83
Struggle for the Land (Churchill), **3:**10
Strychacz, Thomas, **1:**166

Stuart, John T., **3:**261
Stubborn Twig (Kessler), **3:**80
Stuck Rubber Baby (Cruse), **1:**139
Students
- in Cultural Revolution, **1:**161
- deferments for, in Vietnam War, **3:**221
- in movements of 1968, **3:**31–33

Students for a Democratic Society (Buhle et al.), **3:**330
Studies in American Indian Literatures (journal), **1:**23, 70, **3:**109
Studies in English Literature (journal), **2:**231
Studies in the Novel (journal), **1:**313, 314
Studs Turkel Program, The (radio show), **3:**161
Studs Turkel's Working (Buhle and Pekar), **3:**330
Study of the Negro Problem, The (Du Bois), **1:**50
Sturgis, Caroline, **2:**139
Sturgis, Howard, **2:**115
Sturrock, John, **1:**67
Styron, William, **1:205**
- *The Confessions of Nat Turner*, **1:**204, 206
- *Darkness Visible*, **1:204–206**
- *Lie Down in Darkness*, **1:**204, 206
- *Set This House on Fire*, **1:**206
- *Sophie's Choice*, **1:**204, 206, **3:**36
- on *Stop-Time* (Conroy), **1:**165

Suárez, Virgil, *Spared Angola*, **1:**296
Subjectivity, in oral histories, **3:**162, 173, 186
Submission, in Islam, Hirsi Ali (Ayaan) on, **1:**208
Submission, Part 1 (film), **1:**207, 208
Suenaga, Shizuko, *Japanese War Brides in America*, **3:127–130**
Suffolk (England), oral histories of village life in, **3:**59–61, 63–65
Suffrage. *See* Voting rights
Sugarmill, The (Moreno Franglinal), **3:**7
Sugawara no Michizane, **2:**189
Sugawara no Takasue, daughter of. *See* Sarashina, Lady
Sugiman, Pamela, **3:**178

Suicide
- of Hitler (Adolf), **2:**281
- of Levi (Primo), **1:**204, 205
- of Plath (Sylvia), **2:**47
- Styron's (William) battle with, **1:**204–205
- of Woolf (Virginia), **2:**268
- Xie Bingying's idealization of, **1:**339

Sukhu, Gopal, **3:**288
Suleri, Sara
- *Boys Will Be Boys*, **1:**88
- *Meatless Days*, **1:87–89**
- *The Rhetoric of English India*, **1:**87–88

Sullivan, Anne, **1:**43–46
Sullivan, Walter, **1:**165
Sully, Thomas, **2:317**
Sumerians, letter writing by, **2:**94
Summerfield, Penny, **2:**237, **3:**336
Summers, Carol, **3:**253
Summerskill, Edith, **2:**235
Summing Up, The (Maugham), **2:**183
Sumner, Fort. *See* Bosque Redondo Reservation
Sun Also Rises, The (Hemingway), **2:**259
Sun Dance ceremony, **1:**23, 96, 97
Sunday Times (newspaper), **2:**85
Sunrise Tomorrow (Mitchison), **2:**237
Sun Yat-sen, **1:**338, **2:**170
Suppression of Communism Act of 1950 (South Africa), **1:**27
Supreme Court, U.S.
- *Amistad* case in, **2:**70, 71
- on conscientious objectors, **3:**223
- on interracial marriage, **1:**72, 78
- on labor arbitration, **3:**153
- on racial quotas in higher education, **3:**20
- on racial segregation, **1:**37, 50, 122, 249, **3:**44
- on slavery, **2:**38

Survival, literature of
- *The Story of a Shipwrecked Sailor* (García Márquez) as, **3:**183–185
- *They Say in Harlan County* (Portelli) as, **3:**96–97
- *The Unwanted* (Nguyen) as, **1:**170

SUBJECT INDEX

Survival in the Killing Fields (Ngor), **1:**306
Surviving the Slaughter (Umutesi), **3:**258
Survivors: An Oral History of the Armenian Genocide (Miller and Miller), **3:40–43,** 50
Survivors: The Story of Ireland's Struggle (MacEoin), **3:**27, 315
Suter, Thomas, **2:**271
Sutherland, John, **2:**311
Sutherland, Sibyl, **3:**78
Sutton, Roger, **1:**162
Sutzkever, Abraham, **1:**255
Su Xuelin, *Ninety-Four Years of a Floating Life,* **1:**338
Suyeoshi, Amy, **3:**84
Suzuki, Mihoko, **2:**64
Sweeney, Joseph, **3:**29
Sweet and Sour Milk (Farah), **1:**207
Sweeter the Juice, The (Haizlip), **1:**73
Swiftwater People (Russell), **3:93–95**
Swinburne, Algernon Charles, **2:**82, 147
Swinnerton, Frank, **2:**138
Symmachus, **2:**94–95
Symons, Julian, **2:**42–43
"Sympathy" (Dunbar), **1:**50
Symposium (journal), **1:**183
Synethesia, **1:**272
Synge, John Millington, **2:**126, 128
Syria, Greater, Usāmah ibn Munqidh on history of, **1:**285–286
Syrian Thunderbolt, The (Imad al-Din), **1:**286
Syrkin, Marie, **2:**22–23, 24
Szadziuk, Maria, **1:**110

T

Taccola, Mariano, **2:161**
Tacitus, Cornelius, **2:**94, **3:**186
Taggart, Cynthia, **3:**95
Taine, Hippolyte, **2:**82
Taino people, **2:202**
Tait's Edinburgh Magazine, **2:**178
Takaki, Shintaro, **3:**82
Takasue's daughter. *See* Sarashina, Lady

Takeshita, Ben, **3:**196
Takooshian, Harold, **3:**41
Talcott, Samuel, **1:**325
Tale of Genji, The (Murasaki), **2:**59, 60, 189, 190, 290–292, *291*
Tales for Cottagers (Leadbeater), **2:**157
Taliban, rise of, **1:**40
Talking to Myself (Terkel), **3:**214
Tallichet, Suzanne E., **3:**338–339
Talmadge, Herman, **1:**5
Talmage, Thomas de Witt, **1:**150
Tamai Kōsuke, **2:**189, 190–191
Tamari, Salim, **2:**104, 105, 106
Tamura, Keiki, *Michi's Memories,* **3:**127
Tamura, Linda
    The Hood River Issei, **3:80–82**
    Nisei Soldiers Break Their Silence, **3:**80
Tan, Amy, **1:**159
Tanzania
    establishment of borders of, **1:**114
    Ruete (Emily) on life in, **1:**90–92
    Saitoti (Tepilit Ole) on life in, **1:**114–116
Taplin, George, **1:**149, 150
Tappes, Shelton, **3:**101
Tarhan, Mehmet, **3:**229
Tatars, **3:**17, 19
Tateishi, John, *And Justice for All,* **3:195–198,** 224
Tateishi, Yuri, **3:**197
Tavalaro, Julia, *Look up for Yes,* **1:**6
Taylor, Barbara, **2:**111
Taylor, Charles G., **1:**312
Taylor, Craig, **3:**59, 60, 61
Taylor, Elizabeth, **2:**261
Taylor, Ethel Barol, **3:**269, 270–271
Taylor, Jeremy, *Rule and Exercises of Holy Living and Dying,* **2:**195
Taylor, Paul F., *Bloody Harlan,* **3:**96
Taylor, Phyllis, **3:**119
Taylor, Richard, *Destruction and Reconstruction,* **2:**250
Taylor, Sandra, *Jewel of the Desert,* **3:**80
Taylor, Steven J., *Acts of Conscience,* **3:**227
Taylor, Telford, **3:**212
Taylor, Vic, **3:**103

Tchaikovsky, Pyotr Ilyich, **2:**143
Tcheng, Soumay. *See* Cheng Yu-hsiu
Teacher Man (McCourt), **1:**119
Teachers, U.S., oral histories of, **3:**77–79
Teachers College Record (periodical), **3:**77
Teaching a Stone to Talk (Dillard), **1:**279
Tears before the Rain (Engelmann), **3:**210, 265, **279–281**
Tebutt, Melanie, **3:**178
Technological advances
    Adams (Henry) on, **1:**132–134
    in agriculture, in England, **3:**59, 63
    Emerson (Ralph Waldo) on, **2:**139
    in medicine, **3:**170
    in oral history field, **3:**181
    Thoreau (Henry David) on, **1:**233
    in World War I, **2:**180
Technological Revolution, **1:**134
Teel, Witcher, **3:**78
Teenagers. *See* Adolescents
Telegraph (newspaper), **1:**7–8, **2:**153, 261
Telegraph, invention of, **1:**233
Television adaptations. *See also specific programs*
    of *Go Ask Alice* (anonymous), **2:**294, *295*
    of *Nella Last's War* (Last), **2:**265, 266
    of *Testament of Experience* (Brittain), **1:**330
    of *Working* (Terkel), **3:**343
Telling Identities (Sánchez), **3:**115, 121–122
Telling Maya Tales (Gossen), **3:**167
Tell Me Africa (Olney), **1:**246
Tell My Horse (Hurston), **1:**9, 11
Temple, Mary "Minny," **2:**113
Temple, William, **2:**324–327
Ten Africans (collected stories), **1:**64
"Tenir un journal" (Lejeune). *See* "Practice of the Private Journal" (Lejeune)
Tennyson, Alfred, **1:**264, **2:**140, 271, 335
Ten Thousand Sorrows (Kim), **1:102–104**

Ten Years of Madness (Feng), **3:**287
Ten Years' War (1868–1878), **3:**7
Teorey, Matthew, **1:**311
Teresa of Ávila, **1:**212
 Interior Castle, **1:**212
 The Life, **1:**211–213
 The Way of Perfection, **1:**212
Terkel, Louis "Studs," **3:**213, *344*
 on *AIDS Doctors* (Oppenheimer and Bayer), **3:**274
 American Dreams, **3:**300
 Chinese Lives (Zhang and Sang) inspired by, **3:**299, 300
 Division Street, **3:**161, 299, 343
 "*The Good War*", **3:**161, 199, 202, **212–214,** 234, 343
 Hard Times, **3:161–163,** 179, 199, 212, 279, 343
 in origins and rise of oral history, **3:**173, 179, 279, 345
 Talking to Myself, **3:**214
 Touch and Go, **3:**214
 Working, **3:**161, 300, **343–345**
Terni (Italy), oral histories of working class in, **3:**157–159
Terrorism. *See* September 11 terrorist attacks
Terry, Ellen, **2:**335
Terry, Wallace, *Missing Pages,* **3:**199–200. *See also* Bloods (Terry)
Tertullian, **2:**94
Testament of Experience (Brittain), **1:**330
Testament of Friendship (Brittain), **1:**330, 331
Testament of Youth (Brittain), **1:329–331, 2:**247–248, 259, 269, **3:**176
Testimonios. *See also specific works*
 definition of, **3:**7, 322
 origins of, **3:**7
 tradition of, **3:**73–74, 114–115, 164, 322
Testimonios: Early California Through the Eyes of Women (Senkewicz and Beebe), **3:**116
Testimony Films, **3:**313
Tet Offensive (1968), **3:**275
Texas, oral histories of teachers in, **3:**77–79, *78*

Texas Studies in Literature and Language (journal), **1:**213, 316
Textual Cultures (journal), **2:**252
Textual Practice (journal), **2:**182
Thackeray, William, **2:**335
 Vanity Fair, **2:**312
Thames Television, **3:**234
Theater, Hansberry's (Lorraine) writing for, **1:**273–275
Theatre History Studies (journal), **2:**153
Their Eyes Were Watching God (Hurston), **1:**11
Thelen, David, **3:**181
Themistius (orator), **1:**218, 220
Theobald, Paul, **3:**78
Theoharis, Jeanne, **3:**101
Theological Studies (journal), **3:**309
Theology. *See* Religion
Thérèse Raquin (Zola), **1:**6
There Was This Goat (Krog et al.), **3:**242
These Are Our Lives (Federal Writers' Project), **3:**86
They Say in Harlan County (Portelli), **3:**87, **96–98,** 158
Thirteenth Amendment, **1:**50
This Boy's Life (Wolff), **1:47–49**
This Was Not Our War (Hunt), **3:**268
Thomas, Caitlin, **1:**127
Thomas, David, **2:**247, 248
Thomas, Dylan
 A Child's Christmas in Wales, **1:125–127**
 Eighteen Poems, **1:**125
 The Love Letters of Dylan Thomas, **1:**127
 Quite Early One Morning, **1:**125
Thomas, John Peter (Piri), *Down These Mean Streets,* **1:**109
Thompson, Dorothy, **2:**278
Thompson, Paul
 on *Akenfield* (Blythe), **3:**59–61
 on *The Death of Luigi Trastulli* (Portelli), **3:**159
 The Edwardians, **3:**176, 186, 311
 Hooligans or Rebels? (Humphries) influenced by, **3:**311–312
 on *In the Mansion of Confucius' Descendants* (Kong and Ke), **3:**126

 Living through the Soviet System, **3:**331
 Oral History, Health and Welfare, **3:170–172**
 on *The Saga of Coe Ridge* (Montell), **3:**92
 Vietnam War literature influenced by, **3:**209
 The Voice of the Past, **3:**59–61, 92, **186–189,** 209, 311–312
Thompson, Stephen, **3:**126
Thompson, Thea, *Edwardian Childhoods,* **3:**312
Thomson, Alistair
 "ANZAC Memories," **3:**177, 178
 on internationalization of oral history, **3:**129
 The Oral History Reader, **3:**173, 178, 179, 181
 on origins of oral history, **3:**135
 on Portelli (Alessandro), **3:**267
 on *The Voice of the Past* (Thompson), **3:**188
 on *Women's Words* (Gluck and Patai), **3:**192
Thomson, David, **3:**65
Thorberg, Raymond, **2:**115
Thoreau, Henry David, **1:**234
 conscientious objectors influenced by, **3:**228
 Dillard (Annie) influenced by, **1:**279
 Emerson (Ralph Waldo) and, **1:**233, **2:**139, 140
 Gandhi (Mohandas) influenced by, **1:**242
 Hawthorne (Nathaniel) and, **2:**223
 James (Henry) compared to, **2:**115
 "Resistance to Civil Government," **1:**242
 Walden, **1:233–236, 2:**140, 215
 A Week on the Concord and Merrimack Rivers, **1:**233, 234, 235, **2:**140
Thoreau, John, **1:**233
Thornbrough, Emma Lou, **3:**91
Thornhill, James, **2:325**
Thornton, Alice, *Autobiography,* **1:**230
Thornton, Margaret Bradham, **2:**153, 154

SUBJECT INDEX

Thornton, Michael, **2:**261
Thorpe, Charles, **3:**240
Those Devils in Baggy Pants (Carter), **3:**212
Thoughts and Sentiments on the Evil and Wicked Traffic of the Slavery and Commerce of the Human Species (Cugoana), **1:**81
Thoughts without Cigarettes (Hijuelos), **1:**75
Thrasher, Max, **1:**50
Thrasher, Sesali Storm, **3:**233
Three-Inch Golden Lotus, The (Feng), **3:**289
Three Minus One (Kilani), **2:**52
Threepenny Review (journal), **1:**168
Through the Brazilian Wilderness (Roosevelt), **2:**220
Thura's Diary (Al-Windawi), **2:275–277**
Tieck, Ludwig, *Franz Sternbalds Wanderungen*, **1:**276
Tiefenbrun, Susan, **2:**33
Tighe, C., **1:**216
Ti Jean L'Horizon (Schwarz-Bart), **1:**64
Tiller, Emma, **3:**162
Tilley, M. P., **2:**228
Tilton, Theodore, **2:**239
Time (magazine)
    on *Bloods* (Terry), **3:**201
    on *I, Rigoberta Menchú* (Menchú), **3:**165
    on *A Long Way Gone* (Beah), **1:**312, 313, 314
    on *Red Azalea* (Min), **1:**159
    Terry (Wallace) at, **3:**199
Time, and memory
    Conroy (Frank) on, **1:**164, 165, 166
    Nabokov (Vladimir) on, **1:**271, 272
Times Higher Education (magazine), **3:**247
Times Literary Supplement
    on *Akenfield* (Blythe), **3:**59, 61
    on *A Country Parson* (Woodforde), **2:**288
    on *The Dark Child* (Laye), **1:**129
    on *De Profundis* (Wilde), **2:**10

    on *Diaries, 1915–1918* (Sassoon), **2:**248
    on *An Experiment in Autobiography* (Wells), **1:**253
    on *The Journals of Jonathan Carver and Related Documents* (Carver), **2:**206
    on *Testament of Youth* (Brittain), **1:**330
    on *Working-Class Childhood* (Seabrook), **3:**54
    on *The Worlds of a Maasai Warrior* (Saitoti), **1:**115
    on *The Writing Life* (Dillard), **1:**280
Times of London (newspaper), **1:**32, 141, 191, **2:**75, 275
Timmons, Stuart, *Gay L.A.*, **3:**83–84
Tin mining, in Bolivia, oral histories of, **3:**322–324
Tippett, Mehetable, **2:**213
'Tis (McCourt), **1:**119
Tishler, Jennifer, **3:**285
Titcomb, Caldwell, *Blacks at Harvard*, **3:**21
Tito, **3:**135
Titon, Jeff, **3:**88
Tlatelolco massacre of 1968 (Mexico), **3:**31–33
To Bear Any Burden (Santoli), **3:**210
To Be Young, Gifted and Black (Hansberry), **1:273–275**
Tocqueville, Alexis de, **2:**214
Todd, Janet, **2:**109, 110, 111
"To His Excellency General Washington" (Wheatley), **2:**44
Tohono O'odham culture, Chona (Maria) on life in, **1:**69–71
Tóibín, Colm, **1:**79–80
Toilet paper, prisoners writing on, **1:**214, **2:**12, 13, 54
Toki, Tanaka, **3:**216
Toklas, Alice B., **1:**332, 333, 334
Tollefson, James W., *The Strength Not to Fight*, **3:221–223,** 227, 276
Tolstoy, Leo, **1:**194
    Anna Karenina, **1:**193
    A Confession, **1:193–195,** 270
    conscientious objectors influenced by, **3:**228

    Gandhi (Mohandas) influenced by, **1:**242
    Investigation of Dogmatic Theology, **1:**194
    Kafka (Franz) influenced by, **2:**120
    Rilke (Rainer Maria) and, **2:**151
    Translation and Harmony of the Four Gospels, **1:**193–194
    What I Believe, **1:**194, 195
Tolstoy, Sonya, **1:**195
Tolui Khan, **1:**107
Tomalin, Claire, **2:**73
Tomasini, Giacomo Filippo, **2:**160, 161
Tomberlin, Joseph, **1:**38
Tomko, Steve, **3:**87
Tommaso da Milano, **2:**160
Tomorrow (magazine), **1:**10
Tompkins, Sally, **2:**273
Tone, Theobald Wolfe, **2:**159
Tonghak religion, Kim Ku influenced by, **1:**322, 323, 324
To Nicocles (Isocrates), **2:**94
Tonna, Charlotte, **2:**335
Tonomura, Hitomi, **2:**61
Too Long Been Silent (Axford), **3:**196
Top Girls (Churchill), **2:60**
Torkington, Richard, **2:**227
Totah, Khalil, **2:**106
To the Edge of the Sky (Gao), **1:**159
To the Lighthouse (Woolf), **1:**146
Touch and Go (Terkel), **3:**214
Toulouse, Teresa A., **1:**328
Touré, Sékou, **1:**130
Towazugatari (Nijo). *See Confessions of Lady Nijo* (Nijo)
Townsend, Francis G., **1:**265
Townsend, Sue, **2:**338
Trade, between West and East
    expansion of, **1:**90, 105
    Gama's (Vasco da) exploration and, **2:**198–200
Trade routes, in colonial U.S., **2:**205
Tragic Life (Bai), **1:**338
"Tragic mulatto" tradition, **1:**72
Trail of Broken Tears Caravan (1972), **1:**21
Trajan (Roman emperor), **2:**94
Tramp Abroad, A (Twain), **1:**146

Transcendental fiction, **1**:281
Transcendentalism
    Dillard (Annie) influenced by, **1**:279
    Emerson (Ralph Waldo) in, **2**:140
    James's (Henry) views on, **2**:113
    Thoreau (Henry David) in, **1**:233–236
    utopian societies inspired by, **1**:235
Transforming State-Society Relations in Mexico (Craig), **3**:302
Transition (journal), **1**:88
Translation and Harmony of the Four Gospels (Tolstoy), **1**:193–194
Transnational autobiography, *Dreams from My Father* (Obama) as, **1**:79
Trask, Michael, **1**:260
Trastulli, Luigi, **3**:157, 158
Trauma, autobiographies of
    by Africans, **1**:313–314
    definition of, **1**:102
    Ten Thousand Sorrows (Kim) as, **1**:102
    The Unwanted (Nguyen) as, **1**:170–171, 172
Traveling Heavy (Behar), **1**:297
Travel narratives. *See also specific works and writers*
    The Autobiography of Ben Franklin (Franklin) as, **1**:179
    borrowing from other sources in, **2**:227, 229
    Life on the Mississippi (Twain) as, **1**:146–147
    A Long Way from Home (McKay) as, **1**:84–86
    Memoirs of an Arabian Princess from Zanzibar (Ruete) as, **1**:90–92
    Motorcycle Diaries (Guevara) as, **2**:220–221
    The Pylgrymage of Sir Richarde Guylforde (Guylforde) as, **2**:226–228
    rise in popularity of, **1**:90, **2**:229
    The Travels of Dean Mahomet (Mahomet) as, **2**:229–231
    The Travels of Marco Polo (Polo) as, **1**:105–107
    Western biases in, **1**:90
    The Wonderful Adventures of Mrs. Seacole (Seacole) as, **1**:111
Travels in West Africa (Kingsley), **2**:335
Travels of Dean Mahomet, The (Mahomet), **2**:229–232
Travels of Marco Polo, The (Polo), **1**:105–107, *106*, **2**:198, 201
Travels of Sir John Mandeville, The (Mandeville), **2**:198, 227
Travels through the Interior Parts of North America (Carver), **2**:205
TRC. *See* Truth and Reconciliation Commission
Treadwell, James, **2**:179
Treason
    Slingsby (Henry) convicted of, **2**:257, 258
    in Treason Trials of South Africa, **1**:24
Treasonable Growth, A (Blythe), **3**:61
Treasures in the Dust (Porter), **1**:161
Treaties. *See specific treaties*
Treister, Kenneth, **3**:51
Trelawney, Edward John, **2**:143, 154
Trembling of the Veil, The (Yeats), **2**:126, 127
Trench warfare, in World War I, **2**:247
Trenka, Jane Jeong, *The Language of Blood*, **1**:102
Trent, Council of, **1**:211
Trevelyan, G. O., **2**:143
Trial, The (Kafka), **2**:120, 121–122
Trials
    of anarchists, **3**:4
    Nuremberg, **2**:54, 56, **3**:293–295
    of Peltier (Leonard), **1**:96
    Treason, of South Africa, **1**:24
    of Wilde (Oscar), **2**:9, 183, 185
Tribune Books, **2**:338
Tricknor, William D., **2**:224
Trickster stories
    African, **2**:3
    Chinese, **1**:163
Trill, Suzanne L., **1**:316, 317
Trilling, Lionel, **1**:123
Trilogy Principle, **1**:248
Trimmer, Sarah, **2**:300
Triple Alliance (1668), **2**:324
Tripmaster Monkey (Kingston), **1**:173
Trippa, Elchide, **3**:158
Tristes Tropiques (Lévi-Strauss), **3**:37
Troide, Lars, **2**:314
Trollope, Anthony, **2**:101, 320
Trollope, Frances, *Domestic Manners of the Americans*, **2**:223
Tropes, racial, in *Dreams from My Father* (Obama), **1**:80
Tropic of Cancer (Miller), **2**:123
Trotsky, Leon, **1**:84, **2**:172
Trouble I've Seen, The (Gellhorn), **2**:101
Troubles, The (Ireland), **3**:27, 29
Trouble with Diversity, The (Michaels), **1**:16
Trouble with Islam Today, The (Manji), **1**:207
True Relation of My Birth, Breeding, and Life, A (Cavendish), **1**:229–232
Truman, Harry, **3**:199, 248, 249, 293
Trumpener, Katie, **2**:305
Truth
    authors' pact regarding, Lejeune (Philippe) on, **1**:239–240, **2**:174
    of *Biography of a Runaway Slave* (Barnet and Montejo), **3**:8
    of *Bloods* (Terry), **3**:199, 201
    in Cartesian rationalism, **1**:183
    of *Dust Tracks on a Road* (Hurston), **1**:9–11
    of *Everything We Had* (Santoli), **3**:211
    of *Go Ask Alice* (anonymous), **2**:294, 295
    of *The Good Man of Nanking* (Rabe), **2**:19, 20–21
    of *The History of Mary Prince* (Prince), **3**:25
    of *I, Rigoberta Menchú* (Menchú), **3**:164, 165–166
    of *The Journal of Marie Bashkirtseff* (Bashkirtseff), **2**:307
    of *Journal of the First Voyage to America* (Columbus), **2**:203
    Lessing (Doris) on nature of, **1**:167
    of *Letters of a Woman Homesteader* (Stewart), **2**:92
    of *A Long Way from Home* (McKay), **1**:85

SUBJECT INDEX

Truth, *continued*
- of *A Long Way Gone* (Beah), **1:**313
- in *Memories of a Catholic Girlhood* (McCarthy), **1:**259–260
- of *A Million Little Pieces* (Frey), **2:**296
- of *Night* (Wiesel), **1:**319, 320
- in postmodernism, **1:**168
- of *Roots* (Haley), **1:**262
- of *Spandau* (Speer), **2:**54–55
- of *Survivors* (Miller and Miller), **3:**42
- of *Ten Thousand Sorrows* (Kim), **1:**103
- of *The Travels of Marco Polo* (Polo), **1:**107
- of *A True Relation of My Birth, Breeding, and Life* (Cavendish), **1:**230
- of *The Unwanted* (Nguyen), **1:**172
- of *A Woman in Berlin* (anonymous), **2:**281, 282
- of *The Woman Warrior* (Kingston), **1:**175
- of *Zlata's Diary* (Filipovic), **2:**340

Truth, Sojourner, *Narrative of Sojourner Truth,* **1:**37

Truth and Fiction Relating to My Life (Goethe), **1:276–278**

Truth and Reconciliation Commission (TRC), oral histories of, **3:**242–244

Try to Remember (Gomez), **1:**108

Tso, Mae, **3:**11

Tsuchino (Forrester), **3:**127–128

Tsukamoto, Mary, **3:**197

Tuberculosis
- Bashkirtseff's (Marie) struggle with, **2:**306, 307, 308
- Mansfield's (Katherine) struggle with, **2:**133

Tubman, Harriet, **2:**29

Tuchman, Barbara, **3:**186

Tuhami (Crapanzano), **3:**47

Tulsa Studies in Women's Literature (journal), **2:**111, 124

Tulugarjuk, Leo, *Ilagiinniq,* **3:**138

Tunisia, Amrouche (Fadhma Aïth Mansour) in, **1:**93, 94

Tuqan, Fadwa
- *The Harder Journey,* **1:**226
- *A Mountainous Journey,* **1:225–228**
- *My Brother Ibrahim,* **1:**227

Tuqan, Ibrahim, **1:**226, 227

Turgenev, Ivan, **2:**183

Turkey
- Armenian genocide denied by, **3:**40, 42
- in Crimean War, **1:**113

Turkish Embassy Letters (Montagu), **2:**35, 37

Turkish Lover, The (Santiago), **1:**108

Turner, D. R., **3:**255

Turner, Frederick W., III, **1:**304

Turner, J. M. W., **2:**143

Turner, Nat, **1:**206, **2:**238

Tuskegee Airmen, oral histories of, **3:**248–250

Tuskegee Airmen, The (film), **3:249**

Tuskegee Airmen, The (Francis), **3:**212

Tuskegee Institute, **1:**50, 51, *51*, 52

Tute, James, **2:**205

Tutsi people, **3:**257–259

Tutu, Desmond
- *No Future without Forgiveness,* **3:**244
- on Peltier's (Leonard) imprisonment, **1:**96
- in Truth and Reconciliation Commission, **3:243**, 244

Twain, Henry, **1:**147

Twain, Mark, **1:**147
- *Adventures of Huckleberry Finn,* **1:**146, 147–148
- *The Innocents Abroad,* **1:**146
- "The Late Benjamin Franklin," **1:**181–182
- *Life on the Mississippi,* **1:146–148**
- "Old Times on the Mississippi," **1:**146
- in realist movement, **2:**240
- *Roughing It,* **1:**146
- *A Tramp Abroad,* **1:**146

Twelve Years a Slave (Northup), **1:**50

Twentieth-Century Literary Criticism (journal), **2:**24

Twentieth Century Literature (journal), **2:**134

27 Wagons Full of Cotton (Williams), **2:**152

Twice Born (Lifton), **1:**102

Twichell, Joseph, **1:**147

Two Gentlemen of Verona (Shakespeare), **2:**226, 228

Two Sides to Everything (Scott), **3:**96

Two Years before the Mast (Dana), **1:**234

Ty, Eleanor, **2:**111

Tyminski, Dan, **3:**159

Tyndale, William, **2:**97

Typhus, in German concentration camps, **2:**253

Tzotzil language, **3:**167

U

UAW. *See* United Automobile Workers

Ubico, Jorge, **1:**99, 101

UC. *See* University of California

Uchida, Yoshiko, **1:**300
- *Desert Exile,* **1:**309
- *The Invisible Thread,* **1:309–311**

UDI. *See* Unilateral Declaration of Independence

Ukraine
- Bashkirtseff's (Marie) emigration to France from, **2:**306–308
- Chernobyl nuclear disaster in, **3:**282–285
- Great Famine of 1932–1933 in, **3:**19
- independence of (1991), **3:**340
- miners in, oral histories of, **3:**340–342, *341*

Ulin, David, **2:**118

Ulrich, Laurel Thatcher
- *Good Wives,* **2:**331–332
- *A Midwife's Tale,* **2:331–334**

Ulysses (Joyce), **1:**146, **2:**67, 180

Umara al-Hakami al-Yamani, **1:**286

Umkhonto we Sizwe (MK), **1:**27

Umutesi, Marie Béatrice, *Surviving the Slaughter,* **3:**258

UMW. *See* United Mine Workers

UMWA. *See* United Mine Workers of America

UN. *See* United Nations

SUBJECT INDEX

Unabridged Journals of Sylvia Plath, The (Plath), **2:**49
Unaipon (ballet), **1:**149
Unaipon, David, **1:**150
   "Leaves of Memory," **1:**149
   My Life Story, **1:**149–151
   Myths and Legends of the Australian Aboriginals, **1:**149
Unaipon, James, **1:**149, 151
Una Storia Segreta (DiStasi), **3:**224
Unbound (Maathai), **1:**114
Uncertain Travelers (Agosín), **1:**75
UnCivil Liberties (Fox), **3:**226
Uncle Tom's Cabin (Stowe), **1:**33, 144
Uncomfortable Wars (Manwaring), **3:**207
Uncomfortable Wars Revisited (Manwaring and Fishel), **3:**207
Underhill, Evelyn, **1:**191
Underhill, Ruth
   The Autobiography of a Papago Woman, **3:**318
   Chona, **1:**69–71
   The Navajos, **3:**290
   Red Man's Religion, **1:**70
   Singing for Power, **1:**70
Under My Skin (Lessing), **1:**167–169
Undertones of War (Blunden), **1:**329
Underwood, Thomas, *Blacks at Harvard,* **3:**21
Unemployment (Seabrook), **3:**54
Unemployment, during Great Depression, **3:**161, 212
UNESCO, **3:**334
Unfinished Conquest (Perera), **1:**99
Ung, Loung, *First They Killed My Father,* **1:**306
Unger, Harlow Giles, **2:**71
Ungo, Guillermo M., **3:**205
UNICEF, **1:**312, 314, **2:**338
Uniformitarianism, **1:**65
Unilateral Declaration of Independence (UDI), **3:**251
Union Maids (film), **3:**179
Union of Automobile Workers, **3:**99
Unions. *See* Labor movement
Unitarian movement, in England, **2:**76
United Automobile Workers (UAW), **3:**153

United Kingdom. *See* Britain
United Mine Workers (UMW), **3:**98
United Mine Workers of America (UMWA), **3:**337, 339
United Nations (UN)
   First International Children's Parliament at, **1:**314
   Historical Clarifications Commission of, **3:**166
   International Law Commission of, **2:**56
   in International Women's Year Tribunal, **3:**322
   on Iraqi invasion of Kuwait, **2:**278
   on Rwandan genocide, **3:**257, 258
   Siv (Sichan) as U.S. ambassador to, **1:**306, *307*
   on workers' rights, **3:**157
United Nations and Economic Sanctions against Rhodesia, The (Kapungu), **3:**251
United Nations Children's Fund (UNICEF), **1:**312, 314, **2:**338
United Nations Educational, Scientific and Cultural Organization (UNESCO), **3:**334
United Negro College Fund, **1:**273, 274
United States. *See also* American *entries*
   anarchism in, **3:**3–5
   censorship in, **1:**20, **2:**123
   Cheng Yu-hsiu in, **1:**152
   coal mining in, **3:**66–69, 86, 87, 96–98, 157
   colonial era of (*See* United States, colonial)
   containment policy of, **3:**205
   economy of (*See* Economy)
   education in (*See* Education)
   expansion of (*See* Westward expansion)
   flu pandemic of 1918 in, **1:**258
   gender roles in, eighteenth-century, **2:**316
   gender roles in, twentieth-century, **2:**47
   in Guatemalan Civil War, **3:**166
   homosexuality in, attitudes toward, **1:**139
   immigration to (*See* Immigration)

   industrialization of, **1:**233
   interracial adoption in, **1:**102–104
   interracial relationships in, attitudes toward, **1:**72–74
   labor movement in (*See* Labor movement)
   Latin American culture in, **1:**109
   letter writing in, **2:**223
   midwifery in, **2:**331–333
   minorities in (*See* Assimilation; Civil rights; *specific groups*)
   national progress of, Emerson (Ralph Waldo) on, **2:**139, 140
   Native American treaties with, **1:**69, **3:**107, 110, 290, 327
   nuclear weapons of, **1:**293–294, **3:**239–241
   Pakistani relations with, **1:**87
   poverty in, **1:**122, **3:**66, 67, 254–256
   presidential election of 1860 in, **3:**261
   presidential election of 1992 in, **3:**221
   Puerto Rico as territory of, **1:**108
   Puritanism in, **1:**325–327
   Reconstruction in, **1:**50–52, **2:**238
   Saitoti's (Tepilit Ole) education in, **1:**114, 115
   in Salvadoran Civil War, **3:**205–207
   slavery in (*See* Slavery)
   on Vietnamese human rights violations, **1:**171, 172
   Vietnamese relations with, **1:**335
   wars of (*See* Military; *specific wars*)
   women of (*See* American women)
United States, colonial
   Afro-Atlantic writers in, **2:**44
   in Alta California, **3:**114–116
   Condict (Jemima) on life in, **2:**78–80
   Crèvecoeur (Michel-Guillaume Saint-Jean de) on life in, **2:**213–215
   French and Indian War in, **2:**205, 213
   Great Awakening in, **1:**179, **2:**197
   idealization of, **2:**213–215
   King Philip's War in, **1:**325–328

SUBJECT INDEX

United States, colonial, *continued*
    Rowlandson (Mary) on life in, **1:**325–328
    Wesley's (John) mission to, **2:**195, 196
    women's autobiographical writing in, **2:**78–79
University of California (UC), Mark Twain Project of, **1:**148
University of California at Berkeley, **3:**21
    African Americans at, oral histories of, **3:**20–22
    student movements of 1968 at, **3:**33
University of Iowa Writers' Workshop, **1:**164, 165
University of London, **2:**77
University of Nairobi, **2:**12, 13
University of Pennsylvania, **2:**275, 276
University of Toronto Quarterly, **3:**140
Unknown Internment, The (Fox), **3:**215, **224–226**
Unlawful Organizations Act of 1960 (South Africa), **1:**25
Unprivileged, The (Seabrook), **3:**55
Unquiet Mind, An (Jamison), **1:**204
Untold Tales, Unsung Heroes (Moon), **3:99–101**
Unto This Last (Ruskin), **1:**242
Unwanted, The (Nguyen), **1:170–172**
Unwinding Threads (Bruner), **1:**94
Up (documentary series), **3:**53
Upcott, William, **2:**65
Updike, John, **3:**59–60
Up from Slavery (Washington), **1:**3, 15, **50–53**
Upon Their Shoulders (Ota), **1:**309
"Up-river Book" (Conrad), **2:**194
Up the Swiftwater (Crowell and Asleson), **3:**93
Uqalurait (Bennett and Rowley), **3:**107, **138–140**
Urban Anthropology (journal), **3:**122
Urban II (pope), **1:**285
Urchin, The (Bedoukian), **3:**40
Urey, Harold, **3:**239
Urogi (witchcraft), among Meru people, **3:**141–143

Urrea, José de, **1:**304
Urrutia, Matilde, **1:**222, 223
Ury, Marian, **2:**60, 292
Usāmah ibn Munqidh, *An Arab-Syrian Gentleman and Warrior in the Period of the Crusades,* **1:285–288**
USA Today (newspaper), **1:**172
U.S. Catholic Historian (journal), **3:**309
Uses of Literacy, The (Hoggart), **1:**16
Utopian societies, **1:**14, 235
Utopian Studies (journal), **2:**255

V

Vaarzon-Morel, Petronella, *Warlpiri Women's Voices,* **3:**107, **334–336**
VAD. *See* Voluntary Aid Detachment
Valerius (bishop), **1:**196
Valéry, Paul, **2:**150
Vallejo, César, **1:**224
Valley of Shadows and Dreams (Light and Light), **3:**67
Vambe, Lawrence Chinyani
    From Rhodesia to Zimbabwe, **3:**251
    An Ill-Fated People, **3:251–253**
Van Brunt, H. L., **3:**87
Vance, Kevin, **2:**40
Van Derlinder, Jean, **3:**291
Van der Veen, Jon, **3:**181
Van Donzel, Emeri, **1:**91, 92
Van Horssen, Jessica, **3:**181
Vanity Fair (magazine), **1:**204, 205, **2:**118
Vanity Fair (Thackeray), **2:**312
Van Orman, Richard A., **3:**91
Van Vechten, Carl, **1:**84
Van Vorst, Mrs. John, **1:**154
Vanzan, Anna, **3:**219
Vargas Llosa, Mario
    A Fish in the Water, **1:**168
    Letters to a Young Novelist, **2:**150
VaShawasha people, oral histories of, **3:**251–253
Vasquez, Jose "Pepe," **3:**122
Vasvári, Louise, **1:**76–77
Vatican Council, Second (Vatican II), **3:**308, 309

Vaughan, Benjamin, **1:**180
Vega, Ed, **1:**108
Vega, Jaime, **2:**222
Vega-González, Susana, **1:**251
Veganism, of Gandhi (Mohandas), **1:**243
Velasco, Luis Alejandro, **3:**183–185
Velho, Álvaro, **2:**198
Velikova, Rumiana, **1:**5
Venice, Republic of, **2:**198
Veracity. *See* Truth
Verene, Donald P., **1:**183
Verisimilitude. *See* Truth
Versailles, Treaty of (1919)
    Chinese disappointment with, **1:**338, **3:**126, 147, 149
    Germany after, **1:**30, **3:**234
Vesey, Denmark, **2:**238
Vesuvius, Mount, eruption of, **2:**94, 95
Veterans, oral histories of
    by African Americans, **3:**199–201, 248–250
    from Iraq War, **3:**231–233, *232*
    from Vietnam War, **3:**199–201, 209–211, 275–277
    from World War II, **3:**202–204, 248–250
Veterans History Project, **3:**128
Vettini, Amanda, **3:**171–172
Viareggio Book Prize, for *The Order Has Been Carried Out* (Portelli), **3:**265
Vico, Giambattista, **1:184**
    The Autobiography of Giambattista Vico, **1:183–185**
    Dell'antichissima sapienza italica, **1:**183
    New Science, **1:**183, 184, 185
Victoria (queen of Great Britain), **2:210**
    expansion of empire under, **2:**16
    Leaves from the Journal of Our Life in the Highlands, **2:209–212**
    More Leaves from the Journal of Our Life in the Highlands, **2:**209
    Seacole (Mary) and, **1:**112
Victorian era (1837–1901)
    autobiographies in, traits of, **1:**65, 67

biographies in, approach to, **2:**143
end of, **1:**329–330
expansion of empire in, **2:**16
Gissing (George) on culture of, **2:**320–322
literary marketplace of, **2:**320–322
social inequality in, **1:**252, **2:**16
social mobility in, barriers to, **1:**252
social reform at end of, **1:**329, **2:**16
women in, Webb (Beatrice) on, **2:**16–18
working-class youth in, **3:**311–312

Victorian Literature and Culture (journal), **2:**210
Victorian Studies (journal), **2:**17, 322, 337, **3:**313
Victory at Sea (television show), **3:**234
Vidal, Gore, **2:**152, 153
Videla, Jorge Rafael, **3:**185
Vien, Joseph Marie, **1:**219
Vietnam
French rule of, **1:**335, **3:**279
history of occupations of, **1:**335
partition of (1954), **1:**335
postwar social conditions in, **1:**170–172
racism against multiracial individuals in, **1:**170, 171
reunification of (1975), **1:**170, 171
U.S. relations with, **1:**335
in Vietnam War, oral histories of, **3:**279–281
Vietnamese American(s)
autobiographical tradition of, **1:**170–171
Hayslip (Le Ly) on experience of, **1:**335–337
Nguyen (Kien) on experience of, **1:**170–172
racism against, **1:**171
Vietnam Veterans Memorial, **3:**200, 223
Vietnam Veterans Memorial Fund, **3:**223
Vietnam War, **1:**171, **3:**210
antiwar movement against, **3:**221, 222, *269,* 275, 277

conscientious objectors in, **3:**221–223
and drug use, rise of, **2:**294
escalation under Johnson (Lyndon Baines), **3:**254, 256
fall of Saigon in, **3:**209
fall of South Vietnam in, **3:**279–281
Hayslip (Le Ly) on life during, **1:**335–337
literature on consequences of, **1:**335
media coverage of, **2:**280, **3:**199
mistakes made in, **3:**275–276
Nguyen (Kien) on life after, **1:**170–172
refugees from, **1:**306, 337
start of, **1:**335, **3:**275, 279
Tet Offensive in, **3:**275
U.S. entry into, **1:**335, **3:**209, 275
U.S. withdrawal from, **3:**275, 279
Vietnam War oral histories
by African American veterans, **3:**199–201
by American civilians, **3:**275–277, *276*
by American veterans, **3:**199–201, 275–277
by conscientious objectors, **3:**221–223
on fall of South Vietnam, **3:**279–281
by Vietnamese civilians and veterans, **3:**279–281
View in Winter, The (Blythe), **3:**60
Viezzer, Moema, *Let Me Speak!,* **3:**74, 114–115, **322–324**
Vigne, Thea, **3:**311
Villa, Pancho, **3:**167, 302
Village Voice (newspaper), **1:**119, 313
Vindication of the Rights of Women, A (Wollstonecraft), **2:**314
Violence
in British gangs, **3:**311–313
domestic (*See* Domestic violence)
in Guatemala, Perera (Victor) on, **1:**99–100
in Israeli–Palestinian conflict, Ghazzawi ('Izzat) on, **2:**50–51

sexual, in Guatemala, **1:**100 (*See also* Rape)
against women, in Islam, **1:**207–209
Violence against Women (journal), **2:**282
Violent Adventure (Wesley), **1:**48
Virginia
in Civil War, **2:**38
coal mining in, oral histories of, **3:**86–87
interracial marriage in, **1:**72
Virginia Magazine of History and Biography, **2:**38
Virginia Quarterly Review, **2:**137
Vision or Villainy (Hoffaman), **3:**102
Visions, divine, of Teresa of Ávila, **1:**211, 212
VISTA. *See* Volunteers in Service to America
Visual elements, in *The Way to Rainy Mountain* (Momaday), **1:**54, 55, *55*
Vitier, Cintio, **2:**220
Vizgalova, Irina, **3:**332
Voice. *See* Narrative voice
Voice of the Past, The (Thompson), **3:186–189**
on *Akenfield* (Blythe), **3:**59–61
Hooligans or Rebels? (Humphries) influenced by, **3:**311–312
on *The Saga of Coe Ridge* (Montell), **3:**92
Vietnam War literature influenced by, **3:**209
Voice of Witness (Eggers and Vollen), **3:**161
Voices from Chernobyl (Alexievich), **3:**265, **282–286**
Voices from the Grave (film), **3:**29
Voices from the Third Reich (Steinhoff), **3:**215
Voices from the Whirlwind (Feng), **3:287–289,** 301
Voices from this Long Brown Land (Wehrey), **3:102–104**
Voices Long Silent (Hansen and Mitson), **3:**195
Voices of Freedom (Hampton and Fayer), **3:44–46**
Voices of Resistance (Baker), **3:47–49**

SUBJECT INDEX

Voices of the Holocaust (Rothchild), **3:**50
Vollen, Lola, *Voice of Witness,* **3:**161
Voltaire, **2:**37, 329
Voluntary Aid Detachment (VAD), **1:**329, **2:**259–261
Volunteers in Service to America (VISTA), **3:**254
Vo Nguyen Giap, **3:**279
Voss, Barbara L., **3:**116
Voter registration drives, **1:**20
Voting rights
    for African Americans, **1:**50, **2:**238
    for women, **1:**12, 13, 14
Voting Rights Act of 1965 (U.S.), **1:**20
Voyage and Travels of Sir John Mandeville, The, **1:**105
Voyages: The Trans-Atlantic Slave Trade Database, **1:**263
Voyage to the East Indies (Grose), **2:**229
V-2 rockets, **2:**270
Vu, Tran Tri, *Lost Years,* **1:**170
Vuic, Kara Dixon, **3:**277

W

Wada, Ernest, **3:**85
Wagenknecht, Edward, **2:**137
Waggoner, Hyatt, **2:**225
Waheenee (Wilson), **1:**69–70
Wainwright, Loudon, **3:**213
Waiting for Snow in Havana (Eire), **1:**296–297
Waka (Japanese poems), **2:**189, 191, 292
Wakatsuki, George Ko, **1:**300, 301
Wakatsuki, Riku, **1:**301
Wakefield, Priscilla, **2:**300
Wakeman, Stephen H., **2:**224
Walden (Thoreau), **1:233–236,** **2:**140, 215
Waldron, Philip, **2:**134
Waldsteicher, David, **2:**45
Wales, Thomas (Dylan) on life in, **1:**125–126
Walker, Alice
    Angelou's (Maya) influence on, **1:**18–19
    The Color Purple, **1:**18, 175

    on Hurston (Zora Neale), **1:**11
The Way Forward Is with a Broken Heart, **1:**18–19
Walker, Pierre, **1:**20
Walker, Reuben, **1:**149
Walker, Robert, **2:66**
Walking in the Shade (Lessing), **1:**167
Walking Purchase of 1737, **3:**327
Walkowitz, Daniel J., *Workers of the Donbass Speak,* **3:**157, **340–342**
Wall, Irwin, **2:**263
Wallace, Alfred Russel, **1:**67
Wallace, John R., **2:**191
Waller, P. J., **3:**313
Wallington, Nehemiah, **2:**74
Walls, Jeanette, **1:**251
Walls, Laura Dassow, **1:**236
Wall Street Journal, **2:**20, **3:**164
Walmsley, Jan, *Oral History, Health and Welfare,* **3:170–172**
Walpole, Horace, **2:**97, 146, 195, 196
Walpole, Hugh, **2:**115
Walton, Edith, **2:**260
Walton, John, *Western Times and Water Wars,* **3:**102
Walton, Martin, **3:**28
Wang, Jing M., **1:**340
Wang Zheng, *Women in the Chinese Enlightenment,* **3:147–149**
Wansink, Hans, **1:**207
War(s). *See also specific wars*
    childhood during, memoirs of, **1:**312–314
    "low-intensity," **3:**207
    realism in depictions of, **2:**240
War brides, Japanese, **3:**127–129, *128*
War Brides of World War II (Shukert and Scibetta), **3:**127
War correspondents
    Chapelle (Dickey) as, **2:**280
    Gellhorn (Martha) as, **2:**101–103
    in Gulf War, **2:**278–280
    in Iraq War, **2:**278, 280
    in Vietnam War, **2:**280, **3:**199
War crimes
    in Sierra Leone civil war, **1:**312
    in World War II, **1:**77, **2:**54–56, **3:**293–295

Ward, Fumiko, **3:**128
Ward, Hiley, **2:**279
War Department, U.S., **3:**248
Wardle, Ralph M., **2:**109, 111
Ware, Ann Patrick, *Midwives of the Future,* **3:**308
Warhol, Robyn, **1:**141
Warlpiri people, oral histories of, **3:**334–336
Warlpiri sign language, **3:**335–336
Warlpiri Women's Voices (Vaarzon-Morel), **3:**107, **334–336**
Warner, Edith, **3:**241
Warner, Fara, **2:**20
War of 1812, **1:**233, **2:**69
War on drugs, U.S., **2:**294
War on poverty, U.S., **3:**254–256
War Reminiscences (Mosby), **2:**250
Warrior, Robert Allen, **1:**56
Wars I Have Seen (Stein), **1:332–334**
War Walks (television series), **3:**236
Washington, Booker T.
    and Du Bois (W. E. B.), debate between, **1:**186
    The Story of My Life and Work, **1:**37
    Up from Slavery, **1:**3, 15, **50–53**
Washington, D.C.
    Adams (Abigail) on life in, **2:**87–90
    establishment of, **2:**87
Washington, George, **2:**44, 87
Washington Post (newspaper), **1:**16, **2:**56, 278, 331
Washington Post Book World, **3:**213
Washington Times (newspaper), **2:**40
Wasserman, George, **1:**269
Waswo, Richard, **2:**309–310
Wat, Eric, *The Making of a Gay Asian Community,* **3:83–85**
Watching Seagulls (Saliba), **1:**161
Watergate scandal, **3:**279
Waterloo, Battle of (1815), **2:**312
Water Margins (Chinese novel), **1:**338
Water resources
    in Australia, **3:**334
    in California, **3:**102, 103
    on Native American reservations, **1:**69, **3:**11

SUBJECT INDEX

Waters, Chris, **3**:72
Waters, Ethel, **1**:10
Water Seekers, The (Nadeau), **3**:102
Watkins, Gloria Jean. *See* hooks, bell
Watson, James, **3**:37
Watson, Nora, **3**:343
Watson, Reginald, **1**:74
Wattenberg, Miriam, **2**:253
Watts, William, **1**:196
Waverly (Scott), **2**:309
Way Forward Is with a Broken Heart, The (Walker), **1**:18–19
Wayne, John, **1**:100
Way of Perfection, The (Teresa of Ávila), **1**:212
Way to Rainy Mountain, The (Momaday), **1**:54–57, *55*
Wealth
  in Ireland, **1**:119–120
  of Native Americans, **3**:290
Wealth of Nations (Smith), **2**:200
Weapons of mass destruction (WMD), in Iraq, **2**:275
Webb, Beatrice
  Diaries of Beatrice Webb, **2**:16–18
  The Letters of Sidney and Beatrice Webb, **2**:172
  Minority Report to the Commission of the Poor Law, **2**:16
  My Apprenticeship, **2**:17
  Our Partnership, **2**:17, 172
Webb, Richard Davis, **2**:157–158
Webb, Sidney, **2**:16, 17, 172
Webs of Power (Maurer and Mirow), **3**:277
Webster, Daniel, **2**:75
Webster, Robert, **2**:195
Wedderburn, Alexander, **1**:265
"We Don't Want Crumbs" (Luthuli), **1**:25
Weekly Anglo-African, **1**:144
Week on the Concord and Merrimack Rivers, A (Thoreau), **1**:233, 234, 235, **2**:140
Weglyn, Michi, *Years of Infamy*, **3**:212
"We Have Just Begun to Not Fight" (Frazer and O'Sullivan), **3**:227–230
Wehrey, Jane
  Manzanar, **3**:102

The Owens Valley, **3**:102
Voices from this Long Brown Land, **3**:102–104
Weil, Simone, **2**:22, 24
Weinberg, Bill, *Our Appalachia*, **3**:66, 86–89
Weinberg, Sidney J., **3**:163
Weinberg, Sydney Stahl, *The World of Our Mothers*, **3**:305
Weiner, Marli, **2**:273
Weise, Robert, **3**:96, 97
Weisiger, Marsha L., *Dreaming of Sheep in Navajo Country*, **3**:10
Weiss, Brad, **3**:142–143
Weiss, Cora, **3**:269
Weiss, Gillian, **3**:334
Wei Tao-Ming, **1**:152, 154
Wei Tao-Ming, Madame. *See* Cheng Yu-hsiu
Weitzman, Lenore J., **3**:35
Welcher, Jeanne K., **2**:67
Weld, Theodore, *American Slavery as It Is*, **1**:33, 142
Wellcome Trust, **3**:170
Wellesley, Arthur, **2**:217
Wells, G. P., **1**:252, 254
Wells, H. G., **1**:253
  Bennett (Arnold) compared to, **2**:136
  on *A Diary without Dates* (Bagnold), **2**:260
  An Experiment in Autobiography, **1**:252–254
  Gellhorn (Martha) and, **2**:101
  H. G. Wells in Love, **1**:252, 253, 254
  letters of, **1**:252, 253
  London and the Life (Gissing) on, **2**:320
  Woolf (Virginia) on novels of, **2**:138
  A Writer's Notebook (Maugham) on, **2**:183
Wells, Ida B., *Southern Horrors*, **1**:50
Wells, Sarah, **1**:253
Welsh, Michael, **3**:240
Welsh autobiographical writing, by Thomas (Dylan), **1**:125–127
Welsh v. United States, **3**:223

Wen, Chihua, *The Red Mirror*, **3**:287
We of Nagasaki (Nagai), **1**:293
Werfel, Franz, **2**:120
Werner, Craig, **1**:247–248
Werner, Marta L., **1**:45–46
Wesley, Charles, **2**:195
Wesley, John, *Journals of John Wesley*, **2**:195–197, *196*
Wesley, Marilyn, *Violent Adventure*, **1**:48
West, E. Bernard, *Living Atlanta*, **3**:44
West, Geoffrey, **1**:253
West, Kanye, **1**:312
West, Russell, **2**:174
West, U.S., Carver's (Jonathan) exploration of, **2**:205–207. *See also* Westward expansion
West Bank, **2**:51
  Darwish (Mahmoud) in, **1**:255
  Israeli occupation of, **1**:225
  Tuqan (Fadwa) on life in, **1**:225
Westerbork concentration camp, **2**:22–24, *23*, 253
Western Folklore (journal), **2**:92
Western Historical Quarterly, **2**:163, **3**:12, 133, 225
Western Humanities Review (journal), **1**:56
Western Times and Water Wars (Walton), **3**:102
Westfall, Joseph, **2**:168
Westfall, Suzanne, **2**:99
West Indies
  Columbus's (Christopher) voyage to, **2**:201–203, *202*
  slavery in, **3**:23–25
Westoff, Clara, **2**:151
West Virginia
  coal mining in, **3**:66–69, *67*, 91
  colonial era in, **3**:66
  statehood for, **3**:66
Westward expansion, U.S.
  Adams (John Quincy) on history of, **2**:69
  Black Elk on experience of, **3**:110
  Chona (Maria) on experience of, **1**:69
  Emerson (Ralph Waldo) on potential of, **2**:139

SUBJECT INDEX

Westward expansion, U.S., *continued*
   Geronimo on experience of, **1:**302–304
   Ray (Annie) on experience of, **2:**163–164
   Stewart (Elinore Pruitt) on experience of, **2:**91–93, *92*
   Thoreau's (Henry David) critique of, **1:**233
Wey, William, **2:**226
Weyer, Edward Moffat, *The Eskimo,* **3:**138
Wharton, Edith, **2:**113
"What, to the Slave, Is the Fourth of July?" (Douglass), **1:**79
What I Believe (Tolstoy), **1:**194, 195
What's a Woman Doing Here? (Chapelle), **2:**280
What Was Asked of Us (Wood), **3:231–233,** 276
Wheatley, Phillis, **2:**45
   Equiano (Olaudah) compared to, **1:**81, **2:**44
   "Letter to the Reverend Samson Occom," **2:44–46**
   "On Being Brought from Africa to America," **2:**46
   Poems on Various Subjects, **2:**44
   Prince (Mary) compared to, **3:**23
   "To His Excellency General Washington," **2:**44
Wheatley, Susanna, **2:**44, 46
Wheelock, Eleazar, **2:**46
Whelan-Stewart, Wendy, **2:**49
When Bodies Remember (Fassin), **3:**272
When Broken Glass Floats (Him), **1:**306
When Heaven and Earth Changed Places (Hayslip), **1:**170–171, **335–337**
When I Was Puerto Rican (Santiago), **1:108–110**
When the Mill Whistle Blew (Strobel), **3:**93
When We Began, There Were Witchmen (Fadiman), **3:141–143**
Which Side Are You On? (Hevener), **3:**96
Whitaker, Katie, **1:**229
White, E. B., **1:**234, 235

White, Gilbert, **2:**300
White, Jerry, **3:**54
White, Mike, **2:**255
White, Raymond O., **3:**107, 108
White, Thomas Willis, **2:**41
White audience
   of *Dust Tracks on a Road* (Hurston), **1:**9, 11
   of *Incidents in the Life of a Slave Girl* (Jacobs), **1:**142, 143
   of "Letter from the Birmingham Jail" (King), **2:**33
   of *Up from Slavery* (Washington), **1:**50–52
White colleges, African Americans at, **3:**20–22
Whitefield, George, **2:**46, 197
White Revolution (Iran), **3:**218
Whitesinger, Pauline, **3:**11
Whither India? (Nehru), **1:**290
Whitley, Glenna, **3:**201, 211
Whitlock, Gillian, **1:**40, **3:**25
Whitman, Walt, **1:**173, 234, 265
Whitsitt, Novian, **1:**144
Whittier, John Greenleaf, **2:**29
Wickert, Erwin, **2:**19
Widder, Keith, **2:**207
Wiesel, Elie, **1:319**
   Dawn, **1:**319
   Day, **1:**319
   Night, **1:318–321**
Wiggins, Sarah Woodfolk, **2:**246
WikiLeaks, **3:**229
Wilburn, Oleson, **3:**92
Wilde, Oscar
   The Ballad of Reading Gaol, **2:**9
   De Profundis, **2:9–11**
   indecency trial of, **2:**9, 183, 185
   Maugham (W. Somerset) influenced by, **2:**183, 184, 185
   on *Memoirs of an Arabian Princess from Zanzibar* (Ruete), **1:**91
   The Picture of Dorian Gray, **2:**9
   Salomé, **2:**183
Wilde-Menozzi, Wallis, **2:**255
Wild Swans (Chang), **1:**158–159
Wilenski, R. H., **1:**265
Wilford, Hugh, **3:**5

Wilhelm Meister's Apprenticeship (Goethe), **1:**30
Wilkins, William Henry, **2:**217
Wilkinson, Edmund L., **3:**248–249
Wilkinson, James, **1:**202
Wilkinson, Jane, **2:**14
Will. *See* Divine will; Free will
Will, Herman, **3:**228
Willenson, Kim, *The Bad War,* **3:**275
William and Mary Quarterly, **1:**134
William of Orange, **2:**324, *325*
Williams, Ben Ames, **2:**250
Williams, Bill, **3:**186
Williams, David, **2:**207
Williams, Gweno, **1:**230, 231
Williams, Lynne, **3:**175
Williams, Ronald, **1:**96
Williams, Rowan, **1:**212
Williams, Tennessee, **2:153**
   Camino Real, **2:**154
   The Glass Menagerie, **2:**152
   Memoirs, **2:**152, 153
   Notebooks, **2:152–154**
   A Streetcar Named Desire, **2:**152
   27 Wagons Full of Cotton, **2:**152
Willis, Lord, **2:236**
Willison, George, **2:329**
Wills, Garry, **1:**197, 198
WILPF. *See* Women's International League for Peace and Freedom
Wilsey, Sean, **1:**141
Wilson, August, **1:**273
Wilson, Bee, **2:**289
Wilson, Douglas L., *Herndon's Informants,* **3:**264
Wilson, Edmund, **2:**246
Wilson, Gilbert L., *Waheenee,* **1:**69–70
Wilson, Harriet E., *Our Nig,* **1:**142
Wilson, Jean Moorcroft, **2:**249
Wilson, Kathleen, **1:**159
Wilson, Sonia, **2:**81, 307
Wilson, Woodrow, **3:**29, 153
Winder, Robert, **3:**59, 61
Windham, William, **2:**217
Winfrey, Oprah, **2:**296
Wing, Sandra Koa, **2:**265, 267

Wings of the Dove, The (James), **2:**113, 115
Winkler, Allan, *Life under a Cloud,* **3:**239
Winkler, Michael, **2:**151
Winn, Mathew, **3:**233
Winter, Naomi, **2:**27
Winter Soldier (Iraq Veterans against the War), **3:**232
Winterthur Portfolio (journal), **3:**320
Wirzba, Norman, **3:**67–68
Wisconsin Magazine of History, **3:**329
Wise, Christopher, **1:**23
Wise, R. Todd, **1:**23
Wister, Sally, **2:**78–79
Witchcraft
    among Meru, **3:**141–143
    among Navajo, **3:**290–291
Witch Purge of 1878, The (Blue), **3:**290–292
With Wings (Saxton and Howe), **1:**8
Witke, Roxanne, **3:**147
Witnesses, memory of, **3:**265, 266
Witnesses to Nuremberg (Stave et al.), **3:**293–295
Witnesses to the Holocaust (Lewin), **3:**50–52
WMD. *See* Weapons of mass destruction
Wobblies, **3:**93, 328–330
Wobblies, The (documentary), **3:**328
Wobblies!: A Graphic History (Buhle and Schulman), **3:**330
Woerner, Fred F., **3:**205
Wolcott, Reed, *Rose Hill,* **3:**86
Wolf, Benjamin, **3:**155
Wolfe, Charles, **3:**159
Wolff, Tobias
    Back in the World, **1:**47
    The Barracks Thief, **1:**47
    In Pharaoh's Army, **1:**47
    In the Garden of North American Martyrs, **1:**47
    This Boy's Life, **1:**47–49
Wolford, John B., **3:**266
Wolfson, Susan, **2:**147
Wollett, Jan, **3:**280
Wollstonecraft, Mary
    The Collected Letters of Mary Wollstonecraft, **2:**109–112
    on *The Interesting Narrative of the Life of Olaudah Equiano* (Equiano), **1:**82
    Letters Written during a Short Residence in Sweden, Norway, and Denmark, **2:**111
    A Vindication of the Rights of Women, **2:**314
Wolpert, Stanley, **1:**290
Woman (periodical), **2:**136
Woman at War, A (Moore), **2:**278–280
Woman in Berlin, A (anonymous), **2:**281–283
Woman of Peace (Hayslip), **1:**335
Woman Prisoner, The (Ghazzawi), **2:**50
Woman's Bible, The (Stanton), **1:**12, 13
Woman Soldier's Own Story, A (Xie), **1:**338–340
Woman's Place, A (Roberts), **3:**144, 145, 146
Woman's "True" Profession (Hoffman), **3:**77
Woman's World (magazine), **1:**91
Woman Warrior, The (Kingston), **1:**75, 100, **173–176**
Women. *See also specific countries, ethnicities, and religions*
    in abolitionist movement, **1:**142
    education of (*See* Education)
    oral histories of, feminist approach to, **3:**190–192, *191*
    religious roles of, Stanton (Elizabeth Cady) on, **1:**12
    Renaissance, **2:**160–162
    social roles of (*See* Gender roles)
Women Activists (Garland), **3:**268
Women and Families (Roberts), **3:**144–146
Women and the Holocaust (Fuchs), **3:**35
Women in the Chinese Enlightenment (Wang), **3:**147–149
Women in the Mines (Moore), **3:**157, 328, **337–339**
Women of Algiers in Their Apartment (Djebar), **1:**207
Women of Coal (Norris and Cyprès), **3:**337
Women religious, oral histories of, **3:**308–310
Women's International Congress, **3:**268
Women's International League for Peace and Freedom (WILPF), **3:**268, 269, 270
Women's Peace Oral History Project, **3:**268–270
Women's Review of Books (journal)
    on *Bone Black* (hooks), **1:**251
    on *A Mountainous Journey* (Tuqan), **1:**226
    on *My Life Story* (Amrouche), **1:**94
    on *Songs My Mother Sang to Me* (Preciado Martin), **3:**133
    on *Under My Skin* (Lessing), **1:**169
    on *Voices of Resistance* (Baker), **3:**48
    on *A Woman Soldier's Own Story* (Xie), **1:**340
    on *Women in the Mines* (Moore), **3:**338
Women's rights movement. *See also* Feminism
    in Britain, **1:**329, 331, **2:**109
    in China, **1:**338
    in France, **2:**306
    in Iran, **3:**218
    in U.S., **1:**12–14, **2:**47
Women's studies, *Letters of a Woman Homesteader* (Stewart) in, **2:**91
Women's Studies Quarterly, **1:**141
Women Strike for Peace (WSP), **3:**268
Women's Voluntary Service, **2:**265
Women's Words (Gluck and Patai), **3:**190–192
Women's Writing (journal), **2:**325
Wonderful Adventures of Mrs. Seacole in Many Lands, The (Seacole), **1:**111–113
Wong, Alan, **3:**181
Wong, Hertha D., **1:**71
    Sending My Heart Back across the Years, **1:**56
Wong, Sharon, **1:**175
Wood, Frances, **1:**107
Wood, Gordon S., **1:**181
Wood, John, **3:**25
Wood, Trish, *What Was Asked of Us,* **3:231–233**, 276

Woodforde, Anna Maria, **2:**289

Woodforde, James, *A Country Parson,* **2:287–289**

Woodland Indians, oral histories of, **3:**107–109, *108*

Woodley, Arthur E., Jr., **3:**200

Woodson, Dorothy C., **1:**25

Woodward, Comer Vann, **2:**250, 251

Woodworth-Nay, Laura, **3:**12

Wooldridge, E. T.
- *Carrier Warfare in the Pacific,* **3:202–204**
- *Into the Jet Age,* **3:**203

Woolf, Leonard, **2:**180, 181, 182, 235, 268

Woolf, Virginia, **2:181**
- on Bennett's (Arnold) novels, **2:**137, 138
- in Bloomsbury group, **2:**180, 268
- Clifford (Anne) as inspiration for, **2:**64
- on *A Country Parson* (Woodforde), **2:**287, 288, 289
- *Diaries of Beatrice Webb* (Webb) on, **2:**16
- on *The Diary of John Evelyn* (Evelyn), **2:**66, 67
- *The Diary of Virginia Woolf,* **2:**133, 163, 180–182
- Hogarth Press of, **2:**268
- *Jacob's Room,* **2:**138
- Kingston (Maxine Hong) influenced by, **1:**173
- *Moments of Being,* **1:**249, **2:**182
- Nin (Anaïs) compared to, **2:**123
- *Orlando,* **1:**173, **2:**64, 181
- on Osborne (Dorothy), **2:**324, 325
- *A Pacifist's War* (Partridge) on, **2:**268
- *Second Common Reader,* **2:**289
- suicide of, **2:**268
- on *Testament of Youth* (Brittain), **1:**330
- *To the Lighthouse,* **1:**146
- *A Writer's Diary,* **2:180–182**

Woolman, John, *The Journal of John Woolman,* **2:**213

Worde, Wynken de, **1:**189, 191

Wordsworth, Christopher, **2:**301

Wordsworth, Dorothy
- *Grasmere Journals,* **2:**16, **300–302**
- Osborne (Dorothy) compared to, **2:**324

Wordsworth, William
- Byron (George Gordon Noel) compared to, **2:**143
- *Grasmere Journals* (Wordsworth) and, **2:**300–302
- *Journals of Ralph Waldo Emerson* (Emerson) on, **2:**141
- Keats (John) and, **2:**146
- *The Prelude,* **1:**201, 264, **2:**302
- Robinson (Henry Crabb) and, **2:**75

Workers of the Donbass Speak (Siegelbaum and Walkowitz), **3:**157, **340–342**

Workforce, English women's entry into, **2:**266, **3:**145

Work in America report, **3:**343

Working (Terkel), **3:**161, 300, **343–345**

Working class
- in Bolivia, oral histories of women in, **3:**322–324
- in Italy and Kentucky, oral histories of, **3:**157–159
- in Ukraine, oral histories of, **3:**340–342

Working class, in Britain
- education of, **3:**311–313
- social change in, **3:**53, 144
- in Victorian era, **2:**16
- women in, oral histories of, **3:**144–146
- youth in, oral histories of, **3:**53–54, 311–313

Working-Class Childhood (Seabrook), **3:53–55**

Works of John Ruskin, The (Ruskin), **1:**265

Works Progress Administration (WPA), **1:**35, **3:**99

World Affairs (journal), **1:**32

World as Will and Representation, The (Schopenhauer), **1:**193

World at War, The (Holmes), **3:234–236**

World at War, The (television series), **3:**234, 236

World I Live In, The (Keller), **1:**44, 45

World in the Evening, The (Isherwood), **2:**152

World Literature Today (journal), **1:**76, 128, 137, 247, **2:**191

World of Our Mothers, The (Weinberg), **3:**305

World of the Defeated, The (Revelli), **3:**61

Worlds of a Maasai Warrior, The (Saitoti), **1:114–116**

Worlds of Color (Du Bois), **1:**5

World Today (journal), **2:**33

World War I
- Australian military in, **3:**177
- Bagnold's (Enid) service in, **2:**259–261
- conscientious objectors in, **3:**223
- in England, Brittain (Vera) on life during, **1:**329–331, **3:**176
- Germany after defeat in, **1:**30, **3:**234
- Japanese nationalism after, **3:**234
- lost generation of, **1:**329
- Mansfield's (Katherine) writing during, **2:**133
- in modernism, rise of, **2:**180
- nursing in, **1:**329, 330, **2:**259–261, *260*
- Sassoon's (Siegfried) service in, **2:**247–249
- Stein (Gertrude) on experience of, **1:**332
- technological advances in, **2:**180
- war crimes trials after, **3:**293
- women's experience of, **1:**329–331, **2:**259

World War II. *See also* Holocaust; Japanese American internment; Nazi Germany
- autobiographies after, rise of interest in, **1:**239
- China during, **1:**152, 153, **3:**14–16
- conscientious objectors in, **2:**268–269, **3:**223, 227–229
- and *Dust Tracks on a Road* (Hurston), changes to, **1:**9
- end of, **2:**281, **3:**239

England during, Last (Nella) on life in, **2**:265–267

England during, Partridge (Frances) on life in, **2**:268–269

in France, Stein (Gertrude) on experience of, **1**:332–334

Gellhorn's (Martha) reporting on, **2**:101–103

German bombardment of Britain in, **2**:265, 269, 270

German occupation of France in, **1**:332–334

in Germany, Klemperer (Victor) on experience of, **2**:303–305

Iran in, **3**:218

Italian American relocation in, **3**:224–226

Italy in, Nazi occupation of, **3**:265–267

Japanese bombing of Pearl Harbor in, **1**:299, 300, 309, **3**:195, 202, 212, 215, 234

Japanese names for, **3**:215

Korea after, division of, **1**:322

Nuremberg trials after, **2**:54, 56, **3**:293–295

oral histories of (*See* World War II oral histories)

Palestine during, **2**:104

propaganda in, **2**:117, 118, 270, *282*

rape in, **2**:281–283

Scotland during, Mitchison (Naomi) on life in, **2**:235–237

Soviet occupation of Berlin in, **2**:281–282

start of, **3**:215, 234

U.S. entry into, **1**:299, 309, **3**:161, 202, 212, 234

U.S. liberation of France in, **1**:332, 333

U.S. naval aviation in, **3**:202–204

U.S. occupation of Japan after, **3**:127–129

U.S. use of nuclear weapons in, **1**:293–294, **3**:239

war crimes in, **1**:77, **2**:54–56, **3**:293–295

women's autobiographical writing during, **2**:235, 237

World War II oral histories. *See also* Holocaust oral histories
  international, **3**:234–236
  Italian, **3**:265–267
  Japanese, **3**:127–129, 215–217

World War II oral histories, U.S.
  by conscientious objectors, **3**:227–230
  by Italian Americans, **3**:224–226
  by Japanese Americans, **3**:80–81, 102–104, 195–197
  by naval veterans, **3**:202–204
  by ordinary people, **3**:212–214
  by Tuskegee Airmen, **3**:248–250
  by war brides, **3**:127–129

Worst of Times, The (Hoggart), **3**:53

Wotton, Edward, **2**:256

Wounded, literature of the, *Voices from the Whirlwind* (Feng) as, **3**:287

Wounded Knee (South Dakota)
  AIM occupation of (1973), **1**:21, 22–23, 96
  massacre at (1890), **3**:110, 111

Wounds of Passion (hooks), **1**:250, 251

WPA. *See* Works Progress Administration

Wren, Christopher, **2**:65

Wretched of the Earth, The (Fanon), **1**:207, **2**:263

Wright, Esmond, **1**:182

Wright, John Michael, **1**:316

Wright, Richard
  Black Boy, **1**:122–124
  A Father's Law, **1**:124
  Native Son, **1**:122, 123, 273

Writer's Chronicle (journal), **1**:167–168

Writer's Diary, A (Woolf), **2**:180–182

Writer's Notebook, A (Maugham), **2**:183–185

Writing
  Dillard (Annie) on vocation of, **1**:279–281
  Gissing's (George) struggle to earn living with, **2**:320, 321
  Mansfield (Katherine) on process of, **2**:133
  Poe's (Edgar Allan) struggle to earn living with, **2**:41

Woolf (Virginia) on process of, **2**:180–182

Writing Black (Rive), **1**:25

Writing Life, The (Dillard), **1**:168, 279–281

Wrong Turn (film), **3**:68

Wroth, Mary, **2**:62

WSP. *See* Women Strike for Peace

Wudunn, Sheryl, **2**:20–21

Wunyabari, Maloba, **3**:142

Wurts, Jay, **1**:335

Wyman, Leland, **3**:320

Wynn, Antony, **3**:220

Wyoming, homesteaders in, **2**:91–93, *92*

X

X, Malcolm. *See* Malcolm X

Xavier, Silvia, **2**:30

Xie Bingying
  Girl Rebel, **1**:338
  New War Diary, **1**:339–340
  Selected Autobiographies by Women Writers, **1**:340
  A Woman Soldier's Own Story, **1**:338–340

Xu Guangping, *Letters between Two*, **2**:170–173

Xu Xin, **2**:20

Y

Yablonski, Jock, **3**:98

Yacine, Kateb, **1**:95
  Nedjma, **2**:262

Yaddo artists' colony, **2**:129

Yale Law Journal, **3**:197

Yale Review (periodical), **2**:193

Yale University, **1**:251

Yamamoto, Tak, **3**:84

Yardley, Jonathan, **3**:213

Yasgur, Batya, *Behind the Burqa*, **1**:40

Yasutomi, Shigeyoshi, **3**:129

Ye, Weili, **1**:339, **3**:149

Yearbook of English Studies, **2**:322

Year of Consolation, A (Kemble), **2**:336

SUBJECT INDEX

Years of Infamy (Weglyn), **3:**212
Yeats, Elizabeth, **2:**126
Yeats, William Butler, **2:**127
 The Autobiography of William Butler Yeats, **2:**127–128
 The Collected Works of W. B. Yeats, **2:**126, 128
 The Death of Synge, **2:**126, 127
 Estrangement, **2:126–128**
 Reveries over Childhood and Youth, **2:**126, 127
 The Trembling of the Veil, **2:**126, 127
Yellin, Jean Fagan, **1:**144, 145
Yen Mah, Adeline, *Falling Leaves,* **1:**159
Yglesias, José, **1:**223
Yiddish language, *Night* (Wiesel) in, **1:**318
Yim, Louise, *My Forty Year Fight for Korea,* **1:**323
Yoda, Tomiko, **2:**292
Yoruba people, **1:**214, 216
Yoselevska, Rivka, **3:**235
You May Well Ask (Mitchison), **2:**235
Young, Andrew, **3:**45
Young, Filson, *The Relief of Mafeking,* **2:**241
Young, Jennifer Rene, **2:**45
Young, John Wesley, **2:**305
Young, Marilyn, **3:**280, 281

Young Palestinian's Diary, A ('Amr), **2:104–106**
Young Turk Revolution (1908), **2:**106
Young Turks, **3:**40
Youth. *See* Adolescents; Children
Yurechko, John, **2:**279
Yurovsky, Yakov, **2:**84

Z

Zahn, Gordon, **3:**228
Zaleski, Jeff, **1:**294
Zambia Must Be Free (Kaunda), **1:**290
Zami (Lorde), **1:**9, 37, 39, 249, **2:**5
Zane, Paolo, **2:**161
Zanjani, Sally Springmeyer, *A Mine of Her Own,* **3:**337
Zanzibar, Ruete (Emily) on life in, **1:**90–92
Zapata, Emiliano, **3:**302, 303, 304
Zapatistas, **3:**304
Zen Buddhism, **2:**59, 61
Zerbini, Euricledes, **2:**6
Zeuske, Michael, **3:**7, 8, 9
Zhang Kijian, *China Remembers,* **3:**301
Zhang Xinxin, *Chinese Lives,* **3:288, 299–301**
Zhang Ya-Jie, **1:**175
Zhu Su'e, **3:**148
Ziegler, Philip, **2:**266, **3:**235

Zimbabwe
 British colonial rule of, **1:**167, **3:**251–253
 VaShawasha people of, oral histories of, **3:**251–253
Zimmerman, Lee, **1:**205–206
Zinzendorf, Nikolaus Ludwig von, **2:**197
Zionism, Palestinian views on, **2:**104, 105, 106
Zlata's Diary (Filipovic), **2:275, 338–340**
Zola, Émile
 Bashkirtseff (Marie) influenced by, **2:**306
 The Complete Notebooks of Henry James (James) on, **2:**113
 Journal des Goncourt (Goncourt and Goncourt) and, **2:**82, 83
 Thérèse Raquin, **1:**6
Zong (slave ship), **1:**83
Zora Neale Hurston: Jump at the Sun (documentary), **1:**18
Zorzi, Rosella Mamoli, **2:**115
Zoya, *Zoya's Story,* **1:**40
Zoya's Story (Zoya), **1:**40
Zuma, Jacob, **1:**29
Zunes, Stephen, **1:**25–26
Zunigha, Curtis, **3:**108
Zwick, Edward, **1:**312
Zylska, Ruchel. *See* McBride, Ruth

Author Index

The author index includes author names represented in *The Literature of Autobiographical Narrative*. Numbers in **Bold** indicate volume, with page numbers following after colons.

A

Abrams, Lynn, **3**: 173
Adams, Abigail, **2**: 87
Adams, Henry, **1**: 132
Adams, John Quincy, **2**: 69
Adams, Judith Porter, **3**: 268
Agosín, Marjorie, **1**: 75
Ahmedi, Farah, **1**: 40
Alexievich, Svetlana, **3**: 282
Al-Windawi, Thura, **2**: 275
Amr, Sāmī, **2**: 104
Amrouche, Fadhma Aïth Mansour, **1**: 93
Angelou, Maya, **1**: 18
Augustine, **1**: 196
Aurelius, Marcus, **1**: 218
Avrich, Paul, **3**: 3

B

Bagnold, Enid, **2**: 259
Baker, Alison, **3**: 47
Barnard, Anne, **2**: 217
Barnet, Miguel, **3**: 7
Barrett, S. M., **1**: 302
Barrios de Chungara, Domitila, **3**: 322
Barthes, Roland, **1**: 267
Bashkirtseff, Marie, **2**: 306
Bauby, Jean-Dominique, **1**: 6
Bayer, Ronald, **3**: 272
Beah, Ishmael, **1**: 312
Bechdel, Alison, **1**: 139
Benally, Malcolm D., **3**: 10
Bennett, Arnold, **2**: 136
Bennett, John, **3**: 138
Bird, Stewart, **3**: 328
Black Elk, **3**: 110
Blue, Martha, **3**: 290
Blythe, Ronald, **3**: 59
Bornat, Joanna, **3**: 170
Boswell, James, **2**: 328
Brighton Ourstory, **3**: 70
Brittain, Vera, **1**: 329
Brown, James W., **3**: 325
Bruce, Gary, **3**: 245
Buck, Lucy, **2**: 271
Bugul, Ken, **1**: 61
Burlingame, Michael, **3**: 261
Burney, Fanny, **2**: 312
Byron, George Gordon Noel, **2**: 143

C

Carver, Jonathan, **2**: 205
Cavendish, Margaret, **1**: 229
Cereta, Laura, **2**: 160
Cheng Yu-hsiu, **1**: 152
Chesnut, Mary Boykin Miller, **2**: 250
Chona, Maria, **1**: 69
Clifford, Anne, **2**: 62
Columbus, Christopher, **2**: 201
Condict, Jemima, **2**: 78
Conrad, Joseph, **2**: 192
Conroy, Frank, **1**: 164
Cook, Haruko Taya, **3**: 215
Cook, Theodore F., **3**: 215
Craig, Ann L., **3**: 302
Crawford, Miki Ward, **3**: 127
Crévecoeur, Michel-Guillaume Saint-Jean de, **2**: 213

D

Darwin, Charles, **1**: 65
Darwish, Mahmoud, **1**: 255
De Jesus, Carolina Maria, **2**: 6
Dillard, Annie, **1**: 279
D'Israeli, Isaac, **2**: 177
Dog, Mary Crow, **1**: 21
Douglass, Frederick, **1**: 33
Du Bois, W. E. B., **1**: 3
Dyk, Walter, **3**: 318

E

Edward VI, **2**: 97
Emerson, Ralph Waldo, **2**: 139
Engelmann, Larry, **3**: 279
Equiano, Olaudah, **1**: 81
Evans, George Ewart, **3**: 63
Evelyn, John, **2**: 65

F

Fadiman, Jeffrey A., **3**: 141
Fayer, Steve, **3**: 44
Feng Jicai, **3**: 287

AUTHOR INDEX

Feodorovna, Alexandra, **2**: 84
Feraoun, Mouloud, **2**: 262
Filipovic, Zlata, **2**: 338
Fox, George, **2**: 26
Fox, Stephen, **3**: 224
Frank, Anne, **2**: 253
Frank, Leslie, **3**: 293
Franklin, Benjamin, **1**: 179
Frazer, Heather T., **3**: 227
Friedman, Clara, **3**: 153
Frisch, Michael, **3**: 179
Frommer, Harvey, **3**: 118
Frommer, Myrna Katz, **3**: 118

G

Gandhi, Mohandas, **1**: 242
García Márquez, Gabriel, **3**: 183
Gellhorn, Martha, **2**: 101
Georgakas, Dan, **3**: 328
Geronimo, **1**: 302
Ghazzawi, 'Izzat, **2**: 50
Gheith, Jehanne M., **3**: 17
Gillette, Michael L., **3**: 254
Gissing, George, **2**: 320
Gluck, Sherna Berger, **3**: 190
Goethe, Johann Wolfgang von, **1**: 276
Goncourt, Edmond de, **2**: 81
Goncourt, Jules de, **2**: 81
Griffith, Kenneth, **3**: 27
Grimké, Charlotte Forten, **2**: 29
Guevara, Ernesto "Che," **2**: 220
Gurewitsch, Brana, **3**: 34
Guylforde, Richarde, **2**: 226

H

Haley, Alex, **1**: 261
Halkett, Lady Anne, **1**: 315
Hampton, Henry, **3**: 44
Hansberry, Lorraine, **1**: 273
Haskins, Jim, **1**: 37
Hatzfeld, Jean, **3**: 257
Hawthorne, Nathaniel, **2**: 223
Hayashi, Katie Kaori, **3**: 127

Hayslip, Le Ly, **1**: 335
Hickey, Margaret, **3**: 315
Higginson, Thomas Wentworth, **2**: 238
Hillesum, Etty, **2**: 22
Hirsi Ali, Ayaan, **1**: 207
Hitler, Adolf, **1**: 30
Hochstadt, Steve, **3**: 14
Holmes, Richard, **3**: 234
hooks, bell, **1**: 249
Houston, James D., **1**: 299
Houston, Jeanne Wakatsuki, **1**: 299
Humphries, Stephen, **3**: 311
Hurston, Zora Neale, **1**: 9
Hussein, Taha, **1**: 135

J

Jacobs, Harriet A., **1**: 142
James, Daniel, **3**: 73
James, Henry, **2**: 113
Jefferson, Thomas, **2**: 316
Jiang, Ji-li, **1**: 161
Jolluck, Katherine R., **3**: 17

K

Kafka, Franz, **2**: 120
Keats, John, **2**: 146
Ke Lan, **3**: 124
Keller, Helen, **1**: 43
Kemble, Fanny, **2**: 335
Kempe, Margery, **1**: 189
Kierkegaard, Søren, **2**: 166
Kim, Elizabeth, **1**: 102
Kim Ku, **1**: 322
King, Martin Luther, Jr., **2**: 32
Kingston, Maxine Hong, **1**: 173
Klemperer, Victor, **2**: 303
Kohn, Rita, **3**: 107, 325
Kong Demao, **3**: 124
Krause, Corinne Azen, **3**: 305
Krog, Antjie, **3**: 242

L

Ladjevardi, Habib, **3**: 218
Last, Nella, **2**: 265
Laye, Camara, **1**: 128
Leadbeater, Mary, **2**: 157
Lee, Robert E., **2**: 38
Left Handed, **3**: 318
Lejeune, Philippe, **1**: 239, **2**: 174
Lessing, Doris, **1**: 167
Lewin, Rhoda, **3**: 50
Light, Kenneth, **3**: 66
Light, Melanie, **3**: 66
Lorde, Audre, **2**: 3
Luthuli, Albert, **1**: 24
Lu Xun, **2**: 170

M

Mahomet, Dean, **2**: 05
Malcolm X, **1**: 186
Mandela, Nelson, **1**: 27
Manning, Diane, **3**: 77
Mansfield, Katherine, **2**: 133
Manwaring, Max G., **3**: 205
Martin, Patricia Preciado, **3**: 131
Mason, Katrina, **3**: 239
Maugham, W. Somerset, **2**: 183
Maurer, Harry, **3**: 275
McBride, James, **1**: 72
McCarthy, Mary, **1**: 258
McCourt, Frank, **1**: 119
McKay, Claude, **1**: 84
Medina, Pablo, **1**: 296
Menchú, Rigoberta, **3**: 164
Michitsuna No Haha, **2**: 297
Milich, Zorka, **3**: 135
Miller, Donald E., **3**: 40
Miller, Lorna Touryan, **3**: 40
Min, Anchee, **1**: 158
Mitchison, Naomi, **2**: 235
Momaday, N. Scott, **1**: 54
Montagu, Lady Mary Wortley, **2**: 35
Montejo, Esteban, **3**: 7

Montell, William Lynwood, **3**: 90, 107
Moon, Elaine Latzman, **3**: 99
Moore, Marat, **3**: 337
Moore, Molly, **2**: 278
Morris, Gabrielle, **3**: 20
Moye, J. Todd, **3**: 248

N

Nabokov, Vladimir, **1**: 270
Nakazawa, Keiji, **1**: 293
Neihardt, John G., **3**: 110
Nehru, Jawaharlal, **1**: 289
Neruda, Pablo, **1**: 222
Nguyen, Kien, **1**: 170
Nijo, Lady, **2**: 59
Nin, Anaïs, **2**: 123

O

Obama, Barack, **1**: 78
O'Conner, Flannery, **2**: 129
O'Grady, Timothy, **3**: 27
Olney, James, **1**: 246
Oppenheimer, Gerald M., **3**: 272
Orwell, George, **2**: 117
Osborne, Dorothy, **2**: 324
O'Sullivan, John, **3**: 227
Owsley, Beatrice Rodriguez, **3**: 121

P

Palmer, Michele, **3**: 293
Patai, Daphne, **3**: 190
Parks, Rosa, **1**: 37
Partridge, Frances, **2**: 268
Peltier, Leonard, **1**: 96
Pepys, Samuel, **2**: 72
Perera, Victor, **1**: 99
Perks, Robert, **3**: 170
Plaatje, Solomon Tshekisho, **2**: 241
Plath, Sylvia, **2**: 47
Pliny the Younger, **2**: 94
Poe, Edgar Allan, **2**: 41

Polo, Marco, **1**: 105
Poniatowska, Elena, **3**: 31
Popular Memory Group, **3**: 176
Portelli, Alessandro, **3**: 96, 157, 265
Pozas, Ricardo, **3**: 167
Prince, Mary, **3**: 23
Prisk, Court, **3**: 205

R

Rabe, John, **2**: 19
Raleigh, Donald J., **3**: 331
Rilke, Rainer Maria, **2**: 149
Roberts, Elizabeth, **3**: 144
Robinson, Henry Crabb, **2**: 75
Rodriguez, Richard, **1**: 15
Rogers, Carole Garibaldi, **3**: 308
Rousseau, Jean-Jacques, **1**: 200
Rowlandson, Mary, **1**: 325
Rowley, Susan, **3**: 138
Ruete, Emily, **1**: 90
Ruskin, John, **1**: 264
Russell, Bert, **3**: 93

S

Saitoti, Tepilit Ole, **1**: 114
Sang Ye, **3**: 299
Santiago, Esmeralda, **1**: 108
Santoli, Al, **3**: 209
Sarashina, Lady, **2**: 189
Sassoon, Siegfried, **2**: 247
Satrapi, Marjane, **1**: 155
Savage, Thomas, **3**: 114
Scott, Sir Walter, **2**: 309
Seabrook, Jeremy, **3**: 5301
Seacole, Mary, **1**: 111
Shackelford, Laurel, **3**: 86
Shaffer, Deborah, **3**: 328
Shikibu, Lady Murasaki, **2**: 290
Shostak, Marjorie, **3**: 37
Siegelbaum, Lewis H., **3**: 340
Sinor, Jennifer, **2**: 163
Siv, Sichan, **1**: 306
Slingsby, Sir Henry, **2**: 256

Soyinka, Wole, **1**: 214
Speer, Albert, **2**: 54
Stanton, Elizabeth Cady, **1**: 12
Stave, Bruce M., **3**: 293
Stein, Gertrude, **1**: 332
Stewart, Elinore Pruitt, **2**: 91
Stone, Kate, **2**: 244
Styron, William, **1**: 204
Suenaga, Shizuko, **3**: 127
Suleri, Sara, **1**: 87

T

Tamura, Linda, **3**: 80
Tateishi, John, **3**: 195
Teresa of Ávila, **1**: 211
Terkel, Louis "Studs," **3**: 161, 212, 343
Terry, Wallace, **3**: 199
Thiong'o, Ngũgĩ wa, **2**: 12
Thomas, Dylan, **1**: 125
Thompson, Paul, **3**: 170, 186
Thoreau, Henry David, **1**: 233
Tollefson, James W., **3**: 221
Tolstoy, Leo, **1**: 193
Tuqan, Fadwa, **1**: 225
Twain, Mark, **1**: 146

U

Uchida, Yoshiko, **1**: 309
Ulrich, Laurel Thatcher, **2**: 331
Unaipon, David, **1**: 149
Underhill, Ruth, **1**: 69
Usāmah ibn Munqidh, **1**: 285

V

Vaarzon-Morel, Petronella, **3**: 334
Vambe, Lawrence Chinyani, **3**: 251
Vico, Giambattista, **1**: 183
Victoria, Queen, **2**: 209
Viezzer, Moema, **3**: 322

W

Walkowitz, Daniel J., **3**: 340
Walmsley, Jan, **3**: 170
Wang Zheng, **3**: 147
Washington, Booker T., **1**: 50
Wat, Eric, **3**: 83
Webb, Beatrice, **2**: 16
Wehrey, Jane, **3**: 102
Weinberg, Bill, **3**: 86
Wells, H. G., **1**: 252
Wesley, John, **2**: 195
Wheatley, Phillis, **2**: 44
Wiesel, Elie, **1**: 318
Wilde, Oscar, **2**: 9
Williams, Tennessee, **2**: 152
Wolff, Tobias, **1**: 47
Wollstonecraft, Mary, **2**: 109
Wood, Trish, **3**: 231
Woodforde, James, **2**: 287
Wooldridge, E. T., **3**: 202
Woolf, Virginia, **2**: 180
Wordsworth, Dorothy, **2**: 300
Wright, Richard, **1**: 122
Wurts, Jay, **1**: 335

X

Xie Bingying, **1**: 338
Xu Guangping, **2**: 170

Y

Yeats, William Butler, **2**: 126

Z

Zhang Xinxin, **3**: 299

Title Index

The title index includes works that are represented in *The Literature of Autobiographical Narrative*. Bolded numbers refer to volumes, with page numbers following colons.

A

Abandoned Baobab, The: The Autobiography of a Senegalese Woman [Ken Bugul], **1**: 61

Akenfield: Portrait of an English Village [Ronald Blythe], **3**: 59

Always a People: Oral Histories of Contemporary Woodland Indians [Rita Kohn and William Lynwood Montell], **3**: 107

Among You Taking Notes: The Wartime Diary of Naomi Mitchison, 1939–1945 [Naomi Mitchison], **2**: 235

Anarchist Voices: An Oral History of Anarchism in America [Paul Avrich], **3**: 3

And Justice for All: An Oral History of the Japanese American Detention Camps [John Tateishi], **3**: 195

Angela's Ashes [Frank McCourt], **1**: 119

Annals of Ballitore, The [Mary Leadbeater], **2**: 157

Arab-Syrian Gentleman and Warrior in the Period of the Crusades, An: Memoirs of Usāmah ibn Munqidh [Usāmah ibn Munqidh], **1**: 285

Army Life in a Black Regiment [Thomas Wentworth Higginson], **2**: 238

As I Crossed a Bridge of Dreams [Lady Sarashina], **2**: 189

Ask the Fellows Who Cut the Hay [George Ewart Evans], **3**: 63

Autobiographical Pact, The [Philippe Lejeune], **1**: 239

Autobiography, An, or The Story of My Experiments with Truth [Mohandas Gandhi], **1**: 242

Autobiography, An, with Musings on Recent Events in India [Jawaharlal Nehru], **1**: 289

Autobiography: Essays Theoretical and Critical [James Olney], **1**: 246

Autobiography of Ben Franklin, The [Benjamin Franklin], **1**: 179

Autobiography of Charles Darwin, The [Charles Darwin], **1**: 65

Autobiography of Giambattista Vico, The [Giambattista Vico], **1**: 183

Autobiography of Malcolm X, The [Malcolm X], **1**: 186

Autobiography of W. E. B. Du Bois, The: A Soliloquy on Viewing My Life from the Last Decade of Its First Century [W. E. B. Du Bois], **1**: 3

B

Barefoot Gen: A Cartoon Story of Hiroshima [Keiji Nakazawa], **1**: 293

Between Management and Labor: Oral Histories of Arbitration [Clara Friedman], **3**: 153

Biography of a Runaway Slave [Miguel Barnet and Esteban Montejo], **3**: 7

Bitter Water: Diné Oral Histories of the Navajo-Hopi Land Dispute [Malcolm D. Benally], **3**: 10

Black Boy [Richard Wright], **1**: 122

Black Elk Speaks: Being the Life Story of a Holy Man of the Oglala Sioux [Black Elk and John G. Neihardt], **3**: 110

Bloods: An Oral History of the Vietnam War by Black Veterans [Wallace Terry], **3**: 199

Boer War Diary of Sol Plaatje, The: An African at Mafeking [Solomon Tshekisho Plaatje], **2**: 241

Bone Black: Memories of Girlhood [bell hooks], **1**: 249

Book of Margery Kempe, The [Margery Kempe], **1**: 189

Brokenburn: The Journal of Kate Stone, 1861–1868 [Kate Stone], **2**: 244

C

Californio Voices: The Oral Memoirs of José María Amador and Lorenzo Asisara [Thomas Savage], **3**: 114

Cancer Journals, The [Audre Lorde], **2**: 3

Carrier Warfare in the Pacific: An Oral History Collection [E. T. Wooldridge], **3**: 202

Child of the Dark: The Diary of Carolina Maria de Jesus [Carolina Maria de Jesus], **2**: 6

Children of Los Alamos: An Oral History of the Town Where the Atomic Bomb Began [Katrina Mason], **3**: 239

461

TITLE INDEX

Child's Christmas in Wales, A [Dylan Thomas], **1**: 125

Chinese Lives: An Oral History of Contemporary China [Zhang Xinxin and Sang Ye], **3**: 299

Chona: The Autobiography of a Papago Woman [Maria Chona and Ruth Underhill], **1**: 69

Coal Hollow: Photographs and Oral Histories [Kenneth Light and Melanie Light], **3**: 66

Collected Letters of a Renaissance Feminist [Laura Cereta], **2**: 160

Collected Letters of Mary Wollstonecraft, The [Mary Wollstonecraft], **2**: 109

Color of Water, The: A Black Man's Tribute to His White Mother [James McBride], **1**: 72

Complete Notebooks of Henry James, The [Henry James], **2**: 113

Confession, A [Leo Tolstoy], **1**: 193

Confessions [Augustine], **1**: 196

Confessions [Jean-Jacques Rousseau], **1**: 200

Confessions of Lady Nijo [Lady Nijo], **2**: 59

Congo Diary, The [Joseph Conrad], **2**: 192

Country of My Skull: Guilt, Sorrow, and the Limits of Forgiveness in the New South Africa [Antjie Krog], **3**: 242

Country Parson, A: James Woodforde's Diary, 1759–1802 [James Woodforde], **2**: 287

Cross and a Star, A: Memoirs of a Jewish Girl in Chile [Marjorie Agosín], **1**: 75

D

Daring Hearts: Lesbian and Gay Lives of the 50s and 60s Brighton [Brighton Ourstory], **3**: 70

Dark Child, The: The Autobiography of an African Boy [Camara Laye], **1**: 128

Darkness Visible [William Styron], **1**: 204

Death of Luigi Trastulli and Other Stories, The [Alessandro Portelli], **3**: 157

De Profundis [Oscar Wilde], **2**: 9

Detained: A Writer's Prison Diary [Ngũgĩ wa Thiong'o], **2**: 12

Diaries, 1915–1918 [Siegfried Sassoon], **2**: 247

Diaries, 1931–1949 [George Orwell], **2**: 117

Diaries of Beatrice Webb [Beatrice Webb], **2**: 16

Diaries of Franz Kafka, The [Franz Kafka], **2**: 120

Diaries of Lady Anne Clifford, The [Lady Anne Clifford], **2**: 62

Diary, Reminiscences and Correspondence of Henry Crabb Robinson, Barrister-at-Law [Henry Crabb Robinson], **2**: 75

Diary from Dixie, A [Mary Boykin Miller Chesnut], **2**: 250

Diary of Anaïs Nin, The [Anaïs Nin], **2**: 123

Diary of Anne Frank, The [Anne Frank], **2**: 253

Diary of John Evelyn, The [John Evelyn], **2**: 65

Diary of John Quincy Adams, The [John Quincy Adams], **2**: 69

Diary of Lady Murasaki, The [Lady Murasaki Shikibu], **2**: 290

Diary of Samuel Pepys, The [Samuel Pepys], **2**: 72

Diary of Sir Henry Slingsby, The [Sir Henry Slingsby], **2**: 256

Diary without Dates, A [Enid Bagnold], **2**: 259

Diving Bell and the Butterfly, The [Jean-Dominique Bauby], **1**: 6

Doña María's Story: Life History, Memory and Political Identity [Daniel James], **3**: 73

Dreams from My Father: A Story of Race and Inheritance [Barack Obama], **1**: 78

Dust Tracks on a Road [Zora Neale Hurston], **1**: 9

E

Education of Henry Adams, The [Henry Adams], **1**: 132

Egyptian Childhood, An [Taha Hussein], **1**: 135

Eighty Years and More, Reminiscences 1815–1897 [Elizabeth Cady Stanton], **1**: 12

El Salvador at War: An Oral History of Conflict from the 1979 Insurrection to the Present [Max G. Manwaring and Court Prisk], **3**: 205

Estrangement, Being Some Fifty Extracts from a Diary Kept in 1909 [William Butler Yeats], **2**: 126

Everything We Had [Al Santoli], **3**: 209

Exiled Memories: A Cuban Childhood [Pablo Medina], **1**: 296

Exodus to Shanghai: Stories of Escape from the Third Reich [Steve Hochstadt], **3**: 14

Experiment in Autobiography, An [H. G. Wells], **1**: 252

Extraordinary Work of Ordinary Writing, The: Annie Ray's Diary [Jennifer Sinor], **2**: 163

F

Farewell to Manzanar [Jeanne Wakatsuki Houston and James D. Houston], **1**: 299

Firm: The Inside Story of the Stasi, The [Gary Bruce], **3**: 245

First Agraristas, The: An Oral History of a Mexican Agrarian Reform Movement [Ann L. Craig], **3**: 302

Freedom Flyers: The Tuskegee Airmen of World War II [J. Todd Moye], **3**: 248

Fun Home: A Family Tragicomic [Alison Bechdel], **1**: 139

G

Geronimo: His Own Story [Geronimo and S. M. Barrett], **1**: 302

Go Ask Alice [Anonymous], **2**: 294

Golden Bones: An Extraordinary Journey from Hell in Cambodia to a New Life in America [Sichan Siv], **1**: 306

Good Man of Nanking, The: The Diaries of John Rabe [John Rabe], **2**: 19

"Good War, The": An Oral History of World War II [Louis "Studs" Terkel], **3**: 212

Gossamer Years, The [Michitsuna No Haha], **2**: 297

TITLE INDEX

Grandmothers, Mothers, and Daughters: Oral Histories of Three Generations of Ethnic American Women [Corinne Azen Krause], **3**: 305

Grasmere Journals [Dorothy Wordsworth], **2**: 300

Growing Up Jewish in America [Myrna Katz Frommer and Harvey Frommer], **3**: 118

Gulag Voices: Oral Histories of Soviet Incarceration and Exile [Jehanne M. Gheith and Katherine R. Jolluck], **3**: 17

H

Habit of Being, The: Letters of Flannery O'Connor [Flannery O'Conner], **2**: 129

Habits of Change: An Oral History of American Nuns [Carole Garibaldi Rogers], **3**: 308

Hard Times: An Oral History of the Great Depression [Louis "Studs" Terkel], **3**: 161

Head of the Class: An Oral History of African American Achievement in Higher Education and Beyond [Gabrielle Morris], **3**: 20

Hill Country Teacher: Oral Histories from the One-Room School and Beyond [Diane Manning], **3**: 77

Hispanic-American Entrepreneur, The: An Oral History of the American Dream [Beatrice Rodriguez Owsley], **3**: 121

History of Mary Prince, a West Indian Slave, Related by Herself, The [Mary Prince], **3**: 23

Hood River Issei, The: An Oral History of Japanese Settlers in Oregon's Hood River Valley [Linda Tamura], **3**: 80

Hooligans or Rebels?: An Oral History of Working-Class Childhood and Youth, 1889–1939 [Stephen Humphries], **3**: 311

Hunger of Memory: The Education of Richard Rodriguez [Richard Rodriguez], **1**: 15

I

I, Rigoberta Menchú: An Indian Woman in Guatemala [Rigoberta Menchú], **3**: 164

I Know Why the Caged Bird Sings [Maya Angelou], **1**: 18

Ill-Fated People, An: Zimbabwe before and after Rhodes [Lawrence Chinyani Vambe], **3**: 251

Incidents in the Life of a Slave Girl, Written by Herself [Harriet A. Jacobs], **1**: 142

Infidel [Ayaan Hirsi Ali], **1**: 207

Interesting Narrative of the Life of Olaudah Equiano, The, or Gustavus Vassa, the African, Written by Himself [Olaudah Equiano], **1**: 81

Interrupted Life, An: The Diaries of Etty Hillesum [Etty Hillesum], **2**: 22

In the Mansion of Confucius' Descendants: An Oral History [Kong Demao and Ke Lan], **3**: 124

In the Presence of Absence [Mahmoud Darwish], **1**: 255

Invisible Thread, The [Yoshiko Uchida], **1**: 309

Ireland's Unfinished Revolution: An Oral History [Kenneth Griffith and Timothy O'Grady], **3**: 27

Irish Days: Oral Histories of the Twentieth Century [Margaret Hickey], **3**: 315

I Will Bear Witness: A Diary of the Nazi Years, 1933–1945 [Victor Klemperer], **2**: 303

J

Japan at War: An Oral History [Haruko Taya Cook and Theodore F. Cook], **3**: 215

Japanese War Brides in America: An Oral History [Miki Ward Crawford, Katie Kaori Hayashi, and Shizuko Suenaga], **3**: 127

Jemima Condict: Her Book, Being a Transcript of the Diary of an Essex County Maid during the Revolutionary War [Jemima Condict], **2**: 78

Journal, 1955–1962: Reflections on the French-Algerian War [Mouloud Feraoun], **2**: 262

Journal des Goncourt: Mémoires de la vie littéraire [Jules de Goncourt and Edmond de Goncourt], **2**: 81

Journal of George Fox [George Fox], **2**: 26

Journal of Katherine Mansfield [Katherine Mansfield], **2**: 133

Journal of Marie Bashkirtseff, The [Marie Bashkirtseff], **2**: 306

Journal of Sir Walter Scott, The [Sir Walter Scott], **2**: 309

Journal of the First Voyage of Vasco da Gama, 1497–1499, A [Author Unknown], **2**: 201

Journal of the First Voyage to America [Christopher Columbus], **2**: 201

Journals of Arnold Bennett, 1896–1928, The [Arnold Bennett], **2**: 136

Journals of Charlotte Forten Grimké, The [Charlotte Forten Grimké], **2**: 29

Journals of John Wesley [John Wesley], **2**: 195

Journals of Jonathan Carver and Related Documents, 1766–1770, The [Jonathan Carver], **2**: 205

Journals of Ralph Waldo Emerson [Ralph Waldo Emerson], **2**: 139

Journals of Søren Kierkegaard [Søren Kierkegaard], **2**: 166

Juan the Chamula: An Ethnological Re-creation of the Life of a Mexican Indian [Ricardo Pozas], **3**: 167

L

Lakota Woman [Mary Crow Dog], **1**: 21

Last Diary of Tsaritsa Alexandra, The [Alexandra Feodorovna], **2**: 84

Launching the War on Poverty: An Oral History [Michael L. Gillette], **3**: 254

Leaves from the Journal of Our Life in the Highlands, from 1848 to 1861 [Queen Victoria], **2**: 209

Left Handed, Son of Old Man Hat: A Navajo Autobiography [Left Handed and Walter Dyk], **3**: 318

Let Me Speak!: Testimony of Domitila, a Woman of the Bolivian Mines [Moema Viezzer and Domitila Barrios de Chungara], **3**: 322

Let My People Go [Albert Luthuli], **1**: 24

"Letter from the Birmingham Jail" [Martin Luther King Jr.], **2**: 32

Letters and Journals of Fanny Burney [Fanny Burney], **2**: 312

TITLE INDEX

Letters and Journals of Lord Byron, with Notices of His Life [George Gordon Noel Byron], **2**: 143

Letters between Two [Lu Xun and Xu Guangping], **2**: 170

Letters from an American Farmer [Michel-Guillaume Saint-Jean de Crévecoeur], **2**: 213

Letters from Jefferson to His Daughter [Thomas Jefferson], **2**: 316

Letters Home [Sylvia Plath], **2**: 47

Letters of a Woman Homesteader [Elinore Pruitt Stewart], **2**: 91

Letters of John Keats, 1814–1821, The [John Keats], **2**: 146

Letters of Lady Anne Barnard to Henry Dundas, from Cape and Elsewhere, The [Anne Barnard], **2**: 217

Letters of the Younger Pliny, The [Pliny the Younger], **2**: 94

Letters to a Young Poet [Rainer Maria Rilke], **2**: 149

Letters Underway ['Izzat Ghazzawi], **2**: 50

"Letter to Her Daughter" [Lady Mary Wortley Montagu], **2**: 35

"Letter to Her Daughter from the New White House" [Abigail Adams], **2**: 87

"Letter to His Son" [Robert E. Lee], **2**: 38

"Letter to Maria Clemm" [Edgar Allan Poe], **2**: 41

"Letter to the Reverend Samson Occom" [Phillis Wheatley], **2**: 44

Life, The [Teresa of Ávila], **1**: 211

Life on the Mississippi [Mark Twain], **1**: 146

Literary Remains of Edward VI, The [Edward VI], **2**: 97

London and the Life of Literature in Late Victorian England: The Diary of George Gissing, Novelist [George Gissing], **2**: 320

London Journal, 1762–1763 [James Boswell], **2**: 328

Long Journey Home: Oral Histories of Contemporary Delaware Indians [James W. Brown and Rita T. Kohn], **3**: 325

Long Walk to Freedom, The [Nelson Mandela], **1**: 27

Long Way from Home, A [Claude McKay], **1**: 84

Long Way Gone, A: Memoirs of a Boy Soldier [Ishmael Beah], **1**: 312

Love Letters of Dorothy Osborne to Sir Wiliam Temple, 1652–54, The [Dorothy Osborne], **2**: 324

M

Machete Season: The Killers in Rwanda Speak [Jean Hatzfeld], **3**: 257

Making of a Gay Asian Community, The: An Oral History of Pre-AIDS Los Angeles [Eric Wat], **3**: 83

Man Died, The: Prison Notes of Wole Soyinka [Wole Soyinka], **1**: 214

Massacre in Mexico [Elena Poniatowska], **3**: 31

Meatless Days [Sara Suleri], **1**: 87

Meditations of the Emperor Marcus Aurelius Antoninus, The [Marcus Aurelius], **1**: 218

Mein Kampf [Adolf Hitler], **1**: 30

Memoirs [Pablo Neruda], **1**: 222

Memoirs of an Arabian Princess from Zanzibar [Emily Ruete], **1**: 90

Memoirs of Fatemeh Pakravan [Habib Ladjevardi], **3**: 218

Memoirs of Lady Anne Halkett, The [Lady Anne Halkett], **1**: 315

Memories of a Catholic Girlhood [Mary McCarthy], **1**: 258

Midwife's Tale, A: The Life of Martha Ballard, Based on Her Diary, 1785–1812 [Laurel Thatcher Ulrich], **2**: 331

Mothers, Sisters, Resisters: Oral Histories of Women Who Survived the Holocaust [Brana Gurewitsch], **3**: 34

Motorcycle Diaries [Ernesto "Che" Guevara], **2**: 220

Mountainous Journey, A: A Poet's Autobiography [Fadwa Tuqan], **1**: 225

"My Furthest-Back Person—'The African'" [Alex Haley], **1**: 261

My Life Story [Fadhma Aïth Mansour Amrouche], **1**: 93

My Life Story [David Unaipon], **1**: 149

My Revolutionary Years: The Autobiography of Madame Wei Tao-Ming [Cheng Yu-hsiu], **1**: 152

N

Narrative of the Life of Frederick Douglass [Frederick Douglass], **1**: 33

Nella Last's War: The Second World War Diaries of Housewife, 49 [Nella Last], **2**: 265

Night [Elie Wiesel], **1**: 318

Nisa: The Life and Words of a !Kung Woman [Marjorie Shostak], **3**: 37

Notebooks [Tennessee Williams], **2**: 152

Notebooks and *Letters* [Nathaniel Hawthorne], **2**: 223

O

Oral History, Health and Welfare [Joanna Bornat, Robert Perks, Paul Thompson, and Jan Walmsley], **3**: 170

Oral History of Abraham Lincoln, An: John G. Nicolay's Interviews and Essays [Michael Burlingame], **3**: 261

Oral History Theory [Lynn Abrams], **3**: 173

Order Has Been Carried Out, The: History, Memory, and Meaning of a Nazi Massacre in Rome [Alessandro Portelli], **3**: 265

Our Appalachia [Laurel Shackelford and Bill Weinberg], **3**: 86

P

Pacifist's War, A: Diaries 1939–1945 [Frances Partridge], **2**: 268

Paekpom Ilchi: The Autobiography of Kim Ku [Kim Ku], **1**: 322

Peacework: Oral Histories of Women Peace Activists [Judith Porter Adams], **3**: 268

Persepolis [Marjane Satrapi], **1**: 155

"Popular Memory: Theory, Politics, Method" [Popular Memory Group], **3**: 176

"Practice of the Private Journal" [Philippe Lejeune], **2**: 174

Praeterita [John Ruskin], **1**: 264

Prison Writings: My Life Is My Sun Dance [Leonard Peltier], **1**: 96

Pylgrymage of Sir Richarde Guylforde, The [Richarde Guylforde], **2**: 226

R

Records of a Girlhood [Fanny Kemble], **2**: 335

Red Azalea [Anchee Min], **1**: 158

Red Scarf Girl: A Memoir of the Cultural Revolution [Ji-li Jiang], **1**: 161

Rites: A Guatemalan Boyhood [Victor Perera], **1**: 99

Roland Barthes [Roland Barthes], **1**: 267

Rosa Parks: My Story [Rosa Parks and Jim Haskins], **1**: 37

S

Saga of Coe Ridge, The: A Study in Oral History [William Lynwood Montell], **3**: 90

Selected Letters of Martha Gellhorn [Martha Gellhorn], **2**: 101

Shadows on My Heart: The Civil War Diary of Lucy Rebecca Buck of Virginia [Lucy Buck], **2**: 271

Shared Authority, A: Essays on the Craft and Meaning of Oral and Public History [Michael Frisch], **3**: 179

Shattered Dreams?: An Oral History of the South African AIDS Epidemic [Gerald M. Oppenheimer and Ronald Bayer], **3**: 272

Solidarity Forever: An Oral History of the IWW [Stewart Bird, Dan Georgakas, and Deborah Shaffer], **3**: 328

"Some Observations on Diaries, Self-Biography, and Self-Characters" [Isaac D'Israeli], **2**: 177

Songs My Mother Sang to Me: An Oral History of Mexican American Women [Patricia Preciado Martin], **3**: 131

Sovereignty and Goodness of God, The [Mary Rowlandson], **1**: 325

Soviet Baby Boomers: An Oral History of Russia's Cold War Generation [Donald J. Raleigh], **3**: 331

Spandau: The Secret Diaries [Albert Speer], **2**: 54

Speak, Memory: An Autobiography Revisited [Vladimir Nabokov], **1**: 270

Stop-Time [Frank Conroy], **1**: 164

Story of a Shipwrecked Sailor, The [Gabriel García Márquez], **3**: 183

Story of My Life, The: An Afghan Girl on the Other Side of the Sky [Farah Ahmedi], **1**: 40

Story of My Life, The: Helen Keller [Helen Keller], **1**: 43

Strange Ground: Americans in Vietnam 1945–1975: An Oral History [Harry Maurer], **3**: 275

Stranger's Supper, A: An Oral History of Centenarian Women in Montenegro [Zorka Milich], **3**: 135

Strength Not to Fight, The: An Oral History of Conscientious Objectors of the Vietnam War [James W. Tollefson], **3**: 221

Survivors: An Oral History of the Armenian Genocide [Donald E. Miller and Lorna Touryan Miller], **3**: 40

Swiftwater People: Lives of Old Timers on the Upper St. Joe & St. Maries Rivers [Bert Russell], **3**: 93

T

Tears before the Rain: An Oral History of the Fall of South Vietnam [Larry Engelmann], **3**: 279

Ten Thousand Sorrows: The Extraordinary Journey of a Korean War Orphan [Elizabeth Kim], **1**: 102

Testament of Youth [Vera Brittain], **1**: 329

They Say in Harlan County: An Oral History [Alessandro Portelli] **3**: 96

This Boy's Life [Tobias Wolff], **1**: 47

Thura's Diary: A Young Girl's Life in War-Torn Baghdad [Thura Al-Windawi], **2**: 275

To Be Young, Gifted and Black: An Informal Autobiography of Lorraine Hansberry [Lorraine Hansberry], **1**: 273

Travels of Dean Mahomet, a Native of Patna in Bengal, through Several Parts of India, While in the Service of the Honourable the East India Company Written by Himself, in a Series of Letters to a Friend, The [Dean Mahomet], **2**: 229

Travels of Marco Polo, The [Marco Polo], **1**: 105

True Relation of My Birth, Breeding, and Life, A [Margaret Cavendish], **1**: 229

Truth and Fiction Relating to My Life [Johann Wolfgang von Goethe], **1**: 276

U

Under My Skin: Volume One of My Autobiography, to 1949 [Doris Lessing], **1**: 167

Unknown Internment, The: An Oral History of the Relocation of Italian Americans during World War II [Stephen Fox], **3**: 224

Untold Tales, Unsung Heroes: An Oral History of Detroit's African-American Community, 1918–1967 [Elaine Latzman Moon], **3**: 99

Unwanted, The [Kien Nguyen], **1**: 170

Up from Slavery [Booker T. Washington], **1**: 50

Uqalurait: An Oral History of Nunavut [John Bennett and Susan Rowley], **3**: 138

V

Voice of the Past, The: Oral History [Paul Thompson], **3**: 186

Voices from Chernobyl: The Oral History of a Nuclear Disaster [Svetlana Alexievich], **3**: 282

Voices from the Whirlwind: An Oral History of the Chinese Cultural Revolution [Feng Jicai], **3**: 287

Voices from this Long Brown Land: Oral Recollections of Owens Valley Lives and Manzanar Pasts [Jane Wehrey], **3**: 102

Voices of Freedom: An Oral History of the Civil Rights Movement from the 1950s through the 1980s [Henry Hampton and Steve Fayer], **3**: 44

Voices of Resistance: Oral Histories of Moroccan Women [Allison Baker], **3**: 47

TITLE INDEX

W

Walden; or, Life in the Woods [Henry David Thoreau], **1**: 233

Warlpiri Women's Voices: Our Lives, Our History [Petronella Vaarzon-Morel], **3**: 334

Wars I Have Seen [Gertrude Stein], **1**: 332

Way to Rainy Mountain, The [N. Scott Momaday], **1**: 54

"We Have Just Begun to Not Fight": An Oral History of Conscientious Objectors in Civilian Public Service during World War II [Heather T. Frazer and John O'Sullivan], **3**: 227

What Was Asked of Us: An Oral History of the Iraq War by the Soldiers Who Fought It [Trish Wood], **3**: 231

When Heaven and Earth Changed Places: A Vietnamese Woman's Journey from War to Peace [Le Ly Hayslip and Jay Wurts], **1**: 335

When I Was Puerto Rican [Esmeralda Santiago], **1**: 108

When We Began, There Were Witchmen: An Oral History from Mount Kenya [Jeffrey A. Fadiman], **3**: 141

Witch Purge of 1878, The: Oral and Documentary History in the Early Navajo Reservation Years [Martha Blue], **3**: 290

Witnesses to Nuremberg: An Oral History of American Participants at the War Crimes Trials [Bruce M. Stave, Michele Palmer, and Leslie Frank], **3**: 293

Witnesses to the Holocaust: An Oral History [Rhoda Lewin], **3**: 50

Woman at War, A [Molly Moore], **2**: 278

Woman in Berlin, A: Eight Weeks in the Conquered City: A Diary [Anonymous], **2**: 281

Woman Soldier's Own Story, A [Xie Bingying], **1**: 338

Woman Warrior, The: Memoirs of a Girlhood among Ghosts [Maxine Hong Kingston], **1**: 173

Women and Families: An Oral History, 1940–1970 [Elizabeth Roberts], **3**: 144

Women in the Chinese Enlightenment: Oral and Textual Histories [Wang Zheng], **3**: 14703

Women in the Mines: Stories of Life and Work [Marat Moore], **3**: 337

Women's Words [Sherna Berger Gluck and Daphne Patai], **3**: 190

Wonderful Adventures of Mrs. Seacole in Many Lands, The [Mary Seacole], **1**: 111

Workers of the Donbass Speak: Survival and Identity in the New Ukraine, 1989–1992 [Lewis H. Siegelbaum and Daniel J. Walkowitz], **3**: 340

Working: People Talk about What They Do All Day and How They Feel about What They Do [Louis "Studs" Terkel], **3**: 343

Working-Class Childhood: An Oral History [Jeremy Seabrook], **3**: 5301

World at War, The [Richard Holmes], **3**: 234

Worlds of a Maasai Warrior, The: An Autobiography [Tepilit Ole Saitoti], **1**: 114

Writer's Diary, A [Virginia Woolf], **2**: 180

Writer's Notebook, A [W. Somerset Maugham], **2**: 183

Writing Life, The [Annie Dillard], **1**: 279

Y

Young Palestinian's Diary, 1941–1945, A: The Life of Sāmī 'Amr [Sāmī 'Amr], **2**: 104

Z

Zlata's Diary: A Child's Life in Sarajevo [Zlata Filipovic], **2**: 338